CASES AND MATERIALS ON SOCIAL JUSTICE: PROFESSIONALS, COMMUNITIES, AND LAW

By

Martha R. Mahoney
Professor of Law
University of Miami School of Law

John O. Calmore
Reef C. Ivey II Research Professor of Law
University of North Carolina School of Law

Stephanie M. Wildman
Professor of Law and Director,
Center for Social Justice and Public Service
Santa Clara University School of Law

AMERICAN CASEBOOK SERIES®

Mat # 18234845

ISBN 0–314–25713–6

Preface

This book is born of its historic context, and in truth its time has come. Community activists and lawyers across the nation have worked together for transformative social change. Members of the legal academy—in classrooms and clinics—have sought to teach about social justice in law schools because students want to know how they can work with the people who most need them. The Society of American Law Teachers has encouraged the development of materials for a social justice curriculum to ensure that lawyers who work with marginalized, subordinated, and underrepresented clients and causes have the necessary knowledge and skills to assist their clients. Hence, this book brings together cases and materials on lawyers, law, and social justice movements, including many voices and visions of social justice and presenting contexts and contents of social justice practice.

This book celebrates diversity. The text presents a wealth of quite varied voices whose common ground is that they are taking social justice seriously. The rich field of materials on social justice, much of recent vintage and some of long-standing influence, offered contributions from many viewpoints and areas of work. The consolidated, substantive diversity of these voices reflects inspiring scholarship and advocacy. For each author, therefore, this project has been a true labor of love.

This book has also been developed through work with students whose energy has helped it grow. Martha R. Mahoney has been teaching Public Interest Law at the University of Miami since 1992; since 1995 the course has been a large section first-year elective. John O. Calmore taught Ethics, Counseling, and Negotiation for many years at Loyola Law School in Los Angeles and now teaches Social Justice Lawyering at the University of North Carolina School of Law. Stephanie M. Wildman was founding director of the Boalt Center for Social Justice (University of California at Berkeley School of Law) where she taught Law and Social Justice; she now directs the Center for Social Justice and Public Service at Santa Clara University School of Law and continues to teach Law and Social Justice.

Many people have made this book possible. We thank the colleagues, practitioners, judges, and students who have increased our understanding of this emerging field. Many of them appear excerpted or quoted within this book; many more, who are not visible here, continue to work for social justice in evolving, creative ways. We hope this volume contributes significantly to that good work. We give special recognition to Paul Crockett, Joan Graff, Michael Harris, Paul Harris, Sharon Hartmann, Mary Howell, Alan McSurely, john powell, Bill Quigley, and Bob Weisberg.

Thank you to the University of Miami School of Law, the University of North Carolina School of Law, and Santa Clara University School of Law for providing generous support for this project. We particularly appreciate the contribution of the Reef C. Ivey II Research Professorship's scholarship fund at the University of North Carolina School of Law.

We also thank the following colleagues and research assistants for reading chapters, giving us ideas, teaching these materials in various versions, or providing important project support: Josiane Abel, Sasha Abele, Margalynne Armstrong, Jack Boger, Sue Ann Campbell, Kenneth Casebeer, Donna Coker, Amanda Crockett, Chris Daley, Jon Davidson, Charles Daye, Marc Fajer, Emily Fisher, Bryan Ford, Mary Louise Frampton, Angela Harris, Nik Hua, Chine Hui, Grace Hum, Myvan Khuu, Ayn Lowry, Donna Maeda, Holly Maguigan, Gene Nichol, James O'Fallon, Kim Pederson, Mack Player, Jennifer McCloskey Quezada, Eva Raczkowski, Angela Riley, Steve Rosenbaum, Jeff Selbin, Jessica Sharpe, Marge Shultz, Viva Stowe, Steve Sugarman, Eleanor Swift, Sam Thompson, Kerri Utter, Deborah Weissman, Edith Wildman, Michelle Williams, and Tasha Winebarger.

Special appreciation is due to the people whose patience and good humor sustained this project and made its completion possible: Bonita Summers for superlative secretarial assistance, Felicia Martin for exceptional editorial and administrative assistance, Priscilla Battis for outstanding copyediting, and Melanie E. Esquivel for extraordinary administrative support.

Finally to our families whose love, patience, understanding, and sacrifice made it possible to complete this book, thank you Ken, Jeff, Amanda, and Bill; Alyce, Canai, and Jonathan; and Michael, Becky, and Ben.

MARTHA R. MAHONEY
JOHN O. CALMORE
STEPHANIE M. WILDMAN

February 2003

Copyright Acknowledgments and Reprint Permissions

We gratefully acknowledge the authors and publishers who have allowed us to reprint copyrighted materials. Excerpts from the following materials appear with the permission of the copyright holders.

Richard L. Abel, *Big Lies and Small Steps: A Critique of Deborah Rhode's* Too Much Law, Too Little Justice: Too Much Rhetoric, Too Little Reform, 11 Geo. J. Legal Ethics 1019, 1023–27 (1998). Copyright © 1998 by the Georgetown Journal of Legal Ethics. Reprinted by permission of the publisher, Georgetown Journal of Legal Ethics, and Richard L. Abel.

Richard L. Abel, *Law Without Politics: Legal Aid Under Advanced Capitalism*, 32 UCLA L. Rev. 474, 595–96, 600–01 (1985). Reprinted by permission of Richard L. Abel.

Shirley S. Abrahamson, *The Ballot and the Bench*, 76 N.Y.U. L. Rev. 973, 975–77 (2001). Reprinted by permission of the New York University Law Review and Shirley S. Abrahamson, Chief Justice of the Wisconsin Supreme Court.

Kathryn Abrams, *Some Realism About Electoralism: Rethinking Judicial Campaign Finance*, 72 S. Cal. L. Rev. 505, 512–13, 516–17, 519–22, 533–34 (1999). Reprinted by permission of the Southern California Law Review and Kathryn Abrams.

Robert S. Adler and Elliot M. Silverstein, *When David Meets Goliath: Dealing with Power Differentials in Negotiation*, 5 Harv. Negotiation L. Rev. 1, 5–6, 8–10, 13–22, 105–10 (2000). Reprinted by permission of the Harvard Negotiation Law Review, Robert S. Adler, and Elliot M. Silverstein.

Jane H. Aiken, *Provocateurs for Justice*, 7 Clinical L. Rev. 287, 287–99, 305–06 (2001). Reprinted by permission of the Clinical Law Review and Jane H. Aiken.

Linda L. Ammons, *Dealing with the Nastiness: Mixing Feminism and Criminal Law in the Review of Cases of Battered Incarcerated Women—A Tenth-Year Reflection*, 4 Buff. Crim. L. Rev 891, 892, 909–12, 914–17 (2001). Reprinted by permission of the Buffalo Criminal Law Review and Linda L. Ammons.

Fran Ansley, *Inclusive Boundaries and Other (Im)possible Paths Toward Community Development in a Global World*, 150 U. Pa. L. Rev. 353, 361–66, 371–72, 374–75, 377–80, 388–92, 396–97, 400–01, 406 (2001). Reprinted by permission of the University of Pennsylvania Law Review and Fran Ansley.

Keith Aoki, *Space Invaders: Critical Geography, the "Third World" in International Law and Critical Race Theory*, 45 Vill. L. Rev. 913, 917–24, 938–39, 956 (2000). Reprinted by permission of the Villanova Law Review and Keith Aoki.

Harry Arthurs, *Reinventing Labor Law for the Global Economy*, 22 Berkeley J. Emp. & Lab. L. 271, 273–74 (2001). Copyright © 2001 by the Berkeley Journal of Employment and Labor Law. Reprinted by permission.

Jerold S. Auerbach, *Unequal Justice: Lawyers and Social Change in Modern America* vii–viii, 99–100 (1976). Copyright © 1976 by Oxford University Press, Inc. Reprinted by permission.

Jack M. Balkin and Sanford Levinson, *Understanding the Constitutional Revolution*, 87 Va. L. Rev. 1045, 1045–53, 1066–67, 1083–88, 1094–97, 1099–1103, 1107–09 (2001). Copyright © 2001 by the Virginia Law Review. Reprinted with permission of the Virginia Law Review in the format Textbook via Copyright Clearance Center, Jack M. Balkin, and Sanford Levinson.

Mary E. Becker, *Double Binds Facing Mothers in Abusive Families: Social Support Systems, Custody Outcomes, and Liability for Acts of Others*, 2 U. Chi. L. Sch. Roundtable 13, 13-15, 20–32 (1995). Reprinted by permission of the University of Chicago Law School Roundtable and Mary E. Becker.

Derrick A. Bell, Jr., *Serving Two Masters: Integration Ideals and Client Interests in School Desegregation Litigation*, 85 Yale L. J. 470, 471–72, 488–90, 492–93, 512–16 (1976). Reprinted by permission of the Yale Law Journal, William S. Hein Company, and Derrick A. Bell, Jr.

Gary Bellow, *Steady Work: A Practitioner's Reflections on Political Lawyering*, 31 Harv. C.R.–C.L. L. Rev. 297, 301–05, 309 (1996). Copyright © 1996 by the President and Fellows of Harvard College and the Harvard Civil Rights–Civil Liberties Law Review. Reprinted by permission.

Donald L. Beschle, *The Supreme Court's IOLTA Decision: Of Dogs, Mangers, and the Ghost of Mrs. Frothingham*, 30 Seton Hall L. Rev. 846, 848–49, 853–55 (2000). Reprinted by permission of the Seton Hall Law Review and Donald L. Beschle.

David A. Binder, Paul Bergman, and Susan C. Price, *Lawyers as Counselors: A Client-Centered Approach* 17–23 (1991). Reprinted by permission of West Group.

William J. Brennan, Jr., *State Constitutions and the Protection of Individual Rights*, 90 Harv. L. Rev. 489, 498 (1977). Copyright © 1977 by the Harvard Law Review Association. Reprinted by permission.

Paul Brest and Linda Hamilton Krieger, *Lawyers as Problem Solvers*, 72 Temp. L. Rev. 811, 811–19, 822, 824–26, 831–32 (1999). Reprinted by permission of the Temple Law Review, Paul Brest, and Linda Hamilton Krieger.

Stephen B. Bright, *Political Attacks on the Judiciary: Can Justice Be Done Amid Efforts to Intimidate and Remove Judges from Office for Unpopular Decisions?*, 72 N.Y.U. L. Rev. 308, 310–11 (1997). Reprinted by permission of the New York University Law Review and Stephen B. Bright.

Kenneth S. Broun, *Black Lawyers, White Courts: The Soul of South African Law* xv–xvi (2000). Reprinted by permission of the Ohio University Press, Athens, Ohio.

James W. Button, Barbara A. Rienzo, and Kenneth D. Wald, *The Politics of Gay Rights at the Local and State Level*, in *The Politics of Gay Rights* 269, 272–74 (Craig A. Rimmerman, Kenneth D. Wald & Clyde Wilcox eds., 2000). Copyright © 2000 by the University of Chicago Press. Reprinted by permission.

Patricia A. Cain, *Litigating for Lesbian and Gay Rights: A Legal History*, 79 Va. L. Rev. 1551, 1557–59, 1561–65, 1567, 1580–84, 1586, 1587–89 (1993). Copyright © 1993 by the Virginia Law Review. Reprinted with permission of the Virginia Law Review in the format Textbook via Copyright Clearance Center.

John O. Calmore, *A Call to Context: The Professional Challenges of Cause Lawyering and the Intersection of Race, Space, and Poverty*, 67 Fordham L. Rev. 1927, 1927–29, 1932–46, 1955–56 (1999). Reprinted by permission of the Fordham Law Review and John O. Calmore.

John O. Calmore, *Close Encounters of the Racial Kind: Pedagogical Reflections and Seminar Conversations*, 31 U.S.F. L. Rev. 903, 924–926 (1997). Reprinted by permission of the University of San Francisco Law Review and John O. Calmore.

John O. Calmore, *Race-Conscious Voting Rights and the New Demography in a Multiracing America*, 79 N.C. L. Rev. 1253, 1257–62, 1265–76, 1279–80 (2001). Reprinted by permission of the North Carolina Law Review and John O. Calmore.

John O. Calmore, *Spatial Equality and the Kerner Commission Report: A Back-to-the-Future Essay*, 71 N.C. L. Rev. 1487, 1487–88, 1490–1501, 1504–09 (1993). Reprinted by permission of the North Carolina Law Review and John O. Calmore.

Devon W. Carbado, *Black Rights, Gay Rights, Civil Rights*, 47 UCLA L. Rev. 1467, 1468–69, 1472–75, 1478–89, 1492–97 (2000). Reprinted by permission of Devon W. Carbado.

Kenneth M. Casebeer, *The Empty State and Nobody's Market: The Political Economy of Non-Responsibility and the Judicial Disappearing of the Civil Rights Movement*, 54 U. Miami L. Rev. 247, 248–57, 289–91, 297, 309–14 (2000). Copyright © 2000 by the University of Miami Law Review. Reprinted by permission.

Laura L. Castro, *The Future is Now*, ABA Journal, July 1999, at 72. Copyright © 1999 by the ABA Journal. Reprinted by permission.

David Chambers, *Couples: Marriage, Civil Union, and Domestic Partnership*, in *Creating Change: Sexuality, Public Policy, and Civil Rights* 281, 296 (John D'Emilio, William B. Turner & Urvashi Vaid eds., 2000). Reprinted by permission of David Chambers and John D'Emilio.

David L. Chambers and Nancy D. Polikoff, *Family Law and Gay and Lesbian Family Issues in the Twentieth Century*, 33 Fam. L.Q. 523, 532–35, 539–40, 542 (1999). Copyright © 1999 by the American Bar Association. Reprinted by permission.

Wendy Chavkin, Tammy A. Draut, Diana Romero, and Paul H. Wise, *Sex, Reproduction, and Welfare Reform*, 7 Geo. J. on Poverty L. & Pol'y 379, 380–83, 388–33 (2000). Copyright © 2000 by the Georgetown Journal on Poverty, Law and Policy. Reprinted by permission.

Sumi Cho and Robert Westley, *Critical Race Coalitions: Key Movements that Performed the Theory*, 33 U.C. Davis L. Rev. 1377, 1392–93, 1404 (2000). Copyright © 2000 by the Regents of the University of California. Reprinted by permission.

James A. Cohen, *Lawyer Role, Agency Law, and the Characterization "Officer of the Court,"* 48 Buff. L. Rev. 349, 349–50, 353–58, 406–09 (2000). Copyright © 2000 by the Buffalo Law Review. Reprinted by permission.

Donna Coker, *Crime Control and Feminist Law Reform in Domestic Violence Law: A Critical Review*, 4 Buff. Crim. L. Rev. 801, 802–05, 811, 823–27, 830–32, 840–46, 849, 858–60 (2001). Reprinted by permission of the Buffalo Criminal Law Review and Donna Coker.

Luke W. Cole, *Macho Law Brains, Public Citizens, and Grassroots Activists: Three Models of Environmental Advocacy*, 14 Va. Envtl. L.J. 687, 692–98 (1995). Reprinted by permission of the Virginia Environmental Law Journal and Luke W. Cole.

Luke W. Cole and Sheila R. Foster, *From the Ground Up: Environmental Racism and the Rise of the Environmental Justice Movement* 14–15 (2001). Copyright © 2001 by New York University Press. Reprinted by permission.

Dalton Conley, *Being Black, Living in the Red: Race, Wealth, and Social Policy in America* 25, 33 (1999). Copyright © 1999 by the University of California Press. Reprinted by permission.

Virginia P. Coto, *LUCHA, The Struggle for Life: Legal Services for Battered Immigrant Women*, 53 U. Miami L. Rev. 749, 753–58 (1999). Reprinted by permission of the University of Miami Law Review and Virginia P. Coto.

Charles B. Craver, *Negotiation Ethics: How to Be Deceptive Without Being Dishonest/ How to Be Assertive Without Being Offensive*, 38 S. Tex. L. Rev. 713, 713–34 (1997). Reprinted by permission of the South Texas Law Review and Charles B. Craver.

Kimberlé Crenshaw, *Mapping the Margins: Intersectionality, Identity Politics, and Violence Against Women of Color*, 43 Stan. L. Rev. 1241, 1244–46, 1252–53, 1255–61 (1991). Copyright © 1991 by The Board of Trustees of Leland Stanford Junior University and the Stanford Law Review. Reprinted with permission of the Stanford Law Review in the format Textbook via Copyright Clearance Center.

Paul Hampton Crockett, *A Law School Education: Learning the Vocabulary of Power*, Address delivered at the University of Miami School of Law (1999). Reprinted by permission of Paul Hampton Crockett.

Nathan M. Crystal, *Professional Responsibility: Problems of Practice and the Profession* 1–7 (2d ed. 2000). Reprinted by permission of Nathan M. Crystal.

Scott L. Cummings and Ingrid V. Eagly, *A Critical Reflection on Law and Organizing*, 48 UCLA L. Rev. 443, 443, 460–69, 479–93, 498, 500, 502–17 (2001). Reprinted by permission of Scott L. Cummings and Ingrid V. Eagly.

Karen Syma Czapanskiy, *Parents, Children, and Work-First Welfare Reform: Where Is the C in TANF?*, 61 Md. L. Rev. 308, 314–15, 361–62 (2002). Reprinted by permission of Karen Syma Czapanskiy.

Mary C. Daly, Bruce A. Green, and Russell G. Pearce, *Contextualizing Professional Responsibility: A New Curriculum for a New Century*, 58 Law & Contemp. Probs. 192, 194–98 (1995). Reprinted by permission of Law and Contemporary Problems, Mary C. Daly, Bruce A. Green, and Russell G. Pearce.

Julie Davies, *Federal Civil Rights Practice in the 1990s: The Dichotomy Between Reality and Theory*, 48 Hastings L.J. 197, 207–10, 231–36 (1997). Copyright © 1997 by the University of California, Hastings College of the Law. Reprinted by permission.

Charles E. Daye, Marilyn V. Yarbrough, John O. Calmore, Adrienne D. Davis, and Kevin V. Haynes, *Statement by African-American Faculty of the UNC School of Law Regarding the Visit of Justice Clarence Thomas* (February 28, 2002) (www.unc.edu/student/orgs/blsa/documents/Thomas_Final.pdf). Reprinted by permission of Charles E. Daye, Marilyn V. Yarbrough, John O. Calmore, Adrienne D. Davis, and Kevin V. Haynes.

Nancy A. Denton, *The Persistence of Segregation: Links Between Residential Segregation and School Segregation*, 80 Minn. L. Rev. 795, 819–22 (1996). Reprinted by permission of the Minnesota Law Review and Nancy A. Denton.

Michael Diamond, *Community Lawyering: Revisiting the Old Neighborhood*, 32 Col. Hum. Rts. L. Rev. 67, 67, 75, 89–90, 101, 109–26 (2000). Reprinted by permission of Michael Diamond.

Robert D. Dinerstein, *Client-Centered Counseling: Reappraisal and Refinement*, 32 Ariz. L. Rev. 501, 502–04, 588–89 (1990). Copyright © 1990 by Robert D. Dinerstein. Reprinted by permission.

Jay Dixit, *This Firm Won National Recognition for its Commitment to Providing Affordable Legal Service*, L Magazine, Summer 2001, 9-10. This article is reprinted by permission from the Summer 2001 Edition of L Magazine. Copyright © 2001 NLP IP Company. All Rights Reserved. Further duplication without permission is prohibited.

Elizabeth Dvorkin, Jack Himmelstein, and Howard Lesnik, *Becoming a Lawyer: A Humanistic Perspective on Legal Education and Professionalism* 1-3 (1981). Reprinted by permission of West Group.

John S. Dzienkowski, *Professional Standards, Rules & Statutes* 5-7 (1998). Reprinted by permission of West Group.

James R. Elkins, *The Legal Persona: An Essay on the Professional Mask*, 64 Va. L. Rev. 735, 737, 739-41 (1978). Copyright © 1978 by the Virginia Law Review. Reprinted with permission of the Virginia Law Review in the format Textbook via Copyright Clearance Center and James R. Elkins.

Stephen Ellmann, *Client-Centeredness Multiplied: Individual Autonomy and Collective Mobilization in Public Interest Lawyers' Representation of Groups*, 78 Va. L. Rev. 1103, 1112-13, 1135-39, 1163-66, 1170-73 (1992). Copyright © 1992 by the Virginia Law Review. Reprinted with permission of the Virginia Law Review in the format Textbook via Copyright Clearance Center and Stephen Ellmann.

Russell Engler, *Out of Sight and Out of Line: The Need for Regulation of Lawyers' Negotiations with Unrepresented Poor Persons*, 85 Calif. L. Rev. 79, 79-82, 84, 105-14, 158 (1997). Reprinted by permission of the California Law Review and Russell Engler.

Marc A. Fajer, *A Better Analogy: "Jews," "Homosexuals," and the Inclusion of Sexual Orientation as a Forbidden Characteristic in Antidiscrimination Laws*, 12 Stan. L. & Pol'y Rev. 37, 41, 42-43 (2001). Reprinted by permission of Stanford Law and Policy Review and Marc A. Fajer.

Elizabeth Felter, *A History of the State's Response to Domestic Violence*, in *Feminists Negotiate the State: The Politics of Domestic Violence* 5, 16–19 (Cynthia R. Daniels et al. eds., 1997). Reprinted by permission of the University Press of America.

Martha Albertson Fineman, *Cracking the Foundational Myths: Independence, Autonomy, and Self-Sufficiency,* 8 Am. U. J. Gender Soc. Pol'y & L. 13, 14–29 (1999). Reprinted by permission of the American University Journal of Gender, Social Policy, and the Law and Martha Albertson Fineman.

Linda E. Fisher, *Anatomy of an Affirmative Duty to Protect: 42 U.S.C. Section 1986*, 56 Wash. & Lee L. Rev. 461, 461–64 (1999). Reprinted by permission of the Washington and Lee Law Review and Linda E. Fisher.

Eric Foner, *Reconstruction: America's Unfinished Revolution 1863–1877*, at 50, 51, 68–71, 158–64 (1988). Copyright © 1988 by Eric Foner. Reprinted by permission of Harper Collins Publishers Inc.

William E. Forbath, *Constitutional Welfare Rights: A History, Critique and Reconstruction*, 69 Fordham L. Rev. 1821, 1832–38 (2001). Reprinted by permission of the Fordham Law Review and William E. Forbath.

Sheila Foster, *Justice from the Ground Up: Distributive Inequities, Grassroots Resistance, and the Transformative Politics of the Environmental Justice Movement*, 86 Calif. L. Rev. 775, 776–80, 786–89, 791, 807–11, 826, 838–41 (1998). Copyright © 1998 by the California Law Review. Reprinted by permission.

Jerome Frank, *Why Not A Clinical Lawyer-School?*, 81 U. Penn. L. Rev. 907, 909–11, 916–17, 923 (1933). Copyright © 1933 by the University of Pennsylvania Law Review and William S. Hein & Company. Reprinted by permission.

Darlene Furey, *Foreword*, in *Feminists Negotiate the State: The Politics of Domestic Violence* vii–viii (Cynthia R. Daniels et al. eds., 1997). Reprinted by permission of the University Press of America.

Peter Gabel and Paul Harris, *Building Power and Breaking Images: Critical Legal Theory and the Practice of Law*, 11 N.Y.U. Rev. L. & Soc. Change 369, 375–76, 379–81, 389–94, 405 (1982–83). Reprinted by permission of New York University Review of Law and Social Change, Peter Gabel, and Paul Harris.

Marc Galanter, *Why the "Haves" Come Out Ahead: Speculations on the Limits of Legal Change*, 9 Law & Society Review 95, 95–104, 114–17, 123–24, 149–51 (1974). Reprinted by permission of the Law and Society Association and Marc Galanter. This article was originally published in the Law and Society Review, Vol. 9 (1974). It has recently been republished, with corrections, bibliography, and extended commentary by several authors, in Herbert Kritzer and Susan Silbey, eds., *In Litigation: Do the 'Haves' Still Come Out Ahead?* (Stanford University Press, 2003).

Steven H. Goldberg, *Bringing* The Practice *to the Classroom: An Approach to the Professionalism Problem*, 50 J. Legal Educ. 414, 414–15, 418–21, 429–30 (2000). Copyright © 2000 by the Association of American Law Schools. Reprinted by permission.

Jennifer Gordon, *We Make the Road by Walking: Immigrant Workers, the Workplace Project, and the Struggle for Social Change*, 30 Harv. C.R.–C.L. L. Rev. 407, 428–32 (1995). Copyright © 1995 by the President and Fellows of Harvard College and the Harvard Civil Rights–Civil Liberties Law Review. Reprinted by permission.

William B. Gould IV, *The Idea of Job as Property in Contemporary America: The Legal and Collective Bargaining Framework*, 1986 B.Y.U. L. Rev. 885, 886–87, 892, 900, 902–03, 904–08, 908 (1986). Reprinted by permission of the Brigham Young University Law Review and William B. Gould IV, William M. Ramsey Distinguished Professor of Law, Willamette University College of Law and Charles A. Beardsley Professor of Law, Emeritus, Stanford University Law School.

Joseph R. Grodin, *In Pursuit of Justice: Reflections of a State Supreme Court Justice* 3–10 (1989). Reprinted by permission of Joseph R. Grodin.

Lani Guinier, *Lift Every Voice: Turning a Civil Rights Setback into a New Vision of Social Justice* 68 (1998). Copyright © 1998 by Lani Guinier. Reprinted by permission of Simon and Schuster and Lani Guinier, Bennet Boskey Professor, Harvard Law School.

Lani Guinier, *More Democracy*, 1995 U. Chi. Legal F. 1, 1–22 (1995). Reprinted by permission of Lani Guinier, Bennet Boskey Professor, Harvard Law School.

Robert L. Hale, *Bargaining, Duress, and Economic Liberty*, 43 Colum. L. Rev. 626, 626–28 (1943). Reprinted by permission of the Columbia Law Review.

Janet E. Halley, *Sexual Orientation and the Politics of Biology: A Critique of the Argument from Immutability*, 46 Stan. L. Rev. 503, 528, 567–68 (1994). Copyright © 1994 by The Board of Trustees of Leland Stanford Junior University and the Stanford Law Review. Reprinted by permission of Stanford Law Review in the format Textbook via Copyright Clearance Center and Janet E. Halley.

Joel F. Handler, *"Constructing the Political Spectacle": The Interpretation of Entitlements, Legalization, and Obligations in Social Welfare History*, 56 Brook. L. Rev. 899, 899–922 (1990). Reprinted by permission of the Brooklyn Law Review and Joel F. Handler.

Cheryl Hanna, *No Right to Choose: Mandated Victim Participation in Domestic Violence Prosecutions*, 109 Harv. L. Rev. 1849, 1850–54, 1859–68, 1873, 1892, 1897 (1996). Copyright © 1996 by the Harvard Law Review Association. Reprinted by permission.

Angela P. Harris, *Equality Trouble: Sameness and Difference in Twentieth-Century Race Law*, 88 Cal. L. Rev. 1923, 1931–33 (2000). Copyright © 2000 by the California Law Review. Reprinted by permission.

Paul Harris, *The San Francisco Community Law Collective*, 7 Law & Pol'y 19, 19–27 (1985). Copyright © 1985 by Blackwell Publishing. Reprinted by permission.

Philip Harvey, *Human Rights and Economic Policy Discourse: Taking Economic and Social Rights Seriously*, 33 Colum. Hum. Rts. L. Rev. 363, 371–72, 380–82 (2002). Copyright © 2002 by Philip Harvey. Reprinted by permission.

Geoffrey C. Hazard. Jr., Susan P. Koniak, and Roger C. Crampton, *The Law and Ethics of Lawyering* 3–4 (3d ed. 1999). Reprinted by permission of Foundation Press.

Laura Ho, Catherine Powell, and Leti Volpp, *(Dis)Assembling Rights of Women Workers Along the Global Assembly Line: Human Rights and the Garment Industry*, 31 Harv. C.R.–C.L. L. Rev. 383, 383–400, 405–06, 411–12 (1996). Copyright © 1996 by the President and Fellows of Harvard College and the Harvard Civil Rights–Civil Liberties Law Review. Reprinted by permission.

Sharon K. Hom and Eric K. Yamamoto, *Collective Memory, History, and Social Justice*, 47 UCLA L. Rev. 1747, 1748–50, 1752–54, 1756–59, 1764–65 (2000). Reprinted by permission of Sharon K. Hom and Eric K. Yamamoto.

Nan D. Hunter, *Lawyering for Social Justice*, 72 N.Y.U. L. Rev. 1009, 1011–13, 1017–22 (1997). Reprinted by permission of the New York University Law Review and Nan D. Hunter.

Darren Lenard Hutchinson, *Identity Crisis: "Intersectionality," "Multidimensionality," and the Development of an Adequate Theory of Subordination*, 6 Mich. J. Race & L. 285, 285–88 (2001). Copyright © 2001 by Darren Lenard Hutchinson. Reprinted by permission.

Sherrilyn A. Ifill, *Racial Diversity on the Bench: Beyond Role Models and Public Confidence*, 57 Wash. & Lee L. Rev. 405, 468-69 (2000). Reprinted by permission of the Washington and Lee Law Review and Sherrilyn A. Ifill.

Elizabeth M. Iglesias, *Institutionalizing Economic Justice: A LatCrit Perspective on the Imperatives of Linking the Reconstruction of "Community" to the Transformation of Legal Structures That Institutionalize the Depoliticization and Fragmentation of Labor/Community Solidarity*, 2 U. Pa. J. Lab. & Emp. L. 773, 785-86, 798-99 (2000). Copyright © 2000 by the University of Pennsylvania. Reprinted by permission.

Peter Irons, *Michael Hardwick v. Michael Bowers*, in *The Courage of Their Convictions*, 392-403 (1988). Copyright © 1988 by Peter Irons. Reprinted by permission of The Free Press, a Division of Simon & Schuster Adult Publishing Group.

Michelle S. Jacobs, *People from the Footnotes: The Missing Element in Client-Centered Counseling*, 27 Golden Gate U. L. Rev. 345, 345–48, 377–85, 388–90, 401–02, 409–12 (1997). Reprinted by permission of the Golden Gate University Law Review and Michelle S. Jacobs.

Michelle S. Jacobs, *Pro Bono Work and Access to Justice for the Poor: Real Change or Imagined Change?*, 48 Fla. L. Rev. 509, 513–15, 521 (1996). Copyright © 1999 by the Florida Law Review. Reprinted by permission.

Alex M. Johnson, *The Underrepresentation of Minorities in the Legal Profession: A Critical Race Theorist's Perspective*, 95 Mich. L. Rev. 1005, 1007–08, 1011 (1997). Copyright © 1997 by the Michigan Law Review Association. Reprinted by permission.

Greg Johnson, *Vermont Civil Unions: The New Language of Marriage*, 25 Vt. L. Rev. 15, 20–22, 24–35 (2000). Reprinted by permission of the Vermont Law Review and Greg Johnson.

Justice Earl Johnson, Jr., *Equal Access to Justice: Comparing Access to Justice in the United States and Other Industrial Democracies*, 24 Fordham Int'l L.J. S83, S83–S84, S86, S89, S91, S99–S100 (2000).

Reprinted by permission of the Fordham International Law Journal and Earl Johnson, Jr., Justice, California Court of Appeal and former Professor of Law, University of Southern California.

Pamela S. Karlan, *Nothing Personal: The Evolution of the Newest Equal Protection from* Shaw v. Reno *to* Bush v. Gore, 79 N.C. L. Rev. 1345, 1347–48 (2001). Reprinted by permission of the North Carolina Law Review.

Kenneth L. Karst, *The Coming Crisis of Work in Constitutional Perspective*, 82 Cornell L. Rev. 523, 523–28, 530–32, 534–41, 551–55, 557–58, 570–71 (1997). Reprinted by permission of the Cornell Law Review and Kenneth L. Karst.

Duncan Kennedy, *Legal Education and the Reproduction of Hierarchy: A Polemic Against the System* i–ii (1983). Reprinted by permission of Duncan Kennedy.

William C. Kidder, *Affirmative Action in Higher Education: Recent Developments in Litigation, Admissions and Diversity Research*, 12 Berkeley La Raza L.J. 173, 174–86, 188–90 (2001). Reprinted by permission of the Berkeley La Raza Law Journal and William C. Kidder.

Judith Koons, *Fair Housing and Community Empowerment: Where the Roof Meets Redemption*, 4 Geo. J. on Fighting Poverty 75, 77–90, 92–105, 109, 118–20, 123 (1996). Copyright © 1996 by the Georgetown Journal of Poverty Law and Policy. Reprinted by permission.

Lewis A. Kornhauser and Richard L. Revesz, *Legal Education and Entry into the Legal Profession: The Role of Race, Gender, and Educational Debt*, 70 N.Y.U. L. Rev. 829, 833, 835–36 (1995). Reprinted by permission of the New York University Law Review.

Zenobia Lai, Andrew Leong, and Chi Chi Wu, *The Lessons of the Parcel C Struggle: Reflections on Community Lawyering*, 6 Asian Pac. Am. L. J. 1, 2–3, 23–31, 34 (2000). Reprinted by permission of Zenobia Lai, Andrew Leong, and Chi Chi Wu.

Sylvia A. Law, *Families and Federalism*, 4 Wash. U. J.L. & Pol'y 175, 226–27, 232–33 (2000). Reprinted by permission of the Washington University Journal of Law and Policy and Sylvia A. Law.

Sylvia A. Law, *The Messages of Legal Education*, in *Looking at Law School* 155–57, 168–171 (Stephen Gillers ed., 4th ed. 1997). Copyright © 1997 Society of American Law Teachers. Reprinted by permission of the Society of American Law Teachers and Sylvia A. Law.

Charles R. Lawrence III, *Two Views of the River: A Critique of the Liberal Defense of Affirmative Action*, 101 Colum. L. Rev. 928, 965–66 (2001). Reprinted by permission of the Columbia Law Review and Charles R. Lawrence III.

Nancy K. D. Lemon, *Statutes Creating Rebuttable Presumptions Against Custody to Batterers: How Effective Are They?*, 28 Wm. Mitchell L. Rev. 601, 604–07 (2001). Reprinted by permission of the William Mitchell Law Review and Nancy K. D. Lemon.

Anthony Lewis, *The Quiet of the Storm Center*, 40 S. Tex. L. Rev. 933, 933–39 (1999). Reprinted by permission of the South Texas Law Review and Anthony Lewis.

Jules Lobel, *Losers, Fools & Prophets: Justice as Struggle*, 80 Cornell L. Rev. 1331, 1384–87 (1995). Reprinted by permission of the Cornell Law Review and Jules Lobel.

Gerald P. López, *The Work We Know So Little About*, 42 Stan. L. Rev. 1, 1–2, 6–11 (1989). Copyright © 1989 by The Board of Trustees of Leland Stanford Junior University and the Stanford Law Review. Reprinted with permission of Stanford Law Review in the format Textbook via Copyright Clearance Center and Gerald P. López.

Gerald P. López, *Rebellious Lawyering: One Chicano's Vision of Progressive Law Practice* 11–14, 17–18, 20–21, 23, 30–38 (1992). Copyright © 1992 by Westview Press. Reprinted by permission of Westview Press, a member of Perseus Books, L.L.C.

Catherine A. MacKinnon, *Disputing Male Sovereignty: On* United States v. Morrison, 114 Harv. L. Rev. 135, 136–37, 141–44 (2000). Copyright © 2000 by the Harvard Law Review Association. Reprinted by permission of the Harvard Law Review and Catherine A. MacKinnon.

Martha R. Mahoney, *Victimization or Oppression? Women's Lives, Violence, and Agency*, in *The Public Nature of Private Violence: The Discovery of Domestic Abuse* 59, 60–64, 73–79 (Martha Albertson Fineman & Roxanne Mykitiuk eds., 1994). Copyright © 1994 by Routledge, Inc., part of The Taylor and Francis Group. Reprinted by permission.

Martha R. Mahoney, *Constructing Solidarity: Interest and White Workers*, 2 U. Pa. J. Lab. & Emp. L. 747, 748–51, 763–71 (2000). Reprinted by permission of the University of Pennsylvania Law School Journal of Labor and Employment Law and Martha R. Mahoney.

Martha R. Mahoney, *Segregation, Whiteness, and Transformation*, 143 U. Pa. L. Rev. 1659, 1659–69, 1677–80 (1995). Reprinted by permission of the University of Pennsylvania Law Review and Martha R. Mahoney.

Deborah Maranville, *Changing Economy, Changing Lives: Unemployment Insurance and the Contingent Workforce*, 4 B.U. Pub. Int. L.J. 291, 292–99, 301–02, 330–32, 337 (1995). Reprinted by permission of The Boston University Public Interest Law Journal and Deborah Maranville.

Douglas Massey, *Housing Discrimination 101*, 28 Population Today 1, 4 (Aug. 1, 2000). Reprinted by permission of the Population Reference Bureau.

Mari J. Matsuda, *Beside My Sister, Facing the Enemy: Legal Theory Out of Coalition*, 43 Stan. L. Rev. 1183, 1189–90 (1991). Copyright © 1991 by The Board of Trustees of Leland Stanford Junior University and the Stanford Law Review. Reprinted with permission of the

Stanford Law Review in the format Textbook via Copyright Clearance Center and Mari J. Matsuda.

Daniel J. McDonald, *A Primer on 42 U.S.C. § 1983*, 12 Utah B.J. 29, 29-30 (1999). Reprinted by permission of the Utah Bar Journal and Daniel J. McDonald.

Kevin C. McMunigal, *The Costs of Settlement: The Impact of Scarcity of Adjudication on Litigation Lawyers*, 37 UCLA L. Rev. 833, 844-47, 849-50, 852, 855-70, 872, 875-77, 880-81 (1990). Reprinted by permission of Kevin C. McMunigal.

Carrie Menkel-Meadow, *Aha? Is Creativity Possible in Legal Problem Solving and Teachable in Legal Education?*, 6 Harv. Negotiation L. Rev. 97, 98-99, 109-10, 112-14, 125-34 (2001). Copyright © 2001 by Carrie Menkel-Meadow. Reprinted by permission.

G. Kristian Miccio, *Male Violence—State Silence: These and Other Tragedies of the 20th Century*, 5 J. Gender Race & Just. 339, 346-49, 356-58 (2002). Reprinted by permission of the Journal of Gender, Race, and Just. and G. Kristian Miccio, Professor of Law, University of Denver.

Linda G. Mills, *Killing Her Softly: Intimate Abuse and the Violence of State Intervention*, 113 Harv. L. Rev. 550, 552–56, 563–68, 696, 697, 612 (1999). Copyright © 1999 by the Harvard Law Review Association. Reprinted by permission.

Dale Minami, *Asian Law Caucus: Experiment in an Alternative*, 3 Amerasia Journal 28–36, 38–39 (1975). Reprinted by permission of the UCLA Asian-American Studies Center and Dale Minami.

Martha Minow, *Interpreting Rights: An Essay for Robert Cover*, 96 Yale L.J. 1860, 1866–67 (1987). Reprinted by permission of the Yale Law Journal Company, William S. Hein Company, and Martha Minow.

Martha Minow, *Political Lawyering: An Introduction*, 31 Harv. C.R.–C.L. L. Rev. 287, 287–88 (1996). Copyright © 1996 by the President and Fellows of Harvard College. Reprinted by permission.

Thomas W. Mitchell, *From Reconstruction to Deconstruction: Undermining Black Landownership, Political Independence, and Community Through Partition Sales of Tenancies in Common*, 95 Nw. U. L. Rev. 505, 526–27 (2001). Reprinted by special permission of the Northwestern University School of Law, *Law Review* and Thomas W. Mitchell.

Raymond A. Mohl, *Planned Destruction: The Interstates and Central City Housing* in *From Tenements to the Taylor Homes: In Search of an Urban Housing Policy* 226–29, 236–41 (John F. Bauman et al. eds., 2000). Copyright © 2000 by the Pennsylvania State University. Reprinted by permission.

Carolyn Jin-Myung Oh, *Questioning the Cultural and Gender-Based Assumptions of the Adversary System: Voices of Asian-American Law Students*, 7 Berkeley Women's L.J. 125, 125–127, 129–132, 167–172

(1992–93). Copyright © 1992 by the Berkeley Women's Law Journal. Reprinted by permission of the University of California, Berkeley.

Melvin Oliver, *The Social Construction of Racial Privilege in the United States: An Asset Perspective* in *Beyond Racism: Race and Inequality in Brazil, South Africa and the United States* 251, 255, 258–59 (Charles V. Hamilton, Lynn Huntley & Neville Alexander eds., 2001). Copyright © 2001 by The Southern Education Foundation, Inc. Reprinted by permission of Lynne Rienner Publishers, Inc.

Nancy K. Ota, *Queer Recount*, 64 Alb. L. Rev. 889, 893–96 (2001). Reprinted by permission of the Albany Law Review and Nancy K. Ota.

Nancy D. Polikoff, *Am I My Client? The Role Confusion of a Lawyer Activist*, 31 Harv. C.R.–C.L. L. Rev. 443, 443–52, 458–65, 470–71 (1996). Copyright © 1996 by the President and Fellows of Harvard College and the Harvard Civil Rights-Civil Liberties Law Review. Reprinted by permission.

Francesca Polletta, *The Structural Context of Novel Rights Claims: Southern Civil Rights Organizing, 1961–1966*, 34 L. & Soc'y Rev. 367, 367–78, 377–78 (2000). Copyright © 2000 by The Law and Society Association. Reprinted by permission of the Law and Society Association and Francesca Polletta.

Robert C. Post and Reva B. Siegel, *Equal Protection by Law: Federal Antidiscrimination Legislation after* Morrison *and* Kimel, 110 Yale L.J. 441, 441–44, 446–55, 474–77, 481–82, 485–86, 496–97, 501–02, 506, 508, 523–26 (2000). Reprinted by permission of the Yale Law Journal Company, William S. Hein Company, Robert C. Post, and Reva B. Siegel.

john a. powell, *The Tensions Between Integration and School Reform*, 28 Hastings Const. L.Q. 655, 660–65, 667–71, 681–85, 695–97 (2001). Copyright © 2001 by University of California, Hastings College of the Law. Reprinted by permission.

Fran Quigley, *Seizing the Disorienting Moment: Adult Learning Theory and the Teaching of Social Justice in Law School Clinics*, 2 Clinical L. Rev. 37, 37–39, 46–47, 51–52, 57, 59–60, 62–64, 72 (1995). Reprinted by permission of the Clinical Law Review and Fran Quigley.

William P. Quigley, *The Demise of Law Reform and the Triumph of Legal Aid: Congress and the Legal Services Corporation from the 1960's to the 1990's*, 17 St. Louis U. Pub. L. Rev. 241, 241–46, 248, 250–51, 253–56, 259–64 (1998). Copyright © 1998 by St. Louis University School of Law, St. Louis, Missouri. Reprinted by permission of the Saint Louis University Public Law Review and William P. Quigley.

William P. Quigley, *Reflections of Community Organizers: Lawyering for Empowerment of Community Organizations*, 21 Ohio N.U. L. Rev. 455, 455–79 (1994). Reprinted by permission of the Ohio Northern University Law Review and William P. Quigley.

Charles A. Reich, *Beyond the New Property: An Ecological View of Due Process*, 56 Brook. L. Rev. 731, 731–45 (1990). Reprinted by permission of the Brooklyn Law Review.

Judith Resnik, *Trial as Error, Jurisdiction as Injury: Transforming the Meaning of Article III*, 113 Harv. L. Rev. 924, 926–27, 969, 974–76, 993–95, 1003–08, 1035 (2000). Copyright © 2000 by the Harvard Law Review Association. Reprinted by permission.

Deborah L. Rhode, *Access to Justice*, 69 Fordham L. Rev. 1786–88, 1790–98, 1804–06, 1808, 1814–19 (2001). Reprinted by permission of the Fordham Law Review and Deborah L. Rhode.

Deborah L. Rhode, *Cultures of Commitment: Pro Bono for Lawyers and Law Students*, 67 Fordham L. Rev. 2415, 2419–23 (1999). Reprinted by permission of the Fordham Law Review and Deborah L. Rhode.

Deborah L. Rhode, *Professional Responsibility: Ethics by the Pervasive Method* 4–8 (1994). Reprinted by permission of Deborah L. Rhode. *See also* Deborah L. Rhode, *Professional Responsibility: Ethics by the Pervasive Method* 4–7 (2nd ed. 1998).

Jenny Rivera, *The Violence Against Women Act and the Construction of Multiple Consciousness in the Civil Rights and Feminist Movements*, 4 J.L. & Pol'y 463, 464–66, 492–97, 503–08, 510–11 (1996). Reprinted by permission of the Journal of Law and Policy and Jenny Rivera.

Dean Hill Rivkin, *Reflections on Lawyering for Reform: Is the Highway Alive Tonight?*, 64 Tenn. L. Rev. 1065, 1065–69, 1072 (1997). Reprinted by permission of the Tennessee Law Review Association, Inc. and Dean Hill Rivkin.

Dorothy E. Roberts, *Welfare and the Problem of Black Citizenship*, 105 Yale L.J. 1563, 1569–74, 1576, 1578, 1588–91 (1996). Reprinted by permission of the Yale Law Journal Company, William S. Hein Company, and Dorothy E. Roberts.

Florence Wagman Roisman, *Teaching About Inequality, Race, and Property*, 46 St. Louis U. L. J. 665, 667–86 (2002). Reprinted by permission of the St. Louis University Law Journal and Florence Wagman Roisman.

Daria Roithmayr, *Deconstructing the Distinction Between Bias and Merit*, 85 Calif. L. Rev. 1449, 1452, 1475–92 (1997). Copyright © 1997 by the California Law Review. Reprinted by permission.

William B. Rubenstein, *Divided We Litigate: Addressing Disputes Among Group Members and Lawyers in Civil Rights Campaigns*, 106 Yale L.J. 1623, 1623–33, 1635–44, 1680 (1997). Reprinted by permission of the Yale Law Journal Company, William S. Hein Company, and William B. Rubenstein.

Margaret M. Russell, *McLaurin's Seat: The Need for Racial Inclusion in Legal Education*, 70 Fordham L. Rev. 1825, 1827–28 (2002). Copyright © 2002 by the Fordham Law Review. Reprinted by permission.

Joan E. Schaffner, *Approaching the New Millenium with Mixed Blessings for Harassed Gay Students*, 22 Harv. Women's L.J. 159, 159–61, 164, 171–76 (1999). Copyright © 1999 by the President and Fellows of Harvard College and the Harvard Women's Law Journal. Reprinted by permission.

Patrick J. Schiltz, *On Being a Happy, Healthy, and Ethical Member of an Unhappy, Unhealthy, and Unethical Profession*, 52 Vand. L. Rev. 871, 871–73, 881–920 (1999). Copyright © 1999 by Vanderbilt Law Review. Reprinted by permission of the Vanderbilt Law Review and Patrick J. Schiltz.

Elizabeth M. Schneider, *Battered Women and Feminist Lawmaking* 21–24, 27–28 (2001). Copyright © 2001 by the Yale University Press. Reprinted by permission.

Elizabeth M. Schneider, *Resistance to Equality*, 57 U. Pitt. L. Rev. 477, 483, 488, 489–90 495–99, 505–08 (1996). Reprinted by permission of the University of Pittsburgh Law Review and Elizabeth M. Schneider.

Vicki Schultz, *Life's Work*, 100 Colum. L. Rev. 1881, 1883–86, 1914–16, 1930–38 (2000). Copyright © 2000 by Vicki Schultz. Reprinted by permission.

William H. Simon, *Lawyer Advice and Client Autonomy: Mrs. Jones's Case*, 50 Md. L. Rev. 213, 213–16, 222–26 (1991). Reprinted by permission of William H. Simon.

Joseph William Singer, *The Reliance Interest in Property*, 40 Stan. L. Rev. 611, 611, 664, 699, 711–12, 750–51 (1988). Copyright © 1988 by The Board of Trustees of Leland Stanford Junior University and the Stanford Law Review. Reproduced with permission of Stanford Law Review in the format Textbook via Copyright Clearance Center and Joseph William Singer.

Gregory C. Sisk, *A Primer on Awards of Attorney's Fees Against the Federal Government*, 25 Ariz. St. L.J. 733, 739, 740–42, 748, 750–51, 757, 760, 764 (1993). Reprinted by permission of Gregory C. Sisk.

Mark Spiegel, *The Case of Mrs. Jones Revisited: Paternalism and Autonomy in Lawyer-Client Counseling*, 1997 B.Y.U. L. Rev. 307, 315–20, 332–38 (1997). Reprinted by permission of the Brigham Young University Law Review and Mark Spiegel.

Clyde Spillenger, *Elusive Advocate: Reconsidering Brandeis as People's Lawyer*, 105 Yale L.J. 1445, 1448–49, 1528–29 (1996). Reprinted by permission of the Yale Law Journal Company, William S. Hein Company, and Clyde Spillenger.

Evan Stark, *Mandatory Arrest of Batterers, A Reply to Its Critics*, in *Do Arrests and Restraining Orders Work?*, 115, 120–24, 145 (Eve S. Buzawa & Carl G. Buzawa eds., 1996). Copyright © 1996 by Sage Publications, Inc. Reprinted by permission.

Thomas B. Stoddard, *Bleeding Heart: Reflections on Using the Law to Make Social Change*, 72 N.Y.U. L. Rev. 967, 969–89, 990–91 (1997). Reprinted by permission of New York University Law Review.

Julie A. Su, *Making the Invisible Visible: The Garment Industry's Dirty Laundry*, 1 J. Gender Race & Just. 405, 405–17 (1998). Reprinted by permission of the Journal of Gender, Race, and Justice and Julie A. Su.

Louise Trubek, *Embedded Practices: Lawyers, Clients, and Social Change*, 31 Harv. C.R.–C.L L. Rev. 415, 418–25, 428–33, 436–37 (1996). Copyright © 1996 by the President and Fellows of Harvard College and the Harvard Civil Rights Civil Liberties Law Review. Reprinted by permission.

Louise Trubek and Jennifer J. Farnham, *Social Justice Collaboratives: Multidisciplinary Practices for People*, 7 Clinical L. Rev. 227, 228–29 (2000). Reprinted by permission of the Clinical Law Review, Louise Trubek, and Jennifer J. Farnham.

David S. Udell, *The Legal Services Restrictions: Lawyers in Florida, New York, Virginia, and Oregon Describe the Costs*, 17 Yale L. & Pol'y Rev. 337, 338, 357–60, 363–64 (1998). Reprinted by permission of the Yale Law and Policy Review and David S. Udell.

Urvashi Vaid, *Virtual Equality* 37–38, 141–43, 146. Copyright © 1995 by Urvashi Vaid. Reprinted by permission of Doubleday, a division of Random House, Inc.

Francisco Valdes, *Sexual Minorities in the Military: Charting the Constitutional Frontiers of Status and Conduct*, 27 Creighton L. Rev. 381, 406–11 (1994). Copyright © 1994 by Creighton University. Reprinted by permission.

Richard Wasserstrom, *Lawyers and Revolution*, 30 U. Pitt. L. Rev. 125, 129–33 (1968). Reprinted by permission of the University of Pittsburgh Law Review and Richard Wasserstrom.

Richard Wasserstrom, *Lawyers as Professionals: Some Moral Issues*, 5 Human Rights 1, 2–3, 5–6, 8, 13, 17–18, 21 (1975). Copyright © 1975 by the American Bar Association. Reprinted by permission.

Peter D. Webster, *Selection and Retention of Judges: Is There One "Best" Method?*, 23 Fla. St. U. L. Rev. 1, 35–36 (1995). Copyright © 1995 by the Florida State University Law Review. Reprinted by permission.

Margaret Weir, *Politics and Jobs: The Boundaries of Employment Policy in the United States*, 131, 134–36 (1992). Copyright © 1992 by Princeton University Press. Reprinted by permission.

Robin West, *Rights, Capabilities, and the Good Society*, 69 Fordham L. Rev. 1901, 1901–05 (2001). Copyright © 2001 by the Fordham Law Review. Reprinted by permission.

Gerald B. Wetlaufer, *The Ethics of Lying in Negotiation*, 75 Iowa L. Rev. 1219, 1220–21, 1223–24, 1272 (1990). Reprinted by permission of the Iowa Law Review and Gerald B. Wetlaufer.

Lucie E. White, *To Learn and Teach: Lessons from Driefontein on Lawyering and Power*, 1988 Wis. L. Rev. 699, 747–52, 754–65, 768–69. Copyright © 1988 by the Board of Regents of the University of Wisconsin System. Reprinted by permission of the Wisconsin Law Review and Lucie E. White.

Lucie White, *Symposium, Constitutional Lawyering in the 21st Century, March 4, 2000, Panel Three: Creating Models for Progressive Lawyering in the 21st Century*, 9 J.L. & Pol'y 297, 309–10 (2000). Reprinted by permission of the Journal of Law and Policy and Lucie White.

Stephanie M. Wildman, *The Classroom Climate*, in *Looking at Law School* 75–76, 89 (Stephen Gillers ed., 4th ed.1997). Copyright © 1997 Society of American Law Teachers. Reprinted by permission of the Society of American Law Teachers and Stephanie M. Wildman.

Joan Williams, *Do Women Need Special Treatment? Do Feminists Need Equality?*, 9 J. Contemp. Legal Issues 279, 288–91 (1998). Copyright © 1998 San Diego Law Review. Reprinted by permission.

Marilyn V. Yarbrough, *Minority Students and Debt: Limiting Limited Career Options*, 39 J. Legal Educ. 697, 697–701, 703–07 (1989). Copyright © 1989 by the Association of American Law Schools. Reprinted by permission.

Robert Yazzie, *"Hozho Nahasdlii"—We Are Now in Good Relations: Navajo Restorative Justice*, 9 St. Thomas L. Rev. 117, 119–20, 123–24 (1996). Reprinted by permission of the St. Thomas Law Review.

Iris Marion Young, *Justice and the Politics of Difference* 15–16 (1990). Copyright © 1990 by Princeton University Press. Reprinted by permission.

Joan Zorza, *The Criminal Law of Misdemeanor Domestic Violence*, 83 J. Crim. L. & Criminology 46, 47–54, 56–60 (1992). Reprinted by permission of Joan Zorza.

Christine Zuni Cruz, *[On The] Road Back In: Community Lawyering in Indigenous Communities*, 24 Am. Indian L. Rev. 229, 229–31 (2000). Reprinted by permission of the Clinical Law Review and Christine Zuni Cruz. Originally published in 5 Clinical Law Review 557 (1999).

*

Summary of Contents

*

Table of Contents

Table of Cases

The principal cases are in bold type. Cases cited or discussed in the text are roman type. References are to pages. Cases cited in principal cases and within other quoted materials are not included.

*

Table of Authorities

Ansley, Fran, Standing Rusty And Rolling Empty: Law, Poverty, and America's Eroding Industrial Base, 81 Geo. L.J. 1757 (1993), 467

Ansley, Frances Lee, Race and the Core Curriculum in Legal Education, 79 Cal. L. Rev. 1511 (1991), 856

Aoki, Keith, Space Invaders: Critical Geography, the "Third World" in International Law and Critical Race Theory. 45 Vill. L. Rev. 913 (2000), **880**, 884

Aristotle, The Ethics (E.V. Riev ed., J.A.K. Thomson trans., 1955), 49

Armstrong, Margalynne, Desegregation through Private Litigation: Using Equitable Remedies to Achieve the Purposes of the Fair Housing Act, 64 Temp. L. Rev. 909 (1991), 876

Armstrong, Margalynne, Privilege in Residential Housing, in Stephanie M. Wildman with contributions by Margalynne Armstrong, Adrienne D. Davis & Trina Grillo, Privilege Revealed: How Invisible Preference Undermines America (1996), 843

Armstrong, Margalynne, Race and Property Values in Entrenched Segregation, 52 U. Miami L. Rev. 1051 (1998), 878

Aron, Nan, Liberty and Justice for All: Public Interest Law in the 1980s and Beyond (1989), 3, 4

Arthurs, Harry, Reinventing Labor Law for the Global Economy, 22 Berkeley J. Employment & Lab. L. 271 (2001), 481

Atkinson, A.B., Social Justice and Public Policy (1983), 59

Auerbach, Jerold S., Unequal Justice: Lawyers and Social Change in Modern America (1976), **10**

Austin, Regina, Nest Eggs and Stormy Weather: Law, Culture, and Black Women's Lack of Wealth, 65 U. Cin. L. Rev. 767 (1997), 434

Bachmann, Steve, The Hollow Hope: Can Courts Bring About Social Change?, 19 N.Y.U. Rev. L. & Soc. Change 391 (1992), 790

Baker, Lynn, Bargaining for Public Assistance, 72 Denv. U. L. Rev. 949 (1995), 109

Balkin, Jack M., Bush v. Gore and the Boundary Between Law and Politics, 110 Yale L.J. 1407, 1407 (2001), 724

Balkin, Jack M. & Sanford Levinson, Understanding the Constitutional Revolution, 87 Va. L. Rev. 1045 (2001), **715**

Balos, Beverly & Mary Louise Fellows, Law and Violence Against Women: Cases and Materials on Systems of Oppression (1994), 1120

Bandes, Susan, The Negative Constitution: A Critique, 88 Mich. L. Rev. 2271 (1990), 530

Barndt, Joseph, Dismantling Racism: The Continuing Challenge to White America 83 (1991), 877

Baron, Jane B. & Richard K. Greenstein, Constructing the Field of Professional Responsibility, 15 Notre Dame J.L. Ethics & Pub. Pol'y 37 (2001), 335

Basseches, Michael, Dialectical Thinking and Adult Development (1984), 224

Bastress, Robert M. & Joseph D. Harbaugh, Interviewing, Counseling, and Negotiating: Skills for Effective Representation (1990), 277, **407**, 408

Baynes, Leonard M., The Haywood Burns/Shanara Gilbert Award, 31 New Eng. L. Rev. 967 (1997), 43

Beck, Paula, Fighting Section 8 Discrimination: The Fair Housing Act's New Frontier, 31 Harv. C.R.-C.L. L. Rev. 155 (1996), 878

Becker, Mary, Caring for Children and Caretakers, 76 Chi.-Kent L. Rev. 1495 (2001), 539, 540

Becker, Mary E., Double Binds Facing Mothers in Abusive Families: Social Support Systems, Custody Outcomes, and Liability for Acts of Others, 2 U. Chi. L. Sch. Roundtable 13 (1995), **1092**

Been, Vicki, Locally Undesirable Land Uses in Minority Neighborhoods: Disproportionate Sting or Market Dynamics?, 103 Yale L.J. 1383 (1994), 902

Bell, Derrick A., Jr., Brown v. Board of Education and the Interest–Convergence Dilemma, 93 Harv. L. Rev. 518 (1980), 874

Bell, Derrick, Ethical Ambition: Living a Life of Meaning and Worth (2002), 213

Bell, Derrick, "Here Come de Judge": The Role of Faith in Progressive Decision–Making, 51 Hastings L.J. 1 (1999), 705

Bell, Derrick, Race, Racism and American Law (4th ed. 2000), 194, 425

Bell, Derrick A., Jr., Serving Two Masters: Integration Ideals and Client Interests in School Desegregation Litigation, 85 Yale L.J. 470 (1976), 183, 184, **328**

Bellow, Gary, Steady Work: A Practitioner's Reflections on Political Lawyering, 31 Harv. C.R.-C.L. L. Rev. 297 (1996), 277, **309**, 312

Bellow, Gary, Turning Solutions into Problems: The Legal Aid Experience, 34 NLADA Briefcase 106 (1977), 171

Bellow, Gary & Bea Moulton, The Lawyering Process: Materials for Clinical Instruction in Advocacy (1978), 156, 245, 246, 272

Bennett, Susan, Little Engines That Could: Community Clients, Their Lawyers, and Training in the Arts of Democracy, 2002 Wis. L. Rev. 469, 930

Bernstein, Nina, In Control Group, Most Welfare Recipients Left the Rolls Even

Without Reform, N.Y. Times, Feb. 20, 2002, at B5, 558

Beschle, Donald L., The Supreme Court's IOLTA Decision: Of Dogs, Mangers, and the Ghost of Mrs. Frothingham, 30 Seton Hall L. Rev. 846 (2000), 112, 113, 114

Bezdek, Barbara L., Contractual Welfare: Non-Accountability and Diminished Democracy in Local Government Contracts for Welfare-to-Work Services, 28 Fordham Urb. L.J. 1599 (2001), 558

Bezdek, Barbara, Silence in the Court: Participation and Subordination of Poor Tenants' Voices in Legal Process, 20 Hofstra L. Rev. 533 (1992), 73

Binder, David & Susan Price, Legal Interviewing and Counseling: A Client-Centered Approach (1977), 272

Binder, David A., Paul Bergman & Susan C. Price, Lawyers as Counselors: A Client Centered Approach (1991), **273**

"Black Power"—A Statement by the National Committee of Negro Churchmen, July 31, 1966, in The Black Power Revolt (Floyd B. Barbour ed., 1968), 390

Blasi, Gary, Advocacy and Attribution: Shaping and Responding to Perceptions of the Causes of Homelessness, 19 St. Louis U. Pub. L. Rev. 207 (2000), 803

Blasi, Gary, The Homeless Seminar at U.C.L.A., 42 Wash. U.J. Urb. & Contemp. L. 85, 86 (1992), 209

Bloch, Frank S., The Andragogical Basis of Clinical Legal Education, 35 Vand. L. Rev. 321 (1982), 223

Blocker, H. Gener & Elizabeth H. Smith, Preface to John Rawls' Theory of Social Justice: An Introduction (H. Gene Blocker & Elizabeth H. Smith eds., 1980), 59

Boger, Charles, Race and the American City: The Kerner Commission Report, in Race, Poverty, and American Cities (John Charles Boger & Judith Welch Wegner eds., 1996), 840

Bok, Marcia, Civil Rights and the Social Programs of the 1960s: The Social Justice Functions of Social Policy 15 (1992), 49, 59

Booker, Salih & William Minter, Global Apartheid, The Nation, July 9, 2001, at 11, 856

Bork, Robert, Civil Rights—A Challenge, The New Republic, Aug. 31, 1963, at 22, 845

Bowman, Cynthia Grant & Eden Kusmiersky, Praxis and Pedagogy: Domestic Violence, 32 Loy. L.A. L. Rev. 719 (1999), 1048

Boxill, Bernard R., Blacks and Social Justice (revised ed., 1992), 59

Branch, Taylor, Parting the Waters: America in the King Years 1954–63 (1988), 577

Breemer, J. David, IOLTA in the New Millenium: Slowly Sinking Under the Weight of the Takings Clause, 23 U. Haw. L. Rev. 221 (2000), 112

Brennan, William J., Jr., State Constitutions and the Protection of Individual Rights, 90 Harv. L. Rev. 489 (1977), 624, 694

Brest, Paul & Linda Hamilton Krieger, Lawyers as Problem Solvers, 72 Temp. L. Rev. 811 (1999), **367**

Bright, Stephen B., Political Attacks on the Judiciary: Can Justice Be Done Amid Efforts to Intimidate and Remove Judges from Office for Unpopular Decisions?, 72 N.Y.U. L. Rev. 308 (1997), 696

Brittain, John C., Direct Democracy by the Majority Can Jeopardize the Civil Rights of Minority or Other Powerless Groups, 1996 Ann. Surv. Am. L. 441, 635

Brittain, John C., Educational and Racial Equity Toward the Twenty-First Century—A Case Experiment in Connecticut, in Race in America: The Struggle For Equality (Herbert Hill & James E. Jones, Jr. eds., 1993), 635

Brittain, John C., Why Sheff v. O'Neill Is a Landmark Decision, 30 Conn. L. Rev. 211 (1997), 635

Bronfenbrenner, Kate, Final Report: The Effects of Plant Closing or Threat of Plant Closing on the Right of Workers to Organize (September 30, 1996), 479

Brookfield, Stephen, Developing Critical Thinking (1987), 223

Brooks, Rachelle, Feminists Negotiate the Legislative Branch: The Violence Against Women Act, in Feminists Negotiate the State: The Politics of Domestic Violence (Cynthia R. Daniels et al. eds, 1997), 1062, 1068, 1069

Brophy, Alfred L., The World of Reparations: Slavery Reparations in Historical Perspective, 3 J.L. & Soc'y 105 (2002), 929

Broun, Kenneth S., Black Lawyers, White Courts: The Soul of South African Law (2000), 226

Brown, Dorothy A., The LSAT Sweepstakes, 2 J. Gender Race & Just. 59 (1998), 646

Bryan, Penelope Eileen, Women's Freedom to Contract at Divorce: A Mask For Contextual Coercion, 47 Buff. L. Rev. 1153 (1999), 1099

Bryan, Sophie, Personally Professional: A Law Student in Search of an Advocacy Model, 35 Harv. C.R.-C.L. L. Rev. 277 (2000), 193, 345

Bryant, Susan, The Five Habits: Building Cross-Cultural Competence in Lawyers, 8 Clinical L. Rev. 33 (2001), 287

Buchanan, Ruth Margaret, Context, Continuity, and Difference in Poverty Law

Gaventa, John, Power and Powerlessness: Quiescence and Rebellion in an Appalachian Valley (1980), 792

Geoghegan, Thomas, Which Side Are You On?: Trying to Be for Labor When It's Flat on Its Back (1992), 170, 469

George, Tracey E., Court Fixing, 43 Ariz. L. Rev. 9 (2001), 695

Gilkerson, Christopher P., Poverty Law Narrative: The Critical Practice and Theory of Receiving and Translating Client Stories, 43 Hastings L.J. 861 (1992), 156

Gilman, Michele Estrin, Legal Accountability in an Era of Privatized Welfare, 89 Cal. L. Rev. 569 (2001), 519

Glater, Jonathan D., Law Firms Are Slow In Promoting Minority Lawyers to Partner Role, N.Y. Times, Aug. 7, 2001, at A1, C2, 267

Goldberg, Steven H., Bringing The Practice to the Classroom: An Approach to the Professionalism Problem, 50 J. of Legal Educ. 414 (2000), **340**, 345

Goldfarb, Phyllis, A Theory–Practice Spiral: The Ethics of Feminism and Clinical Education, 75 Minn. L. Rev. 1599 (1991), 355

Goldfarb, Sally F., "No Civilized System of Justice": The Fate of The Violence Against Women Act, 102 W. Va. L. Rev. 499 (2000), 1068

Goldman, Sheldon, Picking Federal Judges: Lower Court Selection From Roosevelt Through Reagan (1997), 694

Gondolf, Edward N. & Ellen R. Fisher, Battered Women as Survivors: An Alternative to Treating Learned Helplessness (1988), 1053

Goodman, Diane, Promoting Diversity and Social Justice: Educating People from Privileged Groups (2000), 58

Gordon, Jennifer, We Make the Road by Walking: Immigrant Workers, the Workplace Project, and the Struggle for Social Change, 30 Harv. C.R.-C.L. L. Rev. 407 (1995), **819**

Gorman, Robert A., Assessing and Reforming the Current Law School Curriculum, 30 N.Y. L. Sch. L. Rev. 609 (1985), 223

Gould, William B., IV, The Idea of the Job as Property in Contemporary America: The Legal and Collective Bargaining Framework, 1986 B.Y.U. L. Rev. 885 (1986), **468**

Granfield, Robert, Making Elite Lawyers: Visions of Law at Harvard and Beyond (1992), 17, 62

Greenberg, Mark, Welfare Restructuring and Working–Poor Family Policy: The New Context, in Hard Labor, Women and Work in the Post–Welfare Era (Joel F. Handler & Lucie White eds., 1999), 549, 550

Grillo, Trina, The Mediation Alternative: Process Dangers for Women, 100 Yale L.J. 1545 (1991), 420

Grillo, Trina & Stephanie M. Wildman, Obscuring the Importance of Race: The Implication of Making Comparisons Between Racism and Sexism (or Other-Isms), in Stephanie M. Wildman with contributions by Margalynne Armstrong, Adrienne D. Davis & Trina Grillo, Privilege Revealed: How Invisible Preference Undermines America (1996), 1027

Grodin, Joseph R., Pursuit of Justice: Reflections of a State Supreme Court Justice (1989), **702**, 705

Guill, Terenia Urban, Environmental Justice Suits Under the Fair Housing Act, 12 Tul. Envtl. L.J. 189 (1998), 874, 878, 902

Guinier, Lani, Lift Every Voice: Turning a Civil Rights Setback into a New Vision of Social Justice (1998), **10**, 391, 392, 578

Guinier, Lani, More Democracy, 1995 U. Chi. Legal F. 1, **598**

Guinier, Lani, Michelle Fine, & Jane Balin, Becoming Gentlemen: Women, Law School, and Institutional Change (1997), 27

Guinier, Lani & Gerald Torres, The Miner's Canary: Enlisting Race, Resisting Power, Transforming Democracy (2002), 390, 804

Haddon, Phoebe A., Coalescing With SALT: A Taste for Inclusion, 11 S. Cal. Rev. Law & Women's Stud. 321 (2002), 56, 206

Hafetz, Jonathan L., Almost Homeless, Legal Affairs, July–August 2002, at 11, 73

Hair, Penda D., Louder than Words: Lawyers, Communities and the Struggle for Justice (A Report to the Rockefeller Foundation, 2001), 2, 4, 497

Hale, Robert L., Bargaining, Duress, and Economic Liberty, 43 Colum. L. Rev. 603 (1943), 54

Halley, Janet E., Don't: A Reader's Guide to the Military's Anti–Gay Policy (1999), 971

Halley, Janet E., Reasoning about Sodomy: Act and Identity in and After Bowers v. Hardwick, 79 Va. L. Rev. 1721 (1993), 959

Halley, Janet E., Romer v. Hardwick, 68 U. Colo. L. Rev. 429 (1997), 996

Halley, Janet E., Sexual Orientation and the Politics of Biology: A Critique of the Argument from Immutability, 46 Stan. L. Rev. 503 (1994), 982

Handler, Joel F., "Constructing the Political Spectacle": The Interpretation of Entitlements, Legalization, and Obligations in Social Welfare History, 56 Brook. L. Rev. 899 (1990), **498**

Handler, Joel F., Questions about Social Europe by an American Observer, 18 Wis. Int'l L.J. 437 (2000), 49

Handler, Joel F., Welfare Reform: Is it for Real?, 3 Loy. Poverty L.J. 135 (1997), 551

Handler, Joel F., Welfare-to-Work: Reform or Rhetoric?, 50 Admin. L. Rev. 635 (1998), 558

Handler, Joel F. & Yeheskel Hasenfeld, We the Poor People: Work, Poverty, and Welfare (1997), 551

Haney López, Ian F., Institutional Racism: Judicial Conduct and a New Theory of Racial Discrimination, 109 Yale L.J. 1717 (2000), 877

Hanna, Cheryl, No Right to Choose: Mandated Victim Participation in Domestic Violence Prosecutions, 109 Harv. L. Rev. 1849 (1996), **1070**

Harden, Blaine & Sandra Torry, N.Y. Law Firm to Advise Swiss Bank Accused of Laundering Nazi Loot, Wash. Post, Feb. 28, 1997, at 3, 269

Harris, Angela P., Equality Trouble: Sameness and Difference in Twentieth-Century Race Law, 88 Cal. L. Rev. 1923 (2000), **424**

Harris, Angela P., Race and Essentialism in Feminist Legal Theory, 42 Stan. L. Rev. 581 (1990), 235

Harris, Angela, Reforming Alone?, 54 Stan. L. Rev.1449 (2002), 270

Harris Angela P. & Marjorie M. Shultz, "A(nother) Critique of Pure Reason": Toward Civic Virtue in Legal Education, 45 Stan. L. Rev. 1773 (1993), 23, 24

Harris, Cheryl I., Whiteness as Property, 106 Harv. L. Rev. 1709 (1993), **874**

Harris, Paul, The San Francisco Community Law Collective, 7 Law & Policy 19 (1985), **131**

Hart, Barbara J., Gentle Jeopardy: The Further Endangerment of Battered Women and Children in Custody Mediation, 7 Mediation Q. 317 (1990), 1054

Harvey, Alice E., Comment, Ex-Felon Disenfranchisement and Its Influence on the Black Vote: The Need for a Second Look, 142 U. Pa. L. Rev. 1145 (1994), 596

Harvey, David, Class Relations, Social Justice and the Politics of Difference, in Place and the Politics of Identity (Michael Keith & Steve Pile eds., 1993), 839

Harvey, Philip, Human Rights and Economic Policy Discourse: Taking Economic and Social Rights Seriously, 33 Colum. Hum. Rts. L. Rev. 363 (2002), 480

Havard, Cassandra Jones, African-American Farmers and Fair Lending: Racializing Rural Economic Space, 12 Stan. L. & Pol'y Rev. 333 (2001), 878

Havard, Cassandra Jones, Invisible Markets Netting Visible Results: When Sub-Prime Lending Becomes Predatory, 26 Okla. City U. L. Rev. 1057 (2001), 878

Hazard, Geoffrey C., Jr., After Legal Aid Is Abolished, 2 J. Inst. for Study Legal Ethics 375 (1999), 71

Hazard, Geoffrey C., Jr., Ethics in the Practice of Law (1978), 236

Hazard, Geoffrey C., Jr., Law and Justice in the Twenty-First Century, 70 Fordham L. Rev. 1739 (2002), 49

Hazard, Geoffrey C., Jr., Susan P. Koniak & Roger C. Crampton, The Law and Ethics of Lawyering (3d ed., 1999), 236, 344, **346**

Heinz, John P. & Edward O. Laumann, Chicago Lawyers: The Social Structure of the Bar (1982), 265

Heise, Michael, State Constitutions, School Finance Litigation, and the "Third Wave": From Equity to Adequacy, 68 Temp. L. Rev. 1511 (1995), 624

Henderson, Lynne N., Legality and Empathy, 85 Mich. L. Rev. 1574 (1987), 956

Herman, G. Nicholas, Jean M. Cary & Joseph E. Kennedy, Legal Counseling and Negotiating: A Practical Approach (2001), 271

Higginbotham, A. Leon, Jr., An Open Letter to Justice Clarence Thomas from a Federal Judicial Colleague, 140 U. Pa. L. Rev. 1005 (1992), 725

Hing, Bill Ong, In the Interest of Racial Harmony: Revisiting the Lawyer's Duty to Work for the Common Good, 47 Stan. L. Rev. 901 (1995), 194

Ho, Laura, Catherine Powell & Leti Volpp, (Dis)Assembling Rights of Women Workers along the Global Assembly Line: Human Rights and the Garment Industry, 31 Harv. C.R.-C.L. L. Rev. 383 (1996), **490**

Hochschild, Jennifer L., Facing Up to the American Dream: Race, Class and the Soul of the Nation (1995), 875

Hom, Sharon K. & Eric K. Yamamoto, Collective Memory, History, and Social Justice, 47 UCLA L. Rev. 1747 (2000), **444**

hooks, bell, Theory as Liberatory Practice, 4 Yale J.L. & Feminism 1 (1991), 25

Hopkins, Kevin, Forgive U.S. Our Debts? Righting the Wrongs of Slavery, 89 Geo. L.J. 2531 (2001), 929

Houck, Oliver A., With Charity for All, 93 Yale L.J. 1415 (1984), 3, 4

Houseman, Alan W., Restrictions by Funders and the Ethical Practice of Law, 67 Fordham L. Rev. 2187 (1999), 114

Howarth, Joan, Teaching in the Shadow of the Bar, 31 U.S.F. L. Rev. 927 (1997), 24

Howe, Irving, Steady Work: Essays in the Politics of Democratic Radicalization, 1953–1966 (1966), 312

Hunter, Nan D., Lawyering for Social Justice, 72 N.Y.U. L. Rev. 1009 (1997), **832**

Kenn, Deborah, Instituionalized, Legal Racism: Housing Segregation and Beyond, 11 B.U. Pub. Int. L.J. 35 (2001), 878

Kennedy, Duncan, Distributive and Paternalistic Motives in Contract and Tort Law, With Special Reference to Compulsory Terms and Unequal Bargaining Power, 41 Md. L. Rev. 563 (1982), 299

Kennedy, Duncan, Legal Education and the Reproduction of Hierarchy: A Polemic Against the System (1983), 22

Kennedy, Duncan, Legal Education as Training for Hierarchy, in The Politics of Law (David Kairys ed., 1990), 24

Kepros, Laurie Rose, Queer Theory: Weed or Seed in the Garden of Legal Theory?, 9 Law & Sex. 279 (1999–2000), 939

Kidder, William C., Affirmative Action in Higher Education: Recent Developments in Litigation, Admissions and Diversity Research, 12 La Raza L.J. 173 (2001), **647**

Kidder, William C. & Jay Rosner, How the SAT Creates "Built-in Headwinds": An Educational and Legal Analysis of Disparate Impact, 43 Santa Clara L. Rev. 131 (2002), 646

Kilwein, John, Still Trying: Cause Lawyering for the Poor and Disadvantaged in Pittsburgh, Pennsylvania, in Cause Lawyering: Political Commitments and Professional Responsibilities (Austin Sarat & Stuart Scheingold eds., 1998), 126

King, Martin Luther, Jr., The Ethical Demands for Integration, in A Testament of Hope: The Essential Writings and Speeches of Martin Luther King, Jr. (James Melvin Washington ed., 1986), 846

Kinoy, Arthur, Rights on Trial: The Odyssey of a People's Lawyer (1983), 156

Kitching, Gavin, Seeking Social Justice Through Globalization: Escaping a Nationalist Perspective (2001), 58

Klarman, Michael J., Bush v. Gore Through the Lens of Constitutional History, 89 Cal. L. Rev. 1721 (2001), 725

Kluger, Richard, Simple Justice: The History of Brown v. Board of Education and Black America's Struggle for Equality (1975), 573, 574

Kocks, Dorothee E., Dream a Little: Land and Social Justice in Modern America (2000), 58

Koons, Judith, Fair Housing and Community Empowerment: Where the Roof Meets Redemption, 4 Geo. J. on Fighting Poverty 75 (1996), 879, **903**

Koppelman, Andrew, The Gay Rights Question in Contemporary America (2002), 1016

Kornhauser, Lewis A. & Richard L. Revesz, Legal Education and Entry into the Legal Profession: The Role of Race, Gender, and Educational Debt, 70 N.Y.U. L. Rev. 829 (1995), 26, 27, 33, 266

Korobkin, Russell & Chris Gutherie, Psychological Barriers to Litigation Settlement: An Experimental Approach, 93 Mich. L. Rev. 107 (1994), 420

Kost, Kathleen A. & Frank W. Munger, Fooling All of the People Some of the Time: 1990's Welfare Reform and the Exploitation of American Values, 4 Va. J. Soc. Pol'y & L. 3 (1996), 551

Kotkin, Minna J., Reconsidering Role Assumption in Clinical Education, 19 N.M. L. Rev. 185 (1989), 356

Kramer, John R., Will Legal Education Remain Affordable, by Whom, and How? 1987 Duke L.J. 240, 25

Krane, Steven, Regulating Attorney Conduct: Past, Present, and Future, 29 Hofstra L. Rev. 247 (2000), 354

Kraw, George M., Behind Closed Doors the "Nonpartisan" Plan for Picking California's Federal Judges Is Nonsensical, Recorder, May 9, 2001, at 4, 725

Kreisher, Otto, Wait May Be Over For Two California Judge Nominees, Copley News Service, Mar. 3, 2000, 695

Kruse, Becky, Luck and Politics: Judicial Selection Methods and Their Effect on Women on the Bench, 16 Wis. Women's L.J. 67 (2001), 695

Kruse, Katherine R., Biting Off What They Can Chew: Strategies for Involving Students in Problem–Solving Beyond Individual Client Representation, 8 Clinical L. Rev. 405 (2002), 376

Kuehn, Robert R., Denying Access to Legal Representation: The Attack on the Tulane Environmental Law Clinic, 4 Wash. U. J.L. & Pol'y 33 (2000), 111

Kushner, James A., Apartheid in America: An Historical and Legal Analysis of Contemporary Racial Segregation in the United States, 22 How. L.J. 547 (1979), 879

Kushner, James, Discrimination in Real Estate, Community Development and Revitalization (2d ed., 1995), 840

Kushner, James, The Fair Housing Amendments Act of 1988: The Second Generation of Fair Housing, 42 Vand. L. Rev. 1049 (1989), 841

Kwan, Peter, Complicity and Complexity: Cosynthesis and Praxis, 49 DePaul L. Rev. 673 (2000), 1028, 1029

La Grande, Walter, Getting There, Staying There, ABA Journal, Feb. 1999 at 54, 267

LaFrance, Arthur B., Clinical Education: "To Turn Ideals into Effective Vision," 44 So.Cal. L. Rev. 624 (1971), 356

Lai, Zenobia, Andrew Leong & Chi Chi Wu, The Lessons of The Parcel C Struggle: Reflections on Community Lawyering, 6 Asian Pac. Am. L.J. 1 (2000), **320**

Pizer, Jennifer C. & Doreena P. Wong, Arresting "The Plague of Violence": California's Unruh Act Requires School Officials to Act Against Anti-Gay Peer Abuse, 12 Stan. L. & Pol'y Rev. 63 (2001), 1003

Pleck, Elizabeth, Domestic Tyranny: The Making of Social Policy Against Family Violence from Colonial Times to the Present (1987), 1033

Poindexter, Georgette C., Collective Individualism: Deconstructing the Legal City, 145 U. Pa. L. Rev. 607 (1997), 894

Polikoff, Nancy D., Am I My Client?: The Role Confusion of a Lawyer Activist, 31 Harv. C.R.-C.L. L. Rev. 443 (1996), **290**

Polikoff, Nancy D., Raising Children: Lesbian and Gay Parents Face the Public and the Courts, in Creating Change: Sexuality, Public Policy, and Civil Rights (John D'Emilio, William B. Turner & Urvashi Vaid eds., 2000), 1003

Polletta, Francesca, The Structural Context of Novel Rights Claims: Southern Civil Rights Organizing, 1961–1966, 34 Law & Soc'y Rev. 367 (2000), 439, 443

Porter, Aaron, Norris, Schmidt, Green, Harris, Higginbotham & Associates: The Sociolegal Import of Philadelphia Cause Lawyers, in Cause Lawyering: Political Commitments and Professional Responsibilities (Austin Sarat & Stuart Scheingold eds., 1998), 126

Porter, Eduardo, Janitors Draw Unions' Support of California Suit, Wall St. J., Dec. 1, 2000, at B5, 170

Post, Robert C. & Reva B. Siegel, Equal Protection by Law: Federal Antidiscrimination Legislation After Morrison and Kimel, 110 Yale L.J. 441 (2000), **745**

powell, john a., Addressing Regional Dilemmas for Minority Communities, in Reflections on Regionalism (Bruce Katz ed., 2000), 894

powell, john a., Living and Learning: Linking Housing and Education, 80 Minn. L. Rev. 749 (1996), 847

powell, john a., The "Racing" of American Society: Race Functioning as a Verb Before Signifying as a Noun, 15 Law & Ineq. 99 (1997), 194

powell, john a., Segregation and Educational Inadequacy in Twin Cities Public Schools, 17 Hamline J. Pub. L. & Pol'y 337 (1996), 625

powell, john a., The Tensions Between Integration and School Reform, 28 Hastings Const. L.Q. 655 (2001), 611, **625**, 636

Practicing Therapeutic Jurisprudence: Law as a Helping Profession (Dennis Stolle, David B. Wexler & Bruce J. Winick eds., 2000), 1089

Price, Loretta & Melinda Davis, Seeds of Change: A Bibliographic Introduction to Law and Organizing, 26 N.Y.U. Rev. of L. & Soc. Change 615 (2000–01), 153

Pulido, Laura, Environmentalism and Econmoic Justice: Two Chicano Struggles in the Southwest (1996), 902

Quigley, Fran, Seizing the Disorienting Moment: Adult Learning Theory and the Teaching of Social Justice in Law School Clinics, 2 Clinical L. Rev. 37 (1995), **218**, 224

Quigley, William P., Backwards into the Future: How Welfare Changes in the Millenium Resemble English Poor Law of the Middle Ages 9 Stan. L. & Pol'y Rev. 101 (1998), 551

Quigley, William P., The Demise of Law Reform and the Triumph of Legal Aid: Congress and the Legal Services Corporation from the 1960's to the 1990's, 17 St. Louis U. Pub. L. Rev. 241 (1998), **89**

Quigley, William, Ending Poverty: Amending the Constitution to Create a Right to a Job at a Living Wage (forthcoming, Temple University Press 2003), 490

Quigley, William P., Five Hundred Years of English Poor Laws, 1349–1834: Regulating the Working and Nonworking Poor, 30 Akron L. Rev. 73 (1996), 558

Quigley, William, Full–Time Workers Should Not Be Poor: The Living Wage Movement, 70 Miss. L.J. 889 (2001), 490

Quigley, William P., Reflections of Community Organizers: Lawyering for Empowerment of Community Organizations, 21 Ohio N.U. L. Rev. 455 (1995), 175, **776**

Raack, David W., Law School and the Erosion of Student Idealism, 41 J. Legal Educ. 121 (1991), 344

Raphael, Jody, Saving Bernice: Battered Women, Welfare, and Poverty (2000), 1099

Ratner, Michael & Eleanor Stein, W. Haywood Burns: To Be of Use, 106 Yale L.J. 753 (1996), 43

Rawls, John, A Theory of Justice (1971), 49, 59

Reader on Race, Civil Rights, and American Law, A: A Multicultural Approach (Timothy Davis, Kevin R. Johnson & George A. Martinez eds., 2001), 194

Reagon, Bernice Johnson, Coalition Politics: Turning the Century, in Home Girls: A Black Feminist Anthology (Barbara Smith ed., 1983), 206

Reese, Roy W. & Carolyn A. Eldred, Legal Needs Among Low–Income and Moderate–Income Households: Summary of Findings for the Comprehensive Legal Needs Study (1994), 70

Reich, Charles A., Beyond The New Property: An Ecological View of Due Process, 56 Brook. L. Rev. 731 (1990), **519**

Reich, Charles, Individual Rights and Social Welfare: The Emerging Legal Issues, 74 Yale L.J. 1245 (1965), 511

Simon, William H., The Community Economic Development Movement, 2002 Wis. L. Rev. 377, 930

Simon, William, The Ideology of Advocacy: Procedural Justice and Professional Ethics, 1978 Wisconsin L. Rev. 29 (1978), 225

Simon, William H., Lawyer Advice and Client Autonomy: Mrs. Jones's Case, 50 Md. L. Rev. 213 (1991), 299, **300**

Sinden, Amy, "Why Won't Mom Cooperate?": A Critique of Informality in Child Welfare Proceedings, 11 Yale J.L. & Feminism 339 (1999), 1112

Singer, Joseph William, The Reliance Interest in Property, 40 Stan. L. Rev. 611 (1988), 444, **475**, 478

Sisk, Gregory S., A Primer on Awards of Attorney's Fees Against the Federal Government, 25 Ariz. St. L.J. 733 (1993), 138, 139

Smith, David, Geography and Social Justice (1994), 50

Smith, David Marshall, Geography of Social Justice (2002), 58

Smith, Linda F., Interviewing Clients: A Linguistic Comparison of the "Traditional" Interview and the "Client–Centered" Interview, 1 Clinical L. Rev. 541 (1995), 272, 289

Smith, Reginald Heber, Justice and the Poor (1919), 62

Sniderman, Paul M. & Thomas Piazza, The Scar of Race (1993), 845

Social Justice: From Hume to Walzer (David Boucher & Paul Kelly eds., 1998), 58

Soifer, Aviam, Moral Ambition, Formalism, and the "Free World" of DeShaney, 57 Geo. Wash. L. Rev. 1513 (1989), 666

Soja, Edward, Thirdspace: Journeys to Los Angeles and Other Real-and-Imagined Places (1996), 877

Southworth, Ann, Taking the Lawyer Out of Progressive Lawyering, 46 Stan. L. Rev. 213 (1993), 159

Spann, Girardeau A., The Law of Affirmative Action: Twenty–Five Years of Supreme Court Decisions on Race and Remedies (2000), 438

Sparer, Ed, Fundamental Human Rights, Legal Entitlements, and the Social Struggle: A Friendly Critique of the Critical Legal Studies Movement, 36 Stan. L. Rev. 509 (1984), 156

Spaulding, Norman W., The Prophet and the Bureaucrat: Positional Conflicts in Service Pro Bono Publico, 50 Stan. L. Rev. 1395 (1998), 73

Spiegel, Mark, The Case of Mrs. Jones Revisited: Paternalism and Autonomy in Lawyer–Client Counseling, 1997 B.Y.U. L. Rev. 307 (1997), **305**

Spielman, Fran, Firms Must Come Clean on Slavery, City's Insurers to Be Subject to Requirement, Chi. Sun–Times, Sept 13, 2002, at 3, 929, 930

Spillenger, Clyde, Elusive Advocate: Reconsidering Brandeis as People's Lawyer, 105 Yale L.J. 1445 (1996), **236**

St. Joan, Jacqueline & Nancy Ehrenreich, Putting Theory into Practice: A Battered Women's Clemency Clinic, 8 Clinical L. Rev. 171 (2001), 1048

Stanley, Richard C., The Restatement of the Law Governing Lawyers: Lawyer Regulation Coming of Age, Louisiana Bar Journal, June 2000, at 22, 345

Stapleton, M.A., County's Filing Fees Top Nation; Boost Sought to Fund Legal Aid, Chicago Daily Law Bull. Dec. 26, 1995, at 1, 115

Stark, Barbara, Economic Rights in the United States and International Human Rights Law: Toward an "Entirely New Strategy," 44 Hastings L.J. 79 (1992), 480

Stark, Evan, Mandatory Arrest of Batterers, A Reply to Its Critics, in Do Arrests and Restraining Orders Work? (Eve S. Buzawa and Carl G. Buzawa eds., 1996), **1085**, 1090

Stark, Evan, Re–Presenting Woman Battering: From Battered Woman Syndrome to Coercive Control, 58 Alb. L. Rev. 973 (1995), 1046

Stefancic, Jean & Richard Delgado, No Mercy: How Conservative Think Tanks and Foundations Changed America's Social Agenda (1996), 4, 646

Stevens, Robert, Law School: Legal Education in America from the 1850s to the 1980s (1983), 17, 18

Stoddard, Thomas B., Bleeding Heart: Reflections on Using the Law to Make Social Change, 72 N.Y.U. L. Rev. 967 (1997), **822**, 1009

Stone, Adrienne, The Public Interest and the Power of the Feminist Critique of Law School: Women's Empowerment of Legal Education and its Implications for the Fate of Public Interest Commitment, 5 Am. U. J. Gender & L. 525 (1997), 27

Stover, Robert, Making It and Breaking It: The Fate of Public Interest Commitment During Law School (1989), 15, 16, 17

Strauss, David A., Bush v Gore: What Were They Thinking? 68 U. Chi. L. Rev. 737 (2001), 725

Strickland, Rennard, Tonto's Revenge: Reflections on American Indian Culture and Policy (1997), 51

Su, Julie A., Making the Invisible Visible: The Garment Industry's Dirty Laundry, 1 J. Gender Race & Just. 405 (1998), 9, **195**, 497

Sullivan, Kathleen M., Unconstitutional Conditions, 102 Harv. L. Rev. 1413 (1989), 109

Unequal Protection: Environmental Justice and Communities of Color (Robert D. Bullard ed., 1994), 902

Urbanization of Injustice, The (Andy Merrifield & Erik Swyngedouw eds., 1997), 839

Vaid, Urvashi, Virtual Equality (1995), 836, 837, 937, 939, 960

Valdes, Francisco, Sexual Minorities in the Military: Charting the Constitutional Frontiers of Status and Conduct, 27 Creighton L. Rev. 381 (1994), 959, **968**

Valdes, Francisco, Queers, Sissies, Dykes, and Tomboys: Deconstructing the Conflation of "Sex," "Gender," and "Sexual Orientation" in Euro-American Law and Society, 83 Calif. L. Rev. 1 (1995), 931, 997

Voices Focus: Litigation and Community Empowerment, 4 Geo. J. on Fighting Poverty 199 (1996), 880

Volpp, Leti, Court-Stripping and Class-Wide Relief: A Response to Judicial Review in Immigration Cases after AADC, 14 Geo. Immigr. L.J. 463 (2000), 726

Volz, Gregory L., Keith W. Reeves & Erica Kaufman, Higher Education and Community Lawyering: Common Ground, Consensus, and Collaboration for Economic Justice, 2002 Wis. L. Rev. 505, 930

Waits, Kathleen, Battered Women and Family Lawyers: The Need for an Identification Protocol, 58 Alb. L. Rev. 1027 (1995), 1056

Walker, Lenore, The Battered Woman Syndrome (1984), 1046

Walker, Vernetta L., Legal Needs of the Public in the Future, Florida B.J., May 1997, at 42, 80

Walt, Carmen DeNavas, et al., United States Census Brueau, Money Income in the United States 2000 (2001), 857

Wasserstrom, Richard, Lawyers and Revolution, 30 U. Pitt. L. Rev. 125 (1968), 227

Wasserstrom, Richard, Lawyers as Professionals: Some Moral Issues, 5 Human Rights 1 (1975), **246**

Webster, Peter D., Selection and Retention of Judges: Is There One "Best" Method? 23 Fla. St. U. L. Rev. 1 (1995), 705, 706

Weinstein, Henry, Funding Mechanism for Legal Aid Upheld, Los Angeles Times, Nov. 15, 2001, Part 2, 1, 112

Weir, Margaret, Politics and Jobs: The Boundaries of Employment Policy in The United States (1992), **464**

Weissman, Deborah M., Gender-Based Violence as Judicial Anomaly: Between "The Truly National and the Truly Local," 42 B.C. L. Rev.1081 (2001), 1063

Weithorn, Lois A., Protecting Children from Exposure to Domestic Violence: the Use and Abuse Of Child Maltreatment Statutes, 53 Hastings L.J. 1 (2001), 1112

Wells, Catharine Pierce, Improving One's Situation: Some Pragmatic Reflections on the Art of Judging, 49 Wash. & Lee L. Rev. 323 (1992), 712

Wells, N. Douglas, Thurgood Marshall and "Individual Self-Realization" in First Amendment Jurisprudence, 61 Tenn. L. Rev. 237 (1993), 49

Wendel, W. Bradley, Value Pluralism in Legal Ethics, 78 Wash. U. L. Q. 113 (2000), 207

West, Cornel, Race Matters (1993), 847

West, Robin, Rights, Capabilities, and the Good Society, 69 Fordham L. Rev. 1901 (2001), **434**, 675, 676

Westley, Robert, Many Billions Gone: Is it Time to Reconsider the Case for Black Reparations?, 40 B.C. L. Rev. 429 (1998), 434, 929

Wetlaufer, Gerald B., The Ethics of Lying in Negotiation, 75 Iowa L. Rev. 1219 (1990), **405**

Wexler, Stephen, Practicing Law for Poor People, 79 Yale L.J. 1049 (1970), 775, 776

What is a Hero?, Esquire, Nov. 1998, at 104, 313

Which Direction for Organized Labor?: Essays on Organizing, Outreach, and Internal Transformations (Bruce Nissen ed., 1999), 170

White, Lucie, Remarks, Symposium, Constitutional Lawyering in the 21st Century, March 4, 2000: Panel Three: Creating Models for Progressive Lawyering in the 21st Century, 9 J.L. & Pol'y 297 (2000), 194

White, Lucie E., Subordination, Rhetorical Survival Skills, and Sunday Shoes: Notes on the Hearing of Mrs. G, 38 Buff. L. Rev. 1 (1990), 156

White, Lucie E., To Learn and Teach: Lessons from Driefontein on Lawyering and Power, 1988 Wis. L. Rev. 699, **793**

Wiggins, Mary Jo, Race, Class, and Suburbia: The Modern Black Suburb As a "Race-Making Situation," 35 U. Mich. J. L. Reform 749 (2002), 894

Wildman, Stephanie M., The Classroom Climate in Looking at Law School (Stephen Gillers ed., 4th ed., 1997), 23

Wildman, Stephanie M., Ending Male Privilege: Beyond the Reasonable Woman, 98 Mich. L. Rev. 1797 (2000), 689, 690

Wildman, Stephanie M. with contributions by Adrienne D. Davis, Margalynne Armstrong & Trina Grillo, Privilege Revealed: How Invisible Preference Undermines America (1996), 47, 287, 713

Wildman, Stephanie M., Propositions Are the Wrong Way for Tort Reform, L.A. Daily J., Nov. 7, 1988, Col. 3, 6, 127

Zorza, Joan, The Criminal Law of Misdemeanor Domestic Violence, 1970–1990, 83 J. Crim. L. & Criminology 46 (1992), **1059**, 1091

Zuni Cruz, Christine, [On The] Road Back In: Community Lawyering in Indigenous Communities, 24 Am. Indian L. Rev. 229 (2000), **11**

CASES AND MATERIALS

ON

SOCIAL JUSTICE: PROFESSIONALS, COMMUNITIES, AND LAW

*

INTRODUCTION

As the United States declared national independence, it claimed a vision of democracy in which "life, liberty, and the pursuit of happiness" are inalienable rights, "consent of the governed" legitimates the power of government, and all citizens are "created equal." *The Declaration of Independence of 1776*, para. 2. Today, the achievement of these ideals remains relevant to advocates for social justice. Speaking about democracy in the United States on the occasion of the bicentennial of the Constitution, Justice Thurgood Marshall observed:

> [Anniversary celebrations take] particular events and hold them as the source of all the very best that has followed. * * * [Such celebrations invite] a complacent belief that the vision of those who debated and compromised in Philadelphia yielded the "more perfect Union" it is said we now enjoy. * * * To the contrary, the government they devised was defective from the start, requiring several amendments, a civil war, and momentous social transformation to attain the system of constitutional government, and its respect for individual freedoms and human rights, that we hold as fundamental today.

Thurgood Marshall, *Reflections on the Bicentennial of the United States Constitution*, 101 Harv. L. Rev. 1, 1–2 (1987). As Robert Bullard notes, "Social justice and the elimination of institutionalized discrimination were the major goals of the civil rights movement." Robert D. Bullard, *Dumping in Dixie: Race, Class, and Environmental Quality* 3 (1994). Promoting individual and collective well-being, enhancing human dignity, and correcting imbalances of power and wealth are also social justice concerns.

Social justice lawyering seeks to give material meaning to these ideals in the daily lives of individuals and communities that are marginalized, subordinated, and underrepresented. This book brings together the systems of lawyers, law, and politics that connect legal work and communities that seek to meet basic human needs, create and sustain environments of viable opportunity, and undertake the practice of democracy. How do people who need lawyers find them, and how do lawyers who wish to serve people in need structure practices to meet these goals? How has the law addressed basic human needs and recognized the protections necessary for democratic practice? How can lawyers work with individuals and communities who are engaging in the struggle for a better life and social change?

In taking social justice as its subject matter and exploring these themes, this book recognizes that lawyers, in collaboration with others, have an important role to play in assuring that there is a positive correlation between social justice practice and those founding ideals guaranteeing "life, liberty, and the pursuit of happiness," "consent of the governed," and equality. The book sets forth multiple visions of legal practice and professional commitments for social justice. Situating social justice in varied contexts from diverse perspectives broadens the ability to think critically and creatively about its meaning and also suggests methods to achieve social justice more effectively in practice.

In 2001, a report prepared for the Rockefeller Foundation analyzed six recent case studies of social justice lawyering. Penda D. Hair, *Louder Than Words: Lawyers, Communities and the Struggle for Justice* (A Report to the Rockefeller Foundation, 2001) (describing the struggle for racial diversity at the University of Texas, garment worker advocacy in Los Angeles, the Mississippi redistricting campaign to ensure democratic voice, efforts to ensure that transit revenue in Los Angeles met community needs, organizing to achieve sustainable community in North Carolina through a labor dispute, and decisions about land use in Boston's Chinatown) [hereinafter Rockefeller Report]. The case studies revealed several patterns.

- Community involvement and engagement with local governing institutions take high priority as a consistently reliable tool for solving pressing community problems and sustaining the struggle for justice;
- The attorney/client relationship is fluid, collaborative and multilateral, as the legal arena becomes one among several dynamically interrelated venues in which claims for justice are played out;
- Advocates on the national level are cognizant of the need to nurture and sustain local movements for justice, while maintaining and expanding the federal rights infrastructure upon which local work often builds; and
- Issues of race are defined and addressed in new ways. Popular discussion frames racial exclusion in terms of individual prejudice that causes whites to treat minorities differently. The cure is to treat everyone the same. By contrast, the racial-innovation approach seeks to reveal the deeper structural causes of racial exclusion and make connections between racial exclusion and broader kinds of institutional and social dysfunction.

Id. at 141.

The Rockefeller Report case studies cover a "broad range of issues, constituencies, geographic settings, lawyer roles and visions of racial justice," *id.* at 3, and suggest the emergence of themes in contemporary social justice lawyering. "The lawyers were innovators and problem solvers, bringing a range of skills and techniques to serve the goals of the communities that were their clients." *Id.* at 11. The Rockefeller Report also noted the importance to social justice lawyering of addressing issues of race and revealing the linkage between racial exclusion and other societal ills.

This book brings together materials and cases with the goal of training social justice lawyers to have a grasp of law and lawyering that will enhance their resourcefulness in working with communities as well as the ability to think creatively about the intertwined issues of oppression that appear in the case studies in the Rockefeller Report.

The twenty-first century marks a challenging but exciting time to become a lawyer. Great social movements in the last century brought dramatic changes in society and law. The labor movement won the right to organize collectively, representing at its height about one-third of the American workforce. The civil rights movement ended state-sanctioned racial segregation and renegotiated societal values in the worlds of education, employment, housing, public accommodation, and voting. The women's movement also changed the face of education and work, as well as the notion of a subordinate role for women in society. Activism by lesbian, gay, bisexual, and transgendered people fighting for equality continues. These movements as well as those for disability rights, environmental justice, consumer rights, and criminal justice have all involved both national trends and local manifestations.

Legal work for social justice has been part of these social movements, building on models of public interest law practice that began developing in the first half of the twentieth century. Legal aid organizations represented immigrants and poor people in cities; the American Civil Liberties Union represented dissenters on free speech issues beginning in World War I; and the National Association for the Advancement of Colored People (NAACP) Legal Defense and Educational Fund built a brilliant litigation strategy as part of its opposition to segregation. Nan Aron, *Liberty and Justice for All: Public Interest Law in the 1980s and Beyond* 7–10 (1989). According to one observer:

> These three large movements in poverty, civil liberties, and civil rights practice changed more than the law of the their respective fields. As they evolved, particularly into the 1960's, these organizations changed the way lawyers approached the law. Their lawyers had clients and the clients were injured, but so also was a larger sense of justice which is as difficult to define precisely as it would be to deny. Most importantly, they did not simply seek compensation for their clients; increasingly they sought to change the law.

Oliver A. Houck, *With Charity for All*, 93 Yale L.J. 1415, 1441 (1984). The organizations and institutions working on public interest law multiplied rapidly. Aron, *supra* at 27 (in 1969 there were 23 public interest law centers staffed by fewer than 50 full time attorneys; by 1984, there were 158 groups employing 906 lawyers).

In 1975, Justice Thurgood Marshall described the contribution of these lawyers:

> The new wave of public interest law is built on the successes of civil rights and civil liberties lawyers who for decades have been working through private non-profit organizations. It was given further impetus by the legal services program of the Office of Economic Opportu-

> nity. The development of the newer public interest law firms was a natural outgrowth of the expansion of public interest law into new areas. Public interest lawyers today provide representation to a broad range of relatively powerless minorities—for example, the mentally ill, children, and the poor of all races. They also represent neglected but widely diffuse interests that most of us share as consumers and as individuals in need of privacy and a healthy environment.

Thurgood Marshall, *Advancing Public Interest Law Practice: The Role of the Organized Bar*, ABA Journal 1975, in *Thurgood Marshall: His Speeches, Writings, Arguments, Opinions, and Reminiscences* 242–43 (Mark V. Tushnet ed., 2001). According to Aron:

> Influenced by the activism of the antiwar, civil rights, feminist, and environmental movements of the late 1960s and early 1970s, public interest lawyers * * * developed a common set of goals: to make government more accountable to the public and more responsive to the concerns and needs of unrepresented persons; to increase the power of citizens' groups; to insist on a place at the bargaining table; and to ensure that the development of public policy be open to public scrutiny.

Aron, *supra* at 3–4.

As legal practice for social justice grew, new institutes and "public interest law firms" formed with the orientation of opposing many of the gains of the civil rights, consumer, and environmental movements and protecting business against regulation: "[The] overlay of conservative philosophy on an enterprise largely created, funded, and directed by profit-making corporations is the earmark of the business PILFs [public interest law firms]." Houck, *supra* at 1455. Moreover, in Aron's view:

> Public interest groups have been tagged "liberal" because they were originally identified with causes generally regarded as such. Today, public interest law can no longer be thought of as a monolithic movement dedicated to any one political agenda. It is practiced by organizations that span the ideological spectrum. Groups calling themselves public interest law firms * * * have become increasingly visible and active in pushing a conservative program. * * * While focusing almost exclusively on the needs and concerns of the business community, these groups nonetheless operate under the mantle of a public interest law firm and benefit from its favorable tax-exempt status.

Aron, *supra* at 4; *see also* Jean Stefancic & Richard Delgado, *No Mercy: How Conservative Think Tanks and Foundations Changed America's Social Agenda* (1996). "Advocates on the front lines of the fight for racial and social justice find themselves exhausted from defensive battles against much-better financed and coordinated opposition." Rockefeller Report, *supra* at 10. While fine work for social justice continues to take place through public interest law firms and public interest organizations, the broad term "public interest law" no longer fully captures either the commitment to work on behalf of marginalized, subordinated, and underrepresented clients and communities or the value placed on transformation that characterizes lawyering for social justice.

In addition to "public interest" law, advocates for marginalized, subordinated, and underrepresented clients and communities have described their work as cause lawyering (*see, e.g., Cause Lawyering: Political Commitments and Professional Responsibilities*) (Austin Sarat & Stuart Scheingold eds., 1998); rebellious lawyering (*see, e.g.,* Gerald P. López, *Rebellious Lawyering: One Chicano's Vision of Progressive Law Practice* (1992)); or through the use of many other phrases. Carrie Menkel-Meadow lists the following variations that reflect the idea of "lawyering for the good" of others:

> "activist" lawyering, progressive lawyering, "transformative" lawyering, equal justice lawyering, "radical" lawyering, lawyering for social change, "critical" lawyering, socially conscious lawyering, lawyering for the underrepresented, lawyering for the subordinated, "alternative" lawyering, political lawyering, and "visionary" lawyering * * *.

Carrie Menkel-Meadow, *The Causes of Cause Lawyering: Toward an Understanding of the Motivation and Commitment of Social Justice Lawyers* in Sarat & Scheingold, *supra* at 33. Thus, ultimately, work in law for social justice will require you to think about your own values and your understanding of society.

This book portrays the dynamic development process that involves professionals, communities, and law. Lawyers and activists seeking social justice operate within systemic constraints, while seeking to push the boundaries of those constraints. Social justice lawyering envisions the practice of law both on behalf of and alongside of subordinated peoples, with the efforts and achievements of members of the community a crucial aspect of the work.

Social justice lawyering involves questions about the professional role of lawyers, legal rights and the ability to bring legal claims to courts, and developing ways of working toward the empowerment of clients and communities. For example, consider the issues surrounding an African-American or Latina/o community in a rural area that is threatened by the proposed location of a toxic waste dump. The government has not invested in services and development for this community, and the system of voting districts allows the white or Anglo majority to consistently defeat minority candidates for the school board and county commission. If they get help from a legal services agency serving low-income people, will government funding restrictions affect the ability of their attorney to bring a class action suit, speak to government agencies about the impact of proposed environmental regulations, or sue under the federal Voting Rights Act to change the electoral system so that the community will have a fair opportunity to elect candidates of its choice? They need laws that can be invoked, or the ability to persuade courts or legislatures to make rules that will help protect their community and enable their democratic participation. Will they be shielded by environmental regulation, by civil rights acts, or by state or federal constitutions? What sorts of voting systems will best achieve democracy? They live with economic as well as political inequality. Can they demand development to attract more employers, or public works programs to provide employment, or other measures to transform poverty? If they do find a lawyer to help them, will they rely on the lawyer to file an environmental lawsuit and wait to learn the outcome of the suit, or will the legal action be only part of the community's mobilization? If the community faced tensions between their goals and the potential for changing state or federal law, how will their lawyer advise them? This community needs a lawyer, but many of its needs cannot be addressed with lawsuits unless the law is changed first; many structural problems will not be solved even if some claims succeed. Will the community find this mobilization empowering, so that greater access to the electoral system is part of achieving a set of goals related to racial equality and political transformation? What role might the lawyer play in working through these choices and moving toward community empowerment?

This book brings together the structural, doctrinal, and political aspects of social justice lawyering. The text is organized into three parts. Part I, A System of Lawyers: The Legal Profession and Work for Social Justice, addresses the aspirations that lead students to study law, the delivery of legal services, the transition to becoming a lawyer, the lawyer-client relationship, and professional responsibility and ethics in a social justice context. This part also introduces examples of lawyers working for social justice and discusses how they developed and sustained their practices.

Part II, A System of Law: Shaping Claims in Social Justice Cases, addresses rights claims and access to courts. It begins by examining the efficacy of the discourse of legal rights as a tool of transformation and then provides a survey of claims that have been brought in the attempt to achieve social justice and civil rights through litigation. Sustaining human life requires a means of support, so livelihood, including work and dependency, is a key social justice issue. Voting, education, and the right to make claims on the state for protection against harm are also basic questions for participation in a democratic society. Part II then covers judicial selection and access to federal courts.

Part III, A System of Politics: Legal Work and Social Change, explores issues and achievements of lawyers working with communities toward transformation in the contemporary United States. In addition to an overview of empowerment and lawyering for social change, three areas receive extended attention: the quest for racial equality and a just urban environment; the struggle for gay and lesbian liberation; and the movement against domestic violence. These three areas incorporate the important identity categories of race, sexual orientation, and gender. They also reveal different ways of understanding community and shared goals in social movements. Struggles toward legal change are happening in all these areas, involving victories, defeats, debates, and continuing evolution as social justice lawyers and communities work together.

PART I

A SYSTEM OF LAWYERS: THE LEGAL PROFESSION AND WORK FOR SOCIAL JUSTICE

Advocates who practice social justice lawyering operate within the traditional system of lawyers. For those pursuing traditional career paths, a system of lawyers may be taken for granted, apparently a reality that poses few conflicts. Law students and advocates committed to social justice lawyering, however, often swim against the tide of dominant understandings that drive their professional socialization. Many do not recognize that the process of socialization and the values it promotes are integral parts of a system. But professional socialization entails a process through which all lawyers create their professional selves. Lawyers become part of the system and enable business to be performed as usual. Thus, professional socialization is a process by which lawyers internalize the norms and values of the profession, and each lawyer simultaneously learns what her role is and how to perform it.

The social justice lawyer must find a professional path within an adversary system that values extreme partisanship and moral non-accountability as preeminent norms. Because professional socialization is not fixed, it is possible to carve out norms, values, roles, and behaviors that are better suited to social justice work. Encouraging reflection and reevaluation of values and roles, this text examines issues of professional responsibility in many selected social justice contexts that face lawyers and law students.

The system of lawyers also includes the structures through which legal services can be provided to people who need them and lawyers can be connected with the clients to whom they are committed. The shortage of lawyers for low-income people places constraints on justice within the legal system. The text therefore explores issues of funding for legal services and also addresses alternatives such as attorney fees awarded pursuant to federal civil rights statutes. Dynamic examples from lawyers who have built self-sustaining practices, worked with non-profit agencies, and organized independent community-based law centers introduce the challenges and possibilities of social justice practice.

The exploration of the profession begins in Chapter 1 with law school, the gateway to the profession. This chapter examines the ideals that entering lawyers bring to the profession and the obstacles that they face in shaping their education to meet their goals. Chapter 2 addresses the delivery of legal services, particularly to people who cannot afford to pay their own attorneys; structural inequality in the process of litigation; and the highly contested field of funding legal work for social justice. Chapter 3 introduces issues faced by lawyers who work with activists and communities and explores the theoretical underpinning for that work.

Social justice lawyers face particular tensions between their professional roles and their personal identities. Chapter 4 therefore explores whether lawyers have a justified role morality that differs from ordinary morality. It considers role morality problems that arise within the contexts of professional socialization, practice within the adversary system, and the prospect of entering the profession as a happy and healthy human being. Chapter 5 turns to building a viable lawyer-client relationship. It investigates methods of work among social justice lawyers, including client-centered approaches to counseling and the complications that arise in the representation of groups. This chapter explores these issues and the ways in which models such as facilitative, client-centered, and community-based lawyering understand the professional role of the attorney.

Committing to social justice may clash with dominant understandings of professional responsibility. Chapter 6 considers ethical issues facing both lawyers and law students in the practice of social justice lawyering. Supplementing traditional courses in professional ethics, this chapter emphasizes the importance of context in order to sensitize students to some of the particular ethical issues they may confront as social justice advocates. For example, during law school, social justice lawyering is experienced primarily through clinical legal education courses, whether conducted in-house or through externships, and ethical issues arise in both settings. After law school, particular ethical issues may arise when legal advocates are involved with grass-roots organizers. Because the first professional responsibility of any lawyer is competence, chapter 6 explores building that competence through problem solving skills in traditional ways as well as through legal creativity and community building. This chapter looks, finally, at the special role of negotiation, the special ethics of negotiation, and at the possible costs of settlement when 80% of civil cases are settled.

Following this introduction to the system of lawyers, Part II of this text, A System of Law: Shaping Claims in Social Justice Cases, explores rights to livelihood and participation in democracy; it also addresses the efficacy of rights claims and issues surrounding access to federal courts. Part III, A System of Politics: Legal Work and Social Change, reviews patterns of legal work and activism as lawyers work with social movements to secure a racially just and sustainable urban environment, to advance lesbian and gay equality and liberation, and to end domestic violence.

Chapter 1

ENTERING THE PROFESSION: IDEALS AND OBSTACLES

This chapter addresses the aspirations and ideals that animate work for social justice as well as the obstacles faced by lawyers who choose this professional path. Julie Su, a lawyer working for social justice for garment workers in Los Angeles, writes:

> I have learned more, gained more, cared more, smiled and cried more by sharing my life, work, and passion with the Thai and Latina garment workers, who live with the violence of poverty and suffer the brutality of sweatshops, than I thought I could by choosing to become a lawyer. The workers have inspired me, personally and professionally, to be more than I ever imagined. My work with them has been more gratifying than anything I thought possible during law school. Working not *for* them, but *with* them, it is not only their lives, but mine that has been changed.

Julie A. Su, *Making the Invisible Visible: The Garment Industry's Dirty Laundry*, 1 J. Gender Race & Just. 405, 417 (1998).

Preparing for a social justice practice involves mastering the skills in research, writing, analysis, and problem solving that are required of all law students. Social justice-oriented students also need to connect the sense of purpose that they brought into law school with the actual practice of law. While many law students arrive with that clear sense of direction, others must both develop a sense of their social justice priorities and gain work experience in the social justice arena. Some obstacles to social justice legal practice are personal. But structural and systemic obstacles, such as the cost of education to obtain a law degree or the nature of legal education itself, also create roadblocks. Students often encounter and must overcome these obstacles as they move toward fulfilling their visions of public interest or social justice lawyering. Chapter 3 elaborates on the multiple visions of social justice lawyering and chapter 4 critically addresses the tensions between personal values and professional socialization.

SECTION 1. ASPIRATIONS: WHY DID YOU CHOOSE LAW SCHOOL?

Have you known for years that you wanted to be a lawyer? Did you go to law school because you couldn't decide what else to do? Did you know any lawyers before coming to law school?

LANI GUINIER

Lift Every Voice: Turning a Civil Rights Setback into a New Vision of Social Justice 68 (1998)

I was twelve years old when I first thought about becoming a civil rights lawyer. It was September 1962. Constance Baker Motley was on the television news, escorting a black man named James Meredith into a building of the University of Mississippi. Meredith was about to become the first black to attend that school. The cameras looked out from the doors of the building as Motley and Meredith walked calmly up the stairs and through a howling white mob in order to register for classes. Or so I remember. I could be wrong, but what I did know was that Constance Baker Motley was a black woman lawyer working for the NAACP Legal Defense Fund.

I don't remember anything that Attorney Motley might have said. I don't know that I even watched her speak. It was her erect and imposing figure that caught my notice. Her proud image spoke to me. Her stately bearing said it all. She was a large-boned woman, but it was less her size than her manner. She did not flinch even as the crowd yelled epithets. She was flanked by U.S. Marshals, as I remember, but she could, for all I cared, have been alone. She was that determined.

I thought: I can do that. I can be a civil rights lawyer.

JEROLD S. AUERBACH

Unequal Justice: Lawyers and Social Change in Modern America vii–viii (1976)

In 1957 I entered Columbia Law school as a first-year student. Although mine was the silent generation, and I embraced its values (silently), I nonetheless intended to become a civil liberties lawyer who would vindicate constitutional principles for embattled defendants who were noisier than I could be. I cannot account for this commitment. There were no lawyers in my family to emulate. Certainly I was ignorant of those great moments in American history when, as though by divine favor, a lawyer miraculously appeared to defend political pariahs: Andrew Hamilton for Zenger; John Adams for the British soldiers implicated in the Boston Massacre; Charles Evans Hughes for Socialists expelled from the New York legislature. (I am equally certain that I was unaware of all those other moments, less conspicuous in our folklore if more characteristic of our national experience, when no such miraculous intervention had occurred.) I would like to think that my course was set by attorney Joseph Welch, whose televised indignation at the recklessness of Senator Joseph R. McCarthy during the Army–McCarthy hearings still remains vivid two decades later, or by Martin Luther King, Jr., whose visit to Oberlin College during the Montgomery bus boycott heightened my awareness of conflicts between law and justice. But I cannot be certain. Something about protesting against illegitimate authority drew me to law school.

CHRISTINE ZUNI CRUZ

[On The] Road Back In: Community Lawyering in Indigenous Communities
24 Am. Indian L. Rev. 229, 229–31 (2000)

As a communications major in film and broadcasting, I * * * [made a film] based on the lyrics, "You're my lawyer, you're my doctor, yeah, but somehow you forgot about me," from the song by Gil Scott Heron and Brian Jackson. These lyrics spoke to me of professionals who forget their communities or at least their communities' perspectives, needs, and sometimes their own roots. In turn, they are not respected and become despised for their indifference by those people who had different hopes and aspirations for what these professionals could do to help the general conditions of others in the community.

* * * At the time I produced the student film, I had no idea I would eventually become a lawyer, but I did know that whatever I did do, that I would consider working apart from or without relation to the Indian community and my own tribal community, in particular, as unconscionable. The idea of professional success, especially in the elite legal profession, as being closely linked to community or having corresponding value to the community has directly affected my view of individual lawyering. This idea runs counter to the norm.

SYLVIA A. LAW

The Messages of Legal Education
in *Looking at Law School* 155–57, 168–171
(Stephen Gillers ed., 4th ed. 1997)

I am always pleased when people I like and respect decide to go to law school. The study and practice of law can illuminate our understanding of the collective arrangements that define our individual and social life. Legal training enables people to support themselves doing work that includes rich human relationships and intellectual challenge. Legal skills can help realize our visions of a just society. Although these possibilities make the study and practice of law attractive, the reality of practice is often different. Most lawyers report that they are unhappy with their work. Many work for the relatively privileged to preserve a status quo in which material wealth and political power are distributed unfairly and *everyone* is oppressed by hierarchical and alienated relationships.

One fact, more than any other, influences the personal and professional choices facing lawyers and law students today and the collective choices that we face as a society. It is that we live in a world in which there are gross disparities in the distribution of money, political power, and personal opportunity for significant life choices. In the United States, the richest fifth of the population receives 40 percent of the personal income, whereas the poorest fifth receives 5 percent of the personal income. On a world scale the disparities are greater still. Unearned wealth, political power, and personal power over important life choices are distributed even more unevenly than income. Government policies of the 1980s and 1990s have increased the wealth of the rich and insecurity of the majority.

Despite the gross disparities in the distribution of resources and opportunities, Americans, and increasingly the world, share a common culture. We all see the same ads urging us to buy the same products. We all have similar desires to have those things that we believe will make life more beautiful and comfortable. We share common desires for interesting, creative, and useful work for ourselves and our children. Because we share a common culture, we feel the disparities in wealth, power, and opportunity acutely.

Gross inequality in the distribution of material resources produces a situation of insecurity for everyone. People at the bottom are the most insecure; they face the daily uncertainty of not knowing where the next meal will come from or whether they can keep a roof over their children's heads. Any unexpected expense is a disaster. Most "middle-income" Americans also face economic uncertainty. Jobs that were once secure and well-paying are now disappearing as multinational corporations seek the highest profits, without regard to the consequences for jobs or communities. In 1993, almost one-fifth of Americans under age sixty-five had *no* health insurance. In 1995, that number was increased dramatically when Congress slashed the Medicaid program for the poor and Medicare for the aged. The disparity is growing wider: A typical chief executive of a large American company earns 120 times more than a typical manufacturing worker, compared to a mere 35 times more in 1974. Even the rich are insecure. God forbid that you should not make it to the top. Or that, having made it to the top, you should somehow make a misstep that will cause you to slip from a position of privilege.

The disparity in the distribution of wealth and power, particularly in a time of deep economic insecurity, is a major factor motivating people to go to law school. These disparities also pose a central challenge to our social and legal arrangements. Are democracy, equality, personal security, self-actualization, or solidarity possible in a world in which material goods and political power are distributed in such a wildly uneven way? Are these disparities the inevitable cost of material growth, progress, and innovation?

Unfortunately, thought about the legal profession and legal education often mystifies rather than illuminates our understanding of these social relations, and increases, rather than decreases, perceptions of personal insecurity. * * * [The author discusses five characteristics of the first year of law school that "engender a sense of personal insecurity in students and hinder them from using the study of law as a means of understanding and affecting the world in which we live." These include: emphasis in the first year curriculum on the private and the individualistic, large classes, evaluation based on written exams and anonymous grading, the early start of the "placement" process, suggesting an ordained world, and excessive work pressure.]

* * *

The messages implicit in the way that law school is organized and in theoretical thought about the nature of the law are also reflected in principles of legal ethics. The prevalent view of legal ethics is that an individual attorney is entirely free to represent anyone he or she chooses, without fear of criticism from within the profession. Abe Fortas, former Supreme Court Justice, put it like this:

> Lawyers are agents not principals; and they should neither criticize nor tolerate criticism based upon the character of the client whom they represent or the cause that they prosecute or defend. They cannot and should not accept responsibility for the client's practices. Rapists, murderers, child-abusers. General Motors, Dow Chemical—and even cigarette manufacturers and stream polluters—are entitled to a lawyer; and any lawyer who undertakes their representation must be immune from criticism for so doing.

Furthermore, the conventional view is that a lawyer is free to determine, in the exercise of professional expertise, the way in which the client's interests are to be represented. Fortas argues that the client should not be "permitted to dictate or determine the strategy or substance of the representation, even if the client insisted that his prescription for the litigation was necessary to serve the larger cause to which he was committed."

I could not disagree more strongly with this prevailing view of legal ethics. A lawyer should be responsible in choosing the clients for whom he or she will work. Once having entered into an attorney-client relationship, the lawyer should seek to promote the client's vision of best interest.

In deciding for whom you are going to work, particularly in a period of history in which there are real and sharp divisions of values in society, you must make a personal moral choice. Lawyers and nonlawyers alike should have some sort of philosophy of life and work to make their life have meaning within that philosophy. * * * [N]either professional education nor professional ethics provides any answer to the question "To what ends should I use my legal skills?" Indeed, the prevalent view of legal ethics would seem to say, because everyone is entitled to as much legal talent as they can buy, you can work for anyone you choose and meet your obligation as a professional. Even if this is all that is required of you as a professional, we all have an obligation to ourselves and to each other to try to make sense of our lives in deciding to what ends we will use our legal skills. In becoming a professional, we do not stop being human. As humans we have some responsibility to work toward objectives that seem to us useful.

* * * [L]awyers have a special ability to enhance human autonomy and self-control. Far too often, however, professional attitude, rather than serving to enhance individual autonomy and self-control, strips people of autonomy and power. Rather than encouraging clients and citizens to know and control their own options and lives, the legal profession discourages client participation and control of their own legal claims. Rather than exposing the social and personal value judgments inherent in legal decisions, professionals tend to mask decisions as technical and to make decisions for the client. Lawyers have no particular expertise in making social or value judgments for their clients. In general, the bar has about as much or as little in the way of coherent social philosophy, and personal self-interest, as anyone else.

The lawyer does, however, have a special skill and ability in dealing with the legal system. Perhaps the most important job of a lawyer at this point in history is to build, or to rebuild, democratic processes—to enable individuals to exercise more power and control over their own lives. However, if lawyers are to serve this function, they must recognize that selecting a client or a job is a personal moral choice, and once having agreed to represent a person or organization, the lawyer should work to enable the client to do what she sees as important rather than simply imposing the lawyer's decision on the client.

It is unrealistic, or at least unsympathetic, to recognize, on the one hand, that law students today are subject to enormous pressures growing out of the insecurity and injustice generated by gross disparities in the distribution of wealth and power, and to suggest, on the other hand, that law students have a high degree of responsibility in addressing these issues and making decisions about their own careers? Maybe. However, I am as certain as I am of anything in this world that there will be more joy in your life and a greater day-to-day sense of personal and professional satisfaction if you develop a personal and political philosophy and try to work in accordance with it.

Notes and Questions

1. Lani Guinier was certain she would become a lawyer from the age of twelve. Christine Zuni Cruz did not imagine she would become a lawyer, even when she was in college. Jerold Auerbach was drawn to law by "embattled defendants" who could be "noisier" than he could imagine himself. When did you decide to attend law school? Why did you choose law school? What values influenced you to select the law school you attend?

2. Many students choose to attend law school because they are concerned about justice. During their first year of study they often ask

themselves and their friends, "Where is the class about justice?" Have you found that concern for justice and an interest in legal ethics permeates every law school class? Do you feel that your legal education is helping you toward your goals? Could law school or the legal profession be more helpful? Have your goals changed since you arrived in law school? If so, how?

3. Sylvia Law describes the economic disparities in the late 20th century United States. Are these economic inequalities relevant to legal ethics? Law disagrees with the commonly held view that lawyers should determine the client's best interests. Is she persuasive? Do new ethical obligations arise for the lawyer who follows her view?

4. Law states that she is proud when someone she respects chooses to attend law school. This view seems dissonant from the enormous unpopularity of lawyers. The statement most often cited as the quintessential anti-lawyer sentiment is Shakespeare's, "The first thing we do, let's kill all the lawyers." William Shakespeare, *Henry VI*, Part 2, Act 4, Scene 2. But in the play the statement is uttered by the villains who want to kill the lawyers in order to establish a tyrannical government. Without the lawyers, who will protect civil liberties? Might the lack of respect for the legal profession be connected to the perception that lawyers do not uphold the role of protectors of social justice?

Zuni Cruz notes that "working apart from or without relation" to her community was unthinkable. Would the public perception of lawyers be higher if more lawyers shared her view? Are you motivated by the idea of a community to which you belong?

5. What personal philosophy did you bring to law school? Are you seeking to develop that philosophy through your legal studies?

SECTION 2. LEGAL EDUCATION AND ITS IMPACT ON IDEALS

Social scientists have observed changing aspirations in students during their path through law school. Robert Stover, a political scientist who attended the University of Denver Law School, conducted a study of his classmates (class of 1980) and published his findings in *Making It and Breaking It: The Fate of Public Interest Commitment During Law School* (1989). Stover's study included data gathered from three sources: questionnaires completed by 103 Denver students at the beginning and the end of their time in law schools; a more in-depth series of interviews he conducted with nine students who began law school with a strong commitment to working in public interest jobs after graduation; and Stover's own experiences while a law student. *Id.* at 1–7.

Stover found that 1/3 of beginning first-year law students said they hoped to work in public interest jobs and 1/6 of graduating third years expressed the same hopes: in other words, the number of students who expressed commitment to public interest jobs dropped by half during law school. The number of public interest jobs rated among the most desirable jobs by students also fell dramatically. Data gathered at other law schools showed similar phenomena. *Id.* at 16–17. Stover proposed several interrelated explanations.

The drop in public interest could not be explained by the orientation of the school, which was deeply concerned with producing compassionate, responsible professionals. The school had not failed to emphasize the lawyer's professional obligation to serve the disadvantaged. A significant number of faculty members had public interest backgrounds themselves. But "evidence of this commitment to serving the underrepresented was virtually absent in the classroom." *Id.* at 3.

Another important factor was changing values and expectations among students. Student expectations that they would be able to fulfill their career goals in public interest jobs dropped. Correspondingly, their expectations that they would be able to find interesting work in private sector jobs increased. For example, a student who had not been interested in corporate work—a woman who originally planned to work in a small firm of feminist attorneys—was impressed by a woman professor who taught corporate law and decided corporate work would be more intellectually challenging and satisfying than she had previously believed. *Id.* at 34–35.

Stover described both the hectic first year and the distraction-filled second year as each having a significant impact on the students' career ideals. First-year anxiety and frustration, while not intended to dehumanize or degrade students, had the impact of making students think less about idealism and career goals as they struggled to get through. The stress was produced by a set of factors: (1) the difficult task of mastering a new and confusing body of knowledge; (2) the minimal (at best) feedback regarding success as the year progressed; (3) the challenge of Socratic classroom discussion and the attendant threat of embarrassment; (4) the fact that half the class will now have "below average" grades when previously all applicants were considered highly successful as undergraduates; and, finally, (5) the necessity of adjusting to and becoming part of a new social environment in which academic success is one way of winning respect. Second year found the students more professionally dressed, less anxious, and more absorbed in activities outside the classroom (including part-time legal work). *Id.* at 45–46.

Stover's study also explored alternative explanations. First, age itself could have an impact as students matured. Second, political beliefs could change. The nature of legal education itself might heighten conservatism and discourage altruism because of a pro-business orientation in law school or because law school increased social conservatism among its students in a variety of ways. Finally, the job market might discourage commitment to public interest work. Stover found some support for these concepts and did not rule them out as contributing factors but emphasized the importance of changes in values and expectations. He found that students became more optimistic about employment in small private firms but more pessimistic about employment at big firms and about employment in public interest jobs. *Id.* at 90–100.

Overall, students who did not change their ideals during these periods were more likely to have worked at public interest jobs during law school and to have been involved in organizations supportive of idealistic goals. Student organizations and subculture proved important at promoting continued interest in and commitment to public interest work. *Id.* at 103–120.

Robert Granfield, surveying Harvard law students, also found "the daily experiences of students in law schools are deeply imbricated with contradictions pertaining to their future practice, knowledge of the law, and their views of justice." Robert Granfield, *Making Elite Lawyers: Visions of Law at Harvard and Beyond* 3 (1992). Granfield describes a Harvard 2L who conveyed a passionate interest in doing work related to health care for the elderly. This student described herself as progressive and scoffed at classmates seeking corporate jobs. When Granfield interviewed this student again, at the end of her third year, she reported she was "going to Wall Street to do commercial transactions and there is nothing better I would like to do." *Id.* Granfield describes his shock at the compromise of belief that this student had made in such a short time to justify her career decision.

How well do the patterns of continued and/or changed commitment among students described by Robert Stover and Robert Granfield fit with the experience of law students whom you know? Have your classmates changed? Have you? How?

How well do you feel you understand the legal job market and the employment possibilities you may find?

What do you think is the impact of legal work done while students are in law school on their hope for or interest in public interest and social justice employment after graduation?

How likely do you think it is that you will find the work that you hope to do? How have your ideas on this subject changed during law school?

Does the structure of legal education, beyond the dynamics described by Stover, promote the status quo or discourage work on social justice issues? Robert Stevens describes the development of law schools within American universities during the 19th century. The case method, introduced at Harvard by Christopher Columbus Langdell, was based on the idea of law as a science. This science supposed discoverable principles and rules, which were best revealed in appellate cases. The neutral, value-free, consistent principles taken from these cases could be applied to new cases as they arose. The case method and the Socratic teaching method based on discussion of appellate cases were gradually adopted among American law schools by the early 20th century. Robert Stevens, *Law School: Legal Education in America from the 1850s to the 1980s* 52–64 (1983).

As the case method spread from Harvard across the country, a simultaneous movement to raise standards in law schools brought pressures to bear against part-time programs and night schools which tended to serve immigrants and lower-income applicants. Some scholars have remarked that these developments are related:

> Jerold Auerbach argued, from the perspective of a social historian, that the ideology of the case method as a "science" led legal educators to believe that they could reform society and its evils ultimately through their skills as scientists. Envisioning themselves as leaders of society, they felt they could allow into the field only those who upheld the same moral values and ideology and had the same intellectual background as they did; they had to keep out "the poorly educated, the ill-prepared, and the morally weak candidates," which inevitably included non-native-born Americans. The efforts to raise standards, in Auerbach's view, were primarily concerned with keeping out Jews, blacks, and immigrants.

Id. at 99–100. Stevens reviews evidence for and against Auerbach's thesis regarding prejudice and concludes that "the attack on night and part-time schools that opened the twentieth century seems to have been a confusing mixture of public interest, economic opportunism, and ethnic prejudice" as well as another factor, "professional pride." *Id.* at 101.

Are there changes in legal education that could enhance the commitment of students to social justice work? Is legal education aimed at producing lawyers with the skills necessary for social justice work? Consider this early critique of the application of the case method in legal education, written in the early 1930s.

JEROME FRANK

Why Not a Clinical Lawyer–School?
81 U. Penn. L. Rev. 907, 909–11, 916–17, 923 (1933)

The method of teaching still used in some university law schools (and accepted by them as more or less sacrosanct) is founded upon the ideas of Christopher Columbus Langdell. It may be said, indeed, to be the expression of that man's peculiar temperament.

Langdell unequivocally stated as the fundamental tenet of his system of teaching *"that all the available materials ... are contained in printed books."* The printed opinions of judges are, he maintained, the *exclusive* repositories of the wisdom which law students must acquire to make them lawyers.

* * *

A brief outline of the history of legal education in American universities is helpful as a preliminary to some tentative suggestions for changes:

It began with the apprentice system. The prospective lawyer "read law" in the office of a practicing lawyer. He saw daily what courts were doing. The first American law school, founded by Judge Reeves, in the 1780's was merely the apprentice system on a group basis. The students were still in intimate daily contact with the courts. Then (about 1830) came the college law school with teaching on the college pattern of lectures and text-books. This step is ordinarily pictured as progress. For the student now devoted full time to his books and lectures and the distractions of office and court work were removed. A more unpleasant story could be told: The student was cloistered; he learned of court doings from books and lectures only; the *false* aspects of theory could no longer be compared by him with the actualities of practice.

There followed the period when the leading law schools were dominated by the great systematic text-book writers, the makers of so called (American) "substantive law," substantive law which was divorced and living apart from procedure. The rift widened between theory and practice.

Then came Langdell. Noting his plea for induction, his efforts to avoid the glib generalities of text books, one cannot help feeling that he was seeking obliquely and fumblingly to return to some limited extent to court-room actualities. But he was patently thinking of the lawyer as brief-writer and nothing more. Consequently, the material on which he based his so-called "induction" was hopelessly limited.

Ostensibly, the students were to study cases. But they did not and *they do not study cases.* They do not even study the printed records of cases (although that would be little enough), let alone cases as living processes. Their attention is restricted to judicial *opinions. But an opinion is not a decision.* A decision is a specific judgment, or order or decree entered after a trial of a specific lawsuit between specific litigants. There [is] a multitude of factors which induce a jury to return a verdict, or a judge to enter a decree. Of those numerous factors, but few are set forth in judicial opinions. And those factors, not expressed in the opinions, frequently are the most important in the real causal explanation of the decisions.

As stated above, the Langdell system (even in its revised version) concentrates attention on the so-called legal rules and principles found in or spelled out of the printed opinions. Now no sane person will deny that a knowledge of those rules and principles, of how to "distinguish" cases, and of how to make an argument as to the true *ratio decidendi* of an opinion, is part of the indispensable equipment of the future lawyer. For such knowledge is of some limited aid in guessing what courts will do. And in arguments made to courts lawyers are required to employ terminology in accordance with the fictitious assumption that the rules and principles are the principal bases of all decisions.

* * *

For the law student to learn whatever can be learned of (1) the means of guessing what courts will decide and (2) of how to induce courts to decide the way his clients want them to decide, he must observe carefully what actually goes on in court-rooms and law-offices. * * *

* * *

The case-system should be revised so that it will in truth and fact become a case-system and not a mere sham case-system.

A few of the current type of so-called case-books should be retained to teach dialectic skill in brief-writing. But the study of cases which will lead to some small measure of real understanding of how cases are won, lost and decided, should be based to a very marked extent on reading and analysis of *complete records of cases*—beginning with the filing of the first papers, through the trial in the trial court and to and through the upper courts. *Six months properly spent on one or two elaborate court records, including the briefs (and supplemented by reading of text-books as well as upper court opinions) will teach a student more than two years spent on going through twenty of the case-books now in use.*

In medical schools, "case histories" are used for instruction. But they are far more complete than the alleged case-books used in law schools. *It is absurd that we should continue to call an upper court opinion a case.* It is at most an adjunct to the final step in a case (*i.e.*, an essay published by an upper court in justification of its decision).

But even if legal case-books were true case-books and as complete as medical case histories, they would be insufficient as tools for study. What would we think of a medical school in which students studied no more than what was to be found in such written or printed case-histories and were deprived of all clinical experience until after they received their M.D. degrees? Our law schools must learn from our medical schools. *Law students should be given the opportunity to see legal operations.* Their study of cases should be supplemented by frequent visits, accompanied by law teachers, to both trial and appellate courts. The cooperation of judges could easily be enlisted. * * *

* * *

Medical schools rely to a very large extent on the free medical clinics and dispensaries. There exist today legal clinics in the form of the Legal Aid Society. Today that agency is by no means the equivalent of the medical clinics and dispensaries. The ablest physicians devote a considerable portion of their time to medical clinics while Legal Aid Society is, on the whole, staffed by men who are not outstanding in their profession. The leading lawyers of the community do not actively participate in its activities. The Society is limited in the kinds of cases it can take, and the law teachers have little, if any, direct contact with its efforts.

Suppose, however, that there were in each law school a legal clinic or dispensary. As before indicated, a considerable part of the teaching staff of a law school should consist of lawyers who already had varied experience in practice. Some of these men could run the law school legal clinics assisted by (a) graduate students; (b) undergraduate students; and (c) leading members of the local bar.

The work of these clinics would be done for little or no charge. The teacher-clinicians would devote their full time to their teaching, including such clinical work, and would not engage in private practice.

In sum, the practice of law and the deciding of cases constitute not sciences but arts—the art of the lawyer and the art of the judge. Only a slight part of any art can be learned from books. Whether it be painting or writing or practicing law, the best kind of education in an art is usually through apprentice-training under the supervision of men some of whom have themselves become skilled in the actual practice of the art. That was once accepted wisdom in American legal education. It needs to be rediscovered.

Notes and Questions

1. Frank asserts that lawyers learn legal rules and principles as if the knowledge in printed opinions provides the bases of all decisions. He states:

> But the tasks of the lawyer do not pivot around those rules and principles. The work of the lawyer revolves about specific decisions in definite pieces of litigation. When he draws a will or passes on a mortgage to secure a bond issue, organizes a corporation, negotiates the settlement of a controversy, reorganizes a railroad, or drafts a legislative bill, the lawyer is as truly concerned with how the courts will act in some concrete case as when he is trying such a case. A lawyer tries to answer these questions: "What will happen if these specific documents or transactions should hereafter become a part of the drama of a lawsuit? What will a court decide is their meaning and effect?" For the legal rights and duties of the client, Jones, under any given document (a promissory note, a deed, contract, etc.) or in connection with any given transaction, mean simply what some court, somewhere, some day in the future, will decide (not what it will say in its opinion) in a future concrete lawsuit relating to Jones' specific rights under that specific document or in connection with that specific transaction.

Frank, *supra* at 910.

Does Frank's definition of the lawyer's task illuminate key aspects of lawyering? Might the work of a transactional lawyer aim at helping clients to avoid conflicts? Is Frank's definition adequate when applied to lawyers working for social justice? Is concerning oneself only with individual clients a luxury? Is representation centered on one's own client required by professional ethics? How can the social justice practitioner resolve the dilemma between representing needs of individual clients and avoiding the creation of "bad law" that might affect similarly situated clients adversely? *See* chapters 3, 4, 5, and 6, for an expanded discussion of ethics and social justice practice.

2. Is Frank's critique of legal education still valid today? How many modifications in legal education, including the availability of

clinical study, externships, and other forms of training-in-practice at many schools, alter the main points in Frank's criticisms? If the critique remains valid, why has so little changed in the academy in the past century?

3. In another critique Duncan Kennedy described legal education as "training for hierarchy":

> [L]aw schools are intensely *political* places in spite of the fact that the modern law school seems intellectually unpretentious, barren of theoretical ambition or practical vision of what social life might be. The trade school mentality, the endless attention to trees at the expense of forests, the alternating grimness and chumminess of focus on the limited task at hand, all these are only a part of what is going on. The other part is ideological training for willing service in the hierarchies of the corporate welfare state.
>
> To say that law school is ideological is to say that what teachers teach along with basic skills is wrong, is nonsense about what law is and how it works. It is to say that the message about the nature of legal competence, and its distribution among students, is wrong, is nonsense * * * that the ideas about the possibilities of life as a lawyer that students pick up from legal education are wrong, are nonsense. But all this is nonsense with a tilt, it is biased and motivated rather than random error. What it says is that it is natural, efficient, and fair for law firms, the bar as a whole, and the society the bar services to be organized in their actual patterns of hierarchy and domination.
>
> Because students believe what they are told, explicitly and implicitly, about the world they are entering, they behave in ways that fulfill the prophecies the system makes about them and about that world. This is the link-back that completes the system: students do more than accept the way things are, and ideology does more than damp opposition. Students act affirmatively within the channels cut for them, cutting them deeper, giving the whole a patina of consent, and weaving complicity into everyone's life story.
>
> Resist!

Duncan Kennedy, *Legal Education and the Reproduction of Hierarchy: A Polemic Against the System* i–ii (1983). How can a law student combat complicity?

4. Do the silences in legal education about hierarchy and systems of privilege curtail classroom conversation to the educational detriment of all? Consider this description of the effect of these silences on the classroom climate:

> The foremost issue raised by the law school classroom climate is silence, the silence of students in the class. While silence can be a strength when it is freely chosen, law students often feel compelled to be silent because of the intimidating atmosphere of the law school classroom. One type of student silence is born of fear, given the

hierarchical nature of the law school classroom. This fear is an "equal opportunity" problem; women and men, people of all races and sexual orientation may feel intimidated upon entering law school. But another form of silence may come from a heart-stabbing awareness of assumptions not challenged and issues not discussed.

Legal education needs to understand * * * [the power line. Consider our location as to race, gender, sexual orientation, and other categories.] Those above the line are privileged with respect to those below it. * * * This distribution of power means that a system of white privilege reinforces the existing racial status quo. This system of privilege overlaps and interacts with other systems of privilege, including those based on gender, sexual orientation, economic wealth, physical ability, and religion. In part these systems continue to operate because the unwritten rule is not to discuss them. The result is a deafening silence.

* * *

When we challenge racism, sexism, or homophobia, we give up a little piece of our privileged position in this society, whether we have felt that privilege by being smart, white, male, straight, or just accepted. Perhaps that is why it feels so hard to do it. * * * Sheila O'Rourke has said that she "tries to practice on other people's oppression." So if someone says something racist, she, as a white person, tries to speak out. She hopes others will also speak out when the remark is sexist or homophobic, so that she won't be surrounded by silence.

Stephanie M. Wildman, *The Classroom Climate* in *Looking at Law School* 75–76, 89 (Stephen Gillers ed., 4th ed. 1997). *See also* Margaret E. Montoya, *Silence and Silencing: Their Centripetal and Centrifugal Forces in Legal Communication, Pedagogy and Discourse*, 5 Mich. J. Race & L. 847 (2000) ("[O]ne's use of silence is an aspect of communication that, like accents, is related to one's culture and may correlate with one's racial identity. * * * [S]ilence can be a force that disrupts the dominant discourse within the law school classroom, creating learning spaces where deeper dialogue from different points of view can occur. * * * [S]ilencing of racial issues within legal discourse and public policy debates * * * is a mechanism for racial control and hegemony." *Id.* at 847.)

Have you tried to raise issues of hierarchy or privilege in your classes? What was the reaction from the professor? From other students? Would you recommend to other students that they try to raise these issues? What implications for legal education do your answers suggest?

5. Have you been told that the goal of legal education is to make you "think like a lawyer?" Have you considered what such thinking might mean? Angela Harris and Marjorie Shultz suggest that in many contexts " 'thinking like a lawyer' means suppressing or denying one's feelings and personal experience while putting forth a 'cold' analysis of the 'facts.' " Angela P. Harris & Marjorie M. Shultz, *"A(nother) Critique*

of Pure Reason": Toward Civic Virtue in Legal Education, 45 Stan. L. Rev. 1773, 1774 (1993).

Harris and Shultz continue:

> Classical legal education celebrates reason and devalues emotion. Seeking to remove legal reasoning both from "the political" and from "the personal," law professors traditionally shun openly-expressed emotions in the classroom. When classroom discussions raise deeply emotional issues, students who are able to dispassionately discuss both sides of the argument are the ones admired.

Id. at 1773–74. Harris and Shultz argue that "emotions can never successfully be eliminated from any truly important intellectual undertaking, in the law or elsewhere." *Id.* at 1774.

How might the avoidance of emotion in legal education impact the training of advocates for social justice? For one view, see Ann L. Iijima, *Lessons Learned: Legal Education and Law Student Dysfunction*, 48 J. Legal Educ. 524 (1998) (describing the contribution of legal education to emotional dysfunction and substance abuse in the legal profession). *See also* Duncan Kennedy, *Legal Education as Training for Hierarchy* in *The Politics of Law* 41 (David Kairys ed., 1990) (describing training students to reject emotional reaction of outrage as "naive, nonlegal, irrelevant").

For a description of the role of bar examinations in permeating and controlling significant aspects of legal education, see Joan Howarth, *Teaching in the Shadow of the Bar*, 31 U.S.F. L.Rev. 927 (1997).

6. Describing a quite different aspect of "thinking like a lawyer," Chris K. Iijima describes his own "shock of recognition" when his mentor, Anthony G. Amsterdam, said: "[I]deally no case should be taught to a student without the student first asking him or herself the question, 'Who am I?' " Iijima calls this "the 'who' of legal analysis." He continues: "[Amsterdam] asserted that it was only from the perspective of the lawyer's context—i.e., the particular interest of the client, the stage of the litigation, the jurisdiction of the court, etc.—that a student could appreciate the real meaning of the authority." Chris K. Iijima, *Separating Support from Betrayal: Examining the Intersections of Racialized Legal Pedagogy, Academic Support, and Subordination*, 33 Ind. L. Rev. 737, 738 (2000).

7. Frank expresses concern about the widening rift between theory and practice. For a modern day lament that the gap between theory and practice hampers legal education, see Harry T. Edwards, *The Growing Disjunction Between Legal Education and the Legal Profession*, 91 Mich. L. Rev. 34 (1992). Edwards asserts:

> [L]aw schools and law firms are moving in opposite directions. The schools should be training ethical practitioners and producing scholarship that judges, legislators, and practitioners can use. The firms should be ensuring that associates and partners practice law in an ethical manner. But many law schools—especially the so-called "elite" ones—have abandoned their proper place, by emphasizing

> abstract theory at the expense of practical scholarship and pedagogy. Many law firms have also abandoned *their* place, by pursuing profit above all else.

Id. at 34.

Do you agree with Frank and Edwards that a gap between theory and practice is at the heart of what ails legal education? For another view, urging that theory and practice are inseparable, see bell hooks, *Theory as Liberatory Practice*, 4 Yale J.L. & Feminism 1 (1991).

SECTION 3. DEBT AND SOCIAL JUSTICE IDEALS: FINANCING LEGAL EDUCATION AND ENSURING A REPRESENTATIVE BAR

Professional education is expensive. For many students, that expense makes it necessary to borrow extensively. Does the debt of law students affect their education, daily life, and career choices? Even before law students shouldered the heavy debt loads that are now common, Stover and Granfield observed that students came to law school with social justice aspirations and then moved away from those ideals during the course of their legal educations. Therefore, financial issues do not fully account for student career choices. *See* section 2, discussing the impact of legal education on ideals.

Yet debt remains a critical issue for all students. Large debt poses a substantial structural obstacle to career choices that do not maximize financial rewards. In an early vision of the problems inherent in financing legal education, John Kramer described the ways in which shifting the burden of financing professional education from parent to student had spawned a debt-driven regime. *See* John R. Kramer, *Will Legal Education Remain Affordable, by Whom, and How?*, 1987 Duke L.J. 240. Kramer's concerns proved prophetic. By 1999, 86% of law school graduates had borrowed money for their legal education; the average debt of graduates from private law schools was estimated at between $56,324 and $63,078 for all students; and, for heavier borrowers, law school loans alone (not counting undergraduate debt) averaged $79,851.55. At one law school, average law school debt for graduating students had increased from $30,000 to $71,000 in just eight years. Phillip G. Schrag, *The Federal Income-Contingent Repayment Option For Law Student Loans*, 29 Hofstra L. Rev. 733, 742, 746–47 (2001). Does debt create fears about money for you or your classmates?

Given the high debt burden that accompanies professional education for most law graduates, debates continue about how to facilitate entry into social justice legal work, which is usually low-paying in relation to corporate practice. Several questions are embedded in these debates. How great is the impact of student debt on ideals and career choices? Which policy choices best respond to the economic pressures faced by students who wish to pursue social justice work? How might these choices impact diversity in the legal profession?

A. The Impact of Debt on Ideals and Career Choices

Determining the impact of debt on career choice can be complicated. Students who plan to work at high-paying jobs may borrow more freely and therefore have higher debts. Many students change their plans during law school whether or not their decisions are affected by debt.

Equal Justice Works (formerly The National Association for Public Interest Law (NAPIL)) states that student debts are a serious obstacle to careers in public interest law. States which have instituted Loan Repayment Assistance Programs (LRAPs) also express concern with the impact of debt on the careers of lawyers. *See, e.g.,* the North Carolina program, at <http://www.ncleaf.org> and the Minnesota program, at <http://www.lrapmn.org> (visited September 30, 2002). Some empirical studies have found that debt has an impact on the interest of students in jobs in government or legal services and on the likelihood that students will make plans to work in those sectors. *See* David L. Chambers, *The Burdens of Educational Loans: The Impacts of Debt on Job Choice and Standards of Living for Students at Nine American Law Schools*, 42 J. Legal Educ. 187 (1992); Schrag, *supra* at 779–82.

In a study of the impact of debt on legal education, Lewis A. Kornhauser and Richard L. Revesz emphasized the changes in the proportion of the profession engaged in public sector and public interest work and the great differentials in salaries that developed between public and private sector employment between the early 1970s and the 1990s. The legal profession grew after World War II both in proportion to the population of the United States as a whole and also in terms of the value it added to the gross domestic product. "Between 1950 and 1991, the number of lawyers almost quadrupled, but the size of the population did not even double. Thus, while there was one lawyer for every 679 people in 1950, by 1991 this ratio stood at one lawyer for every 313 people." Lewis A. Kornhauser & Richard L. Revesz, *Legal Education and Entry into the Legal Profession: The Role of Race, Gender, and Educational Debt*, 70 N.Y.U. L. Rev. 829, 835–36 (1995).

Kornhauser and Revesz emphasize the importance of increasing pay differentials within the profession to student choices about social justice work. They found that salaries in private sector employment rose dramatically over time in relation to government sector work. The gap between public interest jobs and private practice jobs grew even more sharply. Kornhauser and Revesz argued that "The greater the income gap between the for-profit and not-for-profit sectors, the more likely it is that graduates will choose the former." Kornhauser & Revesz, *supra* at 833. Their empirical studies of graduating students from the law schools at New York University and the University of Michigan found that several factors predicted entry into private practice or public interest practice better than debt. Career plans and participation in public-interest oriented organizations were also important to subsequent career choices. *Id.* at 891–942.

Kornhauser and Revesz found, after controlling for other relevant factors, "African American and Latino students are more likely to take not-for-profit positions than their white and Asian American classmates." *Id.* at 833. They also found that, after controlling for relevant factors, "women are more likely than men to enter law school with not-for-profit career plans, but law school disproportionately shifts their preferences towards for-profit jobs. *Id.* One commentator suggests that the particular impact of law school on women is a hidden factor in the tendency for students to move away from commitment to social justice lawyering." Adrienne Stone, *The Public Interest and the Power of the Feminist Critique of Law School: Women's Empowerment of Legal Education and its Implications for the Fate of Public Interest Commitment*, 5 Am. U. J. Gender & L. 525 (1997). For a description of the impact of law school on women, see Lani Guinier, Michelle Fine & Jane Balin, *Becoming Gentlemen: Women, Law School, and Institutional Change* (1997).

In a recent examination of the problem of educational debt, Michael Olivas found a "dire threat to professional education" and expressed concern that financing graduate studies "will become as substantial a transaction for many students as purchasing their first home. This certainly does not bode well for higher education's traditional inequity-reducing powers." Michael A. Olivas, *Paying for a Law Degree: Trends in Student Borrowing and the Ability to Repay Debt*, 49 J. Legal Educ. 333, 333 (1999).

Do you feel that pressure from educational debt is influencing your career choice? *See* Marilyn Yarbrough, *Financing Legal Education*, 51 J. Legal Educ. 457, 461 (2001) (describing costs of legal education, sources of financial aid for law students, and speculating that indebtedness means "fewer students can afford to take on starting positions with the lower salary strata, particularly in the area of public interest law.")

Do students at your school talk freely about social justice career plans and how best to achieve them? Or is it common for students to discuss their fears about grades and the ability to get jobs at law firms—without directly confronting their questions about the impact of debt on career choice?

Is it possible that *fear* of debt, not only the *practical effect* of debt, influences the way students consider career choices? How can students interested in working for social justice address these issues constructively?

Sylvia Law argues that the most important tasks for law students interested in social justice are to understand the legal work they want to do, acquire the skills to do it, and create a basis of mutual support that will make the path possible:

> Ralph Nader suggests that while in law school you should simply ignore the question of how you are going to make a living,

and rather try to figure out how, assuming that you had a source of support, you could use your legal talents and skills in the most effective way to do work that seems to you important. I think this is good advice. Nicholas Johnson, former Commissioner of the FCC, suggests that the question of how to support yourself is essentially a legal question. If you have developed your legal skills with the enthusiasm and passion that can only come if you are working in a context that makes sense to you, when the time comes to support yourself, you will be able to figure out how to do it. I think that this is also good advice. Most important, nurture a group of friends who share your values. Friendship requires time and effort; lawyers and law students are crippled when the organization of their lives leads them to believe that they do not have time for friendship. We need our friends to help us figure out who we are, what we think, and what sort of world we want to help to create. None of us can do it alone.

Law, *supra* at 171.

B. Debt and Diversity in the Legal Profession

Several articles have explored the underrepresentation of people of color in elite law firms. One commentator discusses the importance of racial diversity to the profession:

Minority attorneys are underrepresented in prestigious corporate law firms. Before turning to the numbers, however, it is important to note what this means for the state of the profession. The paucity of minority attorneys in large corporate law firms is important because of what these firms represent. The perception within the profession is that these larger firms represent the elite practitioners of the private practice bar. Employment by one of these firms indicates that the lawyer so employed is part of the legal elite. Moreover these lawyers who practice in elite firms not only represent the elite of the profession, to a large degree they control the profession and its development.

* * *

* * * [A]lthough the numbers of minority attorneys are increasing, and although their numbers are also increasing (although not proportionally) as associates in elite law firms, they are still underrepresented among the ranks of such law firms as associates and they are making little or no progress toward increasing their numbers as partners in these same elite firms.

What does this mean for the profession? It means that a profession that prides itself on promoting equal opportunity under the law is failing to adhere to its own standards. It means that a profession that gains prestige and relative preference over other occupations because of its identification as the promoter and guarantor of civil liberties will or should be at risk of losing that prestige when the reality of its abysmal hiring practices is publicized and becomes well-known to the outside world. * * *

Alex M. Johnson, Jr., *The Underrepresentation of Minorities in the Legal Profession: A Critical Race Theorist's Perspective*, 95 Mich. L. Rev. 1005, 1007–08, 1011 (1997). *See also* James W. Pearce, JoAnn S. Hickey & Debra D. Burke, *African Americans in Large Law Firms: The Possible Cost of Exclusion*, 42 How. L.J. 59 (1998) (concluding that large law firms' failure to attract and keep minority lawyers not only perpetuates social inequities, but also negatively impacts firm performance).

The National Association for Law Placement (NALP) website states: "Research released in December of 2001 revealed that attorneys of color accounted for 3.55% of the partners in major law firms and women accounted for 15.80% of the partners in these firms. Nationally, 41.94% of associates and staff/senior attorneys were women, while 13.70% were attorneys of color. Women attorneys and attorneys of color were best represented among summer associates; 17.26% of summer associates were of color, while women accounted for about 48% of summer associates." (http://www.nalp.org/nalpresearch/mw_indx.htm) (visited May 12, 2002). Another study in the 1990s found that minorities were a disproportionate number of graduating law students who did not say that they had secured jobs and did not identify what sort of employment they expected to get in responses to a survey. David L. Chambers, *supra* at 187, 188.

Does the underrepresentation of people of color in elite firms operate to discredit the legal profession? Is the lack of representation by people of color in the bar a concern that the profession needs to address? If so, what steps should be taken and who should take them? The California Bar Board of Governors reviewed a report that indicated the State Bar would remain disproportionately white when compared to the percentage of whites in the state population. Suggestions for addressing the issue included increasing the number of people of color admitted to law school, funding legal education, subsidizing the cost of taking the bar exam, and examining the pipeline that leads students to a legal education. *See* Mike McKee, *A "Disproportionately White" Bar; Bar Study: Even as State's Diversity Grows, Minorities Will Still Struggle to Become Lawyers*, S.F. Recorder 1, Feb. 11, 2000. How might lawyers play a role in implementing these ideas?

Johnson, *Underrepresentation of Minorities, supra*, and others agree that job choices for minority law students are constrained by the continuation of discrimination. *See, e.g.*, David B. Wilkins, *Rollin' On the River: Race, Elite Schools, and the Equality Paradox*, 25 Law & Soc. Inquiry 527, 529–30 (2000) (observing "race continues to *structure* the careers of minority lawyers, including those from the nation's top law schools, in complex ways that, once again on average, make it more difficult for these talented women and men to succeed in certain professional environments.").

In one of the early studies of the growing burdens of law student debt, Marilyn Yarbrough considered the particular impact of debt on minority students.

MARILYN V. YARBROUGH

Minority Students and Debt: Limiting Limited Career Options
39 J. Legal Educ. 697, 697–701, 703–07 (1989)

The provision of higher education to all who qualify for it intellectually has been a social ideal in this country for the last forty years. Until relatively recently, attempts to provide educational opportunity for those who could not afford it took the form of tuition grants and scholarships or tuition waivers, with little reliance on educational loans. In the last decade, however, student loans have come to comprise the major method of funding students in postsecondary education.

* * *

[T]he financing of legal education by means of loans represents a problem for all law students. Minority students, however, already limited by discriminatory employment patterns and salary differentials, are disproportionately disadvantaged by the problems associated with the repayment of educational debts. * * *

* * *

* * * Taking into account the limited job opportunities minority law school graduates have, does it make good economic sense for minority students to borrow in order to pay continually increasing tuition rates? The repayment options available to minority graduates are limited because of their lack of opportunity to obtain higher paying jobs, the self selection of some into low-salaried public interest and public service careers, and the resulting salary differential they suffer, whether by choice or otherwise.

* * *

* * * [G]rants cover less than five percent of the aid awarded to help finance enrollment in law school. Other available sources of funds, e.g., parental support and employment during the academic year and in the summer, add only a small fraction of the money necessary for law school tuition and living expenses. Further, minority students have less access to these non-loan resources because of the lack of opportunities to compete for jobs and the lack of funds from family contributions.

For students with genuine career options, the existence of significant amounts of debt is likely to influence the choices made. There are little persuasive data, however, to verify the *degree* of influence on law-student career choices and none that address the influence on minority law students specifically. * * *

* * *

With regard to low-income students, Pye and Kramer noted that "students from low income backgrounds who attend the highest cost private law schools will have even more debt * * * to the extent that they obtain * * * [federal], state or school loans." * * * [Some graduates on low salaries repaying on current terms would] end up paying close to twenty-five percent of their gross salary even with interest rates as low as eight percent. Although there is a lack of consensus among experts as to what level of debt is manageable, one-quarter of gross salary clearly is not. Estimates of manageable debt range from three to fifteen percent of pre-tax income depending on lifestyle and other factors, and from six to nine percent of after-tax income.

* * * [T]here are no hard data linking loan burden with job choice. Instinct and some random student narratives indicate that debt burden is an important element in job choice for those who have a choice, an option less available to minority graduates than others. * * *

The basic debt/job cause-and-effect question, suggested by surveys sponsored by the Carnegie Foundation and the American Council on Education, was posed in the recent Joint Economic Committee report: "[D]o students borrow more when they expect to enter high paying fields or do they enter high paying fields because they have large debts to repay?" Most evidence would suggest that students actually do not know what manageable debt is and, until recently, have not had the tools even to estimate that amount with any degree of assurance. * * *

* * *

There are data to suggest that disadvantaged students, especially minority students, find large loans onerous. At least one survey has documented that minority undergraduate students graduating from private prestigious colleges are more likely to report that loans were a major source of funds to them than they were to other students. Further, some speculate that black enrollment has declined because many black students are discouraged from enrolling because they wish to avoid a heavy debt burden. * * *

* * *

[The author described statistical evidence of the disparity between employment options for minority and non-minority students, noting] the options for minority students are limited. * * * Access to the profession continues to be differentially available to significant numbers of minority graduates. * * *

* * *

* * * [I]f more minorities were afforded equal access to legal positions with higher salaries, the problems of differential ability to repay debt would not be significant. The fact is that those jobs are not presently available and salary differentials do exist. If the question is how one can limit the discriminatory impact of debt burden created by

salary differentials, a number of solutions have been proposed and some in fact implemented.

* * *

Although none of the programs presently in force focus solely on minority group status, a persuasive argument can be made for public subsidies to groups likely to contain significant numbers of minority graduates (the focus of my concern): persons practicing in lawyer-deficient areas, persons entering low paying jobs with a high social utility such as legal aid, and others who satisfy some public policy objective.

* * *

We have not been as innovative in dealing with the educational debt problems as some other countries. For instance, in Sweden borrowers entering jobs paying below average wages may defer payments for one year at a time and are given until the age of fifty, if necessary, to repay the loans. In return, the amount due is increased each year by an inflation index. In West Germany loans carry no interest, repayment starts five years after students leave school, students have a maximum of twenty years in which to repay, there is a deferment for low income wage earnings, and the debt is canceled after twenty years. * * *

An obvious solution to the problem of excessive borrowing by minority law students is the provision of a greater proportion of grant dollars while students are in school. To the extent a grant program is not narrowly focused on students who are most likely to be unable to repay debts because of limited income, the solution may be overinclusive. Better counseling, with a more realistic assessment by individual students of their own future ability to repay, is also needed. An argument also can be made for the provision of public subsidies through loan forgiveness to persons practicing in lawyer-deficient areas, persons entering low paying jobs of high social utility such as legal aid, and others who satisfy some public policy objective.

* * * Existing deferment options related to public service careers could be expanded. Internships in public service similar to those extant in the public health area could provide for repayment deferment or partial forgiveness. * * *

Notes and Questions

1. Are the burdens of debt that Yarbrough describes for students of color experienced by students from a variety of backgrounds? How do opportunity and job choice affect the burden of debt and students' perceptions of that burden?

2. Should legal educators and members of the profession be concerned about debt load for those seeking to enter the profession? What do you think would be a reasonable ratio of debt to income? Should the profession help aspiring lawyers to achieve a reasonable ratio, or are

these financial matters simply problems of concern to individuals? Could law schools initiate programs to help students further reduce living expenses while in school? Should they?

3. Should the debt issue be addressed by decreasing debt or by assisting with repayment? Equal Justice Works has worked to promote Loan Repayment Assistance Programs (LRAPs) to provide assistance with debt repayment to students in low-paying public service positions. These programs, which have been established by law schools, states, and some employers, provide money to help graduates with loan payments and gradual forgiveness of the loan assistance that has been provided as lawyers remain in public interest positions over a period of years.

Kornhauser and Revesz have criticized LRAPs as the major solution to student debt, based in part on their findings that debt had a less significant impact on career choice than salaries:

> These conclusions lead us to question the increasing reliance by law schools on LRAP as a tool of financial aid policy. Instead, we propose a program of public-service scholarships, under which students would obtain grants simply by certifying that they have a strong commitment to a career in the not-for-profit sector. In order to discourage individuals without strong commitments from seeking such grants, penalties would be applied to recipients taking higher paying jobs within the first ten years after graduation.
>
> The desirability of this program is enhanced by a recently obtained ruling of the Internal Revenue Service, which provides that such scholarships are not taxable to the beneficiaries. Allocating financial aid through this program rather than through LRAP thus results in savings of up to 40% of the funds disbursed. We believe that this difference in tax treatment of two programs that essentially achieve the same objective is, by itself, sufficient reason for law schools to rethink their use of LRAP.
>
> We also propose that more careful attention be paid to moral-obligation grants, under which a moral obligation to repay the economic value of the assistance would attach if the recipient took a for-profit job. Such programs might be more successful than they have been so far if the precise nature of the financial obligation is clearly specified.

Kornhauser and Revesz, *supra* at 833–34.

Kornhauser and Revesz recognize that LRAPs are also important. Some students become interested in social justice work during law school and will not have sought special scholarships in advance. Their program assumes that a law school would maintain its loan forgiveness program and add targeted scholarships as an additional alternative. *Id.* at 954–55.

Would moral obligation grants be preferable to loan forgiveness as a means of financing legal education? What reasons might law schools have for preferring loan forgiveness or grants?

4. Equal Justice Works reported in a study "Financing the Future," released in October 2000, that the "number of LRAPs in existence has remained disappointingly flat." Equal Justice Works found forty-seven LRAP programs nationwide compared to forty-eight in 1994. The report noted that although the number of LRAPs is slightly lower since 1994, the payments made by these programs has more than doubled to roughly $7.6 million in 1999. Six law schools, Yale, New York University, Harvard, Columbia, Stanford, and Georgetown provide the majority of funds allocated nationally, accounting for 70% of LRAP spending. *See* Victoria Rivkin, *Little Progress Seen in Financing Loan Repayments*, N.Y. L.J., Oct. 11, 2000, at col. 5, 1. The Equal Justice Works website gathers information on LRAPs and a variety of other programs that assist students with law school debts. *See* <http://www.napil.org> (visited May 12, 2002).

5. In an attempt to assist students with burgeoning loan repayments, Congress created a federal direct lending program in 1993. The Department of Education can now issue its own loans to students. The legislation requires that the Secretary of Education must offer borrowers four repayment plans: (1) a standard ten-year repayment plan; (2) extended repayment plan over a longer period of time; (3) "graduated repayment" plan wherein the amount to be repaid increases as the loan ages; and (4) income-contingent repayment plan. Under the income-contingent repayment plan, annual loan repayment amounts are based on the income of the borrower. This legislation does not reduce the amount of debt for any student. The fixed low payments are spread over a greater number of years and result in a greater amount to be repaid.

This legislation may offer an option in loan repayment to heavily indebted, socially conscious law graduates, among others, enabling borrowers to consider lower-paying community service jobs. However, the income-contingent option is not widely known among students and has not been widely used by graduates. A recent examination of the program, which makes proposals for legislative reform to heighten effectiveness, suggests many possible reasons for the low rates of utilization of the program, including high cumulative interest figures, the daunting effect of extremely long repayment periods, and questions about its usefulness compared with other forms of loan repayment assistance. *See* Schrag, *supra* at 742–47.

6. What are the methods by which attorneys working for social justice and public interest might be paid? Attorney fees provided by statute and contingency fees are discussed in chapter 2, as are the legal services movement and the Legal Services Corporation.

SECTION 4. ENVISIONING SOCIAL JUSTICE LAWYERING

Students who survive their legal education with an aspiration to work for social justice must then consider work options that follow graduation. This section introduces visions of social justice practice. What is your vision of working for social justice? *See* chapter 3 for a discussion of legal practice for social justice with an emphasis on working with communities. *See* chapters 11, 12, 13, and 14 for an extended discussion of lawyers working with communities in the struggle to face contemporary issues relating to race, sexual orientation, and gender.

GERALD P. LÓPEZ

The Work We Know So Little About
42 Stan. L. Rev. 1, 1–2, 6–11 (1989)

I met someone not long ago who too many of us regrettably have come to regard as unremarkable, someone who might well find herself, along any number of fronts, working with a lawyer in a fight for social change. I'll call her Maria Elena. She lives with her two children in San Francisco's Mission District. She works as a housekeeper. She works as a mother too. And as a tutor of sorts. And as a seamstress. And as a cook. And as a support for those other women—those other Irish-American women, African-American women, Chinese-American women, and most especially those other Latinas—with whom she finds herself in contact. * * *

How Maria Elena and her children make it from day to day tells us all a great deal about where we live, whom we live with, and even about how peoples' actual experiences measure up to the "American dream" * * * . Indeed, our own lives are tied inescapably to the Maria Elenas in our communities. These women are important parts of our economy, indispensable parts of certain of our worklives, and even intimate parts of some of our households. In a very palpable way, Maria Elena's struggles implicate us. More perhaps than we acknowledge and more perhaps than feels comfortable, she and we help construct one another's identities. We're entangled.

Historically, you'd think that how the Maria Elenas of our communities make it from day to day should have played an obvious and central role in training those whose vocation is to lawyer in the fight for social change. After all, the lives in which these lawyers intervene often differ considerably from their own—in terms of class, gender, race, ethnicity, and sexual orientation. Without laboring to understand these lives and their own entanglements with them, how else can lawyers begin to appreciate how their professional knowledge and skills may be perceived and deployed by those with whom they strive to ally themselves? How else can they begin to speculate about how their intervention may affect their clients' everyday relationships with employers, landlords, spouses and the state? And how else can they begin to study whether proposed strategies actually have a chance of penetrating the social and economic situations they'd like to help change?

But, as my niece might say, "Get a clue!" Whatever else law schools may be, they have not characteristically been where future lawyers go to learn about how the poor and working poor live. Or about how the elderly cope. Or about how the disabled struggle. Or about how gays and lesbians build their lives in worlds that deny them the basic integrity of identity. Or about how single women of color raise their children in the midst of underfinanced schools, inadequate social support, and limited job opportunities. Indeed, in many ways both current and past lawyers fighting for social change and all with whom they collaborate (both clients and other social activists) have had to face trying to learn how largely to overcome rather than to take advantage of law school experience. What's ultimately extraordinary, I think, is that these relationships work at all and that we can even sometimes fully realize an allied fight for social change.

* * *

For all her problems, for all the oppressive circumstances she has confronted and continues to confront with employers and about employment, for all her concerns about working conditions, health benefits and child care, Maria Elena just can't see herself seeking a lawyer's help, even at places with so positive a reputation as, say, the Immigrant Legal Resource Center, the Employment Law Center, or California Rural Legal Assistance. "Being on the short end and being on the bottom is an everyday event in my life," she says, usually half-smiling. "What can a lawyer do about that?" That doesn't make it all right, she admits. But she says she's learned to live with it—to deal with it in her own ways. In any event, lawyers and law all seem to conjure up for her big, complicated fights—and these fights, as she sees it, would pit her against a social superior, her word against the word of a more respected someone else, her lack of written records against the seemingly infinite amount of paper employers seem able to come up with when they must. Because she retains her sense of order by focusing on keeping her family's head above water, lawyers and law most often seem irrelevant to and even inconsistent with her day-to-day struggles.

Were Maria Elena alone in these sentiments, lawyers in the fight for social change might have little cause for general concern. But you may be surprised to learn that Maria Elena is hardly without support in her views about lawyers and law—though, to be sure, some of her problems may well be peculiarly the product of her immigration status. In fact, we are beginning to discover that many other low-income women of color—Asian-Americans, Native-Americans, Latinas, Blacks—apparently feel much the same way as Maria Elena, even if they were born here and even when their families have been in this country for generations. Much else may well divide these women—after all, political and social subordination is not a homogeneous or monolithic experience. Still, their actions seem to confirm Maria Elena's impulses and their words seem to echo Maria Elena's own.

The little thus far uncovered about whether and how people translate perceived injuries into legal claims seems to confirm what apparently the Maria Elenas in our communities have been trying to tell us for quite some time, each in her own way. Low-income women of color seldom go to lawyers, and they institute lawsuits a good deal less frequently than anybody else. More particularly, they convert their experiences of oppression into claims of discrimination far less often than they (and everybody else) press any other legal claim. Indeed, most learn never even to call oppressive treatment an injury; if they do, many simply "lump it" rather than personally pressing it against the other party, much less pressing a formal claim through a lawyer. For all the popular (and I might add exaggerated) descriptions bemoaning how litigious we've all become, nearly all careful observers concede that low-income women of color seek legal remedies far too infrequently, perhaps most notably about the discriminatory treatment they experience. * * *

* * *

Instead of using law and lawyers, most low-income women of color apparently often deal with oppressive circumstances through their own stock of informal strategies. Sometimes they tend to minimize or reinterpret certain obvious discrimination they experience. Maria Elena, for example, tells me she often chalks up bad treatment to personal likes or dislikes or denies that it could really be about her. At the same time, these women also employ certain more proactive devices in an effort to alter the situations in which they work. For example, the loose network of housekeepers of which Maria Elena is a part (including both formal work cooperatives and informal support groups), seems to be trying to transform their relationship with employers from master/servant to customer/skilled service provider, all in the somewhat vague but hardly irrational hope that current wages, conditions and benefits will improve along the way.

Yet for the most part, these low-income women of color have fewer illusions about these strategies than you might first presume. They know that you can't explain away all discriminatory treatment and that you can't alter every oppressive situation through informal devices. And they even seem to sense that while they may perceive their own less formal approach to their problems as self-sustaining, it often turns out to be self-defeating. After all, they know better than the rest of us that too many of them still get paid too little, for too many hours of work, in terrible conditions, with absolutely no health benefits or care for their children, and with little current hope of much job mobility over the course of their lifetimes.

Still, you shouldn't facilely condemn the sense of skepticism many low-income women of color feel about the intervention of lawyers and law, particularly if you appreciate (as no doubt you do) that lawyers and law can hardly ensure them the help they need. These women simply find themselves drawn to those informal strategies more within their control and less threatening than subjecting the little they have to the invasive experience and uncertain outcomes of the legal culture. Their collective past has taught them that seeking a legal remedy for their problems will not likely improve their position, and may well disassemble their fragilely constructed lives. If low-income women of color and the very best lawyers at places like the Immigrant Legal Resource Center and the East Palo Alto Community Law Project would seem to offer one another special possibilities, they simultaneously present reciprocally enigmatic challenges. Each potentially threatens the very aspirations that hooking up with the other is meant in part to fulfill.

Somehow in the midst of all this, the Maria Elenas of our communities and at least the very best lawyers with whom they work still manage more than occasionally to make contact, to get things done, and even to find credible self-affirmation in the collective effort. In some instances, no doubt, they join together out of desperation. If you need help badly enough and if you want to help badly enough, you can often figure out ways to hook up and make the relationship other than dysfunctional. That endeavor is nothing to scoff at. It may well suggest how most things get done in this world, and it certainly says something about the human spirit under pressure.

At its best, this joint effort at fighting political and social subordination can be a story of magnificent mutual adaptation. At those times, both the Maria Elenas of our communities and those lawyers with whom they work face the enigma of their relationship head on. Both try to be sensitive to, without uncritically acquiescing in, their respective needs and concerns. Both depend on the other to make some sense of how their overlapping knowledge and skills might inform a plausible plan of action. Both try to connect their particular struggle to other particular struggles and to particular visions of the state and the political economy. And both inevitably challenge the other as together they put a part of themselves on the line. In short, when things go well they seem capable of favorably redefining over time the very terms that otherwise circumscribe their capacity to take advantage of one another's will to fight.

If you realize that there's sometimes real genius to be found in this mutual adaptation, you should also appreciate that it happens little thanks to legal education. Characteristically, law schools have not been places where future lawyers go to learn about the stuff of Maria Elena's life, and historically, they have not been places where future lawyers go to find out about most other intimately related aspects of lawyering for social change. About how to work *with* and not just for clients and allies. About how to help sustain and build the coalitions of which they inevitably become a part. About how to help imagine and orchestrate the strategies they help choose or at least find themselves pursuing. About how to understand and be self-critical about the theories of the political economy to which they respond. About how to make concrete and to pursue the provisional visions of the future to which they apparently claim some allegiance.

* * *

* * * Whether or not legal education likes it, the study of women in all their heterogeneous complexity is no longer just a curiosity. Neither is the study of people of color. Nor the study of gays and lesbians. Nor

the study of power. Nor the study of quiescence and rebellion. Nor the study of economic democracy and development. Nor the study of the secondary labor market. Nor the study of cultural production and identity. These people and these dynamics pervade our legal and social and political and economic world. * * * [E]ven market researchers appreciate this. What [retailers] Lucky and Levi Strauss know and labor to learn about the Maria Elenas of our communities puts to shame our own accumulated wisdom and institutional commitment.

Notes and Questions

1. Social justice lawyering necessitates study of the dynamics and connections that López describes. Is López's critique of legal education as a vehicle for this study harsh or accurate?

2. López believes that "fighting political and social subordination" is the "work we know so little about?" Do you agree? If so, what steps can increase that knowledge? Have you worked against subordination before you came to law school or while in law school, on a personal or institutional level?

3. Why does López believe it is difficult for lawyers to connect with Maria Elena? *See* chapter 2 (discussing access to justice, restrictions on legal services, and alternative social justice practice).

4. Consider the power that students can exercise in the struggle for social change. Sumi Cho and Robert Westley explain how critical race theory emerged from the dynamic interaction between theory and practice that marked student activism for racial justice. Sumi Cho & Robert Westley, *Critical Race Coalitions: Key Movements That Performed the Theory*, 33 U.C. Davis L. Rev. 1377 (2000). Cho and Westley describe dramatic changes in faculty composition that occurred in a context of student activism:

> In fall of 1987, BCDF [U.C. Berkeley's Boalt Coalition for Diversified Faculty] highlighted the lack of progress over the decades in diversifying the law faculty. BCDF widely publicized that from 1967 to 1987, there was only one tenured faculty member of color at the law school. Moreover, there had been an increase over the same time period of the number of tenured (white) female faculty members from one to merely two and one-half. This appalling record graphically symbolized what was clearly a racial and gender caste system at Boalt. The following year, 1988, the school responded to the diversity demands and publicity of its straight, white, male faculty identity with an unprecedented four diversity hires out of five total hires. Adding to the pressure to diversify, Boalt faced the threat of a pending lawsuit from Eleanor Swift's tenure denial. In the fall of 1988, after Swift announced that the Title IX coordinator at U.C. Berkeley had made an unprecedented prima facie finding of sex-based discrimination in her case, the Boalt

> faculty abruptly voted to reverse its denial of tenure to Marge Shultz.
>
> * * *
>
> The activism at Boalt for faculty diversity in the late 1970s and late 1980s should be understood not as episodic, but as part of a tradition of race-conscious resistance at U.C. Berkeley. This Berkeley tradition, beginning with the Free Speech Movement of 1964, valorized political self-historicization and, thereby, promoted a positive culture of coalitional activism among its student body. At Boalt Hall, the student diversity movement constituted itself as a membership organization committed to diversity in three primary spheres: faculty, student body, and curriculum. In part that focus reflected a practical strategy, which we might call "continuous diversity mobilization." To achieve this goal, a coalition model developed among student groups that required us as students to bridge lines of difference through self-education, cooperation, risk-taking, and solidarity.

Id. at 1392–93, 1404.

Do the tactics ascribed to BCDF suggest lessons for "the work we know so little about?" What hurdles hinder self-education, cooperation, risk-taking, and solidarity? Should these tactics inform social justice lawyering?

In providing an alternative assessment of the origins of critical race theory, some scholars emphasize the development of an alternative course on race, racism, and law at the Harvard Law School in 1980. Kimberlé Crenshaw, Neil Gotanda, Gary Peller & Kendall Thomas, *Introduction,* in *Critical Race Theory: The Key Writings That Formed the Movement* xiii, xxi (1995) (observing, "The Alternative Course was in many ways the first institutionalized expression of Critical Race Theory."). The course "was one of the earliest attempts to bring scholars of color together to address the law's treatment of race from a self-consciously critical perspective." *Id.* Moreover, the course reflected the need to "build an oppositional community of left scholars of color within the mainstream legal academy" and to acknowledge "racial power to be at stake across the social plane—not merely in the places where people of color are concentrated but also in the institutions where their position is normalized and given legitimation." *Id.* at xii. Do you feel any need to develop an alternative course at your law school? Does the current curriculum facilitate the development of your vision of social justice lawyering?

5. Consider these comments by attorney Paul Crockett, reflecting on his practice and the importance of learning "the vocabulary of power."

> How many of you are brave enough to admit that you have no idea what you are doing in law school? While at the University of Florida, I wondered what I was doing in law school. I would like to

say that I knew what I was doing when I got there and where I was going, but I cannot. I did realize my purpose, as most law students do, in time. This is the story of integrating my personal and professional lives, and the realization of my sense of purpose. God help you if all you are is a lawyer.

A law school education is great. Even if you are not going to be a lawyer, the education makes you literate in the vocabulary of power. It opens up all your options. The hope is that you find something to be passionate about.

I'm with a four-lawyer firm. This is a "gay and lesbian" niche firm: we have three gays, a lesbian, and a transgendered person in this office. Lawyers are a dime a dozen. There are a million lawyers out there; so to the extent you are going to be successful, you're going to have to find a niche, and work on it. Those that generate business are the ones that are really valued in a firm, because the "grunts" are a dime a dozen. The people who can generate the business are always the highest paid. Ideally, your professional life and personal life are both part of you; you become engaged in what you are doing.

I started as a lawyer in 1988, and I was not yet out to my employers. I had a sense that litigation was wasteful and inherently loathsome, and I had a sense that I wanted to do something positive with my life—but I wasn't sure what it was. [So I went to a small firm and began work in estate planning.] Subsequently, the lawyer who hired me has come out as gay. I think that's part of the reason he hired me. He was teaching me to be an attorney and I was teaching him to be gay. (Actually, he didn't need any lessons; he took to it quite naturally.) I had to come out to these people because there was a steady stream of gays and lesbians coming into my office, and an explanation seemed warranted.

I am openly HIV positive, and I have been for several years. It has been both a blessing and a curse. I started practicing at roughly the same time that AIDS was really taking off among the gay community in Miami. I began getting calls in my office from people who were anguished by the loss of their loved ones. A lot of people were dying, a lot of people were getting sick. My peers, and people a little older than me, were facing challenges that their grandparents had to face: burying all your friends, burying your life partner—the people you thought you would grow old with. I had to pick up the mess, and I realized that this was a part of life, my life. * * *

There's more than educating people about the law and respect for gay people. * * * It's important to find something that works for you, whatever makes it more real than something you just do from nine-to-five; find something that allows you to put your heart into it. * * *

I have been involved with HIV issues since 1988. In a bizarre way, HIV has become a bridge between me, and people with whom I would have not been perceived to have anything in common. We all have different color skin; we all have different backgrounds, but we're one soul. What do I have in common, as a fairly privileged, white, gay man, with a struggling black mother or a Hispanic HIV drug addict? I have HIV, a common challenge. My concept was to establish a framework for AIDS advocacy, since the issues do overlap, because HIV involves homelessness; it involves racial issues, gender issues. Why did it take so long before they studied the effects of inhibitors in women? Why did it take so long for them to realize that women had symptoms that were unique? The answer was [that the medical establishment and the pharmaceutical research companies] did not care. * * *

A lot of people ask me, "Why do you need to talk about it?" And I tell them, "Excuse me, I really need to talk about it. This is who I am." Heterosexual men hold hands with their wives when they walk down the street. People have photographs of their spouses in their office. Are they flaunting their heterosexuality? When did they *choose* their heterosexuality? * * *

* * * I am uncomfortable walking down the street with my partner holding hands, because it's asking for trouble. So, that is a constant reality. There are certain things you learn as a matter of survival. * * *

Even when crusading for something so worthy, there comes a time where you need to step back for a minute and have a life. Having a life has always been very important to me. I think it's a primary duty for all of us.

If you are going to be an effective lawyer you've got to be creative. You need to find out what is it that you individually have, as a result of your experience, to bring to the client's benefit? And, do you really care, why are you doing it? If you're doing it just for the money, it's probably a bad decision, because it is not an easy way to make a living. We all need to make a living. Our landlords don't get paid on good will; you don't walk into a restaurant or a grocery store and pay with your positive wishes. But sometimes you actually get a feeling that you're helping somebody with the case that you are arguing, and then that makes it all worthwhile. You get caught up in learning to be a lawyer; studying for the bar exam. Why are you here? That is the fundamental question; that's a good question, a question you need to keep on asking yourselves.

I think there is a big thirst for meaning generally, in our society, where people realize that just making money is not everything. What is prestige at the end of the day? Nothing, it's dust. * * *

I have spent 10 years doing this. There is a while where you can take your passion and you burn like a flame, as you try to shed light on an area. Then your flame feels like it is dying. But it is better to get burnt out on something with meaning, than to waste your existence and a brilliant, powerful education.

Paul Hampton Crockett, *A Law School Education: Learning the Vocabulary of Power*, Address delivered at the University of Miami School of Law, 1999.

Is passion or outrage at injustice an important aspect of social justice lawyering?

6. There are many models of social justice lawyering and the long-term commitment it entails. In April 1996, law professors Haywood Burns and Shanara Gilbert died tragically in an automobile accident in Capetown, South Africa. As activists, scholars, and teachers, both of these social justice workers "fought for equality, working passionately, relentlessly and unceasingly." Charles J. Ogletree, Jr., *A Tribute to W. Haywood Burns and M. Shanara Gilbert: Revolutionaries in the Struggle for Justice*, 2 Clinical L. Rev. v, vi (1996). In paying tribute to Burns and Gilbert, the Northeast People of Color Legal Scholarship Conference presents an annual award in their name. Among the recipients are Derrick Bell, Cruz Reynoso, and Adrien Katherine Wing. *See* Leonard M. Baynes, *The Haywood Burns/Shanara Gilbert Award*, 31 New Eng. L. Rev. 967 (1997) (discussing the criteria for the award). In advancing civil and human rights around the world, Haywood Burns personified the profound value in "being of use" to the enduring quest for social justice:

> * * * In a divided society that exploits difference, his voice has been one of the strongest in saying we could live together. He did not underestimate the difficulty in doing so and understood that major injustices had to be remedied. His unique voice was strong, but not strident. He spoke with civility and great feelings of love.
>
> Studying Haywood's life, we aspire to be less harsh, more willing to listen to those with whom we disagree. We realize one can adhere to principle without alienating those around us—and that one *must* adhere to principle, consistently. * * *
>
> Haywood understood that change would not be brought about solely by bringing an important case to trial. He knew that schools, organizations, and community institutions were urgently needed, and he built them, brick by brick. He knew that professionals from the "underserved" were needed, to be trained to represent the "underserved." And these professionals had to remember from where they came * * *. For this work he will be remembered as a builder; out of this work have come several generations of black, Hispanic, Asian-American, and women lawyers.

Michael Ratner & Eleanor Stein, *W. Haywood Burns: To Be of Use*, 106 Yale L.J. 753, 776–77 (1996). Burns mused that social justice advocates must "carry on [our] work from crisis to crisis, from liberation struggle to liberation struggle, from arena of injustice to arena of injustice, with a constancy of principle and a commitment to right that is unfailing." *Id.* at 777. In varied ways this book, at bottom, examines how "to be of use" to the clients and communities trying to advance social justice and how to work "with a constancy of principle and a commitment to right that is unfailing." *See also* Haywood Burns, *Bad News, Good News: The Justice Mission of U.S. Law Schools*, 40 Clev. St. L. Rev. 397 (1992).

7. This text uses the phrase social justice lawyering to recapture the progressive spirit historically embodied in public interest lawyering (*see* Introduction). Commentators use many phrases to describe this progressive lawyering spirit, including cause lawyering, community lawyering, left-activist lawyering, and rebellious lawyering, as well as social justice lawyering. Do these phrases have different meanings or interpretations?

JOHN O. CALMORE

A Call to Context: The Professional Challenges of Cause Lawyering at the Intersection of Race, Space, and Poverty
67 Fordham L. Rev. 1927, 1932–36 (1999)

According to Austin Sarat and Stuart Scheingold, our legal profession both needs and at the same time is threatened by cause lawyering. On the one hand, the profession needs lawyers who commit themselves and their legal skills to furthering a vision of the good society so that "moral activism" can put a humane face on lawyering and "provide[ ] an appealing alternative to the value-neutral, 'hired-gun' imagery that often dogs the legal profession." On the other hand, however, cause lawyers are not simply a minority of the bar, but they represent "a deviant strain within the legal profession." Cause lawyering presents a profound professional threat to the dominant bar and its forms of legal practice:

> [Cause lawyers] threaten the profession by destabilizing the dominant understanding of lawyering as properly wedded to moral neutrality and technical competence.... By rejecting nonaccountability, if not partisanship, cause lawyers establish a point from which to criticize the dominant understanding from inside the profession itself. They denaturalize and politicize that understanding. Cause lawyering exposes the fact that it is contingent and constructed and, in so doing, raises the political question of whose interests the dominant understanding serves. The result is a threat to ongoing professional projects and the political immunity of the legal profession and the legal process.

As a deviant strain of the legal profession, cause lawyers must continually threaten and challenge dominant understandings of the professional role and the larger process within which that role is performed. Nowhere is this more crucial than in representing the inner-city poor.

All cause lawyers appear to focus primarily on the broad stakes involved in representing their client community. Sometimes the cause conflicts with representing narrower client interests. Cases are primarily important for their significance to the cause: Is what is at stake something that the cause lawyer deems worth fighting for? Although cause lawyering can be associated with causes of both the political left and right, this Article associates it with leftist progressive lawyering. Progressive lawyering is a subject that began to receive scholarly attention during the 1980s as the viability of liberal legal advocacy diminished, within both antidiscrimination law and poverty law. Left-activist lawyering is driven by a conviction and commitment to oppose the forces of domination and to support activities of resistance. This lawyering is not motivated by a desire to defend and protect rights in the abstract. Instead, rights are means to political ends. Far from asserting rights, the false legitimization function of the law is constantly challenged. This is important, because "[t]he law is a major vehicle for the maintenance of existing social and power relations by the consent or acquiescence of the lower and middle classes." As a consequence, left-activists tend to push their professional role and their organizations into areas that are politically and professionally risky, confrontational, and controversial.

In 1992, Gerald López wrote an important book that contrasted two modes of delivering legal services to the poor that he described as "regnant" and "rebellious." As the name would suggest, regnant lawyers tend to maintain a disassociated power over their clients, embracing the traditional lawyer-client paradigm. By contrast, "the rebellious idea of lawyering demands that lawyers (and those with whom they work) nurture sensibilities and skills compatible with a collective fight for social change." In representing the inner-city poor, it is arguably more important that advocates disassociate themselves from regnant lawyering than it is that they adopt the latter mode. There may be other conceptions of effective representation that do not incorporate the wholesale features of rebellious lawyering. Indeed, effective representation stems from intervening and confronting the array of opportunity-denying circumstances that oppress the client community. There is no grand theory to instruct lawyers how to advocate. Thus, my focus is on what lawyers should not do, because regnant lawyering blocks efforts to recognize and develop alternative approaches that are more effective.

Regnant lawyering is directly tied to the professional socialization and orientation of attorneys. Consider some of the characteristics of regnant lawyers:

- Lawyers "formally represent" others.
- Lawyers choose between "service" work (resolving individual problems) and "impact" work (advancing systemic reforms), largely dichotomous categories.
- Lawyers set up their offices to facilitate formal representation in service or impact work.
- Lawyers litigate more than they do anything else.
- Lawyers understand "community education" as a label for diffuse, marginal, and uncritical work (variations on the canned "after-dinner talk about law"), and "organizing" as a catchword for

sporadic, supplemental mobilization (variations on sit-ins, sit-downs, and protests).

- Lawyers consider themselves the preeminent problem-solvers in most situations they find themselves trying to alter.
- Lawyers connect only loosely to other institutions or groups in their communities, and these connections almost always focus on lawyers' use of institutions or groups for some aspect of the case in which they serve as formal representatives.
- Lawyers have only a modest grasp on how large structures—regional, national, and international, political, economic, and cultural—shape and respond to the status quo.
- Lawyers suspect that subordination of all sorts cyclically recreates itself in certain subcultures, thereby preventing people from helping themselves and taking advantage of many social services and educational opportunities.
- Lawyers believe that subordination can be successfully fought if professionals, particularly lawyers, assume leadership in pro-active campaigns that sometimes "involve" the subordinated.
- Lawyers do not know and try little to learn whether and how formal changes in law penetrate the lives of subordinated people.
- Lawyers understand their profession as an honorable calling and see themselves as aesthetic if not political heroes, working largely alone to make statements through *their* (more than their clients') cases about society's injustices.

Leftist cause lawyers are inclined to smugly dismiss these features as foreign to their personal and professional orientation, values, and commitment. But a genuine, good-faith commitment to antisubordination work does not necessarily insulate one from regnant lawyering. Indeed, the regnant mode of lawyering is cultivated under the pressing circumstances of practice. Those circumstances include the social and cultural distance between lawyers and clients, the occasional but significant mutual distrust and disrespect between lawyers and clients, the overwhelming crush of client demand, the burn-out of practice, the differing, sometimes contradictory worldviews of lawyers and clients, and lawyers' self-righteous arrogance. Moreover, its cultivation takes place regardless of whether the practice emphasizes individual client cases, group or institutional impact cases, or mobilization advocacy. It takes place whether the lawyer is non-white or white, male or female, gay or straight, or a stranger to the community or a former resident who has now moved on.

The first step for most of us in becoming effective advocates, then, is to break away from the regnant idea of lawyering. The client community, as well, must unequivocally indicate that regnant lawyers are not welcome. This strong client stand will not be made in the desperate cases of individual clients facing evictions, welfare cuts, consumer fraud, employment discrimination, and the like. It can and should be made, however, whenever lawyers attempt impact litigation, legislative or administrative advocacy, base-building and mobilization, or other aspects of lawyering that extend beyond resolving private disputes. In other words, at the cutting edges of practice, there is no room for regnant lawyering. It is out of place.

In contrast to regnant lawyers, rebellious lawyers connect with the community they serve and make collaborative advocacy a key premise: lawyers must know how to work *with* the client community, not just on its behalf. There must be collaboration with professional and lay allies, including a willingness to be educated by them. Rebellious lawyers must "ground their work in the lives and in the communities of the subordinated themselves." They must continually assess probable interaction between both legal and non-legal approaches to problems. They must adopt a problem-solving orientation, learning "how to work with others in brainstorming, designing, and executing strategies aimed at responding immediately to particular problems and, more generally, at fighting social and political subordination." Finally, this orientation toward advocacy must nurture the appropriate sensibilities and skills that are "compatible with a collective fight for social change."

Notes and Questions

1. Is "cause lawyering" as described by Calmore synonymous with "social justice lawyering" or "rebellious lawyering?" Might someone be a cause lawyer and not a social justice lawyer?

2. Karen Loewy describes multiple definitions for lawyering for social change and political lawyering. Karen L. Loewy, *Lawyering for Social Change*, 27 Fordham Urb. L. Rev. 1869 (2000). Characteristics she offers from commentators include having concern with the best life for a human being, fighting the status quo, representing the voiceless, altering allocations of power, creating shifts in the cultural imagination, mobilizing and empowering the public, engaging the morality of the underlying issue, and curing historical amnesia. Do these characteristics describe a social justice lawyer?

3. The framework of democratic liberalism, in which social justice study and practice take place, emphasizes the individual over the community. Within that framework, "[w]e think in terms of individual rights, individual achievement, individual merit, rarely of connection, community, and responsibility." Stephanie M. Wildman (with contributions by Margalynne Armstrong, Adrienne D. Davis & Trina Grillo), *Privilege Revealed: How Invisible Preference Undermines America* 159 (1996). Can one practice social justice lawyering within this liberal framework?

Charles R. Lawrence writes of this dilemma in the context of the debate surrounding affirmative action. Charles R. Lawrence III, *Two Views of the River: A Critique of the Liberal Defense of Affirmative Action*, 101 Colum. L. Rev. 928 (2001). Lawrence criticizes the liberal defense of affirmative action, which promotes the importance of diversity, as entrenching a privileged elite. *Id.* at 960. The more progressive solution to the affirmative action debate would involve a reconceptualization of merit. *Id.* at 968–75. Yet Lawrence recognizes that the increased racial integration that affirmative action brings to elite institutions benefits society, even when affirmative action is accepted based on the diversity rationale. *Id.* at 960. Should he support this liberal defense of affirmative action, when he believes that the progressive critique is the proper response? Lawrence finds the progressive and liberal theories reconcilable if activism is directed toward transformation.

> Transformative politics requires looking beyond winning or losing the particular legal dispute or political battle and asking how one's actions serve to reinforce people's awareness of our interdependence and mutual responsibility as members of the human family. Critical legal theorists have typically focused their attention on how best to expand the political consciousness of members of subordinated communities, urging progressive lawyers to use the legal system to increase people's "sense of personal and political power." They have argued that the lawyer who adopts this "power-oriented" approach to justice advocacy "should always attempt to reshape the way legal conflicts are represented in the law, revealing the limiting character of legal ideology and bringing out the true socioeconomic and political foundations of legal disputes." This admonition is directed primarily to the lawyer who is representing clients and political movements seeking to subvert the power of an oppressive state.
>
> Transformative politics also seeks to change the political consciousness of those privileged by systems of subordination. The task is to help the privileged comprehend the profound costs associated with inequality—the public costs of prisons, crime, illiteracy, disease, and the violence of an alienated underclass—as well as the personal costs of loneliness and anomie in a world where no one is responsible for the pain of any other person.
>
> * * * [W]hen we reshape the presentation of legal conflicts to reveal the injury that inequality of power and privilege does to the subordinated, we may discover a concomitant injury to the privileged as well. Those with power, including the liberal defenders of affirmative action, may rely on the mystifying power of law to make their privilege seem legitimate to themselves as well as to subordinated others, and it surely unsettles them when subordinated people challenge the legitimacy of the very system that defines justice. But once the mask comes off, and liberals must resolve the conflict between justice and privilege, they may find that privilege in an unjust world has few comforts.

Id. at 965–66.

Can you think of similar situations where, as a student or lawyer, you have faced the dilemma that Lawrence describes, needing to work for social justice within a liberal framework? What actions did you take to resolve the dilemma? Can it be resolved? *See also* Richard Abel, *Big Lies and Small Steps: A Critique of Deborah Rhode's* Too Much Law, Too Little Justice: Too Much Rhetoric, Too Little Reform, 11 Geo. J. Legal Ethics 1019 (1998) (describing the fallacy of liberalism as "the belief that it is possible to achieve equality in one circumscribed realm without addressing other structural inequalities"), excerpted in chapter 2.

4. Consider how your definition of social justice relates to your vision of lawyering. Theorists from Aristotle to Kant to John Rawls have debated the meaning of justice. *See, e.g.*, Aristotle, *The Ethics* (E.V. Riev ed., J.A.K. Thomson trans., 1955); Immanuel Kant, *Fundamental Principles of the Metaphysics of Morals* (Marvin Fox ed., Thomas K. Abbott trans., 1949); John Rawls, *A Theory of Justice* (1971). *See also* Geoffrey C. Hazard, Jr., *Law and Justice in the Twenty-First Century*, 70 Fordham L. Rev. 1739 (2002). Judith Shklar has suggested that only by understanding the face of injustice can one understand justice. *See* Judith Shklar, *The Faces of Injustice* (1990).

There is no single vision of social justice among the theorists who use this term. Some use the phrase social justice interchangeably with justice, *see, e.g.*, Martha C. Nussbaum, *Sex and Social Justice* (1999). Some use the concept as a counterpoint to injustice, to convey idealistic, humanitarian goals. Some view social justice as requiring a higher moral ground than self-interest, *see, e.g.*, Menkel-Meadow, *supra* at 31 (examining creation and sustenance of motivation in cause lawyers), and others use it as a counterpoint to economic efficiency, *see, e.g.*, Joel F. Handler, *Questions about Social Europe by an American Observer*, 18 Wis. Int'l L.J. 437 (2000) (describing European efforts attempting to harmonize economic efficiency and social justice). Others use the term to describe particular aspects of freedom, such as freedom of expression, *see, e.g.*, N. Douglas Wells, *Thurgood Marshall and "Individual Self-Realization" in First Amendment Jurisprudence*, 61 Tenn. L. Rev. 237 (1993) (describing Justice Marshall's vision of social justice), or freedom from arbitrary searches, seizures, and detention, *see, e.g.*, Anthony E. Cook, *Beyond Critical Legal Studies: The Reconstructive Theology of Dr. Martin Luther King, Jr.*, 103 Harv. L. Rev. 985 (1990) (describing Dr. Martin Luther King's view of elements of the rule of law necessary for social justice). But social justice is often understood to capture something other than justice in general or claims about basic rights.

Usually, social justice invokes substantive rather than formal equality. Some theorists define social justice as involving "the goals of equality of access, opportunity, and outcome." Marcia Bok, *Civil Rights and the Social Programs of the 1960s: The Social Justice Functions of Social Policy* 15 (1992) (citing David Gil, *Unravelling Social Policy* (1976) and comparing Gil with Rawls, *supra*). This approach "presupposes a conception of social justice that provides a standard for assessing the distributive aspects of the basic structure of society." *Id. See also* Tom Tyler et al., *Social Justice in a Diverse Society* 10 (1997) (exploring justice in the context of social psychology and noting that "[m]ost social justice research deals with issues of allocation").

The term can include issues of economic or distributive justice and also of human dignity and solidarity. The meaning of social justice may be "simultaneously distributional and relational":

> The term social justice is taken to embrace both fairness and equity in the distribution of a wide range of attributes, which need not be confined to material things. Although the primary focus is on attributes which have an immediate bearing on people's well-being or the quality of their lives, our conception of social justice goes beyond patterns of distribution, general and spatial, to incorporate attributes relevant to how these come about. While fairness is sometimes applied to procedures and justice to outcomes, we are concerned with both. Preference for the term social justice rather than justice in general is explained not by preoccupation with the distribution of attributes which might be labelled as social, but by concern with something which happens socially, among people in a society.

David Smith, *Geography and Social Justice* 26 (1994) (noting that questions of "who gets what where and how" point to central issues of social justice, but that social justice involves more than a narrow, individualistic and materialistic framework that might be implied by "getting").

5. With all these different uses and views of social justice, what does social justice mean to you? How do the values you bring to law school shape your concept of social justice? Recall how Julie Su, at the beginning of this chapter, describes learning from the garment workers who were her clients. Will work for social justice help you to grow and to develop your values?

> A story is told of a Hasidic Rabbi in a Polish shtetl accosted one evening by a sentry, who demands: "Who are you, and what is your business?" The rabbi inquires of the sentry, "How much do they pay you to do this?" "Five zlotys a week," replies the sentry. "Then I will pay you ten zlotys a week if you will work for me," says the rabbi. "What do I have to do?," asks the sentry, incredulously. "Whenever you see me," replies the Hasid, "I want you to stop me and ask me, 'Who are you, and what is your business?' "

Stephen Wizner, *Beyond Skills Training*, 7 Clinical L. Rev. 327, 340 (2001).

While Wizner uses this story to urge reflection on the work of teaching law, his questions remind us to continue to ask ourselves, "What is social justice? Are my actions furthering the goal of social justice?"

Support for resisting a single, immutable definition of social justice comes from Rennard Strickland:

> Immutable definitions are rare in Native America. Where Westerners classify quantitatively, American Indians evaluate qualitatively; where Western thinking tends toward all-or-nothing absolutism, American Indian thought turns on relative status. Western oppositional thinking with its north/south, day/night, good/evil, sacred/secular, contrasts markedly with the accumulative integrative perception of Native Americans. To the Hopi, for example, the fine tuning of sensory reality is explained by *Enevoqa* and *Nananivoqa*, or directions between directions, "going all directions," or colors between colors. This is not the same as the concept of "northeast" or "magenta," but is an infinitely incremental accounting of qualities that tend more or less toward dominant expressions.

Rennard Strickland, *Tonto's Revenge: Reflections on American Indian Culture and Policy* 90 (1997).

Consider the following vision of social justice offered by Iris Marion Young.

IRIS MARION YOUNG

Justice and the Politics of Difference 15–16 (1990)

Thousands of buses converge on the city, and tens of thousands of people of diverse colors, ages, occupations, and life styles swarm onto the mall around the Washington Monument until the march begins. At midday people move into the streets, chanting, singing, waving wild papier-mâché missiles or effigies of government officials. Many carry signs or banners on which a simple slogan is inscribed: "Peace, Jobs, and Justice."

This scene has occurred many times in Washington, D.C., * * * and many more times in other U.S. cities. What does "justice" mean in this slogan? In this context, as in many other political contexts today, I suggest that social justice means the elimination of institutionalized domination and oppression. Any aspect of social organization and practice relevant to domination and oppression is in principle subject to evaluation by ideals of justice.

Contemporary philosophical theories of justice, however, do not conceive justice so broadly. Instead, philosophical theories of justice tend to restrict the meaning of social justice to the morally proper distribution of benefits and burdens among society's members. * * * While distributive issues are crucial to a satisfactory conception of justice, it is a mistake to reduce social justice to distribution.

[Young later explains: The distributive paradigm defines social justice as the morally proper distribution of social benefits and burdens among society's members. Paramount among these are wealth, income, and other material resources. The distributive definition of justice often includes, however, nonmaterial social goods such as rights, opportunity, power, and self-respect. What marks the distributive paradigm is a tendency to conceive social justice and distribution as coextensive concepts.]

I find two problems with the distributive paradigm. First, it tends to focus thinking about social justice on the allocation of material goods such as things, resources, income, and wealth, or on the distribution of social positions, especially jobs. This focus tends to ignore the social structure and institutional context that often help determine distributive patterns. Of particular importance to the analyses that follow are issues of decisionmaking power and procedures, division of labor, and culture.

One might agree that defining justice in terms of distribution tends to bias thinking about justice toward issues concerning wealth, income, and other material goods, and that other issues such as decisionmaking power or the structure of the division of labor are as important, and yet argue that distribution need not be restricted to material goods and resources. Theorists frequently consider issues of the distribution of such nonmaterial goods as power, opportunity, or self-respect. But this widening of the concept of distribution exhibits the second problem with the distributive paradigm. When metaphorically extended to nonmaterial social goods, the concept of distribution represents them as though they were static things, instead of a function of social relations and processes.

In criticizing distributively oriented theories I wish neither to reject distribution as unimportant nor to offer a new positive theory to replace the distributive theories. I wish rather to displace talk of justice that regards persons as primarily possessors and consumers of goods to a wider context that also includes action, decisions about action, and provision of the means to develop and exercise capacities. The concept of social justice includes all aspects of institutional rules and relations insofar as they are subject to potential collective decision. The concepts of domination and oppression, rather that the concept of distribution, should be the starting point for a conception of social justice.

Notes and Questions

1. Nancy Fraser has criticized Iris Marion Young's work for focusing on identity politics and failing to address the political economy. Iris Marion Young, *Unruly Categories: A Critique of Nancy Fraser's Dual Systems Theory,* New Left Review 147 (March/April 1997) (discussing Fraser's critique). In response, Young wrote: "[Fraser] claims that some recent political theory and practice privilege the recognition of social groups, and that they tend to ignore the distribution of goods and the division of labour." *Id.* at 147. Young refuses to accept the dichotomization of culture and economy, observing:

> * * * From Zapatista challengers to the Mexican government, to Ojibwa defenders of fishing rights, to African-American leaders demanding that banks invest in their neighbourhoods, to unions trying to organize a Labor Party, to those sheltering battered women, resistance has many sites and is often specific to a group

> without naming or affirming a group essence. Most of these struggles self-consciously involve issues of cultural recognition and economic deprivation, but not constituted as totalizing ends. None of them alone is 'transformative,' but, if linked together, they can be deeply subversive. Coalition politics can only be built and sustained if each grouping recognizes and respects the specific perspective and circumstances of the others * * * .

Id. at 160.

Is Fraser correct that recent theorists have not paid enough attention to the material conditions of society, emphasizing, rather, group identities? *See* Richard Delgado, *Two Ways to Think about Race: Reflections on the Id, the Ego, and Other Reformist Theories of Equal Protection*, 89 Geo. L.J. 2279 (2001) (urging consideration of the material side of race and racism, including socioeconomic competition, immigration pressures, the search for profits, and changes in the labor pool).

2. Has the allocation of material goods been ignored as a social justice concern? Should more attention be paid to it? Louis Brandeis remarked, "You can have wealth concentrated in the hands of a few, or democracy. But you cannot have both." Chuck Collins & Felice Yeskel, *Economic Apartheid in America: A Primer on Economic Inequality and Insecurity* 69 (2000). Collins and Yeskel comment that while the power of large corporations and the wealthy has increased, those societal building blocks that historically provided a countervailing balance to that power, such as unions, political parties, and civic institutions, have declined in influence. *Id.*

What is the role of law and the legal system in the shifting balance of economic power? Consider this observation by Robert Hale:

> * * * [T]he degree to which men surrender liberty in the sphere of production, in order to increase their freedom to consume, varies. * * * [One who can provide services which are scarce and in great demand may be able to insist on a high salary from his employer or may organize a business of his own, and the surrender of his liberty to be idle may involve little if any sacrifice.] * * * And he may have a large measure of discretion (or liberty) in deciding just *how* he is to perform his work, whereas those who have to take inferior jobs may have to do just what they are told by superiors throughout the working day. The liberty of these people as producers is more closely restricted than is that of those who can bargain for supervisory positions, or who can become entrepreneurs, and for this greater sacrifice of liberty in the process of production, they generally gain less freedom as consumers, being able to bargain only for low wages. The market value of their labor may be low, reflecting the low degree of compulsion they can bring to the bargaining process, as compared to the compulsion brought to bear by the employer.
>
> The employer's power to induce people to work for him depends largely on the fact that the law previously restricts the liberty of these people to consume, while he has the power, through the

payment of wages, to release them to some extent from these restrictions. He has little power over those whose freedom to consume is relatively unrestricted, because they have large independent means, or who can secure freedom to consume from other employers, because of their ability to render services of a sort that is scarce and in great demand. Those who own enough property have sufficient liberty to consume, without yielding any of their liberty to be idle. Their property rights enable them to exert pressure of great effectiveness to induce people to enter into bargains to pay them money. The law endows them with the power to call on the governmental authorities to keep others from using what they own. For merely not exercising this power, they can obtain large money rewards, by leasing or selling it to someone who will utilize it. These rewards may in many instances amount only to postponed payments for services which the owners have rendered in the past in the process of production, but frequently they greatly exceed any such amount. In fact the owner may have rendered no services whatever himself, but may have acquired his property by government grant or by virtue of the fact that the law assigns property rights to those named in the will of the previous owner, or, if he makes no will, according to the intestacy laws. Bargaining power would be different were it not that the law endows some with rights that are more advantageous than those with which it endows others.

It is with these unequal rights that men bargain and exert pressure on one another. These rights give birth to the unequal fruits of bargaining. There may be sound reasons of economic policy to justify all the economic inequalities that flow from unequal rights. If so, these reasons must be more specific than a broad policy of private property and freedom of contract. With different rules as to the assignment of property rights, particularly by way of inheritance or government grant, we could have just as strict a protection of each person's property rights, and just as little governmental interference with freedom of contract, but a very different pattern of economic relationships. Moreover, by judicious legal limitation on the bargaining power of the economically and legally stronger, it is conceivable that the economically weak would acquire greater freedom of contract than they now have—freedom to resist more effectively the bargaining power of the strong, and to obtain better terms.

Robert L. Hale, *Bargaining, Duress, and Economic Liberty*, 43 Colum. L. Rev. 603, 626–28 (1943). Does the legal system create inequality by choosing whose rights to protect?

3. This text uses "marginalized, subordinated, and underrepresented clients and causes" as representative of some of the constituencies and concerns included within "social justice." What other characteristics should be associated with social justice?

4. "Is it possible to speak of democracy without speaking of social justice?" A Cuban law student asked President Jimmy Carter this question on Carter's historic trip to Cuba, when he urged the integration of Cuba into "a democratic hemisphere." Marion Lloyd, *Carter Criticizes Cuba, Calls on US to Lift Embargo*, Boston Globe, May 15, 2002, at A.1. The relation between democracy and social justice remains an issue for legal theorists. *See* Bruce Ackerman, *Social Justice and the Liberal State* (1980). Democratic inclusion is an important social justice goal.

5. How might race, culture, and ethnicity influence visions of social justice? Native Americans are generally not as concerned with distributive justice (equitable distribution of resources) or rough and wild justice (revenge, punishment, control, determination of who is right) as they are with sacred justice (healing of broken relationships). Diane LeResche, *The Reawakening of Sacred Justice*, 27 Clearinghouse Rev. 893, 899 (1993).

Chief Justice Robert Yazzie of the Navajo Supreme Court criticizes the hierarchical Western model of justice, which he describes as a vertical system based upon "power, force, and authority," in which laws are often made by the elite and enforced by police who are not from poor communities.

> Adjudication is the method of justice which typifies the vertical police model. In this system, the parties submit what they claim to be the true "facts" and the correct "law" to a wise person who makes decisions for others. Vertical justice is adversarial, and some people are unhappy with the resulting confrontation that is part of the process. Adjudication becomes a "win-lose" method where, the common adage is, "one party leaves the courtroom with his tail in the air, and the other leaves with his tail between his legs." The product of adjudication is punishment or liability. * * *
>
> The vertical system of justice in America can best be symbolized by a triangle. It represents a pyramid of power, where the weak and powerless are at the bottom, with the strong and power elite at the top. Justice flows from the top of the triangle to the bottom: from the legislature, police, and court systems, down to the common people.
>
> * * *
>
> * * * [T]he Navajo system of justice is based upon discussion, consensus, relative need, and healing. It is "restorative justice," which puts people in good relations with each other, and in continuing relationships. The Navajo system is "horizontal" or egalitarian law. It is illustrated as a circle where everyone is equal. * * *
>
> * * * Navajo justice methods utilize relationships, talking things out, teaching, and consensus to adjust the interaction of parties. * * * [Payment to someone who has been injured is not like damages in the tort sense of compensation; instead] the parties

discuss what is needed to make the injured person feel better and compensation can be symbolic.

The Honorable Robert Yazzie, *"Hozho Nahasdlii"—We Are Now in Good Relations: Navajo Restorative Justice*, 9 St. Thomas L. Rev. 117, 119–20, 123–24 (1996).

The methods and beliefs of Native Americans and other indigenous peoples have influenced some contemporary international debates about law reform. *See, e.g.,* Robert Yazzie & James W. Zion, *Navajo Restorative Justice: The Law of Equality and Justice*, in Burt Galaway & Joe Hudson, *Restorative Justice: International Perspectives* 157 (1996) (describing Navajo conceptions of justice and their application). Should Native American ideals of "sacred justice," LeResche, *supra*, inform work for social justice?

6. Are coalition politics a necessary component of work for social justice? *See* Phoebe A. Haddon, *Coalescing With SALT: A Taste for Inclusion*, 11 S. Cal. Rev. Law & Women's Stud. 321 (2002) (describing the priority placed on coalition-building and inclusion strategies).

Mari Matsuda explains how recognizing intersecting issues can build the consciousness that informs coalitions and furthers social justice:

> The way I try to understand the interconnection of all forms of subordination is through a method I call "ask the other question." When I see something that looks racist, I ask, "Where is the patriarchy in this?" When I see something that looks sexist, I ask, "Where is the heterosexism in this?" When I see something that looks homophobic, I ask, "Where are the class interests in this?" Working in coalition forces us to look for both the obvious and non-obvious relationships of domination, helping us to realize that no form of subordination ever stands alone.
>
> If this is true, we've asked each other, then isn't it also true that dismantling any one form of subordination is impossible without dismantling every other? And more and more, particularly in the women of color movement, the answer is that "no person is free until the last and the least of us is free."
>
> In trying to explain this to my own community, I sometimes try to shake people up by suggesting that patriarchy killed Vincent Chin.[24] Most people think racism killed Vincent Chin. When white

24. Vincent Chin, a Chinese American, was murdered in Detroit by assailants who shouted racial slurs while attacking Chin with a baseball bat. See *Detroit's Asian Americans Outraged by Lenient Sentencing of Chinese American Man's Killer*, Rafu Shimpo, May 5, 1983 (on file with the Stanford Law Review). For other accounts of anti-Asian violence, see, for example, William Wong, *Anti-Asian Violence*, Forum, June 1989 (reflections on the Stockton, California massacre of Asian-American school children and the Vincent Chin case); *L.A. Group Says Skinheads Tied to Anti-Asian Violence*, Asian Week, Feb. 23, 1990, at 3; Arnold T. Hiura, *The Unfortunate Case of Jim Loo*, The Hawaii Herald, July 6, 1990, at A-13, col. 1 (racially motivated murder of Chinese-American man in Raleigh, North Carolina); Asian Pacific American Coalition USA, *Report: Stockton Killings Racially Motivated*, APAC Alert, Oct. 1989, at 1. [*See also* the annual audits of violence against Asian Pacific Americans conducted by the men with baseball bats, hurling racist hate speech, beat a man to death, it is obvious that racism is a cause. It is only slightly less obvious, however, when you walk down the aisles of Toys R Us, that little boys grow up in this culture with toys that teach dominance and aggression, while little girls grow up with toys that teach about being pretty, baking, and changing a diaper. And the little boy who is interested in learning how to nurture and play house is called a "sissy." When he is a little older he is called a "f—g." He learns that acceptance for men in this society is premised on rejecting the girl culture and taking on the boy culture, and I believe that this, as much as racism, killed Vincent Chin. I have come to see that homophobia is the disciplinary system that teaches men that they had better talk like 2 Live Crew or someone will think they "aren't real men," and I believe that this homophobia is a cause of rape and violence against women. I have come to see how that same homophobia makes women afraid to choose women, sending them instead into the arms of men who beat them. I have come to see how class oppression creates the same effect, cutting off the chance of economic independence that could free women from dependency upon abusive men.

I have come to see all of this from working in coalition: from my lesbian colleagues who have pointed out homophobia in places where I failed to see it; from my Native American colleagues who have said, "But remember that we were here first," when I have worked for the rights of immigrant women; from men of color who have risked my wrath to say, "But racism *is* what is killing us. Why can't I put that first on my agenda?"

The women of color movement has, of necessity, been a movement about intersecting structures of subordination. This movement suggests that anti-patriarchal struggle is linked to struggle against all forms of subordination. It has challenged communities of color to move beyond race alone in the quest for social justice.

Mari J. Matsuda, *Beside My Sister, Facing the Enemy: Legal Theory Out of Coalition,* 43 Stan. L. Rev. 1183, 1189–90 (1991).

7. Reconsider the discussion earlier in this chapter on the ideals with which students choose to attend law school and the obstacles to achieving those ideals. How can students strengthen their commitment to social justice? Noting that some theorists have argued that a commitment to social justice arises from self-interest or empathy, Dorothy Roberts disagrees:

* * * These flaws in both self-interest and empathy as sources of commitment to social justice lead me to conclude that a shared *political* commitment is needed to eradicate systems of domination and to institute more egalitarian ones.

National Asian Pacific American Legal Consortium available at http://napalc.org.]

> This political commitment requires people in privileged places to examine their own position far more than that of their neighbor. More important than a white woman imagining she is her Latina nanny; a male executive putting himself in the place of his secretary; or a well-educated Black woman pretending to be a welfare recipient is the recognition that their whiteness, gender and wealth give them a privilege that the others do not have. This task requires *self*-examination, not empathy. The next step requires a willingness to join in political solidarity with their fellow citizens to create more egalitarian institutions that will erode the positions of privilege that they now enjoy.

Dorothy E. Roberts, *Sources of Commitment to Social Justice*, 4 Roger Williams U. L. Rev. 175, 195–96 (1998).

Creating more egalitarian institutions, eroding privilege, and promoting equality of opportunity are goals of social justice lawyering.

Noting that the mission of clinical teaching includes both social justice and skills training, Antoinette Sedillo Lopez explains:

> The pursuit of social justice involves working to provide access to justice and understanding and addressing inequities in our justice system. In a clinical setting, providing access to justice means designing a program to address needs for legal service in our communities. * * *

Antoinette Sedillo Lopez, *Learning Through Service in a Clinical Setting: The Effect of Specialization on Social Justice and Skills Training*, 7 Clinical L. Rev. 307, 316–17 (2001). *See also*, Mark Tushnet, *Research and the Justice Mission of Law Schools*, 40 Clev. St. L. Rev. 463, 465 (1992) (Considering "To what extent do—or can—law schools advance justice?").

Sedillo Lopez links social justice to addressing community needs. Is that link essential to a definition of social justice? Is it part of your own definition?

8. For further reading on social justice see *Learning to Teach for Social Justice* (Linda Darling-Hammond, Jennifer French & Silvia Paloma Garcia-Lopez eds., 2002); David Marshall Smith, *Geography of Social Justice* (2002); Diane Goodman, *Promoting Diversity and Social Justice: Educating People from Privileged Groups* (2000); William K. Tabb, *The Amoral Elephant: Globalization and the Struggle for Social Justice in the Twenty-First Century* (2001); Cynthia Willett, *The Souls of Justice: Social Bonds and Racial Hubris* (2001); Gavin Kitching, *Seeking Social Justice Through Globalization: Escaping a Nationalist Perspective* (2001); Dorothee E. Kocks, *Dream a Little: Land and Social Justice in Modern America* (2000); David Miller, *Principles of Social Justice* (2001); Martha C. Nussbaum, *Sex and Social Justice* (1999); *Interrogating Social Justice: Politics, Culture and Identity* (Marilyn Corsianos & Kelly Amanda Train eds., 1999); *Social Justice: From Hume to Walzer* (David Boucher & Paul Kelly eds., 1998); *Social Justice in a Diverse Society*

(Tom R. Tyler et al. eds., 1997); Cass R. Sunstein, *Free Markets and Social Justice* (1997); Marcia Bok, *Civil Rights and the Social Programs of the 1960s: The Social Justice Functions of Social Policy* (1992); Bernard R. Boxill, *Blacks and Social Justice* (revised ed., 1992); A.B. Atkinson, *Social Justice and Public Policy* (1983); H. Gener Blocker & Elizabeth H. Smith, *Preface* to *John Rawls' Theory of Social Justice: An Introduction* (H. Gene Blocker & Elizabeth H. Smith eds., 1980); Rawls, *supra*.

*

Chapter 2

THE LEGAL PROFESSION, LEGAL SERVICES, AND ACCESS TO JUSTICE

Power in any society includes effective access to its legal system. This chapter explores the relationship between a system of lawyers and a system of justice. Who needs a lawyer? Can people find lawyers when they need them? Can lawyers who want to work with people in the interest of social justice find ways to do so? If government funds the provision of legal services for some people in need, what special limits (beyond the usual guidelines for the profession) can government place on the ways in which those lawyers can speak and act on behalf of their clients? How would placing special limits on lawyers for low income people affect issues of social and economic power?

As you read, ask yourself how economic structures in society and the legal profession affect social justice lawyering. Are any limits on advocacy consistent with political democracy? With aspirations toward equality and social justice? If people cannot get a lawyer when they need one, how can they seek justice and equality?

SECTION 1. LAW IN WHOSE INTEREST? THE NEED FOR LAWYERS AND LEGAL SERVICES

In 1919 Reginald Heber Smith wrote:

> Freedom and equality of justice are twin fundamental conceptions of American jurisprudence. Together they form the basic principle on which our entire plan for the administration of justice is built. They are so deep-rooted in the body and spirit of our laws that the very meaning which we ascribe to the word justice embraces them. A system which created class distinctions, having one law for the rich and another for the poor, which was a respecter of persons, granting its protection to one citizen and denying it to his fellow, we would

unhesitatingly condemn as unjust, as devoid of those essentials without which there can be no justice.

Reginald Heber Smith, *Justice and the Poor* 3 (1919).

During the late 1960s through the mid-1970s, the Legal Services Program established poverty law fellowships for young attorneys in the name of Reginald Heber Smith. Smith Fellows, affectionately known as "Reggies," were identified with "the new wave of progressive professionalism." David Luban, *The Noblesse Oblige Tradition in the Practice of Law*, 41 Vand. L. Rev. 717, 731–32 (1988). For many, the experience gained as a Reggie developed abiding concerns about law and social justice. *See, e.g.*, Joyce London Alexander, *Aligning the Goals of Juvenile Justice with the Needs of Young Women Offenders: A Proposed Praxis for Transformational Justice*, 32 Suffolk U. L. Rev. 555, 556 (1999) (a former Reggie and current federal magistrate describing her work in juvenile law at Greater Boston Legal Services and how she "still maintains an inveterate concern for more just treatment of juvenile offenders").

Was Smith correct that freedom and equality of justice are inextricably intertwined? Would we condemn today a system that created one law for the rich and one for the poor? How might such a condemnation be voiced?

Echoing Smith, President Jimmy Carter also charged that legal resources are not appropriately distributed. He complained that lawyers served only 10% of the population and that 90% of lawyers served that 10%. Robert Granfield, *Making Elite Lawyers: Visions of Law at Harvard and Beyond* 4 (1992). Contemporary studies confirm that the legal profession is falling short of meeting society's legal needs.

DEBORAH L. RHODE

Access to Justice

69 Fordham L. Rev. 1785, 1786–88, 1790–92, 1794–98, 1804–06, 1808, 1814–19 (2001)

"Equal justice under law" is one of America's most firmly embedded and widely violated legal principles. It embellishes courthouse entries, ceremonial occasions, and occasionally even constitutional decisions. But it comes nowhere close to describing the justice system in practice. Millions of Americans lack any access to the system, let alone equal access. An estimated four-fifths of the civil legal needs of the poor, and the needs of an estimated two- to three-fifths of middle-income individuals, remain unmet. Governmental legal services and indigent criminal defense budgets are capped at ludicrous levels, which make effective assistance of counsel for most low-income litigants a statistical impossibility. We tolerate a system in which money often matters more than merits and equal protection principles are routinely subverted in practice.

This is not, of course, the only legal context in which rhetoric outruns reality. But it is one of the most disturbing, given the fundamental nature of the individual rights at issue. It is a shameful irony that the nation with the world's most lawyers has one of the least adequate systems for legal assistance. It is more shameful still that the inequities attract so little concern. Over the last two decades, national spending on legal aid has been cut by a third, and increasing restrictions have been placed on the cases and clients that government-funded programs can accept. Entire categories of the "unworthy poor" have been denied assistance, and courts have largely acquiesced in these limitations. The case law governing effective assistance of counsel and access to nonlawyer services is a conceptual embarrassment. Yet neither the public nor the profession has been moved to respond in any significant fashion. Access to justice is the subject for countless bar commissions, committees, conferences, and colloquia, but it is not a core concern in American policy decisions, constitutional jurisprudence, or law school curricula.

* * *

II. Policy Failures

Part of the reason that we are reluctant to confront these problems involves the scale of subsidies that would be necessary for solutions. Unlike most other industrialized nations, the United States recognizes no right to legal assistance for civil matters. Although courts have discretion to appoint counsel where necessary to assure due process, they have done so only in a narrow category of cases, and legislatures have guaranteed compensation for a still more limited number of matters. The nation has only about one legal aid lawyer or public defender for every 4300 persons below the poverty line compared with a ratio of one lawyer for every 380 Americans in the population generally. The federal government, which provides about two-thirds of the funding for civil legal aid, now spends only about $300 million for such assistance. This works out to roughly $8 per year for those officially classified poor and less than 1% of the nation's total expenditures on lawyers.

Recent estimates suggest that well over ten times that amount, on the order of three to four billion dollars, would be required to meet the civil legal needs of low-income Americans. Such estimates substantially understate the magnitude of expenditures necessary to guarantee adequate access, since they do not include either the unmet needs of middle-income Americans who are now priced out of the legal process, or collective concerns such as environmental risks, community economic development, and racial discrimination in public education or political reapportionment plans.

Nor do these access-to-justice projections take into account the cost of providing truly adequate assistance in criminal cases and in the limited number of civil proceedings where indigents are already entitled to court-appointed counsel. Hourly rates and statutory caps on compensation for private lawyers are set at utterly unrealistic levels. Rates for out-of-court work are as low as $20 or $25 per hour, which does not even cover overhead in cities like New York.

* * *

* * * Our failure to develop any conceptually coherent strategies for reconciling our ideals and institutions has contributed to corresponding failures at both the political and doctrinal level.

III. Political Failures

Much of the problem in securing broader access to justice stems from the public's failure to recognize that there is, in fact, a problem. A wide gap persists between popular perceptions and daily realities, particularly for criminal cases. Most Americans are convinced that the legal system coddles criminals and that defense lawyers get far too many defendants off on technicalities. The trials featured in entertainment media reinforce this perception. In the courtrooms that the public sees, zealous advocacy is the norm. O.J. Simpson's lawyers left no stone unturned. But they were charging by the stone. Most defense counsel cannot—and it matters. In recent studies, between half and four-fifths of counsel entered guilty pleas without interviewing any prosecution witnesses, and four-fifths did so without filing any defense motions.

The rationalizations for such inadequate efforts occasionally surface with chilling candor. In one Texas case, a defendant managed to win release after seven years of imprisonment. His court-appointed attorney had seen no reason to go to "sleazy bars to look for witnesses," since he assumed, without investigation, that his client was guilty. In a recent North Carolina case, a court-appointed lawyer acknowledged that he had deliberately failed to file a timely appeal because he felt that his client "deserved to die."

Similar rationalizations are apparent among legislators who refuse to support adequate funding for court-appointed counsel. Their position is understandable, given an electorate more interested in getting tough on criminals than in subsidizing their defense. * * * Although recent exonerations of wrongfully convicted defendants through DNA evidence have increased public concerns about the adequacy of their defense, budget priorities have rarely changed in response.

With respect to civil legal assistance, the public is more supportive, but equally misinformed. As an abstract matter, the vast majority of Americans favors providing legal assistance for the poor in civil cases. * * * However, most would prefer the assistance to come from volunteer lawyers rather than from government-funded attorneys, half believe that legal aid lawyers contribute to frivolous litigation, and 40% favor providing only advice, not advocacy in court. Public attitudes also vary considerably depending on the kinds of cases and clients at issue. Assistance in cases involving domestic violence, divorce, child custody, and fraud against elderly victims attracts broad support. For other claims, such as those involving challenges to welfare legislation or prison conditions, one

Denver legal aid attorney aptly noted that "[t]he only thing less popular than a poor person these days is a poor person with a lawyer."

Not only are Americans ambivalent about ensuring legal assistance, they are ill-informed about the assistance currently available. Almost four-fifths incorrectly believe that the poor are currently entitled to legal aid in civil cases. Only a third think that the poor would have a very difficult time obtaining assistance; a quarter think it would be easy. Such perceptions are wildly out of touch with reality. Legal services offices can handle less than a fifth of the needs of eligible clients and often are able to offer only brief advice, not the full range of assistance that is necessary. In some jurisdictions, poor people must wait over two years before seeing a lawyer for matters like divorce that are not considered emergencies, and other offices exclude such matters entirely. Legal aid programs that accept federal funds also may not accept entire categories of cases or clients who seldom have anywhere else to go, such as prisoners, undocumented immigrants, or individuals with claims involving abortions, homosexual rights, or challenges to welfare legislation.

* * *

* * * [Criticisms of Legal Services Corporation by the political right] build on longstanding objections both to government-subsidized legal services and to required pro bono assistance by private lawyers. In critics' view, much of this aid in fact worsens the plight of its intended beneficiaries. The most commonly cited example involves representation of tenants with "marginal" cases; landlords forced to litigate such matters allegedly pass on their costs in the form of increased rents to the non-litigious poor. Other illustrations of assertedly counterproductive legal assistance involve welfare claims that promote dependency; efforts to prevent evictions of drug dealers or expulsions of disruptive students; and farmworkers' lawsuits that encourage mechanization and increase unemployment.

A related objection is that even if some legal services do help the poor, it is inefficient to provide those services in kind rather than through cash transfers. Earmarking government or pro bono funds for legal aid assertedly encourages overinvestments in law, as opposed to other purchases that the poor might value more, such as food, medicine, education, or housing. * * *

There are a number of difficulties with these claims that do not emerge clearly in public debate. To begin with, the value of legal assistance cannot be gauged by what the poor are currently willing to pay. The poor also invest very little in expensive private education for their children, but that hardly suggests that they do not value first-rate schools. Those who cannot meet their most basic subsistence needs often are unable to make purchases that would prove cost-effective in the longer term. That is part of what traps them in poverty. Legal services are often a more efficient use of resources than subsistence goods. A few hours of legal work may result in benefits far exceeding their costs. In its

"Access to Justice" series defending the LSC, the Brennan Center offers a host of examples: domestic violence victims in need of protective orders; brain-damaged children and senior citizens on fixed incomes erroneously denied medical coverage; and impoverished nursing mothers exposed to dangerous pesticides. For many forms of legal assistance, it would be difficult, if not impossible, to attach a precise dollar value, but the benefits may be enormous and enduring. For millions of poor people, government subsidized or pro bono services make it possible to divorce and remarry, to adopt a child, and to terminate an unwanted pregnancy.

Moreover, law is a public good. Protecting legal rights often has value beyond what those rights are worth to any single client. Holding employers accountable for unsafe farm working conditions, or making landlords liable for violations of housing codes and eviction procedures can provide a crucial deterrent against future abuse. Contrary to critics' claims, it is by no means clear that the costs of defending such lawsuits will all be passed on to other poor people, or that those costs are excessive in light of the deterrent value that they serve. Whether the landlord will in fact raise the rent is a complicated empirical question that depends on local market conditions. And whether such increases would be worth incurring is equally complicated, particularly if, as some research suggests, tenants represented by legal aid attorneys typically have valid claims. Understaffed legal services offices have no reason to spend substantial, scarce resources litigating the "marginal" or meritless cases that critics' arguments assume.

* * *

IV. Judicial Failures

In 1956, in *Griffin v. Illinois*, [351 U.S. 12 (1956)], the Supreme Court observed that "[t]here can be no equal justice where the kind of trial a man gets depends on the amount of money he has." Over the next half century, American courts have repeatedly witnessed the truth of that observation, and have repeatedly failed to address it. These failures have occurred along multiple dimensions. Courts have declined to recognize a right to appointed counsel in civil cases except under highly limited circumstances. In the civil and criminal proceedings where courts have recognized a right to assistance, they have failed to insure that representation meets acceptable standards. Judicial oversight has been equally lacking for the substantive and financial restrictions that legislatures have established for legal services. And despite the overwhelming shortages of affordable or government-subsidized legal assistance, courts have failed to establish structures that would enable most Americans to represent themselves effectively.

* * *

In "poor peoples' courts" that handle housing, bankruptcy, small claims, and family matters, parties without lawyers are less the exception than the rule. Cases in which at least one side is unrepresented are far more common than those in which both sides have counsel. In some of these courts, over four-fifths of the proceedings involve pro se litigants. Yet the systems in which these parties operate have been designed by and for lawyers, and courts have done far too little to make them accessible to the average claimant.

Innovative projects and reform proposals are not in short supply. Examples include: procedural simplification; standardized forms; increased educational materials; self-service centers with interactive kiosks for information and document preparation; free in-person assistance from volunteer lawyers or court personnel; and judicial intervention to prevent manifest injustice. Yet few jurisdictions have attempted systematic implementation of such reforms. A majority of surveyed courts has no formal pro se assistance services. Many of the services that are available are unusable by those who need help most: uneducated litigants with limited competence and English language skills. All too often, these litigants are expected to navigate procedures of bewildering complexity, and to complete forms with archaic jargon left over from medieval English pleadings. Court clerks and mediators are instructed not to give legal advice, since that would constitute "unauthorized practice of law." Even pro se facilitators are cautioned against answering any "should" questions, such as "which form should I file?"

Judges vary considerably in their willingness to fill the gaps and to assist unrepresented parties. * * * While some judges attempt to prevent exploitation of the ignorance of pro se litigants, others decline to do so out of concern that such efforts will compromise their impartiality or encourage more individuals to proceed without lawyers. Some courts are openly hostile to unrepresented parties, whom they view as tying up the system or attempting to gain tactical advantages. * * *

V. Failures of the Bar

* * *

* * * The profession has both resisted efforts to provide qualified nonlawyer assistance for * * * [unrepresented] parties, and has tolerated exploitation of their vulnerability by opponents.

* * * Bar leaders have long insisted that such prohibitions are motivated solely by concerns to protect the public rather than the profession. But virtually no experts, including the ABA's own Commission on Nonlawyer Practice, share that view. * * * [M]ost research finds that lay specialists can effectively provide routine services where legal needs are greatest. For many of these needs, retaining a lawyer is like "hir[ing] a surgeon to pierce an ear." Other countries generally permit nonlawyers to give legal advice and to provide assistance on routine matters, and no evidence suggests that these lay specialists are inadequate. A case on point involves Great Britain's Citizen's Advice Bureaus, which rely on nonlawyer volunteers to provide effective low-cost assistance involving some ten million matters yearly.

* * * At its meeting in February of 2000, the ABA approved a resolution to increase enforcement of unauthorized practice prohibitions, and some state and local bars have launched similar efforts.

A profession truly committed to public protection would not only reverse this position, it would also rethink the rules governing lawyers' dealings with unrepresented parties. In response to bar opposition, the commission that drafted the Model Rules of Professional Conduct deleted provisions enjoining lawyers who appeared against pro se opponents from "unfairly exploiting ... ignorance of the law" and from "procur[ing] an unconscionable result." According to opponents, "parties 'too cheap to hire a lawyer' should not be 'coddled' by special treatment." Under the draft ultimately approved, lawyers' sole responsibility is to avoid implying that they are disinterested and to "make reasonable efforts to correct ... misunderstanding[s]" concerning their role.

Such minimal obligations have proven totally inadequate to curb overreaching behavior in contexts involving many unrepresented and uninformed parties. Counsel for more powerful litigants in landlord-tenant, consumer, and family law disputes often mislead opponents into waiving important rights and accepting inadequate settlements. Since these individuals typically do not know or cannot prove that they were misinformed by opposing counsel, such conduct rarely results in any disciplinary or judicial sanctions.

* * *

VI. An Alternative Aspiration: Adequate Access to Justice

* * * To make significant progress, we will first need to identify realistic objectives and to mobilize the profession and the public in their support. Despite the conceptual difficulties surrounding access to justice, several principles seem likely to command broad agreement. While equal access to justice may be an implausible ideal, adequate access should remain a societal aspiration. To that end, courts, bar associations, law schools, legal aid providers, and community organizations must work together to develop comprehensive, coordinated systems for the delivery of legal services. Under such systems, legal procedures and support structures should be designed to maximize individuals' opportunities to address law-related problems themselves, without expensive professional assistance. Those who need, but cannot realistically afford, lawyers should have reasonable opportunities for competent services. Opportunities for assistance should be available for all individuals, not just citizens or those meeting some political litmus test.

Reducing the need for professional assistance calls for strategies along several dimensions: increased simplification of the law; more self-help initiatives; better protection of unrepresented parties; greater access to nonlawyer providers; and expanded opportunities for informal dispute resolution in accessible out-of-court settings. As critics have long noted, American legal procedures are strewn with unnecessary formalities, archaic jargon, and cumbersome rituals that discourage individuals from resolving legal problems themselves. Simplified forms and streamlined procedures could expand ordinary Americans' opportunities to handle routine matters such as governmental benefits, probate, uncontested divorces, landlord-tenant disputes, and consumer claims.

More assistance for self-representation would serve similar objectives. All jurisdictions should have comprehensive services such as free or low-cost workshops, hotlines, court-house advisors, and walk-in centers that provide personalized multilingual assistance at accessible times and locations. Courts and bar ethical rules should also provide unrepresented parties with greater protection. Judges should assume affirmative obligations to prevent manifest injustice, modeled on precedents from small-claims courts and administrative agencies. Lawyers should be enjoined from knowingly exploiting the ignorance of an unrepresented party. More specifically, they should be held to standards analogous to those governing ex parte proceedings, which require lawyers to disclose facts and claims necessary for an informed decision.

Individuals should also have greater access to nonlawyer providers of legal services. * * * Where the risk of injury is substantial, in contexts such as immigration involving unsophisticated and vulnerable consumers, lay practitioners could be subject to licensing requirements. In other fields, it might be adequate to register practitioners and to allow voluntary certification of those who meet certain established standards. Moreover, "[s]tates also could require all lay practitioners to carry malpractice insurance, to contribute to client security funds," and to observe basic ethical obligations governing confidentiality, competence, and conflicts of interest.

* * *

Other eligibility restrictions also require rethinking. Most European nations guarantee legal assistance for a much broader category of individuals than those entitled to legal aid in this country. Under the eligibility structures of other nations, relevant considerations include: Does the claim have a reasonable possibility of success? What would be the benefits of legal assistance or the harms if it is unavailable? Would a reasonable lawyer, advising a reasonable client suggest that the client use his or her own money to pursue the issue? In assessing financial eligibility, these systems typically operate with sliding scales. This approach permits at least partial coverage for a broader range of clients than American legal aid offices, which serve only those below or just over the poverty line. These more liberal eligibility structures avoid a major limitation of the United States model, which excludes many individuals with urgent problems and no realistic means of addressing them.

* * *

It is a national disgrace that civil legal aid programs now reflect less than 1% of the nation's legal expenditures. And it is a professional disgrace that pro bono service occupies less than 1% of lawyers' working hours. We can and must do more, and our greatest challenge lies in persuading the public and the profession to share that view. More education and research needs to focus on what passes for justice among the have-nots. Law schools have a unique opportunity and a corresponding obligation to insure that issues concerning access to legal services occupy a central place in their curricula, and that pro bono activity plays a central role in their students' educational experience.

This country has come a considerable distance since 1919, when Reginald Heber Smith published his landmark account of *Justice and the Poor*. At that time, the entire nation had only about forty legal aid organizations, with sixty full-time attorneys and a combined budget of less than $200,000. Yet despite our substantial progress, we are nowhere close to the goal that Smith envisioned: "that denial of justice on account of poverty shall forever be made impossible in America." That ideal should remain our aspiration, and occasions like this can serve as reminders of all that still stands in the way.

Notes and Questions

1. What does Rhode mean by stating that "law is a public good"? Is it possible to calculate the value to society of protecting rights of individuals? Is the "public good" made up of the sum of the values gained by many individual clients, or is Rhode describing a larger vision of the role of law in society? Why would money spent on legal resources for low-income people be more efficiently spent than money spent on substantive needs such as food or shelter?

2. Middle-income people have trouble finding lawyers in the United States; although they can pay some amount for legal services, often they cannot afford the rates charged by lawyers in their area. The unmet needs of middle-income consumers are addressed in ABA Consortium on Legal Services and the Public, *Agenda for Access: The American People and Civil Justice* (1996), and Roy W. Reese & Carolyn A. Eldred, *Legal Needs Among Low-Income and Moderate-Income Households: Summary of Findings for the Comprehensive Legal Needs Study* (1994).

3. In Gideon v. Wainwright, 372 U.S. 335 (1963), the Supreme Court held that the due process clause of the Fourteenth Amendment mandated application to the states of the right to appointed counsel in criminal matters. *See* Anthony Lewis, *Gideon's Trumpet* (1964). In 1967, the Court held that in "proceedings to determine delinquency which may result in commitment to an institution in which the juvenile's freedom is curtailed," the juvenile has a right to appointed counsel even though the commitment proceedings may be civil and not criminal. In re Gault, 387 U.S. 1, 41 (1967). But the Court has found no comparable right to counsel in civil cases. In Lassiter v. Department of Social Services, 452 U.S. 18 (1981), the Court stated that its precedent only recognized a right to counsel in cases in which a person could lose his or her personal liberty. Although the Court recognized the importance of parental relationships, it found no due process violation in terminating Lassiter's parental rights even though she had no lawyer and could not afford one.

Many states do, however, require representation in such cases by statute.

David Luban has argued that a right to civil legal services for the poor is implicit as a matter of political morality in a constitutional democracy, because "to deny someone equality before the law delegitimizes our form of government." David Luban, *Lawyers and Justice: An Ethical Study* 251 (1988). Richard Abel comments that the primary legitimation function of our current system of legal aid must be to make the legal system seem legitimate to the privileged and the holders of wealth, because the inadequacy of the system cannot make it seem legitimate to the poor. Richard L. Abel, *Law Without Politics: Legal Aid Under Advanced Capitalism,* 32 UCLA L. Rev. 474, 601–607 (1985). Recently, a federal judge called for a "civil *Gideon*"—for the reversal of *Lassiter* and the requirement that lawyers be available to all in civil cases. Robert W. Sweet, *Civil* Gideon *and Confidence in a Just Society*, 17 Yale L. & Pol'y Rev. 503 (1998); *see also* John McKay, *Federally Funded Legal Services: A New Vision of Equal Justice Under Law*, 68 Tenn. L. Rev. 101 (2000) (president of Legal Services Corporation asserts that justice for low-income Americans is "devoid of social policies, political considerations, and partisan agendas," *id.* at 102; defends the "new vision" of legal services after recent cuts and restrictions on legal services, *id.;* but asserts that, "In the absence of adequate federal, state, and private investment in civil legal services, the courts could well entertain a Civil *Gideon* constitutional challenge and mandate representation by an attorney when individual health, safety, or welfare is found at issue," *id.* at 105). *But c.f.* Geoffrey C. Hazard, Jr., *After Legal Aid Is Abolished*, 2 J. Inst. for Study Legal Ethics 375 (1999) (arguing that the expense of legal aid prevents courts from requiring civil legal assistance).

Are lawyers responsible for making sure that the legal needs of the public are met? If the legal profession cannot or does not provide legal representation sufficient to the needs of the public, should society ensure that those needs are met? How?

4. People who confidently believe in the superiority of access to justice in the United States may be surprised by the resources available in other legal systems:

> * * * Like most U.S. citizens, I assumed the United States had the most commitment to equal justice for its citizens of any nation in the world. After all, the U.S. national rhetoric is replete with guarantees the United States provides equal justice. The Pledge of Allegiance that U.S. children start reciting in kindergarten says the United States is a country "with ... justice for all," not just for those who can afford lawyers. The U.S. Constitution purports to guarantee "due process" and "equal protection of the laws." The entrance frieze of the U.S. Supreme Court building bears the promise of "Equal Justice Under Law," which appears constantly on television and other media. * * *
>
> * * *

> * * * [Most] Western European countries, like the United Kingdom, enacted a statutory right to counsel in civil cases over a century, or at least decades, ago. France enacted such a right in 1851; Germany in 1877; the Scandinavian countries and most other Northern European nations in the early 20th Century. Austria, Greece, Italy, and Spain enacted statutory rights to counsel in the late 19th or early 20th Century. In the 1960s and 1970s several members of the U.K. Commonwealth including Hong Kong, New Zealand, and some Australian states and Canadian provinces followed suit.

Justice Earl Johnson, Jr., *Equal Access to Justice: Comparing Access to Justice in the United States and Other Industrial Democracies*, 24 Fordham Int'l L.J. S83, S86, S89 (2000).

In 1979, in the case of an indigent Irish woman who sought separation from her husband, the European Court of Human Rights held that the guarantee of "fair hearing" in the European Convention on Human Rights and Fundamental Freedoms created an affirmative obligation on the government to provide equal justice for lower income citizens:

> The Convention is intended to guarantee not rights that are theoretical or illusory but rights that are practical and effective. This is particularly so of the right to access to the courts in view of the prominent place held in a democratic society by the right to a fair trial.... The court concludes ... that the possibility to appear in person before the [trial court] does not provide the applicant with an effective right of access.... * * *
>
> [H]indrance in fact can contravene the Convention just like a legal impediment. Furthermore, fulfillment of a duty under the Convention on occasion necessitates some positive action on the part of the State; in such circumstances, the State cannot simply remain passive and "there is ... no room to distinguish between acts and omissions." The obligation to secure an effective right of access to the courts falls into this category of duty.

Id. at S90–91, quoting Airey v. Ireland, 32 Eur. Ct. H.R. (ser. A) (1979).

5. Where legal representation is mandated by constitution or statute, are inadequate attorney fees a constitutional problem? In 2001, rates for lawyers for indigent clients in New York were as low as $25 for out of court work and $40 for work in court. The low rates were found to interfere with constitutional and statutory rights to counsel and were raised to $90 per hour by court order. *See* Nicholson v. Williams, 203 F.Supp.2d 153 (E.D.N.Y.2002) (federal order raising fees in representing clients in family court and in child neglect proceedings); Daniel Wise and Tom Perrotta, *18-B Fees for Lawyers Raised to $90 an Hour, Judge Rules Low Rates Imperil Rights of Indigent*, N.Y.L.J., May 6, 2002, Col. 5, 1 (state order raising fees for representing indigent clients).

6. Russell Engler argues that lawyers in adversarial negotiations with unrepresented people routinely violate the ethical prohibition on giving them legal advice. Russell Engler, *Out of Sight and Out of Line: The Need for Regulation of Lawyers' Negotiations with Unrepresented Poor Persons*, 85 Calif. L. Rev. 79 (1997), excerpted in chapter 6. Engler recommends internal regulation by the profession, such as changes in ethical rules and the undertaking of disciplinary actions against lawyers; increased oversight by court personnel, including judges and their clerks; and increasing the availability of counsel in civil cases. *Id.* at 158. *See also* Jonathan L. Hafetz, *Almost Homeless*, Legal Affairs, July-August, at 11 (2002) (describing the case of a woman who became homeless because, without a lawyer, she did not understand her right to keep her apartment); Barbara Bezdek, *Silence in the Court: Participation and Subordination of Poor Tenants' Voices in Legal Process*, 20 Hofstra L. Rev. 533 (1992) (describing Baltimore housing court, where tenants' voices are silenced or treated as disruptive; most tenants are not represented by lawyers; and most landlords are represented by agents who are repeat players in the courts).

7. Judges and bar associations continue to exhort lawyers, pressing the urgency of pro bono work as a tenet of professional responsibility. Bob Egelko, *14 S.F. Law Firms Pledge Free Work for Poor Clients: Judicial Nudge Prompts Commitment*, S.F. Chron., Dec. 15, 2000 (describing successful effort of Chief Judge Marilyn Hall Patel, U.S. District Court in San Francisco, and Chief Justice Ronald George, California Supreme Court, with the Bar Association of San Francisco to encourage law firms to commit a percentage of attorney time to pro bono work). But lawyers are divided over "whether the profession has some special responsibility to help provide that assistance, and if so, whether the responsibility should be mandatory." Deborah L. Rhode, *Cultures of Commitment: Pro Bono for Lawyers and Law Students*, 67 Fordham L. Rev. 2415, 2419 (1999); *see also*, Norman W. Spaulding, *The Prophet and the Bureaucrat: Positional Conflicts in Service Pro Bono Publico*, 50 Stan. L. Rev. 1395 (1998) (examining institutional barriers to pro bono work).

There are many justifications for mandatory pro bono programs, including the monopoly held by the legal profession on the provision of essential services, the special role of law and lawyers in providing justice and the importance of justice in the governance structure, and the benefits to lawyers in exposing them to the way the justice system "functions, or fails to function, for the have nots." Rhode, *Cultures of Commitment*, *supra* at 2419–20. Rhode observes:

> Opponents [of mandatory pro bono] raise both moral and practical objections. As a matter of principle, some lawyers insist that compulsory charity is a contradiction in terms. From their perspective, requiring service would undermine its moral significance and compromise altruistic commitments.

> There are several problems with this claim, beginning with its assumption that pro bono service is "charity." * * * [P]ro bono work is not simply a philanthropic exercise; it is also a professional responsibility. Moreover, in the small number of jurisdictions where courts now appoint lawyers to provide uncompensated representation, no evidence indicates that voluntary assistance has declined as a result. Nor is it self-evident that most lawyers who currently make public-service contributions would cease to do so simply because others were required to join them. As to lawyers who do not volunteer but claim that required service would lack moral value, David Luban has it right: "You can't appeal to the moral significance of a gift you have no intention of giving."
>
> Opponents' other moral objection to mandatory pro bono contributions involves the infringement of lawyers' own rights. From critics' vantage, conscripting attorneys undermines the fundamental rights of due process and just compensation; it is a form of "latent fascism" and "involuntary servitude."
>
> The legal basis for such objections is unconvincing. A well-established line of precedent holds that Thirteenth Amendment prohibitions extend only to physical restraint or a threat of legal confinement. They do not apply if individuals may choose freedom at a price. * * *
>
> * * *
>
> Not only are lawyers' takings and involuntary-servitude objections unpersuasive as a legal matter, they are unconvincing as a moral claim. Requiring the equivalent of an hour a week of uncompensated assistance hardly seems like slavery. * * *

Id. at 2421–23.

The debate about pro bono also concerns the best way to provide legal services to low-income people. There are many advantages to staffed legal services offices, including the development of skills and specialized knowledge about the needs of low-income individuals and communities. But Congress has cut funds, eliminated support for impact litigation, and placed severe restrictions on legal services offices. Furthermore, the funding programs that support most state-based legal aid work are currently subject to constitutional challenge. *See* section 3.

8. Michelle Jacobs criticizes arguments about access to justice and mandatory pro bono for missing the most important questions about power and inequality that face low-income people:

> * * * [R]egardless of whether * * * [pro bono plans] are mandatory in nature * * * [s]uch plans focus on providing access to a legal system which in many ways is ineffective in dealing with the complexities and realities of poverty. Pro bono programs attempt to place poor citizens in the same seats in the courtroom as those citizens who have the means to hire an attorney. In overly simplistic

terms, the plans hope to assist the poor person in having her day in court.

A clear example of the ineffective results of one such plan is supplied by Professor Michael Millemann from the University of Maryland School of Law. In an article supporting mandatory pro bono, Millemann describes a common scene occurring now in Baltimore City Rent Court where tenant after tenant, each unrepresented by counsel, lines up to receive items called "white slips." These tenants are present because they have received notices of eviction. They are accepting put-out orders and getting the slips so that they can obtain emergency Aid for Dependent Children (AFDC). By agreeing to the put-out, the tenant gives up certain legal rights and remedies that she may have against the landlord. In Millemann's vision of Baltimore City Rent Court several years after imposition of mandatory pro bono, tenants receiving notices for eviction still will line up for white slips, but there will be a lawyer present to explain the rights they are giving up and to counsel them on their ability to proceed on various claims against the landlord.

The problem with this vision is that it still begins with many tenants lined up, after receiving notices of eviction, in Baltimore City Rent Court. The new presence of the lawyer, either in the advising role on the "white slip" line or as assigned counsel to handle the eviction case at trial, will not impact the ongoing inability of the tenant to pay the rent. Representation of the client's counterclaims at trial will mean nothing if the tenant has no way to compel the landlord to make repairs or to ensure that the repairs are made correctly with materials of appropriate quality. In truth, the individual client's battle with housing will be delayed for another day, but the question of whether a net benefit will have been achieved in providing access to justice must be asked. Having one's day in court may be a hollow victory for a poor person.

Traditional notions of "access to justice" entertained by the majority in the profession narrowly embrace only helping the poor to have a voice in court. There is no commitment to alter fundamentally the legal structures which help institutionalize poverty. * * * Neither our society nor legal professionals have accepted the necessity of guaranteeing basic human needs.

In order to fundamentally change access to law and justice for poor people, lawyers would need to accept the premise that the conditions which produce poverty must change. If pro bono work is to matter in any real sense, the work would need to be focused on eliminating the conditions, both legally and otherwise, which produce and institutionalize poverty. In other words, pro bono work would need as one of its goals the accomplishment of social justice. On this point, there is clear disagreement within the bar. The disagreement has been explicitly stated as well as demonstrated in the ambivalence of lawyers toward programs aimed at truly assisting the poor. Whether mandated or not, our view of work performed on behalf of the poor is that it is "charity" work.

* * *

The social and legal needs of the poor are complex at the same time they are incredibly simple. The poor need to have a standard of living that allows them to escape the clutches of poverty. The law impacts on the ability of the poor to escape poverty in many ways, both by institutionalizing the poverty and by denying that the poverty itself shapes the way law is applied to the poor. The desire to provide access to justice for the poor is a laudatory one, which I support wholeheartedly. However, before our profession can make lasting and permanent progress toward providing that access, we must come to grips with the reality of our own divisions and diversity of opinion.

If the profession wants to provide a measure of social justice to the poor, mandatory pro bono, as we are envisioning it now, will not accomplish this goal. We cannot lull ourselves into feeling good about support for mandatory programs when we know that realistically they are too narrowly constructed to accomplish social justice. If our view of access to justice is closer to the individual representation model, then mandatory pro bono will not help ensure that poor people receive quality representation any more than does the existence of formal legal services organizations. The minimal hours proposed can do little more than help the clients stay in place. Until we can agree as a profession that it is social justice and access to legal justice that we are trying to achieve, mandatory pro bono requirements ring false.

Michelle S. Jacobs, *Pro Bono Work and Access to Justice for the Poor: Real Change or Imagined Change?*, 48 Fla. L. Rev. 509, 513–15, 521 (1996). *See also* Stuart Scheingold, *The Struggle to Politicize Legal Practice: A Case Study of Left-Activist Lawyering in Seattle*, in *Cause Lawyering: Political Commitments and Professional Responsibilities* 118 (Austin Sarat & Stuart Scheingold eds., 1998); Richard Abel, *Speaking Law to Power*, in *Cause Lawyering*, *supra* at 60 (emphasizing challenges to power in social justice lawyering).

RICHARD ABEL

Big Lies and Small Steps: A Critique of Deborah Rhode's Too Much Law, Too Little Justice: Too Much Rhetoric, Too Little Reform
11 Geo. J. Legal Ethics 1019, 1023–27 (1998)

America may be unusually dependent on law because the institutions of civil society are relatively underdeveloped: political parties, trade unions, religious loyalties, long-term employment, and stable residential neighborhoods. If America has too many laws, lawyers, and lawsuits, why are we so determined to foist our legal system on countries blessed with fewer? American lawyers sought to do that during the first law and development movement of the 1960s and 1970s (itself a pale imitation of the great wave of eighteenth-and nineteenth-century European imperialism). Now, American law schools, bar associations, law firms, and governments, aided by the World Bank, are trying to impose the "rule of law" on the former communist world. Those efforts to reduce judicial delay and corruption can only increase litigation. Even countries whose rapid economic growth is often attributed to their ability to do without law and lawyers, notably Japan and Taiwan, are expanding their legal professions. Indeed, Britain, which always ridiculed contingent fees as a typically American abomination, has begun to legalize what long had been a covert practice.

If the real issue is justice, not excessive or inappropriate litigation, how can we promote it? The basic fallacy of liberalism ensures that the steps toward justice will be small, halting, and self-limiting (as recently illustrated in the backlash against affirmative action, as well as welfare "reform," and anti-immigrant measures). That fallacy is the belief that it is possible to achieve equality in one circumscribed realm without addressing other structural inequalities. Thus, the liberal state offers public services such as education and health care for the elderly and is surprised when race or class correlates with student performance on standardized tests or morbidity and mortality rates. It abolishes *de jure* segregation and is surprised that de facto segregation persists in housing, education, employment, and social and cultural life. It creates formal democracy and is surprised when money shapes elections, legislation, and executive action (even burial in Arlington National Cemetery). And it is surprised that formal equality before the law, symbolized by blindfolded justice, does not translate into equal access or outcomes. By contrast, Marxism, virtually forgotten since the collapse of "actually existing socialism," located the problem of inequality in relations of production and insisted equality could not be attained anywhere until that was democratized.

What can we do to promote "equal justice under law" within the constraints of liberalism? There seem to be only three alternatives. We can give lawyers to the un- or under-represented. We can take them away from the over-represented. And we can seek ways of delivering justice without lawyers.

We seem to have abandoned the first strategy. Can anyone today imagine the political environment in which a distinguished lawyer (who later became Eisenhower's Attorney General) could say of legal aid: "the service should be equal in quality to that of the private law offices of the community." [Emery A. Brownell, *Legal Aid in the United States* 121 (1951).] Or, can anyone believe that only two decades ago the chairman of the Legal Services Corporation (LSC), a sophisticated law professor, declared: "the board intends .. to ensure that the poor receive the same quality and range of service that is provided to the rich." Reagan's draconian cuts in legal services have never been reversed, even though another LSC chair [became] First Lady and the federal budget is in surplus for the first time in decades. Other nations far more committed to welfare services (for example, England) also have curtailed and reversed the growth of legal aid. That is hardly surprising; every program limited to the poor is politically vulnerable, especially when its recipients are largely disenfranchised.

Taking lawyers away from existing clients has always been a nonstarter. Nearly twenty years ago, in an article that sank from sight even faster than most, I reflected on why such a strategy was politically unfeasible and ideologically unimaginable.

That leaves deprofessionalization of advocates, arbiters, or both. Self-help is the ultimate deprofessionalization. Some see it as empowering, but more than two centuries ago Adam Smith convincingly demonstrated the superior efficiency of the division of labor.

What about paraprofessionals? Such workers often have emerged in response to market forces: nurse practitioners, pharmacists diagnosing and even prescribing some medicines, dental hygienists, midwives, psychotherapists, purveyors of alternative medicine, notaries (especially in the Latino community), immigration and tax consultants, claims adjusters, just to name a few. Third-party payers increasingly encourage or demand such deprofessionalization through their reimbursement schedules. Professionals willingly delegate tasks they prefer not to handle (such as emotional or physical messes to nurses) and welcome the chance to enhance profits by extracting surplus labor from subordinates (dental hygienists). Likewise, law firms, legal clinics, and legal aid offices are making increasing use of paralegals.

Although the market can encourage the emergence of paraprofessionals, it cannot ensure the quality of them. Even the strongest proponents of deprofessionalization worry that it relegates clients to second-class justice, prompted by a passion for parsimony rather than a dedication to better quality. Given a choice unconstrained by resources, how many of those seeking vindication of a right would choose a paralegal over a lawyer or a legally-untrained mediator over a judge?

* * *

Most attention has focused on non-professional arbiters rather than representatives. Professor Rhode and others have noted the dangers of abandoning public adjudication. Even if most cases, criminal and civil, are settled, they are settled in the shadow of the law, which is fainter in alternative dispute resolution. In the absence of state norms and coercive power, the outcome is more likely to reflect and reproduce existing power inequalities.

* * * Choices are never free. How can we ensure that clients have the resources and information to maximize their autonomy? How do we address the problem of false consciousness and socially constructed preferences? Patients respond to the bedside manner of physicians, not their technical expertise. We know that lawyers' clients are profoundly affected by such qualities as courtesy (returning phone calls, keeping

them informed) and the ability to listen. If we are queasy about allowing patients to "choose" between doctors and alternative medicine, what about "choices" between lawyers and paralegals? Milton Friedman has argued that professional self-regulation increases cost, thereby lowering average quality by depriving those who would have chosen lower quality paraprofessionals for services. What of the concern that allowing the poor to purchase inferior services lets the profession and the state evade responsibility for providing superior services?

At the end of the day, however, I agree with Professor Rhode. If we cannot equalize professional representation, we should try to increase access to paraprofessional services. The legal profession is likely to be the greatest obstacle. Even though the omnipresent and powerful bar association committees on "unauthorized practice of law" have disappeared, the profession still vigorously polices its boundaries, resisting both independent practice by paraprofessionals and lawyer subordination to other professions through multidisciplinary partnerships. It endlessly repeats the shibboleth: professionals must supervise the quality of subordinates and preserve their own autonomy. Yet, we know that paraprofessionals work with little or no supervision in lawyers' offices. Moreover, employed lawyers display just as much, or as little, autonomy as self-employed. Furthermore, the profession's record of ensuring quality is so abysmal that its arguments have lost all credibility. Still, it probably is prudential to try to enlist bar associations as allies by beginning the deprofessionalization project in areas where lawyers make little money, or those who do are politically powerless. It may even be worthwhile allowing lawyers to enjoy some monopoly rents, ostensibly to ensure paraprofessional quality, as the price of defusing opposition. Finally, it may be possible to convince lawyers that it is cheaper to satisfy their professional obligation for altruism by letting paraprofessionals perform those services than by doing so themselves.

Notes and Questions

1. Abel suggests that "America may be unusually dependent on law because the institutions of civil society are relatively underdeveloped: political parties, trade unions, religious loyalties, long-term employment, and stable residential neighborhoods." What would dependence on law have to do with these "institutions of civil society" being weak or fluid in the United States? Would the great and still unmet need for legal assistance described by both Rhode and Abel change if political parties drew more direct involvement of citizens or spoke to a greater variety of their beliefs and needs? If trade unions were better developed? If residential neighborhoods or employment were more stable?

2. Abel criticizes as a fallacy of liberalism "the belief that it is possible to achieve equality in one circumscribed realm without addressing other structural inequalities." Do you agree with this characterization? What can be done to promote equal justice under law within the "constraints of liberalism" identified by Abel?

3. Rhode argues that the need for *adequate* access to justice is so acute that society needs to expand nonlawyer assistance (such as legal help by paralegals) and pro se access to courts, even if these services cannot fulfill the aspiration to *equal* access to justice. Abel agrees: "If we cannot equalize professional representation, we should try to increase access to paraprofessional services." Alternative possibilities include facilitating pro se representation, "unbundling" legal services so that lawyers represent a client on only one aspect of a matter rather than with regard to the entire case, and allowing greater scope for legal assistance by paralegals. Unbundling legal services means pulling apart the various services lawyers normally provide (e.g., consultation, writing letters, drafting court documents, representing the client in front of the court) and allowing the client or a nonlawyer to perform some of these services. Louise Trubek & Jennifer J. Farnham, *Social Justice Collaboratives: Multidisciplinary Practices for People,* 7 Clinical L. Rev. 227, 228, n.4 (2000) "[T]he new limited representation rules allow an attorney to provide discrete legal services to an otherwise pro se party and to charge the client accordingly. Thus, a low-income individual who cannot afford full-fledged representation by an attorney can now 'order' certain legal services 'à la carte.' " Marcus J. Lock, Comment, *Increasing Access to Justice: Expanding the Role of Nonlawyers in The Delivery of Legal Services to Low-Income Coloradans*, 72 U. Colo. L. Rev. 459, 461 (2001) (arguing for expanded role for nonlawyers as the more viable alternative than mandatory pro bono and explaining that the Colorado Supreme Court amended the rules of civil procedure and professional conduct to allow limited representation of clients at about the same time that mandatory pro bono was rejected in Colorado). *See also* Vernetta L. Walker, *Legal Needs of the Public in the Future,* Florida B.J., May 1997, at 42 (describing unbundled legal services, pre-paid legal plans, and self-service centers).

Is it possible to reconcile these concerns about access to justice with Michelle Jacobs' argument that questions of social justice and inequality must be part of meeting the vast needs of the public? How can the role of nonlawyers be expanded while maintaining demands for social justice? Louise Trubek and Jennifer Farnham describe "social justice collaboratives":

> Multidisciplinary practice[s] for low and moderate income people * * * emphasize working closely with other professions, lay advocates and community agencies to meet a variety of needs and overcome barriers. This type of practice recognizes the centrality of nonlegal as well as legal needs and the barriers clients face in accessing legal services. The concept of social workers, social service agencies and lawyers working together is a longstanding but contested aspiration of many interested in the positive use of law to help people of low income. The creation of Legal Aid in the early twentieth century, for example, incorporated a struggle between social workers and reform-minded lawyers. There were disagreements about where lawyers should be situated: the settlement house

versus the independent law office. There were also conflicts about strategy: separation of social values from legal representation versus an integrated approach.

In current times many practices are again seeking to work in an interdisciplinary manner. The relationship to the client and among collaborators ranges from short-term service provision to a deeply integrated relationship. These relationships are characterized by frequent, ongoing interaction, commitment to the relationship and trust. Such MDPs have a clearly defined client group and a vision of how to meet the needs of that group. We dub these practices "social justice collaboratives." * * *

Trubek & Farnham, *Social Justice Collaboratives*, *supra* at 228–29. The social justice collaboratives described by Trubek and Farnham include practices involving at-risk children, battered women, and community economic development. Multidisciplinary practice is currently undergoing extended debate by lawyers and legal scholars; the outcome of these debates will affect the possibilities for interdisciplinary social justice collaboration. *Id.* at 272.

4. The availability of lawyers to bring social justice cases on behalf of individuals and communities affects both the nature of cases that are brought into court and the legal rules that prevail. Cruz Reynoso gives an example of the importance of lawyers to social justice:

> * * * I can point to the program established in New Mexico fifteen to twenty years ago to bring Native Americans into the legal profession. When that program was first established you could count on the fingers of one hand the number of Native American lawyers nationwide. Yet some people got together in New Mexico, where there is a large percentage of Native Americans, and said, "This is not right. There are Indian courts in the Indian nations, but they don't have any lawyers. We really ought to do something about this." They formed a program, trained Native Americans, and each year placed between thirty and fifty Native Americans in law schools around the country. In but a few years, there were literally hundreds of Native American lawyers.
>
> Soon we started seeing cases coming out of Arizona, for example, in which Native American tribes sued to receive water that they were entitled to under treaties. Rights mean nothing if nobody enforces them. Barry Goldwater is an honorary chief of every tribe in Arizona. But did he fight for Native American water rights? Absolutely not. That was not "his constituency." These things have started changing because, as I have indicated, lawyers have knowledge, and that gives them power. And this program showed us that we can produce lawyers from all walks of life, lawyers that people can talk to and have confidence in.

Cruz Reynoso, *Educational Equity*, 36 UCLA L. Rev. 107, 111 (1988).

Could access to help from paralegals or better pro se representation have enforced treaty rights effectively for Native American tribes? What are the trade-offs—and do you find them acceptable—if the absence of legal representation is addressed through these methods? How *should* society address the tension between "adequate" access to justice and "equal" access to justice?

SECTION 2. LITIGATION AND INEQUALITY

In addition to issues relating to access to attorneys, litigants seeking social justice may be structurally disadvantaged by constraints on their lawyers or by their own resources relative to the resources of their opponents. In a landmark article, Marc Galanter describes how the legal system is stacked against the "have-nots" in society:

MARC GALANTER

Why the "Haves" Come Out Ahead: Speculations on the Limits of Legal Change
9 Law and Society Review 95, 95–98, 103–04, 114–15, 123–24, 150–51 (1974)

* * * [T]he basic architecture of the legal system creates and limits the possibilities of using the system as a means of redistributive (that is, systematically equalizing) change. Our question, specifically, is, under what conditions can litigation be distributive, taking litigation in the broadest sense of the presentation of claims to be decided by courts (or court-like agencies) and the whole penumbra of threats, feints, and so forth, surrounding such presentation.

For purposes of this analysis, let us think of the legal system as comprised of these elements:

A body of authoritative normative learning—for short, RULES

A set of institutional facilities within which the normative learning is applied to specific cases—for short, COURTS

Persons or groups with claims they might make to the courts in reference to the rules, etc.—for short, PARTIES

Let us also make the following assumptions about the society and the legal system:

It is a society in which actors with different amounts of wealth and power are constantly in competitive or partially cooperative relationships in which they have opposing interests.

This society has a legal system in which a wide range of disputes and conflicts are settled by court-like agencies which purport to apply pre-existing general norms impartially (that is, unaffected by the identity of the parties).

The rules and the procedures of these institutions are complex; wherever possible disputing units employ specialized intermediaries in dealing with them.

The rules applied by courts are in part worked out in the process of adjudication (courts revise interstitial rules, combine diverse rules, and apply old rules to new situations). There is a living tradition of such rule-work and a system of communication such that the outcomes in some of the adjudicated cases affect the outcome in classes of future adjudicated cases.

Resources on the institutional side are insufficient for timely full-dress adjudication in every case, so that parties are permitted or even encouraged to forego bringing cases and trying to "settle" cases,—that is, to bargain to a mutually acceptable outcome.

* * *

Most analyses of the legal system start at the rules end and work down through institutional facilities to see what effect the rules have on the parties. I would like to reverse that procedure and look through the other end of the telescope. Let's think about the different kinds of parties and the effect these differences might have on the way the system works.

Because of differences in their size, differences in the state of the law, and differences in their resources, some of the actors in the society have many occasions to utilize the courts (in the broad sense) to make (or defend) claims; others do so only rarely. We might divide our actors into those claimants who have only occasional recourse to the courts (one-shotters or OS) and repeat players (RP) who are engaged in many similar litigations over time. The spouse in a divorce case, the auto-injury claimant, the criminal accused are OSs; the insurance company, the prosecutor, the finance company are RPs. * * * Typically, the RP is a larger unit and the stakes in any given case are smaller (relative to total worth). OSs are usually smaller units and the stakes represented by the tangible outcome of the case may be high relative to total worth, as in the case of the injury victim or the criminal accused. Or, the OS may suffer from the opposite problem: his claims may be so small and unmanageable (the shortweighted consumer or the holder of performing rights) that the cost of enforcing them outruns any promise of benefit.

* * * [An "ideal type" of the repeat player would be] a unit which has had and anticipates repeated litigation, which has low stakes in the outcome of any one case and which has the resources to pursue its long-run interests.

* * * [A repeat player would play the litigation game differently from one-shot player, because he would have several advantages, including: the ability, based on past experience, "to structure the transaction and build the record"—such as writing the form contract, or requiring the security deposit; "expertise," "economies of scale," and "low start-up costs for any case"; a need to invest in his own credibility as a

combatant—to strengthen his "bargaining reputation" for other cases; the ability to play the odds and "adopt strategies calculated to maximize gain over a long series of cases, even where this involves the risk of maximum loss in some cases"; the ability to "play for rules as well as immediate gains"—armed with the resources to spend on influencing the making of the rules by such methods as lobbying, and the accumulated expertise which will enable him to do this persuasively. Further, the repeat player can also use litigation to try to shape the rules for the next litigation, whereas the one shotter is unlikely to do so. Therefore, repeat players can settle cases in which they expect unfavorable rule outcomes, and select to litigate or appeal "those cases which they regard as most likely to produce favorable rules"; on the other hand, one shotters would be "willing to trade off the possibility of making 'good law' for tangible gain. Thus, we would expect the body of precedent cases—that is, cases capable of influencing the outcome of future cases—to be relatively skewed toward those favorable" to repeat players. RPs have experience and expertise that makes them more likely to be able to discern which rules are more likely to be effective and trade off symbolic defeats for tangible gains; also, they "are more likely to be able to invest the matching resources necessary to secure the penetration of rules favorable to them."]

* * *

It is not suggested that RPs are to be equated with "haves" (in terms of power, wealth and status) or OSs with "have-nots." In the American setting most RPs are larger, richer, and more powerful than are most OSs, so these categories overlap, but there are obvious exceptions. RPs may be "have-nots" (alcoholic derelicts) or may act as champions of "have-nots" (as government does from time to time); OSs such as criminal defendants may be wealthy. What this analysis does is to define a position of advantage in the configuration of contending parties and indicate how those with other advantages tend to occupy this position of advantage and to have their other advantages reinforced and augmented thereby. This position of advantage is one of the ways in which a legal system formally neutral as between "haves" and "have-nots" may perpetuate and augment the advantages of the former.

* * *

What happens when we introduce lawyers? Parties who have lawyers do better. Lawyers are themselves RPs. Does their presence equalize the parties, dispelling the advantage of the RP client? Or does the existence of lawyers amplify the advantage of the RP client? We might assume that RPs (tending to be larger units) who can buy legal services more steadily, in larger quantities, in bulk (by retainer) and at higher rates, would get services of better quality. They would have better information (especially where restrictions on information about legal services are present). Not only would the RP get more talent to begin with, but he would on the whole get greater continuity, better record-keeping, more anticipatory or preventive work, more experience and specialized skill in pertinent areas, and more control over counsel.

One might expect that just how much the legal services factor would accentuate the RP advantage would be related to the way in which the profession was organized. The more members of the profession were identified with their clients (i.e., the less they were held aloof from clients by their loyalty to courts or an autonomous guild) the more the imbalance would be accentuated. The more close and enduring the lawyer-client relationship, the more the primary loyalty of lawyers is to clients rather than to courts or guild, the more telling the advantages of accumulated expertise and guidance in overall strategy.

* * *

We assume here that rules tend to favor older, culturally dominant interests. This is not meant to imply that the rules are explicitly designed to favor those interests, but rather that those groups which have become dominant have successfully articulated their operations to pre-existing rules. To the extent that rules are evenhanded or favor the "have-nots," the limited resources for their implementation will be allocated, I have argued, so as to give greater effect to those rules which protect and promote the tangible interests of organized and influential groups. Furthermore, the requirements of due process, with their barriers or protections against precipitate action, naturally tend to protect the possessor or holder against the claimant. Finally, the rules are sufficiently complex and problematic (or capable of being problematic if sufficient resources are expended to make them so) that differences in the quantity and quality of legal services will affect capacity to derive advantages from the rules.

* * *

Our analysis suggests that breaking the interlocked advantages of the "haves" requires attention not only to the level of rules, but also to institutional facilities, legal services and organization of parties. It suggests that litigating and lobbying have to be complemented by interest organizing, provisions of services and invention of new forms of institutional facilities.

The thrust of our analysis is that changes at the level of parties are most likely to generate changes at other levels. If rules are the most abundant resource for reformers, parties capable of pursuing long-range strategies are the rarest. The presence of such parties can generate effective demand for high grade legal services—continuous, expert, and oriented to the long run—and pressure for institutional reforms and favorable rules. This suggests that we can roughly surmise the relative strategic priority of various rule-changes. Rule changes which relate directly to the strategic position of the parties by facilitating organization, increasing the supply of legal services (where these in turn provide a focus for articulating and organizing common interests) and increasing the costs of opponents—for instance authorization of class action suits, award of attorneys fees and costs, award of provisional remedies—these are the most powerful fulcrum for change. The intensity of the opposition to class action legislation and autonomous reform-oriented legal services such as California Rural Legal Assistance indicates the "haves" own estimation of the relative strategic impact of the several levels.

The contribution of the lawyer to redistributive social change, then, depends upon the organization and culture of the legal profession. * * * The more that lawyers view themselves exclusively as courtroom advocates, the less their willingness to undertake new tasks and form enduring alliances with clients and operate in forums other than courts, the less likely they are to serve as agents of redistributive change. Paradoxically, those legal professions most open to accentuating the advantages of the "haves" (by allowing themselves to be "captured by recurring clients") may be most able to become (or have room for, more likely) agents of change, precisely because they provide more license for identification with clients and their "causes" and have a less strict definition of what are properly professional activities.

Notes and Questions

1. The existence of public interest law firms and litigation centers brings some repeat player strengths to one-shot litigants. However, as Galanter points out, it would be unethical for these lawyers to compromise the interests of a one-shot, individual client in pursuit of strategic rule changes that would benefit the entire group of their clients. Therefore, *attorneys* who repeatedly represent one-shot litigants will never match the strategic flexibility of well-funded repeat-player *clients* and their attorneys, who can choose to pursue most vigorously those cases most likely to establish legal rules that favor their long-term interests.

2. Galanter recently commented on the ways in which society has changed since he first wrote about the "haves." Public consciousness about the power of corporations to manipulate law has decreased. By the mid 1970s, a "recoil" against law was taken up by business and political elites, who were "offended and outraged by the shrinking of the leeways and immunities that the system had always afforded them and who now found themselves the targets of an onerous new accountability." Galanter argues that the reaction against that "new accountability" and against legal remedies for "have-nots" is "an important component of the movements for deregulation and tort reform." Marc Galanter, *Farther Along*, 33 Law & Soc. Rev. 1113, 1115–16 (1999).

> Although the rhetoric is often expansive, indicting all lawyers and the entire legal system, the proposals that emerge from this recoil are more patterned: the features of the system under attack are legal services for the poor, contingency fees, the "American Rule" on costs (i.e., no "loser pays"), "trial lawyers," class actions, punitive damages, awards for pain and suffering, and the civil jury. We have seen a 20-year barrage of attacks on rules and devices that give some clout to "have nots" and nothing that impairs in the slightest

> the capacity of corporate entities to use the legal system either defensively or offensively.

Id. at 1116.

3. "Haves" may win for many reasons. Repeat player status is only one factor among many social and economic advantages and disadvantages that are built into the operation of the legal system. Structural advantages include the protection of wealth in the form of corporations, the transmission of wealth between generations, the advantages conferred by wealth in every area of education and the leverage provided by lobbyist and by campaign contributions to legislators and to the executive branch of government. In contrast, legal services lawyers are now prohibited from engaging in lobbying or consulting with legislatures on behalf of their low-income clients. The following section discusses both funding for legal services and restrictions that have been placed on advocacy for low income people.

SECTION 3. THE POLITICS OF FUNDING LEGAL WORK FOR SOCIAL JUSTICE

Funding legal work for social justice remains a political battleground in at least three major areas today: the adequacy of resources to the need; the constitutionality of restrictions on lawyers who are funded by the government to serve poor clients; and the constitutionality of additional sources of funding for services for low-income people raised through legislation.

The total resources available to legal work for low-income Americans are vastly disproportionate to those available for the wealthy. In 1999, one law firm earned more than three times the entire budget of the Legal Services Corporation:

> A single law firm, which represents maybe a hundred or so corporate clients, earned * * * [one billion dollars] while the U.S. Federal government was only willing to spend * * * [300 million dollars] on legal services for forty million poor U.S. citizens. * * *
>
> A half dozen law firms in the United States each took in more than the * * * [total budget] that the U.S. federal, state and local governments now spend on legal representation for the poor.

Justice Earl Johnson, Jr., *Equal Access to Justice: Comparing Access to Justice in the United States and Other Industrial Democracies*, 24 Fordham Int'l L.J. S83, S83–S84 (2000). Countries that recognize a right to civil legal assistance devote a much greater proportion of their resources to funding it than does the United States: France and Germany invest two and one-half times as much of their gross national product, and England invests seventeen times as much, for access to justice for their lower income population. *Id.* at S96. To match the investment made in civil legal assistance by other countries, the total federal, state and local investment in the United States would have to be multiplied: to more than three billion dollars a year to match the three largest Canadian provinces; to 3.5 billion dollars to match the Netherlands; to 4.26 billion dollars to match New Zealand; or to more than ten billion dollars to match England's commitment to equal access to justice. *Id.* at S96–S97 (2000).

A. The Contested Roles of the Legal Services Corporation

The history of the Legal Services Corporation reflects the identity crisis over its central mission. One legendary legal services attorney, Ralph Santiago Abascal, described lawyers standing by a river trying to throw life preservers to the hordes of people being washed away. The legal services lawyer, according to Abascal, would walk upstream, find the culprit who was throwing people into the river, and make him stop. José Padilla, Ralph Abascal Memorial Lecture, Los Gatos, California (March 24, 2000).

Justice Earl Johnson, Jr. of the California Court of Appeal, a former director of the Legal Services program of the Office of Economic Opportunity, compares legal assistance to health care for the poor:

> [Los Angeles] is the most populous U.S. county with over 10,000,000 (ten million) people and almost 2,000,000 (two million) of those are poor in the sense they are *financially* eligible for civil legal services. Los Angeles County has over 40,000 lawyers, yet there are fewer than a hundred government-funded legal services lawyers to meet the legal needs of that 2,000,000 (two million) poor people.
>
> By analogy, the dimensions of the problems legal services lawyers face is similar to expecting a hundred doctors to take care of all the health care needs of two million people. Imagine what you would do if handed the assignment of putting together a health care program with only a hundred doctors to somehow make this population of two million healthier. It is likely you would emphasize "public health" measures such as mass vaccinations calculated to reduce deadly diseases dramatically across the entire population and focus other resources on the treatment of life-threatening conditions like heart disease and cancer, before worrying about patients with colds and backaches. By so doing, you would produce the most improvement in death rates and overall health in that population group, as opposed to randomly treating whatever complaints might be brought to your tiny health service by the one in ten or one in twenty sick people your handful of doctors might be able to see.
>
> For similar reasons, when we can only put a hundred lawyers in a community with two million poor people, it makes sense to try the rough equivalent of a "public health" approach. A class action or a favorable legislative change is like a mass inoculation program against a disease that infects thousands every year because it can improve the lives of thousands at a comparatively minimal cost. For example, if thousands of poor people in the community are being evicted in retaliation for reporting housing code violations to the

authorities, the logical course of action is to seek legislation that would ban retaliatory evictions or perhaps a class action aimed at achieving the same goal. A favorable appellate precedent can do the same, but is also often similar to treatment of heart disease or cancer because it tends to address the most serious legal conditions the poor experience. In essence, the absence of a legally enforceable right to counsel and the resultant shortage of resources virtually compels U.S. legal services programs to practice "triage" and makes it most sensible to emphasize measures like appellate litigation, class actions, and legislative advocacy.

* * *

* * * Taking the problems of poor people one client at a time simply is not a viable strategy when you only have enough lawyers to help a small percentage of those clients.

Johnson, *Equal Access to Justice, supra* at S99–S100.

The following articles describe political battles over the role of legal services; the impact of recent restrictions on law reform work such as class actions, appellate litigation, and legislative advocacy; and a project undertaken since the restrictions were imposed by Congress.

WILLIAM P. QUIGLEY

The Demise of Law Reform and the Triumph of Legal Aid: Congress and the Legal Services Corporation from the 1960's to the 1990's

17 St. Louis U. Pub. L. Rev. 241, 241–46, 248, 250–51, 253, 255–56, 260–64(1998)

Any program * * * which enables the poor to do battle with the forces that oppress them at government expense, has a high potential for conflict with the officials who make public policy affecting the poor. This is especially true where it is governmental action, often in programs designed to aid the poor, that is found to be oppressive. These conflicts have indeed arisen. [Sargent Shriver, Law Reform and the Poor, 17 Am.U.L.Rev. 1, 5 (1967).]

From the very inception of the legal services program up until today, the controversies which marked the program have been the same. In the name of helping the poor, program resources were used to promote political and ideological causes. Lobbying, congressional redistricting cases, abortion litigation and legal attacks on welfare reform and laws against welfare fraud all served to mark this program as being a far cry from the traditional legal aid offered to the poor by the legal profession over the years. [Hearing Before the Subcomm. on Com. and Admin. Law of the House Comm. on the Judiciary, 104th Cong., 2nd Sess. 36 (1996)(statement of Kenneth F. Boehm, Chairman, National Legal and Policy Center).]

In 1996 Congress gave in to long-time critics of the Legal Services Corporation and all but eliminated the ability of lawyers for poor people to use the law as an instrument for reform, legal work usually described as law reform. Congress also dramatically reduced the number of lawyers for poor people but allowed those who remained to continue a century-old tradition of providing legal assistance in individual legal matters, usually called legal aid. The 1996 restrictions had been sought for three decades by opponents of legal services. Since the 1960's, federally funded legal services for the poor has suffered a legislative identity crisis as Congress fought over the extent to which it would allow lawyers for the poor to engage in law reform. While law reform has been a key element of publicly funded legal services since its inception, opposition to law reform has also been a key element of legal services throughout its existence. In 1996, Congress chose to fund only legal aid, refusing to also fund law reform. * * *

[[L]egal aid and law reform will be defined as follows: Proponents of legal aid believe that the legal system works well but has a problem in that more people, usually poor people, need better access to it. As a consequence, the goal of legal aid is to provide individuals with improved access to lawyers to handle individual legal needs. Advocates of law reform do not agree that current systems, including the legal system, are fair. Thus law reform works to change legal, political, social, and economic system to the advantage of its clients by using the tools of the lawyer such as test case or class action litigation, lobbying, or legal support to organizations seeking change. Joel F. Handler, *Social Movements and the Legal System: A Theory of Law Reform and Social Change* 26 (1978).]

* * *

In the United States, for most of this nation's history, "the courts were open to all, but only the well to do could afford the lawyer who was necessary for the vindication of rights." * * *

* * *

As the nation entered the 1960s, legal aid was the norm. Legal aid remained small, local, restricted to the largest cities and, when available, usually provided by private or municipal organizations which served the immediate individual legal needs of the poor. At this time it was estimated that the equivalent of 400 full-time legal aid lawyers were available to serve nearly fifty million poor people.

Legal Services Program of the Office of Economic Opportunity

* * * In 1964, as a part of the War on Poverty launched by President Lyndon B. Johnson, Congress created the Office of Economic Opportunity (OEO) to directly operate some anti-poverty programs and coordinate other programs. As a result of OEO, legal services for the poor grew rapidly. * * * [The OEO was authorized to undertake and fund a wide variety of community activities for the poor because its early legislative history included an express recognition that legal services for the poor were within the scope of its permitted activity.] By 1966, the OEO had allocated over twenty-five million dollars to over 150 legal

services programs [LSP] under the general authority for community action programs.

While the historical legal aid movement was primarily based on the widest possible provision of individual legal services to the poor, the LSP, while continuing the service goal of legal aid, also placed a high priority on reform of the law to make it more responsive to the poor. This effort to change laws to make them more responsive and fair to the poor was called law reform. Interest in law reform increased due to the war on poverty's goal of assisting the poor and changing the nature of society to make it possible for less people to be poor.

* * *

In order to support law reform efforts, the LSP created and funded a number of national law reform centers, affiliated with law schools, to bring test cases and to support the lawyers working in local legal services offices who took on the challenge of law reform. Class actions were consciously used to try to bring about reforms in the law for large numbers of people. Lobbying increased to impact the laws affecting poor people outside the judicial process.

* * *

[Despite the proclamations from its leaders seeking to prioritize law reform, reform work was but a small part of the legal services offered in the initial years of LSP. Local lawyers, like their legal aid counterparts before them, remained overwhelmed with individual legal needs of the poor. However, the first substantive challenges to LSP were aimed at its law reform efforts. In a highly publicized attack on legal services, California Governor Ronald Reagan attempted to curtail the advocacy of the California Rural Legal Assistance (CRLA), and governors in some other states also vetoed LSP funding. Despite opposition, however, the Legal Services Program continued to grow and provide a wider range of legal services to greater numbers of the poor.]

LSP now offered poor people access to more comprehensive legal services than the prior legal aid system. Despite the time and case limitations which prevented a large commitment to law reform efforts, LSP lawyers did manage to do significant law reform. While legal aid lawyers in the 1950s litigated only six percent of their cases and only rarely appealed, LSP lawyers took seventeen percent to court and appealed over 1,000 cases annually. Most telling was the fact that no legal aid staff attorney ever took a case to the U. S. Supreme Court in its entire eighty-nine year history, while in five years of the LSP, from 1967 to 1972, LSP staff lawyers took 219 cases to the Court, had 136 decided on the merits, and won seventy-three of them. Among the significant cases brought by legal services lawyers were those which eliminated welfare residency requirements and others that developed the law of due process in ways that gave more effective remedies to recipients of public assistance, residents of public housing, as well as debtors, mental patients and juveniles.

* * *

Legal Services Corporation

* * *

In 1973, [President] Nixon began to dismantle OEO and appointed Howard Phillips, a known critic of the war on poverty and legal services, to head OEO. Philips unilaterally canceled law reform as a goal of legal services and defunded the back up centers essential to law reform litigation. This effort to eliminate law reform was stopped by federal court action which removed Philips from office and continued funding.

Finally on July 25, 1974, on the eve of his resignation, President Nixon signed a compromise LSC bill that eliminated funding for independent back up centers, imposed some restrictions on the scope of authorized legal work, but did allow group representation. The restrictions imposed included prohibition on litigation involving abortion, school desegregation, and selective service, and also placed some limitations on class actions and some types of juvenile representation. As created by Congress, the LSC would not itself provide any direct legal representation but would rather provide financial assistance to qualified local programs pursuant to annual congressional appropriation.

* * *

[The years from 1975 to 1981 were later called the "heyday of legal services success." Legal aid and law reform coexisted as goals in LSC.] * * * Legal services became even more of a national program with 323 local programs funded by LSC. Poor people in every state in the country were to have access to legal services, and their lawyers were to have increased training and support. LSC enjoyed support in Congress, the organized bar, and the general public. [The 1981 appropriation of $321 million would prove to be the highest annual funding of LSC over the next ten years.]

* * *

With the election of Ronald Reagan as President in 1980, the political climate for LSC abruptly became more harsh, and the controversy over law reform flared anew. * * *

[An] * * * effort to abolish LSC proved impossible, in part, because of support by a number of groups including fourteen past presidents of the ABA, 187 local bar groups, deans of 141 law schools, and hundreds of judges. But the fact that LSC survived did not end the crisis of how it would operate. Since they were unable to terminate the program, the Reagan administration used other strategies like reduced funding, increased restrictions, and unsympathetic leadership by the board to try to bring about a "slow, painful death" of LSC.

* * *

[Yet LSC remained an effective and productive program. Although hobbled by the restrictions, legal services lawyers continued to provide essential legal advice and representation to poor people, if in a more limited fashion. In the 1990s, the financial health of LSC began to improve]

[In 1995, the Congressional forces which had opposed law reform in LSC gained enough legislative power to finally have their way.] Congress ultimately damaged the LSC by a combination of drastic funding cuts and the most severe restrictions on law reform activity. The 1996 LSC appropriation reduced its funding from $400 million to $278 million and severely tightened the restrictions on the activities of legal services programs. * * * The cuts resulted in LSC programs closing over 100 offices, laying off fourteen percent of their legal services lawyers and sixteen percent of the paralegals; Mississippi alone shut down twelve of the state's twenty-five offices.

Equally damaging to LSC were the new Congressional restrictions on the law reform activities permitted. While many of these restrictions are a continuation of prior restrictions, several are newer and tougher restrictions on the legal activities afforded to poor people. The 1996 law prohibited the use of LSC funds for programs which engaged in redistricting, lobbying, class action suits, legal assistance for many aliens, training for political activities, including picketing, boycotts, strikes or demonstrations, attorney fee claims, abortion litigation, prisoner litigation, any activities to reform federal or state welfare systems, except for individual assistance to obtain benefits as long as the assistance does not seek to change the rule or law involved, or defending persons facing eviction from public housing because they were charged with the sale or distribution [of] drugs.

The restrictions on class actions are the toughest ever imposed on the LSC. Section 504(a)(7) of the new law prohibits funds of the Legal Services Corporation to be used to provide financial assistance to any person or entity "[t]hat initiates or participates in a class action suit."

The LSC board moved quickly to implement the prohibition on class actions. Their final rule clearly attempts to bar all types of involvement in any class action, federal or state, at any stage. * * * [The regulations also barred almost all legal action involving welfare, other than individual representation of an individual client in an action that did not challenge the validity of the underlying welfare regulation.]

* * *

As a result of the 1996 Congressional actions, LSC has withdrawn from all class action litigation, ceased challenging the changes in the welfare program and has returned to a docket overwhelmingly consisting of direct legal services to individual people. Law reform by poor people's lawyers has all but ceased and LSC has been returned to the legal aid model of the first half of this century.

* * *

Congress has decided that legal aid alone and not legal aid and law reform will be available to the poor. As a consequence, poor people's lawyers will not be allowed access to all the tools available to the lawyers for the rest of the population.

In 1951, Emery Brownell suggested that, "[i]t cannot seriously be argued that in a democracy there should be one kind of system for the poor and another for those who are better off." Apparently he was wrong.

DAVID S. UDELL

The Legal Services Restrictions: Lawyers in Florida, New York, Virginia, and Oregon Describe the Costs
17 Yale L. & Pol'y Rev. 337, 357–60, 363–64 (1998)

One of Florida Rural's most successful collaborations with clients and community groups was its Voting Rights Project which was initiated with a special IOTA [Interest on Lawyers Trust Accounts] grant in 1991. While many of Florida's coastal counties have been desegregated over the last thirty years, discrimination in its crudest forms still pervades many of the inland rural communities. Conditions for minorities in large areas of rural Florida differ little from those that preceded desegregation. One method of maintaining white ascendance is to elect county commissioners and school board members on an at-large basis. In such a system, minorities might comprise forty percent of a county's population but be governed by a county commission consisting of five white members, all elected in county-wide at-large elections.

The Florida Rural Voting Rights Project began in response to frequent client complaints about discrimination and unresponsive government in rural areas. Working with local community people, advocates implemented a litigation strategy that would compel the creation of single-member districts, each of which would elect its own county commissioner. During the first half of the 1990s, they applied this strategy to great effect. Even as the U.S. Supreme Court was deciding cases that limited the impact of the Voting Rights Act on Congressional districts, the Florida Rural strategy continued to secure a string of successes for its rural minority clients.

In one typical case, the county's African-American population was concentrated in an unincorporated area immediately adjacent to a sugar cane processing plant. The community to this day is referred to as "Harlem" on official highway maps. Though African Americans comprised seventeen percent of the county's population, an at-large election system had prevented the election of any black representatives to the five-person county commission or to the school board. Due to governmental inattention and poverty, Harlem had the appearance of an impoverished third-world village. When the community did draw the attention of county government, it was to be selected as a candidate for a toxic waste transfer facility. Community concern over the toxic waste proposal and other issues reached a crescendo in 1991. In response, Florida Rural filed suit under the Voting Rights Act of 1965 against the county commission and the school board. Before the end of the year, the county signed a consent decree establishing single member districts. Shortly thereafter, the county's first African-American commissioner was elected from the district that included Harlem. Before the new legislation halted this work, similar results were obtained or were in the process of being obtained in other cases.

Unfortunately, much work remains to be done in securing the rights of Florida's rural minorities to full participation in the democratic process. But Florida Rural now must turn away requests for such assistance. It is anticipated that future requests will also come from Latino and Haitian clients as more of them become part of the electorate. Currently, no one in Florida is doing this work which is highly specialized, quite risky, and expensive. Not confronting this ongoing problem, however, may ultimately prove even more costly.

Another source of pride for Florida Rural has been its legal representation of immigrants. Florida is home to over two million non-citizens, a disproportionate number of whom are poor. Although representation of many classes of immigrants had not been permitted with LSC funds since the early 1980s, Florida Rural used IOTA money to offer representation to all immigrants, "no questions asked." Over the years, Florida Rural's racially and ethnically diverse staff, which included twenty-two Spanish speakers and seven Creole speakers, worked with this isolated and vulnerable population. A track record of important impact cases, as well as countless individual service cases, was built in areas such as employment, housing, food stamps, immigration, education law, and farmworker rights. However, when the 1996 legislation applied the LSC alien restriction to IOTA funds, much of this work ended.

The Florida Immigrant Advocacy Center provides high-quality representation to many immigrants who can no longer be served by Florida Rural. However, the wide variety of legal problems experienced by this population not because they are immigrants, but because they are poor, is now going largely unaddressed. Florida Rural can no longer help large numbers of immigrants with their routine civil legal problems. Thus in tying LSC restrictions to non-LSC dollars, the 1996 legislation has left us with a system that responds to immigrants only as immigrants, not as people with the same legal needs as U.S. citizens.

The prohibition on recovering attorneys' fees also has dramatically affected the system of civil justice for the poor. The most obvious consequence for legal services programs is loss of revenue. Florida Rural, for example, received in excess of $2,000,000 in attorneys' fees during the first half of the 1990s and used the money in part to buy a computer system. The 1996 legislation has wiped out this substantial source of support for legal services, appropriately financed by those who engaged in unlawful actions against poor people.

More importantly, the attorneys' fees ban has affected the balance of rights and powers in civil litigation. In the past, parties wishing to bring questionable legal actions against a poor person might be constrained by the prospect of paying substantial attorneys' fees if they did not prevail. However, with the ban on attorneys' fees, the disincentive to harassing litigation has been removed. An example from Florida Rural's case files illustrates this point.

Rose lived in a public housing project with her two children and her sometimes abusive husband. At one point, she felt the need to obtain a restraining order against her husband and did so on her own. The order prohibited the husband from having any contact with the children. When Rose subsequently allowed him to visit, the housing authority attempted to evict her for "criminal conduct." Florida Rural represented Rose in the eviction and had it dismissed on procedural grounds. Under Florida law, Rose was entitled to attorneys' fees, but under the 1996 legislation Florida Rural was prohibited from seeking them for her. Having lost nothing in the first attempt, the housing authority filed a new eviction action against Rose based on the same facts. This time, the case was resolved on the merits, and Rose again prevailed with the help of Florida Rural. As before, she was entitled to an award of attorneys' fees against the housing authority, but again none could be sought or collected.

Finally, the housing authority brought a third eviction action against Rose, on slightly different facts, at a time when Florida Rural did not have the resources available to represent her. As a result of this war of attrition, Rose and her children were evicted shortly thereafter.

It is impossible to know with certainty whether an award of attorneys' fees against the housing authority in the earlier eviction cases would have produced a more just outcome. However, with an attorney on retainer and a cheap, routine procedure available, the housing authority had reason to persist, whatever the merits of its case, because such persistence cost it virtually nothing and was likely to wear down eventually the opposition. In situations like this, the attorneys' fees restriction will cause the system to suffer more rather than less litigation, almost always to the detriment of the poor.

* * *

One [evolving] strategy [in response to the restrictions] is a renewed emphasis on listening to and working with our client community through the representation of both embryonic and full-grown groups. For new groups, initial work simply may involve the preparation of articles of incorporation, bylaws, and board trainings. Even if nothing further is done for the group in the short term, the resulting relationship gives Florida Rural a new set of eyes and ears in the community. The reason for a group's formation may highlight a need that would otherwise be difficult to discover. This approach anticipates that as the group grows, more issues of importance to the community as a whole can be expected to come to light. When the group has matured, it will be able to rely more on its membership. Florida Rural's role will be to provide legal advice and support for the members' chosen actions.

Florida Rural's work with the Coalition of Immokalee Workers (The Coalition) offers one example of this approach. The Coalition is an 800-member, multicultural, community-based organization made up of farm and other low-wage workers. It is centered in Immokalee, Florida, a community created from wilderness as a labor camp. The Coalition's stated purpose is to improve the working conditions and living environment of both its members and their surrounding communities, and it believes that meaningful change will only occur through the efforts of the workers themselves. Florida Rural helped the Coalition incorporate and attain § 501(c)(3) status as a tax-exempt charitable organization and has worked with the group over the past three years as an alternative to Florida Rural's traditional and current representation of individual farmworkers who have experienced job-related problems.

The ongoing representation of the Coalition has led to a close working relationship beneficial to both organizations. It has also improved the lives of many farmworkers in ways that could not have been achieved by a legal services program representing a single client. Workers have successfully campaigned to rein in price-gouging by local merchants by establishing a non-profit food cooperative, eliminated the reported use of violence against workers by marching 400-strong to the home of a feared offender, and won a twenty-five percent pay increase for over 450 workers from the area's largest tomato grower through a thirty-day hunger strike that drew national attention.

It is hard to envision how any of these improvements in the lives of farmworkers could have been achieved through individual client representation. The results are primarily due to the Coalition's hard work and strategic planning. Nonetheless, as general counsel, Florida Rural has taken an active, though intentionally backstage, role in its representation. Florida Rural quietly does the Coalition's increasingly complicated corporate work when feasible and recruits outside counsel for matters better handled by specialists. Florida Rural monitored the Coalition's actions during the hunger strike, for example, to insure that the campaign was consistent with the group's corporate and tax-exempt status. By threatening a libel suit at one heated moment during the anti-violence campaign, Florida Rural forced a local newspaper to print a front-page retraction of a derogatory article about the Coalition and also the group's multi-page response. With this approach, as opposed to one based on litigation, the community group conveys its own message.

This approach has produced results that neither Florida Rural nor the Coalition might have achieved independently. An example is the recent conviction of a powerful farm labor recruiter on federal peonage charges. The crew leader and his henchmen had a long history of flagrant mistreatment of farmworker employees, including beatings, rape, shootings, and the stacking of workers in vans for nonstop transportation to South Carolina. Only through the persistent efforts of

Florida Rural was the Justice Department persuaded to pursue the case. Even so, without the additional assistance of members of the Coalition in tracking down, interviewing, and gaining the trust of necessary witnesses, the prosecution would have gone nowhere. Instead, both the labor recruiter and his chief henchman received fifteen-year federal sentences.

Notes and Questions

1. Legal services offices were restricted from doing outreach—they could not do educational work in the community to inform people of their rights and then represent them when people learned that their rights were being violated. "A lawyer cannot, for example, make a presentation at a homeless shelter regarding the residents' rights to apply for food stamps, inform the residents that he or she is available to represent them if they have been denied this right, and then represent those people who accept the lawyer's offer of assistance." Laura K. Abel & David S. Udell, *If You Gag the Lawyers, Do You Choke the Courts? Some Implications for Judges When Funding Restrictions Curb Advocacy by Lawyers on Behalf of the Poor*, 29 Fordham Urb. L.J. 873, 879 (2002).

The restrictions were imposed at the same moment that Congress enacted immigration reform, prison reform, and welfare reform legislation, affecting the lives of immigrants and the poor. "Congress disabled LSC-funded lawyers from participating in cases involving the many constitutional and statutory issues which the scope of that legislation raised." Burt Neuborne & David Udell, *Legal Services Corporation v. Velazquez*, 35 Clearinghouse Rev. 83, 84 (2001). The 1996 changes in welfare are discussed in chapter 8.

2. Congress made the legal services restrictions apply to any program that received Legal Services Corporation funds. Funding recipients could not engage in the restricted activity, even if it were funded from other sources, including private donors or attorneys' fees. Under a regulation issued in 1997, an LSC program may enter into a relationship with a non-LSC organization. The non-LSC organization is free to use the LSC program's non-LSC funds to conduct restricted activities, called a companion delivery system. The LSC program must maintain "objective integrity and independence," which is measured by whether organizations are "legally separate," whether the non-LSC organization received any LSC funds, and whether the organizations are "physically and financially separate." LSC also considers the extent of restricted activities in which the non-LSC organization engages. Udell, *The Legal Services Restrictions*, *supra* at 338. Setting up companion delivery systems imposed both practical problems and expenses that drained resources from legal work. *Id.* at 337.

3. The restrictions on lobbying and consulting with legislatures and administrative bodies mean that the interests of low-income people cannot be represented with those authorities by the lawyers most familiar with their needs and issues. There are no comparable restric-

tions on lawyers retained by wealthy individuals and corporations. For example, if a county government is considering adopting a new ordinance affecting landlords and tenants, attorneys for developers and landlords will be free to speak at local hearings, but legal services lawyers—most familiar with the housing needs of low-income tenants—will not. If the state considers changing criteria for assistance to disabled children, nursing home operators and representatives from health maintenance organizations will be able to speak about their business needs; parents will be able to speak as individuals; but the lawyers who best know the needs of low-income parents will have no input in the legislative drafting process. Laws and regulations will therefore come into being without this expertise, even if legislators want to consider it and lawyers could provide it.

Consider the effect of the legal services restrictions on the structural questions raised by Marc Galanter in discussing repeat players and the advantages in litigation of the "haves." Legal services is a repeat player on behalf of low-income people, but the lawyer's duties to each one-shot client make it difficult to effectively "play" for better rules in individual cases. Before the restrictions, legal services lawyers could seek to change the rules for groups of clients through class actions or through speaking to legislatures about changing the legal rules.

Why should lawyers be barred from speaking to government on behalf of their clients on any matter? If another Congress might repeal the restrictions, is the ultimate fate of representation for low-income citizens purely a political matter? What do these restrictions mean to the role of lawyers in a democracy? Do these restrictions challenge your belief in lawyers, in the legislature that passed the restrictions, or in democracy?

4. Do the restrictions create a greater responsibility for individual lawyers and the organized bar to ensure the provision of those services? Quigley notes that law deans and bar associations defended legal services when it was under attack. Commenting on the role of the bar in supporting lawyers in social justice work, Louise Trubek observed:

> In the 1960s, the bar often expressed a conservative position in the definition of appropriate lawyering for subordinated people and was viewed as an obstacle to social justice lawyering. However, in recent years, the bar has emerged as the leading advocate for funding legal services for subordinated people. The bar's role is significant both in providing legitimacy to the concept of lawyers as ethically obliged to assist those unable to pay for services and, even more importantly, as the major defender of government funding for lawyers for subordinated people.

Louise G. Trubek, *Embedded Practices: Lawyers, Clients, and Social Change,* 31 Harv. C.R.-C.L L.Rev. 415, 439 (1996).

5. The 1996 restrictions on the Legal Services Corporation were first reviewed in the Ninth Circuit Court of Appeals in 1998, in Legal Aid Society of Hawaii (LASH) v. Legal Services Corporation, 145 F.3d 1017

(9th Cir.1998), *cert. denied*, 525 U.S. 1015 (1998). The LASH opinion focused on the "unconstitutional conditions" doctrine—the question of whether the government could attach conditions in a bill funding an organization that it could not otherwise impose. The Ninth Circuit upheld the restrictions, and the Supreme Court denied certiorari. The opinion was written by retired Supreme Court Justice Byron White, author of the majority opinion in Rust v. Sullivan, 500 U.S. 173 (1991), and relied heavily on the holding in *Rust* that upheld prohibitions on use of federal family-planning funds for abortion counseling as not unduly restrictive of an individual's right to choose abortion. LASH had also raised additional arguments regarding rights to fair and equal access to courts and the clients' right to retain a lawyer of his or her choice to engage in meaningful advocacy. These issues were not decided, because the court of appeals held that LASH did not have standing to pursue these claims on behalf of their indigent clients.

In 2001, the Supreme Court addressed directly the validity of the restrictions on advocacy in relation to welfare law.

LEGAL SERVICES CORPORATION v. VELAZQUEZ

531 U.S. 533 (2001)

Justice KENNEDY delivered the opinion of the Court.

In 1974, Congress enacted the Legal Services Corporation Act, 88 Stat. 378, 42 U.S.C. § 2996 *et seq*. The Act establishes the Legal Services Corporation (LSC) as a District of Columbia nonprofit corporation. LSC's mission is to distribute funds appropriated by Congress to eligible local grantee organizations "for the purpose of providing financial support for legal assistance in noncriminal proceedings or matters to persons financially unable to afford legal assistance." § 2996b(a).

LSC grantees consist of hundreds of local organizations governed, in the typical case, by local boards of directors. In many instances the grantees are funded by a combination of LSC funds and other public or private sources. The grantee organizations hire and supervise lawyers to provide free legal assistance to indigent clients. Each year LSC appropriates funds to grantees or recipients that hire and supervise lawyers for various professional activities, including representation of indigent clients seeking welfare benefits.

This suit requires us to decide whether one of the conditions imposed by Congress on the use of LSC funds violates the First Amendment rights of LSC grantees and their clients. For purposes of our decision, the restriction, to be quoted in further detail, prohibits legal representation funded by recipients of LSC moneys if the representation involves an effort to amend or otherwise challenge existing welfare law. As interpreted by the LSC and by the Government, the restriction prevents an attorney from arguing to a court that a state statute conflicts with a federal statute or that either a state or federal statute by its terms or in its application is violative of the United States Constitution.

Lawyers employed by New York City LSC grantees, together with private LSC contributors, LSC indigent clients, and various state and local public officials whose governments contribute to LSC grantees, brought suit in the United States District Court for the Southern District of New York to declare the restriction, among other provisions of the Act, invalid. The United States Court of Appeals for the Second Circuit approved an injunction against enforcement of the provision as an impermissible viewpoint-based discrimination in violation of the First Amendment, 164 F.3d 757 (1999). We granted certiorari, and the parties who commenced the suit in the District Court are here as respondents. The LSC as petitioner is joined by the Government of the United States, which had intervened in the District Court. We agree that the restriction violates the First Amendment, and we affirm the judgment of the Court of Appeals.

I

From the inception of the LSC, Congress has placed restrictions on its use of funds. For instance, the LSC Act prohibits recipients from making available LSC funds, program personnel, or equipment to any political party, to any political campaign, or for use in "advocating or opposing any ballot measures." 42 U.S.C. § 2996e(d)(4). See § 2996e(d)(3). The Act further proscribes use of funds in most criminal proceedings and in litigation involving nontherapeutic abortions, secondary school desegregation, military desertion, or violations of the Selective Service statute. §§ 2996f(b)(8)–(10) (1994 ed. and Supp. IV). Fund recipients are barred from bringing class-action suits unless express approval is obtained from LSC. § 2996e(d)(5).

The restrictions at issue were part of a compromise set of restrictions enacted in the Omnibus Consolidated Rescissions and Appropriations Act of 1996 (1996 Act), § 504, 110 Stat. 1321–53, and continued in each subsequent annual appropriations Act. The relevant portion of § 504(a)(16) prohibits funding of any organization

> "that initiates legal representation or participates in any other way, in litigation, lobbying, or rulemaking, involving an effort to reform a Federal or State welfare system, except that this paragraph shall not be construed to preclude a recipient from representing an individual eligible client who is seeking specific relief from a welfare agency if such relief does not involve an effort to amend or otherwise challenge existing law in effect on the date of the initiation of the representation."

The prohibitions apply to all of the activities of an LSC grantee, including those paid for by non-LSC funds. We are concerned with the statutory provision which excludes LSC representation in cases which "involve an effort to amend or otherwise challenge existing law in effect on the date of the initiation of the representation."

In 1997, LSC adopted final regulations clarifying § 504(a)(16). 45 CFR pt. 1639 (1999). LSC interpreted the statutory provision to allow indigent clients to challenge welfare agency determinations of benefit ineligibility under interpretations of existing law. For example, an LSC grantee could represent a welfare claimant who argued that an agency made an erroneous factual determination or that an agency misread or misapplied a term contained in an existing welfare statute. According to LSC, a grantee in that position could argue as well that an agency policy violated existing law. § 1639.4. Under LSC's interpretation, however, grantees could not accept representations designed to change welfare laws, much less argue against the constitutionality or statutory validity of those laws. Even in cases where constitutional or statutory challenges became apparent after representation was well under way, LSC advised that its attorneys must withdraw.

After the instant suit was filed in the District Court alleging the restrictions on the use of LSC funds violated the First Amendment, the court denied a preliminary injunction, finding no probability of success on the merits.

On appeal, the Court of Appeals for the Second Circuit affirmed in part and reversed in part. As relevant for our purposes, the court addressed respondents' challenges to the restrictions in § 504(a)(16). It concluded the section specified four categories of prohibited activities, of which "three appear[ed] to prohibit the type of activity named regardless of viewpoint, while one might be read to prohibit the activity only when it seeks reform." The court upheld the restrictions on litigation, lobbying, and rulemaking "involving an effort to reform a Federal or State welfare system," since all three prohibited grantees' involvement in these activities regardless of the side of the issue.

The court next considered the exception to § 504(a)(16) that allows representation of " 'an individual eligible client who is seeking specific relief from a welfare agency.' " The court invalidated, as impermissible viewpoint discrimination, the qualification that representation could "not involve an effort to amend or otherwise challenge existing law," because it "clearly seeks to discourage challenges to the status quo."

Left to decide what part of the 1996 Act to strike as invalid, the court concluded that congressional intent regarding severability was unclear. It decided to "invalidate the smallest possible portion of the statute, excising only the viewpoint-based proviso rather than the entire exception of which it is a part."

Dissenting in part, Judge Jacobs agreed with the majority except for its holding that the proviso banning challenges to existing welfare laws effected impermissible viewpoint-based discrimination. The provision, in his view, was permissible because it merely defined the scope of services to be funded. (opinion concurring in part and dissenting in part).

LSC filed a petition for certiorari challenging the Court of Appeals' conclusion that the § 504(a)(16) suits-for-benefits proviso was unconstitutional. We granted certiorari, 529 U.S. 1052 (2000).

II

The United States and LSC rely on *Rust v. Sullivan*, 500 U.S. 173 (1991), as support for the LSC program restrictions. In *Rust*, Congress established program clinics to provide subsidies for doctors to advise patients on a variety of family planning topics. Congress did not consider abortion to be within its family planning objectives, however, and it forbade doctors employed by the program from discussing abortion with their patients. Recipients of funds under Title X of the Public Health Service Act, §§ 1002, 1008, as added, 84 Stat. 1506, 1508, 42 U.S.C. §§ 300a, 300a–6, challenged the Act's restriction that provided that none of the Title X funds appropriated for family planning services could "be used in programs where abortion is a method of family planning." The recipients argued that the regulations constituted impermissible viewpoint discrimination favoring an antiabortion position over a proabortion approach in the sphere of family planning. They asserted as well that Congress had imposed an unconstitutional condition on recipients of federal funds by requiring them to relinquish their right to engage in abortion advocacy and counseling in exchange for the subsidy.

We upheld the law, reasoning that Congress had not discriminated against viewpoints on abortion, but had "merely chosen to fund one activity to the exclusion of the other." The restrictions were considered necessary "to ensure that the limits of the federal program [were] observed." Title X did not single out a particular idea for suppression because it was dangerous or disfavored; rather, Congress prohibited Title X doctors from counseling that was outside the scope of the project.

The Court in *Rust* did not place explicit reliance on the rationale that the counseling activities of the doctors under Title X amounted to governmental speech; when interpreting the holding in later cases, however, we have explained *Rust* on this understanding. We have said that viewpoint-based funding decisions can be sustained in instances in which the government is itself the speaker, see *Board of Regents of Univ. of Wis. System v. Southworth*, 529 U.S. 217, 229, 235 (2000), or instances, like *Rust*, in which the government "used private speakers to transmit information pertaining to its own program." *Rosenberger v. Rector and Visitors of Univ. of Va.*, 515 U.S. 819, 833 (1995). As we said in *Rosenberger*, "[w]hen the government disburses public funds to private entities to convey a governmental message, it may take legitimate and appropriate steps to ensure that its message is neither garbled nor distorted by the grantee." The latitude which may exist for restrictions on speech where the government's own message is being delivered flows in part from our observation that, "[w]hen the government speaks, for instance to promote its own policies or to advance a particular idea, it is, in the end, accountable to the electorate and the political process for its advocacy. If the citizenry objects, newly elected officials later could espouse some different or contrary position." *Board of Regents of Univ. of Wis. System v. Southworth*, *supra* at 235.

Neither the latitude for government speech nor its rationale applies to subsidies for private speech in every instance, however. As we have pointed out, "[i]t does not follow ... that viewpoint-based restrictions are proper when the [government] does not itself speak or subsidize transmittal of a message it favors but instead expends funds to encourage a diversity of views from private speakers." *Rosenberger, supra* at 834.

Although the LSC program differs from the program at issue in Rosenberger in that its purpose is not to "encourage a diversity of views," the salient point is that, like the program in *Rosenberger*, the LSC program was designed to facilitate private speech, not to promote a governmental message. Congress funded LSC grantees to provide attorneys to represent the interests of indigent clients. In the specific context of § 504(a)(16) suits for benefits, an LSC-funded attorney speaks on the behalf of the client in a claim against the government for welfare benefits. The lawyer is not the government's speaker. The attorney defending the decision to deny benefits will deliver the government's message in the litigation. The LSC lawyer, however, speaks on the behalf of his or her private, indigent client. Cf. *Polk County v. Dodson*, 454 U.S. 312, 321–322 (1981) (holding that a public defender does not act "under color of state law" because he "works under canons of professional responsibility that mandate his exercise of independent judgment on behalf of the client" and because there is an "assumption that counsel will be free of state control").

The Government has designed this program to use the legal profession and the established Judiciary of the States and the Federal Government to accomplish its end of assisting welfare claimants in determination or receipt of their benefits. The advice from the attorney to the client and the advocacy by the attorney to the courts cannot be classified as governmental speech even under a generous understanding of the concept. In this vital respect this suit is distinguishable from *Rust*.

The private nature of the speech involved here, and the extent of LSC's regulation of private expression, are indicated further by the circumstance that the Government seeks to use an existing medium of expression and to control it, in a class of cases, in ways which distort its usual functioning. Where the government uses or attempts to regulate a particular medium, we have been informed by its accepted usage in determining whether a particular restriction on speech is necessary for the program's purposes and limitations. In *FCC v. League of Women Voters of Cal.*, 468 U.S. 364 (1984), the Court was instructed by its understanding of the dynamics of the broadcast industry in holding that prohibitions against editorializing by public radio networks were an impermissible restriction, even though the Government enacted the restriction to control the use of public funds. The First Amendment forbade the Government from using the forum in an unconventional way to suppress speech inherent in the nature of the medium. See *id.*, at 396–397. In *Arkansas Ed. Television Comm'n v. Forbes*, 523 U.S. 666, 676 (1998), the dynamics of the broadcasting system gave station programmers the right to use editorial judgment to exclude certain speech so that the broadcast message could be more effective. And in *Rosenberger*, the fact that student newspapers expressed many different points of view was an important foundation for the Court's decision to invalidate viewpoint-based restrictions. 515 U.S., at 836.

When the government creates a limited forum for speech, certain restrictions may be necessary to define the limits and purposes of the program. *Perry Ed. Assn. v. Perry Local Educators' Assn.*, 460 U.S. 37 (1983); see also *Lamb's Chapel v. Center Moriches Union Free School Dist.*, 508 U.S. 384 (1993). The same is true when the government establishes a subsidy for specified ends. *Rust v. Sullivan*, 500 U.S. 173 (1991). As this suit involves a subsidy, limited forum cases such as *Perry*, *Lamb's Chapel* and *Rosenberger* may not be controlling in a strict sense, yet they do provide some instruction. Here the program presumes that private, nongovernmental speech is necessary, and a substantial restriction is placed upon that speech. At oral argument and in its briefs the LSC advised us that lawyers funded in the Government program may not undertake representation in suits for benefits if they must advise clients respecting the questionable validity of a statute which defines benefit eligibility and the payment structure. The limitation forecloses advice or legal assistance to question the validity of statutes under the Constitution of the United States. It extends further, it must be noted, so that state statutes inconsistent with federal law under the Supremacy Clause may be neither challenged nor questioned.

By providing subsidies to LSC, the Government seeks to facilitate suits for benefits by using the state and federal courts and the independent bar on which those courts depend for the proper performance of their duties and responsibilities. Restricting LSC attorneys in advising their clients and in presenting arguments and analyses to the courts distorts the legal system by altering the traditional role of the attorneys in much the same way broadcast systems or student publication networks were changed in the limited forum cases we have cited. Just as government in those cases could not elect to use a broadcasting network or a college publication structure in a regime which prohibits speech necessary to the proper functioning of those systems, see *Arkansas Ed. Television Comm'n*, *supra*, and *Rosenberger*, *supra*, it may not design a subsidy to effect this serious and fundamental restriction on advocacy of attorneys and the functioning of the judiciary.

LSC has advised us, furthermore, that upon determining a question of statutory validity is present in any anticipated or pending case or controversy, the LSC-funded attorney must cease the representation at once. This is true whether the validity issue becomes apparent during initial attorney-client consultations or in the midst of litigation proceedings. A disturbing example of the restriction was discussed during oral argument before the Court. It is well understood that when there are two reasonable constructions for a statute, yet one raises a constitutional question, the Court should prefer the interpretation which avoids the constitutional issue. *Gomez v. United States*, 490 U.S. 858, 864 (1989);

Ashwander v. TVA, 297 U.S. 288, 346–348 (1936) (Brandeis, J., concurring). Yet, as the LSC advised the Court, if, during litigation, a judge were to ask an LSC attorney whether there was a constitutional concern, the LSC attorney simply could not answer.

Interpretation of the law and the Constitution is the primary mission of the judiciary when it acts within the sphere of its authority to resolve a case or controversy. *Marbury v. Madison*, 1 Cranch 137, 177 (1803) ("It is emphatically the province and the duty of the judicial department to say what the law is"). An informed, independent judiciary presumes an informed, independent bar. Under § 504(a)(16), however, cases would be presented by LSC attorneys who could not advise the courts of serious questions of statutory validity. The disability is inconsistent with the proposition that attorneys should present all the reasonable and well-grounded arguments necessary for proper resolution of the case. By seeking to prohibit the analysis of certain legal issues and to truncate presentation to the courts, the enactment under review prohibits speech and expression upon which courts must depend for the proper exercise of the judicial power. Congress cannot wrest the law from the Constitution which is its source. "Those then who controvert the principle that the constitution is to be considered, in court, as a paramount law, are reduced to the necessity of maintaining that courts must close their eyes on the constitution, and see only the law."

The restriction imposed by the statute here threatens severe impairment of the judicial function. Section 504(a)(16) sifts out cases presenting constitutional challenges in order to insulate the Government's laws from judicial inquiry. If the restriction on speech and legal advice were to stand, the result would be two tiers of cases. In cases where LSC counsel were attorneys of record, there would be lingering doubt whether the truncated representation had resulted in complete analysis of the case, full advice to the client, and proper presentation to the court. The courts and the public would come to question the adequacy and fairness of professional representations when the attorney, either consciously to comply with this statute or unconsciously to continue the representation despite the statute, avoided all reference to questions of statutory validity and constitutional authority. A scheme so inconsistent with accepted separation-of-powers principles is an insufficient basis to sustain or uphold the restriction on speech.

It is no answer to say the restriction on speech is harmless because, under LSC's interpretation of the Act, its attorneys can withdraw. This misses the point. The statute is an attempt to draw lines around the LSC program to exclude from litigation those arguments and theories Congress finds unacceptable but which by their nature are within the province of the courts to consider.

The restriction on speech is even more problematic because in cases where the attorney withdraws from a representation, the client is unlikely to find other counsel. The explicit premise for providing LSC attorneys is the necessity to make available representation "to persons financially unable to afford legal assistance." 42 U.S.C. § 2996(a)(3). There often will be no alternative source for the client to receive vital information respecting constitutional and statutory rights bearing upon claimed benefits. Thus, with respect to the litigation services Congress has funded, there is no alternative channel for expression of the advocacy Congress seeks to restrict. This is in stark contrast to *Rust*. There, a patient could receive the approved Title X family planning counseling funded by the Government and later could consult an affiliate or independent organization to receive abortion counseling. Unlike indigent clients who seek LSC representation, the patient in *Rust* was not required to forfeit the Government-funded advice when she also received abortion counseling through alternative channels. Because LSC attorneys must withdraw whenever a question of a welfare statute's validity arises, an individual could not obtain joint representation so that the constitutional challenge would be presented by a non-LSC attorney, and other, permitted, arguments advanced by LSC counsel.

Finally, LSC and the Government maintain that § 504(a)(16) is necessary to define the scope and contours of the federal program, a condition that ensures funds can be spent for those cases most immediate to congressional concern. In support of this contention, they suggest the challenged limitation takes into account the nature of the grantees' activities and provides limited congressional funds for the provision of simple suits for benefits. In petitioners' view, the restriction operates neither to maintain the current welfare system nor insulate it from attack; rather, it helps the current welfare system function in a more efficient and fair manner by removing from the program complex challenges to existing welfare laws.

The effect of the restriction, however, is to prohibit advice or argumentation that existing welfare laws are unconstitutional or unlawful. Congress cannot recast a condition on funding as a mere definition of its program in every case, lest the First Amendment be reduced to a simple semantic exercise. Here, notwithstanding Congress' purpose to confine and limit its program, the restriction operates to insulate current welfare laws from constitutional scrutiny and certain other legal challenges, a condition implicating central First Amendment concerns. In no lawsuit funded by the Government can the LSC attorney, speaking on behalf of a private client, challenge existing welfare laws. As a result, arguments by indigent clients that a welfare statute is unlawful or unconstitutional cannot be expressed in this Government-funded program for petitioning the courts, even though the program was created for litigation involving welfare benefits, and even though the ordinary course of litigation involves the expression of theories and postulates on both, or multiple, sides of an issue.

It is fundamental that the First Amendment "was fashioned to assure unfettered interchange of ideas for the bringing about of political and social changes desired by the people." *New York Times Co. v. Sullivan*, 376 U.S. 254, 269 (1964) (quoting *Roth v. United States*, 354 U.S. 476, 484 (1957)). There can be little doubt that the LSC Act funds constitutionally protected expression; and in the context of this statute there is no programmatic message of the kind recognized in *Rust* and which sufficed there to allow the Government to specify the advice deemed necessary for its legitimate objectives. This serves to distinguish § 504(a)(16) from any of the Title X program restrictions upheld in *Rust*, and to place it beyond any congressional funding condition approved in the past by this Court.

Congress was not required to fund an LSC attorney to represent indigent clients; and when it did so, it was not required to fund the whole range of legal representations or relationships. The LSC and the United States, however, in effect ask us to permit Congress to define the scope of the litigation it funds to exclude certain vital theories and ideas. The attempted restriction is designed to insulate the Government's interpretation of the Constitution from judicial challenge. The Constitution does not permit the Government to confine litigants and their attorneys in this manner. We must be vigilant when Congress imposes rules and conditions which in effect insulate its own laws from legitimate judicial challenge. Where private speech is involved, even Congress' antecedent funding decision cannot be aimed at the suppression of ideas thought inimical to the Government's own interest. *Regan v. Taxation With Representation of Wash.*, 461 U.S. 540, 548 (1983); *Speiser v. Randall*, 357 U.S. 513, 519 (1958).

For the reasons we have set forth, the funding condition is invalid. The Court of Appeals considered whether the language restricting LSC attorneys could be severed from the statute so that the remaining portions would remain operative. It reached the reasoned conclusion to invalidate the fragment of § 504(a)(16) found contrary to the First Amendment, leaving the balance of the statute operative and in place. That determination was not discussed in the briefs of either party or otherwise contested here, and in the exercise of our discretion and prudential judgment we decline to address it.

The judgment of the Court of Appeals is

Affirmed.

Justice SCALIA, with whom THE CHIEF JUSTICE, Justice O'CONNOR, and Justice THOMAS join, dissenting.

* * *

Today's decision is quite simply inexplicable on the basis of our prior law. The only difference between *Rust* and the present case is that the former involved "distortion" of (that is to say, refusal to subsidize) the normal work of doctors, and the latter involves "distortion" of (that is to say, refusal to subsidize) the normal work of lawyers. The Court's decision displays not only an improper special solicitude for our own profession; it also displays, I think, the very fondness for "reform through the courts"—the making of innumerable social judgments through judge-pronounced constitutional imperatives—that prompted Congress to restrict publicly funded litigation of this sort. The Court says today, through an unprecedented (and indeed previously rejected) interpretation of the First Amendment, that we will not allow this restriction—and then, to add insult to injury, permits to stand a judgment that awards the general litigation funding that the statute does not contain. I respectfully dissent.

Notes and Questions

1. Many people perceive funding restrictions to be an entitlement of those who control the purse strings. The *Velazquez* opinion distinguishes the conditions imposed upon speech regarding abortion in *Rust* from those restricting legal representation.

The "unconstitutional conditions" doctrine has been the subject of extended scholarly debate because of the unpredictability with which the Court has upheld and struck down conditions.

> [T]he doctrine of unconstitutional conditions is riven with inconsistencies. The Court has concluded, for example, that the selective exemption of some magazines from state taxation on the basis of subject matter unconstitutionally infringes speech, but that the selective subsidy of the medical expenses of childbirth but not abortion does not unconstitutionally infringe reproductive autonomy. Having held that using funding conditions to induce public broadcasters to segregate editorializing activity would violate freedom of speech, the Court held that using tax benefit conditions to induce nonprofit organizations to spin off their lobbying activities to a separate affiliate poses no similar infringement. Having held that denial of unemployment compensation to Saturday sabbatarians unconstitutionally burdens freedom of worship, the Court has rejected every other claim that conditions on food stamps or welfare payments unconstitutionally burden rights to speech, expressive association, intimate association, or freedom from unwarranted searches. And having held that the federal government may not use its spending power to pressure state governments into yielding constitutionally protected autonomy, the Court has nevertheless rejected every federalism-based challenge to conditions on federal subsidies since the New Deal. * * *

Kathleen M. Sullivan, *Unconstitutional Conditions*, 102 Harv. L. Rev. 1413, 1416–17 (1989). *See also* Lynn Baker, *Bargaining for Public Assistance,* 72 Denv. U. L. Rev. 949 (1995).

2. The Court says "Congress funded LSC grantees to provide attorneys to represent the interests of indigent clients." According to the court it is this "vital aspect" that distinguishes this case from *Rust*. Can this distinction be used in future challenges to funding restrictions for legal services?

Burt Neuborne and David Udell describe the implications of *Velazquez* on three levels:

> First it limits *Rust v. Sullivan* to a narrow category of settings in which the government is attempting to convey a particular message. By drawing a bright-line distinction between subsidies aimed at conveying the government's message, and subsidies designed to empower private speakers, the decision frees subsidized speakers from the specter of widespread government censorship.
>
> Second, the opinion posits an extremely protective First Amendment standard that prevents the government from imposing viewpoint-based conditions on speech subsidies that are inconsistent with the inherent nature of the medium in which the speech will take place. The opinion prevents the government from using restrictions on subsidized speech to undermine the integrity of the free market in ideas * * *. It protects subsidized speakers specifically in the classroom, museums, and public radio and television against government manipulation in an effort to advance the government's favored viewpoint. It is a charter of free speech for subsidized speakers.
>
> Third, the opinion recognizes that a combination of separation-of-powers principles and the First Amendment insulates both judges and subsidized counsel from viewpoint-based funding restrictions that prevent the courts from hearing all arguments relevant to the making of an informed judgment on what the law is. The opinion assures that subsidized counsel are free to make all arguments necessary to permit a court to make a decision on the law. By linking principles of separation of powers with the First Amendment, the opinion reinforces the concept of an independent judiciary and offers significant constitutional protection against efforts to muzzle lawyers for the poor.

Burt Neuborne and David Udell, *Legal Services Corporation v. Velazquez*, J. of Poverty L. and Pol'y 83, 91 (May-June 2001).

Is their view of the opinion optimistic, or has it laid "the foundation for an argument that any case in which counsel represents the government cannot go forward in a judicial forum in the absence of counsel for the other side"? *Id.* at 92.

B. Restrictions on Law School Clinical Practice

Can restrictions be placed on legal education in retaliation for social justice advocacy? The Tulane Environmental Law Clinic successfully represented a group of community residents who sought to block construction of a chemical factory which had been supported by the governor of Louisiana and by local businessmen. The clinic represented the community group at hearings before the Louisiana Department of Environmental Quality, in state court, and by filing objections to the proposed plant with the EPA, ultimately succeeding in defeating the construction of the plant at that location. The governor made public complaints about the role of the Tulane clinic, asking business leaders at a Chamber of Commerce meeting to apply pressure to Tulane University; business leaders also wrote to the Louisiana Supreme Court to urge restrictions on the activities of the clinic.

The Louisiana Supreme Court revised its rules on student practice with stringent regulations that effectively barred students from taking similar cases, including a rule against student representation if any clinical program supervising lawyer, staff person, or student practitioner had initiated contact for the purpose of representing the person or organization. Students could represent only people who met the definition of "indigent" with reference to federal poverty guidelines used by the Legal Services Corporation. (After significant protest, the Court amended this restriction to allow representation of individuals whose income was up to 200% of the federal poverty guideline.) Student clinics could not represent a community organization unless the organization certified that a majority of its members were eligible for representation under federal poverty guidelines. *See* Robert R. Kuehn, *Denying Access to Legal Representation: The Attack on the Tulane Environmental Law Clinic*, 4 Wash. U. J.L. & Pol'y 33 (2000).

A former supervising lawyer of the Tulane Environmental Clinic explained that these regulations have destructive effects on community struggles. Community activism is particularly important in the environmental justice movement, but funds for lawyers are seldom available. Potential community group clients seldom meet the requirement that more than 50% of their members must fall within federal poverty guidelines. Furthermore, the requirement itself hinders organization: community groups are reluctant to ask their members to share sensitive information about personal income, for fear that it will discourage participation in the group. *Id.* at 97–99.

The U.S. Court of Appeals for the Fifth Circuit held that the restrictions did not discriminate on the basis of viewpoint. Unlike the LSC restrictions at issue in *Velazquez*, the Louisiana restrictions on students did not discriminate between arguments that could be made on behalf of clients and were facially neutral. The court acknowledged the existence of "legal authority" for the proposition that facially neutral rules may be viewpoint discriminatory if they are enacted for retaliatory reasons, but upheld the restrictions. The court stated:

> * * * Although the Plaintiffs have certainly alleged animus on the part of the Governor and various business groups, there is no express allegation, nor do the facts alleged tend to suggest, that the [Louisiana Supreme Court] itself bore any particular ill will towards any of the Plaintiffs. Instead, the complaint in essence alleges that the [Court] gave in to pressure from others to restrict the activities of the student clinics. The Plaintiffs allege that Rule XX was enacted to silence the TELC [Tulane Environmental Law Clinic], but the rule is of wholly general and prospective application—it applies to all student legal clinics in Louisiana, not just TELC. Plaintiffs can be understood to have asserted that the [Louisiana Supreme Court]

> ultimately bore some character of ill will towards the TELC, at least on account of its activities having generated unwanted political pressure on the [Court] and that the [Court] accordingly desired to defuse the political pressure, and to diminish the likelihood of the recurrence of similar activities in the future, by enacting the challenged amendments to Rule XX. Such an alleged motivation on the part of the [Louisiana Supreme Court] does not, however, transform Rule XX into an unconstitutional state action.

Southern Christian Leadership Conference v. Supreme Court of Louisiana, 252 F.3d 781, 794–95 (5th Cir.2001), *cert. denied* 534 U.S. 995 (2001). *See also* Bill Schackner, *Pitt Law Clinic Sparks Debate*, Pittsburgh Post-Gazette, Nov. 18, 2001 (reporting similar debate over a law clinic at the University of Pittsburgh).

C. Funding Legal Aid Programs Through the Workings of the Legal System: Interest on Lawyers Trust Accounts (IOLTA)

The Interest on Lawyers Trust Accounts (IOLTA) programs run by the states provide the second-largest source of funds for legal aid for low-income people, but these programs are currently undergoing constitutional challenge. IOLTA grantees include legal services to the elderly; housing law projects representing low-income people in evictions and other landlord-tenant matters; equal justice fellowships run by the National Association for Public Interest Law; projects helping immigrants and refugees; disability rights and juvenile rights projects; and advocacy centers for victims of domestic violence. In 2001, IOLTA programs provided $134 million, second only to the $329 million in Legal Services funding. Henry Weinstein, *Funding Mechanism for Legal Aid Upheld*, L.A. Times, Nov. 15, 2001, Part 2, at 1.

IOLTA funds are generated by pooling sums of money held by lawyers which would not otherwise generate interest. "Lawyers often hold client funds for short periods of time in order to pay filing fees, cover real estate transaction costs and to carry out settlements. In each of these situations, professional ethical standards require that client money be held apart from an attorney's own funds and remain available to clients on demand." J. David Breemer, *IOLTA in the New Millenium: Slowly Sinking Under the Weight of the Takings Clause*, 23 U. Haw. L. Rev. 221, 224–25 (2000). Therefore, client funds were traditionally deposited in separate checking accounts. Once banks had developed interest-bearing checking accounts, funds held for clients by their attorneys were capable of earning interest. Often, however, "the sums held for an individual client are so small, or are held for so short a time, that the interest earned is less than the transaction costs of establishing and administering the account. Thus, in reality, the client's net interest is zero." Donald L. Beschle, *The Supreme Court's IOLTA Decision: Of Dogs, Mangers, and the Ghost of Mrs. Frothingham*, 30 Seton Hall L. Rev. 846, 848 (2000).

In the processes of legal work in the United States, a great deal of money is routinely held in small amounts for short periods:

> If these small sums * * * were aggregated into a single account, and the costs of allocating interest to each individual client were eliminated, that account would generate some net interest. The attorneys would have no legitimate claim to this interest because it would be generated by clients' funds. Also, the administrative costs of carving the interest up among clients would exceed the value of the interest itself. The obvious alternative course of action would be to have the bank pay no interest at all or, to put it another way, to retain the interest itself. The creators of the IOLTA concept, however, realized that another option existed; the interest could be diverted toward a program to help fund legal assistance for low-income clients. In this modern version of alchemy, a public good could be funded without depriving individuals of anything that they had or reasonably expected to obtain.
>
> Prior to 1981, United States banking regulations prohibited the payment of interest-on-demand deposits held by for-profit entities, including law firms. * * * In that year, however, the regulations were modified to permit interest-bearing demand deposits in cases in which a charitable organization would receive "the entire beneficial interest."

Id. at 848–49.

The crucial definition in IOLTA programs concerns the monies to be placed in pooled accounts. Funds are to be placed in IOLTA accounts only when they cannot be expected to generate any interest for clients after paying administrative costs. Therefore, if programs are properly administered, no client would be deprived of money he would have received if the account had been maintained separately.

The American Bar Association Committee on Ethics and Professional Responsibility issued a formal opinion finding that participation in IOLTA was consistent with an attorney's ethical obligations to assist in improving the legal system. Erin E. Heuer Lantzer, *IOLTA Lost the Battle but Has Not Lost the War*, 33 Ind. L. Rev. 1015, 1018 (2000). By the year 2000, all fifty states had created IOLTA programs. The programs may be mandatory, involving all client funds not expected to generate interest; voluntary, meaning that attorneys choose whether to open an IOLTA account or keep money in non-interest bearing checking accounts; or structured to permit attorneys to opt out of IOLTA participation during an annual review period. *Id.* at 1017. The mandatory programs raise significantly more money than voluntary ones. *See, e.g.*, Washington Legal Foundation v. Texas Equal Access to Justice Foundation, 270 F.3d 180 (5th Cir.2001) (voluntary program in Texas generated $1 million annually in 1980s; "recent earnings approximate more than $5 million annually" under a mandatory program). Twenty-seven states have mandatory IOLTA programs. Brent Salmons, *IOLTAS: Good Work or Good Riddance?*, 11 Geo. J. Legal Ethics 259, 263 (1998). Some states placed restrictions on IOLTA funds similar to those on Legal Services funding. *See* Alan W. Houseman, *Restrictions by Funders and the Ethical Practice of Law,* 67 Fordham L. Rev. 2187, 2196–97 (1999).

Mandatory IOLTA programs have been challenged under the theories that they are an unconstitutional taking of private property and that they violate the First Amendment's protection of freedom of expression. For years, IOLTA survived challenges in state and federal courts. The Eleventh Circuit court of appeals found that the client had no claim of entitlement to the funds, Cone v. State Bar of Florida, 819 F.2d 1002 (1987), and the First Circuit found that IOLTA did not pose problems with freedom of expression, Washington Legal Foundation v. Massachusetts Bar Foundation, 993 F.2d 962, (1st Cir.1993). However, in 1998, in a case dealing with the Texas IOLTA program, the United States Supreme Court held that clients had a property interest in the interest, however small in amount, generated on their funds: "interest follows principal."

> Most significantly, the Court addressed the contention that, because the IOLTA funds could not generate net interest for the owners of the principal, the program could not constitute a taking. The Court stated:
>
> > We have never held that a physical item is not "property" simply because it lacks a positive economic or market value.... Our conclusion in this regard was premised on our long-standing recognition that property is more than economic value; it also consists of "the group of rights which the so-called owner exercises in his dominion of the physical thing," such "as the right to possess, use and dispose of it."
>
> Thus, the Supreme Court affirmed the Fifth Circuit's determination that the interest earned on the client funds placed in IOLTA accounts constituted private property. The Court, however, declined to rule on the ultimate questions of "whether [those] funds have been 'taken' by the State," or "the amount of 'just compensation,' if any, due respondents."

Beschle, *supra* at 853–54 (quoting Phillips v. Washington Legal Foundation, 524 U.S. 156, 169–70, 172 (1998)).

Four justices dissented, arguing that there had been no economic loss, no expectation of economic gain, and that principal followed interest only when the principal could produce interest for whoever held it. Beschle, *supra* at 854–55, citing *Phillips*, 524 U.S. at 180.

In 2001, two federal circuits reached opposite holdings on the constitutionality of IOLTA. The Court of Appeals for the Ninth Circuit upheld IOLTA and found no unconstitutional taking of property, reasoning that the Fifth Amendment did not proscribe taking property; rather, it forbade taking property without just compensation, and in this case, no compensation was due because of the value of the property. Washington Legal Foundation v. Legal Foundation of Washington, 271 F.3d 835

(9th Cir.2001), *cert. granted* 122 S.Ct. 2355 (2002). The Fifth Circuit, on the other hand, found that IOLTA violated the Fifth Amendment but found the notion of compensation irrational, treating it as the necessity to pay 1 dollar for each dollar that went into public funds through the IOLTA program. Washington Legal Foundation v. Texas Equal Access to Justice Found., 270 F.3d 180 (5th Cir.2001).

Notes and Questions

1. Is the use of IOLTA funds comparable to the use of activity fees paid by all students at a university to support activities of which individual students disapprove? *See* Board of Regents of the University of Wisconsin System v. Southworth, 529 U.S. 217 (2000) (holding that in the context of a public university, as long as the distribution of fees was viewpoint neutral, students' rights of free expression were not violated by using their fees to advance views of which they disapproved.) Can free speech interests at a university be compared to the workings of a legal system and society's interest in representation for all parties within it? Was the students' claim stronger because they had actually paid something of value into the university's funds?

2. Talbot "Sandy" D'Alemberte describes the different programs which must be combined to provide legal representation to low income people as "tributaries feeding a mighty river." Talbot "Sandy" D'Alemberte, *Tributaries of Justice: The Search for Full Access*, 25 Fla. St. U. L. Rev. 631, 633–34 (1998). The list of tributaries includes federally funded legal services, which he describes as "the most efficient" program in providing legal services to the poor, *id.* at 634; interest on lawyers trust accounts (IOLTA); state funding for services given to counties through a filing fee surcharge; a comprehensive lawyer pro bono plan; a fee-shifting statute for poor people who must challenge the actions of government agencies; and three methods of raising substantial money for a civil Gideon fund, including a service tax on for-profit legal services, *id.* at 638–39 (quoting estimate that expanding sales tax to services would raise $20 million per year for civil legal assistance); distribution to a civil Gideon fund of a portion of punitive damage awards and unclaimed money from class action suits, *id.* at 639–40; and a filing fee surcharge imposed by the state, *id.* at 637–68 (estimating that state-wide imposition of a $10 surcharge would raise a total of $16 million per year).

Many states provide some support to legal aid programs through filing fees imposed in all court cases, although these fees generate less money for legal aid than IOLTA does. If fees were raised to levels that attempted to generate the amounts of money gained through IOLTA, those fees would then create obstacles to access to courts for people of moderate income. *See* M.A. Stapleton, *County's Filing Fees Top Nation; Boost Sought to Fund Legal Aid*, Chicago Daily Law Bull. Dec. 26, 1995, at 1 (legal services foundation opposes additional fee, which would raise money for legal services for the poor, because fee would impose undue burden on poor clients who do not qualify for indigent status).

SECTION 4. DEVELOPING AND SUSTAINING SOCIAL JUSTICE PRACTICES

Creative lawyers continue to invent ways to practice law that sustain their social justice ideals. They build connections with community organizations and find like-minded attorneys and staff with whom to build a practice. They also find ways to finance their practices, including charging fees on a sliding scale, or using grants to underwrite practice for underserved communities. Contingency fees awarded in personal injury cases have also provided financial support for civil rights and social justice legal work. Awards of attorneys' fees, particularly in civil rights cases, are another method of funding. Just as funding for legal services has been a political battlefield, attorneys' fee awards are part of the contemporary legal and political movement to facilitate social justice work.

A. Structuring Alternative Visions of Legal Practice: Nonprofit Agencies and Social Justice Law Firms

Students aspiring to work for social justice are often daunted by the task of figuring out how to practice law and sustain these ideals. As Sylvia Law advised (*see* chapter 1), sustaining friends are an important part of the equation. Professional networks, through bar associations, provide important opportunities to learn about social justice lawyers in your own community. This section describes examples of practices developed by lawyers to support social justice goals.

LOUISE G. TRUBEK

Embedded Practices: Lawyers, Clients, and Social Change
31 Harv. C.R.-C.L L.Rev. 415, 418–25, 428–33, 436–37 (1996)

* * * Because prospects for state funding are dimming, opportunities for government employment are declining, and our ideas about the best approach to lawyering for subordinated groups are changing, alternative practices for social change lawyering should be identified and encouraged. Recent studies have identified alternative practices, including social justice law firms, law school clinical programs, pro bono models, and client nonprofits, at work in several different geographic locations. These social change practices display an alternative ideological and institutional vision for practicing law for subordinated people. These practices illustrate the viability of models that use diverse funding sources and depend upon a commitment to collaborative lawyer-client relationships. Alternative practices both create and reflect ideological and institutional frameworks for social justice. Ironically, these same elements also create conflicts that may jeopardize the survival of these practices. The success of such practices is crucial as they assist clients, redeem lawyers, and expand the realm of social change lawyering. * * *

The Client Non–Profit

There are a growing number of nonprofit organizations that work with subordinated people; they range from support groups to housing rehabilitative services to homeless shelters. The ascendancy of the client nonprofit during the 1980s "stemmed from the preference of government funders for using private groups to deliver new services rather than expanding government agencies."

These nonprofits view their mission as strengthening the collective and individual power of their clients. Law, lawyers, and legal institutions emerge as both enablers and obstacles in the achievement of their goals. * * *

The Coalition of Wisconsin Aging Groups (CWAG) is a nonprofit corporation founded in 1978. It is the leading Wisconsin-based service and advocacy organization for older people. CWAG's central missions are advocating for the special needs of older persons, assuring that older persons are recognized as people of dignity and worth, and affirming that older persons are partners in building the Wisconsin of tomorrow for people of all ages. CWAG provides its members with services and programs ranging from legislative lobbying to counseling on home equity mortgages to sponsoring a Medicare supplement insurance policy.

CWAG understands the impact of law on the lives of its members. The drastic reduction of the number of elderly poor is directly related to the creation of Medicare and the increases in Social Security during the 1960s. But these programs also generated rules and bureaucracy that negatively impact the lives of older persons. An increasing concern of older people is autonomy and control in their lives; laws and legal institutions influence access to home-based, long-term care and determine medical right-to-die decisions.

From its inception, CWAG's law-related program has provided legislative lobbying, grassroots activism, and client education. CWAG substantially expanded its legal services commitment in 1991 when its Board approved a merger with a well-respected legal project serving the elderly. Funded by federal and state funds, the project is an innovative legal services delivery system serving thousands of older persons throughout the state. Nonlawyers, called "benefit specialists," are located in county offices and provide public benefits counseling and advocacy to older people. Staff lawyers from the legal unit provide backup to these field benefit specialists.

* * *

In addition to the field benefit specialists, there are now four lawyers on the CWAG staff. The scope of legal services provided has expanded to include a guardianship support center and an elder abuse project. While most of the services are provided by the staff attorneys and benefit specialists, several of the projects use pro bono attorneys. The benefit specialist system produces high-quality client service for two reasons. First, the advocates understand the needs of elderly clients such as the need to provide legal services through home visits to the disabled. Second, the benefit specialists are experts in the legal concerns of the elderly such as Medicare and Social Security.

Collaboration between the lawyers and other CWAG staff members has positive effects. The statewide client casework provides the CWAG legislative lobbyists with personal, local stories for their discussions with legislators. The extensive casework also creates a statistical base to establish areas of concern for legislation, administrative agency reform, and class actions. The addition of the lawyer staff also creates what the executive director terms "synergy," arising from the combination of the expertise of the legal staff with concerns identified by the rest of the staff and Board.

The placement of a law unit within the client organization creates an organic client-constituency-lawyer relationship. Such a relationship results in the respectful treatment of clients, more efficient collaboration between the client group and the lawyers, and an overall strengthening of the organization.

* * * In Wisconsin, the sites providing services to battered women are community-based shelters, which are nonprofit organizations funded through a mixture of government grants, foundation support, and individual and corporate contributions. The shelters also belong to the Wisconsin Coalition Against Domestic Violence (WCADV), a state-wide coalition that provides education and advocacy for battered women and support for the shelters.

The movement against domestic violence has involved substantial interaction among movement activists, clients, and lawyers. * * *

Each Wisconsin shelter provides a variety of legal services to its clients. Interviews with the directors of these shelters indicate different combinations of legal service providers, including staff lawyers, lay advocates, lawyer board members, LSC lawyers, pro bono attorneys, and private bar referrals. * * *

Advocacy for protective orders is provided by a "legal advocate," a nonlawyer who assists battered women in court by aiding in the petitioning process, accompanying victims to court, and educating the court and police about the needs of battered women. The shelters rely on the legal advocate to walk the women through the protective order process. The advocates are often part-time, sometimes pro bono; several shelters employ former deputy sheriffs with criminal justice degrees as legal advocates.

Representation in family law matters varies with the shelter's resources. One shelter employs a full-time staff attorney to provide family law services to clients who cannot qualify for the local LSC program. The shelter hired the lawyer because it was unable to locate private attorneys to provide the services. The director explained:

> We worked hard to develop a pro bono network, but it's been very difficult.... Most lawyers are reluctant to take pro bono work

in this area. This is partly because the cases often evolve into messy custody disputes or other messy areas. Also, there may be a stigma attached, and the lawyers would lose other work in the community if strongly associated with victims of domestic violence.

Another shelter uses the local LSC office for family law cases. The shelter does the screening and makes referrals to that office. If the client is above income limits, the LSC office uses a referral service under which the client pays a private lawyer a reduced fee. Even where the LSC office is providing the legal work, clients are directed to the shelter for nonlegal support while going through a divorce. The LSC office relies on this support. * * *

The shelters' work on behalf of battered women extends beyond individual assistance; they integrate policy action with case representation. Advocacy by the shelters in the legislature is coordinated through WCADV. The shelters' local base assists in providing effective lobbying. One shelter director states: "I have earned and worked for a good relationship with my state senator and representatives. They call me and say 'You are my adviser on this issue.' " Action on public and community issues also creates a sense of empowerment in clients. One shelter indicated that "it encourages victims to contact WCADV directly. The most common progression is to see women who were once clients become volunteers and then stay active in their community."

A nonhierarchical workplace environment for staff and clients can be a key aspect of the shelters' missions. Respect and shared responsibility at the shelters can reduce psychological and emotional battering in our society by modeling alternative forms of interaction. One approach to a nonhierarchical workplace is maintaining a collegial and humane office. * * * The shelters' organizational structure can also promote equality. One shelter experimented with a collective model but has moved to a more structured environment where the director, though the final decision maker, employs a participatory management style.

* * *

CWAG and the battered women's shelters realize that lawyers, legal institutions, and laws are significant factors in advancing the interests of their clients and their own organizational goals. They attempt to operationalize a system that will improve their clients' experience with the law. They provide empowering client representation and collaboration between lawyers and client groups. The organizations understand that providing individual case representation is critical to the goals of the group; they believe that collective power increases through successful individual client representation. [The] * * * nonprofits also engage in more traditional collective action such as group organizing, legislative lobbying, and class actions. Each organization has been able to generate funding for its legal program by combining federal and state government funds, organized bar and individual lawyer contributions, foundation and business grants, and charitable donations.

* * * The use of lay advocates for representation is a striking feature of the client nonprofit model. Locally based lay advocates provide a significant portion of the services, working closely with the lawyers associated with the nonprofits. * * *

The Social Justice Law Firm

The model of the full-time public interest practitioner in a legal assistance office is of limited attraction to many recent law school graduates who want to do social justice work. The private sector appears to be more economically viable than the shrinking public arena. The new approaches to lawyering for subordinated people articulated by critical lawyering theorists also interest these young lawyers. Thus, changes in economic realities and new theoretical insights render alternative private practice an appealing option for social change lawyering.

* * * [T]wo firms that have succeeded in developing such practices * * * exemplify the tenets supported by critical lawyering theory: commitment to community and collective action, collaboration with clients, and an alternative workplace environment. They have succeeded in creating socially conscious practices by selecting an appropriate substantive law specialty, combining individual case representation with collective action, and working with social movements. Because of their ability to fund their alternative practice creatively, these firms have remained in existence for quite a while, suggesting that the model is sustainable.

Strickland & Caldwell is a law firm consisting of two white women partners, a junior attorney, and one paralegal. Currently the practice primarily focuses on family law, including divorce actions and child custody cases, supplemented by estate planning, appellate, and general practice. Both women's interest in family law stems from their early involvement in women's rights issues; they were lobbyists and litigators involved in shaping Wisconsin's no-fault divorce legislation in the 1970s. Both were also part of the dramatic upsurge in women attending law school in the early 1970s, and their feminist consciousness reflects some of their law school experiences.

The lawyers started the practice in reaction to the anti-family law attitudes in the large firm where they originally initiated a successful family law practice. Strickland notes:

> [T]here are a lot of problems with a family law practice: you have more accounts receivable, you have more complaining clients, a lot of things that lawyers hate.... Because of the messiness of it, people didn't really like it, and because it reflected on their status. They didn't like being thought of as a family-law firm.

The lawyers express their commitment to advancing civil rights through involvement in feminist and bar organizations. As president of the local YWCA, Strickland is developing the "Y" into the only local organization providing housing and services to single women and their children. During her term as president, she plans to develop a volunteer legal assistance program to provide residents with legal representation and information. She is also a leading activist on issues that advance interests of women lawyers and women clients. Active in both the traditional state bar as well as the local women lawyers group, she thinks bar groups are useful for networking and support, but believes that she must use her position to battle against their traditionalist viewpoints. Caldwell's commitments include substantial pro bono cases, referred by the local domestic violence shelter. Last year, for example, the firm represented clients in two complex cases, which resulted in the firm's income declining by thirty percent. Caldwell notes that they consider this sort of sacrifice as a reason for the creation of the firm and have no regrets.

The lawyer-client interaction is an important aspect of Strickland & Caldwell's alternative practice. The lawyers stress their collaborative relationship with clients. Caldwell describes her approach to lawyer-client relationships as holistic; she collaborates with her clients and tries to make the situation that necessitated contact with the legal system a positive experience. She notes, "I see my role with the client as being a resource, but not a decision maker."

The creation of a humanistic environment is a key aspect of a feminist law firm. The firm sees the importance of a workplace that reflects the institutional statement of a consensual office. Caldwell reports: "[T]here is no place in this law firm for someone who is not a feminist in terms of working relationships." The creation of their own firm is a demonstration of these attorneys' commitment to a workplace that expresses client collaboration, social commitment, and humanistic interaction.

[James] Smith, an African American man, is the lead partner of the firm Smith & Associates. He cofounded the firm with well-known civil rights and employment discrimination attorneys. Smith & Associates' practice comprises work with local economic development clients as well as civil rights and employment discrimination cases. Smith also represents consumers in class actions.

Smith has been greatly influenced by his Virginia roots; inspired by Patrick Henry and James Madison, Smith wanted to play a role in American history. His college experience at Hampton Institute politicized him in terms of the African American struggle. As a young African American growing up in the national political activism of the 1960s, Smith recognized that the United States had to change to meet the demands of a changing society. He states: "I wanted to do what I could to promote civil and social issues. I wanted to help in the advancement of African–Americans and hopefully that has translated into helping the collective [community]." His job as an associate at a large law firm allowed him to work with an attorney who for many years combined a successful social justice practice with corporate clients.

Smith's practice enables him both to represent clients in a manner consistent with their social values and to advocate for groups on broad social issues. The firm's work includes a substantial minority business practice made possible by expertise Smith acquired in the corporate and tax practices of his former firm. Collaborative interaction between lawyer and client allows for a realization of their shared commitment to the goals of community advancement. He sees his firm as allied with the African American community's struggle for respect and economic viability.

Smith describes his practice, nonetheless, as a struggle to keep the rent and overhead paid while carrying contingency-based employment discrimination and class action cases. His aspirations to accept some cases regardless of fees is proving more difficult than he anticipated.

Smith & Associates' aim is to create a humane environment within the office. Smith says: "One of the goals of the firm is to have a firm where people are treated in a respectful manner. We don't have an office where people are expected to make coffee and do grunt work." He sees a humanistic environment as an essential component of the firm's social values.

The attorneys in these two firms search for consonance between their professional roles and their personal identities by combining social change lawyering with fee-for-service work. The lawyers' commitment to or concern for a specific social movement is the essential element: women's rights for Strickland & Caldwell and African American community development for Smith. They express their commitment by engaging in community and collective action, collaborating with clients, and developing humanistic offices.

The ability of the firms to participate in community and collective action while remaining viable is striking. They succeed by selecting an appropriate substantive law specialty, combining individual case representation and collective action, and working with social movements.

Family and community development law are viable areas for practice on behalf of subordinated people; as specialty practices that attract clients who can pay fees, they contribute to the sustainability of the firms. Family law practice places the lawyer in a key position both to assist clients who are restructuring their lives and to represent women's groups seeking to reform family law through court challenges, legislation, and community programs. Community economic development assists the economic well-being of inner-city neighborhoods by combining business and tax counseling with community development interests.

Due to their specialized practices, the lawyers in social justice law firms are able to maintain productive relationships with the social movements that inspired their legal careers. Strickland and Caldwell are actively involved with local battered women's shelters and women's bar associations. Smith works closely with the National Association for the Advancement of Colored People (NAACP) and an African American bar association. He also works with groups such as "One Hundred Black Men," a national and local effort to ally successful African American men with central city youth. The lawyers realize that collective action is essential for their social practices. Since their firms are small and isolated, they locate or create organizations that can provide connections and size.

These lawyers struggle to keep their practices economically viable while achieving their social and personal goals. The social justice law firms use funding from diverse sources to maintain financial viability. Strickland & Caldwell, while primarily relying on client fees, uses government revenue for guardian ad litem appointments and representation of paternity cases. Smith & Associates uses hourly rate charges, contingency fees, and court awards to keep afloat. Smith consciously constructed his firm to function with diverse clients and diverse revenue sources in order to maximize its chances for survival. Contingent fee arrangements contribute to the "constant financial tension" that the social justice law firms experience.

The values to which these practitioners are committed—social change, collaboration with clients, and collegial workplaces—must be negotiated within the broader context of legal practice. The economics of the market and new technologies affect the ability of the social justice law firms to continue their practices. Large firms may successfully compete for economic development business based on their breadth of expertise, undercutting the social justice law firms' years of dedicated involvement with community organizations. Emerging techniques within legal practices may also present challenges to the values of social justice law firms. For example, routinized divorce systems could cut against the empowerment goals of Strickland and Caldwell by removing the client from an active part in defining the legal problem, goals, and strategy. The continual struggle to maintain values in a competitive market creates tensions in a social justice law firm. The lawyers in social justice law firms seek daily to balance and combine client-centered representation, collective action, and economic viability.

* * *

Both the client nonprofit and the social justice law firm are viable means of pursuing the use of law for social justice. Each advances a conception of "lawyering [that] is no longer a unidirectional professional service." The two models share similar elements: a local base with connection to larger networks, client collaboration, and diverse funding. These factors are crucial for the economic viability and the transformative potential of the practices.

* * *

In a period of shrinking government resources and antipathy toward lawyers, financial support for legal services requires strategic planning. Additional funding for legal services for subordinated people can be encouraged by the existence of diverse practice sites. New funding sources can include client contributions, client-based government funding, and new legal claims.

* * *

Social justice law firms could benefit by allowing and encouraging practices that serve a larger community. The financial viability of the social justice law firms is increased if they are eligible for financial assistance through grants to underwrite their low-income client and group advocacy.

CWAG and the domestic violence shelters receive government funding for their legal programs. The Older Americans Act funds legal services for older persons and the Violence Against Women Act funds the law program of the battered women's organizations. Other client groups could organize to create such resources. Specialized funding proposals are attractive to government and foundation donors. * * *

* * *

Social justice law firms and client nonprofits have an incentive to create legal claims that provide attorney fees; they rely on this income for their viability. Lead paint tort actions are an example of a legal claim for the poor developed by social justice law firms to advance client interests and to achieve revenue. Nonprofits in cooperation with private law firms often generate class actions against discriminating businesses. These collaborative ventures unite client group activism with the expertise of litigators. These claims, however, may be developed by any lawyer; the style of the pursuit of the claim and the revenue received may not be linked to client empowerment, group mobilization, or pro bono service. Nonetheless, the development of new legal claims is crucial to the financial viability of social justice law firms.

JAY DIXIT

This Firm Won National Recognition for its Commitment to Providing Affordable Legal Services

L Magazine, Summer 2001, 9–10

Miguel Negron was teaching at an elementary school in the Bronx when he had a life-changing experience. Born to Puerto Rican parents, raised in the Bronx, and educated at CUNY College, Negron taught a "bilingual" class made up of students from Central America, Mexico, and Puerto Rico, teaching all the subjects himself, and conducting all the lessons in Spanish. One day he had to come to class late because of a doctor's appointment, and a teacher's aide supervised his students until he arrived.

Negron's class was an underfunded "bridge class," meaning that fourth, fifth, and sixth graders were crammed together in one classroom. When he got to class, Negron realized that all the older kids were gone. Nobody knew where they were. When he finally tracked the missing kids, he found them in an empty classroom—painting the walls.

Negron was livid that the administration would exploit Spanish-speaking students for manual labor. After all, he thought, white kids never got stuck doing upkeep on the school. Negron raised a fuss, the administration eventually apologized, and Negron was labeled a troublemaker. But he never forgot about it. "That one incident really pissed me off," recalls Negron. At the same time, he felt powerless to affect real change in the administration's practices. "I thought, how much can I do with just a B.A.?" he says. I figured I would get a degree with some bite.

Today, along with his two partners, Negron runs Marcos & Negron, which just won the prestigious American Bar Association's 2001 Pro Bono Publico award, an honor established "to recognize lawyers and law firms for extraordinarily noteworthy contributions to extending free legal services to the poor and disadvantaged." The nod specifically recognized the low-cost legal help the firm provides to the working poor in the underserved communities of New York; it services roughly 4,500 families.

The firm was nominated for the award by Fred Rooney, project director for the Community Legal Resource Network at CUNY School of Law, which supports solo and small-firm lawyers trying to build practices while helping underserved communities. "The nomination was something of a long shot, because in many instances, the firms that are more apt to get recognition are very large firms that also have a pro bono component," says Rooney.

Marcos & Negron is not a large firm—it's made up of just three lawyers. Jim Marcos works on criminal cases, divorce, and real estate; Kenji Akaike handles employment and immigration matters, particularly those relating to Japanese nationals; and Negron deals in immigration law, particularly refugee cases and requests for asylum. They specialize in offering a form of pro bono work that is often overlooked: they provide legal services not for free, but as cheaply as possible without going broke themselves. The firm uses a sliding scale system of payment—charging less, for instance, to illegal immigrants seeking asylum in the U.S., and charging more, for instance, to the banks that Akaike sometimes represents in order to obtain visas for Japanese workers. The firm also welcomes barter and has accepted payment in the form of wood shelving, pizza-making lessons, and mangos.

The firm's clientele consists primarily of poor and working people of color, 90 percent of whom are Latinos, mostly from El Salvador, Guatemala, Honduras, Nicaragua, the Dominican Republic, Columbia, Peru, and Mexico. Most clients are just trying to establish legal residency in the U.S. Negron, for instance, represented an HIV-positive man from El Salvador who was facing imminent deportation. He had a wife, who was a green-card holder from El Salvador, and a child. Negron showed that being HIV positive in El Salvador, the man would be in danger of being shot (by soldiers, off-duty police, or paramilitary "death squads"), and he would not receive proper medical care. The man was granted asylum and allowed to stay. "We can sit down and get people green cards—that's just like factory work—but every now and then you have a case where you see that you really made a difference, so that's the big payoff," says Negron. That particular case really motivated me to continue to work long hours and do all the other crazy stuff that I'm doing right now.

Because of the earthquake in El Salvador, the firm has recently been overwhelmed by El Salvadorans who cannot go home and are seeking asylum. In a period of 40 days in April and early May, Negron took on 3,000 new clients. "I've been practicing law for 15 years," says Rooney, "And I have never seen anyone whose dedication to the law and to serving communities is as great as Miguel's."

The partners met at CUNY law school. Marcos was a former U.S. Marine with a business degree, born in Ecuador and raised in Brooklyn. Akaike was a Japanese national who'd just graduated from NYU's Tisch School for the Arts with a degree in playwriting and screenwriting. "I had a bet with my grandmother, who was footing the bill, that I would publish something before I got out, and if I lost I had to do something worthy," says Akaike. "I lost the bet, so I went to law school."

To students aspiring to do what his firm does, Negron shares his story. "I got out of law school broke, my credit was ruined, it was in the middle of the recession. Enrollment at law schools was down, lawyers were being laid off, all these firms were downsizing," he says. "It was kind of like, hey, you'd better do it on your own, because you're not going to get a shot at it otherwise." But eventually, the partners got a loan and started the firm. "It's going to look impossible," says Negron. "But if you really believe in working hard and following it through, you can actually go out there with very little money and start a practice."

Notes and Questions

1. There are many examples of law practice for social justice. A non-profit center may support its work through a creative combination of affordable fees and grants; a law firm may develop a small but consistent base monthly income by providing contracts for legal insurance plans for public and private labor unions. *See* Louise Trubek & M. Elizabeth Kransberger, *Critical Lawyers: Social Justice and the Structures of Private Practice*, in *Cause Lawyering*, *supra* at 201 (describing the transformative aspects of several law practices and the fee structures for El Centro and Urban Legal Advocates); *see also* John Kilwein, *Still Trying: Cause Lawyering for the Poor and Disadvantaged in Pittsburgh, Pennsylvania*, in *Cause Lawyering*, *supra* at 181 (describing the work of twenty-nine lawyers in private practice in Pittsburgh).

Aaron Porter describes an African-American law firm in Philadelphia, founded in the 1950s, when "African Americans were virtually excluded from white law firms, state and federal clerkships, and professional opportunities in the corporate mainstream," Aaron Porter, *Norris, Schmidt, Green, Harris, Higginbotham & Associates: The Sociolegal Import of Philadelphia Cause Lawyers*, in *Cause Lawyering*, *supra* at 151, comprising a group of lawyers who "gradually moved into distinguished positions of power and influence," *id.* at 152. The lawyers at the Norris firm remained deeply connected to "the infrastructure of a poor, black community as they developed and expanded the law practice" and crystallized a vision of racial and social equality. *Id.* at 174.

2. Because many social justice lawyers have funded their practices through contingency fees in tort litigation, recent attacks on contingency fees are relevant to funding social justice practices. Elihu Inselbuch describes the social and economic divisions over contingency fees:

> Many consumer organizations, public advocates, labor unions, and plaintiffs' lawyers view the United States' system of contingent fees as nothing less than the average citizen's "key to the courthouse door," giving all aggrieved persons access to our system of justice without regard to their financial state. Others, including some defense counsel and academics funded by or speaking for corporations and their insurers, view them as the bane of our legal system, the source of frivolous and expensive litigation that lines the pockets of the claimants' lawyers with unwarranted and extravagant fees. Despite a 1994 formal opinion of the American Bar Association finding contingent fees to be squarely within the bounds of American legal ethics, they remain subject to attack by their critics. As Congress and some state legislatures continue to debate the subject of "tort reform," however its advocates may define it, contingent fees will almost certainly remain among the primary targets of the cries for change.

Elihu Inselbuch, *Contingent Fees and Tort Reform: A Reassessment and Reality Check*, 64 Law & Contemp. Probs. 175, 175–76 (2001). *See also* Marc Galanter, *Anyone Can Fall Down a Manhole: The Contingency Fee and Its Discontents*, 47 DePaul L. Rev. 457, 462–63 (1998) (arguing that cultural attitudes toward lawyers and contingency fees are not a new development; recounting 19th and early 20th century jokes about lawyers still current at the end of the 20th century); Stephanie M. Wildman, *Propositions Are the Wrong Way for Tort Reform*, L.A. Daily J., Nov. 7, 1988, Col. 3, at 6 (critiquing a state ballot initiative that sought to abolish contingent fees); Richard L. Abel, *The Real Tort Crisis—Too Few Claims*, 48 Ohio St. L.J. 443 (1987) (urging that the real tort crisis is "underclaiming rather than overclaiming").

3. The following articles describe visions of social justice legal practice by the Asian Law Caucus, founded as a part of community struggles in the 1970s, and by the San Francisco Community Law Office, founded in about the same period.

DALE MINAMI

Asian Law Caucus: Experiment in an Alternative
3 Amerasia Journal 28–31, 34–35, 38–39 (1975)

The usually festive celebration of Chinese New Year had a particularly disquieting air in 1969. The tourists still swarmed the streets and alleys and the residents of Chinatown turned out to witness the pageantry. But the police were in attendance for different reasons. Before the night had ended, a number of Chinese youth found themselves in jail on charges ranging from illegal sale of firecrackers to assault on a police officer. Many of those arrested were immigrants who could not understand English. They were left confused and disoriented in jail.

Ken Kawaichi, an Asian American attorney who had defended strikers at San Francisco State and UC Berkeley during the Third World strikes, was called to assist the arrestees. He recognized the lack of resources available to aid non-English speaking people and approached several law students at Boalt Hall, UC Berkeley's law school. With interpreters from the community and legal resources from Boalt Hall, he was able to defend those arrested.

Thereafter, whenever an Asian American youth was arrested in the community, he or his family was apt to call Ken for legal assistance. This reaction led Ken to believe that perhaps a more organized effort to represent Asian Americans could be developed. Thoughts coalesced when he began teaching the "Asian American Communities and the Law" course at UC Berkeley's Asian Studies Department. He and law students who assisted in teaching the course began discussing the idea of an Asian American legal organization, which was later realized in the form of the Asian Law Caucus.

Ken's idea was to create a new legal organization committed to practicing law for Asian American people, not for profit. Because federally funded legal aid programs and public defender offices served only the superpoor and since most private attorneys cost upwards of $60 per hour, we hoped to bridge the chasm between the options of government legal programs for the poor and private attorneys. Governmental agencies, in addition, lacked bilingual staff and sensitivities to the cultural and linguistic problems of Asian Americans. Above all, we expected to exercise law with a political emphasis—defending "political" cases, attacking racism in institutions, highlighting society's neglect of Asian American concerns, and supporting the work of progressive community organizations. We especially hoped to be responsive and accountable to the Asian American communities, using law to promote and protect their interests.

Disparaged as idealists, we nevertheless maintained astronomical ambitions for ourselves and our organization. We wanted to provide free and low-cost legal services for Asian Americans, initiate broad suits attacking institutional racism, forge close ties with community groups, participate in community struggles, publish articles and pamphlets designed to inform Asian Americans of their rights, de-mystify the law and legal processes through seminars and workshops, train law students for future community-oriented legal work, democratize the traditional law firm and create a model to encourage others to join in community law practice. Later, we regretted our presumptuousness.

In August 1972, we found an office in Oakland, paid our first and last months' rent of $500, and spent the remainder of our savings of $86.70 on supplies. The furniture came from a Kaiser Industry storehouse, $1400 from the University's student fund, and $3000 from Glide Memorial Church. Six law students, three law graduates and a number of undergraduates and drop-outs painted the office, developed proposals and set up the bookkeeping and filing systems.

* * *

In another case involving police harassment in Chinatown, political support developed and played a critical role in the criminal defense. The defendant was Harry Wong, a vendor of progressive newspapers and magazines at a small sidewalk table on the corner of Jackson and Grant Streets. In early 1973, he was arrested and beaten by the police, charged with obstructing the sidewalk, battery on a police officer, resisting arrest and peddling without a permit. Eleven eye-witnesses declared that the police version of the event was false. Later, a defense committee formed to publicize the case and assist in the defense. During the next several months, the committee garnered hundreds of signatures on petitions demanding dismissal of the charges and circulated leaflets and news articles protesting the treatment of Mr. Wong. The committee's efforts culminated with a demonstration on Central Station which was carried by local media into the homes of district attorneys, police officers, and the public at large.

The political pressure on the District Attorney's office combined with legal challenges to the arrest convinced the prosecutor to negotiate an uneasy truce. Two days after the demonstration, the deputy district attorney in charge of the case offered to drop the three most serious charges in exchange for a guilty plea to the technically supportable charge of peddling without a permit. After several meetings, Harry Wong and the defense committee decided to plead nolo contendere (plea of "no contest" although effective as a guilty plea) to the peddling charge. The judge then fined Harry Wong $10.00 and, in the same breath, awarded $10.00 in interpreter fees to a defense committee member.

* * *

The importance of using legal expertise to defend picketers, strikers, demonstrators and people like Harry Wong is obvious. Criminal proceedings drain time and energy away from the primary struggles in communities and work places, and convictions may steal freedom from political activists. The significance of educational lawsuits is less apparent. We have felt that unjust laws, official misconduct and unresponsive institutions should be exposed and that lawsuits are *one* method for bringing a particular problem to the public's scrutiny.

* * *

* * * [T]he bulk of our caseload and work revolves around day-to-day problems and requests for consultation. * * *

Up to September 1974, the Asian Law Caucus had handled approximately 400 consultations and 360 cases. Approximately 90% of these cases involved Chinese, Japanese and Pilipino clients. The criminal cases were the most frequent everyday encounter; immigration was second; and a fast-rising number of employment discrimination and family cases was third. Geographically, 36% of the cases came from San Francisco,

23% from Oakland, and 19% from Berkeley. The majority of clients had incomes between $0 and $300 per month, and the age group was split—66% of our clients were between the ages of 19 to 33, 22% between 34 and 54.

We have accepted virtually every case that came into our office, including child custody battles, marriage dissolutions, bankruptcies, and administrative hearings, as well as criminal cases involving murders, unlawful assemblies, and petty theft. If the files of the petty theft cases which we have taken over the years were aligned end-to-end, they would form a ten-inch path which could encircle the world twice.

Within three months after we began, our heavy case load became a burden. Every new case brought in a new problem which demanded new research and new approaches. Our law school education proved embarrassingly deficient in the practical aspects of legal work, and office efficiency was often a study in anarchism. Without guidance from the consulting attorneys, we would still be struggling to complete simple tasks such as filing motions, which is no easy matter for the uninitiated. In fact, the support we received from consulting attorneys was crucial at our early stages, for we were able to push legal demands knowing that such experienced lawyers as Ken Kawaichi and Joe Morozumi would always be around to help us by providing indispensable legal expertise.

With the crushing case load, an uncomfortable resemblance between ourselves and Legal Aid developed. The major distinguishing feature, however, was our relationship with community organizations. Over the years, we have worked with many community groups on various issues and have performed legal work for many of them, including advice on incorporations, consultations on law-related questions, participation in demonstrations and pickets as legal observers and assistance in negotiations. The differences between ourselves and legal aid were just as striking: as Asian Americans, we were more sensitive to problems and feelings of Asian American clients. We either had bilingual staff or access to bilingual legal workers, and we would drive to community organizations and agencies to meet immobile clients. We maintained odd hours (late-nights through weekends) for working people and others who could not make appointments during the week. Finally, our educational activities, though underdeveloped as a program, were quite extensive. We gave talks concerning various aspects of the topic of Asian Americans and Law at schools, colleges, law schools, churches and community workshops and radio and television programs.

The last point underscores a major shortcoming of the Asian Law Caucus—the failure to consolidate and develop a systematic and coherent educational program. We initiated suits but neglected one of our stated objectives: to institute a legal education program to inform the Asian American communities of their rights under the law and to avert unnecessary encounters with law enforcement officers.

Easy to say, difficult to do—we realized that law was exceedingly complex but should be translated into a comprehensible form for people.

We knew that lawyers tend to cloud issues with technical jargon and rapid speech patterns; if those techniques failed to confuse people, then lawyers resorted to the use of Latin. While we were able to bring publicity to a particular legal issue through lawsuits, we never followed up the issue with more in-depth analysis.

* * *

Because the role of law in social change is limited, legal challenges and legal work must complement the efforts of progressive organizations. First, legal action can be defensive in that it can protect and expand civil liberties and rights which nurture political organizing and education, such as the freedoms of speech and assembly. As long as these freedoms maintain their vitality, it is necessary to take advantage of their promises to encourage political activity. Thus, when picketers get arrested for some legal transgression, a successful objection to the constitutionality of the law will make arbitrary enforcement of the law more difficult, thereby supporting the political activity. In the defense of political activists, too, use of the law is obviously necessary. The job of the attorney is simple: get the client out of the courtroom or prison and back into the community or organization where his or her real value lies.

Secondly, an affirmative use of the law serves an educational function. For Asian Americans who harbor understandable reluctance to deal with the legal system, it is necessary to assist in their understanding of the law. Whether by seminars, articles, television, radio or word-of-mouth, people should be informed of their rights, the nature of the legal system and its limitations in effecting social change. Employing litigation to highlight injustices and raise issues also serves an educational purpose. * * *

Inevitably, the defensive and affirmative uses of the law should be applied in the support of organizations dedicated to "social change." Legal resources can assist these organizations in other ways: legal advice on particular issues, legal support for political activity such as demonstrations (i.e., as legal observers), assistance with incorporations of groups, and participation in negotiations.

However, it is crucial that attorneys do not labor under the illusion that their work in isolation will produce the massive material changes needed in this society. But the public at large must understand the same about attorneys and the legal system—their limits and potential for contribution at this time. With this understanding, we can place law in its proper perspective, utilize its strengths, understand and avoid its weaknesses and begin to move forward toward a new society.

PAUL HARRIS

The San Francisco Community Law Collective
7 Law & Policy 19, 20–22, 25–27 (1985)

The formation of a collective in itself was a message to the client that lawyers were people not superhumans, that workers (legal secretaries) were equal to bosses (lawyers), and that the law was a tool to be used, not a mysterious force to be feared or idealized. Collectives also consciously attempted to create structures and work patterns that would demystify the law. Legal self-defense courses were taught, legal workers handled administrative hearings, offices often were set up in storefronts, the interior of the collectives was filled with political posters, lawyers spent time explaining the law to their clients, and sometimes (usually in political cases) we were able to work hand-in-hand with our clients in developing our political and legal tactics.

Our goal was to build the power of community groups. The preferred tactics were working as house counsel to organizations and advising them how to avoid the law and, when appropriate, how to use it. We also defended clients against criminal prosecution. We did not rely on test cases. Rather, we attempted to help people recognize their own potential and stood behind them when they exercised that power. In this way the human being goes through a transformation—is empowered—and does not look to the legal system as a savior.

By 1970 the People's Law Office was established in Chicago and handling major political cases. The Menlo Park Commune had developed out of student activism at Stanford University. The Bar Sinister in Los Angeles was providing new political leadership in the National Lawyers Guild, and the San Francisco Community Law Collective was acting as house-counsel for radical community groups. * * *

Stan Zaks and Paul Harris organized the San Francisco Community Law Collective in the multi-racial, primarily Latino, Mission district of San Francisco. * * *

* * *

[During and after law school,] Stan and I worked for civil rights lawyer C.B. King during the summers of 1966 and 1968, respectively. C.B. King was the only black lawyer in southwest Georgia, a man of great dignity and courage. LSCRRC [Law Students Civil Rights Research Council] and the National Lawyers Guild placed law students in his office every summer. It was a significant experience, showing Stan and me how the law could be used to give people breathing space for their organizing efforts. It also helped us shape the notion of a law practice centered in a specific community, related to indigenous groups fighting for social change.

* * *

The collective was dedicated to equal salaries and equal decision-making; but in order to foster long-term stability we felt that transitory participants should not have the same power to change the direction of the office. Consequently, we distinguished between permanent and non-permanent members. Permanent members had to make at least a two-year chronological commitment, as well as a total emotional commitment during that time. Non-permanent members were paid the same monthly salary as permanent members but did not share in long-term assets, such as the law office building or the pension fund. Non-permanent members had an equal vote on any cases or projects in which they were involved but not on long-term decisions, such as hiring and economics.

* * *

[Harris describes the lives and experience of lawyers and legal workers of diverse backgrounds who joined the collective. A description of the practice of the Law Collective as "house counsel" to community organizations appears in chapter 11.]

Our object was to build an enduring model of radical law practice. We wanted to avoid the syndrome, so prevalent among the new left, of several years of intense radical activity and then either a return to the establishment or dropping out. When Stan Zaks settled a big personal injury case in 1976, we used the money to buy a building for the law collective instead of dispersing the money among ourselves, even though our salaries were very low.

* * *

The dynamics of day-to-day legal practice push towards capitalist work relations. How to collectives, started by white radicals become multiracial? How do legal workers attain real equality with lawyers? How do we maintain a balance between political education and handling the ever-present caseload? How are law students developed into community lawyers instead of being used in the most cost-efficient manner? How do we demystify the law yet look like a "real" law firm? * * *

The reality of law practice is that lawyers have more power than legal workers. Lawyers bring in most of the money! Lawyers receive recognition from the media, their peers, and their clients, while legal workers usually remain in the background or in the office. Lawyers are assumed to have the precious legal information; legal workers are assumed to be typists and receptionists. Most lawyers are white men; most legal workers are women. Lawyers have seven years of college; some legal workers have none. All these facts of life create a power imbalance in a collective.

Equal salaries, or salaries based on need, are a bottom line for any collective and fairly easy to attain. But equality in decisionmaking power presupposes that each member is capable of exercising relatively equal power. This presupposition flies in the face of the above realities. Therefore, structures and policies have to be built into the collective to endow legal workers with the sense of power that allows them to interact with lawyers as true equals.

Some collectives had all members do their own typing, freeing the legal workers to do legal work. This succeeds if the legal workers want to do legal work and can learn to do it with approximately the same efficiency as the lawyers. Other collectives, like ours, had the lawyers do a quarter of their own typing and the legal workers do secretarial and legal community work.

Legal secretarial work is invaluable and should be recognized as an integral part of an office. Legal secretaries take pride in their work and resent the implication that it is not important. * * *

The legal workers in our office found that they did not like researching the law, shepardizing cases, and writing memos. But they did enjoy client contact and wanted the skills necessary to help friends, family, and clients with legal problems. Consequently, we taught them how to interview and how to deal with police brutality. The legal workers pointed out that they needed more time to handle both the client interviewing they enjoyed and the typing they felt was necessary. In response, the collective established a schedule in which each person sits at the front desk and answers the phone half a day per week. Although we tried twice to implement this program, we failed. The lawyers felt that their work pressures and court calendars did not allow for rigid scheduling.

We developed other ways to build the skills, confidence, and power of our legal workers. We ensured that they had the opportunity to attend court whenever it was hearing major political cases or cases that they had prepared. This was extremely worthwhile even if it was not cost-efficient. A different member chairs each weekly meeting, so that those without experience in public speaking can become more comfortable in speaking their minds in group discussions. We also encouraged the legal workers to represent the collective at law school seminars and legal conferences. This took time but has been very successful. * * * Many of the decisions entailed sacrificing some office efficiency in order to enhance equality in the law form. But there is no doubt that the end result has been a law collective that is politically more effective and also more human.

Our collective has an equal distribution of wealth and decisionmaking. But there is not an equal division of labor. Some lawyers do more court work than others; some do more administrative tasks. Frankly, the legal workers spend most of their time on legal secretarial tasks. However, we constantly stress the principle that we are a single functioning unit and that all parts must perform in harmony. * * * All our varied skills, whether learned in school or through life, are necessary for that unit called the law collective to function effectively.

Notes and Questions

1. Minami pays homage to the attorney mentors who helped the young caucus develop. Paul Harris and Stan Zaks learned from working for C.B. King. How might you develop such mentors?

2. How important is the nonlawyer staff to the organization of a law office? How important to the work of the law office in the community? *See* Gerald P. López, *Rebellious Lawyering: One Chicano's Vision of Progressive Law Practice*, 87–102 (1992) (discussing staff engagement with clients in a not-for-profit firm).

3. The Asian Law Caucus website can be found at www.asianlawcaucus.org. The mission statement states in part: "Since the vast majority of Asians and Pacific Islanders in America are immigrants and refugees, the Caucus strives to create an informed and educated community empowered to assert their rights and to participate actively in American society. This perspective is reflected in our broad strategy which integrates the provision of legal services, educational programs, community organizing initiatives and advocacy." Does this description of their work match your own idea of social justice lawyering? Does it match the idea of social justice lawyering that you had at the beginning of the semester?

Along with the Asian American Legal Defense and Education Fund in New York City and the Asian Pacific American Legal Center of Southern California in Los Angeles, the Law Caucus is a founding affiliate of the National Asian Pacific American Legal Consortium (NAPALC) whose mission is "to advance and protect the legal and civil rights of Asian Pacific Americans through litigation, advocacy, public education, and public policy development." Established in 1993, NAPALC's programs have included anti-Asian violence prevention and education, voting rights, affirmative action, welfare reform, immigration, naturalization, language rights, and census issues. Additional information about the consortium is available at www.napalc.org.

4. Edgar Cahn, who helped develop the national legal services program in the 1960s, argues that subordinated communities can and must participate in supporting social justice law practices that serve them. "We have to find ways that enable the poor to increase the pie, not just fight for a larger piece of a fixed pie." Edgar S. Cahn, *Reinventing Poverty Law*, 103 Yale L.J. 2133, 2137 (1994). "Increasing the pie," in Cahn's proposal, involves bringing together resources from the market economy and the nonmarket economy, a term that describes the "vast realm of nonmonetarized economic activity contributed by the family, extended family, neighbors, volunteers, neighborhood-based institutions, and others." Clients make contributions in return for legal services through a system of community service credits (Time Dollars), thereby helping community development. Clients are empowered through their contributions to the community and through their shared role in producing legal work for social justice.

Cahn acknowledges that "[m]any poor people—for example children, mothers of newborn infants, dropouts, or the homeless—seem ill-equipped or unsuitable for the work force. Others, such as seniors and people with criminal records, are excluded from the work force. Still others are the working poor who, despite their best efforts, cannot earn enough to escape poverty." Based on successful Time Dollar experiments in several cities, however, Cahn argues that service credits have proven functional for poor people and their families.

Cahn's proposal depends on finding or creating a Time Dollar or service credit program in the community to be served, so that clients have many opportunities to earn credits with which to pay for legal work. Assuming that a program like this existed in your community, what are the arguments for and against requiring clients to contribute something in return for legal services? Cahn argues that the work ethic is so fundamental in the United States that such a program enhances dignity. Is he correct? Do you agree that his approach combats the helplessness and marginalization that characterize poor communities?

5. Since the late 1990s, some law schools have created networks among alumni to support practitioners doing social justice work in small firms. Community Legal Resource Networks (CLRNS) create networks of "like-minded lawyers who can share ideas and advice and help each other through legal and business challenge ... forging a kinship that eases the challenge of doing public interest work in a private practice setting." Seth Olman, *The Double Bottom Line*, L Magazine, January 2001, at 47, 48. Northeastern University School of Law has two CLRNs, one serving low income, inner-city neighborhoods with economic development services, and the other focused on domestic violence that joins "senior family law practitioners and those who are less experienced with students who have a background in domestic violence advocacy." *Id.* The University of Maryland School of Law project links a CLRN with a "demonstration law office," Civil Justice, Inc., which has specialties in consumer law and economic development. Civil Justice, Inc. handles pro bono cases and refers fee generating cases to the network members. *Id.* The CLRN organized by the City University of New York School of Law has five practice groups linking fifty of the school's alumni: two General Practice Groups, a Family Law Group, and Immigration Practice Group, and an Employment Discrimination Group. It has provided internet access, a web community including bulletin board, and computer training including training in office and legal software. *Id.* at 48, 52. One CUNY graduate remarked that support from the CLRN made it "easier for people to do public service work and to make money while they're doing it." *Id.* at 52. The CLRN also links students at the school with practicing lawyers, providing mentors and practical experience. *Id.* at 50.

How might your school create support for social justice work by alumni/ae? How can students begin to build ties with alumni/ae or ties with each other that will continue after graduation?

B. Civil Rights Cases and Shifting Attorney Fees

In the United States, the traditional approach to attorney fees—the "American Rule"—holds that each party generally bears its own expenses in litigation. In a variety of cases, exceptions to the American Rule have been created by statute or in equity to promote the public good. The "private attorney general" doctrine recognizes the importance of private litigation in enforcing law and the need to pay for that benefit to society.

The Supreme Court explained the role of attorney fee awards in a lawsuit brought to desegregate five drive-in restaurants and a sandwich shop:

> When the Civil Rights Act of 1964 was passed, it was evident that enforcement would prove difficult and that the Nation would have to rely in part upon private litigation as a means of securing broad compliance with the law. A Title II suit is thus private in form only. When a plaintiff brings an action under that Title, he cannot recover damages. If he obtains an injunction, he does so not for himself alone but also as a "private attorney general," vindicating a policy that Congress considered of the highest priority. If successful plaintiffs were routinely forced to bear their own attorneys' fees, few aggrieved parties would be in a position to advance the public interest by invoking the injunctive powers of the federal courts. Congress therefore enacted the provision for counsel fees—not simply to penalize litigants who deliberately advance arguments they know to be untenable but, more broadly, to encourage individuals injured by racial discrimination to seek judicial relief under Title II.

Newman v. Piggie Park Enterprises, Inc., 390 U.S. 400, 402 (1968).

Under the "private attorney general" doctrine, many states permit a court, in its discretion, to award attorneys' fees to plaintiffs who have vindicated important public rights. The California Supreme Court explained the need for the doctrine:

> In the complex society in which we live it frequently occurs that citizens in great numbers and across a broad spectrum have interests in common. These, while of enormous significance to the society as a whole, do not involve the fortunes of a single individual to the extent necessary to encourage their private vindication in the courts. Although there are within the executive branch of the government offices and institutions (exemplified by the Attorney General) whose function it is to represent the general public in such matters and to ensure proper enforcement, for various reasons the burden of enforcement is not always adequately carried by those offices and institutions, rendering some sort of private action imperative. Because the issues involved in such litigation are often extremely complex and their presentation time-consuming and costly, the availability of representation of such public interests by private attorneys acting *pro bono publico* is limited. Only through the appearance of "public interest" law firms funded by public and foundation monies, argue plaintiffs and amici, has it been possible to secure representation on any large scale. The firms in question, however, are not funded to the extent necessary for the representation of all such deserving interests, and as a result many worthy causes of this nature are without adequate representation under present circumstances. One solution, so the argument goes, within the equitable powers of the judiciary to provide, is the award of substantial attorneys fees to those public-interest litigants and their attorneys (whether private attorneys acting *pro bono publico* or members of "public interest" law firms) who are successful in such cases, to the end that support may be provided for the representation of interests of similar character in future litigation.

Serrano v. Priest, 20 Cal.3d 25, 44 (1977).

The California court explained three factors influenced the decision whether to apply the doctrine: "(1) the strength or societal importance of the public policy vindicated by the litigation, (2) the necessity for private enforcement and the magnitude of the resultant burden on the plaintiff, (3) the number of people standing to benefit from the decision." 20 Cal. 3d at 45.

In the early 1970s, a trend developed in lower federal courts, under the "private attorney general" rationale, to award fees to prevailing parties in private litigation brought to enforce statutory and constitutional rights. In 1975, however, the Court held in Alyeska Pipeline Serv. Co. v. Wilderness Soc'y, 421 U.S. 240 (1975), that federal courts could not make equitable fee awards under the private attorney general doctrine because Congress had reserved that power to itself; the attorneys' fees of a successful plaintiff could only be shifted to the defendant for payment if a statute specifically authorized such an award, or if certain other traditional exceptions, such as "bad faith," applied.

Congress responded to the *Alyeska Pipeline* decision by enacting the Civil Rights Attorney's Fees Awards Act of 1976, 42 U.S.C. § 1988, authorizing the district courts to award a reasonable attorney's fee to prevailing parties in civil rights litigation. A court, in its discretion, may include expert fees as part of the attorney's fee. This statute ensured an incentive to bring litigation that could vindicate important federal rights. The legislative history recognizes that plaintiffs in such cases act in society's best interest by serving as "private attorneys general" and enforcing legal norms. As Justice Brennan wrote: "Congress decided that it would be better to have more vigorous enforcement of civil rights laws than would result if plaintiffs were left to finance their own cases." Hensley v. Eckerhart, 461 U.S. 424, 444, n. 4 (1983).

Gregory S. Sisk provides an overview of attorney fees:

> Congress in the last twenty years has enacted a number of statutes that both waive the sovereign immunity of the United States and make the government liable for attorney's fees under certain circumstances. There has been an exponential increase in attorney's fee shifting statutes, with separate statutory fee waivers attached to many congressional enactments. In addition, Congress has enacted a general provision shifting fees against the federal government in the Equal Access to Justice Act [28 U.S.C. § 2412 (1988)].

Gregory S. Sisk, *A Primer on Awards of Attorney's Fees Against the Federal Government*, 25 Ariz. St. L.J. 733, 739 (1993).

Sisk points out that, "With respect to any attempt by a party and counsel to collect attorney's fees from an opponent in any form of civil litigation where fee-shifting is authorized, the same set of basic questions must be asked," including eligibility for fees; entitlement to fees, including factors such as the unreasonableness of government action or the benefit to the public derived from the case; the methods of measuring fees; and the timing and procedure of obtaining the fee award. *Id.* at 740–42.

> The basic concept of the "lodestar" is simple: the value of an attorney's work on a case is measured by (1) the number of hours that were reasonably expended on the litigation, multiplied by (2) a reasonable hourly rate. However, defining each of these two elements is somewhat more difficult.
>
> In general, an attorney is allowed compensation for time spent on any activity reasonably associated with the pursuit of the plaintiff's action for relief. This includes necessary administrative proceedings, pre-litigation activities, travel time, appellate work, post-judgment enforcement work, and time spent obtaining the attorney's fee award.
>
> * * *
>
> This is a case-by-case determination. The hours reasonably required to handle a matter will vary according to the novelty of the legal theories, the difficulty of the legal and factual issues, the complexity of the case, and the nature of the opposition. For example, it is appropriate to staff a complex case with more than one attorney, while a simple case may not justify employing the services of more than one attorney.
>
> * * *
>
> * * * [In] *City of Burlington v. Dague*, [505 U.S. 557 (1992),] the Supreme Court ruled that the lodestar may never be adjusted upward to compensate for the contingent risk of loss. * * *
>
> * * *
>
> Although the Supreme Court apparently has closed the door on upward adjustments of the lodestar, the Court emphatically has retained the option of adjusting the fee downward to reflect a plaintiff's limited success. Indeed, the Court has said that the degree of success obtained is "the most critical factor" in determining the reasonableness of a fee award. Unfortunately, the Court has provided little guidance on when less than perfect success triggers an adjustment or on how partial success should affect the lodestar figure. * * *
>
> * * *
>
> Just as fees are available for work performed in bringing the case on the merits to a successful conclusion, compensation also is available for legal fees incurred in applying for and securing an award of fees—what is sometimes called "fees for fees." * * *

Id. at 748, 750–51, 757, 760, 764.

Congress provides for the award of attorney fees as a matter of public policy. The following case illustrates the contrast between civil rights cases and the relationship between fees and damages in tort litigation and other areas of law.

CITY OF RIVERSIDE v. RIVERA

477 U.S. 561 (1986)

Justice BRENNAN announced the judgment of the Court and delivered an opinion in which Justice MARSHALL, Justice BLACKMUN, and Justice STEVENS join.

The issue presented in this case is whether an award of attorney's fees under 42 U.S.C. § 1988 is *per se* "unreasonable" within the meaning of the statute if it exceeds the amount of damages recovered by the plaintiff in the underlying civil rights action.

Respondents, eight Chicano individuals, attended a party on the evening of August 1, 1975, at the Riverside, California, home of respondents Santos and Jennie Rivera. A large number of unidentified police officers, acting without a warrant, broke up the party using tear gas and, as found by the District Court, "unnecessary physical force." Many of the guests, including four of the respondents, were arrested. The District Court later found that "[t]he party was not creating a disturbance in the community at the time of the break-in." Criminal charges against the arrestees were ultimately dismissed for lack of probable cause.

On June 4, 1976, respondents sued the city of Riverside, its Chief of Police, and 30 individual police officers under 42 U.S.C. §§ 1981, 1983, 1985(3), and 1986 for allegedly violating their First, Fourth, and Fourteenth Amendment rights. The complaint, which also alleged numerous state-law claims, sought damages and declaratory and injunctive relief. * * * The jury returned a total of 37 individual verdicts in favor of the respondents and against the city and five individual officers, finding 11 violations of § 1983, 4 instances of false arrest and imprisonment, and 22 instances of negligence. Respondents were awarded $33,350 in compensatory and punitive damages: $13,300 for their federal claims, and $20,050 for their state-law claims. [Respondents did not request injunctive relief, believing it redundant to ask that police obey the law. The Court indicated that the police behavior would have warranted an injunction.]

Respondents also sought attorney's fees and costs under § 1988. They requested compensation for 1,946.75 hours expended by their two attorneys at a rate of $125 per hour, and for 84.5 hours expended by law clerks at a rate of $25 per hour, a total of $245,456.25. The District Court found both the hours and rates reasonable, and awarded respondents $245,456.25 in attorney's fees. The court rejected respondents' request for certain additional expenses, and for a multiplier sought by respondents to reflect the contingent nature of their success and the high quality of their attorneys' efforts.

* * *

Hensley v. Eckerhart announced certain guidelines for calculating a reasonable attorney's fee under § 1988. *Hensley* stated that "[t]he most useful starting point for determining the amount of a reasonable fee is the number of hours reasonably expended on the litigation multiplied by a reasonable hourly rate." This figure, commonly referred to as the "lodestar," is presumed to be the reasonable fee contemplated by § 1988. The opinion cautioned that "[t]he district court . . . should exclude from this initial fee calculation hours that were not 'reasonably expended' " on the litigation.

Hensley then discussed other considerations that might lead the district court to adjust the lodestar figure upward or downward, including the "important factor of the 'results obtained.' " The opinion noted that where a prevailing plaintiff has succeeded on only some of his claims, an award of fees for time expended on unsuccessful claims may not be appropriate. In these situations, the Court held that the judge should consider whether or not the plaintiff's unsuccessful claims were related to the claims on which he succeeded, and whether the plaintiff achieved a level of success that makes it appropriate to award attorney's fees for hours reasonably expended on unsuccessful claims:

> "In [some] cases the plaintiff's claims for relief will involve a common core of facts or will be based on related legal theories. Much of counsel's time will be devoted generally to the litigation as a whole, making it difficult to divide the hours expended on a claim-by-claim basis. Such a lawsuit cannot be viewed as a series of discrete claims. Instead the district court should focus on the significance of the overall relief obtained by the plaintiff in relation to the hours reasonably expended on the litigation."

Accordingly, *Hensley* emphasized that "[w]here a plaintiff has obtained excellent results, his attorney should recover a fully compensatory fee," and that "the fee award should not be reduced simply because the plaintiff failed to prevail on every contention raised in the lawsuit." Petitioners argue that the District Court failed properly to follow *Hensley* in calculating respondents' fee award. We disagree. The District Court carefully considered the results obtained by respondents pursuant to the instructions set forth in *Hensley*, and concluded that respondents were entitled to recover attorney's fees for all hours expended on the litigation. First, the court found that "[t]he amount of time expended by counsel in conducting this litigation was reasonable and reflected sound legal judgment under the circumstances." The court also determined that counsel's excellent performances in this case entitled them to be compensated at prevailing market rates, even though they were relatively young when this litigation began. See *Johnson*, 488 F.2d, at 718–719 ("If a young attorney demonstrates the skill and ability, he should not be penalized for only recently being admitted to the bar").

The District Court then concluded that it was inappropriate to adjust respondents' fee award downward to account for the fact that respondents had prevailed only on some of their claims, and against only some of the defendants. The court first determined that "it was never actually clear what officer did what until we had gotten through with the

whole trial," so that "[u]nder the circumstances of this case, it was reasonable for plaintiffs initially to name thirty-one individual defendants ... as well as the City of Riverside as defendants in this action."
* * *

* * *

The District Court also considered the amount of damages recovered, and determined that the size of the damages award did not imply that respondents' success was limited:

> "[T]he size of the jury award resulted from (a) the general reluctance of jurors to make large awards against police officers, and (b) the dignified restraint which the plaintiffs exercised in describing their injuries to the jury. For example, although some of the actions of the police would clearly have been insulting and humiliating to even the most insensitive person and were, in the opinion of the Court, intentionally so, plaintiffs did not attempt to play up this aspect of the case."

The court paid particular attention to the fact that the case "presented complex and interrelated issues of fact and law," and that "[a] fee award in this civil rights action will ... advance the public interest:"

> "Counsel for plaintiffs ... served the public interest by vindicating important constitutional rights. Defendants had engaged in lawless, unconstitutional conduct, and the litigation of plaintiffs' case was necessary to remedy defendants' misconduct. Indeed, the Court was shocked at some of the acts of the police officers in this case and was convinced from the testimony that these acts were motivated by a general hostility to the Chicano community in the area where the incident occurred. The amount of time expended by plaintiffs' counsel in conducting this litigation was clearly reasonable and necessary to serve the public interest as well as the interests of plaintiffs in the vindication of their constitutional rights."

Finally, the District Court "focus[ed] on the significance of the overall relief obtained by [respondents] in relation to the hours reasonably expended on the litigation." The court concluded that respondents had "achieved a level of success in this case that makes the total number of hours expended by counsel a proper basis for making the fee award,"

> "Counsel for plaintiffs achieved excellent results for their clients, and their accomplishment in this case was outstanding. The amount of time expended by counsel in conducting this litigation was reasonable and reflected sound legal judgment under the circumstances."

Based on our review of the record, we agree with the Court of Appeals that the District Court's findings were not clearly erroneous. We conclude that the District Court correctly applied the factors announced in *Hensley* in calculating respondents' fee award, and that the court did not abuse its discretion in awarding attorney's fees for all time reasonably spent litigating the case.

Petitioners, joined by the United States as *amicus curiae*, maintain that *Hensley*'s lodestar approach is inappropriate in civil rights cases where a plaintiff recovers only monetary damages. In these cases, so the argument goes, use of the lodestar may result in fees that exceed the amount of damages recovered and that are therefore unreasonable. Likening such cases to private tort actions, petitioners and the United States submit that attorney's fees in such cases should be proportionate to the amount of damages a plaintiff recovers. Specifically, they suggest that fee awards in damages cases should be modeled upon the contingent-fee arrangements commonly used in personal injury litigation. In this case, assuming a 33% contingency rate, this would entitle respondents to recover approximately $11,000 in attorney's fees.

The amount of damages a plaintiff recovers is certainly relevant to the amount of attorney's fees to be awarded under § 1988. It is, however, only one of many factors that a court should consider in calculating an award of attorney's fees. We reject the proposition that fee awards under § 1988 should necessarily be proportionate to the amount of damages a civil rights plaintiff actually recovers.

As an initial matter, we reject the notion that a civil rights action for damages constitutes nothing more than a private tort suit benefiting only the individual plaintiffs whose rights were violated. Unlike most private tort litigants, a civil rights plaintiff seeks to vindicate important civil and constitutional rights that cannot be valued solely in monetary terms. * * * Regardless of the form of relief he actually obtains, a successful civil rights plaintiff often secures important social benefits that are not reflected in nominal or relatively small damages awards. In this case, for example, the District Court found that many of petitioners' unlawful acts were "motivated by a general hostility to the Chicano community," and that this litigation therefore served the public interest. * * *

In addition, the damages a plaintiff recovers contributes significantly to the deterrence of civil rights violations in the future. This deterrent effect is particularly evident in the area of individual police misconduct, where injunctive relief generally is unavailable.

* * *

A rule that limits attorney's fees in civil rights cases to a proportion of the damages awarded would seriously undermine Congress' purpose in enacting § 1988. Congress enacted § 1988 specifically because it found that the private market for legal services failed to provide many victims of civil rights violations with effective access to the judicial process. * * *

A rule of proportionality would make it difficult, if not impossible, for individuals with meritorious civil rights claims but relatively small potential damages to obtain redress from the courts. This is totally inconsistent with Congress' purpose in enacting § 1988. Congress recognized that private-sector fee arrangements were inadequate to ensure sufficiently vigorous enforcement of civil rights. In order to ensure that lawyers would be willing to represent persons with legitimate civil rights grievances, Congress determined that it would be necessary to compensate lawyers for all time reasonably expended on a case.

This case illustrates why the enforcement of civil rights laws cannot be entrusted to private-sector fee arrangements. The District Court observed that "[g]iven the nature of this lawsuit and the type of defense presented, many attorneys in the community would have been reluctant to institute and to continue to prosecute this action." The court concluded, moreover, that "[c]ounsel for plaintiffs achieved excellent results for their clients, and their accomplishment in this case was outstanding. The amount of time expended by counsel in conducting this litigation was reasonable and reflected sound legal judgment under the circumstances." Nevertheless, petitioners suggest that respondents' counsel should be compensated for only a small fraction of the actual time spent litigating the case. In light of the difficult nature of the issues presented by this lawsuit and the low pecuniary value of many of the rights respondents sought to vindicate, it is highly unlikely that the prospect of a fee equal to a fraction of the damages respondents might recover would have been sufficient to attract competent counsel. Moreover, since counsel might not have found it economically feasible to expend the amount of time respondents' counsel found necessary to litigate the case properly, it is even less likely that counsel would have achieved the excellent results that respondents' counsel obtained here. Thus, had respondents had to rely on private-sector fee arrangements, they might well have been unable to obtain redress for their grievances. It is precisely for this reason that Congress enacted § 1988.

We agree with petitioners that Congress intended that statutory fee awards be "adequate to attract competent counsel, but ... not produce windfalls to attorneys." However, we find no evidence that Congress intended that, in order to avoid "windfalls to attorneys," attorney's fees be proportionate to the amount of damages a civil rights plaintiff might recover. Rather, there already exists a wide range of safeguards designed to protect civil rights defendants against the possibility of excessive fee awards. * * *

* * *

In the absence of any indication that Congress intended to adopt a strict rule that attorney's fees under § 1988 be proportionate to damages recovered, we decline to adopt such a rule ourselves. The judgment of the Court of Appeals is hereby

Affirmed.

[The concurring opinion by Justice POWELL is omitted.]

* * *

Chief Justice BURGER, dissenting.

I join Justice REHNQUIST's dissenting opinion. I write only to add that it would be difficult to find a better example of legal nonsense than the fixing of attorney's fees by a judge at $245,456.25 for the recovery of $33,350 damages.

The two attorneys receiving this nearly quarter-million-dollar fee graduated from law school in 1973 and 1974; they brought this action in 1975, which resulted in the $33,350 jury award in 1980. Their total professional experience when this litigation began consisted of Gerald López' 1-year service as a law clerk to a judge and Roy Cazares' two years' experience as a trial attorney in the Defenders' Program of San Diego County. For their services the District Court found that an hourly rate of $125 per hour was reasonable.

* * *

Justice REHNQUIST, with whom THE CHIEF JUSTICE, Justice WHITE, and Justice O'CONNOR join, dissenting.

In *Hensley v. Eckerhart*, 461 U.S. 424, 433 (1983), our leading case dealing with attorney's fees awarded pursuant to 42 U.S.C. § 1988, we said that "[t]he most useful starting point for determining the amount of a reasonable fee is the number of hours reasonably expended on the litigation multiplied by a reasonable hourly rate." As if we had foreseen the case now before us, we went on to emphasize that "[t]he district court . . . should exclude from this initial fee calculation hours that were not 'reasonably expended' " on the litigation. * * *

* * *

[In a title dispute between A and B over Blackacre, surely] * * * a court would start from the proposition that, unless special arrangements were made between the client and the attorney, a "reasonable" attorney's fee for researching the title to a piece of property worth $10,000 could not exceed the value of the property. Otherwise the client would have been far better off never going to an attorney in the first place, and simply giving A $10,000 for a worthless deed. * * *

* * * If A has a claim for contract damages in the amount of $10,000 against B, and retains an attorney to prosecute the claim, it would be both extraordinary and unjustifiable, in the absence of any special arrangement, for the attorney to put in 200 hours on the case and send the client a bill for $25,000. Such a bill would be "unreasonable," regardless of whether A obtained a judgment against B for $10,000 or obtained a take-nothing judgment. And in such a case, where the prospective recovery is limited, it is exactly this "billing judgment" which enables the parties to achieve a settlement; any competent attorney, whether prosecuting or defending a contract action for $10,000, would realize that the case simply cannot justify a fee in excess of the potential recovery on the part of either the plaintiff's or the defendant's attorney. All of these examples illuminate the point made in *Hensley* that "the important factor" in determining a "reasonable" fee is the "results obtained." The very "reasonableness" of the hours expended on a case by a plaintiff's attorney necessarily will depend, to a large extent,

on the amount that may reasonably be expected to be recovered if the plaintiff prevails. * * *

Notes and Questions

1. Does the enactment of fee shifting provisions signal a tacit understanding by Congress of the power imbalance between "haves" and "have nots," described earlier by Galanter? Do such provisions, even with the inclusion of expert fees, go far enough to right that imbalance?

2. Is the dissent's example regarding contract damages relevant to the facts of this case? Should a case to vindicate constitutional rights require the same cost-effectiveness? Should the amount of damages recovered be central in evaluating reasonable attorney's fees in civil rights litigation? Should the legal energy expended on civil rights suits be proportionate to the compensatory damages available? What is the relationship between the compensatory damages available and the nature of harm to the individual and to society in a discrimination case or a case involving police brutality?

3. Does Justice Burger, dissenting, have a valid point that it is "legal nonsense" to fix attorney's fees at over $245,000 when the damage recovery was close to $33,000? Might he be peeved that young lawyers were recovering such fees? Should young lawyers recover fees at the same standard as more experienced attorneys?

4. Gerald López was one of the young lawyers who brought this case. As lawyers follow López's model of work with communities on social justice issues, what role might fee awards play in their decisions about legal practice?

Julie Davies interviewed civil rights lawyers to determine how Supreme Court decisions regarding rules fees for civil rights cases affected the practice of law and their ability to pursue civil rights claims. Davies explains that uncertainty about fees affects the decisions of attorneys despite the existence of fee-shifting statutes.

JULIE DAVIES

Federal Civil Rights Practice in the 1990's: The Dichotomy Between Reality and Theory
48 Hastings L.J. 197, 207–10, 231–36 (1997)

* * * Although many attorneys do pro bono work, attorneys who want to practice civil rights law must be able to earn a living. Thus, attorney compensation issues are central to gaining an understanding of how private enforcement works in addressing the problems that civil rights legislation was meant to tackle.

When Congress passed the Civil Rights Attorney's Fees Awards Act of 1976, the intent of the legislation was to encourage private attorneys to undertake representation of civil rights plaintiffs, and Congress thought that attorneys' fees would provide the needed incentive. This legislative modification of the "American Rule" made attorneys' fees available to prevailing plaintiffs who brought suit under a number of civil rights statutes, including 42 U.S.C. section 1983, which dates from the Reconstruction era, and more modern legislation, such as Title VI of the Civil Rights Act of 1964. Other modern civil rights legislation, such as the Voting Rights Act of 1965, Title VII, and the Americans with Disabilities Act, specifically authorizes attorneys' fees awards under provisions contained in those statutes. While the Reconstruction era civil rights statutes differ greatly from modern civil rights statutes, the economic viability of litigation under these statutes coalesces to the extent that suits under both types of statutes are financed by awards of attorneys' fees paid by losing defendants. In addition, the case law interpreting the Attorney's Fees Awards Act has been applied to the other statutory fee-shifting provisions.

Over the years, since Congress enacted the Attorney's Fees Awards Act, the Supreme Court has decided many cases dealing with attorneys' fees in civil rights cases, and in recent years, the Court has increased the number of cases it hears dealing with fees, rendering decisions on discrete issues. Although the Court has furthered fee awards in unanimous or nearly unanimous opinions in some instances, other decisions reveal deep divisions between the justices and have resulted in majority rulings that seem at odds with Congress' intent to encourage attorneys to take civil rights cases. * * * Knowing in theory the impact these decisions would have, I designed a study to evaluate whether they have affected the willingness and ability of attorneys to undertake federal civil rights litigation.

* * *

Many types of civil rights actions seek damages from the defendant. In the area of constitutional litigation, the Supreme Court held in *Carey v. Piphus* [435 U.S. 247 (1978)] that compensatory damages are to be awarded for constitutional violations only on proof of actual injury. Juries may not assume damage or award damages simply to vindicate a right. * * *

In theory, constraints on damages should not deter plaintiffs' attorneys from agreeing to represent plaintiffs with low damages. The availability of statutory attorneys' fees should serve to reassure counsel that they will be compensated even if the plaintiff recovers little. The Supreme Court confirmed that attorneys' fees need not be proportional to the plaintiff's damages in City of *Riverside v. Rivera*. * * * The decision was crucial to civil rights litigators because monetary awards in civil rights claims are often lower than claims in tort actions due to the lack of large compensatory damages.

In the context of constitutional litigation, it can be difficult to obtain compensatory damages for what many jurors view as dignitary injuries. * * * Injuries like those sustained by the *Rivera* plaintiffs may appear less serious to jurors because they do not involve personal injury or at least not injury of the magnitude that makes for lucrative personal injury claims.

* * * [E]mployment practitioners interviewed unequivocally asserted that the amount of damages is a primary consideration in deciding whether to take a case. It is entirely possible that a low or middle income individual could suffer job discrimination that would create some economic loss and constitute a significant career barrier yet not present enormous emotional distress damage or warrant punitives. * * * [P]laintiffs with low value cases may have difficulty obtaining an attorney due to the relationship between fees and damages in the settlement context.

Even in cases where the plaintiff prevails at trial, low damages can bear some relationship to an award of statutory fees. In *Farrar v. Hobby*, [506 U.S. 103 (1992)] the Supreme Court held that in some circumstances a plaintiff who formally "prevails" under 42 U.S.C. section 1988 but receives only nominal damages should receive no attorneys' fees at all. The Court believed that, in a case like *Farrar*, where equitable relief was not at issue, the plaintiff's success had to be measured in monetary terms. The jury's failure to award more than nominal damages thus suggested that the plaintiff was not successful, despite the nominal victory. Although the facts of *Farrar* were somewhat unique,[204] the decision suggests that perhaps the Court is retreating from the non-proportionality rule of *Rivera*. * * * In light of the damages rules themselves and the emerging glimmer of doubt regarding the non-proportionality rule in *Rivera*, I asked participants if a plaintiff's low damages would deter them from taking an otherwise meritorious case, and if they thought the decision would have any effect on the practice of civil rights law or in their practice in particular.

The responses of participants in this study indicate that the damages rules profoundly limit the willingness of attorneys to take cases with low damages. This is so despite the non-proportionality rule in *Rivera*. Attorneys not only mentioned their reluctance to handle cases regarding employment, police misconduct, and prisoner litigation, but also expressed such reluctance in connection with First Amendment and other constitutional litigation and cases brought under Title VII. The reason for the apparent disparity between theory (plaintiff's damages should not affect fees) and reality (they do) is that many cases will settle, and despite the Supreme Court decisions, the amount of money allocated for the attorneys' fee award is, in fact, somewhat proportional to the damages in issue. Thus, while defense lawyers add fees to a settlement offer, they figure them as part of a lump sum package, and the lower the compensatory damages in issue, the lower the fee award. While plaintiffs' attorneys, of course, retain and sometimes exercise the prerogative of counseling a client not to accept a settlement offer because any award for fees would be extremely low, ethical constraints, pessimism about the

204. In *Farrar*, the plaintiff filed a lawsuit seeking 17 million dollars from six defendants. After ten years of litigation, including two appeals, he received one dollar from one defendant. The Court found that the suit would benefit no one besides the plaintiff.

prospects of full payment if fees are awarded by a court, the prospect of lengthy delays in payment, and the risk of not prevailing at all, often lead the attorney to concur that settlement is a better option.

Again, from a theoretical perspective, the fact that these trade-offs are made is not unique to civil rights litigation. Settlements necessarily involve compromise—a goal specifically embraced by the Supreme Court in cases like [*Evans v.*] *Jeff D.* [475 U.S. 717 (1986), in which the Supreme Court held that civil rights lawyers could, within the rules of ethics, be asked to waive their fees as part of negotiating the settlement of a case]. In actuality, the damages rules, combined with the propriety of partial fee waivers, produce a result in some cases that seems contrary to what the Supreme Court intended. Lawyers in a variety of practices unequivocally assert that some types of civil rights cases are not economically feasible and that they will not take them unless they are interested in pro bono work. For example, in the area of employment discrimination, a number of lawyers stated that cases of low wage earners (typically blue collar workers) are not considered economically feasible unless there is excellent proof of emotional distress or a potential for punitive damages. Sexual harassment of a low wage earner might present a promising claim, but denial of a promotion or termination would not. The claim that low damages make it very difficult to represent potential plaintiffs was asserted in differing contexts as well: prisoner litigation, police misconduct litigation, and other types of constitutional litigation.

A number of the attorneys I interviewed indicated that they do represent plaintiffs with low damages. Non-profit organizations litigating for impact clearly take such cases. For them, the significance of rules limiting damages to actual injury is that cases are difficult to refer to the private bar. Class action attorneys also are able to represent people in the working class who have low individual damages claims. However, there are not many firms doing class action work. Barring these options, blue collar workers terminated from employment or people who have suffered police brutality but emerged with soft tissue injuries must find private lawyers who are willing to take their cases despite the low potential recovery. Some lawyers will undertake this work, although I did not encounter many.

The lawyers I met who are willing to represent low wage earners or other plaintiffs with low damages in a non-class action context appeared to operate very close to the margin of economic survival. * * * More commonly, attorneys take a small number of low damage cases on principle or diversify their workload so that they can subsidize the cases that they know will not make money. Despite the existence of individual attorneys whose choice of cases is driven more by ideological commitment than money, the plaintiffs' damages were a factor many survey participants viewed as extremely important in determining what cases they wanted to accept.

* * *

If *Rivera* is undermined, attorneys will be even less likely to take cases in which the injuries suffered are not severe and in which damages awarded are not high. As one city attorney defending section 1983 police misconduct cases noted, even in the event of a death, damages may be low because the plaintiffs may have no earning history or other factors to substantiate an award under current damages rules. Attorneys' fees often comprise the largest part of such claims. If these fees can be reduced, or made proportionate to recovery, civil rights attorneys will have little incentive to bring the cases. Defense attorneys who now settle such cases because the attorneys' fees component is a wild card may instead opt to try them and hope for the best.

Notes and Questions

1. A central theme in *Rivera* and in Davies' argument is that damages in civil rights violations differ from tort damages. Constitutional violations may affect freedom, privacy, or equality without generating the scale of damages often seen in tort suits. Does society face particular dangers if civil rights lawyers have incentive only to bring cases that are rich in tort-like damages?

2. In Buckhannon Board and Care Home, Inc. v. West Virginia Department of Health and Human Resources, 532 U.S. 598 (2001), the Supreme Court defined "prevailing party" narrowly to bar the shifting of attorney fees in cases in which the plaintiff's lawsuit was the "catalyst" that forced the defendant to change the challenged practice.

> In designating those parties eligible for an award of litigation costs, Congress employed the term "prevailing party," a legal term of art. * * *
>
> In *Hanrahan v. Hampton*, 446 U.S. 754, 758 (1980) (*per curiam*), we reviewed the legislative history of § 1988 and found that "Congress intended to permit the interim award of counsel fees only when a party has prevailed on the merits of at least some of his claims." Our "[r]espect for ordinary language requires that a plaintiff receive at least some relief on the merits of his claim before he can be said to prevail." *Hewitt v. Helms*, 482 U.S. 755, 760 (1987). We have held that even an award of nominal damages suffices under this test.
>
> In addition to judgments on the merits, we have held that settlement agreements enforced through a consent decree may serve as the basis for an award of attorney's fees. See *Maher v. Gagne*, 448 U.S. 122 (1980). Although a consent decree does not always include an admission of liability by the defendant, it nonetheless is a court-ordered "chang[e][in] the legal relationship between [the plaintiff] and the defendant." *Texas State Teachers Assn. v. Garland Independent School Dist.*, 489 U.S. 782, 792 (1989). These decisions, taken together, establish that enforceable judgments on the merits and court-ordered consent decrees create the "material alteration of the

> legal relationship of the parties" necessary to permit an award of attorney's fees. * * *
>
> We think, however, the "catalyst theory" falls on the other side of the line from these examples. It allows an award where there is no judicially sanctioned change in the legal relationship of the parties. Even under a limited form of the "catalyst theory," a plaintiff could recover attorney's fees if it established that the "complaint had sufficient merit to withstand a motion to dismiss for lack of jurisdiction or failure to state a claim on which relief may be granted." This is not the type of legal merit that our prior decisions, based upon plain language and congressional intent, have found necessary. Indeed, we held in *Hewitt* that an interlocutory ruling that reverses a dismissal for failure to state a claim "is not the stuff of which legal victories are made." 482 U.S., at 760. A defendant's voluntary change in conduct, although perhaps accomplishing what the plaintiff sought to achieve by the lawsuit, lacks the necessary judicial *imprimatur* on the change. Our precedents thus counsel against holding that the term "prevailing party" authorizes an award of attorney's fees *without* a corresponding alteration in the legal relationship of the parties.

Buckhannon, 532 U.S. at 603–05.

How will *Buckhannon* affect the ability of social justice lawyers to take on civil rights cases? Will defendants simply engage in illegal behavior until they are sued, change their behavior, and refuse to negotiate further, forcing civil rights attorneys into uncompensated law enforcement?

The *Buckhannon* opinion rejected the plaintiff's argument that the "catalyst theory" was important to prevent defendants from changing challenged practices and making challenges moot, even though that was precisely what had happened in that case. The Court stated that a defendant would still have an incentive to enter settlement agreements, which could include negotiating attorney fees, because it was "well settled that a defendant's voluntary cessation of a challenged practice does not deprive a federal court of its power to determine the legality of the practice" unless it is "absolutely clear that the allegedly wrongful behavior could not reasonably be expected to recur." *Id.* at 1842–43 (quoting Friends of Earth, Inc. v. Laidlaw Environmental Services (TOC), Inc., 528 U.S. 167, 189 (2000)).

How much effort goes into the preparation of a civil rights lawsuit? Would a less thoroughly prepared suit be as likely to cause a defendant to change practices and comply with civil rights laws? If attorney fees become uncertain or impossible because of a change in defendants' practices induced by the lawsuit—and if low-income plaintiffs cannot pay attorney fees on their own—how will social justice lawyers be able to afford to do the work involved in these lawsuits? Does *Buckhannon* mean simply that civil rights lawyers must attend to the formality of a consent decree, or has it strengthened the negotiation position of defendants?

3. Herbert Eastman, a former civil rights attorney, comments on the special pleading obligations in civil rights cases. He writes "from the recurring disappointment and frustration I have felt after consultation with clients in cases presenting outrages that * * * cried out to heaven." Herbert A. Eastman, *Speaking Truth to Power: The Language of Civil Rights Litigators*, 104 Yale L.J. 763, 766 (1995). Eastman argues that pleading should present a thicker, more detailed story on behalf of the clients. In reviewing an inadequate complaint, he observed:

> * * * I could barely see over the chasm separating what those clients told me about their lives and what I wrote to the court as factual allegations in the complaint—sterile recitations of dates and events that lost so much in the translation. [What is missing?] Details, of course. Passion, certainly, but more than that. We lose the identity of the person harmed, the story of [the clients' lives]. But even more is lost. This was a class action aimed at remedying a systemic problem harming thousands, over generations. The complaint omits the social chemistry underneath the events normally invisible to the law—events that create the injury or compound it. In this complaint, we lose the fullness of the harm done, the scale of the deprivations, the humiliation of the plaintiff class members, the damage to greater society, the significance of it all.

Id. Eastman includes his original, traditional complaint, *id.* at 865–79, to demonstrate the contrast between that document and his revised, thicker complaint, *id.* at 836–49. The thicker complaint includes stories from the lives of the plaintiffs, sometimes told in their own words, and stories from the history of the community. Compare Eastman's complaints and consider how you would feel about filing a similar complaint in federal court. How would you feel about proposing such a complaint to your supervisor? Eastman enumerates obstacles that you would face, including constraints of: (1) pleading rules, (2) professional standards and practice, (3) legal education, (4) professional roles, (5) culture, (6) hierarchy, (7) language, and (8) self-preservation. *Id.* at 789–805. Regardless of the type of representation, social justice lawyers often face these constraints. Thus, it is important to consider how you can overcome them.

4. Should attorneys' fees be awarded to prevailing *defendants* in civil rights cases? In Hensley v. Eckerhart, 461 U.S. 424, 429, n. 2 (1983), the Court explained: "A prevailing defendant may recover an attorney's fee only where the suit was vexatious, frivolous, or brought to harass or embarrass the defendant." Does this standard provide sufficient protection to plaintiffs? Might the American rule, leaving parties to bear their own costs, have originated to avoid protracted fee litigation, adding litigation to litigation?

Chapter 3

SOCIAL JUSTICE LAWYERS IN CONTEXT

Legal practice for social justice takes many forms. Whether serving individual clients, like Maria Elena, introduced by Gerald López in chapter 1, or helping community organizations opposing toxic waste dumps or evictions, or seeking community economic development, or performing any other of the myriad representational tasks associated with social justice, lawyers engaged in this practice face issues about their own roles in relation to the work. This chapter presents different models of legal practice for social justice and discusses the ongoing issues that lawyers engaged in this practice encounter. *See* chapter 2 for a discussion of the legal services movement, private practices aimed at social justice, and issues related to funding those practices. *See* chapter 11 for further reflection on the roles of lawyers involved with social change and transformation.

Recurrent issues for lawyers interested in practice for social justice include: definition of the parameters of the lawyers' role; identification of the client; the challenge of assisting in community empowerment; how to make strategic choices between legislative action, litigative remedies, and other bureaucratic or administrative options; and how to measure the effectiveness of the chosen strategy. For an excellent compilation of resources on legal work and social change, see Loretta Price & Melinda Davis, *Seeds of Change: A Bibliographic Introduction to Law and Organizing*, 26 N.Y.U. Rev. of L. & Soc. Change 615 (2000–01).

SECTION 1. REFLECTIONS ON SOCIAL JUSTICE LAWYERING

Consider as you read this chapter, what your own vision of legal practice for social justice might be. Dean Hill Rivkin introduces social justice lawyering, with an historic perspective and look to the future. Rivkin describes three unresolved themes for lawyers working with communities: the lawyer-client relation, the role of rights-based litigation, and the direction of the next generation of community advocacy.

Chapter 5 more fully explores the lawyer-client relation. Chapters 7, 8, and 9 consider the efficacy of framing claims in the language of rights and the role that litigation and organizing can play in social justice struggles. This chapter explores directions for community lawyering. The following section examines issues faced by social justice lawyers, particularly those who represent communities, groups, and organizations.

DEAN HILL RIVKIN

Reflections on Lawyering for Reform: Is the Highway Alive Tonight?
64 Tenn. L. Rev. 1065, 1065–69, 1072 (1997)

There is a kaleidoscope of images about the roles that lawyers have played over the years in social reform litigation. I think of civil rights lawyers, ACLU lawyers, poverty lawyers—those who practiced in an era not too long ago when these terms and the vocations they described were not contested. It was not that there was no room at the time for serious critique, but there seemed to be an unproblematic understanding of mission and purpose. Not only were there accepted assumptions about strategies and tactics, but also there were unspoken understandings about the way those who practiced in these fields would evolve. Thus, Arthur Kinoy's "people's lawyer," "movement" lawyers, and law collectives gave way—though not in any linear sense—to public interest lawyers, to Lucie White's third dimensional lawyers, to Louise Trubek's critical lawyers, and to Gerald López's rebellious collaborative lawyers. A clinical colleague from Pakistan calls such lawyers "saint lawyers."

These lawyers engaged in law reform litigation, political lawyering, grassroots advocacy, case aggregation strategies, anti-regnant lawyering, focused case representation, and even "petty disturbances." * * * Using well-accepted rhetoric these lawyers—and I include myself among them—lawyered to vindicate rights, to empower people, to change institutions * * * , and to achieve social change and social justice. We were accused by many of trying to save the world, of being lawyers for causes, not clients.

We strove to write elegant complaints and briefs that told compelling stories, believing that a good story, told with passion, could liberate its subject. We used discovery to bring CEOs to the table. We tried to use legal rules expressively. We were share-bargaining negotiators, furious advocates for our causes and, usually, for our clients. We became players in events that we thought we could (and sometimes did) control. In the office, we worked to be anti-hierarchical, reflective, consensus builders, people who valued community. Our values shaped our aspirations, which in turn shaped our values.

Where are we today? The first observation to make is that there may not be a "we." By this I do not mean to say that we do not exist, or that the survival of activist lawyers depends on government funding, which is in jeopardy in insidious ways. What I mean when I question the cohesiveness of today's reform lawyers is that the concept often does not capture in a meaningful way the diversity that is slowly evolving in the settings where lawyering for reform must take place today—in communities, in neighborhoods, or in familiar institutions, such as schools. Today, there are * * * interlocking themes about lawyering for reform that remain in deep tension, but whose resolution is central if lawyers who care about social change are to transform themselves to adapt to the complex needs of clients, communities, and democracy.

Let me discuss what I perceive to be some of the most important unresolved themes. First, the heightened struggle over our relationships with our clients is a perplexing theme. In days past, reform lawyers genuinely believed that, by virtue of the lawyer-client relationship, they were entitled to be their client's voice. * * * Today, we question anyone's right * * * to speak for those who have not spoken for themselves. Nonetheless, in spite of our sensitivity, we find it enormously hard not to silence and disable clients through our empathy and compassion, much less our distance and, yes, despair. There are theories of empowerment, strategies for dealing with differences, empathy training—they help—but the tensions in the lawyer-client relationship in reform litigation—whether in a class action or an individual case—persist.

Second, rights-based litigation strategies to achieve reform, at least in the academy, have achieved the status of a dysfunctional family member, but one who often speaks the truth. We have absorbed the critique of rights, how the assertion of rights alienates, polarizes, and, in the end, creates a backlash that nullifies the gains that the litigation achieved. Painfully, we see years of work in prisoners' rights litigation, for example, dissipate in the face of escalating rates of incarceration, disproportionately for African-American youth and men, prison construction programs that are the centerpiece of the new New Deal, and a deluge of punitive criminal and juvenile legislation * * * that mock notions of change that informed the agenda supporting prisoners' rights. In field after field—mental health, death penalty defense, welfare—the paradigms of reform that we thought we had constructed have crumbled.

But for litigators who have real clients with immediate issues, abandoning rights-based strategies just is not acceptable in the short run. Rights still possess strong symbolic meaning for people who are in trouble, and, frankly, the denigration of lawyers who assert rights in litigation often comes across as a bit elitist. This is an area where we need much more collaboration among academic theorists, lawyers on the front line, and, yes, clients and communities.

Finally, there is a growing feeling that the reform lawyering of the past should be supplanted by a versatile, multi-layered advocacy more characterized by community, compromise, and conversation; that the ethic of resistance that characterized reform litigation in the past should be replaced by an ethic of connections—one of building alliances and creating alternative institutions, not engaging in guerrilla warfare.

* * *

[The author discusses a project, based on his representation of the Yellow Creek Concerned Citizens, a citizens' organization in far southeast Kentucky, that formed in 1980 to halt toxic pollution. The project will explore issues and dynamics in community-based litigation.]

* * * Charting a new course down the highway, and always questioning whether the road needs to be built and how, are the challenges.

Notes and Questions

1. Rivkin names a number of well-known "saint lawyers." *See* Arthur Kinoy, *Rights on Trial: The Odyssey of a People's Lawyer* (1983). Lucie White's discussion of third dimensional lawyers and Gerald López's of rebellious lawyers appear later in this chapter. Louise G. Trubek discusses critical lawyering in Louise G. Trubek, *Critical Lawyering: Toward a New Public Interest Practice*, 1 B.U. Pub. Int. L.J. 49, 50–56 (1991). *See* the Trubek excerpt in chapter 2, for a description of practices representing subordinated people. *See also* Ed Sparer, *Fundamental Human Rights, Legal Entitlements, and the Social Struggle: A Friendly Critique of the Critical Legal Studies Movement*, 36 Stan. L. Rev. 509 (1984); Gary Bellow and Bea Moulton, *The Lawyering Process: Materials for Clinical Instruction in Advocacy* (1978); and Anthony V. Alfieri, *Practicing Community*, 107 Harv. L. Rev. 1747 (1994).

2. Literature on the theoretics of practice discusses how legal education may fail to prepare lawyers to deal with differences between community and client goals, the legal and administrative structures in which disputes are resolved, as well as the dynamics between lawyers and clients. *See, e.g.*, Anthony V. Alfieri, *The Antinomies of Poverty Law and a Theory of Dialogic Empowerment*, 16 N.Y.U. Rev. L. & Soc. Change 659 (1989); Lucie E. White, *Subordination, Rhetorical Survival Skills, and Sunday Shoes: Notes on the Hearing of Mrs. G*, 38 Buff. L. Rev. 1 (1990); Christopher P. Gilkerson, *Theoretics of Practice: The Integration of Progressive Thought and Action—Poverty Law Narrative: The Critical Practice and Theory of Receiving and Translating Client Stories*, 43 Hastings L.J. 861(1992); Robert D. Dinerstein, *A Meditation on the Theoretics of Practice*, 43 Hastings L.J. 971 (1992).

3. Rivkin questions whether there is a "we" of activist lawyers, noting even on a definitional basis that many competing titles describe the work that they do. The lack of agreement about titles reflects a lack of consensus about the work itself. Michael Diamond offers this definition, characterizing these lawyers as "community lawyers:"

> The practice is located in poor, disempowered, and subordinated communities and is dedicated to serving the communities' goals. The community lawyer is one whose commitment to this practice includes collaborative interaction with members of the community.

Michael Diamond, *Community Lawyering: Revisiting the Old Neighborhood*, 32 Colum. Hum. Rts. L. Rev. 67, 75 (2000).

Shauna Marshall concurs, defining community lawyering as practice "premised upon the belief that one way to remedy certain types of problems in poor communities is for the community to be an integral part of the development and implementation of the solutions to those problems." Shauna I. Marshall, *Mission Impossible?: Ethical Community Lawyering*, 7 Clinical L. Rev. 147, 147 (2000).

4. Michael Diamond describes three models of community lawyers. The collaborative model seeks to break down "barriers between the 'professional' and the client from within subordinated groups. The characteristic of the collaborative model is that attorneys become, as much as possible, a part of the community they serve, and they educate clients to be able to advocate for themselves. At the same time, clients educate attorneys about how to use their skills more effectively to meet client goals." Diamond, *supra* at 89–90.

Proponents of the client-centered model, Diamond's second category, believe it offers "the greatest opportunity to achieve the benefits of collective action while protecting the autonomy of group members." *Id.* at 99. *See* chapter 5 for additional discussion of client-centered lawyering.

Facilitative lawyering, the third model Diamond describes, seeks to provide "only the specific legal assistance sought by the client without creating client dependency. By restricting the lawyer's activities to legal and indirect supportive tasks, the facilitative model purports to maintain client autonomy." *Id.* at 101.

Diamond critiques these models and offers a fourth: "the more active activist." *Id.* at 109. He notes:

> There is substantial agreement among progressive commentators that political, economic, and social factors are inherent in the problems of subordination and so intertwined with the legal issues as to be inseparable from them. Thus, by identifying these problems as discretely "legal," one either condemns the resulting attempts at resolution or provides only piecemeal and temporary respite from their effects.

Id. Diamond's activist lawyer:

> includes several aspects of the collaborative and client-centered models but it goes further in describing the role of a community lawyer. The activist lawyer not only interacts with the client on a non-hierarchical basis, but also participates with the client in the planning and implementation of strategies that are designed to build power for the client and allow the client to be a repeat player at the political bargaining table. The activist lawyer views the client's world in broader terms than merely its legal implications. He or she not only considers the political, economic, and social factors of the client's problem, but assists the client in developing and implementing enduring solutions, legal and non-legal, to these problems and to similar problems that may arise in the future.

> It is not enough for lawyers merely to be non-hierarchical professionals who engage with clients on terms of social equality. Nor is it enough for lawyers merely to be technicians correcting the legal defects in the structure of a client's existence. It is not even enough for a lawyer to act aggressively to enforce a client's legal rights or to create new ones. The law, on its own, fails to provide the kind of long term relief that the poor and subordinated client needs. Activist lawyers must recognize this fact and shift their focus from the limited prospect of the law to the greater potential of a truly cross-disciplinary and pro-active political assault on oppression. While the law may be a necessary weapon in that struggle, it is not a sufficient one.

Id. at 109–10.

Do Diamond's models describe all the potential roles for lawyers seeking social justice? Which roles do you view as essential? Is the community element a critical component? Which models would you reject?

5. Rivkin mentions the American Civil Liberties Union (ACLU) lawyer as one example of lawyers who have played a role in social reform litigation. Diamond expressly excludes ACLU lawyers from his definition of progressive lawyers. Diamond describes ACLU lawyers as public interest lawyers, but defines a progressive lawyer as one who "employs a particular set of political values in his or her practice to empower the poor or subordinated." Diamond, *supra* at 67, n. 1. What do you make of these different views about the meaning of progressive or social change lawyers? Does it reflect a tempest in a teapot or is it a dispute about values in community lawyering?

SECTION 2. WORKING WITH COMMUNITIES AND ORGANIZATIONS

The lawyers in this section are all committed to working with communities as their clients struggle to change their lives. Why do these lawyers believe that the community is central to lawyering for social justice? What special problems do lawyers face because they have a community orientation? On what aspects of this work do they agree or disagree?

A. Contrasting Conventional and Unconventional Roles

Margaret Russell observes:

> Lawyers working for social change have always yearned to "make a difference" in people's lives as well as in the legal systems in which they must operate. From the underground railroad to the civil rights movement, from struggles for suffrage to coalitions for reproductive choice, progressive lawyers have grappled with the structural and ideological contradictions of their roles as both insurgents and gatekeepers of the status quo.

Margaret M. Russell, *Entering Great America: Reflections on Race and the Convergence of Progressive Legal Theory and Practice*, 43 Hastings L.J. 749, 749 (1992).

How can lawyers balance the contradictions in these insurgent and gatekeeper roles, while working with communities struggling for social change?

This section contrasts traditional and nontraditional attorney roles. Gerald López presents five attorneys through the eyes of a law student, seeking her place in social justice practice. Sophie and Amos, his examples of social justice lawyers worth emulating—"rebellious lawyers"—generated much dialogue on the lawyer's role. *See, e.g.*, Marshall, *supra*; Anthony V. Alfieri, *Practicing Community*, 107 Harv. L. Rev. 1747 (1994) (reviewing Gerald P. López, *Rebellious Lawyering: One Chicano's Vision of Progressive Law Practice* (1992)); Ruth Margaret Buchanan, *Context, Continuity, and Difference in Poverty Law Scholarship*, 48 U. Miami L. Rev. 999 (1994); Ann Southworth, *Taking the Lawyer Out of Progressive Lawyering*, 46 Stan. L. Rev. 213 (1993).

GERALD P. LÓPEZ

Rebellious Lawyering: One Chicano's Vision of Progressive Law Practice 11–14, 17–18, 20–21, 23, 30–38 (1992)

Let me tell you about Catharine. * * * [Catharine was a student who would] fit right in with some of the best progressive students that I've had over the years. She's young, smart, industrious, unassuming, motivated, and vocationally committed to doing left activist work as a lawyer. * * * She unashamedly describes herself as wanting to help radically change the world.

[She had volunteered, while in high school, at a local soup kitchen. In college she tutored low-income middle school students, and after graduation she worked in a homeless shelter. After two summers during law school working with progressive organizations she is] * * * at a loss as to where to begin her career.

* * *

* * * Catharine receives advice. Look for a job with one of the high-profile groups that focus on impact litigation—they do good, important work, and besides, after that, a lot of doors will open to you. (Her father a private big-firm attorney with liberal leanings, supports her decision to go into public interest law, but he thinks she should work first for a large firm, "just for a few years, 'so that she can get "proper training." ' ")

One way to approach her dilemma, Catharine decided, is to think about the lawyers she knows, in terms of what she admires about them and their practice and, conversely, what she hasn't found so impressive. Through her work, she's certainly met a lot of different types of lawyers. Some are nationally known and widely respected in their fields; others are far less noticed, but nonetheless remarkable in the work that they do. Of these, there are five she has particularly admired. * * *

* * * Three of them practice in ways that come to mind when we imagine left, liberal, or progressive legal work. But the other two are certainly less seen, certainly less known, and rarely if ever appreciated outside of the world in which they work. And yet to them and to those with whom they work, that doesn't seem to make a bit of difference. [López describes the three lawyers, Teresa, Abe, Jonathan, whose practices illustrate the regnant view of lawyering for underrepresented and subordinated groups. Recall John Calmore's description of regnant lawyers, excerpted in chapter 1.]

* * *

* * * [Teresa works for Advocates for Justice, a public interest law firm, and] remains thoroughly dedicated to winning legal rights for the poor, people of color, and other oppressed groups. She works long hours preparing and litigating cases, she enjoys mastering and presenting highly intricate legal arguments, and she often appears before prestigious federal courts. Although she used to win all the time, she has found it increasingly difficult to get decisions that really serve as landmark cases. * * *

Teresa is committed to the idea of broad-based social change through representation of subordinated groups in the courts. Though she started out representing mainly Latino clients, Advocates for Justice now aims to secure rights and attract attention to a wide range of progressive causes. She and her colleagues facilitate group representation through class actions and other large-scale "test case" litigation, and they are justifiably proud of the numerous cases they have brought on behalf of accused criminals, welfare recipients, victims of school segregation, mentally disabled patients, women seeking abortions, and undocumented children. * * *

[Advocates for Justice mobilizes litigation resources behind the legal claims of the weak, but Teresa says that linking litigation with other strategies is a luxury she cannot regularly afford. She lacks knowledge of social welfare agencies, grassroots organizations, research centers, self-help groups, and other potential resources.]

* * * [Abe, partner in a small union-side labor firm is committed to defending the rights and expanding the power of organized labor.] Abe feels real sympathy for the individuals who call his firm with employment problems. At the same time, however, he feels a constant pressure to maintain the firm's profits. His firm accepts clients based largely on the ability to pay up front and the potential for a long-term relationship with the firm, and he feels badly that he and his co-workers often have to refer needy workers elsewhere. Over the years, the firm has represented mostly local labor unions. Though the firm prides itself in taking only labor side cases, the degree to which Abe and the other partners are insiders with union leadership—and what that connection seems to mean to them and their work—came as a surprise to Catharine.

Abe and his colleagues do nearly all the legal work that unions generate: They provide legal advice; negotiate collective bargaining agreements; represent the union in arbitration and proceedings before the National Labor Relations Board (usually against the employer, but sometimes against workers who sue the union for breach of the duty of fair representation); manage the pension fund; and litigate as it becomes necessary and if it doesn't swallow up too much of the firm's limited resources. The firm once did a fair amount of wrongful termination work for non-union workers but over the years decreased this part of the practice because it wasn't very profitable.

* * * When all is said and done, Abe finds himself regularly doing almost exactly what union leadership wants. [It does not bother Abe that union leadership sometimes resists rank-and-file initiatives, such as a recent effort by women of color to organize a reproductive rights workshop. While he views the needs and interests of workers as his ultimate concern, time pressures confine his attention to what is "legally relevant" to the particular matter at hand. He does not work with the union on education projects. Like Teresa, he dismisses or fails to notice opportunities for collaboration with others.]

* * *

* * * Jonathan is what Catharine has always imagined a "real poverty lawyer" to be. He works very hard under serious time constraints, and he effectively handles cases for a number of different clients at the same time. He is numbed by the repetitive nature of the problems he faces and irritated (often unconsciously) by the fact that he is not taken seriously by society or the legal community. * * *

Jonathan is 29, thoroughly committed to helping poor people, and zealous in his dislike of those strongly implicated in the oppression—welfare bureaucrats, landlords, and the like. He feels overwhelmed by the number of people who come into his office with housing problems. Most of them face evictions that cannot be legally prevented. The single mother of two being evicted because she cannot pay the rent; the man of 80 against whom a default judgment has already been obtained. Jonathan has deep sympathy for all of the people who come in with housing problems. Yet, because of the sheer numbers involved, he told Catharine he has to accept clients by the "triage" method, selecting the "healthiest" cases for representation but commiserating with those who have no defense.

Jonathan sees part of his mission as educating the community about housing law. He does this in several ways. With those he cannot help, Catharine has often seen him spend time explaining in plain, lay language what has happened to them, how they can try to forestall eviction for a few days, and how to avoid having this happen to them again. With cases that he does accept for representation, he always takes time with the client (usually right before settlement) to make sure that the client understands her or his legal rights, the legal issues in the case, and what to do if faced again with an eviction (usually to get to a lawyer as quickly as possible).

But because of time pressure and, frankly, his own low opinion about the good sense or intelligence of some of his clients, he hardly ever asks them to help him gather information, to identify and choose among strategies, to read the materials he prepares for them, to look at the law, to help fill out any of the forms, to take part in (much less lead) meetings and negotiations. In fact, when Catharine attempted to involve clients actively in their cases, Jonathan discouraged her, saying, "It never works—they can't do it right," and "It's much faster if you do it yourself." Even when the client performed well, Jonathan brushed it off as a "rare exception."

* * *

It's not obvious to Catharine that Teresa, Abe, and Jonathan have much in common with each other. Their philosophies on how to change the world diverge considerably. Their methods vary widely. And those with whom they work come from different walks of life, however much they all purport to help those subordinated by social and political life (though they might not use those terms). Still, it may be that these lawyers share more than she might be able to put her finger on. It may be that it is exactly those things that they share that best capture what I call the regnant idea of practice. And it may be those very commonalities that Catharine is struggling against.

Catharine's anxieties are similar to those faced by a number of beginning practitioners trying to find their place in activist circles. Just feeling that you want to change the world doesn't always mean that there's a simple way to know where or how to start. As a beginning practitioner, you expect your vocation to animate and fit quite neatly into your radical ambitions. Yet, in exploring options and thinking about how through your own work you can best help change the world, you run up against a deeply rooted conception of activist lawyers and activist lawyering that seems pretty fundamentally at odds with your own gut sense of what it means to live out your vocation. Even when you try to fight off this dominant conception, you most often find yourself lacking both practical opportunities and the inspiration of mentors within your field. * * *

Everyone who enters the fight for social change must contend with this idea of the lawyer for the subordinated that reigns over the contemporary practice of trying to change the world. This idea defines a lawyer's connection to her job, to what she knows, to those who work with and around her, to the institutions in which she functions, and to the society she desires to change. * * * If you struggle to change the world, you decide in small ways every day whether (like most) to acquiesce in the idea's reign, or whether * * * to elaborate a different idea of practice.

* * *

* * * [López introduces Sophie and Amos as two lawyers whose practices contrast with the reigning view of public interest lawyering. They represent the rebellious idea of lawyering against subordination.] Sophie is a woman whom Catharine first met at the end of the summer when Sophie was translating for Spanish speakers at the workshop on reproductive rights. Catharine was initially intrigued by the nature of her work, and impressed by her gentle and confident manner. Continuing to work closely with Sophie over this school year, she has discovered far more about Sophie and her work that she can only describe as inspiring.

In fact, when all is said and done, Sophie is probably the lawyer whom Catharine would most like to emulate in her own practice. But specifying exactly what it is about Sophie that seems so very remarkable has proven difficult. * * * She knows she admires Sophie's firm convictions. About racism. About economic inequalities. About the importance of understanding the political nature of neighborhoods as well as the politics of multinational decisionmaking. About how what goes on locally reflects and, in turn, affects what goes on regionally and nationally.

But what Catharine may admire most is that Sophie's firm convictions don't mean that she's closed-minded. Sophie listens. And those who work closely with her find her willing to adapt, compromise, experiment, even with ideas she initially considered wrongheaded. They don't think she's just another well-educated "do-gooder" or do-nothing "lefty." She's someone who's with them, who's got a stake in their fight. That makes it all the easier for community residents to respect Sophie when her views run counter to theirs, as they sometimes do, of course, on issues ranging from anti-abortion legislation to flag burning. Yet when Catharine relates these things about Sophie to her father, he seems unimpressed. "What are you, kidding?" her father has asked skeptically. "Three years of law school for that?"

Sophie works out of the neighborhood center of a legal aid organization, under the auspices of its Immigration Project. Though other attorneys are involved with the project, she is the only one housed in her particular office. She is in her mid-30s, one of ten red-headed Irish Catholic kids in her family. * * * She speaks great Spanish (a few years ago, she told Catharine, she and her husband spent some time in Mexico assisting start-up worker cooperatives and just traveling around), and she's just about the most down-to-earth person Catharine has ever met. A real "granola head," you might say.

Sophie lives in the neighborhood where she works, and to Catharine that appears to make all the difference in the world. The community is a small one of predominately low-income people, largely of color, part of the metropolitan mosaic that is Oakland. Getting stuck in the role of "permanent outsider" is a real possibility here—this community has had more than its share of so-called friends flitting in and out trying to make changes. Yet Sophie lives just a few blocks from where she works. She walks to her office each morning and gets her lunch from *La Frontera* (the local taco truck) nearly every day. She has been an active and interested resident throughout the three years she has lived and worked in the community. She and her husband are members of the local Tenants' Council, and they regularly attend as well as help organize and support community events. Their son is in the first grade at the local elementary school, and they participate in the school's Parent Support Network.

Living in her neighborhood is not all cheery or romantic, though. Like everyone else, Sophie has to watch out for her safety. She has to put up with a local library that is small and understaffed. She has no neighborhood park to take her son to on the weekends, no nearby recreation center where he can play with other kids. She has to travel a long way to get to the bank, or even to a sizable grocery store. With everyone else, she has to fight for more resources in local schools. She has to challenge Pacific Gas & Electric rate hikes seemingly every quarter. And she constantly has to battle with the local rentboard to get the rent-control ordinance enforced.

Sophie always has things going on all burners. Even so, she is remarkably good at following through on the commitments she makes. Take her work with a group of immigrant families in her community. The group started out with some parents who individually sought Sophie's advice. They each had taken advantage of the 1986 Immigration Reform and Control Act (IRCA) to become legal residents of this country. But their children remained ineligible to apply for legal status because they arrived after 1982 and therefore hadn't been in the United States for the duration of time required by IRCA. Organizational efforts by both Sophie and these parents have slowly disclosed a number of families with children in the same precarious position. An immigration paralegal from another organization put the group in touch with a Bay Area alliance that's part of a broader-based national coalition trying to mobilize and lobby around this issue. Meanwhile, the group members meet regularly on their own, too, not only to plan strategies but also to help each other cope with the ever-present fear that their children will be discovered and subjected to deportation.

Don't misunderstand me. Sophie does indeed appreciate litigation as a strategy and sometimes helps people in her community pursue individual claims—through federal and state court, administrative hearings, and small claims court proceedings. Even when she's helping out with this litigation, and certainly in the rest of her work, she systematically tries to encourage local people to share experiences and to develop the know-how that will enable them to better anticipate and address their needs over time. She seems to look for opportunities in what others experience only as routines.

During the opening months of the legalization program, for example, Sophie spent a great deal of time helping a paralegal from her office develop a group workshop model for processing claims and then train lay volunteers to staff the workshops. At the beginning, Sophie told Catharine, she was challenged and criticized by other lawyers in her office for spending so much time on these "high-octane ideas" that don't get much work done. As it turned out, the Immigration Project was able to assist far more applicants than it could have if each claim had required individual appointments, so the other lawyers begrudgingly acknowledged the value of her efforts. Sometimes they even praised her. At the same time, as Sophie had hoped, participants were not only more involved with their cases than they probably would have been otherwise, but they also developed bonds with one another that have endured long past the filing of their claims.

But, for Sophie, establishing opportunities for people to help themselves and others isn't limited to imaginative case processing. She keeps a constant watch, often spending a lot of time outside of her office, for news of efforts that she can learn from and contribute to. When she heard about a group of recently documented women who wanted to start a housekeeping cooperative, for example, she let them know through a mutual friend that she'd be interested in working with them—offering them what she knew from her own earlier experiences in Mexico and getting a chance to learn from this kind of entrepreneurial effort here in the United States. Such overtures don't often pan out, as Sophie herself told Catharine, but this time these women really hit it off. Together they got the cooperative started, assembled a modest handbook about cooperatives as an organizational arrangement, and put on a series of workshops sharing their own experiences with other housekeepers in the Bay Area.

From all Catharine has seen, Sophie works most regularly with people in her own community—individuals, groups, lay advocates, and professionals. Still, she seems never to miss a chance to capitalize on opportunities in other parts of the Bay Area, in Sacramento, and even in Washington, D.C. She makes it her business to keep abreast of a wide range of activist coalitions, not only participating herself when it seems necessary or possible but strongly encouraging the involvement of other community members as well. She also makes it her business to maintain contact with policymakers, lobbyists, think-tank types, and others working in seemingly remote bureaucracies, always doing her best to link what these folks do with what's happening at the grassroots level. Her careful attention to detail makes for a rich and intimate knowledge of her own community and the way in which it fits into the broader scheme of things—a knowledge she uses wisely to identify emerging interests, to avoid duplication of efforts, and to help mobilize for increased resources and participation.

Sophie experiences a curious dynamic with the other lawyers with whom she works, especially those in her organization. They all seem to know their own "area of law," and Sophie does rely on them from time to time for their expertise. But when she tries to infuse her ideas of community-based lawyering into their practices, she is often met with confusing responses. A few of the attorneys seem intrigued by her ideas and sometimes even try to implement them. But their individual reactions to her and her work don't seem to have much influence on what appears to be a pretty powerful institutional resistance to her ideas about practice. They regard what she does, she believes, with a mixture of skepticism, bewilderment, and even occasional admiration. Maybe that's one reason that she has found herself working more and more closely with Irma, an immigration paralegal employed by her neighborhood office whose basic sense of problem-solving parallels Sophie's own.

Before Sophie started working, "staff meetings" entailed a kind of ad hoc case review for lawyers. At Sophie's insistence, these meetings now include all members of the staff and sometimes a broader agenda. For the first time, discussions have touched on intake procedures, file maintenance, and scheduling—what used to be thought of as the concerns of only the secretaries and the receptionist. And when it is Sophie's turn to run the rotating "Free Time" portion of the staff meetings (which she also implemented), she and Irma make the most of the opportunity, introducing recent immigration and labor market studies, and offering practical examples of how to incorporate self-help and community education into legal work. Still, Sophie admits that these changes in staff meetings may only be concessions to her and Irma and a few other kindred spirits, rather than real evidence of the beginnings of a practice redefined. But she keeps insisting on them every chance she gets.

Amos is a very different sort from Sophie—at least that's what Catharine thought when she first laid eyes on him. He's a large Black man with big meaty hands, a deep, resonant voice, a jowly face, wrinkly, very 45–ish eyes, and a few white-tipped hairs. Anything but a redheaded Irish Catholic granola head. If Sophie's the kind whose leadership skills sneak up on you, Amos is just the sort you anticipate would dominate any group. Not necessarily because he needs to, but because everyone expects him to—maybe because they don't quite know what to do with this "presence" that seems to fill every room he enters.

But whatever the apparent differences between Sophie and Amos, Catharine quickly found that their firmly held convictions and notions of practice are remarkably alike. Though he carries himself proudly and speaks confidently, he has a gentle, inquisitive nature that is evident when he is working. When Catharine saw him interviewing the director of the women's shelter where she was volunteering, she noticed how he was all eyes and ears—carefully assimilating new information, patiently pursuing trajectories that the director hinted at, no matter how provisional or uncertain. He didn't mechanically follow a script in conducting his needs-assessment survey of those in the community who work most closely with families and children. Rather, he seemed to have a broad and accommodating view of what he was trying to learn about. He expected his survey and his methods to be revised constantly as he met with folks such as the shelter's director.

That sort of embracing curiosity seems to inform Amos' thoughts not only about his survey but also about the whole new project he was then trying to define more concretely. When Catharine first met Amos, he had just begun as coordinator of United Help for Families (UHF), a brand new non-profit organization in the East Bay. UHF's founders had envisioned an entity that would respond to their frustrations over the (dis)array of resources and assistance available for children and families in their community—over turf battles, gaps in and duplications of services, strategic ruts, mindless referrals, organizational mayhem. They had given the entity enough definition to raise considerable funds. But they had deliberately waited to hire a coordinator and staff whose first task would be to ground and, if necessary, reconfigure the project after a more systematic assessment of East Bay needs and of federal, state, and private support for services. They obviously thought Amos was "their man."

And from all Catharine learned, they certainly got it right. Amos had grown up in the East Bay. And his early life seemed to show all the signs of someone with real fire. When he was young, he told Catharine, people thought him a "rabble rouser." That may be an understatement, even a euphemism. Amos was certainly out there. In the playgrounds, in the streets, in church, and at school—people knew him everywhere. He cruised, he danced, he ran with an "in-crowd," he taught Sunday school, he coached kids at the "Y." He "even" liked school, and a school counselor seemed to take a liking to him, which is why he all of a sudden found himself at a state college far away in L.A.—not a place where East Bay home boys usually ended up.

But L.A. is where he stayed for the next seventeen years. Hard to believe, says Amos now, but lots of things kept him there. He got married, taught at a parochial school, got divorced, consumed the work of Malcolm X, lived as a counselor in a home for runaway Black youths, directed an early Head Start program in South Central, went to law school, worked as a public defender in juvenile court, and finally moved back up to the Bay Area when his daughter went away to college. Nothing in particular drove him from L.A. He just realized he missed "home." And taking a job in the family-law unit of a legal services office in San Francisco got him pretty close.

He spent the next eleven years in the office, working his way up through the hierarchy and eventually serving as managing attorney. Over those years, he told Catharine, he saw a whole lot while providing services, raising money, going to conferences, and pushing legislation in San Francisco, in Sacramento, in New York, in Washington, D.C.: struggling families, thoroughly screwed-up families, courageous families; well-intentioned but clueless lawyers, impatient and bossy lawyers, and even some wonderful lawyers; lazy social workers, frustrated and cynical social workers, gifted and caring social workers; self-promoting policy-makers, capable but misguided policymakers, down-to-earth, discerning, and farsighted policymakers; and a whole host of other people involved in or with control over the lives of these families, sometimes for the better, sometimes for the worse. Each of the efforts he witnessed, for all their diversity, suffered to some degree from the glaring lack of coordination among those purportedly helping out—not just disorder between the national, state, and local efforts but a hodgepodge at each and every level.

That's what first struck him about UHF: Its founders were trying to remedy precisely those problems of organization and cooperation that he had been struggling with for years. Maybe that's just how his friend Jeanette characterized UHF for him. She'd known him since they were kids, she ran a youth shelter in his old neighborhood, she wanted him back in the East Bay; so it made sense that she would know what he needed to hear to get interested in the job. Anyway, her description was right on the money. And Amos relished the opportunity, even with a small pay cut, to help give life to an organization that from its inception and at its core understood practice—a lawyer's practice, a social worker's practice, a client's practice—as anything but isolation.

Catharine met him during the initial stages of his work, just as he was trying to reacquaint himself with the neighborhood, the faces that give it, some of his old running mates, some new hangouts. Sometimes she'd find him on his way to the park to check out a Little League game. Sometimes he'd be busily reading through back issues of the weekly community newspaper. ("I feel like I've been gone for so long," he told Catharine, "it takes all my time just trying to catch up on all that's been happening around here since I left.") Sometimes he'd be heading off to another interview as he went through the list of the local family services outfits.

When Catharine offered to help Amos administer some of the surveys, she began to get a glimpse of just how purposefully he approached every part of his work. Instead of jumping on the chance to unload some work, he took the time to explain very carefully how he devised the survey and what he hoped to learn. (Jeanette was a big influence. As he put it, "After all, who should know better about gaps in service provision than a woman who works with kids so fed up with it all that they've left their families?") He reminded her that people probably aren't used to having others come around asking questions about their work, that they may understandably be circumspect, leery, or defensive. He also matter-of-factly broached the issues of race, class, and gender, and how they might bear on her getting out there into the community.

To Catharine, Amos seemed filled with small surprises. When his neighbor raved about her son's teacher, Amos made it a point to go meet this woman—to discuss the survey questions and to get a list of other teachers who might be willing to help. Teachers, says Amos, know a lot more about kids and resources than people give them credit for, or at least take advantage of. When Amos asked Catharine to attend a school board meeting with him, she quickly agreed to go, thinking perhaps he might need a show of support for an idea he was presenting. But as it turned out, he just sat quietly throughout the meeting, unnoticed by most until the end when one of the board members (an old high school buddy) warmly greeted him. He was just "checking it out," as he later told Catharine, trying to get a feel for what was on people's minds about education and how they talked about it with the board.

Amos breaks down social life and activist practice into basic parts. Coordinating services for children and families would necessarily involve the schools, after all, so why not get school folks involved at the ground level, helping to shape the effort? Why not tap into the resources and expertise of each and every university department in Berkeley, Oakland, San Francisco, of each and every "think tank" in Chicago, Atlanta, Raleigh-Durham-Chapel Hill, and of anyplace else that is willing to help and not just use the community as a laboratory? Why not go directly to those in need of services, and find out what the hell they think about all this? For that matter, why not get Rickey Henderson to feel appreciated by the A's not through the organization's purchase of a gift Ferrari but through the donation of three or four mini-vans to Big Brothers/Big Sisters in his name?

Both negotiating with bureaucratic institutions and engaging street-wise people at the grassroots seemed well within Amos's expertise, and he struck Catharine as particularly sensitive to the challenge presented. These institutions and people, he kept repeating, have hard jobs, little time, and already feel stretched to the limit. They may not take lightly to questions or suggestions from outsiders. And, whatever Amos's past, he's hardly the insider he once was. Lots of things have changed in the East Bay. He's been gone for a long time. And, of course, he is now a lawyer.

Maybe Amos' travels and achievements shouldn't change the way others perceive him and imagine working with him. But he learned time and again in San Francisco and L.A. what he always knew—that being a person of color and an old home boy doesn't automatically make you an insider, *especially* if you're a lawyer. Expectations differ, and trust is sometimes hard to reestablish. Only time and shared experiences, he keeps telling Catharine, will renegotiate the terms of his relationship with those in the East Bay and ultimately help him integrate his status and his know-how.

If you asked Sophie and Amos, they'd probably say they see themselves as only beginning to work through what their practices ought to look like. Still, if you study what they think and do in everyday circumstances, the outline of a rarely articulated idea of lawyering begins to emerge. In this idea—what I call the rebellious idea of lawyering against subordination—lawyers must know how to work with (not just on behalf of) women, low-income people, people of color, gays and lesbians, and disabled, and the elderly. They must know how to collaborate with other professional and lay allies rather than ignoring the help that these other problem-solvers may provide in a given situation. They must understand how to educate those with whom they work, particularly about law and professional lawyering, and, at the same time, they must open themselves up to being educated by all those with whom they come in contact, particularly about the traditions and experiences of life on the bottom and at the margins.

To move in these directions, those who would "lawyer rebelliously" must, like Sophie and Amos, ground their work in the lives and in the communities of the subordinated themselves, whether they work for local outfits, regional offices, or national policymaking agencies. They must, like Sophie and Amos, continually evaluate the likely interaction between legal and "non-legal" approaches to problems. They must, like Sophie and Amos, know how to work with others in brainstorming, designing, and executing strategies aimed at responding immediately to particular problems and, more generally, at fighting social and political subordination. They must understand how to be part of coalitions, as well as how to build them, and not just for purposes of filing or "proving up" a lawsuit (as Teresa, Abe, or Jonathan might do). They must appreciate how all that they do with others requires attention not only to international, national, and regional matters but also to their interplay with seemingly more mundane local affairs. At bottom, the rebellious idea of lawyering demands that lawyers (and those with whom they work) nurture sensibilities and skills compatible with a collective fight for social change.

Notes and Questions

1. Is López's view of traditional public interest law, represented by Teresa, Abe, and Jonathan, too harsh? Have you had any experience with lawyers who resemble López's archetypes? Do you have any observations about the lawyers you have seen?

2. Does López's portrayal of Abe, the labor lawyer, match your own image of the work labor lawyers do? Do you have any image of labor lawyers?

In recent years, several unions have undertaken campaigns to organize immigrant workers to ensure protection of their rights. For example, nonunion janitors sued three of the largest supermarket chains in California and their cleaning contractor, claiming a violation of labor laws relating to overtime pay, Social Security contributions, and medical leave. The suit was filed by the Mexican American Legal Defense and Educational Fund (MALDEF) and Service Employees International Union (SEIU), which represents 1.4 million janitors, healthcare workers and other service-sector employees. Eduardo Porter, *Janitors Draw Unions' Support of California Suit*, Wall St. J., Dec. 1, 2000, at B5. For a description of the role of a labor lawyer, see Thomas Geoghegan, *Which Side Are You On?: Trying to Be for Labor When It's Flat on Its Back* (1992). For information on recent developments in the labor movement as several unions expand their efforts to organize the unorganized, see *Organizing to Win: New Research on Union Strategies* (Kate Bronfenbrenner et al. eds., 1998); Bruce Nissen ed., *Which Direction for Organized Labor?: Essays on Organizing, Outreach, and Internal Transformations* (1999); *The Transformation of U.S. Unions: Voices, Visions, and Strategies from the Grassroots* (Ray M. Tillman & Michael S. Cummings eds., 1999).

3. MALDEF, founded in 1968, "is the leading nonprofit Latino litigation, advocacy and educational outreach institution in the United States. MALDEF's mission is to foster sound public policies, laws and programs to safeguard the civil rights of the 35 million Latinos living in the United States and to empower the Latino community to fully participate in our society. * * *

"Through the years, MALDEF has been at the forefront of civil rights litigation, setting precedent in many cases and establishing new systems to elect officials, hire and promote employees, and educate children." <http://www.maldef.org/about/index.htm> (visited July 13, 2002).

MALDEF and many other public interest organizations aspire to change rules through precedent setting litigation. Marc Galanter (*see* excerpt chapter 2), explains that attorneys who are repeat players within the system, such as an established public interest organization, have an advantage over one-time players. Landmark lawsuits also attract media attention and may inspire other community organizations to keep fighting for their beliefs. Many of the cases in this book were brought by public interest organizations seeking to change existing law.

Given the noble aspirations of public interest law firms and the advantages of their experienced role, why is López so tough on Teresa and Advocates for Justice?

4. Consider Jonathan, the overworked legal services attorney. How do his clients perceive him? Would his clients prefer receiving more of his time and attention if it meant he could serve fewer clients? For a thoughtful discussion of the legal services experience, see Gary Bellow, *Turning Solutions Into Problems: The Legal Aid Experience*, 34 NLADA Briefcase 106 (1977) (describing how lawyers tried to do law reform work based in legal services and encountered systemic constraints from pressure to settle, financial cutbacks, attorney inexperience, and huge caseloads).

5. Is living in the same community as one's clients an essential component to López's idea of rebellious lawyering? What characteristics make rebellious lawyering different from the more traditional model?

6. Would you want to emulate any of these lawyers? Why or why not?

7. Does the critique of regnant lawyering suggest that clients should be more "in control" of the decision-making driving litigation? What skills then does a lawyer add? Notice López did not describe rebellious lawyers as limited to using technical knowledge in their roles.

8. Luke Cole describes three models of social justice lawyering in the context of environmental advocacy—the professional model, the participatory model, and the power model.

LUKE W. COLE

Macho Law Brains, Public Citizens, and Grassroots Activists: Three Models of Environmental Advocacy
14 Va. Envtl. L.J. 687, 692–98 (1995)

* * * Before a company applies for a local land-use permit, it sends a letter of intent to the local agency. The agency then holds a *pre-application hearing*. The purpose of this hearing is to explain the project and the permitting process. Next, the company files a formal *application* with the agency. At this point, the agency evaluates potential environmental effects of the project. If the project will have a potentially significant effect on the environment, state law directs the agency to prepare an *environmental impact report* (EIR). The local agency holds a meeting to determine the scope of the EIR. This *scoping meeting* is open to the public, but is often attended exclusively by officials from other government agencies. The agency then prepares an EIR (or contracts with a consultant to produce such a report) detailing the potential effects of the project. This EIR is circulated for *public comment* to anyone requesting it. Thereafter, the local agency prepares a *response to public comments*. Local agencies will often hold *public hearings* on the EIR. Finally, the local agency will decide whether to permit the project, theoretically basing its decision on the EIR and public comment. If a proponent or opponent of the project is unhappy with that decision, he or she can then file a lawsuit.

The Professional Model

The professional model is grounded in the idea that the attorney is an expert and will best represent a group's interests during the permitting process. Because of his or her training and skills, the attorney plays a central role in the permitting process, representing the client group in all fora. * * *

The attorney may first advance the client group's interests and opinions at the pre-application meeting. This stage allows the attorney to gather more information about the project. The attorney can then analyze the permit itself in preparation for scoping meetings. For those experienced in the field, scoping meetings are a routine exercise where relatively obvious potential environmental impacts are raised so that they can be addressed in the EIR.

When an EIR is issued, the professional swings into action. As an expert, or working with experts, the attorney carefully parses the environmental review documents and provides expert written testimony (''comment'') for the client group. The agency, in turn, must respond to filed comments. The comment—often the basis for later lawsuits on the project—is essential because all issues raised in a later lawsuit must have been raised previously in the EIR process.

The public hearing creates another forum for the use of experts. Typically, many of the same experts that evaluated the EIR will testify on behalf of the client group at the hearing.

Finally, if the decisionmakers decide against the client group, the attorney can sue to block the project. Adherents to the professional model enjoy this phase of the process the most, and often look for "test cases" in order to influence the law. A quick glance through any environmental law casebook will reveal the names of the nation's most prominent and leading environmental groups, many of which use the professional model of advocacy.

The Participatory Model

While the professional model essentially revolves around the attorney, the participatory model aims to maximize community involvement in the administrative permitting process. This model seeks to present client voices at every opportunity afforded by the process. * * *

As in the professional model, the pre-application hearing presents the first opportunity for client participation. The hearing is an educational opportunity for everyone involved. Clients can hear about the project and can often ask questions of agency officials. Officials often gauge the time they will need to spend overseeing the permit process according to the turnout at the pre-application hearing. In my experience, officials are far more likely to review an application carefully, and document its potential impacts adequately, if they know the community is actively involved in the permitting process. Bureaucrats in state and local environmental agencies respond to pressure, and when deciding between the desires of a community and those of a company, they will usually favor the interest putting the most pressure on them. The pre-application hearing also gives the company a chance to evaluate potential opposition to the facility. If there is overwhelming opposition, a company may reconsider or modify the project.

The scoping meeting is the next opportunity for public involvement. At the meeting, local agency officials receive information from the public and other agencies about the scope of the review. For example, an EIR for a parking garage in a downtown area will generally consider different impacts (traffic, air pollution, congestion, etc.) than one for an irrigation canal through a wilderness area (wildlife, water quality, etc.). The scoping meeting is another opportunity for client input and for environmental justice advocates to help a community group recognize the value of its own expertise. After all, the people who will actually experience the impact are home-grown experts—no one knows better how truck traffic down a main street will affect a community than neighbors who live on that street. The scoping meeting is one place to recognize and exercise that community knowledge.

Public comment on the EIR itself is perhaps the most important public input and offers the greatest opportunity for client involvement in the environmental review process. The EIR enables a community group to educate itself while building broad opposition to (or support for) the proposed project. The EIR is usually a dense, technical document and is largely incomprehensible to the public and sometimes even to lawyers.

This is especially true of EIR sections discussing human health impacts. Lawyers and other technical consultants may be needed in order to translate the document into plain English.

Use of the EIR in a study-group fashion is one way to maximize public education and organization value. In such a situation, members take different chapters of the EIR and analyze them, learning as much as possible about a particular topic (e.g., air pollution, traffic impacts, waste management projections) and comparing that knowledge to the information found in the EIR. Often, a community's knowledge and experience will clash with the "knowledge" found in the EIR. When a community group engages in such a study-group, the group often points out serious flaws in the project, indicates alternatives, and helps educate decisionmakers and the public. Well-educated community groups are often able to demand changes in the proposed project, additional mitigation measures, different environmental tests, or independent studies of potential environmental impacts.

In other situations, a community group may not be sufficiently prominent or organized to run a full campaign around an EIR. Nonetheless, the EIR can still be a useful organizational tool. The community may hold neighborhood house meetings during which community leaders discuss the campaign against (or for) a particular project. If one member of the community group (or the group's technical consultant or lawyer) explains the findings of the EIR, then the group can discuss their hopes, concerns, and fears about the project. The process of articulating individual concerns encourages group members to recognize their common concerns and allows those present to move from isolated individual fear toward empowered community action. Those present at the meeting can then write letters of comment on the EIR, setting out their thoughts on the project.

The last opportunity for client input is the public hearing. The public hearing serves an educational function—the community and its experts educate both decisionmakers and other audience members about the flaws in a project. Attendance sends an important message to the decisionmakers: the bigger the turnout, the greater the consequences the decisionmakers can expect to suffer if they vote against the will of the group. Finally, public hearings serve as organizing tools for client groups, and provide relatively easy ways to bring people together to learn about a project.

The community has little opportunity for input after the public hearing. The decisionmakers render a decision, and those dissatisfied with it have only the courts for recourse. At this point, a community group must use a lawyer if it wishes to proceed. However, as in the professional model, if a community group actively participated at every opportunity, it has likely built a good administrative record, thus enhancing the chances for a successful lawsuit.

The participatory model essentially accepts the system and encourages participation in it. An adherent might believe that environmental decision making would be fairer if people had more access to the system. Citizen victories in siting battles reinforce a sense that the system works and a belief that the voices of the people can be heard. This belief in the system contrasts with the skepticism felt by advocates of the power model.

The Power Model

Adherents of the power model believe that the system is stacked and that no amount of participation *by itself* will change the relations of power that give rise to environmental degradation. Advocates of the power model are convinced that more access to the system means nothing without power within that system. If it is used at all, the public participation process is viewed as a vehicle for organizing communities and a means to community empowerment. By bringing people together to realize and exercise their collective strength, practitioners of the power model target the root of community problems—powerlessness.

Three central ideas define the power model. First, it eschews the public participation process as co-optive. Second, it focuses on the actual leverage point in the process—the decision by officials. Third, it emphasizes strategies to influence the decisionmakers. * * *

[With the power model strategy] all attention is focused on the actual decision, even to the exclusion of participation in the rest of the process. However, this does not mean that the client group is only active *at the time of the decision*. Rather, the group must be active in trying to influence the decision from the first moment it learns that the process is underway.

Notes and Questions

1. Cole concludes that the participatory or power models can both be used: "Pressuring decisionmakers through the power model makes decisionmakers more receptive to hearing alternatives put forward by those utilizing the participatory model." *Id.* at 709. How should a lawyer advise clients about which model to pursue?

2. Is the environmental justice movement unique or do these models of lawyering for social justice apply to other kinds of practice? How do these models compare with descriptions of lawyering for social justice discussed by López? Do you believe that "the professional model is a waste of time from the perspective of the community," *id.* at 708, as Cole asserts? For comments on this model by community organizers, see William Quigley, *Reflections of Community Organizers: Lawyering for Empowerment of Community Organizations*, excerpted in chapter 11.

B. Understanding Communities: Goals, Context, and Conflicts

Lawyers representing communities, groups, and organizations face issues related to group representation. Michael Diamond explores how to define the community and its goals. John O. Calmore calls for special attention to the context in which this work is done; attention to context may lead to unnoticed choices. Julie Su shows creativity in joining communities. Consider how each of these authors views the lawyers' role.

MICHAEL DIAMOND

Community Lawyering: Revisiting the Old Neighborhood
32 Col. Hum. Rts. L. Rev. 67, 110–26 (2000)

A developer purchases all of the apartment buildings on one square block of a city. He announces his intention to demolish the buildings and to erect a nursing home on the site, an enterprise that will not serve local residents either in terms of the care it provides nor the jobs it will create. Its development is opposed by much of the community due to the loss of housing and community disruption that will result. The developer seeks to remove residents from the buildings, at first by requesting that they vacate their apartments, but later with ever-escalating intimidation and violence. In response to the developer's demands, the residents establish a "Save Our Homes Committee." It achieves broad membership among the residents and elects an executive board to speak for the Committee. The Committee's goal is to force the developer to change his plans and to preserve the housing on the block.

As the struggle intensifies, the developer resorts to guerilla tactics in his attempts to remove the tenants. He terminates essential services such as heat and hot water during the winter months. He allows, even encourages, neighborhood teenagers to hold parties that run late into the night in vacant units in the buildings. Rent collections are conducted door to door by employees who display firearms to residents. Finally, the developer makes vacant apartments available to heroin addicts who use them as "shooting galleries," locations in which to inject heroin and then sleep off its effects.

Conditions on the site deteriorate to devastating proportions. The Save Our Homes Committee continues to fight but residents are more and more concerned about their immediate safety and that of their children. The group and its attorney have taken a number of legal actions and the attorney has been involved in planning several legal and political responses, many of which have been successful and which show promise of further success in the future. Nevertheless, several residents seek out the attorney. They indicate their commitment to the Save Our Homes cause but tell the attorney that they can no longer endure the conditions in which they have been forced to live. They seek her help in getting relocated, perhaps with a financial settlement from the developer.

This story suggests how dissimilar the activist community lawyer's territory is from that of the traditional lawyer. In fact, the territory may even differ from that in which the rebellious lawyer functions. The community setting and representation of grass roots groups raises issues for lawyers absent in these other practices. The conflicts presented in the "Save Our Homes" story are examples of those that commonly arise in communities and within community groups.

There are other challenges that an activist lawyer will face. These include discerning a defensible set of community goals, reconciling these goals with his or her own interests, choosing clients or cases that comport with these interests, recognizing and resolving tensions surrounding the existence of competing community interests, addressing internal conflicts within client groups, and meeting the need to organize new community groups or build the capacity of emerging ones.

Each of these problems raises questions and presents choices as to the role the community lawyer should play in advancing the interests and welfare of the community. They are among those that invariably will confront the community lawyer. * * *

One of the most difficult issues facing the community lawyer is determining who or what is the community. The statement that one is a community lawyer, now a highly recognizable catchphrase, masks a series of philosophical problems as well as some very complicated practical ones. In this context the term "community" could mean the residents of a geographic area. It might mean people with a common religion, political persuasion or profession, or people with a shared interest, all without regard to geography. Or it might indicate merely the speaker's subjective perception of the term. Consider also: is a community, once formed, fixed and immutable or fluid and changing; who is authorized to speak for a community; how does a community spokesperson obtain authority to speak; and how does an attorney verify the authority?

As this brief rumination suggests, the concept of "community" is intricate and elusive. In the context of community lawyering, the term almost certainly connotes a specific and limited geographic location. Nevertheless, it cannot be understood without taking account of its social and political aspects. Consider the typical situation where people living in the same geographic area have completely different goals and aspirations for themselves and for their neighborhood. Take, for example, the common issue of physical and economic redevelopment. Some residents might advocate the demolition of dilapidated housing and the gentrification of commercial and economic activity. They would attempt to attract people with higher incomes to the area and would encourage the building of more expensive housing and the concomitant social and economic amenities. Others might desire to retain the current resident mix in the neighborhood and to improve the stock of existing housing while keeping it affordable. This group would attempt to preserve the flavor of the neighborhood as it exists and would resist any attempt to gentrify it. While these viewpoints are incompatible with each other, each might command substantial support among neighborhood residents. Many of those who oppose each other on this point might be allies on other community matters, such as improving city services for the neighborhood, community control of local schools, or changing the traffic patterns on the main street. Such shifting constituencies demonstrate the complexity of community politics, and underscore the difficulty faced by an attorney in developing a coherent political view and activist philosophy. They also underscore the difficulty in identifying potential spokespersons for a "community," much less authoritative voices.

Despite the inherent difficulties of doing so, the community lawyer must identify the community in which he or she works and discern its overarching goals and aspirations. Since we are addressing "community" as a geographically bounded area with something that is transcendent, even in the face of particular internal disagreements as to objectives and methods, we have to come to grips with the fact that a "community" may speak with several voices and give rise to apparently competing goals. Thus, "community" is greater than any single group within the geographic bounds and longer-lived than any particular manifestation of a perceived problem.

This is an important distinction because a lawyer might view his or her calling as representing "the community" rather than any particular group in it. Yet the lawyer, as an autonomous agent, also has views and principles that deserve recognition and expression. This raises for the community lawyer the thorny problem of representing "community" interests while remaining true to his or her own beliefs. This may not be a problem for a market-driven attorney who normally sells legal services to whomever is willing to pay and who typically invests little in analyzing the social benefits of a prospective client's goals. Nor may it be a problem for the salaried attorney who is expected to adopt the views, at least professionally, of his or her employer. The community lawyer, however, needs to ascertain clearly the principles to which he or she will adhere. As we will see, it is the recognition of a defensible set of community goals that will inform the community lawyer in determining which clients to accept and which projects and cases to pursue.

The appropriate role for an activist community lawyer is quite different from that of an attorney in a more traditional setting. * * * Each of these problems raises questions and presents choices as to the role the community lawyer may play in advancing the interests and welfare of the community.

Discerning a Defensible Set of Community Goals

One's capacity to discern a set of community goals presumes one's capacity to define and to recognize the "community" in its most expansive sense. To do so, a community lawyer must become immersed in the activities and personalities of the neighborhood. This means * * * getting out of the office, going to community meetings, and talking to and getting to know the people and groups in the neighborhood. It is necessary for one who aspires to be a community lawyer to understand the issues confronting the community and the goals and aspirations of its residents.

This is not an easy task, particularly for an outsider. One way to overcome this difficulty is for a new attorney to have a "guide" to introduce him or her to the community. Choosing an appropriate guide is, itself, a difficult task because merely choosing has political ramifications. The guide chosen will influence the attorney's view of the community's structure, its problems and activities. Moreover, the choice might alienate some in the community by suggesting the attorney already has a partisan view of community issues.

Once an attorney has identified goals in a community, he or she should carefully examine his or her own goals as a lawyer and as an activist. An activist lawyer must recognize his or her self-motivation and what values make the occupation attractive. For the lawyer to be effective, there must be a confluence of the goals of the community and of the lawyer. For a lawyer merely to accept whatever goals are adhered to by the community not only deprives the attorney of his or her voice and autonomy but also suggests the same uncritical acceptance of clients that is the hallmark of the attorney for hire, who is likely to accept any paying client whose cause is not morally repugnant.

Choosing Among Competing Goals Within a Community

As I have suggested, the members of a community are not likely to be homogeneous in their goals and aspirations. Since several competing goals might stake a legitimate claim to being "community" goals, the lawyer may have to choose among conflicting possibilities. These may compete not only as to their substance but also as to the allocation of scarce representational resources. In the latter situation, an attorney's choice of one set of goals may be seen as a political statement of the attorney's own view of community benefit. Once an attorney articulates to which goals he or she will adhere, the attorney can evaluate each potential client or matter in relation to these goals and determine whether any new client or matter has the potential for furthering them. This involves choices by the attorney about the goals themselves and the clients espousing those goals.

Consider a community lawyer with a long-term commitment to community improvement. Assume the attorney sees his or her purpose as assisting local community groups to achieve some element of independence and control over the community's environment, to enhance community "empowerment." When representatives of a local group seek the attorney's assistance for a project, with what issues will the community lawyer have to be concerned in order to decide whether to take on the project? These are likely to include a fundamental assessment of whether there is merit in the group's claim. But the attorney must also ask who in the community supports the goals being pursued. Does the project further the goals the attorney has identified as the "community's" and adopted as his or own? Will representation in this project conflict with the attorney's ability to represent wider community interests in the future?

These seemingly straightforward and basic questions are, in fact, deceptive and fraught with danger. In making a decision without information about broader issues in the community and the participants, the attorney risks political calamity. The resulting political situation may affect the attorney's credibility with neighborhood residents and groups well into the future. In the community setting, certain groups and their members may be repeat players who constantly re-evaluate the attorney's political bona fides. In fact, each decision to accept a new project or client has an impact on the attorney's ability to represent a coherent set of community interests in the future.

Choosing Among Competing Interests Within a Group

Community groups often have within them several competing factions. Power competitions often draw the group's attorney into the fray. At that point, issues arise as to which of the competing factions should have the attorney's support. Sometimes the answer is relatively straight forward. For instance, as a matter of legal ethics, the attorney who represents a group may not take another client whose interests are in actual conflict with those of the group. Therefore, the attorney owes his or her allegiance to the group, and not a competing faction. If the management is compromised of one of the factions or supports one of the factions, the attorney's obligation normally is to follow the validly selected management or, in an appropriate case, to withdraw from the representation.

In other situations, the answer is less obvious. For example, how should an attorney act when the management of a client group is no longer recognizable? Or consider what the attorney should do when a functioning management changes a group's purpose to such an extent that it deviates from the defensible community goals that were to guide the attorney's actions. Here, the attorney's position is more difficult and perilous, regardless of whether he or she agrees with a particular faction. In fact, a particularly insidious aspect of this problem involves the attorney who does not take sides. If the lawyer remains neutral, can he or she maintain sufficient credibility to be effective once the internal disputes are resolved? Will there be repercussions within the larger community because of the attorney's apparent lack of resolve?

* * *

While I will offer a different view, advocates of both the traditional and the client-centered models would suggest that when the internal disagreement revolves around fundamental issues of the group's purpose, the lawyer generally should defer to the members to resolve the dispute. Proponents of these models would argue that while a lawyer might have personal opinions on the issue, there are at least two significant reasons why that opinion may be better left unexpressed. The first concerns the attorney's inherent competence to render such opinions. They would argue that, as an outsider, the attorney's knowledge and understanding of the issues are likely to be derivative and less sophisticated than that of the members. Moreover, the attorney's involvement was probably sought primarily to provide professional and strategic guidance and advice.

The second reason presented by advocates for reticence involves principles of client autonomy. When the lawyer intrudes on this are of member prerogative and competence, he or she risks alienating the group's membership. In a strong group, such alienation might manifest itself in a dismissal of the attorney or, at least, relegation to a marginal role. In a weaker group, the alienation may lead the membership to abdicate to the attorney its legitimate role in decision-making and execution.

The situation is even more troubling when the lawyer's opinion is sought not to resolve an internal debate, but rather to be used by one faction in its battle against another. Traditional, client-centered lawyers argue that a lawyer taking such an action would usurp a group function and intrude into the group's internal dynamics. The inexperienced or politically naïve lawyer is particularly susceptible to manipulation by members seeking to further personal ends. On the other hand, a calculating lawyer may manipulate a conflict to achieve his or her own sense of the proper direction for the group. Both situations result in a breach of the professional relationship. As a result, the lawyer's effectiveness, and perhaps that of the group, will be compromised.

Even when the attorney adequately understands the political setting in a community and has accepted a client, he or she must deal with the traditional view of the attorney as "other" and manipulator. I have already examined the conflict between those who see the lawyer as participant and proponents of client-centeredness, the essence of which involves the clash between the wishes of clients and the views of attorneys. The controversies associated with this dissonance are both philosophic and practical. From a philosophic point of view, many in society see the lawyer as a neutral technician who should not attempt to influence client decision-making concerning the objectives of the representation. * * * [T]he community lawyer is rarely associated with the community group other than through his or her representation of it. Thus, as an outsider, the dichotomy between the lawyer's role as "professional" and his or her role as "participant" may well be academic.

This debate, however, establishes a false dichotomy. There surely is a need for client autonomy. Community lawyers should foster and maintain it. There is also a need, however, for professional intervention by the community lawyer, particularly where the lawyer is an ongoing collaborator rather than merely a technical adjunct in the group's activities. In this participatory role, the lawyer has information and, perhaps, a perspective that would benefit the client. Therefore, if the lawyer is to participate in client activities, then he or she has a right, if not a duty, to express his or her views about client goals and strategies.

* * *

Contemplating the Activist Attorney as Organizer

Client autonomy and empowerment and the attorney's proper role are issues that arise both in working with established groups, as discussed above, and with new or loosely organized groups. New groups often need organizational support to enable them to undertake programmatic missions. Community organizers often provide this kind of support to new or nascent groups.

An organizer's first job is to assist individuals to come together as a group. The organizer then assists the group in developing its structure and decision-making capacity. A professional organizer may perform these tasks; alternately the organizer could be a lay resident of the area who commands the respect of residents and possesses skills to augment the organizational effort. It is even possible that an attorney can play this role.

Incorporating an organizing function into the attorney's role may produce some tangible benefits, but it also involves some intrinsic difficulties. Among the obvious disadvantages is that the attorney typically lacks training and experience to adopt the organizer role. Even if an attorney has some training or experience, he or she may lack time to fulfill both capacities.

A more subtle difficulty involves concentrating power and visibility in one person. This latter difficulty is not easily overcome. In many situations, members of a group view attorneys with respect. The members often see the attorney as a person who brings access to solutions for many problems confronting the group. Too often, however, lawyers are unaware of how they are perceived, misapprehend the importance of this perception, or disregard it. Nevertheless, an attorney is in a position—wittingly or unwittingly—to misuse this prominence to the detriment of the group.

Group members also view the person in the role of organizer as one who can solve problems. As such, organizers also command a degree of respect. Part of an organizer's job, however, is to help develop internal leadership and decision-making capacity within the group. This often puts the organizer in a visible and central position among the members. The organizer is thus in a position to serve as an effective counterpoint to the authority of the lawyer.

When the functions of attorney and organizer are combined in one person, several difficulties may surface. For instance, the group may lose the benefit of the independent perspectives provided by the lawyer and the organizer. Indeed, there may be no other person to provide an effective counterpoint to the lawyer/organizer's positions. Without this counterpoint, the visibility and centrality of a lawyer increases, along with his or her ability to influence group decision-making.

There are also conflicts between the roles of organizer and attorney that could negatively affect both the attorney and the group. Consider, for example, a situation that calls for the group to stage a sit-in or otherwise violate the law. The lawyer is constrained both by codes of professional responsibility and ethical considerations, which may restrict the lawyer's ability or willingness to advocate such a course. The problem a lawyer could face is compounded when he or she both advises the group of the possibility of such action and also organizes the effort. What role can or should the lawyer play if the group decides to proceed with an activity that would violate the law? The group might reasonably expect the person who advocated and organized the activity to join in carrying out the strategy. A lawyer, however, could face professional disciplinary action for participation in violating the law. While participation is harmonious with the organizer role, any such action would limit the attorney's ability to represent the group as a lawyer, not to mention the risk to his or her future.

On the other hand, being involved in an organizing capacity may put a lawyer in closer touch with the reality of a client's situation, attitudes, and perceptions. It may also permit members of a group to feel more confidence in a lawyer because of this less formal and structured involvement with the group's struggle. Participating in an organizing capacity offers flexibility not generally found in the traditional lawyer-client relationship. In addition, it may be that there is nobody else, at least initially, to take on these tasks. In this case, the lawyer must function as an organizer until outside assistance can be obtained or until internal capacity comes to the fore. An organized group is a precondition to a successful struggle against subordination and to obtain the power to influence the community's environment. The activist lawyer has an important part to play in the organizing effort.

Notes and Questions

1. In a landmark article, Derrick Bell raised the question of the attorney's role in social justice litigation. In the context of school desegregation cases, Bell explains "courts have come to construe *Brown v. Board of Education* as mandating 'equal educational opportunities' through school desegregation plans aimed at achieving racial balance, whether or not those plans will improve the education received by the children affected." Derrick A. Bell, Jr., *Serving Two Masters: Integration Ideals and Client Interests in School Desegregation Litigation*, 85 Yale L.J. 470, 471 (1976) (excerpted in chapter 5). Bell asks:

> How should the term "client" be defined in school desegregation cases that are litigated for decades, determine critically important constitutional rights for thousands of minority children, and usually involve major restructuring of a public school system? How should civil rights attorneys represent the often diverse interests of clients and class in school suits? Do they owe any special obligation to class members who emphasize educational quality and who probably cannot obtain counsel to advocate their divergent views? Do the political, organizational, and even philosophical complexities of school desegregation litigation justify a higher standard of profes-

> sional responsibility on the part of civil rights lawyers to their clients, or more diligent oversight of the lawyer-client relationship by the bench and bar?

Id. at 471.

Bell explains that civil rights attorneys in these cases focus on desegregation and racially balanced schools. Bell's view is that the equal educational opportunities mandated by *Brown* could be more effectively "obtained, if the creative energies of the civil rights litigation groups could be brought into line with the needs and desires of their clients." *Id.* at 488.

Ron Edmonds names the different masters served by the civil rights attorneys as first, clients, on behalf of whom the suit is filed, and, second, constituents, to whom the attorney must answer. In Edmonds' view, the civil rights attorney is isolated from clients and answers to constituents who have access to the attorney during the litigation process. Ron Edmonds, *Advocating Inequity: A Critique of the Civil Rights Attorney in Class Action Desegregation Suits*, 3 Black L.J. 176 (1974).

How can a lawyer set priorities in cases involving social justice issues? To whom is the lawyer's primary allegiance owed? Is the lawyer's first obligation to represent the client? How should a lawyer decide who the client is? When representing a community organization or group, how should a lawyer resolve divergent member opinions?

2. Diamond describes several ways in which activist lawyers can be part of community organizing. How can the lawyer play a role which will strengthen the internal organization of community groups and avoid creating dependence on the lawyer? Can lawyers be part of changing consciousness within a community in processes that are not related to litigation or other legal efforts? *See* chapter 11 exploring these questions.

3. Dale Minami, a founder of the San Francisco-based Asian Law Caucus, comments on the often overlooked significance of educational lawsuits, brought by lawyers working with community groups:

> * * * [U]njust laws, official misconduct and unresponsive institutions should be exposed and * * * lawsuits are *one* method for bringing a particular problem to the public's scrutiny.
>
> In conjunction with the San Francisco Neighborhood Legal Assistance Foundation, we brought such a suit against Evelle Younger, Attorney General of California, for his publication of a sensationalistic, pseudofactual confidential bulletin to state law enforcement personnel entitled *Triad: Mafia of the Far East*. Some examples of the bulletin's lowlights:
>
> "Drugs are a way of life in the Orient."
>
> "Paying off the police is as everyday as eating rice."
>
> "The only way they (immigrants) know how to make a living is to continue to pursue the same occupations here as they did in the

streets of Hong Kong. This means trafficking in drugs, gambling and prostitution."

The innuendos, insinuations and implications passed on as intelligence information pictured Chinese as brigands, law-breakers, smugglers and opium-smokers—the same stereotypes which justified assaults on the lives and civil liberties of Chinese one hundred years ago.

The reaction of the Chinese community in the Bay Area was explosive: community organizations, newspapers, and leaders voiced their strong objections to the report to the press and to Younger himself. The coalition which formed around the issue distributed petitions, published a thirty-seven page point-by-point refutation of the report and organized a press conference denouncing the racism of the bulletin. Eventually, Younger, then a Republican gubernatorial candidate, issued a reluctant apology to the Chinese community for his department's release of the report to the general public.

The educational value of the issue was not created by the lawsuit itself, but by the community groups and individuals who organized distribution of the bulletin, set up the press conference, communicated with interested persons in Los Angeles and other areas, and amassed petitions. The lawsuit did, however, attract media attention and raise the issue of racism in the courts.

Since race defamation is not a wrong recognized by the courts, making a legal case for enjoining distribution of the bulletin was difficult. But race discrimination in other situations is illegal, and lawsuits directed toward those situations can be effective in alleviating the manifestations of racism (though not the racism itself) and in raising the community's awareness of racism.

* * *

* * * As attorneys and legal workers, however, we are careful to explain the limitations of legal relief—that courts are not empowered nor inclined to afford consistent and complete relief for a given problem. * * * Lawsuits should not become substitutes for political organizing and education. In fact, lawsuits are often destructive because they absorb the attention and energies which could have been channeled into political action. For some, legal actions even create the illusion that real and permanent solutions to socio-political problems can be achieved through the courts, thus building reliance upon the attorneys and reducing community interest to court watching. Used correctly as a tactic in a larger political strategy, however, lawsuits can defend victims of racism, educate people about it, and attack its symptoms. When employing law in light of a political stance, it is important to link up with a stable coalition willing and able to carry their political work through to completion.

Dale Minami, *Asian Law Caucus: Experiment in an Alternative*, 3 Amerasia Journal 28, 31–34 (1975).

JOHN O. CALMORE

A Call to Context: The Professional Challenges of Cause Lawyering at the Intersection of Race, Space, and Poverty
67 Fordham L. Rev. 1927, 1927–29, 1936–46, 1955–56 (1999)

Traditional legal analysis and advocacy are too often plagued by the tendency to * * * [extract] issues from their history and the broader social and normative contexts that bear so heavily on them. Seldom will a client's legal problem be just a legal problem. By issuing a call to context, I am directing attention to the inner-city poor's lived experiences, including the interconnection of legal and non-legal issues they confront, the web of experiences within which they live * * * .

In considering why we describe law as a "profession," many focus on the practice of law as a "public calling." From this perspective, perhaps, the most profound issue in providing effective legal services to the poor is whether legal advocacy on their behalf can maintain a positive, operational connection between rights and justice. With or without lawyers, for the inner-city poor, justice is hard to find. In the quest for justice, representing the poor has generally attracted "cause lawyers." Broadly speaking, cause lawyering encompasses various law-related activities, from rights assertion to legal counseling, that * * * [rely] on law-related means to achieve social justice for individuals and subordinated or disadvantaged groups. Whether representing individuals or groups, cause-oriented poverty lawyers often adopt an orientation of antisubordination advocacy. This requires legal advocates, especially attorneys, to cross traditional boundaries * * * . This lawyering, moreover, must confront the difficulties and contradictions that are part of working for social change within and outside of the legal system's conventional framework.

* * * In this line of work, we must appreciate that poverty has multiple dimensions. In terms of time, there is persistent poverty; in terms of space, there is neighborhood poverty; and in terms of behavior, there is underclass poverty. Sometimes, these dimensions coalesce and those in poverty experience both stigmatizing and oppressive constraints. This predicament is worsened by societal imposition of negative racial characteristics as an overlay. In other words, poverty and space become *racialized* to the detriment of these poor. This marks the intersection of race, space, and poverty.

[The author here describes cause lawyers and contrasts the role of regnant lawyers. Review the excerpt of this discussion which appears in chapter 1.]

* * *

Left-activist, non-regnant cause lawyering must first be community-based, because the poverty we confront is primarily situated at the intersection of race, space, and poverty. Individuals, in this context, are poor primarily because their families and neighborhoods are poor. Although "community" is a problematical term, it is nonetheless apt in the context of the client poverty to be addressed here. Community, here, is not a romantic abstraction, but rather the site of material deprivation and relations that are formed to cope with oppressive circumstances. It is not, however, simply an adaptation to a culture of poverty or a culture of segregation. It is homeplace. As George Revill argues:

> The value of community as a concept in this context is that it throws into prominence the tensions between ... peoples and places. It is not that it enables us to identify a stable or even dominant set of social and cultural characteristics by which a particular place or group of people might be identified. *Rather, community focuses interest on the processes that create a sense of stability from a contested terrain in which versions of place and notions of identity are supported by different groups and individuals with varying powers to articulate their positions.*

The community-based notion of cause lawyering not only allows us to situate our clients as a social group, but also compels us to confront their problems as public issues that reflect systemic "contradictions" or "antagonisms" rather than as "personal troubles." This in turn directs us to adopt a mission of social justice that redresses oppression. Thus, social justice furthers liberation and entails establishing freedom from the features of oppression. These features, as identified by Iris Young, are exploitation, marginalization, powerlessness, cultural imperialism, and violence. David Harvey would add "a further dimension concerning freedom from the oppressive *ecological consequences* of others' actions." Significantly, within the context of inner-city poverty, these multiple forms of oppression often coalesce in synergistically interlocking ways. They constitute the packaged opportunity-denying circumstances that must be redressed. They direct our responsive intervention as legal advocates and they map our social justice projects.

Our social justice project's primary focus must be on helping people to break free from the interlocking features of oppression. Oppression is at the heart of a condition-directed orientation toward redress. According to Marilyn Frye, a ubiquitous feature of oppression is "the double bind—situations in which options are reduced to a very few and all of them expose one to penalty." Over the years of practicing poverty law from Roxbury to Watts, I was continually struck by the apparently optionless world that most of my clients inhabited. I never associated it with oppression, but rather I saw it as a lack of social and monetary capital. I continued to believe in the myth of Horatio Alger. I simply failed to see the predicament of my clients as oppression—as something that was group-based, structured, and systemic. The life of the oppressed "is confined and shaped by forces and barriers which are not accidental or occasional and hence avoidable, but are systematically related to each other in such a way as to catch one between and among them and restrict or penalize motion in any direction.'' The constraint is analogous to that of living within a cage where, in Frye's view, "all avenues, in every direction, are blocked or booby trapped.'' Thus, many of the problems my clients brought to me were recurring: another eviction, another welfare cut, another police beating, another inability to pay bills, an endless and miscellaneous list of booby traps. I did not see that they were linked problems that represented a cage-like structure.

When I represented white working-class clients in Hayward, California in the mid–1970s, I did not really appreciate the race-based exacerbation of poverty that distinguished them from my black and Latino clients. At that time, I was not sharp enough to see the intersection between race and class that I came to see much later in the 1980s. I saw my minority clients as being in a similar boat as the white poor. I knew that Appalachian poverty was different from Harlem poverty, but it was still primarily a class experience that was being played out in different locations. It is the feature of racialized poverty, however, that calls attention to group specificity and the fact that oppression is primarily a function of social group association. The compounded oppression of race-class is the qualitative difference between black-brown poverty and white poverty. My white clients certainly experienced the hardships of poverty. But they generally did not experience these hardships as a social group that was oppressed at the intersection of race *and* poverty. Almost never did they experience them at the tripartite intersection of race, space, and poverty. When we look at oppression, we must look at the specific social group experience and respond accordingly.

We must also pay attention to the structured aspect of poverty. Clearly poor people must take responsibility for their lives and battle the forces that might compel them to engage in dysfunctional behavior. But this responsibility is not enough, because, as Young points out:

> Oppression in the structural sense is part of the basic fabric of a society, not a function of a few people's choice or policies. You won't eliminate this structural oppression by getting rid of the rules or making some new laws, because oppressions are systematically reproduced in major economic, political, and cultural institutions.

The inner-city poor are oppressed by "the normal ongoing processes of everyday life.'' When we speak of empowerment and transformation, we should be referring not only to disrupting stark hierarchy and power imbalances, but also to changing the processes of everyday life as lived by those within the client community.

Finally, cause lawyering must develop a critical vocabulary to present race and racism as part of the poverty story. Here, critical race theory can be useful to the practice. It informs us that race and racism are always concepts in formation. Our notion of race and our experience with racism do not represent fixed, static phenomena. Racism is more than the intentional behavior of the occasional bad actor. Racism mutates and multiplies, creating a range of racisms. We must be able to bring up issues of race and racism without the terms always leading to fear, alienation, and off-point debate. There is no such thing as color-blind poverty. We must appreciate that because the inner-city poor are approximately seventy-five percent black and brown, inner-city poverty itself is "raced." One simply cannot seek economic justice and equal treatment for the poor by separating the quest from considerations of the raced aspects of context, history, social organization, institutional arrangements, and culture.

As Michael Omi notes, "racial and ethnic categories are often the effects of political interpretation and struggle and those categories in turn have political effects." Additionally, Omi reminds us that while we often correlate race with such matters as residential patterns, job qualifications, culture, academic achievement, criminal behavior, welfare dependency, and intelligence, we do so "without problemetizing the concept of race itself." Thus, we fail to appreciate the shifting parameters that mark the consideration of race—"how group interests are conceived, status is ascribed, agency is attained and roles performed." If our advocacy on behalf of the inner-city poor fails to incorporate this understanding, we are likely not only to be ineffective, but also to provide a disservice to the client community. We will disrespect the fullness of their predicament. The changes we seek will not be sufficiently fundamental.

A key aspect of cause lawyering is understanding that individual clients cannot be treated as separate from their racial, geographical, and class identities. Rather, as this part demonstrates, race, class, and "place" often converge to inform both individual client identity and societal perceptions of certain groups.

* * *

The issues confronting the inner-city poor point to a series of problems that we can trace to the inter-connected dynamics of racialized poverty, residential segregation, and the long history of racism. In order to understand the range of racisms in the United States we must appreciate the role that class plays and the relationship between race and class. The most constraining aspect of this relationship may be the way in which it is manifested in ghetto and barrio life. Thus, we must have a comprehensive view of the conditions to be redressed. We must recognize, as john powell observes, that "[r]ace and racism have had, and continue to have, a profound impact not only on who is poor in our society but also on the meaning of poverty and the policies that we adopt and fail to adopt."

In looking at the racial and ethnic data regarding neighborhood poverty, I am struck by two things. First, it is really not a significant problem for whites, as only one percent of all non-Hispanic whites live in poor neighborhoods. Second, for this reason, racism may continue to cultivate broad societal neglect and block efforts at grand-scale redress. As John Payne observes: "Racial discrimination is not far below the surface of economic discrimination. Our society simply would not tolerate the amount of poverty found in black and other minority communities if whites were proportionally as poor as these less-favored groups." I believe that Payne's observation is an accurate reflection of today's neglect of race-based need. Worse, his observation reflects on a legacy where the intersection of race and poverty has dampened the nation's commitment to bold anti-poverty redress.

Indeed, Hugh Heclo explicitly ties a retreat from fundamental anti-poverty policy to the disproportionate numbers of blacks to be affected. He observes that during the 1960s "[t]he minority status of all blacks left antipoverty policy highly vulnerable to white liberal doubts and antiblack racist sentiment." White support for racial justice remained strong as long as moral issues were salient in the civil rights movement—issues associated with addressing such matters as state-sanctioned segregation, political disenfranchisement, and antiblack violence, largely in the South. Support waned, however, when the movement's attention was redirected to the economic aspects of racial inequality. Heclo states, "[a]s the civil rights movement moved north after 1964 and pressed demands for open housing, busing, and affirmative action, the northern white civil rights constituency began melting away and undermining the political foundations of antipoverty policy." Many, perhaps most, Legal Services attorneys and other lawyers for the poor may have been deterred or detoured by the right-wing backlash against challenging the economic aspects of racial inequality. Too often we have simply treated poverty law practice as redressing the problems of poor people who were largely fungible clients who stood on common ground, as poor people. We have shied away from interjecting a racial element into the advocacy. This has been, and continues to be, a terrible flaw in our practice.

* * * [T]here are many ways in which inner-city poverty is different from other poverty. Those who experience it live under harsh and interlocking circumstances that reinforce the elements of poverty in ways that are very different from those of other poor people. Not only is their space generally racialized, but also they are socially isolated, geographically constrained, and, for many, their poverty is concentrated within high-poverty neighborhoods. Thus, they experience poverty not simply as individuals, but as members of a poor community, which is why I refer to them as clients in poverty *and* place.

The racialized inner-city poor, particularly African Americans and Puerto Ricans, experience concentrated poverty in their neighborhoods that is compounded by a spatial and geographic marginalization that deepens their intersectional racist and economic subordination. Within this context of ghetto and barrio poverty, geographic racism operates in a way that manifests the effects of what Michael Harrington has called "the new poverty." In the context of past poverty, the poor suffered from deprivation, constrained opportunity, and exploitation. These marked their economic inequality. A significant segment of today's poor, in contrast, are superfluous not only to the economy, but also to the nation's societal organization. * * *

The condition to be redressed under these circumstances is the face of oppression that Iris Young calls marginalization: "Marginalization is perhaps the most dangerous form of oppression. A whole category of people is expelled from useful participation in social life and thus potentially subjected to severe material deprivation and even extermination." Young also notes that "increasingly in the United States racial oppression occurs in the form of marginalization rather than exploitation. Marginals are people the system of labor cannot or will not use." Similarly, Katz characterizes marginalization as "the process whereby some combination of factors—for instance, technological change, racial competition, or government action—pushes groups to the edges of the labor force, leaving them redundant, unwanted, or confined to the worst jobs." As a fundamental criticism, marginalization theory must be recognized before society can attempt to redress the conditions and lived experiences of a significant number of the inner-city poor. Moreover, marginalization should direct the attention of cause lawyering in seeking to redress particular injustices.

* * * Urban space is now arranged in a hierarchy that reflects new patterns of increased economic, social, and political separation. Legal advocacy on behalf of the inner-city poor must recognize the interrelationships at work here and our practice must be responsive to them. Within the spatial hierarchy, at bottom is the largely abandoned city, in between is the suburban city, and at top is the luxury city. These spatial developments include the transformation of earlier racial and ethnic ghettos, whose white-ethnic occupants experienced the ghetto as a point of departure, into the present ghettos that society now excludes, abandons, and separates from others by social, economic, and often physical barriers.

A second development is a qualitatively new phase of suburbanization. No longer dependent on the central city for employment, services, or cultural or entertainment outlets, there is an increasing "totalizing suburban development, in which 'edge cities' are created combining residential, business, social, and cultural areas, removed from older central cities, overlaid on earlier patterns of suburbanization." While white suburbs have historically represented racial and class exclusion, there has been some dependence on central cities and some relation to a region as metropolitan. The totalizing environment of the suburb is a new and dramatic increase in localistic insularity and self-sufficiency. This development parallels the transformation of upper-class living areas, which are similarly totalizing, as separate, often gated communities. In Marcuse's view, "[t]he three developments are intimately connected with each other and mutually reinforcing." While not entirely new, these developments "are new phenomena that represent a combination of old and well-known processes with elements that are substantively new."

Traditional ghettos were sites of opportunity through exploitation. The residents were confined by dominant interests not only to facilitate a strong measure of social control but also to channel ghetto activities in a way to further dominant economic interests. The new ghetto of the excluded is very different. * * * [H]ere race and class intersect "in a spatially concentrated area where residents' activities are excluded from the economic life of the surrounding society, which does not profit significantly from its existence." Society is less inclined to use these residents, even under circumstances of exploitation, because "of fear that their activities, not controlled, may endanger the dominant social peace."

* * *

If we enter the context of poverty described here, it is not enough to direct intervention efforts at what occurs within poor communities. Rather, we must affect inter-spatial relationships. Spatial organization within the ghetto is now in a new relationship to related spatial organization. This geographic separation of blacks primarily, but also some Latinos, has important political consequences. Through the process of racialization it transforms many urban problems, particularly those associated with living in the city, into black and Latino problems. Indeed, the array of problems associated with city life get reduced to the black and brown poor, so that they become the problem. As Margaret Weir notes, "[t]his geo-political separation exacerbates the disconnection of the black [and brown] poor from whites, as the fate of the city becomes not a shared interest, but part of a battle over how resources will be distributed across political boundaries."

* * *

To all advocates, I wonder whether we can really "do good" without respecting the client community's voice, vision, and humanity. I know we pay lip service to issuing that respect, but nonetheless I wonder if our practice genuinely reflects it. It is our professional responsibility to do so. In responding to the actual conditions of the racialized, inner-city poor, we must direct our quest for the cause of social justice with respectful regard and comprehensive understanding of a world that is foreign to us, even as we practice within it. Practicing law in the community is not a tourist adventure and, therefore, we must eschew the routine of the autonomous, interloping advocate who dreams up cases in the home office and then tests them on the community. That is, we must search for invitation, opportunity, and connection that legitimate our very presence and committed practice. An open mind and a correct sensibility may be more important than the command of technical craft, because often we must learn as we go. We must approach that learning in non-linear, non-laboratory ways. Learning within our client communities will likely respond to these places as "eco-system[s] of knowledge" where learning is "multi-dimensional, often messy and confusing." Only through this approach will advocates effectively become incorporated within the client community.

Notes and Questions

1. What strategies can a lawyer use in order to follow Calmore's advice and avoid treating social justice practice as a "tourist adventure"? Is tourism inescapable when the lawyer returns home to a different neighborhood and social structure? Some commentators have urged a "law and organizing" model. *See, e.g.*, Scott L. Cummings & Ingrid V. Eagly, *A Critical Reflection on Law and Organizing*, 48 U.C.L.A. L. Rev. 443 (2001) (advocating a model that privileges community mobilization); Christine Parker, *Just Lawyers: Regulation and Access to Justice* (2000) (urging a model that incorporates both courtroom and informal everyday justice as well as social movement politics). *See also* Sophie Bryan, *Personally Professional: A Law Student in Search of an Advocacy Model*, 35 Harv. C.R.-C.L. L. Rev. 277 (2000) (describing one student's struggle with these issues).

2. Calmore comments that "the inner city poor are oppressed by 'the normal processes of everyday life.' " Can regnant lawyering change those processes? Can rebellious lawyers like Sophie and Amos?

3. Calmore underlines the importance of addressing race and racism as an aspect of social justice lawyering. *The Rockefeller Report*, discussed in the introduction to this book, agreed.

Lucie White elaborates on the importance of recognizing racial oppression, particularly as it links with poverty in the context of social justice practice:

> * * * [T]he overriding goal of attacking the link between race and poverty—between racialized institutional practices and the increasingly bipolar distribution of income, wealth, status, and power [is central]. This * * * lawyer's tactics may be all over the map—she may be involved in litigation, or in transactional work that seeks to develop enterprises or build community institutions. She may be involved in drafting legislation or lobbying for its enactment. She may be involved with all kinds of clients, groups, organizations, and social movements. But no matter where, how, or for whom she works, her overriding cause is to represent the most disempowered in today's world: to expose, historicize, denaturalize, and challenge the linkage between racial formations and the increasing north-south polarization of wealth and power. By challenging this linkage repeatedly, in big and small ways, she seeks to help disrupt the complacent coupling of race subordination and wealth division, the way that a swarm of gnats might disturb the peace of an sleeping lion. * * *
>
> Furthermore, no matter what this * * * lawyer's specific business is, she always seeks to activate political action, and thus build the capacity for more powerful political intervention. * * * What are the dimensions of political capacity that the progressive lawyer wants to draw forth and thus build up, through every move that she

> makes? There are six on my list: (1) every person's capacities for voice, for relating and caring for others, for maintaining well-being, for moral imagination; (2) the people's capacities for forming and working effectively in action groups; (3) for forming effective coalitions; (4) for staging cultural performances and kicking off social movement; (5) for critical deliberation and astute strategic planning; and (6) for democratically constituted leadership.

Symposium, Constitutional Lawyering in the 21st Century, March 4, 2000, Panel Three: Creating Models for Progressive Lawyering in the 21st Century, 9 J.L. & Pol'y 297, 309–10 (2000) (remarks by Lucie White).

4. While agreeing that addressing race and racial issues is important, john a. powell notes the difficulty of recognizing racial issues in neutral discourse:

> [A]s explicitly racist discourse has been discredited, a new discourse consistent with conventional understandings of race has emerged to maintain White supremacy. Many of the race-neutral terms that are popular in today's discourse have overtly racist historical underpinnings and practical racial implications. For example, terms like "individualism," "working class" and "equal opportunity" all hearken back to explicitly racist exclusionary practices.

john a. powell, *The "Racing" of American Society: Race Functioning as a Verb Before Signifying as a Noun*, 15 Law & Ineq. 99, 109 (1997). *See also* Naomi R. Cahn, *Representing Race Outside of Explicitly Racialized Contexts*, 95 Mich. L. Rev. 965 (1997) (exploring the gendered and raced images in the welfare reform debate and urging that the stereotypes embedded in the discussion be made explicit).

Do racial issues require special attention from lawyers working with communities? *See* Kevin Johnson, *Lawyering for Social Change: What's a Lawyer to Do?*, 5 Mich. J. Race & L. 201 (1999) (considering the lawyer's role in easing interracial tension); Eric K. Yamamoto, *Critical Race Praxis: Race Theory and Political Lawyering Praxis in Post-Civil Rights America*, 95 Mich. L. Rev. 821 (1997) (describing litigation as critical race praxis); and Eric K. Yamamoto, *Interracial Justice: Conflict and Reconciliation in Post-Civil Rights America* 128–49 (1999). *See also* Bill Ong Hing, *In the Interest of Racial Harmony: Revisiting the Lawyer's Duty to Work for the Common Good,* 47 Stan. L. Rev. 901 (1995) (urging that an ethical goal for community lawyering should be racial justice).

For further readings on race and racial theory see Derrick Bell, *Race, Racism and American Law* (4th ed., 2000); *A Reader on Race, Civil Rights, and American Law: A Multicultural Approach* (Timothy Davis, Kevin R. Johnson & George A. Martinez eds., 2001); and Juan F. Perea, Richard Delgado, Angela P. Harris & Stephanie M. Wildman, *Race and Races: Cases and Resources for a Diverse America* (2000). Over the last decade, scholars have also relied on critical race theory to examine the relationship between law and subordination. *See Critical Race Theory:*

The Key Writings That Formed the Movement (Kimberlé Crenshaw, Neil Gotanda, Gary Peller & Kendall Thomas eds., 1995); *Critical Race Theory: The Cutting Edge* (Richard Delgado & Jean Stefancic eds., 2d ed. 2000); *Crossroads, Directions, and a New Critical Race Theory* (Francisco Valdes, Jerome McCrystal Culp & Angela P. Harris eds., 2002); and *Critical Race Feminism: A Reader* (Adrien Katherine Wing ed., 1997).

JULIE A. SU

Making the Invisible Visible: The Garment Industry's Dirty Laundry
1 J. Gender, Race & Just. 405, 405–17 (1998)

This is the story of some garment workers very dear to my heart who were enslaved in El Monte, California. From their homes in impoverished rural Thailand, these garment workers dared to dream the immigrant dream, a life of hard work with just pay, decency, self-sustenance for themselves and their families, and hope. What they found instead in America was an industry—the garment industry—that mercilessly reaps profits from workers and then closes its eyes, believing that if it refuses to see, it cannot be held responsible. What these workers also found were government bureaucracies so inhumane and so impersonal that such agencies confuse their purpose to serve the people with a mandate merely to perpetuate themselves.

* * *

On August 2, 1995, modern slave labor in America emerged from invisibility with the discovery of seventy-one Thai garment workers, sixty-seven of whom were women, in a suburb of Los Angeles: El Monte, California. These Thai workers were held in a two-story apartment complex with seven units where they were forced to work, live, eat and sleep in the place they called "home" for as long as seven years. A ring of razor wire and iron inward-pointing spikes, the kind usually pointed outward to keep intruders out, surrounded the apartment complex. They ensured the workers could not escape.

The workers lived under the constant threat of harm to themselves and their families. They were told that if they tried to resist or escape, their homes in Thailand would be burned, their families murdered, and they would be beaten. As proof, the captors caught a worker trying to escape, beat him, and took a picture of his bruised and battered body to show the other workers. They were also told that if they reported what was happening to anyone, they would be sent to the Immigration and Naturalization Service (INS). The workers were not permitted to make unmonitored phone calls or write or receive uncensored letters. Armed guards imposed discipline. Because the workers were not permitted to leave, their captors brought in groceries and other daily necessities and sold them to the workers at four or five times the actual price. When the workers were released and we first took them to the grocery store, they were shocked by the prices of toiletries, toothpaste, shampoo, fruits and vegetables. They had, of course, no way to know that they had been price gouged at the same time that they were making less than a dollar an hour for their eighteen-hour work days.

Hundreds of thousands of pieces of cloth, spools of thread, and endless, monotonous stitches marked life behind barbed wire. Labels of brand name manufacturers and nationwide retailers came into El Monte in boxes and left El Monte on blouses, shorts, shirts and dresses. Manufacturer and retailer specifications, diagrams, details and deadlines haunted the workers and consumed their lives.

The workers tell me that though eighteen-hour days were the norm, they sometimes worked more depending on how quickly the manufacturers and retailers wanted their orders. The workers had to drink large quantities of coffee or splash water on their faces to stay awake. When they were finally permitted to go upstairs to sleep, they slept on the floor, eight or ten to a bedroom made for two, while rats and roaches crawled over them. The Thai workers were denied adequate medical attention, including care for respiratory illnesses caused by poor air, eye problems including near blindness, repetitive motion disorders, and even cancerous tumors. One of the workers extracted eight of his own teeth after periodontal disease went untreated. Today, we are still dealing with many of the health effects of the long years of neglect and physical and psychological torture. Freedom from imprisonment has not meant freedom from its many tragic effects.

Once the El Monte complex was discovered, however, the workers were not freed. The INS immediately took them and threw them into detention at a federal penitentiary where they found themselves again behind barbed wire. The INS forced the workers to wear prison uniforms while in detention. "Due process" consisted of reading an obscure legal document that the workers were compelled to sign, making them deportable. Each day, an INS bus shuttled the workers back and forth from the detention center to the downtown INS facility, where they waited interminably in holding tanks that felt like saunas. As if this were not horror enough, the INS shackled them like dangerous criminals each time the INS transported them. A small group of activists, mostly twenty-something-year-old Asian Americans, demanded their release. As a policy matter, we insisted that the continued detention of the Thai workers was wrong; it sent the message to abused and exploited workers that if they reported the abuse and exploitation, they would be punished—that the INS would imprison and then deport them. Sweatshop operators use this fear as a tool for their cruel and unlawful practices. Workers are commonly told, "If you resist or if you report me, I will call the INS." Garment industry manufacturers and retailers profit by the millions by employing such workers and exploiting their vulnerability. The INS's role in furthering the imprisonment of the Thai workers could only serve to discourage workers from reporting labor law, civil rights, and human rights abuses, and push operations like El Monte further underground. The INS, we asserted, ought not conspire with exploitative employers.

We quickly learned that the INS is not convinced by sound policy arguments. So we resorted to aggression and street tactics. We set up a makeshift office in the basement waiting room of INS detention. We used their pay phones, banged on windows, and closed down the INS at one or two in the morning, refusing to accept "paperwork" and bureaucracy as an excuse for the continued detention of the Thai workers. By the end of the nine long days and nights before the workers' release, both pay phones were broken, as we had slammed them back onto the receivers in frustration each time we received an unsatisfactory and unjust response.

I am convinced that we succeeded in getting the workers released in just over a week in part because we did *not* know the rules, because we would not accept procedures that made no sense either in our hearts or to our minds. It was an important lesson that our formal education might, at times, actually make us *less* effective advocates for the causes we believe in and for the people we care about.

Soon after the workers were freed from INS detention, they filed a civil lawsuit in federal district court in Los Angeles. Their lawsuit charged the immediate operators of the El Monte compound with false imprisonment, civil RICO, labor law and civil rights violations. The suit also brought these charges against the manufacturers and retailers who ordered the clothes and who control the entire garment manufacturing process from cut cloth to sewn garment to sale on the racks. At the same time, the United States Department of Justice, through the U.S. Attorney's office in Los Angeles, brought a criminal case against the operators, charging them with involuntary servitude, criminal conspiracy, kidnaping by trick, and smuggling and harboring individuals in violation of U.S. immigration law.

The criminal case was the first of many conflicts I would see between the mandates of traditional legal avenues for achieving justice and the goals of nontraditional political and social activism. The criminal case highlighted the tension between the limited redress that forms the model for most (though certainly not all) traditional litigation, and the achievement of justice broadly defined. Because the workers were the key witnesses in the criminal case, the prosecutors at the U.S. Attorney's office warned them not to speak out about the abuses they had endured. Whereas this restriction may have made sense in the context of the criminal prosecution, it served to silence, indeed make invisible again, the Thai workers at a time when their own voices needed to be heard. Thus, a conflict existed between the criminal law's narrow focus on punishing the workers' captors and a larger hope that subordinated individuals and communities could increase control over their own lives.

In February 1996, the captors pleaded guilty and were sentenced to prison terms of two to seven years. Yet the workers' struggles were just beginning. Upon conclusion of the criminal case, the workers' civil lawsuit could now proceed.

On one level, the civil lawsuit is significant simply because workers have accessed the legal system. In the large majority of cases, the notion of legal protections for exploited workers and redress for violations is illusory. Workers too seldom find the legal system open to them. The significance of the workers' civil lawsuit, however, is greater still than the fact that workers have gained access. The suit is also significant because it names the manufacturers and retailers whose clothes the garment workers sewed. Rather than limiting its theories of liability to the immediate captors of the Thai workers, this lawsuit seeks to establish corporate accountability.

The theories against the manufacturers and retailers fall into four categories. First, they are joint employers of the workers, and therefore subject to all federal and state labor laws governing employers. The manufacturers and retailers defend themselves by maintaining that the manner in which they practice, and the way the industry has been structured, allows manufacturers and retailers to "independently contract" with sewing shops who make their clothes, insulating them from employer status.

Second, the manufacturers and retailers acted negligently in hiring and supervising the workers. The El Monte operation was structured so that more than seventy Thai workers were held against their will and forced to work eighteen hours a day, while a couple [of] "front shops" in downtown Los Angeles employed seventy some Latina and Latino garment workers in "typical" sweatshops—the kind that characterize the Los Angeles garment industry. The manufacturers and retailers sent their goods to the front shops. Many of the workers at the front shops performed finishing: ironing, sewing buttons and buttonholes, cutting off thread, packaging and hanging and checking finished clothes. The manufacturers and retailers sent quality control representatives to the front shops to ensure that their clothes were being made to specification. The turnaround time the manufacturers demanded was much too fast for the downtown locations to have been furnishing all of the work. Such large quantities of high quality garments could not have been filled by workers making the requisite minimum wage and overtime.

Third, the manufacturers and retailers violated various provisions of state law requiring all those engaged in the business of garment manufacturing to register with the California Labor Commissioner and to avoid the use of industrial homeworkers for garment production. Federal law also provides that any person or corporation that places products in the stream of commerce for sale for profit must ensure that its products are not produced in violation of minimum wage and overtime laws. Manufacturers' and retailers' failure to comply with these laws constitutes negligence per se.

Fourth, the lawsuit charges that manufacturers and retailers violated California law in engaging and continuing to engage in unfair and unlawful business practices.

One of the most legally significant, politically important, as well as personally gratifying aspects of the workers' lawsuit is the inclusion of the Latina and Latino garment workers as plaintiffs. The Latina workers are entitled to redress for the hundreds of thousands of dollars in minimum wage and overtime payments they were denied. While not held physically against their will, they lived in economic servitude. Despite working full-time, year-round, they were still unable to rise above poverty. The inclusion of the Latina workers is also significant for another reason. The discovery of slave labor in the California garment industry had, I feared, set a new standard for how bad things had to be before people would be outraged. We would no longer be horrified by conditions that are standard throughout the garment industry: overcrowded conditions and dark warehouses, endless hours for subminimum wage, constant harassment, and degrading treatment. The reasoning would be, ironically, "at least they weren't held and forced to work as slaves; at least we don't see barbed wire." The workers united in their civil suit send a clear message to garment manufacturers and retailers: this case is not just about slave labor. You are not only responsible for involuntary servitude; this case is also about the hundreds of thousands of garment workers, primarily Latina, laboring in sweatshops throughout the United States.

The strategic value of this move has been confirmed again and again, both by the defendants' continual efforts to distinguish and separate the Thai and Latino workers, and also by the pressure other manufacturers and retailers in the industry have placed on the defendants because the potential impact on the garment industry is enormous.

The struggle the workers are engaged in challenges us and challenges various elements of our society in at least five ways. The first is a challenge the workers issue to the corporate powers in the garment industry. The lawsuit has the potential to transform the way manufacturers and retailers do business. The workers' lawsuit forces us to view abuses such as these not as isolated incidents, but as structural deficiencies. Unless and until corporations are held accountable for exploitation, abuse of workers will continue and sweatshops will remain a shameful reality—the dirty laundry of the multi-billion dollar fashion industry.

The second challenge is to workers themselves and to their advocates. The workers have had to learn that even in this country, nothing is won without a fight, no power is shifted without struggle, and no one is more powerful to stand up for them than they themselves. They—and I—have learned that mere access to the legal system and to lawyers does not ensure that justice will be served. No one will give you a social and economic structure governed by principles of compassion and equality over corporate profit, particularly if you are poor, non-English speaking, an immigrant, a woman of color, a garment worker—unless you fight for it yourself. It is also a challenge to the workers and to me to maintain and build the coalition between Asian and Latina workers. These are workers who share neither a common language nor cultural and national roots. When we have had joint meetings with all the workers, each meeting takes three times as long because every explanation, question, answer and issue needs to be translated into three languages. But its rewards are so precious. A Thai worker says in Thai, "We are so grateful finally to be free so we can stand alongside you and to struggle with you, to make better lives for us all," and her words are translated from Thai into English, then from English into Spanish. At the moment when comprehension washes over the faces of the Latina workers, a light of understanding goes on in their eyes, and they begin to nod their heads slowly in agreement, you feel the depth of that connection.

Working across racial lines has also posed challenges for me as an Asian American woman. As such, the Latino workers who first came to see me were skeptical and a bit suspicious of me. "¿Si ayuda los Thailandeses, porque quiere ayudarnos?" ["If you are helping the Thai workers, why would you want to help us?"] I answered the best I could in Spanish, "Porque creo in justicia, y la lucha es muy grande. Si no luchamos juntos, no podemos ganar." ["Because I believe in justice and the struggle is a big one. If we do not fight together, we will not succeed."] The garment industry's structure magnifies ethnic and racial conflict at the bottom—workers against factory operators. Workers, who are primarily Latino and Latina, see their daily subjugation enforced by factory operators who are primarily Asian; Asian owners transfer the pressure and exploitation they experience from manufacturers and retailers to the garment workers. Ironically, Asian owners learn Spanish to enable them to communicate, but often little more than "rapido, mas rapido." Poverty and helplessness experienced by immigrants, Asian and Latino, combine with language and racial differences to make the garment industry a source of racial tension. Meanwhile, manufacturers and retailers, like puppet masters high above the scene they create and control, wield their power with impunity.

Third, the workers' struggles and their strength have challenged the government. The workers' case says to the INS that its way of doing business as usual is totally unacceptable. The INS cannot be a tool of exploitative employers to keep workers from bettering their lives. The workers in the garment industry further challenge the narrow ways in which government compartmentalizes the lives of subordinated individuals. Garment workers' cases are about labor law violations, so they fall under the purview of the Department of Labor. But in an industry like the garment industry, where almost all the workers are poor women of color, we have a civil rights problem. Why are manufacturers and retailers not investigated for rampant civil rights abuses? Why is the State Department not involved, where issues of foreign policy, and manufacturer and retailer conduct in countries around the world, so clearly impact the human rights of poor workers in other countries and immigrant workers in the United States? Where is the Presidential

Commission on rooting out the shameful existence of sweatshops in this country? Such a commission ought to call on manufacturers and retailers, who create and profit from such conditions, to take responsibility and change their practices.

Fourth, the workers' lawsuit challenges our legal system. It says that our legal system has to be able to bridge the gap between reality and justice. Manufacturers and retailers cannot simply walk into court with an argument that on its face looks like an independent contracting relationship without looking at the reality of what they have done. Manufacturers and retailers have created a structure intended to get around existing law and to perpetuate subordination of workers.

The lawsuit also challenges the legal system's primary focus on lawyers. The legal system is a forum for lawyers—a place where we write our briefs, argue in court, play our game and go home. The question for me as a lawyer is this: how are the workers made better off, even if we win this suit, if they do not feel like they have been participants in the process? The fact that the workers often want to rely on lawyers makes the struggle more difficult. Moreover, whether through an inflated sense of self-importance, or a desire for self-preservation, we all too often want to monopolize control and power. We are told in law school that we and only we understand this system. But even if they receive thousands of dollars once the case is over, the workers are not necessarily better off if they have not gained some control over their lives and access to a system that has largely been closed off to them and to people like them.

I avoid referring to the workers as "clients." To me, it impersonalizes the workers and places them in a dependent relationship. As "clients," the relationship is defined by my education and skills as their "lawyer"; instead, by referring to them as "workers," their experiences define our work together. I talk with them not just in terms of legal rights, but in terms of basic human dignity. For many people, when language is framed as "law," I have seen an immediate shift in their willingness to engage in the dialogue; many people think the discussion is suddenly taking place in a language they do not and cannot understand. What workers do understand is a language of human dignity. They desire to be treated as human beings, not as animals or machines. Human dignity must be the measure of what we recognize as legal rights.

Finally, the question of not only what particular words we use, but *which* language we use is critical. The workers will often ask me to tell their story for them, both because I can tell it in English and because they believe my knowledge of the law instills in me instant efficacy as a spokesperson. However, they are wrong. Forced into English or into the narrow confines of legal terminology, the workers become speechless. But when I listen to them tell their stories in their own language, listen to them describe their suffering, their pain, their hope through the long, dark days, they become poetic and strong. We as lawyers and advocates must always encourage those who have lived the experiences to tell them, in whatever language they speak.

The final challenge of this lawsuit and the workers' struggle is to the paradigms by which we operate and through which we engage social justice issues. The garment industry and the lives of these garment workers give reality to concepts such as intersectionality and multi-layered oppression. Within racial justice movements there are classist notions; among workers' rights advocates there is racism. These workers embody characteristics of almost every disaffected group in our society today. Women of color, the poor, non-English speaking immigrants, and workers are all under attack in our mainstream national discourse.

It is not enough to see their struggles through one lens or through limited models of racial justice, immigrants rights, or workers rights. They challenge us to view the achievement of a just society far more broadly than these paradigms permit.

The media's role, both news and entertainment, has been such a big part of the work involving the El Monte Thai workers. Without question, the media can be an ally. The local, national and international coverage of the slave conditions under which the Thai workers were held brought public sympathy to and knowledge of their suffering. Accurate portrayal of the context in which it occurred—the garment industry—sheds light on a highly exploitative and lawless industry in which human lives pay the price of corporate greed. The media has helped us particularly because those against whom we struggle, big corporations whose names have financial value and government agencies both state and federal, care very much about public opinion and thrive on their public images. In short, the media plays a critical role in making the invisible visible.

But the struggle, related to media visibility, is how we keep our stories from becoming distorted. The media has resisted covering the union of Asian and Latina workers in this struggle. While racial discord between communities of color is newsworthy, particularly in Los Angeles, interracial solidarity is not. The Latina workers have thus remained largely invisible to the public.

The media likes simplistic stories. I have learned that they portray isolated "heroes" and nameless groups of "victims." The continuous victim status imposed on the workers gives the false impression that they are not full human beings engaged in a struggle for justice, committed to a better world, and intent on ensuring that others do not suffer what they have.

More recent coverage of exploitative conditions and inhumane treatment of workers in the garment industry further highlights this problem. Morning television talk show host Kathie Lee Gifford and her reaction to the discovery that her private label was being sewn by child laborers in Honduras and sweatshop workers in New York received extensive news coverage. Just as legal education might have us believe that lawyers solve the problems of an inequitable society through lawsuits, news coverage paints a picture of celebrity goodwill as the antidote to exploitation. When Gifford and her former football-star husband handed out $300 cash to workers denied minimum wage and overtime in New York, major newspapers and news stations across the country reported it in the headlines.

This kind of news coverage suggests that workers want handouts. Again, the worker as independent actor is made invisible by worker as passive, powerless recipient. From my experience, they do not want one-time handouts. What they want is a just day's pay for a just day's work. The workers continually attend court hearings, get on buses to come to meetings, spend hours responding to discovery requests and the other demands of litigation. They have gone with me to retail stores to see garments they made selling for a price they could never afford. People who question, or ignore altogether, the value of this level of participation by the workers utterly miss the power of litigation to teach and to change. The workers continue to fight, not for the far-off possibility of collecting money, but for the sense of control it gives them over their lives and out of a fundamental belief that social justice demands it.

Finally, I want to share one story about the media that illuminates the many facets of the struggle for justice. Several months ago, I received a call from a Hollywood producer. The producer had called before, soon after the Thai workers were discovered. At that time, I had told her that the workers' story was not mine to sell, and she would have to wait until the workers were in a position to decide for themselves if they wanted their story told this way. She was calling again now because the criminal case was over and the suit against the manufacturers and retailers was going well. She billed it as a huge Hollywood movie that would get the workers' story out to millions of people, and then she said, "To make this really work, we need a hero."

I interrupted this familiar refrain with, "The workers are the heroes; they are the ones who endured, who were resilient, who have worked to rebuild their lives and who continue to engage in the fight for justice."

"No, no, no," she insisted. "I have read all the newspaper accounts and you've really been a hero. But what we need is an *American* hero."

Now I had spent many months dealing with unreasonable, often ignorant, even offensive people and positions, but I was momentarily stunned. After she repeated herself, I responded, "You must mean a white hero then, because I am an American."

It was her turn to pause, no doubt realizing, even without understanding why, that she had said something wrong. She countered, "Oh, of course you are . . . and I'm not a bad person" and proceeded to list the movies she and her company had produced to show they were an "issues-oriented" company—a movie about domestic violence, one on the Watts riots. But she just wanted me to understand "what sells" in the entertainment world. Then she added, "Now if you had a romance, that would make a great angle." So the movie script would read: white man saves Asian woman, and in the process, rescues all the Thai workers too.

As an Asian American woman and an advocate, I have been confronted with ignorance, racism, preconceptions, stereotypes and multiple challenges. This story leads me to conclude with some of the tensions I feel in the work that I do.

First, the tension embodied in the question, what is the purpose of the lawsuit? Is the purpose to win the lawsuit or is the lawsuit a process by which workers, immigrant workers, women, women of color become more empowered and politicized? Are these mutually exclusive purposes? And do we take this case all the way through to a judgment or do we accept manufacturers' and retailers' small offers to settle? If we take this case to trial and win, the precedent-setting impact would be enormous. On the other hand, the risk of an adverse judgment may not be one the workers are willing to or should be counseled to take. They live in poverty, need to pay rent, buy clothing and food for themselves and their children. There is an ongoing tension between the immediate needs of particular workers and the larger, social justice ends to which we are committed.

Second, with regard to the idea of invisibility, I have suggested that even if you gain visibility through the media, you can still be made invisible again. Similarly, even after you have filed a lawsuit, you can be made invisible by the way the legal system operates. The question really is how do we listen to and tell the stories of these workers—bring them out of invisibility—without distorting their stories at the same time? The legal terms at our disposal are wholly inadequate to describe and address what these workers have been through and continue to experience. We stay away from the immigration aspect of their case because we fear backlash in this climate. When the workers were first discovered, the news media referred to them as "Thai nationals" or "illegal immigrants." We insisted on calling them "workers," thus shifting the focus from their immigration status to their experiences in the United States in the garment industry. But when United States immigration policies contribute directly to the vulnerability of immigrant workers and facilitate the kind of exploitation workers suffer, have we not distorted the workers' experience by downplaying that aspect of their lives and of their struggle?

Third, workers face risks for their actions that we as their advocates do not. What do I say to a worker after I have informed her of the rights she has—to minimum wage and overtime, to organize, to work without harassment or intimidation, to seek redress without retaliation, and to speak out—and I tell her, I will fight with you if you want to fight for these rights; then she goes out on a picket line and marches for corporate accountability, her employer sees it on the six o'clock news and she gets fired the next day? There are real dangers for people who stand up and fight; is it right or sufficient for us to say, "This is an important struggle and we think it is something we all need to be a part of together?"

Finally, I experience tensions as a community lawyer, or lawyer activist. As an Asian American woman, I embody traits traditionally excluded from the environments, the profession, and the system to which I have sought access. I engage in my own struggle to be heard, to find words that describe my life and vision and make my experiences resonate within the narrow language of the law, and to change a legal system and a society that does not recognize my experience of injustice or exclusion. Other lawyers treat and view the lawyer activist as an outsider. Here, I am not just talking about the times I have been ignored, when a white male attorney representing a garment manufacturer reached directly past me to shake the hands of my white male co-counsel, for example. I am not talking about those many instances.

I am talking about the attorneys *on our side* who say, "If you want to do all that political and educational stuff, organize meetings with the workers and visit them in their homes at night, go ahead and do that. But leave the 'real' lawyering—the hard-core strategizing, brief writing and arguing—to the real lawyers." But to me, the traditional, so-called "real" lawyers, who are not engaged in the workers' lives, cannot represent them in the lawsuit in a way that is true to the workers. The lawyer activist has to be an active participant in the litigation to ensure that the workers' lives guide the litigation. Lawyer activists have to be active participants in litigation to transform the practice of law.

Lawyer activists are often marginalized by non-lawyers as well. Many progressive activists with whom I have worked refer to lawyers as "necessary evils." They feel that lawyers distort and destroy a struggle, wanting to speak for the workers and take over the cause, insisting on leading rather than joining. Non-lawyer activists often seek to limit the role of the lawyer activist to that more suited to a traditional lawyer—at the margins of the struggle.

So what is our role as lawyers? How can we make transformative work—both in our profession and our communities—real? I do not know the answers to these difficult questions. I do not even know if finding answers is the ultimate goal. But I believe that anyone who tells you these tensions are not worth struggling over misses the essence of what it means to be an advocate for people *and* an advocate for justice. Law school does a good job of telling you that all of these tensions are really nonsense, or at best, that they make for interesting discussions in those "soft, fuzzy" courses but have no place in the real practice of law. I want to tell you that is absolutely wrong.

* * *

The workers say that they are engaged in the struggle not for money, and not necessarily even because they think we will win the lawsuit or radically alter the corporate power structure. They are engaged, they say, because their humanity depends on it. And I would say we engage in the struggle with them not for their humanity, but for ours.

Notes and Questions

1. What tensions exist for lawyers representing communities from which they don't come? Do Su's experiences in representing different communities across racial/cultural lines suggest strategies to assist lawyers representing communities different from their own?

2. Su uses the phrases "community lawyer" and "lawyer activist" to identify her work. Are these phrases synonymous? Must a community lawyer be an activist? Is the identity "activist" incompatible with the identity "lawyer?" Have you been involved in strategies for social change that were effective or in any political work that you might describe as organizing, activism, or direct action? Do you have any feelings about the word "activism"?

3. Coalition work may be an important part of social justice lawyering, as lawyers work with communities and with each other:

> "[T]he success of social justice work depends upon the ability of those committed to the fight—whether conceiving of themselves as insiders or outsiders—to come together, to work and to listen to each other."

Phoebe A. Haddon, *Coalescing With SALT: A Taste for Inclusion*, 11 S. Cal. Rev. Law & Women's Stud. 321 (2002) (describing the priority placed on coalition-building and inclusion strategies). *See also* Bernice Johnson Reagon, *Coalition Politics: Turning the Century* in *Home Girls: A Black Feminist Anthology* 356–68 (Barbara Smith ed., 1983) (explaining "Most of the time you feel threatened to the core and if you don't you're not really doing no coalescing."). *See also* Sumi Cho & Robert Westley, *Critical Race Coalitions: Key Movements That Performed the Theory*, 33 U.C. Davis L. Rev. 1377 (2000) (urging a race-centered coalitional model as essential for moving toward inclusion in education).

Can protest enhance efforts toward inclusion and coalition or does it undermine those goals?

4. Su depicts struggles she has faced with other lawyers and the media about her own identity and how she is perceived. How will you respond to similar tensions? Have you ever felt invisible? How have you combated that invisibility? For further discussion, see chapter 4 on becoming a lawyer and staying yourself.

5. Do the authors in this section trust that lawyers drawn to social justice work will have political instincts to guide them? Might this assumption be true for some law students, but not all?

6. The articles in this chapter describe work by lawyers that is not typically highlighted as part of legal education. How can you develop your own skills and find support for that development at your law school? Su commented that formal education might have made her a less effective advocate. Might it be an advantage not to know the rules?

Chapter 4

PERSONAL IDENTITY, ROLE, AND VALUES: BECOMING A LAWYER, STAYING YOURSELF

Deborah Rhode and David Luban ask, "To what extent can the idea that lawyers have a *role morality* different from ordinary morality be justified?" Deborah L. Rhode & David Luban, *Legal Ethics* 137 (1992). This puzzle is illustrated by the following story:

> A parishioner approaches a priest and says, "Father, I don't understand how, if God is good and loves us, He can permit so much pain in the world." The priest hesitates, then replies: "God has to do a lot of things in his professional capacity that He would never do if it were up to him personally."

Id. at 138. In three sections, this chapter explores this role morality problem within the respective contexts of professional socialization, practicing within the accepted and challenged assumptions of the adversary system, and joining the profession as a happy and healthy human being.

Advocates who practice social justice lawyering operate within a traditional system of lawyers. Yet, committing to social justice may clash with dominant understandings of professional responsibility. Austin Sarat & Stuart Scheingold, *Cause Lawyering and Reproduction of Professional Authority*, in *Cause Lawyering: Political Commitments and Professional Responsibilities* 3, 7 (Austin Sarat & Stuart Scheingold eds., 1998). As Bradley Wendel observes, when social justice advocacy takes on the contours of political activity, which it often must, then practicing law may amount "to tickling the dragon's tail. One is playing around with the instrumentalities of one's own corruption, but these same means are necessary in order for any good to come through the rule of law administered by lawyers." W. Bradley Wendel, *Value Pluralism in Legal Ethics*, 78 Wash. U. L. Q. 113, 190 (2000).

Law students and advocates committed to social justice lawyering often swim against the tide of dominant understandings that drive their professional socialization. Many tend not to recognize that the process of socialization and the values it promotes are integral parts of a system: "We are generally not socialized to understand systems as systems, to analyze how they actually work and their consequences. Instead, we come to understand systems as a taken-for-granted reality that is simply as it seems to be." Allan G. Johnson, *The Blackwell Dictionary of Sociology: A User's Guide to Sociological Language* 267 (1995). Law school is part of the socialization process for the legal profession. As you consider what the commitment to social justice entails, ask whether it requires that law students must undergo *re-socialization*?

For those pursuing traditional career paths, a system of lawyers may appear to be simply a taken-for-granted reality that poses few conflicts. But for all lawyers, professional socialization entails a process through which we create our professional selves. We attach ourselves to that system and we enable it to function in a business-as-usual fashion. Like every social system, the system of lawyers "depends upon people who are motivated to perform the various roles that it encompasses." *Id.* Thus, professional socialization describes a process by which we learn to become members of the bar—our profession—through internalizing the norms and values of the profession, and also by learning what our roles are and how to perform those roles. Because professional socialization is not fixed, but continues throughout our professional lives, it is subject to contestation. It is possible, therefore, to carve out norms, values, roles, and behaviors that are well suited to working to secure justice. According to Robert Nelson and David Trubek, "Conceptions of lawyer professionalism reflect 'the arenas' in which they are produced, that is, the particular institutional settings in which groups construct, explicitly or implicitly, models of the law and of lawyering. The arenas perspective allows for the possibility that different groups will develop different versions of the professional ideal in response to a variety of political, ideological, and situational concerns." Robert L. Nelson & David M. Trubek, *Arenas of Professionalism: The Professional Ideologies of Lawyers in Context*, in *Lawyers' Ideals/Lawyers' Practices: Transformations in the American Legal Profession* 177, 179 (Robert L. Nelson & David M. Trubek eds., 1992). Moreover, as Jane Aiken suggests, for instance, educators can work to cultivate among students a "justice readiness" and "ensure that the future lawyers we are training have an appreciation for justice and work to inspire them to use their legal skills to bring about a more just society." Jane H. Aiken, *Provocateurs for Justice*, 7 Clinical L. Rev. 287, 306 (2001).

Thus, section 1 explores Aiken's concept of becoming ready for justice, starting with an examination of the process that transforms a lay person into a lawyer. Some of the material refers to clinical pedagogy in particular. At first blush, a student may remark: "Yes, good idea—tell my professor that." But the professional behavior of law school graduates and students is greatly affected by their legal education, and clinical education may play a particularly significant role for those who engage in social justice lawyering. Stephen Wizner, for example, states: "Today, outside of a relatively small number of academic purists, the majority of law teachers would subscribe to the notion that law teachers have at least some responsibility for the socialization and acculturation of law students into the norms and values of the legal profession. The law school clinic provides an educational setting in which that is a primary objective." Stephen Wizner, *The Law School Clinic: Legal Education in the Interests of Justice*, 70 Fordham L. Rev. 1929, 1936 (2002).

As indicated in section 2, in examining the relation of law, lawyers, and professional responsibilities, the particular role of the social justice advocate within the adversary system is a fundamental consideration. Traditionally, the professional role is divorced from the individual's values and moral principles. The standard conception of the lawyer's role is characterized by the ideological features of "extreme partisanship" and "moral non-accountability." Murray L. Schwartz, *The Professionalism and Accountability of Lawyers*, 66 Calif. L. Rev. 669, 671 (1978). Where does the social justice lawyer fit within an adversary system that values extreme partisanship and moral non-accountability as preeminent norms?

Section 3 explores aspects of entering the profession, focusing particularly on the connection between role conceptualization and professional socialization within large-firm legal practice.

SECTION 1. BECOMING JUSTICE READY

Law school is a primary institutional site of professional socialization. For better or worse, students are being socialized through a legal methodology in much the same way now as when Christopher Columbus Langdell "discovered" a new way to teach law by using the case method. While clinical education has made some inroads as an alternative, the case method continues to dominate the first year of law school. What impact does this socialization—assimilating the conventional lessons of advocacy and analysis—have on students' social justice aspirations? Does legal training reinforce what Gary Blasi describes as "the professional myopia of lawyers," a condition that blinds lawyers to all issues that do not present themselves as issues of litigation? Gary Blasi, *The Homeless Seminar at U.C.L.A.*, 42 Wash. U.J. Urb. & Contemp. L. 85, 86 (1992).

ELIZABETH DVORKIN, JACK HIMMELSTEIN & HOWARD LESNICK

Becoming a Lawyer: A Humanistic Perspective on Legal Education and Professionalism 1–3 (1981)

* * * We believe that a subtle process of professionalization occurs during law school without being addressed or even acknowledged. This learning by inadvertence means that the participants often fail to consider fundamental questions about the identity they are assuming, and its relation to their values. These questions about professional identity are difficult and elusive, hard to capture as they arise moment-

to-moment in the classroom or practice, and hard to respond to. They are also vital, it seems to us, to anyone who is choosing to spend three years in law school, and anywhere from a few years to a lifetime in the practice of law. Their importance also extends to the greater community; the construction of a professional identity for lawyers helps determine what the practice of law, and law itself, will mean for society.

The lawyer's professional identity is shaped in part by the boundaries we adhere to in deciding what is appropriate and inappropriate to legal education. In general we emphasize the ability to analyze and advocate, placing a high value on the capacity to be precise, logical and objective. Law students learn that because the legal system is proof-oriented, they should make statements that can be defended through objective criteria. In order to identify and then respond to the specific legal issues posed by the problems presented, they develop and refine their ability to set aside their personally-held beliefs. When it is time to argue "policy" the frame of reference moves from what objectively "is" to what "ought to be," but this "ought" is still largely determined by outside forces; there is no necessary connection between the lawyer's (or the client's) beliefs and the legal argument.

The task of learning these skills is a difficult, perhaps never-ending one, and it is not surprising that it absorbs most of the energy of teachers and students. Legal argument has a narrowing and focusing nature and when issues are put beyond the scope of what is legally relevant, by such concepts as precedent, justiciability or procedure, it does not seem fruitful to put class time into them. From accepting their irrelevance to the argument, we often move imperceptibly to thinking them irrelevant altogether. Questions of the sort we deal with here—the nature of the lawyer's role, the relationship between an individual's values and who he or she is as a lawyer, what legal issues mean to a client in the context of his or her life—do not, in general, fit into this accepted analytic scheme.

We become acculturated to an unnecessarily limiting way of seeing and experiencing law and lawyering, a way which can separate lawyers (as well as the other actors in the legal system) from their sense of humanity and their own values. When that separation occurs, the profession easily becomes experienced as only a job or role, and human problems as only legal issues. Care and responsibility yield to exigencies and stratagems; and legal education, instead of reflecting the aspiration and searching that embody law and lawyering, can all too easily become an exercise in attempted mastery and growing cynicism. In short, the search for competence can lead lawyers and law students to become constricted by the roles and patterns of thinking they have adopted and unable to move beyond these confines when they work.

This limiting way of professional life is not, of course, solely the result of the professionalization process that occurs in law schools. There are strong economic, cultural and psychological forces at work within the profession and the larger society that influence both the experience of the practicing attorney and the direction of legal education, making it all the more difficult to bring meaningful change to law schools. These forces are supported by, and reinforce, an atomistic and manipulative view of our relation to the world. The focus on the parts to the exclusion of the whole results in peoples' becoming cut off from their own sense of humanity, aspirations and values, and from their responsibility towards self and others.

An example is the prevalent assumption that clients' only needs are to maximize their wealth or freedom of action. Similar assumptions are made for lawyers, that their significant needs in professional life are for financial earnings, prestige and autonomy. The professional model justifies satisfaction of these ends, while other needs, such as the expression of concern or regard for others, are assumed to be non-existent or of minimal importance. As law students became professionalized they tend not to consider the possibility that other models of legal professionalism can exist. A resistance to creative change and development is thus built into the profession. We do not mean to suggest that the legal profession is devoid of recognition of the underlying aspirations and values of all persons, both members of the profession and the general public, whose lives are affected by law. The history of the profession and its underlying ideals evidence the humanistic base of the law and the lawyer's role. We do believe that we can move much closer than we are to having that humanistic base as the principal force guiding conduct and content in education and in practice.

A humanistic perspective on learning and teaching law * * * broadens the scope of traditional education to include a focus upon the persons of teachers and students, the human dimensions underlying the subject matter, and the experience of learning. The goal of this perspective is not to replace the traditional strengths of the profession but to include them in a larger context. For example, the point is not that concern with human aspirations and values should replace technical mastery and analytic rigor. What is needed is a way of bringing together mastery with aspiration, intellect with experience, rigor with value, pragmatism with idealism, competence and skill with caring and a sense of meaning. We are searching for ways of experiencing and thinking in law school and lawyering inclusive of these different poles of human life. When we look at legal education in this light we see several issues of importance: the need to complement the traditional focus of legal education on intellectual analytic skill with attention paid to moral sensitivity, personal values and social awareness; the proper role of authority in education; the importance of encouraging the assumption of personal responsibility by teacher and student and by lawyer, client and others in the practice of law; and the difficulties we face in developing the ability and will to adhere to a sense of personal integrity and value within the rewards, demands and pressures of the educational environment, the profession and society.

JOHN O. CALMORE

Close Encounters of the Racial Kind: Pedagogical Reflections and Seminar Conversations
31 U.S.F. L. Rev. 903, 924–26 (1997)

* * * The fact that legal education is primarily preparing students to enter the profession and practice of law raises a number of complexities that center on the tension, if not conflict, between our students' role and identity. As Thomas Shaffer observes, "[i]f I close my eyes and imagine a lawyer, I expose myself to a *role*. If I close my eyes and see me, I expose myself to an *identity*. And if I close my eyes and see myself as a lawyer, I expose myself to the conflict between my role and my identity." What happens when our students open their eyes and direct their lives in light of what their imaginations have exposed while their eyes were closed? * * *

Law students generally yield to intense pressure to conform to the professional expectations that seem to be associated with the imperatives of the lawyer's role. Too often this is done with little thought or critical examination. The overall legal profession to which the students aspire sidesteps the question "Who are we as a people?" But learning the craft of lawyering should not be separated from who one is as a person and one's core values. I wish more lawyers would seek justice, not in lieu of practicing law, but, rather, as they practice law. I wish there were less disconnection from the practice/business of law and the quest for attaining a more just society. Here, I am not speaking about justice in some abstract jurisprudential manner, but as a reflection of lived experience across color lines and other lines that mark an unfairly established and maintained social order. As law teachers we must intervene to bring about a more satisfying, humanistic, and holistic integration of our student's personal values, identity, and professional role. Consider this observation in detailing our professional challenge:

> [Law students] assume roles as students and seek a way to become comfortable with roles they are about to assume as attorneys, often separating themselves in the process from some of their own aspirations about law and humanity. In the face of difficult questions about what it means to be a lawyer in society, they are understandably moved to settle for learning the mores and the attitudes that will identify them as legal professionals. With the added external emphasis that law school, the legal system and our society place upon performance, it is understandable that concern over role is so paramount and the deeper questions of who we are as a people move into the background, and there are forgotten.

Notes and Questions

1. In discussing a "humanistic perspective," Dvorkin, Himmelstein, and Lesnick claim that during the process that changes one from a lay person to a lawyer, professionalization entails "learning by inadver-

tence." Has that been your experience? If so, what aspects of your professional education have been learned by inadvertence? How might the search for professional competence adversely affect one's humanity, aspirations, and values? They claim that "a resistance to creative change and development is * * * built into the profession." Have you seen evidence of this assertion?

2. Calmore indicates that professional training subverts an examination of deeper questions, such as "Who are we as a people?" Why should a lawyer, especially, be concerned with such questions? Should practicing law be connected to concern for a more just society? *See generally* Derrick Bell, *Ethical Ambition: Living a Life of Meaning and Worth* (2002).

JANE H. AIKEN

Provocateurs for Justice
7 Clinical L. Rev. 287, 287–98, 305–06 (2001)

* * * *We must provoke a desire to do justice in our students. As provocateurs, we determine where our students are in the developmental process toward "justice readiness."* * * * *Being "justice ready" requires sensitivity to the ways in which assumptions color all aspects of our cases.* * * *

Clinical legal education offers students direct experience as lawyers working for social justice. * * * Nevertheless, I am not at all sure that I am teaching enough about justice by merely ensuring that my students experience the fight for it.

A "justice experience" is too often like that trip to Paris: it was an exciting trip that one occasionally reflects upon and that provides fodder for good stories. It makes me interesting but not a Parisian. Mere exposure to substance is insufficient to train good lawyers. Relying on pure case-handling as the medium in which we teach about justice reflects a belief that we communicate values through our content choices rather than by engaging the student in the moral and ethical discourse about those choices. * * * If we truly are going to fulfill our justice mission, we must determine what skills and content make our students more likely to be able to identify injustice and develop teaching interventions that will increase the probability that our students will acquire those skills.

I aspire to be a provocateur for justice. A provocateur is one who instigates, a person who inspires others to action. A provocateur for justice actively imbues her students with a lifelong learning about justice, prompts them to name injustice, to recognize the role they may play in the perpetuation of injustice and to work toward a legal solution to that injustice. * * * One of the special problems that clinicians face is the urge to try to do it all—often within the space of one semester of law school. We want our students to come away from the clinic with a more varied understanding of what it means to be a lawyer serving a client, with strong lawyering skills including negotiation, counseling, interviewing, and fact investigation. We hope to give them opportunities to develop their trial preparation and presentation of evidence skills and to gain an understanding of effective legal writing. On top of this, we want to expose our students to the deep injustices of poverty and abuse of power. We want to instill in them an abiding desire to use their legal skills to remedy these injustices and the wisdom to know the limitations of the legal system in effectuating comprehensive change in the conditions within which they operate. Needless to say, this is a set-up for failure.

Most of us have learned that we cannot do it all. Most of us have recognized that we cannot expect our students to leave our clinics with well-developed client and litigation skills. Instead we have developed teaching interventions that attempt to identify what the student's level of skill is and provide opportunities to improve. We have learned that if we can teach students, at best, how to reflect on their experience, engage in meaningful self-criticism and learn lessons on their own, then we have accomplished a great deal. We have launched the student on his way toward being that skillful lawyer we would like to produce. * * *

* * * It is time we recognize that our success as social justice educators is not determined by how many Thurgood Marshalls or Marion Wright Edelmans we produce. We would be far better off if our students learned how to reflect on their experience, place it in a social justice context, glimpse the strong relationship between knowledge, culture and power, and recognize the role they play in either unearthing hierarchical and oppressive systems of power or challenging such structures. I call this "justice readiness." If we can move our students toward "justice readiness" through their clinical experience, then we should count that as success. It is then up to them what choices they make about the kind of lawyers they want to be. We have pulled back the curtain and dethroned neutrality.

Just as with differing levels of lawyering skills, our students come to us with differing awareness of social justice and differing levels of commitment. Our job is to become effective diagnosticians of our students' "justice readiness" and to employ a wide range of interventions that will enhance the likelihood that they will appreciate the role they play in promoting or inhibiting justice as they act as lawyers.

* * * The first step in moving our students toward a commitment to justice is for teachers to understand that the ability to recognize injustice and participate in creative solutions involves a developmental process that usually occurs in sequence. First, a student must develop effective critical thinking skills. Critical thinking in the law is the ability to see that law is constructed rather than discovered. The law does not exist "out there" to be found; rather it is a reflection of a complex interplay of information, expertise, and value choice. Being "justice ready" takes critical thinking one step further: the student sees that she can play an active role in exposing the inherent biases in law. She can use that

understanding to construct legal challenges that will enhance human dignity and move toward a more just society. As teachers we can become competent diagnosticians of where our students fall within the developmental sequence and foster movement toward "justice readiness."

* * * The first stage of intellectual development, right-wrong dualism, is very familiar to legal educators. Students often begin their legal education with the idea that they are learning the "facts" of law. The role of the law professor is to be the "authority" who conveys to the student the "truth." Students believe that once they know what the law/truth is, they can apply it and act as lawyers. Students believe that this is what we mean when we say we are training them to "think like lawyers." If one applies precedent from similar fact situations to current facts, then one can arrive at an "answer" or argument that is likely to be persuasive to a court. "Thinking like a lawyer" suggests that the lawyer's own values play no role in the analysis, that the process is neutral. This inculcated belief in the possibility of neutrality ensures the triumph of the status quo. Indeed, students coming from traditional law school courses are often imbued with values that promote established economic and social interests. The students themselves are often unaware of this inculcation.

* * *

* * * We cannot expect our students to embrace a justice agenda if they do not understand the degree to which power and privilege affect how law is created and enforced. Understanding that legal issues are grounded in decisions about what we value, what we believe matters, permits students to understand that they must choose what to value when they practice law. They cannot avoid the choice. Students modify their idea that there are right and wrong answers for everything when they are required to accommodate those situations where there are multiple solutions to a problem or the possibility of uncertainty.

* * *

In law, the recognition that there are multiple approaches to a legal problem usually occurs in the first year, when students recognize that when applying precedent, one must choose which precedent to apply and, based on the facts of the case, argue appropriate outcomes. Despite the fact that students are beginning to be able to identify cases on the margins and the ways in which arguments can be made for either party in a case, they frequently take the position that there is no nonarbitrary basis for determining what is right. Law school reinforces this "relativism" by teaching students that the right outcome will result from the efficient functioning of the adversary system. In the educational setting, students begin to think of their task as figuring out the "teacher's games," that is, reflecting back on exams what they believe the teacher wants to hear as the "right" answer. Many students remain at that level of thinking about the law, taking essentially a "hired gun" approach to what it means to be a lawyer. If any opinion can be just as valid as any other opinion, it is not surprising that the law appears chaotic and lacking in principle to students at this stage of intellectual development.

One way to move the student at this stage toward "justice readiness" is to structure their learning experience so that they have cases that require creative solutions to clients' problems. Cases that require the student to create causes of action or legal remedies otherwise unavailable might be appropriate. The fact that there is no "outside authority" from which to draw a remedy may force the student to draw from her own knowledge base and to draw connections based on context. These challenges require the student to assert his own values and not merely echo the law's authority. Such cases are not so rare: the gay partnership that needs legally created "familial protections" that are not available if relying on the default protection of the law; the battered woman/parent who needs her seemingly acquiescing behavior translated into a reasonable coping response to the violence in her life; the civil rights challenge that transforms a factual situation into something that arguably can be redressed under the law. There is no shortage of opportunities for students to face the fact that they cannot rely on "the way things are" and meet the needs of their clients. Reliance on authority may work unfair results for the client. Our choice of cases also allows the teacher to be a role model by demonstrating a lawyer taking a stand grounded in values despite uncertainty and complexity.

* * * If we are successful in bringing the student to a realization of her own power to shape the law to achieve justice, we have brought her to the threshold of "justice readiness." All too often we leave our students there: poised and ready, but not committed. That is the trip to Paris. As provocateurs for justice, we can usher them through that door and support them in actually making a commitment to justice. * * *

Once our students develop this appreciation for the role values play in the justice system, we can help them identify that they can play a role in the delivery of justice and teach them ways in which they can mediate their actions and values through that identity. Teaching an appreciation of and desire to do justice focuses on a process. That process is one step beyond critical thinking to becoming "justice ready." One educational theorist calls this the development of "critical consciousness." A provocateur for justice assists in the development of this "critical consciousness." It is a difficult and complex task.

Provocateurs do not punish those who do not share this value. Our job is not to produce automatons spouting "justice rhetoric." Students will only make a true commitment to justice if they are aware of what it means to think about their role in the delivery of justice. It is only then that they can choose this value in the face of alternatives. We do not have to worry about ensuring that students know that there are many alternative identities that they can embrace as lawyers. If there is one thing with which law school confronts our students, it is the value choice of how they want to be as lawyers. We call this "Career Services." Our problem will be ensuring that the justice alternative is clear. It is not enough to offer public interest commitment as an alternative to corporate practice. We need to assist the student in making an initial commitment to justice as an essential part of their identity as lawyers. We can help them understand the implications of the commitment and the responsibilities that such a commitment imposes.

Provocateurs share their passion so that students can see the value of such a choice. Provocateurs also validate that a sincere commitment to justice is difficult for virtually any person graced with a professional education. A commitment to justice is affirmed through multiple responsibilities and is always unfolding throughout one's life. Therefore, in addition to teaching our students to be critical thinkers who are active makers of meaning, we must teach in such a way as to have them develop a sensitivity to injustice and learn how to synthesize solutions that move toward justice. We must focus on the student's ability to identify the value conflicts that are a necessary component of a justice-oriented value system.

What things do I want students to consider when thinking about justice? Justice has no absolute meaning because it, too, like all knowledge, is grounded in context. At a minimum, however, those of us who dedicate ourselves to social justice must ask ourselves if our proposed action as a lawyer will support and increase human dignity. We must also educate our students about the obstacles they are likely to face while seeking social justice. Therefore, understanding how oppression manifests itself in the law is critical to the educational process. I assume in my clinic that oppression is pervasive, restricting, hierarchical, complex, and internalized. Understanding how oppression operates assists in making sense out of many of the phenomena that my students experience. Many of the students in the clinic have given little or no thought to these ideas. Soon enough they will encounter evidence of the effects of oppression in their case handling. It is helpful during our supervision sessions to focus our students on questions such as: "Where do you see resistance to the solution you seek for your client?" and "Who benefits if this solution is denied?"

The step from critical thinking to "justice readiness" cannot be made if we merely rely on the issues that the cases raise. At every point, we must intervene to enhance the experience for our students. At this particular stage of intellectual and ethical development, our interventions should be directed toward uncovering the values that underlie the law, the limits of what law has to offer our clients and the consequences of using law in the particular context in which we operate. Perhaps our biggest obstacle to achieving these insights is legal training's pervasive insistence that the law is "neutral." The cases we choose are likely to rebut that presumption, but their teaching impact can be enhanced by focusing the student's attention on questions such as: "What are the interests that the client has that underlie the legal problem?" "What options might respond to those interests?" "What are the relative benefits of those options?" "What values underlie the legal solutions to this problem?" "Are those values consistent with the values of the client?" "What values are reflected in your particular suggested solution?" These questions will assist the student in combating that ingrained notion that the law is neutral (and the playing field is level).

Once we have introduced values as a legitimate source of knowledge and a critical component of lawyerly thinking, we can begin the process of helping our students recognize that they must make choices among conflicting values, and that necessarily means taking "stands." As provocateurs for justice, we can play critical roles in helping our students make the transition from being able to identify the values content of their choices to making a commitment to social justice.

* * *

It is not enough to look at each individual case for its possibilities for teaching about justice. We need to look at the bigger picture as well. We should encourage our students to evaluate whether the legal options that we offer our clients are merely designed to reduce the intensity of the injustice or whether they assist in a long-term strategy of social transformation. If our legal work is merely a short term solution to our clients' problems, our discussion should move on to activities in which we can work toward the elimination of the structures of injustice. We need to create occasions for discourse on the essential attributes of just societies. By making that space, we communicate the importance of social justice, the opportunity to make a difference that their law degree creates, and the responsibility that they bear as lawyers for the delivery of justice in our society.

FRAN QUIGLEY

Seizing the Disorienting Moment: Adult Learning Theory and the Teaching of Social Justice in Law School Clinics
2 Clinical L. Rev. 37, 37–39, 46–47, 51–52, 57, 59–60, 62–64, 72 (1995)

#1: I couldn't believe what I saw in court yesterday. While we were waiting for our trial to start, dozens of people were getting evicted by the judge without even having a real chance to defend themselves. A lot of these tenants seemed to have good cases, but just because they were poor and didn't know the system the landlords' lawyers were getting anything they wanted from the judge. I just never realized how poor people get railroaded in what I thought was a fair system.

#2: So if my client receives less than $300 a month in A.F.D.C. and can't afford transportation to look for a job, much less day care and health care if she finds a low-paying job, how is her family supposed to survive? I didn't know people like her were stuck in such a no-win situation.

#3: You could tell what was really happening during that custody hearing. The judge saw my client as less able to care for her kids than their father just because her income is limited to a disability payment, while he has a good-paying job. My client is real upset and she keeps saying she doesn't see the system as fair. I have to say that I agree with her.

Variations of the above statements are repeated so often by students in clinical law courses that clinical teachers may be tempted to take such reactions for granted. However, when clinical students' experiences representing poor, disabled, elderly or otherwise marginalized clients cause the students to question their prior notions of social justice, an important educational dilemma is presented: Should clinical teachers treat these reactions as a natural byproduct or even a happy accident of a poverty-oriented clinical course, or should the teachers and the institutions they represent adopt an active role in facilitating clinical students learning lessons of social justice? Further, if an active role is to be adopted, do clinical teachers know what triggers this type of social justice learning and how they can facilitate the learning?

* * *

A significant body of literature has developed in support of the notion that instruction in the law is fundamentally lacking unless it includes as a core component significant opportunities for learning about the social setting which shapes the practice of law and issues of justice in the adoption and application of the law. The core of these arguments questions the Langdellian model of legal instruction based on the concept of law as reason-based, abstract, and value-free, and thus best studied in a detached and scientific method. The Langdellian method, the argument goes, ignores the impact of social and political factors on law and therefore presents a picture of the legal system and lawyers' place in it that is, at best, hopelessly naive, and at worst, dangerously misleading.

* * *

Opportunities for social justice learning in legal education can best be provided through application of principles of adult learning theory in the clinical setting, where experiential learning is central to the teaching methodology. The learner's clinical experience of representing victims of injustice often includes a "disorienting moment" for the learner, in which her prior conceptions of social reality and justice are unable to explain the clients' situations, thus providing what adult learning theory holds is the beginning stage of real perspective transformation. * * *

* * * Central to the philosophy of adult learning is that the instruction of adult students, whether they be enrolled in law school courses or community quilting class, must be framed by a methodology that acknowledges the vast differences between the cognitive processes of adults and children.

[Malcolm] Knowles articulates four characteristics of adult learners that separate them from child learners, thus mandating different instructional approaches. First, adults see themselves as self-directing human beings, as opposed to child learners whose self-concept is one of depending on an instructor's will. Second, adults' greater reservoir of personal experience can be used as a basis for learning. Third, adults' readiness to learn is quite high if the subject of learning is related to their developmental tasks, i.e., the performance expected from them in their social role. Finally, adult learners are much more inclined than child learners to acquire knowledge that is able to be immediately applied rather than acquiring knowledge that has some future benefit. In other words, adults approach learning with a "problem-centered" frame of mind.

* * *

Adult learning theory maintains that when a learner begins describing an experience with the phrase, "I just couldn't believe it when I saw. . . . ," an opportunity for significant learning has been opened. This phenomenon is called the "disorienting moment," when the learner confronts an experience that is disorienting or even disturbing because the experience cannot be easily explained by reference to the learner's prior understanding—referred to in learning theory as "meaning schemes"—of how the world works. The process that begins with the disorienting moment has been described as follows:

> Psychologists and educators thus have some understanding about how adults learn from life experience. If an experience is unsettling or puzzling or somewhat incongruous with our present meaning structure, it captures our attention. If the gap is too great between how we understand the world and ourselves in it and the experience, we may choose to ignore it or reject it. If however we choose to grapple with it, learning results. Some of this learning affects us more than others. Powerful learning experiences may even transform how we think and act.

Jack Mezirow is the adult learning theorist most often associated with the notion that transformative learning can be produced from a disorienting moment. He calls the change that can result from the disorienting moment "perspective transformation," where such trigger events cause the learner to engage in critical thinking focusing on reassessment of societal and personal beliefs, values, and norms.

Mezirow and others describe this learning pattern as possessing at least three stages: First, the "disorienting experience," second, the "exploration and reflection," and finally, "reorientation." Upon reorientation, the learner's perspective is transformed in such a way that the previously disorienting experience is explained. Mezirow's description of the perspective transformation learning process has been empirically confirmed, most recently by a large-scale study of adult learners.

The role of the instructor in "disorienting moment" learning is to provide a proper environment for these three stages to unfold. Initially, the instructor must design learning experiences that will provide the opportunity for such disorienting moments to occur. Thereafter, the instructor facilitates the productive assimilation of the experience through reflection and exploration of other information related to the disorienting experience so that the final stage, "reorientation" occurs. Thus, learning, rather than confusion and retreat, is the product of the disorientation.

* * *

Research on adult learners has revealed that cooperative learning—learning that takes place when peers share experiences and insights—is not only the most common type of adult learning, it is perhaps the most effective style. These findings are consistent with the very foundation of adult learning theory, namely that self-directed adult learners will draw upon their own experience and motivation to learn by gaining information from a variety of sources, a habit which follows the oral tradition of informal learning through tales of shared experiences. * * *

* * *

Although group-oriented reflection has considerable merit in learning potential, the term "reflection" often connotes private meditation on the meaning of experiences. Such personal reflection can be spurred by journal writing and/or asking for students to conduct a formal self-evaluation. * * *

Journal writing is a highly-valued tool for reflection in a variety of adult educational contexts because journals have been shown to facilitate adults in the process of organizing their thoughts about sometimes chaotic experiences. This process has been described as "sorting, naming and framing" the experiences, thus setting the stage for reorientation of the learners' perspectives. When students are asked to use a journal to answer specific questions such as, "The most surprising thing I learned this week was . . ." or generally reflect upon their experiences, students can express their feelings in a less intimidating forum than classroom discussion. Through journal writing, students can also take a break from the results-oriented pressure of actual student practice and reflect on the meaning of their sometimes whirlwind clinical experiences.

Similarly, formal self-evaluation can spur reflection. Self-evaluation is an accepted tenet in clinical methodology in terms of skills training, however, self-evaluation exercises can also lay the groundwork for a lifetime of regular consideration of the learner's place in the society. Students asked to comment on their relative success in establishing a productive attorney-client relationship may use the opportunity to reflect on the cultural boundaries between themselves and their clients. Students asked to assess the "impact" of their client representation can hardly help but consider the structural constraints faced by their clients and by themselves in their roles as advocates. A self-evaluative process contemplates the type of critical thinking about one's perceptions of the world and her place within it that is urged by "liberation" adult learning theorists such as Friere and Mezirow.

* * *

Adult learning theory holds that disorienting information is most powerful in its potential to inspire real learning when it is experientially-based and/or is provided by the narratives of fellow learners. However, just as there are limits to the experiential knowledge possessed by any one individual learner, the learning group also has significant limits on its experiential knowledge base. Therefore, broad-based objective empirical data on social justice issues, as well as cross-cultural and comparative perspectives on justice issues from a variety of disciplines, often must be presented to students to fully inform their reflection after their disorienting moments.

It is of course possible that confrontation with disturbing data on social justice can itself inspire the disorienting moment and thus open the window for significant learning, although there is much more potential for such an event when the knowledge is gained experientially. Surprising information provided in classroom presentations or reading assignments, when combined with experiential learning, can provide the impetus for disorientation with the learner's prior perspective on poverty, race, or other social justice issues. At a minimum, such information certainly informs the reflection process following the disorienting moment.

* * *

However, presentation of uninterpreted data may well leave the clinical student confused about the cause and effect of the paucity of social justice available to their clients. Theoretical context can be supplied by a discussion of different perspectives on the relationship between law and society, including critical legal studies' "rule-skepticism" view of law in American society, feminist jurisprudence, critical race theory, or theories about the relationship between law and cultural norms. Reference to justice theories of sociology, political science, anthropology, and psychology should also give broader meaning to the raw data provided through the student/client experiences or through instructor-provided empirical data.

* * *

History tells us that today's law students, including clinical students, will play key roles in determining the level of justice provided to the poor and disempowered members of our society. Clinical instructors should use well-established adult learning techniques to seize the disorienting moments so often provided by these students' clinical experiences, and accept the obligation to teach lessons of social justice.

These future policy-makers clearly deserve such enlightened instruction. A just society clearly demands it.

Notes and Questions

1. In Aiken's view, what is "justice readiness"? How do traditional first-year law school courses affect justice readiness? Did your course in constitutional law, property, or torts, for examples, orient you to a form of justice readiness?

2. Aiken aspires to be a provocateur for justice who inspires her students to action and "imbues her students with a lifelong learning

about justice, prompts them to name injustice, to recognize the role they may play in the perpetuation of injustice and to work toward a legal solution to that injustice." Aiken, *supra* at 288. From both teaching and learning viewpoints, she asks many questions: "What kinds of interventions with students can make this happen? Are there particular kinds of cases that make such interventions more potent? How do we relate to our students as peers and experts in order to maximize the chance that they will be faithful trustees of justice? How do we teach students to recognize injustice when they see it, engage in meaningful analysis of the causes and potential cures for that injustice, and develop an abiding desire to use their legal skills to ensure that justice is done? How do we do this and still accomplish other pedagogical goals?" *Id.* Does your law school experience, within and without clinical education, provide any thoughts or perspectives in response to these questions? What does it mean to become "a faithful trustee of justice"? Do you see how you may play a role in the perpetuation of injustice even as you work toward becoming such a trustee? Does one need to be a law professor in order to be a provocateur for justice or might students and lawyers also be teachers?

3. For other discussions advocating a central place for justice instruction in legal education see the symposium, *The Justice Mission of American Law Schools*, 40 Clev. St. L. Rev. 277–531 (1992).

4. Adult learning theory suggests that critical thinking induces calling "into question the assumptions underlying our customary, habitual ways of thinking and acting and then being ready to think and act differently." Stephen Brookfield, *Developing Critical Thinking* 258–59 (1987). How might this critical thinking relate to becoming justice ready? *See also* Frank S. Bloch, *The Andragogical Basis of Clinical Legal Education*, 35 Vand. L. Rev. 321 (1982).

5. Although the first year of law school traditionally promises to teach students "to think like a lawyer," the law school teaching methodology and curriculum are often disconnected from the students' future role in the legal profession, a concept stressed by adult learning theory as central to effective adult instruction:

> At a more general level, our students have an inadequate appreciation of what lawyers actually do. In the largest sense, they have little understanding of what it means to be a professional and to be part of a profession—what the profession's obligations are to society, how legal services are delivered today and will be delivered twenty years from now, or how standards of professional conduct are maintained and elevated. In a more situational sense, our students learn too little of how lawyers interact with clients, develop sensitivity to ethical issues, sharpen skills other than critical analysis of primary source materials, and contribute actively in the non-litigious resolution of social conflict.

Robert A. Gorman, *Assessing and Reforming the Current Law School Curriculum*, 30 N.Y. L. Sch. L. Rev. 609, 611 (1985). Quigley notes, "The law school-imbued notion that the practice of law is a technical matter of value-free representation of a client's best interests—without regard to societal implications—prevails among practicing lawyers. Legal education needs to confront this narrow vision of legal advocacy not only because it is in error, but because critical analysis of one's role in the social and legal systems should be an essential part of any higher education experience." Quigley, *supra* at 41. Where have you learned about your future role within the profession and how effective were the lessons? In your law school experience, have you participated in adult-learning as described by Fran Quigley?

6. Have you undergone any significant experiences of perspective transformation regarding your professional role or personal identity during law school? Jack Mezirow describes the phenomenon as follows:

> Perspective transformation can occur either through an accretion of transformed meaning schemes resulting from a series of dilemmas or in response to an externally imposed epochal dilemma such as death, illness, separation or divorce, children leaving home, being passed over for a promotion, failing an important exam or retirement. A disorienting dilemma that begins the process of transformation also can result from an eye-opening discussion, book, poem, or painting or from efforts to understand a different culture with customs that contradict our previously accepted suppositions. Any major challenge to an established perspective can result in a transformation. These challenges are painful; they often question deeply held personal values and threaten our very sense of self.

Id. at 52, n. 55, quoting Jack Mezirow et al., *Fostering Critical Reflection in Adulthood: A Guide to Transformative and Emancipatory Learning* 168 (1990).

7. Do you find that disorienting moments are primarily negative rather than helpful in facilitating your learning lessons of social justice? Michael Basseches discusses the role of the instructor after a disorienting experience: "What then becomes important in educational settings is for instructors to promote adults' development through engaging with existing structures of thought, challenging those structures to their limits, being careful not to reach the point where learners experience this as an attack and react defensively." Quigley, *supra* at 54, n. 61, quoting Michael Basseches, *Dialectical Thinking and Adult Development* (1984). Do Quigley's teaching suggestions seem helpful in reflecting positively on the disorienting moment—e.g., student-to-student discussions, personal reflections mechanisms such as journal entries or self-evaluations, and supervisor-student discussions? Have her learning techniques or others helped you through disorienting moments?

8. Although adult learning theory can be an effective teaching basis, there are problems in some settings. Despite its attractive humanistic underpinnings, the application of the theory was frustrating in a particular externship program "because our students have not always reached the stage of 'adulthood' the * * * method requires, and also

because we feel it necessary to teach specific content." Linda Morton, Janet Weinstein & Mark Weinstein, *Not Quite Grown Up: The Difficulty of Applying an Adult Education Model to Legal Externs*, 5 Clinical L. Rev. 469, 470 (1999). If you came to law school right out of college, how adult do you feel? Beyond chronology, what does "adulthood" mean to you and to adult learning theory's assumptions?

SECTION 2. ADVOCACY WITHIN THE ADVERSARY SYSTEM: TRADITIONAL ASSUMPTIONS AND CONTEMPORARY CHALLENGES

In addressing the advocate's role in an adversary system, William Simon describes two guiding principles, neutrality and partisanship. William Simon, *The Ideology of Advocacy: Procedural Justice and Professional Ethics*, 1978 Wisconsin L. Rev. 29, 36. The first principle "prescribes that the lawyer remain detached from his client's ends. The lawyer is expected to represent people who seek his help regardless of his opinion of the justice of their ends. * * * Even if the lawyer happens to share [his client's] purposes, he must maintain his distance. In a judicial proceeding, for instance, he may not express his personal belief in the justice of his client's cause." *Id.* Thus, this first principle requires the lawyer to divorce her own morality from that of the client. The second principle of advocacy is that of partisanship, requiring the lawyer to serve as the client's zealous advocate. According to Simon, "[t]his principle prescribes that the lawyer work aggressively to advance his client's ends. The lawyer will employ means on behalf of his client which he would not consider proper in a nonprofessional context even to advance his own ends." *Id.* The principle of partisanship, or zealous advocacy, is qualified, however: "A line separates the methods which a lawyer should be willing to use on behalf of a client from those he should not use. Before the lawyer crosses the line, he calls himself a representative; after he crosses it, he calls himself an Officer of the Court. Most debates within the Ideology of Advocacy concern the location of this line." *Id.* at 36–37.

A strong defender of the adversary system, Monroe Freedman, argues that a lawyer's special obligation to act in the interest of justice requires faithful adherence to traditional notions of the adversary system: "In a free society * * * we lawyers act in the interests of justice not by acting as a self-appointed moral elite, but by serving our clients zealously within the rule of law * * * by counseling our clients about the moral as well as the legal consequences of what they want to do * * * [and] by using all means that are lawful and reasonably available to help our clients to advance and to protect their interests as the clients, after proper counseling, perceive their interests to be." Monroe H. Freedman, *How Lawyers Act in the Interests of Justice*, 70 Fordham L. Rev. 1717, 1727 (2002). Some critics of the traditional rationales of the adversary system argue that, in pursuing social justice, obligations to clients may need to be undertaken with consideration of personal and social values that conflict with the traditional role of zealous advocate. Thus, the material presented in section 2 looks at being a lawyer while balancing the tension between one's professional role on one hand, and one's personal values on the other hand. *See* Robert C. Crampton, *Furthering Justice by Improving the Adversary System and Making Lawyers More Accountable*, 70 Fordham L. Rev. 1599 (2002), and Alan W. Scheflin, *Professional Responsibility for California Lawyers* (2003)(describing in chapter 6 debates about representing unpopular clients or causes).

KENNETH S. BROUN

Black Lawyers, White Courts: The Soul of South African Law xv-xvi (2000)

When I think of the black lawyers of South Africa, I sometimes visualize them as lawyers doing things that lawyers do everywhere—going to court, winning and losing cases, struggling to get clients and to make a living. The[se] lawyers * * * certainly have done and continue to do all those things. But these are South African black lawyers and my image of them is altered by the unique situation in that nation. So I think about Godfrey Pitje in the Johannesburg suburb of Boksburg refusing to sit at a table in the courtroom specially reserved for blacks. I see Ismail Mahomed moving from room to room in his advocates' chambers because the Group Areas Act prevented him from having his own office. I envision Dullah Omar calling a wife or parent of a Robben Island prisoner as a witness in a trial on the island, not because her testimony had any value to the case at hand, but rather to give his client the opportunity to see a loved one.

Because it is South Africa, I also have mental images of these same lawyers in circumstances not directly related to the practice of law. I visualize Dikgang Moseneke on Robben Island, sixteen years old or so, breaking up rocks and conjugating Latin verbs with his teacher, Stanley Mogoba. I see Yvonne Mokgoro thrown into a township police van after having her baby ripped from her arms because she came to the defense of a man being arrested for no cause. I again see Grodfrey Pitje, this time not as a lawyer, but rather as a father forced to sit in a car rather than be at the graveside for the funeral of his ten-year-old son.

* * * [T]hese individuals and other lawyers * * * [struggle] to deal with a society that openly and systemically discriminated against them because of their race. Their histories demonstrate their importance to the protection of whatever meager rights the apartheid government offered to individuals. The same stories also show the significance of the experience of these men and women in the old legal system to the success of the new South Africa. Their words also give some insight into these individuals as people. How could they become professionals under an educational system diabolically structured to keep them as hewers of wood and drawers of water? What enabled their spirit to persevere under

circumstances where most of us would have resigned ourselves to our governmentally designed destiny?

RICHARD WASSERSTROM

Lawyers and Revolution
30 U. Pitt. L. Rev. 125, 129–33 (1968)

* * * [Lawyers] and revolution don't mix especially well. * * * [T]he legal system—any legal system—is an essentially conservative institution [in a fundamental sense]. * * * First, the law is conservative in the same way in which language is conservative. It seeks to assimilate everything that happens to that which has happened. * * * Thus, the lawyers' virtually instinctive intellectual response when he is confronted with a situation is to look for the respects in which that situation is like something that is familiar and that has a place within the realm of understood legal doctrine. * * *

> [P]ersons who are genuinely concerned with far-reaching and radical * * * solutions to social ills ought to be on guard against and ought to mistrust this powerful tendency on the part of the lawyer to transmogrify what is new into what has gone before or to reject as unworkable or unintelligible what cannot be so modified.
>
> * * *

The second way in which the law is conservative comes about through the very basic character of the lawyer *qua* lawyer. * * * First, there is the obvious, but important, fact that when an individual is a lawyer he is playing an institutional role. As such, there are all sorts of explicit and implicit constraints upon his thought and action. As a *lawyer*, there are some things he simply cannot do—without ceasing to play the role of a lawyer.* * * Second, the lawyer *qua* advocate plays an essential non-critical role. The very essence of the lawyer's institutional role is to submerge himself in his clients' position and to represent that interest in the legal arena as forcefully as possible. * * * [B]eing an advocate in our legal system—where one does not or need not choose one's causes—encourages a non-critical, non-evaluative, uncommitted state of mind. * * *

* * * The attorney's role is intimately connected with securing for his client the greatest possible advantage that can be wrung for him from the institutional system. Paradoxically enough, this leads not to the single-mindedness of purpose that so typically characterizes the revolutionary and the radical, but leads rather to a penchant for compromise, accord and accommodation. The attorney is in many respects the system's broker. * * * [T]he processes of litigation and adjudication derive from and are infected by the model of the market place in which a good bargain consists in each of the parties making concessions and compromises.

* * * [The lawyer's cast of mind] is at best neutral and more typically uncongenial to that of the revolutionary's. * * * The revolu-

tionary may, for instance, simply not be interested in winning in any conventional sense. Or, he may be interested in winning if and only if certain very special conditions obtain. In either case, the tension that is latent in the lawyer's whole approach to problems becomes manifest and intense.

* * * [T]he lawyer's ambitions to try to get the best he can for his client *within the legal order* can be not so much inconsistent with his client's interest as genuinely corruptive of them. For there are innumerable situations in which the lawyer's inclination to take what he can get leads to the compromise of interests and rights about which no accommodation ought ever be tolerated.

* * *

[T]he third major issue that falls within the heading of the lawyer and revolution * * * [is] whether we ought to be radical in respect to the law, and if so, of what such radicalism would consist.

* * * [I]t is [not] very easy or very sensible to be radical in respect to the *idea* of a legal system. * * *

The trouble begins * * * when we move beyond * * * [ameliorative] proposals to genuinely radical suggestions for social innovation and change. * * *

* * *

* * * [We can't get along without law or lawyers and intermediate steps, such as getting rid of the adversary system, are] an extraordinarily difficult undertaking, particularly for lawyers. * * *

Notes and Questions

1. In Broun's story, consider the instance of Dullah Omar calling on the wife of an inmate of Robben Island not to give relevant testimony, but, rather, in order for the inmate to have the opportunity to see a loved one. As an officer of the court, do you think that was the right thing to do? Was Omar engaging in a revolutionary aspect of legal practice? Was he at least acting as a radical toward the *idea* of the legal system? In considering the black South African lawyers, is a new model of advocacy necessary to describe their actions?

2. According to Naomi Cahn:

> Lawyers, as individuals, take their places within many different types of communities. They may identify with communities formed by family, religion, race, gender, sexual orientation, and/or other characteristics. Either explicitly or implicitly, these communities influence lawyers in defining their moral orientation towards their lawyering responsibilities and influence outsiders in their perceptions of their lawyers. At the same time, regardless of and in addition to the impact of these other influences, all lawyers are subject to rules propounded by the legal professional self, a "community" of which each lawyer is, by definition, a member. These rules

may seem to encourage lawyers to separate their professional identities from their personal identities within their communities.

Naomi R. Cahn, *Foreword: Responsible Lawyers*, in *Symposium: Community, Pluralism, and Professional Responsibility*, 63 Geo. Wash. L. Rev. 921, 921 (1995). Do the factors of moral non-accountability, detachment from clients, and partisanship work together to help keep a lawyer on track and avoid the role confusion that may result from the influence of various communities?

CAROLYN JIN–MYUNG OH

Questioning the Cultural and Gender-Based Assumptions of the Adversary System: Voices of Asian-American Law Students
7 Berkeley Women's L. J. 125, 125–27, 129–32, 167–72 (1992–93)

The political and legal institutions of a country inevitably reflect the ethos of its dominant culture. The legal system of the United States is no exception. * * *

The legal system's focus on the protection of individual rights and personal liberties reflects the essential and pervasive cultural value of individualism. The American values of free-market competition, decentralized and minimized government intervention, and laissez-faire economics are mirrored in the adversary process. Hence, it is not surprising that the American legal model, including the "rules of the game," fosters competition between largely autonomous and self-interested, zealous advocates in a winner-take-all scheme. Insofar as the legal system reflects the particular characteristics of the dominant culture, tensions and value conflicts may arise for those of a minority cultural background. * * *

* * *

Since the legal system embodies the cultural values of a specific group, people from different cultural and experiential backgrounds may have different perceptions of the legal system. People previously excluded from the legal arena may perceive the system somewhat differently than do members of the mainstream white male culture. In addition, those holding different values may experience role conflict and tension both as law students and as lawyers when seeking to adapt and conform to the preexisting legal structure with its normative elements. Asian culture, for example, is a culture whose values are largely inconsistent with the pluralist, individualist, self-oriented ethos that forms the foundation of the adversary system. Moreover, Asian cultural values of avoiding confrontation and maintaining harmonious relationships directly conflict with the overtly competitive and combative nature of the adversary system.

* * *

The term "adversary system" refers to a "method of adjudication characterized by three things: an impartial tribunal of defined jurisdiction, formal procedural rules, and ... assignment to the parties of the responsibility to present their own cases and challenge their opponents." In theory, advocates are partisan representatives who bring the issues and all relevant legal principles and arguments to the attention of the fact-finder and decision-maker. The jury or judge, who is passive in the investigation and presentation of the dispute, then determines which arguments are more persuasive and declares its proponent the winner. These features make the adversary system closely analogous to a battle or sporting event where litigants' advocates are the players and the judge or jury is the umpire.

The key participants in the adversarial process are the advocates on either side, whose primary obligation is to present their client's case in the most favorable light. David Luban argues that the adversary system requires the lawyer to present his side as forcefully as possible on the justification that anything less would subvert the operation of the system. Luban alleges that this justification is a presupposition accepted by all parties before the arguments begin. The basis and rationale for this underlying "presupposition" is the belief that the best outcome (the truth) will emerge if two sides vigorously fight to win. Consequently, the adversary's goal is not to help the court uncover the truth of the matter, but rather to maximize his or her side's interests and thereby reach the byproduct of truth. Monroe Freedman eloquently portrays this classic justification of the adversary system:

> Before we will permit the state to deprive any person of life, liberty, or property as the state does even when it enforces a civil judgment against a defendant, we require that certain processes be duly followed which ensure regard for the dignity of the individual, irrespective of the impact of those processes upon the determination of truth. By emphasizing that the adversary process has its foundations in respect for human dignity, even at the expense of the search for truth, I do not mean to deprecate the search for truth or suggest that the adversary system is not concerned with it.... Nevertheless, the point that I now emphasize is that in a society that honors the dignity of an individual, the high value that we assign to truth-seeking is not an absolute, but may on occasion be subordinated to even higher values. It is precisely these "higher values" in the American culture that account for the distinctive characteristics of our adversary system and set our system apart from those of other countries.

Some have argued that a connection exists between the political and economic culture of the United States and the attributes of the adversary system. Commentators have noted a correlation between the adversary system and the theory of the free market. Judge Richard Posner extolls the virtues of the adversary system because of its similarity to the free market system, while Judge Jerome Frank criticizes the adversary system precisely because its laissez-faire approach hinders the discovery of truth and justice. The adversary system also closely parallels classic liberal political theory which exalts individual autonomy and allows for state intervention only insofar as it is necessary to ensure individual choice and opportunity. Malcolm Feeley, in *The Adversary System*, comments:

* * *

If the judge in an adversarial system can be likened to a consumer assessing the positions of competitive salesmen, the judge in an inquisitorial system might be likened to a leader of a seminar, the collective goal of which is to get at the truth and each of whose members is expected to volunteer what they know. In the criminal process . . . this difference is underscored by the fact that in inquisitorial systems, there are fewer safeguards of a defendant's interests and the judge assumes a more active role in questioning witnesses.

Second, liberal theorists distrust public power because they believe that such power will have a corrupting influence on society. Hence, state power should be limited to intervention in a live case or controversy. Similarly, the adversary system distrusts non-interested parties' involvement in the process. For example, the standing doctrine requires that litigants be self-interested in a suit and personally affected by its outcome. This doctrine flows from the belief that the pursuit of intense individual self-interest will not only promote the litigant's own interest, but also benefit the public at large by fostering "just" outcomes. Again, Malcolm Feeley contrasts the United States' adversary system to the inquisitorial systems in Europe:

The dominant theoretical traditions in Europe do tend to place considerably more emphasis on the importance of community and relatively less on the interests and rights of individuals. . . . This concern with community informs traditions of European political theory, both liberal and conservative, and this concern stands in sharp contrast to the British and American traditions, which are preoccupied with the individual and individual rights.

Feeley also comments that many socialist and so-called primitive cultures are likely to have legal processes that emphasize communal concerns. Hence, these cultures rely less heavily on the self-interest of the disputants to guide the proceedings and facilitate the outcome. In addition, since the advocate's self-interest is intimately connected with the litigant's self-interest, it is not surprising that the advocate's role requires undivided devotion and loyalty to the client. Again, this feature stems from American culture's strong emphasis on individual rights. Deborah Rhode, in *Ethical Perspectives on Legal Practice,* asserts, "the second premise of adversarial ideology is that lawyers' undivided client allegiance serves fundamental interests of individual dignity, privacy, and autonomy."

The foregoing reveals how the adversary process, the foundation of the legal system, reflects the predominant political and cultural views of this country. Hence, those who are part of the dominant white male culture are most likely to experience comfort and success in this system. The relative discomfort of those who are not part of the dominant culture is borne out in feminist literature which has criticized the established legal norms and theories which serve, in part, to exclude women and to validate the established hierarchy. * * *

* * *

[T]he adversary system inherently reflects and perpetuates American cultural values, especially values held by white men in power. The Asian culture is an example of a culture whose predominant values of community, relational harmony, and consensus clash with American values of individualism, competition, and self-orientation. * * * I hypothesized that, as a result of this biculturalism, Asian-American law students would experience greater tension and role conflict in the adversary system than their Caucasian counterparts. Moreover, I anticipated that Asian-American women would experience greater dissonance than Asian-American men because of the dual effect of Asian and American gender socialization.

The personal narratives gathered from the interviews of twenty-two law students partially supported the hypothesis. Both Asian-American men and women articulated similar perceptions of Asian cultural values and noted Asian culture's divergence from American values. However, Asian-American men did not express or anticipate tension or role conflict as the women did. In fact, most of the Asian-American men felt that they would confront little personal dissonance in working within the adversary system. In spite of this positive perception of the system, most of the Asian-American men chose transactional work rather than litigation.

In contrast, Asian-American women were quite concerned about the ways in which the adversary system contradicted their Asian values. For example, the adversary system requires one to focus solely on the client's needs while Asian culture advocates a focus on the needs of others in the community (for example, one's family). The Asian-American women perceived that Asian cultural emphasis on showing respect for others, sacrificing oneself, and maintaining harmonious relationships conflicted with the aggressive, self-oriented, and confrontational mode embodied in the adversary system.

Surprisingly, the responses of Asian-American women were more similar to the responses of Caucasian women than to the responses of Asian-American men. Feminist literature indicates that women are less sympathetic to the hostile and combative nature of the adversary system and prefer to find solutions that maintain the relationship between the parties and enable both parties to win. This was borne out in the comments by both groups of women, who expressed dissatisfaction with the competitiveness in the process and the limitations of the win/lose result. Hence, the women tended to prefer mediation because they felt that it promoted more compromises and yielded more satisfying results for both parties involved. The majority of the women did not particularly admire or value aggressiveness and confrontativeness as personality traits. Nevertheless, both groups of women were very concerned that the gender and racial stereotypes of being less assertive and combative would limit their effectiveness and advancement in the profession.

Likewise, Asian-American men seemed to have more in common with Caucasian men than with Asian-American women. They tended to be more supportive of the adversary system as an effective method of conflict resolution, and were more favorably inclined toward the competitive adversarial process. These results indicate that gender may be a more determinative characteristic of role tension in the legal profession than is race.

This preliminary finding appears to be at odds with [Angela] Harris' and [Kimberlé] Crenshaw's claims that the combination of race- and gender-based discrimination is not merely additive, but is qualitatively different from either race- or gender-based discrimination alone. However, there are tantalizing hints that there may be fundamental differences in the students' perceptions of the adversary system that grow out of the intersection of race and gender. For example, while Asian-American and Caucasian men express similar support for the adversary system, this surface similarly may be misleading. After all, unlike the Caucasian counterparts, Asian-American men consistently choose legal roles that are relatively non-adversarial. It is possible that the demands of gender may prompt Asian-American men to adopt the rhetoric of adversarialism while the demands of race and culture prompt them to make alternative career choices. Therefore, it would be inappropriate to rule out too quickly the possible importance of the intersection of race and gender in constructing a legal professional identity.

Even assuming that the preliminary finding that gender is more significant than race is accurate, however, many factors may explain this gender distinction. Asian-American men may have assimilated more American values and fewer Asian values than Asian-American women and hence, may have responded similarly to Caucasian men. Asian-American men may have also been less expressive, and may not have articulated their concerns as well as the students in other groups. Moreover, it is possible that Asian-American men are less aware of issues surrounding race and gender than their female counterparts, and are therefore less conscious of the impact of these issues on their lives. One Asian-American male student indicated that another likely reason for this result is the need to protect the male ego. He commented that most men would not feel comfortable about admitting that they are not aggressive, since aggressiveness is such a highly valued masculine trait. Asian-American men may also have had trouble admitting that they would experience problems in the adversary system because this admission would indicate that they were not strong and in control, contrary to masculine cultural values.

In addition, men in Asian cultures have historically been in a superior position and have been granted greater power, deference, and value than women. To a large extent, Asian-American families have continued to treat males differently than females, according them higher status. The hierarchy in most Asian-American families still reflects the picture of the father as the head and the sons as the preferred children. Perhaps this practice has empowered Asian-American men and given them greater self-confidence in their abilities to succeed in other arenas of life, including the legal sphere. While Asian-American men feel empowered, at least in Asian society, through sexist cultural norms, Asian-American women are disempowered and devalued in both Asian and American cultures.

The significant overlap between the Asian culture and the female culture in America accounts, in part, for the similarity between the responses of Asian-American women and Caucasian women. Both cultures focus on maintaining relationships, being sensitive to the need of others, and being diplomatic rather than confrontational. Given the similarity in the stereotypes of Asians and women in America, Asian-American women are doubly alienated from the values and processes of the adversary system. As a result, perceptions by others and by selves reinforce these stereotypes in two spheres—race and gender—and produce greater tension in playing the adversarial role. One Asian-American woman captures this tension by stating that at home she will be the traditional Asian motherly type whereas at work she will be "more Caucasian—more aggressive, assertive, and outspoken." Asian-American women already play multiple roles as Asians, as Americans, as women, and now as Asian-American women lawyers. Every time the situational context changes, the roles shift and the Asian-American woman has to adjust to the different norms and rules of a particular sphere, which may cause dissonance and tension.

This inquiry indicates that there are issues related to the intersection of race and gender which remain to be explored in future studies. The following are suggestions of ways that these theories could be tested and explored further. Future studies should be conducted with a large, random, and diverse group which has been separated by specific countries of origin. Since there are significant cultural differences among the Asian countries, a diverse cross-section of students of different nationalities should be interviewed. This would make it possible to study the similarities and differences among the various Asian groups.

* * *

The adversary structure which forms the cornerstone of the American legal system is neither culture-neutral nor gender-blind. We need to recognize that the adversary system embodies and perpetuates the values of a narrow group of people. Hence, it needs to be modified to better reflect the values present in an increasingly dual-gender and multicultural community of lawyers and clients. As a start, law schools should encourage students to question the cultural and gender-based assumptions of the legal system and affirm the students' diverse views and experiences. This inquiry revealed that personal tension and role conflict exists for Asian-American and Caucasian women and to a lesser extent for Asian-American men. To become thoughtful and progressive agents of institutional change, we need to listen to the voices of these groups, acknowledge the existence of inequalities within the profession, and seek to remove the barriers that they face. In doing so, both the legal community and the greater public will be better served.

Notes and Questions

1. In an increasingly multicultural nation, cultural analysis of the law, such as Oh's, is likely to become more significant. As Austin Sarat and Jonathan Simon observe: "Cultural study of law is important * * * as a way of unpacking what Rosemary Coombe calls 'the signifying power of law and law's power over signification.' It invites us to acknowledge that legal meaning is found and invented in the variety of locations and practices that comprise culture, and that those locations and practices are themselves encapsulated, though always incompletely, in legal forms, regulations, and symbols." Austin Sarat & Jonathan Simon, *Beyond Legal Realism?: Cultural Analysis, Cultural Studies, and the Situation of Legal Scholarship,* 13 Yale J.L. & Human. 3, 21 (2001).

2. Essentialism seeks to identify the essence of things, searching "for the intrinsic 'nature' of things as they are, in and of themselves. The opposite strategy is relationalism." Stephen Fuchs, *Against Essentialism: A Theory of Culture and Society* 12 (2001). Thus, in making either/or distinctions, it "posits polar opposites, instead of gradations." *Id.* at 13. Operationally, essentialism fails "to allow for variation. Where nothing is allowed to vary, nothing can be explained." *Id.* at 15. *See also* Angela P. Harris, *Race and Essentialism in Feminist Legal Theory*, 42 Stan. L. Rev. 581 (1990). Interestingly, although Justice Clarence Thomas is black, he sees race-conscious voting as essentializing, arguing that "[o]f necessity, in resolving vote dilution actions we have given credence to the view that race defines political interest." Holder v. Hall, 512 U.S. 874, 903 (1994) (Thomas, J., concurring in the judgment). On the other hand, Patricia Williams claims that "the simple matter of color of one's skin so profoundly affects the way one is treated, so radically shapes what one is allowed to think and feel about this society, that the decision to generalize from this division is valid." Patricia J. Williams, *The Alchemy of Race and Rights* 256 (1991). Oh makes many racial and gender generalizations. Does she essentialize racial and gender groups or does she draw valid generalizations?

3. Do you think that as more people of color enter into the legal profession, they will renegotiate the profession's institutional culture? Or will they most likely embrace it, adversary system and all?

4. In Oh's study, were you surprised by the finding that "Asian-American men seemed to have more in common with Caucasian men than with Asian-American women?" What might explain this commonality?

5. Do you think that the American legal system generally, and the adversary aspects particularly, need to be modified "to better reflect the

values present in an increasingly dual-gender and multicultural community of lawyers and clients"? *See* Kimberly E. O'Leary, *Using "Difference Analysis" to Teach Problem–Solving*, 4 Clinical L. Rev. 65 (1997).

6. The following article by Clyde Spillenger critically examines a challenge to the adversarial system that was personified by Louis Brandeis. He personified the "lawyer for the situation"—one who "often preferred to facilitate a comprehensive resolution to a dispute rather than represent a single party in adversarial negotiations. * * * Acting in this role involves either joint representation or a mediatory role, both a departure from advocacy of a single client's interest—the role primarily envisioned by the lawyer codes." Geoffrey C. Hazard, Jr., Susan P. Koniak & Roger C. Crampton, *The Law and Ethics of Lawyering* 634 (3d ed., 1999). Hazard elaborates on the meaning of a lawyer for the situation:

> [N]o other lawyer is involved. Hence the lawyer is no one's partisan and, at least up to a point, everyone's confidant.... [H]e undertakes to discern the needs, fears, and expectations of each [client] and to discover the concordances among them.... He can contribute historical perspective, objectivity, and foresight into the parties' assessment of the situation [and] discourage escalation of conflict.... He can articulate general principles and common custom as standards by which the parties can examine their respective claims. He is advocate, mediator, entrepreneur, and judge, all in one. He could be said to be playing God.

Id. at 635, quoting Geoffrey C. Hazard, Jr., *Ethics in the Practice of Law* 64–65 (1978).

CLYDE SPILLENGER

Elusive Advocate: Reconsidering Brandeis as People's Lawyer
105 Yale L.J. 1445, 1448–49, 1522, 1528–29 (1996)

No one holds a surer place in American legal iconography than Louis D. Brandeis. And, unlike most celebrated jurists, Brandeis is almost as revered for his exploits as a lawyer as for his judicial works. Brandeis's biographers regularly call attention to the public spirit and daring he displayed as "the people's attorney." Scholarly critics of mainstream legal professionalism likewise point approvingly to Brandeis's approach to the practice of law, sometimes citing it as an alternative to the crabbed and uninspiring ethic that is said to dominate American legal practice. * * *

* * *

He was the original "counsel for the situation," an appealing phrase whose provenance I will explore in some detail. His 1905 address "The Opportunity in the Law"—urging lawyers to stand "between the wealthy and the people, prepared to curb the excesses of either"—is cited or excerpted in virtually every introductory casebook on professional responsibility. And, most significantly, a good deal of detail adorns the account of Brandeis's heroics. In general, we have little information about the dilemmas lawyers face in their day-to-day encounters with clients and others, and the way in which they navigate those dilemmas. But, largely because the 1916 hearings aired many episodes in Brandeis's lawyering career, we may learn about his lawyering methods from fact rather than myth.

* * *

In offering a less celebratory account of Brandeis's political and lawyerly persona, I have tried to suggest, not that Brandeis misbehaved, but that his style in politics and lawyering had as much to do with a chosen mode of self-presentation as with larger ideals of the good lawyer or the public-spirited citizen. That choice necessarily came at the expense of competing values, those of dialogue and engagement with others. In interpreting his actions as I have, I am not so much devaluing Brandeis's choice as I am underscoring the dilemma that awaits anyone faced with the alternatives of aloneness and solidarity. That dilemma has tended to drop out of sight in the invariably admiring scholarly evaluations of Brandeis's lawyering. Ultimately, Brandeis would not be worth all the attention he has received had he been as uncomplicated and as stultifyingly wise as is the Brandeis of the textbooks.

Reconsideration of Brandeis's approach to lawyering, however, begets other questions. The first entails a more general examination of our lawyering ideals. If one is to assess his approach critically, one must at least outline a more general theory of legal representation that mediates between the ideals of autonomy and engagement. Second, why has so partial a Brandeis made its way into the standard scholarly accounts? What interpretive process explains the ingenuous manner in which he had been portrayed?

* * *

Stated with the requisite generality, or embedded in a sufficiently poignant scenario, the lawyering traits attributed to Brandeis have unquestionable appeal. For example, when Robert W. Gordon advocates lawyerly independence and points to Brandeis as an inspiring example thereof, concededly he is not calling for lawyers to adopt an attitude of contempt or neglect toward their clients. What he has in mind is Brandeis's willingness to guide his business clients, forcefully if necessary, toward morally acceptable behavior and to engage in public interest work of his own, regardless of what they might think. Luban's conception of "moral activism" and Simon's phrase "ethical autonomy" speak to the same point. Likewise, a subtly different ethic associated with Brandeis—that of "counsel for the situation"—has clear and fruitful application to the more nuanced portrait of lawyers as counselors, negotiators, and intermediaries that has partially supplanted the image of lawyers as adversarial litigators that structured the set of legal-ethical norms prevalent in Brandeis's day. Thomas Shaffer's argument concerning the responsibilities of lawyers to represent *relationships* and not merely individuals is only one example of the invocation of Brandeisian imagery to support the notion of the lawyer-as-intermediary. * * *

These visions of lawyering differ in some respects, but they share one important feature: They ascribe to the lawyer a responsibility for articulating larger values (whether those of the "public interest" or of the "situation" or "relationship") that must structure or qualify the ends desired by an individual client. In this sense, Brandeis is indeed an apt source of inspiration for modern critiques of the ideology of lawyering. No lawyer ever assumed this responsibility with fewer qualms. But this seemingly salutary principle is itself the source of my ambivalence concerning Brandeis and his meaning for the ethos of lawyering.

The problem is this: The lawyerly autonomy that Luban and Simon counterpose to the principle of nonaccountability is usually framed as the "Lysistratian prerogative"—the lawyer's right to "withhold services from those of whose projects he disapproves." The prerogative is one of withdrawal, of refusal to assist. And the disapproval is an expression not merely of private preference, but of values that are public and categorical. The Lysistratian prerogative is concerned not with saving the lawyer's soul, nor with minimizing her sense of cognitive dissonance by permitting her to act as she believes, but with ending the lawyer's exemption from the citizen's duty to uphold public values. The principle of nonaccountability that underwrites this exemption is problematic because it rationalizes the lawyer's obligation to perform acts on behalf of a client that, as Richard Wasserstrom has put it, "an ordinary person need not, and should not do." It is this image of disengagement from the act condemned by common morality that gives the Lysistratian prerogative its picturesque and compelling character.

Accordantly, Simon and Luban leave the impression that the circumstances that called forth Brandeis's characteristic assertions of lawyerly independence involved clients hell-bent on evil deeds, from whose dictation Brandeis extricated himself, or whom Brandeis persuaded to take a different path. But the truth is more complicated. No doubt in some instances Brandeis prevailed upon clients to abandon wrongheaded plans of action. But it is one thing to speak of the lawyer's "ethical autonomy" or her "moral activism" as a basis of declining, in specific instances, to assist in the furtherance of the client's goals. It is another for a lawyer to conceive an attorney-client relationship primarily to further her own. Anyone attending closely to Brandeis's actions * * * must sense that they were assertions not simply of ethical autonomy for its own sake, of withdrawal or abnegation, but of individual political aspiration.

Therefore, while critiques of the nonaccountability principle and the concomitant exaltation of moral activism are inspiring in the abstract, the more complex kind of autonomy exhibited by Brandeis seems more troubling. * * * But what might be an alternative to Brandeis's approach? The traditional lawyerly ideal is "loyalty," but to adhere to this ideal in its unqualified form would be merely to reinscribe the "hired gun" vision of lawyering that critics have so effectively castigated as morally untenable. (Brandeis, of course, cuts a dashing figure in our histories of lawyering partly because he was the antithesis of a "hired gun.") To have one's own articulated view on a matter of public concern determined entirely by the identity or the views of another impoverishes the very notion of political belief and action. In challenging Brandeis's mode of independence, I am not thereby accepting the defense of the extreme form of the lawyerly duty of loyalty that has been articulated by Charles Fried and others.

Yet the phrase used by Fried, "The Lawyer as Friend," does capture an image that grounds a compelling alternative to Brandeisian detachment in legal representation. * * * The most glaring weakness of Fried's *The Lawyer as Friend* is not its analogy between lawyering and friendship, but its impoverished conception of what real friendship involves. Friendship connotes a duty of remonstration, of interpersonal challenge, and not simply the unquestioning adoption of another's ends as one's own. Perhaps the image that best captures this idea is that of *dialogue*—the notion that in any meaningful relationship, questions of ends are not determined solely in an anterior way by one party but are made the subject of a joint inquiry.

This way of looking at relationships, including lawyer-client relationships, is an apt critique not only of Fried's vision but of Brandeis's as well. No doubt the image of friendship, and of joint exploration of ends, can appear artificial or inapt in a variety of lawyering contexts. The criminal defense lawyer, the counsel to a major corporation, the attorney for a mentally incompetent person might find such a portrait of representation unrecognizable. But Brandeis's representations, at least those that I have chosen to highlight here, did not fall into these categories. Precisely because so many of his representations involved larger questions of public policy, they *did* lend themselves to deliberation or dialogue between lawyer and client about ends. There is thus some irony in Luban's commendable emphasis on the "moral requirement on the lawyer . . . to engage the client in moral dialogue," a requirement that lies at the heart of the "moral activism" he sees embedded in the figure of Brandeis. But dialogue usually involves two people talking and two people listening. The fixation among legal ethicists upon the *figurae* of the immoral client and the amoral lawyer has almost concealed the possibility that moral dialogue might be edifying for the lawyer as well as the client. Brandeis's very lack of interest in this enterprise of dialogue takes us beyond the question of whether the lawyer should be a frictionless conduit for the client's views and ends, a question to, which few would now give an unqualifiedly affirmative answer. It raises the question as well of whether the client should constitute the pedestal from which the lawyer attains political "standing."

* * *

But I do not challenge the legitimacy of the public interest law movement, whose source Luban finds in Brandeis's "moral activism."

The question raised by Brandeis in his roles as lawyer and reformer is, rather, how political meaning—the identification of ends and means, in the smallest dispute as well as thc largest conflict—is created. I am less troubled by the "arrogation of power" of which some accuse the activist lawyer than by the implications of an ideal of withdrawal, the aspiration to an Emersonian autonomy, embodied in Brandeis's quest to have his political voice wholly self-defined. Anyone for whom the application of critical intelligence to the larger world partakes of a *creative* individual act understands, at least dimly, the allure if not the compulsion of that aspiration: To say only what one thinks, to advocate only the precise thing that one believes to be just and true. That ideal is an indispensable part of the tradition of conscience and dissent suggested by the figure of Emerson himself (who maintained a famous remoteness from the political controversies of his time).

But in nurturing "devotion to a thought," one eventually encounters a world of others, some bearing claims that conflict with such a devotion. To join with others in political action, or to stand up for a client in court or elsewhere, may entail some surrender of individual prerogative if those others are not to be made simply role players in one's own script. For those of us tempted to look back wistfully on him, fixation upon the larger public good that is transcendently embodied by a figure like Brandeis is poignant, not because no one has the right to define the public good, but because that fixation can hide from us the virtues of dialogue, negotiation, and accommodation as politics. It is no coincidence that the person most often revered as a modern-day Brandeis, Ralph Nader, seems as little committed to a communal or "dialogic" approach to the substance and process of politics as Brandeis was. It may be that Brandeis and Nader represent an essential type in the realm of rebellious or dissenting politics—charismatic figures who bear an inspiriting and egalitarian message, but whose effectiveness is due in part to the very aloofness that makes them uninterested in accommodating dialogue even with followers. Whether this is an equally essential type in the realm of client representation is another question.

JAMES A. COHEN

Lawyer Role, Agency Law, and the Characterization "Officer of the Court"

48 Buff. L. Rev. 349, 349–50, 353–58, 406–09 (2000)

The law of agency has governed American lawyers since before the Revolution, but recent scholarship about legal ethics and professional role almost entirely ignores it. Most commentators would concede that attorneys are agents, but would quickly add that the lawyer is also an "officer of the court" who has obligations to seek justice. However, analysis of the phrase "officer of the court" reveals that it has surprisingly little content; it is mostly rhetoric, caused by self-love and self-promotion. What little content it has points to a role of the attorney as agent whose obligations to the court are almost identical to those owed by non-lawyers and almost entirely consistent with duties to clients.

By largely ignoring agency law, and failing to thoroughly examine the attorney's role as an "officer of the court," commentators have mistakenly grounded wide ranging arguments that lawyers must seek "justice" because they are officers of the court who have a special obligation to seek justice. Indeed, they argue that the lawyer's duty to seek justice is superior to the obligation of loyalty and zealous advocacy on behalf of the client. In their view, there are situations in which the lawyer's duty as an "officer of the court" empowers her to disobey the client's lawful instructions because following them would not promote justice. Proponents of this "moral activist" role have overlooked or misapprehended the importance of agency law and uncritically exaggerated the role of lawyer as an "officer of the court." Acceptance of their arguments would, moreover, profoundly change the attorney's role from that of agent for a client to that of agent for "justice." This would create a system that would allow the lawyer to substitute her moral beliefs for her client's lawful instructions.

As it applies to the representation of clients, analysis of the characterization "officer of the court" reveals that the term consists of process obligations, which are wholly consistent with fundamental principles of agency law including the duty of zealous advocacy. Therefore, in our adversary system the lawyer's duty to the court is almost entirely harmonious with the lawyer's duty as agent for her client.

* * *

The image of lawyer as loyal and zealous client protector (also bedeviled by its own rhetoric) is normally juxtaposed against rhetoric about attorneys as "officers of the court," leaving attorneys not knowing which master to serve and when. Tension is said to exist because zealous advocacy on behalf of clients on occasion conflicts with the lawyer's responsibilities to the court and the public. When there is a conflict, the attorney's duty as an "officer of the court" trumps the lawyer's duty to the client. Attempts to reconcile the purported conflict between zealous advocacy and the duty to the court to seek justice have absorbed commentators on professional role for many years. Discovering the meaning of the concept and separating it from its rhetorical use is the task which we are about to undertake.

Attempting to resolve the purported conflict in the lawyer's role, commentators argue that lawyers owe a substantive duty to the judicial system and the public to seek justice because they are "officers of the court." This duty is separate from, and sometimes inconsistent with, the duties a lawyer owes to her clients. This so-called "role-differentiation thesis" posits a separation between personal morality and the conduct required of the lawyer thus permitting the erroneous claim that lawyers are not morally accountable for their client's goals. Moral non-accountability is seen as the "central harm" of the standard conception of lawyering. To solve this problem requires a substantive duty to do justice obligation. "Moral activism" is the phrase that has captured the notion that lawyers have a substantive duty to seek justice even when it is at odds with the client's lawful instructions. According to proponents, moral activism is needed because the traditional or standard conception of lawyer role makes it impossible to be both a good person and a good lawyer. The crux of the argument is that the lawyer's most important role is as an "officer of the court" and, therefore, the substantive duty to seek justice is paramount. Professors William H. Simon and David Luban are among the most prominent and prolific writers on this subject. Professor Simon grounds his proposal for "ethical discretion" on the lawyer's role as an "officer of the court." Professor Luban's "ordinary morality" proposal is justified by the attorney's role as "minister of justice."

But what if lawyers do not owe duties to the court or the public that are inconsistent with duties owed to clients nor greater than duties owed by non-lawyers to the legal system? If the duties to the court and the public are merely rhetorical, the role certainly can not bear the weight of these moral activist schemes no matter how well intentioned or appealing such a role may be to some. Moreover, if lawyers are agents, such proposals may be so fundamentally incompatible with agency law that acceptance would require reconsideration of the current basic understanding of the attorney's role within the adversary system.

* * *

The proposals of the moral activists differ in some respects, but they share the common view that the lawyer has the right to refuse to follow the client's lawful instructions regarding objectives when the lawyer believes the objectives are immoral. Proponents of moral activism have simply ignored or misapprehended the application of agency law to the lawyer role and grossly exaggerated the lawyer's role as an "officer of the court." The lawyer's role as officer of the court does not (and could not) embrace a substantive duty to seek justice because, as agents, lawyers owe their clients the duty of obedience. Once the lawyer role permits the lawyer's views about morals and values to be the basis for refusing to obey lawful client instructions, the role of lawyer had been transformed from that of agent to that of judge.

Without seeking to trivialize the discomfort felt by some commentators and lawyers caused by a conflict between their morals and obedience to lawful client instructions, allowing lawyers to act on their own beliefs at the expense of the client's rights is not the solution. One solution is law reform. For example, reforming the Statute of Limitations and other laws whose applications are perceived by the moral activists to be unfair would be a great public service (if you agree). Another answer for lawyers who experience discomfort is to find positions such as a prosecutor or judge that are less likely to cause discomfort. Finally, perhaps these individuals should consider another line of work.

Lawyers should not be allowed to determine for themselves where justice lies and then impose it on the client (or withdraw). This would in the words of Judge Sharswood, be "unjust and indefensible, [and] usurp . . . the functions of both judge and jury" or in the words of Professor

Wasserstrom: "The private judgement of individual lawyers would in effect be substituted for the public, institutional judgement of the judge and jury."

* * *

> As professional trial lawyers, hired courtroom gladiators, they cannot always expect to be favored with heartwarming luxury of knowing for a fact that their clients are the ones in the right. They simply get hired to go into court and fight the good fight. That they might not be on the side of right is no more their concern than that of a literally hired gun—a soldier of fortune—who finds himself employed purely for the purpose of waging and winning a war, and for whom the underlying political and philosophical merits of that war are of no great concern.... *Lawyers serve not as a judge or jury, but as stewards of their clients cause, and as such, in our adversary system, they serve a vital purpose, giving litigants the process that is their due.* They need not like the client, or the client's cause, any more than a surgeon need like the patient or the patient's self-inflicted disease, in order to perform their task as professionals.

* * *

Lawyers are agents and have been so for quite some time. Lawyers owe a duty of loyalty and obedience to the client as agents. Lawyers in our adversary system can not be burdened with special responsibilities to seek justice that are inconsistent with duties to clients and greater than those of non-lawyers without profoundly changing the basic nature of the lawyer's role.

Notes and Questions

1. How does "moral activism" seem to be reflected by Brandeis? How does moral activism stand as an alternative to nonaccountability? According to David Luban, moral activism is "a vision of law practice in which the lawyer who disagrees with the morality or justice of a client's ends does not simply terminate the relationship, but tries to influence the client for the better." David Luban, *Lawyers and Justice: An Ethical Study* 160 (1988). Luban suggests, however, that there are certain situations in which, in order to vindicate important principles, lawyers should represent "abhorrent clients with repellent projects." *Id.* at 161. He provides the examples of the ACLU's defense of the Nazi's right to march in Skokie or of a pornographer's right to publish and distribute *Bitches in Boots.* Why isn't this zealous advocacy driven by the nonaccountability principle? Luban argues the lawyers in these cases are fighting for the First Amendment more than the interests of the clients. They "*are* morally accountable for their representation—not to be sure, for promoting their clients' projects, but for advocating the political and legal principles they are trying to vindicate." *Id.* If you were an attorney for the ACLU in one of these situations, would you represent the Nazis or the pornographers? Why or why not?

2. How might racial or gender issues complicate your consideration? A decade ago Anthony Griffin, a black attorney, was working as NAACP general counsel in Texas. He also served as a cooperating counsel for the ACLU and represented the KKK in a free speech case. Deborah L. Rhode & David Luban, *Legal Ethics* 150 (3d. ed., 2001), citing Sue Ann Pressley, *Klan Leader and NAACP Make an Odd Couple of Civil Rights*, Wash. Post, Sept. 29, 1993, at A3. Does this representation mark a clash between principles of civil rights versus civil liberties? Reportedly, the NAACP fired Griffin. *Id.*, citing Jerry Thomas, *NAACP Fires Black Lawyer in Klan Case*, Chi. Trib., Oct. 3, 1993, at C21. Was the NAACP response appropriate?

3. Spillenger's essay on Brandeis, in spite of the critique of his lawyerly vision, associates many positives with it. What are they? What are the principal critiques lodged against Brandeis? Does Spillenger appropriately link Brandeis and Ralph Nader?

4. Upon admission to the bar, attorneys become "officers of the court." What does this mean? Does it have substantive content? Is it necessarily either associated with, or divorced from, seeking justice? As a normative matter, should being "an officer of the court" mean more than Cohen argues? Research the term "officer of the court" in the state where you attend law school or intend to practice and present support for, or rebuttal to, Cohen's view.

SECTION 3. JOINING THE PROFESSION

What does becoming a lawyer mean to you? This section examines a number of related questions: What is the nature of the legal profession? What behavioral norms for individuals and the bar affect an individual's values and identity? In short, what are the expressions of the self in lawyering? *See* Howard Lesnick, *Being a Lawyer* 328 (1992).

JAMES R. ELKINS

The Legal Persona: An Essay on the Professional Mask
64 Va. L. Rev. 735, 737, 739–41 (1978)

* * * The lawyer's perception of himself as a lawyer and his perception of his role in society begin to crystallize during his first days in law school. Confronted with the Socratic method of teaching that obliges him to master a new form of reasoning, the law student begins to adjust his view of the world to accord with his changed environment. And through the persuasive efforts of law professors and older law students, the prospective lawyer realizes that he must learn to "talk like a lawyer" and to "think like a lawyer" to *become* a lawyer.

* * *

What attributes of lawyers and lawyering create a special "world view"? Simply stated, the lawyer considers himself a neutral, rational, and objective problem solver. As a rational thinker, the lawyer perceives client problems, clients, and self through the mist of legal rules and legal problems. In essence, a lawyer's way of thinking and representing certain events in the world consists of a dislike of vague generalities, the structuring of all possible human relations into the form of claims and counterclaims, and the belief that human conflicts can be settled under established rules in a judicial proceeding.

Judith Shklar has labeled this professional view of the world "legalism." She defines it as "the ethical attitude that holds moral conduct to be a matter of rule following, and moral relationships to consist of duties and rights determined by the rules." In the final sense, legalism is "a way of thinking about social life, a mode of consciousness" that structures the lawyer's social experience and prescribes a code of conduct for individual lawyers.

Legalism also creates and molds the lawyer's legal persona. "The legal view is no more narrowing than any other unidimensional explanation of the world"; yet it is "more deluding than some other world views" in "its covert character." Law professors and lawyers erroneously believe that their legal training and their intellectual tools will enable them "to strip a problem, any problem, down to its essentials." The socialization process begun in law school creates and provides the lawyer with a new model of the world—a world of rights and obligations, liabilities, and causes of action—which excludes much from its vision. As Professor Scheingold has noted: "When we accuse someone of being legalistic, we suggest an excessive zeal for purely formal details which becloud rather than clarify the *real* issue. The legalist is someone who is lost among the trees and cannot *or will not* consider the overall shape of the forest." The process of "thinking like a lawyer" thus provides no basis for critically analyzing and assessing the assumptions underlying the lawyer's peculiar view of the world.

Notes and Questions

1. Has "legalism," the professional view of the world discussed by Elkins, had any impact in your developing a "persona"? What is your legal persona? As a law student, is it too early to tell if you have one or need one? For further reflections upon professional masks, see Leslie G. Espinoza, *Masks and Other Disguises: Exposing Legal Academia*, 103 Harv. L. Rev. 1878 (1990), and Margaret E. Montoya, *Máscaras, Trenzas, y Greñas: Un/masking the Self While Un/braiding Latina Stories and Legal Discourse*, 15 Chicano-Latino L. Rev. 1, 17 Harv. Women's L. J. 185 (1994). How does the legal persona relate to one's professional role? How does personal identity interact with professional role? According to Gary Bellow and Bea Moulton, "In simple terms, a fully-socialized individual is one who is, does, and believes pretty much what society asks him or her to be, do and believe." Gary Bellow & Bea Moulton, *The*

Lawyering Process: Materials for Clinical Instruction in Advocacy 11 (1978).

2. Bellow and Moulton focus on three interrelated concepts that explain socialization: "*role*—a socially generated set of expectations about one's behavior in specific situations; *reference group*—the audience (or audiences) to whom one looks for approval, support, acceptance, reward and sanction; and *ideology*—the constellation of beliefs, knowledge, and ideas which, in a given situation, serve to justify, legitimate and explain both role definitions and the allocation of reward and sanction power among reference groups." *Id.* at 12. How might these three factors—role definitions, reference groups, and ideology—produce a distinct legal subculture that influences the "professionalization" of young lawyers?

3. In the following article, Richard Wasserstrom discusses the concept of "role-differentiated behavior." In reading it, consider these questions: What effect does the adversary system have on role-differentiated behavior? Does it justify the role-differentiated amorality of the lawyer? How might the adversary system and role-differentiated behavior affect lawyer-client relationships?

RICHARD WASSERSTROM

Lawyers as Professionals: Some Moral Issues
5 Human Rights 1, 2–3, 5–6, 8, 13, 17–18, 21 (1975)

* * * The primary question that is presented is whether there is adequate justification for the kind of moral universe that comes to be inhabited by the lawyer as he or she goes through professional life. For at best the lawyer's world is a simplified moral world; often it is an amoral one; and more than occasionally, perhaps, an overtly immoral one.

* * *

* * * [O]ne central feature of the professions in general and of law in particular is that there is a special, complicated relationship between the professional and the client or patient. For each of the parties in this relationship, but especially for the professional, the behavior that is involved is to a very significant degree, what I call, role-differentiated behavior. And this is significant because it is the nature of role-differentiated behavior that it often makes it both appropriate and desirable for the person in a particular role to put to one side considerations of various sorts—and especially various moral considerations—that would otherwise be relevant if not decisive. * * *

* * *

Consider, more specifically, the role-differentiated behavior of the lawyer. Conventional wisdom has it that where the attorney-client relationship exists, the point of view of the attorney is properly different—and appreciably so—from that which would be appropriate in the absence of the attorney-client relationship. * * * Once a lawyer represents a client, the lawyer has a duty to make his or her expertise fully available in the realization of the end sought by the client, irrespective, for the most part, of the moral worth to which the end will be put or the character of the client who seeks to utilize it. Provided that the end sought is not illegal, the lawyer is, in essence, an amoral technician whose peculiar skills and knowledge in respect to the law are available to those with whom the relationship of client is established. The question, as I have indicated, is whether this particular and pervasive feature of professionalism is itself justifiable. At a minimum, I do not think any of the typical, simple answers will suffice.

* * *

* * * The job of the lawyer, so the argument typically concludes, is not to approve or disapprove of the character of his or her client, the cause for which the client seeks the lawyer's assistance, or the avenues provided by the law to achieve that which the client wants to accomplish. The lawyer's task is, instead, to provide that competence which the client lacks and the lawyer, as professional, possesses. In this way, the lawyer as professional comes to inhabit a simplified universe which is strikingly amoral—which regards as morally irrelevant any number of factors which nonprofessional citizens might take to be important, if not decisive, in their everyday lives. * * *

* * *

* * * [I]t is clear that there are definite character traits that the professional such as the lawyer must take on if the system is to work. What is less clear is that they are admirable ones. Even if the role-differentiated amorality of the professional lawyer is justified by the virtues of the adversary system, that also means that the lawyer *qua* lawyer will be encouraged to be competitive rather than cooperative; aggressive rather than accommodating; ruthless rather than compassionate; and pragmatic rather than principled. This is, I think, part of the logic of the role-differentiated behavior of lawyers in particular, and to a lesser degree of professionals in general. * * *

* * *

* * * [T]o be a professional is to have been acculturated in a certain way. It is to have satisfactorily passed through a lengthy and allegedly difficult period of study and training. It is to have done something hard. Something that not everyone can do. * * * It is hard, I think, if not impossible, for a person to emerge from professional training and participate in a profession without the belief that he or she is a special kind of person, both different from and somewhat better than those nonprofessional members of the social order. It is equally hard for the other members of society not to hold an analogous view of the professionals. And these beliefs surely contribute, too, to the dominant role played by a professional in any professional-client relationship.

* * *

Thus it is, for example, fairly easy to see how a number of the features already delineated conspire to depersonalize the client in the eyes of the lawyer *qua* professional. * * *

* * *

The forces that operate to make the relationship a paternalistic one seem to me to be at least as powerful. If one is a member of a collection of individuals who have in common the fact that their intellects are highly trained, it is very easy to believe that one knows more than most people. If one is a member of a collection of individuals who are accorded high prestige by the society at large, it is equally easy to believe that one is better and knows better than most people. If there is, in fact, an area in which one does know things that the client doesn't know, it is extremely easy to believe that one knows generally what is best for the client. All this, too, surely holds for lawyers.

* * * [T]he client often establishes a relationship with the lawyer because the client has a serious problem or concern which has rendered the client weak and vulnerable. This, too, surely increases the disposition to respond toward the client in a patronizing, paternalistic fashion. The client of necessity confers substantial power over his or her wellbeing upon the lawyer. Invested with all of this power both by the individual and the society, the lawyer *qua* professional responds to the client as though the client were an individual who needed to be looked after and controlled, and to have decisions made for him or her by the lawyer, with as little interference from the client as possible.

PATRICK J. SCHILTZ

On Being a Happy, Healthy, and Ethical Member of an Unhappy, Unhealthy, and Unethical Profession
52 Vand. L. Rev. 871, 872–73, 881–920 (1999)

Dear Law Student:

I have good news and bad news. The bad news is that the profession that you are about to enter is one of the most unhappy and unhealthy on the face of the earth—and, in view of many, one of the most unethical. The good news is that you can join this profession and still be happy, healthy, and ethical. I am writing to tell you how.

Lawyers play an enormously important role in our society. "It is the lawyers who run our civilization for us—our governments, our business, our private lives." Thus you might expect that a lot of people would be concerned about the physical and mental health of lawyers. You would be wrong. Contrary to the old joke, scientists have not replaced laboratory rats with lawyers, and medical literature has little to say about the well-being of attorneys. At the same time, many law professors—at least those teaching at the fifty or so schools that consider themselves to be in the "Top Twenty"—do not care much about lawyers. Increasingly, faculties of elite schools and aspiring elite schools consist of professors who have not practiced law, who have little interest in teaching students to practice law, and who pay scant attention to the work of practicing lawyers. Even law professors like me—law professors who practiced law for several years, who love teaching, and who are intensely interested in the work of lawyers—often do not have the training or resources to conduct empirical research about the legal profession. As a result, legal scholarship also has little to say about the well-being of attorneys.

* * *

* * * [P]eople who suffer from depression, anxiety, alcoholism, drug abuse, divorce, and suicide to this extent are almost by definition unhappy. It should not be surprising, then, that lawyers are indeed unhappy, nor should it be surprising that the source of their unhappiness seems to be the one thing that they have in common: their work as lawyers. * * *

A study of California lawyers by the RAND Institute for Civil Justice found that "only half say if they had to do it over, they would become lawyers." On the whole, California lawyers were reported to be " 'profoundly pessimistic' about the state of the legal profession and its future." A survey of the North Carolina bar produced similar results. Almost a quarter of North Carolina lawyers said that, if given the choice, they would not become attorneys again; almost half said that they hope to leave the practice of law before the end of their careers; and over 40% said that they would not encourage their children or other qualified persons to enter the legal profession. Along the same lines, a nationwide poll of attorneys conducted by the *National Law Journal* found that less than a third of those surveyed were "very satisfied" with their careers.

For almost thirty years, the University of Michigan Law School has been surveying its former students five years after they graduate. The last survey for which results have been reported was conducted in 1996. Given the stellar reputation of their alma mater, Michigan graduates would presumably have more employment options available than graduates of most other law schools and thus would presumably be among the most satisfied practitioners in America. Yet annual surveys have discovered surprisingly low levels of career satisfaction in general and a marked decline in career satisfaction over time, at least for lawyers in private practice.

* * *

Taken together, the surveys show a substantial decline in the job satisfaction of attorneys. In 1984, 41% of lawyers said that they were "very satisfied" with their jobs; in 1990, only 33% of all lawyers surveyed were "very satisfied," a decline of one-fifth in just six years. At the same time, the number of lawyers who were "very dissatisfied" with their jobs rose from 3% in 1984 to 5% in 1990. The dissatisfaction was widespread. In the words of the 1990 study:

> In the past six years, the extent of lawyer dissatisfaction has increased throughout the profession. It is now reported in significant numbers by lawyers in all positions—partners as well as junior associates. It is now present in significant numbers in firms of all sizes, not just the largest and the smallest firms.

* * *

I should note two things about these statistics on career satisfaction. First, although most surveys suggest that career satisfaction is relatively low among attorneys and has been declining, there are studies to the contrary. Prominent among them is a recent study of the Chicago bar by John Heinz, Kathleen Hull, and Ava Harter. The Chicago study was not a career satisfaction study as such; rather, attorneys were subject to lengthy personal interviews and, in the course of being interviewed about numerous subjects, were asked a few questions about career satisfaction. Chicago lawyers reported levels of job satisfaction that were similar to those reported by Americans in other lines of work. Eighty-four percent of Chicago lawyers were "very satisfied" or "satisfied," about 10% were "neutral," 5% were "dissatisfied," and less than 2% were "very dissatisfied."

* * *

The second thing to note about the data described above is that all of these statistics relate to the overall level of career dissatisfaction among lawyers. It is important to understand, though, that career dissatisfaction is not distributed equally throughout the profession. Lawyers in some practice settings are happier than lawyers in others. And "[l]awyers in large law firms are often among the least happy." This appears to be true for both associates and partners.

* * *

It is also telling that lawyers who leave big firms rarely go to other big firms.* * *

Many big firm partners are also dissatisfied. Indeed, "[h]appy law partners are a small minority these days." A 1997 survey of partners in the 125 largest American law firms found that one third of those partners—lawyers who, in the eyes of many, have reached the pinnacle of their profession—would choose a different career if they could do it over again. Almost one third of them thought that they would probably or definitely not remain at their firms until retirement, and over 80% said that the nature of private practice in big firms had changed for the worse. Hildebrandt reports that despite the fact that 1997 was "the best year ever" for many firms "due to record demand for legal services in almost all practice areas," big firm partners are unhappy: "Mo[st] disturbing is the low morale (and almost a disdain for their own profession) we see in partners who wonder whether continuing to practice is worth the effort."

Why are lawyers so unhealthy and unhappy? Why do so many lawyers, in the words of Judge Laurence Silberman, "hate what the practice of law has become"? Lawyers give many reasons. They complain about the commercialization of the legal profession—about the fact that practicing law has become less of a profession and more of a business. They complain about the increased pressure to attract clients in a ferociously competitive marketplace. They complain about having to work in an adversarial environment "in which aggression, selfishness, hostility, suspiciousness, and cynicism are widespread." They complain about not having control over their lives and about being at the mercy of judges and clients. They complain about a lack of civility among lawyers. They complain about a lack of collegiality and loyalty among their partners. And they complain about their poor public image. Mostly, though, they complain about the hours.

In every study of the career satisfaction of lawyers of which I am aware, in every book or article about the woes of the legal profession that I have read, and in every conversation about life as a practicing lawyer that I have heard, lawyers complain about the long hours they have to work. Without question, "the single biggest complaint among attorneys is increasingly long workdays with decreasing time for personal and family life." Lawyers are complaining with increasing vehemence about "living to work, rather than working to live"—about being " 'asked not to *dedicate,* but to *sacrifice* their lives to the firm.' "

* * *

A study conducted by William Ross in 1991 discovered that almost half of the associates in private practice billed at least 2000 hours during both 1989 and 1990, and a fifth billed at least 2400 hours in 1990. Another study conducted by Ross three years later discovered that 51% of associates and 23% of partners billed at least 2000 hours in 1993. Seventy percent of those responding to the Michigan Law School survey worked an average of fifty or more hours per week; over a quarter of the respondents worked more than sixty hours per week. The ABA's 1990 study found that 45% of attorneys in private practice billed at least 1920 hours per year, and 16% billed 2400 or more hours. The same study also found that, although 70% of attorneys are permitted to take more than two weeks of vacation every year, only 48% actually do so. Finally, an extensive survey by Altman Weil Pensa, a prominent legal consulting firm, found that the median number of billable hours for associates in firms of all sizes in 1995 was 1823; 25% of associates billed 1999 hours or more, and 10% billed at least 2166 hours. Not long ago, billable hours at these levels "would have [been] thought unbearable."

Workloads, like the job dissatisfaction to which they so closely relate, are not distributed equally throughout the profession. Generally speaking, lawyers in private practice work longer hours than those who work for corporations or for the government. In the 1990 ABA survey, for example, only 56% of those in private practice agreed that they had enough time to spend with their families, compared to 74% of corporate lawyers and 79% of government lawyers. Similarly, only 46% of private practitioners said that they had enough time for themselves, compared to 53% of corporate lawyers and 66% of government lawyers. In the words of the study, "[t]ime for family and self is a real problem for lawyers in private practice. Far fewer lawyers in corporate counsel and government settings have insufficient time." The findings of the Michigan Law School survey were similar: Only 20% of the respondents working in private practice were "quite satisfied" with "[t]he balance of their family and professional life," as compared to 35% of those working in corporations, 45% of those working for the government, and 50% of those doing public interest work.

Within private practice, the general rule of thumb is the bigger the firm, the longer the hours. For example, a recent study found that over 41% of associates in firms of under 101 lawyers billed fewer than 1800 hours, as compared to about 16% of associates in firms of over 250 lawyers. At the same time, almost 27% of associates in the smaller firms billed over 1900 hours, as compared to approximately 36% of associates in the larger firms. At the biggest firms in the biggest cities, associates commonly bill 2000 to 2500 hours per year. Big firm partners do not have it much better. Junior partners at the nation's 125 largest law firms average 1955.5 billable hours per year, almost 300 hours per year more than partners in small firms. At some big firms, the average number of hours billed by partners and associates alike is 2000.

The long hours that big firm lawyers must work is a particular source of dissatisfaction for them. While roughly half of all attorneys in private practice complain about not having enough time for themselves and their families, in big firms the proportion of similarly disaffected lawyers is about three quarters. The ABA's survey of young lawyers in 1995 found that 62% of those working in firms of at least 150 lawyers were dissatisfied with the amount of time they had to work, while only 28% of those working in firms of fewer than seven lawyers had the same complaint. Among respondents to the Michigan Law School survey, 37% of those working as solo practitioners or in firms of ten or fewer lawyers were quite satisfied with "[t]he balance of family and professional lives," while only 14% of those working in firms of 150 or more lawyers were similarly satisfied. Finally, young attorneys in large firms who are interested in finding a new job are more likely than similarly situated associates in small firms to be motivated by "a desire for more personal time."

The unhappiness of lawyers may puzzle you. At first blush, these billable hour requirements may not seem particularly daunting. You may think, "Geez, to bill 2000 hours, I need to bill only forty hours per week for 50 weeks. If I take an hour for lunch, that's 8:00 a.m. to 5:00 p.m., five days per week. No sweat." Your reaction is common among law students—particularly among law students who are in the process of talking themselves into accepting jobs at big firms. Your reaction is also naive.

There is a big difference—a painfully big difference—between the hours that you will *bill* and the hours that you will *spend at work.* If you're honest, you will be able to bill only the time that you spend working directly on matters for clients. Obviously, you will not be able to bill the time that you spend on vacation, or in bed with the flu, or at home waiting for the plumber. But you will also not be able to bill for much of what you will do at the office or during the workday—going to lunch, chatting with your co-workers about the latest office romance, visiting your favorite websites, going down the hall to get a cup of coffee, reading your mail, going to the bathroom, attending the weekly meeting of your practice group, filling out your time sheet, talking with your spouse on the phone, sending e-mail to friends, preparing a "pitch" for a prospective client, getting your hair cut, attending a funeral, photocopying your tax returns, interviewing a recruit, playing Solitaire on your computer, doing pro bono work, reading advance sheets, taking a summer associate to a baseball game, attending CLE seminars, writing a letter about a mistake in your credit card bill, going to the dentist, dropping off your dry cleaning, daydreaming, and so on.

Because none of this is billable—and because the average lawyer does a lot of this every day—you will end up billing only about two hours for every three hours that you spend at "work." And thus, to bill 2000 hours per year, you will have to spend about sixty hours per week at the office, and take no more than two weeks of vacation/sick time/personal leave. If it takes you, say, forty-five minutes to get to work, and another forty-five minutes to get home, billing 2000 hours per year will mean leaving home at 7:45 a.m., working at the office from 8:30 a.m. until 6:30 p.m., and then arriving home at 7:15 p.m.—and doing this *six days per week,* every week. That makes for long days, and for long weeks. And you will have to work these hours not just for a month or two, but year after year after year. That makes for a long life.

Now do you understand why so many attorneys are unhappy? And why, generally speaking, the more lawyers work, the less happy they are? What makes people happy is the *nature* of the work they do and the quantity and quality of their lives outside work. Long hours at the office have no relationship to the former and take away from the latter. Every hour that lawyers spend at their desks is an hour that they do not spend doing many of the things that give their lives joy and meaning: being with their spouses, playing with their children, relaxing with their friends, visiting their parents, going to movies, reading books, volunteering at the homeless shelter, playing softball, collecting stamps, traveling the world, getting involved in a political campaign, going to church, working out at a health club. There's no mystery about why lawyers are so unhappy: They work too much.

Why do lawyers work too much? * * *

* * *

In one sense, the answer to the question of why so many lawyers work so much is easy: It's the money, stupid. It begins with law students, who, like most Americans, seem to be more materialistic than they were twenty-five or thirty years ago. In 1970, 39% of students entering college said that "being very well off financially" was either an "essential" or a "very important" life goal; in 1993, the figure had almost doubled to 75%. Of the nineteen possible life goals suggested to incoming college students, getting rich was selected most often—even more often than "raising a family." Not surprisingly, then, "the most coveted jobs amongst [law students] are high-paying large law firm jobs. The vast majority of law students—at least the vast majority of those attending the more prestigious schools (or getting good grades at the less prestigious schools)—want to work in big firms. And the reason they want to work in big firms is that big firms pay the most."

Of course, students deny this. Students—many of whom came to law school intending to do public interest work—don't like to admit that they've "sold out," so they come up with "rationalizations, justifications, accounts, and disclaimers" for seeking big firm jobs. They insist that the real reason they want to go to a big firm is the training, or the interesting and challenging work, or the chance to work with exceptionally talented colleagues, or the desire to "keep my doors open." They imply that the huge salaries are just an afterthought—mere icing on the cake. Or they reluctantly admit that, yes, they really are after the money, but they have no choice: Because of student loan debt, they *must* take a job that pays $80,000 per year. $60,000 per year just won't cut it.

Most of this is hogwash. * * * [A]lmost all of the purported nonmonetary advantages of big firms either do not exist or are vastly overstated. Moreover, there are few lawyers who could not live comfortably on what most corporations or government agencies pay, whatever their student loan debt. Students are after the money, pure and simple. The hiring partner of any major firm will tell you that if his firm offers first year associates a salary of $69,000, and a competitor down the street offers them $72,000, those who have the choice will flock to the competitor—even if the competitor will require them to bill 200 hours more each year.

I realize that I am not exactly flattering law students. But if this were not true, would big firms get into bidding wars for the services of the best law school graduates? Of course not. But big firms do get into bidding wars—all the time—and, as a result, the salaries of first year associates get pushed to extraordinary levels. * * *

As the salaries of first year associates go up, the salaries of senior associates must rise to keep pace. After all, no sixth year associate wants to be paid less than a first year associate. And as the salaries of senior associates go up, the salaries of junior partners must rise to keep pace. After all, no junior partner wants to be paid less than a senior associate. And, of course, as the salaries of junior partners go up, so must the salaries of senior partners.

How do firms pay for this ever-spiraling increase in salaries? In theory, they have two options: First, they can raise billing rates. Instead of charging, say, $100 per hour for the time of first year associates, they can charge $115, and instead of charging, say, $225 per hour for the time of junior partners, they can charge $250. Second, they can bill more hours. Instead of demanding 2000 billable hours per year from first year associates, they can demand 2100, and instead of demanding 1900 billable hours per year from junior partners, they can demand 1950.

In reality, though, firms have only one option: They have to bill more hours. * * *

I am leaving out one wrinkle—an important wrinkle that you should know about if you are contemplating joining a large law firm (or a firm that acts like a large law firm). The partners of a big firm have a third option for making more money. This option involves what big firm partners euphemistically refer to as "leverage." I like to call it "the skim." Richard Abel calls it "exploitation." The person being exploited is you.

It is common for the top partners in the biggest firms to earn upwards of $2 million per year. At some firms, profits per partner approach or exceed $2 million per year, meaning that some partners are paid more than $2 million (because profits are not divided equally among partners). Not one of these highly paid partners could personally generate the billings necessary to produce such an income. * * * So how can big firm partners take home double or triple or quadruple the revenue they generate? They can do so because partner compensation reflects not only the revenue that partners themselves generate, but also "the surplus value law firms extract from associates." Alex Johnson puts the point more dramatically: "[T]he blood and sweat of new associates line[] the pockets of the senior members of the firm."

Basically, what happens is that big firms "buy associates' time 'wholesale and sell it retail.' " Here's how it works: As a new associate in a large firm, you will be paid about one-third of what you bring into the firm. If you bill, say, 2000 hours at $100 per hour, you will generate $200,000 in revenue for your firm. About a third of that—$70,000 or so—will be paid to you. Another third will go toward paying the expenses of the firm. And the final third will go into the pockets of the firm's partners. Firms make money off associates. That is why it's in the interests of big firms to hire lots of associates and to make very few of them partners. The more associates there are, the more profits for the partners to split, and the fewer partners there are, the bigger each partner's share.

After you make partner (*if* you make partner—your chances will likely be about one in ten), you will still be exploited, although somewhat less. You may take home 40% or so of what you bring into the firm as a junior partner. Your take will gradually increase with your seniority. At some point, you will reach equilibrium—that is, you will take home roughly what you bring into the firm, minus your share of the firm's overhead. And, if you stick with it long enough, some day you will reach Big Firm Nirvana: You will take home more than you bring into the firm (minus your share of overhead). You will become the exploiter instead of the exploited.

* * *

* * * The result? Long hours, large salaries, and one of the unhealthiest and unhappiest professions on earth.

But something is wrong here. Something doesn't make sense.

As I have tried to convey, the profession that you are about to enter is absolutely obsessed with money. "[M]oney is not just incidental to the practice, but at its core." Money is at the root of virtually everything that lawyers don't like about their profession: the long hours, the commercialization, the tremendous pressure to attract and retain clients, the fiercely competitive marketplace, the lack of collegiality and loyalty among partners, the poor public image of the profession, and even the lack of civility. Almost every one of these problems would be eliminated or at least substantially reduced if lawyers were simply willing to make less money. * * *

* * *

* * * At the same time that lawyers are enjoying these fantastic incomes, many are dissatisfied with their professional lives, and their single biggest complaint is the long hours they have to work. Lawyers could enjoy a lot more life outside work if they were willing to accept relatively modest reductions in their incomes. Take, for example, a partner who is billing 2000 hours and being paid $200,000. If we assume that a 20% reduction in billable hours will translate into a 20% reduction in pay (an assumption that is unlikely to be exactly true, but that is close enough for our purposes), this lawyer could trade $40,000 in income for 600 more hours of life outside work (assuming that three hours at work translates into two hours billed).

Our hypothetical partner has a choice, then: He can make $200,000 per year and work many nights and most weekends—routinely getting up early, before his children are awake, driving to the office, eating lunch at his desk, leaving the office late, picking up dinner at the Taco Bell drive-through window, and then arriving home to kiss the cheeks of his sleeping children. Or he can make $160,000 per year and work few nights and weekends. He can spend time with his spouse, be a parent to his children, enjoy the company of his friends, pursue a hobby, do volunteer work, exercise regularly, and generally lead a well-balanced life—*while still making $160,000 per year.* If all such lawyers making $160,000 per year sat down and asked themselves, "What will make me a happier and healthier person: another $40,000 in income (which, after taxes, will mean another $25,000 or so in the bank) or 600 hours to do whatever I enjoy most?," it is hard to believe that many of them would take the money.

But many of them do take the money. Thousands of lawyers choose to give up a healthy, happy, well-balanced life for a less healthy, less happy life dominated by work. And they do so merely to be able to make seven or eight times the national median income instead of five or six times the national median income. Why? Are lawyers just greedy?

Well, some are, but it is more complicated than that. For one thing, lawyers don't think in these terms. They don't see their lives as crazy. Lawyers don't see any of this. Lawyers don't sit down and think logically about why they are leading the lives they are leading any more than buffalo sit down and think logically about why they are stampeding.

* * * I hope that you *will* sit down and think about the life that you want to lead before you get caught up in the stampede.

* * * [V]ery few lawyers are working extraordinarily long hours because they need the money. They are doing it for a different reason.

Big firm lawyers are, on the whole, a remarkably insecure and competitive group of people. Many of them have spent almost their entire lives competing to win games that other people have set up for them. First they competed to get into a prestigious college. Then they competed for college grades. Then they competed for LSAT scores. Then they competed to get into a prestigious law school. Then they competed for law school grades. Then they competed to make the law review. Then they competed for clerkships. Then they competed to get hired by a big law firm.

Now that they're in a big law firm, what's going to happen? Are they going to stop competing? Are they going to stop comparing themselves to others? Of course not. They're going to keep competing—competing to bill more hours, to attract more clients, to win more cases, to do more deals. They're playing a game. And the money is how the score is kept in that game.

Why do you suppose sixty year old lawyers with millions of dollars in the bank still bill 2200 hours per year? * * *

It is not because the lawyers *need the money*. * * * What's driving these lawyers is the desire to *win the game*. These lawyers have spent their entire lives competing against others and measuring their worth by how well they do in the competitions. And now that they are working in a law firm, money is the way they keep score. Money is what tells them if they're more successful than the lawyer in the next office—or in the next office building—or in the next town. If a lawyer's life is dominated by the game—and if his success in the game is measured by money—then his *life* is dominated by money. For many, many lawyers, it's that simple.

At this point, I should say a few words about ethics. * * *

There are many reasons why ethics course are so unpopular, but the most important is probably that law students do not think that they will become unethical lawyers. Students think of unethical lawyers as the sleazeballs who chase ambulances * * *. Students have a hard time identifying with these lawyers. When students think of life after graduation, they see themselves sitting on the 27th floor of some skyscraper in a freshly pressed dark suit (blue, black, or gray) with a starched blouse or shirt (white or light blue) doing sophisticated legal work for sophisticated clients. Students imagine—wrongly—that such lawyers do not have to worry much about ethics, except, perhaps, when the occasional conflict of interest question arises.

If you think this—if you think that you will not have any trouble practicing law ethically—you are wrong. Dead wrong. In fact, particularly if you go to work for a big firm, you will probably begin to practice law unethically in at least some respects within your first year or two in practice. This happens to most young lawyers in big firms. It happened to me, and it will happen to you, unless you do something about it.

Let's first be clear on what I mean by practicing law ethically. I mean three things.

First, you generally have to comply with the formal disciplinary rules—either the Model Rules of Professional Conduct, the Model Code of Professional Responsibility, or some state variant of one or the other. As a law student, and then as a young lawyer, you will often be encouraged to distinguish ethical from unethical conduct solely by reference to the formal rules. Most likely, you will devote the majority of the time in your professional responsibility class to studying the rules, and you will, of course, learn the rules cold so that you can pass the Multi-State Professional Responsibility Exam ("MPRE"). In many other ways, subtle and blatant, you will be encouraged to think that conduct that does not violate the rules is "ethical," while conduct that does violate the rules is "unethical."

It is in the interests of your professors, the organized bar, and other lawyers to get you to think about ethics in this way. It is a lot easier for a professor to teach students what rules say than it is to explore with students what it means to behave ethically. * * * Defining ethics with reference to rules puts tremendous power in the hands of the organized bar that writes those rules. And many lawyers want "the absence of disciplinary measures and adherence to the profession's own Model Rules of Professional Conduct" to be sufficient to qualify a lawyer as "ethical," simply because it is easy to avoid disciplinary measures and to adhere to at least the letter of formal rules.

I don't have anything against the formal rules. Often, they are all that stands between an unethical lawyer and a vulnerable client. You should learn them and follow them. But you should also understand that the formal rules represent nothing more than "the lowest common denominator of conduct that a highly self-interested group will tolerate." For many lawyers, "[e]thics is a matter of steering, if necessary, just clear of the few unambiguous prohibitions found in rules governing lawyers." But complying with the formal rules will not make you an ethical lawyer, any more than complying with the criminal law will make you an ethical person. Many of the sleaziest lawyers you will encounter will be absolutely scrupulous in their compliance with the formal rules. In fact, they will be only too happy to tell you just that. Complying with the rules is usually a necessary, but never sufficient, part of being an ethical lawyer.

The second thing you must do to be an ethical lawyer is to act ethically in your work, even when you aren't required to do so by any rule. To a substantial extent, "bar ethical rules have lost touch with ordinary moral intuitions." To practice law ethically you must practice law consistently with those intuitions. For the most part, this is not complicated. Being an ethical lawyer is not much different from being an ethical doctor or mail carrier or gas station attendant. Indeed, long before you applied to law school, your parents had probably taught you all that you need to know to practice law ethically. You should treat others as you want them to treat you. Be honest and fair. Show respect and compassion. Keep your promises. Here is a good rule of thumb: If you would be ashamed if your parents or spouse or children knew what you were doing, then you should not do it.

The third thing you must do to be an ethical lawyer is to live an ethical life. Many big firm lawyers—who can be remarkably "smug[] about the superiority of the ethical standards of large firms"—ignore this point. So do many law professors who, when writing about legal ethics, tend to focus solely on the lawyer at work. But being admitted to the bar does not absolve you of your responsibilities outside of work—to your family, to your friends, to your community, and, if you're a person of faith, to your God. To practice law ethically, you must meet those responsibilities, which means that you must live a balanced life. If you become a workaholic lawyer, you will be unhealthy, probably unhappy, and I would argue, unethical.

* * *

It is hard to practice law ethically. Complying with the formal rules is the easy part. * * *

Acting as an ethical lawyer in the broader, non-formalistic sense is far more difficult. I have already given you some idea of why it is hard to practice law in a big firm (or any firm that emulates a big firm) and live a balanced life; I will return to that point in a moment. But even practicing law ethically in the sense of being honest and fair and compassionate is difficult. To understand why, you need to understand what it is that you will do every day as a lawyer.

Most of a lawyer's life is filled with the mundane. It is unlikely that one of your clients will drop a smoking gun on your desk or ask you to deliver a briefcase full of unmarked bills or invite you to have wild, passionate sex (or even un-wild, un-passionate sex). These things happen to lawyers only in John Grisham novels. Your life as a lawyer will be filled with the kind of things that drove John Grisham to write novels: dictating letters and talking on the phone and drafting memoranda and performing "due diligence" and proofreading contracts and negotiating settlements and filling out time sheets. And because your life as a lawyer will be filled with the mundane, whether you practice law ethically will depend not upon how you resolve the one or two dramatic ethical dilemmas that you will confront during your entire career, but upon the hundreds of little things that you will do, almost unthinkingly, each and every day.

Because practicing law ethically will depend primarily upon the hundreds of little things that you will do almost unthinkingly every day, it will not depend much upon your thinking. You are going to be busy. The days will fly by. When you are on the phone negotiating a deal or when you are at your computer drafting a brief or when you are filling out your time sheet at the end of the day, you are not going to have time to reflect on each of your actions. You are going to have to act almost instinctively.

What this means, then, is that you will not practice law ethically—you *cannot* practice law ethically—unless acting ethically is *habitual* for you. You have to be in the habit of being honest. You have to be in the habit of being fair. You have to be in the habit of being compassionate. These qualities have to be deeply ingrained in you, so that you can't turn them on and off—so that acting honorably is not something you have to *decide* to do—so that when you are at work, making the thousands of phone calls you will make and writing the thousands of letters you will write and dealing with the thousands of people with whom you will deal, you will *automatically* apply the same values in the workplace that you apply outside of work, when you are with family and friends.

Here is the problem, though: After you start practicing law, nothing is likely to influence you more than "the culture or house norms of the agency, department, or firm" in which you work. If you are going into private practice—particularly private practice in a big firm—you are going to be immersed in a culture that is hostile to the values you now have. The system does not *want* you to apply the same values in the workplace that you do outside of work (unless you're rapaciously greedy outside of work); it wants you to replace those values with the system's values. The system is obsessed with money, and it wants you to be, too. The system wants you—it *needs* you—to play the game.

Now, no one is going to say this to you. No one is going to take you aside and say, "Jane, we here at Smith & Jones are obsessed with money. From this point forward the most important thing in your life has to be billing hours and generating business. Family and friends and honesty and fairness are okay in moderation, but don't let them interfere with making money." No one will tell you, as one lawyer told another in a Charles Addams cartoon, "I admire your honesty and integrity, Wilson, but I have no room for them in my firm." Instead, the culture will pressure you in more subtle ways to replace your values with the system's.

Here is an example of what I mean: During your first month working at the big firm, some senior partner will invite you and the other new associates to a barbeque at his home. The "barbeque" will bear absolutely no relationship to what your father used to do on a Weber grill in your driveway. You will drive up to the senior partner's home in your rusted Escort and park at the end of a long line of Mercedeses and BMWs and sports utility vehicles. You will walk up to the front door of the house. The house will be enormous. The lawn will look like a putting green; it will be bordered by perfectly manicured trees and flowers. Somebody wearing a white shirt and black bow tie will answer the door and direct you to the backyard. You will walk through one room after another, each of which will be decorated with expensive carpeting and expensive wallpaper and expensive antiques. Scattered throughout the home will be large professional photographs of beautiful children with tousled, sun-bleached hair.

As you enter the partner's immaculately landscaped backyard, someone wearing a white shirt and black bow tie carrying a silver platter will approach you and offer you an appetizer. Don't look for cocktail weenies in barbeque sauce; you will more likely be offered pâté or miniature quiches or shrimp. A bar will be set up near the house; the bartender (who will be wearing a white shirt and black bow tie, of course) will pour you a drink of the most expensive brand of whatever liquor you like. In the corner of the yard, a caterer will be grilling swordfish. In another corner will stand the senior partner, sipping a glass of white wine, holding court with a worshipful group of junior partners and senior associates.

The senior partner will be wearing designer sunglasses and designer clothes; the logo on his shirt will signal its exorbitant cost; his shorts will be pressed. He will have a tan—albeit a slightly orange, tanning salon enhanced tan—and the nicest haircut you've ever seen. Eventually, the partner will introduce you to his wife. She will be beautiful, very thin, and a lot younger than her husband. She, too, will have a great tan, and not nearly as orange as her husband's. You and the other lawyers will talk about golf. Or about tennis. After a couple hours, you will walk out the front door, slightly tipsy from the free liquor, and say to yourself, "This is the life."

In this and a thousand other ways, you will absorb big firm culture—a culture of long hours of toil inside the office and short hours of conspicuous consumption outside the office. You will work among lawyers who will talk about money constantly and who will be intensely curious about how much money other lawyers are making. * * *

* * *

Big firm culture also reflects the many ways in which lawyers who are winning the game broadcast their success. A first year male associate will buy his suits off the rack at a department store; a couple years later, he will be at Brooks Brothers; a few years after that, a salesperson will come to his office, with tape measures and fabric swatches in hand. Similar ostentatious progress will be demonstrated with regard to everything from watches to cell phones to running shoes to child care arrangements to private social clubs. When lawyers speak with envy or admiration about other lawyers, they do not mention a lawyer's devotion to family or public service, or a lawyer's innate sense of fairness, or even a lawyer's skill at trying cases or closing deals, nearly as much as they mention a lawyer's billable hours, or stable of clients, or annual income.

It is very difficult for a young lawyer immersed in this culture day after day to maintain the values she had as a law student. Slowly, almost imperceptibly, young lawyers change. They begin to admire things they did not admire before, be ashamed of things they were not ashamed of before, find it impossible to live without things they lived without before. Somewhere, somehow, a lawyer changes from a person who gets intense pleasure from being able to buy her first car stereo to a person enraged over a $400,000 bonus.

As the values of an attorney change, so, too, does her ability to practice law ethically. The process that I have described will obviously push a lawyer away from practicing law ethically in the broadest sense—that is, in the sense of leading a balanced life and meeting non-work-related responsibilities. When work becomes all-consuming, it consumes all. To succeed in today's big firm, a lawyer must live without a single "compelling, time consuming, and deeply valued interest outside the practice of law." If you are working all the time, you will not—you cannot—meet any other responsibilities that require any appreciable commitment of time or energy. This much is obvious. However, absorbing the values of big firm culture will also push a lawyer away from practicing law ethically in the narrower sense of being honest and fair and compassionate. In the highly competitive, money-obsessed world of big firm practice, "[m]ost of the new incentives for lawyers, such as attracting and retaining clients, push toward stretching ethical concerns to the limit."

Unethical lawyers do not start out being unethical; they start out just like you—as perfectly decent young men or women who have every intention of practicing law ethically. They do not become unethical overnight; they become unethical just as you will (if you become unethical)—a little bit at a time. And they do not become unethical by shredding incriminating documents or bribing jurors; they become unethical just as you are likely to—by cutting a corner here, by stretching the truth a bit there.

Let me tell you how you will start acting unethically: It will start with your time sheets. One day, not too long after you start practicing law, you will sit down at the end of a long, tiring day, and you just won't have much to show for your efforts in terms of billable hours. It will be near the end of the month. You will know that all of the partners will be looking at your monthly time report in a few days, so what you'll do is pad your time sheet just a bit. Maybe you will bill a client for ninety minutes for a task that really took you only sixty minutes to perform. However, you will promise yourself that you will repay the client at the first opportunity by doing thirty minutes of work for the client for "free." In this way, you will be "borrowing," not "stealing."

And then what will happen is that it will become easier and easier to take these little loans against future work. And then, after a while, you will stop paying back these little loans. You will convince yourself that, although you billed for ninety minutes and spent only sixty minutes on the project, you did such good work that your client should pay a bit more for it. After all, your billing rate is awfully low, and your client is awfully rich.

And then you will pad more and more—every two minute telephone conversation will go down on the sheet as ten minutes, every three hour research project will go down with an extra quarter hour or so. You will continue to rationalize your dishonesty to yourself in various ways until one day you stop doing even that. An, before long—it won't take you much more than three or four years—you will be stealing from your clients almost every day, and you won't even notice it.

You know what? You will also likely become a liar. A deadline will come up one day, and, for reasons that are entirely your fault, you will not be able to meet it. So you will call your senior partner or your client and make up a white lie for why you missed the deadline. And then you will get busy and a partner will ask whether you proofread a lengthy prospectus and you will say yes, even though you didn't. And then you will be drafting a brief and you will quote language from a Supreme Court opinion even though you will know that, when read in context, the language does not remotely suggest what you are implying it suggests. And then, in preparing a client for a deposition, you will help the client to formulate an answer to a difficult question that will likely be asked—an answer that will be "legally accurate" but that will mislead your opponent. And then you will be reading through a big box of your client's documents—a box that has not been opened in twenty years—and you will find a document that would hurt your client's case, but that no one except you knows exists, and you will simply "forget" to produce it in response to your opponent's discovery requests.

Do you see what will happen? After a couple years of this, you won't even notice that you are lying and cheating and stealing every day that you practice law. None of these things will seem like a big deal in itself—an extra fifteen minutes added to a time sheet here, a little white lie to cover a missed deadline there. But, after a while, your entire frame of reference will change. You will still be making dozens of quick, instinctive decisions every day, but those decisions, instead of reflecting the notions of right and wrong by which you conduct your personal life, will instead reflect the set of values by which you will conduct your professional life—a set of values that embodies not what is right or wrong, but what is profitable, and what you can get away with. The system will have succeeded in replacing your values with the system's values, and the system will be profiting as a result.

Does this happen to every big firm lawyer? Of course not. It's all a matter of degree. The culture in some big firms is better than in others. Every year I steer students who are intent on big firm practice toward some firms and away from others, precisely because some large firms are better places to work than others. I could tell you many stories about big firms going out of their way to show compassion to a partner with a drinking problem or a loyal client who could not pay its bills or a rival attorney who is over the hill and on the verge of embarrassing himself. The big firm at which I practiced was as decent and humane as a big firm can be. Similarly, some big firm lawyers have better values than others. I owe a lot to a partner who sacrificed hundreds of hours of his time and tens of thousands of dollars of income to act as a mentor to me and to many other young lawyers like me.

At the same time, you should not underestimate the likelihood that you will practice law unethically. It is true, for example, that not every lawyer knowingly and blatantly lies on his time sheets. But there is a reason why padding time sheets has been called "a silent epidemic." Lots of lawyers pad time sheets in ways that are less obviously dishonest and more socially accepted. For example, a lawyer who needs to fly from Los Angeles to New York for one client may do the work of another client during the five hour flight, and bill both clients five hours—the first for five hours of travel, the second for five hours of work. Another common practice is for lawyers not to fill out their time sheets until the end of the day—or end of the week—or even end of the month. When a lawyer sits down on July 31 and tries to remember how much time she devoted to a client's work on July 9, it is only natural that she will underestimate the amount of time wasted on coffee breaks and personal phone calls and overestimate the amount of time devoted to client's work.

Another widely accepted way of padding time sheets is to bill in minimum increments of, say, .25 hours or .30 hours. This permits the enterprising lawyer to engage in four two-minute phone calls and bill one hour. I cannot tell you how many times I have seen a lawyer bill a client fifteen minutes for the ninety seconds it took him to leave a voice mail message or to read a one paragraph deposition notice. I recall one occasion on which I sent a letter to an attorney who was representing my client in connection with a lawsuit filed in a distant state. I included in the same envelope copies of two other letters about the lawsuit that I had mailed other people. I later learned that this lawyer had billed my client .90 hours for reading three letters that I had billed my client .50 hours for writing. How? He billed in .30 minimums and billed separately for each of the three letters he read, while I billed only for the time that I actually devoted to writing the letters. Many lawyers would admire this as clever and creative (if perhaps a bit aggressive) billing.

Likewise, not every big firm lawyer is a workaholic. This, too, is a matter of degree. I know big firm lawyers who make a good living and still eat dinner with their families most nights and spend most weekends away from the office. Unfortunately, though, these lawyers are almost invariably regarded by their partners as "deadwood" or as "semi-retired." If you think I am exaggerating, I challenge you to find *one* big firm partner who lives a balanced life—that is, who does not work regularly on nights or weekends (at home or at the office)—and yet is well respected and considered successful by his peers. And I challenge you to find *one* big firm lawyer who lived anything like a balanced life as an associate and still made partner. I do not know of such a lawyer. Not one. In the last couple years, I have given speeches to various groups of lawyers and judges, and I have challenged my audiences to identify one such big firm lawyer for me. I have yet to be given a name. At best, such partners are rare. They may be nonexistent.

As I say, neither big firms nor big firm lawyers are all alike. But what you need to understand is that they are *becoming* more alike. One of the most consistent findings of the social scientists involved in a recent ABA study of the ethics of big firm litigators was that the cultures of individual firms are weakening, leaving a "void of guidance to junior lawyers." The void, in turn, is being "filled by other powerful systemic or environmental influences," especially influences from outside the firm. In other words, the distinctive cultures of individual big firms are influencing young lawyers less and less, while generic big firm culture is influencing young lawyers more and more. That is why, no matter which big firm you join, there is a good chance that working at the firm will make you unhealthy, an even better chance that it will make you unhappy, and an almost 100% chance that it will make you unethical—at least if you accept that practicing law ethically includes practicing law in a manner that permits you to meet your responsibilities to someone besides your firm and clients.

Notes and Questions

1. Marc Galanter and Thomas Palay express skepticism about the premise, explanation, and implications of the Schiltz argument. Regarding the latter, they wonder if it would be such a bad thing that big-firm lawyers are obsessed with money and more miserable than other lawyers. They ask: "Should we be concerned to have happy and fulfilled corporate lawyers?" They suggest, "The presence of that cost may prevent the corporate sector from siphoning off even more of the best legal talent and aggravating still further the disparity in the quality of lawyering between individuals and organizations." Marc S. Galanter & Thomas M. Palay, *Large Law Firm Misery: It's the Tournament, Not the Money,* 52 Vand. L. Rev. 953, 968 (1999). They argue that the prestige associated with representing establishment clients fuels a "promotion-to-partner tournament" that motivates associates buying into the firm orientation of law practice. This is more important than the obsession with money. Moreover, service to the poor, for instance, takes away from professional prestige. Therefore, "a profession made up of lawyers going all out to maximize professional prestige, as currently allotted, would be far worse than one obsessed by money." *Id.* at 969. Do you agree? *See generally Symposium: Attorney Well–Being in Large Firms: Choices Facing Young Lawyers*, 52 Vand. L. Rev. 868 (1999), and Dennis Curtis, *Can Law Schools and Big Law Firms be Friends?*, 74 S. Cal. L. Rev. 65 (2000).

2. If both prestige and monetary reward are associated with big-firm practice, are social justice lawyers who do not work in a big-firm "left-over" lawyers? Are the big-firm pro-bono lawyers able to have their cake and eat it too when it comes to practicing social justice law *and* having a lot of prestige and a lot of money? In a study of lawyers who ranked thirty fields of law by their relative prestige, big business law was ranked at the top, while at the other end of the prestige ranking were the types of work undertaken on behalf of individuals, such as general family practice, divorce, personal injury, consumer, and criminal law.

John P. Heinz & Edward O. Laumann, *Chicago Lawyers: The Social Structure of the Bar* 92–93 (1982). Within prestige rankings, where would you place working for a legal services office, the ACLU, the Mexican American Legal Defense and Educational Fund, the National Organization of Women, or the NAACP Legal Defense and Educational Fund? What about a social justice private practice like those described by Louise Trubek in chapter 2? Given the relatively low prestige and relatively low salaries, why would you want to work for a social justice law office? Is it simply a matter of default? If not, what commitments motivate you?

3. How do you respond, practically, to Schiltz's invitation: "Make the decision now that *you* will be the one who defines success for you"? Is this basically asking the question, "Who am I?" *See* Howard Lesnick, *Speaking Truth to Powerlessness,* 52 Vand. L. Rev. 995, 997 (1999).

4. Aside from money and prestige, some argue that the most meaningful experiences of law practice are found in a large firm: "[I]f you are excited by being involved in some of the most important issues facing our society today and in some of the most important cases, and if you get excited by writing a great brief, negotiating a transaction for a client, or standing up before the United States Court of Appeals, then the practice of law in a big firm is your best chance of having an exciting legal practice." Mary A. McLaughlin, *Beyond the Caricature: The Benefits and Challenges of Large-Firm Practice*, 52 Vand. L. Rev.1003, 1014 (1999). Do you agree?

5. McLaughlin declares, moreover, that "the most unfair and inaccurate assertion [that Schiltz makes] is that the big-firm lawyers regularly act unethically." *Id.* at 1005. Schiltz replies that he has not claimed that big-firm lawyers regularly violate the formal rules of professional responsibility: "Those rules require so little that I doubt that many lawyers violate them 'regularly'." Patrick J. Schiltz, *Reply—Provoking Introspection: A Reply to Galanter & Palay, Hull, Kelly, Lesnick, McLaughlin, Pepper, and Traynor*, 52 Vand. L. Rev. 1033, 1041 (1999). Moreover, "I do think big firm lawyers act unethically in permitting work to consume their lives, and in failing to meet their responsibilities to their families, friends, communities, and others." *Id.* Is this a fair characterization of acting "unethically"? Does this claim of unethical conduct have anything to do with professional responsibility? Or is this another way of asking the more introspective questions, "What is my definition of professional success?" and "Who am I?"

6. In light of the Schiltz article, responses, and reply, consider the issues of big-firm practice a person of color or a woman might face. How might race and gender complicate the issues? How might issues related to big-firm practice be complicated if you were disabled? What impact might your being gay or lesbian have? For one thing, law school debt may especially affect job choices among some social groups. *See* Lewis A Kornhauser & Richard L. Revesz, *Legal Education and Entry into the Legal Profession: The Role of Race, Gender, and Educational Debt*, 70

N.Y.U. L. Rev. 829 (1995), and David B. Wilkins & G. Mitu Gulati, *Why Are there So Few Black Lawyers in Corporate Law Firms?: An Institutional Analysis*, 84 Cal. L. Rev. 493 (1996). *See also* Jonathan D. Glater, *Law Firms Are Slow in Promoting Minority Lawyers to Partner Role*, N.Y. Times, Aug. 7, 2001, at col. 2, A1. Glater reports that since 1990, even though more than 20% of the students at some elite schools have been people of color, their promotion to partner lags: "[A] survey of the 12 highest-grossing law firms in the United States by *The New York Times* shows that minority lawyers accounted for about 5% of the new partners in recent years at the seven firms that supplied such data. And at some firms the percentage was much lower." At Sullivan & Cromwell, among the thirty-three new partners since 1997 none was a person of color. At Sherman & Sterling, of the seventeen lawyers who became partner in 2001, only one was a person of color while none of the twelve who made partner in 2000 was a person of color. *Id.* According to a 1999 ABA survey, 41% of whites, but only 8% of blacks, believed that law firms had a genuine commitment to diversity. Walter La Grande, *Getting There, Staying There,* ABA Journal, Feb. 1999, at 54.

7. Deborah Rhode and David Luban identify the following barriers for women in the legal profession: (1) gender stereotypes, (2) inadequate access to informal networks of mentoring, contacts, and client development, (3) workplace structures that do not accommodate substantial family responsibilities and pro bono commitments, (4) persistent sexual harassment in spite of workplace policies prohibiting it, and (5) gender bias in the justice system. Deborah L. Rhode & David Luban, *Legal Ethics* 34–39 (3d ed., 2001). Have you experienced, observed, or heard of these or other barriers?

Women are disproportionately affected by the time demands of the profession: "Most male attorneys have spouses who assume the bulk of family responsibilities; most female attorneys do not. Almost half of women in legal practice are currently unmarried, compared with 15% of men, and few women have partners who are primary caretakers." Deborah L. Rhode, Report Prepared for the ABA Commission on Women and the Profession, *Balanced Lives: Changing the Culture of Legal Practice* 17 (2001). Many law firms now provide for part-time work schedules, and a few firms provide access to childcare, emergency back-up care, and flexible schedules; however, working part-time can affect opportunities for promotion and career advancement. *See generally* Cynthia Fuchs Epstein et al., *The Part-Time Paradox: Time Norms, Professional Lives, Family, and Gender* (1999); *see also* Rhode, *Balanced Lives, supra* at 16–18. How can law schools and the profession address issues of time demands and family responsibilities to help students and young lawyers plan their careers?

8. In spite of the prospects of becoming unhappy and unhealthy, what are some of the reasons, particularly associated with underrepresented groups, to join a large law firm? Consider the challenges and opportunities for Latina/o lawyers discussed in Laura L. Castro, *The Future Is Now*, ABA Journal, July 1999, at 72:

While many Latino lawyers acknowledge efforts by some institutions and employers to diversify, most agree that the progress is too slow.

"There's just so little mobility," says Antonia Hernandez, president and general counsel of the Mexican American Legal Defense and Educational Fund in Los Angeles. Hernandez remembers that when she entered law practice 25 years ago, "You either went into public service or you hung your own little shingle out there because the law firms weren't going to hire you. I don't see very much changing."

A lack of networks and support systems are often cited as the biggest barrier for Latinos across the profession, particularly in large law firms. With few exceptions, there are only one or two Hispanic attorneys employed at any large firm, says Maribel Medina, a Los Angeles attorney who is president of the Latino Lawyers Association, an informal networking and support group for Latinos in large law firms.

Most Latino associates find it hard to find a mentor in such an environment. Medina, who graduated from law school in 1995, recalls her first job at a 360-lawyer firm in New York City that had no Latino partners. She left after two years. It was a very difficult existence, she recalls. "The firm I'm with now has a Latino partner who has taken it upon himself to mentor me and make sure I'm getting the right assignments." Another barrier at law firms for Latino lawyers, who are often first-generation professionals, is developing business for the firm without the availability of family and business connections. Fortunately, Medina says, some in-house counsel positions at large corporations are now held by Latinos who have the power to contract work out to Latinos at law firms.

Despite their struggles to advance in larger firms, Latino lawyers say the effort is worth it. "It's important for us to be partners because individually that's where the money is and it's an indication of being successful in your career," says Alfredo Silva, a partner at Strasburger & Price in Dallas. "And more importantly for the community, law firms are a source of political and social power."

Martin R. Castro, a partner at Chicago's Baker & McKenzie, says there are many Latinos working to break stereotypes and increase diversity. "What it takes is a critical mass of people or an individual who is willing to put the effort in to get the system to change internally," says Castro, the first Latino hired at the firm not to work in its Latin American practice. "It's not an easy thing in a lot of law firms, but it's something that every Latino lawyer who is at a law firm has an obligation to attempt to do."

If the struggle to advance in the higher reaches of the profession is a challenge for all Hispanic Lawyers, it may be particularly difficult for women. "There's still the perception that we're not as competent," says Elsa Leyva, a solo practitioner in Los Angeles who helped form the Latina Lawyers Bar Association in 1997. "So most of us feel that we really have to prove ourselves and do better than others in order to have someone take us seriously."

Achieving a stronger presence at law firms may help Hispanics gain a greater foothold in the judiciary, at both the federal and state levels. "We probably need to get some Hispanic attorneys working at getting into firms where judges tend to come from, as well as maybe broadening the search for minority attorneys when appointments to judgeships are being made," suggests Judge Jorge A. Solis, the first Hispanic to serve as a federal judge in the Northern District of Texas, based in Dallas.

9. David Wilkins argues that blacks in corporate firms have obligations to the black community, because "[c]ertain relationships create special moral obligations." David B. Wilkins, *Two Paths to the Mountaintop? The Role of Legal Education in Shaping the Values of Black Corporate Lawyers*, 45 Stan. L. Rev. 1981, 1996 (1993). For racial and ethnic groups of color, membership in an "identifiable culture" constitutes this kind of relationship. *Id.* Do you agree? Wilkins also lists a number of reasons why it is important for blacks to have a presence among corporate lawyers: (1) it undermines stereotypical notions of black intellectual inferiority; (2) it may inspire others to high achievement and it may open doors of opportunity; (3) it provides access to money and other resources that can support community projects; (4) it traditionally has served as a stepping stone to political office and influence, which may enable black corporate lawyers "to translate their power into public power in ways that benefit the black community"; and (5) "the very fact that corporations have such power to impose costs on the black community underscores the benefits that could accrue if black lawyers are able to persuade corporations to act in ways that are less harmful (and perhaps even beneficial) to the black community." *Id.* at 1991.

What does "community" mean to you? Is there a womens' community that suggests an obligation to decline to represent clients alleged to have engaged in sexual discrimination or sexual harassment?

10. In 1997, Cravath, Swaine & Moore, the prestigious New York law firm, was retained to represent Credit Suisse to defend allegations that it laundered Nazi gold that was stolen from Jews. Blaine Harden & Sandra Torry, *N.Y. Law Firm to Advise Swiss Bank Accused of Laundering Nazi Loot*, Wash. Post, Feb. 28, 1997, at 3. Can any lawyer, and especially a Jewish lawyer, at the firm morally agree to this representation? What does the concept of "legal ethics" mean in this context?

11. Angela Harris writes:

> Along with my then-colleague Stephanie Wildman, I recently taught a seminar on "Law and Social Justice" that examined the practice of lawyering in the service of "social justice" goals, however defined. One of the most striking observations to come from teaching that course was the increasing polarization of the student body between those who had committed themselves to a "public interest"

> career and those who were choosing corporate jobs (whether out of a genuine desire to do such work, the notorious desire for "training," the pressure of student loans, or because offers from large firms—like large salaries among associates—are the coin of the realm in the law student hierarchy of prestige). As entry-level associate salaries skyrocket and law school tuition inexorably rises, public-interest-bound students feel increasingly caught in an untenable material situation, and also feel put on the psychological defensive.

Angela Harris, *Reforming Alone?*, 54 Stan. L. Rev.1449, 1459 (2002). Has it been your experience or observation that social justice law students are put on the psychological defensive? What manifestations of that have you noticed? If you are inclined to pursue social justice lawyering, do you feel like a sucker? According to Harris, "One reaction to feeling like a sucker is a Nietzschean strategy: Social justice-oriented students, in order to justify their choices to themselves, their peers, their class 'reference group,' and their worried parents, increasingly identify themselves as morally good and their big-firm-bound friends as morally evil." *Id.* This strategy has a drawback, however, in that the students who intend to work, and associates who do work, for a large law firm are then permitted, if not encouraged, "to stop worrying about pro bono work or professional ethics." *Id.* Whether or not you intend to work for a large firm, do you see the polarization that Harris describes? If you intend to pursue a social justice lawyering career, are you tempted, self-righteously, to see yourself as morally superior to the large-firm lawyer? Does Schiltz, *supra*, do that? Finally, Harris notes that at least at her law school, the University of California, Berkeley (Boalt Hall), there is anecdotal evidence of racial polarization as well among the students, "with public-interest-identified students more likely to be white and students of color more likely to cite financial need as a reason for rejecting social justice work." *Id.* at 1460, n. 47. Given the difficulty people of color may have in succeeding in large law firms, how do students from these racial and ethnic groups decide which way to go?

12. Devise your own personal balance sheet, assessing the costs and benefits, challenges and opportunities, that are associated with working for, or aspiring to work for, a large law firm. In light of the readings above, has your view or understanding of this option changed? If so, how? What are some of the views of your classmates regarding the balancing of pros and cons of working for a large firm? What are the views of your law school's placement or career services office? Is it unduly biased toward accommodating on-campus interviewing by large law firms? How effectively does it accommodate students who seek an alternative placement to large-firm practice? Does your school's placement office work especially to accommodate social justice careers? *See* Douglas Phelps, *Law Placement and Social Justice,* 53 N.Y.U. L. Rev 663 (1978).

Chapter 5

FROM INDIVIDUAL CLIENTS TO GROUPS AND COMMUNITIES: ESTABLISHING AND SUSTAINING A VIABLE LAWYER-CLIENT RELATIONSHIP

A substantial body of classic and recent literature addresses the complexities of relationship-building between the lawyer and the client. This chapter focuses on some of the particular difficulties that are associated with progressive advocacy of subordinated individuals, groups, and communities. It begins with the model of client-centered representation that attempts to resolve the tension between professional paternalism and client autonomy. Then it turns to alternatives to client-centered representation and, finally, to the special issues that arise when lawyers represent groups and communities.

Clients primarily come to the lawyer for help solving a problem. Moreover, as discussed in chapter 3, collaborative work with client communities is an important part of social justice lawyering. The popular images of the lawyer at trial and the client sitting passively at the counsel table are far too narrow. Along with litigation, counseling and negotiation represent key processes by which lawyers facilitate the resolution of client disputes and issues. Most lawyers generally spend more time on these aspects of advocacy and representation than on any other particular aspect of legal work. The estimated total time that lawyers spend resolving disputes for individual clients through legal counseling and negotiation is approximately 44%. G. Nicholas Herman, Jean M. Cary & Joseph E. Kennedy, *Legal Counseling and Negotiating: A Practical Approach* 3–4 (2001). Thus, effective representation often depends on building advocacy from a positive working relationship between the lawyer and the client.

SECTION 1. THE CLIENT-CENTERED MODEL OF REPRESENTATION

According to Deborah Rhode, "Paternalism in lawyer-client relationships is seldom preached but often practiced." Deborah L. Rhode, *Professional Responsibility: Ethics by the Pervasive Method* 411 (1994). When a lawyer acts paternalistically, she imposes restrictions on her client's freedom of choice in order to further the client's own good. When such restrictions are imposed, competition arises between the principles of autonomy and benevolence: "Our respect for personal liberty and dignity counsels deference to a client's own choices; our desire to do good sometimes argues for overriding a client's choices for his or her own benefit." *Id.* This observation illustrates a significant tension between professional paternalism and client autonomy.

This tension, as expected, is seen in the two major approaches to interviewing and counseling clients. The traditional attorney-client relationship, reflecting the paternalistic approach to interviewing and counseling clients, prompts the lawyer to take the role of expert decision maker. While the client makes "the critical decisions concerning the overall goals of the representation," the lawyer exercises great influence over what options are presented to the client and how the decisions are made. Robert D. Dinerstein, *Client-Centered Counseling: Reappraisal and Refinement*, 32 Ariz. L. Rev. 501, 504 (1990). The lawyer's job is to present all the relevant legal considerations to the client and then recommend, in his professional capacity, a course of action that the lawyer feels the client should follow. In this scenario, the lawyer has a duty to persuade the client to make the decision that the lawyer feels is in the client's best interest.

In 1974, Douglas Rosenthal proposed a model where the client had a more active, participatory role in the lawyer-client relationship. Douglas E. Rosenthal, *Lawyer and Client: Who's in Charge?* (1974). This view originated primarily from the experience of public interest lawyers who worked with poor and oppressed clients. Many of these lawyers expressed "a pressing concern with clients' experience of powerlessness and their need for greater participation in both societal institutions and the lawyer-client relationship." *Id.* at 520. The traditional model was criticized as promoting a severe imbalance of power between the attorney and his or her client. Rosenthal argued that a "participatory" attorney-client model "promotes the dignity of citizens as clients," increases the chances for client satisfaction, and encourages effective problem solving. *Id.* The theory behind this model came to be known as the client-centered approach to client counseling. For two early works endorsing this approach to client counseling and interviewing, see David Binder & Susan Price, *Legal Interviewing and Counseling: A Client-Centered Approach* (1977), and Gary Bellow & Bea Moulton, *The Lawyering Process: Materials for Clinical Instruction in Advocacy* (1978). These texts quickly became the most widely used materials for teaching clinical skills in American law schools. *See* Michael Diamond, *Community Lawyering: Revisiting the Old Neighborhood*, 32 Colum. Human Rights L. Rev. 67, 91 (2000), and Linda F. Smith, *Interviewing Clients: A Linguis-*

tic Comparison of the "Traditional" Interview and the "Client-Centered" Interview, 1 Clinical L. Rev. 541, 543 (1995). The following text builds on the earlier work of Binder and Price and provides an overview of client-centered counseling.

DAVID A. BINDER, PAUL BERGMAN & SUSAN C. PRICE

Lawyers as Counselors: A Client-Centered Approach 17–23 (1991)

The client-centered approach encompasses conceptions of both problems and clients. Insofar as problems are concerned, the approach is anchored on the reality * * * that problems have both legal and nonlegal dimensions.

Contrast the client-centered conception of problems with a more traditional view. Under the traditional conception, lawyers view client problems primarily in terms of existing doctrinal categories such as contracts, torts, or securities. Information is important principally to the extent the data affects the doctrinal pigeonhole into which the lawyer places the problem. Moreover, in the traditional view, lawyers primarily seek the best "legal" solutions to problems without fully exploring how those solutions meet clients' nonlegal as well as legal concerns.

Next, compare client-centered and traditional conceptions of clients. A client-centered conception assumes that most clients are capable of thinking through the complexities of their problems. In particular, it posits that clients are usually more expert than lawyers when it comes to the economic, social and psychological dimensions of problems. The client-centered conception also assumes that, because any solution to a problem involves a balancing of legal and nonlegal concerns, clients usually are better able than lawyers to choose satisfactory solutions. Moreover, the approach recognizes that clients' emotions are an inevitable and natural part of problems and must be factored into the counseling process. Finally, the approach begins with the assumption that most clients seek to attain legally legitimate ends through lawful means.

Clients are less well regarded in the traditional conception. Lawyers adhering to the traditional view have often muttered, "The practice of law would be wonderful if it weren't for clients." Such lawyers tend to regard themselves as experts who can and should determine, in a detached and rational manner, and with minimal client input, what solution is best. Three common attributes that lawyers who hold a traditional view tend to ascribe to clients are: (1) Clients lack sophistication; (2) Clients are too emotionally wrapped up in their problems; and (3) Clients do not adequately consider the potential long-term effects (risks) of decisions.

As you might imagine, despite these differing conceptions, client-centered and traditional conceptions of lawyering have much in common. Both, for example, recognize the critical importance of legal analysis and have as their ultimate goal maximum client satisfaction. Moreover, most lawyers do not follow one conception to the complete exclusion of the other. However, the client-centered conception "fills in" the traditional approach by stressing that problems have nonlegal as well as legal aspects, and by emphasizing the importance of clients' expertise, thoughts and feelings in resolving problems. In a client-centered world, your role involves having clients actively participate in identifying their problems, formulating potential solutions, and making decisions. Thus, client-centered lawyering emanates from a belief in the autonomy, intelligence, dignity and basic morality of the individual client.

Client-centered lawyering does not, however, place you at the mercy of every client caprice and demand. Admittedly, the approach may from time to time require you to support client values and decisions with which you disagree. But when clients seek to go beyond the bounds of what is legal or just, a client-centered approach does not dictate that you disregard fundamental legal concepts and moral values. Nor does it suggest that you close your eyes and mouth to a client's desire to adopt a course of action fraught with the likelihood of disaster. Finally, when a client's values conflict with fundamental moral precepts and positive legal rules, the approach does not require that you become a blind instrumentalist.

The complexity of human interaction makes a precise definition of client-centered lawyering impossible. However, a client-centered approach has at least the following attributes.

A. The Lawyer Helps Identify Problems from a Client's Perspective

Central to the client-centered approach is the idea that you are most helpful to clients if from the outset you try to understand a problem from a client's point of view. Clients vary enormously in regard to such matters as their cultural-religious-ethnic characteristics; socio-economic status; financial needs; prior experience with lawyers and the legal system; willingness to take risks; desire to win; desire to establish harmonious working relationships; desire to prove a point, get revenge, or avoid conflict altogether; level of anxiety, anger or depression; and willingness to consider long-range as well as short-term consequences. Such factors almost inevitably influence a client's perception of what the problem is and what solutions are possible and worth pursuing.

Moreover, the context (environment) in which problems arise will be no less unique than the clients themselves. For example, a problem that arises at a time when inflation is low and social concern about "runaway jury verdicts" nonexistent will be different from one that arises at a time when inflation is higher and many people think jurors are awarding large windfalls to undeserving litigants. And, even at the same point in time, the facially similar problems (e.g., two manufacturing companies preparing dealership contracts) of two personally similar clients will very likely be quite unique. If one client is in the computer business in a small town and the other is in the furniture business in a big city, the different contexts will inevitably affect the nature and scope of their problems. Geographic areas and industries vary according to such factors as growth potential, custom and trade practices, standard operating procedures, composition of the labor force, capital needs, and the like. Hence, two problems which might in the traditional conception be housed in the same legal pigeonhole will, because of differing environments, often be viewed differently by individual clients.

B. The Lawyer Actively Involves a Client in the Process of Exploring Potential Solutions

This aspect of client centeredness involves two features. First, since there is rarely only one obvious solution to a client's problem, you try to make sure that the client considers the broadest range of options. You both suggest potential solutions and encourage a client to develop additional ones. Second, you encourage a client to identify the potential nonlegal consequences of each potential solution so that ultimately a solution is fashioned which takes into account the client's unique needs and goals.

C. The Lawyer Encourages a Client to Make Those Decisions Which Are Likely to Have a Substantial Legal or Nonlegal Impact

The client-centered approach emphasizes the value and importance of clients' taking the role of primary decision maker. It adopts the emphasis for two reasons. First, decisions having significant impact on a client are best based on an evaluation of which potential solution is most likely to satisfy the client. Second, because each client generally has unique values and goals, a client is typically in a better position than you to choose which potential solution is best.

For example, clients are generally in the better position to know how willing they are to spend money and how big a risk they are willing to take to achieve a particular goal. Assume that a client who has been fired is considering whether to file suit for wrongful termination, and if so, whether to seek reinstatement. The decision will rest on such factors as how willing the client is to incur attorney's fees, to relive his or her employment history in open court, and to bear the discomfort that may attach to returning to work in a possibly unfriendly environment. Since any one client is likely to weigh these factors differently, this pivotal decision is best left to the client.

Of course, you need not remain silent during the decision-making process. You must provide clients with an assessment of the likely legal (and sometimes nonlegal) consequences of following potential courses of action. Indeed, as the next section suggests, at times you may even recommend what course of action a client should adopt. Nonetheless, the basic point remains. Usually only a client can decide how willing he or she is to run the risks and bear the potential costs of adopting a particular course of action. Therefore, a client should make critical choices whenever possible and practical.

D. The Lawyer Provides Advice Based on a Client's Values

No amount of wishing for a world filled with fully autonomous clients—clients who make decisions on their own—can eliminate the reality that many clients will not feel comfortable making a decision until they hear your advice. Hence, while clients usually are best off making their own decisions, a client-centered conception recognizes that you may provide advice in many instances. However, your advice should generally be based on your understanding of the client's values. Giving advice based on the consequences you personally think important would impose your values on a client and would be antithetical to client-centeredness.

E. The Lawyer Acknowledges a Client's Feelings and Recognizes Their Importance

Client-centered counseling also requires that you understand and respond to clients' feelings. Legal problems do not exist in an emotionless vacuum. Clients' emotional reactions to situations are as significant an aspect of problems as are the facts which generate the problems. Recall * * * that feelings are an inherent part of legal problems. Worries and concerns form the heart of problems and motivate clients to seek help in the first place. It is not surprising, then, that clients *want* and *need* to talk about their feelings. Thus, by focusing on both feelings as well as facts, you can build rapport, elicit detailed and accurate information, and help fashion solutions that best meet clients' needs.

F. The Lawyer Repeatedly Conveys a Desire to Help

Another aspect of a client-centered approach consists of an amazingly simple step. Convey, explicitly, that you want to help a client. For example, you might say, "I really want to help you decide whether incorporating the business makes sense." Perhaps this suggestion seems fatuous. After all, won't a client assume that you are there to provide help? Maybe. But a formal attorney-client relationship does not always assure a client that you are personally committed to providing help. Asserting your desire to help is an explicit form of reassurance that clients often find comforting and motivating.

* * *

Through the foregoing attributes, the client-centered approach encourages clients to participate actively in the description and resolution of their problems. As the discussion of the attributes suggests, the advantages of active client participation are substantial. Active client participation enhances the likelihood of producing satisfactory resolutions. It does so by (1) embracing both the legal and nonlegal dimensions of a client's problem; (2) employing the combined expertise of lawyer and client in identifying and evaluating potential solutions; and (3) encouraging decisions to be made by clients, who are generally better able than lawyers to assess whether solutions are likely to be satisfactory.

Moreover, active client participation respects the autonomy of the person who "owns" the problem. A client does not lose the right to make decisions which are likely to have a substantial impact on his or her life for having sought legal assistance.

Notes and Questions

1. Along with the technical skills of a lawyer, the client-centered approach demands that the lawyer possess very good interpersonal skills. During an initial interview session, the helper role is emphasized as the lawyer gathers facts, establishes rapport, and sets the bounds of the lawyer-client relationship. Here, the necessary interpersonal skills would include active listening, empathy, genuineness, and probing. These same skills would be used in counseling sessions. Robert M. Bastress & Joseph D. Harbaugh, *Interviewing, Counseling, and Negotiating: Skills for Effective Representation* 7–8 (1990).

2. Bastress and Harbaugh suggest that client-centered representation must respond to a number of basic themes: "How should you relate to your clients? How does the nature of your relationships with clients affect your ability to interview, counsel, and represent them? What is the appropriate relationship between your professional life and your private life? Should you personally judge the social and moral propriety of your clients' cases? Why or why not?" *Id.* at 6.

3. How do prejudices, stereotypes, and social distance from "others" affect the ability to follow a client-centered approach? How does lawyer arrogance and myopia affect this approach? Michelle Jacobs laments, "As a practicing lawyer assigned to indigent clients, I was sometimes disturbed by comments made by my colleagues about the clients to whom they were assigned. Their voices would often be tinged with disrespect and, frankly, disgust towards their clients. * * * [D]uring my tenure as a clinical professor I have also heard many students express similar attitudes toward their clients. I find the phenomenon deeply disturbing." Michelle S. Jacobs, *Full Legal Representation for the Poor: The Clash Between Lawyer Values and Client Worthiness*, 44 How. L. J. 257, 258 (2001). Have you observed—or worse, represented—this "disturbing" phenomenon? How can this problem, the clash between professional values and client worthiness, be overcome? *See also* Paul E. Lee & Mary M. Lee, *Reflections from the Bottom of the Well: Racial Bias in the Provision of Legal Services to the Poor*, 27 Clearinghouse Rev. 311 (Special Issue 1993).

4. Paternalism may not be the main obstacle to effective lawyer-client relations. In Gary Bellow's view, the main problems are indifference, distance, drift, and visionlessness. Gary Bellow, *Steady Work: A Practitioner's Reflections on Political Lawyering*, 31 Harv. C.R.-C.L.L.

Rev. 297, 304 (1996). Is vision a quality that can be taught? Bellow's view is explored more fully in section 2.

MICHELLE S. JACOBS

People from the Footnotes: The Missing Element in Client-Centered Counseling
27 Golden Gate U. L. Rev. 345, 345–48, 377–85, 388–90, 401–02, 409–12 (1997)

The development of a client-centered approach to counseling was fueled by a concern that under the traditional approach to lawyering, the client came into the relationship with her lawyer in an unequal and/or subordinate position. As a result, the client was thought to be overwhelmed by the power represented in the lawyer's position and, therefore, subject to manipulation by the lawyer. Manipulation has been described as having two principal elements. First, it is an effort by one person to guide another's thoughts or actions in a direction desired by the person guiding. Second, the manipulator seeks this goal by means that undercut the other person's ability to make a choice that is truly his own. The goal of client-centered counseling was to create an "interactive dynamic that facilitates the development of mutual trust, confidence and respect." It was thought that behavior which was sensitive to communication dynamics would facilitate disclosure of complete and accurate information and ultimately result in making the lawyer pursue client, rather than lawyer, objectives.

Currently, many clinical programs have adopted models of lawyer-client relationship which employ one of two prevailing client-centered models. Both models recognize the importance of lawyer-client interaction in decision-making on a non-manipulative basis. It was perceived that in a traditional lawyer-client relationship the client is manipulated into doing what the lawyer wished, regardless of whether it was what the client actually desired. On the whole, both models provide a good framework for the lawyer (and in our realm, law student) to learn and hone some of the skills of effective communication with his/her clients. However, a major weakness of both models is that they fail to address, in any significant way, the effects of race, class and, to a lesser extent, gender on the interaction between lawyer and client. In addition, neither the models' creators nor the clinical community acknowledge that the models may not be applicable for use with clients of color in the lawyer-client counseling relationship or by lawyers of color in the clinical supervisor-student relationship. Indeed, there are no references in the texts to how a lawyer's race or gender may affect counseling. Both models of lawyer-client relationships caution lawyers not to "color" the process with personal feelings, biases or values.

In both models client characteristics are essentially presented as interchangable. The gender of the clients are alternated and sometimes the reader is given enough bare boned facts to enable her to designate class status but rarely anything more. In light of the growing recognition accorded to the importance and validity of client narratives among clinicians as well as traditional academics, the absence of client context within the models seems strangely out of step with prevailing clinical thought. If, after all, the clients are interchangeable, what difference does it make that they each come with their own narrative, with their own individual views of the legal system and different sets of expectations based on their cultural experiences and personal values?

The irony of the models is that they were constructed to return the client to the centrality of the lawyer's work. Yet, even with the best of intentions, lawyers most concerned with preserving the autonomy of client decision-making have, by adopting the "client-centered" model of counseling, continued to place the client, especially the client of color, out at the margin.

* * *

Lawyers, law students and law professors, like every other member of society, carry with them preconceived notions rooted in the lawyer's own cultural background. If the lawyer in question is white, which according to statistics is the norm, and is working in a legal services, clinical or public interest position, the client-participants are likely to be people of color and/or individuals from a lower socio-economic background than the lawyer or law student. It is also likely that the lawyer or law student carries with him/her elements of unconscious racism. What we, as clinicians, have failed to examine is how the unconscious racism, or, in other words, the lawyer's or law student's preconceived cultural notions will impact both the lawyer's expectations of the client as well as the lawyer's interpretation and understanding of the client's actions and ultimate objectives.

The potential impact of preconceived notions is demonstrated in a phenomenon known as the self-fulfilling prophecy. In this phenomenon, an originally false definition of a situation can influence the believer of the false definition to act in such a way as to bring about that situation. More specifically, the principle establishes that one person's attitudes and expectations about another may influence the believer's actions, which in turn, may induce the other to behave in a way that confirms the original false definition. In their study, the authors focused on detecting possible nonverbal mediators of this phenomenon and on the resulting performances of the interactants. The participants in the study were both black and white job applicants being interviewed by whites. The authors reported data which suggested that attitudes toward individuals are linked with nonverbal behaviors emitted toward the individual. For instance, positive attitudes led to more immediate behaviors. Discrediting characteristics were treated with less immediate behaviors. The authors sought to determine whether the white interviewers would exhibit nonverbal behavior as well as whether the target (job applicants) would be influenced by the interviewer's nonverbal behavior.

In the first study, the interviewers were naive as to the study's purpose. The "applicants," however, were not; the applicants were confederates. The authors found that the white interviewers spent twenty-five per cent less time with the black applicants versus the white applicants. For example, the white interviewers physically placed themselves further away from the black applicants versus the white ones, which indicated negative reactions to the black applicants. Overall, the black applicants received a negative total immediacy score while the white applicants received a positive one. In the second study, the authors attempted to determine whether a white applicant, treated similarly to the way black applicants were treated, would reciprocate with less immediacy. In this test, the white applicants did not know the study's purpose. The authors found that white applicants who were treated similarly to the original black applicants had been treated in the first study, performed less well, reciprocated with less immediacy and perceived their interviews to be less adequate. The authors concluded that the actions of the interviewer could, therefore, influence the behavior of the applicant and have ramifications on the applicant's ability to secure employment. This finding is significant because issues such as black unemployment were frequently examined from the perspective of the "disposition of the disinherited" (black person), thus casting blame on the peculiarities of the victim, rather than on an examination of the black-white interaction itself.

The concept of self-fulfilling prophecy can certainly provide illumination in the area of client-centered counseling. The lawyer or student unaware of her own behavior perceives the client to be exhibiting negative behavior. One of the insidious dangers of the self-fulfilling prophecy is that since individuals are seldom able to monitor their own behavior, they are more likely to attribute negative behavior from the client, not to their own original nonverbal behavior, but instead to some disposition inherent in the client. Presently, except in one isolated area, skills training material devotes no attention to negative nonverbal behaviors that students and white lawyers in general might be exhibiting toward their clients. Nor, do we have any idea how clients may decode and reciprocate such behavior.

Client-centered counseling materials do discuss extensively, however, the significance of the physical lay-out of offices to enhance the appearance of lawyer-client proximity to encourage a more positive attorney-client dynamic. In accordance with the Word, Zanna and Cooper study, proper office lay-out reduces the likelihood of several negative nonverbal behaviors like lack of eye contact and physical distancing.

While factors such as office layout, positioning of chairs, and so forth, are important in the overall scheme, it strikes me as unfortunate that so much effort is directed to this topic, without exploring the ways unconscious racism creates the distancing factors. * * * [T]he unconscious predispositions to which the student and lawyer are blind and are, therefore, unable to guard against [must be addressed]. Similarly, client-centered attempts to employ active listening and empathetic responses, as presently advocated, do not address problems of the nature of the self-fulfilling prophecy. As the phenomenon is based on perceptions, the lawyer/student may be unaware of the nonverbal behaviors which her/his expectations produce. S/he is, therefore, unable to compensate for the effects of her/his own nonverbal behavior.

The issue of expectancies on the part of the provider of counseling is quite complicated. Expectancy refers to a belief, hypothesis, theory, assumption or accessible construct that is brought from a previous experience and is used either consciously or unconsciously as a basis for interpreting or generating behavior in the present context. In the medical field, Ditto and Hilton demonstrated in a study that physician expectancy regarding the patient can impact on the physician's ability both to hear what the patient is communicating about his/her symptoms, and also, the physician's ability to convey a diagnosis and plan treatment. In the Ditto and Hilton study it was shown that physicians suffer from a double assumption problem. The double assumption is as follows: the physician first assumes that the patient does not have the sophistication to understand the intricacies of her/his condition. Yet, when the physician explains the condition to the client, the physician relies on medical jargon that the patient, in fact, cannot understand. In relying on the jargon, the physician overestimates the patient's ability to absorb information about her/his medical conditions. This leads to confusion on the patient's part which affirms the physician's original assumption that the patient could not understand the details of the medical condition. The authors also suggested the physicians assumed that their patients did not want to hear bad news about their conditions. Therefore, the physicians did not completely and thoroughly discuss the patient's condition with the patient. In fact, the authors suggest the physician misinterpreted patient anger over receiving bad health news as not wanting to hear the news. Similarly, Ditto and Hilton found that doctors may also misinterpret a patient's intimidation due to the physician's level of education and socio-economic status as apathy toward her/his medical condition.

The results of the Ditto and Hilton study are particularly relevant to client-centered counseling. One of the frequent complaints heard from the students is that the clients seem apathetic. The students feel that they care more about the client's well-being than does the client himself. Yet, the student/lawyer and the physician share the traits of high levels of education and higher socio-economic status. These factors may be producing, in the legal services client, the same level of intimidation that the lower socio-economic patient feels when visiting a doctor. In fact, it is generally accepted, in client-centered counseling material, that clients may be intimidated by the difference in status between the client and the lawyer. The Ditto and Hilton study demonstrates the importance of examining the impact of this status difference from the perspective of the behavior of the service provider, in our case the student/lawyer behavior, and not just from the perspective of client behavior, as is advocated by the client-centered models.

Similarly, the student/lawyer's expectancy can influence how she diagnoses or frames her client's legal problem; it may also affect how she plans what steps to pursue in the legal strategy. * * * [In one study] expectancies about the client *and* the legal system led [the lawyers] to frame the case purely as a Fourth Amendment suppression issue without regard to the racial dynamics being played out.

Further, enlightenment on the way race may unconsciously affect the provider of services can be gleaned from a study involving physician breaches of patient confidentiality. In this study, 628 white male physicians were asked to complete a survey which sought to determine how frequently physicians breach the confidentiality of patients who were HIV positive by reporting them to public health authorities. There were eight "patients" in the study. Each patient had a different combination of sex, race, and sexual preference. The eight patient histories were identical except for the description of the hypothetical patient. The study found that white male physicians would violate the confidentiality of black homosexual and heterosexual males more often than they would hypothetical patients in other categories. While the authors would not conclusively state that the results were a result of racism, they asserted that the results were consistent with racial prejudice. The results are also consistent with studies that show, in hospital emergency room treatment situations, physicians provide different levels of service to black patients than they do to white patients.

* * * To date, there have been no empirical studies which seek to determine how the perceptions of white law students impact on their ability to represent clients of color, especially black clients. Yet, if we can glean anything from the works in other disciplines, it is that such studies could provide lawyers and students interested in client-centered counseling with a wealth of information about how negative nonverbal behavior exhibited by the lawyer and student/lawyer expectancies can influence the nature and quality of the interaction with the client and hamper our ability to give effective representation.

* * * [O]ne of the characteristics of the difficult client is his reluctance to participate in the interviewing process. As discussed, the authors of the client-centered counseling models provided suggestions to encourage client participation. These suggestions, according to the authors, should be successful if the client is not in need of more serious psychological assistance. There are many reasons, however, why clients may be reluctant to participate in the information-gathering process. Although psychological studies examining the client's cultural perceptions are numerous, social scientists of African descent argue that there are not enough studies and that many of the existing studies are not properly focused. Nevertheless, there are studies which present valid data concerning the psyche of the black client, in particular. The issues studied which are most pertinent to the counseling relationship have included the levels of mistrust black clients have for white counselors, black self-disclosure, black client expectations of white counselors, and black clients' perceptions of the competence of white counselors.

Francis and Sandra Terrell have both authored or co-authored numerous studies concerning black clients and mental health counseling. One of their earliest works involved developing a scale to measure a black client's level of mistrust of a white counselor. Later, the Terrells sought to determine whether the race of the counselor would lead black clients with a high mistrust level to prematurely terminate therapy. Previous psychological studies established that ethnic differences between client and counselor were related to premature termination of counseling. One explanation for the high drop-out rate among black clients was that black clients did not trust white counselors and as a result often failed to establish a therapeutic alliance with white counselors.

The Terrells studied black clients at a local community mental health center. Each client in the study was asked to complete the Terrells' Cultural Mistrust Inventory (CMI). Based on the results, each client was assigned to either the low cultural mistrust category or the high cultural mistrust category. The groups were then randomly assigned for intake by either a white counselor or a black counselor. The study demonstrated that black clients with a high level of cultural mistrust and who were seen by white counselors, had a higher rate of premature termination than did highly mistrustful clients seen by a black counselor. One result which surprised the authors was that highly mistrustful black clients seen by black counselors also demonstrated premature termination though at lesser rates than those seen by white counselors. The authors suggest that a plausible explanation may be that even though the counselor was black, the client may have perceived the situation to be one that was white-oriented.

* * *

* * * Several studies have examined the level of distrust in black communities in America. * * * Because of the socialization process in America, black people exhibit a "healthy cultural paranoia." Alternatively, this phenomenon has been described as "eco-system distrust." Eco-system distrust means that most of the elements in an individual's environment are perceived as being potentially harmful. Furthermore, the person perceives no possibility of improving the situation. * * *

* * * Charles Ridley discusses the inhibiting effect an interracial situation may create. Because of mutual fear and distrust, a black person may not open up to a white person. Conversely, a white person may not provide the type of feedback that is most accurate in describing the black individual. Among the problems cited, which exacerbated nondisclosing behavior of black people, are therapist insensitivity, stereotyping, lack of specialized training and failure to establish rapport.

Once again, the issue of nondisclosure bears directly upon the relationship established by the student/lawyer and the client. Failure of the client to disclose completely to the lawyer, particularly after the student/lawyer has "assured" the client of confidentiality, leads the student to feel the client has been less than honest with the student/lawyer. The student/lawyer may misinterpret apparent sullenness or hostility on the part of the client as an indication that the client is unwilling to establish a relationship with the student/lawyer. Ridley warns against adopting the view, now discredited in his field, that difficulty in therapy results merely from client resistance. Ridley notes that the theory is no longer viable in explaining away interactive difficulties. This is an insight which lawyers engaged in client-centered counseling would do well to consider since the client-centered counseling models focus so heavily on the client's behavior.

Using a different approach, a study was conducted to determine whether a black student's racial identity affected the student's perceptions of white counselors' cultural sensitivity. The authors accepted the argument that it is important for counselors working with ethnic minority clients to be sensitive to each client's cultural identity. They wanted to determine the extent to which black students' own racial identity impacts on their evaluation of a counselor who failed to be culturally sensitive. Results of the study showed not only that culturally sensitive counselors' behavior was considered more competent than culture blind behaviors, but also that such perceptions were influenced by the racial identify of the perceivers.

Similar empirical studies have been performed using Asian-Americans, Native-Americans and Latinos (of both American and foreign descent) as subjects. All showed that, on some level, race or culture played a role, not only in the clients' behaviors, but also in their evaluation of white counselors.

* * *

* * * Adherence to the client-centered counseling models in their present race neutral constitution have not and can not cure the problem of client-manipulation. Nor, can they provide a solid blueprint for client empowerment, because the clients and their world views are not truly valued within the models. In fact, as previously noted, in many cases, the use of client-centered counseling resulted in further silencing of our clients. It is imperative that we move away from the essentialist construction, not only of our client, but of our students as well. We have discovered that our clients can resist, do resist and have a rich and full history of resistance. As lawyers and students, we must now find ways to understand and to use the client's resistance on their behalf. We can do this by using their resistance to reframe legal issues and to assist in developing legal strategy. We can use their resistance to challenge stereotypical characterizations made by the courts and administrative agencies of our clients and their lives. We must also begin to understand the causes of clients' resistance to their lawyers, and where possible, eliminate the lawyer-created causes of resistance. * * *

* * * I am struck by the notion that so frequently we excuse lawyer distortion of client narrative, claiming we are constrained to represent the client in a particular doctrinal way. We claim we are forced to distort the narrative because the court will only recognize and value our clients'

legal claim if it is presented in the right doctrinal form. And yet, we admit at the same time that courts are not seeing our clients in the proper light, nor hearing their stories correctly. We need to begin educating the courts about our clients' lives and stories, outside of the adversarial context, so that our attempts to "empower" our clients do not become empty rhetoric. We need to help the bench and bar recognize that the indigent clients we serve are not just rich clients dressed in cheaper clothes, but are people who have problems that are uniquely their own, problems which until now the legal system has refused to acknowledge.

* * *

* * * The Counseling Section of the American Psychological Association [APA] urged the adoption of several measures to increase effectiveness in counseling minorities. Among the recommended measures was the establishment of a threshold for cross-cultural counseling therapy competencies. The areas of cross-cultural competency were broken into Beliefs/Attitudes, Knowledge and Skills. While the areas are basic, the mere fact that they were recognized as essential to cross-cultural counseling was instructive. For example, among the items mentioned in Beliefs/Attitudes competency was that the counselor be aware of his/her own values and biases and how they may affect minority clients. The competent counselor was urged to avoid prejudices, unwarranted labeling and stereotyping. A culturally competent counselor was defined as not holding preconceived * * * notions about their minority clients. The culturally skilled counselor was one who monitored his functioning through consultation, supervision, and continual education.

In the Knowledge section, cross-culturally competent counselors were defined as counselors who have knowledge of the role cultural racism plays in the identity and world views among minority groups. We can compare this racially specific language with the vague reference in our own client-centered materials, which encourage the lawyer/student to take the client's world view into account during the interview process. The competent counselor was further defined as one possessing specific knowledge and information about the particular group he/she is working with.

In the Skills category, the competent counselor was defined as one who could generate a wide variety of verbal and nonverbal responses and send them accurately and appropriately. Further, the skilled counselor must be able to exercise institutional intervention skills on behalf of the client, when appropriate.

In its position paper, the counseling committee defined "cross-cultural counseling/therapy" as any counseling relationship in which two or more of the participants differ with respect to cultural background, values, and lifestyle. The committee explored the history of the APA and its own failures to address the needs of minorities in health counseling. The recommendation of minimal competencies in cross-cultural skills was the latest in a series of steps aimed at increasing both the knowledge of the minority communities by mental health counselors as well as ongoing training in skills to be employed in delivering services to minorities.

Clinicians are uniquely situated within * * * legal education to develop some aspirational goals for cross-cultural counseling competency. The clinics have frequently been the place where experimentation and bold ventures are tried. We can be the first in the law school to squarely face the issues of racism and the legal profession and start moving toward realistic ways of eliminating limitations artificially set on both ourselves and our clients by racism. Hopefully, we can demonstrate that we are capable of empowering our clients and raising our own consciousness as well.

Both psychologists and physicians have noted the need within their own communities to increase their knowledge about the lives and environmental conditions of their patients/clients. The call for increased knowledge is made, not so much to help resolve an individual, specific problem, but rather, to assist the provider of services in formulating a context that makes sense to the patient/client's reality of existence. As practitioners involved in the client-centered counseling process, we fall behind our peers in other counseling settings in that we have dedicated next to no resources to study our own motivations and reactions in the counseling setting. The subject of counselor behavior in the application of counseling skills comports well with the methodology of empirical research. Moreover, within our walls, we have a pool of subjects who are in the process of completing their final steps toward the ultimate goal of becoming a lawyer. Law students presently are required to demonstrate knowledge in numerous areas before they are sanctioned to represent themselves to the public as competent professionals. Upon entering the profession, most lawyers will spend a significant amount of their professional lives interviewing, counseling and negotiating. Yet, there are no mechanisms to test or evaluate whether they have acquired a level of skill sufficient to enable them to perform these tasks. Not a surprising thought, in view of the fact one could finish three years of law school without any one even mentioning that this was an area lawyers should be concerned about. Though legal educators appear to assume counseling skills are innate, clinicians would agree that in fact they are difficult to learn and effectively employ. * * *

Notes and Questions

1. Why and how does Michelle Jacobs claim that client-centered counseling has marginalized people of color? How have empirical studies reflected professional-client or professional-patient relationships that illustrate this marginalization?

2. In describing oppression, Iris Marion Young identifies its five faces, one of which is "cultural imperialism." Iris Marion Young, *Justice and the Politics of Difference* 53 (1990).

Cultural imperialism applies the dominant meanings of society to render a group's particular perspective invisible, while at the same time stereotyping its members as the deviant, inferior others. The injustice of cultural imperialism, then, is that "the oppressed group's own experience and interpretation of social life finds little expression that touches the dominant culture, while that same culture imposes on the oppressed group its experience and interpretation of social life." *Id.* at 60. At one point Jacobs refers to "cross-cultural counseling/therapy" as practiced by mental health workers. Should lawyers engage in an analogous practice? Would cross-cultural legal counseling counter the practice of cultural imperialism? Is the answer that black lawyers should represent blacks, Asian lawyers should represent Asians, Latina/o lawyers should represent Latina/os? Aside from the limited supply of lawyers of color, what other limits do you see in having similar-race lawyers and clients working together? Would such racially paired representation, at least, mitigate the damage of cultural imperialism? If not, why not? *See also* Susan Bryant, *The Five Habits: Building Cross-Cultural Competence in Lawyers*, 8 Clinical L. Rev. 33 (2001).

3. Stephanie Wildman has analyzed white privilege, both systemic and individually held. Stephanie M. Wildman, with contributions by Margalynne Armstrong, Adrienne D. Davis & Trina Grillo, *Privilege Revealed: How Invisible Preference Undermines America* (1996). Can you see how white privilege's invisibility adversely affects the relationship between clients of color and white lawyers? According to Wildman, "The invisibility of privilege strengthens the power it creates and maintains. The invisible cannot be combated, and as a result privilege is allowed to perpetuate, regenerate, and re-create itself. Privilege is systemic, not an occasional occurrence. Privilege is invisible only until looked for, but silence in the face of privilege sustains its invisibility." *Id.* at 8. One way that privilege—race, class, gender, sexuality—interferes with establishing a viable lawyer client relationship is through its normalization. According to Wildman, the characteristics and attributes of the privileged identity or status are deemed to personify or represent societal norms—"as the way things are and as what is normal in society." *Id.* at 14. Thus, "members of society are judged, and succeed or fail, measured against the characteristics that are held by those privileged." *Id.* In what ways are you privileged? How aware are you of your privilege? *See generally Displacing Whiteness: Essays in Social and Cultural Criticism* (Ruth Frankenberg ed., 1997).

4. As Peggy McIntosh has observed, because whites are socialized to not recognize white privilege, describing it "makes one newly accountable." Peggy McIntosh, *White Privilege and Male Privilege: A Personal Account of Coming to See Correspondences Through Work in Women's Studies*, in Leslie Bender & Daan Braveman, *Power, Privilege and Law: A Civil Rights Reader* 22, 23 (1995). She views her white privilege as "an invisible package of unearned assets which [she] can count on cashing in each day, but about which [she] was 'meant' to remain oblivious. White privilege is like an invisible weightless knapsack of special provisions,

assurance, tools, maps, guides, codebooks, passports, visas, clothes, compass, emergency gear, and blank checks." *Id.* If you are white, how do you view your skin-color privilege? If you are nonwhite, do you ever see yourself as having skin-color privilege in a manner similar to that which McIntosh describes? Do other privileges operate the same way as her description of white privilege?

ROBERT D. DINERSTEIN

Client-Centered Counseling: Reappraisal and Refinement
32 Ariz. L. Rev. 501, 502–04, 588–89 (1990)

Of all the skills that good lawyers must possess, the ability to counsel clients effectively may be the most critical. To counsel clients about their legal problems, lawyers must be knowledgeable about substantive and procedural law. They must be able to engage in strategic planning. They must have well developed interpersonal skills. They must be able to predict with some degree of certainty the likelihood of certain results occurring as a result of particular action(s) or failure(s) to act. They must effectively communicate to the client the many nuances of their craft in understandable and non-technical language. They must have a breadth of vision that enables them to present to clients a wide range of alternatives and options to consider and weigh. Yet the lawyer's vision must be deep as well as wide, for the counselor must be able to assist the client in examining the underlying reasons for her goals and contemplated actions. In Anthony Kronman's terms, "[t]he wise counselor is one who is able to see his client's situation from within and yet, at the same time, from a distance, and thus to give advice that is at once compassionate and objective."

Definitions of legal counseling abound, from the deceptively simple, through the relatively technical, and the highly specialized, to the almost lyrical. But under any definition of the term, an examination of legal counseling must address the complex interactions and negotiations between lawyers and clients concerning the variety of decisions within the lawyer-client relationship. Legal counseling inevitably raises questions about the proper role of the lawyer with respect to her client and the degree of the client's participation in the decisionmaking process. Who should decide what actions to take—lawyer, client, or a combination of the two? Is the lawyer's professional role to make decisions for the client, advise the client about what decision the client should make, or simply lay out the options and let the client decide? Should client decisions be judged by an informed consent standard? These questions are not unique to the lawyer-client relationship—in some sense they arise in all professional/layperson relationships—but they have particular salience within that relationship.

* * *

Ultimately, the primary contributions of the [client-centered] model are its strong emphasis on the need for the lawyer to pay more than lip service to the ideology of client choice and its concrete description of techniques designed to effectuate that ideology and the attitude that animates it. The importance of technique is critical because it allows the examination of the complex questions of client choice and lawyer behavior in a specific, non-abstract context. If the theory is sound and the technique suspect, we might conclude that the technique needs refinement. Alternatively, we could conclude that the difficulties of technique suggest conceptual flaws in the theoretical underpinnings of the model itself and therefore call for its reassessment.

My concern with the technique of client-centered counseling and its relationship to the concept's core values lead me to examine the * * * model from a perspective that differs from that of the client-centeredness discussion that has proceeded thus far. In particular, assuming that * * * in many circumstances client-centered counseling is a viable approach to legal counseling, do the techniques of the * * * model foster client-centeredness in all respects? I conclude that in one aspect of the counseling process, the lawyer's initial discussion with the client about the client's alternatives, the Binder and Price model is too law- (and lawyer-) centered. * * * [T]he model, by focusing in the "alternative" stage almost exclusively on lawyer-perceived choices, unnecessarily undercuts the powerful client-centeredness message that the authors otherwise wish to convey. * * *

Notes and Questions

1. What are some of the practical difficulties in attempting to adopt a client-centered approach? How and when might attorney dominance threaten or displace client autonomy? How do the client-centered techniques in the interview possibly differ from those in the counseling session? According to Linda Smith, "[A] comparison between the 'legal interview' and the 'legal counseling session' strongly suggests that the tendency for attorney control and dominance may be closely related to the analytical and counseling functions. Therefore, the counseling session or the advice-giving portion of the meeting should become a major focus of our inquiries in studying attorney dominance and client self-determination." Linda F. Smith, *Interviewing Clients: A Linguistic Comparison of the "Traditional" Interview and the "Client–Centered" Interview*, 1 Clinical L. Rev. 541, 591 (1995).

2. Smith sees that the biggest benefit of the client-centered interview is that it provides an opportunity for the client to give an uninterrupted narrative about her problem. Do you see any constraints that may negate this opportunity? From an interviewing standpoint, a crucial task is for the lawyer to probe and ask more pointed follow-up questions. In allowing an uninterrupted narrative, how does the interviewer obtain the details she needs?

NANCY D. POLIKOFF

Am I My Client?: The Role Confusion of a Lawyer Activist
31 Harv. C.R.-C.L. L. Rev. 443, 443–52, 458–65, 470–71 (1996)

Like many progressive lawyers of my generation, I was an activist before I became a lawyer. I marched in demonstrations, participated in a consciousness-raising group, and supported radical social change long before I had any understanding of what role a lawyer could play in furthering economic, political, and social justice. It is now more than twenty years since my law school graduation. I spent five of those years in practice with a feminist law collective that I helped to create and then five more in a policy and advocacy position in a national women's rights legal organization. For the past nine years I have worked as a clinical law teacher. Even now, twenty years after the start of my legal career, I still struggle with the question of how to use my lawyering skills to advance the issues and movements in which I believe.

I am a lesbian activist. I support and engage in a variety of activities designed to change the fundamental way in which American society views homosexuality. Some of this work entails changing the law, especially in the area of gaining respect and recognition for lesbian and gay families. Other aspects of this work fall outside the legal system, including organizing and attending demonstrations and conferences, public speaking, fundraising for groups involved in cultural change and political and economic empowerment, and writing for nonlegal audiences.

Since 1987, I have represented demonstrators arrested for committing acts of civil disobedience in support of lesbian and gay rights and acquired immunodeficiency syndrome (AIDS) issues. This work has allowed me to combine my lawyering skills with my conviction that direct action, including civil disobedience, is often an effective strategy for changing society. I do this work because I know that the legal system alone will not produce the fundamental changes I seek.

* * *

In October 1987, two days after more than 500,000 people marched in the National March on Washington for Lesbian and Gay Rights, hundreds of people were arrested for civil disobedience in front of the United States Supreme Court. While different groups engaged in various forms of action, most protestors were arrested for unlawfully demonstrating on the plaza in front of the main building. I was one of the two legal coordinators for this protest action and the only one who attended planning meetings during the months before it took place. The Supreme Court protest transformed the lesbian and gay rights movement by making civil disobedience a widely accepted form of protest against injustice, bigotry and discrimination based upon sexual orientation or human immunodeficiency virus (HIV) status.

Since the Supreme Court action, I have represented numerous lesbians and gay men arrested in smaller actions, and I have trained other lawyers to do the same. Organizers designed each of these actions to call attention to lesbian and gay issues and influence public opinion and the political process in ways I strongly support. Because of our common concerns, I have always felt connected to clients arrested during these protest actions: although as a lawyer I represent them, through their actions, they represent me. They speak for me and advocate the changes that would improve my life and the lives of those I love.

Even so, this welcome feeling of connection can be problematic. During the 1987 protest, I realized that my role as a lawyer distinguished me from my clients. There is a boundary between us created by our different roles, and * * * [here I explore] the conflicts I have experienced as a result of desiring connection across this divide.

* * * The first set of conflicts occurs because, as an attorney, I have legitimacy within the legal system that my clients, as lawbreakers, lack. This legitimacy disconnects me from my clients in several ways. I must behave in a manner consistent with a lawyer's designated role, even if this distinguishes, and therefore distances, me from my clients. Additionally, to be an effective advocate, I need to capitalize upon my relationships with those in positions of authority, such as judges, prosecutors, and police. My ability to sustain these relationships, however, depends precisely upon the differences between me and my clients—I am the lawyer, and they are the lawbreakers; I am an insider, and they are outsiders. Finally, I recognize that some of my clients have had experiences with lawyers who used their legitimacy within the legal community to emphasize their distance from clients and that as a result of their experiences, these clients may not treat me as a trusted comrade.

The second set of conflicts I experience occurs because I believe that a good lawyer must be a client-centered counselor who does not make decisions for her clients. This approach undermines my feeling of connection to my clients in various ways. If my clients feel as connected to me as I feel to them, they may want me to make decisions that I feel are theirs to make. My resistance, often followed by their insistence, can open a gulf between us. On the other hand, I am perhaps most profoundly troubled when my clients make choices with which I disagree. Although all lawyers have had this experience, the impact of such disagreement is minimized when the lawyer understands that the client must have the final say about his or her life. Yet my persistent sense that these activists represent me as much as I represent them inspires my wish for us to have common values and priorities.

* * *

I share with my civil disobedience clients a common experience of marginality as a lesbian or gay person in an overwhelmingly heterosexual world. This common experience of marginality blurs, however, when I function as their lawyer. As a lawyer I am an officer of the court, an insider entitled to civility of treatment, sometimes even respect, by virtue of my occupation and its role, regardless of my political beliefs or sexual orientation. At the moment my clients intensify their outsider status as lesbians and gay men by becoming lawbreakers, I remove a layer of my own outsider status as a lesbian and gain legitimacy by acting within the legal system as their attorney.

My legitimacy grants me access within the legal system that my clients do not have. Indeed my clients usually view this access as essential to representing their interests, and my ability to serve them is dependent upon my retaining legitimacy in the eyes of those who confer it, namely, judges and police officers. This act of maintaining legitimacy, however, often requires behavior that separates me from my clients, behavior I adopt because it is essential to my effectiveness, perhaps even my survival, as a lawyer. Yet in the acts that reinforce this separation, I feel disintegrated, sometimes dishonest, unable to be seen by those in authority for all of me, never both a lawyer and a lesbian activist at the same time.

Clients who see their lawyers behaving as lawyers rather than as activists, as legitimate insiders rather than as daring outsiders, may associate their representatives with the very system they are challenging rather than with the particular civil disobedience action itself. I want my clients to feel that we are all challenging the system together and that, although I have a distinct role, I am their comrade in a common struggle.

* * *

Civil disobedience activists misbehave: they break the law, breach decorum, and disregard order. Lawyers behave: they uphold the law, maintain decorum, and cooperate in preserving order. I cannot be in both groups at the same time.

In 1991, I represented approximately sixty demonstrators who had been arrested for blocking a Washington D.C. street in a protest against government AIDS policy. All but one of the protestors paid a fine at the police station and were released. The one remaining demonstrator, however, chose to go to court in order to plead guilty, make a statement, and request that he be permitted to pay the equivalent of his fine to an AIDS service organization. I spoke to him in jail before he was brought before a judicial officer of the D.C. Superior Court and then waited in the courtroom for his case to be called. Most of his fellow demonstrators were in the courtroom to support him.

As we were waiting, one of the demonstrators seated behind me leaned over and asked, "Can we applaud and cheer when he comes in the courtroom?" The first thought that came to my mind was, "Of course you can't do that in a courtroom." The second though was, "That's the wrong answer, Nancy. You are the lawyer; they are the clients. Just tell them the consequences of their actions so that they can make a decision that best meets their goals." My third thought was, "Get me away from these people." I was in a courtroom where I often appear, and a part of me could not bear to be associated with a major breach of courtroom decorum. If they were going to cheer and clap, I wanted to say, "It's not me; it's them," even though I was there as their lawyer precisely because they are me and because we represent each other.

I would have been less troubled by this scenario had I felt less connected to and less associated with my clients. As I think back on other activist groups I have represented, I realize that I would not have felt uncomfortable sitting near them during their disruptive courtroom behavior as a statement of professional connection. I would have expected the judge to see me as their lawyer, nothing more and nothing less. Had a judge suggested that it was my job to enforce rules of courtroom decorum, I would have resisted while still feeling that I was separate from my clients.

With lesbian and gay clients, however, I feel vulnerable. I do not know what the judges think about me when I represent such activists. Some certainly know I am a lesbian, as I have never been secretive about my sexuality. In these situations, however, my need to preserve the judge's ongoing respect for my professional judgment compels me to distance myself from my clients. Otherwise, I assume the judge will see me in the way that I see myself: as connected to my clients and in some way represented by them. If, however, the judge does not know that I am a lesbian and therefore sees me as being merely their lawyer, then I stand before the court absolved of my clients' misbehavior but also as a fraud—labeled as separate when in fact I am not.

To distance myself is to betray both myself and my relationship with my clients. To allow myself to be distanced by the system also feels dishonest. Nonetheless, I am not prepared to throw my lot in with those who disregard the rules of courtroom behavior by which I must live if I am to have any credibility or respect within the judicial system.

That day in 1991, I acted as a lawyer should. I explained the possible consequences of disruptive behavior to my clients without making their decision for them. They chose to remain quiet, so I had no further discomfort. Yet, I felt in that moment the inevitability of role confusion.

* * *

The above examples illustrate the separation that occurs between my clients and me as a result of the lawyer-client relationship both during civil disobedience actions and afterwards in court. Further distancing occurs before an action, if, as activists' lawyer, I also act as the negotiator with the police and court personnel, informing them of the protest plans. The conversation with the police and/or court representatives is carried on under the guise of, "I'm doing my job. You're doing your job." As the lawyer, I am speaking for others, not myself. It is "they," not "we," who are planning for a certain number of people to be arrested, who will stage the action at a particular location, and who plan whether to stay in jail. This rational, professional, "I'm doing my job" conversation covers up the rage and pain that motivate me, as well as my clients, to work against injustice.

As the negotiating lawyer discusses the plans of her clients, from whom she is necessarily separate, she cannot use the negotiation as an opportunity to engage in honest discussion about the conditions that make civil disobedience imperative because this is not her role. In much literature about nonviolent civil disobedience, however, honest discussion with police officers, prison guards, and court personnel is described as an integral part of the protest action because it can educate these groups about the protestors' motivation to break the law. Thus, the ideology of civil disobedience comprehends that individuals, regardless of their position as agents of an oppressive state, can and should be reached through conversation. A lawyer—whose role is separate and distinct from that of a participant—often must forgo this opportunity for sincere conversation. Indeed, if her clients have asked her to obtain as much information as possible while revealing as little information as possible, the lawyer may be approaching dishonesty and disingenuousness. When I experience this dynamic, I do not feel as though I am playing a separate role within an action I share in common with my clients; instead, I feel as though I am completely separate from the action and its goals. "They" and "I" remain distinct categories.

* * *

* * * I am a strong proponent of client-centered counseling. This model of lawyering rests upon the conviction that clients bear the consequences of their decisions and are in the best position to understand the full nonlegal as well as legal significance of their choices. Accordingly, lawyers counsel clients best by helping them to explore all of the possible consequences of their actions so that the clients can make decisions that best suit their needs.

My sense that my clients represent me as much as I represent them, however, complicates the implementation of client-centered counseling. When I feel that I, as a member of the group that my clients represent, also bear the consequences of their choices, it is difficult maintaining my role as a counselor. My feelings of connection to my clients imply that we have a common cause, and unless I am careful, may deny my clients the client-centered assistance that they should receive.

* * * I conclude that political lawyers should follow a client-centered model when representing activists and should work for the implementation of their own goals and strategies only when they are participating as activists, not lawyers, in political organizations.

In speaking around the country about representing activists, I have found a good deal of resistance to the client-centered counseling model. Some lawyers, especially young ones, went to law school to become part of a movement, and they do not want any distance between themselves and their clients; they want to be full participants in their clients' political decision making. Other lawyers hold a belief with which I entirely disagree: that by virtue of being a lawyer they have specialized knowledge that allows them to exert control over the political decision-making process.

I do believe that lawyers can be political activists and can make decisions about civil disobedience actions, but I do not believe that they should do so as lawyers. Rather, I support the position articulated by Martha Minow that "if the lawyer wants to make or help make the choice to violate the law for political reasons, then the lawyer should join the client as a comrade rather than serve in the role of legal advisor." When acting as a lawyer, one should participate in the decision-making process as a client-centered counselor rather than as a decision maker.

* * *

Clients who feel connected to me and who appreciate that connection may be inclined to defer to me more than they might defer to another, less connected, lawyer. This observation is especially true of my activist clients who know me well. Even so, clients will bear consequences that I will not, so I must resist their requests to make decisions that I do not feel are mine to make.

As previously discussed, during the 1987 courtroom incident, I experienced conflict about both my association with and my disassociation from clients considering disruptive courtroom behavior. The client who consulted me about clapping and cheering did not ask me about the consequences of various courses of action. He asked me a direct yes-or-no question about whether he could engage in certain behavior. His question deferred to my authority and gave me permission to make this decision for him. I thus had to reinterpret his question as a request for an explanation of consequences.

Lawyers are often asked questions the answers to which must be informed as much, if not more, by the client's goals, values, and priorities as by the legal consequences of the decision. * * *

* * * Some of my closest friends, for example, were among the first group of demonstrators arrested and processed at the 1987 Supreme Court disobedience action. In the District of Columbia, plea bargaining does not include a determination of the sentence. Thus, only after the first person pled guilty before the judicial officer would any of us know what sentence would be imposed. The demonstrators had to choose between paying a $100 fine without pleading guilty, pleading not guilty, and pleading guilty and facing an unknown fine or jail sentence.

After the initial paperwork was completed, we learned the name of the protestor whose case would be called first. It was "Jenifer," a friend of mine. As we stood together in the cell block, she and her fellow demonstrators (including my lover and other close friends) behind the bars and me outside of them, she tried every way imaginable to have me make a decision for her. First, she asked directly what I thought she should do. Then she asked what I would do if I were she. Resolutely, I maintained my role as client-centered counselor. I explained consequences and helped her articulate her goals. I engaged in active listening and reflected back what I heard.

My responses were somewhat frustrating to Jenifer. We had common personal and political bonds, but our relationship in this situation was really no different from that of any client trying to get her lawyer to make a decision and any lawyer resisting with the knowledge that it is the client, not the lawyer, who must live with the consequences of that decision. Jenifer had been arrested in other demonstrations and was not customarily deferential to lawyers. It was because she trusted me both personally and politically that she looked to me to make her decision to her.

My friends and political comrades have often told me how much they like having me as their lawyer. They too like the connection and the ability to rely on someone whom they can trust. It then falls on me, however, to maintain the distance required by the lawyer's role. Jenifer was not asking me what to do solely because I was her lawyer, but she was not asking me what to do solely because I was her friend, either; she had many friends in jail with her. As long as she turned to me as her *lawyer*, I felt a strong obligation to respond as her lawyer. In that situation—she was behind bars, I was free to leave—we were not just two friends, one helping the other make a decision. * * *

A different set of conflicts occurs when a lawyer and her client have different values. These differences may result from the lawyer's self-interest in maintaining professional legitimacy, or they may result from political differences, thus making a lawyer uncomfortable with, or even unwilling to accept, client choices. For example, among those who organize and participate in civil disobedience, there is disagreement about whether to prepare police, prosecutors, and court personnel for mass arrests by informing them of an upcoming protest action. Those who favor discussion and negotiation usually hope to ease the process for those arrested. If some of those arrested take frequent medication, such as people with HIV infection, organizers may also wish to negotiate for the ability to take medicine while in custody and for other issues related to health care. Those who oppose advance discussion with official are often offended by the concept of negotiating with the very people who embody the value system that they are opposing. They also point out that advance discussion produces the illusion, but not the reality, of smooth processing and safety.

Court officials like advance warning. It permits them to arrange for the presence of necessary personnel and facilitates the adjustment of normal procedures. Court personnel may be grateful to the individual lawyers for providing advance warning and, conversely, may be hostile toward lawyers who were aware of mass arrest plans but failed to notify them.

This dynamic can make it difficult for a lawyer to provide client-centered advice to civil disobedience organizers about whether to discuss plans in advance with court personnel. For example, a paper prepared by a North Carolina lawyer for a National Lawyers Guild Southern Regional Conference, which was client-centered in most respects, cautions that "the group may give the lawyer limited authority to negotiate preliminary matters with the government, and it is very important for the lawyer to understand the limit of the authority." In the next sentence, however, the lawyer writes:

> If the group understands the consequence of no prior negotiations, i.e., amounts of bail unknown, long in-custody wait for processing, adverse attitude of law enforcement who are called in without notice, and prosecutor's ability to schedule demonstrators to be in court numerous times before finally calling the cases for trial, then at least some prior negotiating will occur except in the rarest circumstances.

This statement indicates the lawyer's firmly held view that lawyers should negotiate with government representatives prior to a civil disobedience action, a view he is certain to convey to clients. This perspective may even cause the lawyer to reveal information to court officials without the authority to do so from clients on the assumption that revealing such information will benefit the clients and therefore could not possible be opposed by them. Such a view minimizes or ignores the strongly held convictions of some clients that negotiation or even cooperation with representatives of the system betrays their fundamental principles.

Civil disobedience clients sometimes make other choices that seem incomprehensible to lawyers—choices that place them at greater risk of physical or emotional abuse, that are likely to result in longer detention and greater isolation, and that try the patience of judges, prosecutors, police, jail guards, and the lawyers themselves. During the processing of the 1987 Supreme Court arrests, for example, some lawyers did not understand that self-representation was a priority for some of those arrested. One protestor asked a lawyer what she and her colleagues had to do to represent themselves before the court. According to her account, the lawyer responded by telling the activists to "sign these." "These" turned out to be court documents indicating that the lawyer was representing the woman and her colleagues. When they were called to the courtroom, the judicial officer honored the document, effectively precluding the clients from representing themselves.

I accept client decisions that impede orderly processing of their cases, although I have experienced frustration and impatience with extra work that these decisions create for me. I have found it both difficult and confusing to preserve an atmosphere of legitimacy and integrity in my dealings with court personnel while honoring my clients' wishes. The conflicts that challenge me the most, however, are those that arise between my political judgment about the effectiveness of a particular action and my clients' choices.

During the Supreme Court action, my ability to balance and to resolve these internal conflicts was taxed by the "affinity groups" of "radical faeries," men who got arrested and went to jail in skirts. Defiant gender incongruity forces people to confront their deepest fears of the subversiveness of same sex love, and those who provoke such fear subject themselves to the brutality of those who fail to control their hatred and anger. While I feared for the men in skirts, I found myself thinking that they were going too far, that their visual display was unnecessary. "No one will understand you," I thought to myself. "They will see you as freaks, and they will write us all off as freaks."

Thus the radical faeries forced me to face my own limits in defining acceptable confrontation. As a lawyer practicing client-centered counseling, I respected their choices. This decision, in turn, helped me to see them as comrades in the struggle to end gay and lesbian oppression. By the time they were out of jail, my view of them had changed dramatically. I now saw their bravery and courage to be true to their innermost selves.

Although through the course of this representation I came to respect the radical faeries, it is possible for the activist lawyer to confront an action that surpasses her limits. Here I refer to an action that contradicts the lawyer's own political beliefs or judgment to the extent that she no longer wishes to be connected to it. A lawyer who begins representation from a stance of political distance is less likely to be troubled by client decisions. On the other hand, a lawyer with a political connection to her work may face the choice of either assuming the distanced stance of the "hired gun" or withdrawing from representation.

* * *

The title of this Article poses the question that I have repeatedly asked myself in the course of representing lesbian and gay civil disobedience activists: Am I my client? The answer is a resounding, and sometimes agonizing, "No."

Every civil disobedience action needs a lawyer who does not blur the role between counselor and decision maker. Sometimes a lawyer will choose to be a comrade, to get arrested, or at least to shape the political dimension of the action, but on those occasions, someone else must act formally as the lawyer. Every client and every activist group must have a person who can inform them of their options and help them to evaluate the consequences of their actions.

Client-centered counseling and participation in political decision making cannot occur simultaneously. The dynamics that I have described—lawyers who impose their values on clients or activists who defer to the judgment of a lawyer—are dangers that can be avoided only when a lawyer adheres to the client-centered counseling model.

Lawyering can be a lonely endeavor for an attorney desiring connection with a movement because of the inevitability of separation across the divides that I have described. The belief that one can live one's activism within the confines of the lawyer's role is probably misguided, and those who try may be most likely to experience both role confusion and a blurring of the separation between lawyer and client necessary for effective client counseling.

It may be, however, that by periodically engaging in political activism outside of the lawyer role, it is possible when working within the lawyer role to live with the accompanying loneliness. * * * By engaging in political activism as an activist rather than as a lawyer, it is possible to feel the connection to a larger movement—a connection that for me has always felt attenuated when I have functioned as a lawyer.

Notes and Questions

1. Why does Nancy Polikoff ask the question, "Am I my client?" and why does she say, "No!"? For extended discussion of issues that revolve around advocating for lesbian and gay liberation, see chapter 13.

2. How does the activist role complicate adopting a client-centered approach? Contrast the views of Polikoff with those of Michael Diamond, who argues, "The activist lawyer not only interacts with the client on a non-hierarchical basis, but also participates with the client in the planning and implementation of strategies that are designed to build power for the client and allow the client to be a repeat player at the political bargaining table." Michael Diamond, *Community Lawyering: Revisiting the Old Neighborhood*, 32 Col. Hum. Rts. L. Rev. 67, 109 (2000). Does Diamond satisfactorily resolve the role confusion Polikoff describes?

SECTION 2. ALTERNATIVES TO CLIENT-CENTEREDNESS

While counselors have voiced approval of the client-centered approach to interviewing and counseling, others have posed alternatives that refine paternalism. According to William H. Simon, the two most influential advocates of the paternalistic approach today are David Luban and Duncan Kennedy. William H. Simon, *Lawyer Advice and Client Autonomy: Mrs. Jones's Case,* 50 Md. L. Rev. 213, 223 (1991). Luban has argued that the paternalistic approach can be justified "when, among other conditions, the client's articulated goal fails to meet a minimal test of objective reasonableness." *Id. See* David Luban, *Paternalism and the Legal Profession*, 1981 Wis. L. Rev. 454, 474–92 (1981). Kennedy has argued that paternalism is needed when the lawyer is convinced that "the [client's] articulated choice [does] not truly express his identity, for example, because of fear and depression." Duncan Kennedy, *Distributive and Paternalistic Motives in Contract and Tort Law, With Special Reference to Compulsory Terms and Unequal Bargaining Power*, 41 Md. L. Rev. 563, 638 (1982). In the following material, William Simon and Mark Spiegel examine the paternalistic approach, while Gary Bellow proposes that lawyers and clients form an alliance that furthers "political lawyering."

WILLIAM H. SIMON

Lawyer Advice and Client Autonomy: Mrs. Jones's Case
50 Md. L. Rev. 213, 213–16, 222–26 (1991)

In one influential view, the lawyer's most basic function is to enhance the autonomy of the client. The lawyer does this by providing the information that maximizes the client's understanding of his situation and minimizes the influence of the lawyer's personal views.

This autonomy or "informed consent" view is often contrasted with a paternalist or "best interest" view most strongly associated with official decisions about children and the mentally disabled. Here the professional's role is to make decisions for the client based on the professional's view of the client's interests.

I am going to argue against the autonomy view that any plausible conception of good practice will often require lawyers to make judgments about clients' best interests and to influence clients to adopt those judgments. The argument, however, does not amount to an embrace of paternalism. The issue of paternalism remains moot until we can clearly distinguish a judgment that a client choice is autonomous from a judgment that a choice is in the client's best interests, and my argument is that in practice we often cannot make such distinctions. The argument takes the form of an illustration from my own experience followed by an analysis of it.

The only criminal case I ever handled involved defending a woman who worked as a housekeeper for the senior partner in the firm where I worked. The client, Mrs. Jones, was charged with leaving the scene of a minor traffic accident without stopping to identify herself.

According to her, she *had* stopped to identify herself, it was the other driver—the complainant—who had both caused the accident by hitting her car in the rear and who had left the scene without stopping. The other driver then called the police and reported Mrs. Jones as leaving the scene.

Mrs. Jones was black; the other driver was white. The police, without investigation, had taken the other driver's word for what had happened, and when Mrs. Jones came down to the station at their insistence, they reprimanded her like a child, addressing her—a sixty-five year old woman—by her first name while referring to the much-younger complainant as "Mrs. Strelski."

Mrs. Jones lived near Boston in a lower middle class black neighborhood with a history going back to the Civil War. She was a homeowner, a church-goer, and a well known and respected member of the community. This was her first brush with the police in her sixty-five years. Nervous and upset as her experience had made her, she was obviously a charming person. As far as I was concerned, her credibility was off the charts.

Moreover, I had a photograph of her car showing a dent and a paint chip of the color of the other driver's car in the rear—just where she said the other driver had struck her. When we got to the courthouse, we located the other car in the parking lot, found the dent and a paint chip of the color of my client's car in the front, and I took a Polaroid picture of that.

The case seemed strong, and the misdemeanor procedure gave us two bites at the apple. First, there would be a bench trial. If we lost that, we were entitled to claim a trial de novo before a jury.

Thus, things looked fairly good. Mrs. Jones's main problem was that her lawyer—me—was incompetent. I had never tried a case and had never done any criminal work. But I tried to remedy that by getting a friend with a lot of experience in traffic cases to co-counsel with me. The first thing my friend did was to dismiss, with a roll of his eyes, my plan to expose the police's racism through devastating cross-examination. The judge and the police were repeat players in this process who shared many common interests, he told me. We could never get a dismissal on a challenge to prosecutorial discretion, and if an acquittal would imply a finding of racism against the police, it would be all that harder for the judge to give one. The second thing my friend did was to start negotiation with the prosecutor, which he told me was the way nearly all such cases were resolved. He told the prosecutor some of the strengths of our case and showed him my photographs, but he didn't say a word about racism.

The prosecutor made the following offer. We would enter a plea of, in effect, nolo contendere. Under the applicable procedure, this, if accepted by the judge, would guarantee a disposition of, in effect, six months probation. Mrs. Jones would have a criminal record, but because it would be a first offense, she could apply to have it sealed after a year.

We considered the advantages: It would spare her the anxiety of a trial and of having to testify. In the unlikely but possible event that we lost this trial, the plea bargain would have spared her six further months of anxious waiting, and the anxiety of a second trial. In the even more unlikely but still possible event that we lost both trials, it would have spared her certain loss of her driver's license, a probably modest fine, and a highly unlikely but theoretically possible jail term of up to six months.

What was the downside? I couldn't say for sure that the criminal record Mrs. Jones would have for at least a year wouldn't adversely affect her in some concrete way, but I doubted it. (She was living primarily on Social Security and worked only part-time as a housekeeper.) What bothered me was that the plea bargain would deprive her of any sense of vindication. Mrs. Jones struck me as a person who prized her dignity, deeply resented her recent abuse, and would attach importance to vindication.

Mrs. Jones had brought her minister to the courthouse to support her and serve as a character witness. Leaving my friend with the prosecutor, I went over to her and the minister to discuss the plea bargain. I spoke to them for about ten minutes. For about half this time, we argued about whether I would tell her what I thought she should do. She and her minister wanted me to. "You're the expert. That's what we come to lawyers for," they said. I insisted that, because the decision was hers, I couldn't tell her what to do. I then spelled out the pros and cons, much as I've mentioned them here. However, I mentioned the cons last, and the last thing I said was, "If you took their offer, there probably wouldn't be any bad practical consequences, but it wouldn't be total justice." Up to that point, Mrs. Jones and her minister seemed anxiously ambivalent, but that last phrase seemed to have a dramatic effect on them. In unison, they said, "We want justice."

I went back to my friend and said, "No deal. She wants justice." My friend stared in disbelief and then said, "What? Let me talk to her." He then proceeded to give her his advice. He didn't tell her what he thought she should do, and he went over the same considerations I did. The main differences in his presentation was that he discussed the disadvantages of trial last, while I had gone over them first; he described the remote possibility of jail in slightly more detail and than I had, and he didn't conclude by saying, "It wouldn't be total justice." At the end of his presentation, Mrs. Jones and her minister decided to accept the plea bargain, and as I said nothing further, that's what they did.

Let's consider some descriptions of the contrasting approaches to counseling in the autonomy and paternalist views. Begin with a crude but nevertheless influential version of the autonomy view: the lawyer's job is to present to the client, within time and resource constraints, the information relevant to the decision at hand. The lawyer discharges her function when this information has been presented, and whatever decision the client then articulates is deemed autonomous.

This crude formulation is unworkable and implausible. It is unworkable because it does not provide any criteria of relevance, and because it ignores that the most obvious criteria—the client's goals and values—are not immediately accessible to the lawyer. It is implausible because it measures autonomy simply in terms of the information the lawyer presents without regard to whether the way she presents it influences the decision or whether the client is emotionally or cognitively able to make effective use of the information. * * *

Thoughtful autonomy proponents do not argue for this crude view. In their refined version, the lawyer's duty is to present the information a typical person in the client's situation would consider relevant except to the extent the lawyer has reason to believe that the particular client would consider different information relevant, in which case she is to present that information. The lawyer has to start by imputing the goals of a typical client to the actual client because before she knows the client she has no other basis for understanding.

But in this refined autonomy view the lawyer has a duty both to educate herself about the particular client's concerns and to assist the client in making use of the information the lawyer provides. Here the client's autonomy is as much a goal as a premise of the counseling relation. The refined view contemplates a dialogue in which the lawyer adjusts her presentation as she learns more about the client's concerns and abilities and in which she is as much concerned with relieving the client's disabling anxieties and enhancing her cognitive capacities as she is with simply delivering information.

Now consider the paternalist view—first in a crude version. In this view, the lawyer simply consults her own values; she asks what she would do in the client's circumstances or what she thinks a person with some general characteristic of the client should do and tries to influence the client to adopt that courses.

Two versions of more refined paternalist views are associated with the University of Maryland School of Law. David Luban has argued that paternalist coercion is justified when, among other conditions, the client's articulated goal fails to meet a minimal test of objective reasonableness. On the other hand, * * * Duncan Kennedy argued for paternalistic coercion on the basis of "lived intersubjectivity." He justified paternalism where the actor was convinced that the subject's articulated choice did not truly express his identity, for example, because of fear and depression.

In contrast to Luban's, Kennedy's approach is triggered by a concrete sense of the particular subject. Here the paternalist judgment does not hold the subject to an external standard such as reasonableness, but holds him to an interpretation of the subject's own projects and commitments. The paternalist works for the choice that seems most consistent with her understanding of who the client is. When she disregards the client's articulated choice, she has concluded that the client has misunderstood either himself or how the options relate to his deeper goals. The Luban and Kennedy approaches are not incompatible, and the refined view should make room for them both.

The two aspects of the refined paternalist view can be readily applied to Mrs. Jones's case. The concerns about Mrs. Jones's request for me to make the decision for her seem to resonate with Luban's perspective. It wasn't reasonable for her to want to put her fate in the hands of someone as inexperienced and ignorant as me. On the other hand, the concerns about her ultimate decisions seem to resonate with the Kennedy perspective. There's nothing unreasonable in any general sense about the decision to accept the plea bargain. It would be the right choice for many people—for example, for someone with no strong sense of dignity, with no respect for authoritative public pronouncements, and with no tolerance for conflict or the stress of self-presentation in public. But Mrs. Jones seemed to be a different person. There's at least a suspicion that I let her make the wrong choice, *given who she was*.

My claim is that, once we get beyond the crude versions, it is hard to distinguish the autonomy and paternalist views. Each refined view contemplates a dialogue with the client that it recognizes is both essential to understanding the client and fraught with dangers of oppressing or misunderstanding him. Each refined view involves a dialectic of objective constructs (the "typical client" presumption or the minimal reasonableness test) and efforts to know the client as a concrete subject. The paternalist view is intensely individualistic to the extent that it aspires to deep knowledge of the clients as a concrete individual and grounds the lawyer's decision in the client's self-realization. Even where it disregards client choices because they fail the minimum reasonableness test, it is not denying the value of autonomy, just that the particular client has the capacity for autonomous choice. Conversely, the refined autonomous view is quite collectivist to the extent that it licenses the application of objective "typical" client presumptions to the particular client. And to the extent that it differs from the paternalist view in failing to apply a minimum reasonableness test, that difference, though perhaps defensible on other grounds, is not plausibly grounded in the value of autonomy, since that value presupposes a capacity for rational choice.

David Luban suggests that the defining and problematical feature of paternalism is its commitment to particular "conception[s] of the good life." But the most notable theory of "the good" to come out of the law schools in recent years defines the good in terms of the "choices" people make when not under "domination." This sounds very much like a theory of autonomous choice.

A genuine conflict between autonomy and paternalism would require a view that contained both a thick theory of the good that did not depend on individual choice and a notion of individual choice capable of envisioning choices that violate the good as autonomous. It is not hard to find examples of such views—for example, in most versions of Christianity and other scriptural religions—but they seem to have little direct influence within the legal profession.

If the debate between the autonomy and paternalist views is so often moot, why does it inspire so much energy and emotion? My guess is that the debate expresses the anxiety that lawyers, especially those who represent clients socially distant from themselves, feel about getting to know their clients and about assuming responsibility for them. The process of learning to understand and communicate with a stranger is usually difficult and often scary. Moreover, as I've emphasized, in this process the lawyer inescapably exercises power over the client. The issues that have to be decided are tremendously difficult, and the stakes are often very high. In these circumstances, lawyers often find the demand of connecting with the client and the responsibilities of power emotionally overwhelming.

The crude autonomy view is attractive to lawyers because it absolves them of the burdens of connection and the responsibilities of power by suggesting that they can perform their duties simply by presenting a professionally defined package of information. Both the crude and the refined paternalist views are frightening because both emphasize the inescapability of lawyer power, and the latter emphasizes as well the duty to connect with the client. So of course does the refined autonomy view, but perhaps the rhetorical association of the refined autonomy view with the crude one evokes some of the psychologically comforting associations of the latter and makes it more palatable than refined paternalism, even when they are functionally indistinguishable.

I don't claim that we can never plausibly conceive of a meaningfully autonomous choice that is not in the chooser's best interests. But I would argue, at least, that there is a large category of cases involving legal decisions, where, given the circumstances in which the decisions must be made, we have no criteria of autonomy entirely independent of our criteria of best interests. Many of the best reasons we have for thinking that Mrs. Jones's choice was not autonomous are the reasons we have for thinking that it was not in her best interests.

MARK SPIEGEL

The Case of Mrs. Jones Revisited: Paternalism and Autonomy in Lawyer-Client Counseling
1997 B.Y.U. L. Rev. 307, 315–20, 332–38 (1997)

Paternalism can be defined in a number of ways, but common elements include the substitution of one person's judgment for another's for the benefit of the latter person. In the refined version, as stated above, the goal is to ascertain what the client truly wants to do and influence her decision making to reach that decision. I call this a weak version of paternalism because, in theory, it does not attempt to impose the paternalist's values upon the client, but to implement the client's own values.

* * *

In conclusion, Simon is correct that the refined autonomy view and the paternalist view he describes are similar in theory because the refined autonomy view is a weak version of autonomy and the refined paternalist view is a weak view of paternalism. This is not surprising. Weak views of any theory usually attempt to incorporate objections or opposing viewpoints. Simon may have shown that these refined or weak views are points on a spectrum or continuum rather than distinct categories, but does that mean they are the same? The differences in theory described above may still lead to differences in practice. Evaluating this claim requires further exploration of how each of these two theories works in practice. * * *

Even if Simon is correct that the refined autonomy view and the refined paternalist view are very similar in practice and that there are no differences in implementation between the two views, there still may be important differences if we focus on the intentions of the lawyers who implement these views in practice. Assume that we have transcripts of a skilled practitioner of the refined autonomy view and a skilled practitioner of the refined paternalist view counseling the same client under the same circumstances, and that these transcripts look quite similar. Does that mean there are no significant differences between the two? In order to answer this question, we have to address the difficult question of whether intentions or motives matter.

Simon's explanation of why he was justified in refusing to give Mrs. Jones his opinion about what to do provides a good test. Simon feels he was correct in not providing Mrs. Jones with advice she wanted because he doubted his legal competence in criminal law and because he did not know Mrs. Jones very well. But he does not see this decision as distinctively supported by his respect for Mrs. Jones's autonomy. Rather it could as easily be supported because "it was not in Mrs. Jones's best interests for her to delegate the decision to someone as ignorant about both the law and her." Arguably, an exponent of the autonomy view might also refrain from giving an opinion to Mrs. Jones, but the motive would be different. Presumably, the motive would be to allow the client the time to think about delegating the decision, or to override the client's short-run autonomy in the interests of the client's long-run autonomy. Are these differences in motive merely semantic? Even if they are not, do they matter? From the client's perspective it is the same information being denied—the lawyer's opinion.

It is a familiar principle in law that intentions do matter. The criminal-law requirement of mens rea expresses that viewpoint. In the law of torts, intentional actions justify higher damages through the availability of punitive damages than ordinary negligence. In both these cases, however, the act is wrongful, and one might argue that this distinguishes these situations from the discussion of the refined paternalist's intent. At least within Kantian ethics, however, the reasons for action are critical. Doing the right thing for the wrong reasons is not of the same moral worth as doing the same act for the correct reasons. Moreover, one does not have to be a Kantian to argue that reasons for actions matter. Ethical theories that have virtue or character as their basis also focus upon the motives of agents. Virtuous character depends not only upon morally correct actions, but requires correct motives as well.

Still there might be nothing wrong in the intentions Simon expressed. This depends to some extent upon why one values autonomy. An important component of autonomy and its expressive value is that it treats the other person as an autonomous agent. Howard Lesnick * * * expressed this idea another way. He stated:

> I honestly do not think it matters which position the attorney takes—to leave the final decision with the client or insist on keeping it—so much as I think it matters whether the attorney makes either decision in a way that respects the concerns of both attorney and client, and treats the client as an understanding independent person....

When confronted with a request for an opinion, the dilemma for the autonomy practitioner is deciding whether acceding to that request or ignoring it, in the hope the client will make the decision, shows more respect for the client's capacities as an independent agent. The lawyer's motive is not to prevent the client from making a wrong decision. Her fear is that the client will fail to make any decision at all. The autonomy practitioner may get it wrong, but if she takes her task seriously, it is out of respect for the client. Simon's reasons for denying the client this information do not show respect for Mrs. Jones's capacities. Rather they reveal fear that she will make the wrong decision, i.e., she will rely upon an ignorant lawyer.

The impact or harm, however, is not only to the client. Harm is also done to the lawyer. This suggests another reason intentions matter. Intentions as well as actions shape character. And although virtue theory raises difficult questions about what the appropriate virtues are in modern society, Amy Gutmann argues convincingly that a necessary virtue for lawyers is what she calls the deliberative virtues—"the disposition and capacity of lawyers to deliberate with nonlawyers.... about the practical implications of legal action and its alternatives." Much of Simon's essay can be read as arguing that refined paternalism is consistent with the exercise of deliberative virtue. Yet his own examples do not support this reading. As stated above, Simon suggests that refusing to give Mrs. Jones his opinion can be justified by the likelihood that she would make the wrong decision by relying upon him. In his discussion of the possibility that talk of jail might disable Mrs. Jones. Simon states he would be justified in telling her there was no possibility that she could go to jail. Neither of these options is an exercise of deliberative virtue; rather, they constitute exercises of power to achieve a particular end.

Simon, at the least, needs further argument to establish that there is no difference in moral quality between the refined paternalist and the practitioner of the refined autonomy view. Only if one thinks that reasons for acting are irrelevant, or that there is no significant difference between a refined paternalist's reasons for acting in a particular way and the reasons of the autonomy practitioner, can it be claimed that the refined paternalist and the refined practitioner of autonomy view are the same by showing their behavior is similar. Otherwise, there has to be debate as to whether the differences in motives or intentions matter. Moreover, virtues viewed as preconceptions or dispositions inevitably affect behavior. To that extent, even if we have an example of similar behavior in a particular instance, there will inevitably be significant differences over time between the practitioner of the refined autonomy view and the refined paternalist.

Professor Simon states that for the thoughtful autonomy proponent "the client's autonomy is as much a goal as a premise of the counseling relation." I agree. We disagree on the significance of having that goal. There are still significant differences in practice between the refined autonomy view and the refined paternalist view because the goals and intent of the lawyer affect both the meaning and the texture of relationships between lawyer and client. Lawyers who believe in refined paternalism will act differently at critical moments from lawyers who believe the decision belongs to the client. Mrs. Jones's story illustrates these differences. Finally, even if Mrs. Jones's story shows that there is similarity in behavior between the two viewpoints, the intentions of the lawyers matter. Even if we accept that the behavior of the refined paternalist and the practitioner of sophisticated views of autonomy are very similar, the lawyer's intentions in each case have moral significance.

Nevertheless, Simon has made a valuable contribution by reminding us that both in theory and in practice the refined autonomy view and refined paternalism may not be as far apart as is sometimes claimed. Moreover, by focusing on the inevitability of lawyers influencing clients, he forces us to consider not only whether lawyers should influence clients, but under what conditions and in what situations we should recognize such influence and to what extent we should be concerned about it. Finally, Simon's willingness to break down these categories suggests further focus on ways in which influence and power travel in both directions, even with lawyer interactions with individuals. Lawyers not only have influence and power over their clients, but clients have influence and power over their lawyers. All this makes attention to context vital. It also may make it unrealistic to adopt general models or theories for application to all lawyer-client interactions. I believe it is important, however, to face those issues directly rather than by suggesting that there is no meaningful difference between autonomy and paternalism.

At the end of his essay, Simon switches the focus to ourselves. "Ourselves" includes both academics who write about these issues and lawyers who are concerned about justifying their behavior. Simon speculates as to why the debate between the autonomy view and the paternalist view inspires so much energy even though in his view it is "so often moot." His answer is that "[t]he crude autonomy view is attractive to lawyers because it absolves them of the burdens of connection and the responsibilities of power." Paternalist views are frightening because they emphasize "the inescapability of lawyer power." Finally, according to Simon, the refined autonomy view through its rhetorical association with the crude autonomy view "evokes some of the psychologically comforting associations of the latter and makes it more palatable than refined paternalism, even when they are functionally indistinguishable."

One obvious response to the above is that the refined paternalist position and the refined autonomy view are not the same. * * * The attractiveness of the autonomy view can stem from its denial of responsibility and that is a substantial problem. We need a way for lawyers to accept responsibility for their actions without controlling the lives of others. * * * [S]ome of the newer literature about poverty lawyers and their clients seems to romanticize poor clients and to assume that the only problem is lawyer domination. Simon is correct about these problems of the autonomy view. He ignores, however, the parallel problems or difficulties of the paternalistic view. Just as the autonomy view can be psychologically comforting because it allows lawyers to refuse responsibility for their actions, the refined paternalist view can be comforting because it allows lawyers to exercise paternalism while claiming only to be implementing what the client truly desires. Furthermore, although the crude autonomy view may be the easiest stance, the hardest position is to accept responsibility for one's power in a relationship without dominating or asserting power over the other. Ultimately, however, both Professor Simon and I believe that whether one is a proponent of the autonomy view or a paternalist, good lawyering involves more than following mechanical models. It requires serious dialogue with one's client. * * *

Notes and Questions

1. Do you think Mrs. Jones received effective legal representation? Did she get want she really wanted—"justice?" In light of this expressed client objective, how would you have counseled her? Recall Michelle Jacobs' suggestion that lawyers must understand and use the client's resistance on her behalf: "We can do this by using their resistance to reframe legal issues and to assist in developing legal strategy. We can use their resistance to challenge stereotypical characterizations made by courts and administrative agencies of our clients and their lives." Did the case of Mrs. Jones present a very good opportunity to practice this advice?

2. What are the features of the crude views of autonomy and paternalism? Simon suggests that once one gets beyond crude versions, there really are few distinguishing features between the autonomy and paternalist views. Do you agree? If so, why is there so much debate over which view is preferable?

3. In revisiting the case of Mrs. Jones, how does Mark Spiegel differentiate the two views? What does he cite as the problems with each of the refined views of autonomy and paternalism? Do you see some value in adopting the latter view? In what context and why?

4. In the following excerpt, Gary Bellow presents an "alliance model" of lawyer-client relationship to animate what he calls "political lawyering." Consider how his model differs from the client-centered model. Does it resolve satisfactorily the tension between lawyer paternalism and client autonomy?

GARY BELLOW

Steady Work: A Practitioner's Reflections on Political Lawyering
31 Harv. C.R.-C.L. L. Rev. 297, 301–05, 309 (1996)

* * * [T]the practice of law always involves exercising power. Exercising power always involves systemic consequences, even if the systemic impact is a product of what appear to be unrelated cases pursued individually over time. Lawyers influence and shape the practices and institutions in which they work, if only to reinforce and legitimate them. Clients, similarly, bring to their legal advisers and representatives claims

and concerns that arise from and are examples of underlying institutional arrangements and culturally created controls. It would be a poor corporate lawyer who did his or her work without regard to the long-term systemic and aggregate effects on clients and others of any particular course of action or strategy. In many ways, we did no more than that, and we argued with those of our contemporaries who shared our politics and our commitments that they should do no less.

Social vision is part of the operating ethos of self-conscious law practice. The fact that most law practice is not done self-consciously is simply a function of the degree to which most law practice serves the status quo. Self-conscious practice appears to be less important, and is always less destabilizing, when it serves what is, rather than what ought to be. The kind of political lawyering embedded in the foregoing examples is distinguishable from general law work by the degree to which it was fueled by a more dissatisfied and change-oriented self-consciousness than the law practice of most of our contemporaries. Whether the goals and projects we pursued were right or "progressive" I leave to others. It surely requires a new generation to define an adequate social vision and self-consciousness for today's complicated times. It seems enough here to say that "vision-making" work is fundamental to the activist strategies political lawyering inevitably embodies.

Any animating social vision held by a lawyer inevitably shapes and influences relations with those whom she serves. Particularly where those served are poor or otherwise vulnerable, the patterns of influence in the relationships formed can be asymmetrical and even exploitative. Power is always a heady experience, even, or especially, for those who serve the "greater good." Similarly, choice in any lawyer-client undertaking is never equally allocated. Choice often follows the power dynamics that frame and shape it. My colleagues who have written eloquently about the potential abuse of power relations in political lawyering have done all of us a service in pointing out this pervasive problem.

Nevertheless, at least for me, an emphasis on lawyer influence and authority in politicized legal work does not fully capture the sort of mutuality between myself and those I served that I experienced * * * [in practicing law]. I did, in a sense, choose my clients and could withdraw from most cases if I wished. But I also made commitments to my clients and their ends, commitments that were supported by life choices concerning where I lived and with whom I spent my time. Those commitments made my choices far more constrained and dependent than a less contextualized analysis would suggest. I surely influenced and argued with those I served, often loudly and long. But I, in turn, was influenced and argued with as well, and felt justified in asserting my views only because I also felt open to being overruled or outvoted.

Alliance seems as good a word as any to describe this relationship because alliance generates bonds and dependencies and is grounded, at least in aspiration, in forms of respect and mutuality that are far more personal and compelling, for many of us who do political legal work, than the demands of some notion of client-centered lawyering, no matter how strongly held. Alliance also seems to offer an ideal that permits us to talk seriously about purposive judgment—when and whether to intervene or to seek influence—in situations in which one has unequal power in a relationship. The ideal of alliance avoids oversentimentalized and categorical attitudes—my client, the victims, the hero—toward clients. Such an orientation seems necessary in any honestly mutual relationship and is especially important when working with groups in which issues of which faction one serves constantly arise, and where humor, patience, and a genuine fondness for and realism about the individuals involved are often all one has to maintain one's bearings until some particular storm subsides.

Nor is such a notion of common cause with clients an unfamiliar phenomenon in ordinary legal work. Alliance, as a descriptive term, aptly fits many lawyer-client interactions. Most lawyers share the aspirations, financial circumstances, and general world view of their clients, whatever their disagreement on particular actions. The influence of lawyers on their clients is a familiar characteristic of most lawyer-client relationships, explicitly supported in the profession's ethical codes. Indeed, influence is a fundamental element of respect and mutuality, not its adversary. What distinguishes alliance in political lawyering is the social distance that often must be bridged between lawyer and client, and perhaps, the greater danger of excessive influence. Only a conception of clients as much weaker and manipulable, however, dictates a level of subservience that leaves the lawyer without her own vision and stake in the outcomes being pursued.

Although paternalism can be real and ugly, I do not believe it is the primary issue with which the next generation of political lawyers will have to deal. Indifference and distance, drift and visionlessness are much more salient concerns. If these barriers are overcome, alliance with clients seems an appropriate model for the kind of relationships that will be needed, despite or because of the differential circumstances, commitments, and needs that will bring new opportunities for political lawyering into being.

* * *

In various forms, I think this idea of connection and continuity, and the emotions it evokes, transcends and unifies all of the complexities I have described here. Political lawyering, or whatever we choose to call it, simply describes a medium through which some of us with law training chose to respond to the need for change in an unjust world. Of course, the values and the faith that drive such efforts go well beyond law and lawyers. They embrace a community of men and women who try to make things "better than they found them."

Notes and Questions

1. How does Bellow distinguish his alliance model of lawyer-client relationship, as an alternative to the client-centered model? Bellow says, "Gerald López's vision of 'rebellious' practice most closely approximates my hope for an 'alliance' 'between lawyer and client.' " Bellow, *supra* at 303, n.11. *See also* Gerald P. López, *Rebellious Lawyering: One Chicano's Vision of Progressive Law Practice* 1–10 (1992).

2. Does the political lawyering that Bellow describes necessarily involve representing groups or communities? Does political lawyering suggest a tension between cause lawyering and client-centered lawyering? Bellow denies such a conflict. He attempts to reconcile individual and collective ends in politically motivated legal work, stating: "I have always been so attracted to case-by-case focused litigation rather than class actions. The former strategy makes any individual representation far less charged with group responsibilities than does lawyer work for groups and large aggregates." Bellow, *supra* at 303, n. 12.

3. Consider the following comment by former President Nixon's Vice President Spiro Agnew: "What we may be on the way to creating is a federally funded system manned by ideological vigilantes, who owe their allegiance not to a client, not to the citizens of a particular state or locality and not to the elected representatives of the people, but only to a concept of social reform." Bellow, *supra* at 301, n. 9, quoting Spiro Agnew, *What's Wrong with the Legal Services Program*, 58 A.B.A.J. 930, 931 (1972). Does his description of legal services lawyers apply to political lawyers? Are other social justice or cause lawyers subject to the characterization of "ideological vigilantes"? Keep this question in mind as you read the following section that looks at the lawyer client-relationship in representing groups and communities.

SECTION 3. THE LAWYER-CLIENT RELATIONSHIP IN THE CONTEXT OF REPRESENTING GROUP AND COMMUNITY CLIENTS

Social justice lawyering, at its best, entails a commitment toward long-haul lawyering. Gary Bellow's reference to "steady work" derives from the following story of a man who was sitting on a box outside the gates of a Jewish ghetto in 16th century Poland. He was approached by a recent visitor to the settlement:

> "Every day I see you sitting here," the visitor said, "are you waiting for someone?" "Oh yes," the man replied, "I'm waiting for the Messiah. It is my job here." "Your job?," said the visitor. "Are you happy with your job?" "Well," the man replied, "the job has its ups and downs. But it's steady work, you know."

Bellow, *supra* at 301, n. 1. *See* Irving Howe, *Steady Work: Essays in the Politics of Democratic Radicalization, 1953–1966* (1966). The quality of steadfastness is also illustrated by civil rights hero and Georgia Congressman John Lewis's self-description: "I'm more like a pilot light than a firecracker. I burn low, but I burn long and strong. I don't just pop off then go away." *What is a Hero?*, Esquire, Nov. 1998, at 104, 108. Whatever model of lawyer-client relationship is established, sustaining it may well entail steady work and pilot-light persistence. And, as suggested in the material that follows, this is perhaps particularly the case in representing groups and communities. As indicated in chapter 3, many social justice advocates see this form of representation as a necessary component of implementing transformative social change. Indeed, though particularly addressed in chapter 11, the themes of engaging in community struggle and group empowerment recur throughout the book.

STEPHEN ELLMANN

Client-Centeredness Multiplied: Individual Autonomy and Collective Mobilization in Public Interest Lawyers' Representation of Groups
78 Va. L. Rev. 1103, 1112–13, 1135–39, 1163–66, 1170–73 (1992)

* * * Where individual representation is the model, the lawyer must assiduously work for each individual client, but may well have to withdraw altogether if the clients develop conflicts of interest. In group representation, on the other hand, the lawyer's fidelity to each individual is considerably curtailed, but her ability to help the individuals to achieve their collective ends is enhanced. * * *

* * *

A basic lesson of client-centered practice is that clients do not automatically trust their lawyers, or communicate frankly and fully with them. Such trust and cooperation must be won, because there are strong reasons for clients not to speak frankly to their lawyers. Clients may fear that revealing the truth will hurt their cases. Perhaps more important, clients are people, and so they are interested in obtaining their lawyers' approval; the more the facts or concerns of the client's situation cast him in what he perceives as a bad light, the less willing he will be to reveal them fully. In individual client-centered practice, a central tool for overcoming these obstacles is the very carefully nurtured attorney-client "community of two." Like lawyers for individual clients, lawyers representing groups should certainly try to win the group members' trust—but they will not be able to make such free use of the "community of two."

Lawyers for individual clients address their clients' mistrust in a number of ways. Such a lawyer promises her client confidentiality, a promise that professional codes suggest is crucial to lawyer-client communication, presumably because it will be taken to mitigate the danger that the lawyer will use what she learns in a way that damages the client. She speaks to this same danger further by assuring her client of her desire to help (and then proceeding to act helpfully). At the same time, she takes account of her client's emotional needs by listening attentively, and by responding to what she hears with empathy or nonjudgmental acceptance. She also applauds her client's efforts to provide information. She may even, however unintentionally, give her client the sense that she actually approves of and concurs in the client's feelings and views. Wielding these techniques and assurances, the lawyer seeks to build a community of two in which the client feels safe, nurtured and vindicated.

Like lawyers representing individuals, the lawyer who represents groups must also nurture her clients' trust. The lawyer for a group can promise the members confidentiality—as a group. She can also affirm her desire to help, applaud the group's working together, listen attentively, and respond empathetically. But her use of these techniques is subject to important constraints. So long as she meets with the group members only as a group, the lawyer *cannot* forge exclusive communities of two, because the other members of the group form a constant and potentially competitive audience for her encounter with any one of their number. The lawyer who responds to a client's expression of strong feelings by saying emphatically "I certainly understand how upset you feel" risks saying to the listening group that she considers the contrary position of other members provocative and even wrong. As a result, she may often have to temper the empathetic responses that would be appropriate in individual representation. The impact of this restraint on the individual to whom the lawyer responds would be less potentially significant if the members of the group were themselves conveying to each other the degree of unhesitating support and acceptance that the lawyer can give to a single client. Some group members, even some entire groups, may behave this way—but surely most do not. The result can easily be that even as the lawyer attempts to convey a measure of empathetic regard for a group member who has voiced an unpopular opinion, other members are offering much more confrontational responses.

The lawyer for a group may also face another barrier to her formation of communities of two—namely, the prior existence of another community, with its own members and norms: the client group itself. This community may be long established and firmly organized. Even if its members are quire diffuse, however, and have actually been brought together by the lawyer, a set of people who are capable of coming together for some shared purpose as likely to find they have much in common already—and are likely to create more. Moreover, as much as the lawyer may want to serve this group, she will often not be seen automatically as "one of us," for she may not share a culture, a class, a gender, or a race with the bulk of the group's members. Members of the group may be far from eager to put their faith in her.

By contrast, the lawyer for an individual—even an individual with whom the lawyer shares little by way of background—is much better situated to generate this influential community of two. It is true, of course, that each individual client is probably a member of a variety of groups and communities outside the lawyer's office, and that many clients may *not* readily trust a lawyer whom they consider an outsider. But even these clients may be deeply dependent on their lawyers for advice, and may well be guided by norms of deference to the powerful and prestigious, norms that counterbalance or outweigh their feelings of suspicion. Perhaps most important, the lawyer dealing with an individual client typically deals with him alone, and faces no direct challenge to her efforts to mold their relationship. The lawyer who attends a meeting of her client group is never more than one of the contending (or cooperating) personalities on the scene.

The lawyer might respond to such barriers by meeting with individual group members outside the confines of group meetings. Doing so, however, may be taken by some members as a sign that the lawyer is trying to manipulate them and to undercut what they have done as a group. Even in this setting, in any case, she cannot establish exclusive communities of two. Legally, she owes a duty of loyalty to the entity or to the other members (depending on the definition of the client), which constrains her ability to promise confidentiality to the individual with whom she speaks. Psychologically, she is constantly in danger—in this individual's eyes, and in the eyes of the others—of entering unwittingly into an alliance with the individual with whom she speaks or of seeming to want to do so. Unless she wants such an alliance, she needs to be particularly careful not to imply that she does. This may make it essential to hold comparable meetings with the other members, and to make sure that everyone knows of the lawyer's impartial distribution of her time. It may also make it essential to tone down the degree of empathy that the lawyer offers to any one group member, even outside the presence of the others, so as to limit the danger that the recipient of the lawyer's empathy will report it to his fellow members as alliance.

Even if the lawyer who relies on such nonexclusive communities of two to elicit clients' thoughts manages to escape the danger of inadvertent partisanship, she runs another risk—of acquiring dominance over the members. I have touched on this danger already, in criticizing the idea that the lawyer should try to determine her group client's wishes by carefully interviewing and counseling each of the individual members separately. The result of that, I suggested, would be to diminish the group members' influence on each other, and enhance the role of the lawyer. Even if the lawyer tries to use individual sessions only as a buttress for later interaction and decision by the members as a group, she may tacitly signal to the members that she is not confident of their ability to decide fairly and wisely for themselves. The more the members come to depend on the lawyer as an intermediary, the more they may concur in this assessment of their own group processes.

The lawyer considering how prominent a role to play in the group's interactions should take seriously this danger of inadvertently weakening the group members' own sense of responsibility and capacity for dealing with each other. Nonetheless it must be emphasized that the possibility of direct communication between the lawyer and individual members may be essential to protecting those individuals. As one lawyer put it:

> [There are] some people who are just so beaten down that they are not going to be taking part [in] any process, and we represent a lot of people like that, who have been just through absolute hell time after time, and have been through rotten tenants' associations, they've been through rotten landlords and winters without heat, and this, that and the other thing. Sometimes there are people who are just not going to take part, who are not going to feel empowered, who are not going to try to empower themselves, and I think that we can't have their opinions and their voices be lost. So it's those people I really try to get involved with on an individual basis.

This comment points to the members' individual needs; these needs may be all the greater if the group's characteristic ways of functioning pay little heed to the silent voices around the table.

In short, the lawyer for a group faces a painful dilemma in seeking to build a community encompassing herself and her clients: the very techniques that may be most effective in building such ties with individual clients may damage her connection to the client group as a whole. To some extent, * * * the lawyer can "split the difference," employing such tools as individualized expressions of empathy in somewhat muted, but hopefully still efficacious, form. But to some extent the lawyer forging a relationship with a group client will likely need to look to other, distinctively group-focused, techniques to win her client's confidence. Among these techniques, I suggest, will be * * * approaches by which the lawyer can both enhance the group's functioning so as to diminish the need for her special intervention with particular members, and build her relationship with the group so as to enjoy more latitude for intervention when it is needed.

* * *

[A] client-centered lawyer must address the substantive choices before her client as well as the procedures to be used in making those choices. Most prosaically, she must provide the client with the information the client needs in order to make a decision based on an accurate understanding of the available options and their likely consequences. Somewhat more controversially, she may tell the client what she thinks the client ought to do. Binder, Bergman, and Price now accept—in my judgment, correctly—the propriety of the lawyer's giving advice, and indeed take the view that "reject[ing] requests for advice ... demeans clients' ability to make independent judgments." Though they suggest that normally the lawyer should give advice based on the client's values, discerned through the counseling process, they also affirm the propriety of the lawyer's expressing her own moral or political perspective when she disagrees with the client's intentions. So, too, a client-centered lawyer for a group can give advice based on the priorities the group has articulated during her work with it, and she can speak based on values she holds but that the group may not. But the implications of the advice-giving role change in certain respects when the client is a group rather than an individual.

First, the lawyer will often be unable to take a clearly defined set of client values and give advice that simply applies those values to the situation the client faces. To be sure, individual clients rarely present their lawyer with entirely clear sets of values either, and the lawyer who tries to give advice based on the client's values may not so much be telling the client what his values suggest he should do as helping him to reflect further on just what his values are. Nevertheless the lawyer's uncertainty about the client's values is often bound to be greater with a group client, for a straightforward reason: the group is unlikely to be unanimous about its values. In addition, because of the multiplicity of individual sentiments within the group and the impossibility of fully eliciting them, the lawyer often may not achieve as precise a feel for whatever values the group does shares as she can attain when she deals with a single individual. As a result, the lawyer may be unable to give advice of the form, "Since you feel this is an important consideration, it makes sense to take this action." Instead, her advice may need to be, "*If* you decide that this is an important consideration, then this action makes sense." Sometimes she will need to add, "But if you decide that another consideration is also important, then a second course of action makes sense." Her advice, in short, may have to be even more tentative than when she speaks with an individual client, and the role of her advice frequently may be more to inform further debate them to bring the client to a quick resolution of uncertainty.

Second, if a lawyer contemplates giving advice based on her own values to a group, she must weigh against the benefit of her advice the risk of contributing to the disunity of the group. As we have seen, the lawyer for a group can have a special responsibility for promoting group harmony around decisions, a concern that disappears in individual representation. When the lawyer gives advice based on her own values, she inevitably runs the risk of being seen as a partisan, and very possibly also as an ally of one segment of the group against others. She may then be less able to win the conflicting members' trust in a process, whether of mediation or of structured discussion, that is meant to lead the members to see the logic of each others' positions and find common ground among them. If agreement is never achieved, moreover, the lawyer may have sacrificed some part of her credit with the dissenters, and thus be less able to assist them in their decision either to stay with the group or to abandon it.

Third, the lawyer who gives advice based on her own values when the group itself does not share those values is not likely to see her views prevail, at least unless she resorts to methods of persuasion that are emotive, and sometimes manipulative, rather then merely reasoned. It may never be easy for a lawyer to persuade a client to follow her values rather than his own. A group's values represent the confluence of many people's thinking, however, and may well be part of the very foundation of the group's existence. The chances of the lawyer's overcoming the group's contrary inclinations seem limited. It might seem, in sum, that there is little to be gained, and much to be lost, by lawyers who go beyond giving advice carefully keyed to the values of the group members.

When a lawyer gives only this modest advice and bends her efforts to promoting group harmony from a stance of neutrality, she *is* playing a valuable role, but there is another, much more assertive, possible part for the lawyer to take. If the lawyer who gives advice based on her own values risks alienating or dividing the group, perhaps she can partially overcome these dangers by showing the group members that she in fact shares their core convictions. Then her supporting one side rather than the other in an internal dispute might be couched in the context of her fellowship with all of the members, and even her arguing against a consensus of the group might be framed as an argument from a dependable ally rather than from a disengaged critic. To be sure, this visibly shared commitment will not always be a way to preserve credibility with the group's members. Some groups will be too divided for the lawyer to present herself as everyone's ally, and some issues will be too divisive for disagreement not to be seen as fundamental. In those cases, in fact, the lawyer's more active commitment might even make her a more divisive force than someone who, however irritating, was not seen as directly involved. But in some groups, the more engaged the lawyer is, the greater the impact she may make with her advice.

* * *

The guidelines for group client-centeredness * * * are meant in large measure to encourage lawyering behavior that fosters the organization, effectiveness and survival of client groups. It is quite reasonable, however, to hope for even more—to hope that groups of disadvantaged people might grow into spearheads of much broader community activity. Political mobilization of disadvantaged communities is a crucial goal, crucial both for the individual men and women in those communities who find a voice through the process of shared struggle and for their communities, for which such efforts may win political victories that alter the broad relations between them and the larger society. It is very tempting, therefore, to ask whether lawyers can contribute to this process even more effectively if they abandon some of the constraints of client-centeredness. Much of political life, after all, is vastly more manipulative than anything that a client-centered lawyer might undertake; politics is the domain of the rough-and-tumble, and sometimes of the demagogue.

I remain unpersuaded that allowing lawyers to borrow the norms of politics in dealing with their clients is necessary for political change. On the contrary, the norms of group client-centeredness appear to offer lawyers a pathway by which they can contribute to community mobilization while still providing substantial protection for the autonomy of the individual members of client groups. If these guidelines have their desired effect, after all, they will foster not only groups' survival but also their growth. Although it must be admitted that undemocratic groups controlled by charismatic leaders may enjoy even greater success (perhaps at a terrible price), groups that make wise decisions through democratic processes and enjoy cohesive memberships are well positioned to spread the ideas they espouse in the larger communities of which they are a part. Client-centeredness alone, therefore, is potentially a boon to the political mobilization of client communities—the very large, very loosely organized collectivities within which the client groups we have been discussing are to be found. The lawyer's impact can be particularly great, moreover, when she joins with her client group in ideological agreement, and then uses, hopefully with self-restraint, the new opportunities for influence that this alliance gives her.

The lawyer wielding such influence can promote political mobilization in a range of ways that do not flout, though they may well alter, group members' autonomy. In doing so, she will be helping the members to change, for political mobilization is a process of change. The kinds of change involved, however, undoubtedly vary from person to person. For some, who are ready to act but are not experienced in doing so, the lawyer's role may simply be instructional. With others, who hesitate out of self-doubt, apathy, and cynicism that are the fruit of the very disadvantages that frame their position in society, the lawyer may seek to instill in them—or better yet, to elicit from them—the desire to act. Perhaps she will do this by exposing them to catalyzing experiences—although she will always need to scrutinize carefully the justifiability of immersing people in experiences whose impact they do not fully understand in advance. Perhaps she will encourage them directly, by exhorting them, and there will be room for some passion in her words to such group members—room given to the lawyer by people who have accepted alliance with her. But the danger of overdoing this rhetoric will always be present, and there is much to be said for a less flamboyant, sustained interaction between lawyer and client, in which the lawyer helps the members to find together their own ways of expressing themselves, and so discover both abilities they did not know they possessed and desires they had not dared to have.

The spectrum of lawyer roles in such change thus runs from mere instruction in skills to participation in client self-revelation. It might be argued that as the lawyer begins to play a role that goes beyond informing her clients to transforming them, she has definitively breached the boundaries of respect for client autonomy. But transformation is part of what happens in groups, and membership in groups is a crucial part of our selfhood. We ought not to reject the possibility of such transformation, nor of lawyers' participation in it. Instead, we should seek to insure that the groups to which lawyers lend their support are collectivities that respect and protect, as well as change, their individual members.

ZENOBIA LAI, ANDREW LEONG & CHI CHI WU

The Lessons of the Parcel C Struggle: Reflections on Community Lawyering
6 Asian Pac. Am. L. J. 1, 2–3, 23–31, 34 (2000)

Chinatowns are some of the most vibrant ethnic neighborhoods in America's landscape. Home to recent immigrants and old-timers alike, a city's Chinatown is the heart of many urban Asian American communities. But Chinatowns are often found in city centers and in crowded and polluted environments. Boston's Chinatown, the fourth largest in the United States, is no exception.

What explains a Chinatown's location and circumstance? Is it pure chance? Unfortunately, no. At least not with Boston's Chinatown. Since the 1950s, urban planning has given Boston's Chinatown two massive highways, land-hungry medical institutions, and a red-light district. Half a century of such policy came to a head in 1993, when the city of Boston tried to sell open land in the heart of Chinatown to build a mammoth garage. The proposed sale of this land, known as "Parcel C," sparked protest and organized resistance.

The Parcel C struggle combined grassroots community organizing and community lawyering. As attorneys who joined the campaign, we share the community's story of struggle and victory. Based on this experience, we explore what "community lawyering" means in practice, especially when the community is disenfranchised, immigrant, and not fluent in English. We also address how to go beyond the limitations of traditional lawyering, which focuses too narrowly on legal remedies granted by a court of law. The struggle succeeded only because legal strategies were supplemented with political protests, media campaigns, neighborhood coalition-building, and political alliances with powerful environmental groups. It is our hope that the Parcel C story will help produce a better model of community lawyering that is useful across communities and crises. * * *

* * *

In particular, we address those lessons especially important for lawyers serving the Asian Pacific American immigrant communities.

* * *

Lawyers are often needed because the community faces some serious problem. However, once lawyers enter the picture, the community often jumps to the conclusion that all its problems are solved because they think, "we have a lawyer on our side now who will take care of everything." But the community should not surrender responsibility for the struggle because only the community itself can decide what its goals are. To be sure, lawyers can help achieve those goals; however, they should not be the ones deciding what they are in the first instance. This is the first step to community empowerment. It requires community lawyers to engage in the following:

Educate the community about the problem's context.

Community lawyers can help frame the problem. For instance, few within the community knew that Parcel C was once the home of Chinatown residents. Some basic history about the legacy of urban renewal on Chinatown provided the context the community needed to evaluate NEMC's [New England Medical Center's] garage proposal. The community learned that Parcel C was not an isolated incident but was simply the most recent episode in the long saga of institutional expansion. They understood that institutional expansion would not end even if the community acquiesced to the Parcel C garage. This recognition helped mobilize broad support for the Parcel C struggle. In addition, it produced concrete payoffs during the environmental impact review process. The resident's testimonies effectively invoked history to challenge NEMC's attempt to portray the Parcel C garage as an isolated construction project with limited community impact.

Educate the community about the law.

Community lawyers need to convey legal knowledge to the community so that they "may become aware of their rights, guarding and wielding them, as symbols of inclusion, participation and respect." But this requires plain talk, not legalese. The language of the law is not readily accessible to non-lawyers, especially if they are non-English-speaking immigrants. Community lawyers must overcome this obstacle. In the Parcel C struggle, we always tested our "translation" of legal concepts on the Steering Committee first and only afterwards presented them to the community at large. Instead of using jargon such as "summary judgment," "motions," "scoping," "Clean Air Act," and "Massachusetts Environmental Policy Act," we presented the more basic ideas underlying these terms. By not focusing on technical details, we helped the community connect the legal concepts with examples from their daily lives.

Explain to the community that the law is not a panacea.

The community should not have unrealistic expectations about legal solutions. For example, the Legal Committee clearly explained that the environmental review process was only procedural. That is, if NEMC fulfilled the technical requirements laid down by the Secretary of Environmental Affairs, it could eventually build the garage. The community then realized that the law was not the "end all" and that they had to pursue other solutions, which included the media, politics, and coalition building with other neighborhoods.

Let the community speak for itself.

When the press sought comment about the Parcel C struggle, we, as the community lawyers, often responded "Why don't you speak to someone who lives here?" The press assumes that the lawyer is the leader and designated spokesperson. And in many community struggles, lawyers tend to take over such positions. However, we challenged this conventional wisdom during the Parcel C fight. Instead of appointing ourselves the community spokespersons, we helped the Political Mobilization Committee identify residents, organizers, and directors of community-based organizations to be spokespersons. To make clear that this was a community struggle, no lawyers were designated as spokespersons. There can be no better spokesperson than a member of the aggrieved community itself.

Respect the community's judgment, even on legal strategy.

It is often tempting for lawyers who work for subordinated communities to assume that they alone are able to make the most educated choice among legal strategies. This patronizing attitude is even more prevalent among lawyers who work with immigrants uncomfortable with English. But if the goal of community lawyering is to empower the community by bringing out its own talents, enhanced with legal knowledge, then community lawyers must learn to respect the community's strategic choices. In addition, lawyers must remember that it is the community that ultimately bears both the benefits and costs of any legal strategy.

In the Parcel C struggle, for example, the Legal Committee had to choose between using its limited resources to complete the state environmental review process or to join a class-action lawsuit filed by the Conservation Law Foundation against building unwanted garages throughout Boston. Instead of telling the community which option to take, the Legal Committee learned the relevant law and shared its findings with the community. After a careful weighing of the pros and cons, the community opted to complete the environmental review, which kept the community a full player in the legal process. The Legal Committee fully respected this decision.

In the Parcel C struggle, the Coalition's initial reception of the Legal Committee ranged from distant to lukewarm. Many on the Coalition had prior bad experiences with lawyers in other community struggles. From their perspective, certain lawyers had hijacked the community's struggles for their own professional gains; other lawyers, especially those who were "home-grown," had ridiculed progressive ideologies, goals, and methods. Assistance from these sorts of lawyers had rarely produced systemic benefits to the community. Thus, instead of welcoming the Legal Committee with open arms, the Coalition's Steering Committee adopted a "wait and see" attitude, testing out this group's commitment.

Members of the Legal Committee had varying degrees of working relationships and histories with the Coalition's members. Some knew more about the Boston Chinatown history than others, but all shared a deep appreciation of Asian American history and were committed to turning this understanding into activism. Therefore, whether consciously or unconsciously, we took the following steps to make ourselves welcome in the Coalition:

Do not assume "trust" exists simply because of shared ethnicity, race, or language ability.

Lawyers who share the linguistic, ethnic, or cultural background of their clients assume, often correctly, that they will be more adept in observing subtle cues and be admitted more quickly into the clients' confidences. But automatic "trust" should not be presumed. Regardless of the similarities between lawyer and client, the client sees the lawyer first as a "lawyer." For many, the legal profession represents the hostile, inaccessible, and the insensitive legal system that permeates and complicates their lives. In addition, as suggested above, the community may have had bad encounters with lawyers who offered their "help" in the past. Therefore, community lawyers should not assume too much: Trust must be earned.

Build trust by participating respectfully in all aspects of the community struggle.

In addition to serving on the Legal Committee, the Parcel C legal team participated in all the other Coalition committees to help strategize and share the work. We assisted with literature distribution, publicity tabling, fundraising, media coordination, interpreting at meetings, and coalition building. We immersed ourselves in this work to join the struggle as members of the community, not merely as lawyers. We participated in most of the Steering Committee meetings, in which we did not chair or vote. We also took part in the community meetings and offered our opinions only when asked. Our relatively inconspicuous but regular presence helped us become accepted by the Coalition.

Build trust by learning about the community.

By getting to know the community, we do not mean merely going there to shop, eat, play, or socialize. We mean learning about its history, its geography, and the various players, institutions, and organizations that constitute the community. We also mean interacting with the residents and learning about their individual histories, including their immigration and socio-economic backgrounds, their political identification, their financial and employment status, and their perspectives of the community. Such in-depth knowledge enabled us to identify what sorts of strategies, both legal and non-legal, might be viable and appropriate during the Parcel C struggle.

Build trust by establishing a permanent presence within the community.

Community lawyers need to be available to the community beyond the instant struggle. Besides serving on boards of community-based organizations, they need to volunteer their time and skills and use their legal training to further the best interests of the community on myriad issues. Examples include conducting community legal education on relevant topics such as immigration, workers' rights and American government structure; mentoring community youth; and assisting community functions. An informal survey of community-based organizations found that visibility at community functions was especially important. This way the community could get to know the lawyers and to see them as members of the community, not merely as outsiders who specialize in legal problems.

Address lawyer biases and community prejudice.

To be effective, community lawyers should be cognizant about presumptions they may have about the community they serve. On the other hand, community lawyers should also be aware that communities of subordinated people are not immune from the prejudices and biases that permeate the broader society. The following are several lessons that we learned during the Parcel C struggle:

1. Address lawyer biases against the community.

Regardless of whether or not they share the linguistic, ethnic, or cultural background of the community, all community lawyers need to engage in a personal identification process. Community lawyers need to be conscious of how their class, race, ethnicity, culture, gender, sexual orientation, physical disability, and age affect their interactions with their clients and community base. For instance, community lawyers should recognize that as lawyers, they belong to a socio-economic class quite different from their clients, even though they may share the same ethnic or racial identity. Therefore, community lawyers must be conscious of their manner of speech, the setting in which they meet their clients, and even the subject matter of small talk.

2. Address community biases against lawyers: race, gender, and age.

The 1994 Final Report of the Commission to Study Racial and Ethnic Bias in the Courts reported that among Massachusetts' 25,466 attorneys, 95.9 percent were White, 2 percent were Black/African American, 1.2 percent were Hispanic, and 0.8 were Asian American. Nearly three-quarters of all the lawyers were men, though a slight majority among the attorneys of color were women. The study also found that because racial minorities began to enter the legal profession in substantial numbers only recently, the majority of the attorneys of color practicing in Massachusetts were young. These demographics reinforce the image—held even by the client community—of the consummate lawyer as an older, White man. Anyone who does not fit this bill is presumed to be less effective.

For example, during the initial phase of the Parcel C struggle, as the two young Asian American women attorneys (Lai and Wu) leading the Legal Committee, we were repeatedly mistaken by community members as interpreters, students, secretaries to the lawyers, and occasionally youth helpers. Instead of judging our presentation on its merits, we felt that it was sometimes rejected simply because it delivered through a female voice. When members of the Coalition repeatedly exclaimed how youthful their lawyers were, we could not tell whether they were marveling at our educational accomplishment or doubting our abilities.

To overcome this bias, as the two women attorneys on the Legal Committee, we asserted our voices in discussions and delivered regular legal services, alongside the Parcel C struggle. By exposing the community to other facets of our work, and being able to deliver results, we somewhat overcame the initial bias against our age, gender, and race. When the community won the Parcel C struggle in October 1994, there was little doubt within the Coalition that their young Asian American female attorneys were just as good as the abstract "White, older male" attorneys.

3. Address community biases against public interest lawyers.

Legal services lawyers are treated differently by the community than corporate and law firm lawyers. The Coalition had initially retained two teams of lawyers: the pro bono corporate counsel retained exclusively for the BRA [Boston Redevelopment Authority] project review process and the Legal Committee for the environmental review process and other matters. Some members of the Parcel C Legal Committee sensed that the community was willing to "bend over backwards" to accommodate the firm lawyer's requests, even at the risk of compromising the community empowerment goal of the struggle.

Further support for this theory is found in our survey of community-based organizations. The respondents characterized firm lawyers as more professional and more business-like. Some believed that firm lawyer contribute more resources and deliver better services, although they may not take the community's issues at heart. Shortcomings of corporate lawyers engaged in pro bono representation were forgiven because they faced the economic reality of billable hours. For this reason, none of the respondents felt that they should or could expect the firm lawyers to be equally accessible or to take on the various non-legal tasks as community lawyers. Moreover, community lawyers are generally affiliated with agencies such as legal services that pay their salaries, and their services are offered free of charge to the community groups. Implicit in their responses is that the time and commitment of community lawyers are taken for granted.

We admit that the community lawyer's need to establish a permanent presence in the community often conflicts with their desire to impress upon the community that their time is also valuable. Unfortunately, the amount of time one spends working with the community is often taken as the measure of one's level of commitment. There is no shortcut to establishing a permanent presence in the community. Furthermore, the community will not necessarily always appreciate the community lawyers' efforts. The advice here is that community lawyers need to be aware of the competing demands within their practice and make appropriate adjustments.

In setting priorities, one should examine whether the "non-legal" work that a community lawyer performs is for the community or for individual clients. Non-legal work for community-related causes such as leafleting, attending and speaking out at community meetings, and staffing informational tables often results in building trust between the community and the lawyer. "Favors" to an individual such as filling out a financial aid form, making a phone call on a non-legally related matter, and reading junk mail, however, only benefit one person. They do not advance the community's cause of fostering trust between the community lawyer and the community.

C. *Translating Across Language and Culture*

Working with an immigrant community with limited English ability poses special problems. From our struggle with Parcel C, we learned the following:

Try to retain bilingual, bicultural lawyers.

Because the Legal Committee members could speak Chinese (both Cantonese and Mandarin) and understand Chinatown's culture, we were able to convey legal information in understandable terms and talk directly with average community members. This yielded numerous benefits, such as: allowing community participation in strategy discussions; observing the community's reaction, unfiltered by interpreters or community leaders; facilitating trust critical to the attorney-client relationship; enhancing the community's sense of ownership over the struggle; and clarifying the lawyers' accountability to the entire community, not just its leaders. In our survey of community-based organizations, the respondents almost unanimously pointed out the significance of having bilingual and bicultural community lawyers.

Be careful when using interpreters.

Simultaneous, bidirectional interpretation is not easy. Simply because one is fluent in both languages does not mean that one is a successful interpreter. Community lawyers must take precautions to make certain that interpreters are faithfully conveying messages in both directions and that they are not injecting their own perspectives, biases, or judgments. One way to do this is for community lawyers to bring their own interpreter incognito into meetings to assess the accuracy and completeness of the interpretation. Another way is to make clear to ad hoc interpreters from the community what their job entails and that they should strive to be as accurate as possible, even with complex legal information. If an interpreter is uncertain, she should ask the lawyers for clarification before making a half-correct interpretation. Finally, community lawyers should make the intepreter's job easier by breaking up complicated thoughts into short segments, with pauses.

Do not let interpreters disrupt your relationship with your client.

Working with interpreters is a skill. Instead of talking to the interpreter, community lawyers should talk directly to their clients. For example, instead of telling the interpreter to "ask her this" or "tell him that," lawyers should speak to the client in the first person, almost as if the interpreter were not there.

Change communication styles to reduce the need for interpreters.

Instead of speaking in long, complicated sentences, try simpler sentences that clients with even limited English ability can understand. Lawyers should also not underestimate the value of non-verbal communication, such as a handshake, a nod, a smile, or picture drawing to interact with their clients.

* * *

The success of Parcel C as a community movement and as a demonstration of good community lawyering grew out of a synergy of good fortune and good practice. It took place when the community was ready to fight, with the assistance of a group of energetic, young, daring, and committed lawyers, law students, and activists. No one participated in the Parcel C struggle intending to make it a demonstration project of community lawyering. It was through a process of learning to work with community activists, residents, and other professional that we developed a road map for community lawyering. Our inexperience made it easier for us to let go of the law in "solving" problems and enabled us to pursue non-legal strategies. However, it is by repeating the practice, reflecting on its efficacy, and refining it over time that we may expand the components and strategies to make community lawyering effective.

Community lawyering is about returning power to the community by supplementing their skills with the tools of legal information, so that they know how and when to wield the knowledge, to protect their life, liberty, and property. Its goal is to make lasting changes and bring about social justice.

Community lawyers must recognize the limitations of the law. We need to make intelligent use of the community's assets and ensure that our practice stays innovative, energetic, and adaptive. Our success as community lawyers lies in building tools for subordinated people to negotiate with the dominant society, making room for them to sit at the negotiation table, facilitating their say in decisions that affect their lives, and encouraging them to capitalize on their talents and assets.

There is nothing especially rebellious in the concept of community lawyering. It is merely asking lawyers committed to social change to sustain the youthful idealism, energy, and creative vision that they possessed when they first entered the law. What we did during the Parcel C struggle was simple to live up to the vision that beckoned us to become community lawyers in the first place.

Notes and Questions

1. When representing groups and communities, the involvement of lawyers is quite extensive and seems to suggest a risk of throwing off any healthy balance between work and family. While the time commit-

ment is not like the law firm problem of "billable hours," does the elaborate guidance here suggest a risk of early lawyer burn-out?

2. How can lawyers gain the trust of the client group? How can client-centeredness guide lawyers' contribution to mobilization, for instance, by giving advice without defeating the autonomy of the individual members of client groups? How can the lawyer be an activist and still remain client-centered? As the lawyer goes beyond informing her clients to transforming them, has she breached the boundaries of respect for client autonomy? In pushing the envelope, how far should the attorney go? To be effective must the activist lawyer recognize that it is not enough to act aggressively to enforce a client's legal rights or to create new ones? Must she shift her focus "from the limited prospect of the law to the greater potential of a truly cross-disciplinary and pro-active political assault on oppression"?

3. Review and evaluate the guidelines for representing groups and communities. Do you have additional suggestions that should be on such a list? *See* excerpts by Sheila Foster and Judith Koons in chapter 12.

4. Social justice ideals can supplant client autonomy, giving rise to a conflict between the lawyer and the client. This problem is illustrated in Derrick Bell's classic piece on school desegregation.

DERRICK A. BELL, JR.

Serving Two Masters: Integration Ideals and Client Interests in School Desegregation Litigation
85 Yale L. J. 470, 471–72, 488–90, 492–93, 512–16 (1976)

How should the term "client" be defined in school desegregation cases that are litigated for decades, determine critically important constitutional rights for thousands of minority children, and usually involve major restructuring of a public school system? How should civil rights attorneys represent the often diverse interests of clients and class in school suits? Do they owe any special obligation to class members who emphasize educational quality and who probably cannot obtain counsel to advocate their divergent views? Do the political, organizational, and even philosophical complexities of school desegregation litigation justify a higher standard of professional responsibility on the part of civil rights lawyers to their clients, or more diligent oversight of the lawyer-client relationship by the bench and the bar?

As is so often the case, a crisis of events motivates this long overdue inquiry. The great crusade to desegregate the public schools has faltered. There is increasing opposition to desegregation at both local and national levels (not all of which can now be simply condemned as "racist"), while the once vigorous support of federal courts is on the decline. New barriers have arisen—inflation makes the attainment of racial balance more expensive, the growth of black populations in urban areas renders it more difficult, an increasing number of social science studies question the validity of its educational assumptions.

Civil rights lawyers dismiss these new obstacles as legally irrelevant. Having achieved so much by courageous persistence, they have not waivered in their determination to implement *Brown* using racial balance measures developed in the hard-fought legal battles of the last two decades. This stance involves great risk for clients whose educational interests may no longer accord with the integration ideals of their attorneys. Indeed, muffled but increasing criticism of "unconditional integration" policies by vocal minorities in black communities is not limited to Boston. Now that traditional racial balance remedies are becoming increasingly difficult to achieve or maintain, there is tardy concern that racial balance may not be the relief actually desired by victims of segregated schools.

* * *

Whether based on racial balance precedents or compensatory education theories, remedies that fail to attack all policies of racial subordination almost guarantee that the basic evil of segregated schools will survive and flourish, even in those systems where racially balanced schools can be achieved. Low academic performance and large numbers of disciplinary and expulsion cases are only two of the predictable outcomes in integrated schools where the racial subordination of blacks is reasserted in, if anything, a more damaging form.

The literature in both law and education discusses the merits and availability of educational remedies in detail. The purpose here has been simply to illustrate that alternative approaches to "equal educational opportunity" are possible and have been inadequately explored by civil rights attorneys. Although some of the remedies fashioned by the courts themselves have been responsive to the problem of racial subordination, plaintiffs and courts seeking to implement such remedies are not assisted by counsel representing plaintiff classes. Much more effective remedies for racial subordination in the schools could be obtained if the creative energies of the civil rights litigation groups could be brought into line with the needs and desires of their clients.

Civil rights lawyers have long experience, unquestioned commitment, and the ability to organize programs that have helped bring about profound changes in the last two decades. Why, one might ask, have they been so unwilling to recognize the increasing futility of "total desegregation," and, more important, the increasing number of defections within the black community? A few major factors that underlie this unwillingness can be identified.

1. *Racial Balance as a Symbol*

For many civil rights workers, success in obtaining racially balanced schools seems to have become a symbol of the nation's commitment to equal opportunity—not only in education, but in housing, employment, and other fields where the effects of racial discrimination are still present. As Dean Ernest Campbell has observed, "[T]he busing issue has acquired meanings that seem to have little relevance for the education of children in any direct sense." In his view, proponents of racial balance fear that the failure to establish busing as a major tool for desegregation will signify the end of an era of expanding civil rights. For them the busing debate symbolizes a major test of the country's continued commitment to civil rights progress. Any retreat on busing will be construed as an abandonment of this commitment and a return to segregation. Indeed, Dr. Campbell has suggested that some leaders see busing as a major test of black political strength. Under a kind of domestic domino theory, these leaders fear that failure on the busing issue would trigger a string of defeats, ending a long line of "major judicial and administrative decisions that substantially expanded the civil rights and personal opportunities of blacks in the post-World War II period."

2. *Clients and Contributors*

The hard-line position of civil rights groups on school desegregation is explained in part by pragmatic considerations. These organizations are supported by middle class blacks and whites who believe fervently in integration. At their socioeconomic level, integration has worked well, and they are certain that once whites and blacks at lower economic levels are successfully mixed in the schools, integration also will work well at those levels. Many of these supporters either reject or fail to understand suggestions that alternatives to integrated schools should be considered, particularly in majority-black districts. They will be understandably reluctant to provide financial support for policies which they think unsound, possibly illegal, and certainly disquieting. The rise and decline of the Congress of Racial Equality (CORE) provides a stark reminder of the fate of civil rights organizations relying on white support while espousing black self-reliance.

Jack Greenberg, LDF [NAACP Legal Defense and Educational Fund] Director-Counsel, acknowledges that fund-raising concerns may play a small role in the selection of cases. Even though civil rights lawyers often obtain the clients, Greenberg reports, "there may be financial contributors to reckon with who may ask that certain cases be brought and others not." He hastens to add that within broad limits lawyers "seem to be free to pursue their own ideas of right, . . . affected little or not at all by contributors." The reassurance is double-edged. The lawyers' freedom to pursue their own ideas of right may pose no problems as long as both clients and contributors share a common social outlook. But when the views of some or all of the clients change, a delayed recognition and response by the lawyers is predictable.

* * *

NAACP General Counsel Nathaniel Jones denies that school suits are brought only at the behest of middle class blacks, and points out what he considers to be the absurdity of attempting to pool the views of every black before a school desegregation suit is filed. But at the same time he states that his responsibility is to square NAACP litigation with his interpretation of what Supreme Court decisions require.

3. *Client-Counsel Merger*

The position of the established civil rights groups obviates any need to determine whether a continued policy of maximum racial balance conforms with the wishes of even a minority of the class. This position represents an extraordinary view of the lawyer's role. Not only does it assume a perpetual retainer authorizing a lifelong effort to obtain racially balanced schools. It also fails to reflect any significant change in representational policy from a decade ago, when virtually all blacks assumed that integration was the best means of achieving a quality education for black children, to the present time, when many black parents are disenchanted with the educational results of integration. Again, Mr. Jones would differ sharply with my evaluation of black parents' educational priorities, but his statement indicates that it would make no difference if I were correct. The Supreme Court has spoken in response to issues raised in litigation begun and diligently pursued by his agency. The interpretation of the Court's response by him and other officials has then determined NAACP litigation policies.

This malady may afflict many idealistic lawyers who seek, through the class action device, to bring about judicial intervention affecting large segments of the community. The class action provides the vehicle for bringing about a major advance toward an idealistic goal. At the same time, prosecuting and winning the big case provides strong reinforcement of the attorney's sense of his or her abilities and professionalism. Dr. Andrew Watson has suggested that "[c]lass actions . . . have the capacity to provide large sources of narcissistic gratification and this may be one of the reasons why they are such a popular form of litigation in legal aid and poverty law clinics." The psychological motivations which influence the lawyer in taking on "a fiercer dragon" through the class action may also underlie the tendency to direct the suit towards the goals of the lawyer rather than the client.

* * *

There is nothing revolutionary in any of the[se] suggestions * * * . They are controversial only to the extent they suggest that some civil rights lawyers, like their more candid poverty law colleagues, are making decisions, setting priorities, and undertaking responsibilities that should be determined by their clients and shaped by the community. It is essential that lawyers "lawyer" and not attempt to lead clients and class. Commitment renders restraint more, not less, difficult, and the inability of black clients to pay handsome fees for legal services can cause their lawyers, unconsciously perhaps, to adopt an attitude of "we know what's best" in determining legal strategy. Unfortunately, clients are all too willing to turn everything over to the lawyers. In school cases, perhaps more than in any other civil rights field, the attorney must be more than a litigator. The willingness to innovate, organize, and negotiate—and the ability to perform each with skill and persistence—are of crucial importance. In this process of overall representation, the apparent—and sometimes real—conflicts of interest between lawyer and client can be resolved.

Finally, commitment to an integrated society should not be allowed to interfere with the ability to represent effectively parents who favor education-oriented remedies. Those civil rights lawyers, regardless of race, whose commitment to integration is buoyed by doubts about the effectiveness of predominantly black schools should reconsider seriously the propriety of representing blacks, at least in those school cases involving heavily minority districts.

This seemingly harsh suggestion is dictated by practical as well as professional considerations. Lacking more viable alternatives, the black community has turned to the courts. After several decades of frustration, the legal system, for a number of complex reasons, responded. Law and lawyers have received perhaps too much credit for that response. The quest for symbolic manifestations of new rights and the search for new legal theories have too often failed to prompt an assessment of the economic and political condition that so influence the progress and outcome of any social reform improvement.

In school desegregation blacks have a just cause, but that cause can be undermined as well as furthered by litigation. A test case can be an important means of calling attention to perceived injustice; more important, school litigation presents opportunities for improving the weak economic and political position which renders the black community vulnerable to the specific injustices the litigation is intended to correct. Litigation can and should serve lawyer and client as a community-organizing tool, an educational forum, a means of obtaining data, a method of exercising political leverage, and a rallying point for public support.

But even when directed by the most resourceful attorneys, civil rights litigation remains an unpredictable vehicle for gaining benefits, such as quality schooling, which a great many whites do not enjoy. The risks involved in such efforts increase dramatically when civil rights attorneys, for idealistic or other reasons, fail to consider continually the limits imposed by the social and political circumstances under which clients must function even if the case is won. In the closest of lawyer-client relationships this continual reexamination can be difficult; it becomes much harder where much of the representation takes place hundreds of miles from the site of litigation.

Professor Leroy Clark has written that the black community's belief in the efficacy of litigation inhibited the development of techniques involving popular participation and control that might have advanced school desegregation in the South. He feels that civil rights lawyers were partly responsible for this unwise reliance on the law. They had studied "cases" in which the conflict involved easily identifiable adversaries, a limited number of variables, and issues which courts could resolve in a manageable way. A lawyer seeking social change, Clark advises, must "make clear that the major social and economic obstacles are not easily amenable to the legal process and that vigilance and continued activity by the disadvantaged are the crucial elements in social change." For reasons quite similar to those which enabled blacks to win in *Brown* in 1954 and caused them to lose in *Plessy* in 1896, even successful school litigation will bring little meaningful change unless there is continuing pressure for implementation from the black community. The problem of unjust laws, as Professor Gary Bellow has noted, is almost invariably a problem of distribution of political and economic power. The rules merely reflect a series of choices by the society made in response to these distributions. " '[R]ule' change, without a political base to support it, just doesn't produce any substantial result because rules are not self-executing: they require an enforcement mechanism."

In the last analysis, blacks must provide an enforcement mechanism that will give educational content to the constitutional right recognized in *Brown*. Simply placing black children in "white" schools will seldom suffice. Lawyers in school cases who fail to obtain judicial relief that reasonably promises to improve the education of black children serve poorly both their clients and their cause.

* * *

The tactics that worked for civil rights lawyers in the first decade of school desegregation—the careful selection and filing of class action suits seeking standardized relief in accordance with set, uncompromising national goals—are no longer unfailingly effective. In recent years, the relief sought and obtained in these suits has helped to precipitate a rise in militant white opposition and has seriously eroded carefully cultivated judicial support. Opposition to any civil rights program can be expected, but the hoped-for improvement in schooling for black children that might have justified the sacrifice and risk has proven minimal at best. It has been virtually nonexistent for the great mass of urban black children locked in all-black schools, many of which are today as separate and unequal as they were before 1954.

Political, economic, and social conditions have contributed to the loss of school desegregation momentum; but to the extent that civil rights lawyers have not recognized the shift of black parental priorities, they have sacrificed opportunities to negotiate with school boards and petition courts for the judicially enforceable educational improvements which all parents seek. The time has come for civil rights lawyers to end their single-minded commitment to racial balance, a goal which, standing alone, is increasingly inaccessible and all too often educationally impotent.

Notes and Questions

1. Is Bell critiquing more than an apparent conflict of interest between lawyer ideals and client interests? Is he also challenging the liberal civil rights consensus and its sacred text of *Brown v. Board of Education*. Is he challenging integration *per se*? Was this courageous?

According to a leading text on critical race theory, "In fact, by the mid-1970s, when Bell was writing, the norms of racial integration had become so powerful that they were taken to define the difference between being enlightened and being backward. In other words, only racists—both black and white—could possibly oppose *Brown*." *Critical Race Theory: The Key Writings That Formed the Movement* 3 (Kimberlé Crenshaw, Neil Gotanda, Gary Peller & Kendall Thomas eds., 1995). For further discussion of social justice lawyering in the context of education, see chapter 9.

2. Even outside of the class action context, do you view a risk of social justice law to be a conflict between "the cause" and "client interests"? Can you think of possible examples where social justice lawyers were at risk of engaging in zealous advocacy that is more on behalf of the cause than the client? How should a lawyer handle the representational role when client goals change during litigation?

3. Conflicts can be a big problem within the context of social justice lawyering whenever the advocacy involves groups. *See* William B. Rubenstein, *Divided We Litigate: Addressing Disputes Among Group Members and Lawyers in Civil Rights Campaigns*, 106 Yale L. J. 1623 (1997). For an excellent discussion of conflicts of interests within the context of legal services practice, see Peter Margulies, *Multiple Communities or Monolithic Clients: Positional Conflicts of Interest and the Mission of the Legal Services Lawyer*, 67 Fordham L. Rev. 2339 (1999). Other relevant articles include, Esther F. Lardent, *Positional Conflicts in the Pro Bono Context: Ethical Considerations and Market Forces*, 67 Fordham L. Rev. 2279 (1999); Adrienne Thomas McCoy, *Law Student Advocates and Conflicts of Interest*, 73 Wash. L. Rev. 731 (1998); and Tracy N. Zlock, *The Native American Tribe as a Client: An Ethical Analysis*, 10 Geo. J. Legal Ethics 184 (1996).

Chapter 6

PROFESSIONAL RESPONSIBILITIES IN CONTEXT: THE SOCIAL JUSTICE CHALLENGE

A decade ago, a survey of 130 leading texts found that the median amount of coverage on professional responsibility was less than 2% of the total pages and much of that coverage simply reprinted bar rules. Deborah L. Rhode, *Ethics by the Pervasive Method*, 43 J. Legal Educ. 31, 41 (1992). While matters have improved over the decade, the subject of professional responsibility stands isolated from most of the curriculum. Worse, the subject of legal ethics often emphasizes the rules of professional responsibility as compilations of minimum standards of disciplinary rules. According to Jeffrey Maine, "Rather than having an ethical system based on ideals and aspirations, we have produced and cultivated a system in which lawyers can do whatever they want, as long as within the rules. If we want to increase the level of lawyer professionalism, more focus should be given to the aspirational values underlying lawyer professionalism and less on the minimum standard ethical disciplinary rules that govern lawyer conduct." Jeffrey A. Maine, *Importance of Ethics and Morality in Today's Legal World*, 29 Stetson L. Rev. 1073, 1080 (2000).

Sections 1 and 2 discuss the teaching of professional ethics in law school, the emergence of professional responsibility as a legal discipline, and the law of lawyering—the structure of professional responsibility and regulation. In traditional courses the emphasis on the rules of professional responsibility cheats an extensive consideration of the issues of professionalism and role. Jane B. Baron & Richard K. Greenstein, *Constructing the Field of Professional Responsibility*, 15 Notre Dame J.L. Ethics & Pub. Pol'y 37, 53 (2001) ("Most books focus on the *Model Rules* or the *Model Code*; indeed, the stronger the focus on the rules, the better the book seems to sell.").

The material that follows seeks to move beyond traditional pedagogy and to examine professional responsibility in selected contexts of social justice lawyering. While the material may augment and reinforce traditional survey courses in professional responsibility, the design here emphasizes context. As indicated in the first excerpt, the material attempts to nurture the development of reflective ethical judgment and to sensitize students to the ethical issues they will confront within the settings and practice of social justice lawyering. *See* Mary C. Daly, Bruce A. Green & Russell G. Pearce, *Contextualizing Professional Responsibility: A New Curriculum for a New Century*, 58 Law & Contem. Probs. 192 (1995).

Section 3 focuses on issues of ethics as they arise in clinics, because social justice lawyering, while in law school, is primarily experienced in clinical legal education courses, whether in-house or extern. The section also looks at ethical issues that arise beyond a traditional clinic setting—the legal advocacy involved with grass-roots organizing.

The largest section of this chapter, section 4, looks at developing the first professional responsibility—competence. In part A, building that competence through problem solving is explored. In considering the development of problem solving skills, traditional models are discussed along with the role of legal creativity, complex problem solving, and community building. Part B looks at the pros and cons of negotiation. It begins with a consideration of the special need for social justice lawyers to develop an ability to deal with power differentials in negotiation and to be effective when representing David against Goliath. Then, the material addresses the issue of lawyers negotiating with unrepresented poor persons. Subsequently, the section considers "negotiation ethics," exploring why it is not an oxymoron. Finally, section 4 closes by looking at the costs of settlement in a culture where over 80% of civil disputes reach a settlement without a trial.

SECTION 1. PEDAGOGICAL NOTES

MARY C. DALY, BRUCE A. GREEN & RUSSELL G. PEARCE

Contextualizing Professional Responsibility: A New Curriculum For A New Century
58 Law & Contem. Probs. 192, 194–95, 197–98 (1995)

The teaching of professional responsibility in U.S. law schools is entering a new age. A relative newcomer to the traditional curriculum, professional responsibility has struggled over the past twenty-one years to establish its intellectual legitimacy. It has evolved from a cramped course on the codes of lawyer conduct adopted by the American Bar Association ("ABA") to an expansive course on the law of lawyering. * * *

The richness and complexity of the subject matter demand an exploration greater than most law school curricula presently offer. * * *

* * *

Prior to 1974, professional responsibility was a cipher in most law school curricula. If a school did offer a course, neither the faculty nor the students took it seriously. Readings and discussions rarely went beyond platitudes about professionalism and warnings against commingling funds. In response to the Watergate scandal, the ABA adopted Standard 302(a)(iii) in 1974, mandating the teaching of professional responsibility in all ABA-accredited law schools. Most law school faculties responded in a manner that psychologists would label "passive-aggressive." Like John Dean [Legal Counsel to President Nixon during the Watergate scandal] himself, the faculties doubted that attendance at an ethics course would have altered the behavior of the lawyer-participants in the scandal. At a more primitive, political level, they resisted the ABA's assertion of curricular authority for territorial reasons, viewing it as a threat to academic autonomy. As one prominent law school dean commented, "I resent it. I resent the imposition of the bar, telling us *how* to do it." Rather than formally objecting to the ABA's directive, however, law schools signaled the course's second-class status within the curriculum by assigning it minimal credit, by making it a rite-of-passage course for junior faculty, or by hiring local attorneys as adjunct faculty members to teach the course.

* * *

Until recently, two methods of instruction dominated most law school classrooms: the pervasive method and the survey-course method. Proponents of the pervasive method argue that the most effective way to expose students to their future ethical responsibilities is to raise professional responsibility issues and discussions in all substantive courses. For example, civil procedure professors are encouraged to talk about the genuineness of the attorney-client relationship in the context of class actions; insurance professors are invited to discuss conflicts of interest between insurers and insureds; contracts professors are asked to analyze the ethical parameters of negotiations; and tax professors are urged to address the ethics of estate planning. Even legal writing can be an occasion for professional responsibility instruction. The opportunities for ethical reflection are legion in clinical instruction.

* * *

Proponents of the survey-course method argue that the pervasive method is well intentioned but fatally flawed. First, it would be impossible to monitor each full-time and adjunct faculty member's classroom without excessive intrusion. Second, to be effective, it would require extraordinary cooperation among faculty members to ensure that students were exposed to a complete curriculum before graduation and to avoid repetition of the same issues in different courses. Third, the amount of time devoted the ethical issues would inevitably be a function of the pace of each year's courses, with no guarantee of similar coverage from year to year. Finally, to implement a pervasive curriculum successfully, teachers would have to invest substantial time in mastering the subject matter and keeping abreast of the latest developments. Their criticisms have carried the day, according to a 1985 nationwide survey of professional responsibility teaching, which showed that 95 percent of all ABA-accredited law schools required the successful completion of a separate professional responsibility course as a condition of graduation.

The pedagogic assumption underlying survey courses is that law schools can best prepare students to wrestle with the multitude of law-of-lawyering dilemmas they will encounter by exposing them to ethical and liability conundrums in a deliberate mix of practice environments. The standard survey-course curriculum is all-embracing in two senses. The substantive-law units contain material in an array of practice settings (such as criminal, corporate, or matrimonial law) and employment sectors (such as solo-, small-, and mega-firms, government offices, and corporate counsel). [The authors advocate "contextualization of the curriculum" through "a studied examination of ethical dilemmas in a single practice area."]

DEBORAH L. RHODE

Professional Responsibility: Ethics by the Pervasive Method 4–8 (1994)

What is the "ethics" in legal ethics? That in itself is a matter of ethical debate. In a narrow sense, the term refers to the law of lawyering—the formal rules governing attorney's conduct. In a broader sense, legal ethics is an application of ethical theory and implicates deeper questions about the moral dimensions of our professional lives. * * *

The traditional view in most law schools has been that instruction in professional responsibility is someone else's responsibility. Although ethical issues arise in all substantive areas, such issues have received little coverage in standard courses or casebooks. Legal ethics classes have been regarded as intellectual interlopers, taught to "vacant seats and vacant minds." Such classes have often been criticized as too theoretical and not theoretical enough: too removed from the actual context of practice, and too uninformed by historical, philosophical, and social science materials.

* * *

[S]ome measure of skepticism about the effectiveness of professional responsibility instruction remains common. It thus makes sense at the outset to confront the two most common bases of resistance. One objection is that ethics courses do not significantly affect ethical values; the other is that ethical values do not significantly affect ethical conduct.

Legal Education and Ethical Values. The first argument takes several forms. One variation assumes that professional responsibility is largely a matter of moral integrity, which is determined through early socialization. Adherents of this view question (most often rhetorically) whether it is possible to alter in a few classroom hours the values that individuals have acquired over long periods from family, friends, schools, churches, and popular culture. A second variation of this argument builds on still more skeptical premises. Its assumption is that ethical questions worth discussing have no "right" answers and that faculty have no business trying to turn their podiums into pulpits. Alternatively, if professors studiously avoid imposing their views, an ethics course can lapse into a form of "values clarification" that erodes values. If everyone's view is as good as everyone else's, what is the point of classroom debate?

* * *

Ethical Reasoning and Ethical Conduct. The extent to which enhanced capacities for ethical analysis affect ethical conduct is more difficult to assess. Both historical experience and psychological research make clear that moral conduct is highly situational. Individuals may differ in their responses to temptation, but contextual pressures have a substantial effect on moral conduct independent of any generalized "integrity" or stated principles. One sobering survey found no significant differences in the moral beliefs characteristic of Chicago ministers and inmates of the state penitentiary. And in Stanley Milgram's well-known experiment, two-thirds of the subjects complied with directions to administer apparently dangerous electric shocks to co-participants despite their cries of pain.

Moreover, self-interest often skews interpretation of moral action. Individuals selectively perceive information that is consistent with their desires, discount contrary evidence, and adopt euphemistic labels to validate preferred conduct. Diffusion of responsibility and distance from victims also affect moral perceptions, priorities, and perseverance.

These patterns suggest reasons to avoid overstating the potential contributions of ethical instruction, but not reasons to avoid including it in professional school curricula. Despite the importance of situational pressures, most psychological research finds some modest relationship between moral judgment and moral behavior. How individuals evaluate the consequences of their actions can be critical in shaping conduct, and education can affect those evaluative processes. It can also make individuals aware of ways that economic and peer pressures, structures of authority, and diffusion of responsibility skew judgment. * * *

* * * A well-constructed ethics curriculum addresses issues of far greater personal relevance than much of what is tested in law courses or bar exams. Many practitioners will never encounter a shifting (or springing) executory interest; almost all will confront questions of loyalty, confidentiality, and conflicts of interest. Practitioners who have taken legal ethics courses, even in early, ill-developed forms, have credited them with helping to resolve ethical issues. And surveyed lawyers have generally favored maintaining or expanding ethics coverage. There is, in short, more evidence on the effectiveness of professional responsibility instruction than there is on the effectiveness of most legal education.

For law schools to refuse, explicitly or implicitly, to address ethical issues that arise throughout the curriculum encourages future practitioners to do the same. Our primary cause of unethical conduct, particularly in organizational settings, is the assumption that moral responsibility lies elsewhere. We cannot afford to mirror this approach in our classroom priorities. Although professional education cannot fully simulate, or insulate us from, the pressures of practice, it can provide a setting to explore their causes. Particularly in areas where the interests of professionals and the public do not coincide, future lawyers can benefit from analyzing the gap before they have a vested interest in ignoring it.

Historically, advocates of greater ethical instruction in professional schools have both overstated its likely effect and understand its necessary scope. Contrary to proponents' expectations, a class in ethics cannot itself instill integrity, ensure virtue, or prevent the proverbial decline of a profession into a business. Nor is a single required course likely to achieve even the more modest goals of sharpening moral perceptions and reinforcing moral commitments. But a collective effort to make ethical issues more central throughout the educational experience could bring us somewhat closer to those ends. And if ethics by the pervasive method remains the aspiration, perhaps ethics as a continuing presence will be the result.

STEVEN H. GOLDBERG

Bringing the Practice to the Classroom: An Approach to the Professionalism Problem

50 J. of Legal Educ. 414, 414–15, 418–21, 429–30 (2000)

In the 1980s many leaders of the organized bar and a few academic commentators began to complain that the legal profession was in a decade-long process of losing its professionalism. As the dialog grew, there were disagreements about whether anything was lost; if so, what it was; and whether it was worth finding. Nevertheless, concern about the "professionalism problem" has kept the profession in an uproar for close to twenty years. I doubt that we will see, in our lifetimes, any agreement on defining the problem, much less a solution to it, but three observations seem beyond argument.

- There has been a dramatic diminution over the last twenty years in the time practicing lawyers spend tending to the acculturation of new lawyers into the profession.
- The organized bar has focused on law schools as a primary resource for solving the professionalism problem—however it is defined.
- The faculties responsible for law school curricula have not thought much about professionalism, have not agreed about the existence or the nature of the problem when they have thought about it, and would have little idea of what to do if they could agree.

* * *

Professionalism remains a label in search of content. With no attempt to resolve which "professionalism" is the subject that law school should teach, here are some of the suggested "solutions" for the professionalism problem.

- Do more to teach the skills and values needed to be a competent professional.
- Teach less about esoteric theory and more about the kind of doctrinal issues that make up the day-to-day concern of the living law.
- Teach more about what it takes to be a good lawyer and a good person.
- Teach more about the philosophy of the law.
- Teach about how the profession can be changed so the legal system will better serve society.
- Study and teach more about the organization and structure of the legal profession.
- Do more to acquaint students with the life of a lawyer.

The first two are less about teaching professionalism as a course or a body of understanding than they are competing critiques of a perceived general educational gap between the legal academy and the profession. * * *

The five remaining "solutions," though different in approach, have in common that they are specific areas of inquiry, with the last two aimed directly at helping students to anticipate the world they will enter after law school and to understand the life they will lead in that world. Which of the five professionalism "solutions" is attempted in the curricula of American law schools? With very few exceptions, the answer is none of the above. David B. Wilkins contends that this state of affairs is "more than just a pedagogical oversight or a scholarly shortcoming" and characterizes it as "nothing less than an ethical failure by the legal academy." * * *

Professionalism receives hardly a mention in law school courses other than Professional Responsibility. To be sure, professional responsibility instruction has done no better. Despite a sustained professorial lobbying campaign to infuse professional responsibility throughout the curriculum and at least one text designed to facilitate that, the pervasive approach is pervasive only in the long list of schools in which professional responsibility remains locked in a single classroom. If an already well-defined subject involving rules, laws, and discipline cannot squeeze into a teacher's favorite doctrinal course, what chance has professionalism, a subject without definition, rules, doctrine, or text?

Professionalism, unfortunately, does not do substantially better inside the Professional Responsibility classroom than it does outside. While professionalism and Professional Responsibility both focus on lawyers, professionalism receives only a fleeting glance in a course that after thirty years is still a kind of stepchild with law school faculty and is even less well regarded by law students. As one of my students wrote, "I believe that professionalism is neglected. Generally, it is only addressed in Professional Responsibility, which is treated as a joke class among students here." Most PR teachers will confirm, with regret, that even if students do not think of the course as a "joke," they are uninterested at best, and they hate it at worst. They take PR because it is required, which they resent. It is the course in which they will memorize as much of the Code or the Rules as they think will get them through the Multi-State Professional Responsibility Examination. They resent the MPRE too. The result is a group of students, ranging from discontented to aggravated, who will resist with inattention and silence anything beyond black letter recitation calculated to help them successfully traverse the MPRE. * * * .

* * *

The reluctance of teachers to address professionalism, either because they know their captive PR students will not respond to it or because they are not willing to sacrifice any part of their syllabi in other courses, is not the only impediment to the introduction of professionalism into the curriculum. Most law faculty do not have extensive practice experience. This is particularly important for those approaches to professionalism that focus on the structure of the world students will enter and the lives they will lead in it. Concerns about personal/professional relationships and conduct, or about the problem of squaring the practice of law with personal values, do not have rules or guidelines around which a course syllabus is easily constructed. The combination of faculty practice inexperience and the lack of rules or doctrinal guidelines makes a course in professionalism difficult to produce. One need not agree with the Professionalism Committee's suggestions that the legal academy must hire a "significant number of experienced practitioners" in order to have "excellent role models for students" or agree that "only faculty with extensive practice experience . . . teach the basic and advanced ethics and professionalism courses," to acknowledge that the paucity of law teachers with substantial practice experience has an indirect influence on the failure of law schools to do much with professionalism. Law teachers are responsible for academic culture and curriculum. Professionalism, particularly the approach that explores personal values and relationships, is not the normal grist of the law school mill. It does not suggest the analytic rigor, the policy perspective, or the doctrinal analysis that are the core concerns of the legal academy. * * *

Stories of the practice of law that provide a context for student understanding are the indispensable material for addressing professionalism. Ask those often dispirited souls stomping around in the vineyard of law school Professional Responsibility—making more vinegar than wine—and they will tell you that PR classes fail largely because students have no understanding of the context in which the ethical issues arise. The same subject matter and the same issues are red meat for practitioners in continuing legal education courses. Throw out just one good legal ethics hypothetical and practitioners will chew on it for hours. Why are practitioners so interested in something that law students ignore or despise? Context and personal involvement. The practitioners can fill in the spaces of the hypothetical, spaces that students without experience cannot even see. Practitioners understand the subtle human dynamics that make a factual scenario a real-life problem. They can visualize the impact of a suggested theoretical resolution on the lawyer, the client, or the society. Practitioners know that the most difficult and absorbing ethics issues are not those addressed by the Code or the Rules, but those that slip between the cracks, leaving the lawyer with nothing on which to rely but judgment and a sense of professionalism. * * *

* * *

While the profession is right to insist that the academy take professionalism more seriously, it might be yet another example of the truth that you should be careful what you ask for—you might get it. The professionalism addressed in the law schools is unlikely to be a prescriptive list of appropriate manners and proper attitudes or a call for another Code of Civility. We need to tell our students more realistic stories about the profession—its heroes as well as its villains, its contributions to society as well as the damage it inflicts, its professional aspirations as well as its economic reality, and then encourage them to critique and improve what they see. We need to describe in its rich detail the practice on Wall Street and the practice on Main Street and let our students make their choices. They need to understand the horrendous hours of work and poor chances of partnership that accompany the big-money offer from the major firms, just as they must understand the failure rate for those who hang out a shingle right after law school.

Notes and Questions

1. How do you see yourself fitting into the system of lawyers? Do you perceive a need for re-socialization, for focusing more precisely on "the history and sociology of the legal profession[] and * * * the morality of the lawyer's role"? *See* Ian Johnstone & Mary Patricia Treuthart, *Doing the Right Thing: An Overview of Teaching Professional Responsibility*, 41 J. Legal Educ. 75, 90 (1991) (suggesting that an archetypical ethics course would encompass this focus along with a study of doctrine). According to some:

> * * * Aside from the bar examination, the major shared experience of American lawyers is law school. To the extent that all lawyers, whatever work they do, share a common culture and ideology, legal education is a critical aspect of the common socialization of the bar.
>
> Criticism of legal education has been constant and repetitious for many years. The four principal categories of criticism * * * are: (1) Law school does not adequately prepare its graduates for the practice of law; (2) the educational experience has a destructive effect upon the character or values of students; (3) law school fails to

produce public-spirited and socially responsible lawyers; and (4) legal education is not accessible to all sectors of American society.

Geoffrey C. Hazard, Jr., Susan P. Koniak & Roger C. Crampton, *The Law and Ethics of Lawyering* 971 (3d ed., 1999). *See also Symposium, Maximizing the Law School Experience II*, 29 Stetson L. Rev. 1009–1327 (2000). Bridget Maloney identifies the sources of law school stress: the Socratic method of teaching—"the distinctive characteristic of law school," time pressures, difficulty of the material, lack of meaningful feedback, fear of failure, and the importance of first-year grades. Bridget A. Maloney, *Distress Among the Legal Profession: What Law Schools Can Do About It*, 15 Notre Dame J. Legal Ethics & Pub. Pol'y, 323, 328 (2001). What particular sources of stress may be associated with an ambition to do social justice advocacy? *See* David W. Raack, *Law School and the Erosion of Student Idealism*, 41 J. Legal Educ. 121 (1991) (book review of Robert V. Stover, *Making It and Breaking It: The Fate of Public Interest Commitment During Law School* (1989)).

2. Consider the messages about legal ethics that law schools and the legal profession send: "How does law school communicate messages about the importance of legal ethics? If professional responsibility issues have come up in other courses, how has the subject been treated by the professor? Is professional responsibility a theme that runs through your law school career? How do legal employers treat the subject? Fellow students? How have these messages affected your attitude toward legal ethics?" Hazard et al., *supra* at 987. What has been your experience?

3. Goldberg offers five solutions to the "professionalism problem." Do you perceive a problem? If so, what is it? What would be effective responses to the problem as you perceive it?

4. Robert Nelson and David Trubek write of the importance of agency: "that the actions of lawyers reflect choices that are neither totally unconstrained nor totally determined structurally." Robert L. Nelson & David M. Trubek, *Introduction: New Problems and New Paradigms in Studies of the Legal Profession,* in *Lawyers' Ideals/Lawyers Practices: Transformations in the American Legal Profession* 1, 22 (Robert L. Nelson, David M. Trubek & Rayman L. Solomon eds., 1992). Drawing from Pierre Bourdieu's theory of practice, they rely upon his concept of "habitus" to mediate between structure and consciousness. They state that "habitus is the set of orderly predispositions actors possess as a result of their historical and social locations. While individual actors may be only partially aware of them, these predispositions manifest in many ways, including styles of dress, speech, and bodily presentation. They form a schema in which individuals instantiate the status-class composition of society." *Id.* at 23. Although habitus is dynamic, varying across time and space, "habitus tends to produce behavior in individuals that reproduces the very system from which it emerged." *Id.* As you prepare to enter the profession of law, what does this interpretive framework suggest about the challenges and opportunities before you? For a description of one student's experience in an

attempt to close the gap between the traditional law school curriculum and practice-based training, see Sophie Bryan, *Personally Professional: A Law Student in Search of an Advocacy Model*, 35 Harv. C.R.-C.L. L. Rev. 277, 278 (2000) ("What professional aspirations are realistic for an attorney? Does my desire to connect with people evidence a constitution ill suited for the analytical rigors of practicing law? Is providing direct service and advocating for systemic change, in truth, an either/or proposition? Is collaboration with clients a panacea for professional-status guilt rather than a feasible and useful possibility?").

5. Do you perceive any ways that your law school training contributes to negative public perceptions of the legal profession? *See* Roger E. Schechter, *Changing Law Schools to Make Less Nasty Lawyers*, 10 Geo. J. Legal Ethics 367 (1997). For a recent overview of the profession, see the *Symposium on Legal Professionalism*, 32 Wake Forest L. Rev. 613–992 (1997).

6. Steven Goldberg, *supra*, declares that most law faculty do not have extensive practice experience. He sees this as an impediment to introducing professionalism into the study of law. Do you know if many of your law professors have had extensive practice backgrounds? Do you see the lack of such a background as an impediment to professionalism? Would you find it to be odd that many of your professors lack such a background? Why do you think a background in the actual practice of law is not highly regarded in preparing one to teach students to become lawyers?

SECTION 2. THE EMERGENCE OF PROFESSIONAL RESPONSIBILITY AS A LEGAL DISCIPLINE

There are many sources of rules and standards that govern legal ethics. Professional codes of ethics for lawyers first appeared in the United States in Alabama in 1887. The ABA promulgated its original Canons of Ethics in 1908. According to Attorney Richard Stanley, however, "it was not until 1969, with the passage of the ABA's comprehensive Code of Professional Responsibility, including its DRs (disciplinary rules) and ECs (ethical considerations), that legal ethics began to gain recognition as its own discipline of study." Richard C. Stanley, *The Restatement of the Law Governing Lawyers: Lawyer Regulation Coming of Age*, Louisiana Bar Journal, June 2000, at 22. As doubt grew around the effectiveness of the Code, the ABA overhauled the regulatory project and, in 1983, published the Model Rules of Professional Conduct. Nancy Moore refers to three new influences on the professional responsibility of lawyers: the American Law Institute's recently published *Restatement of the Law Governing Lawyers* (2000); the proceedings of the ABA Commission on the Evaluation of Rules of Professional Conduct ("The Ethics 2000 Commission"), and the work of the ABA Commission on Multijurisdictional Practice ("the MJP Commission"). Nancy J. Moore, *Symposi-*

um Foreword: Lawyering for the Middle Class, 70 Fordham L. Rev. 623, 624, n.15 (2001). Professor Moore serves as the Chief Reporter for the Ethics 2000 Commission and she notes that the Commission responded to three recent developments: "(1) the adoption of the ABA Model Rules of Professional Conduct by forty-four states but with significant variations; (2) the newly recognized legal framework for law practice reflected in the ALI Restatement; and (3) the dramatic changes in the organization and structure of law practice, including significant developments in the technologies available to lawyers and clients." *Id.* at 624–25, n.16.

Nathan Crystal cites three ways in which the ABA's Model Rules of Professional conduct are incomplete. They are incomplete, because they merely establish rules to discipline attorneys and generally ignore professional aspirations; they focus on general principles at the expense of the problems that are associated with specific areas of practice; and they assume and often incorporate, by reference, legal principles. Crystal concludes, "The diverse movement to develop standards of professional conduct, sponsored by many organizations, extending over many decades, and continuing to grow in scope, responds to the three ways in which the Model Rules are incomplete." Nathan M. Crystal, *The Incompleteness of the Model Rules and the Development of Professional Standards,* 52 Mercer L. Rev. 839, 854 (2001).

GEOFFREY C. HAZARD, JR., SUSAN P. KONIAK & ROGER C. CRAMPTON

The Law and Ethics of Lawyering 3–4 (3d ed., 1999)

The profession's codes of legal ethics govern a number of matters that are very important to the public interest but either trivially obvious or largely irrelevant to ethics as such. These include:

- Rules requiring that a lawyer be truthful and honest.
- Rules regulating competition among lawyers (advertising, solicitation, etc.), which are subsumed under the rubric of assisting "the legal profession in fulfilling its duty to make legal counsel available."
- Rules regulating competition from outside the profession. The substance of these rules is that lawyers should prevent nonlawyers from doing anything that is the "practice of law," whatever that may include.

Putting these aside, the ethics codes * * * deal with essentially four problems.

- Prohibited assistance: What kinds of things is a lawyer prohibited from doing for a client?
- Competence: What measures will assure competent lawyering?
- Confidentiality: What information learned by a lawyer should she treat as secret, and from whom, and under what conditions may the secrecy be lifted?

- Conflicts of interest: When and to what extent is a lawyer prohibited from acting because there is a conflict of interest between her clients or between herself and a client?

These are all tough problems, and not only for lawyers. What is perhaps not fully appreciated, by lawyers and lay people alike, is that similar problems arise in everyday life. If this fact were appreciated by lawyers, they might be able to perceive and to discuss the problems free of the introverted assumption that lawyers alone can appreciate their complex and stressful nature. If lay people recognized the similarity, they might regard the lawyers' ethical dilemmas with greater comprehension and perhaps even greater sympathy.

Many illustrations might be suggested from other walks of life, at work and at home, of problems involving prohibited assistance, confidentiality and conflict of interest. A few will suffice to make the point. Thus, regarding prohibited assistance: Do you help a friend by lying to the police? Omit adverse information when asked to evaluate a former student or employee? Help sell stock that may be overvalued? Maintain the "character of a neighborhood" by not renting to an African American? Regarding confidentiality: What should a parent do who knows that a child has stolen something from a store? A pediatrician who discovers physical abuse of a child by its parents? A teacher who finds out that a student has been using drugs? An accountant who knows that a client is understating income for tax purposes? Regarding conflicts of interest: Does a parent send a healthy child to college rather than send a sick one to the Mayo Clinic? A plant manager trim on safety systems to keep her company financially afloat? A doctor order hospitalization because medical insurance will not otherwise cover the patient? A supervisor commend a subordinate who may become a rival?

If there is any peculiarity about these problems as they are confronted by lawyers, it is that a lawyer confronts them every day and is supposed to resolve them in a fashion that is compatible with a conception of her professional role. The ethics codes and the law of lawyering undertake to tell her how she should do so.

Notes and Questions

1. Is the term "legal ethics" an oxymoron? According to Richard Zitrin and Carol Langford:

> You may wonder what we mean by the term "ethics" in the context of the practice of law. We believe that there is no one single answer to this complex question. Some commentators believe that legal ethics refers to "the law of lawyering," or the formal body of rules and opinions and cases which govern our behavior. Others agree with us that an understanding of legal ethics involves more—the consideration of both individual and group morality. A lawyer evaluating this moral component might ask questions like "How do I want to live my life as a practitioner?" and "What do I think the legal profession should be, and what is my role in that profession?"

Richard A. Zitrin & Carol M. Langford, *Legal Ethics in the Practice of Law* 4 (1995).

2. Is the concept of "legal ethics" the same as "professional responsibility"? Is it the same as morality? Is any of this effectively subjected to rules of regulation?

3. By the time one comes to law school, one already has a pretty fixed ethical compass. Is a course about ethics in law school a case of "too little, too late"?

4. Do you agree or disagree that ethics courses do not significantly affect ethical values and that ethical values do not significantly affect ethical conduct?

5. What are some of the reasons for unethical conduct: self interest, situational pressures, passing the buck?

6. At the end of the day, how might legal ethics be related to individual and group morality? For an interesting read, see the classic Lon L. Fuller, *The Case of the Speluncean Explorers*, 62 Harv. L. Rev. 616 (1949).

JOHN S. DZIENKOWSKI

Professional Responsibility Standards, Rules & Statutes 5–7 (1998)

[ABA Model Rules of Professional Conduct] Preamble: A Lawyer's Responsibilities

[1] A lawyer is a representative of clients, an officer of the legal system and a public citizen having special responsibility for the quality of justice.

[2] As a representative of clients, a lawyer performs various functions. As advisor, a lawyer provides a client with an informed understanding of the client's legal rights and obligations and explains their practical implications. As advocate, a lawyer zealously asserts the client's position under the rules of the adversary system. As negotiator, a lawyer seeks a result advantageous to the client but consistent with requirements of honest dealing with others. As intermediary between clients, a lawyer seeks to reconcile their divergent interests as an advisor and, to a limited extent, as a spokesperson for each client. A lawyer acts as evaluator by examining a client's legal affairs and reporting about them to the client or to others.

[3] In all professional functions a lawyer should be competent, prompt and diligent. A lawyer should maintain communication with a client concerning the representation. A lawyer should keep in confidence information relating to representation of a client except so far as disclosure is required or permitted by the Rules of Professional Conduct or other law.

[4] A lawyer's conduct should conform to the requirements of the law, both in professional service to clients and in the lawyer's business

and personal affairs. A lawyer should use the law's procedures only for legitimate purposes and not to harass or intimidate others. A lawyer should demonstrate respect for the legal system and for those who serve it, including judges, other lawyers and public officials. While it is a lawyer's duty, when necessary, to challenge the rectitude of official action, it is also a lawyer's duty to uphold legal process.

[5] As a public citizen, a lawyer should seek improvement of the law, the administration of justice and the quality of service rendered by the legal profession. As a member of a learned profession, a lawyer should cultivate knowledge of the law beyond its use for clients, employ that knowledge in reform of the law and work to strengthen legal education. A lawyer should be mindful of deficiencies in the administration of justice and of the fact that the poor, and sometimes persons who are not poor, cannot afford adequate legal assistance, and should therefore devote professional time and civic influence in their behalf. A lawyer should aid the legal profession in pursuing these objectives and should help the bar regulate itself in the public interest.

[6] Many of a lawyer's professional responsibilities are prescribed in the Rules of Professional Conduct, as well as substantive and procedural law. However, a lawyer is also guided by personal conscience and the approbation of professional peers. A lawyer should strive to attain the highest level of skill, to improve the law and the legal profession and to exemplify the legal profession's ideals of public service.

[7] A lawyer's responsibilities as a representative of clients, an officer of the legal system and a public citizen are usually harmonious. Thus, when an opposing party is well represented, a lawyer can be a zealous advocate on behalf of a client and at the same time assume that justice is being done. So also, a lawyer can be sure that preserving client confidences ordinarily serves the public interest because people are more likely to seek legal advice, and thereby heed their legal obligations, when they know their communications will be private.

[8] In the nature of law practice, however, conflicting responsibilities are encountered. Virtually all difficult ethical problems arise from conflict between a lawyer's responsibilities to clients, to the legal system and to the lawyer's own interest in remaining an upright person while earning a satisfactory living. The Rules of Professional Conduct prescribe terms for resolving such conflicts. Within the framework of these Rules many difficult issues of professional discretion can arise. Such issues must be resolved through the exercise of sensitive professional and moral judgment guided by the basic principles underlying the Rules.

[9] The legal profession is largely self-governing. Although other professions also have been granted powers of self-government, the legal profession is unique in this respect because of the close relationship between the profession and the processes of government and law enforcement. This connection is manifested in the fact that ultimate authority over the legal profession is vested largely in the courts.

[10] To the extent that lawyers meet the obligations of their professional calling, the occasion for government regulation is obviated. Self-regulation also helps maintain the legal profession's independence from government domination. An independent legal profession is an important force in preserving government under law, for abuse of legal authority is more readily challenged by a profession whose members are not dependent on government for the right to practice.

[11] The legal profession's relative autonomy carries with it special responsibilities of self-government. The profession has a responsibility to assure that its regulations are conceived in the public interest and not in furtherance of parochial or self-interested concerns of the bar. Every lawyer is responsible for observance of the Rules of Professional Conduct. A lawyer should also aid in securing their observance by other lawyers. Neglect of these responsibilities compromises the independence of the profession and the public interest which it serves.

[12] Lawyers play a vital role in the preservation of society. The fulfillment of this role requires an understanding by lawyers of their relationship to our legal system. The Rules of Professional Conduct, when properly applied, serve to define that relationship.

NATHAN M. CRYSTAL

Professional Responsibility: Problems of Practice and the Profession 1–7 (2d ed., 2000)

Issues of professional responsibility pose some of the most difficult problems that lawyers face in practice. The perplexing nature of these problems usually flows from the fact that troubling issues of professional ethics involve tensions or conflicts between three ideas that are central to the lawyer's role: the lawyer as fiduciary, the lawyer as an officer of the court functioning in an adversarial system, and the lawyer as an individual with personal values and interests. * * *

1. The Lawyer as Fiduciary

* * * Many of the rules of professional ethics can be understood as expressing fiduciary duties of attorneys. In addition, the law of agency, which governs the attorney-client relationship, also defines the nature of fiduciary obligations. Indeed, one leading scholar of professional ethics, Professor Charles Wolfram, has referred to lawyers as "fiduciary agents."

What does it mean to say that a lawyer is a fiduciary? A fiduciary relationship is different from an arm's-length business relationship. In an arm's-length transaction the parties do not have obligations to protect the interests of the other party, although they do owe each other certain obligations, such as the duty not to engage in fraud. Instead, parties to an ordinary business transaction have the responsibility to protect their own interests. By contrast, fiduciaries have special obligations to care for and to protect the interests of their beneficiaries or clients. While fiduciary relationships may have contractual aspects (for example, fee agreements between lawyers and clients), the contractual aspects of fiduciary relationships are secondary to the duties that fiduciaries owe to their clients. What are these fiduciary duties?

The fiduciary obligations that lawyers owe to their clients include three specific duties: First, attorneys owe their clients a *duty of competence*, a duty expressed in American Bar Association (ABA) Model Rule 1.1. See also Model Rule 1.3 (duty to handle matter with reasonable diligence and promptness). * * * Note that the duty of competence expressed in Model Rule 1.1 goes beyond simple knowledge of the law to encompass both skills and character. Lawyers who violate the duty of competence not only commit an ethical transgression but also can be held liable to their clients for damages. Indeed, courts are increasingly willing to hold attorneys liable even to third parties who are not clients.

Second, attorneys owe their clients a *duty of loyalty*. The ethical rules dealing with conflicts of interest express this concept of loyalty. Conflicts of interest can arise in various forms: between current clients in a single matter or in unrelated matters (Model Rule 1.7), between a current client and a former client (Model Rule 1.9), conflicts between the interest of a client and a lawyer's personal or financial interest (Model Rule 1.8(a)).

The rules dealing with conflicts of interest are rarely absolute. For example, a lawyer is not necessarily precluded under Model Rule 1.9 from undertaking representation against a former client. The lawyer may do so, even without the former client's consent, if the current and former matters are not "substantially related." The fact that the rules do not adopt a per se prohibition on representation against a former client shows that the issue involves interests in addition to those of the former client. * * *

Third, attorneys owe their clients a *duty of confidentiality*. While closely related to the duty of loyalty, the obligation of confidentiality is important enough to warrant separate treatment. Attorneys have an ethical obligation to maintain confidentiality of information. Model Rule 1.6 broadly expresses this duty as follows: "A lawyer shall not reveal information relating to representation of a client unless the client consents after consultation ...."

Like the rules dealing with conflicts of interest, the duty of confidentiality is not absolute. Rule 1.6 provides a number of exceptions to the duty, exceptions that express interests thought to be sufficiently important to override the general duty of confidentiality.

The scope and limitations of the duty of confidentiality have been one of the most controversial issues facing the profession in recent years. Debate continues to rage over issues such as whether lawyers should be required to reveal perjury committed by criminal defendants, and whether lawyers must reveal information showing that clients have committed fraud in business transactions.

2. *The Lawyer as an Officer of the Court Functioning in an Adversarial System of Justice*

Professional obligations would be difficult enough if lawyers simply owed fiduciary obligations to their clients. However, lawyers serve not only as fiduciaries but also as officers of the court functioning in an adversarial system of justice.

What is meant by an *adversarial system of justice*? In broad terms an adversarial system is characterized by (1) a neutral decisionmaker, (2) competent advocates zealously presenting the positions of each of the interested parties, and (3) rules of procedure fairly designed to allow the presentation of relevant evidence to the decisionmaker. A number of rules of professional conduct are designed to preserve the integrity and proper functioning of the adversarial system. For example, lawyers may not make false statements of law or fact to tribunals (Model Rule 3.3); try to influence judges, jurors, or other officials by improper means (Rule 3.5); or engage in trial publicity that has a substantial likelihood of materially prejudicing a proceeding (Rule 3.6).

Like other rules of professional conduct, the rules dealing with the maintenance of the adversarial system are subject to exceptions and qualifications. For example, consider the possibility of what could be called a "pure" adversarial system. Under such a system, lawyers would have no obligation to evaluate the merits of their clients' cases. If a client wished to bring a case in court, the lawyer could do so. Indeed, we might even go further, viewing lawyers as, in essence, common carriers, required to bring an action in court if clients wanted to employ their services. The prevailing conception of the adversarial system is not, however, this pure version. Under the standard view of the adversarial system, the lawyer may not bring an action, indeed may not file any document in court, when the claim would be frivolous. See Model Rule 3.1 and Federal Rule of Civil Procedure 11. * * *

Many lawyers function in capacities that do not involve litigation. A growing body of law and commentary is now focusing on the role of the lawyer as what might be called "an officer of the regulatory system." For example, lawyers who engage in securities transactions may not continue to represent a client if the lawyer knows that the client is perpetrating a fraud on investors. At a minimum, the lawyer would be required to withdraw from representation. * * *

3. *The Lawyer as a Person with Personal and Financial Interests*

Our lives have many dimensions: work, family, religion, community. As a professional occupation, law is or will soon be an important part of your lives, but most of us hope that the law will not become our entire life. Personal interests and professional obligations interact in various and complex ways. Since the practice of law is both a profession and a livelihood for most lawyers, the relationship between the business and professional aspects of practice is significant. The practice of law has become more competitive in recent years. Solo practitioners, small-to-medium sized firms, and mega-firms practicing throughout the country and the world face growing economic pressures. In part, the pressure flows from changes in the market for legal services, including increased advertising and solicitation by lawyers and greater scrutiny of fees by clients such as insurance companies.

The rules of professional conduct deal to a limited degree with the business aspects of legal practice. The rules contain some regulation of fee agreements and business transactions between lawyers and clients (Model Rules 1.5 and 1.8(a)), limitations on advertising and solicitation (Model Rules 7.1–7.5), and prohibitions on unauthorized practice of law (Model Rule 5.5). But the formal rules only touch the surface of the degree to which business considerations shape a whole range of issues of professional ethics, such as conflicts of interest, establishment of legal fees, and marketing of legal services. Moreover, the rules barely hint at the relationship between the business pressure of practice and the personal lives of lawyers.

* * *

4. *The Concept of a Philosophy of Lawyering*

The tensions among these central aspects of a lawyer's role generate the need for what can be called a "philosophy of lawyering" a general approach to dealing with conflicts among these fundamental ideas. A philosophy of lawyering operates at three interrelated levels: the personal, the practice, and the institutional.

At the personal level a philosophy of lawyering focuses on how lawyers integrate their personal and professional lives. For example, consider the dilemma facing lawyers who wish to advance their professional careers without sacrificing the needs of their families in the process. Or think about the problem facing lawyers who may be asked by clients or senior lawyers to engage in conduct that they find personally distasteful although not illegal.

Lawyers choose how they integrate their personal and professional lives. These choices can be made intelligently, based on thoughtful analysis of the relevant considerations, or they can be made haphazardly, by default, or even by others on the lawyer's behalf. An important aspect of how you decide to integrate the personal and the professional is your choice of type of practice. Different types of practice will make distinctive demands on your time and energies and will provide disparate forms of rewards. In addition, the nature of the ethical problems and the tensions you face will vary depending on the type of practice you choose. For example, in private business or commercial practice you will usually not encounter problems of pretrial publicity, but you will certainly face issues of conflicts of interest, and you may face difficult questions of how to deal with client fraud. You cannot avoid difficult ethical problems regardless of your choice of type of practice, but you can shape the nature of the problems you face. Thus, as you begin to develop a philosophy of lawyering, you will want to consider a number of questions:

1. What type of practice do I see myself going into: plaintiff's litigation, corporate law, prosecution or defense, legal services? Large or small organization? What area of the country or the world?

2. What types of ethical problems am I likely to encounter in this type of practice?

3. What level of income do I aspire to have? Will the practice that I plan to undertake meet this goal?

4. What kind of personal life do I wish to have? Will the demands of the type of practice that I envision allow me to have the kind of personal life I desire?

5. Do I have enough information about the type of practice that I envision to answer these questions? If not, how am I going to get this information? If the type of practice that I contemplate will not allow me to meet either my income or personal desires, are there alternatives that I should consider?

Notes and Questions

1. How would you answer the "Philosophy of Lawyering" questions raised immediately above?

2. Consider the following comment.

> * * * Is there anything wrong with our fundamental approach to attorney regulation? Our approach, going back to the 1800s, proceeds on a fundamental fallacy * * * of the monolithic attorney-client relationship. Each of our rules purports to address one issue for all walks of lawyers, regardless of the nature of their practice or of the clients they represent. Commentary sometimes diverges but the DRs treat all lawyers the same and all clients the same. But all lawyers are not the same, all clients are not the same, and all factual situations are not the same. Lawyers work in a broad variety of practice settings. Clients are very different. They have different needs, different expectations, and different relationships with their lawyers. Does it make any sense to treat all of these lawyers, clients, and relationships the same way?

Steven Krane, *Regulating Attorney Conduct: Past, Present, and Future*, 29 Hofstra L. Rev. 247, 262–63 (2000). What do you think? Review the Preamble to the ABA Model Rules, *supra*. How instructive is it in introducing you to your professional responsibilities?

SECTION 3. CLINICS, ORGANIZING, AND ETHICS

Law school clinics are often a student's first exposure to live clients and the ethical issues that may arise in providing representation. According to two experienced clinicians, "Early in the development of law school clinics, it became clear that students' cases often presented challenging ethical issues, and that clinicians could encourage students to struggle with those issues while working on cases. Exploring ethical dilemmas before they are resolved, and while students and teachers must make agonizing decisions and then live with the consequences, makes this aspect of clinic work lively." Philip G. Schrag & Michael Meltsner, *Reflections on Clinical Legal Education* 250 (1998). In clinics, however, a tension may exist between the twin goals of serving a client community and providing a first-rate educational experience. Supervisorial intervention may be necessary in the client's best interest, but that intervention may undercut student learning. Further conflicts of interest and confidentiality may also raise ethical issues in the clinical setting. *See* James E. Moliterno, *In-House Live-Client Clinical Programs: Some Ethical Issues*, 67 Fordham L. Rev. 2377 (1999) (urging that professional norms of protecting client confidences, maintaining loyalty to clients, and avoiding or fairly resolving conflicts of interest be modeled, even if those norms undercut the education mission of the clinic).

Clinical education provides a unique opportunity both to teach ethical behavior and to engage discussion about difficult ethical questions. *See* Joan L. O'Sullivan et al., *Ethical Decisionmaking and Ethics Instruction in Clinical Law Practice*, 3 Clinical L. Rev. 109 (1996). Is identifying the client's perspective essential in order to act ethically and to reach client goals? Consider the following assessment of what feminism adds to clinical education:

> Clinic students' perceptions, judgments, strategies, and communications as lawyers—the components of lawyering technique—may differ qualitatively from their clients' perceptions, judgments, strategies, and communications. In part, these differences may result from the fact that law students typically come to clinics from different race, culture, and class backgrounds than their indigent clients. Students and clients also may differ on criteria such as gender, physical health, and mental health. These powerful socializing forces systematically influence what people come to know and understand about law, ethics, justice, and the world. As a consequence, the student lawyer's knowledge, like all knowledge, is partial and value-laden, and by uncritically applying technical skills that do not account for such structural influences, the student lawyer will likely reproduce the dominant and distinctive world view at the expense of the client's. Feminist thinkers would rivet their attention on the impact of professional interaction across powerful socially constructed divides.

Phyllis Goldfarb, *A Theory-Practice Spiral: The Ethics of Feminism and Clinical Education*, 75 Minn. L.Rev. 1599, 1675 (1991). Recall that Gerald López, in chapter 1, concurred that understanding difference is crucially important. Beyond being attentive to these divides, what should students do to overcome them?

Chapter 4 explored professional socialization. Do you see law school clinics playing any special role in that process? According to Stephen Wizner, a clinical law professor at Yale Law School, "Skills-training through the representation of clients was to be the methodology of clinical legal education. But its educational goal was far more ambitious * * * . It was to teach law students about the actual functioning (and malfunctioning) of the legal system, and to instill in them the value and duty of public service." Stephen Wizner, *The Law School Clinic: Legal Education in the Interests of Justice*, 70 Fordham L. Rev. 1929, 1934 (2002). He adds, "Today, outside of a relatively small number of academic purists, the majority of law teachers would subscribe to the notion that law teachers have at least some responsibility for the socialization and acculturation of law students into the norms and values of the legal profession. The law school clinic provides an educational setting in which that is a primary objective." *Id.* at 1936. Do you see any difficulties for law school professors seeking to carry out this responsibility for socialization and acculturation? Does the clinic play a potentially unique role?

In addition to in-house clinical instruction, many students have a clinical experience through externship programs. This text will not review legal educators' long-standing debate over the value of "in-house" versus "externship" experiences. *See, e.g.*, Minna J. Kotkin, *Reconsidering Role Assumption in Clinical Education*, 19 N.M.L.Rev. 185, 198–99 (1989); Arthur B. LaFrance, *Clinical Education: "To Turn Ideals into Effective Vision,"* 44 So.Cal. L. Rev. 624, 640–43 (1971); William R. Trail & William D. Underwood, *The Decline of Professional Legal Training and a Proposal for its Revitalization in Professional Law Schools*, 48 Baylor L. Rev. 201, 238–39 (1996). At present, externship programs continue to develop in a variety of ways. *See, e.g.*, Stephen T. Maher, *The Praise of Folly: A Defense of Practice Supervision in Clinical Legal Education*, 69 Neb. L. Rev. 537 (1990), and Robert F. Seibel & Linda H. Morton, *Field Placement Programs: Practices, Problems and Possibilities*, 2 Clin. L. Rev. 413 (1996) (discussing a nationwide survey of externship programs and describing the diversity of models).

Lisa Lerman believes: "Clinical experience in law school (whether in a live-client clinic or an externship) provides students with opportunities to think carefully about issues that might not get such attention in a busy practice." Lisa G. Lerman, *Professional and Ethical Issues in Legal Externships: Fostering Commitment to Public Service*, 67 Fordham L. Rev. 2295 (1999).

Lerman poses a series of hypothetical situations, faced by student externs, with implications for the attorneys and instructors who work with them.

1. Isiah, working for the county prosecutor, overhears a police officer in the courthouse hallway brag that his testimony had just convicted a known drug dealer, when in fact the officer had lied about finding drugs in the defendant's possession. Isiah tells this story to his

externship class. What professional responsibility does Isiah have? the clinical instructor? the prosecutor? *Id.* at 2299–2303.

2. Aleah begins working for a solo practitioner who does immigration work. The lawyer gave her a file and instructed her to go to an immigration hearing as everyone else in the office had other court appearances. What is the student's professional responsibility? *Id.* at 2304–06.

3. Drake delivers a presentation to his extern class in which he poses as his client, interviewed by other students. He uses a real client's medical records, which he provides to the class with the name blacked out. Following the mock interview he discusses his own difficulty in communicating with the client and several times slips, using the client's real name. Has this student breached the confidentiality of the lawyer-client relationship? *Id.* at 2310.

4. Carrie externs for legal services and also works part-time as a law clerk in a private law office. In her externship she worked on a case for a client who complained that a house painter never finished the promised second coat of paint. Then she learned that her law office represented the paint company in that case and several others. What steps should be taken now? *Id.* at 2313–15.

Often the rules of professional misconduct provide inadequate guidance for resolving these ethical dilemmas. How can the profession develop skills to address these issues, besides the ability to cope with stress? Lerman suggests: "Student externs can cultivate their skills as reflective practitioners. Even if the students become busy lawyers who have little time to ruminate, they will carry with them the skill of reflective observation."

Jane Aiken, excerpted in chapter 4, also emphasizes reflection as a tool to help professionals focus on justice. She observes: "Clinical legal education has long valued reflection as a key to effective teaching. Our supervisory questions should be directed to fostering reflection rather than eliciting information. As teachers, we must deviate from system-reinforcing behaviors and challenge the students to examine and reflect upon the prevailing social, political, and cultural realities that affect their own and their clients' lives." Jane H. Aiken, *Provocateurs for Justice*, 7 Clinical L. Rev. 287, 298 (2001). She further notes, "Critical reflection has at its root an attempt to tease out or hunt down assumptions. Perhaps the most powerful tool for lawyers dedicated to social justice is the ability to identify assumptions and expose them. There are essentially three kinds of assumptions that we want our students to be good at identifying: paradigmatic, prescriptive, and causal assumptions." *Id.* at 298–99.

Paradigmatic assumptions are the most difficult to unmask. They represent "the very structural assumptions we use to put our experience into fundamental categories * * * the bedrock of our understanding." *Id.* at 299. According to Aiken, identifying these assumptions may enable students not only to remedy resistence to clients who personify difference, but also may help in developing case theories. She provides the following illustration:

> Our clinic represented a female client who was formerly a male and the father of the child who was the subject of the custody dispute. The students prepared for the trial and struggled with their feelings about the problems that our client created for her son by having a sex-change operation. It was not until we were in trial that we fully appreciated the paradigmatic assumptions that we and everyone in the courtroom were making. At base, we treated our client's sex change as a "luxury" rather than a necessity. It was as if our client had decided to spend her afternoons engaging in a hobby rather than working with her child on his homework. Such a choice would not be in the best interests of the child and would pose problems for us in arguing that she was a dedicated mother. We had to confront that assumption and make the court understand that our client's surgery was essential to her as a person and as a parent.

Id.

Might critical reflection be applied to resolve some of the ethical issues presented in clinical settings? In one national survey in 1992, 44% of the externship programs used journals to facilitate reflection. J.P. Ogilvy, *The Use of Journals in Legal Education: A Tool for Reflection*, 3 Clinical L. Rev. 55, n.2 (1996). *See* Charles R. Lawrence, III, *The Word and the River: Pedagogy as Scholarship as Struggle*, 5 Cal. L. Rev. 2231 (1992) (discussing the use of reflection pieces). Recall the philosophy of lawyering questions raised by Nathan M. Crystal, *supra*. Revisit them and answer them as a "reflective practitioner."

Today, across the board the practice of law grows increasingly complex. *See* James W. Jones, *The Challenge of Change: The Practice of Law in the Year 2000*, 41 Vand. L. Rev. 683, 686–92 (1988). Beyond teaching students "to think like a lawyer," social justice lawyering must focus on what lawyers do. This is, in a sense, an offshoot from clinical legal education. *See* Carrie Menkel-Meadow, *The Legacy of Clinical Education: Theories About Lawyering*, 29 Clev. St. L. Rev. 555, 555 (1980) ("[The developing clinical legal education movement] has been concerned with the central question 'What is it that lawyers do?' "). The following excerpt discusses the law of organizing. An elaborate discussion of the features of this lawyering paradigm is presented in chapter 11. Here, the text asks: "What special ethical issues arise in this context?"

SCOTT L. CUMMINGS & INGRID V. EAGLY

A Critical Reflection on Law and Organizing
48 UCLA L. Rev. 443, 443, 502–17 (2001)

Over the last decade, poverty law scholars and practitioners have engaged in a lively debate about the relationship between law and social change. What has emerged from this dialogue is a new community-based *approach to progressive lawyering that combines legal advocacy and grassroots action in a form of practice that this Article terms "law and organizing." The law and organizing model privileges movement politics over law reform efforts and suggests that lawyers should facilitate community mobilization rather than practice in the conventional mode.* * * *

Surprisingly absent from the growing dialogue on law and organizing is any examination of the ethical challenges created by this form of practice. Some might consider any discussion of ethical restrictions in the context of progressive legal work to be inherently regnant and stifling of creative advocacy on behalf of marginalized clients. Indeed, commentators have argued that public interest lawyers should not be bound by the ethical rules, which were designed with traditional modes of practice in mind. Nonetheless, as lawyers become more involved in organizing movements, it would be irresponsible to ignore the ethical implications of this practice. Indeed, it has long been held that the same ethical standards apply to lawyers working in legal services programs as to lawyers in law firms. This part highlights several of the most prominent ethical challenges that arise in the context of law and organizing: determining when an attorney-client relationship is established, maintaining client confidentiality, addressing conflict of interest and scope of representation problems, and avoiding the unauthorized practice of law.

1. Establishing an Attorney-Client Relationship

Lawyers working in an organizing context often confront issues related to the difficulty of determining when an attorney-client relationship has been established. This is especially true for lawyers engaged in the type of law and organizing practice in which significant organizing responsibilities are assumed by the lawyer. Unlike traditional legal services lawyers who work within the confines of their legal offices, only meeting potential clients during intake interviews, attorneys operating in the field as organizers come into contact with potential clients on a daily basis. Precisely because of the fact that lawyer-organizers have increased community contact in a variety of settings—including at meetings, trainings, social events, protests, and pickets—they are more frequently approached by community members with questions of a legal nature. To complicate matters even further, it is often unclear whether community members approaching these attorneys are seeking legal advice.

Lawyer-organizers must be extremely careful in their interactions with community members because their conversations, however brief, might establish an attorney-client relationship. In general, when a lawyer gives specific legal advice that is reasonably relied on by a layperson, most courts have found that the provision of such advice is sufficient to establish an attorney-client relationship. Even in cases in which the attorney did not intend to establish such an obligation, did not charge any fees, and did not sign a retainer, courts have found that an attorney-client relationship, or, at least, a fiduciary obligation, existed. Once such a relationship is established, lawyers are required to conform to the range of duties inherent in the attorney-client relationship, including confidentiality, competence, and loyalty.

Consider the complications that can arise when a lawyer, acting as an organizer, is asked a question that requires legal knowledge. For example, what would happen if, in the context of an organizing drive, a worker approaches a lawyer-organizer and asks her what he should do regarding his workplace injury? If the organizer were not a lawyer, the organizer's responsibilities with respect to the question would be limited. However, because the organizer in this situation is a lawyer—and likely was approached by the worker precisely because of her lawyer status—a different set of considerations apply. Any advice given to the worker by the attorney would likely be viewed as legal advice and, if reasonably relied on by the worker, could be sufficient to establish an attorney-client relationship. Accordingly, the attorney would need to explain the range of legal options available to the individual—filing a worker's compensation claim and, if a certain product or machine caused the injury, perhaps also filing a civil claim against the manufacturer. Any relevant restrictions, such as a statute of limitations or notification requirements, should be mentioned. The lawyer would also need to obtain any specific facts relevant to the case that would influence the type of legal advice required. And, of course, the lawyer's ethical obligations, such as confidentiality and conflict of interest, would attach to the conversation with the worker.

Another area in which ambiguity regarding attorney-client relationships occurs is in the context of lawyers providing training for community members to pursue their legal claims on a pro se basis. Law and organizing practitioners frequently offer educational courses that teach self-help strategies for addressing legal problems. Lawyer-organizers working in these contexts should be careful to explain to participants that they are not providing legal advice in order to avoid crossing the line into individualized, fact-specific consultations with participants. Otherwise, the lawyer runs the risk of establishing an attorney-client relationship and being bound by the numerous obligations that such a relationship entails.

2. Confidentiality

Confidentiality is a central tenet of the legal profession. A lawyer is required to maintain the confidentiality of all attorney-client communications and may not reveal any information related to the representation of a client to third parties. The duty of confidentiality applies to all information obtained during the course of representation, regardless of the source. Confidentiality rules can apply even in situations in which the lawyer receives confidential information, but does not take on representation or perform legal services for the prospective client.

Perhaps the most perplexing confidentiality issues emerge when lawyers and organizers collaborate on a common project. A good illustration of how such ethical tensions could arise is found in the Workplace

Project, which uses a multidisciplinary staff to provide legal services. When an individual comes to the Workplace Project for assistance, he first meets with an organizer and describes his workplace problem, which may or may not be amenable to a legal solution. The organizer describes the way that the Workplace Project operates, including its organizing mission. Next, the client meets with a nonlawyer counselor who also listens to the client's problem. In deciding how to respond to the client's concerns, the counselor might consult with a lawyer on staff. If the client is found to have a complex problem, the client will meet with a team of advisors, including the attorney, organizer, and counselor. Through the course of these strategy sessions, the team decides whether legal action is necessary. If the client's case is accepted for legal representation, the team continues to work together on the matter.

While the interdisciplinary team approach to working with the client is appealing for a variety of reasons, this form of advocacy raises serious questions regarding the protection of client confidentiality. In order to include nonlawyer organizers within the scope of confidentiality protections, strict procedures—similar to those in place at a law firm—must be established before collaboration begins. Protocols regarding how confidential information must be handled should be reduced to writing so that all parties involved, including clients, organizers, and lawyers, understand the rules that apply to the collaboration. A lawyer who fails to create such procedures exposes herself to possible discipline. Furthermore, lawyers working together with organizers on legal matters must provide training for the nonlawyer organizers regarding confidentiality rules and explain that their work on legal matters must comply with the lawyer's ethical responsibilities. At all times, the attorney must carefully supervise and remain responsible for the organizer's work product and conduct.

Lawyers collaborating with organizers in this manner might ask the client to sign a waiver of confidentiality. However, consent to disclosure of confidential information is extremely problematic because such consent may only be sought if it is in the best interests of the client, there is full disclosure, and the client's consent is knowing and voluntary. Not only will it be difficult to explain to a client the many possible scenarios that could arise as a result of such a waiver, but it is also questionable whether such a waiver is voluntary when made in a situation in which organizing is a required condition to receiving legal services.

One solution to the client confidentiality dilemma is to entirely separate the legal work from that of the organizing work and not involve any organizers in the lawyering process. Under such a model, clients must be informed of the potential consequences of sharing their confidential information with individuals outside the attorney-client relationship, such as organizers. In addition, steps should be taken to ensure that other aspects of the representation, such as the physical setup of client meetings and the location of client's files, are conducive to maintaining the client's privacy.

3. Conflict of Interest and Scope of Representation

The ethical rules of conflict of interest and scope of representation provide important guidance for law and organizing practitioners in determining the proper path to follow when working with community members and organizations. It has long been held that the lawyer has a duty of loyalty to her clients. Accordingly, the lawyer may not allow her personal interests, the interests of other clients, or the interests of third parties to interfere with her representation of the client. If interests of a third party potentially conflict, the lawyer may accept representation only if the lawyer reasonably believes that the client's interests will not be negatively affected and if the client consents after full disclosure. Even if a third party is paying for the client's legal services, the third party may not interfere with the attorney-client relationship.

Under the scope of representation rules, the attorney must allow the client to articulate his objectives and to make any key decisions regarding his substantive legal rights. In contrast, the attorney has the responsibility of making final decisions regarding questions of legal strategy. However, the attorney must consult with the client regarding the means by which client objectives will be pursued. In general, "the lawyer should assume responsibility for technical and legal tactical issues, but should defer to the client regarding such questions as the expense to be incurred and concern for third persons who might be adversely affected."

Tension between the interests of the client and the interests of the organizers is one of the principal ways in which ethical dilemmas arise. Consider, for example, a situation in which lawyers and organizers are working together on a matter and a decision must be made regarding whether to file an action on behalf of a client in state or federal court. Each option offers advantages and disadvantages, but after learning that the potential for recovering damages is greater in federal court, the client expresses his desire to pursue the federal remedy. The attorney also feels that, as a matter of strategy, federal court is preferable because the federal law on the matter is more favorable to the client and the judges in federal court have a history of finding in favor of clients in similar situations. However, the organizers do not agree. The federal court is a good distance away from the community in which the events occurred, and the organizers believe that this will prevent mass mobilization around the suit. The organizers are adamant that the suit be filed in the local state court so that it can be used as the centerpiece of an organizing campaign.

The attorney in the hypothetical is in a difficult situation. If she decides to file in state court, despite the fact that both she and the client believe that federal court is the preferable forum, she risks violating her ethical duties as an attorney. Although the state filing might be best from the organizing standpoint, the attorney must properly give the authority to make decisions regarding the goals and objectives of the case to the client, not to the organizers. Furthermore, she must not allow a third party to influence the course of the litigation and must insist on pursuing the client's goals zealously, within the bounds of the law, applying her best tactical judgment as an attorney.

Lawyers working with community-based organizations or organized groups of community residents are also likely to encounter conflicts of interest in their work. Although the rules are clear that lawyers representing entities are obligated by the dictates of the organization's "authorized constituents," commentators have noted that discerning who those constituents are in grassroots organizations can be difficult. This difficulty is heightened when lawyers representing organizations face situations in which members who once agreed on the group's direction divide into competing factions with conflicting agendas. These internecine battles can escalate into power struggles over the group's leadership. Lawyers advising groups in this scenario are often approached by group members complaining of the machinations of a competing faction and asking for advice on how to oust their rivals. If the lawyer in this case is not careful—which may happen if she has developed strong relationships with all of the group members over a long period of time and has a personal stake in the organization's work—she might find that her attempts to broker a truce place her in the middle of an irresolvable conflict.

It has been suggested that conflict of interest problems could be avoided by carefully crafted client retainers. For example, the attorney could draft a "limited retainer" explaining to the client that the attorney will only continue to represent him so long as the client's interests do not diverge from broader public interest or community organizing goals. Alternatively, the client could be asked to sign a "prospective waiver" in which the client would waive any conflicts of interest that might evolve in the future between the lawyer-organizer and the client. Yet, whether such contracts would be found valid by a court of law remains unclear. The simplest strategy for averting conflicts is for the lawyer to avoid simultaneously serving as an organizer and a legal representative.

4. Unauthorized Practice of Law

The growing collaboration between lawyers and organizers on both legal and nonlegal matters necessitates a discussion of what is known as the "unauthorized practice of law" (UPL).

UPL proscriptions consist of both state laws criminalizing UPL activities on the part of nonlawyers as well as ethical rules that create disciplinary sanctions against attorneys who facilitate UPL. Almost all states have UPL statutes that limit "the practice of law to those who have been licensed by the government and admitted to the state's bar association after meeting certain requirements of education, examination, and moral character." * * * "UPL statutes usually proscribe three broad categories of activity: (1) representing another in a judicial or administrative proceeding, (2) preparing legal instruments or documents that affect the legal right of another, and (3) advising another of their legal rights and responsibilities." Under the ethical rules, the lawyer is prohibited from assisting nonlawyers in the performance of any activity that constitutes UPL.

Several different aspects of law and organizing practice raise UPL concerns. First, UPL issues emerge when lawyers train lay organizers on legal topics. For instance, several law and organizing projects provide educational courses that teach community leaders about the law. When conducting these programs for nonlawyers, attorneys must be aware of their obligation to avoid facilitating UPL. Although attorneys can provide the nonlawyer students with valuable background information on legal issues, they must be careful not to engage in proscribed activities, such as instructing nonlawyers on how to provide legal representation in court, prepare legal documents, or advise others regarding their legal rights. UPL can also occur when attorneys provide backup support for organizers advising community members through means such as telephone hotlines, radio call-in programs, or community fairs. If the lawyer finds that the organizer is dispensing individualized legal advice in these forums and does nothing to prevent it, this could constitute the facilitation of UPL in violation of the ethical rules. Finally, UPL concerns arise when lawyers and organizers collaborate on a legal matter. Although an organizer can legitimately work with a lawyer as a legal assistant, the lawyer must carefully delegate tasks and remain ultimately responsible for the organizer's work product. Moreover, the attorney must ensure that the nonlawyer complies with the lawyer's ethical standards. If the lawyer fails to do this and the nonlawyer engages in unsupervised legal practice, the lawyer exposes herself to possible disciplinary sanctions.

* * * [A]ttorneys working in interdisciplinary law and organizing contexts face significant ethical challenges. Indeed, as many commentators have noted, the ethical rules are so restrictive that they have largely inhibited lawyer collaboration with persons trained in other areas. Under such an ethical regime, law and organizing practitioners must pay close attention to how they structure relationships with their organizing counterparts and vigilantly monitor their involvement in grassroots activities.

The law and organizing movement has energized discussions of progressive lawyering by outlining a community-oriented approach to social change that links legal advocacy with grassroots organizing efforts. The theoreticians and practitioners of law and organizing have developed a model that privileges movement politics over litigation strategies and locates the seeds of social transformation squarely within marginalized communities. Rather than remaining entrenched in traditional poverty law practice, law and organizing proponents have highlighted innovative techniques designed to foster community empowerment.

* * * Specifically, in the areas of workers' rights, environmental justice, and community development, the combination of organizing techniques with more traditional forms of legal advocacy has led to the

development of strategies that have effectively redressed problems faced by low-income constituencies. For example, law and organizing practitioners have succeeded in increasing the wages of poor workers, creating job training and placement programs for the unemployed, and protecting communities of color from environmental contaminants.

However, despite the broad appeal of law and organizing, the movement is still in its early stages. Although the advantages of law and organizing have been presented in the academic literature, the actual practice has not yet been tested in a variety of contexts, scrutinized by reflective practitioners, and evaluated by critical scholars. This paucity of analysis has resulted in wasted resources, client dissatisfaction, and lawyer disillusionment.

* * * [L]aw and organizing practitioners need to pay special attention to the distinctions between different forms of organizing strategies, develop mechanisms to connect local organizing to broader institutional reform, and be aware of the possibility that organizing practice can reinforce group hierarchy. Additionally, advocates must negotiate tensions in law and organizing practice that can lead to decreased client services, lawyer-organizer role confusion, and client coercion. Finally, law and organizing practitioners confront a series of practical and ethical dilemmas in implementing their programs that demand creative and well-informed responses.

As law and organizing continues to evolve as a form of poverty law practice, a more focused effort must be made to evaluate its strengths and weaknesses, examine its tensions, and use these analyses to chart new directions for practice. * * * In the end, the dynamism generated by law and organizing advocates should continue to infuse debates about the future of progressive lawyering and the contours of legal pedagogy. However, this dynamism should be tempered by a thoughtful consideration of the difficulties of this approach.

Most significantly, law and organizing should not be promoted as an idealized model for producing meaningful social change. Instead, law and organizing should be viewed as an important tool—albeit one fraught with its own inherent limitations and contradictions—that practitioners can use to complement more conventional legal strategies. With this understanding, progressive lawyers can begin to move away from one-dimensional modes of advocacy and toward a more pragmatic, multifaceted vision of social change practice.

Notes and Questions

1. Alexander Scherr writes, "Lawyering is decision-making in phases and is strongly dependent on the bond between lawyer and client. The phases of lawyering process—assessment, decision and action—bear a dynamic relation to each other. They rarely separate into distinct tasks. When they do, it is never for very long. Indeed, this decision-making process centers and guides the characteristic legal tasks of

negotiation, advocacy and planning. These jobs bring realities to bear that further shape the lawyer's mind and the lawyer's decisions." Alexander Scherr, *Lawyers and Decisions: A Model of Practical Judgment*, 47 Vill. L. Rev. 161, 163–64 (2002). How is this observation reflected in the particular type of legal advocacy described above by Scott Cummings and Ingrid Eagly? *See* Scott L. Cummings, *Community Economic Development as Progressive Politics: Toward a Grassroots Movement for Economic Justice*, 54 Stan. L. Rev. 399 (2001).

2. The complexity of social justice lawyering often places a lot of pressure on the advocate to exercise practical judgment. According to Scherr, "Throughout, the lawyer accommodates influences well beyond legal doctrine. Doctrine remains a necessary, distinctive part of a lawyer's thought, but it is neither sufficient nor always dominant. Instead, it serves as one among many 'topics' which surface regularly in a lawyer's handling of decisions. Other topics include narrative, emotion, relational realities, power, interests and resources. These topics comprise internal and external influences and engage both conceptual and affective dimensions. The lawyer's ability to integrate these influences, and to act on them within practical constraints, constitutes a distinctive capacity, for which I use the term 'practical judgment.' " Sherr, *supra* at 164. How does one develop this distinctive capacity of practical judgment? Is it primarily a function of experience? How might it affect your sense of professional responsibility? Does law school help to develop it? Sherr states,

> I suspect that we may not be able to teach practical judgment, at least not fully, although we can talk about it, and suggest ways to guide what we do when we exercise it. This learning would ask the student to exert self-direction and responsibility for her own learning: an adult learning model of education. * * * To the extent we do try to teach it, we need to recognize the qualities which it requires: awareness of the dimensions of our own inner life, and the lives of our clients and others; an appreciation of the limitations on our power and influence; care and planning in assessing and integrating opportunities and goals; alertness to differences of experience, perception and value; skepticism coupled with a willingness to act on incomplete, even unreliable information; recognition and creative acceptance of practical constraints; combined respect and suspicion of the power of law; and balancing of personal values and professional restraint.

Id. at 277–78.

SECTION 4. BUILDING SOCIAL JUSTICE LAWYERING COMPETENCE

A. The Necessity and Propriety of Developing Problem-Solving Skills

As Paul Brest and Linda Hamilton Krieger note in the following excerpt, the ABA MacCrate Report has listed problem solving as the number one fundamental lawyering skill. *See* American Bar Association Section on Legal Education and Admission to the Bar, *Legal Education and Professional Development—An Educational Continuum (Report of the Task Force on Law Schools and the Profession: Narrowing the Gap)* 135 (1992) (known as the "MacCrate Report" after the chair of the task force, Robert MacCrate). The Report orders both law-related skills and general skills. In the order listed in the Report, the former are (2) legal analysis and reasoning, (3) legal research, (8) litigation and alternative dispute-resolution procedures, and (10) recognizing and resolving legal ethical dilemmas. The more general skills, in order, are (1) problem solving, (4) factual investigation, (5) communication, (6) counseling, (7) negotiation, and (9) the organization and management of legal work. *Id. See also* Russell Engler, *The MacCrate Report Turns 10: Assessing Its Impact and Identifying Gaps We Should Seek to Narrow*, 8 Clinical L. Rev. 109 (2001).

PAUL BREST & LINDA HAMILTON KRIEGER

Lawyers as Problem Solvers
72 Temp. L. Rev. 811, 811–12, 819, 822, 824–26, 831–32 (1999)

A client with a problem consults a lawyer rather than, say, a psychologist, investment counselor, or business advisor because he perceives the problem to have a significant legal dimension. But few real world problems conform to the boundaries that define and separate different professional disciplines. It is therefore a rare client who wants his lawyer to confine herself strictly to "the law." Rather, most clients expect their lawyers to integrate legal considerations with other aspects of their problems. Solutions are often constrained or facilitated by the law, but finding the best solution—a solution that addresses all of the client's concerns—usually requires more than technical legal skill.

* * * In a recent survey of the partners of American law firms, "problem solving" was reported as the single most attractive aspect of the respondents' work. The primacy of problem solving reflects how lawyers view themselves and would like to be viewed by others—especially in the face of much popular rhetoric to the contrary.

* * * At their best, lawyers serve as society's general problem solvers, skilled in avoiding as well as resolving disputes and in facilitating public and private ordering. They help their clients solve problems flexibly and economically, not restricting themselves to the cramped decision frames that "legal thinking" tends to impose on a client's situation. Good lawyers bring more to bear on a problem than legal knowledge and lawyering skills. They bring creativity, common sense, practical wisdom, and that most precious of all qualities, good judgment.

* * *

In sum, real-world problem solving and decision making inevitably require tradeoffs between the importance of the decision, its urgency, and the costs of engaging in the process. By definition, a good problem-solving process maximizes the satisfaction of the parties' interests, all things considered, including the costs of the process itself.

* * *

* * * Experts differ from laypersons not merely in the quantity of detailed knowledge, but in the quality of its organization. They possess domain-specific schemas that describe the attributes of problems and contain solutions to them. As Gary Blasi writes:

> The knowledge of experts is organized in ways that permit the expert to recognize patterns that are entirely invisible to novices in complex situations. In routine cases, this organized knowledge permits an expert merely to match a problem situation to a stored "problem schema" and to retrieve from memory the associated solution procedure. In more complex and uncertain situations, the schematic knowledge permits experts to construct mental models that capture much of the complexity of the situation, and to "run" the mental models in simulation in order to evaluate the likely consequences of alternative courses of action.

* * *

* * * [T]he fundamental process of problem solving in a professional context is not essentially different from problem solving in everyday life. The main differences are that lawyers are typically involved in a representative role and that they possess professional expertise. * * * But precisely what does legal expertise comprise? How is it acquired and improved? As background, consider some vignettes of the tasks that lawyers perform:

- An appellate lawyer seeks to influence the course of legal doctrine by persuading a court that settled doctrine with respect to race and sex discrimination forbids discrimination on the basis of sexual orientation.
- * * * A trial lawyer seeks to discover, organize, and present evidence to persuade the jury to return a verdict for her client. * * *
- An estate planner assists a client in transferring wealth to her family and to charitable organizations in ways that are both tax-efficient and assure that she will have adequate income during her retirement years.
- A company's general counsel works with its chief operating officer to develop a procedure for responding to sexual harassment claims if any should arise, or responds to the crisis occasioned by a particular accusation of harassment.
- A lawyer for a tenants' organization seeks to persuade a regulatory agency to tighten standards and enforcement regarding lead paint.

- An environmental lawyer representing a local government agency negotiates an agreement with neighboring jurisdictions involving the quality of drinking water in their common watershed.

Lawyers bring different kinds of professional expertise to these diverse tasks. It is useful to differentiate among (1) knowledge about the law, legal institutions, and actors; (2) knowledge about particular substantive domains; and (3) expertise in problem solving as such.

* * * [T]he lawyer's task of persuading an appellate court to extend settled case law to a new area calls for creative problem solving with respect to both analogical reasoning and advocacy. The task draws on the skills of doctrinal analysis, legal research, writing, and advocacy—many of which play a background role in the other tasks as well. The foundations for these skills are laid in the traditional law school curriculum, which also prepares students to acquire specialized knowledge of new areas of doctrinal and statutory law as the need arises during their careers.

* * * [There are] other kinds of legal expertise, such as knowing how to persuade judges, juries, administrative officers, and other actors in the legal system. The traditional law school curriculum does not address the psychology of advocacy or prepare graduates to deal with masses of unorganized facts, to present factual narratives, or to deal persuasively with various legal actors other than, perhaps, appellate judges. In view of the uneven mentoring our graduates receive, we might well do more to lay foundations for acquiring these skills.

* * *

* * * While we do not see any real downsides to the idea of lawyers as problem solvers, we would like to express two cautions. First, lawyers who think they are more skillful problem solvers than they actually are, or who are overly impressed with their comparative expertise, may lure or press their clients into poor decision processes with bad outcomes. Second, being a good problem solver does not obviate the moral complexities of legal representation. The best interests of the client are not necessarily those of society at large, and even the brilliantly negotiated, "win-win" solution to a multiparty dispute may inflict harm on nonparties. On the flip side, the lawyer who views herself as "counsel to the situation," rather than her clients, may deprive the clients of the unqualified commitment they have reason to expect.

This said, however, the aspiration of lawyers to be problem solvers seems unequivocally good. Many lawyers are already quite successful in this enterprise. Their task, and the task of legal educators, is to disseminate their knowledge—and their aspirations—to others in or entering the profession.

CARRIE MENKEL-MEADOW

Aha? Is Creativity Possible in Legal Problem Solving and Teachable in Legal Education?
6 Harv. Negotiation L. Rev. 97, 98–99, 109–10, 112–14, 125–34 (2001)

* * * In the last twenty years we have come a long way in the teaching and practice of negotiation in law schools, law offices and other legal institutions. At the same time, we still have a long way to go in the conceptualization and operationalizing of teaching all the elements of good legal problem solving and judgment, including the "creation" of solutions to legal problems. Where do good, interesting, creative and workable solutions to legal problems come from? Can law students, lawyers, clients and other legal actors be taught to frame legal problems effectively and to seek innovative and implementable solutions? Are solutions to legal problems to be found exclusively within the currently existing domain of legal resolutions (cases and settlements) or boilerplate clauses?

* * * As structured problem solving requires interests, needs and objectives identification, so too must creative solution seeking have its structure and elements in order to be effectively taught. Because research and teaching about creativity and how we think has expanded greatly since modern legal negotiation theory has been developed, it is now especially appropriate to examine how we might harness this new learning to examine and teach legal creativity in the context of legal negotiation and problem solving. * * *

* * * We can explore needs, interests and objectives in categories: (1) legal, the need for a ruling, judgment, legal status, or precedent; (2) economic, including transaction costs and present and future values; (3) social, including dealing with the parties' group or membership needs and objectives such as family, workplace, organizational, joint responsibility or community; (4) psychological, including all individually important needs or objectives including risk preferences, reputational, emotional, mental and physical health concerns, needs to assert, fear of shame, guilt, publicity; (5) political, such as rule change, justice, internal or public organizational concerns, precedent setting, relation to other problems, constituents, and finally; (6) moral, ethical or religious, including concerns about traditions, and fairness. Canvassing needs, objectives and goals in these and other categories, for both present and future desired states, is usually effective in bringing to the fore issues that may be of concern to a party in a negotiation context.

Like the pieces of puzzles and brainteasers * * * , the creative problem solver lines up the needs and interests of the different parties and examines what solutions may be possible in reconciling and meeting all parties' needs and objectives. These solutions will eventually have to be tested against what is really possible within our domain—law.

* * *

Although much of the theory and social psychology of creativity has focused on grand creativity—those who are really inventive or who have radically altered our thinking in some artistic or scientific domain, much of what has been learned about creativity may be applicable to those smaller domains of everyday legal problems rather than more grand "Constitutional moments." Specifically, to the extent that some forms of creative activity are social, and not merely individual, and that certain conditions may be more or less likely to foster, encourage or exploit creativity, there may be things we can do in our thinking processes, working environments, social behavior and educational processes to facilitate more creative legal problem solving. Thus, * * * expanding modes of what counts as legal thinking might actually improve the number and quality of solutions to legal problems.

Psychologists have defined creativity as "a process by which a symbolic domain in the culture is changed," "any act, idea or product that changes an existing domain or that transforms an existing domain into a new one," "how the new comes into being," "the quality of products or responses judged to be creative by appropriate observers and . . . also be regarded as the process by which something so judged is produced," and "that process which results in a novel work that is accepted as tenable or useful or satisfying by a group at some point in time." * * * In the words of Howard Gardner:

> People are creative when they can solve problems, create products or raise issues in a domain in [a] way that is initially novel but is eventually accepted in one or more cultural settings. Similarly, a work is creative if it stands out at first in terms of its novelty but ultimately comes to be accepted within a domain. The acid test of creativity is simple: In the wake of a putatively creative work, has the domain subsequently been changed? . . . Creativity includes the additional category of asking new questions [or creating new fields or domains].

* * *

Scholars of creativity distinguish between big "C" breakthrough creativity, such as Einstein's relativity theory, and more incremental creativity such as the patterns of social research and the development of legal doctrine. Some argue there is no big "C" creativity in the law, precisely because Anglo-American law, at least, is based on adherence to precedent and incrementalism. On the other hand, overruling major doctrines, such as changes in liability rules (non-privity) and recognition of new rights (privacy) may have the effects of big "C" creativity on those governed by law and rules. It is also possible to see law as having benefitted from the communal big "C" creativity that produced the Constitution—a template for stability and elasticity that has been replicated in different forms throughout the world.

* * *

[M]any of the creative processes described by creativity scholars and practitioners in other disciplines have, in fact, been used in law to create new concepts or ideas by interpreting or characterizing words, the constituent element of all law (by creatively reading and "misreading" prior concepts or tropes), expanding, aggregating, disaggregating, rearranging and altering existing ideas and concepts, borrowing or translating ideas from one area of law to another or from other disciplines, and finally, by use of re-design or architecture of words and concepts to build both new legal theories at the abstract level and new institutions at the practical level. * * *

Law as a discipline has contributed to the solution of human problems with the creation of institutions designed to preserve order and reduce or eliminate violence through the development of both governing principles and processes. Whether particular regimes or institutions are legitimate within a particular society, law and the institutions it creates are the glue which holds the society together by resolving disputes at both system-wide and individual levels. Law can be used illegitimately, as the Nazi and other fascist regimes demonstrated, but more commonly, law appeals to legal principles or processes are legitimately used to get things done. To the extent that we continue to view our own Constitution as the ultimate creative act, in its creation of a structure of government with checks and balances, separation of powers and federalism that places great emphasis on the process of governance, it is not surprising that negotiation theorists want to claim for lawyers the moniker of process architects. Our Constitution and much American law has also created substantive legal concepts and ideas, which in turn influence the legal behavior of those regulated or acted upon. Where do the ideas for these substantive legal concepts come from and how do new ones arise and become recognized? Virtually all of our legal ideas have been negotiated, whether in the august chambers of constitutional conventions or the more common locations of law offices and conference rooms.

Except for those rare revolutionary moments, when legal ideas are plentiful and debated by many, we tend to think of the development of legal concepts and principles as gradual, incremental and not necessarily creative. A limited number of cognitive processes are thought to govern the development of new legal ideas, such as reasoning by analogy, or its converse, differentiation, and the use of inductive logic, as well as deductive logic. Some would argue that as one of the most creative breaks in legal intellectual history, law and economics has added some further cognitive processes to the mix. We utilize rational choice theory, wealth maximization and efficiency concerns to affect that more ambiguous form of legal reasoning—policy analysis—in making choices among possible rules or creation of new ones. More recently, some use of statistical and empirical ideas (such as logical-mathematical intelligences) have found their way into legal reasoning (e.g. antitrust, employment discrimination) and even the economists have begun to take note of the psychological forces affecting rational man. * * *

Lawyers work with words, so most of our creative acts involve the construction of new language and interpretation of existing language, creating new concepts from whole cloth or from the interstices of statutory, regulatory or contractual gaps. Our words have the force of law behind them, however, so that powerfully creative words in law have been known to create whole new institutions. Examples of new legal and real entities that have been created are corporations, trusts, regulatory agencies, condominiums, unions and tax shelters. In addition, our words have created new legal rights and constructs like leases, sexual harassment, probation—and also have recognized (sometimes from conflicting ideologies) new claims like civil rights, privacy, free speech and emotional distress.

Words have also been creatively interpreted or "misread" by lawyers or judges, seeking to alter, expand, contract or even radically change a legal concept or doctrine. David Cole, for example, has suggested that "creative misreadings" by several notable justices of First Amendment doctrine creatively fashioned our First Amendment jurisprudence. * * * Dissents, in particular, offer an opportunity for oppositional ideas to be expressed and gradually to become less shocking and more acceptable. Cole traces the development of First Amendment law through Justice Holmes, Brandeis, Black and Brennan's "creative misreadings" of precedent to develop such legal memes as "clear and present danger," "free trade in ideas" which became the "marketplace of ideas," and the resultant change in legal doctrine from one restricting speech to one increasingly tolerant of even subversive speech. As Cole artfully argues, Justice Holmes, by dissenting from himself, used the common forms of legal reasoning by employing background philosophical principles derived from Blackstone, Smith and Mill, expressed in pithy metaphors which are themselves altered by context and by interpretations of subsequent readers (other judges). Constitutional adjudication has been particularly subject to this form of creative literary process as words and metaphors are used to break from the past and legal memes are needed to build legitimacy and acceptance for breaks from the past. As *Brown v. Board of Education* ushered in an era of "separate is not equal," the requirement to integrate "with all deliberate speed" was an effort to use the lawyer's tools of words to effectuate a more gradual compliance with a revolutionary and creative newly announced principle. Note that the choices of language or metaphors can be problematic as well. As Justice Blackmun chose "viability" of the fetus as a way of finessing religion by using science in *Roe v. Wade*, a new justifying principle is needed as science moves viability ever forward. Thus, a judge's and lawyer's creativity may be measured by the "viability" of the legal meme or trope that he creates.

At the opposite end of "creative misreadings" is the cognitive process of extension. One of the major legally creative acts in modern times is Charles Reich's "new property," an application or extension of traditional property principles to the new forms of property—employment expectations, welfare and other entitlements provided by the government. Current efforts to expand the Nuremberg War Tribunals and the current War Crimes Tribunal to build an International Criminal

Court demonstrate the expansion of an entire legal institution by changing levels of regulation and exposing the difficulties and opportunities of creating legal institutions and laws across jurisdictional domains.

Related to expansion of legal concepts is the common legal creative act of transfer from one legal domain to another. Another important creative act is the variety of contributions made to legal scholarship by Joseph Sax—the use of public trust doctrine in environmental law, the treatment of "slumlordism" as a tort, both of which were developed by exporting or importing one area of the law to another. This juxtaposition of seemingly unrelated things, or combining, explains much of innovative product development. Catherine MacKinnon's treatment of pornography as a civil rights or torts claim and the recognition of sexual harassment as employment discrimination illustrates this important principle—that given a body of law designed to remedy particular harms or wrongs, either the harms or wrongs covered by the law, or the remedies available, may be extended as we recognize appropriate new members of a category. This type of transfer occurs when we creatively borrow from other domains or systems. Many creative legal theories and institutions actually have their roots in other legal systems (e.g., European social insurance regimes, civil law models of comparative negligence, and Asian and African systems of dispute resolution). As a method of challenging assumptions, looking at how others of different cultures and domains solve problems demonstrates how our legal constructs are chosen, not given, and how they may be altered.

A form of creativity somewhat unique to legal reasoning, though similar to our related linguistic intelligences, is the process of characterization or argumentation in which we use our words to re-categorize facts, claims, arguments and rules, which disturb the linguistic purity desired by those outside of our domain. Consider how patent lawyers successfully assimilated the architecture of software to the vocabulary of a machine in order to obtain patent protection for what were thought to be unpatentable "mental processes, abstract intellectual concepts" or ideas. Or, in a form of creative reversal, consider how conservatives reclaimed takings law to render many land use regulations compensable events under the Fifth Amendment. In another example, defense counsel who initially resisted plaintiffs' class actions in mass torts captured the device when seeking global settlements with plaintiffs and insurers.

* * *

[L]egal professionals demonstrate creativity when they create whole new institutions like the "problem solving courts" of drug courts, vice courts, and integrated family courts that are seeking to work interdisciplinarily with both individuals and families to combine treatment with punishment. Similarly, creative clinical programs in law school have moved from totally litigation-oriented strategies to transactional work, developing venture capital and investments in housing and economic development projects, and multi-disciplinary problem solving, such as legislative advocacy connected to public health professionals for needle exchange programs.

Legal creativity has its own special structure. The adversary system itself may spark certain forms of creativity by requiring reversals and responses to arguments and characterizations of facts. To respond is to think and to deny as well as to explain. Thus, new explanations must be found, new defenses created, and new causes of action and new transactional forms to be discovered. Some adversarial creativity may be exercised in the spirit of law avoidance. The decision of *Buckley v. Valeo* and its attempts to sustain limits on campaign contributions produced the legally creative Political Action Committee (PAC), a cure that some think is worse than the original problem. Recall that Howard Gardner warns that intelligences have no morality and can be exercised for good or ill. Law's creativity may be somewhat limited by the bounds of law and legal ethics rules, but there still remains a fair amount of problem space to be manipulated within our adversarial culture. At the same time, the adversarial culture may also constrain and cabin our thinking unnecessarily by structuring it in polarized and oppositional terms. Are transactional lawyers more creative by being less constrained? Corporations and trusts, for example, were created legally to accomplish many different goals, some adversarial (tax delay, minimization or avoidance), but also to permit different power and control arrangements and to bundle and unbundle interests of wealth, time and assets to permit great flexibility of action.

* * * Legal creativity is necessarily limited by its need to work within the law, or at least within the foreseeable boundaries of legal change, but for optimal problem solving it would seem we should try to push the boundaries of little "c" creativity as much as we can to produce at least a greater number of choices about how best to accomplish legal results.

In searching for big "C" creativity in law, beyond perhaps the group act of drafting the Constitution, we should consider the contributions of legal scholars to the development of overarching theories or legal frameworks that attempt to reorient the development of law. One cannot avoid the remarkable achievement of Richard Posner and the law and economics movement in creating a legal meme that has been quite powerful in its transmission into the legal culture and law (with so many of its proponents now on the bench). Additionally, how can we ignore the legal memes created by Christopher Columbus Langdell as we generally labor in both the same physical and intellectual architecture that he created over one hundred years ago? Legal realism, critical legal studies, legal feminism and critical race theory are all group acts of legal creativity, seeking to develop new frames for thinking about legal problems, creating theories, new causes of action and new remedial schemes. What Weber called charismatic leadership demonstrates another form of creativity—intellectual or motivational leadership to rethink existing paradigms, evident in both intellectual and political realms. * * * Those of us who are laboring on the concept of problem solving or constructive lawyering hope that we have launched another legal meme—that of the problem solving lawyer and the integrative, interest-based negotiator.

Notes and Questions

1. How do these authors describe the nature of a problem? How does lawyer expertise direct her role in problem-solving? Does the lawyer's reliance on her expertise threaten to diminish the effectiveness of client-centered counseling described in chapter 5?

2. In the view of Brest and Krieger, how does problem solving differ from decision making?

3. Menkel-Meadow discusses the concepts of "creativity" and "multiple intelligences." How can these be applied to legal problem solving? As she asks, "Is it possible to speak of legal creativity or is the phrase itself an oxymoron?"

4. Problem solving is typically taught in the context of representing individual clients in small, pretty routine cases that students are able to manage and retain primary control over. Additional challenges to the traditional model of problem solving exist when students are involved in broader advocacy that goes beyond individual service cases. Thus Katherine Kruse asks: "But how can law school clinics meaningfully involve students in framing and brainstorming solutions to problems that are large, complex, and difficult to grasp? How can students gain a sense of ownership in a problem-solving enterprise that spans several semesters, or even several years? How can law students gain the context and perspective needed to meaningfully define goals, evaluate possible options or measure the success of initiatives they undertake?" Katherine R. Kruse, *Biting Off What They Can Chew: Strategies for Involving Students in Problem-Solving Beyond Individual Client Representation,* 8 Clinical L. Rev. 405 (2002).

B. Negotiating Social Justice

ROBERT S. ADLER & ELLIOT M. SILVERSTEIN

When David Meets Goliath: Dealing with Power Differentials in Negotiation

5 Harv. Negotiation L. Rev. 1, 5–6, 8–10, 13–22, 105–10 (2000)

As teachers of negotiation both to law and business students, we have long sought to understand and explain the proper use of power in negotiation settings. In particular, we have tried to prepare our students for situations in which they perceive themselves to face significantly more powerful opponents. To our surprise, few useful sources address this critical topic. We find this distressing because we believe the proper use of power to be one of the most valuable lessons that one can learn about negotiation. This topic is particularly important because certain common assumptions about the use of power turn out, upon close scrutiny, to be flawed. For instance, greater power, by itself, does not necessarily produce more favorable agreements for the powerful.

* * *

To effectively address the challenges presented by power disparities, one first needs to understand the basic concept of power. In the broadest and most elemental sense, power is the "ability to act or produce an effect." But what does it mean when we say that a person has power? Most observers agree that the critical element of power is the ability to have one's way, either by influencing others to do one's bidding or by gaining their acquiescence to one's action. This necessarily includes the ability to achieve one's ends even in the face of opposition. Power does not exclude the ability to persuade or to inspire others. Although the ability to persuade and inspire is an important element of power, the critical test of power is whether one's goals can be met even when charm and persuasiveness prove inadequate to the task. This is a decidedly unsentimental view of power. Yet, we cannot see any other way to capture its essence and to distinguish it from closely related, but less compelling, concepts such as influence or charisma.

The type of power that most of us are concerned with is social in nature. We are routinely influenced by power in a social context: negotiating with bosses, colleagues, business associates and family members. Thus, power * * * is a relational concept, pertaining to use between two or more people. Without social relationships, power becomes a fairly limited and uninteresting topic.

* * *

* * * The critical test of one's effectiveness in a negotiation is what one has convinced an opponent that one can do, whether or not one can actually do it. Unless exposed as bluffers, parties that convince their opponents that they have more power than they really do will generally be able to exercise the power they have asserted. As a practical matter, the successful bluffer has the power that his or her opponent cedes in the negotiation. This phenomenon extends to an almost infinite number of settings: from the "poker-faced" card player who defeats a full house with a hand that holds a mere pair to the timid soul who manages to convince the playground bully that he has studied a lethal form of karate and will not hesitate to use it.

Why is negotiation power such a matter of perceptions? We believe it is because negotiation substitutes for the actual exercise of power, leaving each party to calculate, without knowing, the other's resources, determination, skill, and endurance. Absent the actual contest, each side must guess about the other's power. This "guess," mistaken though it may be, becomes the reality in each negotiator's mind. Thus, power becomes a perception "game." Depending on the situation, this can either work for or against a party. If one has successfully bluffed, one gains leverage in the situation, while if the other party has successfully bluffed, one loses leverage.

Perceptions can also play a critical and confounding role even when no bluffing occurs. One of the most common and deadly perception traps is what we call a "negotiator's bias" in bargaining situations. By this, we mean that the natural tendency of negotiators to enter deliberations with trepidation often leads to judgments, based on little or no evidence, that their opponents are negotiating aggressively and competitively, despite the negotiators' sincere efforts to bargain cooperatively. These judgments, in turn, may be used to rationalize combative behavior against an opponent that would otherwise not be justifiable.

In a similar fashion, negotiators too often perceive, without good reason, that their opponents enter into a deliberation with substantially more power than the opponents actually have. Effective negotiators must learn to avoid these common perception traps and instead substitute clear and rational assessments. One must always seek to determine in as accurate a manner as possible the strength of the other side and whether the other side understands and appreciates its strength.

To have effective power, one must be willing to use it or be able to convince an opponent that one will use it[.]

* * *

* * * *Having greater power does not guarantee successful bargaining outcomes*[.]

Repeated studies confirm that power symmetry, rather than disproportionate power, is the most favorable condition for reaching agreement. Disproportionately greater power on the part of one party in a negotiation often reduces the likelihood of a favorable outcome for the powerful party, producing what Professor William Ury calls the "power paradox": "[t]he harder you make it for them to say no, the harder you make it for them to say yes." Several reasons seem to account for this phenomenon. First, parties with greater power are often tempted to achieve their goals through coercion rather than persuasion, and this leads to resistance from those with less power. Second, those with less power and under pressure to acquiesce often will scuttle agreements perceived to be demeaning—even to the point of rejecting deals that give them more benefits than no agreement. Third, while weaker parties are initially more likely to employ conciliatory tactics in negotiation, they may feel provoked to shore up their positions by making threats, adopting stubborn positions, or using punitive tactics in response to power plays by stronger parties. Finally, weaker parties may be so suspicious of the stronger parties' intentions that they will refuse to agree even to terms that most observers would characterize as reasonable.

Why is it that interactions between parties of equal bargaining power are more likely to produce favorable outcomes than those with disparate power? In addition to removing the negative factors detailed above, symmetrical power tends to encourage good feelings between the parties, open parties to creative, deal-enhancing suggestions, and remove the temptation to use force and threats. Of course, there is no guarantee that power equality will result in favorable agreements, but it does tend to produce optimal conditions for such agreements.

* * *

Power in negotiations typically arises from the dependence that each party has on the other[.]

* * *

Negotiation power depends less on the other side's strength than on one's own needs, fears, and available options[.]

As a corollary to the previous point, we note that the essence of determining the relative power of the parties in a negotiation depends less on how powerful each party is in any absolute sense than on how badly each party needs or fears the other. This is where the concept of BATNA (Best Alternative To a Negotiated Agreement) proves useful. If one has a number of attractive alternatives to a deal with one's opponent, one has great power regardless of the tremendous resources that the other side might have within its control.

A full assessment of the parties' power, however, requires a look beyond their BATNAs. Alternatives give negotiators leverage by establishing ways they can function without one another. But a proper power calculus also includes an assessment of what each party can do *for* and *to* the other. Professor Richard Shell calls the former "positive leverage" and the latter "negative leverage." Positive leverage is "needs based" and negative leverage is "threat-based." Positive leverage arises when one party can satisfy the other's desires, especially if one has the unique ability to do so. For example, owning a particular plot of highly desired land or a record-setting homerun ball hit by a famous baseball player would make even the lowliest citizen powerful in the eyes of one who desperately craves that particular item. Negative leverage arises when one can inflict damage on another or reduce his or her alternatives. For example, one of the ways that the Wal-Mart Department store chain has proved powerful in business is by drawing so many customers from small local stores in rural areas that the small competitors become unprofitable and go out of business. Thereafter, given the lack of convenient alternatives, even shoppers who might otherwise wish not to shop at Wal-Mart become customers out of necessity.

In short, those who calculate the parties' relative power by comparing one side's strength to the other's miss the subtleties of the power dynamic. Power in negotiation stems from what each side can do *for* and *to* each other, not from what each side can do *compared to* one another.

Power is neither inherently good nor bad[.]

Although ever mindful of Lord Acton's admonition that "[p]ower tends to corrupt, and absolute power corrupts absolutely," we do not view the exercise of power as inherently bad or good. The ability to do good things may require the use of power just as much as the ability to do bad things. During World War II, the Allies defeated the Nazis through their greater military and industrial might, not their superior moral standing. Similarly, those who have committed war crimes in the Balkans in recent years will face justice only if a suitably powerful force is deployed to arrest, indict, and try them. Much the same point can be made regarding negotiation. Those who lack power (or the appearance of power) in negotiation are unlikely to attain much success when they bargain.

* * *

[The authors identify the sources of power as personal, organizational, informational, and moral. They also offer a number of suggestions for one who is negotiating with a more powerful party, some of which follow.]

Form an Alliance Against the More Powerful Party[.]

The adage that there is strength in numbers holds particularly true for negotiations. One way to equalize or exceed the power of a stronger party is to form an alliance with others who share an interest in working against the stronger party. This principle extends from those who are friendly allies through those who dislike a common enemy only slightly more than they dislike one another.

Organizing a coalition against a common adversary requires careful planning and openness, particularly if one is seeking allies from unlikely sources. For example, one may ask what the American Paper Institute, National Coffee Association, Milk Industry Foundation and American Council on Education ever had in common. The answer in this case is: opposition to "sewer user charges." At one time, all of these groups objected to the industrial cost recovery provisions of the Federal Water Pollution Control Act. Acting jointly, they worked effectively to oppose the federal government's method of imposing charges. In similar fashion, we suggest that those who face a powerful adversary in an upcoming negotiation consider whether it would be useful to organize a coalition against the other side. In particular, one needs to consider approaching even those with whom one does not have a good relationship if they might be inclined to put aside their hostility in the interest of facing a common enemy.

There is a step short of coalition building that one should consider in negotiating with a powerful opponent. Sometimes it helps to organize a team of negotiators or, at a minimum, to have a friend or colleague attend the negotiation as a source of advice and as an extra set of eyes and ears. In addition to providing valuable emotional support, teams can bring a measure of objectivity and fresh ideas to the negotiation. Research suggests that teams produce better agreements, not so much because of the extra threat of power that they bring to the table, but rather because team members can identify overlooked ways of expanding the total value of the deal to both sides.

Appeal to a Powerful Adversary's Sense of Justice and Fairness[.]

People do not operate exclusively on the basis of economic efficiency, notwithstanding the economic models that would suggest otherwise. Nor do most people act exclusively on the basis of pure, brutal power. To the contrary, most individuals carry internal values, standards, and norms that govern how they interact with others and which limit their willingness to take advantage of particular situations.

As we earlier discussed, moral power can function as effectively in negotiation settings as other, rawer forms of power. The fact that one has the ability to overwhelm the other side does not automatically mean that one will do so. Appeals to fairness and justice can operate powerfully under the proper circumstances. In fact, we suspect that most negotiations involve elements of moral appeals to a greater or lesser extent.

In some cases, virtually an entire claim rests upon a moral foundation. For example, fifty years after the end of World War II, a number of Nazi-era slave laborers have pressed claims for compensation against the corporations (or their successor entities) that "employed" them during the war. Given the passage of time, one might consider these demands legally dubious, but the horror of the practice, as well as the moral stigma that companies would suffer from rejecting the claims, has led a group of roughly sixty-five companies to contribute to a 10 billion mark ($5.19 billion) fund to compensate the laborers.

Use Weakness as a Source of Strength[.]

Few things better illustrate the situational nature of power than the point that weakness can sometimes be a source of power. Weakness provides substantial leverage in several situations. First, a weak party with little or nothing to lose can bring a powerful weapon—indifference—to bear. For example, an indigent debtor faced with demands for payment by a creditor may convince the creditor to accept a settlement of pennies on the dollar by convincing the creditor that the debtor is "judgment proof," i.e., the debtor has few assets against which the creditor could execute a judgment. Second, the plight of a weaker party may trigger feelings of sympathy and concern in the stronger party. This may lead the stronger party to forbear from taking action against the weaker person. We offer a somewhat unusual example to illustrate this point. In 1944, his health rapidly failing, President Franklin Roosevelt implored his daughter Anna to arrange a rendezvous with Lucy Mercer Rutherford, his lover from thirty years before. Although undoubtedly capable of thwarting a reunion and inclined to do so because of loyalty to her mother, Anna, upon reflection, eventually agreed to help. Why? As described by historian Doris Kearns Goodwin:

> Anna knew that her father's strength was failing and she understood how important it would be for him to enjoy some evenings that were, as she put it, "light-hearted and gay, affording a few hours of much needed relaxation." If seeing Lucy again provided the inspiration he needed to assuage his loneliness and buoy his spirits, then who was she to sit in judgment? . . . At thirty-eight years of age . . . she was learning to accept his weaknesses and enjoy his strengths.

Once again, one sees the situational nature of power. In this example, despite being arguably the most powerful person in the world, Roosevelt had to achieve his goal through weakness, not strength.

Third, weakness can trump a stronger party's power if the powerful party faces public criticism for taking action against the weaker. Publicity can often shift the balance of power when television and newspapers treat a powerful party's actions as exploitative. For example, during the Montgomery bus boycott by blacks during the mid-1950s, media coverage from across the country exposed the oppressive nature of segregation in the south, slowly leading to reform efforts. Moreover, the publicity discouraged white violence and emboldened the black boycotters, eventually leading the city government to accede to their demands.

Finally, weakness can lead to desperate acts, which in turn may make coercive behaviors by powerful parties very costly—so much that the battle may not be worth it. Rosa Parks, a black woman in Montgomery whose refusal to move from her seat to permit a white man to sit down triggered the historic boycott, had not sought a confrontation on the day that she was arrested. She was just tired and frustrated. As David Halberstam describes it:

> Perhaps the most interesting thing about her was how ordinary she was, at least on the surface, almost the prototype of the black woman who toiled so hard and had so little to show for it. She had not, she later explained, thought about getting arrested that day. Later, the stunned white leaders of Montgomery repeatedly charged that Park's refusal was part of a carefully orchestrated plan on the part of the local NAACP, of which she was an officer. But that was not true; what she did represented one person's exhaustion with a system that dehumanized all black people. Something inside her finally snapped.

In such acts of desperation by the oppressed are sometimes born mighty movements that forever shift the power dynamics of a community, a city, and, ultimately, a nation. It, therefore, should not surprise that they can easily change the dynamics of a negotiation.

RUSSELL ENGLER

Out of Sight and Out of Line: The Need for Regulation of Lawyers' Negotiations with Unrepresented Poor Persons

85 Calif. L. Rev. 79, 79–82, 84, 105–14, 158 (1997)

Negotiations between lawyers and unrepresented parties are common occurrences. Many litigants appear without counsel, a result not surprising given reports that over eighty percent of the legal needs of the poor and working poor currently are unmet. In some civil courts, as many as ninety percent of the defendants appear without counsel. Given that most civil cases settle, negotiations and communications between lawyers and their unrepresented adversaries occur frequently. Negotiations between lawyers and lay people also occur regularly in situations outside the scope of litigation.

Despite the frequency of such encounters between lawyers and lay people, the ethical rules governing lawyers virtually ignore this scenario. Neither the Model Rules of Professional Conduct ("Model Rules"), nor the Model Code of Professional Responsibility ("Model Code"), contains a provision specifically regulating negotiations between lawyers and lay people. In the Model Rules, only a single rule speaks directly to a lawyer's dealings with an unrepresented adversary. Only a single subsection of one disciplinary rule of the Model Code focuses exclusively on this situation. Thus, a reading of the rules of ethics suggests that cases pitting parties with lawyers against lay people are rare occurrences, or, at a minimum, the exception rather than the rule.

Leading ethics and negotiation textbooks perpetuate the sense that cases involving unrepresented opponents are rare. For example, a sampling of ethics textbooks reveals that scant attention is paid to the lawyer's obligations when facing an unrepresented opponent in litigation. Textbooks for legal negotiation also fail to address ethical constraints on negotiation with an unrepresented litigant. Even articles and textbooks explicitly focusing on the ethics of negotiation either are silent on the issue of the ethics of negotiating with a lay person or provide only a passing reference.

Contrary to the impression created by the ethical rules and ethics texts, lawyer negotiations with unrepresented adversaries occur in vast numbers every day. Though the two rules that address directly lawyers' communications with unrepresented adversaries make clear that there are severe limitations on the permissible scope of negotiations with unrepresented parties, these limitations routinely go unheeded. Compounding the problem, the vast majority of these unrepresented parties already face significant power disadvantages in the legal system; unrepresented litigants often are poor, are women, and are people of color.

* * *

The prohibition of advice-giving significantly limits permissible attorney behavior in the context of negotiations. An attorney must refrain from giving legal advice, but must also refrain from suggesting a proposed course of action to the unrepresented adversary. The attorney must not mislead the unrepresented person, and must refrain from overreaching. The assessment as to whether an attorney's communications constitute impermissible advice must be made from the perspective of the unrepresented litigant. The inquiry depends on the characteristics and legal sophistication of the unrepresented party, as well as the setting in which the attorney's behavior or comment occurs.

* * *

While the prohibition against advice-giving is widely recognized, what constitutes impermissible advice-giving is a source of confusion. * * *

The Housing Court was created by the New York state legislature with the stated purpose of providing adequate judicial procedures for the effective enforcement of proper housing standards in the City of New York and to protect the health, safety and welfare of the citizens of the State. On paper, eviction proceedings—referred to as summary proceedings—comprise only one of the numerous types of housing cases over which the Housing Court has jurisdiction. In reality, summary proceedings dominate the court's docket.

The Housing Court's volume is crushing. The volume of cases filed annually varies from 300,000 to almost 400,000. Such a volume leads to a "jurisprudence of ultimate expedition." By one estimate, each housing judge handles over 12,000 cases per year, or an average of 33 1/3 per day. "These cases are disposed of at an average rate of five to fourteen minutes per case, with many settlements in the range of five minutes or less." According to one study, 34.4% of the cases lasted less than five minutes, while 71.7% of the cases lasted less than fifteen minutes.

* * *

In most cases in New York City's Housing Courts the landlord is represented by counsel, while the tenant is forced to appear without counsel. Landlords are represented in approximately ninety percent of the cases. In contrast, tenants are unrepresented in close to ninety percent of the cases, and, by some estimates, in greater than ninety percent of the cases. Hence, the typical case in Housing Court pits a represented landlord against an unrepresented tenant. Often, the landlord does not actually appear in court, leaving the landlord's lawyer and the unrepresented tenant as the sole participants in the proceeding.

Tenants in Housing Court are overwhelmingly poor women of color. Housing Court itself is typically referred to as a "poor people's court," and the statistics dramatically underscore the poverty of the tenants. Over eighty-five percent of the tenants are African-Americans and Latinos. Women comprise anywhere from two-thirds to four-fifths of the tenant population. Many tenants have a limited understanding of English, let alone legalese. White tenants and male tenants are more likely to be represented than female tenants or tenants of color. Unrepresented tenants therefore disproportionately come from groups that have experienced bias and powerlessness both inside and outside the legal system. This demographic makes unrepresented tenants particularly vulnerable in their encounters with opposing counsel.

Analysis of negotiations that occur in a hallway setting is difficult. The setting is unmonitored: no third party records the communications by the attorneys, and no transcripts exist. As a result, it is difficult to determine precisely the extent to which landlords' lawyers violate the prohibition against advice-giving to unrepresented tenants. The inquiry remains critical, however, because "most cases are settled with only minimal supervision by the court." Observation of New York's Housing Courts compels the conclusion that violations of the prohibition against advice-giving to an unrepresented adverse party are widespread.

The Housing Court setting renders unrepresented tenants particularly susceptible to overreaching landlords' lawyers. The settlements occur "away from the courtroom in the hurly-burly of the hallway." The enormous volume of cases, poor facilities, and high level of stress render the setting burdensome for virtually everyone. Many unrepresented tenants face the additional difficulty of coming to Housing Court with their children in tow. Additionally, some have a limited understanding of English. Even those who do understand English often do not grasp the complexities of the law.

The comments of observers reveal improper attorney behavior even under a narrow interpretation of impermissible advice-giving. A number of observers reported that landlords' attorneys engaged in behavior that is, at a minimum, overreaching:

> Ninety percent of tenants do not have lawyers and many—who may not speak English, much less know their rights—are bullied into signing hallway agreements by landlords' lawyers brandishing cellular phones, calculators and legal papers . . . .
>
> . . . .
>
> On the fourth-floor hallway, some tenants were backed against walls by landlords' lawyers waving a consent document known as a stipulation, or, in the slang of the court, a "stip."

In another account, "Landlord's lawyer . . . went into an interrogation of tenant. *Really* pressuring tenant." Were transcripts of encounters available, it would not be surprising to find statements that would constitute an opinion as to a proposed course of action, an opinion as to the applicability of the law to the facts, or even misleading statements as to the law and facts.

Some observations reflect the tenants' confusion as to whether the attorney was in one case the mediator and in another the judge.

> [A] short, wiry white man in a dark, double knit suit, his tie already loosened at 9:30 in the morning, stands in front of the bench calling out names. The first ten bring no answer. The eleventh yields an eager black man with a mock-fur hat. He rushes up to the white man and identifies himself.
>
> "Yes, that's me, sir," he whispers.
>
> There is some discussion, apparently about money, which I cannot hear completely, then: "Sign this stip, and you can go," the white man explains, not looking at him.
>
> The black man signs quickly, says, "Thank you, Your Honor," and rushes out.
>
> His Honor is not a judge. He is . . . counsel to the landlord in this case. [He] has just gotten his tenant/opponent to sign some sort of stipulation in an eviction proceeding that the tenant had . . . been fighting.

This behavior is, at a minimum, misleading as to the facts. * * * The behavior also violates Rule 4.3 of the Model Rules, which prohibits a lawyer from stating or implying that the lawyer is disinterested and requires the lawyer to make reasonable efforts to correct a misunderstanding as to the lawyer's role. Finally, this encounter illustrates the power disparity between unrepresented tenants and landlords' lawyers. The attorney's authority in the courthouse goes unquestioned by the tenant. Without counsel, disenfranchised parties agree to settlements without knowing their rights or understanding their cases.

The observed attorney comments and behavior effectively propose a course of action to the unrepresented tenant: the signing of a stipulation. The communications attempt to persuade the tenant to sign the stipulation:

> "Just sign this stip, o.k.?"
>
> "If the judge sees this doubtful look on your face or he thinks I'm taking advantage of you, it'll take hours," crooned a lawyer to a young woman. "But if you say you understand, we'll be out of here. You know I'm being a good guy and we're not fighting, right?" She looked doubtful and scared, but signed the stipulation. The lawyer grabbed it and dashed into a courtroom.

Suggesting to an unrepresented tenant how she should behave before the judge, reminding her that "we'll be out of here" if she acts a certain way, and reassuring her that the attorney is a good guy all amount to proposing a course of action: that the tenant sign the stipulation. The comments succeeded in inducing the tenant—looking "doubtful and scared"—to adopt the attorney's proposed course of action and sign the stipulation.

It would be comforting to conclude that the impermissible attorney behavior described above constitutes only an extreme, undertaken by a few isolated attorneys. One could then be content that, while steps need to be taken to deal with a few bad apples, the misconduct does not permeate the court's fundamental structure. The available information, however, indicates that such impermissible behavior is widespread. Moreover, a closer analysis of the negotiation process in New York City's Housing Court reveals that behavior far less extreme than the behavior observed would constitute impermissible advice-giving.

The comments of regular observers of, and participants in, the Housing Court suggest that improper attorney behavior is the rule, rather than the exception. * * * The consistent examples of attorney misconduct underscore the widespread nature of the behavior. The City-Wide Task Force on Housing Court has reported that "[l]andlords' lawyers are in the habit of aggressively approaching tenants in the courtroom (which is usually in chaos) or in hallways, and persuading them to sign stipulations." According to tenant advocates:

> The result is a lopsided system in which unrepresented tenants routinely are approached by landlord attorneys in court hallways

and pressured to sign complicated settlements that in many cases they cannot read, much less understand....

Attorneys from one legal services office have described the hallway negotiations as follows:

> Once the landlord's attorney does appear in the trial part, he will almost always engage in a settlement discussion with the pro se tenant without the judge or the judge's law assistant being present. No court-appointed translators are available to assist *pro se* tenants in these settlement discussions. The landlord's attorney will invariably focus solely on the amount of rent claimed owed by the landlord, and will frequently mislead the *pro se* tenant into believing that she has no option but to agree to the terms he is proposing.

The agreements themselves—the products of the hallway negotiations—provide further evidence of the widespread nature of the observed attorney behavior. An extensive body of law has emerged in which judges vacate stipulations previously entered into by a landlord's lawyer and an unrepresented tenant. The court may exercise its discretion to vacate stipulations that are unduly harsh or one-sided. Since the current ethical rules do not prohibit obtaining an unconscionable or one-sided agreement, the mere existence of an unduly one-sided agreement does not constitute an ethical violation. The agreements, however, result from unmonitored, hallway encounters between lawyers and unrepresented tenants. Landlords' lawyers routinely employ tactics central to negotiation: manipulation, argument, appeals, threats, and promises. These tactics are all designed to persuade the unrepresented tenant quickly to adopt a particular course of action: settlement on terms favorable to the landlord.

Tenants may unwittingly waive significant rights by accepting a hallway settlement agreement. Various New York State and local laws provide that a tenant may raise substantive and procedural defenses to the nonpayment proceeding, including claims such as breach of the warranty of habitability and rent overcharge. Yet, the agreements regularly include provisions regarding payment of rent or vacatur of the premises and ignore concerns of the tenants such as repairs or reductions in rent. Where tenants capitulate to the terms of a settlement agreement dictated by a landlord's lawyer, they often are inadvertently and unknowingly waiving important rights.

This realization underscores the extent to which the attorney misconduct extends far beyond bullying tenants and backing them against the wall. Consider even a well-intentioned landlord's lawyer, negotiating calmly and respectfully, in a relatively quiet corner of the hallway. The negotiation in a typical nonpayment case might include the following exchanges. The lawyer states that the tenant owes a certain amount of rent. If the tenant disputes the amount of rent, the lawyer asks for receipts, and explains that the tenant cannot be credited for payments absent receipts. If the tenant mentions conditions in need of repair, the lawyer agrees to have the landlord inspect the apartment, but tells the tenant that the rent still needs to be paid. The lawyer also tells the tenant that if the parties do not settle, the judge may only give the tenant five days to pay before being evicted.

The lawyer's seemingly innocuous comments are riddled with the lawyer's opinion as to the applicability of the law to the facts, and therefore constitute legal advice. Statements that a certain amount of rent is owed or that rent must be paid in the face of poor conditions are attorney opinions. For example, they include the attorney's opinion of whether the bookkeeping is correct, whether the proper level of rent is being charged, and whether the tenant's offsetting claims, such as the breach of the warranty of habitability, have merit. The statement that the tenant must show receipts reflects the lawyer's opinion that the landlord will carry his burden of proving the arrearage, and that the tenant may only prove her defense of payment of rent by showing receipts. The prediction as to what the court will do similarly includes the lawyer's opinion as to whether the court will recognize and give merit to procedural defenses that could lead to dismissal of the action, rather than judgment for the landlord. The prediction also includes the lawyer's opinion as to how the judge will rule on the substantive defenses.

Each comment comprises the attorney's opinion as to the applicability of the law to the facts of the case and may also be a misleading presentation of the law or the facts. Moreover, the comments, and others that may occur in the course of the negotiation, are intended to push the tenant toward settlement on the proposed terms. The comments therefore must be seen as an effort to influence the unrepresented tenant to take a course of action. The comments constitute improper advice-giving and underscore the extent to which the typical landlord's lawyer, conducting routine negotiations with an unrepresented tenant, may engage in impermissible attorney conduct.

The typical negotiation bears little resemblance to negotiations conducted within the constraints of * * * [the rules of professional responsibility]. Lawyers respecting the limitations on advice-giving should clarify that they are representing the landlord. They may, and perhaps should, advise the tenant to obtain legal counsel, or at least seek independent legal advice. They could inform the tenant of the terms on which the landlord will settle and the steps the lawyer (or the landlord) will take if the parties do not settle, such as going before the judge. If a tenant proposes additional or different terms, lawyers can accept the terms if they have authorization to do so. If the lawyer begins the process of persuasion, however, whether that entails explaining why the landlord is entitled to the terms, what the court might do if there is no settlement, or why the settlement is in the tenant's interest, then the lawyer has crossed the line and is engaging in impermissible advice-giving. Even in rejecting the tenant's proposals, the lawyer must avoid suggesting that the tenant is not entitled to what she is asking.

* * *

* * * [A] number of corrective steps are available to the profession. Given the scope of the problem, and the difficulties likely to arise with each corrective step, the legal profession's overall enforcement strategy must employ a range of options. States should increase enforcement of violations of [the rules of professional responsibility] in the context of negotiations between lawyers and unrepresented litigants. States should adopt additional disciplinary rules that will protect unrepresented parties forced to negotiate against lawyers. Courts must provide additional oversight to ensure that the rights of unrepresented litigants are protected. Finally, the profession must redouble its efforts to expand the provision of counsel in civil proceedings in which lawyers oppose unrepresented parties.

The need for the legal profession to address its own ethical problems, however broadly rooted, goes to the very integrity of the profession's system of self-government. The willingness of the profession to struggle for solutions should flow from the aspirational goals of the profession as well. "A lawyer should assist in improving the legal system."

> [L]awyers are especially qualified to recognize deficiencies in the legal system and to initiate corrective measures therein. Thus they should participate in proposing and supporting legislation and programs to improve the system, without regard to the general interests or desires of clients or former clients.

Notes and Questions

1. According to one commentator, "Power is America's last dirty word. It is easier to talk about money—and much easier to talk about sex—than it is to talk about power." Rosabeth Moss Kantor, *Power Failure in Management Circuits*, 57 Harv. Bus. Rev. 65 (1979). Why do you think she says that? Do you agree with her statement? Betrand Russell observed, "[T]he fundamental concept in social science is power, in the same sense in which energy is the fundamental concept in physics." Bertrand Russell, *Power: A New Social Analysis* 12 (1938). Is power a fundamental concept in legal representation? As a prospective lawyer, do you see yourself as having power because of your professional status? How is power associated with holding rights? During the civil rights struggle, issues of power were constantly addressed through protest: "Throughout the civil rights movement, two struggles were taking place simultaneously: a legal struggle and a protest struggle. * * * Many rights successfully litigated in the courts * * * were not honored in practice until actual conditions of discrimination were shown to the world through mass media coverage of protest activity." National Research Council, *A Common Destiny: Blacks and American Society* 220 (Gerald David Jaynes & Robert M. Williams, Jr. eds., 1989). In the mid-1960s, during the controversy over "black power," a group of African-American churchmen observed, "What we see shining through the variety of rhetoric [about black power] is not anything new but the same

old problem of power and race which has faced our beloved country since 1619.... We are now faced with a situation where conscienceless power meets powerless conscience, threatening the very foundations of our nation." *"Black Power"—A Statement by the National Committee of Negro Churchmen, July 31, 1966*, in *The Black Power Revolt* 264, 264 (Floyd B. Barbour ed., 1968). Few white individuals feel they are powerful in ways that discriminate against various nonwhite groups. Indeed, today's power is manifested primarily by institutions and organizations. How might the powerless negotiate against institutional and organizational power? How would social justice lawyers be of service? Can you think of examples? *See generally* Lani Guinier & Gerald Torres, *The Miner's Canary: Enlisting Race, Resisting Power, Transforming Democracy* (2002).

2. Over 150 years ago, Frederick Douglas wrote:

> The whole history of the progress of human liberty shows that all concessions, yet made to her august claims, have been born of earnest struggle. * * * If there is no struggle, there is no progress. Those who profess to favor freedom, and yet depreciate agitation, are men who want crops without plowing up the ground. They want rain without thunder and lightening. They want the ocean without the awful roar of its many waters. This struggle may be a moral one; or it may be a physical one; or it may be both moral and physical; but it must be a struggle. Power concedes nothing without a demand. It never did, and it never will. Find out just what people will submit to, and you have found out the exact amount of injustice and wrong which will be imposed upon them; and these will continue till they are resisted with either words or blows, or with both.

Frederick Douglas, *No Progress Without Struggle! 1849*, in *Black Power Revolt, supra* at 42. Do you see this observation as more or less obsolete in today's more complex world? Or do these eloquent words still resonate? Is there any way or context where you do see the notion of "struggle" tied to social justice advocacy? In what contexts do you see it manifested? Or is a sense of struggle now inappropriately missing from the orientation of social justice advocacy and movements? *See* chapters 11–14 where the place of struggle is incorporated into the quest for social justice.

3. In negotiating against more powerful forces, should advocates for social justice engage in the strategic use of the media? What are the challenges and opportunities that are presented in media advocacy? Regarding issues of race, for instance, the media matters a great deal in framing issues and presenting them to the public and policy makers. Two commentators state:

> [T]here is nothing in "reality" that compels the presentations of African Americans that the media offer. * * * The news does not usually reflect any conscious effort by journalists to cultivate their audiences' accurate understanding of racial matters. Rather, the news embodies the effects of tacitly obeying norms and following

> cultural patterns of which journalists are only imperfectly aware, and of responding to pressures from elites and markets which news organizations are disinclined to challenge.
>
> We cannot overlook the implications of these inadvertent racial patterns for Whites steeped in mainstream culture, especially for those tending toward racial animosity. The presences and absences of Blacks in key roles and situations create implicit racial comparisons. These construct a sense of the prototypical Black person that fits with anti-Black stereotypes readily served up by the culture. The omissions, along with the different subjects emphasized in stories depicting Blacks and Whites, imply exaggerated, fundamental differences between the two groups. They connote that membership in the category of Black persons reliably predicts that an individual will possess disfavored traits and behave improperly. Even if these intimations trace partially to racial differences in social behavior and role, in America they carry ideologically potent and damaging cultural connotations.

Robert M. Entman & Andrew Rojecki, *The Black Image in the White Mind: Media and Race in America* 77 (2000). Would these observations pertain to Asians and Latina/os as well?

4. Although Gerald López views using the media as an important aspect of progressive lawyering, he also presents a case memo that suggests practical limits to public advocacy. Gerald P. López, *Rebellious Lawyering: One Chicano's Vision of Progressive Practice* 206, 208 (1992). For example, lawyers are advised to seek press coverage only after they have exhausted efforts on behalf of their client with other "power brokers" in the community. Lawyers must be careful that premature press coverage may make a deal difficult to secure, especially if the coverage is excessive. Nonetheless, advocates of groups who are outside of the mainstream often rely on strategic use of the media in an attempt to influence public debate, because they "may feel that many of their legal theories will not get a hearing inside the courtroom without public pressure." Jonathan M. Moses, *Legal Spin Control: Ethics and Advocacy in the Court of Public Opinion*, 95 Colum. L. Rev. 1811, 1834, n.126 (1995). Moses adds, "Public interest clients also need a lawyer with a good sense of legal spin control because victories outside the courtroom may be more important than those inside." *Id.* at 1833.

5. Lani Guinier warns that newspeople too often "are not listening in order to hear a genuinely different or refreshing perspective. They are waiting to get a sound bite, a pithy statement that fits a preexisting frame. As a result, they train us to speak aloud not to be understood, but to be judged." Lani Guinier, *Lift Every Voice: Turning a Civil Rights Setback into a New Vision of Social Justice* 308 (1998). Guinier proposes a national conversation on race that would have multiple objectives: "to raise people's awareness of how race masks issues of resource distribution, to give potential allies a stake in our struggle, and, most important to encourage those with a fighting spirit to remain hopeful." *Id.* at 309.

Regarding these conversations, Guinier views them as "an important part of an ongoing national experiment in that the problem of race touches every nook and cranny of our [nation]. This process will almost certainly not resemble the mass movements of Selma, Alabama, in 1965. Those movements were right for their time, but their time is not now. For now, the objectives are more modest, but the long-range goals are just as ambitious." *Id.* Those goals would include rebuilding communities, reconnecting citizens, and ultimately providing laboratories for social justice. The conversations would "rekindle the sense of struggle and the concept of participatory democracy that was at the heart of the early civil rights mass movement. In this instance, the burgeoning idea that animates these conversations is that democracy—like learning—is often social, interactive, cooperative, and ongoing, as opposed to individualistic, isolated, competitive, and static." *Id.* One way that negotiation can be enhanced is through litigation that gives voice to those who are marginalized, so that they can initiate the type of conversation that Moses and Guinier contemplate. *See* Herbert A. Eastman, *Speaking Truth to Power: The Language of Civil Rights Litigators*, 104 Yale L. J. 763 (1995) (describing the benefits of "thick" pleadings in civil right cases).

6. Russell Engler describes a paradigm case of the powerless confronting the powerful where lawyers negotiate with unrepresented parties. What can be done about this? Ultimately, he suggests:

> An unwillingness or inability on the part of the profession to address ethical problems arising in lawyers' negotiations with the poor would send a powerful and unfortunate message about the efficacy of the rules themselves. It would reveal an inability on the part of the legal profession to regulate itself in a manner that identifies and eliminates attorney misconduct. It would also perpetuate the subordination and silencing of those who are often powerless in our legal system and our society.

Engler, *supra* at 158. What arguments might you make to a local bar association to intervene to correct this problem?

CHARLES B. CRAVER

Negotiation Ethics: How to Be Deceptive Without Being Dishonest/How to Be Assertive Without Being Offensive

38 S. Tex. L. Rev. 713, 713–34 (1997)

When experts discuss alternative dispute resolution procedures, they generally focus on mediation, neutral case evaluation, mini-trials, arbitration, and other forms of third-party intervention. They ignore the most basic form of dispute resolution—negotiation. Most practicing lawyers are not litigators. They handle family and property matters, trusts and estates, business transactions, tax liabilities, and similar situations. They almost never participate in judicial or arbitral adjudications. Most of their interactions with other lawyers involve negotiations. When direct negotiations do not generate mutual accords, they may request mediation assistance. Even litigators rarely participate in formal adjudications, due to the high financial and emotional costs and the unpredictable nature of those proceedings. They thus resolve ninety to ninety-five percent of their cases through direct inter-party discussions or mediator-assisted settlement talks.

Mediation is not a distinct form of dispute resolution. It is *assisted negotiation*. Mediators lack the authority to impose terms on disputants, they only possess the power of personal persuasion. They employ negotiation skills to reopen blocked communication channels and to encourage further inter-party discussions. Each mediator negotiates with the parties—jointly and separately—while the parties negotiate with each other through the mediator and directly with mediator assistance.

* * *

* * * [W]hile I have rarely participated in legal negotiations in which both participants did not use some misstatements to further client interests, I have encountered few dishonest lawyers. I suggest that the fundamental question is not whether legal negotiators may use misrepresentations to further client interests, but when and about what they may permissibly dissemble. Many negotiators initially find it difficult to accept the notion that disingenuous "puffing" and deliberate mendacity do not always constitute reprehensible conduct.

It is easy to exhort legal practitioners to behave in an exemplary manner when they participate in the negotiation process:

> [T]he lawyer is not free to do anything his client might do in the same circumstances .... [T]he lawyer must be at least as candid and honest as his client would be required to be .... Beyond that, the profession should embrace an affirmative ethical standard for attorneys' professional relationships with courts, other lawyers and the public: *The lawyer must act honestly and in good faith*. Another lawyer ... should not need to exercise the same degree of caution that he would if trading for reputedly antique copper jugs in an oriental bazaar....
>
> ....
>
> ... [S]urely the professional standards must ultimately impose upon him a duty not to accept an unconscionable deal. While some difficulty in line-drawing is inevitable when such a distinction is sought to be made, there must be a point at which the lawyer cannot ethically accept an arrangement that is completely unfair to the other side....

Despite the nobility of such pronouncements, others maintain that "[p]ious and generalized assertions that the negotiator must be 'honest' or that the lawyer must use 'candor' are not helpful." They recognize that negotiation interactions involve a deceptive process in which a certain amount of "puffing" and "embellishment" is expected, as the participants attempt to convince their opponents that they must obtain better terms than they must actually achieve.

Observers also note that trustworthiness is a relative concept that is rarely defined in absolute terms, based on different expectations in diverse situations.

> [T]rustworthiness and its outward manifestation—truth telling—are not absolute values. For example, no one tells the truth all of the time, nor is perpetual truth telling expected in most circumstances. To tell the truth in some social situations would be a rude convention. Consequently, when one speaks of the essential nature of trustworthiness and truth telling, one actually is talking about a certain circumstance or situation in which convention calls for trustworthiness or truth telling. Thus, a person considered trustworthy and a truth teller actually is a person who tells the truth at the right or necessary time.
>
> * * *

When students or practicing attorneys are asked whether they expect opposing counsel to candidly disclose their true authorized limits or their actual bottom lines at the beginning of bargaining interactions, most exhibit discernible discomfort. They recall the numerous times they have commenced negotiations with exaggerated or distorted position statements they did not expect their adversaries to take literally, and they begin to understand the dilemma confronted regularly by all legal negotiators.

> On the one hand the negotiator must be fair and truthful; on the other he must mislead his opponent. Like the poker player, a negotiator hopes that his opponent will overestimate the value of his hand. Like the poker player, in a variety of ways he must facilitate his opponent's inaccurate assessment. The critical difference between those who are successful negotiators and those who are not lies in this capacity both to mislead and not to be misled.
>
> ... [A] careful examination of the behavior of even the most forthright, honest, and trustworthy negotiators will show them actively engaged in misleading their opponents about their true positions.... To conceal one's true position, to mislead an opponent about one's true settling point, is the essence of negotiation.

Some writers criticize the use of deceptive negotiating tactics to further client interests. They maintain that these devices diminish the likelihood of * * * optimal results, because "deception tends to shift wealth from the risk-averse to the risk-tolerant." While this observation is undoubtedly true, it is unlikely to discourage the pervasive use of ethically permissible tactics that are designed to deceive risk-averse opponents into believing they must accept less beneficial terms than they need actually accept. It is thus unproductive to discuss a utopian negotiation world in which complete disclosure is the norm. The real question concerns the types of deceptive tactics that may ethically be employed to enhance bargaining interests. Attorneys who believe that no prevarication is ever proper during bargaining encounters place themselves and their clients at a distinct disadvantage, since they permit their less candid opponents to obtain settlements that transcend the terms to which they are objectively entitled.

The schizophrenic character of the ethical conundrum encountered by legal negotiators is apparent in the *ABA Model Rules of Professional Conduct*, which were adopted by the House of Delegates in August of 1983. Rule 4.1(a), which corresponds to EC 7–102(A)(5) under the *ABA Code of Professional Responsibility*, states that "[A] lawyer shall not knowingly . . . make a false statement of material fact or law to a third person." This seemingly unequivocal principle is intended to apply to both litigation and negotiation settings. An explanatory Comment under this Rule reiterates the fact that "[a] lawyer is required to be truthful when dealing with others on a client's behalf. . . . " Nonetheless, Comment Two acknowledges the difficulty of defining "truthfulness" in the unique context of the negotiation process:

> Whether a particular statement should be regarded as one of fact can depend on the circumstances. Under generally accepted conventions in negotiation, certain types of statements ordinarily are not taken as statements of material fact. Estimates of price or value placed on the subject of a transaction and a party's intentions as to an acceptable settlement of a claim are in this category. . . .

Even state bars that have not appended this Comment to their version of Rule 4.1 have appropriately recognized the ethical distinctions drawn in that Comment.

Although the *ABA Model Rules* unambiguously proscribe all lawyer prevarication, they reasonably, but confusingly, exclude mere "puffing" and dissembling regarding one's true minimum objectives. These important exceptions appropriately recognize that disingenuous behavior is indigenous to most legal negotiations and could not realistically be prevented due to the nonpublic nature of bargaining interactions.

> If one negotiator lies to another, only by happenstance will the other discover the lie. If the settlement is concluded by negotiation, there will be no trial, no public testimony by conflicting witnesses, and thus no opportunity to examine the truthfulness of assertions made during the negotiation. Consequently, in negotiation, more than in other contexts, ethical norms can probably be violated with greater confidence that there will be no discovery and punishment.

One of the inherent conflicts with regard to this area concerns the fact that what people label acceptable "puffing" when they make value-based representations during legal negotiations may be considered improper mendacity when uttered by opposing counsel.

Even though advocate prevarication during legal negotiations rarely results in bar disciplinary action, practitioners must recognize that other risks are created by truly dishonest bargaining behavior. Attorneys who deliberately deceive opponents regarding material matters or who withhold information they are legally obliged to disclose may be guilty of fraud. Contracts procured through fraudulent acts of commission or omission are voidable, and the responsible advocates and their clients may be held liable for monetary damages. It would be particularly embarrassing for lawyers to make misrepresentations that could cause their clients additional legal problems transcending those the attorneys were endeavoring to resolve. Since the adversely affected clients might thereafter sue their culpable former counsel for legal malpractice, the ultimate injury to the reputations and practices of the deceptive attorneys could be momentous. Legal representatives who employ clearly improper bargaining tactics may even subject themselves to judicial sanctions.

Even though Model Rule 4.1(a) states that attorneys must be truthful when they make statements concerning material law or fact, Comment One expressly indicates that lawyers have "no affirmative duty to inform an opposing party of relevant facts." In the absence of special relationships or express contractual or statutory duties, practitioners are normally not obliged to divulge relevant legal or factual information to their adversaries. This doctrine is premised upon the duty of representatives to conduct their own legal research and factual investigations. Under our adversary system, attorneys do not have the right to expect their opponents to assist them in this regard. It is only when cases reach tribunals that Model Rule 3.3(a)(3) imposes an affirmative obligation on advocates "to disclose to the tribunal legal authority in the controlling jurisdiction known to the lawyer to be directly adverse to the position of the client and not disclosed by opposing counsel." No such duty is imposed, however, with respect to pertinent factual circumstances that are not discovered by opposing counsel.

Suppose attorneys representing a severely injured plaintiff learn, during the critical stages of settlement talks, that their client has died due to unrelated factors. Would they be under an ethical duty to disclose this fact to defense counsel who are clearly assuming continuing pain and suffering and future medical care for the plaintiff? Although one court held that "[p]laintiff's attorney clearly had a duty to disclose the death of his client both to the Court and to opposing counsel prior to negotiating the final [settlement] agreement," this conclusion is not supported by the Comment to Rule 4.1 pertaining to negotiation discussions. Nonetheless, since the death of the plaintiff would presumably have necessitated the substitution of plaintiff's estate executor, plaintiff's counsel may have been under a duty to notify defense attorneys of this development before concluding any agreement that would have affected the estate. A similar issue would arise if plaintiff lawyers learned that their client had miraculously recovered from the serious condition that provides the basis of the current lawsuit. If plaintiff attorneys in either of these situations had previously answered interrogatories concerning the health of the plaintiff, they would probably be obliged under Federal Rule of Civil Procedure 26(e)(2) to supplement their previous responses. A party is under a duty to seasonably amend a prior response to an interrogatory, request for production, or request for admission if the party learns that the previous response is in some material respect incomplete or incorrect and if the additional or corrective information has not otherwise been made known to the other parties during the discovery process or in writing.

Suppose the party possessing the relevant information regarding the plaintiff is not the plaintiff's attorney, but rather defense counsel. This issue was confronted by the Minnesota Supreme Court in *Spaulding v. Zimmerman*. Plaintiff Spaulding was injured in an automobile accident when defendant Ledermann's car, in which the plaintiff was riding, collided with defendant Zimmerman's vehicle. He suffered multiple rib fractures, bilateral fractures of the clavicles, and a severe cerebral concussion. Several doctors who treated the plaintiff concluded that his injuries had completely healed. As the trial date approached, the defense attorneys had Spaulding examined by a neurologist who was expected to provide expert testimony for the defense. That physician agreed that the ribs and clavicles had healed, but discovered a life-threatening aneurysm on Spaulding's aorta. Defense counsel were never asked by plaintiff counsel about the results of this examination, and the defense lawyers did not volunteer any information about it.

A settlement agreement was achieved, which had to be approved by the trial court since Spaulding was a minor. After the case was settled, Spaulding discovered the aneurysm, which was surgically repaired, and he sued to set aside the prior settlement. The trial court vacated the settlement, and this decision was sustained by the Minnesota Supreme Court. Despite the fact that most people would undoubtedly regard an affirmative duty to disclose the crucial information as the morally appropriate approach, the Minnesota Supreme Court correctly determined that the defense attorneys were under no ethical duty to volunteer the new medical information to plaintiff counsel. In fact, without client consent, the confidentiality preservation obligation imposed by Model Rule 1.6 would preclude volitional disclosure by defense counsel under these circumstances. Comment 5 explicitly states that "[t]he confidentiality rule applies not merely to matters communicated in confidence by the client but also to all information relating to the representation, whatever its source."

The *Spaulding* court circumvented the Rule 1.6 prohibition by holding that as officers of the court, defense counsel had an affirmative duty to disclose the newly discovered medical information to the trial court prior to its approval of the settlement agreement. Had Spaulding not been a minor, the court may have had to enforce the original accord, because of the absence of any trial court involvement in the settlement process. If courts are unwilling to impose affirmative disclosure obligations on advocates who possess such critical information pertaining to opposing clients, they should sustain the resulting settlement agreements despite the lack of disclosure. This would at least permit defense lawyers to divulge the negative information as soon as the settlement terms have been satisfied. By voiding such agreements after plaintiffs learn of the withheld information, courts effectively require defense attorneys to remain silent even after the lawsuits have been finally resolved.

Attorneys can easily avoid these disclosure problems by remembering to ask the appropriate questions concerning uncertain areas before they enter into settlement agreements. Defense lawyers can directly ask if the plaintiff's condition has changed in any way. Plaintiff representatives could not ethically misrepresent the material condition of their client. If they were to use evasive techniques to avoid direct responses, defense lawyers should restate their inquiries and demand specific answers. If plaintiff attorneys know that defense counsel have had the plaintiff examined by a medical expert, they should always ask about the results of that examination. They should also request a copy of the resulting medical report, since they are entitled to that information in exchange for the right of defense counsel to have the plaintiff examined. While defense counsel may merely confirm what plaintiff lawyers already know, it is possible that plaintiff attorneys will obtain new information that will affect settlement discussions.

Suppose plaintiff or defense lawyers are on the verge of a lawsuit settlement based upon a line of State Supreme Court cases favoring their client. The morning of the day they are going to conclude their transaction, the State Supreme Court issues an opinion overturning those beneficial decisions and indicating that the new rule applies to all pending cases. Would knowledgeable attorneys whose position has been undermined by these legal changes be obligated to inform their unsuspecting opponents about these critical judicial developments? Almost all practitioners asked this question respond in the negative, based on their belief that opposing counsel are obliged to conduct their own legal research. Sagacious lawyers would recognize, however, that they could no longer rely upon the overturned decisions to support their afternoon discussions, because these legal misstatements would contravene Rule 4.1. On the other hand, they could probably ask their unsuspecting adversaries if they could cite a single case supporting their position!

Negotiators regularly use selective disclosures to enhance their positions. They divulge the legal doctrines and factual information beneficial to their claims, while withholding circumstances that are not helpful. In most instances, these selective disclosures are expected by opponents and are considered an inherent aspect of bargaining interactions. When attorneys emphasize their strengths, opposing counsel must attempt to ascertain their undisclosed weaknesses. They should carefully listen for verbal leaks and look for nonverbal signals that may indicate the existence of possible opponent problems. Probing questions may be used to elicit some negative information, and external research may be employed to gather other relevant data. These efforts are particularly important when opponents carefully limit their disclosures to favorable circumstances, since their partial disclosures may cause listeners to make erroneous assumptions.

When I discuss negotiating ethics with legal practitioners, I often ask if lawyers are obliged to disclose information to correct erroneous factual or legal assumptions made by opposing counsel. Most respondents perceive no duty to correct legal or factual misunderstandings generated solely by the carelessness of opposing attorneys. Respondents only hesitate when opponent misperceptions may have resulted from misinterpretations of seemingly honest statements made by them. For example, when a plaintiff attorney embellishes the pain being experienced by a client with a severely sprained ankle, the defense lawyer may indicate how painful *broken* ankles can be. If the plaintiff representative has said nothing to create this false impression, should he or she be obliged to correct the obvious defense counsel error? Although a respectable minority of respondents believe that an affirmative duty to correct the misperception may exist here—due to the fact plaintiff embellishments may have inadvertently contributed to the misunderstanding—most respondents feel no such obligation. So long as they have not directly generated the erroneous belief, it is not their duty to correct it. They could not, however, include their opponent's misunderstanding in their own statements, since this would cause them to improperly articulate knowing misrepresentations of material fact.

When opponent misperceptions concern legal doctrines, almost no respondents perceive a duty to correct those misconceptions. They indicate that each side is obliged to conduct its own legal research. If opposing counsel make incorrect assumptions or carelessly fail to locate applicable statutes or cases, those advocates do not have the right to expect their adversaries to provide them with legal assistance. The more knowledgeable advocates may even continue to rely on precedents supporting their own claims, so long as they do not distort those decisions or the opinions supporting the other side's positions.

* * *

* * * When lawyers are asked if negotiators may overtly misrepresent legal or factual matters, most immediately reply in the negative. Many lawyers cite Model Rule 4.1 and suggest that this prohibition covers all intentional misrepresentations. While attorneys are correct with respect to deliberate misstatements by negotiators concerning material legal doctrines, they are not entirely correct with respect to factual issues. Almost all negotiators expect opponents to engage in "puffing" and "embellishment." Advocates who hope to obtain $50,000 settlements may initially insist upon $150,000 or even $200,000. They may also embellish the pain experienced by their client, so long as their exaggerations do not transcend the bounds of expected propriety. Individuals involved in a corporate buy out may initially over- or under-value the real property, the building and equipment, the inventory, the accounts receivable, the patent rights and trademarks, and the goodwill of the pertinent firm.

It is clear that lawyers may not intentionally misrepresent *material facts*, but it is not always apparent what facts are "*material*." The previously noted Comment to Rule 4.1 explicitly acknowledges that "[e]stimates of price or value placed on the subject of a transaction and a party's intentions as to an acceptable settlement of a claim" do not constitute *material* facts under that provision. It is thus ethical for legal negotiators to misrepresent the value their client places on particular items. For example, attorneys representing one spouse involved in a marital dissolution may indicate that their client wants joint custody of the children, when in reality he or she does not. Lawyers representing a party attempting to purchase a particular company may understate their client's belief regarding the value of the goodwill associated with the target firm. So long as the statement conveys their side's belief—and does not falsely indicate the view of an outside expert, such as an accountant—no Rule 4.1 violation would occur.

Legal negotiators may also misrepresent client settlement intentions. They may ethically suggest to opposing counsel that an outstanding offer is unacceptable, even though they know the proposed terms would be accepted if no additional concessions could be generated. Nonetheless, it is important to emphasize that this Rule 4.1 exception does not wholly excuse all misstatements regarding client settlement intentions. During the early stages of bargaining interactions, most practitioners do not expect opponents to disclose exact client desires. As negotiators approach final agreements, however, they anticipate a greater degree of candor. If negotiators were to deliberately deceive adversaries about this issue during the closing stage of their interaction, most attorneys would consider them dishonest, even though the Rule 4.1 proscription would remain inapplicable.

The relevant Comments to Rule 4.1 are explicitly restricted to *negotiations* with *opposing* counsel. Outside that narrow setting, statements pertaining to client settlement objectives may constitute "material" fact. *ABA Commission on Ethics and Professional Responsibility, Formal Opinion* 370 indicated that knowing misrepresentations regarding client settlement intentions to judges during pretrial settlement discussions would be impermissible because the misstatements would not be confined to adversarial bargaining interactions.

When material facts are involved, attorneys may not deliberately misrepresent the actual circumstances. They may employ evasive techniques to avoid answering opponent questions, but they may not provide false or misleading answers. If they decide to respond to inquiries pertaining to material facts, they must do so honestly. They must also be careful not to issue partially correct statements they know will be misinterpreted by their opponents, since such deliberate deception would be likely to contravene Rule 4.1.

A crucial distinction is drawn between statements of lawyer opinion and statements of material fact. When attorneys merely express their opinions—for example, "I think the defendant had consumed too much alcohol" and "I believe the plaintiff will encounter future medical difficulties"—they are not constrained by Rule 4.1. Opposing counsel know that these recitations only concern the personal views of the speakers. Thus, personal view statements are critically different from lawyer statements indicating that they have witnesses who can testify to these matters. If representations regarding witness information is knowingly false, the misstatements would clearly violate Rule 4.1.

A frequently debated area concerns representations about one's authorized limits. Many attorneys refuse to answer "unfair" questions concerning their authorized limits because these inquiries pertain to confidential attorney-client communications. If negotiators decide to respond to these queries, must they do so honestly? Some lawyers believe that truthful responses are required, since they concern material facts. Other practitioners assert that responses about client authorizations merely reflect client valuations and settlement intentions and are thus excluded from the scope of Rule 4.1 by the drafter's Comment. For this reason, these practitioners think that attorneys may distort these matters.

Negotiators who know they cannot avoid the impact of questions concerning their authorized limits by labeling them "unfair" and who find it difficult to provide knowingly false responses can employ an alternative approach. If the plaintiff lawyer who is demanding $120,000 asks the defendant attorney who is presently offering $85,000 whether he or she is authorized to provide $100,000, the recipient may treat the $100,000 figure as a new plaintiff proposal. That individual can reply that the $100,000 sum suggested by plaintiff counsel is more realistic but still exorbitant. The plaintiff attorney may become preoccupied with the need to clarify the fact that he or she did not intend to suggest any reduction in his or her outstanding $120,000 demand. That person would probably forego further attempts to ascertain the authorized limits possessed by the defendant attorney!

In recent years, a number of legal representatives—especially in large urban areas—have decided to employ highly offensive tactics to advance client interests. They may be rude, sarcastic, or nasty. These individuals erroneously equate discourteous actions with effective advocacy. They use these techniques as a substitute for lawyering skill. Proficient practitioners recognize that impolite behavior is the antithesis of competent representation.

Legal representatives should eschew tactics that are merely designed to humiliate or harass opponents. *ABA Model Rule* 4.4 expressly states that "[A] lawyer shall not use means that have no substantial purpose other than to embarrass, delay, or burden a third person . . . ." Demented win-lose negotiators occasionally endeavor to achieve total annihilation of adversaries through the cruel and unnecessary degradation of opposing counsel. When advocates obtain munificent settlement terms for their client, there is no reason for them to employ tactics intended to discomfort their adversaries. Not only is such behavior morally reprehensible, but it needlessly exposes the offensive perpetrators to future recriminations that could easily be avoided through common courtesy.

This approach also guarantees the offensive actors far more nonsettlements than are experienced by their more cooperative cohorts, and it tends to generate less efficient bargaining distributions.

Many practicing attorneys seem to think that competitive/adversarial negotiators—who use highly competitive tactics to maximize their own client returns—achieve more beneficial results for their clients than their cooperative/problem-solving colleagues—who employ more cooperative techniques designed to maximize the joint return to the parties involved. An empirical study, conducted by Professor Gerald Williams, of legal practitioners in Denver and Phoenix contradicts this notion. Professor Williams found that sixty-five percent of negotiators are considered cooperative/problem-solvers by their peers, twenty-four percent are viewed as competitive/adversarial, and eleven percent did not fit in either category. When the respondents were asked to indicate which attorneys were "effective," "average," and "ineffective" negotiators, the results were striking. While fifty-nine percent of the cooperative/problem-solving lawyers were rated "effective," only twenty-five percent of competitive/adversarial attorneys were rated effective. On the other hand, while a mere three percent of cooperative/problem-solvers were considered "ineffective," thirty-three percent of competitive/adversarial bargainers were rated "ineffective."

In his study, Professor Williams found that certain traits were shared by both effective cooperative/problem-solving negotiators and effective competitive/adversarial bargainers. Successful negotiators from both groups are thoroughly prepared, behave in an honest and ethical manner, are perceptive readers of opponent cues, are analytical, realistic, and convincing, and observe the courtesies of the bar. The proficient negotiators from both groups also sought to *maximize* their *own client's* return. Since this is the quintessential characteristic of competitive/adversarial bargainers, it would suggest that a number of successful negotiators may be adroitly masquerading as sheep in wolves' clothing. They exude a cooperative style, but seek competitive objectives.

Most successful negotiators are able to combine the most salient traits associated with the cooperative/problem-solving and the competitive/adversarial styles. They endeavor to maximize client returns, but attempt to accomplish this objective in a congenial and seemingly ingenuous manner. They look for shared values in recognition of the fact that by maximizing joint returns, they are more likely to obtain the best settlements for their own clients. Although successful negotiators try to manipulate opponent perceptions, they rarely resort to truly deceitful tactics. They know that a loss of credibility will undermine their ability to achieve beneficial results. Despite the fact successful negotiators want as much as possible for their own clients, they are not "win-lose" negotiators who judge their results, not by how well they have done, but by how poorly they think their opponents have done. They realize that the imposition of poor terms on opponents does not necessarily benefit their own clients. All factors being equal, they want to maximize opponent satisfaction. So long as it does not require significant concessions on their part, they acknowledge the benefits to be derived from this approach. The more satisfied opponents are, the more likely those parties will accept proposed terms and honor the resulting agreements.

These eclectic negotiators employ a composite style. They may be characterized as competitive/problem-solvers. They seek competitive goals (maximum client returns), but endeavor to accomplish these objectives through problem-solving strategies. They exude a cooperative approach and follow the courtesies of the legal profession. They avoid rude or inconsiderate behavior, recognizing that such openly adversarial conduct is likely to generate competitive/adversarial responses from their opponents. They appreciate the fact that individuals who employ wholly inappropriate tactics almost always induce opposing counsel to work harder to avoid exploitation by these openly opportunistic bargainers. Legal negotiators who are contemplating the use of offensive techniques should simply ask themselves how they would react if similar tactics were employed against them.

* * *

What about seemingly one-sided arrangements that have not been procured through improper means and do not constitute legally unconscionable agreements? Should it be considered unethical or morally reprehensible for attorneys to negotiate such contracts? This concept would place the responsible advocates in a tenuous position. If courts would be unlikely to find the proposed agreements illegal and the opposing parties were perfectly willing to consummate the apparently skewed transactions, should the prevailing legal representatives refuse to conclude the deals merely because they believe the transactions may unreasonably disadvantage their opponents? Why should the subjective personal judgments of these lawyers take precedence over the willingness of their opponents and their attorneys to conclude the proposed exchanges? These individuals may not know—and may never know—why their opponents considered these deals "fair." Their adversaries may have been aware of factual or legal circumstances that either undermined their own positions or bolstered those of the other side.

Some lawyers might reasonably feel compelled to mention the apparently one-sided aspect of the suggested transactions to their own clients. A few might even feel the need to explore this concern at least obliquely with opposing counsel. Would it be appropriate for them to refuse to consummate the agreements even when the other participants still favor their execution? If they continued to sanctimoniously oppose the proposed deals, should they be subject to bar discipline for failing to represent their client with appropriate zeal, or to liability for legal malpractice? Attorneys who are positioned to conclude lawful arrangements that would substantially benefit their clients should be hesitant to vitiate the transactions based solely on their own personal conviction that the proffered terms are "unfair" to their opponents. How many lawyers in these circumstances would inform their clients that they were unwilling to accept offers tendered by opposing parties in response to wholly proper bargaining tactics, merely because they thought the proposed terms were too generous?

Practitioners and law students occasionally ask whether lawyers who represent clients in civil actions arising out of arguably criminal conduct may suggest the possibility of criminal prosecution if the civil suit negotiations are not completed successfully. DR 7–105(A) of the *ABA Code of Professional Responsibility*, still followed in some jurisdictions, states that lawyers shall not "threaten to present criminal charges solely to obtain an advantage in a civil matter." This provision might be read to preclude the mention of possible criminal action to advance civil suit discussions. Courts have appropriately acknowledged, however, that neither DR 7–105(A) nor extortion or compounding of felony prohibitions should be interpreted to prevent civil litigants from mentioning the availability of criminal action if related civil claims are not resolved or to preclude clients from agreeing to forego the filing of criminal charges in exchange for money paid to resolve their civil suits. Nonetheless, legal representatives must be careful not to use the threat of criminal prosecution to obtain *more* than is owed or have their clients agree not to testify at future criminal trials. "Seeking payment beyond restitution in exchange for foregoing a criminal prosecution or seeking any payments in exchange for not testifying at a criminal trial ... are still clearly prohibited."

The Model Rules do not contain any provision analogous to DR 7–105(A), and it is clear that the drafters deliberately chose not to prohibit the threat of criminal action to advance civil suit settlement talks pertaining to the same operative circumstances. As a result, the ABA Standing Committee on Ethics and Professional Responsibility indicated in *Formal Opinion 363*, that it is not unethical under the *Model Rules* for attorneys to mention the possibility of criminal charges during civil suit negotiations, so long as they do "not attempt to exert or suggest improper influence over the criminal process." Nevertheless, legal representatives must still not demand excessive compensation that may contravene applicable extortion provisions or promise that their clients will not testify at future criminal trials.

Despite the contrary impression of some members of the general public, I have generally found attorneys to be conscientious and honorable people. I have encountered few instances of questionable behavior. I would thus like to conclude with the admonitions I impart to my Legal Negotiating students as they prepare to enter the legal profession. Lawyers must remember that they have to live with their own consciences, and not those of their clients or their partners. They must employ tactics they are comfortable using, even in those situations in which other people encourage them to employ less reputable behavior. If they adopt techniques they do not consider appropriate, not only will they experience personal discomfort, but they will also fail to achieve their intended objective due to the fact they will not appear credible when using those tactics. Attorneys must also acknowledge that they are members of a special profession and owe certain duties to the public that transcend those that may be owed by people engaged in other businesses. Even though *ABA Model Rule* 1.3 states that "[a] lawyer shall act with reasonable diligence," Comment One expressly recognizes that "a lawyer is not bound to press for every advantage that might be realized for a client. A lawyer has professional discretion in determining the means by which a matter [shall] be pursued."

Popular negotiation books occasionally recount the successful use of questionable techniques to obtain short-term benefits. The authors glibly describe the way they have employed highly aggressive, deliberately deceptive, or equally opprobrious bargaining tactics to achieve their objectives. They usually conclude these stories with parenthetical admissions that their bilked adversaries would probably be reluctant to interact with them in the future. When negotiators engage in such questionable behavior such that they would find it difficult, if not impossible, to transact future business with their adversaries, they have usually transcended the bounds of propriety. No legal representatives should be willing to jeopardize long-term professional relationships for the narrow interests of particular clients. Zealous representation should never be thought to require the employment of personally compromising techniques.

Lawyers must acknowledge that they are not guarantors—they are only legal advocates. They are not supposed to guarantee client victory no matter how disreputably they must act to do so. They should never countenance witness perjury or the withholding of subpoenaed documents. While they should zealously endeavor to advance client interests, they should recognize their moral obligation to follow the ethical rules applicable to all attorneys.

Untrustworthy advocates encounter substantial difficulty when they negotiate with others. Their oral representations must be verified and reduced to writing, and many opponents distrust their written documents. Their negotiations become especially problematic and cumbersome. If nothing else moves practitioners to behave in an ethical and dignified manner, their hope for long and successful legal careers should induce them to avoid conduct that may undermine their future effectiveness.

Attorneys should diligently strive to advance client objectives while simultaneously maintaining their personal integrity. This philosophy will enable them to optimally serve the interests of both their clients and society. * * *

GERALD B. WETLAUFER

The Ethics of Lying in Negotiation
75 Iowa L. Rev. 1219, 1220–21, 1223–24, 1272 (1990)

If it is true that lawyers succeed in the degree to which they are effective in negotiations, it is equally true that one's effectiveness in negotiations depends in part upon one's willingness to lie. As Professor James J. White has written:

> Like the poker player, a negotiator hopes that his opponent will overestimate the value of his hand. Like the poker player, in a variety of ways he must facilitate his opponent's inaccurate assessment. The critical difference between those who are successful negotiators and those who are not lies in this capacity both to mislead and not to be misled.
>
> Some experienced negotiators will deny the accuracy of this assertion, but they will be wrong. I submit that a careful examination of the behavior of even the most forthright, honest, and trustworthy negotiators will show them actively engaged in misleading their opponents about their true position .... To conceal one's true position, to mislead an opponent about one's true settling point, is the essence of negotiation.

* * * [T]he ethics to which I am here referring are not the rules embodied in the lawyers' code of professional self-regulation but, instead, the broader and, I will argue, distinct inquiry into the principles of right or good conduct.

Many lawyers deny White's claim and assert, one way or another, that honesty is the best policy in the specific sense that in the long run it is the most profitable. They argue that lying in negotiations is ineffective. Others acknowledge the truth of White's claim but then argue that lying in negotiations is not a serious problem because those lies are ethically permissible. This, as I understand it, is White's own position. I will present a third position by arguing that lying in negotiations is instrumentally effective and that most such lies are ethically impermissible.

* * *

For purposes * * * [here], "lying" will be defined to include all means by which one might attempt to create in some audience a belief at variance with one's own. These means include intentional communicative acts, concealments and omissions. * * *

* * *

My definition of lying, it will be noted, does not rely upon the distinction between what is "true" and what is "false." It is drawn instead in terms of "beliefs at variance with one's own." The advantage of this approach is that it permits us to frame our inquiry into the ethics of lying in such a way that we do not become mired in unresolvable and, I think, irrelevant debates over what is true or, worse still, over the nature of truth. * * * [A] particular "lie" may be ethically permissible because its subject is one as to which there is no knowable "truth."

* * *

Effectiveness in negotiations is central to the business of lawyering and a willingness to lie is central to one's effectiveness in negotiations. Within a wide range of circumstances, well-told lies are highly effective. Moreover, the temptation to lie is great not just because lies are effective, but also because the world in which most of us live is one that honors instrumental effectiveness above all other things. Most lawyers are paid not for their virtues but for the results they produce. Our clients, our partners and employees, and our families are all counting on us to deliver the goods. Accordingly, and regrettably, lying is not the province of a few "unethical lawyers" who operate on the margins of the profession. It is a permanent feature of advocacy and thus of almost the entire province of law.

Our discomfort with that fact has, I believe, led us to create and embrace a discourse on the ethics of lying that is uncritical, self-justificatory and largely unpersuasive. Our motives in this seem reasonably clear. Put simply, we seek the best of both worlds. On the one hand, we would capture as much of the available surplus as we can. In doing so, we enrich our clients and ourselves. Further, we gain for ourselves a reputation for personal power and instrumental effectiveness. And we earn the right to say we can never be conned. At the same time, on the other hand, we assert our claims to a reputation for integrity and personal virtue, to the high status of a profession, and to the legitimacy of the system within which we live and work. * * * [The author concludes that lawyers can not convincingly assert both of these claims.]

Notes and Questions

1. Both Charles Craver and Gerald Wetlaufer tolerate a substantial degree of misrepresentation in negotiation. Indeed, Wetlaufer declares, "The problem of lying in negotiations is central to the profession of law." Do you agree? Does your role as a zealous advocate force you to lie on behalf of the client in order to negotiate effectively? Does a problem-solving approach to negotiation reduce the need to lie? Robert Bastress and Joseph Harbaugh compare the process of adversarial and problem-solving negotiation:

> * * * Adversarials proceed linearly to develop their plans, concentrating and defending positions along the bargaining continuum. Planning by problem solvers, on the other hand, focuses on identifying needs and brainstorming to develop solutions for mutual gains. Adversarials engage in positional argument while problem solvers tend to explore interests. Adversarials make offers to which they appear to be committed. Problem solvers advance proposals that invite opponents to accept, reject, or modify based on how the proposals intersect with their interests. Adversarials are more likely to restrict information flow, problem solvers more inclined to exchange data. Adversarials reject the opponents' offers summarily and make concessions along the continuum. Problem solvers explain why solutions are acceptable or unacceptable in whole or in part based on a needs analysis. They also seldom make concessions, as their adversarial colleagues do, but instead shift to another proposal that more completely addresses the parties' mutual problems.

Robert M. Bastress & Joseph D. Harbaugh, *Interviewing, Counseling, and Negotiating: Skills for Effective Representation* 383 (1990). How easy is it to separate these two approaches during a negotiation?

2. Although problem solving seems to be an important instrument in the social justice tool kit, do you see disadvantages in trying to use it as a negotiation strategy? The most obvious disadvantage is that it cannot be employed in a case where the parties are bargaining over a fungible resource, like money. *Id.* at 384. Another downside to problem solving is the great deal of time and energy that it may take and the parties may end up in a relationship that is discomforting. *Id.* at 385. Moreover, some settings simply do not lend themselves to a problem-solving approach: "The parties may be too wealthy, too powerful, or too set in their bargaining ways to consider seriously negotiating for mutual gain. * * * We cannot force an opponent to candidly discuss its needs and interests and then engage in a creative search for mutually satisfactory solutions." *Id.* at 385–86. Finally, do you think that an adversarial negotiator will just out negotiate a problem solver—that is, prove generally to be a more effective negotiator?

3. Respect for others and reinforcing human dignity are social justice values. How might these be incorporated in negotiation? *See* Jonathan R. Cohen, *When People Are the Means: Negotiating with Respect*, 14 Geo. J. Legal Ethics 739, 768 (2001) ("The orientational duty to respect others in negotiation is rooted in the other person's humanity. Derivative upon the conception of fundamental human dignity, we have a general duty to respect other people and the negotiation process does not excuse us of it."). Do you agree that you can take this position and still be an effective advocate? Must there at least be a demonstration of mutual respect, some reciprocity, for Cohen's approach to work? If the other side has done harm to your client, would you "turn the other cheek" and nonetheless proceed with respect for the other side? If you respect the other side, are you likely to be "eaten alive" if the other side is disrespectful toward you and your client and adopts an adverserial posture?

4. While negotiated settlement is the norm empirically, are there costs associated with an over-reliance on settlement at the expense of adjudication? Consider the following article and evaluate the arguments that suggest there are substantial costs involved. Do you agree?

KEVIN C. McMUNIGAL

The Costs of Settlement: The Impact of Scarcity of Adjudication on Litigation Lawyers
37 UCLA L. Rev. 833, 844–47, 849–50, 852, 855–70, 872, 875–77, 880–81 (1990)

Two related questions have generated considerable debate in recent years: Is the degree of our present reliance on settlement desirable? Should that reliance be encouraged and increased? Proponents of settlement answer "yes" to both questions, offering various arguments in favor of settlement and devices aimed at its promotion. Prominent among the proffered merits of settlement are savings of time and money.

Settlement, its advocates argue, avoids much of the delay and financial cost increasingly associated with trial and appeal. These savings are viewed not just as virtues, but as necessities in an era of limited adjudicative resources and expanding court caseloads.

A second theme among settlement advocates is the avoidance of psychological and emotional costs to litigants. Settlement and related processes, with their emphasis on compromise, exact less of a toll on the parties. Some view the process of encouraging settlement as motivated by a spirit of personal reconciliation which rests on values of "religion, community, and work place." Settlement techniques may also "personalize" the process of resolving disputes by allowing more direct participation by the parties than would the formal processes of adjudication.

Finally, settlement outcomes are seen as superior to those of adjudication, in part because settlement avoids the "zero-sum" aspect of adjudication. Moreover, settlement proponents argue that parties are more likely to comply with a resolution they consented to and had a role in shaping than one imposed by a neutral third party. Other advantages claimed for some ADR mechanisms are privacy, procedural flexibility, and the ability of the parties to choose someone with substantive expertise in the area of dispute to facilitate settlement.

These arguments have not gone unchallenged. One critic of settlement captures some of the tone and substance of the opposition in the following passage:

> I do not believe that settlement as a generic practice is preferable to judgment or should be institutionalized on a wholesale and indiscriminate basis. It should be treated instead as a highly problematic technique for streamlining dockets. Settlement is for me the civil analogue of plea bargaining: Consent is often coerced; the bargain may be struck by someone without authority; the absence of a trial and judgment renders subsequent judicial involvement troublesome; and although dockets are trimmed, justice may not be done. Like plea bargaining, settlement is a capitulation to the conditions of mass society and should be neither encouraged nor praised.

Critics of settlement respond to its efficiency claims by arguing that settlement, though often producing speedier and less expensive resolutions than adjudication, does not solve the problems of cost and delay. If distributional inequalities exist between the parties, the cost and delay of adjudication tend unfairly to distort the terms of the settlement in favor of the party with greater resources, preventing the settlement from reflecting the merits of each party's position. Second, the voluntariness of many settlements is subject to question; driven by the costs and delays of adjudication, parties may be coerced to settle. In addition, authoritative consent may be lacking because of conflicts of interest between the party and the lawyer conducting the settlement negotiations or because organizations and groups often lack procedures for generating authoritative consent. Since settlement derives its authority from the consent of the parties, potential coercion or absence of authoritative consent undermines the legitimacy of settlement.

* * *

Perhaps the most fundamental argument against settlement is that overreliance on it both undervalues and undermines the rule of law, because it makes compromise rather than enforcement of factual and legal claims the ascendant value. It elevates peace over our traditional idea of justice. Settlement may compromise not only the rule of law, but also respect for our entire system of justice, since adjudication is basic to a civilized society and is "the means by which society keeps the promises of its substantive law."

* * *

Perhaps the most obvious impact one would expect from scarcity of trial experience is a diminution in lawyer competence in the forensic skills used to try a case, such as cross-examination and closing argument. * * *

* * *

Scarcity of trials may compromise lawyer forensic skills in two distinct ways.

First, such a scarcity reduces the opportunities for lawyers to obtain and retain basic advocacy skills by actually trying cases. * * *

* * *

Scarcity of trials may threaten advocacy skills in a second and different way. Actual trials are not the only way to obtain trial skills. Lack of opportunity to learn through real trials can in part be remedied by providing substitute learning experiences, such as trial simulation courses. Yet, such programs are not perfect substitutes for real trials since they cannot reproduce all of the pressures inherent in a real trial. Nevertheless, certain characteristics which make them unrealistic, such as the opportunity for videotaping and critiquing student performances, actually may make them better teaching devices than real trials. One might expect, then, that lack of opportunity to try real cases might be compensated for in good measure through increased use of other means of acquiring advocacy skills.

* * *

The issue of competence in advocacy skills poses an ethical concern which implicates both the interests of individual clients and broader systemic concerns as well. In an adversary system, the skill of lawyers in developing factual and legal issues is critical to the system's functioning. As long as we retain a system of adjudication which relies on lawyers and their forensic skills to define and develop the issues for adjudication, lack of advocacy skills not only disserves clients, but also inhibits the system's ability to perform, reducing the quality of the results it produces. If there is an imbalance in trial skills between the lawyers on each side of a case, this asymmetry can compound the problems generated by poor trial skills.

Furthermore, the systemic impact of poor advocacy quality will not be limited to those few cases which are adjudicated. A system such as ours, in which settlement is the dominant mode of dispute resolution, relies on the results of the adjudicatory processes of trial and appeal to produce precedents which serve as guides to settlement. It is in the "shadow" of these adjudicated cases that most cases are resolved by settlement. If the adjudicatory process and its results suffer from an inadequate supply of skilled advocates, both adjudicated cases and those settled in their "shadow" suffer.

Proponents of adjudication have criticized settlement on a number of grounds. One point of attack has been the validity of the assumption of settlement proponents that the terms of a settlement accurately reflect the relative merits of each party's position. The tendency of a settlement to reflect the likely outcome on the merits at trial may be distorted, sometimes quite dramatically, by inequalities between the parties in areas other than the strength of their claims or defenses. Imbalance in financial resources, for example, may impair one party's ability to conduct adequate investigation. Consequently, one party's lack of knowledge may render it unable to predict accurately the likely outcome at trial and to bargain on that basis. Even if the party knows the likely outcome, the settlement may be distorted by a different sort of resource imbalance: the ability to tolerate the delay and expense of adjudication. A plaintiff with a good case and aware of a very high chance of success on the merits at trial, for example, may choose to settle for a small fraction of the trial recovery because of either present financial need or a simple inability to finance the litigation. In either case, the resource imbalance results in discounting steeper than is warranted by the merits of the case. Terms of the settlement are thereby "distorted" from reflecting the merits. Lack of trial experience may impose settlement distortions analogous to those imposed by financial inequalities.

The process of settling cases involves both evaluation and bargaining. The element of evaluation requires predictions about liability and damages involving factual issues and tactical considerations such as a jury's likely reaction to particular witnesses, evidence, or arguments. One would expect a lawyer lacking in trial experience to operate at a disadvantage in assessing the prospects at trial in terms of both liability and damages. The broader the range of variation among individual juries, the broader the range of trial experience a lawyer would need to provide truly representative information about likely jury reactions. As in the area of advocacy skills, an ethical issue of competence arises, but this time in the form of competence to render advice on the advisability of settlement. Incompetence resulting in inaccurate predictions may impose the same sort of settlement distortion as lack of financial resources to conduct adequate investigation. Both hinder accurate prediction of the outcome of a trial and thus hamper the ability of the settlement to reflect the relative merits of the parties' positions.

Impairment of the ability to predict outcome at trial might cause a lawyer lacking in trial experience to err either by being more optimistic or more pessimistic in predicting the outcome at trial than the merits of the case actually warrant. Which is the more likely direction of error?

Many factors unrelated to the merits of a case may influence an attorney's outlook toward settlement. Some have noted that attorneys in an adversary system may adopt a "litigation mentality" in which they magnify the legal and factual aspects of the case favorable to their own position, making them more disinclined toward settlement than the merits of the case warrant. Some studies have shown that despite contingent fee arrangements, personal injury plaintiff lawyers often find it in their own economic self-interest to urge their clients toward early and relatively meager settlements. On the other hand, if a plaintiff's lawyer has a portfolio of cases over which to distribute risk of loss at trial, she may be more prone to trial than her client's interests dictate. Analysis of the work of criminal defense lawyers has highlighted the many factors which incline the defense attorney to prefer guilty pleas over trials, such as financial incentives, heavy caseloads, and pressure from prosecutors and judges to process cases efficiently.

Lack of trial experience creates a similar potential for conflict of interest between attorney and client. Take, for example, a young partner in the litigation section of a firm whose experience places her in the category of litigator rather than trial lawyer. Her firm handles exclusively commercial matters usually resolved by settlement. She has "second chaired" a few trials in her ten years of practice but has tried none by herself. She has significant litigation experience, but it has primarily involved discovery, motion practice, and negotiating the settlement of cases. One would expect that such a lawyer would be reluctant to put the client's money as well as her own reputation, ego, and ability to attract future clients at risk on uncertain and untested trial skills and would thus urge settlement. Trial entails a public display of those skills, or the lack thereof, in front of the client, the judge, the firm's associates, and possibly other partners.

It seems more likely that our hypothetical lawyer, confronted with the pressures inherent in this scenario, will evaluate a particular settlement offer by inflating both the advantages of settlement and the risks of trial than if the case were being handled by an experienced trial lawyer. She is more likely to recommend settlement for several reasons. First, she may simply think about the outcome at trial and quite consciously and rationally conclude that her lack of trial experience decreases the chances for success. Or she may unconsciously magnify the risks and uncertainties at trial because of fear of the unknown. In either case, the lawyer's lack of trial competence introduces an additional element of risk unrelated to the merits and decreases the settlement value of the case.

Second, the lawyer may think about her own performance at trial. Fearing her own embarrassment in the process of trying the case—quite apart from an assessment of the likely outcome—she may either consciously or unconsciously inflate the attractiveness of a particular settlement. For a lawyer at any age, willingness to risk mistakes to gain trial skills will depend in part on one's work environment. In a highly evaluative, competitive, and unforgiving work environment, even young lawyers may be reluctant to risk trying cases. As lawyers mature, they may be less dependent on the evaluation of peers, but more is expected of them from clients, judges, and those who work with and for them. As a lawyer becomes more senior and more highly paid, it may become harder to risk the inevitable awkwardness and mistakes inherent in gaining trial skills.

Here, the issue of competence is compounded by ethical issues of conflict of interest and loss of independence of judgment. As with economic self-interest, a lawyer's self-interest in avoiding the risk of trial because of embarrassment and exposure of lack of trial skills may conflict with the client's interests. It also threatens the lawyer's independence of judgment in assessing the desirability of settlement. The easiest way for the lawyer to resolve such a dilemma is to avoid the risks of trial and settle the case. The resulting settlement distortions are particularly insidious because many clients have at best a limited ability to assess a lawyer's settlement advice and the basis for it, particularly given the lawyer's apparent expertise.

For a younger lawyer, the lack of trial experience may create a similar conflict between attorney self-interest and client interest, but one which pushes the lawyer to be less rather than more trial-averse than the client. Take, for example, a young lawyer at a large firm who knows that the opportunities for trial experience in her regular workload are limited. The firm, however, takes on small *pro bono* cases, partly to satisfy the firm's ethical obligations but also to provide their younger lawyers with trial experience. In advising such a *pro bono* client about the relative advantages of accepting a settlement offer versus taking the case to trial, the young lawyer's desire to gain trial experience may put her own self-interest in gaining trial experience at odds with the client's interest in settlement, particularly since the case is one in which the monetary exposure and visibility of the case are much lower than in her regular paying work. This sort of conflict might also arise in a system in which trial experience was abundant, since small cases are an easy way to break into the field of trial practice. But scarcity of trial experience increases the premium put on taking small cases to trial and thus increases the likelihood that such a conflict will occur.

* * *

In settlement negotiations, fear of trial weakens one's bargaining position, since the strength of one's bargaining position is in part a function of one's willingness to try the case. Willingness to proceed with trial turns in part on a comparison of the potential risk and return of trial with the terms of settlement. Reluctance to try a case may stem from the weakness of one's position on the merits, the amount of damages at stake, or, as pointed out above, the cost and delay entailed in pursuing the case through trial and appeal. It may also stem, however, from a lawyer's lack of confidence in her own ability to try a case.

The discounting may be even steeper if the lawyer's opponent is aware of the lawyer's lack of trial experience and consequent reluctance to try the case. The lawyer's opponent may conclude that his own case is worth more since the lawyer's lack of trial experience increases the opponent's chances for success at trial. One experienced trial lawyer summed up the connection between advocacy skill and negotiating value as follows:

> I have to maintain my advocacy in court on trial in order to keep up my settlement value.
>
> Let me lose two in a row, and the value for a case in current negotiations drops precipitously. Let me go into a low verdict center and be successful in achieving an adequate award and immediately, the value of cases, both on settlement and on trial, rises.

Additionally, the opponent's awareness of the lawyer's reluctance to try the case may allow the opponent to drive a harder bargain because that reluctance weakens the lawyer's bargaining position.

The previous sections have shown that lack of trial experience may impair the effective functioning of a lawyer in both the evaluation and bargaining aspects of settlement. This impairment may in turn disadvantage the client in relation to both the decision whether or not to settle and the terms of the settlement. In short, inaccurate prediction and fear of trial can mean the difference between settling and not settling. But it may also affect the amount of the settlement as well as other terms. Like inequalities in other resources, the quality of one's lawyer, including her trial skills, may result in a discounting of the settlement beyond that warranted by the merits of the client's case. Inaccurate predictions about outcome and risk assessments tainted by incompetence and conflict of interest may also undermine the knowledge and voluntariness of the consent which provides settlement with its authority.

* * *

The filing of unwarranted claims is perceived as a pervasive contemporary problem in civil litigation. A recent survey by the New York State Bar Association, for example, revealed that ninety-three percent of judicial officers and seventy-seven percent of the responding lawyers felt that sanctions were needed to discourage meritless filings. Ethical rules impose a duty on lawyers to screen claims for factual and legal merit. This screening obligation is enforced by professional discipline, the tort of malicious prosecution, fee shifting mechanisms, sanctions, and injunctive relief or contempt for repeat offenders. Federal Rule of Civil Procedure 11, which allows the use of sanctions to curb unwarranted filings, is the most prominent of these remedies. * * *

A primary focus of the rapidly expanding Rule 11 literature has been the consequences of sanctions and the comparative costs and benefits of their use. Proponents of sanctions suggest that the Rule discourages frivolous filings by making lawyers "stop and think" before filing. Others have warned of the possible negative effects of expansive Rule 11 sanctions, including the costs of the "satellite litigation" required for enforcement and the chilling effect on creative advocacy and the assertion and expansion of legal rights.

There are doubtless numerous causes for the filing of unwarranted claims. Various financial pressures may play a contributing role. The amount at stake in the case may be too low to allow a substantial investment in thorough legal and factual investigation prior to filing. Alternatively, hourly fees may create pressures for lawyers to file meritless cases to generate hourly fee work in discovery and motion practice. However, scarcity of adjudication may also contribute to unwarranted filings.

Prevalence of settlement and inaccessibility of adjudication create a number of pressures to inflate claims. The first source of inflationary pressure is the fact that settlement normally requires compromise. As noted before, the primary rationale behind Rule 11 is to make lawyers "stop and think." But frivolous claims may have as much to do with what lawyers are thinking about before filing as with their not thinking at all. In today's legal system, the process of negotiation, rather than trial, might quite reasonably be foremost in the minds of rational litigators when drafting claims. It is their most common experience and the fate of the overwhelming percentage of claims.

* * *

A second source of inflationary tendencies is the infrequency with which claims are proven or disproven. In a system predominantly characterized by settlement and inaccessible adjudication, a lawyer rarely proves the merit of claims asserted, while opponents rarely have the opportunity to disprove their merit. Put simply, litigators who settle rather than try cases deal primarily in allegations rather than proof. Actually having to prove what one puts in a pleading, as one does at trial, with an opponent pointing out weaknesses in one's proof and bringing forth contrary evidence, is a chastening experience. It is an experience which enhances a lawyer's modesty in drafting the assertions made in a complaint or answer, and provides a natural check to the psychological tendency of lawyers in litigation to exaggerate the strength of their own positions and the weakness of their adversaries' positions.

In a system in which opportunities to adjudicate are scarce, not only does a litigator lack the experience of adjudication to curb the pressure to inflate, she also faces the prospect of inaccessible adjudication. The prospect of available adjudication works to deter frivolous claims in several ways. Deterrence is generally viewed as a function of the severity and certainty of the imposition of some negative consequence, such as punishment in the criminal law. In adjudication a party with insufficient proof is threatened with the consequence of a negative ruling on the merits. Additionally, it may also lead to other, collateral negative consequences, such as a suit for malicious prosecution. In settlement, by contrast, a lawyer is not called on to prove the validity of a claim or defense. On the contrary, meritless claims may well provide valuable bargaining chips in the settlement process. The more available adjudication is, the more certain is the imposition of negative consequences for filing meritless claims and therefore the greater the deterrence. In short, a lawyer who knows that her opponent can put her to her proof in a timely and cost effective manner has less incentive to file a frivolous claim than one who knows that she will never have to prove her claims and that her opponent's opportunity to disprove those claims is impaired by significant cost and delay. It is not settlement alone which generates these pressures for frivolous claims. Rather, it is settlement coupled with the unavailability of adjudication. The availability of cost-effective adjudication can have a prophylactic effect by deterring frivolous filings even if it is not used in every case.

One way to conceive of Rule 11 sanctions is as a form of deterrence which substitutes for that which accessible adjudication would provide. Viewed in this light, the developments in the Rule 11 area are consistent with the basic premise of much of the "managerial judging" movement: to overcome inappropriate behavior in litigation by relying on judges to detect it on a case-by-case basis and apply counteracting incentives after the fact. The problem with this approach in the Rule 11 context, as elsewhere, is that it "may actually make matters worse by imposing an additional layer of procedural resources that can be used by lawyers for tactical purposes." This concern about strategic manipulation has surfaced in the debate about Rule 11 and its potential to generate "satellite litigation." A more efficient way to modify the behavior at issue, here frivolous filings, would be to change the underlying incentives or build counterincentives into the underlying system. Accessible adjudication, while it cannot cure the problem of frivolous filings, creates such built-in counterincentives.

* * *

The modern rules of discovery are based on the assumption that lawyers and the parties they represent would engage in a period of nonadversarial, open exchange of information prior to and in preparation for trial. The idea was that the competitive forces inherent in the adversary system would be contained within the courtroom for the actual trial of the case, and that they would not spill over into the period of trial preparation.

The adversary character of much of modern discovery makes this assumption seem naive. Even in a system in which most cases were tried rather than settled, it might be unrealistic to think that the pretrial period could be successfully insulated from the competitive pressures of the trial, since the results of discovery play a large role in determining whether cases are tried and how those that are tried will be resolved. In a system in which trials are scarce, however, this very scarcity increases the likelihood that the pretrial phase, including discovery, will become a substitute focal point for the adversary system rather than a prelude to it. Simply put, for many litigators trial never takes place. How could one hope then that trials would focus and contain the adversarial energy of these lawyers? Rather, as pretrial maneuvering, including discovery and settlement negotiations, have become increasingly the "main event" in litigation, it seems only natural, however regrettable, that they have become a focal point for adversariness in a legal and ethical system which is premised on and encourages adversariness. On a systemic level, then, scarcity of trials increases the importance of pretrial activities and makes them more likely to be influenced by adversarial pressures.

In addition to depriving a lawyer of an alternate focal point for her adversarial energy, scarcity of trial experience may encourage overuse of discovery in another way. Discovery is ostensibly aimed at producing the evidence needed for trial. Its parameters are whether or not the information sought is "reasonably calculated to lead to the discovery of admissible evidence." If trial experience is scarce, actually proving anything at trial is a foreign experience to litigators. Though the rules tell litigators that proof at trial provides the ultimate point of reference for discovery, their own experience leaves them unfamiliar with that point of reference. Moreover, lack of trial experience deprives a lawyer of the confidence to trust her own judgment in discriminating between what will be important at trial and what will not.

The experienced trial lawyer understands the ultimate end of the discovery process. He knows that everything he does is directed to the single goal of convincing the judge or jury. When the experienced trial lawyer prepares a case, he never loses sight of the fact that he is structuring the case for trial. In a sense, he is constantly asking what do I need for the trial? how can I get it quickly? and how can I get the information without helping or instructing my adversary? The tendency of the trial lawyer is to constantly aim for the jugular.

All too often the discovery lawyer with little trial experience is uncertain and lacks direction. This is particularly so in large cases where the lawyer who prepares the case not only will not try it but may only be familiar with one small aspect of the case. In such a case the discovery tends to lack direction because the lawyer does not know where he is going or why he's doing certain things. More depositions are taken than needed. Witnesses are deposed who are not needed and who should not have been deposed at all. Objections and evasions are frequent because the discovery lawyer just isn't sure how the senior man will try the case and doesn't want to be criticized for not protecting the client.

> The lawyer's lack of trial experience causes him anxiety and uncertainty. Because he is not confident all too often the tendency is to try to insure that absolutely nothing is left uncovered. The discovery goes on interminably as every conceivable stone is turned.

> The unfortunate result is misused discovery, overdiscovery, expensive discovery, and at times, harmful discovery.

Thus, the lawyer who has limited trial experience may take a broad brush approach to discovery because she lacks the ability and the confidence derived from trial experience to focus on what will be important and unimportant at trial. Our system of civil procedure has been criticized as suffering from an imbalance in which procedural techniques for developing and expanding issues greatly outweigh techniques for narrowing and resolving issues. Not surprisingly, lawyers who operate in that system may reflect a similar asymmetry in their own abilities, in part due to their lack of trial experience.

* * *

* * * In short, the reality of a pending trial may force the trial lawyer to utilize his ability to focus on what is needed to try the case and to evaluate it for settlement, rather than diverting resources into skirmishing on marginal discovery issues.

* * *

* * * Litigating lawyers do not simply act as intermediaries between clients and the system of justice in the same way computer salespeople act as intermediaries between customers and the company. Lawyers and their value, under the conventional view, are much more interstitially connected to the system of adjudication. Under that view, the litigating lawyer's role and function are tied to the process and results of adjudication since the cardinal tenets of legal ethics are most often justified in terms of the function of the adversary system of adjudication. The principles of partisan advocacy are seen under this view as a necessary means of promoting a fully informed and legally sound decision by the neutral decisionmaker who is the focal point of traditional adjudication. If the lawyer's value and role are tied to the results of adjudication, then as adjudicated results become less frequent, the value and justifications for lawyers become more attenuated. With this attenuation may come a lessening of the lawyer's ability to believe in the value of her own role. In short, the experience of adjudication may help lawyers to understand and respect the values embodied in our legal system and thus the value of their own roles as advocates.

Demoralization may occur not only because adjudication is scarce, but may also result from the beliefs and attitudes that have accompanied and perhaps caused the scarcity. Doubts about the moral status of lawyers have long been with us. The recent wave of enthusiasm for settlement, however, has been marked by an extension of these doubts to within the pale of the legal profession, what some have termed a "failing faith" in adjudication and adjudicatory process. The original drafters of the Federal Rules of Civil Procedure, for example, evinced a faith "in adversarial exchanges as an adequate basis for adjudication, in adjudication as the essence of fair decisionmaking, and in fair decisionmaking as essential for legitimate government action." Today considerable evidence demonstrates that such faith is failing, resulting in the devaluation of both the adversarial adjudicatory process and those lawyers whose role and value have been closely identified with adjudicatory process.

* * * Lack of trial experience may compromise competence in the advocacy skills used in trial, the counseling and negotiating skills used in settlement, and the ability to conduct discovery which effectively and efficiently prepares a case for trial. Such scarcity also exerts pressure toward compromise of the lawyer's loyalty to the client and independence of judgment through conflicts between attorney self-interest and client interest. It simultaneously increases the risk of the lawyer's overstepping the bounds of zealous representation by filing inflated claims or defenses and abusing discovery by reducing the counterincentives to engage in such behavior.

Scarcity of adjudication and consequent lack of trial experience may also affect ethical conformity in a broader and more diffuse sense by undermining a primary rationale for our ethical rules. As pointed out above, the lawyer's connection with our system of justice is much more interstitial than merely working in the system and being an intermediary between the system and individual members of society. The lawyer represents the system of justice with its premise of adjudication in a deeper way: the very essence of our traditional view of the meaning of lawyers is tied to adjudication. As our faith in adjudication fails, the ability of an ethical system premised on adjudication to command the respect and adherence of lawyers may diminish. Lawyers then may increasingly ignore both the ethical imperatives and limitations derived from such a system.

* * *

* * * Settlement and adjudication are not simply separate dispute resolution mechanisms, but rather mutually interdependent, what a biologist would term symbiotic, systems of resolving disputes. Settlement, for example, benefits adjudication by freeing procedural resources from some cases and allowing those resources to be devoted to the adjudication of other cases. The cases adjudicated consequently can be handled with more care and attention than if all cases were adjudicated. However, settlement may also have a harmful impact on adjudication. For example, the existence of settlement as an alternative to adjudication may tempt the judge to pressure the parties to settle. If the case is not settled, the judicial neutrality upon which adjudication relies may be undermined. Similarly, adjudication casts a broad shadow over the realm of settled cases. Adjudication can benefit settlement by producing clear factual and legal precedents which provide incentives and guidance for settlement; adjudication can harm settlement when its costs and delays distort settlement terms.

One of the facets of this interdependence which needs to be explored is the optimal balance between the two systems. More work remains in finding the proper balance point, in identifying which cases should be adjudicated and which settled, and in developing mechanisms which will channel cases to the appropriate system. As the previous paragraph makes clear, this Article is not against settlement. Settlement will and probably should continue to dominate as our means of resolving cases. Nor is this Article against alternative dispute resolution mechanisms. Even if we settle fewer cases than we presently do, ADR may well have a growing role to play in making settlements fairer and less costly to achieve. But if we rely on settlement too heavily and ignore reform of our adjudicative process, we risk encountering the problems described in this Article as well as those warned of by other critics of over-reliance on settlement.

Notes and Questions

1. Trina Grillo presented a now classic critique of mandatory mediation, primarily looking at the rise of mandatory child custody mediation in California. She argues that such mediation "provides neither a more just nor a more humane alternative to the adversarial system of adjudication of custody, and, therefore, does not fulfill its promises * * * [of] reliance on context rather than exclusively on abstract rules; the inclusion of emotions along with rational self interest; and the introduction of self-determination in the place of an outside decisionmaker." Trina Grillo, *The Mediation Alternative: Process Dangers for Women*, 100 Yale L. J. 1545, 1549, 51 (1991).

2. Litigation imposes substantial emotional costs on litigants, many of which are unanticipated by the parties themselves: "For plaintiffs and defendants alike, litigation proves a miserable, disruptive, painful experience. Few litigants have a good time or bask in the esteem of their fellows—indeed, they may be stigmatized. Even those who prevail may find the process very costly." Marc Galanter, *The Day After the Litigation Explosion*, 46 Md. L. Rev. 3, 9 (1986).

On the other hand, do you perceive any psychological barriers to settlement? *See* Russell Korobkin & Chris Gutherie, *Psychological Barriers to Litigation Settlement: An Experimental Approach*, 93 Mich. L. Rev. 107 (1994).

3. Can you be a litigator without having trial experience? What costs are associated with the overwhelming number of settled cases? Do you agree with Kevin McMunigal's assessment? What criticisms of his assessment might you lodge? The classic polemic is Owen M. Fiss, *Against Settlement*, 93 Yale L. J. 1073 (1984). Since then the issues of settlement have generated a good deal of scholarly debate. *See* Judith Resnik, *Managerial Judges*, 96 Harv. L. Rev. 374 (1982); Judith Resnik, *Whose Judgment? Vacating Judgments, Preferences for Settlement, and the Role of Adjudication at the Close of the Twentieth Century*, 41 UCLA L. Rev. 1471 (1994); Kent D. Syverud, *The Duty to Settle*, 76 Va. L. Rev. 1113 (1990); and Michael W. Loudenslager, Note, *Erasing the Law: The Implications of Settlements Conditioned upon Vacatur or Reversal of Judgments*, 50 Wash. & Lee L. Rev. 1229 (1993). *See generally A Symposium: Ethical Issues in Settlement Negotiations*, 52 Mercer L. Rev. 807–1002 (2001).

PART II

A SYSTEM OF LAW: SHAPING CLAIMS IN SOCIAL JUSTICE CASES

This part of the book provides a survey of the legal and judicial framework for using litigation to pursue claims for basic human needs and to ensure participation in democratic society. Social justice lawyers have fought for civil rights in cases involving employment, subsistence, caregiving and children, education, and voting, among other issues. The makeup of the judiciary, the jurisdiction of federal courts, and the power of Congress to define federal civil rights claims are also contested areas that shape legal claims and affect their outcomes.

Education presents an example of the interlocking influences of decisional and statutory law and social policy. The terrain on which profound educational inequality developed in this country was affected by 19th century legislative decisions that shrank from redistributing land to the freed slaves who had worked it. Instead, African-American laborers, then mostly located in southern states, were forced into exploitive labor contracts. The institutionalization of poll taxes and other devices denied political power to African Americans and thereby stifled social justice reforms. The entrenchment of segregation extended to the system of education. Court decisions regarding both racial segregation and economic inequality have shaped litigation challenging educational inequality. In another example of these interlocking forces, the situation of homeless people seeking shelter and food was obviously affected by the cases that found no right to housing or subsistence, but it was also shaped by the way in which social insurance had been developed and interpreted in the United States.

The availability of a federal or state court as a forum to seek remedies is also a significant factor in how law can work to meet basic human needs and build democracy. Federal jurisdiction is a product both of statutes and judicial interpretation, subject to expansion or shrinkage as courts review not only the substance of claims but also whether the statutes creating those claims were constitutionally authorized. Consider, as you read the materials in this part, how legal arguments have expanded or limited the ability of courts to think about social problems.

Law students, for the most part, learn the legal regime currently in place. The case method of legal study structures this learning process so that students work hard to synthesize disparate pieces of existing legal doctrine, leaving relatively little time to reflect upon what law might have been or how the present laws came to exist. But laws that failed to pass, as well as laws that were enacted, affect the conceptualization of legal doctrine and its possibilities. Taking only federal legislation as an example, at various times crucial reforms that might have changed history as well as law in the United States were considered but not enacted in Congress. Of course, the list of the most important statutes that failed to pass could be subjected to extended—and interesting—debate. Two such measures include the demand for land reform during Reconstruction (popularly known as the distribution of "40 acres and a mule"), discussed in chapter 7, and the consideration in the 1940s and the 1970s of guaranteed rights to employment for all, discussed in chapter 8. The effect of the failure of these proposals sheds light on the interrelationships between law, society, and politics.

Scholars have debated whether framing human needs in the language of legal rights provides the best avenue toward social transformation, or whether framing social struggles as legal claims for rights may actually limit their scope and potential. Discussion of both the transformative power of rights and their limits is therefore part of considering legal work for social justice. This part of the book, A System of Law: Shaping Claims in Social Justice Cases, first frames the general question of the efficacy of rights and then explores the way those rights have evolved. The chapters explore the interrelated contexts in which social justice lawyers and their clients frame claims into legal arguments. Chapter 7 describes the recent debate about the benefits and detriments of rights discourse. Chapter 8 examines livelihood, including employment, globalization, social insurance, and caregiving and dependency. Chapter 9 recounts social justice battles over voting, education, and rights to protection against harm. Chapter 10 explores the judiciary and access to courts. The final part of this book, A System of Politics: Legal Work and Social Change, will explore the goal of empowering clients and the ways in which rights claims have been advanced as part of political and social movements in specific social justice struggles.

Chapter 7

THE POLITICAL NATURE OF RIGHTS CLAIMS

Think back to your young adult self, as you were graduating from high school. What rights did you think you had? Has legal education altered your views? What rights do you think you should have? What rights do you see as essential to citizens in a democracy to enable democratic practices?

SECTION 1. FRAMING DEMANDS FOR SOCIAL JUSTICE AS CLAIMS FOR LEGAL RIGHTS

Where do claims for rights come from? How do aggrieved parties perceive that they need a lawyer? Legal education focuses on appellate decisions, rarely considering where the legal claim originated. Clinical and skills courses do examine trial practices and the negotiation and counseling that may precede them. But very little attention has been paid to how disputes emerge.

William L.F. Felstiner, Richard L. Abel, and Austin Sarat urge more study of the emergence and transformation of disputes.

> Trouble, problems, personal and social dislocation are everyday occurrences. Yet, social scientists have rarely studied the capacity of people to tolerate substantial distress and injustice. We do, however, know that such "tolerance" may represent a failure to perceive that one has been injured; such failures may be self-induced or externally manipulated.

William L.F. Felstiner, Richard L. Abel & Austin Sarat, *The Emergence and Transformation of Disputes: Naming, Blaming, Claiming*..., 15 Law & Soc'y Rev. 631, 633 (1980–81).

Felstiner, Abel, and Sarat have described three stages in the transformation of a legal dispute: naming, blaming, and claiming. Naming, the first stage, requires the transformation from a lack of awareness to an awareness that an experience has been injurious. *Id.* at 635.

The second stage, blaming, requires transforming the perceived injurious experience into a grievance. *Id.* As to claiming, the authors state: "The third transformation occurs when someone with a grievance voices it to the person or entity believed to be responsible and asks for some remedy. We call this communication *claiming.*" *Id.* at 635–36.

They assert: "The sociology of law should pay more attention to the early stages of disputes and to the factors that determine whether naming, blaming, and claiming will occur. Learning more about the existence, absence, or reversal of these basic transformations will increase our understanding of the disputing process and our ability to evaluate dispute processing institutions. We know that only a small fraction of injurious experiences ever mature into disputes." *Id.* at 636.

Consider, as you read this chapter and the following chapters on livelihood, democratic practice, and courts, how the naming, blaming, and claiming of these rights claims did occur. Can social justice lawyers play a role in facilitating the awareness that leads ultimately to claiming?

A. The Example of Reconstruction

The Reconstruction Era amendments and accompanying legislation forged legal rights that changed U.S. history. The legal structure enacted following the Civil War underlies many of the rights claims of the 20th century examined in chapters 8 and 9. The meaning of these amendments and their interpretation remain central to the debate about constitutional interpretation.

ANGELA P. HARRIS

Equality Trouble: Sameness and Difference in Twentieth-Century Race Law
88 Cal. L. Rev. 1923, 1931–33 (2000)

The Radical Republicans who wielded power in Congress at the end of the Civil War had a new vision for the United States: "the utopian vision of a nation whose citizens enjoyed equality of civil and political rights, secured by a powerful and beneficent national state." Neither equality as a principle nor the notion of a strong national state had been a part of the constitutional framework before the Civil War. It was the task of the Republicans, then, to fundamentally alter American law.

As a legal framework, Reconstruction consisted of three constitutional amendments—the Thirteenth, Fourteenth, and Fifteenth—and a myriad of federal statutes protecting "civil rights." Section one of the Thirteenth Amendment (1865) abolished slavery and gave Congress the power to enforce the prohibition with further legislation. It was widely feared, however, that the Thirteenth Amendment did not go far enough to secure the freed slaves in their new legal existence. Hence, section one of the Fourteenth Amendment (1868), providing that "[a]ll persons born or naturalized in the United States, and subject to the jurisdiction thereof, are citizens of the United States and of the state wherein they reside," made citizenship national for the first time. This Amendment laid to rest the ghost of *Dred Scott*, in which all American descendants of Africans, whether free or slave, had been set outside the bounds of citizenship. The Fourteenth Amendment further prohibited the states from abridging the privileges or immunities of any United States citizen, or depriving any citizen of due process or equal protection of the law. Finally, in 1870, the Fifteenth Amendment, guaranteeing the vote to all men regardless of race or color, was declared ratified.

The Reconstruction Amendments were accompanied by a series of federal statutes directed at dismantling state race law and forestalling the creation of new legal forms of racial oppression. For instance, the Civil Rights Act of 1866 and the Fourteenth Amendment were passed to stop the Southern states from recreating slavery in all but name through the infamous "Black Codes." Around the same time, the Reconstruction Congress also greatly expanded citizens' ability to remove cases to federal court, and abolished peonage, a form of indentured servitude that had oppressed Indians and Mexicans living under Spanish rule in the territory of New Mexico. Two months after the passage of the Fifteenth Amendment, Congress passed the Civil Rights Act of 1870. In addition to giving some substance to the constitutional voting guarantee, the act made illegal the California practice of subjecting Chinese to special taxes, and nullified state legal rules that forbade Chinese persons from testifying in court against white persons. The Reconstruction Congress also passed legislation intended to provide a federal tool against white legal and extralegal violence. In April of 1871, Congress passed the "Ku Klux Klan Act" in response to the widespread terrorism against blacks and white "carpetbaggers" (white emigrants from the North) in the southern states. A final aspect of Reconstruction legislation was the effort to entitle all citizens, regardless of color, to the full enjoyment of public life in the name of equality. In 1875, for example, Congress passed a civil rights act directed toward public accommodations.

Reconstruction transformed the political life of the United States, especially in the South, where African Americans surged to the polls, into political clubs, and into statehouses and houses of Congress. Now subjects rather than objects of the law, the freed slaves organized to learn about and enforce their rights, engaged in strikes, and agitated for land redistribution. They worked with carpetbaggers and "scalawags" (white Southerners who allied themselves politically with the freed slaves) toward economic development, civil rights legislation, and the establishment of public school systems. For a time, a new interracial society seemed on the verge of emerging in the heart of Dixie.

Notes and Questions

1. Modern legal history was built on this legal structure of the First Reconstruction. But legal battles in recent history have also been influenced by rights that were lost or not enacted. *See* Derrick Bell, *Race, Racism and American Law* 21–80 (4th ed., 2000).

Few Americans today are aware that a far-reaching land reform act was debated and came close to being enacted after the Civil War. The people who had done the work that ran the plantations had been enslaved, treated as property and deprived of the fruits of their labor. The planters who had rebelled against the United States government were subject to legal consequences. What would become of the land, and what would become of the people who had worked it? Eric Foner describes the legal debates, laws proposed and enacted, and the ultimate decision not to give property rights in land to the people who had labored to give it value.

ERIC FONER

Reconstruction: America's Unfinished Revolution, 1863–1877, 50, 51, 68–71, 158–64 (1988)

* * * Of the many questions raised by emancipation, none was more crucial to the future place of both blacks and whites in Southern society than how the region's economy would henceforth be organized. Slavery had been, first and foremost, a system of labor. And while all Republicans agreed that "free labor" must replace slave, few were certain how the transition should be accomplished. * * *

As the war progressed, the Union army found itself in control of territory ranging from coastal Virginia and South Carolina to the plantation belt along the Mississippi River. Legal title to land under army control was uncertain. Theoretically, the Second Confiscation Act of 1862 raised the prospect of the wholesale forfeiture of property owned by Confederates. This penalty, however, could be imposed only after court proceedings in individual cases, and a clause added at Lincoln's insistence provided that the loss of property would be limited to the lifetime of the owner, and not his or her heirs. The President had no enthusiasm for large-scale confiscation that, he feared, would undermine efforts to win the support of loyal planters and other Southern whites, and the act remained largely unenforced. Far more land came into federal hands from seizures for nonpayment of taxes (in which case it could be sold at auction) or as abandoned property (which the Treasury Department would then administer). How to dispose of this land, coupled with the organization of its black labor, became points of conflict as former slaves, former slaveholders, military commanders, and Northern entrepreneurs and reformers sought, in their various ways, to influence the wartime transition to free labor.

* * *

* * * Radicals advocat[ed] an act of federal intervention comparable in scope only to emancipation itself—the confiscation of planter lands and their division among the freedmen. * * * [George W. Julian, chairman of the House Committee on Public Lands,] insisted that without land reform, Southern society could not be remade according to the tenets of "radical democracy," and the freedmen would find themselves

reduced to "a system of wages slavery ... more galling than slavery itself." Julian led a fight to amend the Second Confiscation Act so as to authorize the permanent seizure of Confederates' land, and by the end of the war, both houses had approved separate versions, but no joint measure had been enacted. Nonetheless, the creation of the Freedmen's Bureau in March 1865 symbolized the widespread belief among Republicans that the federal government must shoulder broad responsibility for the emancipated slaves, including offering them some kind of access to land.

* * *

* * * The [Freedmen's] Bureau was to distribute clothing, food, and fuel to destitute freedmen and oversee "all subjects" relating to their condition in the South. Despite its unprecedented responsibilities and powers, the Bureau was clearly envisioned as a temporary expedient, for not only was its life span limited to one year, but, incredibly, no budget was appropriated—it would have to draw funds and staff from the War Department. * * * Indeed, at the last moment, Congress redefined the Bureau's responsibilities so as to include Southern white refugees as well as freedmen, a vast expansion of its authority that aimed to counteract the impression of preferential treatment for blacks.

In one respect, however, the Freedmen's Bureau appeared to promise a permanent transformation of the condition of the emancipated slaves. As suggested by its full title—Bureau of Refugees, Freedmen, and Abandoned Lands—it was authorized to divide abandoned and confiscated land into forty-acre plots, for rental to freedmen and loyal refugees and eventual sale with "such title as the United States can convey" (language that reflected the legal ambiguity surrounding the government's hold upon Southern land). Earlier drafts of the bill had envisioned the Bureau's operating plantations itself, with the freedmen as wage laborers. But while hardly a definitive commitment to land distribution, the final version clearly anticipated at least some blacks becoming, with the government's assistance, independent farmers in a "free labor" South.

While Congress deliberated, the gods of war, in the person of Gen. William T. Sherman and his 60,000-man army, dealt slavery its death blow in the heart of Georgia and added a new dimension to the already perplexing land question. Having captured Atlanta in September 1864, Sherman set out two months later on his March to the Sea. To Georgia's slaves the arrival of this avenging host seemed, as one federal officer put it, "the fulfillment of the millennial prophecies." By the thousands, men, women, and children abandoned the plantations to follow the Union army. They cheered the destruction of their owners' estates and refused to obey when the troops, following Sherman's orders, attempted to drive them away. * * *

* * * [In January, 1865] Sherman issued Special Field Order No. 15, setting aside the Sea Islands and a portion of the low country rice coast south of Charleston, extending thirty miles inland, for the exclu-

sive settlement of blacks. Each family would receive forty acres of land, and Sherman later provided that the army could assist them with the loan of mules. (Here, perhaps, lies the origin of the phrase "forty acres and a mule" that would soon echo throughout the South.)

Sherman was neither a humanitarian reformer nor a man with any particular concern for blacks. Instead of seeing Field Order 15 as a blueprint for the transformation of Southern society, he viewed it mainly as a way of relieving the immediate pressure caused by the large number of impoverished blacks following his army. The land grants, he later claimed, were intended only to make "temporary provisions for the freedmen and their families during the rest of the war," not to convey permanent possession. Understandably, however, the freedmen assumed that the land was to be theirs, especially after Gen. Rufus Saxton, assigned by Sherman to oversee the implementation of his order, informed a large gathering of blacks "that they were to be put in possession of lands, upon which they might locate their families and work out for themselves a living and respectability." Certainly, the freedmen hastened to take advantage of the Order. Baptist minister Ulysses Houston, one of * * * [a] group that had met with Sherman, led 1,000 blacks to Skiddaway Island, Georgia, where they established a self-governing community with Houston as the "black governor." By June, in the region that had spawned one of the wealthiest segments of the planter class, some 40,000 freedmen had been settled on 400,000 acres of "Sherman land." Here in coastal South Carolina and Georgia, the prospect beckoned of a transformation of Southern society more radical even than the end of slavery.

* * *

Even though the Lincoln Administration had left the 1862 Confiscation Act virtually unenforced, the Bureau controlled over 850,000 acres of abandoned land in 1865, hardly enough to accommodate all the former slaves but sufficient to make a start toward creating a black yeomanry. Howard's [General O. O. Howard, Commissioner of the Freedmen's Bureau] subordinates included men sincerely committed to settling freedmen on farms of their own and protecting the rights of those (mostly on the "Sherman reservation") who already occupied the land. In Tennessee, General Fisk began locating blacks on the 65,000 acres under his control. In Louisiana, Thomas Conway invited applications from freedmen who wished to "procure land for their own use," and leased over 60,000 acres to blacks (including a plantation owned by the son of former President Zachary Taylor). Orlando Brown, an advocate of "*extensive confiscation,*" urged Howard to "take possession of all the abandoned and confiscated land we require, and permit the negroes to work it on their own behalf." Most dedicated of all to the idea of black landownership was Gen. Rufus Saxton, a prewar abolitionist who directed the Bureau in South Carolina, Georgia, and Florida during the summer of 1865. * * * In June 1865, he announced his intention to use the property under Bureau control to provide freedmen with forty-acre homesteads "where by faithful industry they can readily achieve an independence." Market-oriented farming was Saxon's ideal. "Put in all the cotton and rice you can," he advised black farmers, "for these are the crops which will pay the best." * * * In this way, he argued, blacks tilling their own lands could demonstrate the superiority of free labor to slave.

* * * President Johnson during the summer and fall issued a rash of special pardons, restoring the property of former Confederates. Johnson's actions threw into question the status of confiscated and abandoned land, including the Sherman reservation. At the end of July, without consulting the President, Howard issued Circular 13, which instructed Bureau agents to "set aside" forty-acre tracts for the freedmen as rapidly as possible. Presidential pardons, he insisted, did not carry with them the restoration of land that had been settled by freedmen in accordance with the law establishing the Bureau. Johnson, however, soon directed Howard to rescind his order. A new policy, drafted in the White House and issued in September as Howard's Circular 15, ordered the restoration to pardoned owners of all land except the small amount that had already been sold under a court decree. Soon thereafter, the government suspended land sales scheduled in Virginia and South Carolina. Once growing crops had been harvested, virtually all the land in Bureau hands would revert to its former owners.

Most of the land occupied by blacks in the summer and fall of 1865 lay within the Sherman reservation, where 40,000 freedmen had been settled. "Could a just Government," Saxton asked, "drive out these loyal men?" To Howard fell the task of informing the freedmen that the land would be restored to their former owners, and that they must either agree to work for the planters or be evicted. * * * [He traveled to low-country South Carolina to speak with the freedmen himself.] Blacks * * * had been holding weekly meetings, where issues of "general interest" were discussed and Republican newspapers read aloud. They fully anticipated Howard's message, and when he rose to speak to more than 2,000 freedmen gathered at a local church, "dissatisfaction and sorrow were manifested from every part of the assembly." * * * Howard begged them to "lay aside their bitter feelings, and to become reconciled to their old masters." He was continually interrupted by members of the audience: "No, never," "Can't do it," "Why, General Howard, do you take away our lands?"

Howard requested the assembled freedmen to appoint a three-man committee to consider the fairest way of restoring the planters to ownership. The committee's eloquent response did not augur well for a tranquil settlement:

> General, we want Homesteads, we were promised Homesteads by the government. If it does not carry out the promises its agents made to us, if the government having concluded to befriend its late enemies and to neglect to observe the principles of common faith between its self and us its allies in the war you said was over, now takes away from them all right to the soil they stand upon save such

as they can get by working for *your* late and their *all time* enemies . . . we are left in a more unpleasant condition than our former. . . . You will see this is not the condition of really freemen.

You ask us to forgive the land owners of our island. *You* only lost your right arm in war and might forgive them. The man who tried me to a tree and gave me 39 lashes and who stripped and flogged my mother and my sister and who will not let me stay in his empty hut except I will do his planting and be satisfied with his price and who combines with others to keep away land from me well knowing I would not have anything to do with him if I had land of my own—that man, I cannot well forgive. Does it look as if he has forgiven me, seeing how he tries to keep me in a condition of helplessness?

"The condition of really free men," "I cannot well forgive," "their *all time* enemies," "the war you said was over." In these words, the committee expressed with simple dignity convictions that freedmen throughout the South had come to share—land was the foundation of freedom, the evils of slavery could not be quickly forgotten, the interests of former master and former slave were fundamentally irreconcilable. * * *

* * *

[Within a short time, the Bureau leaders most committed to land reform were gone, and the President's policies had been enforced.] By mid-1866, half the land in Bureau hands had been restored to its former owners, and more was returned in subsequent years. Although in some areas the process of restoration was delayed by court challenges into the 1870s, in the end the amount of land that came into the possession of blacks proved to be minuscule. Johnson had in effect abrogated the Confiscation Act and unilaterally amended the law creating the Bureau. The idea of a Freedmen's Bureau actively promoting black landownership had come to an abrupt end.

The restoration of land required the displacement of tens of thousands of freedmen throughout the South. The army evicted most of the 20,000 blacks settled on confiscated and abandoned property in southeastern Virginia, as well as freedmen near Wilmington, North Carolina, cultivating land assigned them by Gen. Joseph Hawley. The 62,000 acres farmed by Louisiana blacks were restored to their former owners * * * . [Dispossession was disruptive and occasionally violent.] Bureau agents, black and white, bent every effort to induce lowcountry freedmen to sign contracts with their former owners, while federal troops forcibly evicted those who refused.

* * *

* * * The question of land restoration became embroiled in the broader national debate over Reconstruction * * * . President Johnson, working in close consultation with * * * [the Washington representative of the South Carolina governor], successfully blocked efforts to validate

the Sherman land titles. In February, 1866, Johnson's veto killed a bill extending the life of the Bureau that would have granted three-year "possessory titles" to freedmen on the Sherman land and authorized Howard to provide forty acres to those dispossessed. When Congress in July, finally enacted a Freedmen's Bureau law (over another veto), the blacks holding land warrants from General Sherman received only the right to lease or purchase twenty-acre plots on government land.

* * *

The events of 1865 and 1866 kindled a deep sense of betrayal among freedmen throughout the South. Land enough existed, wrote former Mississippi slave Merrimon Howard, for every "man and woman to have as much as they could work." Yet blacks had been left with

> "no *land*, no *house*, not so much as place to lay our head.... Despised by the world, hated by the country that gives us birth, denied of all our writs as a people, we were friends on the march, ... brothers on the battlefield, but in the peaceful pursuits of life it seems that we are strangers."

Long after the end of slavery, the memory of this injustice lingered. * * *

Thus, by 1866, the Bureau's definition of "free labor" had been significantly transformed. Instead of carrying out a two-pronged labor policy, in which some blacks farmed independently, while others worked as hired laborers for white employers, the Bureau found itself with no alternative but to encourage virtually all freedmen to sign annual contracts to work on the plantations. * * *

Notes and Questions

1. Historians have argued that the failure of land reform was crucial in the development of inequality in America.

> In 1865, at the time of the Emancipation Proclamation, African Americans owned 0.5 percent of the total worth of the United States. This statistic is not surprising; most black Americans had been slaves up to that point. However, by 1990, a full 135 years after the abolition of slavery, black Americans owned only a meager 1 percent of total wealth. In other words, almost no progress had been made in terms of property ownership. African Americans may have won "title" to their own bodies and to their labor, but they have gained ownership over little else.
>
> * * *
>
> The importance of the lack of land redistribution cannot be overstated. Historian Paul Cimbala writes, "Once established on property of their own, [the former slaves] believed, they would be truly free to pursue additional goals [such as wealth accumulation and political participation] without constantly worrying about offending those who otherwise would have been paying them wages."

> W.E.B. DuBois argued that if white America had made good on its promise of land reparation to blacks, it "would have made a basis of real democracy in the United States."

Dalton Conley, *Being Black, Living in the Red: Race, Wealth, and Social Policy in America* 25, 33 (1999). Chapter 12 further explores the connection between inequality and the allocation of residential space.

2. The Southern Homestead Act, passed in 1866, did not achieve the goal of land ownership for the freedmen. That Act "allowed all persons who applied for land to swear that they had not taken up arms against the Union or given aid and comfort to the enemies. This opened the door to massive white applications for land. One estimate suggests that over three-quarters (77.1 percent) of the land applicants under the act were white." While high filing fees affected all poor applicants, racial prejudice and discrimination made it difficult for the freedmen to take advantage of the opportunity to acquire land. Melvin L. Oliver & Thomas M. Shapiro, *Black Wealth/White Wealth* 14 (1995).

3. The struggles over land persist up to the present:

> African Americans throughout the South overcame obstacles to land acquisition by demonstrating what can only be described as heroic action. African Americans acquired fifteen million acres of land in the South between Emancipation and 1910 almost completely through private purchase, overcoming discriminatory credit practices, violence perpetuated by anti-black groups, and the refusal of many whites to sell to black people. In the agricultural sector, where the overwhelming number of black landowners were concentrated, black farm owners constituted 16.5% of all southern landowners by 1910. It must be noted, however, that African Americans were never permitted to purchase any significant amount of prime real estate; for the most part, black people could buy land in "areas with less fertile soil, perhaps tucked away in the hills, not too close to the main highways or railroads, nor to white schools or churches."
>
> These remarkable gains in black landownership in the rural South (the poor quality of the land notwithstanding) have almost been wiped out. At the end of the twentieth century, African Americans in the region were losing land almost as rapidly as their forbearers acquired it at the beginning of the century. One study estimates that of the fifteen million acres of land that black people acquired between 1865 and 1910, hardly any land remains under the ownership of the original black families who once owned the land. Fewer than three million acres of land are currently owned by rural African Americans in farming irrespective of when such land was acquired. The dwindling number of black-operated farms today are concentrated in the southeastern states within the Black Belt and in Texas, Oklahoma, and California.
>
> Black land loss closely tracks the steep decline of black farmers since 1920 * * * . In 1920, black farm owners accounted for one out

> of every seven farms in the United States; today these farms account for less than one percent of all U.S. farms. * * *

Thomas W. Mitchell, *From Reconstruction to Deconstruction: Undermining Black Landownership, Political Independence, and Community Through Partition Sales of Tenancies in Common*, 95 Nw. U. L. Rev. 505, 526–27 (2001).

3. The pattern of federal government support for white property ownership continued in policies supporting the suburbanization of the United States. The federal government financed and supported "suburban growth from the 1930s through the 1960s by way of taxation, transportation, and housing policy." Oliver & Shapiro, *supra* at 16. Federal policies excluded African Americans from purchasing property in these areas. *Id.* at 18.

4. Oliver and Shapiro urge an examination of wealth rather than income as a measure of social resources. They explain the distinction:

> Wealth is a particularly important indicator of individual and family access to life chances. Income refers to a flow of money over time, like a rate per hour, week, or year; wealth is a stock of assets owned at a particular time. Wealth is what people own, while income is what people receive for work, retirement, or social welfare. Wealth signifies the command over financial resources that a family has accumulated over its lifetime along with those resources that have been inherited across generations. Such resources, when combined with income, can create the opportunity to secure the "good life" in whatever form is needed—education, business, training, justice, health, comfort, and so on. Wealth is a special form of money not used to purchase milk and shoes and other life necessities. More often it is used to create opportunities * * * .

Id. at 2.

If wealth is as significant a measure as Oliver and Shapiro suggests, why do you suppose its existence is so invisible in the U.S. legal system?

Contemporary society is marked by a widening inequality in economic status. Lawrence Mishel, Jared Bernstein & John Schmitt, *The State of Working America, 2000–2001* 33–109 (2001). "[T]he last few decades have witnessed a historically large shift of economic resources from those at the bottom and middle of the income (or wage or wealth) scale to those at the top. The result has been an increase in inequality such that the gap between the incomes of the well-off and those of everyone else is larger now than at any point in the postwar period." *Id.* at 49.

5. Regina Austin urges particular attention be paid to the obstacles facing black women who seek wealth accumulation.

> [B]lack women are not substantial beneficiaries of the principal forms of government subsidized asset accumulation, nor of other kinds of institutional privileges that facilitate wealth accumulation,

such as beneficial tax treatment of gifts and capital gains or employee-sponsored health and life insurance.

> "One road to wealth is long-term steady employment in the kinds of work organizations that offer job-sponsored benefits and retirement packages." That is, unfortunately, one path to wealth from which black women have been foreclosed until very recently. Black women today earn roughly sixty-three percent of the median weekly earnings of white men. The width of the contemporary gap between black female wage-earners and white men reflects vast improvements in the position of black women in the labor market. Historically, the difference between black female earnings and white male earnings was much greater. This gap has had a devastating impact on black women's wealth. "[O]ver the years these earnings shortfalls have resulted in less savings, less investments, and less transfers to succeeding generations. Over time, less income can result in vast differences in asset accumulation."

Regina Austin, *Nest Eggs and Stormy Weather: Law, Culture, and Black Women's Lack of Wealth*, 65 U. Cin. L. Rev. 767, 773 (1997) (describing the lack of institutional support for saving and money management by black women).

6. Demands for reparations for the harm of slavery and racial subordination continue in the United States today. *See* Randall N. Robinson, *The Debt: What America Owes to Blacks* (2000); Robert Westley, *Many Billions Gone: Is it Time to Reconsider the Case for Black Reparations?*, 40 B.C. L. Rev. 429 (1998) (describing potential for reparations to benefit subordinated communities and to avoid some of the issues inherent in affirmative action); Mari J. Matsuda, *Looking to the Bottom: Critical Legal Studies and Reparations*, 22 Harv. C.R.-C.L. L. Rev. 323 (1987) (emphasizing the need to place the legal imagination at the service of the reparations claims of subordinated groups). Is the demand for reparations a rights claim that can help change popular consciousness?

B. The Efficacy of Rights Claims

Robin West examines the justifications for claiming state responsibility to protect and to help its citizens. She challenges the idea that strong individual rights conflict with the state's role in providing the material conditions for a just society. Consider, as you read this section, whether rights claims serve as an advantage or an obstacle in work for social justice?

ROBIN WEST

Rights, Capabilities, and the Good Society
69 Fordham L. Rev. 1901, 1901–05 (2001)

What is a "good society," as opposed to a just one, and what is demanded of the state by the demand of "goodness" in a good society?

Must a state in a good society ensure for its citizens the minimal material preconditions of a decent life? Is it obligated to do so? Many of course, think not, but of those who think there is such an obligation, there are a variety of reasons, or arguments proffered, as to why. One "civic republican" argument * * * is basically instrumental. A state, in a good society, might be obligated to ensure for its citizens some minimal level of material goods, but if so, it is required to do so in order to instill some threshold level of civic virtue: in a good society, citizens must be able to be free and equal participants in the collective project of self rule, and if some threshold level of material well-being is necessary for that participation, then the state is obligated to provide it.

A quite different and perhaps more basic sort of response, held by scores of liberal, progressive, and radical legal theorists over the last century, as well as innumerable political activists and state actors, might be called a "welfarist" conception—the state, in a good society, is directly, not just instrumentally, obligated to ensure that all citizens enjoy some minimal threshold level of material well-being, or welfare, or met needs, or access to primary goods. They must enjoy this minimal threshold, furthermore, *not* because such a threshold is necessary to the exercise of the various civic virtues required of them if they are to participate as free and equals in a liberal state, nor for any other instrumental reason. More basically, the state must ensure some minimal level of well-being because such a threshold is necessary if citizens are to live fully human lives and have the dignity to which their humanity entitles them. Many citizens of even prosperous democratic states cannot possibly enjoy such a minimal threshold, furthermore, without some state involvement in the distribution of resources, particularly with the inequalities that persist and threaten to worsen today. States are required, by justice and goodness both, to treat citizens with dignity, and with equal dignity at that. Therefore, welfarists conclude, the state is obligated to do whatever it takes to provide that minimal level of well-being to each of its citizens.

In a number of books and articles over the last ten years, Martha Nussbaum and Amartya Sen have carved out a third position, which, they argue, is in greater accord with liberal commitments to individual autonomy, and particularly the autonomous right of individuals to determine their own conceptions of the good. The state, Nussbaum and Sen argue, as a matter of goodness and justice both, must not ensure minimal welfare directly—that would indeed be unduly paternalistic, illiberal, and in important respects, impossible: a state cannot ensure, say, a healthy, long life for each citizen. Rather, a decent and liberal state in a good society must ensure that citizens achieve and enjoy certain fundamental human *capabilities* (thereby leaving to the citizens the choice whether or not to avail themselves of those capabilities)—including the capability to live a safe, well-nourished, productive, educated, social, and politically and culturally participatory life of normal length. Thus, to be "fully human," Nussbaum argues, and to be possessed of the full dignity that one's humanity implies, just *is* to enjoy this minimal threshold level of capability. If they are to have fully human lives, citizens must have access to, and the capability to attain, non-alienating, non-discriminatory and non-humiliating work. They must have, or have the capability to acquire, various welfare goods such as decent health care, adequate food, shelter, and clothing. They must have a good and liberal education, a safe upbringing, protection against physical and sexual assault, and security in their intimate and affiliative associations. Citizens must have access to the material preconditions of these capabilities, if they are to have the ability to live fully human lives.

Furthermore, Nussbaum argues, for many or even all of us, these preconditions cannot be met without considerable state and community assistance, or more pointedly, without considerable state-run redistribution and regulation. These are not preconditions readily satisfied in either a state of nature or a minimally regulated social order. A good society, therefore, Nussbaum concludes, *and* a liberal, just society, is one in which the state is not just permitted, but is obligated to ensure, on behalf of its citizens, that these material preconditions of our fundamental human capabilities are met. All states, particularly liberal states, ought to regard their obligation to secure the preconditions of basic human capabilities as fundamental and as required by justice. Liberal states should regard their obligation to secure the minimal material preconditions of the basic human capabilities to be a basic *constitutional* duty.

I do not want to take issue with the basic welfarist version of the good society thesis, or with Nussbaum's more liberal, antipaternalist, "capabilities-based" (rather than primary goods-based) approach. Rather, I assume the welfarist thesis, and for reasons that I think will become clear, I take Nussbaum's "capabilities" approach to be its best account. * * * I want instead to re-open what some might regard as a stale question: whether individual, constitutional rights, as they have been understood by liberal theorists, and as they have been employed and are now employed in various constitutional liberal democracies, might be a vehicle for securing those state obligations. Briefly, if justice and goodness require that liberal states have an obligation to secure the minimal preconditions of our fundamentally human capabilities, as Nussbaum argues, and also require that states respect citizens' rights, as countless liberals assert, then doesn't it follow that citizens in liberal states have a right to enjoy those capabilities, and a right to a state obligated to commit itself to ensuring them? More to the point, does it not follow that welfare or capabilities advocates should be arguing as much?

In the last twenty-five years, a sort of conventional wisdom has emerged, at least in the legal academy, that the answer to both of these questions must be "no." According to [theorists ranging from Amartya Sen to Richard Epstein to "rights critics" from the critical legal studies movement, among others,] liberal rights, for better or for worse, but virtually by definition, are all obstacles to, rather than a possible vehicle for, any welfarist effort—even Nussbaum's liberalized, capabilities-based version. There is good reason for this remarkably widespread consensus.

Liberal-constitutional rights, as they are now conventionally understood and authoritatively interpreted, at least in the United States, do not obligate the state to ensure anything resembling what welfarist "good society" advocates envision, whether put in terms of primary goods, civic virtue, or fundamental human capabilities—or at least, they have never been construed that way.

Worse, liberal constitutional rights, as they are sometimes authoritatively interpreted in this country and others, actually *limit* the state's authority to take action to secure the material preconditions of the good society. According to some strands of liberal rights theory as construed by at least some United States constitutional and legal theorists, individual rights on the one hand, and the state's obligation to ensure the minimal material preconditions of either well-being, civic virtue, or capabilities on the other, do not support one another but rather inevitably collide. And individual rights trump state's obligations. Essentially and inevitably then, liberal rights undercut, rather than support, efforts to even conceive, much less achieve, an obligatory state role to secure general well-being. As liberal rights expand, any state role, including any obligatory role, contracts. This result would hold were well-being defined in terms of capabilities rather than basic human goods or civic virtue. The good society, and the state's obligation to ensure that citizens have access to the minimal capabilities necessary to participate in it, must then be both conceived and achieved by recourse to some means other than rights.

* * *

* * * [T]wo core rights that a refashioned liberal state, understood as a vehicle for protecting not just the liberty but also the capabilities of citizens, should recognize * * * [are] first, a right to be protected against private violence, and second, a right of caregivers to give care to dependents without incurring the risk of severe impoverishment or subordination * * *. Both rights, I think, are directly entailed by the state's obligation to provide the minimal preconditions for the development of those fundamental human capabilities that are themselves essential to a fully human life. Both rights however, could be and should be conceived in the most traditionally liberal terms. The first such right—the right to protection against private violence—although now disfavored in United States rights discourse, seems fully authorized by both the liberal tradition and the American Constitution itself. The second right for which I will argue—the right to provide care to dependents—has no similar basis of support in either liberal theory or American constitutionalism. It is not incompatible with either, however, and is at least arguably required by the deepest commitments of both. The right to protection and the right to care are rights that can be framed in liberal terms, and both rights would go a long way toward securing for individual citizens the minimal preconditions of a good society.

Notes and Questions

1. Is West persuasive that "a right to be protected against private violence" and "a right of caregivers to give care to dependents without incurring the risk of severe impoverishment or subordination" are necessary for full human life? If so, what role should society play in ensuring those rights to its members? Should social justice lawyers seek to establish these "rights?"

The rights of caregivers and the duty of society to support them are explored in chapter 8. The efforts of social justice activists, theorists, and lawyers to establish rights to protection against private violence are discussed in chapters 9 and 14.

2. Some critical race theorists have challenged the critical legal studies view that the utilization of rights is "one of the ways that law helps to legitimize the social world by representing it as rationally mediated by the rule of law." Kimberlé Crenshaw, Neil Gotanda, Gary Peller & Kendall Thomas eds., *Critical Race Theory: The Key Writings that Formed the Movement* xxiii (1995). Critical legal scholars also "saw legal rights—like those against racial discrimination—as indeterminate and capable of contradictory meanings, and as embodying an alienated way of thinking about social relations." *Id.* For example Mark Tushnet argued:

> [N]othing whatever follows from a court's adoption of some legal rule * * * . Progressive legal victories occur * * * because of the surrounding social circumstances. If those circumstances support material as well as ideological gains, well and good. And, of course, as long as those circumstances are stable, the legal victory will be so as well. But, if circumstances change, the "rule" could be eroded or, more interestingly, interpreted to support *anti*-progressive change.

Mark Tushnet, *The Critique of Rights*, 47 SMU L. Rev. 23, 32–33 (1993).

What does it mean that rights are indeterminate? The term right sounds like a concrete guarantee of protection. Yet the right against racial discrimination—carved out by years of heroic struggle—has for more than a decade been invoked by the Supreme Court mostly to strike down programs aimed at remedying the effects of past racial discrimination. *See* Girardeau A. Spann, *The Law of Affirmative Action: Twenty-Five Years of Supreme Court Decisions on Race and Remedies* (2000). One study found that whites had challenged the gains of the civil rights movement in fourteen cases that reached the Supreme Court between 1987 and 2000, winning outright in nine cases, losing in one case that was later reversed, and losing in three cases on points, such as the standing of a particular plaintiff, that had little effect on the determination of substantive rights against discrimination. Martha R. Mahoney, *Whiteness and Remedy: Under-Ruling Civil Rights in* Walker v. City of Mesquite, 85 Cornell L. Rev. 1309, 1352–54 (2000). This use of a right, here against racial discrimination, to protect the entrenched structures of privilege created by discriminatory practices led scholars to point to the elasticity in the notion of a right.

3. A study of southern civil rights organizing summarized the arguments against an emphasis on rights: " 'It is not just that rights-talk does not do much good,' Mark Tushnet states flatly. 'In the contemporary United States, it is positively harmful.' " Francesca Polletta, *The Structural Context of Novel Rights Claims: Southern Civil Rights Organizing, 1961–1966*, 34 Law & Soc'y Rev. 367, 367 (2000). Francesca Polletta observes that Critical Legal Studies theorists:

> argue that the indeterminacy of rights allows judicial decisionmakers to operate on the basis of idiosyncratic and ideological preferences and allows unmeritorious opponents of progressive interests to invoke legal rights with equal clout. Thinking in terms of rights, moreover, substitutes a mystified notion of human sociability for a more authentic form of unalienated connection. The problem, then, is not only litigation as movement strategy, with its dependence on lawyers, its cost, and its inability to guarantee enforcement, but the very formulation of grievances in terms of rights. As Kelman puts it, "Basically the claim is quite cognitive: to the extent that people are 'afflicted' by legal thinking . . . counterhegemonic thought will simply make less sense, simply be harder to think." * * * While they may not want to junk rights claims altogether, recognizing their value as a motivating source of "imagery and inspiration[,]" activists should concentrate on collectively "unthinking" the ideological distortions that rights-talk reflects and furthers. They should "keep [their] eye on power and not on rights."

Polletta, *supra* at 367–68.

Is the terminology of rights empty, alienating, and essentially meaningless?

4. Might rights discourse hold dangers that are worse than meaningless? Consider Richard Abel's critique of rights in the context of legal aid work:

> Legal aid is at least consistent with, and arguably supportive of, capitalism in several * * * respects. Because it necessarily seeks to enforce legal rights, it forces grievances into a legal, that is, individual, form. Eligibility criteria define the legal aid clientele as a collection of individuals sharing common characteristics—indigence, residence, perhaps nationality—rather than as a group. Legal aid programs create bonds, but among lawyers, not clients. Clients share few experiences except those inherent in the amorphous status of poverty; they are not even united by a visible common enemy. In both respects, they contrast markedly with trade unions, ethnic associations, the feminist movement, even environmentalist groups. Although legal aid clients may be treated as a category for purposes of litigation, this does not build an ongoing collectivity but merely provides a temporary surrogate. Therefore, it is not surprising that efforts to institute community control of legal aid programs

> generally fail, for they presuppose precisely what is missing and what legal aid is unable to create—meaningful community. Indeed, programs often curtail or prohibit efforts to organize groups, although such restrictions seem superfluous since lawyers lack both the skills and the inclination to attempt that task. * * * * * *
>
> * * * To the extent that legal aid alters the balance of power, it does so only within the judicial or quasi-judicial arena, namely the administrative agency. It assumes that the most significant conflicts within society have been translated into a legal form and ignores those that are not or cannot be. Substantive rules give powerless groups and individuals significant leverage within the judicial arena, but those rules also establish limits. More importantly, powerless groups and individuals cannot change the rules, except by appealing to higher rules, nor can they resist rule changes sought by others. Even within the courtroom, equality remains an unattainable chimera. * * * In civil litigation, legal aid clients face adversaries who have structured transactions with an eye toward future legal consequences; the latter enjoy advantages of experience, information, and credibility, possess infinitely greater resources, and can benefit from economies of scale. When legal aid lawyers do win cases, especially test cases, they may secure only paper victories: Some commentators have estimated that enforcement rates vary from fifty percent to as low as ten percent. Yet how could it be otherwise? How could anyone have expected a few dozen, or even a few thousand, lawyers to effect fundamental social change? The illusion shows the enormous power of the myth of rights in liberal ideology.

Richard L. Abel, *Law Without Politics: Legal Aid Under Advanced Capitalism*, 32 UCLA L. Rev. 474, 595–96, 600–01 (1985).

In contrast, for critical race scholars, "rights discourse held a social and transformative value in the context of racial subordination that transcended the narrower question of whether reliance on rights could alone bring about any determinate results." Crenshaw, Gotanda, Peller & Thomas, *supra* at xxiii. Patricia Williams urges that the experience of rights by people of color is different from the privileged mainstream:

> To say that blacks never fully believed in rights is true. Yet it is also true that blacks believed in them so much and so hard that we gave them life where there was none before; we held onto them, put the hope of them into our wombs, mothered them and not the notion of them. And this was not the dry process of reification, from which life is drained and reality fades as the cement of conceptual determinism hardens round—but its opposite. This was the resurrection of life from ashes four hundred years old. The making of something out of nothing took immense alchemical fire—the fusion of a whole nation and the kindling of several generations. The illusion became real for only a few of us; it is still elusive for most. But if it took this long to breathe life into a form whose shape had already been forged by

> society, and which is therefore idealistically if not ideologically accessible, imagine how long the struggle would be without even that sense of definition, without the power of that familiar vision.

Patricia J. Williams, *The Alchemy of Race and Rights* 163 (1991). Is Williams' argument for the use of rights in that historic context persuasive? Does litigation for legal rights remain an important strategy for social justice lawyers? Should litigation be seen as the primary way to claim rights?

Michael Diamond has commented:

> [T]he law is not capable of protecting the interests of the poor and subordinated. While the creation of a legal right is an important symbolic victory in the struggle against subordination, it should not be seen as the culmination of the struggle. Poignantly, creating the legal right to a desegregated school system is not the same thing as having an integrated, non-discriminatory, high-quality school system.

Michael Diamond, *Community Lawyering: Revisiting the Old Neighborhood*, 32 Colum. Human Rights L. Rev. 67, 107 (2000).

5. If creation of legal rights is not the ultimate goal of social justice lawyering, what then should be ultimate goals? Commenting on the debate about goals, Diamond states:

> What is missing in the debate is the recognition of the political possibilities in what clients and their lawyers confront. The goal for community lawyers should include assisting clients to create power and lasting institutions with the ability to influence the clients' environment, rather than solely the creation or enforcement of rights or providing legal remedies to legal wrongs.

Id. at 108–09.

Martha Minow emphasized the difference between legal rules and rights claims that express aspirations about how people should be treated:

> I should try to clarify what I mean by "rights," an overused word in legal, philosophical, and political debates. * * * One meaning is the formally announced legal rules that concern relationships among individuals, groups, and the official state. "Rights" typically are the articulation of such rules in a form that describes the enforceable claims of individuals or groups against the state. Yet * * * [there is a second meaning:] "Rights" can give rise to "rights consciousness" so that individuals and groups may imagine and act in light of rights that have not been formally recognized or enforced. Rights, in this sense, are neither limited to nor co-extensive with precisely those rules formally announced and enforced by public authorities. Instead, rights represent articulations—public or private, formal or informal—of claims that people use to persuade others (and themselves) about how they should be treated and about what they should be granted. * * * [I] include within the ambit of rights

discourse all efforts to claim new rights, to resist and alter official state action that fails to acknowledge such rights, and to construct communities apart from the state to nurture new conceptions of rights. Rights here encompass even those claims that lose, or have lost in the past, if they continue to represent claims that muster people's hopes and articulate their continuing efforts to persuade.

Consciousness, or cognizance, of rights, then, is not simply awareness of those rights that have been granted in the past, but also knowledge of the process by which hurts that once were whispered or unheard have become claims, and claims that once were unsuccessful, have persuaded others and transformed social life. The connections between past and future claims of rights are voiced through interpretations of inherited understandings of rights. Interpretation engages lawyers and nonlawyers in composing new meanings inside and outside of legal institutions. Charges against new rights express opposition to this interpretive process.

Martha Minow, *Interpreting Rights: An Essay for Robert Cover*, 96 Yale L.J. 1860, 1866–67 (1987).

6. In response to the critique of rights, some scholars emphasized "the ways in which rights claims can be linked to claims for power." Elizabeth M. Schneider, *The Dialectic of Rights and Politics: Perspectives from the Women's Movement*, 61 N.Y.U. L. Rev. 589, 629, n. 201 (1986). Schneider argues that rights discourse has "dual possibilities:" it can "reinforce alienation and individualism, and can constrict political vision and debate," but it also has the potential to affirm human values and enhance political growth. *Id.* at 598.

Echoing points made earlier by Stuart Scheingold, Elizabeth Schneider argues that rights, and specifically litigation, can mobilize people by casting grievances as legitimate entitlements and by fostering a sense of collective identity; can help to organize political groups through lawyers' resources of organizational skills and legitimacy; and can contribute to processes of political realignment, though in ways that are less predictable and conclusive than "ideologists" of a rights strategy would suggest. Litigation can force those in power to account for their actions; it renders them less invulnerable, exposes them to evaluation, and challenges the practices implicitly justified by tradition or habit. Together, these can motivate other forms of political action: lobbying for legislation, direct action demonstrations, economic boycotts, and so forth.

Legal victories may not be necessary to realize those benefits. For the targets of litigation, the possibility of a defeat in court may be enough to convince them to institute changes. * * *

Recognizing the multivalent character of rights should not lead us to an overoptimistic faith in the power of challengers to replace hegemonic meanings with subversive ones, however. As Didi Herman cautions, "[T]here is no reason why progressive social movements necessarily rearticulate rights in such a way as to challenge

> power relations. Rights' meanings cannot simply be 're-invented' and disseminated at will." To be sure, people can assert anything as a "right," which can be defined as an "entitlement" without requiring that the entitlement be legally authorized or enforced. But we usually think of rights as claims backed up by the force of law—or *potentially* done so. This conception of rights allows for innovation, but not wild invention. What makes legal rights claims powerful is the conjunction of moral principle and the force of the state. That American courts are unlikely to protect rights to bigamy any time soon, for example, diminishes the power of such claims outside the courts.

Polletta, *supra* at 377–78.

The emphasis on substantive equality over formal equality in critical race theory reflects this understanding of rights discourse:

> The image of a "traditional civil rights discourse" refers to the constellation of ideas about racial power and social transformation that were constructed partly by, and partly as a defense against, the mass mobilization of social energy and popular imagination in the civil rights movements of the late fifties and sixties. To those who participated in the civil rights movements firsthand—say, as part of the street and body politics engaged in by Reverend Martin Luther King, Jr.'s cadres in town after town across the South—the fact that they were part of a deeply subversive movement of mass resistance and social transformation was obvious. Our opposition to traditional civil rights discourse is neither a criticism of the civil rights movement nor an attempt to diminish its significance. On the contrary, * * * we draw much of our inspiration and sense of direction from that courageous, brilliantly conceived, spiritually inspired, and ultimately transformative mass action.

Crenshaw, Gotanda, Peller & Thomas, *supra* at xiv. How might rights claims inspire transformation? If they can, does that possibility answer concerns raised by scholars who argue that in some ways rights claims may also limit transformation?

7. What might it mean to imagine relationships in ways not limited by the structures of rights discourse? Robert Williams reports how the Five Confederated Tribes of the Iroquois responded to European encroachment on their land and personal freedom by " 'link[ing] arms together' with European newcomers through treaties negotiated according to indigenous North American visions of law and peace in a multicultural world." Robert A. Williams, Jr., *Linking Arms Together: Multicultural Constitutionalism in a North American Indigenous Vision of Law and Peace*, 82 Cal. L. Rev. 981, 984 (1994). The Iroquois, "a five nation confederacy of tribes comprised of the Mohawks, Oneidas, Onondagas, Cayugas, and Senecas," *id.* at 988, formed the Covenant Chain to provide trade and collective security. The Covenant Chain positioned the Iroquois to demand and receive "reciprocal treatment and respect as

mutual partners in their alliance with the English colonies." *Id.* at 990. Williams explains:

> As a constitution, the Chain was fundamentally a legal and political text, for both the English and the Iroquois were guided in their relations by its underlying principle of a continually renewed reciprocity of rights and duties. The Chain's imagery and metaphors—of two once-alien groups connected in an interdependent relationship of peace, solidarity, and trust—became the governing legal and political language of English-Iroquois forest diplomacy * * * .

Id. at 991.

Williams quotes Joseph Singer, who argues that "the relation between power and vulnerability should be at the heart of our analysis of property rights. Rather than asking 'who owns the factory?' we should ask 'what relationships should we nurture?' " Joseph W. Singer, *The Reliance Interest in Property,* 40 Stan. L. Rev. 611, 751 (1988) (excerpted in chapter 8). Echoing Singer, Williams challenges us to consider "what it would take to create the kind of society in which we could trust each other enough to place our lives in each other's hands, by linking arms together * * * ." *Id.* at 1048.

Do you want to create a society in which we can trust each other enough to place our lives in each others' hands? Does the use of rights language to claim protection for individuals produce tensions with the goal of building a society that creates new partnerships, protects vulnerability, and chooses which relationships to nurture? Can rights discourse facilitate those goals?

C. The Transformative Potential of Rights Claims

Sharon Hom and Eric Yamamoto explain how claims about rights may be part of mobilizing and defining a public sense of social justice.

SHARON K. HOM & ERIC K. YAMAMOTO

Collective Memory, History, and Social Justice
47 UCLA L. Rev. 1747, 1748–50, 1752–54,
1756–59, 1764–65 (2000)

* * * The dawning of the new century unveils familiar and persistent global and local inequalities, conflict and violence, human suffering and environmental destruction. As the first United Nations High Commissioner for Human Rights recognized, "the world picture of human rights violations continues to display the same disturbing patterns and trends that it did prior to the establishment of the United Nations." Indeed, despite the current rhetoric in foundation, government, and policy circles about the rise of civil society and the rule of law, we live in violent—uncivil—times.

Hundreds of thousands of civilian men, women, and children have been butchered in "internal" ethnic and religious conflicts throughout the world; and the killing continues. More than six million people are exploited in some form of bonded labor or human servitude, including the forced prostitution of children and women, the forced recruitment of child soldiers, and the exploitation of child labor.

Within the United States, the level of violence against people of color, women, and gays and lesbians also signals the uncivility of the times. White supremacists dragged James Byrd behind a truck until his body parts tore off. Gay-bashers beat Matthew Shepard and left him to die on a fencepost. The U.S. Supreme Court invalidated the Violence Against Women Act. Random racial shootings occur with alarming frequency. In New York, Newark, Los Angeles, and other cities, police not only admit to racial profiling of blacks and other dark-skinned minorities, they participate in numerous racial shootings and false prosecutions of innocent people. And while death penalty supporters advocate for more executions more quickly, some judges and politicians are acknowledging not only the racial disparity in death sentencing, but also the startlingly high percentage of death penalty mistakes.

These realities of domestic and international violence are related to the economic violence of a global (dis)order that relegates the majority of humans on the planet to poverty and destroys local communities and cultures. Despite demands by developing countries for a more equitable share of the world's resources, such as those made in the New International Economic Order (NIEO) plan advocated by Third World countries and adopted by the United Nations General Assembly in 1974, the gap between poor and rich countries continues to widen. * * *

* * *

In the United States, where a "rising tide" was supposed to lift all the boats, a recent study by the Center on Budget and Policy Priorities suggests that despite two decades of economic growth, only a small segment has benefited. Economic inequality may now be at its most extreme since the Second World War. This is particularly so at the intersection of race and poverty. Statistics tell part of the story. For instance, 46.3 percent of black children live below the poverty line, compared to 12.3 percent of white children; blacks with Bachelors degrees earn 76 percent of the salary of similarly qualified whites. Disparities such as these are explained in part by the persistence of racism against people of color, particularly African Americans, at all levels of employment. Indeed, a massive study in 1999 by the Russell Sage Foundation, covering four major cities, 10,000 workers, and 3000 businesses, found significant racial discrimination in favor of whites in institutional hiring and promotion practices.

Other parts to this uncivil story lie beyond statistics. Despite entrenched group economic disparities, strident and sometimes virulent political campaigns have succeeded in legally banning affirmative action, cutting off the rights of immigrants and their children, barring bilingual education, prohibiting gay marriage, and paring down welfare benefits. The current Supreme Court also has sharply limited the reach of civil rights laws, except in cases in which whites claim "reverse discrimination," dissociating law from many communities' sense of justice. * * *

* * *

The once potent U.S. civil rights movement of the sixties sought transformation of the spirit, mind, and most of all, the daily material conditions of peoples' lives. From Civil War abolitionists to the Montgomery Boycott to the March on Washington, civil rights mobilized African Americans and communities of all colors, including liberal whites, men and women, to break down racial barriers that created and supported the inequities of existing social and economic hierarchies. Civil rights as a call to action tapped into diverse peoples' moral and ethical cores; "civil rights" meant rectifying deep injustices. * * *

As U.S. society moves into the next century, this progressive civil rights legacy has been undermined by conservative political backlash and rhetorical appropriation of rights language and its moral claims. The equality and affirmative action social transformation goals of the fifties and sixties have been challenged by the rhetoric of color blindness, racial preferences, and reverse discrimination of the late eighties and nineties. Yet, this conservative civil rights rhetoric clearly legitimates continuing inequities—witness California's Proposition 209, the anti-affirmative action "Civil Rights Initiative." Narrow civil rights laws have been largely ineffective against entrenched institutional forms of discrimination. Intraracial conflict and tensions emerge as blacks, Asian Americans, and Latinos charge each other with civil rights violations in disputes over education and government contracting. Amid the emerging demographic and economic fault lines, immigrants, migrant workers, women, gays and lesbians, and the poor are claiming space at the crowded "rights" table.

Beyond the increasingly blurred domestic boundaries of the nation-state, geopolitical shifts and transnational capital redefine meanings of "citizenship," "work," and "fair treatment," and international genocide, ethnic conflict throughout the world, indigenous peoples' claims, and truth commissions reframe understandings of "accountability," "reparation," and "justice." The foundational notion of rights itself is destabilizing. Buffeted by these international and domestic crosscurrents, "civil rights" in these "uncivil" times has not only lost much of its transformative power, it can no longer meaningfully do the progressive theoretical and strategic work it needs to do. * * *

Given this complex material, discursive and theoretical landscape, what is to be done? Do we abandon civil rights altogether and search for something fresh? We think not. Despite its limitations, civil rights still carries enormous purchase. Its rhetoric connects historically to reconstruction and transformation. Its past practices link to mass protests, civil disobedience, and public education. Its roots are embedded in established, although ideologically limited and limiting, antidiscrimination law. And civil rights still signals the moral and ethical power of

African-Americans' struggles for freedom and equality—for a better and fairer life for all.

* * *

Who frames injustice in the law's eye and the public's mind? How and with what societal effects? As these questions imply, in important ways, framing injustice is about social memory.

In an era characterized by a conservative "retreat from justice," many progressive lawyers and activists seeking legal justice define injustice narrowly. They focus on legal doctrine and its definition of a civil rights claim. They then frame the injustice in language that satisfies the requirements of antidiscrimination law—for instance, the disparate impact on racial minorities of discriminatory practices of an Alaskan salmon cannery. That framing, while legally apt, narrows public imagination and debate. In its search for "relevant facts" and crisp argument, it relegates history and community agitation to back-up roles in civil rights struggles.

By contrast, groups seeking social justice tend to define injustice more broadly. To fuel political movements, they expand the law's narrow framing of injustice and focus on historical facts to more fully portray what happened and why it was wrong. In this way, history becomes a catalyst for mass mobilization and collective action aimed at policymakers, bureaucrats, and the American conscience.

Both of these approaches to framing injustice have contributed to ground level justice efforts. But both, in their handling of history, miss something of considerable strategic import. They miss what the 1950s' Civil Rights Congress (CRC) incorporated strategically into its action plans, and what today's conservative think tanks hold as a lynchpin: Social understandings of historical injustice are largely constructed in the present. Those understandings are rooted less in backward-looking searches for "what happened" than in the present-day dynamics of collective memory.

* * * [G]roup identities, social suffering and collective accounts of historical events evade easy description. How are historical memories of group pain and loss formed by group experiences and continually reformed by changing ideology and social circumstances? How, for instance, do group memories of racial grievances inform current conflicts and shape the ways in which racial wounds are aggravated or salved?

Recent international works identify the political dimensions of memory reconstruction by both oppressors and victims, at all levels. Individuals, social groups, institutions, and nations filter and twist, recall and forget "information" in reframing shameful past acts (thereby lessening responsibility) as well as in enhancing victim status (thereby increasing power). Collective memory not only vivifies a group's past, it also reconstructs it and thereby situates a group in relation to others in a power hierarchy.

For instance, the recent investigation of the International Commission on the Balkans (the Commission) revealed a tortuous postcommunist remaking of history integral to the justification of ethnic and religious violence in the Balkan states. The Commission found that Balkan leaders—Serbian president Slobodan Milosevic, Croatian president Fanjo Tudjman, and Bosnian Serb leader Radovan Karadzic—identified ancestral and religious strife as the main sources of recent atrocities. The Commission also found that the political leaders' specific characterizations of ancestral strife were unsupported by historical circumstances. The politicians deployed falsely constructed ancient enmities to justify the unjustifiable. According to the Commission, the politicians "have invoked the 'ancient hatreds' to pursue their respective nationalist agendas and have deliberately used their propaganda machines to justify the unjustifiable: the use of violence for territorial conquest, expulsion of 'other' peoples, and the perpetuation of authoritarian systems."

* * *

The public portrayal of group memory transformed the process of Japanese American redress. For Japanese Americans interned during World War II without charges or trial because of race, the deep, wounded need to tell their story (to remake history from their perspective) drove the 1980s redress movement into the courts, legislatures, schools, and newsrooms. It was only when scores of now-aging Japanese Americans spoke publicly for the first time before a congressional commission in 1982, telling their stories both of loyalty and patriotism and of loss, humiliation, and continuing hardship, did a new story emerge. That story deeply touched even conservatives on the commission. It framed United States-generated injustice in terms of the human suffering of loyal U.S. citizens and thereby grounded $1.6 billion in reparations and a presidential apology.

Yet, that emergent group memory, which so moved mainstream policymakers and the public, was partial. It was partial—that is, incomplete—because the dominant story of patriotic suffering focused only on unquestioning loyalty and acquiescence to governmental abuse. It was partial—that is, ideological—because it erased from history fierce Japanese American resistance to the internment's injustice, including the constitutional challenges, opposition to the military draft, and civil disobedience in the internment prisons. This partial memory, publicly proclaimed and governmentally recognized, split open old wounds of exclusion within the Japanese American community, wounds only now beginning to heal.

* * *

The struggle over recognition of competing collective memories is therefore often a struggle over the supremacy of world views, of colliding ideologies. And through those struggles we have the potential to remake our, and society's, understandings of justice—for good or ill.

This means that the group members, lawyers, politicians, justice workers, and scholars possess often unacknowledged power at the very foundational stages of every redress movement. The power resides in the potential for constructing collective memories of injustice as a basis for redress. * * *

* * *

In light of the importance of power and culture, it is never enough for societal outsiders only to frame the injustice narrowly to satisfy legal norms. Conversely, *it is always important for those outsiders to conceive of law and legal process as contributors to—rather than as the essence of—larger social justice strategies*. This means working with legal process and rights claims with dual goals: to achieve the specific legal result and to contribute to construction of social memory as a political tool.

Notes and Questions

1. For a description of the success of reparations claims for Japanese Americans, linking that struggle with continuation of rights claims for African Americans, see Eric K. Yamamoto, *Racial Reparations: Japanese American Redress and African American Claims*, 40 B.C. L. Rev. 477 (1998). *See also* Chris K. Iijima, *Reparations and the "Model Minority" Idealogy of Acquiescence: The Necessity to Refuse the Return to Original Humiliation*, 40 B.C. L. Rev. 385 (1998) (describing internment of Japanese Americans on Native American land). For an argument that collective memory "should reflect an understanding of the ways in which racial discrimination against one group is connected to racial discrimination against another," see Robert S. Chang, *Closing Essay: Developing a Collective Memory to Imagine a Better Future*, 49 UCLA L. Rev. 1601, 1610 (2002) (urging an examination of differences and convergences in treatments of racial groups).

2. Is contributing to the construction of social memory, as described by Hom and Yamamoto, appropriately a task for a lawyer? Are lawyers trained to perform this aspect of social justice work? Is the task of shaping collective memory related to community empowerment, discussed in chapter 11? How might lawyers acquire the training to empower communities or to shape collective memory?

*

Chapter 8

LIVELIHOOD: WORK, CAREGIVING, AND DEPENDENCY

This chapter explores the efforts to vindicate claims of rights to employment and subsistence in law in the United States. It examines the interrelationships in social policy between work for wages, lack of work or inability to work, and care for those members of society who cannot care for themselves. During the 20th century, a political demand for rights to employment was articulated during the Great Depression and after the Second World War. Should workers have protection against arbitrary and unreasonable discharge from employment? Should government have the responsibility of ensuring that enough jobs exist for the people who need them? If a society chooses *not* to protect workers—indeed, deliberately maintains unemployment among workers as part of managing the economy—then how should that society handle the hardships which will be inevitable for those who have no other resources?

What about the people who could not work even if a job were available because they are too young, too old, or disabled? Are caregivers—people who care for those who cannot care for themselves—as free to work as those who have no similar responsibilities? Should care of the young and disabled be accomplished through paid employment? Or, because society depends on human reproduction to survive, must society find ways to ensure that people who care for others have enough support to meet their fundamental needs?

SECTION 1. THE SEARCH FOR A RIGHT TO EMPLOYMENT

This section examines rights to employment. Kenneth Karst argues that the government already manages the economy with regard to employment, but that it does so to maintain unemployment rather than to provide jobs for all. William Forbath and Margaret Weir describe measures that the United States has considered, but declined to adopt, which would have created statutory recognition of rights to full employment. Although exceptions to the doctrine of employment at will exist in many states, common law has, for the most part, refused to protect rights to jobs for either individuals or communities.

A. The Importance of Work

PRESIDENT FRANKLIN D. ROOSEVELT

The "Economic Bill of Rights"(State of the Union Message to Congress, 1944)
The Public Papers and Addresses of Franklin D. Roosevelt, Vol. 13, Victory and the Threshold of Peace, 1944–45
40–41, 43 (Samuel I. Rosenman ed., 1950)

This Republic had its beginning, and grew to its present strength, under the protection of certain inalienable political rights, among them the right of free speech, free press, free worship, trial by jury, freedom from unreasonable searches and seizures. They were our rights to life and liberty.

As our nation has grown in size and stature, however—as our industrial economy expanded—these political rights proved inadequate to assure us equality in the pursuit of happiness.

We have come to a clear realization of the fact that true individual freedom cannot exist without economic security and independence. "Necessitous men are not free men." People who are hungry and out of a job are the stuff of which dictatorships are made.

In our day these economic truths have become accepted as self evident. We have accepted, so to speak, a second Bill of Rights under which a new basis of security and prosperity can be established for all—regardless of station, race, or creed.

Among these are :

The right to a useful and remunerative job in the industries or shops or farms or mines of the Nation;

The right to earn enough to provide adequate food and clothing and recreation;

The right of every farmer to raise and sell his products at a return which will give him and his family a decent living;

The right of every business man, large and small, to trade in an atmosphere of freedom from unfair competition and domination by monopolies at home or abroad;

The right of every family to a decent home;

The right to adequate medical care and the opportunity to achieve and enjoy good health;

The right to adequate protection from the economic fears of old age, sickness, accident, and unemployment;

The right to a good education.

* * *

ORGANIZATION OF AMERICAN STATES CHARTER

Article 29: * * * Work is a right and a social duty; it shall not be considered as an article of commerce; it demands respect for freedom of association and for the dignity of the worker * * *.

UNIVERSAL DECLARATION OF HUMAN RIGHTS

Adopted by the United Nations General Assembly, December 10, 1948

Article 23.

1. Everyone has the right to work, to free choice of employment, to just and favourable conditions of work and to protection against unemployment.

2. Everyone, without any discrimination, has the right to equal pay for equal work.

3. Everyone who works has the right to just and favourable remuneration ensuring for himself and his family an existence worthy of human dignity, and supplemented, if necessary, by other means of social protection.

4. Everyone has the right to form and to join trade unions for the protections of his interests.

Article 24.

Everyone has the right to rest and leisure, including reasonable limitation of working hours and periodic holidays with pay.

Article 25.

1. Everyone has the right to a standard of living adequate for the health and well-being of himself and his family, including food, clothing, housing and medical care and necessary social services, and the right to security in the event of unemployment, sickness, disability, widowhood, old age or other lack of livelihood in circumstances beyond his control.

2. Motherhood and childhood are entitled to special care and assistance. All children, whether born in or out of wedlock, shall enjoy the same social protection.

KENNETH L. KARST

The Coming Crisis of Work in Constitutional Perspective,
82 Cornell L. Rev. 523, 523–28, 530–32, 534–38,
540–41, 551–55, 557–58, 571 (1997)

Every month the United States Bureau of Labor Statistics issues a report on employment and unemployment. Even if you are not old enough to remember the Great Depression, you may think, as I do, that a decline in unemployment is good news. But when the number of the unemployed goes down month after month, the people who trade in stocks become fearful that interest rates will be raised. The committee of the Federal Reserve System that regulates those rates has tended to interpret a low level of unemployment as a sign that the economy is "overheating" and in need of a cold-water bath to prevent inflation. The regulators often refer to a five or six percent civilian unemployment rate as the "natural" level, and if Mother Nature should fail to produce the right level on her own, they stand ready to help.

No one disputes that there is some trade-off between full employment and the avoidance of inflationary pressures. Nor can one deny that workers who are employed benefit from an anti-inflation policy to the extent that it protects the buying power of their wages against erosion. For the moment, it is enough to recognize that our national employment policy is not a full employment policy but a policy to control the demand for labor, keeping unemployment at a level high enough to prevent wages from rising too much.

* * * [W]e need to consider the ways in which the official unemployment rate—an artifact of counting—understates the difficulty millions of Americans face when they seek steady, adequately paid work. For one thing, many who are wholly unemployed have become so discouraged that they have simply stopped looking for work. These people are not counted in the official unemployment figures; if they were counted, the figures would be much greater. And unemployment for black Americans consistently runs at about twice the rate for whites at any age level. But even this is only part of the story.

The official figures count part-time, temporary, and seasonal workers as employed, even though they may ardently desire steady, full-time work. "Consultants" are counted as employed even when they are self-employed only because they cannot find other work. Despite the * * * creation of millions of new jobs [during the 1990s], a great many of these jobs offer part-time work or work that is temporary or otherwise contingent. These "permanent temporary workers" generally receive lower hourly wages than those paid to full-time, year-round workers. More disturbingly, in a system that largely ties social welfare to jobs, these temporary and contingent jobs typically offer no health insurance, no child care, no pension benefits, and little opportunity for advancement. One can only estimate degrees of underemployment; one of the higher estimates is that as much as one-third of the American labor force wants work, wants more work, or has given up on the possibility of finding work. Ultimately, a greater flexibility of employment, including job-sharing itself, may be part of a sensible response to the crisis of joblessness—but not if part-time workers are still paid lower wages and are still unprotected by private or public health care and pension benefits.

Among the newly created full-time jobs, many pay the minimum wage. Most recipients of the minimum wage are not raising families, and for good reason: even after the increase * * * enacted by Congress [in

1996], one earner's minimum wage is insufficient to bring a family of three up to the poverty line. The purchasing power of the minimum wage declined sharply in the 1980s and early 1990s. With that factor compounded by the depressing effects on wages of the large number of Americans who are looking for work, or for more work, real wages for jobs at the lower skill levels have fallen dramatically in the last quarter-century. These lowest-wage jobs typically offer the slimmest chances for upward movement, especially for minority workers, who are disproportionately represented in those jobs. The poverty rate for *full-time workers* increased by about fifty percent from 1980 to the early 1990s.

The distribution of poverty in American society is not random. It falls most heavily on members of some racial and ethnic minorities, on women, on the young, and on people with limited educational opportunities. Lower-skill manufacturing jobs have disappeared at an alarming rate, giving way to automation and to low-wage competition from overseas workers. Service jobs, once seen as a promising substitute, are becoming automated at a rate that beclouds the earlier optimism. Many Americans have come to fear that their families will fall out of the middle class because relatives or friends have already suffered that fate. In the 1980s, while middle class income and wealth stayed constant, and while the poor were struggling to survive, the rich got much, much richer. The "split society" is here.

* * *

Liberty: Work and the Constitution of Independent Individuals

* * *

* * * Most obviously, jobs are "the entry tickets to provisions." Whatever other meanings work may bear, for most of us it is a crucial means of sustaining ourselves and our families. Work can be a teacher, offering the chance to learn tasks at increasing levels of authority and increasing levels of pay. Central to "the American dream" is the notion that a free and independent individual can rise to a better condition through hard work, and that his or her family can join in the rise. Especially vital to family security today are the health care and pension benefits that attach to many jobs. Where there are young children, decent child care becomes an additional family concern.

* * * [W]ork means much more than a paycheck; it is the exercise of responsibility. The responsibilities involved in work extend not just to our loved ones but to our coworkers, and even to the larger community. Work is still seen as connected to the citizenship values of respect, independence, and participation. In our society, as much as anywhere else in the world, work is a means of proving yourself worthy in your own eyes and in the eyes of others. Even a person who hates his or her job can understand the idea of "[t]he dignity of work and of personal achievement."

* * *

What happens to individuals and families when the formal freedom to work becomes hollow because stable work with a decent wage, decent health and retirement benefits, and access to decent child care just isn't available? Most obviously, family income is sharply reduced. But other harms of unemployment and underemployment are less tangible, growing out of the positive social meanings that Americans have invested in work:

— If stable, adequately paid work is a source of independence, its absence means dependence on others.

— If stable, adequately paid work is an avenue to personal achievement, its absence signifies failure.

— If stable, adequately paid work offers advancement up the socioeconomic ladder, its absence means that one's social station is either fixed or in decline.

— If stable, adequately paid work provides family security, its absence means insecurity.

— If stable, adequately paid work elicits the esteem of others, its absence means shame.

Considerations like these undoubtedly have influenced the Justices who have nourished a number of constitutional guarantees that are not in any formal sense related to the freedom to work. Consider, for example, the application of the Equal Protection Clause to education. When the Supreme Court held [in Plyler v. Doe, 457 U.S. 202, 218–19 (1982), excerpted in chapter 9] that Texas could not constitutionally exclude undocumented alien children from public schools, Justice Brennan's opinion for the Court decried the irrationality of creating a permanent lower caste. One unspoken link in this reasoning is that education is the basis for many employment opportunities, the first step on the occupational ladder for the independent individual. The subject of work was also in the minds of the Justices who first recognized a woman's constitutional right to choose to have an abortion, and who two decades later preserved that right in the face of an assault that almost destroyed it. In the latter case [Planned Parenthood of Southeastern Pa. v. Casey, 505 U.S. 833 (1992)], the plurality opinion was explicit: "The ability of women to participate equally in the economic and social life of the Nation has been facilitated by their ability to control their reproductive lives." Both of these rights are explainable in the constitutional vocabulary of equality; but they also sound in the vocabularies of individual liberty, independence, and free access to work.

Given decisions of this kind, it may seem incongruous that the Supreme Court in the modern era has not given constitutional recognition to a free-standing right to work. Even in the days when the Court was invalidating wage-and-hour laws and other governmental restrictions on the liberty of the employment contract, the Justices gave no hint of any individual right to be afforded work. The liberty in question was a formal freedom from governmental regulation of private bargains, grounded on a formal equality of right—and never mind the huge differences in the bargaining power of employers and workers. But even this formal legal equality could be submerged. For one example among many, a potential worker who claimed a freedom to be idle might be imprisoned because his idleness was made into the crime of vagrancy, but the idea of imposing on potential employers a correlative legal duty to provide work was unthinkable. Any assertion of an employer's constitutional duty would encounter the "state action" limitation that had been read into the Fourteenth Amendment, and a statute imposing a similar duty would be an unconstitutional invasion of the employer's sphere of private liberty. Nor could any comparable duties be imposed on the states or Congress. Government's constitutional duty was noninterference, and no one in authority thought that judges could compel legislators or executive officials either to employ the unemployed or to take other positive action on their behalf.

* * *

In the nineteenth century, American law began to confront two stark systems of dependency, both of which centered on control over work and its rewards. The system of slavery succumbed to constitutional amendment and congressional legislation only after four years of carnage. Married women's economic subordination to their husbands eroded more gradually through legislation and judicial interpretation, in a process that took more than a century. In each of these cases, ending the dependency meant freeing identifiable clients (enslaved persons, married women) from the legal control of identifiable patrons (slaveholders, husbands). * * * In contrast, the victims of today's crisis of work have no one in particular to be independent *from*, no one in particular who has controlled their destinies and whom they have enriched. To put it more abstractly, the shortage of decent work offers no specific legal relation, the abolition of which can lead the unemployed and underemployed from dependence to independence.

* * *

Equality: Work, Status, and the Constitution of Social Groups

The positive social meanings of work in America have survived through four centuries, despite the dependency and degradation of slavery on the plantations and the reduction of workers to cogs in the machinery of the mills and factories that began the industrial era. Even today, the actual experience of work might be meaningless drudgery, might be degradation—might, in fact, be violence—but the *idea* of work retains its strong connections with the liberty-oriented ideas of independence, self-expression, personal satisfaction, security, and even dignity. These are sunshine words, but let us take note of a cloud. Americans have also understood a worker's liberties to be imbued with notions of "getting ahead," of competitive individualism in a zero-sum game of status dominance. If work in America were a food product, the list of ingredients on the label would place individualism first.

* * *

Much of America's history of race relations, and other intergroup relations, could be written with a focus on the world of work. Today, an author who described slavery as a form of workplace discrimination would be understood to be indulging in irony. But the basic rationalization offered for slavery was that the people who were enslaved were inherently dependent, were not qualified for anything better—indeed, were not quite persons in the fullest sense. Their very enslavement was offered as proof that black people as a race were, as Chief Justice Taney said in the *Dred Scott Case* opinion, "an inferior class of beings," incapable of bearing the burdens of free citizenship. This pattern of circular rationalization is familiar even today. By the same sophistry, women can't be "splicers" because they aren't macho enough. In sum, the status of a social group strongly affects the work opportunities of the group's members, and, in turn, the kinds of work allowed to those members affect the group's status.

* * *

The world of work * * * offers vivid evidence of the connections between group status equality and national union—or, conversely, the links between inequality and disunion. * * * Three decades ago, a distinguished national commission captured the economic and social separation of black and white Americans by calling the races "two societies";[147] a substantial racial differential in access to work was identified by the commission as both indicator and cause. Today it is more obvious than it was in 1968 that the "two societies" label oversimplifies, failing to account for the many millions of Americans who identify themselves as neither black nor white. As a characterization of black/white relations, however, the concept of "two societies" retains considerable validity. A generation of advance for the one-third of black Americans who are now in the middle class is something to applaud, but the applause is muffled when we consider the nearly one-third of black Americans who live in poverty—or move in and out of poverty, as unemployment levels wax and wane. Until that number is drastically reduced, we must speak of a national community in the vocabulary of hope.

Race is by no means the only contributor to the group division that threatens national union in our increasingly "split society." * * * A majority of Americans have access to employment at decent wages and, through that employment, access to family security benefits. A smaller but growing number of Americans lack decently remunerative pay and also lack the essentials of family security. This latter group is growing and seems likely to continue growing for years to come. * * *

147. Report of the Nat'l Advisory Comm'n on Civil Disorders 1 (1968).

We confront a social Great Divide, one that endangers the union of citizens that is the foundation of our constitutional order. * * *

A Constitutional Right of Access to Work?

Although it is instructive to look at work and unemployment from the constitutional perspectives of liberty, equality, and national union, I do not suggest that American courts are capable of enforcing a constitutional right to stable and adequately compensated work.* * *

* * *The problems lie not only in the application of remedies but in the definition of substantive claims.

Judicial remedies, even sweeping remedies, are readily conceived when the courts have a clear idea of what constitutes wrongdoing, and who is doing the wrong. Jim Crow was an all-pervading social system, but the basic wrong of racial subordination through race-based exclusion was easy to see for anyone who was looking. The wrong—the constitutional wrong—was committed not only by officers of government but by nongovernmental actors who controlled access to elements of "the public life of the community," and especially the public world of work. When the wrong consists of exclusion, one obvious remedy is to order an end to the exclusion. In furtherance of this end, a positive command to desegregate the workplace is appropriate. Affirmative remedies for employment discrimination were developed early in the Supreme Court's interpretations of Title VII of the Civil Rights Act of 1964 and have become a standard part of the judiciary's remedial repertoire.

* * * [T]he chief difficulties lie in the superabundance of causes for the harm of joblessness in today's economy. This diffusion of responsibility seriously complicates not only the identification of particular defendants and the crafting of judicial remedies, but also the definition of the wrong.

Consider, for example, the multifaceted question of temporary and part-time work. A great many workers who occupy these jobs surely would prefer steady, full-time work, not only for job security and better incomes, but also for the health care and pension benefits that are so vital to family security. What is the wrong here? Who is the wrongdoer? What remedial action should a court command? To the extent that underemployment is aggravated by low wages in a global labor market, most of that factor lies beyond any American judge's writ. * * * Unlike the constitutional litigation that invalidated the Jim Crow laws (or even statute-based litigation against private employers who practice racial discrimination), litigation to enforce a right to decent work does not offer the prospect of standardized lawsuits, against standardized defendants, with demands for standardized forms of relief.

* * *

The idea of a right to work at a living wage, backstopped by the health and pension benefits needed for family security, unquestionably resounds with our constitutional values of liberty, equal citizenship, and national union. But if the courts are not going to enforce the right—and, certainly, they are not—then they should not declare it to be a constitutional right. * * *

The Fourteenth Amendment's guarantees of liberty and equal citizenship, however, do have their own legislative-power "penumbras," with a clear textual basis in Congress's power to enforce the amendment "by appropriate legislation." This power has been interpreted generously by the Supreme Court in the field of voting rights legislation, and a similar generosity ought to extend to congressional laws to promote a right to remunerative work. Access to work, we have seen, is an individual liberty of major importance, and equal access to work has a comparable importance for individuals' enjoyment of equal citizenship, which typically turns on the status of groups. Surely Congress can promote this liberty and this equality, not only in the name of the commerce and spending powers, but also in exercising its Fourteenth Amendment power. * * *

It is entirely appropriate to refer to such legislation as the enforcement of a constitutional right. But the claim of a constitutional status for a right of access to work ought to be left to Congress, to the President, to other political actors, and to commentators on the Constitution. * * *

* * *

If the United States continues its policy of maintaining a permanent pool of unemployed and underemployed citizens, Congress, the President and the state legislatures have the corresponding duty—the moral duty and the political duty—to assure those citizens who are involuntarily unemployed or underemployed that their families will be secure. More specifically, government has the duty to assure that every family has enough resources to live on and has good medical care and decent retirement benefits. Even if no crisis of work were impending, our constitutional commitments to liberty, to equality, and to national union would demand a serious national effort to promote the fair distribution of work and its associated benefits.

WILLIAM E. FORBATH

Constitutional Welfare Rights: A History, Critique and Reconstruction
69 Fordham L. Rev. 1821, 1832–38 (2001)

* * * [D]uring his first year in office, FDR promised a redefinition of the duties of government and a "redefinition of [classical liberal] rights in terms of a changing and growing social order." In the past, FDR explained, quoting Jefferson (and with Jefferson neglecting the black laboring class), America had "no paupers. The great mass of our population [was] of laborers ... [and] [m]ost of the laboring class possess[ed] property." For this yeoman citizenry, Roosevelt observed, the rights "involved in acquiring and possessing property" combined with

the ballot and the freedom to live by one's "own lights" to ensure liberty and equality. "The happiest of economic conditions made that day [of Jeffersonian individualism] long and splendid. [For on] the Western frontier, land was substantially free." The "turn of the tide came with the turn of the century ... [T]here was no more free land and our industrial combinations had become great uncontrolled and irresponsible units of power within the State."

These "conditions impose[d] new requirements upon Government" and new meanings on old texts. A mature industrial society could not be governed by a laissez-faire Constitution, insulating industry and finance from the modern claims of liberty and equality. America needed an "economic constitutional order." The "terms" of our basic rights "are as old as the Republic"; but new conditions demand new readings. "Every man has a right to live," Roosevelt declared, and "this means ... a right to make a comfortable living." The "Government formal and informal, political and economic, owes to everyone an avenue to possess himself of a portion of [the nation's] plenty sufficient for his needs, through his own work."

FDR introduced the "general welfare Constitution" in his 1934 address to Congress announcing the formation of the Committee on Economic Security, which would draft the administration's version of the Social Security Act of 1935. There he also continued to assimilate the new social rights to the "old and sacred possessive [traditional, constitutionally enshrined common law] rights" of property and labor. In pre-industrial America, these common law rights had had rich significance for the "welfare and happiness" of ordinary Americans; now, only the recognition of new governmental responsibilities would enable "a recovery" of the old rights' once robust social meaning.

Repeatedly, FDR and New Dealers in Congress spoke in terms of the non-judicial branches' obligation to redeem the "new social rights" that were the "modern substance" of the old guarantees of constitutional liberty and equality. Always "paramount" was work, or what the Committee on Economic Security called "employment assurance" for "those able-bodied workers whom industry cannot employ at a given time." As the Social Security Act's sponsor in the Senate, Robert Wagner underscored that "[a]t the very hub of social security is the right to have a job." Unemployment insurance was designed "not to supplant, but rather to supplement" the government's obligation to assure work for the "bulk of persons ... disinherited for long periods of time by private industry." The Social Security Act would not work without federal guarantees for those who could not find private employment. Roosevelt concurred. A national guarantee assuring the "opportunity to make a living—a living decent according to the standard of the time" was at the heart of the new understanding of liberty he'd proclaimed. Income security for those who could not work and public employment for those who could not find decent jobs in the private economy had to become the "permanent policy [of] the federal government."

By 1945, when Congress took up the administration's Full Employment Bill, the "all-important right to work" seemed secure, not only in labor movement and reform rhetoric but in the discourse of the liberal legal establishment. That year the American Law Institute appointed a committee of legal luminaries to draft a "Statement of Essential Human Rights." The staff of the Senate committee, holding hearings on FDR's "Full Employment Bill," asked the members of the ALI group to prepare "an analysis of the legal and philosophical considerations that led to the inclusion of the right to work" in the ALI Statement.

Liberal legal notables like these had inscribed FDR's "four freedoms" and "second bill of rights" into the founding documents and machinery—the Atlantic Charter, the UN Charter * * * —of the postwar international order. As they surveyed those new institutions, as well as * * * "the forty nations whose current or recent constitutions contain provisions granting various social and economic rights," and put these alongside the "fundamental legislative measures passed in the United States in the last dozen years to secure such rights to its citizens," they concluded that "the place of social and economic rights in any modern declaration of the rights of man has already been decided." In particular, no "modern understanding or bill of rights" could omit the right to work, whose popular support seemed "irresistible." Yet, this idea of a right, "which requires positive action by government, involving complex organization and the expenditures of public funds" seemed to many "inconsistent with the American tradition," "paternalis[tic]," potentially "tyrann[ical]," and, at the same time, "useless because it is impossible to go into court and force the government ... to insure that a man has a job."

The ALI draftsmen set out to respond, justifying the idea "in the light of these traditional habits of thought." To those who insisted on "the traditional legal habit of looking upon rights as negative," they replied * * * [by suggesting] that conceptions inherited from the "seventeenth and eighteenth centuries" imparted "confusion" and "rigidity to legal thinking about rights" that ill-served "the legislators who must implement" the Constitution. Thus, they pointed out that several of the rights in the Bill of Rights "actually require government to take very positive action indeed ... [entailing] all the involved and expensive machinery for the administration of civil and criminal justice.... In terms of mechanism and trained personnel, a system of social insurance is child's play in comparison with the system that gives effect to due process of law."

To the reproach that the right to work did not lend itself to judicial enforcement, * * * they responded first that "legal invention [could] develop new procedures" and second that, in any case, "immediate judicial enforceability" was not the right test of a right. The framers afforded good authority that the Constitution "was equally binding" on the Congress, and that the latter "had the right to determine for itself the meaning of its provisions." "A Bill of Rights is more than a consolidation of the fractions of freedom already gained.... It is a directive to the whole society and a guide to legislatures and executives in the framing of laws and regulations that will gradually make the rights effective." The reason to recognize social and economic rights in a Bill of Rights is chiefly to erect a standard "around which public opinion can mobilize ... and the acts of legislatures and executives be guided and judged."

What, then, became of the New Deal's robust conception of social citizenship and of its vaunted right to decent work? Between the popular ratification of the New Deal vision of citizenship and its enactment into law fell the shadow of Jim Crow and the nation's betrayal of Reconstruction. Measures instituting rights to decent work and social provision for all Americans enjoyed broad support; yet they expired in Congress. The explanation lies chiefly in what V.O. Key long ago called the "Southern Veto": the hammer lock on Congress that Southern Democrats enjoyed by dint of their numbers, their seniority and their control over key committees. Hailing from an impoverished region with a populist tradition, most Southern Democrats were staunch supporters of the New Deal until the late 1930s. In exchange for their support, however, they insisted on decentralized state administration and local standard setting of all labor measures and demanded that key bills exclude the main categories of Southern labor. Otherwise, how "were they going to get blacks to pick and chop cotton, when Negroes [on federal work programs] were getting twice as much as they had ever been paid" and when old-age insurance and social security bills had provisions that "would demoralize our region," until the Southern committee heads rewrote them.

By allying with Northern Republicans, or by threatening to do so, they stripped all the main pieces of New Deal legislation of any design or provision that threatened the separate Southern labor market and its distinctive melding of class and caste relations, its racial segmentation and its low wages. Consider, for example, the Social Security Act. The Committee on Economic Security had crafted the administration's proposals to propitiate the Southerners. For that reason the proposals favored state-level autonomy—albeit with national minimum standards—in both the unemployment insurance and assistance for the needy, aged, dependent children, and blind programs. Only the old-age benefits program would be purely federal. But the Dixiecrats exacted more concessions from the congressional sponsors of the administration bill. National standards for unemployment and old-age insurance were dropped and the administration's commitment to include all employed persons in the unemployment and old-age insurance schemes was sacrificed. The price of Dixiecrat support included drumming out of the insurance programs agricultural and domestic workers—and thereby the majority of black Americans, who worked in these two occupations.

The AAA, the NRA, the National Labor Relations and Fair Labor Standards Acts, all were tailored in this fashion. More encompassing and inclusive bills, bills with national, rather than local, standards and administration, enjoyed solid support from the Northern Democrats (and broad but bootless support from disenfranchised southern blacks and poor whites); but the Southern Junkers and their "racial civilization" exacted a price, and FDR, willingly at first, paid up. * * * However, as the new industrial unions of the CIO and the black voters of the North loomed large in FDR's 1936 reelection bid and his social and economic rights talk grew more and more robust and universal, the southern attacks began. Governor Talmadge of Georgia convened a "Grass Roots Convention" to "Uphold the Constitution" against "Negroes, the New Deal and Karl Marx," while Senator Carter Glass of Virginia worried if the white South "will have spirit and courage enough to face the new Reconstruction era that Northern so-called Democrats are menacing us with."

By the late 1930s, then, roughly half of the southerners in the Senate voted consistently against FDR. Increasingly, roll call votes in both houses revealed Southern Democrats joining with Republicans to oppose administration measures in the areas of labor reform and social insurance. Even more Dixiecrats "backed Roosevelt on a final vote but fought his program in their respective committees, in conference committees, in supporting crippling amendments, and in block[ing] consideration of many [labor, health, and housing] measures." Then with the coming of War, the "gentleman's agreement" collapsed. During this uncertain moment of war-time labor shortages, national mobilization and rapid economic and central-state expansion, the Solid South redrew its lines of toleration toward New Deal reform. Southern Congressmen openly joined ranks with the minority-party Republicans to defeat those 1940s legislative programs and structural innovations and institutional reforms in the executive branch that looked toward "completing the New Deal" by enacting and implementing FDR's "second Bill of Rights." Thus, the Dixiecrats allied with Northern Republicans to scuttle FDR's executive reorganization plan, they gutted the administration's 1945 Full Employment Act, and took the lead in abolishing the National Resources Planning Board. Together, these would have laid an institutional foundation for active national labor market and full employment policies. These defeated and dismantled laws, agencies and innovations were ones that would have sustained the public rhetoric and generated the new institutional capacities and commitments embodied in the "all-important right to work," in "the right to earn a decent livelihood," "to opportunity and advancement," "to train and retrain."

MARGARET WEIR

Politics and Jobs: The Boundaries of Employment Policy in the United States 131, 134–36 (1992)

In the mid-1970s, unemployment rates not seen since the Great Depression galvanized a heavily Democratic Congress into action. The apparent failure of Keynesian strategies to alleviate joblessness rekindled interest in planning and, for a brief moment, thrust ideas once rejected back into the national spotlight. * * *

* * *

Congressional sponsors of planning * * * [tied] their bill to a broad full employment measure written by the Congressional Black Caucus. The Equal Opportunity and Full Employment Act of 1976 was first proposed in June 1974 by Representative Augustus Hawkins (D. Calif.), an active member of the Congressional Black Caucus. In its earliest and most sweeping form, the Hawkins bill had attracted support primarily from African-Americans, their close allies in Congress, and the labor movement. This first bill, intended as a rallying effort around the employment issue, guaranteed jobs for all who wanted to work. If national economic policies failed to generate sufficient employment, the shortfall would be made up by federally financed jobs on projects designed by local planning councils. * * * Most controversial, the bill made the right to employment legally enforceable, allowing individuals to sue if they were denied a job.

As unemployment began to climb rapidly upward in 1975, Hawkins's bill attracted growing support. It was reintroduced in somewhat revised form in 1975, this time also sponsored in the Senate by [Senator Hubert] Humphrey [of Minnesota]. Still providing a legally enforceable right to employment, the bill established 3 percent unemployment as an interim goal to be achieved in eighteen months. It required the president to present a "Full Employment and National Purposes Budget," much as the original Full Employment bill of 1945 had. It also explicitly called on the Federal Reserve to bring its policies into line with a national effort for full employment and required the board to prepare an annual statement outlining how its policies in the coming year would be consistent with the goal of full employment.

* * *

In March of 1976, the planning proposals of the Initiative Committee and the concern for full employment animating the various Hawkins bills came together in the Full Employment and Balanced Growth Act of 1976. Proposed as an amendment to the 1946 Employment Act, the new bill aimed to fulfill the promise of the original Full Employment Bill of 1945. In Humphrey's words, the bill, "put full employment back in the Employment Act." The new bill kept the 3 percent unemployment goal, to be reached as soon as possible, but within a deadline of four years. The president, the Congress, and the Federal Reserve were all directed to participate with state and local governments in devising a plan to allow "full use of the resources and ingenuity of the private sector of the economy." It made the federal government the "employer of last resort" by establishing public jobs paying the prevailing wage whenever they were necessary but eliminated the legally enforceable job guarantee.

In 1976, the congressional Democratic leadership, seeking to make unemployment a major issue for the upcoming campaign season, threw its support behind the Humphrey-Hawkins bill. For a brief moment, it appeared certain that the bill would pass, forcing President Ford into a politically damaging veto. Instead, congressional leaders refrained from bringing the bill to the floor that year. Its fate remained in doubt for two years, until it finally passed in a form that made it no more than a symbolic gesture.

Notes and Questions

1. Do you find Karst's arguments about the limits on judicial enforcement of a "right to work" persuasive? If judges should not declare such a right "constitutional," why is it appropriate for the legislature (or the president) to do so? What would make political leaders likely to articulate these rights if the burdens resulting from lack of work fall disproportionately on people who lack political power?

Compare Karst's position with the optimistic arguments of the American Law Institute in the 1940s, quoted by Forbath, that legal invention could develop new procedures and that immediate judicial enforceability should not be the test of a right. What is the "right test" of a right?

2. Should the fact that federal regulatory action has a *goal* of maintaining some unemployment create a corresponding responsibility for the federal government? Does your answer depend on the adequacy of unemployment insurance and other avenues of relief for displaced workers? *See* Deborah Maranville, *Changing Economy, Changing Lives: Unemployment Insurance and the Contingent Workforce* 4 B.U. Pub. Int. L.J. 291 (1995) (describing inadequacy of unemployment benefits for contingent workers and particularly for women with children), excerpted in section 3.

3. The lack of a public health insurance program had an interactive effect with employment in America, shaping the politics of work as well as health. Unions negotiated benefits, and this task took up significant negotiating energy. The resulting system of contractual benefits gradually raised standards for many nonunion employers as well—but this system had divisive effects. In countries like Sweden and West Germany, high levels of public benefits maintained unity among workers. In the United States, workers protected by contracts with good benefits tended to become disinterested in political activism for public programs. Robert Zieger, *American Workers, American Unions, 1920–1985*, 152–53 (1986).

4. Would the attitude of courts or Congress toward rights to employment have been different if the nation had previously recognized rights of former slaves to land on the theory that they were owed compensation for their labor, or that they had developed a property right in the land through the labor that made the land profitable? *See* Eric Foner, *Reconstruction: America's Unfinished Revolution, 1863–1877* (1988), excerpted in chapter 7.

B. Employment At Will and Individual Rights in Jobs

Historically, common law in the United States did not recognize the inequality inherent in the employment relationship, nor did it protect workers against arbitrary discharge. Theoretically, both parties were equally free to end the employment relationship at any time. This "equality" is formal, not substantive. It calls to mind the memorable line by Anatole France, "The law, in its majestic equality, forbids the rich as well as the poor to sleep under bridges, to beg in the streets, and to steal bread." Fran Ansley, *Standing Rusty And Rolling Empty: Law, Poverty, and America's Eroding Industrial Base*, 81 Geo. L.J. 1757, 1786, n.91 (1993) (discussing at-will employment and quoting France). *See, e.g.,* Harney v. Meadowbrook Nursing Center, 784 S.W.2d 921, 922 (Tenn. 1990) (noting long-standing rule that "an employee-at-will may be discharged without breach of contract for good cause, bad cause or no cause at all") .

DeMARCO v. PUBLIX SUPER MARKETS, INC.

360 So.2d 134 (Fla. 3d DCA 1978), *affirmed*
384 So.2d 1253 (Fla.1980)

HAVERFIELD, Chief Judge

Anne DeMarco, the minor daughter of Carl DeMarco, while shopping with her mother in one of the stores of the appellee, Publix Super Markets, Inc., sustained a severe eye injury when a soda bottle exploded. At the time of the accident Carl DeMarco was an employee of Publix, whose insurer, Hartford Insurance Company, paid the medical expenses incurred by Anne. After her initial treatment had been completed, Hartford offered the additional sum of $200 as a complete settlement on behalf of Publix. This offer was refused by Carl DeMarco who then filed suit on behalf of his minor daughter against Publix and the manufacturer of the bottle which exploded. Publix informed DeMarco that if he did not withdraw the lawsuit, he would be discharged. DeMarco refused and his employment was terminated. He thereupon filed * * * [a] multi-count complaint against Publix seeking compensatory and punitive damages and reinstatement. He alleged that as a result of this deliberate and malicious termination, Publix was primarily liable in the following respects: (1) interference with the good faith exercise of his rights under Article I, Section 21 and 9, Florida Constitution (1968) * * * [Section 21 guarantees access to courts, and Section 9 guarantees due process of law]; (2) damage to his reputation in that his firing imputed that he was unreliable or incompetent; and (3) severe emotional distress and mental anguish suffered. * * *

The established law is that where the term of employment is discretionary with either party or indefinite, then either party for any reason may terminate it at any time and no action may be maintained for breach of the employment contract. The employment agreement in the case at bar having been for an indefinite time, Publix could terminate DeMarco for *any* reason without incurring liability. Thus, Publix was not liable for firing him for the reason that he was exercising his constitutionally protected rights. Furthermore, there is no civil cause of action for the interference with the exercise of one's right under Article

I, Section 21 of the Florida Constitution [which guarantees access to the courts]. In fact, DeMarco's suit on behalf of his daughter is still pending which contradicts the allegation that he is being denied access to the courts in derogation of this constitutional right. * * *

WILLIAM B. GOULD IV

The Idea of the Job as Property in Contemporary America: The Legal and Collective Bargaining Framework
1986 B.Y.U. L. Rev. 885, 886–87, 900, 902–03, 905 (1986)

Until * * * [the early 1980s] the assumption was that workers who were not represented by trade unions under collective bargaining agreements had no protection—or virtually no protection—against either individual or collective dismissal. This lack of protection existed because America accepted a legal proposition founded in a laissez-faire economy which reached its zenith in the latter part of the previous century and the early part of this one.

The common law of the time, which represented a misreading of British common law, held that absent an explicit provision to the contrary, an employment contract was terminable at will. But the attitudes of * * * [the 1980s] are summarized well by the late Justice Tobriner of the Supreme Court of California who characterized the terminable-at-will doctrine as anachronistic in our contemporary society.

Today a clear majority of jurisdictions have modified or created exceptions to the terminable-at-will principle. * * *

* * *

The first exception to terminable-at-will is the so-called public policy exception which provides that an employee's dismissal is null and void if instituted for a reason inconsistent with public policy. In these cases, the courts have extended protection to employees who have been dismissed even though a statute does not explicitly provide a remedy for dismissal. The employee's dismissal is sometimes in direct violation of the law or a specific statute, but the cases clearly extend much further in most jurisdictions. The cases have protected workers, for instance, who have been retaliated against for protesting illegal behavior, who have engaged in "whistle blowing," and who have publicized or protested the illegal conduct of employers, as in the landmark decision of the Supreme Court of California, *Tameny v. Atlantic Richfield Co.* Indeed, a number of state legislatures have enacted statutes which prohibit dismissal for "whistle blowing" and, in so doing, they have replaced or supplemented common law.

* * * [W]here an employer requires an employee to choose between his or her public obligation, such as serving on a jury when called to do so, and employment, the public policy exception has [also] been applied. The theory is that the purposes of state law will be eroded if employers can flout them so effectively.

* * *

A second line of cases, accepted in far fewer jurisdictions, * * * is the breach of the so-called covenant of good faith and fair dealing. This tort, first recognized in the insurance area, has been applied to employment cases under certain circumstances. * * *

* * *

A third line of cases, in contrast to the covenant of good faith and fair dealing, are contractual in the pristine sense of the word. That is to say, these cases do not create tort liability for defendants. They divide themselves in two parts. The first is the so called implied contract in fact cases. Here, the employee has been employed for some considerable period of time, has received commendations, promotions, and the like, and then is dismissed. The courts have been willing to impose a good cause or good faith limitation under these circumstances.

A second group of cases impose a good cause or just cause standard upon employers by virtue of contractual promises which are deemed to flow from personnel manuals or booklets which have been distributed to employees. * * * [T]hese manuals are frequently designed in response to union organizational campaigns or to thwart the potential for implied promises.

* * *

* * *[M]ost of the employees in the work force have yet to benefit from the newly emerging doctrines. A disproportionate number of the plaintiffs are managerial and professional employees. While this appears to be attributable to the considerable costs of litigation, even prior to trial itself, it also has something to do with the theories employed. Most of the theories developed by the courts are of little help to the average employee—in sharp contrast to just cause provisions in collective bargaining agreements.

Notes and Questions

1. Although organization into a union with collective bargaining would offer greater protection for most employees, union organization has become extremely difficult in the United States. Even when workers do vote for unions, it is difficult to get a contract, and workers who strike lack job protection. *See* Thomas Geoghegan, *Which Side Are You On: Trying to Be for Labor When It's Flat on Its Back* (1991). Would greater individual protection against discharge affect workers who attempt to organize labor unions? Union membership in the United States fell from 35.5% of the work force in 1945 to 15.8% in 1993. Richard Sennett, *The Corrosion of Character: The Personal Consequences of Work in the New Capitalism* 152, 157 (1998). Public sector workers—who often have procedural rights against arbitrary discharge, and whose employers cannot relocate for cheaper wages—have a much higher rate of union membership than do private sector workers. In 2001, 13.5% of wage and salary workers were union members. "Nearly 4 in 10 government workers were union members in 2001, compared with less than 1 in 10

private wage and salary workers." Bureau of Labor Statistics, U.S. Dept. of Labor, *Union Members in 2001.*

For a discussion of the influence of conservative judicial decisions on labor unions and the direction of the labor movement, see William E. Forbath, *The Shaping of the American Labor Movement*, 102 Harv. L. Rev. 1109 (1989). Joel Rogers emphasizes the structure of labor regulation and particularly the negative impact of the Labor Management Relations Act in the situation of capitalist democracy in the United States. Joel Rogers, *Divide and Conquer: Further "Reflections on the Distinctive Character of American Labor Laws,"* 1990 Wis. L. Rev. 1.

2. Most states have more exceptions to the rule of at-will employment than does Florida. Should Mr. DeMarco be protected as a matter of public policy? What would be the effect on the labor market of protecting DeMarco's job?

If individuals had stronger rights to retain their jobs, would the common law be more likely to protect rights in a community to keep an employer from leaving the area? The next section discusses one of many such cases that occurred as industrial plants closed throughout the eastern and midwestern states during the late twentieth century.

C. Community Rights to Employment

JULES LOBEL

Losers, Fools & Prophets: Justice as Struggle
80 Cornell L. Rev. 1331, 1384–86 (1995)

Between 1977 and 1987, the steel industry in the two leading steelmaking cities of the nation, Pittsburgh and Youngstown, declined precipitously. A wave of plant shutdowns ended all steelmaking in Youngstown and decimated the once vibrant industry in Pittsburgh, resulting in the direct loss of approximately 80,000 jobs in basic steel in the two metropolitan areas. A broad coalition of workers, churches, and community activists emerged to fight these mill closings.

Litigation played an important role in this struggle. The major legal challenge to plant shutdowns was a 1979 lawsuit filed by five local steelworker unions, an incumbent Republican Congressman, the Lordstown Local of the UAW, sixty-five individual steelworkers, and the Tri-State Conference on Steel. The suit sought to prevent U.S. Steel's announced shutdown of its Youngstown plants. The broad coalition of plaintiffs reflected the wide array of social forces opposing the plant closings.

The complaint articulated in legal terms the feelings of ordinary steelworkers and a substantial section of the community. U.S. Steel had made a promise to keep the Youngstown mills open if they could be made profitable. The workers had agreed to a variety of concessions, worked hard, and relied on that promise to their detriment, yet U.S. Steel had breached its promise. The workers' contract theory was promissory estoppel. The complaint later added a second, more radical theory, actually suggested by the district court judge trying the cases, that a community "property right has arisen from [the] lengthy, long-established relationship between United States Steel, the steel industry as an institution, the community in Youngstown, the people in Mahoning County and the Mahoning Valley in having given and devoted their lives to this industry." The contract theory could certainly be viewed as falling within well-established law; the community right to property was a more radical interpretation and revamping of property law.

The Youngstown elite generally viewed the lawsuit as futile. The mayor of Youngstown thought it was a ridiculous, silly, pathetic, and contemptible lawsuit. The International Steelworkers Union did not join the plaintiffs, and one important reason for that failure may have been the Union's perception that the lawsuit could not succeed.

Much of the community, however, supported the litigation. Other methods short of litigation had been tried in prior plant closings, and the workers felt that there was virtually no other alternative.

In a preliminary hearing before District Court Judge Lambros, the plaintiffs won a preliminary injunction against the plant closing. Judge Lambros responded to the plaintiffs' argument with a rambling discourse in which he (1) proclaimed sympathy for the workers' plight; (2) expressed grave doubts about the court's ultimate jurisdiction over the case; (3) suggested the radical idea, as yet unproposed by the plaintiffs, that the workers and community might have a property right to the U.S. Steel mills; and (4) granted the injunction.

The trial was held in Youngstown in early March. The judge dismissed the plaintiffs' claims in a thirty-seven-page opinion that expressed great sympathy for the workers' situation, but rejected the promissory estoppel claim and found no community property right. Although he himself had suggested the argument, the judge's opinion held that "this new property right [ ] is not now in existence in the code of laws of our nation."

By the time of the trial, the workers' activist movement to keep the mills open had dissipated, and the lawsuit represented the only significant resistance to the company's decision.

* * *

[The case was appealed to the Sixth Circuit.]

LOCAL 1330, UNITED STEEL WORKERS OF AMERICA v. UNITED STATES STEEL CORPORATION

631 F.2d 1264 (6th Cir.1980)

EDWARDS, Chief Judge:

This appeal represents a cry for help from steelworkers and townspeople in the City of Youngstown, Ohio who are distressed by the prospective impact upon their lives and their city of the closing of two large steel mills. These two mills were built and have been operated by the United States Steel Corporation since the turn of the century. The Ohio Works began producing in 1901; the McDonald Works in 1918. * * * [A]s of the notice of closing, the two plants employed 3,500 employees.

* * *

In the background of this litigation is the obsolescence of the two plants concerned, occasioned both by the age of the facilities and machinery involved and by the changes in technology and marketing in steelmaking in the years intervening since the early nineteen hundreds.

For all of the years United States Steel has been operating in Youngstown, it has been a dominant factor in the lives of its thousands of employees and their families, and in the life of the city itself. The contemplated abrupt departure of United States Steel from Youngstown will, of course, have direct impact on 3,500 workers and their families. It will doubtless mean a devastating blow to them, to the business community and to the City of Youngstown itself. While we cannot read the future of Youngstown from this record, what the record does indicate clearly is that we deal with an economic tragedy of major proportion to Youngstown and Ohio's Mahoning Valley. * * *

In the face of this tragedy, the steel worker local unions, the Congressman from this district, and the Attorney General of Ohio have sued United States Steel Corporation, asking the federal courts to order the United States Steel Corporation to keep the two plants at issue in operation. Alternatively, * * * they have sought intervention of the courts by injunction to require the United States Steel Corporation to sell the two plants to the plaintiffs under an as yet tentative plan of purchase and operation by a community corporation and to restrain the piecemeal sale or dismantling of the plants until such a proposal could be brought to fruition.

Defendant United States Steel Corporation answered plaintiffs' complaints, claiming that the plants were unprofitable and could not be made otherwise due to obsolescence and change in technology, markets, and transportation. The company also asserts an absolute right to make a business decision to discharge its former employees and abandon Youngstown. It states that there is no law in either the State of Ohio or the United States of America which provides either legal or equitable remedy for plaintiffs.

The District Judge, after originally restraining the corporation from ceasing operations as it had announced it would, and after advancing the case for prompt hearing, entered a formal opinion holding that the plants had become unprofitable and denying all relief. We believe the dispositive paragraphs of a lengthy opinion entered by the District Judge are the following:

This Court has spent many hours searching for a way to cut to the heart of the economic reality—that obsolescence and market forces demand the close of the Mahoning Valley plants, and yet the lives of 3500 workers and their families and the supporting Youngstown community cannot be dismissed as inconsequential. United States Steel should not be permitted to leave the Youngstown area devastated after drawing from the lifeblood of the community for so many years.

Unfortunately, the mechanism to reach this ideal settlement, to recognize this new property right, is not now in existence in the code of laws of our nation.

* * *

This Court is mindful of the efforts taken by the workers to increase productivity, and has applauded these efforts * * * . In view of the fact, however, that this Court has found that no contract or enforceable promise was entered into by the company and that, additionally, there is clear evidence to support the company's decision that the plants were not profitable, the various acts of forebearance taken by the plaintiffs do not give them the basis for relief against defendant.

* * *

[The court turned to the community property claim.]

At a pretrial hearing of this case on February 28, 1980, the District Judge made a statement at some length about the relationship between the parties to this case and the public interest involved therein. He said:

> Everything that has happened in the Mahoning Valley has been happening for many years because of steel. Schools have been built, roads have been built. Expansion that has taken place is because of steel. And to accommodate that industry, lives and destinies of the inhabitants of that community were based and planned on the basis of that institution: Steel.
>
> * * *
>
> We are talking about an institution, a large corporate institution that is virtually the reason for the existence of that segment of this nation (Youngstown). Without it, that segment of this nation perhaps suffers, instantly and severely. Whether it becomes a ghost town or not, I don't know. I am not aware of its capability for adapting.
>
> * * *
>
> But what has happened over the years between U.S. Steel, Youngstown and the inhabitants? Hasn't something come out of that relationship, something that out of which—not reaching for a case on property law or a series of cases but looking at the law as a whole, the Constitution, the whole body of law, not only contract

law, but tort, corporations, agency, negotiable instruments—taking a look at the whole body of American law and then sitting back and reflecting on what it seeks to do, and that is to adjust human relationships in keeping with the whole spirit and foundation of the American system of law, to preserve property rights.

* * *

It would seem to me that when we take a look at the whole body of American law and the principles we attempt to come out with—and although a legislature has not pronounced any laws with respect to such a property right, that is not to suggest that there will not be a need for such a law in the future dealing with similar situations—*it seems to me that a property right has arisen from this lengthy, long-established relationship between United States Steel, the steel industry as an institution, the community in Youngstown, the people in Mahoning County and the Mahoning Valley in having given and devoted their lives to this industry.* Perhaps not a property right to the extent that can be remedied by compelling U.S. Steel to remain in Youngstown. But *I think the law can recognize the property right to the extent that U.S. Steel cannot leave that Mahoning Valley and the Youngstown area in a state of waste, that it cannot completely abandon its obligation to that community, because certain vested rights have arisen out of this long relationship and institution.* * * *

[The steelworkers' complaint was amended to assert that a property right had arisen, enforceable in court, from the "long-established relation between the community of the 19th Congressional District, plaintiffs, and the defendant." The right was described as "in the nature of an easement" and it required that the defendant: "[a]ssist in the preservation of the institution of steel in that community; * * * figure into its cost of withdrawing and closing the Ohio and McDonald Works the cost of rehabilitating the community and the workers; [and be] restrained from leaving the Mahoning Valley in a state of waste and from abandoning its obligation to that community."]

This court has examined these allegations with care and with great sympathy for the community interest reflected therein. Our problem in dealing with * * * [this] cause of action is one of authority. Neither in brief nor oral argument have plaintiffs pointed to any constitutional provision contained in either the Constitution of the United States or the Constitution of the State of Ohio, nor any law enacted by the United States Congress or the Legislature of Ohio, nor any case decided by the courts of either of these jurisdictions which would convey authority to this court to require the United States Steel Corporation to continue operations in Youngstown which its officers and Board of Directors had decided to discontinue on the basis of unprofitability.

This court has in fact dealt with this specific issue in *Charland v. Norge Division, Borg–Warner Corp.*, 407 F.2d 1062 (6th Cir.), *cert.*

denied, 395 U.S. 927, *rehearing denied*, 396 U.S. 871 (1969). * * * [That case involved an individual plaintiff, one of many employees thrown out of work by the removal of the Norge Muskegon Heights plant to Fort Smith, Arkansas. The court rejected Charland's argument that it was fundamentally unfair and a deprivation of property rights in his job to force him to choose between a move to another city and a new start as a new employee without accumulated seniority or pension rights, or, in the alternative, $1,500.]

* * *

Appellants, however, cite and rely upon a decision of the Supreme Court of the United States, *Munn v. Illinois,* 94 U.S. 113 (1877), claiming "that a corporation affected by the public interest, which seeks to take action injurious to that interest, may be restrained from doing so by the equitable powers of a court of law." * * *

The case is undoubtedly important precedent establishing power on the part of state legislatures to regulate private property (particularly public utilities) in the public interest. It cannot, however, properly be cited for holding that federal courts have such legislative power in their own hands.

* * *

The problem of plant closing and plant removal from one section of the country to another is by no means new in American history. The former mill towns of New England, with their empty textile factory buildings, are monuments to the migration of textile manufacturers to the South, without hindrance from the Congress of the United States, from the legislatures of the states concerned, or, for that matter, from the courts of the land.

In the view of this court, formulation of public policy on the great issues involved in plant closings and removals is clearly the responsibility of the legislatures of the states or of the Congress of the United States.

JOSEPH WILLIAM SINGER

The Reliance Interest in Property
40 Stan. L. Rev. 611, 664, 699, 750–51 (1988)

The legal system often imposes mutual obligations on persons who enter relationships of mutual dependence. This is true not only in family relationships but in market relationships, too, as in the landlord/tenant relationship. Thus the legal system often requires property rights to be shared from the very beginning of the relationship. Moreover, at crucial points in the development of social relationships—often, but not always, when the relationship breaks up—the legal system requires a further sharing or shifting of property interests to protect the more vulnerable party. This happens, not because the parties have relied on specific promises to their detriment, but because the parties have relied on each other generally and on the continuation of their particular kind of relationship. * * *

* * *

[The author reviews legal doctrines that shift property rights based on reliance, including real property rights such as adverse possession, prescriptive easement, and easements by estoppel, and the equitable distribution of property after a marriage.]

Let us try for a restatement of the doctrine of the reliance interest in property. It would look something like this:

Restatement (Third) of Property § 90: The Reliance Interest in Property

(1) When owners grant rights of access to their property to others, they are not unconditionally free to revoke such access. Non-owners who have relied on a relationship with the owner that made such access possible in the past may be granted partial or total immunity from having such access revoked when this is necessary to achieve justice.

(2) When people create relations of mutual dependence involving joint efforts, and the relationship ends, property rights (access to or control of valued resources) must be redistributed (shared or shifted) among the parties to protect the legitimate interests of the more vulnerable persons.

(3) Property rights are redistributed from owners to non-owners:

(a) to protect the interests of the more vulnerable persons in reasonably relying on the continuation of the relationship;

(b) to distribute resources earned by the more vulnerable party for contributions to joint efforts; and

(c) to fulfill needs of the more vulnerable persons.

* * *

I take as a premise that "human society ought to be organized in such a way as to eliminate useless suffering." How then can we foster desirable economic change without destroying communities and creating unnecessary social misery? When people participate in a common enterprise and rely on the continuation of the relationship to satisfy their needs for work, security and companionship, the legal system should protect the reliance of the more vulnerable persons when the more powerful party seeks to end the relationship. The reliance interest in property is already recognized in the legal rules in force, and we have good reasons to extend its application to plant closings. Imposition of this principle would be economically feasible and would mitigate the otherwise uncompensated losses caused by worker dislocation. Creation of this new property right would be a modest contribution toward the effort to curtail the illegitimate concentration of power in the marketplace.

How can we structure the rules of the marketplace in a way that both ensures adequate freedom for market participants and protects those who are most vulnerable to the vicissitudes of economic change? Answering this question requires us to worry about the distribution of power and wealth and the ways in which the legal system both creates and enforces that distribution. It also requires us to devise ways to protect those who are vulnerable in market relationships, especially when their vulnerability is a product of rules devised by those with power—persons other than themselves. Yet, in providing such protection, we want also to enable members of common enterprises to have the freedom to fashion their relationships with each other, to control collectively their destiny.

* * *

Property rights allocate power, and we are suspicious of power. Those without power are vulnerable. Thus the relation between power and vulnerability should be at the heart of our analysis of property rights. Rather than asking "who owns the factory?" we should ask "what relationships should we nurture?" We should encourage people to rely on relationships of mutual dependence by making it possible for everyone to form such relationships and by protecting those who are most vulnerable when those relationships end. * * *

Notes and Questions

1. Singer argues that, if the reliance interest were recognized, questions of profitability might be transformed:

> [T]he plant may be owned by a conglomerate that includes different kinds of industries as subsidiaries. The company may be able to maximize its profits by using the earnings of one of its subsidiaries to subsidize operations of the others. This is in fact what happened with the Youngstown Sheet and Tube Company in Youngstown, Ohio, which was taken over by the Lykes Corporation. Lykes used the company's profits to finance capital investment in other subsidiaries. It did this rather than re-invest the profits in the steel industry for modernization of obsolete plants. In another example, the Sheller-Globe Corporation bought in 1974 the Colonial Press in Clinton, Massachusetts. Until the plant was closed in 1977, the Press was charged an average of $900,000 yearly in corporate overhead costs with little justification. Companies like Youngstown Sheet and Tube and Colonial Press are referred to as "cash cows", said to be "milked" for the benefit of the conglomerate's other operations. Once the company has been milked for a long enough time, it may become unprofitable because its plant has been run down and because it has not been modernized in ways needed to compete with other producers in the industry. Thus, these plants are closed not because they are inherently unprofitable; they are unprofitable because the parent company has decided to *make* them unprofitable by milking them or by failing to modernize them.

Id. at 711–12.

Is Singer's argument an example of the legal creativity Carrie Menkel-Meadow discusses in chapter 6? Do successful rights claims necessarily involve legal creativity?

2. What is the legacy of lawsuits like the *Local 1330* litigation? When it is difficult to vindicate legal rights, is it worth attempting the effort? Jules Lobel observes:

> Despite the legal loss, the litigation left a legacy. It generated a significant amount of publicity. It allowed the steelworkers of Youngstown to gain the nation's attention, to "make a claim on the reason and conscience of the community." The lawsuit was "one more voice asserting that the mill closings were wrong."
>
> The lawsuit also gave voice to the steelworkers' own stories and aspirations. It was important to [Staughton] Lynd [the attorney who represented the steelworkers] that the legal theory articulate the injustice felt by the ordinary people of Youngstown. For Lynd, the most important thing that a lawyer for a marginalized group of people could do was to articulate their stories and aspirations and to help define their issues in court. He and the other lawyers gave voice to the victims of Youngstown. Both the district court and court of appeals decisions left a strong narrative record of the injustice of the plant closings.
>
> Moreover, the lawsuit provided a focus for a community's affirmation of its identity. As Bob Vasquez, one of the workers' leaders, said, "It saved people's dignity that they made that fight for the mill." Or as John Barbaro put it, "Youngstown sure died hard."

Lobel, *supra* at 1387. *See also* Staughton Lynd, *Towards a Not-for-Profit Economy: Public Development Authorities for Acquisition and Use of Industrial Property*, 22 Harv. C.R.-C.L. L. Rev. 13 (1987).

3. In 1988, Congress passed the Worker Adjustment and Retraining Notification Act (WARN) 29 U.S.C. §§ 2101–02. The act requires employers with 100 or more employees to provide sixty days' notice of plant closings or mass layoffs. Exceptions exist for business circumstances that were not "reasonably foreseeable" at the time notice would have been required and for natural disasters such as floods or earthquakes. Another exception is allowed if the employer was seeking capital or business which might have avoided the shutdown and providing notice would have "precluded the employer from obtaining the needed capital or business."

4. In more than half of union campaigns between 1993 and 1995, employers threatened to close. The threats were effective in reducing the rate of union campaign success, according to a report prepared by Kate Bronfenbrenner of the New York State School of Industrial and Labor Relations at Cornell University for the North American Commission for Labor Cooperation in 1996. The rate at which employers actually did close increased after the passage of the North American Free Trade

Agreement (NAFTA). Kate Bronfenbrenner, *Final Report: The Effects of Plant Closing or Threat of Plant Closing on the Right of Workers to Organize* (September 30, 1996), http://www.ilr.cornell.edu/library/e_archive/gov_reports/naalc/ReportonPlantClosing.pdf (last viewed 9/17/02).

5. International human rights documents provide sources for recognition of a right to work.

> The right to work—generally conceived as an individual entitlement to a freely chosen job paying wages capable of supporting a dignified existence—was first accorded positive recognition as a human right in the French Constitution of 1793. * * * In the confluence of historical events that gave birth to the United Nations at the end of World War II, human rights claims—including right to work claims—attracted more concerted political attention from governments than they ever had before. The result was formal recognition of the right to work in a number of international human rights agreements that impose theoretically binding obligations on the United States government to at least strive to secure the right. * * *
>
> * * *
>
> First, [the right] * * * involves more than freedom from forced labor and an opportunity to compete for available jobs. It is a right actually to be employed. An offer of income support in lieu of a job will not secure the right, nor will assurances of non-discriminatory access to available jobs. The ready availability of suitable opportunities for self-employment might count as contributing to the realization of the right. For example, access to land might secure the right to work for agricultural workers. But these opportunities would have to be as easy to exploit as job offers are to accept.
>
> * * *
>
> Second, the right to work does not include a right to retain a particular job. There is nothing in the U.N. Charter, the Universal Declaration [of Human Rights], or the ICESCR [International Covenant on Economic, Social and Cultural Rights] implicating termination rights if adequate alternative employment opportunities are available to terminated employees. Realization of the right is therefore compatible with legal regimes that make it easy to fire individual workers as well as with those that make it difficult to fire them. Its touchstone is not tenure in a particular job but the availability of enough jobs to eliminate involuntary unemployment.
>
> Third, the entitlement is viewed as including a right to be paid wages sufficient to support a dignified standard of living; the right has not been secured if employment is only made available on terms that leave full-time workers in a condition of poverty. * * * What constitutes an adequate standard of living will depend on local conditions and expectations, of course, but for the right to work to

be fully realized, a minimum wage must be paid that reflects those conditions and expectations.

Fourth, the right can be asserted against governments, but the duty of governments to secure the right is perceived to be limited. They are not viewed as having an obligation to guarantee the right immediately, but only to adopt policies that will secure the right progressively over time. * * *

Philip Harvey, *Human Rights and Economic Policy Discourse: Taking Economic and Social Rights Seriously*, 33 Colum. Hum. Rts. L. Rev. 363, 371–72, 380–82 (2002). *See also* Barbara Stark, *Economic Rights in the United States and International Human Rights Law: Toward an "Entirely New Strategy,"* 44 Hastings L.J. 79 (1992) (discussing The International Covenant on Economic, Social and Cultural Rights).

How can a right be effective if it is difficult to enforce against governments? How can a right to work be enforced?

SECTION 2. GLOBALIZATION, WORK, AND SOCIAL JUSTICE

Harry Arthurs recently defined globalization, explaining why defending the interest of workers often means opposition to the culture and logic of globalizing business arrangements:

Globalization, as we know it today, is an integrated system of business arrangements that seeks to move large volumes of goods, services, information and capital across international borders with low friction and at high velocity. But it is much more. Globalization is also a technological system that uses transportation and communications and manufacturing techniques to make such movements possible.

Moreover, globalization—at least in its current incarnation—is a political system sometimes known as neo-liberalism, a tribute to Adam Smith and the 19th century liberal economists who built on his work. Neo-liberals, like their forebears, believe that market forces are superior to all other forms of social ordering, such as state intervention or community cooperation. Consequently, neo-liberals want to eliminate both domestic market regulation and all barriers to transnational trade. Of course, neo-liberals do not favor markets to the point of utter foolishness. States are still welcome to provide infrastructure, protect commerce from fraud and violence, and discipline obstreperous workers. But at least at the level of rhetoric, globalization as we know it is built on the neo-liberal premise that states should govern to the least extent possible. This neo-liberal political project has succeeded to the point where it has become paradigmatic. It is now generally accepted that the logic of markets sweeps everything before it and that all other logics must give way. Not surprisingly, people who resist market logic—that is, people who persist in thinking and acting as if politics or families or culture or ethics mattered—often become the sworn enemies of neo-liberalism and globalization. Workers who claim rights and dignity despite their lack of market power, farmers who resist destruction of their indigenous stocks by genetically-modified imports, and cultural communities that shelter their books and movies from the great global entertainment conglomerates are all, in their way, fighting the culture of globalization and neo-liberalism.

Finally, I want to stress that globalization is a legal system. It depends upon the willingness of states to repeal old laws that constrain trade, to bring existing laws into alignment with the regulatory and property regimes of international trading partners, to abstain from passing new laws that discriminate against foreign firms or discourage foreign investors, and to accommodate the complex body of contractual and customary legal arrangements that have grown up to facilitate global business transactions.

Harry Arthurs, *Reinventing Labor Law for the Global Economy*, 22 Berkeley J. Employment & Lab. L. 271, 273–74 (2001).

The following section discusses the relationship between the lack of rights in work within the United States—and the lack of rights to control capital investment—and contemporary cross-border issues of social justice for working people.

A. Capital Mobility and Human Mobility: Justice and the Politics of Borders

The plant closing movement fought to strengthen control of capital and investment by the people affected—workers and members of their communities—as well as the owners of capital. Fran Ansley argues that this approach had some important strengths, but that it overlooked the needs of immigrants who were newly arrived in the United States. It also overlooked the need for working people in the United States to learn to work with, not against, the workers in the countries to which capital investment was relocating. Fran Ansley, *Inclusive Boundaries and Other (Im)possible Paths Toward Community Development in a Global World* 150 U. Pa. L. Rev. 353 (2001).

Ansley identifies two poles of a dilemma facing activists as they frame contemporary social justice movements. On one hand, "Social movements interested in strong democracy must assert and defend the holding power of political boundaries, because in a globalizing world, the erosion of a polity's jurisdictional bounds renders democratic social disciplines toothless, increases inequality, and fortifies economic privilege." *Id.* at 376. Defending political boundaries is not a simple question for social justice activists in the United States, however: "Pro-democracy social movements located in wealthy countries must insist on the openness and contingency of their boundaries, and must understand how their own polity relates to others, because in a radically unequal globalizing world, the fortification of a wealthy community's membership bounds renders democratic practices inauthentic, increases inequality, and fortifies economic privilege." *Id.* at 404. She explores the development of that dilemma in both the plant closing movement and activism on issues of globalization. In the excerpt following Ansley, Elizabeth Iglesias discusses issues of inequality that accompany unbalanced development.

FRAN ANSLEY

Inclusive Boundaries and Other (Im)possible Paths Toward Community Development in a Global World
150 U. Pa. L. Rev. 353, 361–66, 371–72, 374–75, 377–80, 388–92, 396–97, 400–01, 406 (2001)

* * * Social movement theory tells us that in order to communicate effectively, movements—like other social and individual actors who undertake to speak and be heard in public fora—must find or construct frames that provide a way for listeners to understand them, cognitive scaffolds that work to organize perception and explain reality. Unlike just any old social actor looking for an audience, however, social movements must use a frame that valorizes and motivates collective action. William Gamson developed a widely cited formulation for what such a "collective action frame" requires. He said it must include three elements: (1) *injustice* (the frame presents the situation as unfair or unequal); (2) *identity* (the frame identifies an "us" and a "them," with the former seen to be suffering as a result of a situation for which the latter are responsible); and (3) *agency* (the frame offers the view that through collective action "we" have the capacity to change the situation).

The plant-closing movement tried to construct and project precisely such a frame. First, it cast its core issue—plant closings—as an instance of social *injustice* rather than some inexorable law of economic development. Second, the movement specified relevant *identities*, naming an "us" and a "them," and generally putting the blame for the core injustice not on workers or local communities, but on corporate decision makers and government officials. Finally, the movement worked to convince its constituents that their own power and *agency* was not a pipe dream, that if they worked together in local plant-closing organizations and coalitions, or in the larger national network, they could change the situation in a meaningful way—both through more and better bargains that could be hammered out in contentious negotiations among corporations, workers, and communities, and through enforcement victories and substantive reforms that could be won in legal arenas.

* * *

* * * [B]road segments of ordinarily quiescent Americans were irate about what corporations were doing. There was a strong feeling among many people that foundational promises were being broken, long-secure arrangements were crumbling, and profound questions about the past and future were in order. In communities all over the country, new

coalitions of labor, religious, and community organizations were emerging with a focus and unity on matters of economic justice that had not been seen for decades. Fundamental questions about the nature and meaning of economic arrangements—and about the values that should guide them—were being debated on the evening news. * * *

* * *

* * * By definition, the frame proposed by a social movement urges change: it seeks to move people out of their current stance and into new sorts of action. Nevertheless, to some extent a movement's framing efforts must draw from collective memories, past experiences, and existing belief structures of the movement's constituency in order to have mobilizing power.

* * *

* * * The plant-closing movement did provide opportunities for direct learning and exchange with people who were undergoing economic crisis. * * * Achievements [in altering public policy] included stronger job security provisions in many collective bargaining agreements, limited legislative protection for workers affected by some types of plant closings, enhanced adjustment programs to help dislocated workers make smoother transitions after mass layoffs, and the creation of a network of labor and community activists who had made each other's engaged acquaintance and who were critical of the corporate attitudes and practices embodied in many plant-closing sagas.

By no stretch of the imagination did the plant-closing movement emerge victorious. In fact, some of the movement's original aspirations to reduce capital flight as a corporate behavior in U.S. industry appear now to have been poignantly—perhaps pathetically—naive. Many industries continued on a crash course of restructuring. They reorganized their production processes and their corporate structures in new post-Fordist ways that radically diminished job security. They engaged in a frenzy of mergers, acquisitions, and disaggregations. In addition, they exponentially escalated their use of co-production across national boundaries.

Foes of plant closings were soon forced to recognize the deep structural character and the broad global scale of the decisions we were trying to influence. Meanwhile, the economic and political clout of labor unions continued to decline, in part because the industries that were closing down were often those with the strongest union base, and in part because even when jobs stayed in the United States, the "threat effect" of globalization exerted severe downward pressure on labor's bargaining position. It was as if plant-closing foes began by trying to put out what they thought was a small kitchen grease fire, only to realize as their efforts continued that arsonists had set the blaze and already the basement was fully involved.

Nevertheless, despite the undeniable disappointments, the plant-closing movement did not go up in flames, metaphorical or otherwise. In fact, the movement and its attendant framing project flowed directly into several important successor currents, including the international agitation against neoliberal "free trade" regimes, college anti-sweatshop coalitions, state and local efforts to curb abuse of corporate subsidies and other development incentives, and the burgeoning patchwork of campus and community campaigns for a living wage. * * *

* * *

* * * [Through] varied efforts to enlist the aid of the state [judicially and legislatively], the movement chalked up some modest successes. For instance, it won a scattering of plant-closing ordinances and statutes aimed at controlling subsidy abuse, it allied with administrators in some locations to begin monitoring the costs and benefits of development incentives, and it convinced some local officials to bring suit against departing employers. In the federal arena, despite vastly overheated opposition and a presidential veto, the movement helped win eventual passage of the Worker Adjustment and Retraining Notification Act (the "WARN Act") in the U.S. Congress. [The movement was less successful at seeking help from the judiciary.]

* * *

* * * Meanwhile, defenders of "flexible" production and corporate freedom were quick to provide their own spin. In most instances, corporations tried to cast state-centered demands by the plant-closing movement as ill-advised attempts to induce government interference with the natural functioning of the market.

This laissez-faire line of argument may have appeared hypocritical when advanced by the same corporations that were quick to demand or accept government subsidies and development incentives, but the inconsistency did not deter them from invoking the powerful free market frame. In many cases, high-toned calls to free market principles were coupled with open or veiled threats of raw power. Companies frequently announced that they would take their production elsewhere even more rapidly, completely, or irrevocably than otherwise if a government entity imposed unwanted rules or refused to provide desired benefits.

These threats promoted regulatory competition, a practice that constituted one of the most powerful obstacles the plant-closing movement faced when it tried to persuade governments to impose stronger popular controls on capital mobility. Local and state governments were acutely aware of the fierce contest to attract scarce investor dollars in an environment where it had become both easier and more profitable to withdraw and move investments with great frequency. Under these circumstances, government officials were often pressed into a race to see which jurisdiction could and would create the most "business friendly" regulatory climate.

* * *

As time went on, * * * the movement encountered more and more cases where production was being shifted not simply from inner cities to suburbs, from the industrial heartland to greenfield locations in right-to-work states, or from one in-state location to another in response to a sweeter deal. Instead, production was moving out of the country altogether, often bound for low-wage locations in nations of the global South. The *maquiladoras* in particular, located so close to the United States, strung out along the northern tier of Mexican states fronting the U.S.-Mexico border, drew increased attention from plant-closing activists and became the topic of animated discussion and apprehension.

When first President George H.W. Bush and then President Clinton took up the banner of the North American Free Trade Agreement (NAFTA), this complex of issues about capital mobility and democratic governance became focused more than ever at the national and international level. Plant-closing veterans were exquisitely primed to see the dangers and the deep power contests embedded in laws that governed and protected freedom of movement for capital. They saw free trade deals as the locking-in of exactly the rules and practices they had been trying so hard to fight, and many plant-closing activists were quick to involve themselves in the emerging mobilizations against NAFTA and free trade.

NAFTA made an easy target because it posed specific and facially evident threats to democracy * * * .

* * * NAFTA imposed prospective substantive limits * * * that constrained the exercise of legislative power in the signatory countries. For instance, under NAFTA, governments can be sanctioned for giving preference to domestic products or for using human rights criteria in government purchasing, and, under the rubric of assuring fairness and stability to foreign investors, a host of other often ill-defined prohibitions are imposed.

* * *

* * * NAFTA's new rights for international investors are supported by powerful new remedies. Trade sanctions, such as countervailing duties, may be invoked by aggrieved governments. More radically, however, NAFTA also created unprecedented avenues by which private corporations themselves may invoke dispute-settlement proceedings against sovereign governments for allegedly violating investor rights set out in the agreement. Although similar language on indirect expropriation has been a feature of bilateral investment treaties for some time, these new investor-to-state dispute settlement procedures break new ground in creating a corporate right of action. Monetary compensation may be ordered in favor of a complaining corporation if a legislative body or other government official or entity in one of the member nations is held to have overstepped the new prohibitions announced in the NAFTA text, as that text comes to be interpreted by the elite international dispute-resolution panels created and empowered by it.

* * *

In * * * [the contexts of free trade agreements and the World Trade Organization,] existing or proposed one-sided investor protections and new international trade and investment regimes significantly restrict the power of governments to set national economic policy or to pursue national development strategies if those policies or strategies are at variance with neoliberal precepts. This new global legal order, a kind of "global constitutionalization" of international investment rights, has reinforced my embrace of the lessons and imagery I have suggested * * * above. Polities do, indeed, need the power to hold economic actors accountable to those who do business within their boundaries.

* * * [But I have come to feel uneasy about this frame and these images in some respects,] at least in the context of a social movement born and bred in the United States. The factor that most profoundly unsettled my equanimity about defending the bounds of home in a global age was my very local encounter with a very global phenomenon: mass labor migration.

* * *

* * * In the expanded context of immigration policy, strongly defended boundaries around the communities of the privileged center seemed to exacerbate rather than to balance power differentials that had begun to yawn so ominously between footloose transnational corporations and nationally grounded workers. Far from protecting the ability of directly affected workers and communities to help set economic ground rules for corporate behavior, strong boundaries in this new context seemed to reinforce privilege and exclude many voiceless people from relevant democratic deliberation. * * *

* * *

* * * [In Tennessee, for example,] Latino and Latina immigrants were showing up in rural and urban counties all over the state. Most of them were from Mexico, but many were from Central America as well. A high proportion of them were undocumented, many were living in families with "blended" immigration status, and they were present, by all accounts, in numbers the region had never seen before.

These newcomers were finding their way into niche employment in the toughest and worst-paying jobs our regional economy has to offer—harvesting tomatoes, washing dishes, processing poultry, digging ditches, hanging dry wall, pruning nursery stock, removing asbestos, and the like. New day-labor agencies and temp services with Spanish-speaking staff began springing up to act as brokers between area businesses and this brand new kind of worker. Latinos could be found searching the men's clothing racks in thrift stores, dropping off kids at school, swelling the pews at Catholic and evangelical church services, seeking help in hospital emergency rooms, forming and playing in new soccer leagues, going to jail, dating the locals, sending money orders home on Friday afternoons by Western Union, and waiting in line at the Greyhound bus station. Eventually, we even got our very own INS office, and some immigrants found themselves detained and sent to Memphis for deportation.

* * *

The reception these immigrants received from others in East Tennessee ranged from cordial and welcoming to overtly racist and xenophobic. * * *

* * *

The most common "pro-immigrant" response to * * * [the charge that Mexicans were stealing American jobs] was to argue that at least north of the border in the United States, immigrants were only taking "the jobs Americans don't want." * * * I view * * * [this argument] as highly problematic. It treats wages and working conditions as somehow essential, inherent, and unchanging features of the jobs themselves, rather than factors that are malleable and under human control. More U.S. workers would be eager to do many of the jobs immigrants do if the wages and working conditions were more reasonable.

This theme of "unwanted jobs" implies there should be nothing troubling about building a labor market on a sub-group of foreign workers with limited legal rights and no political clout—in fact, it suggests it would make for a happy fit, as long as those workers are slotted of their own "free" will. According to this view, it matters not that immigrants' work is more distasteful, dangerous, and poorly paid than the sort of work the rest of the workforce, clothed with the rights and privileges of legal membership, presently prefers or is compelled to undertake. Such a vision implies a segmentation of the labor market that is highly correlated to race and is constructed and policed by immigration law. Further, it suggests that such a market should not only be tolerated by Americans, but welcomed by them. It invites American workers in particular to embrace color-coded and nation-coded labor market segmentation as appropriate and mutually advantageous to different groups of laborers, rather than to reject it as discriminatory toward individual immigrants and destructive of the possibilities for cross-race movement-building and solidarity. * * *

* * *

* * * [W]e frameworkers of the plant-closing movement should have paid sharper attention to the exclusionary potential of the "bounded polities" and "local roots" imagery of the frame we were laboring to construct. Our frame at times cast a falsely simple and rosy light on the democratic practices of the American past, both in the electoral arena and within the American labor movement. On occasion we failed to give sufficient attention to the problem of who had been historically—and who was still presently—left out of the American polity or the house of labor and why. Questions about historical inclusion and exclusion seem especially salient given the geopolitical power relations, the particular channels of commerce and communication, and the material maldistributions that characterize today's global economy. All of these patterns and

relationships bear the clear and present imprint of the colonial past, and suggest that America has never existed as something apart from a thoroughly international context.

In retrospect, it seems to me that we too often and too uncritically invoked a kind of golden age of past American democracy in order to rally people to democracy's contemporary defense. Of course, myths of golden ages are hardly unusual in the framingwork of social movements, and they have often shown their power to motivate and inspire collective action. * * *

* * *

* * * We neglected to include as strongly and vividly as we should have a more critical, inclusive, and internationalist edge to our nostalgic talk of a threatened polity and its righteous powers.

* * *

* * * Unless poor and working-class people in the world's North achieve the capacity to see themselves in a global context, it will be flatly impossible for them to build organizations that are strong enough to defend their interests or to carry out successful campaigns for economic justice. * * *

ELIZABETH M. IGLESIAS

Institutionalizing Economic Justice: A LatCrit Perspective on the Imperatives of Linking the Reconstruction of "Community" to the Transformation of Legal Structures That Institutionalize the Depoliticization and Fragmentation of Labor/Community Solidarity

2 U. Pa. J. Lab. & Emp. L. 773, 785–86, 798–99 (2000)

Plant relocations increase profits by exploiting the relative powerlessness of non-unionized and Third World workers as compared to unionized workers in advanced industrial countries. The story of American plant closings is a particularly instructive window into the politics of division at an international level. Management advocates often characterize plant relocations as a necessary response to increased competition from Third World producers. In this account, the low wages accepted by Third World workers give Third World producers a comparative advantage in labor intensive production. Confronted by cheaper (and often better) foreign products, American companies blamed their lack of competitiveness on the high wages commanded by a militant domestic labor movement. Offshore sourcing was promoted as the obvious solution.

By relocating to low wage areas, American firms seek to internalize the comparative advantage of their Third World competitors, namely a low wage labor force. However, offshore sourcing affords only a temporary advantage because the higher profits are not based on permanent manufacturing improvements or technological innovations. Instead, plant relocations to non-union areas are just another way to increase profits by "sweating" the workforce. This reality is disguised, however, by characterizing plant relocations as a vehicle for Third World economic development. In this context, plant relocations are called "foreign direct investment." The arguments are simple. Foreign direct investment creates employment in underdeveloped countries. Employment generates income. Income stimulates demand, which in turn encourages investment, and eventually results in a diversified local economy. Thus, from this perspective, the relocation of American businesses to Third World countries is cast as an engine of Third World development.

Plant relocations do create employment in the Third World, but at exceedingly low wages. American multinationals operating there have made it clear that their continued presence depends on wages remaining low. Indeed, despite dirt-cheap wages, Ford workers at the plant in Hermosillo, Mexico were forced to strike for thirty-nine days when Ford refused to pay a legally required cost-of-living increase. Ford workers involved in union struggles for higher wages and safer working conditions have also been met with violence. As a result, it is unlikely that this form of "foreign direct investment" will generate any meaningful or sustainable economic development in the Third World.

Foreign direct investment appears even more questionable as a development mechanism when compared to other alternatives—specifically those aimed at encouraging domestic producers. Compared to domestic producers, foreign capitalists routinely tend to repatriate profits for investment or distribution in their home countries, rather than reinvesting in the local economies of the host country. Moreover, foreign investment (especially investment involving plant relocations) is often aimed at establishing production platforms for export markets in the First World, rather than for local consumption needs. In short, plant relocations operate as a profit-maximizing strategy by capitalizing on the relative powerlessness and desperate economic situation of the most vulnerable workers in the world, even as the dominant ideology enables American businesses to represent themselves as the champions of competitive efficiency and economic development against the special interests of an unproductive and parochial labor union aristocracy.

* * *

* * * [U]nion failures to participate reciprocally in community struggles over matters unrelated to the conditions of employment must be analyzed against a history of judicial interpretation that has worked to isolate unions and to narrow the instances in which unionized workers can lawfully exercise economic and political power.

Judicial precedents have imposed significant legal restrictions on union power to conduct secondary boycotts* and political strikes; they have expanded the threat of antitrust liability in instances where labor unions coordinate their concerted activities with non-labor groups; they have imported and arbitrarily applied highly indeterminate obligations of

* In secondary boycotts, unions urge consumers or workers to support the employees of a company by refusing to buy or handle the company's products.

employee "loyalty" to employers; and they have substantially restricted the use of union member dues to promote a broad political agenda and even to organize unorganized sectors of the working class. Through the articulation of these precedents, courts have been deeply implicated in the emergence and consolidation of a narrow minded, apolitical, conformist and isolated brand of unionism. The fact that *some* unions have, nevertheless, taken the risk of engaging broader issues and of acting in solidarity with non-labor groups is as unsurprising as the fact that *many more have not*.

Notes and Questions

1. How can people in the United States come to understand and incorporate perspectives that include global patterns of privilege and power? Is it possible for "poor and working class people in the world's North" to define their interests in common with the interests of lower-paid workers in other countries?

2. What is the responsibility of social justice movement activists and social justice lawyers when confronted with the dilemma Ansley describes, in which emphasizing some interests may fail to confront and even exacerbate other social justice issues?

3. How can social justice activists in the United States strengthen labor-community coalitions under the constraints described by Iglesias? One possibility may be the living wage movement, mentioned by Ansley as one of the successors to the plant-closing movement, which brings together labor and community interests. *See* William Quigley, *Ending Poverty: Amending the Constitution to Create a Right to a Job at a Living Wage* (forthcoming, Temple University Press 2003); William Quigley, *Full-time Workers Should Not Be Poor: The Living Wage Movement*, 70 Miss. L.J. 889 (2001). What are other possibilities?

B. Labor and Human Rights Claims

If human rights declarations and treaties can help support some claims for rights to employment, is it possible to use international law to protect workers both inside and outside the United States? Laura Ho, Catherine Powell, and Leti Volpp discuss the necessity and possibility of protecting workers at different points on the "global assembly line."

LAURA HO, CATHERINE POWELL & LETI VOLPP

(Dis)Assembling Rights of Women Workers Along the Global Assembly Line: Human Rights and the Garment Industry

31 Harv. C.R.-C.L. L. Rev. 383, 383–400, 405–06, 411–12 (1996)

On August 2, 1995, a multi-agency raid found sixty-seven Thai women and five Thai men kept in slave-like conditions in an apartment complex in a Los Angeles community called El Monte. Under the constant surveillance of armed guards and confined behind a ring of razor wire, they had been held for several years and had been forced to work as garment workers up to eighteen hours per day for far less than the minimum wage. They were refused unmonitored contact with the outside world and threatened with rape or harm to themselves and their families if they tried to escape. On one occasion, a worker who tried to escape was brutally beaten, his photograph taken and shown to the other workers as an example of what might happen to them if they too tried to flee.

Such conditions constitute the essence of slavery. An ideological remnant of Black slavery that has survived despite the enactment of the Reconstruction amendments is the misguided notion that certain categories of people can be mistreated through employment arrangements aimed at placing them beyond legal protections as well as through constructs of citizenship that deny them full enjoyment of human rights. * * * [I]mmigrant women, Black women, and women of color generally continue to occupy disproportionately the most degraded positions on the economic ladder * * * .

Some observers would like to explain away sweatshops as immigrants exploiting other immigrants, as "cultural," or as the importation of a form of exploitation that normally does not happen here but occurs elsewhere, in the "Third World." While the public was shocked by the discovery at El Monte, garment workers and garment worker advocates have for years been describing abuses in the garment industry and have ascribed responsibility for such abuses to manufacturers and retailers who control the industry.

Sweatshops, like the one in El Monte, are a home-grown problem with peculiarly American roots. Since the inception of the garment industry, U.S. retailers and manufacturers have scoured the United States and the rest of the globe for the cheapest and most malleable labor—predominantly female, low-skilled, and disempowered—in order to squeeze out as much profit as possible for themselves. Along with this globalization, the process of subcontracting, whereby manufacturers contract out cutting and sewing to contractors to avoid being considered the "employer" of the workers, has made it extremely difficult for garment workers in the United States to assert their rights under domestic law.

* * *

Women workers have formed the backbone of the U.S. garment industry throughout its history. The geographic location and racial composition of this workforce has varied as retailers and manufacturers have shifted location of production to lower their labor costs. During the 1800s and early 1900s, the industry was centered primarily in New York City with a large influx of White immigrants providing a vast supply of inexpensive labor. Following the Triangle Shirtwaist Company fire in 1911 and the exposure of dehumanizing sweatshop conditions, the union movement gained momentum, building on the "Uprising of the Twenty

Thousand" in 1909 when women shirtwaist workers walked off the job to demand better working conditions.

The success of unions in northern industrial centers and immigration restrictions imposed by the 1924 Immigration Act led to the relocation of the garment industry to southern states that offered large economic incentives to firms willing to relocate, as well as a workforce of rural White women who were an unorganized and inexpensive source of labor. After the civil rights movement succeeded in opening up manufacturing jobs previously unavailable to Blacks, companies turned to Black women in the 1970s as the newest source of cheap labor in the U.S. South. Meanwhile, New York and California developed as the twin centers of the U.S. garment industry, where a new influx of immigrants provided low-wage labor. California has capitalized on its large Asian and Latina immigrant populations to become, today, the largest site of garment production in the United States.

In addition, garment facilities along the U.S.-Mexico border in Texas have incorporated immigrant labor, primarily from Mexico and other parts of Latin America. While garment employment in Texas has dropped, the garment sector has expanded on the other side of the border in *maquiladora* factories in Mexico, largely due to the Mexican government's establishment of the Border Industrialization Program in 1965. Lower wages and less stringent labor law enforcement than in the United States make *maquiladoras* in Mexico and Central America attractive sites for offshore production. Drawing from a pool of women of Mexican descent as their primary source of labor, garment factories on both sides of the U.S.-Mexico border are paradigmatic examples of the increasingly transnational nature of corporations and of labor.

While the garment industry has provided women, particularly women of color and immigrants, access to the manufacturing work force, this result has been accompanied by a downward spiral of wages and consistent exploitation. Wages are especially low in thriving "underground" economies in such cities as Los Angeles and New York, where garment workers usually make much less than * * * the current federal minimum wage * * * and work ten to twelve hour days without the overtime compensation mandated by federal law.

As predominantly working-class women of color, garment workers face severe structural barriers to exercising their rights. Positioned at the intersection of oppressions based on race, gender, class, and frequently immigrant status, these women workers must also struggle against the power of international capital. Their organizing attempts are often met by a shift to offshore production, where their counterparts—primarily low-wage women workers in developing countries—are paid even less for the same work.

The garment industry is one of the most global industries in the world. The proliferation of industrial garment production follows broader patterns in trade globalization and economic restructuring. * * * Many developing countries have switched from the model of "import substitution"—industrialization through substituting imports with goods produced domestically—to a model of "export promotion"—export-led industrialization. Export promotion typically involves strategies that attract foreign investment through such incentives as tax holidays, the promise of cheap controllable labor for transnational corporations, and the establishment of export-processing zones (EPZs) that ease importing/exporting restrictions.

In addition to engaging in direct foreign investment (for example, through their own branch offices), TNCs [transnational corporations] also arrange arms' length relationships through subcontracting and licensing agreements, which often allow them to limit their liability for labor violations. TNCs benefit from their ability to scour the globe for the cheapest sources of labor in developing countries, as well as in advanced-industrialized countries, where extensive immigration from less-developed countries has created a "Third World within." Part of this immigration is itself due to globalization, as the new economic order dislocates people, disrupting their livelihoods and causing them to emigrate for survival. On arrival in advanced-industrialized countries, immigrants and refugees are faced with new forms of coercion, including immigration controls, racism, and sexism—practices that often relegate them to positions on the bottom rung of the economic ladder.

These trends in garment production and trade highlight ways in which the concept of the nation-state is becoming an increasingly ineffective model for designing market-controlling mechanisms. States are often unable to control the activities of TNCs, although strong governments exercise considerable influence through trade policies and development assistance. While the nation-state traditionally has been viewed as the locus for the declaration of rights-based norms (through courts) and their enforcement (through police and army), the state cannot adequately respond to dynamics that arise from markets that cut across borders. This effacement of sovereignty at the national level is accompanied by the emergence of regional and world trade agreements and bureaucracies that seek to mediate the new global space where transnational economic transactions rule, and markets generally triumph over government action. The decline of geographic sovereignty and conceptual boundaries such as the traditional public/private, state/market, political/economic, and national/international dichotomies testifies to the fact that simplistic, nationalistic approaches for securing worker rights are no longer viable.

Thus, more sophisticated approaches that are transnational in scope and that explore the interplay of labor rights and free trade must be examined. Labor, environmental, and other types of human rights discourses have begun to penetrate free trade discussions, although purist free traders object to this infiltration. Indeed, more often than not, the free trade debate has a dichotomous quality—in its starkest from breaking down between free traders who value complete economic liberalization and protectionists who want to shield certain industries and their workers from unfettered competition. * * *

An alternative paradigm to the free trade/protectionist paradigm is a post-free trade approach, which posits transnational mechanisms through which to harmonize labor, environmental, and human rights standards. Such mechanisms allow for trade liberalization while offering protections to workers both at home and abroad. They include, among other things, social clauses in trade laws that may be enforced through adjudicatory bodies. While in theory these mechanisms are attractive, in practice they have often failed to live up to their mission because of inadequate resources, investigatory capability, and enforcement powers. * * *

Putting a transnational, post-free trade approach into practice requires thinking *and* acting globally *and* locally, in contrast to the popular aphorism, "Think Globally, Act Locally." But even when restated, the "global-local" distinction does not reflect the way parameters of the "local" and "global" are often indefinable, indistinct, or intermingled, due to the transnational flows of culture and corporations. Any attempts to change working conditions in the "local" will be largely fruitless without improved conditions in other sites. We therefore need to engage in transnational solidarity. In doing so, we must take care to acknowledge differences in women's lives—specifically with regard to the geographic distribution of power and privilege, as well as the ways in which other structures of dominance and subordination, for example, class or race, cross-cut gender. * * *

TNCs have adopted two effective strategies that allow them to maintain sweatshops on the global assembly line. First, TNCs use the contracting system, whether domestically or abroad, to avoid legal liability for the workers' wages or working conditions. Second, TNCs use their ability to relocate production to virtually any country as a threat to all their current workers: if workers demand higher wages, TNCs can move their production to lower wage sites. Combating these two tactics necessitates coupling U.S. legal strategies with transnational ones, such as deploying the extraterritorial application of U.S. laws, public international law, U.S. trade laws, and multilateral trade agreements. * * *

* * * [T]he extraterritorial application of protective provisions of the NLRA [National Labor Relations Act], such as collective bargaining protections, could greatly enhance protections for garment workers laboring for U.S. corporations abroad.

More promising is the extraterritorial application of Title VII, which clearly provides antidiscrimination protection for garment workers in U.S. plants overseas. In 1991, in response to the Supreme Court's refusal to extend Title VII of the Civil Rights Act extraterritorially, Congress specifically amended Title VII to have such reach. For workers employed by U.S. companies in factories outside U.S. borders, the law provides a way to combat the sexual harassment, as well as other forms of discrimination, common in many factories both domestically and abroad.

Garment workers, however, are not always well served by the extraterritorial application of U.S. laws. To the extent U.S. labor law is an amalgamation of corporate and labor interests, specific provisions may be the product of political deal making rather than concern for the protection of workers' rights. Moreover, the extension of U.S. laws to the activities of U.S. companies in other national jurisdictions could be viewed as a form of neocolonialism. As such, more cooperative approaches to developing and enforcing transnational labor standards should be explored.

Internationally recognized worker rights have long been part of the regime of international human rights law. The International Bill of Human Rights, composed of the Universal Declaration of Human Rights, the International Covenant on Civil and Political Rights, and the International Covenant on Economic, Social and Cultural Rights, declares core labor rights, which include freedom from slavery, freedom of association including organizing trade unions, and fair wages and equal pay to be universal human rights. Similarly, according to the International Labor Organization (ILO), "fundamental" or "basic" labor/human rights are: (1) freedom of association (including freedom to organize and bargain collectively), (2) freedom from forced labor, and (3) equality of opportunity and treatment (including equal remuneration and freedom from discrimination).

The ILO, now a part of the United Nations, sets international labor standards through the passage of Conventions and Recommendations, supervision of implementation of those standards, provision of technical assistance, information and aid, and enforcement by means of reporting requirements and moral suasion. Unlike typical international human rights instruments, ILO conventions and recommendations are unique in that they are arrived at by a tripartite structure made up of employer, employee, and government representatives from 152 countries. While the lack of effective enforcement mechanisms is a general weakness of international law, the incorporation and acceptance of these internationally recognized rights into labor-protective regimes in the United States have allowed such rights to be accessed and enforced more effectively by garment workers and their advocates.

Of all U.S. trade laws available to assert labor rights, worker advocates have used the Generalized System of Preferences (GSP) petition process most frequently. The GSP provides duty-free tariff treatment on certain products for designated "beneficiary developing countries" (BDC) in order to promote economic development in those countries. When the GSP program was renewed in 1984, section 502(b) of the Renewal Act added mandatory worker rights criteria to the statute. Furthermore, section 502(b)(7) of the Renewal Act mandated that "the President shall not designate any country a beneficiary developing country under this section ... if such country has not taken or is not taking steps to afford internationally recognized worker rights to workers in the country (including any designated zone in that country)." Those internationally recognized worker rights are: (1) freedom of association; (2) the right to organize and bargain collectively; (3) a prohibition on the use of forced or compulsory labor; (4) a minimum wage for the employment of children; and (5) acceptable conditions of work with respect to minimum wages, hours of work, and occupational safety and health.

Following a review of BDCs in 1985–1986, the United States Trade Representative issued regulations that allow "any person," on an annual basis, to "file a request to have the GSP status of any eligible beneficiary developing country reviewed with respect to any of the designation criteria...." * * * Because the United States imports garments from many BDCs, the GSP can and has been a useful tool for garment workers.

The successor to the General Agreement on Tariffs and Trade (GATT), the World Trade Organization (WTO) is the primary multinational regulator of trade. While neither the provisions of the GATT nor the mandate of the WTO protects workers' rights explicitly, some commentators have suggested utilizing the unfair trade practices provisions under GATT/WTO to vindicate certain labor rights. For instance, the use of forced and child labor, which artificially lowers production costs, arguably violates the antidumping provisions of GATT/WTO and may also be considered a prohibited subsidy, which could lead to countervailing duties. Similarly, the practice of denying labor rights that are otherwise generally applicable in a country in export-processing zones arguably confers an unfair trade advantage by effectively subsidizing exports to other countries.

Such assertions of unfair trade practices, if successful, would thus subject the offending countries to economic sanctions, providing a powerful disincentive to exploit workers in their own countries. * * * [However,] because many trade agreements do not protect worker rights or improve working conditions directly, the solutions they offer usually can do no more than protect U.S. industries generally against lower-priced imports and thus only indirectly protect workers' jobs.

Unlike GATT/WTO, the North American Free Trade Agreement (NAFTA) contains labor and environmental side agreements and thus affords worker rights greater protection. Article I of the labor side agreement identifies one of its objectives as the promotion, "to the maximum extent possible, the labor principles set out in Annex 1." Annex 1 states that each country should promote the following: (1) protection of the rights to organize, bargain, and strike; (2) prohibition of forced labor, child labor, subminimal wages, and employment discrimination; and (3) promotion of equal pay for equal work, occupational safety and health, and equal treatment for migrant workers.

These standards, however, are merely hortatory. The side agreement provides for enforcement of each country's existing labor laws in only three areas: (1) occupational health and safety, (2) child labor, and (3) minimum wages. Significantly, the right to organize and bargain collectively is listed only in the aspirational Annex I rather than as an enforceable obligation governed by the procedures in the side agreement.

The side agreement's enforcement procedures provide for a quasi-judicial system to hear complaints brought by any of the three signatory countries, the United States, Mexico, and Canada, against another signatory that it believes is failing to enforce its labor laws in the three enumerated areas. Within each country, a National Administrative Office (NAO) must be set up to provide information to the Commission for Labor Cooperation, which attempts to resolve the dispute through consultation and cooperation. * * * Ultimately, fines or suspension of NAFTA trade benefits are available for persistent violations of certain defined labor rights and labor standards.

* * *

Unions and other worker advocacy groups have begun to respond to global economic restructuring through transnational organizing. For instance, unions are strengthening ties among workers of different countries so that when a plant announces that it is closing in the United States, workers at the relocation site can put concerted and simultaneous pressure on the manufacturer. * * *

Both unions and nonunionized workers' associations have begun worker exchanges, which encourage workers to see their commonalities and the potential of their combined strength, rather than allowing protectionist impulses, racism, or xenophobia to convince them that they will be well served by competing with the workers of other countries. * * *

* * *

International women's conferences have also served as a site for the creation of transnational solidarity. The growth of the women's human rights movement as a global phenomenon is apparent in the ability of women to engage the U.N. and other multilateral organizations, thereby compelling these institutions to hold themselves accountable to the world's working women. Few practical gains in economic justice, however, have been achieved as a result of such conferences, in part because economic and social rights have not received the same degree of attention as civil and political rights in those fora. * * *

Notes and Questions

1. The lawyers who worked on the El Monte case coordinated innovative legal claims with support for organization among the workers themselves. *See* Julie A. Su, *Making the Invisible Visible: The Garment Industry's Dirty Laundry*, 1 J. Gender Race & Just. 405 (1998), excerpted in chapter 3; Penda D. Hair, *Louder Than Words: Lawyers, Communities, and the Struggle for Justice* 38 (2001).

2. Although remedies for labor violations through the procedures created under NAFTA are very limited, they have been invoked through submissions to NAO offices in Canada, Mexico, and the United States by labor unions and other complainants. "These submissions * * * cannot

contribute substantially to the development of labor standards because the obligation of the United States is only to enforce its own laws. They can, however, serve the purpose of deflating our hubris and focusing our attention on our pervasive failure to effectively enforce our own labor laws." Clyde Summers, *NAFTA's Labor Side Agreement And International Labor Standards*, 3 J. Small & Emerging Bus. L. 173, 186 (1999). Submissions have involved topics such as the failure to protect the right to organize unions in Mexico, the practices of the U.S. Immigration and Naturalization Service, pregnancy discrimination in Mexico, protection of farmworkers in the state of Washington, and delays and inadequacies of the workers compensation process in New York. A summary of submissions can be viewed on the NAALC website, http://www.naalc.org/english/publications/summarymain.htm (last viewed September 19, 2002).

SECTION 3. WORK AND SOCIAL INSURANCE

What is the relationship between a society's approach to work and its policy regarding those who are not working? Should that relationship depend on whether paid work is available or on the reason a person is not working? What if the person is unable to work because of disability or some other condition that prevents work? What if society needs that person to perform some other labor outside the market, such as child bearing or military service?

A. Income Protection and the Labor Market

JOEL F. HANDLER

"Constructing the Political Spectacle": The Interpretation of Entitlements, Legalization, and Obligations in Social Welfare History
56 Brook. L. Rev. 899, 906–22 (1990)

Who the poor are and what to do about their poverty form the basis of welfare policy. The construction of the nature, causes, and remedies for poverty reflects fundamental values about how society should be organized, how people should act, and how to assign blame. Poverty policy is part of the normative order of the political economy. From at least the time of Henry VIII, the overarching tension has been to balance the need to maintain labor discipline with the need to relieve misery. Under liberal capitalism, the state offers protection, comfort, and support for those who participate in the productive system. For those who cannot because of conditions beyond their control, the state provides relief. Thus, the heart of poverty policy centers on the question of who is excused from work. Those who are excused are the "deserving poor"; those who must work are the "undeserving." Ultimately, this is a moral distinction. It involves deciding the nature and significance of the work ethic, the causes and extent of disability, the impact, both real and perceived, of incentives and disincentives on human behavior, and the consequences to the individual, the family, and the community of failing to abide by conventional norms.

The normative order of the political economy involves far more than work. The construction of the family—gender roles, child rearing, and socialization—are integral parts of this political economy, as are race and ethnicity. Thus, poverty policy is influenced by and, in turn, influences labor discipline, gender and family roles, socialization, and race and ethnicity. All are part of the ideological construction of welfare policy.

Central to an understanding of welfare is the role of poor women in the paid labor force. From the earliest days of the country, poor women were *never* morally excused from the paid labor force. During the colonial and early national periods, women from all social classes were encouraged to seek paid labor. Starting about the 1830s, the situation changed. With the rise of the "domestic code," the patriarchal family was defined by the husband in the paid labor force and the wife and mother in the home. The spheres were to be separate; the female role was morally defined in terms of the purer sex, the provider of sanctuary, and the moral educator of the children. Many reasons are given for the rise of the domestic code, including competition from male wage earners, employers who blamed working women for low wages, and social reformers who feared the destruction of the family.

The domestic code had serious, negative effects on poor women and mothers. These women *had* to work; there were no alternatives. Yet, they were severely condemned for working. They were blamed for competition and for undermining working conditions, and they were attacked for bad mothering—neglecting their children, or if married—neglecting their husbands as well. The moral degradation of these women was compounded by additional factors. The poorer the woman, the worse the job—in laundries, in factories, as domestic servants, taking in boarders—jobs that were the least "feminine." African-Americans and immigrants were disproportionately represented at the bottom of the paid labor force. Finally, the number of poor women in the paid labor force was not small. Thus, they were perceived as a social menace. Poor mothers, especially single mothers, were in an inescapable dilemma. They had to work—there were no sources of aid—yet, by working they violated the domestic code and faced the loss of their children. * * *

Why were there no welfare programs for poor mothers? * * *

* * * Because they were part of the paid labor force, giving them aid would undermine labor discipline. The giving of aid would also weaken the family, lessen the husband's obligations, or encourage desertion. The task of social policy, argued the reformers, was to force the husband to return to the family by affirming obligations, not encouraging dependency. * * * From time to time, local work programs were established for "worthy" widows, but these programs were largely unsuccessful. What is important about these programs is that they insisted on work for these

poor women. As Sonya Michel put it: "[I]n the lives of poor women there was no place for the conceit of the non-working wife as a symbol of the husband's ability to maintain his 'angel in the house.' "

Yet, there was the need to relieve misery and to help the blameless poor. The nineteenth century witnessed the rise of categories—aid for particular categories of the poor who were considered blameless. This approach has remained a basic characteristic of American social welfare policy. Institutions were created for the blind, the deaf, and the insane, and later, for orphans. A separate pension system was created for Civil War veterans, which eventually grew into a massive welfare program.

The first of the twentieth century categorical programs—Aid to Dependent Children (ADC)—was enacted in 1911 and quickly spread throughout the country. This program, popularly called "Mothers' Pensions," was designed to provide income support for single mothers to maintain their homes. Thus, the programs were interpreted as a major change in social welfare policy towards poor single mothers: these women were removed from the paid labor force—the hallmark of the deserving poor.

In fact, nothing was further from the truth. At this time, single mothers and their children, as a category, were indistinguishable from the mass of the poor; that is, they were undeserving and required to work. * * * All the programs were very restrictive; only a small number of white widows were enrolled. * * *

Aid to the Blind was enacted during this period but under very different circumstances. * * * The blind were not considered part of the labor force.

Relief for the dependent aged came a bit later, but was much contested. At this time, there was no agreed-upon retirement age; hence, capitalists opposed these programs on labor-supply grounds as well as differing local taxes. Relief for the aged, it was felt, compromised traditional family values of saving and intergenerational responsibility. Accordingly, these programs spread very slowly and were filled with conditions designed to weed out the morally unfit. As a category, the dependent aged were still part of the undeserving poor; they were still part of the labor market.

* * *

This brings us to the New Deal, the great watershed in the American welfare state. * * *

The New Deal consisted of four parts: (1) work relief; (2) unemployment insurance; (3) Social Security for the retired; and (4) the grant-in-aid programs for aid to dependent children, old-age assistance, and aid to the blind. Together, these parts show continuity with the past by the strengthening of the categories.

The first and most immediate crisis facing the new administration was massive unemployment. There was significant local disorder and serious concern about threats to social order at all levels of government.

The initial New Deal reforms were constructed during this state of crisis and widespread poverty. The Roosevelt administration quickly put together an extensive system of public employment. While these programs turned out to be temporary, their brief history tells us much about the future course of the American welfare state.

Within a year, more than 4,500,000 families and single people were receiving some sort of relief. Even though administration was through grants-in-aid to the states, the federal government insisted on separate administrative agencies (to distinguish these programs from welfare), the prohibition of racial, religious, and political discrimination, and uniform benefits. Between 1.4 and 2.4 million people per month worked at wages higher than both direct relief and market wages. Nevertheless, despite the apparent success of the work programs, they were instantly and bitterly attacked, and ultimately seriously crippled by the business community on the grounds that the federal programs did not follow traditional welfare requirements and compromised industrial discipline. Under extreme pressure, Congress rescinded the minimum wage, imposed a means test, and shortly, despite their national popularity, scaled back the programs drastically.

The reasons for the demise of work relief are telling. Despite the fact that the vast number of recipients were the submerged middle class and in no sense the stereotypical malingerer, the perceived need to preserve industrial discipline was overwhelming. Capitalists insisted that employed workers had to be reminded that if they lost their jobs, there was no reliable cushion for them to fall back on.

* * *

President Roosevelt himself was opposed to the work relief programs. He feared the creation of a large, permanent, entrenched bureaucracy and worried about the effects of relief on work incentives. * * *

This was the context in which the Social Security Act was debated. Despite the massive unemployment and the impressive accomplishments of the work programs, traditional attitudes towards relief and labor discipline prevailed. * * * [R]egulating employment was more a matter of industrial discipline and preventing dependency than meeting need. Moreover, the federal government was not to be trusted. Social control was best left to the states and local governments, which were more sensitive to local labor markets. It was this dominant ideology towards work and relief that explains the outcome of the first major task of the Social Security reformers: unemployment insurance.

* * *

The experience of the Civil War pension system [which became infected with political patronage and corruption], the specter of Europe [where unemployment insurance in Britain had yielded to an open-ended system of relief for the unemployed], and the work relief experience helped determine the fate of unemployment insurance. Roosevelt insisted that unemployment insurance be separate from relief, and be actuarily "sound"—that is, financed by contributions and taxes. There would be maximum state control. This was of central importance; in fact, the dispute over the administrative form of unemployment insurance was *the* dominant political issue in 1934. Why were state interests so important? It was in local labor markets that the interests of capitalists and labor were fought out. "Sensitivity" or "control over local labor markets" was the code for the social control of marginal workers; the capitalists insisted that the price and availability of local labor not be disturbed. * * *

In the end, state unemployment insurance laws reflected these positions; programs were state and local and they failed to reach those most in need, the "less deserving" workers such as employees of small firms, agricultural workers, women, African-Americans, and migrants. * * * [U]nemployment insurance was more in the nature of temporary emergency relief. Moreover, it was for the deserving workers—those who worked in steady, reliable, covered employment. Benefits were calibrated to length of employment and rates of pay. There were waiting periods. Workers were excluded if they quit voluntarily, were discharged for cause or a labor dispute, or failed to register at a public employment office and be available for suitable alternative work. All attempts to impose significant, substantive national standards on the states were defeated.

The centerpiece of the Social Security Act was the establishment of a contributory, national pension for the aged—old age insurance (OAI). * * * By 1935, * * * the political climate outside the South had changed. The elderly, along with the working population, were politically active and various radical redistribution plans were being proposed. Nevertheless, Roosevelt was strongly committed to an actuarily sound contributory insurance system and adamantly opposed to anything resembling the dole. He believed that the program would only attain solid legitimacy if it was "earned," if it was financed by contribution, if it had no means test, if it clearly defined the risks, and if it had a fixed retirement age. Benefits would reflect wages, thus strengthening incentives rather than redistribution. Only in this way would recipients avoid the stigma of welfare. The program was (and is) sold on its insurance features. This was a dignified program paying individually earned benefits as of right rather than relief for people who had to demonstrate need.

There was now a strong desire to get older workers out of the labor market. Families had changed, and young people did not want their parents moving back in. In contrast to unemployment insurance, there were strong arguments in favor of a uniform, national scheme. It was in the interests of big business to avoid different state taxes, and the fact that there was a general relationship between wages and benefits (and not much redistribution), meant that wage structures and regional variations would not be disturbed. The South was opposed, and insisted on the exclusion of agricultural and domestic workers, insuring that planter control over African-Americans would not be disturbed. * * *

[T]he vast majority of elderly African-Americans were almost completely excluded.

Why was OAI national while Unemployment Insurance (UI) was not? The arguments in favor of a national OAI applied as well to UI—namely, the mobility of labor and uniform taxes. The reason lies in the differential effects on labor markets. OAI wanted its beneficiaries *out* of the labor market; UI wanted to make sure that its beneficiaries stayed in. And in the United States, the regulation of work tests are invariably at the local level. Local businesses want to keep close control over economic issues (and avoid taxes), and the local community wants to keep control over moral behavior. * * *

* * *

Of course, the plight of poor single mothers worsened during the Depression. Divorce and desertion increased, as did joblessness and homelessness. * * * The old problems continued to dog this category of the poor—the stigma of poor single mothers, labor discipline, and race. "[N]o one in 1935 imagined throwing millions of dollars into broken homes." Some important federal requirements, however, were imposed—for example, programs had to be implemented statewide, eligibility standards were broadened, benefits had to be paid in cash, and there had to be fair hearings.

However, while access to ADC was increased formally, in practice the programs stayed the same. In contrast to Old Age Assistance (OAA), most states lagged in buying into grant-in-aid and did little to encourage enrollments. Congress did not encourage the states to either adopt grant-in-aid or enroll poor single mothers. [OAA and Aid to the Blind were treated more generously than ADC, a pattern of appropriations that continues to the present.] * * *

At the local level, social control of the poor single mother continued. Through the use of "suitable home" and "employable mother" policies, states were able to exclude the unworthy, maintain labor markets, and reduce costs. Even under the Social Security Act, ADC remained small and primarily for white widows.

* * *

The distinctions drawn by the Social Security Act continued in the post-World War II period. * * * Southern opposition lessened when agriculture became mechanized, African-Americans migrated, a poor aged population became an increasing welfare burden, southern congressional power declined, and civil rights took hold.

* * * In 1974, Supplementary Security Income (SSI) was enacted, thus federalizing Old Age Assistance, Aid to the Blind, and Aid to the Totally and Permanently Disabled (which had been established in 1954). SSI is completely federally funded and administered (by the Social Security Administration) with national eligibility standards and a basic uniform grant (there is optional state supplementation). SSI was not

controversial. The aged and the blind are not in the labor force; they are now full members of the deserving poor.

Social Security expanded only slowly; until the 1960s, it was a low-level income-maintenance program. The big changes came in 1968 and 1974 when benefits were raised substantially and indexed to the cost of living * * * . Today, Social Security is a major source of income for the vast majority of the aged in America. It has not only become a retirement wage; it has also become a "citizen's wage," an entitlement that has significant redistribution effects. It has significantly reduced poverty among the elderly, and it is comparable to the most advanced systems in Western Europe.

* * *

* * * [A]s distinguished from the aged, helping the unemployed affects the bargaining power of labor, lessens the pressure to take less desirable jobs, and lessens the pressure to limit strikes. Accordingly, the basic features of UI have remained in place. Various attempts to assert national standards have failed. There is great variation among the states, but in general, benefits remain low. It is estimated that a single worker could meet daily subsistence needs, but not an unemployed worker with a family—probably the most important segment of the work force.

UI is funded entirely through the payroll tax, and employers are experience-rated. These features, unique in the industrialized world, evidence the central relation of this program to the market. Meanwhile, the program remains seriously inadequate. * * * Coverage has declined sharply: since 1985, to less than a third of the unemployed. This means that in an average month, in 1988, 4.6 million jobless workers did not receive any unemployment insurance benefits. Coverage is even worse for African-Americans (21 percent) and Hispanics (14 percent). There are very few alternative income supports for the able-bodied unemployed who are no longer covered by UI. * * * [P]overty rates among the long-term unemployed are very high.

DEBORAH MARANVILLE

Changing Economy, Changing Lives: Unemployment Insurance and the Contingent Workforce

4 B.U. Pub. Int. L.J. 291, 292–99, 301–02, 337 (1995)

* * * [M]any gender-based assumptions underlying the unemployment insurance system are no longer valid. The world contemplated by the architects of the American social welfare system, including unemployment insurance, consisted mostly of white, male breadwinners and their full-time, homemaker wives. With that social framework in mind, the unemployment insurance system in the United States intended to provide the best protection to workers who were available for work on a full-time, year round basis. In addition, unemployment insurance targeted workers in relatively stable jobs structured around the traditional

employer-employee relationships. But because workers and jobs in the United States economy increasingly fail to reflect the assumptions underlying the program as originally designed, the protection afforded by the unemployment insurance system has become increasingly inadequate.

With the entry of a substantial number of women into the workforce, fewer workers fit the traditional male breadwinner script. Yet women continue to bear greater responsibility for family care, and thus are more likely to drop out of the labor force with greater frequency, and for longer time periods than men. Women also are more likely to take part-time employment and to place limits on their availability for work on weekends or for particular shifts. Moreover, labor market segregation continues to result in women holding lower-paying jobs with less security and fewer benefits than men. * * * [E]ach of these factors results in women receiving less favorable treatment under the unemployment insurance system.

* * * [T]he American economy in recent decades has undergone a major transformation away from the assumption of job stability contemplated by those who designed the nation's unemployment insurance system. This transformation has had four primary components: a shift from manufacturing jobs to service jobs, with an accompanying decline in the percentage of the workforce that is unionized; an increasing gap between high-paying jobs requiring significant educational prerequisites and low-paying unskilled jobs; a growing disparity in income, marked by a decrease in the real value of the minimum wage, and a rising differential between average wages and executive salaries; and a trend away from job security and long-term employment toward increased reliance on contract, temporary, and part-time workers. These changes have had a pervasive effect on unemployment insurance, including a steadily decreasing percentage of unemployed workers who receive benefits, an increasing fixation with job training programs, and a rise in eligibility issues affecting contingent workers.

* * * Rapid inflation in the 1970's, combined with high unemployment, strained the solvency of many state unemployment programs, forcing many states to borrow from the federal loan fund available in such emergencies.

The states' fiscal crises coincided with pressures at the federal level to restrict expenditures on unemployment insurance. The early Reagan years were marked by intense efforts to decrease spending on social welfare programs generally. In addition, a unified federal budget was developed for deficit calculation purposes under which unemployment compensation tax revenues were included for the first time, and payments from the unemployment trust fund appeared as an expenditure item.

In response to these pressures, Congress took several measures to create incentives for states to restrict their unemployment insurance programs and placed additional burdens on claimants collecting benefits.

* * * States responded to Congressional pressure and their own fiscal crises by cutting back their unemployment programs, primarily through tightening eligibility standards and imposing stricter penalties on claimants who were fired for misconduct or who voluntarily quit their jobs. These factors—the entry of more women into the labor force, structural changes in the economy, and more restrictive state unemployment insurance statutes—have had significant implications in terms of gender, race and economic class. Women, minorities and low-wage workers tend to fill precisely those jobs that lack the comparatively stable, predictable characteristics contemplated by the architects of the system.

* * *

Unemployment insurance typically imposes four requirements that can create eligibility problems for contingent workers. First, all states make eligibility for unemployment benefits contingent upon satisfying a "work test," whereby a claimant must have worked in statutorily approved employment for a specified number of hours or weeks, or must have earned a prescribed sum during a specified period before becoming unemployed. Thus, the system excludes women following the traditional homemaker script who are forced into the labor market by unexpected necessities until they can satisfy the work test. Similarly, many individuals who combine work and caretaking activities are likely, at times, to fail the "work test" requirement, either because they move in and out of the work force, or because of insufficient part-time earnings. In addition, the number of part-time, seasonal, and temporary workers who qualify for unemployment insurance will vary greatly depending on the specifics of the work test, particularly the requirements covering the number of weeks worked, earnings, and the period(s) of employment.

Second, in all states, workers who "voluntarily quit" their employment without good cause are disqualified from receiving unemployment benefits. To the extent that family reasons are not considered good cause, workers who leave their employment either due to family emergencies or because they are unable to comply with a change in their work schedule are disadvantaged by this requirement. Women, of course, still perform the bulk of family care and disproportionately comprise those quitting for family reasons.

Third, all states require that an individual be "able and available for work" in order to qualify for unemployment benefits. Typically, availability is defined according to standards fitting the male breadwinner script. In other words, an individual is likely to face legal obstacles in receiving benefits unless he or she is available for employment on a full-time, year-round basis, regardless of the assigned shift. A fourth requirement, closely related to the third, is that a worker receiving benefits who refuses an offer of "suitable" employment will be disqualified from receiving further benefits. In addition to monitoring the effect of these specific eligibility requirements, advocates for the poor must also consider the ways in which the legal system in general, and unemployment insurance statutes in particular, create unnecessary incentives for employers to rely on contingent workers.

Traditional gender-based assumptions regarding the American labor force have been severely undermined by the rise of women holding paid employment as well as employers' increased reliance on contingent workers. As a result, it seems increasingly necessary to modify those technical requirements that exclude low-income workers from receiving unemployment benefits as well as reexamine the rationale underlying them.

* * *

* * * In 1976, Congress amended FUTA [the Federal Unemployment Tax Act] in order to extend coverage to domestic workers earning more than $1,000 per quarter and to farmworkers employed on large farms. Again the states followed Congress' lead by quickly extending coverage * * * . However, even in states where farmwork qualifies for coverage, farmworkers do not necessarily receive the benefits which they are entitled to * * * .

* * * [I]ndividual employers of domestic workers often fail to pay payroll taxes on behalf of their employees. Thus, many domestic workers—a group composed disproportionately of women, particularly women of color—remain outside the protections of wage-based social welfare programs, including unemployment insurance. * * *

* * *

To ensure that attachment to the labor force requirements do not exclude "contingent workers," advocates will need to rely on legislation at both the state and federal levels, administrative rulemaking efforts, and major law reform litigation. The definition of "good cause" in voluntary quit cases, as well as the definition of "availability" can be expanded through individual casework in states having only broad statutory provisions. However, efforts at the legislative and agency level will be needed in states with restrictive statutes, and may both affect more claimants and be necessary in order to preserve gains achieved through individual case work. * * *

Notes and Questions

1. What are the strengths and weaknesses of the ways social programs in the United States have separated assistance for old age, disability, unemployment, and families raising children? Can issues of work be effectively separated from issues of bearing children and caring for them? For which workers is this separation possible—those without children, or those without someone else to care for their children? *Cf.* Marion Crain, *Gender and Union Organizing*, 47 Indus. & Lab. Rel. Rev. 227 (1994) (study showing that, although traditional union organizing generally overlooked child care, innovative organizers focusing on women's issues found child care closely related to issues of wages; gender-

conscious approaches were highly successful in organizing unions among women workers in service sector).

2. After most African Americans were excluded from coverage under the Social Security Act and many excluded from unemployment insurance, how could those workers protect themselves when they were unemployed or aged? Would the lack of social insurance programs that were available to whites affect wealth and wellbeing in black communities?

3. Courts originally perceived unemployment benefits as an individual right earned by each worker. Over the following decades, interpretation of the statute gradually shifted. Unemployment insurance became understood as a protection for society—a way to maintain a floor under purchasing power to keep consumers buying and avoid recession—rather than as protection for workers. Kenneth M. Casebeer, *Unemployment Insurance: American Social Wage, Labor Organization and Legal Ideology*, 35 B.C. L. Rev. 259 (1994).

During the 1930s, Congress had considered a far more radical alternative than the Social Security Act. The Workers Bill for a Social Wage would have included maternity leave, provided coverage for agricultural and domestic workers, and involved workers in decision-making bodies. *Id.*

Should social insurance funds routinely provide benefits for maternity leave as temporary disability? Are the legal distinctions between welfare and social insurance rational?

B. The Question of Property Rights in Benefits

The Fifth and Fourteenth Amendments protect against deprivation of life, liberty, or property without due process of law. After a regime of social insurance was created in the United States, courts faced the question of whether individuals had property interests in receiving these benefits that would make termination require due process. If the recipient did have a property interest, the next problem was to determine what process would be constitutionally adequate: Would a trial be necessary, or would an administrative hearing suffice? Must the hearing take place before deprivation of benefits, or would it be sufficient to allow a review after termination and restore any benefits missed if the appellant succeeded?

In Lynch v. United States, 292 U.S. 571 (1934), the Court found it easy to protect a property right in benefits against repeal by Congress when disabled soldiers, who had fought in World War I, held contracts for war risk insurance. But would *Lynch* mean that, when the system of social insurance expanded, workers held property interests in benefits? Under the Social Security Act passed in the New Deal, individuals and employers both contributed taxes toward old age insurance. The employee's contribution might have supported finding a property right in benefits to be paid on retirement.

The Supreme Court faced this question in Flemming v. Nestor, 363 U.S. 603 (1960). Ephram Nestor immigrated from Bulgaria in 1913 and lived in the United States for 43 years. From 1936 to 1939, Nestor was a member of the Communist Party. At the time, his membership was not illegal, and it was not a statutory ground for deportation. A year after Nestor quit the Communist Party, *past* party membership was made a ground for deportation. In 1954, Congress amended the Social Security Act to provide for the termination of old-age, survivor, and disability insurance benefits payable to an alien who was deported after the date the bill was enacted for grounds including past membership in the Communist Party. Nestor began to receive Social Security benefits in 1955. He was deported in July 1956, and his Social Security benefits were terminated pursuant to the statute.

Justice Harlan wrote the majority opinion, holding that Nestor did not have an "accrued property right" in his Social Security benefits.

> The Social Security system may be accurately described as a form of social insurance, enacted pursuant to Congress' power to "spend money in aid of the 'general welfare,' " whereby persons gainfully employed, and those who employ them, are taxed to permit the payment of benefits to the retired and disabled, and their dependents. Plainly the expectation is that many members of the present productive work force will in turn become beneficiaries rather than supporters of the program. But each worker's benefits, though flowing from the contributions he made to the national economy while actively employed, are not dependent on the degree to which he was called upon to support the system by taxation. It is apparent that the noncontractual interest of an employee covered by the Act cannot be soundly analogized to that of the holder of an annuity, whose right to benefits is bottomed on his contractual premium payments.
>
> It is hardly profitable to engage in conceptualizations regarding "earned rights" and "gratuities." The "right" to Social Security benefits is in one sense "earned," for the entire scheme rests on the legislative judgment that those who in their productive years were functioning members of the economy may justly call upon that economy, in their later years, for protection from "the rigors of the poor house as well as from the haunting fear that such a lot awaits them when journey's end is near." But the practical effectuation of that judgment has of necessity called forth a highly complex and interrelated statutory structure. Integrated treatment of the manifold specific problems presented by the Social Security program demands more than a generalization. That program was designed to function into the indefinite future, and its specific provisions rest on predictions as to expected economic conditions which must inevitably prove less than wholly accurate, and on judgments and preferences as to the proper allocation of the Nation's resources which evolving economic and social conditions will of necessity in some degree modify.

> To engraft upon the Social Security system a concept of "accrued property rights" would deprive it of the flexibility and boldness in adjustment to ever-changing conditions which it demands. It was doubtless out of an awareness of the need for such flexibility that Congress included in the original Act, and has since retained, a clause expressly reserving to it "[t]he right to alter, amend, or repeal any provision" of the Act. * * *
>
> We must conclude that a person covered by the Act has not such a right in benefit payments as would make every defeasance of "accrued" interests violative of the Due Process Clause of the Fifth Amendment.

363 U.S. at 609–11.

The Court further held that the statute did not lack rational justification, because Congress could have decided that payments to residents abroad did not have the same productive effects on the economy as payments to those who lived in the United States. Congress could also have concluded that "the public purse should not be utilized to contribute to the support of those deported on the grounds specified in the statute." 363 U.S. at 612. Although Nestor had argued that the deprivation unconstitutionally imposed punishment through an *ex post facto* law, the Court disagreed, stating that, unlike imprisonment, "the mere denial of a noncontractual government benefit" did not impose any affirmative disability or restraint. 363 U.S. at 617.

Justice Black dissented, citing the protection given to war insurance benefits in *Lynch*:

> The Court today puts the *Lynch* case aside on the ground that "It is hardly profitable to engage in conceptualizations regarding 'earned rights' and 'gratuities.' " * * * [They] tell the contributors to this insurance fund that despite their own and their employers' payments the Government, in paying the beneficiaries out of the fund, is merely giving them something for nothing and can stop doing so when it pleases. This, in my judgment, reveals a complete misunderstanding of the purpose Congress and the country had in passing that law. It was then generally agreed, as it is today, that it is not desirable that aged people think of the Government as giving them something for nothing. An excellent statement of this view * * * was made by Senator George, the Chairman of the Finance Committee when the Social Security Act was passed, and one very familiar with the philosophy that brought it about:
>
> > "It comports better than any substitute we have discovered with the American concept that free men want to earn their security and not ask for doles—that what is due as a matter of earned right is far better than a gratuity. . . ."
> >
> > * * *
> >
> > "Social Security is not a handout; it is not charity; it is not relief. It is an earned right based upon the contributions and

> earnings of the individual. As an earned right, the individual is eligible to receive his benefit in dignity and self-respect."

363 U.S. at 622–23.

Justice Black reasoned that Congress could repeal the Social Security Act, stop covering new people, or stop increasing obligations to old contributors, but it could not disappoint "the just expectations of the contributors to the fund which the Government has compelled them and their employers to pay its Treasury." 363 U.S. at 624–25. He also argued that the statute imposed punishment in a classic sense.

> The basic reason for Nestor's loss of his insurance payments is that he was once a Communist. This man, now 69 years old, has been driven out of the country where he has lived for 43 years to a land where he is practically a stranger, under an Act authorizing his deportation many years after his Communist membership. Now a similar *ex post facto* law deprives him of his insurance, which, while petty and insignificant in amount to this great Government, may well be this exile's daily bread, for the same reason and in accord with the general fashion of the day—that is, to punish in every way possible anyone who ever made the mistake of being a Communist in this country or who is supposed ever to have been associated with anyone who made that mistake. * * *

363 U.S. at 626–27.

Justice Brennan also dissented, joined by Chief Justice Warren and Justice Douglas, stating that "common sense" showed that Nestor had been "punished severely for his past conduct." 363 U.S. at 635. "The Framers ordained that even the worst of men should not be punished for their past acts or for any conduct without adherence to the procedural safeguards written into the Constitution." 363 U.S. at 640.

In response to *Flemming v. Nestor*, Charles Reich argued in two influential articles that "property rights" are recognized everywhere in modern society through interactions with government, and that the poor required similar recognition of property rights in income received through government programs. Charles Reich, *Individual Rights and Social Welfare: The Emerging Legal Issues*, 74 Yale L. J. 1245 (1965); Charles Reich, *The New Property*, 73 Yale L. J. 733 (1964). Reich's work was part of a legal movement to seek new recognition in the United States Supreme Court of statutory and constitutional rights for low-income people.

In King v. Smith, 392 U.S. 309 (1968), the Court construed the AFDC statute to strike down an Alabama welfare rule that disqualified families from benefits if a man lived in the home or visited frequently "for purpose of cohabiting." Under this rule, issued in 1964 by Governor George Wallace, Alabama had dropped 16,000 children—90% of them black—from the rolls. Chief Justice Warren reasoned that Congress surely would not have allowed the states arbitrarily to leave one class of destitute children entirely without meaningful protection. Forbath, *Constitutional Welfare Rights*, at 1859–61.

Shortly after *King v. Smith*, the Supreme Court struck down welfare restrictions under the Constitution. Several states and the District of Columbia barred migrants to the state from receiving benefits through the AFDC program until they had lived in the jurisdiction for one year. In Shapiro v. Thompson, 394 U.S. 618 (1969), the Court held that the "nature of our Federal Union and our constitutional concepts of personal liberty unite to require that all citizens be free to travel throughout the length and breadth of our land uninhibited by statutes, rules, or regulations which unreasonably burden or restrict this movement."

> We do not doubt that the one-year waiting-period device is well suited to discourage the influx of poor families in need of assistance. An indigent who desires to migrate, resettle, find a new job, and start a new life will doubtless hesitate if he knows that he must risk making the move without the possibility of falling back on state welfare assistance during his first year of residence, when his need may be most acute. But the purpose of inhibiting migration by needy persons into the State is constitutionally impermissible.

394 U.S. at 629.

In *Shapiro*, the Court distinguished *Flemming v. Nestor* and other cases that required a "mere showing of a rational relationship" between the regulation and permissible state goals. Instead, the Court held, "in moving from State to State or to the District of Columbia appellees were exercising a constitutional right, and any classification which serves to penalize the exercise of that right, unless shown to be necessary to promote a *compelling* governmental interest, is unconstitutional." 394 U.S. at 634. (Thirty years later, faced with a similar regulation, the Court would again affirm that welfare recipients were protected by a right to travel and would locate that protection in the privileges and immunities clause of the Fourteenth Amendment. Saenz v. Roe, 526 U.S. 489 (1999).) In this hopeful context, poverty lawyers framed the question of procedural protection of welfare rights. *See* Martha Davis, *Brutal Need: Lawyers and the Welfare Rights Movement: 1960–1973*, 103–04 (1993).

GOLDBERG v. KELLY

397 U.S. 254 (1970)

Mr. Justice BRENNAN delivered the opinion of the Court.

The question for decision is whether a State that terminates public assistance payments to a particular recipient without affording him the opportunity for an evidentiary hearing prior to termination denies the recipient procedural due process in violation of the Due Process Clause of the Fourteenth Amendment.

This action was brought in the District Court for the Southern District of New York by residents of New York City receiving financial aid under the federally assisted program of Aid to Families with Dependent Children (AFDC) or under New York State's general Home Relief program.[1] Their complaint alleged that the New York State and New York City officials administering these programs terminated, or were about to terminate, such aid without prior notice and hearing, thereby denying them due process of law. At the time the suits were filed there was no requirement of prior notice or hearing of any kind before termination of financial aid. However, the State and city adopted procedures for notice and [a post-termination] hearing after the suits were brought, and the plaintiffs, appellees here, then challenged the constitutional adequacy of those procedures.

* * *

The constitutional issue to be decided, therefore, is the narrow one whether the Due Process Clause requires that the recipient be afforded an evidentiary hearing *before* the termination of benefits. The District Court held that only a pre-termination evidentiary hearing would satisfy the constitutional command * * * . The court said: "While post-termination review is relevant, there is one overpowering fact which controls here. By hypothesis, a welfare recipient is destitute, without funds or assets.... Suffice it to say that to cut off a welfare recipient in the face of ... 'brutal need' without a prior hearing of some sort is unconscionable, unless overwhelming considerations justify it." * * *

Appellant does not contend that procedural due process is not applicable to the termination of welfare benefits. Such benefits are a matter of statutory entitlement for persons qualified to receive them.[8] Their termination involves state action that adjudicates important rights. The constitutional challenge cannot be answered by an argument that public assistance benefits are "a 'privilege' and not a 'right.'" *Shapiro v. Thompson*, 394 U.S. 618, 627 n. 6 (1969). Relevant constitutional restraints apply as much to the withdrawal of public assistance benefits as to disqualification for unemployment compensation; or to denial of a tax exemption; or to discharge from public employment. The

1. * * * Home Relief is a general assistance program financed and administered solely by New York state and local governments. It assists any person unable to support himself or to secure support from other sources.

8. It may be realistic today to regard welfare entitlements as more like "property" than a "gratuity." Much of the existing wealth in this country takes the form of rights that do not fall within traditional common-law concepts of property. It has been aptly noted that "[s]ociety today is built around entitlement. The automobile dealer has his franchise, the doctor and lawyer their professional licenses, the worker his union membership, contract, and pension rights, the executive his contract and stock options; all are devices to aid security and independence. Many of the most important of these entitlements now flow from government: subsidies to farmers and businessmen, routes for airlines and channels for television stations; long term contracts for defense, space, and education; social security pensions for individuals. Such sources of security, whether private or public, are no longer regarded as luxuries or gratuities; to the recipients they are essentials, fully deserved, and in no sense a form of charity. It is only the poor whose entitlements, although recognized by public policy, have not been effectively enforced." Reich, Individual Rights and Social Welfare: The Emerging Legal Issues, 74 Yale L. J. 1245, 1255 (1965). See also Reich, The New Property, 73 Yale L. J. 733 (1964).

extent to which procedural due process must be afforded the recipient is influenced by the extent to which he may be "condemned to suffer grievous loss," and depends upon whether the recipient's interest in avoiding that loss outweighs the governmental interest in summary adjudication. Accordingly, * * * "consideration of what procedures due process may require under any given set of circumstances must begin with a determination of the precise nature of the government function involved as well as of the private interest that has been affected by governmental action."

It is true, of course, that some governmental benefits may be administratively terminated without affording the recipient a pre-termination evidentiary hearing. But we agree with the District Court that when welfare is discontinued, only a pre-termination evidentiary hearing provides the recipient with procedural due process. For qualified recipients, welfare provides the means to obtain essential food, clothing, housing, and medical care. Thus the crucial factor in this context—a factor not present in the case of the blacklisted government contractor, the discharged government employee, the taxpayer denied a tax exemption, or virtually anyone else whose governmental entitlements are ended—is that termination of aid pending resolution of a controversy over eligibility may deprive an *eligible* recipient of the very means by which to live while he waits. Since he lacks independent resources, his situation becomes immediately desperate. His need to concentrate upon finding the means for daily subsistence, in turn, adversely affects his ability to seek redress from the welfare bureaucracy.

Moreover, important governmental interests are promoted by affording recipients a pre-termination evidentiary hearing. From its founding the Nation's basic commitment has been to foster the dignity and well-being of all persons within its borders. We have come to recognize that forces not within the control of the poor contribute to their poverty. This perception, against the background of our traditions, has significantly influenced the development of the contemporary public assistance system. Welfare, by meeting the basic demands of subsistence, can help bring within the reach of the poor the same opportunities that are available to others to participate meaningfully in the life of the community. At the same time, welfare guards against the societal malaise that may flow from a widespread sense of unjustified frustration and insecurity. Public assistance, then, is not mere charity, but a means to "promote the general Welfare, and secure the Blessings of Liberty to ourselves and our Posterity." The same governmental interests that counsel the provision of welfare, counsel as well its uninterrupted provision to those eligible to receive it; pre-termination evidentiary hearings are indispensable to that end.

Appellant does not challenge the force of these considerations but argues that they are outweighed by countervailing governmental interests in conserving fiscal and administrative resources. These interests, the argument goes, justify the delay of any evidentiary hearing until after discontinuance of the grants. Summary adjudication protects the public fisc by stopping payments promptly upon discovery of reason to believe that a recipient is no longer eligible. Since most terminations are accepted without challenge, summary adjudication also conserves both the fisc and administrative time and energy by reducing the number of evidentiary hearings actually held.

We agree with the District Court, however, that these governmental interests are not overriding in the welfare context. The requirement of a prior hearing doubtless involves some greater expense, and the benefits paid to ineligible recipients pending decision at the hearing probably cannot be recouped, since these recipients are likely to be judgment-proof. But the State is not without weapons to minimize these increased costs. Much of the drain on fiscal and administrative resources can be reduced by developing procedures for prompt pre-termination hearings and by skillful use of personnel and facilities. * * * Thus, the interest of the eligible recipient in uninterrupted receipt of public assistance, coupled with the State's interest that his payments not be erroneously terminated, clearly outweighs the State's competing concern to prevent any increase in its fiscal and administrative burdens. * * *

II

We also agree with the District Court, however, that the pre-termination hearing need not take the form of a judicial or quasi-judicial trial. We bear in mind that the statutory "fair hearing" will provide the recipient with a full administrative review. Accordingly, the pre-termination hearing has one function only: to produce an initial determination of the validity of the welfare department's grounds for discontinuance of payments in order to protect a recipient against an erroneous termination of his benefits. Thus, a complete record and a comprehensive opinion, which would serve primarily to facilitate judicial review and to guide future decisions, need not be provided at the pre-termination stage. We recognize, too, that both welfare authorities and recipients have an interest in relatively speedy resolution of questions of eligibility, that they are used to dealing with one another informally, and that some welfare departments have very burdensome caseloads. These considerations justify the limitation of the pre-termination hearing to minimum procedural safeguards, adapted to the particular characteristics of welfare recipients, and to the limited nature of the controversies to be resolved. We wish to add that we, no less than the dissenters, recognize the importance of not imposing upon the States or the Federal Government in this developing field of law any procedural requirements beyond those demanded by rudimentary due process.

"The fundamental requisite of due process of law is the opportunity to be heard." The hearing must be "at a meaningful time and in a meaningful manner." In the present context these principles require that a recipient have timely and adequate notice detailing the reasons for a proposed termination, and an effective opportunity to defend by confronting any adverse witnesses and by presenting his own arguments and evidence orally. These rights are important in cases such as those before us, where recipients have challenged proposed terminations as resting on incorrect or misleading factual premises or on misapplication of rules or policies to the facts of particular cases.

* * *

The city's procedures presently do not permit recipients to appear personally with or without counsel before the official who finally determines continued eligibility. Thus a recipient is not permitted to present evidence to that official orally, or to confront or cross-examine adverse witnesses. These omissions are fatal to the constitutional adequacy of the procedures.

The opportunity to be heard must be tailored to the capacities and circumstances of those who are to be heard. It is not enough that a welfare recipient may present his position to the decision maker in writing or second-hand through his caseworker. Written submissions are an unrealistic option for most recipients, who lack the educational attainment necessary to write effectively and who cannot obtain professional assistance. Moreover, written submissions do not afford the flexibility of oral presentations; they do not permit the recipient to mold his argument to the issues the decision maker appears to regard as important. Particularly where credibility and veracity are at issue, as they must be in many termination proceedings, written submissions are a wholly unsatisfactory basis for decision. The second-hand presentation to the decisionmaker by the caseworker has its own deficiencies; since the caseworker usually gathers the facts upon which the charge of ineligibility rests, the presentation of the recipient's side of the controversy cannot safely be left to him. Therefore a recipient must be allowed to state his position orally. Informal procedures will suffice; in this context due process does not require a particular order of proof or mode of offering evidence.

In almost every setting where important decisions turn on questions of fact, due process requires an opportunity to confront and cross-examine adverse witnesses. * * * Welfare recipients must * * * be given an opportunity to confront and cross-examine the witnesses relied on by the department.

"The right to be heard would be, in many cases, of little avail if it did not comprehend the right to be heard by counsel." We do not say that counsel must be provided at the pre-termination hearing, but only that the recipient must be allowed to retain an attorney if he so desires. Counsel can help delineate the issues, present the factual contentions in an orderly manner, conduct cross-examination, and generally safeguard the interests of the recipient. We do not anticipate that this assistance will unduly prolong or otherwise encumber the hearing. * * *

Finally, the decisionmaker's conclusion as to a recipient's eligibility must rest solely on the legal rules and evidence adduced at the hearing. To demonstrate compliance with this elementary requirement, the decision maker should state the reasons for his determination and indicate the evidence he relied on, though his statement need not amount to a full opinion or even formal findings of fact and conclusions of law. And, of course, an impartial decision maker is essential. We agree with the District Court that prior involvement in some aspects of a case will not necessarily bar a welfare official from acting as a decision maker. He should not, however, have participated in making the determination under review.

Affirmed.

Mr. Justice BLACK, dissenting.

* * *

* * * [I do] not think that the Fourteenth Amendment should be given such an unnecessarily broad construction. That Amendment came into being primarily to protect Negroes from discrimination, and while some of its language can and does protect others, all know that the chief purpose behind it was to protect ex-slaves. The Court, however, relies upon the Fourteenth Amendment and in effect says that failure of the government to pay a promised charitable instalment to an individual deprives that individual of *his own property*, in violation of the Due Process Clause of the Fourteenth Amendment. It somewhat strains credulity to say that the government's promise of charity to an individual is property belonging to that individual when the government denies that the individual is honestly entitled to receive such a payment.

* * * Once the verbiage is pared away it is obvious that this Court today adopts the views of the District Court "that to cut off a welfare recipient in the face of . . . 'brutal need' without a prior hearing of some sort is unconscionable," and therefore, says the Court, unconstitutional. The majority reaches this result by a process of weighing "the recipient's interest in avoiding" the termination of welfare benefits against "the governmental interest in summary adjudication." Today's balancing act requires a "pre-termination evidentiary hearing," yet there is nothing that indicates what tomorrow's balance will be. Although the majority attempts to bolster its decision with limited quotations from prior cases, it is obvious that today's result doesn't depend on the language of the Constitution itself or the principles of other decisions, but solely on the collective judgment of the majority as to what would be a fair and humane procedure in this case.

* * *

The procedure required today as a matter of constitutional law finds no precedent in our legal system. * * * I know of no situation in our legal system in which the person alleged to owe money to another is required by law to continue making payments to a judgment-proof claimant without the benefit of any security or bond to insure that these payments can be recovered if he wins his legal argument. * * * These recipients are by definition too poor to post a bond or to repay the benefits that, as the majority assumes, must be spent as received to insure survival.

* * *

* * * I dissent from the Court's holding. The operation of a welfare state is a new experiment for our Nation. For this reason, among others, I feel that new experiments in carrying out a welfare program should not be frozen into our constitutional structure. They should be left, as are other legislative determinations, to the Congress and the legislatures that the people elect to make our laws.

Notes and Questions

1. In an omitted footnote the Court commented: "[The welfare recipient's] impaired adversary position is particularly telling in light of the welfare bureaucracy's difficulties in reaching correct decisions on eligibility." When balancing rights, should it matter how often bureaucracies make errors? Although the decision is about rights of recipients, what incentives (if any) does it place on the system to avoid error?

2. The Supreme Court clarified its approach to procedural due process and the requirement of a hearing before the deprivation of a benefit in Mathews v. Eldridge, 424 U.S. 319 (1976). Eldridge's Social Security benefits were terminated after the agency reviewed some documents, including reports from his physician and a consultant, and concluded that his disability had ceased. He responded by letter, as permitted by the review procedure, challenging a factual finding that was part of the termination decision; his benefits were terminated anyway. Eldridge sued, claiming that he was entitled to a hearing of the sort provided to welfare recipients pursuant to *Goldberg*.

The Court found no right to a predeprivation hearing. A three-part test determined whether a predeprivation hearing was constitutionally required:

> [I]dentification of the specific dictates of due process generally requires consideration of three distinct factors: First, the private interest that will be affected by the official action; second, the risk of an erroneous deprivation of such interest through the procedures used, and the probable value, if any, of additional or substitute procedural safeguards; and finally, the Government's interest, including the function involved and the fiscal and administrative burdens that the additional or substitute procedural requirement would entail.

424 U.S. at 335.

Applying the factors, the majority distinguished the indigency of welfare recipients from the situation of disabled workers, who might have other sources of income. Disability determinations, in which much of the material relied on by decision-makers would be in a paper record, were distinguished from the evidentiary issues facing recipients in *Goldberg*. In weighing the public interest, rather than focusing on the government's interest in a fair outcome as in *Goldberg,* the court focused on administrative costs of additional proceedings, although it held that financial cost alone was not controlling. The dissent criticized as speculative the reasoning that disability recipients might be able to find additional sources of government assistance, pointing out that after termination of benefits Eldridge and his family had experienced foreclosure on their home and repossession of their furniture, forcing the entire family to sleep in one bed.

3. In *Goldberg v. Kelly,* is the dissent correct that the court's interpretation of the due process clause was based "solely on the collective judgment of the majority as to what would be a fair and humane procedure" in the case before the court? If not, what is interpretation of the due process clause based upon?

4. In *Goldberg*, Justice Brennan noted that "We have come to recognize that forces not within the control of the poor contribute to their poverty." In contrast, the welfare reform act of 1996, the "Personal Responsibility and Work Opportunities Reconciliation Act of 1996" (PRWORA), reflected different attitudes about poverty and welfare recipients. The PROWRA operates through block grants to the states. The Act declares that benefits paid through the Temporary Assistance to Needy Families (TANF) program are not "entitlements." However, "[m]ost scholars who have considered the issue, as well as the only two courts to address it, have concluded that TANF benefits are still entitlements." Michele Estrin Gilman, *Legal Accountability in an Era of Privatized Welfare*, 89 Cal. L. Rev. 569, 606 (2001). They reason that "the existence of an entitlement depends on the substantive standards set forth in the statute, not on the legislature's characterization of those standards." *Id.* TANF requires states to "set forth objective criteria for the delivery of benefits and the determination of eligibility and for fair and equitable treatment," a requirement which becomes the basis for an entitlement to benefits for those who meet the criteria. It is also not clear that Congress intended to extinguish due process protection. *Id.* at 607. With the increasing privatization of welfare administration, however, there remain legal questions about whether decisions made by private agencies administering welfare programs are state action subject to due process review. *Id.* at 609–11.

Before the PRWORA gave rise to renewed debates about entitlements, Charles Reich advocated an ecological approach to constitutional protection.

CHARLES A. REICH

Beyond The New Property: *An Ecological View of Due Process*
56 Brook. L. Rev. 731, 731–45 (1990)

We live in a society where the economic security of the individual is constantly threatened by outside forces. Illness, accident, inflation or recession may wipe out an individual's resources. Remote actions by government or corporate management, wholly beyond the individual's control, can leave a person destitute. Often the victims are children, often the aged, but any individual can be destroyed in this way. The question is: how much responsibility should the community take for the protection of the individual?

The community must choose among three responses. It can deny social responsibility entirely. It can make economic protection of the individual a goal, but balance this goal against other goals which may be given an equal or higher priority. Or the community can make individual security an absolute right. *Goldberg v. Kelly* took the middle ground. It was a modest, moderate decision giving procedural protection to welfare recipients. *Goldberg v. Kelly* was only a beginning, but it deserves recognition as a landmark in the evolution of social justice.

Twenty years later, we must confront the fact that the road opened by *Goldberg v. Kelly* has not been taken. Instead there has been retreat. The goal of individual economic protection has been weakened, subordinated to other goals, and viewed negatively by powerful elements in society. In *Mathews v. Eldridge*, the Supreme Court limited the *Goldberg v. Kelly* principle by holding that an evidentiary hearing was not required prior to the termination of disability benefits. The Court reached this result by a balancing test in which what the Court described as "the private interest" was weighed against "the Government's interest, including the function involved and the fiscal and administrative burdens that the additional or substitute procedural requirement would entail." The Court said that disability benefits are "not based upon financial need" because such benefits are "wholly unrelated to the worker's income or support from many other sources, such as earnings of other family members, workmen's compensation awards, tort claims awards, savings" and the like.

What the Court failed to say is that its entire list of "many other sources" of support is purely speculative; the disability benefits in question might, in fact, be the worker's sole source of support. This is not a serious approach to the question of individual need. Then the Court added this: "Significantly, the cost of protecting those whom the preliminary administrative process has identified as likely to be found undeserving may in the end come out of the pockets of the deserving since resources available for any particular program of social welfare are not unlimited." Again pure speculation is used in place of facts. The Court assumed that the government's resources are so limited that hearings can be held only at a cost to the "deserving."

Mathews v. Eldridge represents an outlook that treats the government's claims as having greater urgency than the claims of individuals—even when there is nothing to justify the government claims. This represents judicial acceptance of the idea that the economic support of individuals may disappear if the government says it has no money. The middle of the road approach cannot survive such judicial indifference.

Today we have the most severe economic insecurity I have seen in my lifetime. Even during the Great Depression, which I remember as a child, there was never the visible and hidden suffering in our cities as now. And what will happen next year, and the year after that? Will there be twice the number of homeless, or ten times the number? Will all of our public spaces be filled by human beings struggling to survive in cardboard boxes? Will even more children be denied an adequate start in life? Will even more old people be abandoned and alone?

Judged by the experience of twenty years, the moderate, due process, cost-benefit approach to individual security must surely be deemed a failure. We have given it a fair trial, and it does not work. We must therefore choose between one of the two other courses. We can allow economic forces unrestrained sway, and take no communal responsibility for individual security. Or we can give economic security the status of a constitutional right which must be honored ahead of the other goals of society. If individual protection is our goal, nothing less than a full constitutional guarantee will do.

The fifth and fourteenth amendments provide that no person shall be deprived of life, liberty or property without due process of law. I believe that in a centrally managed economy, such as we have today, the due process clause gives every person in America a constitutional right to minimum subsistence and housing, to child care, education, employment, health insurance, retirement, and to a clean and healthy natural environment.

This interpretation of the due process clause is contrary to the longstanding view that the clause imposes no affirmative duties on government, a view that the Supreme Court reiterated recently in *DeShaney v. Winnebago County Department of Social Services*. [*See* excerpt in chapter 9.] No doubt the framers would be surprised at my interpretation. But the framers would be even more surprised at the kind of economy we now have in America. They would be shocked at the extreme concentration of economic power, amazed at the way national economic policy is set by government, and stunned by the individual's loss of the capacity to earn a living independent of large organizations. The framers would be dismayed at the impossibility of saving money due to inflation, the astronomical costs of health care, the tight control of housing and the disappearance of open land. They would be aghast at the cumulative loss of the individual's economic independence.

The framers were deeply concerned about any abuse of power by government. They tried to provide protection against the abuses they knew. The great increase of governmental power has brought with it an equal rise in the forms of abuse of power that are possible. The interpretation of due process that I propose is not a claim for "new" rights so much as it is an effort to protect against new wrongs.

The approach I take has much in common with the developing legal protection of the natural environment. The crisis of the natural environment and the crisis of the unprotected individual are similar. Both crises derive from the destructive aspects of our modern economic system. The lakes, trees, and wildlife dying from acid rain and the human beings dying on our city streets are alike in that they are victims of an economic system out of control in that it denies and displaces its costs. Protecting the natural environment and the social environment must go together. But protection of the social environment has lagged behind protection of the natural environment because of outmoded thinking. We do not blame trees or spotted owls for their own demise, but we continue to blame the human victims of the same forces. We realize that the death of nature threatens our own survival, but we continue to believe that the destruction of the more vulnerable members of a human community is not threatening to the community as a whole. It is time we took an ecological approach to the plight of human beings.

An ecological approach to individual economic rights would begin with the question of what kinds of habitat, nurture, and protection from harm are needed to produce a healthy individual. This is the starting point for plants or animals—why not for human beings?

Such an approach has long been taken in constitutional law with respect to governmental powers. From the time of John Marshall, the powers granted to government by the framers have been interpreted so as to ensure that government will possess the means to survive. The approach has been functional, allowing a vast expansion of governmental power in accordance with need. Government, said Marshall, must be able to deal with the unforeseeable crises of the future, not merely with the known needs of 1789. Accordingly, when the Great Depression required national economic regulation, the Court undertook what some have called a constitutional revolution in order to allow governmental powers unimaginable to the framers, but necessary to the survival of the nation. After the Second World War, the Court promulgated yet another constitutional revolution to permit an international security system. Where once the war power was reserved to Congress, the President has been allowed to conduct major and minor wars on his own. Whenever this vast extension of governmental power was challenged, the Court spoke of national security and the ultimate value of self-preservation.

Does it not seem strange that the same Constitution that is capable of unlimited expansion in the name of national self-preservation does not also grant the individual the means to survive? With all the talk about national security is there no equal validity to an adequate concept of individual security? What is the purpose of the security of the state if it does not apply to the security of the individuals for whom the state exists? Can such a Constitution allow the individual to be left isolated, defenseless, cut off from the absolute necessities of life?

Let us invoke the spirit of John Marshall when we read the due process clause. It refers to life, liberty and property; to me it makes sense to run these three words together—"life-liberty-property" because they are overlapping and inseparable. Read together they seem as functional as any other provision of the Constitution. They are more sweeping and general than the word "commerce"; they are more organic than taxing and spending. To me, life-liberty-property represents security and survival. These ancient words can also be seen as modern and functional. They imply the grant of the power to survive.

* * * [*The New Property,* 73 Yale L.J. 733 (1964)] started me on the road to a functional, need-based concept of individual power. I argued that the function of property was to confer power on the individual—power to control one's own life and to provide for one's own survival. Property is to the individual as the enumerated powers are to government. But I also pointed out that traditional property was no longer serving its function. It was being replaced by non-traditional interests, such as government benefits, which represent the individual's share in a society where value derives from relationships with organizations more than it derives from separate ownership of land or other assets. Accordingly, these non-traditional, relational interests should be treated as "new property."

Part of my idea has won acceptance—the idea that government benefits are valuable interests which deserve at least procedural protection. But many commentators have rejected the larger idea that such benefits are the property of the beneficiary—that the beneficiary, not the government, *owns* the benefits. For some of these commentators, the question of who owns the benefits is beside the point. For other scholars the idea of property is even detrimental to what they consider the important issue—the procedural accommodation of individual and governmental interests. On the other hand, I continue to insist that it makes a vital difference whether or not the individual owns and has sovereignty over the economic means of survival.

If we allow these benefits to be the property of government, the result is to give power to government that ought to belong to the individual. There is a world of difference between allowing government to hold in its hands the individual's survival, and vesting this power in the individual. The former is tyranny, even if administered by the most reasonable bureaucrats. The latter is what this country is supposed to be all about.

Those who would permit government to be the "owner" of benefits needed by individuals are overlooking the vital importance of controlling one's own life. Control is as important as food and shelter. Control is necessary to health, critical to self-esteem. The fact that persons are materially needy ought never to be an excuse for denying them control over their own lives. People who are being controlled are out of control. Lack of control is the problem that underlies many of the issues that hold America's attention today. It is out-of-control people who become dependent on drugs or who engage in violent crime and abuse. The purpose of benefits should be to empower people, not to deny them power. People are better off as owners than as clients of a welfare bureaucracy. America should never become a nation of propertyless people.

Thus the idea of the individual's property is ecological. Like an animal's habitat, property represents the individual's means of survival. It is attached to the individual by a biological bond. Indeed, it is a part of the definition of the individual. We would not define a fish in such a way as to exclude the water in which it swims, nor would we define a bird without its nesting site, nor an otter without its food supply. Life does not exist in artificial isolation. If the Constitution protects persons, surely it means to protect viability, not persons as specimens in a museum exhibit. Not for a minute should we concede that existence in a cardboard box on a city sidewalk is "life" in the constitutional sense. Not for a moment should we allow that a person without heat or shelter during a freezing winter possesses life, liberty and property in the constitutional sense. Never should we accept the proposition that a human being can exist disconnected from the human community. Human life developed in organic communities. In primitive societies, the individual is not threatened by starvation or lack of shelter unless the entire community is similarly threatened. Even in societies where existence is at the level of subsistence, the individual is not in danger of starvation as part of a community. The bare or naked individual does not exist in nature. In our so-called "higher" civilization we should recognize that there is no such thing as a "person" without a life support system.

The notion that life support for the individual is the property of the government leads to many unacceptable consequences. It changes the focus of attention from substance to procedure. We become preoccupied with the costs of procedure, the fine points of who is qualified for assistance, the constitutional issue of what "process" is "due." A miserly and grudging attitude develops in which procedure comes first and survival second. Moreover, procedure is in the hands of government, not the individual. Delay matters not at all to the government, whereas it may be fatal to the individual. No matter how fair, reasonable and scrupulous the authorities who administer procedure may be, the result is that "they" are deciding the fate of another human being. Instead of asking if the individual can survive, the question becomes whether the government can "afford" the procedures. These two questions should never be deemed comparable.

If benefits necessary to the survival of the individual are the property of the government, then these benefits become an instrument of social control. The government can impose conditions, supervise the behavior of recipients, or deny them the control over their own lives that most other citizens take for granted. One state has gone so far as to deny welfare benefits to families if one of their children is guilty of unexcused absences from school. Benefits become an instrument of control and domination, a means of meddlesome invasion of autonomy, an opportunity for abuse of power by government officials. Why should the price of survival be submission to arbitrary government power? Such supervision undermines the principles of a free society. It permits a form of inequality in which some families exist under the thumb of government while others do not. This is discrimination in its most obnoxious form. It creates second-class citizenship. It allows government to exercise powers over individual lives that are inconsistent with the spirit of our Constitution. This smothering invasion of the individual zone of life would not be possible if we held life support to be the property of individuals, not the government. To make need the occasion for deprivation of autonomy is pernicious; it further undermines the individual's ability to survive.

A further reason to consider life support to be the property of the recipient involves priorities. This has become very clear in a time of budget deficits and the accompanying claim that there is no money for social programs. This allows the government to prioritize the use of its money in ways that ignore the needs of individuals. Aid to a foreign country, bailing out the savings and loan system, and raising the salaries of government officials are not only put on a par with the life support of members of our own community, they are given a higher priority. I would deny government the power to make such choices. I would say that the money required to sustain the lives of individuals does not belong to the government and cannot be used for any other purpose. There may be room to disagree about where to draw the line marking the border of minimum survival. But within that boundary line, a person who is a member of this community should not be separated from his or her life support.

The most rudimentary idea of the social contract should make clear that when people form a society for mutual protection, they do not give up their individual life supports. If, because of the complex interdependence of modern society, some of that life support, such as the water supply, is entrusted to a central authority, this does not allow the authority to withhold the supply from any individual, or to convert it to other uses. No rational person would make a social contract giving up the means to life. And surely this analysis accords with our deepest instinct—that there is something grotesquely wrong with a society that denies individual life support while spending billions of dollars of public money on anything else. That even one person should be without shelter while the community's wealth is spent elsewhere is an abomination. It violates the natural order, and it cannot pass muster under a Constitution adopted in the name of human rights.

Under the due process clause, there is a second question to be addressed: when does government "deprive" an individual of the life support described above? Like the other major concepts in the Constitution, "deprivation" must be interpreted according to the realities of a changing economic system. In a centrally managed economy, where employment or housing is regulated by policy makers in Washington D.C. or financial managers in New York, "deprive" will have a very different meaning than the framers could have imagined. Where the means of life are controlled by state-sponsored monopolies, the exclusion of any individual from the benefits of the system is today's equivalent of constitutionally prohibited "deprivation."

Suppose that the present trend toward economic concentration were to continue until there was just one large corporation which was both the sole employer and the sole supplier of resources and services. And suppose that outside of this corporate domain no land remained for agriculture, and no other means were available to sustain life. Citizenship would then be quite an empty concept, and only *membership* in the corporate family would enable individuals to sustain life. Suppose further that this corporation excluded some people from membership—anywhere from a few individuals to a substantial fraction of the population. Surely there could be no doubt that the excluded persons had been constitutionally deprived of life, liberty and property. Even if the corporation were not state-owned, the state would be held responsible for giving sanction to such an all-powerful monopoly, and the deprivation would be unconstitutional no matter what justification was advanced. Granted we have not reached this point, but on a scale of one to ten, where one represents the economy of 1789 and ten represents the monopoly conditions I have just described, how far along the way are we?

In recent decades many of the safeguards against economic concentration have ceased to function effectively. The antitrust laws, adopted a century ago to prevent the sort of danger I have described, have for all practical purposes been abandoned. Gigantic mergers have gone forward without any effort to stop them. The next safeguard is the regulatory system, which was perfected in New Deal days and seeks to ensure that the private economy operates in the public interest. Like antitrust, the regulatory protections are now moribund. There is instead a trend toward deregulation. And most of the regulatory agencies have long since become captives of the industries they were supposed to regulate. A third major safeguard was the labor movement, permitting employees a strong voice in decisions affecting workers. In the last ten years the labor movement has largely gone the way of antitrust and regulation. Labor has been battered into submission to the point where the standard of living of workers has fallen despite rising corporate profits. To strike is suicidal; strikers lose their jobs and join the scrapheap of those excluded from the system. Another safeguard, shareholder democracy, never was very effective, but what power shareholders once possessed has steadily lost ground to management. Another safeguard might be the power of consumers. But here too corporations have gained ascendancy. Nor are our democratic institutions, such as Congress, a significant check on corporate power. By means of major contributions for congressional campaigns, Congress has been remade into a body beholden to business.

It is true that in many areas of the economy there are several large companies rather than only one. But their so-called "competition" is limited, while the ways in which they act in concert have grown. In broadcasting, the three major networks put forth identical programming and have similar employment policies. An individual excluded by one network will probably be excluded on the same grounds by the others. So the "competition safeguard" is yet another failure when it comes to limiting corporate power. In summary, on a scale of one to ten we are much closer to the ten than the one. And the long-term trend toward ever greater economic concentration keeps us moving toward the ten.

Now consider the changes in the social environment outside the domain of the corporate giants. No longer is there free land for homesteading, farming, and self-support. No longer is there a large area serviced by independent tradespeople or professionals. The small retail store maintains a marginal existence at best. Not too long ago it could be said that working for the corporate sector was a free choice; the individual could always fall back on independent alternatives. Today, corporate or institutional employment is not a choice but a necessity for most workers. When a corporation lops off five thousand or ten thousand employees, where do they go?

When we consider the situation of persons in need today, we must ask whether their condition is due to choices they made or to choices made by the organized sector of society over which the individuals had no control. Are the needy at fault or are they the dispossessed, refugees, people driven out of their habitat? The whole history of industrialization tells us that we are seeing forced loss of habitat, not a refusal to contribute to society. * * *

* * *

If the world of 1790 had been instantaneously transformed into the world of 1990, so that in a moment people lost the economic independence and opportunity that was considered the backbone of American democracy, then the displaced population would surely have felt "deprived" of life, liberty and property. A system of social support is but a substitute—a rather poor substitute—for what has been taken away. We cannot return to the conditions of 1790. But in today's world of ever more concentrated economic power, denial of substitute support to all who need it should be recognized as an unconstitutional deprivation. It is a denial of history to call social support a "new right." Instead it is the birthright of every American, a part of the original understanding when the nation was formed.

Of course, the due process clause applies only to deprivations by the state, and not to those caused by the private sector. But today the state is engaged in active economic management. The state is itself a large employer, its contracts with the private sector are responsible for another large area of employment, and central decision making by the Federal Reserve, the Treasury, and many other agencies of economic management, as well as tax policy and spending decisions, make the government an active and influential participant in the economy. In these ways the state is responsible for the economy, and if the economy denies participation to any group of individuals, the state's responsibility seems direct and clear. To sum up, in a centralized, managed economy which provides most jobs, owns most resources and supplies most services, where alternate means of survival have been taken away, the due process clause *must* mean that no person can be denied the means to economic survival. Any other interpretation would defeat the purpose of the framers, which was to carry forward the promise of Magna Carta, that no person should be in any manner "destroyed" unless by due process of law.

Paradoxically, the more advanced a society becomes, the more severe the consequences of being excluded from the system. I can remember from my childhood many individuals, both in New York City and in the back woods of upstate New York, who somehow managed to survive with no visible means of support. There was a hermit who lived on Cold River, twenty miles from the nearest road, where he fished and shot game with a bow and arrow. Another hermit went lake fishing for bullheads at twilight. My grandfather, who was a neighborhood doctor in the Chelsea district of New York City, provided health care to the poor, charging one or two dollars for house calls and when necessary charging nothing at all. The world was a more forgiving place then.

Today, by contrast, exclusion is a punishment of such severity that it seems worse than the punishment we mete out to those who break the law. Today the world is like an expensive hotel where even the smallest needs cost money (more every day) and there is not a cranny or a corner that is free or available as a hiding place. Exclusion amounts to a major human rights violation, if measured by suffering.

It is one thing to accept inequality as part of our system, where some enjoy luxury while other lives are comparatively spartan. But what we see today is not the kind of inequality that provides incentive to healthy ambition; it is misery that fills the rest of us with fear and horror. This is too great a punishment for fecklessness or failure; it falls below the line of what any society can morally tolerate.

Suppose that the dispossessed of our society had been sentenced to internal exile because of their political beliefs, because of their religion, or because of their race. If children in foster care, or families in rural poverty, or the people camped out over heating grates were all political dissenters, or Jews, or persons thought dangerous to the regime, we would react very differently to the suffering in our midst.

Suppose that the excluded of our society were chosen by a lottery—a state-wide *negative* lottery—because, as in the game of musical chairs, someone must be left out. Again, we would be up in arms at the outrage, the injustice.

What I want to know is this: if we would never tolerate internal exile for political or religious dissent or by lot, why do we tolerate it for the innocent people, including children, the aged, and the mentally ill, who are out there now?

The answer is that we do not feel responsible ourselves, and we do not feel that society is responsible. The moment I suggest a hypothetical case where the action of government is responsible for the suffering of those in internal exile, we immediately recognize that this would be intolerable. It is the premise of non-responsibility that allows us to look the other way. What we need to consider is how the structure of our society permits this sense of non-responsibility. The key element is distancing. There is such a great distance between the choices we make and the consequences of those choices that responsibility vanishes.

Beginning with the invention of the limited liability corporation, non-responsibility is one of our civilization's most remarkable creations.

I am not seeking to blame someone. My point is just the opposite. Where there is no specific responsibility, an environmental approach is needed. The ecological approach is not concerned with blame. I deplore the prosecution of one individual for the Alaska oil spill when the conditions for disaster were created by many different public and private bodies, if not by all of us. The ecological approach says that in order to have healing one must go beyond blame. The ecological approach is concerned with needs, and with survival.

The environmental principle should warn us that, because all life is interconnected, none of us can escape the consequences of suffering in our midst. Everyone in America is worse off today because schools, health services, child care and urban life are deteriorating. Human deterioration is like the air we breathe—there is no escape.

Our Constitution and the due process clause were drawn up at a time when it was sufficient to be left alone. Government was given specified powers and all the rest was simply left to the people or to nature. But today it is not enough to leave nature alone. Left alone, nature is everywhere at risk. Only affirmative intervention and protection will preserve nature. The same is true of human beings. And so the negative constitutional guarantee of one era becomes the affirmative obligation of another era—not because the words of the Constitution have changed, but because those guarantees can no longer be carried out and the Constitution cannot be given its true meaning without affirmative action. In the areas of racial and gender discrimination, there is widespread recognition that leaving things alone is not good enough. Even though the constitutional words are negative—"no person shall be *denied* the equal protection of the laws"—the obligation imposed may call for affirmative action. By the same principle, today the promise that no person shall be *deprived* can only be fulfilled by affirmative action.

The environmental movement and the many different human rights causes—racial minorities, women, gays, the disabled, children and the aged, all need each other. Each is a part of a larger historical event—the paying of the true costs of our industrial and technological progress. We should welcome the chance to pay our debts, correct our wrongs and injustices, and provide a better future for our posterity. Everyone has a right to a share in the commonwealth. Let the blaming cease, and let the healing begin.

Notes and Questions

1. Whether the United States Constitution contains positive rights mandating affirmative government intervention remains contested:

> The text of the Constitution does not support the idea that, as a whole, it was meant to be solely a charter of negative rights. Although many of the rights it provides are phrased negatively,

> many are also phrased affirmatively. Even as to the rights which are phrased negatively, their enforcement may require the imposition of affirmative obligations on government. The conventional wisdom treats the affirmative rights as exceptions to the general rule, but there is nothing inexorable about this conclusion.
>
> More specifically, the language of the due process clause does not mandate the conclusion that it prohibits only affirmative acts, and not omissions. Although its language prohibits certain deprivations, it affirmatively demands that when the government does deprive, it must *afford* due process of law, something which only the government can provide. Finally, to say that the clause protects against abuse of power says very little about the form such abuse must take, or specifically, about whether government can abuse by its inaction as well as its action.

Susan Bandes, *The Negative Constitution: A Critique*, 88 Mich. L. Rev. 2271, 2311–12 (1990). The legitimacy of the terminology is also challenged. Cass Sunstein observed: "Whether a right is 'positive' or 'negative' turns out to depend largely on whether it calls for alterations in existing practices." Cass R. Sunstein, *Constitutionalism After the New Deal*, 101 Harv. L. Rev. 421, 503 (1987).

2. Frank Michelman suggested in 1969 that the Constitution guaranteed some level of "minimum protection" against the effects of poverty. Frank I. Michelman, *The Supreme Court 1968 Term—Foreword: On Protecting the Poor Through the Fourteenth Amendment*, 83 Harv. L. Rev. 7 (1969). Michelman relied on the work of John Rawls, *A Theory of Justice* (1971), to further develop his argument that justice mandates "minimum protection" rather than "equal protection" for the poor. Frank I. Michelman, *In Pursuit of Constitutional Welfare Rights: One View of Rawls' Theory of Justice,* 121 U. Pa. L. Rev. 962 (1973); *see also* Frank I. Michelman, *Welfare Rights in a Constitutional Democracy*, 1979 Wash. L.Q. 659.

A number of cases in the 1960s and early 1970s indicated that the Supreme Court might interpret the Constitution to guarantee some minimal subsistence. *Goldberg* accorded procedural protection to welfare benefits. In Boddie v. Connecticut, 401 U.S. 371 (1971), the Court held that indigent people who sought divorce must be able to obtain waivers of court fees. In Harper v. Virginia State Board of Elections, 383 U.S. 663 (1966), reproduced in chapter 9, the Court struck down the poll tax as unconstitutional. Inspired by these cases and often funded by legal services, poverty lawyers sought to establish rights to subsistence. This effort and the debates among feminist legal theorists over work, welfare, and social responsibility for dependency are explored in the following section.

SECTION 4. CAREGIVING AND DEPENDENCY

What is the responsibility of society to its members who take care of children? Answering this question raises issues that encompass the social organization of work, care for children and the disabled, and the structure of welfare programs. Child care affects the caregiver's liberty to work, and therefore the emotional and material needs of families. How should work and care be balanced? Some scholars emphasize the moral and practical importance of supporting caregivers, while others emphasize the importance of work in the development of all persons who are able to work. Since both work and caregiving are socially important, why has it been more difficult in the United States than in Europe to develop universal programs to help parents without discouraging labor force participation?

A. Dependency and Subsidy: Identifying Society's Interest

Martha Fineman argues for societal recognition of collective responsibility for dependency. If this responsibility is delegated entirely to the private family, and particularly if it is performed by women within the family, the resulting structures unfairly protect the liberty to work in some members of society while constraining others without compensation.

MARTHA ALBERTSON FINEMAN

Cracking the Foundational Myths: Independence, Autonomy, and Self-Sufficiency
8 Am. U. J. Gender Soc. Pol'y & L. 13, 14–27 (2000)

In economic and other important public policy discussions, we focus on the appropriate relationship between market and state, with the family relegated to the "private" sphere. Discussions proceed as though the policies that are designed to affect these institutions in the public sphere have only few implications for the unexamined private family. Even more fundamental, the discussions fail to grasp the fact that the actual (as contrasted with the assumed) family might profoundly affect the possibilities of success and failure of policies created for the market and the state.

To point out the neglect of the family in legal and policy theory differs from concluding that the family has been considered an unimportant institution. In fact, the importance of the family is asserted in its very segregation from other areas of human endeavor. * * *

Not only is the family perceived as occupying the private sphere, it is also conceptualized as embodying values and norms that are very different from the institutions occupying the public sphere, particularly those of the market. Family relationships are cast as different in function and form than relationships existing in the public world. Families are altruistic institutions held together by bonds of affection. Of course, any serious consideration of the family reveals that it is a very public institution, assigned an essential public role within society. The family is delegated primary responsibility for dependency.

* * * Policy development and social theory considerations should center on assessing the appropriateness of the aspirations and expectations we have for the family. This assessment is crucial to one of the most compelling problems facing society at the end of the Twentieth Century—the increasing inequitable and unequal distribution of societal resources and the corresponding poverty of women and children.

Perhaps the most important task for those concerned with the welfare of poor mothers and their children, as well as other vulnerable members of society, is the articulation of a theory of collective responsibility for dependency. The idea of collective responsibility must be developed as a claim of "right" or entitlement to support and accommodation on the part of caretakers. It must be grounded on an appreciation of the value of caretaking labor. A further important concern is to ensure that any theory of collective responsibility not concede the right of collective control over individual intimate decisions, such as whether and when to reproduce or how to form one's family.

The rhetorical and ideological rigidity with which contemporary policy debates have been conducted makes the claim of collective responsibility a particularly difficult task at the end of the Twentieth Century. Core components of America's founding myths, such as the sacredness of individual independence, autonomy, and self-sufficiency have been ossified, used as substitutes for analysis, and eclipsed rather than illuminated debate.

I do not reject these core concepts. I do, however, insist that we have a responsibility to reexamine them in the context of our present society and the needs and aspirations of people today. * * *

* * *

[In political discourse, d]ependence is negatively compared with the desirable status of independence—subsidy with the meritorious self-sufficiency. Independence and self-sufficiency are set up as transcendent values, attainable aspirations for all members of society. Simplified pejorative notions of dependence and subsidy are joined, and condemnation or pity are considered appropriate responses for those unable to live up to the ideals, particularly those who are dependent and in need of subsidy.

In fact, dependency is assumed if an individual is the recipient of certain governmental subsidies. Furthermore, the mere label of dependency serves as an argument against governmental social welfare transfers. Policy makers argue that the goal should be independence, and favor the termination of subsidy so the individual can learn to be self-sufficient.

It is puzzling, as well as paradoxical, that the term dependency has such negative connotations. Its very existence prompts and justifies mean spirited and ill-conceived political responses, such as the recent welfare "reform." Far from being pathological, avoidable, and the result of individual failings, dependency is a universal and inevitable part of the human development. It is inherent in the human condition.

All of us were dependent as children, and many of us will be dependent as we age, become ill, or suffer disabilities. In this sense, dependency is "inevitable" and not deserving of condemnation or stigma. Note that the examples I have chosen to illustrate this category of inevitable dependency are biological or physical in nature. Biological dependencies, however, do not exhaust the potential range of situations of dependence. For example, in addition to biological dependence, one may be psychologically or emotionally dependent on others. * * * It is the characteristic of universality (which indisputably accompanies inevitable dependence) that is central to my argument for societal or collective responsibility. In other words, the realization that biological dependency is both inevitable and universal is theoretically important. Upon this foundational realization is built my claim for justice—the demand that society value and accommodate the labor done by the caretakers of inevitable dependents.

I argue that the caretaking work creates a collective or societal debt. Each and every member of society is obligated by this debt. Furthermore, this debt transcends individual circumstances. In other words, we need not be elderly, ill, or children any longer to be held individually responsible. Nor can we satisfy or discharge our collective responsibility within our individual, private families. Merely being financially generous with our own mothers or duly supporting our own wives will not suffice to satisfy our share of the societal debt generally owed to all caretakers.

My argument that the caretaking debt is a collective one is based on the fact that biological dependency is inherent to the human condition, and therefore, of necessity of collective or societal concern. Just as individual dependency needs must be met if an individual is to survive, collective dependency needs must be met if a society is to survive and perpetuate itself. The mandate that the state (collective society) respond to dependency, therefore, is not a matter of altruism or empathy (which are individual responses often resulting in charity), but one that is primary and essential because such a response is fundamentally society-preserving.

If infants or ill persons are not cared for, nurtured, nourished, and perhaps loved, they will perish. We can say, therefore, that they owe an individual debt to their individual caretakers. But the obligation is not theirs alone—nor is their obligation confined only to their own caretakers. A sense of social justice demands a broader sense of obligation. Without aggregate caretaking, there could be no society, so we might say that it is caretaking labor that produces and reproduces society. Caretaking labor provides the citizens, the workers, the voters, the consumers, the students, and others who populate society and its institutions. The uncompensated labor of caretakers is an unrecognized subsidy, not only to the individuals who directly receive it, but more significantly, to the entire society.

Society preserving tasks, like dependency work, are commonly delegated. The delegation is accomplished through the establishment and maintenance of societal institutions. For example, the armed services are established to attend to the collective need for national defense. But delegation is not the same thing as abandonment. The armed services are structured simultaneously as both the responsibility of only some designated members (volunteers or draftees) and of all members of society (taxpayers and voters).

This dual and complementary responsibility is consistent with our deeply held beliefs about how rights and obligations are accrued and imposed in a just society—collective obligations have both an individual and a collective dimension. Certain members of society may be recruited, volunteer, or even be drafted for service, but they have a right to be compensated for their services from collective resources. They also have a right to the necessary tools to perform their assigned tasks and to guarantees that they will be protected by rules and policies that facilitate their performance. Caretakers should have the same right to have their society-preserving labor supported and facilitated. Provision of the means for their task should be considered the responsibility of the collective society.

Society has not, however, responded this way to caretaking. The most common form of social accommodation for dependency has been its assignment to the institution of the private family. Within that family, dependency has been further delegated as the individual responsibility of the family equivalent of volunteer or draftee—the person in the gendered role of mother (or grandmother or daughter or daughter-in-law or wife or sister). But the resources necessary for caretaking have not been considered to be the responsibility of the collective society. Instead, each individual private family is ideally and ideologically perceived as responsible for its own members and their dependency. A need to call on collective resources, such as welfare assistance, is considered a family as well as an individual failure, deserving of condemnation and stigma.

The assignment of responsibility for the burdens of dependency to the family in the first instance, and within the family to women, operates in an unjust manner because this arrangement has significant negative material consequences for the caretaker. This obvious observation allows me to introduce an additional, but often overlooked, form of dependency into the argument—"derivative dependency." Derivative dependency arises on the part of the person who assumes responsibility for the care of the inevitable dependent person. I refer to this form of dependency as derivative to capture the very simple point that those who care for others are themselves dependent on resources in order to undertake that care. Caretakers have a need for monetary or material resources. They also need recourse to institutional supports and accommodation, a need for structural arrangements that facilitate caretaking.

Currently, neither the economic nor the structural supports for caretaking are adequate. Many caretakers and their dependents find themselves impoverished or severely economically compromised. Some of their economic problems stem from the fact that within families, caretaking work is unpaid and not considered worthy of social subsidies. There are also, however, direct costs associated with caretaking. Caretaking labor interferes with the pursuit and development of wage labor options. Caretaking labor saps energy and efforts from investment in career or market activities, those things that produce economic rewards. There are foregone opportunities and costs associated with caretaking, and even caretakers who work in the paid labor force typically have more tenuous ties to the public sphere because they must also accommodate caretaking demands in the private. These costs are not distributed among all beneficiaries of caretaking (institutional or individual). Unjustly, the major economic and career costs associated with caretaking are typically borne by the caretaker alone.

Further, most institutions in society remain relatively unresponsive to innovations that would lessen the costs of caretaking. Caretaking occurs in a larger context and caretakers often need accommodation in order to fulfill multiple responsibilities. For example, many caretakers also engage in market work. Far from structurally accommodating or facilitating caretaking, however, workplaces operate in modes incompatible with the idea that workers also have obligations for dependency. Workplace expectations compete with the demands of caretaking—we assume that workers are those independent and autonomous individuals who are free to work long and regimented hours.

In discussing the costs and impediments associated with undertaking the tasks of caretaking, it is important to emphasize that, unlike inevitable dependency, derivative dependency is not a universal experience. In fact, many people in our society totally escape the burdens and costs that arise from assuming a caretaking role, perhaps even freed for other pursuits by the caretaking labor of others. * * * [The notion of individual choice] allows us to avoid general responsibility for the inequity and justify the maintenance of the status quo.[15] We ignore the fact that individual choice occurs within the constraints of social conditions. * * *

As it now stands in this society, derivative dependents are expected to get both economic and structural resources within the family. The market is unresponsive and uninvolved, and the state is perceived as a last resort for financial resources, the refuge of the failed family. A caretaker who must resort to governmental assistance may do so only if she can demonstrate that she is needy in a highly stigmatized process.

In popular and political discourse, the idea of "subsidy" is viewed as an equally negative companion to dependence, the opposite of the ideal

15. In particular, I have been struck by [a quasi-economic response to the point that caretakers should be compensated that I refer to as] the "Porsche Preference." This argument states that if someone prefers a child, this preference should not be treated differently than any other choice (like the choice to own a Porsche). Society should not subsidize either preference. I hope the society-preserving nature of children helps to distinguish that preference from the whim of the auto fan. * * *

of self-sufficiency. But a subsidy is nothing more than the process of allocating collective resources to some persons or endeavors rather than other persons or endeavors because a social judgment is made that they are in some way "entitled" or the subsidy is justified. Entitlement to subsidy is asserted through a variety of justifications, such as the status of the persons receiving the subsidy, their past contributions to the social good, or their needs. Often, subsidy is justified because of the position the subsidized persons hold or the potential value of the endeavor they have undertaken to the larger society.

Typically, subsidy is thought of as the provision of monetary or economic assistance. But subsidy can also be delivered through the organization of social structures and norms that create and enforce expectations. Taking this observation into account, along with the earlier discussion of inevitable and derivative dependency, it seems obvious that we must conclude that subsidy is also universal. We all exist in context, in social and cultural institutions, such as families, which facilitate, support and subsidize us and our endeavors.

In complex modern societies no one is self-sufficient, either economically or socially. We all live subsidized lives. Sometimes the benefits we receive are public and financial, such as in governmental direct transfer programs to certain individuals like farmers or sugar growers. Public subsidies can also be indirect, such as the benefits given in tax policy. Private economic subsidy systems work in the forms of foundations, religions and charities. But a subsidy can also be non-monetary, such as the subsidy provided by the uncompensated labor of others in caring for us and our dependency needs.

It seems clear that all of us receive one or the other or both types of subsidy throughout our lives. The interesting question in our subsidy shaped society, therefore, has to be why only some subsidies are differentiated and stigmatized while others are hidden. In substantial part, subsidies are hidden when they are not called subsidy (or welfare, or the dole), but termed "investments," "incentives," or "earned" when they are supplied by government, and called "gifts," "charity," or the product of familial "love" when they are contributions of caretaking labor.

* * *

* * * In recent decades, it has become apparent that the role of the state has been overtaken by the presumed inevitability of market forces. As more and more is conceded to privatization, we are rapidly losing any sense of public responsibility. Even public education is in danger of falling victim to the privatizing siege. Missing from our discourse is strong support for an active or responsive state of the kind I am trying to imagine—the public as a mediating force against private, obscured excesses, and exploitation.

* * *

* * * Independence from subsidy and support is not attainable, nor is it desirable—we want and need the contexts that sustain us. * * *

Independence is gained when an individual has the basic resources that enable her or him to act consistent with the tasks and expectations imposed by the society. * * *

In order to move from our current situation to a more just resolution for the dilemma of caretaking and dependency, we will need more than a responsive state. * * *

In this endeavor, the state must use its regulatory and redistributive authority to ensure that those things that are not valued or are undervalued in market or marriage are, nonetheless, publicly and politically recognized as socially productive and given value. Conferral of value requires the transfer of some economic resources from the collective society to caretakers through the establishment of mechanisms that tax those who receive the benefits of caretaking in order to compensate those who do the caretaking. Other societies do this in a variety of ways, such as using tax revenues to provide childcare allowances and universal benefits that assist caretakers, or through a basic income guarantee. Money, however, is not enough. The active state must also structure accommodation of the needs of caretaking into society's institutions.

The fact is that today, some workers must shoulder the burdens assigned to the family, while market institutions are relieved of such responsibility (even free to punish workers who have trouble combining market and domestic labor). The state must ensure that market institutions positively respond to dependency burdens. Workers cannot be assumed independent and unencumbered. Quite often, they are dually responsible for economic and caretaking activities. Restructuring workplaces to reflect that reality would more equitably distribute the burdens for dependency, and forge a more just relationship between family and market institutions.

* * *

[This restructuring can take multiple forms. For example, flexible work weeks, job sharing without penalty, paid family leave, and the guarantee of a living wage would contribute to a more sharing and equitable arrangement between the market and the family.]

Notes and Questions

1. How many forms of subsidy, as Fineman defines it, are you receiving as of today? How many have you received over the course of your life?

2. Fineman argues for "an integration of the roles and responsibilities of the family, market, and state for dependency," beginning with the basic premise that "there are certain fundamental social goods that are necessary for survival and for the caretaking of others," including "housing, health care, a basic income, and other necessities that complement and strengthen the civil and political rights we have as citizens of a democracy." *Id.* at 26–27, n.25. Income redistribution can meet the

government's obligation to be sure that basic social goods are delivered, but Fineman also calls for a redistribution of responsibility to make the market and its institutions respond to dependency. Mechanisms of transformation might include "restructuring of the tax and subsidy systems, and crediting (and ultimately taxing) market institutions and actors on the imputed benefits they receive from the uncompensated labor of others." *Id.*

3. What sorts of programs might implement Fineman's ideas? Does her argument ultimately point toward home care of children by primary caregivers (usually mothers)? Or is she criticizing the way society has delegated this collective responsibility to the institution of the family and calling for adequate support for caregivers inside and outside the home?

4. Joan Williams argues that the focus in the United States on redistribution of work within the family fails to address the continuing costs of the marginalization of mothers in the context of employment:

> [E]xclusive reliance on the redistribution of family work [within the household] has proved a failure in the U.S. Many men still do very little, and men as a group still do far less than half. * * * As long as employers are free to marginalize anyone who does not perform as an ideal worker, and the ideal worker is defined as someone with immunity from family work, most men feel little choice but to resist demands to do more household work.
>
> * * *
>
> * * * Latin American feminists are astonished, indeed disbelieving, to learn how recently American women gained the right to maternity leaves, and the fact that such leaves are unpaid. In Chile, for example, an employer must provide a child care facility if he employs more than twenty women workers; in Sweden, parents can work part-time until the child has completed the first year of school. In Norway, employees can take one year's parental leave paid at a rate of eighty percent of their earnings for the past 52 weeks. * * *
>
> * * *
>
> * * * Sweden is the pre-eminent example of socialization strategies designed to destabilize the traditional allocation of family work to women. Sweden has long drafted eligibility for its programs in a sex-neutral way; and when it found that only women used parental leave despite its gender-neutrality, it set aside a specific period of parental leave that was available only if leave was taken by the father.
>
> Although public resources for child care outside the home may not be the whole solution, no doubt exists that an acute need exists for more support for such care. For single parents, and many married ones, child care remains an important part of the solution (even if it is not the magic cure it is sometimes represented to be). Child care in the U.S. is both under funded and under regulated, with the result that the quality of child care is not what it should be:

child care workers are paid less than garbage collectors, and turnover is among the highest for any job in the country.

* * * Currently, mothers' marginalization depresses the wages of women: because families typically compare the costs of child care to the salary potential of the mother, it also keeps child care salaries low.

* * * American feminists' repeated attempts to gain government funding for child care have met with little sustained success. For a long time, the U.S. was the only Western industrialized country with no parental leave; after twelve years of lobbying, the result was the FMLA [Family Medical Leave Act]. While the FMLA is a significant and important accomplishment, it is also a drop in the bucket: it covers only a small percentage of those employed in the U.S., and offers only an unpaid leave that many women cannot afford to take. The long struggle to achieve even this minimal level of coverage dramatizes the difficulties American feminists have faced when they try to shift tasks or funding into the public sphere.

Joan Williams, *Do Women Need Special Treatment? Do Feminists Need Equality?*, 9 J. Contemp. Legal Issues 279, 288–91 (1998).

Is the goal of social support for caregiving to support family life? To recognize the labor that is already carried out in society? Or is caregiver support a way to structure the labor market so that it is usable by all workers—male and female, regardless of whether they are raising children at the time?

5. Mary Becker advocates adopting supports like those in place in France, which create no disincentive to work. Mary Becker, *Caring for Children and Caretakers*, 76 Chi. Kent L. Rev. 1495, 1500 (2001). France makes some supports available to all families and some only to poor families. Although poverty rates are about equal before government supports, only 8% of French adults and less than 5% of French children remain poor after government supports, compared with 16% of American adults and 21% of American children. The French system works better for women: "In the United States, 38% more women than men are poor, whereas in France only 11% more women than men are poor." *Id.*

Free nursery schools are available for all children in France. Parents who use private centers are also subsidized with cash benefits and tax breaks. Daycare workers are well trained and paid better than they are in the United States and also receive free housing or a tax-free allowance. *Id.* at 1501. Allowances similar to American welfare grants are available to all families with children. Some allowances are not income-based but available to all families with new babies, or with more than one child under sixteen; additional allowances are given to poor families, to families of modest means, and to single parents. *Id.* at 1502–03.

These state-provided subsidies for child raising have two important effects: First, by working, even at a minimum-wage job, parents who work can pull their families out of poverty. Good supports provide

> no disincentive to work in France, because families remain poor unless parents work, but can rise above the poverty level if parents work. Second, many of the supports needed by poor families are either available to all families or to all but wealthy families. Because these supports are available to all or most families, they enjoy broad support.

Id. at 1503–04.

Do you believe that people in the United States will continue to work if they are able to be lifted from poverty through government supports? How important is participation in work compared to the well-being of children when government policies regarding the care of children are being determined? Compare Vicki Schultz, *Life's Work*, excerpted below (arguing in favor of bringing caregivers and caregiving within the realm of paid work, rather than supporting in-home care through government payments to parents).

B. Rights to Subsistence

In framing the litigation strategy in *Goldberg v. Kelly*, the plaintiffs' lawyers debated whether to advocate for recognition of a right to subsistence. While some lawyers working on the welfare cases felt that "it was a kooky idea that would never be adopted by the Supreme Court," others argued "that it was imperative that the Center use *Goldberg* to advance this theory," particularly because the theory seemed to be gaining acceptance. Davis, *Brutal Need*, at 103–04. In the end, the lawyers compromised, and the brief did not argue extensively for a right to subsistence but noted that "without 'the bare minimum essential for existence ... our expressed constitutional liberties become meaningless.' " *Id.* at 104.

Shortly after *Goldberg v. Kelly*, the Court considered the application of the Equal Protection Clause to the Maryland AFDC program in *Dandridge v. Williams*.

DANDRIDGE v. WILLIAMS

397 U.S. 471 (1970)

Justice STEWART delivered the opinion of the Court.

[In Maryland, the Aid to Families with Dependent Children (AFDC) program provided for most families according to the standard of need determined by the state, but it imposed an upper limit of $250 on the total amount of money any one family unit could receive per month. Effectively, this meant that large families received much less assistance per child than small families received.]

* * * The appellees urged in the District Court that the maximum grant limitation operates to discriminate against them merely because of the size of their families, in violation of the Equal Protection Clause of the Fourteenth Amendment. * * *

* * *

* * * The argument is that the state regulation denies benefits to the younger children in a large family. * * *

It cannot be gainsaid that the effect of the Maryland maximum grant provision is to reduce the per capita benefits to the children in the largest families. Although the appellees argue that the younger and more recently arrived children in such families are totally deprived of aid, a more realistic view is that the lot of the entire family is diminished because of the presence of additional children without any increase in payments. It is no more accurate to say that the last child's grant is wholly taken away than to say that the grant of the first child is totally rescinded. In fact, it is the *family* grant that is affected. * * *

* * *

* * * [A state] may not, of course, impose a regime of invidious discrimination in violation of the Equal Protection Clause of the Fourteenth Amendment. Maryland says that its maximum grant regulation is wholly free of any invidiously discriminatory purpose or effect, and that the regulation is rationally supportable on at least four entirely valid grounds. The regulation can be clearly justified, Maryland argues, in terms of legitimate state interests in encouraging gainful employment, in maintaining an equitable balance in economic status as between welfare families and those supported by a wage-earner, in providing incentives for family planning, and in allocating available public funds in such a way as fully to meet the needs of the largest possible number of families. The District Court, while apparently recognizing the validity of at least some of these state concerns, nonetheless held that the regulation "is invalid on its face for overreaching,"—that it violates the Equal Protection Clause "(b)ecause it cuts too broad a swath on an indiscriminate basis as applied to the entire group of AFDC eligibles to which it purports to apply. . . . "

If this were a case involving government action claimed to violate the First Amendment guarantee of free speech, a finding of "overreaching" would be significant and might be crucial. For when otherwise valid governmental regulation sweeps so broadly as to impinge upon activity protected by the First Amendment, its very overbreadth may make it unconstitutional. But the concept of "overreaching" has no place in this case. For here we deal with state regulation in the social and economic field, not affecting freedoms guaranteed by the Bill of Rights, and claimed to violate the Fourteenth Amendment only because the regulation results in some disparity in grants of welfare payments to the largest AFDC families.[16] For this Court to approve the invalidation of state economic or social regulation as "overreaching" would be far too reminiscent of an era when the Court thought the Fourteenth Amendment gave it power to strike down state laws "because they may be unwise, improvident, or out of harmony with a particular school of

16. Cf. *Shapiro v. Thompson*, 394 U.S. 618, where, by contrast, the Court found state interference with the constitutionally protected freedom of interstate travel.

thought." *Williamson v. Lee Optical of Oklahoma, Inc.*, 348 U.S. 483, 488. That era long ago passed into history.

In the area of economics and social welfare, a State does not violate the Equal Protection Clause merely because the classifications made by its laws are imperfect. If the classification has some "reasonable basis," it does not offend the Constitution simply because the classification "is not made with mathematical nicety or because in practice it results in some inequality." *Lindsley v. Natural Carbonic Gas Co.*, 220 U.S. 61, 78. "The problems of government are practical ones and may justify, if they do not require, rough accommodations—illogical, it may be, and unscientific." "A statutory discrimination will not be set aside if any state of facts reasonably may be conceived to justify it."

To be sure, the cases cited, and many others enunciating this fundamental standard under the Equal Protection Clause, have in the main involved state regulation of business or industry. The administration of public welfare assistance, by contrast, involves the most basic economic needs of impoverished human beings. We recognize the dramatically real factual difference between the cited cases and this one, but we can find no basis for applying a different constitutional standard.[17] * * * [I]t is a standard that is true to the principle that the Fourteenth Amendment gives the federal courts no power to impose upon the States their views of what constitutes wise economic or social policy.

Under this long-established meaning of the Equal Protection Clause, it is clear that the Maryland Maximum grant regulation is constitutionally valid. We need not explore all the reasons that the State advances in justification of the regulation. It is enough that a solid foundation for the regulation can be found in the State's legitimate interest in encouraging employment and in avoiding discrimination between welfare families and the families of the working poor. By combining a limit on the recipient's grant with permission to retain money earned, without reduction in the amount of the grant, Maryland provides an incentive to seek gainful employment. And by keying the maximum family AFDC grants to the minimum wage a steadily employed head of a household receives, the State maintains some semblance of an equitable balance between families on welfare and those supported by an employed breadwinner.

It is true that in some AFDC families there may be no person who is employable.[20] It is also true that with respect to AFDC families whose determined standard of need is below the regulatory maximum, and who therefore receive grants equal to the determined standard, the employment incentive is absent. But the Equal Protection Clause does not require that a State must choose between attacking every aspect of a problem or not attacking the problem at all. *Lindsley v. Natural Carbonic Gas Co.*, 220 U.S. 61. It is enough that the State's action be rationally

17. It is important to note that there is no contention that the Maryland regulation is infected with a racially discriminatory purpose or effect such as to make it inherently suspect.

20. It appears that no family members of any of the named plaintiffs in the present case are employable.

based and free from invidious discrimination. The regulation before us meets that test.

We do not decide today that the Maryland regulation is wise, that it best fulfills the relevant social and economic objectives that Maryland might ideally espouse, or that a more just and humane system could not be devised. Conflicting claims of morality and intelligence are raised by opponents and proponents of almost every measure, certainly including the one before us. But the intractable economic, social, and even philosophical problems presented by public welfare assistance programs are not the business of this Court. The Constitution may impose certain procedural safeguards upon systems of welfare administration, *Goldberg v. Kelly*, 397 U.S. 254. But the Constitution does not empower this Court to second-guess state officials charged with the difficult responsibility of allocating limited public welfare funds among the myriad of potential recipients.

The judgment is reversed.

Justice MARSHALL, whom Justice BRENNAN joins, dissenting.

* * *

The Court recognizes, as it must, that this case involves "the most basic economic needs of impoverished human beings," and that there is therefore a "dramatically real factual difference" between the instant case and those decisions upon which the Court relies. The acknowledgment that these dramatic differences exist is a candid recognition that the Court's decision today is wholly without precedent. I cannot subscribe to the Court's sweeping refusal to accord the Equal Protection Clause any role in this entire area of the law, and I therefore dissent * * *.

* * *

This classification process effected by the maximum grant regulation produces a basic denial of equal treatment. Persons who are concededly similarly situated (dependent children and their families), are not afforded equal, or even approximately equal, treatment under the maximum grant regulation. Subsistence benefits are paid with respect to some needy dependent children; nothing is paid with respect to others. Some needy families receive full subsistence assistance as calculated by the State; the assistance paid to other families is grossly below their similarly calculated needs.

Yet, as a general principle, individuals should not be afforded different treatment by the State unless there is a relevant distinction between them, and "a statutory discrimination must be based on differences that are reasonably related to the purposes of the Act in which it is found." Consequently, the State may not, in the provision of important services or the distribution of governmental payments, supply benefits to some individuals while denying them to others who are similarly situated.

In the instant case, the only distinction between those children with respect to whom assistance is granted and those children who are denied such assistance is the size of the family into which the child permits himself to be born. * * *

* * *

Under the so-called "traditional test," a classification is said to be permissible under the Equal Protection Clause unless it is "without any reasonable basis." On the other hand, if the classification affects a "fundamental right," then the state interest in perpetuating the classification must be "compelling" in order to be sustained.

This case simply defies easy characterization in terms of one or the other of these "tests." The cases relied on by the Court, in which a "mere rationality" test was actually used are most accurately described as involving the application of equal protection reasoning to the regulation of business interests. The extremes to which the Court has gone in dreaming up rational bases for state regulation in that area may in many instances be ascribed to a healthy revulsion from the Court's earlier excesses in using the Constitution to protect interests that have more than enough power to protect themselves in the legislative halls. This case, involving the literally vital interests of a powerless minority—poor families without breadwinners—is far removed from the area of business regulation, as the Court concedes. Why then is the standard used in those cases imposed here? We are told no more than that this case falls in "the area of economics and social welfare," with the implication that from there the answer is obvious.

In my view, equal protection analysis of this case is not appreciably advanced by the *a priori* definition of a "right," fundamental or otherwise. Rather, concentration must be placed upon the character of the classification in question, the relative importance to individuals in the class discriminated against of the governmental benefits that they do not receive, and the asserted state interests in support of the classification. As we said only recently, "In determining whether or not a state law violates the Equal Protection Clause, we must consider the facts and circumstances behind the law, the interests which the State claims to be protecting, and the interests of those who are disadvantaged by the classification."

It is the individual interests here at stake that, as the Court concedes, most clearly distinguish this case from the "business regulation" equal protection cases. AFDC support to needy dependent children provides the stuff that sustains those children's lives: food, clothing, shelter. And this Court has already recognized several times that when a benefit, even a "gratuitous" benefit, is necessary to sustain life, stricter constitutional standards, both procedural and substantive, are applied to the deprivation of that benefit.

* * * [G]overnmental discrimination between children on the basis of a factor over which they have no control—the number of their brothers and sisters—bears some resemblance to the classification be-

tween legitimate and illegitimate children which we condemned as a violation of the Equal Protection Clause in *Levy v. Louisiana*, 391 U.S. 68 (1968).

* * *

* * * [I]t is perfectly obvious that limitations upon assistance cannot reasonably operate as a work incentive with regard to those who cannot work or who cannot be expected to work. * * *

Even if the invitation of the State to focus upon the heads of AFDC families is accepted, the minimum rationality of the maximum grant regulation is hard to discern. * * * [I]it is clear, although the record does not disclose precise figures, that the total number of "employable" mothers is but a fraction of the total number of AFDC mothers. * * * [N]ot only has the State failed to establish that there is a substantial or even a significant proportion of AFDC heads of households as to whom the maximum grant regulation arguably serves as a viable and logical work incentive, but it is also indisputable that the regulation at best is drastically *overinclusive* since it applies with equal vigor to a very substantial number of persons who like appellees are completely disabled from working.

Finally, it should be noted that, to the extent there is a legitimate state interest in encouraging heads of AFDC households to find employment, application of the maximum grant regulation is also grossly *underinclusive* because it singles out and affects only large families. No reason is suggested why this particular group should be carved out for the purpose of having unusually harsh "work incentives" imposed upon them. * * * There is simply no indication whatever that heads of large families, as opposed to heads of small families, are particularly prone to refuse to seek or to maintain employment. * * *

* * *

* * * [The] asserted state interests * * * are advanced either not at all or by complete accident by the maximum grant regulation. Clearly they could be served by measures far less destructive of the individual interests at stake. Moreover, the device assertedly chosen to further them is at one and the same time both grossly underinclusive—because it does not apply at all to a much larger class in an equal position—and grossly overinclusive—because it applies so strongly against a substantial class as to which it can rationally serve no end. Were this a case of pure business regulation, these defects would place it beyond what has heretofore seemed a borderline case, and I do not believe that the regulation can be sustained even under the Court's "reasonableness" test.

In any event, it cannot suffice merely to invoke the spectre of the past and to recite from *Lindsley v. Natural Carbonic Gas Co.* and *Williamson v. Lee Optical of Oklahoma, Inc.* to decide the case. Appellees are not a gas company or an optical dispenser; they are needy dependent children and families who are discriminated against by the State. The basis of that discrimination—the classification of individuals into large and small families—is too arbitrary and too unconnected to the asserted rationale, the impact on those discriminated against—the denial of even a subsistence existence—too great, and the supposed interests served too contrived and attenuated to meet the requirements of the Constitution. In my view Maryland's maximum grant regulation is invalid under the Equal Protection Clause of the Fourteenth Amendment.

I would affirm the judgment of the District Court.

Notes and Questions

1. Justice Marshall criticizes distinctions based on "the family into which the child permits himself to be born." How important to the dissent is the concept that the state is distinguishing among people based on circumstances of their birth?

2. By applying a deferential standard of review and by drawing a contrast to *Shapiro v. Thompson*, which protected a fundamental right to travel, the majority makes clear that it finds no fundamental right to subsistence in the Constitution. Did Justice Marshall's dissent argue for recognizing a fundamental right to subsistence?

3. How does the majority structure its review of regulations under the equal protection clause? How does the dissent differ on its approach to constitutional review?

4. *Dandridge* was one of a series of defeats for the attempt to expand recognition of constitutional rights to welfare through litigation. In Wyman v. James, 400 U.S. 309 (1971), welfare recipients failed to persuade the Court to protect welfare recipients from losing welfare benefits if they denied authorities permission to search their homes. In Jefferson v. Hackney, 406 U.S. 535 (1972), the Supreme Court found no equal protection problem in the unequal structures of assistance programs in Texas, which paid 100% of the standard of need for predominantly white recipients of Aid to the Aged and less than 70% of need for the predominantly black and Latino recipients of AFDC.

5. Rights to subsistence also failed as a legislative reform strategy. In Congress, the same period saw the failure of attempts to enact a federal guarantee of an minimum income for a family of four, which had at one time drawn support from President Richard Nixon and a variety of forces in Congress. Davis, *Brutal Need*, *supra* at 135–38.

Welfare rolls had vastly expanded beginning in 1964 after decades of restrictive benefit programs. States had not responded with increased benefits to the hardships created by crisis in Southern agriculture, nor to the difficulties faced by millions of African Americans who migrated into the cities of the North and West, encountering job discrimination and the effects of mechanization and recession.

> Instead, the "welfare explosion" occurred during several years of dramatic domestic protest—the greatest moment of civic disorder in the nation's history—marked by the epic confrontation in Birming-

> ham, the wave of civil rights sit-ins, demonstrations, and near-riots that swept the South, and the "long hot summers" of protracted rioting and clashes with police in the North's black urban ghettoes.
>
> Prodded by the Johnson administration, Congress came forward with a series of programs, aimed at eradicating the "poverty amid plenty" that civil rights protests and ghetto riots had put on the national agenda. Among these was the War on Poverty, whose programs would come to employ thousands of attorneys, and tens of thousands of social workers and poor community resident-activists. * * * Centuries-old [welfare] restrictions were broken down by a combination of civic unrest and federally-funded community organizing and litigation.

Forbath, *Constitutional Welfare Rights*, at 1841–42.

In 1970, Frances Fox Piven and Richard Cloward examined this pattern of change in welfare and described it as part of a historical pattern of social control through governmental expansion and contraction of relief:

> The key to an understanding of relief-giving is in the functions it serves for the larger economic and political order, for relief is a secondary and supportive institution. Historical evidence suggests that relief arrangements are initiated or expanded during the occasional outbreaks of civil disorder produced by mass unemployment, and are then abolished or contracted when political stability is restored. * * * [E]xpansive relief policies are designed to mute civil disorder, and restrictive ones to reinforce work norms. In other words, relief policies are cyclical—liberal or restrictive depending on the problems of regulation in the larger society with which government must contend. * * * [T]his view clearly belies the popular supposition that government social policies, including relief policies, are becoming progressively more responsible, humane, and generous * * * .

Frances Fox Piven and Richard Cloward, *Regulating the Poor: The Functions of Public Welfare* xv (2d ed., 1993).

Civil rights leaders had demanded jobs, not welfare. Martin Luther King and other leaders warned repeatedly that both full employment and antidiscrimination law were necessary. "The 'full emancipation and equality of Negroes and the poor,' King repeatedly told rallies and demonstrations, legislative hearings and White House conferences, demanded a 'contemporary social and economic Bill of Rights.' " Forbath, *Constitutional Welfare Rights*, at 1843. Bayard Rustin, chief organizer of the March on Washington in 1963, told Congress that civil rights must be "built on the right to a decent livelihood" or they would rest on sand. *Id.* at 1842.

A few years later, welfare recipients took a different approach, demanding a minimum guaranteed income for all. The National Welfare Rights Organization (NWRO), which organized rapidly between 1967 and 1970, forged a social movement of "the poorest, most powerless Americans." *Id.* at 1853. At its peak, NWRO claimed more than 100,000 dues-paying members in 350 local organizations. As Forbath notes, "rank-and-file members developed some sense of efficacy and entitlement by gaining their demands from the nation's welfare departments." *Id.* at 1850. NWRO leaders were welfare recipients who sought dignity and opposed work programs, which they saw as more likely to be punitive than rewarding.

> For them, a "Guaranteed Adequate Income" was an unconditional citizenship right, essential to equal respect, and an appropriate touchstone of equality in an affluent nation. That income would be available to both men and women regardless of whether they were in the labor market or whether they were raising children. The focus on income and not employment resonated with * * * a widespread view in 1960s America that affluence had diminished the need for universal labor force participation. Income, not employment, also spoke to "modern women's" paradigmatic economic activity, the work of managing family and household through the consumer marketplace.
>
> * * *
>
> * * * Today it seems wildly shortsighted to have spurned all talk of work programs and job training. Welfare rights were essential to meeting the immediate needs of the NWRO's constituents; but welfare rights were no basis for ending the social and economic marginality and stigmatization of the black poor. * * *
>
> * * * [M]imicking AFDC came at a price. It led to the absence of poor men in a movement that claimed to represent the nation's poor and their needs. As a consequence, it led to a rights rhetoric that downplayed the disappearance of decently paid unskilled industrial jobs from the nation's old industrial regions and center cities. This was the social fact that leaders like King and Rustin had highlighted and called on Congress to remedy as a necessary condition for the "full emancipation and equality of Negroes and the poor."
>
> Instead, the War on Poverty provided organizers and attorneys to help wage a struggle for welfare rights. Gaining welfare as a matter of right would relieve unwarranted suffering and indignity. But it would not do enough to help poor blacks make their way into a shared social destiny of work and opportunity. * * *

Id. at 1851–53.

Ultimately, the leaders of the NWRO divided over whether to pursue coalitions with the working poor or to continue to seek rights to subsistence. The organization lost most of its membership as the legal strategy to win recognition of rights to adequate subsistence failed. Davis, *Brutal Need*, *supra* at 140–45.

6. Although the Federal Constitution does not guarantee subsistence, state constitutions may be more protective of rights of their citizens. "The provision of assistance to the needy is not a matter of legislative grace but is specifically mandated by the New York State Constitution * * * [which] provides that the 'aid, care and support of the needy are public concerns and shall be provided by the state and by such of its subdivisions, and by such manner and by such means, as the legislature may from time to time determine.' " Jiggetts v. Grinker, 75 N.Y.2d 411, 416, 553 N.E.2d 570, 572 (1990). In 1995, the Connecticut Supreme Court divided sharply over whether the Connecticut constitution protected subsistence, and also disagreed on the question of whether other states recognized rights to subsistence. Moore v. Ganim, 233 Conn. 557, 660 A.2d 742 (Conn. 1995) (reviewing natural law and common law arguments, but finding no right to subsistence for the poor in Connecticut).

Because of the state's duty under its constitution to care for the poor, *Jiggetts* found that a New York statute imposed a duty on the state to establish shelter allowances for the poor that bore a reasonable relation to the cost of housing in New York. 553 N.E.2d at 575. In contrast, the United States Supreme Court has held that shelter is not a fundamental right in the United States. Lindsey v. Normet, 405 U.S. 56 (1972).

7. In *Dandridge*, the majority found that the regulation limiting benefits to large families had a rational basis because it sought to avoid discriminating between families receiving welfare and the families of the working poor. Is that an appropriate policy goal?

Is it necessary to lower benefits in order to avoid rewarding people who do not work? If people did have a fundamental right to subsistence under either federal or state constitutions, can you think of other ways in which governments might avoid disadvantaging the working poor?

C. Welfare and Work

Until 1996, Aid to Families with Dependent Children (AFDC) was the principal program supporting poor families. State benefits varied from $923 a month for a family of three in Alaska to $120 in Mississippi. In 1995, just before the program ended, cash assistance averaged $377 per month. Families on welfare remained under the poverty line—the combination of food stamps and AFDC benefits brought the average recipient family income to about 65% of the federal poverty level.

"AFDC was not typically thought of as a program of assistance for working-poor families." Mark Greenberg, *Welfare Restructuring and Working-Poor Family Policy: The New Context*, in *Hard Labor, Women and Work in the Post-Welfare Era* 24 (Joel F. Handler & Lucie White eds., 1999). In 1973, about 16% of AFDC families reported earning wages in addition to welfare assistance. The Reagan administration obtained amendments that restricted the eligibility of working poor families, and the percentage of working families declined until, by 1994, only 9% of AFDC families reported earnings in an average month.

> In and before its final years, AFDC was a program in transition, enormously controversial and deeply unpopular. The program was criticized both for failing to provide adequate support to needy families and for providing sufficient support to function as a work disincentive and as an incentive to the formation and maintenance of single-parent families. * * * With [women's] increased participation [in the labor force], it became increasingly problematic to have a program that seemed designed to discourage labor market participation. Thus, an increasing focus of reform efforts became how to redesign AFDC into a program that encouraged, supported, and required employment by parents who were able to enter the work force.
>
> Before 1996, there had been several rounds of initiatives intended to strengthen the linkage between AFDC and employment. The last major federal legislative enactment before the 1996 legislation was the Family Support Act of 1988. The Family Support Act had a number of significant features: it expanded child support enforcement; provided additional funding to states for education, training, and employment-related services for AFDC families; increased the circumstances under which adults and teen parents could be required to participate in employment-related activities [and increased support for child care] * * * .

Id. at 26.

In the early 1990s, through waivers of federal program requirements, some states increased assistance to working poor families to meet a variety of policy concerns: avoiding disincentives to employment created by the loss of benefits upon taking a job, solving the problems in retaining work that can be created by insufficient income, and alleviating the hardships faced by low-income families. Before the effects of these programs had been evaluated, however, Congress ended the AFDC program in 1996 and imposed stringent work requirements without increasing support structures for working poor families who were not welfare recipients.

In 1996, the Personal Responsibility and Work Opportunity Reconciliation Act (PRWORA) replaced AFDC with Temporary Assistance for Needy Families ("TANF") and narrowed access to Supplemental Security Income (SSI). It excluded immigrants from most poverty programs and made receiving food stamps more difficult. The new statute did, however, strengthen child support enforcement, child protection, and child care. TANF allowed states substantial flexibility in determining how to administer their block grant programs. The new federal law imposed comprehensive work requirements and initiated a five year lifetime limit on receipt of assistance. "Nearly all of these legislative changes have made assistance for poor people much more difficult to secure and, if secured, much more difficult to retain." William P.

Quigley, *Backwards into the Future: How Welfare Changes in the Millenium Resemble English Poor Law of the Middle Ages* 9 Stan. L. & Pol'y Rev. 101, 102 (1998). Some states enacted TANF statutes with even shorter time limits on benefits. For summaries of the changes enacted in the Personal Responsibility and Work Opportunity Reconciliation Act (PRWORA), see, e.g., Joel F. Handler, *Welfare Reform: Is it for Real?*, 3 Loy. Poverty L.J. 135 (1997); Joel F. Handler & Yeheskel Hasenfeld, *We the Poor People: Work, Poverty, and Welfare* (1997).

The rhetoric and ideology of the debates that framed welfare reform were hotly contested. Conservative proponents of welfare reform argued that AFDC created disincentives to work and promoted dependency; they also emphasized deviant behavior as a cause of poverty. *See* Charles A. Murray, *Losing Ground: American Social Policy, 1950–1980* (1984); Lawrence M. Mead, *The New Politics of Poverty: The Nonworking Poor in America* (1992). In reply, many scholars emphasized structural causes of poverty, rebutted concepts of welfare recipients that treated poverty as an individual failing, and denounced the race-coded stereotypes of idleness and irresponsible reproduction that characterized public debates. *See, e.g.*, Nancy A. Wright, *Welfare Reform under the Personal Responsibility Act: Ending Welfare as We Know it or Governmental Child Abuse?*, 25 Hastings Const. L.Q. 357 (1998) (describing the Personal Responsibility and Work Opportunity Reconciliation Act of 1996 as a form of child abuse); Risa E. Kaufman, *The Cultural Meaning of the "Welfare Queen": Using State Constitutions to Challenge Child Exclusion Provisions,* 23 N.Y.U. Rev. L. & Soc. Change 301 (1997) (discussing racism in welfare reform debates); Sylvia Law, *Ending Welfare as We Know It*, 49 Stan. L. Rev. 471 (1997) (summarizing welfare debates and identifying stereotypes); Kathleen A. Kost & Frank W. Munger, *Fooling All of the People Some of the Time: 1990's Welfare Reform and the Exploitation of American Values*, 4 Va. J. Soc. Pol'y & L. 3 (1996) (same).

Vicki Schultz framed the discussion of work and caregiving differently, emphasizing both the needs of caregivers and the importance of paid work to human development.

VICKI SCHULTZ

Life's Work

100 Colum. L. Rev. 1881, 1883–86, 1914–16, 1930–38 (2000)

* * * [A] robust conception of equality can be best achieved *through* paid work, rather than *despite* it. Work is a site of deep self-formation that offers rich opportunities for human flourishing (or devastation). To a large extent, it is through our work—how it is defined, distributed, characterized, and controlled—that we develop into the "men" and "women" we see ourselves and others see us as being. Because law's domain includes work and its connection to other spheres of existence, the prospect of who we become as a society, and as individuals, is shaped profoundly by the laws that create and control the institutions that

govern our experiences as workers. I believe that it is only by recognizing the formative power of such forces that we can imagine and invent ourselves as full human agents.

* * * [P]eople are shaped deeply by our work. Our historical conception of citizenship, our sense of community, and our sense that we are of value to the world all depend importantly on the work we do for a living and how it is organized and understood by the larger society. In everyday language, we are what we do for a living.

* * *[O]ur society has been slow to understand this fundamental feature of socialization to be true for women (although we believe it is true for men). Our views of women have been distorted by family-wage ideology, "the sex/gender/family system that prescribes earning as the sole responsibility of husbands and unpaid domestic labor as the only proper long-term occupation for women." Family-wage thinking has left us with a mythologized but misleading image of women as creatures of domesticity—and not of paid work. This view inhabits labor economics, anti-discrimination law, and even some strands of feminist thought. In policy terms, it finds expression in the proposition that it is women's position within families, rather than the workworld, that is the primary cause of women's economic disadvantage, and hence should be the primary locus for redistributive efforts. This view is both empirically inaccurate and theoretically counterproductive; it reifies gender-based patterns of labor and perpetuates class bias. * * * [W]e must move beyond family-wage thinking and instead adopt strategies that promote gender integration across both paid and unpaid work in order to improve the lives of women, men, and children from all social and economic walks of life.

* * *

* * * Paid work has the potential to become the universal platform for equal citizenship it has been imagined to be, but only if we ensure meaningful participation in the workforce by attending to the specific needs of various social groups and individuals. In the past, legal efforts to achieve equality focused on protecting people from identity-based discrimination; we have tended to take the number and quality of jobs, job-holding services, wages, and working conditions produced by the market as a neutral baseline to which no one is to be denied access because of group status. But in order to make paid work the basis for equal citizenship, we will have to take steps to ensure that what the market produces is both substantively adequate and universally available for everyone. This means that, in the future, we will have to supplement employment discrimination law with measures like job-creation programs, wage subsidies, universal child care and health care programs, enhanced employee representation, and a reduced workweek for everyone. * * * [Feminists] must join forces with a broad array of groups—including the labor movement—not simply to advance each other's interests, but to fashion a shared interest in creating a social order in

which work is consistent with egalitarian conceptions of citizenship and care.

* * *

Joint-property approaches * * * [, in which women are compensated by their husbands at divorce for their caregiving work, reproduce] harmful gender- and class-based dynamics; traditional welfare strategies can be detrimental to women as well. Joint property approaches rely on individual breadwinners to fund household labor, while welfare strategies rely on the state. State funding is advantageous for women, because it frees them from serving individual men and sheds class bias by funding household work at a uniform level regardless of the earnings of the family members who support it. Nonetheless, by paying women to stay home with their children rather than providing real support for parents (especially single parents) to work at paid jobs, welfare strategies still encourage women to invest in homemaking and caregiving to the exclusion of their job skills—which may harm women and their families in the long run. For this reason, in the wake of changes to the traditional Aid to Families with Dependent Children (AFDC) system, a number of feminists are proposing alternatives designed to enable low-income mothers and fathers—along with their middle-class counterparts—to participate in parenting and paid work at the same time, and to improve the status of the work they do.

Feminist economist Barbara Bergmann, for example, has criticized the traditional AFDC program for creating a disincentive to employment that hurts women in the long run. She advocates a system more like the French system, which eliminates this disincentive by providing single parents with better support for working at a job while parenting. * * *

Bergmann's analysis shows that, despite its facial neutrality, the traditional American welfare approach has harmful class and gender effects. Single mothers are likely to remain poor no matter what they do, whether they work at paid jobs or not. In addition, Bergmann points out, paying single mothers to care for their children raises demands to support married middle-class women's homemaking, which only exacerbates class differentials and further reinforces the gender-based division of labor. To move the United States in a more promising direction, Bergmann has proposed a program called "Help for Working Parents," which would provide low-income parents (single or married) the resources to combine paid work with parenting. The program would provide universal health insurance (on a sliding scale), child care vouchers (for public or private forms of child care), food stamps, and expanded housing assistance for high-cost areas. Perhaps most importantly, it would also provide government subsidies to bring individual earnings above the poverty level. The proposal contemplates that, like most fathers, mothers will engage in full-time work; however, full-time work is defined as thirty hours a week—a substantial reduction from the current norm for American men and women.

* * *

* * * Ordinary people understand the significance of work and have demanded access to work in broad, inclusive terms. Indeed, over the past forty years, all the major social movements have focused on obtaining equal access to work for those excluded from its rewards. * * *

* * *

Although women, racial and ethnic minorities, older people, and sexual minorities are often characterized as "special interests," many of the rights and remedies for which these groups have struggled have extended the benefits of work more broadly to other people as well. For example, racial minorities' challenges to pencil and paper tests have benefited disadvantaged whites, too, due to the strong correlation between success on these tests and socioeconomic class. Similarly, women's challenges to height requirements have benefited many nonwhite men who are shorter than the average white Anglo-Saxon Protestant male, just as mothers' efforts to win more flexible work schedules to accommodate parenting have benefited everyone who provides care—male and female, father and mother, son and daughter. Gay men's efforts to challenge the workplace harassment their heterosexual counterparts direct at them also helps many women, too, because such challenges make it easier to see that harassment can be motivated not simply by sexual desire, but by a desire to exclude anyone who undermines the dominant composition and image of the work.

The disability rights movement has also emphasized access to work, and they won an important victory with the Americans with Disabilities Act (ADA). At least potentially, the ADA represents an expansion of the traditional civil rights paradigm: It recasts the demand for a "level" playing field into a call for an "accessible" one. At the core of the ADA is a revolutionary idea: People who have disabilities (or who are perceived to have them) have the right to participate in the workforce just like everyone else; and they must be considered for any jobs they can do with reasonable modification or support from the employer. * * *

Once again, making way for "them" helps make way for all of us. The ADA requires both structural transformations—such as building ramps—and individual accommodation—such as allowing employees to work around their treatment schedules. These changes can benefit all of us, not simply those of us who meet the legal definition of "persons with disabilities." People who push baby strollers or ride bicycles appreciate ramps along with people in wheelchairs; and almost everyone can benefit from flexibility in scheduling. Furthermore, the very notion of "them" and "us" is an illusion when it comes to disability. If "disability" is defined sufficiently broadly, as it should be, most of us will be disabled at some point in our lives.

We can also view the transition from welfare to work as part of this trend. I realize that the impetus for welfare-to-work programs has come from the political right, who may not have the best interests of poor people at heart. But it would be a mistake to attribute all of the new emphasis on work to conservatives alone. Some of the demand has come from members of the working poor who do not receive welfare, and who do not have the luxury of keeping a parent at home to take care of their own children. They may understandably resent the fact that their hard-earned tax dollars are used to support other parents who are not much worse off than they are. In this sense, welfare entitlements have divided the welfare class from other members of the working classes.

But even this view is too simplistic. It is not only resentful taxpayers, but welfare recipients themselves who focus attention on work. Poor single parents have long expressed a desire for work that will allow them to support their children; they know that a decent job is the only path that provides real hope for their empowerment in the long run. Most people who receive welfare payments have been working for pay all along, as they must in order to ensure the survival of their families. * * * Women who draw on welfare are overrepresented among classic contingent workers, who fare worse on a variety of dimensions than people in more permanent employment. * * *

Even if many welfare-to-work programs have been adopted for the wrong reasons, their existence does provide a political opening to turn things around. Not only is paid work important to people's ability to get ahead and their sense of community and self-esteem; it is also a more easily politicized setting than the privatized home. By creating social systems that allow poor (and other) parents to combine caregiving with stable employment, we enable them to move into the workforce—a space in which they can more easily engage in collective action to improve their situation. Perhaps this is why, all over the country, poor single parents and their advocates are seeking to convert the duty to work into a *right* to work, with all the social support necessary to make steady employment possible. For instance, * * * one Wisconsin program * * * provides a remarkable array of services designed to facilitate welfare mothers' successful transition to paid work. Everyone in the program who can work receives a job: Although the ultimate goal is private-sector employment, the program provides a series of subsidized private- and public-sector jobs for those who are not "job ready." Clients receive job search assistance and job training. Those who land jobs * * * continue to receive job retention assistance and support. They also continue to receive payments for child care and health care, and caseworkers help with transportation. Perhaps most importantly, the program provides sizable wage subsidies to ensure that those who hold down a job earn more than they did on AFDC. * * *

* * * [T]he best welfare-to-work programs push in the direction of a more expansive set of social programs that guarantee and support a right to work for everyone. * * * There is no reason to find or create jobs exclusively for people who have drawn on welfare, when so many others are struggling to find jobs, often under fiercely competitive conditions. The goal should be to ensure that everyone—mothers on welfare, fathers struggling to pay child support, poor women and men without children, people with disabilities, middle-class homemakers or divorcees, people in temporary jobs who want steady employment, older

people, youth who are trying to finance continuing education, and, yes, even well-educated displaced workers—has work.

Yet, it is not simply a lack of jobs, but a lack of jobs that pay a decent wage that discourages many people. * * * [W]e cannot raise wages only for people who have drawn on welfare, when so many others face jobs with pay so low that they cannot support themselves—let alone their children. We must ensure that everyone has a pathway to sustaining work.

In addition to decent-paying jobs, people must have access to all the services that facilitate finding and keeping employment * * *. As anthropologist Katherine Newman has observed, providing such things as health care and coveted child care slots to welfare recipients may be a worthy goal, but it "leaves the working poor, whose lives have little impact on [cities'] bottom line, out in the cold." We all need health care, for ourselves and our children. And, in an age of dual-career couples and single-parent households, almost everyone needs high-quality, affordable child care in order to work effectively. * * * The only answer is a massive public investment in day-care, preschool, and after-school programs, which in turn could create many new jobs for other people as this form of housework is collectivized and turned into paid employment. * * *

* * * [T]hose of us who believe in gender integration must call for reforms that encourage men and women to work similar—and saner—hours that will allow both to participate more fully in all life's experiences. * * *

Notice that something remarkable has happened: To underscore the importance of paid work as a political and cultural ideal, I began talking about how many different people, from many different walks of life have been demanding equal access to work. I drew from examples of groups who have sought to use anti-discrimination law as a wedge into the mainstream of work. * * * The effort to enable those who traditionally have been excluded from the workforce to participate on equal terms led to broader proposals that would transform the social landscape for everyone. * * * This transformation powerfully conveys how a focus on work can unite us across differences and provide a common foundation for equal citizenship for all.

Notes and Questions

1. How are Schultz and Fineman in agreement on the working lives of caregivers, and how do they differ? Which approach do you find most persuasive?

Schultz argues that an emphasis on work might be transformative, uniting disparate groups as they seek that right and strengthening potential alliances. Is this strategy viable?

2. Karen Czapanskiy criticizes the lack of attention to the needs of children in current welfare reform policies. She describes the case of a

welfare mother who was sanctioned for failure to meet work requirements. She did not complete a homework assignment from her work activity over the weekend when both of her children were ill. The sanction was imposed even though the mother had attended her work activity all week while her children were in child care. Czapanskiy argues for recognizing the importance to children of flexibility in welfare arrangements:

> Work-first welfare reform is a problem for parent-child relationships. It demands that parents dichotomize: either they become self-sufficient by putting work first and children last, or they suffer extreme poverty. What many working parents have been demanding for decades, however, is an abandonment of dichotomous thinking about work and family life. Instead, parents have been seeking a balance—an opportunity to be responsible at home and responsible at work simultaneously. Parents do not want to sacrifice or even put at risk their deep connection with their children in order to make a living. And society at large should not want parents to make that sacrifice because the key to a child's long-term success as an adult is having a deep connection with his or her parent right from the start.
>
> Work-first welfare reform rejects balance as an objective. Single mothers must demonstrate personal responsibility by working for pay. They must stop being economically dependent, at least on public benefits. It is as if parenthood does not exist for people on welfare. Indeed, it is possible to look at state after state, at welfare reform program after welfare reform program, and hear no mention of children at all, except as a "barrier" to work, a barrier that is fully resolved once child care is arranged. Those who fail to comply with work requirements are irresponsible, even if their "failure" occurred because, in their view, they needed to meet the needs of a child.
>
> Outside of work-first welfare reform, dichotomous thinking about work and family life is declining. Most mothers have responsibilities both at home and at work. They spend time, energy, and resources making sure that they can meet their responsibilities in both places without risking the deep connection on which their children's eventual well-being depends. * * * Work-first welfare reform too often ignores the complexities of making paid employment compatible with responsible parenthood.

Karen Syma Czapanskiy, *Parents, Children, and Work-First Welfare Reform: Where Is the C in TANF?*, 61 Md. L. Rev. 308, 314–15, 361–62 (2002).

3. Should the welfare reform statute have required support structures such as child care, health insurance, and paid medical leave to be in place for all families? While these programs are vital to low-income families, they would help middle-class families as well.

4. To increase the gap between the working and nonworking poor, and to increase the relative rewards for people who work, government

can move either to raise wages or lower benefits. *See generally* William P. Quigley, *Five Hundred Years of English Poor Laws, 1349–1834: Regulating the Working and Nonworking Poor*, 30 Akron L. Rev. 73 (1996) (describing history of adjustments in regulation of poor and noting a pattern of "continual, cyclical dissatisfaction with all the methods of providing relief to poor people" in which previous reforms "will be criticized as either too harsh and punitive, or not tough enough to provide an incentive to work, or, frequently, both," *id.* at 127). Why did the United States government choose to lower benefits rather than to raise wages?

5. What should be the goals of welfare-to-work programs, and which criteria should define success when these programs are evaluated: ending poverty; providing a living wage; reducing welfare rolls; moving recipients into steady employment; stabilizing families; protecting children; supporting caregiving; providing education to enhance job skills; creating support structures such as elder care or transportation for the disabled; avoiding errors in administrative decision-making; or other factors? Would changes in the national economy affect your policy choices? *See, e.g.,* Nina Bernstein, *In Control Group, Most Welfare Recipients Left the Rolls Even Without Reform*, N.Y. Times, Feb. 20, 2002, at B5 (noting minor differences in numbers leaving welfare from control group not subject to time limits as those under new rules during same period); Joel F. Handler, *Welfare-to-Work: Reform or Rhetoric?*, 50 Admin. L. Rev. 635 (1998) (questioning causes of changes in welfare rolls and impact on recipients). *See also* Morgan B. Ward Doran & Dorothy E. Roberts, *Welfare Reform and Families in the Child Welfare System*, 61 Md. L. Rev. 386 (2002) (describing interaction of welfare reform and child welfare programs); Barbara L. Bezdek, *Contractual Welfare: Non-Accountability and Diminished Democracy in Local Government Contracts for Welfare-to-Work Services,* 28 Fordham Urb. L.J. 1559 (2001) (criticizing failure to monitor private implementation of programs); Matthew Diller, *Working Without a Job: The Social Messages of the New Workfare,* 9 Stan. L. & Pol'y Rev. 19 (1998) (criticizing workfare programs).

Dorothy Roberts argues that the failure to enact universal programs to benefit working people is rooted in past and present racism in the United States.

DOROTHY E. ROBERTS

Welfare and the Problem of Black Citizenship
105 Yale L.J. 1563, 1569–74, 1576, 1578, 1588–91 (1996) (reviewing Linda Gordon, *Pitied But Not Entitled: Single Mothers and the History of Welfare* (1994) and Jill Quadagno, *The Color of Welfare: How Racism Undermined the War on Poverty* (1994))

Although much of the American public now views welfare dependency as a Black cultural trait, the welfare system systematically excluded Black people for most of its history. * * *

Immigrant women, who [Progressive] reformers incorrectly believed made up a disproportionate share of deserted wives and illegitimate mothers, became the primary objects of reformers' moral concern. Worried about urban immigrants' threat to the social order, the reformers treated welfare as a means of supervising and disciplining recipients as much as a means of providing charity. According to this social work perspective, the cure for single mothers' poverty lay in socializing foreign relief recipients to conform to "American" family standards. Thus, aid generally was conditioned on compliance with "suitable home" provisions and often administered by juvenile court judges who specialized in punitive and rehabilitative judgments.

Black single mothers, on the other hand, were simply excluded. The first maternalist welfare legislation was intended for white mothers only: Administrators either failed to establish programs in locations with large Black populations or distributed benefits according to standards that disqualified Black mothers. As a result, in 1931 the first national survey of mothers' pensions broken down by race found that only three percent of recipients were Black. The exclusivity of mothers' aid programs coincided with the entrenchment of formal racial segregation—another Progressive reform intended to strengthen social order.

* * * [Linda] Gordon demonstrates the welfare movement's *ideological* loss that resulted from excluding Black women by contrasting the elite white reformers' programs with the welfare vision of Black women activists of the era. Although Black women reformers also relied on motherhood as a political platform, their approach to women's economic role differed dramatically from that of their privileged, white counterparts. Black women eschewed the viability of the family wage and women's economic dependence on men. Instead, they accepted married women's employment as a necessity, advocating assistance for working mothers.

* * *

The New Deal solidified welfare's stratification along racial as well as gender lines. * * * In addition [to the systematic exclusion of Blacks from social insurance benefits,] New Deal public works programs blatantly discriminated against Blacks, offering them the most menial jobs and paying them sometimes half of what white workers earned. Even Aid to Dependent Children was created primarily for white mothers, who were not expected to work; the relatively few Black recipients received smaller stipends on the ground that "blacks needed less to live on than whites."

[Jill] Quadagno connects racial politics both to the enactment and to the dismantling of the 1960s welfare programs that followed. She interprets the War on Poverty as an effort to eliminate the racial barriers of the New Deal programs and to integrate Blacks into the national political economy. For example, the Office of Economic Opportunity used federal funds to empower community action groups run by local Black activists; federal affirmative action and job-training programs broke longstanding racial barriers to union jobs; the Department of Housing and Urban Development gave housing subsidies to the poor.

At the same time, the National Welfare Rights Organization, a grassroots movement composed of welfare mothers, joined forces with neighborhood welfare rights centers and legal services lawyers to agitate for major changes in the welfare system's eligibility and procedural rules. This welfare rights movement secured entitlements to benefits, raised benefit levels, and increased availability of benefits to families headed by women. As a result, "by 1967, a welfare caseload that had once been eighty-six percent white had become forty-six percent non-white."

But Black welfare activists won a Pyrrhic victory. As Gordon notes, they got themselves included "not in social insurance but mainly in public assistance programs, which by then had become even stingier and more dishonorable than they had been originally." As AFDC became increasingly associated with Black mothers already stereotyped as lazy, irresponsible, and overly fertile, it became increasingly burdened with behavior modification, work requirements, and reduced effective benefit levels. Social Security, on the other hand, effectively transferred income from Blacks to whites because Blacks have a lower life expectancy and pay a disproportionate share of taxes on earnings. Meanwhile, a white backlash had decimated the War on Poverty programs within a decade.

Supporters of a strong welfare state puzzle over the rejection of evidence that more generous and universal welfare programs would improve the quality of life for everyone. Why have Americans disdained basic protections, such as national health insurance, family allowances, and paid parental leave, that citizens of other industrialized nations take for granted? Why do Americans prefer a stingy welfare system that fosters a society marred by poverty, poor health, crime, and despair? * * *

Quadagno demonstrates that it was precisely the War on Poverty programs' link to Blacks' civil rights that doomed them: Whites opposed them as an infringement of their economic right to discriminate against Blacks and a threat to white political power. President Nixon abolished the Office of Economic Opportunity in 1973, nine years after its creation, when its extension of political rights to Blacks through local community action agencies appeared to foment rebellion in cities such as Newark. At a time when European trade unions were fighting for full-employment policies and more comprehensive welfare provisions, the AFL-CIO defended its "property right" to exclude Blacks from its ranks and opposed the civil rights campaign for an open labor market. Peaking in 1968, federal housing subsidies underwent a precipitous decline when white homeowners backed by the powerful real estate lobby adamantly resisted residential integration.

For Quadagno, our deficient welfare state is "the price the nation still pays for failing to fully incorporate African Americans into the national community." Privileged racial identity gives whites a powerful incentive to leave the existing social order intact. White Americans therefore have been unwilling to create social programs that will facilitate Blacks' full citizenship, *even when those programs would benefit whites*. Even white workers' and feminist movements have compromised their most radical dreams in order to strike political bargains that sacrifice the rights of Blacks. W.E.B. Du Bois explained white resistance to labor and education reform during Reconstruction by the fact that poor and laboring whites preferred to be compensated by the "public and psychological wage" of racial superiority. Derrick Bell has similarly argued that whites in America—even those who lack wealth and power—believe that they gain from continued economic disparities that leave Blacks at the bottom. In his most recent exposition of this thesis, Bell dismally concludes, "Black people will never gain full equality in this country." Thus, opposition to Black citizenship has had a profound impact on our conception of welfare: It not only denied Blacks benefits to which whites were entitled; it also constrained the meaning of citizenship for all Americans.

* * *

Race helps to explain why the maternalist rhetoric that propelled welfare reform during the Progressive Era has lost all its persuasive force. While mothers' aid at the outset of this century supported white women in exchange for their valuable caretaking, welfare reform at the end of the century castigates Black single mothers whose work in the home is devalued. Because the public views Black mothers as "less fit, less caring, and less hurt by separation from their children," it seems inconceivable to compensate their domestic contribution and natural to make them work outside the home. More generally, Black single mothers are the target of measures that cut back benefits to welfare recipients and that attempt to reform their behavior because they are not considered to be citizens.

* * *

* * * Current welfare reform rhetoric condemns mothers who receive AFDC for transmitting a pathology of "welfare dependency" to their children. According to this view, reliance on this form of welfare reflects a lack of work ethic and leads to a myriad of social problems, including crime, unwed motherhood, and long-term poverty. Yet Americans do not view reliance on Social Security as "dependency" at all, despite the program's strong redistributive effects and the millions of nonworking wives and children who in fact depend on its benefits for subsistence. Gordon gives the following example of the downward-spiraling process that results from stigmatizing welfare recipients:

> The stigmas of "welfare" and of single motherhood intersect; hostility to the poor and hostility to deviant family forms reinforce each other. The resentment undercuts political support for the program, and benefits fall farther and farther behind inflation. The resulting immiseration makes poor single mothers even more needy and less politically attractive. The economic downturn of the last

decade has deepened both the poverty and the resentment, and created the impression that we are experiencing a new, unprecedented, and primarily minority social problem. * * *

* * *

Universal programs that benefit all citizens would constitute a significant improvement over the current, inadequate system. National health insurance, for example, would secure desperately needed medical care for the thirty-nine million, mostly working poor, Americans who are currently uninsured. Child allowances would similarly provide an important assurance of children's well-being and eliminate the less visible system of income tax deductions that benefits only those with high enough incomes to take advantage of it. Earned income tax credits offer similar advantages: By subsidizing low-wage jobs, they "blur the distinction between the single parent family moving off welfare, or combining welfare and work, and the non-welfare family."

Faith in universalism, however, underestimates America's problem with Black citizenship. Universalist solutions center on eliminating the stigma that welfare's stratification places on Black Americans, but overlook the degree of white Americans' unwillingness to accept Blacks as full citizens in the first place. Universalism focuses on implementing restructured programs without paying sufficient attention to the social forces that structured the current stratified system and that have similarly stratified every other aspect of American society. Some advocates of universal programs naively believe that the barriers to Black citizenship stem from flaws in welfare policy itself, rather than from the racism that drives those policies.

Universal programs are inadequate for three reasons. First, universal programs alone constitute an improbable guarantee that the poor will receive sufficient benefits. Universal programs have a "trickle-up" effect: Programs designed to benefit all citizens, rich and poor, are likely to benefit rich citizens the most because they have greater political and economic resources to structure programs to their advantage. At the very least, universal benefits must be supplemented with need-based programs to ensure that those at the bottom actually receive adequate aid. Benefits that provide the necessities of a decent life—housing, nutrition, adequate income, jobs for unskilled workers—must be administered directly to those who need them, or the very poor risk falling below the minimum level of welfare.

Second, universal programs do not attempt to dismantle the institutionalized impediments to Blacks' social and economic citizenship. They leave racist social structures in place, relying on the distribution of benefits to relieve the problems these structures create. Universal programs are subject to Iris Marion Young's criticism of the distributive definition of justice: By focusing attention on the allocation of material goods, Young argues, the distributive paradigm fails to scrutinize the institutional context that helps to determine distributive patterns. I have a similar fear about universalism's effort to maneuver around racism.

The process of making programs race-neutral and therefore more palatable to white Americans is likely to weaken their power to eradicate systemic oppression.

Finally, and most devastatingly, universal programs are hindered by their ultimate appeal to the public's self-interest. Strategizing to expand the welfare state has involved devising ways to convince Americans that helping others is in their own interest. Social Security retains its political popularity because it appeals to Americans' individual self-interest: It is perceived as an insurance program in which beneficiaries recoup what they contributed. Social theorists have noted the political attractiveness of using the Social Security model for other welfare programs; even liberal theories of justice rely on a model of self-insurance.

White supremacy, however, complicates reformers' reliance on universalism and self-interest to promote the welfare state. The assumption that universal programs are intrinsically appealing because they benefit everyone crumbles in the face of racism. Many white Americans remain uninterested in advancing the welfare of Black Americans; many others see helping everyone as contrary to their self-interest because they perceive Black people's social position in opposition to their own. Under American racist ideology, universal programs that benefit Blacks are necessarily antithetical to white interests because Blacks' social advancement diminishes white superiority.

Indeed, the popularity of "universal" social insurance programs has hinged on their formal or effective exclusion of Black people. New Deal reformers could promote Social Security as a universal program designed to benefit all classes only by first disqualifying most Black workers. "Instead of a 'universal' welfare state that could create solidarity among workers," Quadagno notes, "the New Deal welfare state instituted a regime that reinforced racial inequality." Ironically, then, while universal programs are advocated as a pragmatic means of racial inclusion, their implementation realistically may depend on racial exclusion. Quadagno defines universalism as "benefits granted as a right of citizenship." Perhaps universalism is the only politically feasible strategy for expanding the welfare state; but until Blacks are counted as citizens, they will never receive purportedly universal entitlements—even if denying entitlements to Blacks means denying needed benefits to everyone.

Notes and Questions

1. Would the vision of black women during the Progressive Era—that working mothers deserved state assistance—have created a better program for all mothers? Do you agree that universal programs that would benefit families in the United States have been defeated by racism—even when those defeats ultimately hurt white people as well as nonwhites?

2. Is Roberts correct that Social Security is not seen as dependency? Do you agree that excluding most African Americans from Social

Security in its early years helped establish it as a "universal" program in the eyes of the public?

3. Roberts attributes to racism the willingness to use welfare—as opposed to Social Security—as a method of controlling the behavior of recipients. The next section explores one of the most controversial provisions enacted by many states under the Temporary Assistance to Needy Families (TANF) program—the exclusion from eligibility for benefits of children conceived after a parent begins receiving welfare.

D. Sex and Dependency

The modern family cap is a provision in some state welfare laws that denies an increase in benefits when children are born into families already on welfare. For example, a family that has three children when first applying for welfare receives assistance for all three children. In contrast, if a family has two children at the time of application and another child is conceived and born after the start of welfare benefits, assistance continues to be paid for only two children.

First enacted through waivers of federal requirements under AFDC, the caps were widely adopted after the passage of the new welfare act in 1996 as the states created TANF programs. The caps differ from the regulation at issue in *Dandridge* in that they explicitly exclude some children in a family while supporting others. Further, they apply whether the family has one child or many when they first receive welfare. The cap is based on two related beliefs: that welfare recipients had children in order to increase the size of their monthly grants and that economic penalties would encourage "responsible" child-bearing decisions.

When these clauses were first implemented, Lucy Williams criticized these beliefs:

> [T]he underlying assumptions of Family Cap proposals—that AFDC mothers have many children, that they have free access to medical options for family planning, and that they get pregnant in order to receive additional benefits—are unsound. In fact, as of 1990, the average AFDC family, including adults, had 2.9 members; 72.5% of all families on AFDC had only one or two children, and almost 90% had three or fewer children. These figures are no larger than those found among two-parent families in the general population. Moreover, AFDC family size has declined substantially; in 1969, 32.5% of AFDC families had four or more children, and in 1990, only 9.9% had four or more children. * * *
>
> Furthermore, for those women who wish to terminate their pregnancies, neither abortion facilities nor government funding are necessarily available.

Lucy A. Williams, *The Ideology of Division: Behavior Modification Welfare Reform Proposals*, 102 Yale L.J. 719, 737–38 (1992).

There are many reasons why AFDC mothers become pregnant or remain pregnant, including among others: unplanned pregnancies, the belief that a child solidifies a relationship with the father, and the meaning of having a child or giving a grandchild to one's own mother. Williams compares these reasons with those of middle-class mothers:

> Most people do not view having a baby as the prize for having made it economically, nor do they have a child to gain an additional tax deduction for a dependent. Just like AFDC recipients, they want to be parents and to share their lives with a child. * * *
>
> Empirical studies have consistently documented the lack of a correlation between the receipt of AFDC benefits and the child-bearing decisions of unmarried women—even for young, unmarried women. * * *
>
> Furthermore, the incremental increase that an AFDC family receives when a new child enters the family is so small that it does not even cover such basic essentials as diapers, clothing, bottles and formula. In Wisconsin, for example, an additional third child adds $100 to the grant; in New Jersey, $64; in Mississippi, $24. Thus if economics were really the driving factor in an AFDC mother's decision to have a child, she would make the "rational" decision not to do so.

Id. at 739–40.

WENDY CHAVKIN, TAMMY A. DRAUT, DIANA ROMERO & PAUL H. WISE

Sex, Reproduction, and Welfare Reform
7 Geo. J. on Poverty L. & Pol'y 379, 380–83, 388–90, 393 (2000)

* * * [E]mbedded in [the Personal Responsibility and Work Opportunity Reconciliation Act (PRWORA) of 1996] is a vision of socially desirable family formation, expressed in terms of individual sexual, reproductive, and childrearing goals. As outlined in § 601 of the law, the purpose of the legislation is to accomplish the following goals:

> 1. Provide assistance to needy families so that children may be cared for in their own homes or in the homes of relatives;
>
> 2. End the dependence of needy parents on government benefits by promoting job preparation, work, and marriage;
>
> 3. Prevent and reduce the incidence of out-of-wedlock pregnancies and establish annual numerical goals for preventing and reducing the incidence of these pregnancies; and
>
> 4. Encourage the formation and maintenance of two-parent families.

PRWORA provided increased flexibility to the states, allowing them to translate these policy aspirations into concrete amendments to their state welfare programs.

Many states have adopted policies intended to mold reproductive and parental decision-making through a series of economic disincentives.

* * * These policies include: family caps on benefits, immunization requirements, family planning mandates, abstinence education, and policies directed toward decreasing out-of-wedlock births. * * *

It is our opinion that the welfare reform law fails to address the underlying issue of poverty. Rather, under the rubric of reform, these policies emphasize change in individual sexual and reproductive behaviors in a manner that raises serious concerns about ethics and efficacy. * * *

* * * Although PRWORA itself is silent on the issue of family caps in that it does not require or prohibit states from adopting the measure, a total of twenty-three states have decided to continue waiver era policies or to create new ones since the passage of the federal law.

During the period preceding passage of PRWORA, nineteen states had received waivers to implement some version of a family cap. Of the fourteen states that were first to receive their waivers, only half have conducted or completed the required evaluations. Only two states, New Jersey and Arkansas, completed evaluations using experimental designs comparing outcomes to AFDC recipients subjected to the family cap with those who were not. * * * [D]ue to the fact that the provisions were embedded in multifaceted program changes, they were difficult to assess in isolation. Arkansas reported no effect on birth rates, nor on other outcome indicators such as paternity identification, income, exits, and entrances to AFDC. The investigators found that approximately half of the women were not even fertile, either because of previous sterilization or postmenopausal status (grandmothers caring for children). The New Jersey analysis revealed a significant decrease in birth rates, especially for those newly joining AFDC, and an increase in both family planning utilization and abortion rates, again especially for new welfare cases. According to the Center for Law and Social Policy, more than 83,000 children in sixteen states have been born to families under the family cap provisions—meaning that these children and their families have to get by on a reduced per capita income.

An additional five of the first fourteen states to implement family cap waivers have surveyed AFDC caseworkers and recipients about their attitudes regarding the family cap. In Arizona, Delaware, and Indiana, many caseworkers reported doubts that the cap would influence fertility as they did not believe recipients' childbearing decisions had ever been motivated by the prospect of a grant increase. Client surveys in Arkansas confirmed this, with over 90% saying that the AFDC grant was not a factor in their decisions about childbearing. The majority of New Jersey respondents reported that financial insecurity was a reason to avoid pregnancy but did not see the loss of a grant increment in this light.

* * * Five states require a parent to return to work sooner when she gives birth to a "capped" child. Specifically, a woman who has a baby once she is a TANF recipient may be required to return to work within 3 months, whereas she might not have to return to work for one year if she already had an infant (*i.e.*, non-capped child) when she applied for

TANF. Most states provide exemptions from family cap sanctions for children born as a result of rape, incest, or domestic violence. One state, California, exempts children born as a result of contraceptive failure. * * *

* * *

There are several dramatic demographic developments that took place over the last several decades (referred to as the second demographic transition): decline in birth rates overall, as well as among teens; later age at first childbirth; a decrease in marriage together with an increase in divorce; and, a concomitant rise in out-of-wedlock childbearing.

While it is true that these patterns vary somewhat across socioeconomic status and racial/ethnic groupings, it is also true that they pertain to all. To wit, in the U.S., while the rate of out-of-wedlock births is higher among poor and Black women, the rate of out-of-wedlock deliveries has increased dramatically among White women—and this latter group contributes the greatest absolute number. * * * Similarly, poor Black and Hispanic women have higher teen birth rates than do White teens—but the rate of teen births to Black women has also declined more steeply than any other group. * * *

Much of the rise in divorce, deferred childbearing, and out-of-wedlock births has been attributed to women's participation in the paid labor force. Whatever the complicated socioeconomic causes may be, these are widespread persistent developments affecting all Western industrialized countries. Out-of-wedlock births rose during the last two decades in the United Kingdom, Germany, and Italy (although Italy's rate remains very low). In fact, the United States' out-of-wedlock birth rate practically mirrors that of the United Kingdom since 1990. * * *

Although the U.S. profile is similar to that of Western European industrialized nations, some features are exaggerated in this country. The teen pregnancy and birth rates here have been much higher and are currently almost double those of the United Kingdom despite the fact that levels of teen sexual activity are similar. The high frequency of teen pregnancy and births in the U.S. has been variously attributed to less access to contraception and to more "religiosity," which in turn may constrict education and comfort with sex.

* * *

[A short period of upward trend in teen births during the economic recession in the late 1980s and early 1990s may have been taken out of context by policymakers and used to justify the policies under discussion here.]

We assert the critical importance of accurately defining the problem and not mistaking symptoms for causes. For example, what is the problem with out-of-wedlock childbearing? The problem is a lack of paternal affection, caretaking, and monetary support which causes hardship for both the child and mother. The solution is not wedlock, as too often these problems arise in marriages, and certainly following divorce.

The Scandinavian countries tackle this concern very differently by trying to create a series of incentives and infrastructural changes to encourage and sustain paternal participation in childrearing.

* * *

The real issue is that too many U.S. women and children live in poverty. These policies have not redressed the grave income inequalities that typify the U.S. Indeed, the number and percentage of children living in poverty has grown. Rather than misdirecting policies and resources toward constricting individuals' sexual and reproductive choices, we should concentrate on bolstering education and employment opportunities. * * *

Notes and Questions

1. Since 1996, about half the states have enacted laws excluding children conceived while their parents receive welfare from benefits or restricting the benefits that can be paid to those children. Family caps have been upheld against initial challenges, with federal and state courts concluding, citing *Dandridge*, that the legislation had a rational basis. *See, e.g.*, C.K. v. Shalala, 883 F.Supp. 991 (D.N.J.1995) *aff'd sub nom* C.K. v. New Jersey Dep't of Health and Human Services, 92 F.3d 171 (3d Cir. 1996) (holding that the family cap did not deprive children of benefits because of parental behavior but "merely imposes a ceiling on the benefits accorded to a AFDC household while permitting an additional child to share in that 'capped' family income.") In N.B. v. Sybinski, 724 N.E.2d 1103 (Ind.App.2000), recipients alleged that capping cash benefits to TANF families but funding the same children if they lived with a qualified caretaker outside the home lacked a rational basis and infringed on the right of family association. The Indiana appellate court found the effect on the family was incidental and did not require heightened review: "The State has merely chosen not to subsidize the parents' fundamental right [to have children] by removing the automatic benefit increase associated with an additional child under the AFDC." *Id.* at 1109.

2. There are differences between the state statutes that may seem technical but can be crucial to the well being of the children and their parents. The child may be disqualified from assistance for life, or for as long as it lives with its biological parents (or with the household into which it was born while receiving welfare). A child who is not disqualified may receive a diminished benefit. If the child lives with caretaker who is not the recipient parent, the child may be qualified for future benefits after a period of time. The mother may be required to work more quickly after the birth of a "capped" child than would have been required after the birth of a child not subject to the cap. Most states that have a clause excluding these children make an exception if the birth was the result of rape or incest. The PRWORA permits but does not require states to enact these exclusionary restrictions. Therefore, the

effect and constitutionality of each state law must be analyzed separately.

The Indiana family cap provides an example:

> Under Indiana's former AFDC program, when an AFDC recipient gave birth to a child, the family's AFDC benefits were increased by approximately $59 a month to provide for the needs of the newborn. The family cap provision, however, eliminates the automatic increase provided under AFDC. Under the family cap rule, TANF assistance is not provided to a child who is born to a TANF recipient ten or more months following the month in which the family began receiving benefits. There are four exceptions in which the welfare grant will be increased upon the birth of an additional child: 1) when the child was conceived through incest or sexual assault; 2) when the child is born to a minor included in an AFDC grant who becomes a first-time minor parent; 3) when the child does not reside with his or her parent; and 4) when the child was conceived in a month that the family was not on TANF. Although they do not receive an increase in cash benefits, children subject to the family cap remain eligible for other benefits including vouchers for food products through the Women-Infants-Children's program, food stamps, and Medicaid payments.

N.B. v. Sybinski, 724 N.E. 2d at 1106.

The Indiana provision is typical in its emphasis on the timing of the conception of the child, in its exception for rape or incest, and in being drafted to permit Medicaid and some non-cash benefits to be available to excluded children. How is the Indiana "family cap" different from the provision at issue in *Dandridge*? How is it similar?

3. The Georgia exclusion clause states that "the recipient family in which the recipient parent *gives birth to an additional child* during the recipient's period of eligibility for TANF assistance * * * may not receive additional assistance," but creates an exception "in cases in which the birth of a child is the result of a *verifiable* rape or incest." Code of Georgia, § 49-4-186 (emphasis added).

Does the phrase "gives birth to" in the Georgia statute apply to both men and women recipients? Do men "give birth to" children? If not, does this language mean that only the children of *female* recipients will be disqualified? Does the emphasis on both birth and rape mean that the state cared most about the behavior of female recipients and was not very concerned about male recipients?

4. Since rape is an exception to the family cap/child exclusion provision, the state law of rape is important to the definition of benefits. Two Indiana cases reveal the difficulty with basing welfare benefits on rape law. In Jones v. State, 589 N.E.2d 241 (Ind.1992), a man came into the room of a young woman who lived with her foster mother in his home. He asked her to have sex with him three times, and she said "no" each time. He turned her over and had sexual intercourse; she did not

resist. The court reversed his conviction, holding there was inadequate force to prove rape. In Gilliam v. State, 509 N.E.2d 815 (Ind.1987), two men broke into the home where a young woman was staying with her mother and children. One of them pushed her down on the bed and had intercourse with her; she did not resist. The court affirmed the defendant's conviction for rape, holding that physical resistance was not required if the victim was in fear of bodily harm. In both cases, the women testified that they had not cried out for help because they were afraid. If the Indiana family cap had applied to welfare benefits for these two women and their families, children born of the act in *Gilliam* would have been qualified for welfare benefits, but children born of the act in *Jones* would not.

Does state assistance to a child turn upon whether its mother consented to sex or on whether she forcibly resisted? Or does eligibility turn on whether a court would have found that, under the circumstances, forcible resistance was not required in order for an aggressive sexual act to be rape? Is rape a rational way for states to distinguish between children? Is it a sex discriminatory standard, because the qualification of children for benefits depends on their *mother's* acts of resistance at the moment of intercourse? If the state does *not* have a rape exception, what circumstances ultimately determine the child's qualification for welfare?

5. Although the great majority of adult recipients of AFDC were women when Congress enacted welfare reform, 13% of adult recipients of AFDC were men in 1995–96. Research and Evaluation Division of Data Collection and Analysis, Administration for Children and Families Office of Planning, Department of Health and Human Services, *Characteristics and Financial Circumstances of AFDC Recipients FY1996, Aid to Families with Dependent Children October 1995–September 1996.* If both male and female welfare recipients might have sex and reproduce, why should it be the woman's consent which is dispositive as to the benefits for the child?

6. If the goal of welfare reform is to build parental responsibility, do time limits on receipt of benefits accomplish that goal without inquiry into the sexual act in which the child was conceived? Indiana allows families to receive benefits for only twenty-four months. Recipients are subject to work requirements. The exclusion provision only applies to children born ten months after the family begins receiving assistance. Therefore, the restriction will affect benefits for a maximum of fourteen months, or even less time for a child conceived after the family has received welfare for more time. Under these circumstances, does the distinction between children whose parents had consensual sex and those who did not actually further the goal of building responsibility in welfare recipients?

7. What political and social messages are sent by the child exclusion clauses? Are these messages aimed only at welfare recipients—or are they part of a larger social and political statement about the

deserving and undeserving poor? If so, do they replace a discussion about the importance to all families of programs like support for child care, currently associated with welfare? Why would working- and middle-class families accept a discourse that condemns welfare recipients rather than one that demands better resources for all? *See* Herbert J. Gans, *The War Against the Poor: The Underclass and Antipoverty Policy* (1995) (arguing that stereotypes of the poor help maintain social control of working- and middle-class people).

*

Chapter 9

PARTICIPATION IN DEMOCRATIC SOCIETY

The United States Constitution originally denied participation in democratic government to women of all races and Native-American and African-American men. Struggles throughout this nation's history, including the Civil War which led to the passage of the Thirteenth, Fourteenth, and Fifteenth Amendments and the suffrage movement which led to the passage of the Nineteenth Amendment, show that participation in democracy was highly contested.

In the modern era, the nation accepts the idea of participation in democracy as a basic right for United States' citizens, and the extension of that right around the world is an aspirational goal. This chapter considers legal developments in three areas that are part of participating in democratic society: voting, which has been recognized as a fundamental right by the United States Supreme Court; education, which has been recognized as a fundamental right by some state supreme courts; and the right to call on the state for protection against harm, which is highly contested in several fields, including child protection and domestic violence. As you read this chapter, consider how social justice lawyers working with communities to bring about legal change may succeed or fail through litigation.

Perhaps the most widely acclaimed success story of using law for social change would be the multi-year litigation strategy, employed by Thurgood Marshall, Charles Hamilton Houston, and the NAACP, culminating in Brown v. Board of Education, 347 U.S. 483 (1954). Theorizing on how to overturn Plessy v. Ferguson, 163 U.S. 537 (1896), and its "separate but equal" doctrine justifying racial segregation, the NAACP developed a litigation plan, using a series of cases involving education, to demonstrate the incompatibility of segregation with equality. Richard Kluger, *Simple Justice: The History of* Brown v. Board of Education *and Black America's Struggle for Equality* 134–37 (1975). (In 1939, a tiny enclave became an offshoot of the parent NAACP organization. According to Kluger, "Set up to take advantage of new laws granting tax-empt status to non-profit organizations that did not have a lobbying function as their principal purpose, the offshoot was formally called the NAACP

Legal Defense and Educational Fund, Inc. That was, everyone agreed, rather a mouthful. For short, it was called the Legal Defense Fund. For shorter, it became 'the Inc. Fund.' In time, it would be just 'the Fund.' " *Id.* at 221. Although initially, the Fund was the litigation arm of the NAACP, today the two entities are independent. Following the lead of the Fund, later groups developed as the Asian American Legal Defense and Education Fund, the Mexican American Legal Defense and Educational Fund, and the Puerto Rican Legal Defense and Education Fund.)

Marshall, Houston, and their allies tackled legal education in several cases, including Sweatt v. Painter, 339 U.S. 629 (1950). The University of Texas Law School had denied admission to Heman Sweatt, who was African American. The State argued that Sweatt could attend another law school, created for African-American students. Examining this contention, Chief Justice Vinson, for the court, considered the meaning of legal education to an aspiring lawyer:

> The University of Texas Law School, from which petitioner was excluded, was staffed by a faculty of sixteen full-time and three part-time professors, some of whom are nationally recognized authorities in their field. Its student body numbered 850. The library contained over 65,000 volumes. Among the other facilities available to the students were a law review, moot court facilities, scholarship funds, and Order of the Coif affiliation. The school's alumni occupy the most distinguished positions in the private practice of the law and in the public life of the State. It may properly be considered one of the nation's ranking law schools.
>
> The law school for Negroes which was to have opened in February, 1947, would have had no independent faculty or library. The teaching was to be carried on by four members of the University of Texas Law School faculty, who were to maintain their offices at the University of Texas while teaching at both institutions. Few of the 10,000 volumes ordered for the library had arrived; nor was there any full-time librarian. The school lacked accreditation.
>
> Since the trial of this case, respondents report the opening of a law school at the Texas State University for Negroes. It is apparently on the road to full accreditation. It has a faculty of five full-time professors; a student body of 23; a library of some 16,500 volumes serviced by a full-time staff; a practice court and legal aid association; and one alumnus who has become a member of the Texas Bar.
>
> Whether the University of Texas Law School is compared with the original or the new law school for Negroes, we cannot find substantial equality in the educational opportunities offered white and Negro law students by the State. In terms of number of the faculty, variety of courses and opportunity for specialization, size of the student body, scope of the library, availability of law review and similar activities, the University of Texas Law School is superior. What is more important, the University of Texas Law School pos-

sesses to a far greater degree those qualities which are incapable of objective measurement but which make for greatness in a law school. Such qualities, to name but a few, include reputation of the faculty, experience of the administration, position and influence of the alumni, standing in the community, traditions and prestige. It is difficult to believe that one who had a free choice between these law schools would consider the question close.

Moreover, although the law is a highly learned profession, we are well aware that it is an intensely practical one. The law school, the proving ground for legal learning and practice, cannot be effective in isolation from the individuals and institutions with which the law interacts. Few students and no one who has practiced law would choose to study in an academic vacuum, removed from the interplay of ideas and the exchange of views with which the law is concerned. The law school to which Texas is willing to admit petitioner excludes from its student body members of the racial groups which number 85% of the population of the State and include most of the lawyers, witnesses, jurors, judges and other officials with whom petitioner will inevitably be dealing when he becomes a member of the Texas Bar. With such a substantial and significant segment of society excluded, we cannot conclude that the education offered petitioner is substantially equal to that which he would receive if admitted to the University of Texas Law School.

It may be argued that excluding petitioner from that school is no different from excluding white students from the new law school. This contention overlooks realities. It is unlikely that a member of a group so decisively in the majority, attending a school with rich traditions and prestige which only a history of consistently maintained excellence could command, would claim that the opportunities afforded him for legal education were unequal to those held open to petitioner. * * *

* * *

* * * [P]etitioner may claim his full constitutional right: legal education equivalent to that offered by the State to students of other races. Such education is not available to him in a separate law school as offered by the State. * * *

We hold that the Equal Protection Clause of the Fourteenth Amendment requires that petitioner be admitted to the University of Texas Law School.

339 U.S. at 632–36. Why did the Court believe the equal treatment of exclusion "overlooks realities?" Does this case support the notion that equal protection requires more than equal treatment?

The argument that a "separate" education was not "equal" finally won recognition from the Supreme Court in the landmark *Brown v. Board of Education* ruling. In finding racial segregation unconstitutional, the United States Supreme Court commented: "[E]ducation is perhaps the most important function of state and local governments. * * * It is required in the performance of our most basic public responsibilities * * *. It is the very foundation of good citizenship." 347 U.S. 483, 493 (1954).

Thus the court, in striking down the separate but equal doctrine, recognized the connection between education and voting. This chapter first examines the recent legal history of the voting rights movement and then returns to examine developments in both education and protection against harm.

SECTION 1. VOTING, COMMUNITY ACTIVISM, AND POLITICAL PARTICIPATION

Dr. Martin Luther King Jr. regarded voting as "the foundation stone for political action." James Thomas Tucker, *Affirmative Action and [Mis]representation: Part I—Reclaiming the Civil Rights Vision of the Right to Vote*, 43 How. L.J. 343 (1999). The history of the struggle over voting reveals a story of community activism using the tool of law. Education was a key component for organizers in the voting rights movement because many southern states required those seeking to register to vote to answer questions about state law. One aspect of the civil rights movement was the development of citizenship schools in southern states to teach aspiring voters the legal background necessary to answer voter registrar's questions. These schools developed through difficult community organizing under a specter of extreme violence.

Septima Clark describes one early effort, in the years following *Brown*, that occurred on Johns Island in South Carolina, where a farmer, Esau Jenkins, drove a bus that transported children to school and tobacco workers and longshoremen to Charleston. A resident, Ms. Alice Wines, asked Jenkins for help:

> "I don't have much schooling, Esau," she said to him. "I wasn't even able to get through the third grade. But I would like to be somebody. I'd like to hold up my head with other people; I'd like to be able to vote. Esau, if you'll help me a little when you have the time, I'll be glad to learn the laws and get qualified to vote. If I do, I promise you I'll register and I'll vote."

Septima Clark, *Septima Clark and the Civil Rights Movement: Ready From Within* 46 (Cynthia Stokes Brown ed., 1986).

Jenkins distributed laws about registration and voting to his passengers. He explained the requirements to those who couldn't read. Ms. Wines memorized the passages and registered to vote. But she wanted to learn to read and write. Jenkins, with help from Highlander Folk School in Monteagle, Tennessee, purchased a building. He established a grocery store in the front "to fool white people" and used two rooms in the back with no windows for teaching. *Id.* at 46–47.

Highlandor continued training teachers to return to their communities and start citizenship schools. By Spring 1961 eighty-two teachers were holding classes in Alabama, Georgia, South Carolina, and Tennessee. *Id.* at 60. *See also* Taylor Branch, *Parting the Waters: America in the King Years 1954–63* 480–95 (1988) (detailing the efforts to register voters in Mississippi).

The drive to register voters and the continued exclusionary practices that prevented African Americans from voting led to the Voting Rights Act of 1965 (with amendments in 1982), 42 U.S.C. § 1973 (1994). The Court described the Voting Rights Act in South Carolina v. Katzenbach, 383 U.S. 301 (1966).

> The Voting Rights Act of 1965 reflects Congress' firm intention to rid the country of racial discrimination in voting. The heart of the Act is a complex scheme of stringent remedies aimed at areas where voting discrimination has been most flagrant. Section 4(a)-(d) lays down a formula defining the States and political subdivisions to which these new remedies apply. The first of the remedies * * * is the suspension of literacy tests and similar voting qualifications for a period of five years from the last occurrence of substantial voting discrimination. Section 5 prescribes a second remedy, the suspension of all new voting regulations pending review by federal authorities to determine whether their use would perpetuate voting discrimination. The third remedy, covered in §§ 6(b), 7, 9, and 13 (a), is the assignment of federal examiners on certification by the Attorney General to list qualified applicants who are thereafter entitled to vote in all elections.
>
> Other provisions of the Act prescribe subsidiary cures for persistent voting discrimination. * * * [The Act] authorizes the appointment of federal poll-watchers in places to which federal examiners have already been assigned * * * [,] excuses those made eligible to vote * * * [by] the Act from paying accumulated past poll taxes for state and local elections * * * [, and] provides for balloting by persons denied access to the polls in areas where federal examiners have been appointed.
>
> The remaining remedial portions of the Act are aimed at voting discrimination in any area of the country where it may occur. Section 2 broadly prohibits the use of voting rules to abridge exercise of the franchise on racial grounds. * * * [Other sections] strengthen existing procedures for attacking voting discrimination by means of litigation. * * * [The Act] excuses citizens educated in American schools conducted in a foreign language from passing English-language literacy tests * * * [,] facilitates constitutional litigation challenging the imposition of all poll taxes for state and local elections * * * [and,] authorize[s] civil and criminal sanctions against interference with the exercise of rights guaranteed by the Act.

383 U.S. at 315–16.

Even after the landmark legal change represented by the passage of the Voting Rights Act, lawyers continued to work with community leaders who were prosecuted for trying to help African-American citizens to vote by absentee ballot. *See* Lani Guinier, *Lift Every Voice* 183–219 (1998). *See also* J.L. Chestnut, Jr. & Julia Cass, *Black in Selma: The Uncommon Life of J.L. Chestnut, Jr.* 257–71 (1990) ("Almost every step of progress for black people required either a confrontation—a lawsuit, a boycott, a march, or the threat of them—or a federal regulation * * * ." *Id.* at 268.).

A. Voting and Equality

The year after the passage of the 1965 Voting Rights Act, the Supreme Court addressed the constitutionality of the poll tax.

HARPER v. VIRGINIA STATE BOARD OF ELECTIONS

383 U.S. 663 (1966)

MR. JUSTICE DOUGLAS delivered the opinion of the Court.

These are suits by Virginia residents to have declared unconstitutional Virginia's poll tax.[1]

* * *

While the right to vote in federal elections is conferred by Art. I, § 2, of the Constitution, the right to vote in state elections is nowhere expressly mentioned. It is argued that the right to vote in state elections is implicit, particularly by reason of the First Amendment and that it may not constitutionally be conditioned upon the payment of a tax or fee. We do not stop to canvass the relation between voting and political expression. For it is enough to say that once the franchise is granted to the electorate, lines may not be drawn which are inconsistent with the Equal Protection Clause of the Fourteenth Amendment. That is to say, the right of suffrage "is subject to the imposition of state standards which are not discriminatory and which do not contravene any restriction that Congress, acting pursuant to its constitutional powers, has imposed." * * *

We conclude that a State violates the Equal Protection Clause of the Fourteenth Amendment whenever it makes the affluence of the voter or payment of any fee an electoral standard. Voter qualifications have no relation to wealth nor to paying or not paying this or any other tax. Our cases demonstrate that the Equal Protection Clause of the Fourteenth Amendment restrains the States from fixing voter qualifications which invidiously discriminate. Thus without questioning the power of a State to impose reasonable residence restrictions on the availability of the

1. [Virginia assessed a poll tax as a precondition for voting.] * * * The poll tax * * * [was] often assessed along with the personal property tax. Those who do not pay a personal property tax are not assessed for a poll tax, it being their responsibility to take the initiative and request to be assessed. * * *

ballot, we held in *Carrington v. Rash*, 380 U.S. 89, that a State may not deny the opportunity to vote to a bona fide resident merely because he is a member of the armed services. * * * Previously we had said that neither homesite nor occupation "affords a permissible basis for distinguishing between qualified voters within the State." We think the same must be true of requirements of wealth or affluence or payment of a fee.

Long ago in *Yick Wo v. Hopkins*, 118 U.S. 356, 370, the Court referred to "the political franchise of voting" as a "fundamental political right, because preservative of all rights." Recently in *Reynolds v. Sims*, 377 U.S. 533, 561–562, we said, "Undoubtedly, the right of suffrage is a fundamental matter in a free and democratic society. Especially since the right to exercise the franchise in a free and unimpaired manner is preservative of other basic civil and political rights, any alleged infringement of the right of citizens to vote must be carefully and meticulously scrutinized." There we were considering charges that voters in one part of the State had greater representation per person in the State Legislature than voters in another part of the State. We concluded:

> "A citizen, a qualified voter, is no more nor no less so because he lives in the city or on the farm. This is the clear and strong command of our Constitution's Equal Protection Clause. This is an essential part of the concept of a government of laws and not men. This is at the heart of Lincoln's vision of 'government of the people, by the people, (and) for the people.' The Equal Protection Clause demands no less than substantially equal state legislative representation for all citizens, of all places as well as of all races." *Id.*, at 568.

We say the same whether the citizen, otherwise qualified to vote, has $1.50 in his pocket or nothing at all, pays the fee or fails to pay it. The principle that denies the State the right to dilute a citizen's vote on account of his economic status or other such factors by analogy bars a system which excludes those unable to pay a fee to vote or who fail to pay.

It is argued that a State may exact fees from citizens for many different kinds of licenses; that if it can demand from all an equal fee for a driver's license, it can demand from all an equal poll tax for voting. But we must remember that the interest of the State, when it comes to voting, is limited to the power to fix qualifications. Wealth, like race, creed, or color, is not germane to one's ability to participate intelligently in the electoral process. Lines drawn on the basis of wealth or property, like those of race, are traditionally disfavored. To introduce wealth or payment of a fee as a measure of a voter's qualifications is to introduce a capricious or irrelevant factor. The degree of the discrimination is irrelevant. In this context—that is, as a condition of obtaining a ballot—the requirement of fee paying causes an "invidious" discrimination that runs afoul of the Equal Protection Clause. * * *

* * *

In a recent searching re-examination of the Equal Protection Clause, we held, as already noted, that "the opportunity for equal participation by all voters in the election of state legislators'' is required. *Reynolds v. Sims, supra,* 377 U.S. at 566. We decline to qualify that principle by sustaining this poll tax. Our conclusion, like that in *Reynolds v. Sims,* is founded not on what we think governmental policy should be, but on what the Equal Protection Clause requires.

We have long been mindful that where fundamental rights and liberties are asserted under the Equal Protection Clause, classifications which might invade or restrain them must be closely scrutinized and carefully confined.

Those principles apply here. For to repeat, wealth or fee paying has, in our view, no relation to voting qualifications; the right to vote is too precious, too fundamental to be so burdened or conditioned.

Reversed.

Notes and Questions

1. How important is wealth in the electoral process? In Georgia State Conference of NAACP v. Cox, 183 F.3d 1259 (11th Cir.1999), voters and candidates for office challenged the Georgia campaign finance system, asserting that it excluded nonwealthy citizens from meaningful participation in the electoral process, thereby violating equal protection, freedom of expression, and freedom of association. Plaintiffs focused on the exemptions from limits on campaign contributions that continued to allow contributions made by a candidate or a member of the candidate's immediate family to the candidate's own campaign; the exemption for bona-fide loans made to a candidate or campaign committee; and the structure that permitted (with certain restrictions) a candidate, campaign committee, or public officer to carry forward funds from one campaign cycle to the next. They argued that the campaign finance system "prevents nonwealthy candidates from raising sufficient funds to run an effective campaign and prevents nonwealthy voters from contributing meaningfully to a candidate." They sought a declaratory judgment as to their rights and an order enjoining the challenged provisions unless the state provided "remedial measures that reduce the dominance of wealth in Georgia State Senate elections and provide an alternative public source of financing as well as meaningful contribution limits to enable non-wealthy voters and candidates to participate on an equal and meaningful basis in the state senate election process and to be heard in that process." 183 F.3d at 1261–62.

The plaintiffs' argument about exclusion from the political process relied on Terry v. Adams, 345 U.S. 461 (1953).

> In *Terry,* the Supreme Court addressed the continuing efforts by white citizens, including state-sanctioned actors, to exclude blacks from exercising their right to vote. Each spring, before the official Democratic Party Primary, the private Jaybird Democratic Association would conduct a pre-primary to endorse candidates for election, using the same process provided for by Texas state law

> governing primary elections, but permitting only whites to vote. Endorsed candidates then entered the democratic primary. These candidates usually went unchallenged because candidates did not enter the race apart from the Jaybird primary system. As the Court noted, the official elections "became no more than perfunctory ratifiers of the choice that [had] already been made [in the Jaybird primary]." In concluding the Jaybird primary violated the Fifteenth Amendment, the Court reasoned "[t]he Jaybird primary has become an integral part, indeed the only effective part, of the elective process that determines who shall rule and govern in the county." 345 U.S. at 469–76.

183 F.3d at 1263.

The Eleventh Circuit Court of Appeals distinguished *Terry* as concerning only access to the ballot, which had not been denied by the Georgia campaign finance system, and held that,

> The ballot access cases * * * do not recognize the right to equal influence in the overall electoral process. *See FEC v. Massachusetts Citizens For Life, Inc.,* 479 U.S. 238, 257 (1986) ("Political 'free trade' does not necessarily require that all who participate in the political marketplace do so with exactly equal resources."); *Buckley v. Valeo,* 424 U.S. at 48–49 ("[T]he concept that government may restrict the speech of some elements of our society in order to enhance the relative voice of others is wholly foreign to the First Amendment.").

183 F.3d at 1263–64.

The court also held:

> * * * [The] alleged inability meaningfully to participate in and influence elections is attributable to the conduct and resources of private individuals, not the state. *See Jones,* 131 F.3d at 1323 (9th Cir.1997) ("Here, there is no state action putting wealthy voters in a better position to contribute to campaigns than nonwealthy voters."). Individual voters remain free to associate and pool their resources to support the candidate of their choosing under Georgia's campaign finance system and candidates remain free to rely on their own resources, which may include fundraising abilities, name recognition, speaking, organizational, and leadership abilities, as well as popular and easily understood positions on the issues, to be successful at the polls. The extent of voter and candidate influence is based on individual efforts, not state action.

183 F.3d at 1264.

How useful is it to low-income people to guarantee that economic conditions cannot be placed on their right to vote, if the election finance system restricts them from running for office and limits the available candidates by wealth? If "individual voters remain free to associate and pool their resources," but the rules favor candidates who have raised money in the past and those who possess or can borrow large sums of money in the present, how can nonwealthy voters ever successfully compete with wealthy voters for political influence? *See* Spencer Overton, *Voices from the Past: Race, Privilege, and Campaign Finance*, 79 N. C. L. Rev. 1541 (2001) (explaining that the current campaign finance system replicates inequality grounded in the existing distribution of property and noting that state-sanctioned discrimination against racial minorities contributed to that disparity).

2. If the judiciary should not or will not force the state to provide a more equal playing field by providing public funding for elections, why would legislators who had successfully navigated a system based on wealth wish to fund future nonwealthy opponents?

3. Although *Harper* commented "Lines drawn on the basis of wealth or property, like those of race, are traditionally disfavored," the Supreme Court later held that wealth is not a suspect classification triggering heightened constitutional review. *See* San Antonio Independent School Dist. v. Rodriguez, 411 U.S. 1 (1973); *Plyler v. Doe*, excerpted later in this chapter. What implications do these rulings have for the use of equality theory in relation to voting and democratic participation?

4. While early litigation used equality theory to establish the right to vote, the enactment of the Voting Rights Act of 1965 changed the litigative focus to statutory interpretation. For a description of this history, see Jose Garza, *History, Latinos, and Redistricting*, 6 Tex. Hisp. J.L. & Pol'y 125 (2001).

5. In the next excerpts, Martha R. Mahoney and John O. Calmore describe contemporary struggles over voting and democracy in the United States. Consider whether equality theory remains viable as an organizing or litigating strategy in the voting arena. Mahoney argues that the disempowerment of nonwealthy voters and the history of racial exclusion of minority voters need to be understood as connected within the framework of equality theory. Calmore considers voting rights in the context of this multiracial nation.

MARTHA R. MAHONEY

Constructing Solidarity: Interest and White Workers

2 U. Pa. J. Lab. & Emp. L. 747, 748–51, 763–71 (1900–2000)

[As a result of a series of cases on voting rights, Greensboro was moved from a mostly black congressional district, represented in Congress by a black Democrat, to a mostly white district represented by a white Republican. The interests of the white working class people of Greensboro are not represented better under the new political system.]

The Greensboro Distribution Center was the only Kmart distribution center with a mostly-African-American work force. Workers at the Greensboro Distribution Center were paid an average of $5.10 per hour less than workers in identical jobs at other centers. Therefore, all the workers, *including* approximately one-third who were white, suffered financial losses because of racism.

The drive to organize a union at the distribution center began with the leadership of black workers and support from the black community. Black ministers voluntarily were arrested in support of the organizing drive, and they organized community support when the company refused to negotiate with the union. When the workers demonstrated at Kmart, blacks met first at the church and whites met first at the union hall. The union was literally the base from which whites entered shared organization with African-Americans. When Kmart sued black workers and black ministers, white workers held a press conference and demanded to know why they too had not been sued. Black community support was crucial in mobilizing community support in general in Greensboro. White workers therefore gained directly from the strength of black community figures during the several years of struggle.

The success of the drive eventually brought union benefits to white workers as well as to blacks. When the union won a contract, it marked the first time in the history of the Kmart corporation that a distribution center had been organized. Although whites were a minority of the union, they had gained considerably from the leadership of black employees and black community figures. Reverend Nelson Johnson and the other black ministers had carefully described their campaign as one for "sustainable community" in part to avoid a double trap: when the struggle was described as a fight for racial justice, white workers did not see it as their problem; and when the struggle was defined in purely economic terms, blacks felt the campaign ignored its racial dimension.

* * *

Most whites understand racism as something that a second party (the racist actor) does to a third party (the subordinated person of a minority race); racism appears to be a phenomenon distinct from themselves. Because whites do not see the dominant norm of whiteness and the mechanisms of its reproduction, bigotry and prejudice—individualized and intentional harms—become the focus of inquiry for whites. Both hostility (in others) and self-consciousness (in ourselves) intervene in the norm of white transparency and the apparently natural state of affairs in which whites prosper. For white Americans above the working class—those who write the books and do most social analysis—racism often appears to be something that working class whites (particularly Southerners) do to African-Americans and other people of color. In the absence of any widely agreed upon concept of class interest, wealthier and more educated whites perceive working class whites only as racists. In the absence of systematic structures to facilitate solidarity, white privilege in the working class will continue to be reproduced whether or not whites are aware of it, as it is in other classes.

Because law and legal theory have difficulty recognizing class interest and are relatively new at recognizing whiteness, the interest of whites in solidarity can be especially difficult to explore. Focusing on *status* rather than *class* as an analytical category leads to the belief that white interest in retaining privilege is natural and essential for all whites, regardless of economic class. * * *

* * *

[Some scholars have suggested that workers of color and women of all races would be empowered if race- and gender-based organizing were permitted under labor law, rather than the current doctrine in which one union, governed by majority rule, represents all the workers. In the context of Kmart, however, the shared space of the union hall was the base from which the white workers joined with black workers; otherwise, given the history of racial division in North Carolina, they might not have joined the drive at all.]

> The South's fabled and endlessly trumpeted "favorable business climate"—read "no unions welcome"—has ... helped make the region, *particularly the Interstate 85 corridor between Richmond and Atlanta* ... the new manufacturing center of America. [Peter Applebome, *Dixie Rising: How the South is Shaping American Values, Politics, and Culture* 186 (1996).]

There is an interactive relationship between low levels of union organization and class consciousness in American society. The *legal* conditions necessary for labor to organize are eroded or lost in part because of the lack of labor's *political* power. As labor's presence in national politics diminishes, challenging legal rules that protect employers becomes more difficult. Low levels of union organization decrease the capacity of workers to pursue their interests as a class and make them increasingly dependent on the state for protection. While local struggles may gain strength from labor-community coalitions, the process of building these mutually fortifying alliances is slow, and moving them toward labor as a community issue is impeded by labor's current general weakness. The decline in union organization reduces labor's organized political presence in the process of government. Working people become disproportionately dependent on the general attentiveness—or lack of it—of their political representatives, who may not be directly responsive to labor at all.

Low levels of labor organization also lead *white* workers to interact less with leaders who have an investment in building antiracist solidarity. As a result of pervasive residential segregation, working class whites often do not live near working class people of color. Since class formation happens outside the workplace as well as within it, and given the history and persistence of racism in America, promoting antiracist class-based mobilization is a practical challenge as well as a theoretical one. Political leaders in mostly-white districts often consolidate voting bases that do not require interracial solidarity. The loss of organized labor's political leadership and the transition to less organized participation within broader civic processes both tend to diminish the total amount of antiracist messages that white workers hear.

Without a labor party, labor interests are only one of many interests of voters, and one of the interests least emphasized in contemporary politics. In the absence of political representation for labor, representational appeals to white working class people are often pitched overtly or covertly to whiteness and threats to whiteness. In the infamous political advertisement during Jesse Helms's senatorial campaign against African-American Harvey Gantt, a pair of white hands crumpled a slip of paper while the narrator said, "You really needed that job, but it went to a minority because of a quota." These types of messages tell white workers that people of color are their real problem, inflicted on them by the intervention of powerful outsiders into the natural state of affairs where white people had access based on their own individual merit. Since neither Democrats nor Republicans are pursuing labor-protective legislation to protect these voters *as workers*, however, nobody claims to speak directly to their self-interest except those who speak to them as *white workers*, as did the "white hands" commercial. In the contested, interrelated construction of race and class in contemporary America, conscious efforts to identify, mobilize, or create antiracist class consciousness have been largely absent. It is particularly important, then, to examine the redistricting struggles in North Carolina in the district within which the Kmart struggle was located.

In the early 1990s, to comply with the Voting Rights Act, North Carolina created a mostly-black district that spanned much of I-85 through the industrial centers of the Piedmont district, which at the time included Greensboro. The district was challenged by white plaintiffs, who complained that they had been placed in a mostly-black district on the basis of their race. [In *Shaw v. Reno*, 509 U.S. 630, 113 (1993), the] Court held that the "bizarre" shape of the district and the fact that it created a black majority district juxtaposed to areas of white majority created the appearance of "racial gerrymander." Justice O'Connor's majority opinion held that the act of classifying by race is itself "odious," without regard to whether the classification creates privilege, subordination, harm, or deprivation.

* * *

* * * Justice O'Connor's assertion that majority-minority districts may "pull us apart" reflects the positioned white belief [typically accompanying white privilege] that there exists a social "we" who are not currently "apart." In 1993, as *Shaw* was being decided, a study revealed that white residents of North Carolina tended to believe that race prejudice and discrimination against blacks were not major problems in North Carolina. African-Americans, in contrast, saw discrimination and prejudice as widespread. Although whites indicated they supported local ordinances that permitted segregation, they rarely showed overt hostility to blacks or expressed openly racist sentiments. It is consistent with Southern history for whites to believe that race relations are comfortable and undivided while blacks perceive division and oppression.

* * *

But the political economy of District Twelve was less mysterious than the Court insisted, and its organization seems to have favored the *labor* interests of white workers who lived within it. The interstate highway through the Piedmont tracks much of the history of labor struggle in North Carolina because it linked the mills and factories. Greensboro was home to the corporate headquarters of Burlington Mills, Cone Mills, and other textile companies; there, paternalism as a labor system disintegrated into labor struggles by the time of the Depression. Further down the highway, in Kannapolis, home of the giant Cannon Mills, the needle trades union UNITE won a National Labor Relations Board (NLRB) election in June 1999 after twenty-five years of organizing.

The placement of highways through the Piedmont is not arbitrary. Roads track the organization of production, as materials and people must be moved from place to place. Along those routes, black and white working people came to work in mills, factories, and the businesses that developed around them. As the textile industry grew through the late nineteenth and twentieth centuries, mill villages became close-knit white working-class communities. Blacks were excluded from all but the heaviest jobs and lived outside the mill villages. Blacks were only able to obtain industry jobs in large numbers after the federal government brought pressure for desegregation of the textile mills. The presence of black workers brought both segmentation of the labor market and a militancy that had been forged from collective action and the civil rights movement into struggles of textile workers. Black support proved fundamental to union successes after 1970. But racism continued to be used as an anti-union strategy in fighting organizing drives, and many textile companies continued to reserve supervisory positions and better jobs for whites.

The Piedmont is the most urbanized area of North Carolina. The black population of the Greensboro area increased between 1960 and 1980, but geographic racial separation also increased during this period. In 1992, the District Director for the Amalgamated Clothing and Textile Workers Union ("ACTWU") described the newly created Twelfth Congressional District in North Carolina as an unparalleled opportunity for his union and for labor in the state: running along Interstate 85, it concentrated more shops organized by ACTWU than any other district in the state.

If the goal of legislative districting in North Carolina were to increase the political strength of working class people, and particularly of organized labor, the Piedmont would need a district through the textile and furniture belt along the interstate. However, North Carolina has never sought to maximize working class strength. Quite the opposite: after the Civil War, a sustained period of coalitional voting by blacks and poor whites, usually in the Republican Party, triggered repeated waves of opposition. Some of the opposition was social and cultural, seeking to mobilize racism in opposition to class solidarity through racist rhetoric and inflammatory denunciation of African-Americans. This was not only a cultural attack. Violence and terror against both blacks and whites, including whippings and killings, was part of the repression of biracial political alliances. * * *

The working class in North Carolina has historically been "politically and economically weak and, as a result of the way in which industrialization has taken place, socially and geographically fragmented." For example, North Carolina deliberately scattered its urban and industrial center rather than develop a unified urban center. Having attracted major industries fleeing union organization, the state energetically pursued anti-union policies, even going as far as declining to assist investment from unionized companies. State policies also kept workers racially divided and helped keep industry dispersed. In the 1970s, the State Department of Administration favored "creation of a network of smaller urban centers [as] the key idea in a settlement pattern for shaping the growth and location of population within the state." The state also sought to attract militantly anti-union employers and was hostile, at the state or local level, toward industries that were high-wage and unionized.

Therefore, "traditional" districting practices in North Carolina could never unite working class districts to gain electoral power. First, state policy had opposed such a development. Second, even if state policy now favored it, the dispersed geography of the region would require crossing through farming districts and other areas to link industrial and urban areas together. There is little hope in the American legal system to force legislators who are dependent on fund raising, answerable to PACs, and who are seldom from working class backgrounds themselves, to redistrict in ways that maximize working class strength. Although the "one man, one vote" decisions brought more democracy to urban areas packed with working-class voters, nothing forced the South to empower workers.

The *Shaw* cases disrupted a district well suited to developing class-based politics that linked industrial locations along an interstate highway while creating a black-majority voting district. In a state that consciously scattered industrial and urban areas, the Court's attack on the black majority weakened the political strength of the labor movement and therefore the potential power of labor-community coalitions. E.P. Thompson defined class as not a "structure" but "something that happens." By moving Greensboro out of District Twelve, the *Shaw* Court made it improbable that white workers would continue to have minority leadership that would help protect their interests. The Court therefore constructed a political theater in which "class," meaning combined mobilization *and* consciousness, is less likely to "happen" at all. * * *

At the end of the nineteenth century, disfranchisement in North Carolina, as elsewhere, had the primary goal of preventing African-Americans from participating in the political process. Some white politicians also sought to disfranchise poor white farmers and workers, while others sought to protect them from disfranchisement, at least temporarily. Disfranchisement virtually eliminated African-Americans from political participation, but also diminished lower-class voting generally. * * *

Working class interest in the voting rights cases would favor strong representation for labor and an end to the myth that black domination is dangerous for white workers. When a white worker desires to pursue class-conscious interests in America today, he or she may be best represented in a minority district. Minority-concentrated districts may serve the class needs of white workers far better than cross-class white majority political districts. White working class people in wealthier suburban districts may discover that their elected leadership consistently opposes their class interest. Because consciousness and organization interact in making class, and because Americans possess little social awareness of class, placing white working class people in wealthy districts may result in their identification with people of "middle class" status. This diminishes class consciousness and opportunities for class mobilization.

The interest of whites in black leadership is seldom explored in law. When racial classification is defined as a harm in itself, or intentional placement in a mostly-minority district is defined as a harm to whites, exploration into the nature of subordination disappears. The reasoning of *Shaw* makes it impossible to hold the searching inquiry into the real nature of harm and interest that is fundamental to increasing *class* consciousness today. When either whiteness or class is ignored, white workers are placed in an inherently more reactionary position than when they are considered together. If we notice only whiteness, then working class whites only identify with those aspects of themselves which they share with whites of other classes and fail to identify those aspects of self which they share with people of color. If we emphasize only class, race does not disappear from American society. Rather, because whites do not perceive white privilege and norms as a matter of course, demands for inclusion from people of color are experienced by white workers as disruptive of the natural state of affairs.

Formalism on race (the *Shaw* approach) combined with the invisibility of class places white workers in the most reactionary position of all. Transformative work requires both the recognition of structures of power and of mutual need. Eventually this includes developing an understanding of the limits that racism places on class advancement. For whites, therefore, transformative identity does *not* lie in separate organization on the basis of their whiteness, nor in emphasizing only privilege and not class solidarity, but rather in the recognition of shared goals on the basis of equality and strength for minorities.

JOHN O. CALMORE

Race-Conscious Voting Rights and the New Demography in a Multiracing America
79 N.C. L. Rev. 1253, 1257–62, 1265–76, 1279–80 (2001)

In 1999, Eric Yamamoto observed that "[b]y the year 2000, the familiar characterization of black versus white will no longer describe race relations in the United States. In crucial respects, the twenty-first century will be a nation of minorities." * * * [A]s we enter the twenty-first century, the new demographic development is so salient that even Nathan Glazer, the former die-hard assimilationist, has declared that "we are all multiculturalists now." In recognizing this fact, however, Glazer also explains why the new demography could manifest itself in a way that profoundly threatens African Americans. In his frightening view, "the two nations for our America are the black and the white, and increasingly, as Hispanics and Asians become less different from whites from the point of view of residence, income, occupation, and political attitudes, the two nations become the blacks and the others." In these words, "the blacks and the others," the new demography could represent a complex development wherein new people of color will consolidate white rule over black. At the heart of that assumption is the idea that to be like white is important, of course, but not as important as to be unlike black.

As individualized opportunity and colorblind race ("symbolic ethnicity") gain increasing currency, being unlike black may entail a very different meaning of "race consciousness" than that which is held by African Americans. Even as the black middle class achieves greater access to the mainstream opportunity structure and experiences a greater variety of integration, it remains stubbornly race-conscious. As I live through this irony myself, I often wonder why we are so race-conscious and what it signifies about the legacy of the civil rights movement. Race consciousness is more than a lived-out refutation of colorblindness. It appears instead to be a fundamental social identifier and group orientation for most of us. Moreover, "blacks are more likely than whites to express high levels of group consciousness" and this often correlates with political participation. * * *

Interestingly, although Justice Clarence Thomas is black, he sees race-conscious voting as essentializing, arguing that "[o]f necessity, in resolving vote dilution actions we have given credence to the view that race defines political interest." In many ways, both the Supreme Court and the new demography challenge the necessity and propriety of race consciousness, which is at the heart of voting rights law. Under the pressures of a colorblind regime, we know that the Court is increasingly hostile to the concept and orientation of race consciousness. Within the Court's colorblind jurisprudence, two key questions emerge pertaining to the context of the changing demographics. First, what does race consciousness mean among Latinos and Asians? Second, will Asians and Latinos politically deploy race consciousness or, instead, adopt a politics of assimilation?

During the civil rights movement, integration and equal opportunity took priority, eclipsing a race-conscious orientation toward justice for black people as a distinct social group. Individual agents from the race were to take advantage of formal equality of opportunity to advance through a colorblind assimilationism. Furthermore, race consciousness was delegitimated within the core culture, because it was associated with militant black nationalists and white supremacists. Over the last thirty-five years, however, as the difficulties of mainstream integration have continued to be problematical, blacks have come to reinforce race consciousness, even though it tends to polarize blacks from whites and to insulate them from mainstream dictates. Asian-Pacific Americans and Latinos may not grip this stubborn race consciousness as firmly. Time will tell.

Because Asian and Latino residential integration and intermarriage with whites are more prevalent than is the case with blacks, race consciousness may simply make less sense. At bottom, each group may question whether race consciousness is an impediment or a spur to social group betterment. Still, at least for now, race consciousness is held tightly by blacks and this feature of social identity explains, in part, why only nine percent of the black vote went to George W. Bush in the 2000 presidential election.

Rather than looking nationally, sometimes we must look regionally to examine the experience and ramifications of the new demography. Demographers now view the nation as divided between "gateway" areas that have a highly diverse population, largely due to immigration, and other areas that remain mostly white, or mostly black and white, such as the South. Thus, in addressing voting rights we must pay more attention to specific space because, as John Hartigan observes, "Racial identities are produced and experienced distinctly in different locations, shaped by dynamics that are not yet fully comprehended." The focus on "racial situations" compels us to acknowledge and work with the recognition of "the distinctive role of places in informing and molding the meaning of race." * * * [C]ommentary about the scope and magnitude of multiracial community development in California, particularly the Los Angeles region, has the effect of downplaying the continued significance and persistence of the black-white paradigm in other regions of the country.

In demographer William Frey's opinion, a national view of the new demography may obscure the fact that America's broad regions differ distinctly in their racial-ethnic makeup. The regional variations in distribution of Asians and Latinos suggest that demographic changes will not undermine the analytical framework of the Voting Rights Act in the South, because in that region the presence of Asian and Latino voters will be small. Indeed, the biracial, black-white paradigm will persist in significance in the South. This conclusion is based, in part, on examining where the people who represent the new demography primarily live now and are likely to live in the next twenty-five years. According to Frey's projections, by 2025, ten states will be significantly racially and ethnically diverse as a function of the new demography, with only Texas and Florida representing the South. * * * Beyond Florida and Texas, the other eight states that will reflect the new demography are Arizona, California, Hawaii, Illinois, Nevada, New Jersey, New Mexico, and New York. The other forty states will remain largely white or black and white. Within these states, there will be multiracial diversity in some metropolitan areas, primarily gateway cities, but for the most part the new demography will be more imagined than experienced, more hearsay than eye-witnessed. California will remain uniquely multiracial. Certainly, in California where non-Hispanic whites only constitute 49.9 percent of the thirty-three million residents and no racial or ethnic group constitutes a majority, the social relations, politics, and evolving culture have already moved beyond the black-white paradigm in dramatic ways.

* * *

Because the South reflects the purest expression of conservative values and politics, its influence transcends its regional borders. Indeed, at present the United States is more the South than it is California. As Peter Applebome argues, "[T]he most striking aspect of American life at the century's end—in a way that would have been utterly unimaginable three decades ago at the height of the civil rights era—is how much the country looks like the South." The South looks back in time for future direction, whereas California has a different orientation. Because of the incorporation of immigrants and others from out of state, it is a place of new beginnings and dreams. In spite of backlash, in California history has less hold and traditional ways are less entrenched. Prior ownership of the place is less secure.

In many ways, while the South is America, California is a foreign country. According to Applebome, the South—becoming America—is a place "that's bitterly antigovernment and fiercely individualistic, where race is a constant subtext of daily life, and God and guns run through public discourse like an electric current." It is a place "where influential scholars market theories of white supremacy, where the word 'liberal' is a negative epithet, where 'hang-em-high law-and-order justice' centered on the death penalty and throw-away-the-key sentencing are politically all but unstoppable." It is "a place obsessed with states' rights, as if it were the 1850s all over again and the Civil War had never been fought." Applebome concludes, "such characteristics have always described the South. Somehow, they now describe the nation."

What makes California exceptional is not that there is no South there, because there really is quite a bit of the South there. However, in California, there are many forces—human agency and other factors—that work to countervail the characteristics that describe the South in Applebome's depiction. Within California, there is no clear hegemony resulting from either race discourse or race politics. Within the South, there is no strong counter hegemony to either the neoconservative/far right race discourse or race politics. Whereas the left's attempt to establish an insurgent multiculturalism has a chance in California, it has no chance in the South. * * *

* * *

As the Republican West and South gain population, a Presidential candidate could now win the election if he or she were to carry exactly those states that Richard Nixon carried in *losing* to John F. Kennedy in

1960. This regional pairing, in terms of population and influence, is South-dominant. * * *

* * *

Finally, in the * * * [2000] Presidential election, George W. Bush gained all the electoral college votes from the southern states—the only region that constituted a solid voting bloc for him. This dilutes the African-American vote, because it "operates to diminish [black] potential voting strength that derives from the group's geographic concentration." This reinforces Matthew Hoffman's prior contention that this form of vote dilution calls into question the legitimacy of the winner-take-all system of the electoral college. From 1948 to 1968, there was a gradual realignment of white southerners, a development that indicates that "the current Republican domination of the electoral college in the South is no accident." As Hoffman demonstrates, this domination "is in large part the result of a conscious effort by white southern politicians—first by segregationist Democrats, and later by racially conservative Republicans—to make race a focal point of Presidential politics." Although only nine percent of blacks nationwide voted for George W. Bush, the electoral college's dilution of the southern black vote emboldened him not simply to ignore black interests, but also to insult black people. * * *

* * *

The racist taint of conservative politics is driven by southern politics and the primary focus has been to subordinate blacks in particular. While the racist messages of this conservatism are masked by code words, its momentum, largely unchecked, contributed to the ascendancy of George W. Bush, who was supported by a majority of voters throughout the South, although not in California. When the Voting Rights Act was passed in 1965, it sought to address the political conflict that raged throughout the South between blacks and whites. The Voting Rights Act imposed provisions on the South that "represented a direct and pervasive federal assault on the deeply-rooted practice of controlling the local political process in order to maintain the economic and social subordination of blacks." The legacy of that conflict continues today, unmitigated by an increasing population of Latinos and Asians. In the foreseeable future, the black-white paradigm will persistently describe race relations in the South even as the country becomes "a nation of minorities." How we think about race relations and how we think about racial justice will have to take this reality into account. This is the racial situation that competes with that of California.

In sum, the recent Presidential election confirms David Abbott and James Levine's view that black voters in the South "have had little more influence on most modern Presidential general elections than Bulgarians. Their votes, although technically cast, have not usually counted." This vote dilution through the electoral college process is a significant reason that blacks were so outraged by the debacle in Florida, because the black vote could have made a real difference this time. For example, one estimate suggests that the ballots of black voters in Florida were rejected 14.1 percent of the time, compared with a 1.6 percent rate of rejection for non-black voters. According to one report, "black voters are outraged. They are filing affidavits, saying they weren't allowed to vote, or, in one case near Tallahassee, that they had to dodge a police roadblock to get to the polls, or that voting equipment in black precincts is old and faulty." Admittedly, a lot of blacks and others experienced confusion during the election, but many African Americans feel that dirty tricks—"something purposeful and foul"—were part of a deliberate effort to disenfranchise them. Black votes should count more than those of the Bulgarians, and the fact that they did not last November is a function of racial subordination. This confirms the black-white paradigm's persistent relevance not only in the South, but also where Dixie rises beyond. Just as systemic political and social forces have produced minority vote dilution in the South, the Supreme Court has provided obstacles as well.

Through an imposition of colorblind *in*justice, the Supreme Court is undermining the Voting Rights Act by rearticulating its antidiscrimination principles to "diminish minority political power." While the Supreme Court majority opinions are death to black race consciousness, they are amazingly naive or intellectually dishonest when it comes to appreciating that whiteness is also deployed in bloc voting ways. This misrecognition of whiteness as individualized and benign steers many Supreme Court cases off-track. The recent voting rights decisions such as *Shaw v. Reno* [509 U.S. 630 (1993)], *Miller v. Johnson* [515 U.S. 900 (1995)], and *Bush v. Vera* [517 U.S. 952 (1996)] emphasize that rights inhere primarily in individuals who are separate from a social group that has a racial identity. These decisions transport the ideology of individualized colorblindness across contexts, from affirmative action to vote dilution. Individualized colorblindness triumphs over social group race consciousness. In the vote-dilution context, however, this is peculiar because, as Chandler Davidson observes, vote dilution is a racialized group phenomenon: "It occurs because the propensity of an identifiable group to vote as a bloc waters down the voting strength of another identifiable group, under certain conditions." As Davidson states, "one individual acting alone could not dilute the vote of another individual or of a group of individuals."

Thus, the vote dilution remedies that white individuals are challenging so successfully were put into place to counter white racial bloc voting that prevented blacks from electing candidates of their choice. Racially polarized voting by whites forced the formulation of a remedy that would allow blacks to fight fire with fire, so to speak. That remedy, race-conscious and group-based, is dismissed as simply as observing that two wrongs do not make a right. * * *

* * * In the context of voting rights, * * * [the Court's] approach fails to appreciate that a right of effective political participation in the election process makes no sense if that right is viewed as undermining the transcending notion that rights are simply individual. An inevitable effect and objective of apportionment, for example, is to treat individual

voters as part of a social group. The Supreme Court has singled out race as the singular, most inappropriate basis for the attribution of group identity and aggregation. Race, other than whiteness, is inappropriate to form the basis for "any sophisticated right to genuinely meaningful electoral participation."

The race opinions of a five-to-four majority on the Supreme Court achieve a false coherence through an incredible process of decontextualization. As a consequence of this radical decontextualization, the Supreme Court majority appears literally blinded by color as it—the same five characters each time—neither acknowledges nor recognizes the degree of racially polarized *white* bloc voting and therefore will not permit black bloc voting in what really amounts to self defense. The Court acts as if black bloc voting is the first move rather than the second, the initial fire rather than the return fire. Through this misrecognition of whiteness, the Court majority subjects this second move to strict scrutiny as it claims to be unable to distinguish invidious from benign racial discrimination. The second move, blacks taking race predominantly into account, violates the equal protection rights of whites, because they are deemed to suffer *individual* "expressive harm." Individual rights trump efforts to redress vote dilution, a group harm.

* * *

As the nation celebrates American Democracy, pointing with triumphant pride to the fact that across the land there is virtually universal suffrage, over four million convicted felons cannot vote under varied circumstances. They constitute the largest single group of citizens who are prohibited by state laws from voting in both state and federal elections. Of this total, 1.5 million, or 37.5 percent, are African Americans. With the exception of Maine, Massachusetts, and Vermont, forty-seven states disenfranchise offenders while they are incarcerated. Thirty-two states go farther and disenfranchise parolees while twenty-nine states disenfranchise probationers. Remarkably, nine states (recently reduced from thirteen) deny felons the right to vote for the rest of their lives.

Despite the real gains in anti-discrimination law made under constitutional amendments and the Voting Rights Act, felons—mostly African-American and Latino males, many of them young—probably remain disenfranchised not only because they are nonwhite, but also because they lack political support. The recent problems in Florida, many pointed out by Walter Farrell and James Johnson, open up a new opportunity to focus on this problem. As Lani Guinier points out, in Florida alone, for example, as a result of permanent disenfranchisement, more than 400,000 ex-felons—almost fifty percent of them black—were ineligible to vote in last November's election. Florida, moreover, "has the largest number of people affected by this rule." Thirty-one percent of the black men in Florida are disenfranchised because of prior felonies.

During the 2000 Presidential election, Florida officials sought to counter voter fraud by purging the rolls of felons. Again, many blacks saw this as another concerted attack on black voters, because forty-four percent of the names on the felon list were black and the felon purge eliminated 8,456 blacks from the voter rolls before the election. Ultimately, too late for the election, of the 4,847 people who appealed, 2,430 were judged not to have been convicted felons. Given the profiles of the felons, disproportionately black and Latino, it is likely that if these voters had not been purged, the outcome of the election may well have been different. As Michael Tomasky observes, "[t]o put it bluntly: A wildly inaccurate purge of voters, which the state of Florida knew to be inaccurate but did nothing to correct, cost Al Gore Florida, and the presidency." This egregious variation on the theme of felon disenfranchisement is outrageous.

This particular injustice aside, the larger problem of felon disenfranchisement demands redress. According to Marc Mauer, "if current criminal justice trends continue, we can expect that thirty to forty percent of black males born today will lose the right to vote for a least part of their adult lives." Because the rate of incarceration has increased so dramatically in the last forty years, social scientists speculate that had the current level existed in 1960, "it is very likely that Richard Nixon would have defeated John Kennedy in the popular vote and possible that Nixon would have won the electoral college vote as well."

Many of the problems in Florida, like felon disenfranchisement, are rooted in a racist history and are fundamentally structural. They predate the recent debacle. According to 1990 census data on the proportion of black and white prisoners to the total black and white population for the state, out of a black population of 1,759,534 there were 25,385 prisoners. Although the white population in Florida totaled 10,749,285 the number of white prisoners was significantly less than the black prisoners, numbering 18,206. That is, while the white population in Florida outnumbered blacks by ten million, black inmates outnumbered white inmates by over seven thousand. As a collateral consequence of incarceration, blacks in Florida have less opportunity than white members of the electorate to participate in the political process and to elect candidates of their choice.

* * *

* * * The United States has the most restrictive, unjust disenfranchisement laws of any democratic nation in the world, particularly those laws that impose lifetime bans. The harsh consequences that can result are excessive, racial injustices. According to Virginia law, for instance, an eighteen year-old convicted of felony drug possession in that state who successfully completes his sentence to a drug treatment program is disenfranchised for life even though he may not have spent a day in jail. We see then that felon disenfranchisement, as a collateral consequence of mass incarceration, not only disproportionately affects nonwhites and their communities, but it also offends racial justice and fundamental fairness. It embarrasses, or ought to embarrass, our Democracy.

Notes and Questions

1. Mahoney describes the successful union organizing drive in Greensboro where white workers aligned with blacks. She asserts that these white workers were harmed by redistricting that denied them black congressional representation. Is she persuasive? Might whites other than those in the working class be harmed by a denial of elected representation from people of color? For one view of how better representation for all groups, whether minority or majority, might be achieved, see Lani Guinier, excerpted later in this chapter.

2. Calmore believes that the subordination of blacks by whites persists. In the conclusion of his essay he thinks of "Dixie rising in time and space beyond the old South." Calmore, *supra* at 1281. He recalls the sentiment of a president of the White Citizens Council who said:

> Some people think the nigger is beneath their dignity. They talk Constitution but they look at the nigger. They talk states' rights but they mean nigger. This will never be a dead issue. Some issues never die.

Id. Calmore concludes:

> Today, among the loudest echoes of the White Citizen's Council are those that disturbingly emanate from the Supreme Court majority, where "They talk Constitution, but they look.... They talk states' rights, but they mean...."

Id. Does this description of black-white race relations that originated in the South persist as the United States becomes a nation of minorities? Is Calmore's assessment of the need to look regionally at racial patterns persuasive? Can a rule of law utilize that kind of context?

3. In Hunter v. Underwood, 471 U.S. 222 (1985), the Supreme Court found racial motivation in legislative speeches surrounding the passage of an Alabama statute disqualifying voters for crimes of moral turpitude. Ten times more blacks than whites had been disenfranchised under the act. *See also* Alice E. Harvey, Comment, *Ex-Felon Disenfranchisement and Its Influence on the Black Vote: The Need for a Second Look*, 142 U. Pa. L. Rev. 1145, 1146 (1994) (describing racial impact of ex-felon disenfranchisement) and Andrew L. Shapiro, Note, *Challenging Criminal Disenfranchisement Under the Voting Rights Act: A New Strategy*, 103 Yale L.J. 537, 538 (1993) (characterizing criminal disenfranchisement as "the most subtle method of excluding blacks from the franchise"). Disenfranchising felons makes any bias in the system of policing, prosecuting, and sentencing criminals translate into bias in the political system.

4. The issue of group identification and its role in elections has been the subject of a series of reapportionment decisions by the Supreme Court. Commenting on the intervention of the Court in these decisions and others involving elections, Pamela S. Karlan writes:

> [T]he "image of democracy" that has informed the contemporary Supreme Court's interventions into the political arena—in contexts as diverse as blanket primaries, ballot access, and candidate debates—is a fear of too much democracy, of too robust and tumultuous a political system. That image underlies the Court's *Shaw* jurisprudence as well: the Court sees itself as the only institution capable of resolving the difficult questions raised by the role of race in American democracy. In the *Shaw* cases, as in *Bush v. Gore* [531 U.S. 98 (2000)], the Supreme Court has radically transformed not only the substantive rules that govern reapportionments and recounts, but also the vertical and horizontal relationships among the various institutional players involved in these intensely political activities. The former concern the connection between the federal government and state governments: for example, what is the extent of congressional power to regulate state elections? The latter concern the interaction among different branches of government: when can courts overturn the choices reached by other branches and when should courts resolve, or pretermit, conflicts among the other branches? And, as *Bush v. Gore* shows, the institutional questions may sometimes seem almost diagonal: what is the relationship between, for example, Article II, section 1 of the Constitution, which provides that "Each State shall appoint" its presidential electors "in such Manner as the Legislature thereof may direct," the federal Electoral Count Act, which confers special responsibilities on Congress, and the powers of the Florida and federal courts? The Supreme Court's newest equal protection manifests a striking mistrust of nearly every other actor in the reapportionment and recount processes. Forty years after the judiciary's first significant foray into the political thicket, we find ourselves ensnared in the political *Bushes*.

Pamela S. Karlan, *Nothing Personal: The Evolution of the Newest Equal Protection from* Shaw v. Reno *to* Bush v. Gore, 79 N.C. L. Rev. 1345, 1347–48 (2001).

B. Voting and Democracy: Moving Toward the Future

Discussions of voting rights typically conflate three distinct issues, identified by Eben Moglen and Pamela Karlan as the mechanics of voting, methods of electing officials, and the way we govern ourselves. *See* Eben Moglen & Pamela S. Karlan, *The Soul of a New Political Machine: The Online, the Color Line and Electronic Democracy*, 34 Loy. L.A. L. Rev. 1089 (2001). In this section Lani Guinier looks at democracy and how methods of electing implicate democracy and the way we govern ourselves.

LANI GUINIER

More Democracy

1995 U. Chi. Legal F. 1, 1–22

I want to suggest the extraordinary notion that democracy means that ordinary people should participate in making the decisions that affect their lives. I want to talk about how we can make democracy more participatory and less alienating. I want to describe a vision of democracy as engaged public communication, democracy that is less about winning a "game" and more about listening, responding, and working through the creative tension of difference. This is democracy in which we strive for a synthesis of component voices rather than the monolithic command of a single or homogeneous majority. This is democracy as participatory public conversation.

My husband and I were sitting around the kitchen table * * * . I was trying to explain the basic idea that people should be participating in the decisions that affect their lives. So I said, "What could I call this in order that people would understand what I am talking about?" My husband said, "Well, what you're really talking about, Lani, is participatory democracy." And I said, "Oh no, participatory democracy, that's too abstract a concept. I need something catchy." So my seven-year-old son, who was eavesdropping as he loaded magnets on the refrigerator door, exclaimed, "Oh, I know what you should call it." Curious, I asked, "What's that?" He announced, "Baseball!"

I paused. "Baseball?" I skeptically repeated his statement. Without missing a beat, my son responded, "Yeah, you know, you said 'catchy,' and when you're playing baseball, you go out into the field and you *catch* the ball." As any good law professor would, I questioned my son further. I asked, "Nikolas, do you know what we're talking about?" He answered proudly, "Yeah, democracy." I continued the Socratic interrogation. I asked, "Well, what is democracy?" He said, "It's this really weird thing where people raise their hands and vote. Now can you imagine doing that all day, just raising your hands and voting? Who would want to do that? That's really weird." I queried him further, "Well, why would people vote?" Nikolas replied, "Well, I guess you vote because otherwise the person who's President would be President for their whole life and that would be really boring."

I was intrigued. I starting thinking about a seven year old's version of democracy. I thought, "Is there some way to use Nikolas's notion that on the one hand, democracy is really weird if it is only about voting, and yet on the other hand, if you don't vote, you give up the chance to hold elected officials accountable? Voting is an essential aspect of democracy but it is 'weird' if it becomes the only condition of a genuine democracy." * * *

PBS just produced a critically acclaimed television series about baseball. An African-American philosopher was interviewed. He predicted that in a thousand years the United States of America will probably be known for three things: its form of constitutional democracy, jazz, and baseball. So, you see, others unrelated to me have perceived some connection between baseball and democracy. Baseball, democracy, and jazz are authentic American pursuits that are part of the ongoing experiment we call the United States. I want to explore with you today another way of viewing the evolution and dynamic interaction of all three indigenous experiments: constitutional democracy, baseball, and jazz.

In one sense, my son was exactly right. Democracy and baseball have a lot in common. Baseball is a highly structured and open-ended game of strategy, skill, and luck. It is often reduced to a confrontation between a pitcher and a batter, but it takes an entire team to execute. Many people say that baseball is fun to play but boring to watch. The same can be said of democracy.

Both baseball and, unfortunately, democracy as we now practice it have become spectator sports. They are games in which the emphasis is on watching others play to win. Voters do not participate; they spectate. Elections in which voters are spectators are elections characterized by high levels of alienation and low levels of turnout. When voters merely spectate, they do not listen, learn, or engage. * * *

Jazz is different. You don't "win" at jazz; you collaborate in order to communicate. Jazz is highly structured—like baseball and American politics. Its goal, however, is not winning or losing but producing something of beauty that is shared as much among the musicians as it is between the musicians and the audience. Its beauty lies in the improvisation that exalts communication over mere performance. The best jazz artists are usually remembered for the way they function in a collaborative setting. The excitement might be generated by a soloist, but the soloist is almost always playing against, and with the support of, the rhythm section and the melodic themes of the piece. Dissonance, double time, improvisation, and extending the melody through different rhythmic ranges produce a new way of hearing and speaking that borrows from European as well as African roots.

I want to discuss whether democracy as we practice it in the United States could become less like a spectator sport and more like a jazz conversation. I want to talk about how we can make political participation *less* like a game of winners and losers and *more* like a medley of diverse voices working together to interpret a theme and to drive it forward. I want to explore whether democracy, like jazz music, can be an evolving experiment in public conversation.

I want to discuss the idea of reconceptualizing democracy as participatory, public conversation in the context of race. The question I ask is: How can we have a democracy in a multiracial society in which everyone feels that they have an opportunity to participate, in which everyone feels that they have access to the forum where the debate is taking place, and in which everyone feels not only that we are playing on a level playing field, but that they have a shot at getting a chance at bat?

Now, I'm talking about race in part because race is such an important political cue in our democracy. Race, in other words, still matters. Race, unfortunately, or fortunately, depending on your perspective, still defines the political interests of many Americans, and it should not surprise us that this is true given the fact that we live in such a racially defined world.

* * *

Times Mirror did * * * a very extensive study, of American attitudes. One of the most interesting results was that 65 percent of white Americans now agree that it would be okay for a member of their family to date an African-American. * * * That is a huge increase from just four years ago; in fact, it is a twenty point increase from just four years ago. And yet, of the same group of white respondents, 51 percent say that we have gone too far in pushing for equal rights in this country. So, on the one hand, people are willing to make exceptions for individuals who may be of a different race, but in terms of groups, in terms of equal rights for African-Americans as a group, we're still thinking very much along different and racialized lines.

Now, in the legal academy, on the Supreme Court, and in public discourse, many people who are committed to contemporary-equality jurisprudence and who believe that equal rights should matter nevertheless say that race should not matter. Many of those people committed to contemporary-equality jurisprudence say that race should not matter and that government must be color-blind as a normative principal. They argue that if we recognize race, we inevitably advantage some and disadvantage others, and that to recognize race in the public sphere simply reinforces existing hostilities or provides a moment at which people who are feeling stigmatized will just feel more so.

Those who say that we have to pursue a color-blind jurisprudence also suggest that we must be color-blind not only as a normative matter, but as an empirical matter. They point out that not all members of a racial group think alike. People who are members of a particular racial group do not all think alike. People do not all think alike whether it is the white majority, the Latino minority, the Asian minority, or the African-American minority. These commentators point out that, indeed, there are a range of viewpoints within each group and that to recognize race ignores the shades and the nuances of differences within those groups. In addition, those who claim that the government should be color-blind suggest that race is socially constructed, that race is not a real category, and that we don't know what race is anymore when we have so many people who don't identify solely as a member of one race or another. They argue that what should matter—these critics of race-conscious policies—is the individual, not the group.

I am here to provide an alternative viewpoint. I believe that talking about race is important to encourage biracial cooperation. I believe that recognizing racial difference is an essential *precondition* to multiracial collaboration. I believe that in talking about race we must acknowledge the complexity of race, but that we cannot talk about democracy in a multiracial society without also talking about race.

I am not saying that race should matter always and I am not saying that race should matter always in the same way. But I am saying that race does matter. And I am saying that in the political sphere, if we are talking about participatory democracy, if we are talking about a democracy in which everyone feels that they have an opportunity to participate in making decisions about things that affect their lives, then we have to be aware of race. We have to be conscious of racial differences because those differences matter to many of the people that we want to participate in the political process. Racial pride, racial identity, and racial solidarity can, of course, be marginalizing "cul-de-sacs." But recognition of race can also be empowering, affirming, and energizing. Racial awareness among racial minority group members can mobilize political participation. And that political participation can become the basis for participation across, not just within, racial groups. Indeed, when racial minority-group members are confident that they are being respected, when they do not feel the need to "racialize" an issue just to be recognized, then they can participate vigorously and confidently in cross-racial majorities. Indeed, I have argued elsewhere that it is often the refusal to recognize race that highlights and cements its salience.

Now, when I argue that race matters, I am not saying that race is monolithic. I am not saying that we should redefine race as a fixed social category. I am not saying that we should reinforce arbitrary distinctions along racial lines. I am not saying that people who disagree or dissent from the prevailing or majority viewpoint of a particular racial group should be excommunicated and booted out of the racial category.

Race does matter. But that does not mean that we have to make race the only thing that matters or that we or any group of elites have to decide for other people how they should racially identify themselves. Nor does it mean that talking about race is a means of empowering only racial minorities. Talking about race and democracy does not mean gaining the opportunity for racial minorities to do to the racial majority what has been done to them. * * *

* * *

* * * [D]emocratic representation cannot be understood purely and exclusively in terms of one person, one vote. One person, one vote suggests that democracy is only about voting and that voting is merely an exercise in individual empowerment and individual scoring or winning. But individuals, meaning individual voters, don't "win." Individuals don't elect people, groups of individuals do. Representative democracy presumably rewards a group for mobilizing politically cohesive voters to participate and elect representatives who advocate their interests. The first question, then, is how do you aggregate individuals into groups to

determine what groups of individuals are going to elect which representatives?

The way that we commonly aggregate individuals in this society, in terms of determining what groups of individuals can elect what representatives, is through something called geographic districting. We allocate representation by drawing physical communities of political representation and we call those physical or geographical communities "districts." And then we give each district one representative. It is a way of presumably assuring that local communities have a voice in our democratic conversation. Districts are geographic groups. Districting reflects the presumption that geography is a suitable proxy, on some level, for community. By community, we mean "community of interests," i.e., territorially defined communities of political interests. We aggregate individuals into a group called a district and we then allow that group to choose a representative to represent them.

Political parties are also a form a group representation. Political parties are ideological groups more or less. Political parties are groups of people who organize along some kind of communal, cooperative, or congenial sense of what their interests are. In our democracy, we acknowledge group representation for at least these two kinds of collective aggregations: geographic collections of people in districts and partisan or ideological collections of people in political parties.

Two of the dominant concepts, at least twentieth-century dominant concepts, of democracy are communitarianism and pluralism. Both assume that groups play an important role. Therefore, in my view, these concepts are consistent with the idea that *in a democracy* individual rights can best be protected and acknowledged when groups of people are provided the opportunity to participate in our democratic conversation.

In communitarianism, the basic assumption is that community is fundamental to democracy. The idea of democracy depends upon a collection of individuals with a collective consciousness or a common cultural or social experience. That collection of people is the essence of democracy; that community is the primary site for citizen participation and involvement. Communitarians would argue that a sense of community and a shared set of values help to legitimate political authority, that democracy is most fruitful where intermediate groups or local communities help to generate a common fund of knowledge and information to facilitate productive and rational debate and promote interaction among citizens. In a sense, for communitarians, political groups become an alternative to neighborhood-based geographic communities, and especially in an era when modern technology permits rapid exchange of information without the constraints of space or physical proximity, voluntary interest groups function as a modern version of community.

As Americans become less tied to, and less identified with, a particular geographic locality, political groups or these voluntary interest groups become surrogate communities. Interest groups or associations of like-minded people are communities of interest or belief rather than communities of geography. Twenty percent of Americans move every year. In an age with that kind of mobility, many communitarians seek to enhance voluntary political groups or associations as a way to strengthen American democracy. Indeed, they argue that it is the absence of healthy political groups and parties that is at the root of much current apathy and skepticism about our democracy. So, communitarians say that communities or groups are the essence of political participation and involvement.

Pluralism, another important twentieth-century concept about democracy, also assumes that groups are an important unit in democratic functioning. In a pluralistic conception, democracy is based on free competition between groups. Individuals join groups based on their perceptions about their group interests. The democratic process becomes a clash among group interests, bargains, compromises, trade-offs, coalitions, and negotiations. Groups are natural competitors because one group's advancement occurs only at the expense of another. There is not an independent common good except the compromise between competing groups. Political life then, as pluralism sees it, is a game with group winners and group losers. And group competition may replicate, on a larger scale, the self-interested individual; or, as pluralism might assert, group solidarity can help individuals transcend their private or passive conceptions of self-interest. But, in any event, groups are an important part of the political process. They provide individuals with an opportunity to organize effectively with other individuals, and they give such groups an incentive to try and win over the majority through bargains and coalitions that promote familiarity with the viewpoints of others and a willingness to work with others, including those with whom one disagrees. So, we have these two conceptions of democracy, both of which enjoy, or at least embrace, the idea of group participation as important to democratic function.

* * *

* * * [I]ndividualized democracy or democracy by public opinion poll allows little room for interactive democratic conversation. So the metaphor that I am using for democracy—democracy as conversation, democracy as public collaboration, democracy as jazz music—really requires more than one person to be involved. And indeed, Hannah Arendt describes democracy as public conversation in a way that on some level tracks my son's version of why voting as the embodiment of democracy is so weird. She said, and I am paraphrasing, "Voting cannot be the essence of democracy. Because if voting is the essence of democracy, it is a very private, not a public, act. Because if you look at the voting booth as the ultimate metaphor for democracy, there is only room enough in that booth for one person. That can't be democracy."

If, as Hannah Arendt suggests, democracy is about people talking to each other and participating collectively in trying to decide public policy, then I would argue that group representation and group participation is essential to a functioning democracy. Group participation, assuming the group is a voluntary association of individuals, is a way of mobilizing individuals. It is a way of dispersing authority and it is a way of creating broad-based access to that conversation.

I would argue that if democracy is a public conversation in which we want broad-based public participation, then we should also ensure representation for racial groups if those groups feel politically congenial and if those groups act in a way that is similar to other voluntary political associations. Group participation or group representation is particularly important for disadvantaged racial groups who have been denied historical access to that democratic conversation. And indeed, in my view, that is what the Voting Rights Act has tried to remedy. The goal of the Voting Rights Act is to undo the exclusion of certain disadvantaged groups who have been denied access, who have been denied the opportunity to participate as equals in our democratic conversation. So the Voting Rights Act justifies intervention, it justifies court or legal intervention to correct certain political arrangements where the majority is hoarding power and not allowing minority groups to participate in the democratic conversation. It allows or promotes intervention where the majority is not acting as a representative of the whole but is acting as a representative of its own natural self-interest.

Now, what am I talking about when I say that the majority is not representing the whole? Well, when we think of democracy, some of us think that democracy is simply winner-take-all, majority rule. Some of us think that democracy simply means that 51 percent of the people get 100 percent of the power. That is democracy, right? You vote. Whoever gets the most votes gets all the power. Well, that is one version of democracy and it is a version of democracy that we assume is fair because we assume that those with the most votes are going to disperse their power not only to benefit themselves but to benefit everybody. We assume that the majority is really a majority or a collection of shifting coalitions. We assume that the majority is a shifting or fleeting collection of individuals, not a monolithic group that is hoarding power permanently.

I like to tell a story that again involves my son Nikolas. This time he was four years old and we were looking at a Sesame Street magazine. I was very excited because the headline on the magazine article stated, "Vote!" So I thought, "Ah, I get to teach a four year old about voting." The magazine pictured six kids and they were trying to decide what game to play. Four of the kids had their hands raised because they wanted to play tag, and two had their hands down because they wanted to play hide and seek. The magazine said to the reader, "What game will the children play? Count the number of hands raised, count the number of hands lowered, and answer the question." My son—the son of a law professor—bucked the hypo! Nikolas said, "First they will play tag, because four kids want to play tag, and then they will play hide and seek because there are two who want to play hide and seek."

Nikolas implicitly challenged the basic premise that those with the most votes should always decide each and every game. Nikolas did not assume that the preference of the majority, the four who wanted to play a particular game, should control every decision. Nikolas declined to award 66 percent of the kids 100 percent of the power. The magazine, by contrast, assumed that the majority should decide for everybody what game to play. The magazine assumed that two-thirds of the children could and should act on behalf of all of the children.

This assumption, that the four who wanted to play tag would be acting democratically by deciding for everybody what game to play, is based on two conditions. First, we assume that the majority is operating on the golden rule. We assume that the tag majority is going to treat the hide and seek players with some respect, that at some point they are going to say, "Okay, we will now play hide and seek because that is what you guys what to play." Second, we assume that the tag majority is not monolithic; we assume the tag majority is not homogeneous; we assume the tag majority is not permanent. We assume that the tag majority is a majority today, but that it has to worry about being a *different* minority tomorrow. The tag majority, we believe, worries about defectors. Some of those who want to play tag may join forces with the hide and seek players on a different issue to forge a *new* majority. We believe, therefore, that today's majority is going to treat today's minority fairly because today's majority does not want to be treated any differently when it becomes tomorrow's minority.

What if these two conditions are absent? What if the majority is disrespectful *and* monolithic? What if the majority of today is also the majority of yesterday and of the year before that and of the year before that and has every likelihood of being the majority of tomorrow? What if the majority of today is not treating the minority of today with respect; what if the majority is not worrying about what the minority thinks because the majority is assured permanent power. In this case, the majority does not have to worry about the minority because the majority is not a group of shifting individuals but is a single monolithic group. I have litigated cases in which that in fact was the problem.

I have litigated many such cases, including * * * a case in which the majority in Phillips County, Arkansas was a monolithic group hoarding power. Even though blacks were about 44 percent of the electorate in that community, they had never been able to elect a representative of their choice to any of the seven countywide governing positions in this century. Blacks were unsuccessful in county elections because voting in the county was racially polarized. Racially polarized voting meant that whites would vote for whites and blacks would vote for blacks. Voting in Phillips County was not only racially polarized, it was extremely polarized. Our expert witness testified that there were some precincts in which no whites voted for any black running for office.

There was also testimony that in this particular community, whites would not publicly support black candidates for office even when they thought those black candidates were the most qualified. One of our witnesses testified that he ran several times without success for public office in Phillips County. Our witness was a black attorney. He described the time he ran in a three-person race. In the primary, the black attorney came in first but with less than 51 percent of the vote. Because there was a majority-vote requirement in Phillips County, whoever won had to get 51 percent of the vote. So, there had to be a run-off because none of the candidates got "a majority" of the vote. Prior to the second election, the majority-vote, run-off election, the losing candidate—the person who came in third in the first primary—came up to the black candidate and said, "You know, Mr. Whitfield, I believe you are the most qualified candidate, but I cannot say that publicly because I am a farmer and my wife is a school teacher and if we are going to continue to live in this community, and we are white—I cannot support you."

So, Phillips County, Arkansas represented a majority that is a self-centered, monolithic *group*. Because of racially polarized voting, winner-take-all majority rule is not working as we assume it should. It is in those instances that I believe the Voting Rights Act suggests that a court should intervene to protect the interests of a minority that is being ignored or excluded by the permanent majority. But, the question becomes, even if a court should intervene because the minority has been excluded and has been excluded because of racial prejudice, what is the remedy? How do you remedy that exclusion? And that is where the issue is joined right now in terms of the debate about group participation in voting and elections and the Voting Rights Act of 1965 as it has been amended in 1982.

It is at that stage—how do you remedy the violation?—that I proposed those remedies that got me into so much trouble. * * * [O]ne of the remedies that I proposed is used in corporations to elect their boards of directors; it is called cumulative voting. It was also used in Illinois; it was called bullet voting. It was used in Illinois to elect members of the state legislature for many years in the middle of this century.

Where the majority is not functioning to protect and include the minority, I have proposed a system of nondistricted elections—basically, a system in which the voters district themselves by the way they cast their ballots. It is a system in which if you have, for example, a seven-person governing body, every voter gets seven votes. The conventional approach would be to divide that governing body into seven single-member electoral districts. The conventional approach would protect the excluded minority by giving that minority a district in which it is the majority. The conventional approach would protect the minority by carving out from control by the governing majority a special district in which the minority becomes the majority and can then elect its own, minority, representative. I have suggested [cumulative voting as] an alternative that does not involve districts. I have suggested giving each voter the same number of votes, in this case seven votes, and letting them district themselves by the way they cast their ballots. If they want to put all seven of their votes on one candidate because that person reflects their most preferred, most deeply held preferences, they can. If they want to put six on one candidate and one on another, they can. If they want to put seven on seven different candidates, they can. It is up to the voter to district him or herself by the way he or she casts or distributes the seven ballots.

Now what does this have to do with the idea of participatory democracy? Well, basically, I believe that if you give voters the choice to district themselves, if you give voters the means of deciding what is important to them, and if you give voters multiple votes to cast, it is a way of including more people in our democratic conversation. It is a way of telling voters, "Your votes do count." It is a way of ensuring a principle that I call "one vote, one value": everyone's vote should count towards the election of someone who has a good chance of getting elected. Not just black voters' votes should count, not just Latino voters' votes should count—all voters' votes should count.

One vote, one value is based on three fundamental democratic principles: (1) all voters should be able to help elect someone; (2) members of self-identified groups should be able to participate in the democratic conversation as a group; and (3) self-identified groups should enjoy the opportunity to exercise a fair share of political power. Everyone should get a chance to vote for representatives of their choice, everyone who identifies with a common and significant set of interests (significant as measured by a locally defined threshold) should get to have those interests articulated and represented in the conversation we call democracy, and everyone should be represented commensurate to their ability to mobilize and organize political support. This principle applies not just to racial minorities, but to any politically cohesive minority; so women, gays, religious minorities, Republicans in Democratic cities, and Democrats in Republican suburbs all can use this approach to gain political representation. In this way, empowering racial minorities opens up democratic participation for many underrepresented groups.

One of the reasons that all voters' votes should count is because democracy is not just about the symbolic ritual of casting a ballot. It is not just about going into that secret space—that anonymous voting booth—and exercising private preferences. Political participation is about joining with other people with whom you have shared interests and trying to see those interests represented in public discourse, in that public space, in that public conversation that we call democracy.

Democracy is not just about voting; it is not just about winning. Democracy is about participating. Participation matters. It matters because the decisions that governments make affect everyone. Respect for those decisions, including those with which we disagree, demands meaningful participation in the decision making process. People have to be able to express their preferences, but more importantly, people have to participate in the formation and the implementation of preferences. In this project, voting is a necessary but hardly sufficient condition to achieve more democracy.

* * *

* * * [D]emocratic participation depends upon opportunities to communicate and opportunities to hear opposing points of view. * * * Cumulative voting may help us see that we may not want to lock people into a particular set of preferences—which we call districts—which must last for ten years between census enumerations. We may need a decision-making process that is more dynamic; we may need to consider a process that allows people to ascertain their preferences—and to organize in conjunction with like-minded other people—based on a full discussion of the issues that emerge at each election.

Many people, not all people, but many people think of their interests along racial lines. If that is true, and that is important to them, and they choose to vote along racial lines, then it is democratic, in my view, to allow them to participate as a racial group. But we must allow people to self-identify so that if they do not want to vote along racial lines, they don't have to. Nobody is forcing them. Cumulative voting or nondistricted elections provide exit opportunities for people who do not want to vote along with the majority of their particular racial-minority group. Cumulative voting provides racial "dissenters" the opportunity to form coalitions, biracial coalitions. But it also provides racial minority groups with a chance to reach out to other groups. Because it minimizes "wasted" votes, meaning votes cast for political losers, cumulative voting enables groups to reach out beyond their racial "cul-de-sac" and negotiate and bargain excess votes on particular issues or at particular elections.

Cumulative voting does not eliminate the need for compromise. It changes, however, the *timing* and the atmosphere of the compromise. Compromises are made in the open; compromises are made after open exchanges of views. Compromises are not hidden in order to confuse voters; compromises are not suppressed in order to pretend one is all things to all people.

Now some people might argue that the problem with cumulative voting, the problem with race-conscious districting, and the problem with any remedy for the exclusion of minorities from the democratic conversation is that it will balkanize the electorate. It will further divide us; it will fragment us. It will reinforce race as a meaningful interest when we should be erasing race.

My response to that is, they may be right. But maybe and *are* are not the same. They may be right, but in my view we are already balkanized. We are not watching the same television shows. We are not living next door to each other. We are not going to the same elementary and high schools together. So we are already balkanized. And the question is, how do you deal with that? Do you deny that the balkanization is there and pretend that everything is fine and that we are all color-blind; do you sacrifice the demonstrated virtues of a robust pluralism for fear of the potential excesses of unbounded factionalism; or do you acknowledge that there are differences, respect those differences, and then, having acknowledged, recognized, and respected those differences, invite everyone into that democratic conversation?

My view is that it is premature to deny those differences when they are so important to so many people. That is not to say that you want ultimately to reinforce those differences as our goal or as our vision. But it does mean that if you are going to get people to the point where they can converse together and communicate across these differences, the first thing that you have to do is respect and recognize those differences. And having respected and recognized those differences, in my experience, you will find that people are much more willing to engage in conversation about the common good and about our common interests because their differences don't become so key to their self-definition. You have already recognized and respected those differences, so every conversation doesn't have to be about those differences which you've already recognized and respected. It's a way of transcending race ultimately. But in order get there, you must first recognize race.

Thinking about democracy in terms of group participation is also important to revive our confidence in democracy as a public, not a private, activity. Group activity in a public space is a way of reclaiming democracy for all of its citizens. Group participation is necessary to overcome the profound alienation that many people observe among members of our electorate. Just as the term-limits movement reflects a desire to mobilize voters "to take back their government," alternative election systems can respond to the profound alienation that is corroding our public discourse.

* * *

Ultimately, what participatory democracy means is that governance must be first and foremost about a well-conducted conversation—a conversation in which we all get a chance to speak, to listen, to be heard, and to collaborate to solve *our* problems. To local citizens, participatory democracy is not just insider talk about or among winners. To make America a genuine democracy, we must all be encouraged to partake actively in its conversation. The challenge is to imagine a democratic system that permits a range of views to be represented—not just in the streets or on talk radio, but in the sturdy halls of the legislatures and other public spaces constructed to house vigorous debate and true deliberation—in order to restore trust, overcome antagonism, regain government's legitimacy, and achieve our collective wisdom.

Notes and Questions

1. Would Guinier's "one vote, one value" promote democratic participation? How would Guinier's cumulative voting apply, for example, in the context of white workers from the Kmart Distribution Center, described by Martha Mahoney in the excerpt above, who are located in a

mostly-black congressional district? Would white and black workers active in the same labor organization be likely to work out shared opinions on some candidates?

2. Jerry Kang predicts that "E-voting is inevitable." Jerry Kang, *E-racing E-lections*, 34 Loy. L.A. L. Rev. 1155, 1155 (2001). He urges paying "close attention to how cyberspace can be specifically designed to alter preferences and attitudes, political as well as social, of its inhabitants in particular ways." *Id.* at 1169. He continues:

> In terms of governing, the spread of the Internet may encourage more instantaneous forms of direct democracy. This is bad news for racial minorities because they are numerical minorities and people vote more in their self-interest than in the public interest. To respond to the possibility of a digital tyranny of an electronically mediated majority, racial minorities must prepare to play smart. We should start right now exploring how information technologies can counter numerical disadvantages. This might require hacking bogus polls. This might require smart electronic voting guides that "get the vote out" in an entirely different sense. It is politics and struggle on a new terrain.

Id. at 1169–70.

Kang defines E-voting as "voting through any computer-mediated device (e.g., desktop computer, cellular telephone, personal digital assistant, Internet appliance) from any geographical location that the voter chooses, through a communications network, such as the Internet." *Id.* at 1155, n.1.

On the differential rates of access to the internet, Kang reports these racial differences in household access to the Internet: Asian-Pacific Islanders (56.8%); whites (46.1%); blacks (23.5%); and Hispanics (23.6%). *Id.* at 1156, n.8.

R. Michael Alvarez and Jonathan Nagler express concern about the consequences of internet voting:

> Some low propensity voters, like non-whites or the unemployed, might see further reductions in the quality and strength of their political representation as a result of the introduction of widespread Internet voting. Some low propensity voters, in particular the younger generations of voters, might see enhanced political representation with the introduction of Internet voting as this might make younger voters more likely to participate in politics. Thus, if Internet voting were widely used in American politics, it would change the character of political representation, with some specific groups behind the digital divide (minorities, the unemployed, and the elderly) losing further political power while other groups (especially the young and those in urban areas) might see increased political power.

R. Michael Alvarez & Jonathan Nagler, *The Likely Consequences of Internet Voting for Political Representation*, 34 Loy. L.A. L. Rev. 1115,

1147–48 (2001) (expressing pessimism about the validity of internet voting in light of the Voting Rights Act).

3. Can "direct" experiences that occur through the internet be comparable to direct experiences in face-to-face communication? What implications will increased internet encounters mean for democratic participation? If e-voting is inevitable as Kang predicts, but its consequences decrease representation among nonwhites or low income populations, what will be the fate of democratic participation? Might part of the answer hinge upon education?

SECTION 2. EDUCATION

Education, like voting, is an important building block in society, ensuring democratic participation. As john a. powell has observed, "All discussions of education are at essence discussions of citizenship." john a. powell, *The Tensions Between Integration and School Reform*, 28 Hastings Const. L.Q. 655, 655 (2001). He continues:

> The Supreme Court has identified "the objectives of public education as the inculcation of fundamental values necessary for the maintenance of a democratic political system." [Bd. of Educ. v. Pico, 457 U.S. 853, 876 (1982).] More, these are discussions on the ability of members of all races to participate fully in democratic structures, and critiques of the formation and sustenance of racially just democratic structures. Molly Townes O'Brien has written that the efficacy of education could be measured by its capacity to "instill moral character, critical thinking ability, and cultural literacy," but it is studied, instead, in terms of "standardized test scores, drop-out rates, or occupational attainment." It is integration, in terms of not merely parity but in terms of the creation of a just space for the constitution of the self, education, and democracy, that must be the measure for the success of our schools.

Id.

Social justice advocates, recognizing this essential connection between the self, education, and democracy, sought to establish education as a fundamental right under equal protection review. Even when that effort failed, they convinced the court that exclusion from education denied the equal protection of the laws under the Fourteenth Amendment. Battles over a right to a quality education shifted to state courts, where theories of equality, educational adequacy, and debates about integration and diversity continued. Contemporary education battles continue to examine the meaning of integration, diversity, and acting affirmatively in order to ensure that merit is not measured by cookie-cutter numbers.

A. Education as a Fundamental Right

Given the importance attributed to education by the court in *Brown*, social justice litigators sought to establish a fundamental interest in education as the next frontier of litigation. The U.S. Supreme Court declined to find that education was a fundamental right under the equal protection clause in San Antonio Independent School District v. Rodriguez, 411 U.S. 1 (1973). The suit had been initiated by Mexican-American parents who sued on behalf of children who were minority group members or poor and resided in school districts with a low property tax base. Affluent school districts spent more money per pupil than poor school districts. The Court had never considered discrimination based on wealth to be constitutionally suspect. While acknowledging the importance of education as bearing "a peculiarly close relationship to other rights and liberties accorded protection under the Constitution," 411 U.S. at 35, the Court declined to apply the strict scrutiny standard of equal protection review, accorded to fundamental rights, to the Texas funding scheme. The court observed:

> Education, perhaps even more than welfare assistance, presents a myriad of "intractable economic, social, and even philosophical problems." The very complexity of the problems of financing and managing a statewide public school system suggests that "there will be more than one constitutionally permissible method of solving them," and that, within the limits of rationality, "the legislature's efforts to tackle the problems" should be entitled to respect. On even the most basic questions in this area the scholars and educational experts are divided. Indeed, one of the major sources of controversy concerns the extent to which there is a demonstrable correlation between educational expenditures and the quality of education—an assumed correlation underlying virtually every legal conclusion drawn by the District Court in this case. Related to the questioned relationship between cost and quality is the equally unsettled controversy as to the proper goals of a system of public education. And the question regarding the most effective relationship between state boards of education and local school boards, in terms of their respective responsibilities and degrees of control, is now undergoing searching re-examination. The ultimate wisdom as to these and related problems of education is not likely to be divined for all time even by the scholars who now so earnestly debate the issues. In such circumstances, the judiciary is well advised to refrain from imposing on the States inflexible constitutional restraints that could circumscribe or handicap the continued research and experimentation so vital to finding even partial solutions to educational problems and to keeping abreast of ever-changing conditions.
>
> * * *
>
> [Justice Marshall dissented, observing:]
>
> In my judgment, the right of every American to an equal start in life, so far as the provision of a state service as important as education is concerned, is far too vital to permit state discrimination on grounds as tenuous as those presented by this record. Nor can I accept the notion that it is sufficient to remit these appellees to the

vagaries of the political process which, contrary to the majority's suggestion, has proved singularly unsuited to the task of providing a remedy for this discrimination. I, for one, am unsatisfied with the hope of an ultimate "political" solution sometime in the indefinite future while, in the meantime, countless children unjustifiably receive inferior educations that "may affect their hearts and minds in a way unlikely ever to be undone."

* * *

* * * I must once more voice my disagreement with the Court's rigidified approach to equal protection analysis. The Court apparently seeks to establish today that equal protection cases fall into one of two neat categories which dictate the appropriate standard of review—strict scrutiny or mere rationality. But this Court's decisions in the field of equal protection defy such easy categorization. A principled reading of what this Court has done reveals that it has applied a spectrum of standards in reviewing discrimination allegedly violative of the Equal Protection Clause. This spectrum clearly comprehends variations in the degree of care with which the Court will scrutinize particular classifications, depending, I believe, on the constitutional and societal importance of the interest adversely affected and the recognized invidiousness of the basis upon which the particular classification is drawn. * * *

* * *

Nevertheless, the majority today attempts to force this case into the same category for purposes of equal protection analysis as decisions involving discrimination affecting commercial interests. By so doing, the majority singles this case out for analytic treatment at odds with what seems to me to be the clear trend of recent decisions in this Court, and thereby ignores the constitutional importance of the interest at stake and the invidiousness of the particular classification, factors that call for far more than the lenient scrutiny of the Texas financing scheme which the majority pursues. Yet if the discrimination inherent in the Texas scheme is scrutinized with the care demanded by the interest and classification present in this case, the unconstitutionality of that scheme is unmistakable.

411 U.S. at 42, 71–72, 98–99, 110.

Why did the *Rodriguez* Court decline to hold that education is a fundamental right? Equal opportunity to education is a basic tenet of international human rights law. *See* Connie de la Vega, *The Right to Equal Education: Merely a Guiding Principle or Customary International Legal Right?*, 11 Harv. BlackLetter L.J. 37 (1994) (urging that international standards be used to convince state courts that a right to equal educational opportunity exists under state constitutions).

B. Exclusion From Education as a Denial of Equal Protection

Although the *Rodriguez* Court held that education was not a fundamental right, the Court treated it as extremely important in *Plyler v. Doe*.

PLYLER v. DOE

457 U.S. 202 (1982)

Justice BRENNAN delivered the opinion of the Court.

The question presented by these cases is whether, consistent with the Equal Protection Clause of the Fourteenth Amendment, Texas may deny to undocumented school-age children the free public education that it provides to children who are citizens of the United States or legally admitted aliens.

Since the late 19th century, the United States has restricted immigration into this country. Unsanctioned entry into the United States is a crime, and those who have entered unlawfully are subject to deportation. But despite the existence of these legal restrictions, a substantial number of persons have succeeded in unlawfully entering the United States, and now live within various States, including the State of Texas.

In May 1975, the Texas Legislature revised its education laws to withhold from local school districts any state funds for the education of children who were not "legally admitted" into the United States. The 1975 revision also authorized local school districts to deny enrollment in their public schools to children not "legally admitted" to the country. These cases involve constitutional challenges to those provisions.

This is a class action * * * on behalf of certain school-age children of Mexican origin residing in Smith County, Tex., who could not establish that they had been legally admitted into the United States. * * *

In considering this motion, the District Court made extensive findings of fact. The court found that neither * * * [the law] nor the School District policy implementing it had "either the purpose or effect of keeping illegal aliens out of the State of Texas." Respecting defendants' further claim that * * * [the law] was simply a financial measure designed to avoid a drain on the State's fisc, the court recognized that the increases in population resulting from the immigration of Mexican nationals into the United States had created problems for the public schools of the State, and that these problems were exacerbated by the special educational needs of immigrant Mexican children. The court noted, however, that the increase in school enrollment was primarily attributable to the admission of children who were legal residents. It also found that while the "exclusion of all undocumented children from the public schools in Texas would eventually result in economies at some level," funding from both the State and Federal Governments was based primarily on the number of children enrolled. In net effect then, barring undocumented children from the schools would save money, but it would "not necessarily" improve "the quality of education." The court further observed that the impact of * * * [the law] was borne primarily by a very small subclass of illegal aliens, "entire families who have migrated illegally and—for all practical purposes—permanently to the United States." [The District Court contrasted this group with those illegal aliens who entered the country alone in order to earn money to send to their dependents in Mexico, and who in many instances remained in this country for only a short period of time.] Finally, the court noted that under current laws and practices "the illegal alien of today may well be the legal alien of tomorrow," and that without an education, these undocumented children, "[a]lready disadvantaged as a result of poverty, lack of English-speaking ability, and undeniable racial prejudices, ... will become permanently locked into the lowest socio-economic class."

* * *

The Fourteenth Amendment provides that "[n]o State shall ... deprive any person of life, liberty, or property, without due process of law; nor deny to *any person within its jurisdiction* the equal protection of the laws." * * * Appellants argue at the outset that undocumented aliens, because of their immigration status, are not "persons within the jurisdiction" of the State of Texas, and that they therefore have no right to the equal protection of Texas law. We reject this argument. Whatever his status under the immigration laws, an alien is surely a "person" in any ordinary sense of that term. Aliens, even aliens whose presence in this country is unlawful, have long been recognized as "persons" guaranteed due process of law by the Fifth and Fourteenth Amendments. Indeed, we have clearly held that the Fifth Amendment protects aliens whose presence in this country is unlawful from invidious discrimination by the Federal Government.

* * *

> "The Fourteenth Amendment to the Constitution is not confined to the protection of citizens. It says: 'Nor shall any state deprive any person of life, liberty, or property without due process of law; nor deny to any person within its jurisdiction the equal protection of the laws.' *These provisions are universal in their application, to all persons within the territorial jurisdiction*, without regard to any differences of race, of color, or of nationality; and the protection of the laws is a pledge of the protection of equal laws."

Yick Wo, [118 U.S.356] at 369.

* * *

Use of the phrase "within its jurisdiction" thus does not detract from, but rather confirms, the understanding that the protection of the Fourteenth Amendment extends to anyone, citizen or stranger, who *is* subject to the laws of a State, and reaches into every corner of a State's territory. That a person's initial entry into a State, or into the United States, was unlawful, and that he may for that reason be expelled, cannot negate the simple fact of his presence within the State's territorial perimeter. Given such presence, he is subject to the full range of obligations imposed by the State's civil and criminal laws. And until he leaves the jurisdiction—either voluntarily, or involuntarily in accordance with the Constitution and laws of the United States—he is entitled to the equal protection of the laws that a State may choose to establish.

Our conclusion that the illegal aliens who are plaintiffs in these cases may claim the benefit of the Fourteenth Amendment's guarantee of equal protection only begins the inquiry. The more difficult question is whether the Equal Protection Clause has been violated by the refusal of the State of Texas to reimburse local school boards for the education of children who cannot demonstrate that their presence within the United States is lawful, or by the imposition by those school boards of the burden of tuition on those children. It is to this question that we now turn.

The Equal Protection Clause directs that "all persons similarly circumstanced shall be treated alike." But so too, "[t]he Constitution does not require things which are different in fact or opinion to be treated in law as though they were the same." * * * In applying the Equal Protection Clause to most forms of state action, we thus seek only the assurance that the classification at issue bears some fair relationship to a legitimate public purpose.

But we would not be faithful to our obligations under the Fourteenth Amendment if we applied so deferential a standard to every classification. The Equal Protection Clause was intended as a restriction on state legislative action inconsistent with elemental constitutional premises. Thus we have treated as presumptively invidious those classifications that disadvantage a "suspect class," or that impinge upon the exercise of a "fundamental right." With respect to such classifications, it is appropriate to enforce the mandate of equal protection by requiring the State to demonstrate that its classification has been precisely tailored to serve a compelling governmental interest. In addition, we have recognized that certain forms of legislative classification, while not facially invidious, nonetheless give rise to recurring constitutional difficulties; in these limited circumstances we have sought the assurance that the classification reflects a reasoned judgment consistent with the ideal of equal protection by inquiring whether it may fairly be viewed as furthering a substantial interest of the State. We turn to a consideration of the standard appropriate for the evaluation of * * * [the law].

Sheer incapability or lax enforcement of the laws barring entry into this country, coupled with the failure to establish an effective bar to the employment of undocumented aliens, has resulted in the creation of a substantial "shadow population" of illegal migrants—numbering in the millions—within our borders. This situation raises the specter of a permanent caste of undocumented resident aliens, encouraged by some to remain here as a source of cheap labor, but nevertheless denied the benefits that our society makes available to citizens and lawful residents. The existence of such an underclass presents most difficult problems for a Nation that prides itself on adherence to principles of equality under law.

The children who are plaintiffs in these cases are special members of this underclass. Persuasive arguments support the view that a State may withhold its beneficence from those whose very presence within the

United States is the product of their own unlawful conduct. These arguments do not apply with the same force to classifications imposing disabilities on the minor *children* of such illegal entrants. At the least, those who elect to enter our territory by stealth and in violation of our law should be prepared to bear the consequences, including, but not limited to, deportation. But the children of those illegal entrants are not comparably situated. Their "parents have the ability to conform their conduct to societal norms," and presumably the ability to remove themselves from the State's jurisdiction; but the children who are plaintiffs in these cases "can affect neither their parents' conduct nor their own status." Even if the State found it expedient to control the conduct of adults by acting against their children, legislation directing the onus of a parent's misconduct against his children does not comport with fundamental conceptions of justice. * * *

Of course, undocumented status is not irrelevant to any proper legislative goal. Nor is undocumented status an absolutely immutable characteristic since it is the product of conscious, indeed unlawful, action. But * * * [the law] is directed against children, and imposes its discriminatory burden on the basis of a legal characteristic over which children can have little control. It is thus difficult to conceive of a rational justification for penalizing these children for their presence within the United States. Yet that appears to be precisely the effect of * * * [the law].

Public education is not a "right" granted to individuals by the Constitution. *San Antonio Independent School Dist. v. Rodriguez*, 411 U.S. 1, 35 (1973). But neither is it merely some governmental "benefit" indistinguishable from other forms of social welfare legislation. Both the importance of education in maintaining our basic institutions, and the lasting impact of its deprivation on the life of the child, mark the distinction. The "American people have always regarded education and [the] acquisition of knowledge as matters of supreme importance." We have recognized "the public schools as a most vital civic institution for the preservation of a democratic system of government," and as the primary vehicle for transmitting "the values on which our society rests." "[A]s . . . pointed out early in our history, . . . some degree of education is necessary to prepare citizens to participate effectively and intelligently in our open political system if we are to preserve freedom and independence." *Wisconsin v. Yoder*, 406 U.S. 205, 221 (1972). And these historic "perceptions of the public schools as inculcating fundamental values necessary to the maintenance of a democratic political system have been confirmed by the observations of social scientists." In addition, education provides the basic tools by which individuals might lead economically productive lives to the benefit of us all. In sum, education has a fundamental role in maintaining the fabric of our society. We cannot ignore the significant social costs borne by our Nation when select groups are denied the means to absorb the values and skills upon which our social order rests.

In addition to the pivotal role of education in sustaining our political and cultural heritage, denial of education to some isolated group of children poses an affront to one of the goals of the Equal Protection Clause: the abolition of governmental barriers presenting unreasonable obstacles to advancement on the basis of individual merit. Paradoxically, by depriving the children of any disfavored group of an education, we foreclose the means by which that group might raise the level of esteem in which it is held by the majority. But more directly, "education prepares individuals to be self-reliant and self-sufficient participants in society." *Wisconsin v. Yoder, supra*, 406 U.S. at 221. Illiteracy is an enduring disability. The inability to read and write will handicap the individual deprived of a basic education each and every day of his life. The inestimable toll of that deprivation on the social economic, intellectual, and psychological well-being of the individual, and the obstacle it poses to individual achievement, make it most difficult to reconcile the cost or the principle of a status-based denial of basic education with the framework of equality embodied in the Equal Protection Clause. * * *

* * * Undocumented aliens cannot be treated as a suspect class because their presence in this country in violation of federal law is not a "constitutional irrelevancy." Nor is education a fundamental right; a State need not justify by compelling necessity every variation in the manner in which education is provided to its population. But more is involved in these cases than the abstract question whether * * * [the law] discriminates against a suspect class, or whether education is a fundamental right. * * * [The law] imposes a lifetime hardship on a discrete class of children not accountable for their disabling status. The stigma of illiteracy will mark them for the rest of their lives. By denying these children a basic education, we deny them the ability to live within the structure of our civic institutions, and foreclose any realistic possibility that they will contribute in even the smallest way to the progress of our Nation. In determining the rationality of * * * [the law], we may appropriately take into account its costs to the Nation and to the innocent children who are its victims. In light of these countervailing costs, the discrimination contained in * * * [the law] can hardly be considered rational unless it furthers some substantial goal of the State.

It is the State's principal argument * * * that the undocumented status of these children *vel non* establishes a sufficient rational basis for denying them benefits that a State might choose to afford other residents. The State notes that while other aliens are admitted "on an equality of legal privileges with all citizens under non-discriminatory laws," the asserted right of these children to an education can claim no implicit congressional imprimatur. Indeed, in the State's view, Congress' apparent disapproval of the presence of these children within the United States, and the evasion of the federal regulatory program that is the mark of undocumented status, provides authority for its decision to impose upon them special disabilities. Faced with an equal protection challenge respecting the treatment of aliens, we agree that the courts must be attentive to congressional policy; the exercise of congressional power might well affect the State's prerogatives to afford differential treatment to a particular class of aliens. But we are unable to find in the congressional immigration scheme any statement of policy that might weigh significantly in arriving at an equal protection balance concerning the State's authority to deprive these children of an education.

* * *

To be sure, like all persons who have entered the United States unlawfully, these children are subject to deportation. But there is no assurance that a child subject to deportation will ever be deported. An illegal entrant might be granted federal permission to continue to reside in this country, or even to become a citizen. In light of the discretionary federal power to grant relief from deportation, a State cannot realistically determine that any particular undocumented child will in fact be deported until after deportation proceedings have been completed. It would of course be most difficult for the State to justify a denial of education to a child enjoying an inchoate federal permission to remain.

We are reluctant to impute to Congress the intention to withhold from these children, for so long as they are present in this country through no fault of their own, access to a basic education. In other contexts, undocumented status, coupled with some articulable federal policy, might enhance state authority with respect to the treatment of undocumented aliens. But in the area of special constitutional sensitivity presented by these cases, and in the absence of any contrary indication fairly discernible in the present legislative record, we perceive no national policy that supports the State in denying these children an elementary education.* * *

Appellants argue that the classification at issue furthers an interest in the "preservation of the state's limited resources for the education of its lawful residents." Of course, a concern for the preservation of resources standing alone can hardly justify the classification used in allocating those resources. The State must do more than justify its classification with a concise expression of an intention to discriminate. Apart from the asserted state prerogative to act against undocumented children solely on the basis of their undocumented status—an asserted prerogative that carries only minimal force in the circumstances of these cases—we discern three colorable state interests that might support * * * [the law].

First, appellants appear to suggest that the State may seek to protect itself from an influx of illegal immigrants. While a State might have an interest in mitigating the potentially harsh economic effects of sudden shifts in population, * * * [the law] hardly offers an effective method of dealing with an urgent demographic or economic problem. There is no evidence in the record suggesting that illegal entrants impose any significant burden on the State's economy. To the contrary, the available evidence suggests that illegal aliens underutilize public services, while contributing their labor to the local economy and tax money to the state fisc. The dominant incentive for illegal entry into the

State of Texas is the availability of employment; few if any illegal immigrants come to this country, or presumably to the State of Texas, in order to avail themselves of a free education. Thus, even making the doubtful assumption that the net impact of illegal aliens on the economy of the State is negative, we think it clear that "[c]harging tuition to undocumented children constitutes a ludicrously ineffectual attempt to stem the tide of illegal immigration," at least when compared with the alternative of prohibiting the employment of illegal aliens.

Second, * * * appellants suggest that undocumented children are appropriately singled out for exclusion because of the special burdens they impose on the State's ability to provide high-quality public education. But the record in no way supports the claim that exclusion of undocumented children is likely to improve the overall quality of education in the State. * * * [A]fter reviewing the State's school financing mechanism, the District Court * * * concluded that barring undocumented children from local schools would not necessarily improve the quality of education provided in those schools. Of course, even if improvement in the quality of education were a likely result of barring some *number* of children from the schools of the State, the State must support its selection of *this* group as the appropriate target for exclusion. In terms of educational cost and need, however, undocumented children are "basically indistinguishable" from legally resident alien children.

Finally, appellants suggest that undocumented children are appropriately singled out because their unlawful presence within the United States renders them less likely than other children to remain within the boundaries of the State, and to put their education to productive social or political use within the State. Even assuming that such an interest is legitimate, it is an interest that is most difficult to quantify. The State has no assurance that any child, citizen or not, will employ the education provided by the State within the confines of the State's borders. In any event, the record is clear that many of the undocumented children disabled by this classification will remain in this country indefinitely, and that some will become lawful residents or citizens of the United States. It is difficult to understand precisely what the State hopes to achieve by promoting the creation and perpetuation of a subclass of illiterates within our boundaries, surely adding to the problems and costs of unemployment, welfare, and crime. It is thus clear that whatever savings might be achieved by denying these children an education, they are wholly insubstantial in light of the costs involved to these children, the State, and the Nation.

If the State is to deny a discrete group of innocent children the free public education that it offers to other children residing within its borders, that denial must be justified by a showing that it furthers some substantial state interest. No such showing was made here. * * *

Affirmed.

* * *

Chief Justice BURGER, with whom Justice WHITE, Justice REHNQUIST, and Justice O'CONNOR join, dissenting.

Were it our business to set the Nation's social policy, I would agree without hesitation that it is senseless for an enlightened society to deprive any children—including illegal aliens—of an elementary education. I fully agree that it would be folly—and wrong—to tolerate creation of a segment of society made up of illiterate persons, many having a limited or no command of our language. However, the Constitution does not constitute us as "Platonic Guardians" nor does it vest in this Court the authority to strike down laws because they do not meet our standards of desirable social policy, "wisdom," or "common sense." We trespass on the assigned function of the political branches under our structure of limited and separated powers when we assume a policymaking role as the Court does today.

* * *

In the end, we are told little more than that the level of scrutiny employed to strike down the Texas law applies only when illegal alien children are deprived of a public education. If ever a court was guilty of an unabashedly result-oriented approach, this case is a prime example.

* * *

Once it is conceded—as the Court does—that illegal aliens are not a suspect class, and that education is not a fundamental right, our inquiry should focus on and be limited to whether the legislative classification at issue bears a rational relationship to a legitimate state purpose.

* * *

Without laboring what will undoubtedly seem obvious to many, it simply is not "irrational" for a state to conclude that it does not have the same responsibility to provide benefits for persons whose very presence in the state and this country is illegal as it does to provide for persons lawfully present. By definition, illegal aliens have no right whatever to be here, and the state may reasonably, and constitutionally, elect not to provide them with governmental services at the expense of those who are lawfully in the state. * * *

It is significant that the Federal Government has seen fit to exclude illegal aliens from numerous social welfare programs, such as the food stamp program, the old-age assistance, aid to families with dependent children, aid to the blind, aid to the permanently and totally disabled, and supplemental security income programs, the Medicare hospital insurance benefits program, and the Medicaid hospital insurance benefits for the aged and disabled program. Although these exclusions do not conclusively demonstrate the constitutionality of the State's use of the same classification for comparable purposes, at the very least they tend to support the rationality of excluding illegal alien residents of a state from such programs so as to preserve the state's finite revenues for the benefit of lawful residents.

* * *

Denying a free education to illegal alien children is not a choice I would make were I a legislator. Apart from compassionate considerations, the long-range costs of excluding any children from the public schools may well outweigh the costs of educating them. But that is not the issue; the fact that there are sound *policy* arguments against the Texas Legislature's choice does not render that choice an unconstitutional one.

Notes and Question

1. Has the Court in *Plyler* followed Justice Marshall's approach to equal protection, discussed in chapter 8 in *Dandridge v. Williams*, resisting the rigid tests of "rational basis" or "strict scrutiny?" How does *Plyler* distinguish the *Rodriguez* holding? In what circumstances might *Plyler* be further extended? Has education turned out to be an *almost*-fundamental right that will merit increasing protection? Or is *Plyler* limited to its facts (helpless children who are subjected to classifications by the state)? Would *Plyler* provide an argument for challenging the exclusion from benefits of children born after their parents begin receiving welfare benefits? *See* chapter 8 for a discussion of welfare benefits.

2. In *Plyler*, plaintiffs introduced testimony that "fifty to sixty per cent . . . of current legal alien workers were formerly illegal aliens." 457 U.S. at 207, n.4. A defense witness testified that " 'undocumented children can and do live in the United States for years, and adjust their status through marriage to a citizen or permanent resident.' The court also took notice of congressional proposals to 'legalize' the status of many unlawful entrants." *Id.* Does the fact that many formerly undocumented people attain legal status explain the Court's decision?

3. The Court rejects the claim that undocumented aliens are a suspect class. 457 U.S. at 223. The Court, in a footnote, examines indicia of suspectness, observing:

> Some classifications are more likely than others to reflect deep-seated prejudice rather than legislative rationality in pursuit of some legitimate objective. Legislation predicated on such prejudice is easily recognized as incompatible with the constitutional understanding that each person is to be judged individually and is entitled to equal justice under the law. Classifications treated as suspect tend to be irrelevant to any proper legislative goal. Finally, certain groups, indeed largely the same groups, have historically been "relegated to such a position of political powerlessness as to command extraordinary protection from the majoritarian political process."

457 U.S. at 216, n.14. What images do the words "alien" and "illegal" suggest? Are these images different from those associated with the words "worker," "child," or "undocumented?" Why does the Court persist in the use of the "illegal alien" language? Why does the Court's language

shift when describing "children" to the adjective "undocumented?" Does this case suggest lessons about language and social justice litigation?

4. In addition to its application in *Plyler*, the Supreme Court has utilized some form of intermediate scrutiny to classifications involving gender, *see* U.S. v. Virginia, 518 U.S. 515 (1996); Mississippi Univ. for Women v. Hogan, 458 U.S. 718 (1982).

C. Educational Adequacy and Equality Under State Constitutions

While the federal constitution provides protection for citizens, states may choose to protect interests at a higher level, to protect interests not protected under the federal scheme, or simply to apply different tests for evaluating equal protection claims under their own constitutions. In one such case, Serrano v. Priest, 18 Cal.3d 728, 557 P.2d 929 (1976), California examined a similar financing scheme under its state constitution:

> [O]ur state equal protection provisions, while "substantially the equivalent of" the guarantees contained in the Fourteenth Amendment to the United States Constitution, are possessed of an independent vitality which, in a given case, may demand an analysis different from that which would obtain if only the federal standard were applicable. We have recently stated in a related context: "(I)n the area of fundamental civil liberties—which includes . . . all protections of the California Declaration of Rights—we sit as a court of last resort, subject only to the qualification that our interpretations may not restrict the guarantees accorded the national citizenry under the federal charter. In such constitutional adjudication, our first referent is California law and the full panoply of rights Californians have come to expect as their due." * * *
>
> * * *
>
> * * * [F]or purposes of assessing our state public school financing system in light of our state constitutional provisions guaranteeing equal protection of the laws (1) discrimination in educational opportunity on the basis of district wealth involves a suspect classification, and (2) education is a fundamental interest. Because the school financing system here in question has been shown by substantial and convincing evidence produced at trial to involve a suspect classification (insofar as this system, like the former one, draws distinctions on the basis of district wealth), and because that classification affects the fundamental interest of the students of this state in education, we have no difficulty in concluding today * * * that the school financing system before us must be examined under our state constitutional provisions with that strict and searching scrutiny appropriate to such a case.

18 Cal.3d at 764–66.

Justice William J. Brennan extolls the virtues of using a state court approach:

> [T]he point I want to stress here is that state courts cannot rest when they have afforded their citizens the full protections of the federal Constitution. State constitutions, too, are a font of individual liberties, their protections often extending beyond those required by the Supreme Court's interpretation of federal law. The legal revolution which has brought federal law to the fore must not be allowed to inhibit the independent protective force of state law—for without it, the full realization of our liberties cannot be guaranteed.

William J. Brennan, Jr., *State Constitutions and the Protection of Individual Rights*, 90 Harv. L. Rev. 489, 491 (1977).

Consider the value of a state court approach as measured by developments in the education arena. As education litigation evolved over two decades, state courts turned to different constitutional approaches to protect rights to equality in education. Michael Heise summarized this history:

> Commentators note three distinct "waves" of school finance court decisions. The first wave, which focused on the federal constitution's Equal Protection Clause, began in 1971 with *Serrano v. Priest* and ended in 1973 with the U.S. Supreme Court's decision in *San Antonio Independent School District v. Rodriguez*. The second wave, which concentrated on equal protection and education clauses found in state constitutions, began in 1973 with *Robinson v. Cahill* [303 A.2d 273 (N.J.), *cert. denied*, 414 U.S. 976 (1973)] and ended in 1989. The third and current wave of decisions, which began in 1989, focuses on education clauses in state constitutions.
>
> Besides its focus on the education clauses of state constitutions, the most recent wave of school finance court decisions is distinguished by another important factor. Specifically, the third wave illustrates the replacement of traditional "equity" court decisions with "adequacy" decisions. The initial two waves of equity decisions typically sought to reduce spending disparities and focused on traditional input measures such as per-pupil and overall educational spending. In contrast, the more recent adequacy decisions concentrate on the underlying sufficiency of school funding and argue that "all children are entitled to an education of at least a certain quality and that more money is necessary to bring the worst school districts up to the minimum level mandated by state education clauses." Adequacy decisions emphasize differences in the quality of educational services provided, rather than the resources provided to the school districts.

Michael Heise, *State Constitutions, School Finance Litigation, and the "Third Wave": From Equity to Adequacy*, 68 Temp. L. Rev. 1151, 1152–53 (1995).

Elaborating on adequacy theories based on state constitutions, john a. powell states:

> Virtually all states, by their constitution or statutes, guarantee some of form of adequate education to their students. Where such provisions are found to be legally binding, the state has an obligation to provide, and students have an entitlement to receive, an adequate education. When the state can take reasonable measures to meet this obligation, and fails to do so, it has breached its constitutional duty. Courts are reluctant to impose definitions of adequacy, but education experts, state promulgated standards, and the opportunities provided by successful schools, can guide the court in defining adequacy. Thus, insufficient funding to support a basic education would violate the adequacy standard. Similarly, if it can be shown that segregation by race and socioeconomic status undermines students' ability to achieve an adequate education, the state violates its duty to provide an adequate education, where it allows such segregation.

john a. powell, *Segregation and Educational Inadequacy in Twin Cities Public Schools*, 17 Hamline J. Pub. L. & Pol'y 337, 362 (1996).

In the next article, john powell argues that "radical integration" rather than recent school reform proposals ought to be the focus of work for social justice. Observing that "[a]ll discussions of education are at essence discussions of citizenship," powell seeks more than parity between schools. In a portion of his article omitted here, he explains that many contemporary school reform measures, including charter schools, standardized testing, tracking, educational choice programs, and vouchers, have had negative effects on integration. Powell seeks the transformation of institutions rather than merely distributive justice. He argues for the importance of integration to the goal of creating a "just space for the constitution of the self, education, and democracy." Consider whether the arena of education offers transformative potential, as he suggests.

john a. powell

The Tensions Between Integration and School Reform
28 Hastings Const. L.Q. 655, 660–65,
667–71, 681–85, 695–97 (2001)

* * * It is important to recognize that advances toward educational parity have been made.

* * * [A]chievement gaps have narrowed considerably between African Americans and whites. There is near equivalency between whites and students of color in high school graduation rates, and college attendance rates have risen dramatically for African American students.

* * *

A criticism I anticipate is that my call for a transformation of education into one that has radical integration as its goal and reform as its armature is idealistic and unrealizable. Even if this model of education is unobtainable, I would respond, if it functions as a regulative ideal and creates real improvements, it will have served the transformative mission. It may also provide a means of measuring our progress beyond the narrow goal of parity.

The goal of public education is not only to provide all children with a mastery of skills and knowledge, but to take them beyond that to full participation in society. Second, it must be acknowledged that public education is the primary mechanism for instilling our societal values.

* * *

Education is a forum in which justice, and not merely choice, is imperative. Neither equality in income, nor ability to pay for education translates into equality of educational access, attainment, or performance. Iris Young concurs, "Money continues to be a major discriminator. Middle-and upper-class children have better schools than poor or working-class children. Thus they are better prepared to compete for college admission. If by chance poor and working-class children qualify for college, they often cannot pay...."

Edmund Gordon has written that an effective education and social justice, a too often disowned democratic ideal, are inextricably linked:

> There may be some educational context/process relationships that are so symbiotic as to defy separation. It appears that education and social justice are so symbiotically related. In modern societies the achievement of universally effective education may not be possible in the absence of contexts in which social justice is valued and practiced. Similarly, the achievement of social justice may not be possible in the absence of achievement of universally effective education.

Since education is a highly important locus for personal development, and effective education cannot occur without social justice at the fore, we should ask what would result if justice were inserted into education. Can the ideas students have about race be changed if education is just? The answer is clear from research on school desegregation: students who are educated in an integrated environment are more likely to live in integrated environments as adults. This evidence shows that individual preferences are not pre-ordained; rather, that schools are a site of formation of the self and the choices made later on in life. That this is true of the self, the site of education, and perceptions on race has great significance for a new model of education and justice.

* * *

To understand the ways in which the citizenship of African Americans has been limited, particularly in the context of educational rights, it is necessary to examine the history of the courts' engagement with the issues of access to educational institutions, broadly defined, and the negative impacts of the racially hierarchical nature of education on African Americans, particularly low-income African Americans.

This story is often told beginning with *Brown*, but it is more appropriate to begin the story with *Dred Scott*. This is because, although *Brown* is often cited by the court for the overturning of *Plessy*, this is too narrow a reading of *Brown*: it can also be read as the overturning of *Dred Scott*. The Court in *Dred Scott* was explicit that African Americans, slaves or otherwise, were not part of the American polity. In the land of the free, even free African Americans were unfree. There were no rights that whites were required to respect for African Americans. They were subordinated and subjugated. They were non-citizens. *Plessy* was a modification of this same logic. *Brown*, however, embodied a pledge on the part of the legal system to alter the systems that educate youth for citizenship—toward a racially just set of systems—indeed, a pledge to grant full citizenship to African Americans.

Though our schools today are the sites of greater equity than in the era preceding *Brown*, schools in this nation have never been truly integrated and are currently rapidly regressing to a state of racial and economic segregation. Equity is not justice. The segregation observed at present is a perpetuation of the denial of the right to the constitution of the self, education and, more largely, democracy, outside of a hierarchical and subordinating setting. When responding to racial segregation, the courts have largely condoned assimilation or striven for desegregation alone, rather than for a transformation of the system of education that radical integrationism calls for.

In the early history of the United States, African Americans and other people of color were wholly denied citizenship. In *Dred Scott v. Sandford*, Chief Justice Taney stated:

> The question is simply this: Can a negro, whose ancestors were imported into this country, and sold as slaves, become a member of the political community formed and brought into existence by the Constitution of the United States, and as such become entitled to all the rights, and privileges, and immunities, guaranteed by that instrument to the citizen?

The Court held that black people were not citizens, and therefore had no rights under the Constitution, stating that a slave "could form no part of the design, no constituent ingredient or portion of a society based upon *common*, that is, upon *equal* interests and powers. He could not at the same time be the sovereign and the slave."

Dred Scott was reconfigured in *Plessy*, but the position of the Court that African Americans should be subjugated to whites strongly remained: a renewed statement about the very limited citizenship rights of people of color. *Plessy v. Ferguson* upheld the segregation of African Americans in "separate but equal" settings. * * *

This pronouncement of jurisprudential support for separate but equal educational systems in *Plessy* caused civil rights advocates to strategically alter their approach, by necessity of this legal framework[,] to a focus on institutional parity rather than racial justice in education. From 1939 to 1954, civil rights activists focused their challenges on the allegedly equal status of legally segregated African American schools, calling for the enforcement of *Plessy*. One result of this tactic, and a demonstration of the willingness of whites to fund segregation, was that financing for African American schools in the South increased 800 percent.

The *Brown* cases * * * exhibited a reversal in the approach of civil rights advocates, who targeted their efforts toward undermining the rationale behind keeping schools separate, having won for a time the battle over equality in funding.

In the landmark 1954 decision of *Brown v. Board of Education*, the Supreme Court ruled that separate educational facilities did indeed provide unequal opportunities, finding against proponents of separate but equal schools. In overruling *Plessy*, the Court in *Brown* acknowledged that the psychological stigma of segregation deprived African American students of an equal education, stating that segregated schools are "inherently unequal." *Brown* can be seen as the first promise of full citizenship to African Americans. With a truly equal and integrated education, African American students would take a substantial step toward full and equal participation in American society. Moreover, students of all races, and our society itself, would benefit from a more fully realized democracy.

That this promise would not be kept, in any way truly transformative of education and other democratic structures, was apparent very early on. Education administrators, politicians, and the judiciary refused to accept the full meaning of the case and generally read *Brown* in its most narrow construction: as a command to make only slight reparations for the exclusion of African Americans from the very structure that would permit participation of African Americans in the shaping and construction of American society. In 1955, one year after their original decision in *Brown*, the Court in *Brown v. Board of Education (No. II)*, placed the implementation of the *Brown I* ruling in the hands of district courts, merely mandating that desegregation be done "with all deliberate speed." The Supreme Court subsequently refused to hear desegregation cases for eight years.

* * *

The 1970's saw a conservative turn in the Supreme Court's school segregation cases, simultaneous with the Nixon administration diminishing the strength of the federal government's desegregation efforts. Exemplifying this turn was the 1973 case *Keyes v. School District Number 1* [413 U.S. 189 (1973)]. There, the Court held that in school districts where no law mandated segregated schools, illegal *de jure* discrimination could still be found if district policies and practices were intended to segregate the schools. By broadly interpreting "*de jure*" segregation to include intentionally segregative policies, rather than just explicitly segregationist laws, the Court in *Keyes* extended the duty to desegregate to many northern cities. But in so doing, the Court forsook the opportunity to abolish altogether the distinction between *de jure* and *de facto*, or "in fact," discrimination. This more progressive move, advocated by only two justices filing separate opinions in *Keyes*, would have imposed on all segregated school districts the obligation to desegregate.

The failure of the *Keyes* Court to set the stage for confrontation of *de facto* segregation has profound relevance * * *. This case disturbingly confirmed that whites were unwilling to accept and examine education as a forum for a racially just democracy, but were only willing to support reparations for explicit, clinically evidenced white supremacy, and only then in a narrowly distributive fashion. This was a lost opportunity for a declaration that systemic racism requires systemic and far-reaching transformation.

In *San Antonio School District v. Rodriguez*, also decided in 1973, the Court ruled that there is no federal constitutional right to an education and that the disparate distribution of school funding in Texas did not violate the Constitution. This was another blow to efforts to advance racial and economic justice in education, and served as a tool for maintaining the isolation of racially and economically marginalized students.

The import of the *de jure/de facto* distinction set out in *Keyes* was demonstrated the following year when the Supreme Court, in a five-to-four decision in *Milliken v. Bradley*, struck down the district court's order requiring interdistrict desegregation of Detroit and fifty-three surrounding suburbs. The Court ruled that cross-district desegregation measures could not be ordered unless it was shown that intentionally racially discriminatory acts of either the state or local officials were a substantial cause of the interdistrict segregation. While this decision did not completely rule out metropolitan-area-wide desegregation efforts, it set a standard of proof that has since been met only twice, both times in metropolitan areas with only a few suburban school districts.

* * *

With the regressive shifts occurring in the federal jurisprudence, advocates have turned for relief to state statutes and constitutions that guarantee an adequate education to students. Adequacy suits not only reject the narrow federal jurisprudence but also breathe new life into Dewey's concept that education is about citizenship. In *Sheff v. O'Neill* [678 A.2d 1267 (Conn.1996)] and a number of other cases, suburban whites have been members of the plaintiff class: if education is constitutive, then a segregated education not only marks minority urban students but white suburban students as well. As Toni Morrison has noted, we have acknowledged how our racist structures and histories have marked African Americans but little attention has been paid to how these phenomena have marked whites. Adequacy suits provide a space for this.

Several cases outside of the adequacy sphere in the past few decades are remarkable in that the courts showed a cognizance of the link between racial isolation in education and patterns of residential segregation, or because the scope of the remedy ordered by the court demonstrated an understanding that only a metropolitan-wide desegregation scheme would effectively begin to address the problem. A resurgence in this type of judicial analysis and remedy-crafting is necessary to prevent further resegregation of the schools, and to open the door to more effective integration-oriented school reforms. That is, a satisfaction of the aspirations of reformists and integrationists.

Successful desegregation for decades was achieved in Charlotte, through the embrace of such broadly reaching remedies. In *Swann v. Charlotte-Mecklenburg* [402 U.S. 1 (1971)], after finding that segregated residential patterns in the city and county resulted from federal, state, and local government action, a unanimous Court authorized district courts to employ a variety of remedial tools as they oversaw the desegregation process, including: the adoption of express racial goals for the student population in each desegregating school, as well as for faculty and staff racial ratios; the "pairing" of neighborhoods within a school district to meet desegregation goals; and busing. This first busing program in the nation caused Charlotte to become one of the most thoroughly desegregated school systems.

In the companion case, *North Carolina State Board of Education v. Swann* [402 U.S. 43 (1971)], the Court unanimously struck down North Carolina's anti-busing law, which had forbidden any assignment of school children by race. Writing for the Court, Chief Justice Burger described race-conscious student assignments as an essential tool to fulfill "the promise of *Brown*" and rebuffed North Carolina's contention that the federal Constitution required "colorblind" student assignments.

Another important case is *Liddell v. City of St. Louis* [491 F.Supp. 351 (E.D.Mo.1980)], because the court considered the effect of patterns of residential segregation on school segregation, and recommended a remedy that addressed the relationship between the two. The court wrote that governmental actions had "intensified racial segregation" and, accordingly: "It is critical that future actions in the housing area of all governmental bodies, federal, state and local, facilitate and not hamper school desegregation."

The vast majority of cases do not evince an understanding of the ways in which political fragmentation creates segregation and undermines democracy. *Sheff* again, is an exception. In *Sheff*, the Connecticut Supreme Court held that the state constitution guaranteed the right to a substantially equal educational opportunity and that the de facto segregation in the public schools in Hartford deprived students of this opportunity. Crucial to the judgment was the fact that municipal and school district lines were identical by statute. This districting statute was called the single greatest contributor to segregation in the opinion. At the time of the suit, the districting statute had left fourteen of Hartford's twenty-five elementary schools with a white enrollment of less than two percent. By considering the fragmented design of the metropolitan region, the court in *Sheff* was able to ascertain the engine behind the segregation and design the appropriate remedy.

These cases are exceptions to a generally very limiting jurisprudence.

* * *

Before turning to the continuing need for educational integration and integration-cooperative reforms, it is important to clarify terminology. Segregation is racial, ethnic, and/or socioeconomic homogeneity of schools. Desegregation has come to mean numeric balance of racial and ethnic groups within a school—as it was originally intended, it was a broader term that encompassed elements of what I will now call integration. In the words of Martin Luther King, Jr.:

> Although the terms desegregation and integration are often used interchangeably, there is a great deal of difference between the two. In the context of what our national community needs, desegregation alone is empty and shallow. We must always be aware of the fact that our ultimate goal is integration, and that desegregation is only a first step on the road to the good society....

Educational integration is the systemic transformation of a school to create a diverse and inclusive environment within the school and the curricula, achieved through a variety of reforms. Importantly, integration is not simply a goal in terms of the schools in which students learn as a static site, but requires a transformation of the setting in which the identities of students are formed and form others. This is a deeper sense of integration. Edmund Gordon has written that we all operate on multiple cognitive levels, and require plurality in our thinking in order to reach full participation in society—this is the idea of integration of the mind:

> [This] refers to the increasing demand that learners develop multiple competencies, some of which ... apply generally while others will [apply in more] idiosyncratic settings. All of us find ourselves increasingly in situations where we must meet other than indigenous standards. Thus it is required that we become multilingual, multicultural, multiskilled, and capable of functioning in multiple environments and settings. So, while education is influenced by and must be responsive to the differences with which learners enter the educational system, the exit characteristics of its students must reflect the pluralistic demands of the society in which they live.

Integration is sometimes confused with assimilation, which forces a conformity to dominate white culture upon minority students. The integration that others in the radical integrationist camp and I are calling for requires a transformation of these privileging and subordinating structures and should not produce assimilation.

A new model for justice and education requires a rejection of a distributive approach. But it is meaningful that we as a society have not even achieved distributional equality in the schools. That is, neither the calls made by the most modest integrationists nor reformists have been answered. * * * Students of color historically have suffered lower academic achievement and depressed life opportunities as compared to white students when they are educated in segregated environments. This conclusion was central to the *Brown* decision, and remains true today: children in racially isolated, high-poverty urban schools face myriad challenges that middle-class suburban children do not face, including substandard or deteriorating facilities, larger demands made on fewer resources which forces the cutting of so-called non-basic opportunities, racial isolation, concentration of poverty, and fewer familial resources.

A profound contributing factor to school segregation and racial and economic inequities generally is housing segregation, but we have not effectively addressed this connection as a society. Housing and school segregation are inextricably linked; the largest central city schools serve an increasingly non-white and poor population, reflecting the housing segregation in these cities. Cities like New York, Los Angeles, and Chicago have schools that have at least 85% students of color. Cities like Detroit and Washington, D.C. serve virtually no white students.

As a result of our failure to acknowledge the forces driving school segregation, and the implications for educational opportunity of school segregation, public schools are resegregating. Between 1980 and 1997, the number of African American students who attended majority white schools declined from 37.1 percent to 31.2 percent. In the South, after showing improvement for over 20 years, the number of African American students attending majority white schools began declining rapidly from 43.5 percent to 36.6 percent between 1988 and 1994. The number of Latino students attending majority white school declined from 45.2 percent to 25.2 percent between 1968 and 1997.

Concentrated poverty that arises along with residential segregation brings with it additional impediments. Schools with high levels of low-income and minority students suffer more intensely the inadequacies many school reforms purport to address, such as parental involvement and poor student performance. And the schools are less equipped to respond to the needs of these students; these students are more likely to experience a fragmented curriculum, large classes, and low teacher expectations.

The education of students in high poverty and racially isolated schools is hindered by the effect of poverty on their families' ability to provide an educationally supportive environment. There is agreement that in both schools and in the larger society education must be valued and encouraged for all children. Families, communities, and schools must provide learning environments that are supportive and inclusive. But this is nearly impossible to achieve when communities and schools are overwhelmed by poverty.

* * * [T]here is disbelief surrounding whether the efforts that have been made in this nation to democratize education through desegregation actually worked. This disbelief fuels the position of certain refor-

mists who would abandon desegregation efforts wholesale in favor of colorblind reforms. Understanding that desegregation has produced both student outcome and societal benefits is imperative to the mission of both the modest and radical integrationists, and should serve to correct misapprehensions on the part of reformists. * * *

The positive effects of desegregation in the schools start with the students but permeate far beyond the immediate environs of students. Students of color "who attend more integrated schools have increased academic achievement and higher test scores." These increases have been credited to, among other factors, better resource access and enhanced motivation or competition. Attending a more desegregated school translates into heightened goals for future educational attainment and career, whereas being educated in a racially segregated environment is associated with lower educational attainment and career goals.

An important benefit of a long-term desegregated education is that students tend more to live in integrated environments as adults. Hence, diverse educational settings contribute to students' ability to participate in a pluralistic society. A fifteen-year longitudinal study comparing similar groups of minority students in Hartford, Connecticut who did or did not transfer to the suburbs under a voluntary desegregation program showed that those attending suburban schools were considerably more likely to live in integrated communities as adults.

The Institute on Race and Poverty conducted a qualitative study that demonstrates many more benefits of an integrated environment than achievement, such as school enjoyment, increased understanding among students, improved student teacher relationships, greater interracial understanding, increased interracial interaction later in life, and better preparation for a diverse work world.

Other research has shown that the benefits of school desegregation extend into housing desegregation. A study of 960 school districts found that cities which implemented metropolitan-wide desegregation plans experienced substantially increased housing integration, an effect evident in districts of all sizes and in all regions of the country. Districts that have experienced desegregation over the longest period of time have the lowest levels of housing segregation as well. School desegregation between 1968 and 1973 doubled the rate of housing integration in twenty-five central cities with an African American population of at least 100,000.

With *Brown*, we as a society recognized the harm implicit in a system ordered on supremacy of some and subordination of others. Indeed, this harm is not limited to negative impacts on students' achievement, but reaches into and damages our democratic structure—reifying racial subordination in employment, health, wealth access, and political participation. Research has shown that the system can be altered for the good. Yet today still, we are in the position of having to ask: Have the negative effects of segregation and subordination ever been truly disestablished? Importantly, we have to consider the harms of segregation on both subordinated groups and whites * * * .

* * *

As we examine the history and current condition of education, and we reestablish what we want our system of public education to achieve for our citizens, we must ask some difficult questions. Is providing a quality education for all children rather than only a specific and ever decreasing segment of our society what we want? Are the crippling issues of racism and socioeconomic bias as they pertain to education worthy of addressing? Surely the answer to both questions must be yes. As Martha Minow exhorts:

> Schools afford an arena for fighting about what kind of society we should be, how the old and new generations should relate, whether commerce should govern democracy or democracy shall govern commerce, and how individual freedoms should be rendered compatible with the common good. It is imperative that the new round of school fights center as much on the symbols of inclusion and equality as upon the rhetoric of individualism and quality. These values need one another so that the whole is at least as worthy as the sum of its parts, if not perhaps more so.

* * *

Educational reform in the U.S. has a tendency to move from one effort to another in a pendular fashion, while retaining little of the beneficial aspects of the prior effort, whether in curriculum (e.g., phonics and whole language) or systemic issues (e.g., desegregation and neighborhood schools). In this pattern of subscribing to the reform in vogue, policy makers and others of influence seem to lose sight of the greater goal of education and what we need to provide for all of our students in order for them to become productive citizens, not just workers or consumers. We need an approach that does not just focus on the next new approach, or how to deal with the latest "crisis,"—what is often a reactionary rather than a thoughtful response. Often these strategies are only available to suburban, wealthier, whiter schools and leave behind the already struggling urban schools. As a society, we need to reestablish our societal goals for education. Perhaps at its most basic, our goal for education is to prepare our children for a full life in our democracy. This can only be accomplished if we create a system that reflects these values, effectively and consistently delivering them.

Notes and Questions

1. John Brittain, part of the *Sheff* litigation team, wrote:

> Today, forty-three years after *Brown*, more segregation exists in public schools than in 1954 at the time of *Brown*. Yet, de jure segregation, though illegal, is nonexistent. However, the prevalent segregation in nearly every urban school district in America—that

makes schools more segregated now than ever in history—has been found by the United States Supreme Court to be legal. Except in Connecticut, where *Sheff v. O'Neill* rises above the entire nation as the only case to prohibit de facto racial and ethnic segregation in education, and to require a city-suburban regional remedy.

In the end, the court recognized two significant public policies. As a moral imperative, "[i]t is crucial for a democratic society to provide all of its schoolchildren with fair access to an unsegregated education." But, argued the court in the last sentence of the majority opinion on legal liability, there is also an economic necessity:

> Economists and business leaders say that our state's economic well-being is dependent on more well-educated citizens. And they point to the urban poor as an integral part of our future economic strength.... So it is not just that their future depends on the State, the state's future depends on them.

John C. Brittain, *Why* Sheff v. O'Neill *Is a Landmark Decision*, 30 Conn. L. Rev. 211, 217–18 (1997). *See also* John C. Brittain, *Educational and Racial Equity Toward the Twenty-First Century—A Case Experiment in Connecticut*, in *Race in America: The Struggle For Equality* (Herbert Hill & James E. Jones, Jr. eds., 1993).

Commenting elsewhere on ballot initiatives and the relation of voting to equality in education, Brittain observed:

> Fortunately, Connecticut has no direct democracy provision. It is widely believed that if it did, the voters, like those in California, would have initiated a ballot measure to change the Connecticut Constitution to effectively reverse the decision and discontinue the de facto segregation legal standard.

John C. Brittain, *Direct Democracy by the Majority Can Jeopardize the Civil Rights of Minority or Other Powerless Groups*, 1996 Ann. Surv. Am. L. 441, 448–49.

Is Brittain's assessment of majority voting correct? Does his comment affect your view of the earlier discussion about the importance of voting to democratic practice? *See* section 1. Does it add force to Guinier's arguments about one vote, one value? What are the implications of Brittain's view for the e-voting that Kang sees likely in our future?

2. The dissenters in the *Sheff* case said:

> There is no question, therefore, that everyone involved in this case shares the same goal: the elimination of racial and ethnic isolation in the public schools of this state. Every desirable or wise policy, even every noble goal, however, is not necessarily embodied in the constitution. The debate, therefore, is over whether that goal is constitutionally mandated under the facts of this case. The majority, by an act of judicial will, without fidelity to the facts of the case or the claims of the parties, has imposed a constitutional

> mandate and has usurped a policy function that legitimately belongs to the legislature.

Sheff v. O'Neill, 238 Conn. 1, 678 A.2d 1267, 1299 (1996). Is the dissent correct that the court majority engaged in social engineering? Recall that the *Plyler* dissenters made a similar objection. Is the majority decision the result of creative social justice lawyering or a usurpation of the legislative role? *See* chapter 11 on the role of community groups. Should courts be the final arbiters of disputes involving public education?

3. Highlighting the overemphasis placed on testing, powell urges transformation in this area as well:

> High stakes standardized tests continue to be touted as reform mechanisms but have been shown to be more detrimental to low-income student of color outcomes than they are beneficial. Research has shown that students of color, those with disabilities, and low-income students tend to have lower passage rates on the standardized tests that determine grade advancement and graduation. Beyond bias in the drafting, a well documented issue, and disparities in outcomes, concerns for students of color are that the institution of high stakes testing may lead students to drop out under self-imposed pressure and be encouraged to drop out by administrations eager to present a positive portrait of testing results. And tests increase the retention rate (i.e., the rate at which students are held back) for students of color in major metropolitan school districts, which is the "single strongest predictor of whether students will drop out." A further concern for students of color attending schools in urban settings is that the pressures associated with poor outcomes may lead experienced teachers to leave these urban schools.
>
> Tests have not even been shown to improve educational outcomes generally. The 1980s experienced a surge of standardized testing and assessment; the largest effort was the New Standards Project (NSP). It was found that these tests offer little to no reliability or generalizability, seldom take into account the variety of learning styles, and are often found to be racially and culturally biased. Despite such evidence, standardized testing as a means to improve educational "excellence" still maintains popular support. Proponents of high stakes testing point to several potential advantages for students of color in public schools: that testing increases teacher and student motivation, functions to eliminate tracking by standardizing expectations of students, and can provide the impetus to targeting for improvement low-performing schools that are attended predominantly by low-income students of color. Evidence to support these claims has not been put forth by proponents, however.

powell, *Integration and School Reform*, 689–91.

Testing has also been a battleground in the affirmative action debate.

D. Affirmative Action: The Current Debate About Diversity and Equality In Education

The litigation leading to *Brown v. Board of Education* represented a struggle for desegregation and equal access to education. In the modern era, where de jure segregation is unconstitutional, de facto segregation remains. The aspirations for integration and diversity have framed debates about education and affirmative action programs in the last several decades. Consider whether desegregation should remain the first justification for affirmative action or whether diversity is a preferable rationale.

Brown successfully challenged the use of racial categories to segregate and stigmatize. Yet it is hard to imagine constructing remedies for racial discrimination in society without taking notice of race. Commenting at the state court level, in dissent on the law suit attacking the admissions program at U.C. Davis Medical School, Justice Mathew O. Tobriner wrote, "There is, indeed, a very sad irony to the fact that the first admission program aimed at promoting diversity ever to be struck down under the Fourteenth Amendment is the program most consonant with the underlying purposes of the Fourteenth Amendment." *Bakke v. Regents of Univ. of Cal.*, 18 Cal.3d 34, 66 (1976).

The use of racial categories remains contested as civil rights advocates have urged that only by acting affirmatively, taking into account racial patterns and white privilege, could true integration be achieved. For early legal and political history on affirmative action, see Joel Dreyfuss & Charles R. Lawrence III, *The Bakke Case: The Politics of Inequality* (1979) and Charles R. Lawrence III & Mari J. Matsuda, *We Won't Go Back: Making the Case for Affirmative Action* (1997).

Reconsider Charles Lawrence's critique of the diversity rationale in chapter 1. Lawrence described the diversity rationale as a liberal reform, preferring instead to reevaluate the meaning of merit. In the next article, Daria Roithmayer examines the bias and merit debate.

DARIA ROITHMAYR

Deconstructing the Distinction Between Bias and Merit
85 Calif. L. Rev. 1449, 1452, 1475–80, 1482–92 (1997)

* * * [T]he conventional understanding of merit assumes that merit standards measure an individual's potential ability to produce something of social value—good lawyering, or high performance in law school, for example—by assessing certain traits, qualities, or skills that reflect potential ability. Law schools admit students on the basis of their grades and LSAT scores—on their "merits"—because admissions committees think that a high score on the LSAT and a high GPA reflect an applicant's potential ability to achieve and produce social value in legal education and the legal profession.

In contrast, bias is understood as the direct opposite of merit. Biased selection standards—those based on race, ethnicity, family connections, social status—are condemned because society does not think that these factors rationally correlate to the ability to produce value in legal education or the legal profession. To the extent that statistical analysis might demonstrate some correlation between race and success in law schools, scholars search for some external and theoretically race-neutral factor—e.g., poor schooling—to explain the correlation. But they begin with the presumption that the standards by which they measure merit are race-neutral, and that merit itself—the ability to produce something of social value—is race-neutral as well. Within that framework of analysis, policy-makers seek to eliminate racism by rooting out bias and ensuring that opportunities are distributed on the race-neutral basis of pure merit standards.

* * *

* * * For as long as law schools have administered aptitude tests, Latino/a and African-American applicants disproportionately have achieved lower scores than white applicants. Many scholars have argued that such results are due to improper procedures or a cultural bias in the test itself. For example, Professor Leslie Espinoza has pointed out that past LSATs have contained questions about culturally specific phenomena, like polo matches and regattas, with which applicants of color are not likely to be familiar. Other scholars contend that Blacks and Latinos/as have disproportionately lower LSAT scores and undergraduate GPAs because they lack comparable educational opportunities and suffer from other forms of disadvantage.

Both arguments assume, however, that there is something "out there" called "merit"—the knack for legal reasoning, smarts, or diligence—that at least in theory is race-neutral. Both arguments also assume that people of color have been unfairly prevented from acquiring "merit" because of discrimination. Finally, both sides appear willing to concede that properly validated tests can theoretically measure an applicant's "true" ability to succeed in law school in a race-neutral way.

But opponents of admissions standards need not concede the standards' theoretical color-blindness quite so quickly. When one situates law school admission standards in their historical context, it appears that merit criteria deferred to and depended on the race-conscious social bias of the time to define what constituted "social value" in the legal profession. * * * [A]dmissions standards reflected the subjective preferences of white male lawyer elites. These leaders had acquired social power or "status" within the legal culture of the early twentieth century, in large part because of their race, given that people of color were affirmatively excluded from the profession at the time. Moreover, the leadership's subjective preferences about "social value" substantially reflected if not embodied the profession's desire to exclude Black and immigrant applicants from the practice of law.

The development of law-school admission standards can be traced to a number of related events occurring in the late nineteenth and early twentieth centuries. First, the number of European immigrants and

African Americans entering into the legal profession and law schools increased dramatically. At the same time, large, elite corporate law firms gained prominence on the Eastern seaboard, and created symbiotic relationships with prestigious Eastern law schools, at least in part to create a "safe haven" from the influx of immigrants. In addition, in an effort to prevent both immigrants and African Americans from gaining admission to practice law, the American Bar Association ("ABA") was formed. The ABA was part of a larger movement to eliminate part-time, night-time, and proprietary law schools, which served the rising numbers of immigrants and African Americans who sought to become lawyers. Reinforcing the hierarchy between prestigious law schools and schools that served immigrants and African Americans, Christopher Columbus Langdell and others introduced the case method into elite law schools, which helped to orient legal education toward abstract legal reasoning and away from practical experience. * * * [T]hese events all were directly or indirectly related to the more general explosion of racist and nativist sentiment in the legal culture and in American society during the period.

* * *

From 1870 to 1920, record numbers of immigrants from Eastern and Southern Europe flooded into the United States, and many began to seek entry into the legal profession. Many first and second generation immigrants saw the practice of law as a gateway to economic opportunity. Free public education at lower levels meant that immigrants could save their money toward tuition for part-time and night-time classes at proprietary schools. In response to new demand, proprietary law schools sprang up almost overnight in large numbers, predominantly in cities with heavy immigrant populations.

Typically, the immigrant student had far less formal education than his native-born counterpart, and the immigrant's parents were less likely to be professionals. The immigrant practitioner was also much more likely to practice in criminal law, real estate, and non-commercial civil law. Jerold Auerbach describes how the professional elite began to create "selective" institutions, based in large part on the profile of the immigrant practitioner, in order to protect their elite status.

> As mass immigration and urbanization inundated the dominant Anglo-Saxon culture, the fortunate few moved to the safety of selected social institutions—Eastern schools, for example, and careers in business and finance—which could protect, or extend, their power and status.... Big business served as "a new preserve of the older Americans, where their status and influence could continue and flourish."

These big business clients, whose numbers increased exponentially as America underwent industrialization, in turn, created a demand for large corporate law firms along the Eastern seaboard. Given the demographic makeup of big business at the time, firms catered to those clients by limiting entry into the firm to Easterners of "old-American stock," whose fathers were, like the firm's clients, wealthy professionals or businessmen. Quite predictably, symbiotic relationships formed between these corporate firms and the elite law schools. Big firms began to court only the top graduates from the "best" schools, and law schools discovered that grades and law review membership were a way to help separate the "appropriate" applicant from others who would not fit into big firm culture. Law schools were enthusiastic participants in the process, because they were able to reinforce their elite status by serving as a pipeline to funnel associates into the most prestigious firms.

In addition to closing ranks between big firms and prestigious law schools, prominent members of the profession also responded to the influx of immigrants by calling for "reform" on many fronts. Leaders of the profession created reform-minded bar organizations that limited their membership to the most affluent lawyers, all of whom were of old-American stock. After much discussion about the downward direction of the profession, in 1878 a group of elite lawyers created the American Bar Association for the purpose of restricting entry into the profession, and they vowed to "admit no men who would not be worthy members." * * *

Strains of nativism and racism were also evident legal education. In 1917, the ABA and the Association of American Law Schools ("AALS") commissioned non-lawyer Alfred Z. Reed to study the state of legal education and to make recommendations for reform. Both organizations had been inspired by the success of the Flexner report, a similar study of medical schools that had called for the medical profession to close many part-time or newly created programs. In 1921, Reed issued his first report, which described the legal profession as stratified along class, racial and ethnic lines. Reed agreed with earlier writers who viewed proprietary schools as supplying the needs of members of the social strata "whose sons [were not] thinking of university education," but who looked to the law school for training in a craft. However, unlike many commentators of the time, Reed proposed creating different tracks for both bar and law schools to coincide with the two strata. He predicted that if the intellectually less fashionable schools were driven out of business, large segments of the practice areas that were most useful for immigrant and racial groups would go unserved.

Reed's report was published only a month after the ABA's Committee on Legal Education had issued their own report on the same matter. Displeased with the ABA's lack of support for legal education, the AALS had pressured the ABA into creating the Committee, to be chaired by former ABA president Elihu Root. Predictably, the Root report pressed for a unitary bar, arguing that the different parts of the profession required the same intellectual training, and that such training could only be provided by law schools, preferably within a university setting. By 1927 the AALS and the ABA had issued lists of approved schools, and had done away with any requirements for office-training or other apprenticeship. The ABA had also increased law school admission requirements to include two years of college training.

Ignoring pressure from the ABA, Reed issued a second report in 1928, denouncing the homogenization of law schools, which he traced in part to the growing use of the case-law method. In keeping with his earlier report, Reed proposed creating two types of schools to match the stratification in the profession. In 1930, the ABA rejected his recommendations and passed a resolution against commercially operated schools. The ABA also created the National Conference of Bar Examiners to centralize the standards for bar examinations; whereupon the conference promptly proposed that bar-exam questions be modeled after questions being tested at the "better" university-affiliated law schools. In 1935, capitalizing on the explosion of racist and nativist sentiment in the bar, the ABA moved to limit the number of lawyers in the bar, citing overcrowding and problems with "moral character."

* * * [The author describes the rise of the case method, discussed in chapter 1.]

In *Unequal Justice*, Jerold Auerbach traces the foregoing events—the ascendance of the elite corporate law firm, the spread of the case-law method, and the ensuing call for "standards"—to virulent anti-immigrant sentiment, Anti-Semitism and racism in the legal profession in the early part of this century. Auerbach contends that middle-class, native-born white lawyers called for "standards," both "moral character" and academic, in order to safeguard their professional respectability and status from what they saw as the threat of dilution by the flood of immigrants and African Americans into the profession.

As chronicled by Auerbach, many reformers made little attempt to disguise the racist, anti-immigrant and anti-Semitic prejudices motivating their call for standards relating to "moral character." One member of the Root Committee, who explicitly equated the values of the legal profession with American cultural values, defended new bar admission requirements as "an instrument of Americanization" needed to protect the profession against "[t]he 'influx of foreigners' in the cities [who] comprised an uneducated mass of men who have no conception of our constitutional government." Surely, he concluded, "the American Bar Association did not wish to 'lower standards simply to let in uneducated foreigners.' "

Auerbach notes that even the most visible and respected professional leaders were not subtle about drawing a connection between professional concerns about "moral character" and ensuing restrictions based on ethnicity and immigrant status. Former ABA president Elihu Root declared, "I do not want anybody to come to the bar which I honor and revere ... who has not any conception of the moral qualities that underlie our free American institutions; and they are coming, today, by the tens of thousands."

Auerbach describes the anti-Semitic undertone of the "moral character" debate:

> Even before the war Theron Strong [an influential New York lawyer and author who wrote about the legal profession] complained sourly

> about "the influx of foreigners." Strong was especially troubled by the rising proportion of Jewish lawyers, which was "extraordinary, and almost overwhelming—so much so as to make it appear that their numbers were likely to predominate, while the introduction of their characteristics and methods has made a deep impression upon the bar."

Auerbach also cites remarks, made by the dean of the University of Wisconsin Law School in 1915, as evidence that concerns about ethics were racially motivated. The dean's statements were quite openly racist and nativist:

> If you examine the class rolls of the night schools in our great cities, you will encounter a very large proportion of foreign names. Emigrants and sons of emigrants remembering the respectable standing of the advocate in their own home, covet the title as a badge of distinction. The result is a host of shrewd young men, imperfectly educated, crammed so they can pass the bar examinations ... viewing the Code of Ethics with uncomprehending eyes. It is this class of lawyers that cause Grievance Committees of Bar Associations the most trouble.

Concerns about immigrant status and ethnicity were not limited to the immigrants' "moral character." Professional leaders also expressed dismay and doubt concerning the academic abilities of their immigrant counterparts. Future Chief Justice Harlan Fiske Stone "referred to 'the influx to the bar of greater numbers of the unfit,' who 'exhibit racial tendencies toward study by memorization' and display 'a mind almost Oriental in its fidelity to the minutiae of the subject without regard to any controlling rule or reason.' " Austen Fox, a prominent lawyer who would later antagonize Louis D. Brandeis during his Supreme Court confirmation hearings, spoke of "the many immigrant boys ... [who] can hardly speak English intelligibly and show little understanding of or feeling for American institutions and government." * * * In response to this outpouring of Anti-Semitism and nativism, in 1909, the Section of Legal Education of the ABA adopted the requirement that lawyers be American citizens, even though the foreign student was a market force to be reckoned with, having created a great demand for proprietary and night schools.

Efforts to restrict admission to the bar targeted African Americans as well as immigrants. Paul Finkelman has documented turn-of-the-century efforts to keep Blacks from practicing law:

> Starting in the 1890s, white-dominated southern governments began to disenfranchise and segregate blacks as a backlash against the Civil War and the goals of the Reconstruction. As blacks lost their newly acquired rights, black lawyers disappeared from the scene. For example, in 1900, Mississippi had twenty-four black lawyers, and South Carolina had twenty-nine. A decade later Mississippi was down to twenty-one black lawyers and South Carolina had seventeen. In 1920, both states had only fourteen black lawyers, and

> by 1930, Mississippi had only six black lawyers, and South Carolina had thirteen. In 1940, there were just three blacks practicing law in Mississippi, and five in South Carolina.

The pervasiveness of racial exclusion during this time period manifested itself in an incident involving the American Bar Association during the early part of the century. In 1912, the ABA unwittingly admitted three Black lawyers. When informed of the error, the organization rapidly passed a resolution rescinding admission. "[S]ince the settled practice of the Association ha[d] been to elect only white men as members," the ABA referred the matter for a vote by the entire association. In discussing the matter, the Association quite openly declared that, from their perspective, the matter posed "a question of keeping pure the Anglo-Saxon race." Eventually, the ABA reached a compromise; it allowed the three black lawyers to keep their memberships, but it imposed a new requirement that all future applicants identify themselves by race.

Of course, racism pervaded legal education during this time period as well. Many law schools, particularly those in the South, formally denied Blacks admission, and most others informally excluded them. As late as 1939, thirty-four of the eighty-eight accredited law schools had formal policies excluding Blacks. * * * As late as 1938, the University of Missouri Law School continued to formally exclude Black applicants on the grounds that "it was 'contrary to the constitution, laws and public policy of the State to admit a negro as a student in the University of Missouri.' "

Although the University of Texas Law School formally excluded Latinos by restricting their admission to white students only, law schools did not need to adopt formal exclusionary policies for Chicanos and other Latinos; pre-existing social and economic constraints alone were sufficient to keep them out. Most Mexicans and Mexican Americans lacked even the requisite high-school degree to apply to proprietary schools, much less the more prestigious university-affiliated law schools. The majority of newly arrived Mexicans in the Southwest and California took jobs in agriculture, where they suffered sub-standard living conditions, chronic underemployment and dramatically low wages. A minority of Mexican immigrants entered the lower ranks of industrial employment in the Northwest and the Midwest as unskilled laborers, but few sought entry into the legal profession.

While racism against Latinos did not manifest itself as explicitly during this time period in legal education, Mexican Americans and Mexican nationals experienced in other ways much of the same nativist and racist sentiment that had been directed against Blacks and immigrants in the legal profession. Although immigrants from Mexico narrowly had escaped the limits on European immigration enacted in the Immigration Restriction Acts of 1914 and 1924, during the 1920s, Congress tried again to restrict Mexican immigration by eliminating Mexico's exemption. In 1926, Representative John C. Box of Texas introduced a bill to remove the exemption. During Senate hearings on the subject in 1928, Box publicly referred to Mexican workers as "peonized, illiterate and unclean." Support for Box's effort to remove the exemption came from many sources, including teachers' organizations and labor unions, as well as the more blatantly nativistic "patriotic societies" and overtly racist groups.

This, then, was the state of legal and social culture when law schools first began to explore the use of competitive admissions standards. In the early twentieth century, law schools first began to require some college attendance beyond a high school degree. By 1921, elite schools insisted on college degrees, while the less elite schools offered legal education as part of their undergraduate curriculum.

Admissions programs also became selective for the first time in the early 1920s, in conjunction with the demands of the case-law method of instruction. Previously, most elite law schools had employed open admissions policies at least for affluent males who had a college degree and could pay their way. However, in the 1926–27 academic year, Harvard failed 250 of its 700 first-year students, and other schools experienced similarly high rates of attrition, largely due to the introduction of the case-law method and the ensuing radical transformation of legal education. * * *

The elite schools sought to limit the high rate of academic failures in another way—through the use of aptitude testing. At Columbia, Dean Harlan Fiske Stone initiated experimental testing for admissions in 1921, and in 1928 Columbia added aptitude testing to its newly selective admissions process. In 1925, the year after enactment of the Immigration Restriction Act of 1924, the West Publishing Company published the first edition of its Ferson-Stoddard aptitude test, which was used through three editions by a number of law schools. Yale's success with aptitude testing encouraged other schools to explore the use of psychometric testing. Through aptitude testing, elite law schools solved the problem of admitting students who were not proficient in case-method analysis. "Rather than cut back on the case method, the schools cut back on the average student."

The use of aptitude testing continued to spread throughout the 1930s and 40s. In the late 1940s, three law schools formed an early version of what is now the Law School Admissions Council ("LSAC") to develop the Law School Aptitude Test ("LSAT"). * * *

* * * In *The Mismeasure of Man*, Steven Jay Gould points out that the same racist and nativist assumptions that had fueled support for anti-immigrant legislation had created a demand for the development of ability testing. Gould notes that ability testing was the practical (and inevitable) offspring of biological determinism, an intellectual movement then coming into its own, one that used genetic and evolutionary theory to justify existing social, racial, and cultural arrangements.

According to Gould, the pioneers of ability testing developed their tests during the early twentieth century expressly to justify on biological grounds certain *a priori* political and social assumptions about race and ethnicity that were then in vogue. For example, Lewis M. Terman, who developed the Stanford-Binet scale in 1916, dreamed of a "rational" society that allocated professional opportunities by IQ scores. Henry H. Goddard, who brought the Binet IQ scale to America, reified its results as concrete representations of innate intelligence. Goddard hoped to use test scores "in order to recognize limits, segregate, and curtail breeding to prevent further deterioration of an endangered American stock, threatened by immigration from without and by prolific reproduction of its feeble-minded from within."

Robert M. Yerkes, who persuaded the Army to test its recruits in World War I, was perhaps the most responsible for developing aptitude testing to perpetuate the notion that immigrants and Blacks were intellectually inferior for genetic reasons. Yerkes' Army data purported to show that dark-skinned Southern and Eastern European immigrants were less intelligent than the light-skinned Northern and Western Europeans, and that the Negro was least intelligent of all. Yerkes' data, along with data from other hereditarian ability testers, led directly to passage of the Immigration Restriction Act of 1924, and to segregation in higher education:

> Other propagandists used the army results to defend racial segregation and limited access of blacks to higher education. Cornelia James Cannon, writing in the *Atlantic Monthly* in 1922, noted that 89 percent of blacks had tested as morons and argued .... "[that] the education of the whites and colored in separate schools may have justification other than that created by race prejudice ...."
>
> But the army data had its most immediate and profound impact upon the great immigration debate, then a major political issue in America, and ultimately the greatest triumph of eugenics.

Carl Brigham, the man who eventually would become the head of the Educational Testing Service, used the Yerkes data to argue publicly for restrictions on immigration and eugenic regulation of reproduction. * * *

Gould's arguments about the racist and nativist sentiments underlying ability testing rest on more than the openly racist motivations of the testers. Indeed, Gould argues that the very idea of ability testing itself rests on racist and nativist assumptions: the key structural components of ability measurement are tied inextricably to social and cultural desires to justify pre-existing distributions of wealth and power on the basis of race and ethnicity. * * *

* * *

* * * Far from being colorblind, law school admissions standards were developed in a context of racial and cultural exclusion, where those professional leaders who developed those standards and values had achieved their leadership status in large part because of their race. Far more troublingly, this critical history raises the possibility that law

schools admissions standards may have been developed as part of a broader professional effort to exclude on the basis of race and ethnicity.

Practically speaking, the history of law school admission may help to explain the admissions standards' disproportionate impact on groups that were excluded from the legal profession at the relevant time. Given the origins of aptitude testing, it is less likely to be mere coincidence that contemporary academic selectivity measures continue to exclude certain people of color disproportionately. For as long as the tests have been administered, Blacks and Latinos have performed at levels significantly below those of white applicants. For example, in 1992–93, 25.7% of white applicants scored at or above 160 on the LSAT, compared to 11.5% of Latino applicants, 12.7% of American Indian applicants, and 2.9% of African-American applicants.

Notes and Questions

1. Do these histories of exclusion in education and professional membership or the origins of intelligence testing surprise you? Does this information lend credence to Roithmayr's assertion that "merit" is not an objective, isolated fact, separable from bias?

2. Should LSAT scores play a significant role in admissions decisions? What "qualifies" a person to attend law school? Did your grades and test scores reflect your qualifications? *See* Dorothy A. Brown, *The LSAT Sweepstakes*, 2 J. Gender Race & Just. 59 (1998) (providing a fictionalized account of a world in which blacks outscored whites on the LSAT) and Leslie G. Espinoza, *The LSAT: Narratives and Bias*, 1 Am. U. J. Gender & L. 121 (1993) (relating how the narrative content of standardized tests contributes to bias).

3. "Standardized" testing remains for many the touchstone of merit. The relationship between the origin of this measure of merit and race is little known:

> In 1923 Carl Campbell Brigham, in *A Study of American Intelligence*, declared that Nordic white intelligence in the United States was being diluted because of the introduction of inferior Negro stock. A few years later, Brigham designed an intelligence test that professed to measure native ability but incorporated a bias that would award high scores for knowledge of facts associated with Anglo culture. Shortly thereafter, Brigham became director of testing for the College Board; his test became known as the Scholastic Aptitude Test and is still given to millions of high school students today. The organization has not repudiated his teaching; as Stanley Fish points out, the library at the College Board's Educational Testing Service still bears Brigham's name.

Jean Stefancic & Richard Delgado, *No Mercy: How Conservative Think Tanks and Foundations Changed America's Social Agenda* 35 (1996). *See also* Nicholas Lemann, *The Big Test: The Secret History of the American Meritocracy* (1999) and William C. Kidder & Jay Rosner, *How the SAT Creates "Built-in Headwinds": An Educational and Legal Analysis of Disparate Impact*, 43 Santa Clara L. Rev. 131 (2002) (describing how the process of selecting and developing SAT questions exacerbates that test's disparate impact on African-American and Chicano test-takers).

WILLIAM C. KIDDER

Affirmative Action in Higher Education: Recent Developments in Litigation, Admissions and Diversity Research
12 Berkeley La Raza L.J. 173, 174–86, 188–190 (2001)

Students of color—not university administrators—have the broadest, deepest and most urgent interests in preserving affirmative action. After all, when race can no longer be a factor in admission decisions, it is minority students who are denied access to higher education opportunities. Yet, students of color have too often been silenced and marginalized in litigation challenging affirmative action, with predictably deleterious consequences. For example, in the landmark *Bakke* case [438 U.S. 265, 320 (1978)], the University of California (UC) had no interest in arguing that Allan Bakke may have been denied admission because the Dean at the UC Davis Medical School had the prerogative to reserve seats for the relatives of wealthy donors. UC also declined to present evidence that affirmative action was necessary to remedy its prior discrimination or to neutralize racial bias in admission criteria like standardized tests, since such evidence might expose the University to litigation from rejected minority applicants.

Despite these clear conflicts of interest, and while for decades leading scholars and advocates have recognized the importance of student intervention in affirmative action cases, it has been a real struggle to get minority student voices heard. Thus, in the Fifth Circuit's *Hopwood* decision—where the University of Texas Law School failed to develop a full record on its own (embarrassing) history of racial discrimination or its misuse of the LSAT—the court denied intervention.

However, in 1999 the Sixth Circuit overturned two district court decisions denying intervention in affirmative action lawsuits against the University of Michigan and its Law School. The Sixth Circuit was persuaded by the Intervenors' argument that the "University is unlikely to present evidence of past discrimination by the University itself or of the disparate impact of some current admissions criteria, and that these may be important and relevant factors in determining the legality of a race-conscious admissions policy." In *Grutter v. Bollinger* [188 F.3d 394 (6th Cir.1999)], the University of Michigan Law School case, students of color and progressive White students intervened in order to have their voices heard, to shape the trial court record, to present their own experts, to contribute to the larger public debate and to build a student movement in support of affirmative action. *Grutter* and *Gratz v. Bollinger* [135 F.Supp. 790 (E.D. Mich. 2001)] (the Michigan undergraduate case) currently have the highest likelihood of being granted certiorari by the U.S. Supreme Court.

During January and February of 2001, Bernard Friedman, the federal district court judge in *Grutter*, conducted a trial on the following three issues:

> (1) the extent to which race is a factor in the law school's admissions decisions; (2) whether the law school's consideration of race in making admissions decisions constitutes a double standard in which minority and non-minority students are treated differently; and (3) whether the law school may take race into account to 'level the playing field' between minority and non-minority applicants.

Judge Friedman limited the Plaintiffs, Defendants, and Defendant-Intervenors to 30 hours each to present their respective cases, but only the Intervenors elected to use their entire allotted time.

* * *

In *Grutter*, the trial court began by reviewing the testimony of key officials and documents related to admissions at the University of Michigan Law School (UMLS) from the 1980s to the present. Judge Friedman concluded, "[T]he evidence indisputably demonstrates that the law school places a very heavy emphasis on an applicant's race in deciding whether to accept or reject." In arriving at this finding of fact, Friedman relied heavily on the report and testimony of statistician Dr. Kinley Larntz, who served as the principal expert for the Center for Individual Rights (CIR). Larntz's primary analysis—indeed the core of the case presented by CIR—consisted of cell-by-cell comparisons for each racial and ethnic group of the different admission odds of applicants with similar LSAT scores and UGPAs. Judge Friedman found Larntz's calculations to be "mathematically irrefutable proof that race is indeed an enormously important factor." * * *

In addition to Larntz's testimony, Judge Friedman found it significant that over the years the Law School's goal was to have entering classes with around 10–17% underrepresented minorities (Black, Latino, and Native American students) in order to attain "critical mass." He also found it significant that the Law School's dean and admissions director monitored the daily admission reports, which were classified by race/ethnicity. Thus, the fact that UMLS had broad targets and the fact that it tracked the admissions process as it crafted an entering class—both common practices at law schools—were transformed into "proof" of an unconstitutional hidden quota system.

In his trial court ruling in *Grutter*, Judge Friedman determined, "[T]he court is persuaded that *Bakke* did not hold that a state educational institution's desire to assemble a racially diverse student body is a compelling government interest." While noting that five Justices in *Bakke* agreed that universities have a substantial, legitimate interest in considering race in admissions, Friedman agreed with CIR's contention that Justice Powell's opinion—upholding the use of race as a plus factor in order to promote the educational benefits of a diverse learning environment—represented his views only, and did not constitute a holding of the case. * * *

* * *

* * * Judge Friedman repudiated the diversity rationale by noting that the Supreme Court's recent affirmative action rulings treat benign racial classification with far greater suspicion than the Court applied in the *Bakke* era. Drawing from two public contracting cases, *Croson* [488 U.S. 469 (1989)] and *Adarand* [515 U.S. 200 (1995)], Friedman concluded, "When read together, *Adarand* and *Croson* clearly indicate that racial classifications are unconstitutional unless they are intended to remedy carefully documented effects of past discrimination."

By ruling that Powell's diversity rationale is not part of *Bakke*'s holding, Judge Friedman largely sidestepped the heart of the University of Michigan Law School's expert witness evidence, in which it sought to establish the educational benefits that accrue from a racially and ethnically diverse learning environment. In *Grutter*, the court acknowledged that racial diversity enhances the educational experience of law school. Nonetheless, Friedman minimized the Defendant's evidence on this issue by tersely opining about the difference between racial diversity and viewpoint diversity. Citing affirmative action critic Terrance Sandalow, Friedman confidently suggested that the racial resegregation of legal education would likely have little impact on the views expressed in law school classrooms.

In *Grutter*, Judge Friedman ruled that even if racial diversity were a compelling interest, the University of Michigan Law School's current affirmative action program nevertheless fails to be narrowly tailored to serve that interest. Friedman cited five considerations weighing against a finding of narrow tailoring: 1) the "critical mass" concept is too amorphous; 2) the University did not specify an ending date; 3) the Law School's enrollment targets amounted to a hidden quota system; 4) there was no articulated, logical explanation why some groups were included in the plan and others were excluded; and 5) the University failed to try "race-blind" alternatives, such as increased recruiting or a lottery system.

After summarizing the Defendant-Intervenors' trial evidence, Judge Friedman found that "the comparatively lower grades and test scores of underrepresented minorities is attributable, at least in part, to general, societal racial discrimination against these groups," but he concluded that these facts provide no constitutional protection for the University of Michigan Law School's affirmative action program. Friedman proclaimed that the "daunting" legal flaw in the Intervenors' case is that "the Supreme Court has held that the effects of general, societal discrimination cannot constitutionally be remedied by race-conscious decision-making." The Intervenors charge that Friedman's characterization grossly misrepresents their core argument in *Grutter*. In their brief to the Sixth Circuit, the Intervenors responded to Judge Friedman's castigation:

> So it has (the Court has disavowed the societal discrimination rationale), but famously enough to ensure that the student intervenors never argued that the affirmative action plan at UMLS is justified on the basis that it remedies general societal discrimination: not in moving to intervene, not in summary judgment proceedings, not at trial, and not in post-trial pleadings. On the contrary, their arguments and evidence about discrimination and bias, while grounded in a broader exposition of the context of race in America, were centered on the two academic criteria at the heart of law school admissions across the country and at the heart of the plaintiff's case . . . The district court set up its concluding magician's moment in the very first words of its section on the intervenors by entitling the section "Remedying Societal Discrimination as a Rationale for Using Race as a Factor in University Admissions: The Intervenors' Case." The rabbit having thus been tucked into the hat, it was there to be pulled out at the end of the opinion.

Additional support for the Intervenors' objection to Friedman's interpretation can also be found in Justice Powell's *Bakke* opinion. Since in the very same opinion Powell both rejected societal discrimination as a justification for affirmative action, and opined that compensating for bias in standardized testing and grades could conceivably justify race-sensitive admissions, Judge Friedman is mistaken to confuse these two issues. Judge Friedman's "top down" legal conclusions and factual findings cannot be understood in isolation from the "bottom up" arguments and evidence presented by the Intervenors. In particular, the Intervenors' arguments about the two primary law school admission criteria (LSAT scores and undergraduate grades) deserve explanation.

In *Grutter*, the district court's finding that race is an "extremely strong factor" in admission to UMLS was largely a function of the court's adoption of CIR expert Kinley Larntz's evidence, which is to say that the LSAT is the standard for "merit" and, by implication, for Equal Protection analysis. The Intervenors' criticism of racial bias on the LSAT are part of an effort to challenge the unquestioned assumption underlying the *Grutter* Plaintiff's case—that the University of Michigan Law School's affirmative action plan involves a preference for "less qualified" students of color. The Intervenors put together a team of several expert witnesses on the issue of the racial/ethnic bias on the LSAT and similar standardized tests, including Martin Shapiro, Jay Rosner, David M. White and Eugene Garcia. * * *

Professor Martin Shapiro, a psychometrician from Emory University with extensive experience testifying in higher education civil rights cases, presented a report and testimony detailing the methods used to develop and pre-test questions appearing on standardized tests. Shapiro argued that discrimination against students of color occurs as an inevitable (though not intentional) byproduct of the manner in which standardized tests like the LSAT are developed and pre-tested. Shapiro testified that the requirement that test items are internally consistent (high scorers should get the item correct and vice versa) produces the following double-bind for under-represented minorities and other lower-scoring groups: items that lessen or reverse the disparate impact of the test are *a priori* defined as poor/unreliable items, and are thus removed from the final version of the test.

Jay Rosner and David M. White amplified Shapiro's criticism—that the LSAT pre-testing process inculcates racial bias. Rosner, Executive Director of the Princeton Review Foundation, testified that the LSAT and similar standardized tests amount to a "White preference test" because the test development process weeds out nearly all the questions that do not favor Whites. Rosner asserts that expensive preparation courses significantly improve students' scores on the LSAT. Rosner also points out that wealth differences and a test-preparation avoidance phenomenon related to racialized (negative) experiences with standardized tests worsen racial and ethnic performance differences on the LSAT.

David White, director of Testing for the Public, a Berkeley-based non-profit educational research organization, likewise testified that several factors cause the LSAT to unfairly exaggerate racial and ethnic differences in academic preparation. One line of evidence White cited was a study I authored (and he oversaw) involving 1996–98 applicants to Boalt Hall, whose main "feeder" schools are substantially similar to those of the University of Michigan Law School. The Testing for the Public study matched applicants possessing equivalent UGPAs and graduation dates within each of fifteen elite feeder schools (Berkeley, Stanford, Harvard, Michigan, etc.). David White testified that among these pools of equally accomplished college students, African Americans trailed their White classmates on the LSAT by 9.2 points, Latinos scored 6.8 points lower, and Native Americans scored 4.0 points lower, and that controlling for these students' choice of major did nothing to lessen these gaps. In the context of a narrow tailoring requirement, it is important to point out that the size of the LSAT differences in this study were remarkably similar to the racial/ethnic differences in LSAT averages among accepted applicants to the University of Michigan Law School. During 1995–2000, the period in question in the *Grutter* litigation, admitted African American applicants averaged 9.6 points lower than Whites, and Mexican Americans averaged 7.0 points lower.

David White testified that the LSAT produces a false impression of reverse discrimination, since the UGPAs of students of color admitted to Michigan were in the same range as Whites, and in recent years the admitted applicants at the Law School who had the lowest UGPAs were usually *Whites*. White argued that race-based affirmative action was an appropriate remedy for a problem with standardized testing that had uniquely racialized consequences, since socioeconomic differences alone do not account for racial/ethnic disparities in LSAT scores. Thus, in appealing Judge Friedman's ruling, the Intervenors argue:

> The caste system in America is not absolute, and there are other kinds of privilege and disadvantage besides those strictly based on race. Nevertheless, racial bias on the LSAT means that the black daughter of bankers will be outscored by the white daughter of municipal employees by an average of 6 points, the difference between attending a competitive law school or none at all.

David White buttressed the Intervenors' argument that the LSAT test construction process contributes to the problem of racial bias. White reviewed the psychometric literature surrounding the LSAT item bias detection method (called differential item functioning, or DIF) and concluded that DIF is an inadequate and ineffective method for rooting out culturally biased test items.

White's report also summarized recent studies documenting the phenomenon of "stereotype threat," a line of research pioneered by psychologists Claude Steele and Joshua Aronson suggesting that the psychosocial milieu of standardized testing can be experienced differently depending on the test-taker's race or ethnicity. In fact, UMLS's sole expert witness on standardized testing was Professor Steele of Stanford University. In his expert report, Steele concluded that stereotype threat can artificially depress test performance of under-represented minorities because they face the added interference and pressure of having one's individual performance confirm a socially salient negative stereotype about one's group. In what turned out to be a serious development, in the middle of the *Grutter* trial UMLS attorneys removed Claude Steele from their "will call" witness list. This made it impossible for the Intervenors to obtain Steele's testimony, and made it easier for Judge Friedman to find that there was insufficient evidence to establish the influence of stereotype threat in contributing to racial and ethnic differences in LSAT scores.

Finally on the testing front, the Intervenors called on the testimony of Eugene Garcia and Richard Lempert. Garcia, dean of UC Berkeley's Graduate School of Education and chair of the UC system's Latino Eligibility Taskforce, addressed why his Task Force led the charge to eliminate the SAT as a UC eligibility requirement. Garcia testified that standardized tests often reward race/class privilege in the form of exposure to "academic English," rather than measuring true merit. He also stated that the end of affirmative action in California has resegregated the UC system—particularly at the Berkeley and UCLA law schools—and that there are simply no workable "race-neutral" alternatives to affirmative action.

Lempert, a professor of law and sociology at the University of Michigan, earlier testified for UMLS about the formation of the Law School's current affirmative action plan. The Intervenors called Lempert to testify about a major empirical study he coauthored that assessed the career success of White, Black, Latino, and Native American UMLS alumni. * * * The authors found that despite lower LSAT scores and UGPAs, under-represented minority alumni of UMLS were equally successful in terms of income and career satisfaction, they had superior civic contributions compared to their White classmates, and that overall, LSATs and UGPAs were not significant predictors of career outcomes in legal practice.

* * *

In *Grutter*, the district court commented that the "gap in LSAT scores between underrepresented minorities and Caucasians is even more difficult to explain" than gaps in undergraduate grades. Judge Friedman ruled, "The court is unable to find that anything in the content or design of the LSAT biases the test for or against any racial group. If such a bias exists, it was not proved at trial." Friedman dismissed the evidence and testimony presented by Shapiro, Rosner, and White, concluding that they did not demonstrate to the court's satisfaction that test design or the selection of LSAT questions contributes to racial/ethnic differences in LSAT scores.

The court did find plausible a couple of the Intervenors' explanations of the LSAT gaps. Dean Garcia's testimony that standardized tests favor students steeped in "academic English" and Rosner's testimony that underrepresented minorities enroll in expensive test preparation courses in "token numbers" were found by Judge Friedman to likely contribute to LSAT performance differences.

Regarding Claude Steele's research on stereotype threat, recall that Judge Friedman blocked the Intervenors' efforts to have Steele testify at trial. Friedman then concluded that the sparseness of the evidence precluded him from determining whether stereotype threat was influential in contributing to LSAT performance differences. Friedman's hostility to the Intervenors' test bias evidence is visible in his characterization of the stereotype threat evidence. Judge Friedman criticized Steele's expert report as follows: "He reports the results of only one experiment he performed using the GRE, and he does not indicate when the experiment was done, how many students participated, whether the results were tested for statistical significance, or whether the results were published and subjected to peer review." Unfortunately, this seriously misstates the record because Steele's *Grutter* deposition and numerous deposition exhibits (both entered into the record by designation) cite to several stereotype threat experiments. Thus, Friedman simply ignored information in the record about stereotype threat research, including specifics available on dates, sample sizes, statistical significance tests performed and the issues of peer-reviewed scientific journals in which the studies appeared.

* * *

[An omitted portion of this article discusses the research presented on bias in undergraduate grades based on campus climate.]

While the Intervenors' case focused mainly on standardized testing and campus climate, their efforts to establish a wider context of historical and policy arguments for affirmative action should also be acknowledged. Many of the nation's foremost experts in their areas of specialty testified at trial. Gary Orfield of Harvard testified about the inferior, segregated K–12 education provided to Black and Latino students (particularly in Michigan), about the consequences of ending affirmative action, and about his recent research with the Harvard Civil Rights Projects on the value of diversity in legal education. Professor Frank Wu (Howard University Law School) testified about the ways in which Asian Pacific Americans benefit from affirmative action and how "model minority" stereotyping is used as a vehicle to limit the opportunities of other minority groups. Likewise, Faith Smith (President, Native American Educational Services College) testified about the importance of affirmative action to Native American students and their communities.

John Hope Franklin, famed historian and Co-Chair of the President Clinton's Initiative on Race, testified for several hours about the history of racism and inequality in America, and how this history is linked to the current struggle over affirmative action. Four students, Erica Dowdell, Concepcion Escobar, Crystal James, and Tania Kappner, testified poignantly about their educational experiences at the University of Michigan and about the post-affirmative action environments of UCLA and Berkeley.

While the thirty-hour time limit prevented other experts for the Intervenors from testifying at trial, they nonetheless produced expert reports that are an important part of the defense of affirmative action. Professor Stephanie Wildman (now at Santa Clara University Law School) addressed the value of affirmative action in creating opportunities for women and in breaking down entrenched systems of privilege. Elizabeth Chambliss (Harvard Law School) reported the results of her research, much of which was commissioned by the American Bar Association, on the status of people of color in the legal profession. Finally, Marcus Feldman (Professor of Biology, Stanford) refuted genetic determinist arguments about the causes of current racial/ethnic differences in educational achievement. Feldman, whom Judge Friedman would not permit to testify, argued that the dubious research of race/IQ scholars needs to be identified as an undercurrent in *Grutter*, given that CIR has repeatedly accepted financial contributions from the Pioneer Fund, a leading White supremacist/eugenics organization.

Notes and Questions

1. The *Grutter* Intervenors included 41 African-American, Latina/o, Asian-American, and other students (from high school to law school), and three pro-affirmative action coalitions: The Coalition to Defend Affirmative Action By Any Means Necessary (BAMN), United for Equality and Affirmative Action (UEAA), and Law Students for Affirmative

Action (LSAA). The intervenors viewed the attacks on affirmative action as part of "a broader attack on those gains won by the first civil rights movement." Miranda Massie, Grutter v. Bollinger: *A Student Voice and a Student Struggle: The Intervention in the University of Michigan Law School Case*, 12 La Raza L.J. 231, 231 (2001).

Believing "[a]ffirmative action is the only way to move toward integration," *id.* at 232, the intervenors sought to dispel "the racist myth of meritocracy," *id.*, by joining the legal and political debates.

> [M]any tens of thousands of students across the country have participated in days of action in defense of affirmative action, in panel discussions, teach-ins, and weeks of education about affirmative action and integration, have participated in a petition campaign started several months ago that has gathered approximately 40,000 signatures thus far in support of the basic points in the student intervenors' case–including those of outgoing University of Michigan President Lee Bollinger, U.S. Representative and Dean of the Congressional Black Caucus John Conyers, United Auto Workers International President Al Yokichand, and film director John Singleton * * * .

Id. at 234.

How do you assess the intervenor's strategy? Would the University of Michigan have been better off defending its affirmative action policy on diversity grounds without intervenors in the case? The Sixth Circuit Court of Appeals decision in *Grutter* held that the law school's admissions policy was valid because it was narrowly tailored to serve the school's claimed compelling interest in achieving a diverse student body. Grutter v. Bollinger, 288 F.3d 732 (6th Cir. 2002), *cert. granted*, 71 U.S.L.W. 3387 (U.S. Dec. 2, 2002) (No. 02–241).

Might desegregation provide a better justification than diversity for affirmative action? Consider Samuel Issacharoff's view.

> Under an integrationist perspective, the black experience in America provides the paradigm for understanding equal protection as a constitutionally-compelled commitment to meet our society's ongoing historic responsibility. Oddly, that legacy now compels defenders of affirmative action to explain what it is about black Americans that requires the continuation of this legal protection.

Samuel Issacharoff, *Law and Misdirection in the Debate Over Affirmative Action* (2002). *See also* Richard Delgado, *1998 Hugo L. Black Lecture: Ten Arguments Against Affirmative Action—How Valid?*, 50 Ala. L. Rev. 135 (1998) (urging reconsideration of reparational justifications for affirmative action, as well as examination of socio-economic status when privileged applicants have underperformed).

2. Is the judicial system the right place to resolve the public debate over affirmative action? Is it the only place? What responsibility do colleges, professional schools, and the professions have? Consider Marga-

ret Russell's suggestions, as she reflects on the small numbers of students of color in her law school classroom:

> With regard to the possibilities for the legal profession as a vehicle for social justice, we need to recognize that our classrooms and our curricula are in a state of crisis. We cannot continue to assume that we can provide competent professional training to any student—whether white or non-white—in the interests of justice unless we openly acknowledge racial injustice within legal education and within the legal profession itself. Our graduates will be ill-equipped to challenge racial inequality on behalf of their clients if they have failed to recognize the racial inequalities that undergird their existence in law school and their entry into the profession.
>
> * * * The first and most obvious solution is to continue to press vigorously toward racial inclusion through the recruitment, admission, and retention of students of color. Beyond admissions and retention reform, however, there is much that we can do in the classroom to encourage a climate of greater racial inclusion and awareness. Rather than skirt issues of race and racial justice because of the embarrassing realities of racial tokenism in the classroom, we should find ways to encourage students to discuss those realities and particularly to understand the institutional and societal dynamics underlying them. Most students, and certainly all students of color, take note of the racial composition of their classes; it is a risk well worth taking to find ways to discuss generally how the lack of racial diversity affects legal professional training without putting individual students "on the spot."
>
> Finally, law schools should consider adding a required unit of materials about diversity in the legal profession as a permanent part of the law school curriculum. Law students (as well as law professors and practicing lawyers) would benefit from an intellectual structure within which to examine the history of discrimination in the legal profession, the present demographics of the legal profession, and how the lack of racial diversity in the profession affects not only their future as lawyers but the future of their clients as well. * * *

Margaret M. Russell, *McLaurin's Seat: The Need for Racial Inclusion in Legal Education*, 70 Fordham L. Rev. 1825, 1827–28 (2002).

SECTION 3. SECURING PROTECTION AGAINST HARM

Social justice lawyers have devoted time to voting and education, which are frequently cited as cornerstones of democracy. Protection against harm and state accountability for that harm have received less attention as social justice issues within the system of law. Yet an important part of life and liberty is the ability to be free of harm inflicted by the state, and an important part of equality is the ability to demand that the state provide protection against harm in the same way to all of its citizens. Recall Robin West's admonition in chapter 7 that "the state must ensure some minimal level of well-being because such a threshold is necessary if citizens are to live fully human lives and have the dignity to which their humanity entitles them."

Why do you suppose that protection against harm has rarely been named as an important requirement for democratic participation? Has violence been seen as a purely private matter, the province of the criminal justice or tort systems, and therefore not viewed as a social justice issue?

Yet as G. Kristian Miccio observes:

> American constitutional and common law principals affirm the centrality of the body in our framework of individual rights. The physical indivisibility of the person is central to conceptions of the self and the rights created to protect the self, and the right to bodily integrity is central to all other liberties.

G. Kristian Miccio, *Notes from the Underground: Battered Women, the State, and Conceptions of Accountability*, 23 Harv. Women's L.J. 133, 162 (2000).

Under which circumstances will harm to an individual be recognized as the product of action by the state? This section first explores state responsibility and then, in the context of domestic violence, examines the challenge of insuring that people have an equal ability to claim state protection. *See* chapter 14 for an exploration of the legal and social movement to end domestic violence.

A. Liberty, Due Process, and State Responsibility

DESHANEY v. WINNEBAGO COUNTY DEPARTMENT OF SOCIAL SERVICES

489 U.S. 189 (1989)

Chief Justice REHNQUIST delivered the opinion of the Court.

Petitioner is a boy who was beaten and permanently injured by his father, with whom he lived. Respondents are social workers and other local officials who received complaints that petitioner was being abused by his father and had reason to believe that this was the case, but nonetheless did not act to remove petitioner from his father's custody. Petitioner sued respondents claiming that their failure to act deprived him of his liberty in violation of the Due Process Clause of the Fourteenth Amendment to the United States Constitution. We hold that it did not.

I

The facts of this case are undeniably tragic. Petitioner Joshua DeShaney was born in 1979. In 1980, a Wyoming court granted his parents a divorce and awarded custody of Joshua to his father, Randy DeShaney. The father shortly thereafter moved to Neenah, a city located in Winnebago County, Wisconsin, taking the infant Joshua with him. There he entered into a second marriage, which also ended in divorce.

The Winnebago County authorities first learned that Joshua DeShaney might be a victim of child abuse in January 1982, when his father's second wife complained to the police, at the time of their divorce, that he had previously "hit the boy causing marks and [was] a prime case for child abuse." The Winnebago County Department of Social Services (DSS) interviewed the father, but he denied the accusations, and DSS did not pursue them further. In January 1983, Joshua was admitted to a local hospital with multiple bruises and abrasions. The examining physician suspected child abuse and notified DSS, which immediately obtained an order from a Wisconsin juvenile court placing Joshua in the temporary custody of the hospital. Three days later, the county convened an ad hoc "Child Protection Team"—consisting of a pediatrician, a psychologist, a police detective, the county's lawyer, several DSS caseworkers, and various hospital personnel—to consider Joshua's situation. At this meeting, the Team decided that there was insufficient evidence of child abuse to retain Joshua in the custody of the court. The Team did, however, decide to recommend several measures to protect Joshua, including enrolling him in a preschool program, providing his father with certain counselling services, and encouraging his father's girlfriend to move out of the home. Randy DeShaney entered into a voluntary agreement with DSS in which he promised to cooperate with them in accomplishing these goals.

Based on the recommendation of the Child Protection Team, the juvenile court dismissed the child protection case and returned Joshua to the custody of his father. A month later, emergency room personnel called the DSS caseworker handling Joshua's case to report that he had once again been treated for suspicious injuries. The caseworker concluded that there was no basis for action. For the next six months, the caseworker made monthly visits to the DeShaney home, during which she observed a number of suspicious injuries on Joshua's head; she also noticed that he had not been enrolled in school, and that the girlfriend had not moved out. The caseworker dutifully recorded these incidents in her files, along with her continuing suspicions that someone in the DeShaney household was physically abusing Joshua, but she did nothing more. In November 1983, the emergency room notified DSS that Joshua had been treated once again for injuries that they believed to be caused by child abuse. On the caseworker's next two visits to the DeShaney home, she was told that Joshua was too ill to see her. Still DSS took no action.

In March 1984, Randy DeShaney beat 4-year-old Joshua so severely that he fell into a life-threatening coma. Emergency brain surgery revealed a series of hemorrhages caused by traumatic injuries to the head inflicted over a long period of time. Joshua did not die, but he suffered brain damage so severe that he is expected to spend the rest of his life confined to an institution for the profoundly retarded. Randy DeShaney was subsequently tried and convicted of child abuse.

Joshua and his mother brought this action under 42 U.S.C. § 1983 in the United States District Court for the Eastern District of Wisconsin against respondents Winnebago County, DSS, and various individual employees of DSS. The complaint alleged that respondents had deprived Joshua of his liberty without due process of law, in violation of his rights under the Fourteenth Amendment, by failing to intervene to protect him against a risk of violence at his father's hands of which they knew or should have known. The District Court granted summary judgment for respondents.

* * *

Because of the inconsistent approaches taken by the lower courts in determining when, if ever, the failure of a state or local governmental entity or its agents to provide an individual with adequate protective services constitutes a violation of the individual's due process rights, and the importance of the issue to the administration of state and local governments, we granted certiorari. We now affirm.

II

The Due Process Clause of the Fourteenth Amendment provides that "[n]o State shall ... deprive any person of life, liberty, or property, without due process of law." Petitioners contend that the State[1] deprived Joshua of his liberty interest in "free[dom] from ... unjustified intrusions on personal security," by failing to provide him with adequate protection against his father's violence. The claim is one invoking the substantive rather than the procedural component of the Due Process Clause; petitioners do not claim that the State denied Joshua protection without according him appropriate procedural safeguards, but that it was categorically obligated to protect him in these circumstances, see *Youngberg v. Romeo*, 457 U.S. 307, 309 (1982).[2]

But nothing in the language of the Due Process Clause itself requires the State to protect the life, liberty, and property of its citizens against invasion by private actors. The Clause is phrased as a limitation on the State's power to act, not as a guarantee of certain minimal levels of safety and security. It forbids the State itself to deprive individuals of life, liberty, or property without "due process of law," but its language cannot fairly be extended to impose an affirmative obligation on the State to ensure that those interests do not come to harm through other

1. As used here, the term "State" refers generically to state and local governmental entities and their agents.

2. Petitioners also argue that the Wisconsin child protection statutes gave Joshua an "entitlement" to receive protective services in accordance with the terms of the statute, an entitlement which would enjoy due process protection against state deprivation under our decision in *Board of Regents of State Colleges v. Roth*, 408 U.S. 564 (1972). But this argument is made for the first time in petitioners' brief to this Court: it was not pleaded in the complaint, argued to the Court of Appeals as a ground for reversing the District Court, or raised in the petition for certiorari. We therefore decline to consider it here.

means. Nor does history support such an expansive reading of the constitutional text. Like its counterpart in the Fifth Amendment, the Due Process Clause of the Fourteenth Amendment was intended to prevent government "from abusing [its] power, or employing it as an instrument of oppression." Its purpose was to protect the people from the State, not to ensure that the State protected them from each other. The Framers were content to leave the extent of governmental obligation in the latter area to the democratic political processes.

Consistent with these principles, our cases have recognized that the Due Process Clauses generally confer no affirmative right to governmental aid, even where such aid may be necessary to secure life, liberty, or property interests of which the government itself may not deprive the individual. As we said in *Harris v. McRae*: "Although the liberty protected by the Due Process Clause affords protection against unwarranted *government* interference . . ., it does not confer an entitlement to such [governmental aid] as may be necessary to realize all the advantages of that freedom." 448 U.S., at 317–318 (emphasis added). If the Due Process Clause does not require the State to provide its citizens with particular protective services, it follows that the State cannot be held liable under the Clause for injuries that could have been averted had it chosen to provide them. As a general matter, then, we conclude that a State's failure to protect an individual against private violence simply does not constitute a violation of the Due Process Clause.

Petitioners contend, however, that even if the Due Process Clause imposes no affirmative obligation on the State to provide the general public with adequate protective services, such a duty may arise out of certain "special relationships" created or assumed by the State with respect to particular individuals. Petitioners argue that such a "special relationship" existed here because the State knew that Joshua faced a special danger of abuse at his father's hands, and specifically proclaimed, by word and by deed, its intention to protect him against that danger. Having actually undertaken to protect Joshua from this danger—which petitioners concede the State played no part in creating—the State acquired an affirmative "duty," enforceable through the Due Process Clause, to do so in a reasonably competent fashion. Its failure to discharge that duty, so the argument goes, was an abuse of governmental power that so "shocks the conscience," as to constitute a substantive due process violation.

We reject this argument. It is true that in certain limited circumstances the Constitution imposes upon the State affirmative duties of care and protection with respect to particular individuals. In *Estelle v. Gamble*, 429 U.S. 97 (1976), we recognized that the Eighth Amendment's prohibition against cruel and unusual punishment, made applicable to the States through the Fourteenth Amendment's Due Process Clause, requires the State to provide adequate medical care to incarcerated prisoners. We reasoned that because the prisoner is unable " 'by reason of the deprivation of his liberty [to] care for himself,' " it is only " 'just' " that the State be required to care for him.

In *Youngberg v. Romeo*, 457 U.S. 307 (1982), we extended this analysis beyond the Eighth Amendment setting, holding that the substantive component of the Fourteenth Amendment's Due Process Clause requires the State to provide involuntarily committed mental patients with such services as are necessary to ensure their "reasonable safety" from themselves and others. As we explained: "If it is cruel and unusual punishment to hold convicted criminals in unsafe conditions, it must be unconstitutional [under the Due Process Clause] to confine the involuntarily committed—who may not be punished at all—in unsafe conditions."

But these cases afford petitioners no help. Taken together, they stand only for the proposition that when the State takes a person into its custody and holds him there against his will, the Constitution imposes upon it a corresponding duty to assume some responsibility for his safety and general well-being. See *Youngberg v. Romeo*, *supra* at 317 ("When a person is institutionalized—and wholly dependent on the State[,] . . . a duty to provide certain services and care does exist"). The rationale for this principle is simple enough: when the State by the affirmative exercise of its power so restrains an individual's liberty that it renders him unable to care for himself, and at the same time fails to provide for his basic human needs—*e.g.*, food, clothing, shelter, medical care, and reasonable safety—it transgresses the substantive limits on state action set by the Eighth Amendment and the Due Process Clause. The affirmative duty to protect arises not from the State's knowledge of the individual's predicament or from its expressions of intent to help him, but from the limitation which it has imposed on his freedom to act on his own behalf. In the substantive due process analysis, it is the State's affirmative act of restraining the individual's freedom to act on his own behalf—through incarceration, institutionalization, or other similar restraint of personal liberty—which is the "deprivation of liberty" triggering the protections of the Due Process Clause, not its failure to act to protect his liberty interests against harms inflicted by other means.

The *Estelle-Youngberg* analysis simply has no applicability in the present case. Petitioners concede that the harms Joshua suffered occurred not while he was in the State's custody, but while he was in the custody of his natural father, who was in no sense a state actor. While the State may have been aware of the dangers that Joshua faced in the free world, it played no part in their creation, nor did it do anything to render him any more vulnerable to them. That the State once took temporary custody of Joshua does not alter the analysis, for when it returned him to his father's custody, it placed him in no worse position than that in which he would have been had it not acted at all; the State does not become the permanent guarantor of an individual's safety by having once offered him shelter. Under these circumstances, the State had no constitutional duty to protect Joshua.

It may well be that, by voluntarily undertaking to protect Joshua against a danger it concededly played no part in creating, the State acquired a duty under state tort law to provide him with adequate protection against that danger. See Restatement (Second) of Torts § 323 (1965) (one who undertakes to render services to another may in some circumstances be held liable for doing so in a negligent fashion); see generally W. Keeton, D. Dobbs, R. Keeton, & D. Owen, Prosser and Keeton on the Law of Torts § 56 (5th ed. 1984) (discussing "special relationships" which may give rise to affirmative duties to act under the common law of tort). But the claim here is based on the Due Process Clause of the Fourteenth Amendment, which, as we have said many times, does not transform every tort committed by a state actor into a constitutional violation. A State may, through its courts and legislatures, impose such affirmative duties of care and protection upon its agents as it wishes. But not "all common-law duties owed by government actors were . . . constitutionalized by the Fourteenth Amendment." Because, as explained above, the State had no constitutional duty to protect Joshua against his father's violence, its failure to do so—though calamitous in hindsight—simply does not constitute a violation of the Due Process Clause.

Judges and lawyers, like other humans, are moved by natural sympathy in a case like this to find a way for Joshua and his mother to receive adequate compensation for the grievous harm inflicted upon them. But before yielding to that impulse, it is well to remember once again that the harm was inflicted not by the State of Wisconsin, but by Joshua's father. The most that can be said of the state functionaries in this case is that they stood by and did nothing when suspicious circumstances dictated a more active role for them. In defense of them it must also be said that had they moved too soon to take custody of the son away from the father, they would likely have been met with charges of improperly intruding into the parent-child relationship, charges based on the same Due Process Clause that forms the basis for the present charge of failure to provide adequate protection.

The people of Wisconsin may well prefer a system of liability which would place upon the State and its officials the responsibility for failure to act in situations such as the present one. They may create such a system, if they do not have it already, by changing the tort law of the State in accordance with the regular lawmaking process. But they should not have it thrust upon them by this Court's expansion of the Due Process Clause of the Fourteenth Amendment.

Affirmed.

Justice BRENNAN, with whom Justice MARSHALL and Justice BLACKMUN join, dissenting.

"The most that can be said of the state functionaries in this case," the Court today concludes, "is that they stood by and did nothing when suspicious circumstances dictated a more active role for them." Because I believe that this description of respondents' conduct tells only part of the story and that, accordingly, the Constitution itself "dictated a more active role" for respondents in the circumstances presented here, I cannot agree that respondents had no constitutional duty to help Joshua DeShaney.

It may well be, as the Court decides, that the Due Process Clause as construed by our prior cases creates no general right to basic governmental services. That, however, is not the question presented here; indeed, that question was not raised in the complaint, urged on appeal, presented in the petition for certiorari, or addressed in the briefs on the merits. No one, in short, has asked the Court to proclaim that, as a general matter, the Constitution safeguards positive as well as negative liberties.

This is more than a quibble over dicta; it is a point about perspective, having substantive ramifications. In a constitutional setting that distinguishes sharply between action and inaction, one's characterization of the misconduct alleged under § 1983 may effectively decide the case. Thus, by leading off with a discussion (and rejection) of the idea that the Constitution imposes on the States an affirmative duty to take basic care of their citizens, the Court foreshadows—perhaps even preordains—its conclusion that no duty existed even on the specific facts before us. This initial discussion establishes the baseline from which the Court assesses the DeShaneys' claim that, when a State has—"by word and by deed,"—announced an intention to protect a certain class of citizens and has before it facts that would trigger that protection under the applicable state law, the Constitution imposes upon the State an affirmative duty of protection.

The Court's baseline is the absence of positive rights in the Constitution and a concomitant suspicion of any claim that seems to depend on such rights. From this perspective, the DeShaneys' claim is first and foremost about inaction (the failure, here, of respondents to take steps to protect Joshua), and only tangentially about action (the establishment of a state program specifically designed to help children like Joshua). And from this perspective, holding these Wisconsin officials liable—where the only difference between this case and one involving a general claim to protective services is Wisconsin's establishment and operation of a program to protect children—would seem to punish an effort that we should seek to promote.

I would begin from the opposite direction. I would focus first on the action that Wisconsin *has* taken with respect to Joshua and children like him, rather than on the actions that the State failed to take. Such a method is not new to this Court. Both *Estelle v. Gamble*, 429 U.S. 97 (1976), and *Youngberg v. Romeo*, 457 U.S. 307 (1982), began by emphasizing that the States had confined J.W. Gamble to prison and Nicholas Romeo to a psychiatric hospital. This initial action rendered these people helpless to help themselves or to seek help from persons unconnected to the government. Cases from the lower courts also recognize that a State's actions can be decisive in assessing the constitutional significance of subsequent inaction. For these purposes, moreover, actual physical restraint is not the only state action that has been considered relevant.

See, *e.g.*, *White v. Rochford*, 592 F.2d 381 (C.A.7 1979) (police officers violated due process when, after arresting the guardian of three young children, they abandoned the children on a busy stretch of highway at night).

* * *

Wisconsin has established a child-welfare system specifically designed to help children like Joshua. Wisconsin law places upon the local departments of social services such as respondent (DSS or Department) a duty to investigate reported instances of child abuse. See Wis.Stat. § 48.981(3) (1987–1988). While other governmental bodies and private persons are largely responsible for the reporting of possible cases of child abuse, see § 48.981(2), Wisconsin law channels all such reports to the local departments of social services for evaluation and, if necessary, further action. § 48.981(3). Even when it is the sheriff's office or police department that receives a report of suspected child abuse, that report is referred to local social services departments for action, see § 48.981(3)(a); the only exception to this occurs when the reporter fears for the child's *immediate* safety. § 48.981(3)(b). In this way, Wisconsin law invites—indeed, directs—citizens and other governmental entities to depend on local departments of social services such as respondent to protect children from abuse.

The specific facts before us bear out this view of Wisconsin's system of protecting children. Each time someone voiced a suspicion that Joshua was being abused, that information was relayed to the Department for investigation and possible action. When Randy DeShaney's second wife told the police that he had " 'hit the boy causing marks and [was] a prime case for child abuse,' " the police referred her complaint to DSS. When, on three separate occasions, emergency room personnel noticed suspicious injuries on Joshua's body, they went to DSS with this information. When neighbors informed the police that they had seen or heard Joshua's father or his father's lover beating or otherwise abusing Joshua, the police brought these reports to the attention of DSS. And when respondent Kemmeter, through these reports and through her own observations in the course of nearly 20 visits to the DeShaney home, compiled growing evidence that Joshua was being abused, that information stayed within the Department—chronicled by the social worker in detail that seems almost eerie in light of her failure to act upon it. (As to the extent of the social worker's involvement in, and knowledge of, Joshua's predicament, her reaction to the news of Joshua's last and most devastating injuries is illuminating: " 'I just knew the phone would ring some day and Joshua would be dead.' " 812 F.2d 298, 300 (C.A.7 1987).)

Even more telling than these examples is the Department's control over the decision whether to take steps to protect a particular child from suspected abuse. While many different people contributed information and advice to this decision, it was up to the people at DSS to make the ultimate decision (subject to the approval of the local government's Corporation Counsel) whether to disturb the family's current arrangements. When Joshua first appeared at a local hospital with injuries signaling physical abuse, for example, it was DSS that made the decision to take him into temporary custody for the purpose of studying his situation—and it was DSS, acting in conjunction with the corporation counsel, that returned him to his father. Unfortunately for Joshua DeShaney, the buck effectively stopped with the Department.

In these circumstances, a private citizen, or even a person working in a government agency other than DSS, would doubtless feel that her job was done as soon as she had reported her suspicions of child abuse to DSS. Through its child-welfare program, in other words, the State of Wisconsin has relieved ordinary citizens and governmental bodies other than the Department of any sense of obligation to do anything more than report their suspicions of child abuse to DSS. If DSS ignores or dismisses these suspicions, no one will step in to fill the gap. Wisconsin's child-protection program thus effectively confined Joshua DeShaney within the walls of Randy DeShaney's violent home until such time as DSS took action to remove him. Conceivably, then, children like Joshua are made worse off by the existence of this program when the persons and entities charged with carrying it out fail to do their jobs.

It simply belies reality, therefore, to contend that the State "stood by and did nothing" with respect to Joshua. Through its child-protection program, the State actively intervened in Joshua's life and, by virtue of this intervention, acquired ever more certain knowledge that Joshua was in grave danger. These circumstances, in my view, plant this case solidly within the tradition of cases like *Youngberg* and *Estelle*.

* * *

As the Court today reminds us, "the Due Process Clause of the Fourteenth Amendment was intended to prevent government 'from abusing [its] power, or employing it as an instrument of oppression.'" My disagreement with the Court arises from its failure to see that inaction can be every bit as abusive of power as action, that oppression can result when a State undertakes a vital duty and then ignores it. Today's opinion construes the Due Process Clause to permit a State to displace private sources of protection and then, at the critical moment, to shrug its shoulders and turn away from the harm that it has promised to try to prevent. Because I cannot agree that our Constitution is indifferent to such indifference, I respectfully dissent.

Justice BLACKMUN, dissenting.

Today, the Court purports to be the dispassionate oracle of the law, unmoved by "natural sympathy." But, in this pretense, the Court itself retreats into a sterile formalism which prevents it from recognizing either the facts of the case before it or the legal norms that should apply to those facts. As Justice BRENNAN demonstrates, the facts here involve not mere passivity, but active state intervention in the life of Joshua DeShaney—intervention that triggered a fundamental duty to aid the boy once the State learned of the severe danger to which he was exposed.

The Court fails to recognize this duty because it attempts to draw a sharp and rigid line between action and inaction. But such formalistic reasoning has no place in the interpretation of the broad and stirring Clauses of the Fourteenth Amendment. Indeed, I submit that these Clauses were designed, at least in part, to undo the formalistic legal reasoning that infected antebellum jurisprudence, which the late Professor Robert Cover analyzed so effectively in his significant work entitled Justice Accused (1975).

Like the antebellum judges who denied relief to fugitive slaves, the Court today claims that its decision, however harsh, is compelled by existing legal doctrine. On the contrary, the question presented by this case is an open one, and our Fourteenth Amendment precedents may be read more broadly or narrowly depending upon how one chooses to read them. Faced with the choice, I would adopt a "sympathetic" reading, one which comports with dictates of fundamental justice and recognizes that compassion need not be exiled from the province of judging. Cf. A. Stone, Law, Psychiatry, and Morality 262 (1984) ("We will make mistakes if we go forward, but doing nothing can be the worst mistake. What is required of us is moral ambition. Until our composite sketch becomes a true portrait of humanity we must live with our uncertainty; we will grope, we will struggle, and our compassion may be our only guide and comfort").

Poor Joshua! Victim of repeated attacks by an irresponsible, bullying, cowardly, and intemperate father, and abandoned by respondents who placed him in a dangerous predicament and who knew or learned what was going on, and yet did essentially nothing except, as the Court revealingly observes, "dutifully recorded these incidents in [their] files." It is a sad commentary upon American life, and constitutional principles—so full of late of patriotic fervor and proud proclamations about "liberty and justice for all"—that this child, Joshua DeShaney, now is assigned to live out the remainder of his life profoundly retarded. Joshua and his mother, as petitioners here, deserve—but now are denied by this Court—the opportunity to have the facts of their case considered in the light of the constitutional protection that 42 U.S.C. § 1983 is meant to provide.

Notes and Questions

1. Do the differences between the majority and dissenting justices turn on the distinction between action and inaction? Did the state act? If the state did not act, did it violate a duty to act?

Is the majority's result persuasive? *DeShaney* has been roundly criticized by the commentators. *See, e.g.*, "Chief Justice Rehnquist's opinion for the majority in *DeShaney* is an abomination. It is illogical and extremely mechanistic; it also abuses history, fails to consider practical impact, and demonstrates moral insensitivity. Not only that, it is wrong." Aviam Soifer, *Moral Ambition, Formalism, and the "Free World" of* DeShaney, 57 Geo. Wash. L. Rev. 1513, 1514 (1989).

2. Does the argument raised in note 2 of the majority's opinion, suggesting that Wisconsin's child protection statutes may have given Joshua an entitlement to receive protective services, have merit? Why do you suppose that argument was not raised? Have social justice litigators neglected state statutory and constitutional arguments that may not have been given centrality in their legal educations?

3. What if the state fails to follow its own laws and orders an employee into a position of danger? On October 21, 1988, Larry Michael Collins, an employee in the sanitation department of the City of Harker Heights, Texas, "died of asphyxia after entering a manhole to unstop a sewer line." His widow sued the city, alleging:

> [Collins] "had a constitutional right to be free from unreasonable risks of harm to his body, mind and emotions and a constitutional right to be protected from the city of Harker Heights' custom and policy of deliberate indifference toward the safety of its employees." Her complaint alleged that the city violated that right by following a custom and policy of not training its employees about the dangers of working in sewer lines and manholes, not providing safety equipment at jobsites, and not providing safety warnings. * * * [The complaint made two other important allegations: (1)] that a prior incident [in which Collin's supervisor had been rendered unconscious in a manhole several months before Collins began working there] had given the city notice of the risks of entering the sewer lines, and [(2)] that the city had systematically and intentionally failed to provide the equipment and training required [by law.]

Collins v. City of Harker Heights, Texas, 503 U.S. 115, 117–18 (1992). One state law required education and training that had not been provided, including a requirement that new employees be provided training before working in an area containing hazardous chemicals. Another law mandated information for employees about hazardous chemicals, training about chemical hazards, and provision of protective equipment. 503 U.S. at 129.

Citing *DeShaney*, the Supreme Court held that the behavior of the city government had not been "arbitrary in a constitutional sense." 503 U.S. at 129.

Is this outcome required under *DeShaney*? Would it change your analysis if *no* state tort remedy is available because of the state workers' compensation law? How can any employee compel Texas to follow its own laws?

4. Consider this assessment of the Court's jurisprudence that could culminate in a decision like *DeShaney*.

KENNETH M. CASEBEER

The Empty State and Nobody's Market: The Political Economy of Non-Responsibility and the Judicial Disappearing of the Civil Rights Movement
54 U. Miami L. Rev. 247, 248–57, 289–91, 297, 310–14 (2000)

This essay * * * is about how the Court during this period [1975–1998] restructured the system of Constitutional interpretation in such a profound manner as to lay to rest once and for all the conservative canard that judges neutrally decide cases based on legal text and that therefore there is any such fictional beast as a non-activist judge. Law is politics, or more correctly, political-economics in this period of constitutional history.

By political economy, I mean the interdependence of the political structure and actions of the State, with the structure and actions of relations associated with production and distribution of resources. This article is an argument about the production of power. While the social construction of power in the United States is by no means limited to the adjudication of legal conflict, and the United States Supreme Court is not immune to formal and informal influences of power directed towards it, neither is the Court powerless, in conjunction with other power holders, to substantially alter the type and meaning of our democratic experience. Any such production and deployment of power in society must be judged by the democratic accountability which such force demands in any authentic, that is, participatory democracy. By the standard of democracy measured by the experience of all in our society, the present United States Supreme Court fails in this democratic accountability, its most basic responsibility.

The constitutional law of the present Supreme Court is systematically undemocratic in content. It represents a danger for all the people even as the Court cynically celebrates majoritarian democratic form in the denial of civil and constitutional rights for minorities. This experientially false, rhetorical legal strategy deployed as power depends on two key concepts. One political and the other economic, seemingly opposed yet presupposing each other—the doctrine of the Empty State and of Nobody's Market.

* * *

In reality, the past twenty years of the Court's business has been a more focused but unannounced systematic dismantling of the decision, legal reasoning, and social assumptions of *Brown v. Board of Education*. The Court has so thoroughly manipulated the technical doctrines of constitutional rights litigation, that, taken together, these developments can be explained only as a judicial war against the Civil Rights Movement. But while the veneer of this transformation has been Federalism, and the main mechanisms of change have been doctrines affecting the litigation of rights, backed by fraudulent concern over judicial legitimacy, the driving ideas of this change in the relation of the State to the organization of social relations has been the constitutional installation of a specific political economy. As a result, anti-discrimination rights, especially on grounds of race and gender, under the Constitution and federal statutes have been magically detached from economic development. At the same time, a particular set of legal relations allocating racial and gender power seemingly naturally reduce the power of government to overcome racial and gender injustices. In this manner, an ideology of the production of power and the legal/political deployment of power reflect and shape the material conditions and social experiences of power in a system of production.

The general consequence of this attack insulates increasingly walled, suburban, white, and largely wealthy local communities from any political forum that includes the mass of the population and virtually all minorities who reside in our large urban cities. These populations historically sought political power through Congress and enforcement of individual rights against wholesale exclusions from power through the federal courts. Now they are to be abandoned as an underclass, maintained as a continuous low wage labor pool to increase propertied wealth.

The liberty served by Rehnquist's Court is the liberty of exclusion from voluntary propertied relations and geography. The Supreme Court thus abandons enforcing rights that embody the "liberty of inclusion in fair political processes" rationale that underlies the post-depression understanding of the Constitution, formulated in footnote four of *United States v. Carolene Products*, and exemplified by the *Brown* decision. Rewriting *Brown* to get rid of Court responsibility to end invidious subordination of current minorities, by turning *Brown* into a demand for "colorblindness" freezes existing majority race use of law to preserve the majority's gains and exclusivity of geographical location. Conveniently, this preserves the white majority's gains against their coming twenty-first century minority status in the larger, more diverse polity that is to come.

The construction of the new version of a constitutional system of social power is deeply defended and multiply masked. First, it is doctrinally masked in the name of individual mobility among diverse enclaves protected by legal gate keepers. Second, it is institutionally masked in the name of "judicial restraint." The inter-connection of race, gender, and other subordination to economic development within the legal conceptualization of power will require two things: (1) a mapping of the political content of judicial decisions that permit government to wash its hands of responsibility for historical or social domination and (2) the tying of this political constitution to a particular form of economic organization.

* * *

The Empty State presupposes a sharp separation of public and private responsibility. This is true although its proponents deny this possibility and even as the Rehnquist majority purports to hold that all property consists of legally permitted bundles of resource uses. This is thus not a return to the strong State separation of central and local functions defined by the regime of a "dual sovereignty" in the nineteenth century and built on the exhaustion of liberty as liberty of voluntary contract. Rather, the Empty State is a new legal construction that denies public accountability for subordination—the focus of much of the Civil Rights Movement—and simultaneously protects the current distribution of wealth and market leverage as just or natural.

* * *

The new argument continues * * * that surely government cannot be liable for every person's power simply because power is only what the government is willing to enforce. Some kind of distinction must be drawn, no longer to protect individual right, but to limit public responsibility. Purely negative constitutional rights designed to prevent excess by direct governing officials, combined with the need to limit the scope of governmental responsibility, allow the courts to fashion a fictional public-private distinction in legal doctrine where power is divorced from legally accountable government responsibility for its use.

Legal enforcement of legal permissions, and by extension all patterns and practices of governmental policies, are not State action. Note carefully that law as general policy (such as the Uniform Commercial Code) is not State action unless a government official directly carries out the policy producing the direct consequences to a complaining person. More and more governance is carried out by delegation to private institutions, by subsidy, by tax incentive or disincentive, by private enforcement, by the nod and the wink, or by intentional inaction. All such law is not State or government action subject to the responsibilities of constitutional rights or enforceable limits. Unless a government official is inextricably necessary to the fulfillment of the consequences of law, there is no State. Only private individuals exist. The private sector did it. The Market did it. But who is the Market?

In the cartoons, when the parent asks the innocent child, "Who broke the vase, Who let the dog out, Who took the cookies?", the child's response is, "Nobody did it." Sure enough, in the background the barely invisible gremlin, the "Nobody," is seen snickering away.

Just as the State is empty, so the Market is comprised of Nobody's. Presupposing the Empty State and Nobody's Market to be manifestations of each other distributes power in a particular way. The State distributes power as an option to accept or reject personal responsibility for the social risks associated with production, both economic and cultural. Market actors, who have little access to productive capital of their own, face market pressure to accept a low market value for social risks supposedly compensated by their private wages. Thus, citizens with fewer personal resources end up in the worst position along with those who suffer high costs of work participation. Both categories often describe women and minorities, and especially minority women.

Why would a constitutional system that systematically insulates power from accountable responsibility for its delegation and deployment represent an acceptable vision of social organization? * * *

A more realistic understanding of the State encompasses the totality of power deployed as legitimate because of the law within a community. The State is not empty of distributions of power to specific interests any more than market practices are ordained by faceless fuzzy spirits. * * *

The 1983 action in *Flagg Brothers, Inc. v. Brooks* [436 U.S. 149 (1978)] raises the question of who has the constitutional responsibility * * * to protect the plaintiff's procedural due process rights. Treating responsibility as a component of the substantive content of the fourteenth amendment's state action requirement limits who can be sued in the same way justiciability screens out potentially liable actors under a similar threshold question of who are the proper plaintiffs:

> A claim ... under § 1983 must embody at least two elements. Respondents are first bound to show that they have been deprived of a right "secured by the Constitution and the laws" of the United States. They must secondly show that Flagg Brothers deprived them of this right acting "under color of any statute" of the State of New York.

Although the Flagg Brothers plaintiff demonstrated that the warehouseman's authorization to sell her goods for nonpayment of a disputed bill stemmed from the Uniform Commercial Code (U.C.C.) in New York, she could not identify a "secured" right by a showing that the injury was properly attributable to the State of New York. Because no State actor sold Mrs. Brooks's goods there was no State action although the sale was permitted only by the (U.C.C.) The U.C.C. is mere authorization. Law as policy is not State action!

* * *

Because no specific governmental actor directly contributed to the specific action of the warehouseman, by either delegating an exclusively sovereign function ordering the choice leading to the plaintiff's deprivation, or specifically approving the action taken as policy, the Court found no state action present. Although the sheriff removed Mrs. Brooks' possessions during an eviction and placed them in a private warehouse, the warehouseman's self-help was simply permitted by the background rules of public order available to all private decisions. The sharp line drawn between public and private power prevents a private individual from using constitutional rights to interfere with other private individuals' state-permitted choices. Such interference, if allowed, would be a seemingly perverse use of court protections of the boundaries of public power. By limiting liability to direct causation, the individualization of public responsibility allows the creation of a sharp conceptual division of public and private power through the doctrine of state action. Not surprisingly, it does more. Beyond doctrinal symmetry, * * * *Flagg*

Brothers evidence[s] an identical understanding of federal courts as limited institutions.

The fact that conduct is private does not insulate it from government control. The fourteenth amendment shields it only from federal court review. Such conduct will be supervised, if so desired, by state or local legislative majorities in the name of the public good. * * * [T]he State is not responsible for individual choices. It simply limits the scope of responsibility to that of individual governmental actors. Despite lip service in string cites, *Shelley v. Kraemer* has been overruled in its reasoning and limited almost completely to preventing judicial enforcement of racially restricted covenants.

* * *

DeShaney v. Winnebago Co. is the most explicit embodiment of the new Rehnquist liberty in the substance of constitutional rights. After numerous trips to the emergency room with severe but suspicious bruises, toddler Joshua DeShaney was removed from the custody of his father, Randy, by social workers acting under state law authorization. The county department returned Joshua to his father. Shortly thereafter, on the next visit to the emergency room, Joshua's skull was found fractured, leaving the four-year-old profoundly impaired for the rest of his life. The case was not dismissed on standing or state action grounds. By the time of *DeShaney*, the new regime is in place sufficiently to allow the doctrine of due process to be limited to wrongs of intentional and strict causation. The State did not beat Joshua; his father, Randy, swung the club.

The State's decision to return Joshua to Randy, while discretionary, was not the cause of Joshua's harm in any way because constitutional rights consist purely of negative orders not to do specific acts. Any other subsequent actor relieves the state of responsibility. Any alternative would have to stem from non-existent affirmative obligations on government impossible under the Constitution. Ironically, as a result of the litigation, Winnebago County ultimately responded by ceasing all voluntary removals of child custody in cases of suspected abuse and will now only intervene under court order.

* * *

* * * As in *Plessy*, we must not be individually judged by our voluntary encounters and exclusions, but contrary to *Plessy*, the primacy of racial status need never be legalized. It merely needs to be tolerated in the lack of constitutionalized power in an Empty State mechanically servicing free market merit. We are now equal before the law because we are employees, regardless of our wealth or lack of it, regardless of our homes or access to bridges for shelter, but not simply equal before the law because we are members of differing races.

This is the double bind of our oppression—both the fact of injustice, and the systematic denial of responsibility for those realities oppress. Under the Empty State, we can only try to prevent discrimination, help mobility of all, help choices now that market risks have been internalized as the cost of entering the market, and are presumably reflected in the market wage. These very solutions, however, cover up the historical responsibility of the state's production of power and the law's distribution of productive capacity that underlies access to resources and other social empowerment. Once the solutions directed against past oppression are limited to "individual rational choice" and "individual opportunity," the ability to trace state responsibility and complicity disappears into Nobody's Market, freezing the already acquired fruits of past discrimination and making further attempts at attacking past inequality a new cost to someone else. In effect, now all are innocents in the new regime. The Empty State pardons all market participants.

* * *

Law should be practiced in ways that do not defeat democracy, and in such practices, for the need to recover possible suppressed alternative political economies, particularly in the legal strategies most directly related to work and production. Of necessity, the meaning of a lived democracy will be contested. Such interdependent struggles, after all, establish the very justice of *democratic* claims to the power to mediate social conflicts. The key is to demand that constitutional interpretation by unelected judges be rationally linked to constitutional structure, and then rationally linked to justifications based on democracy. Of course, no changes will be objective or neutral, including the massive rewriting done by the present Court. Like all exercises of power, strategic content must be defended.

* * *

* * * Authentic democracy demands participation in the construction of power in the name of society.

Three distinct changes would increase the democratic accountability of constitutional adjudication and may be loosely captured by the label, "Substantive Carolene Products." First, and at a minimum, the courts should be forced to justify the inevitable distribution of power contained in every adjudication by explaining the decision's contribution to and effect on democracy or democratic accountability.

Second, judicial interpretation must focus on the facts of the conflict over power within society represented by the parties to any case. The current Supreme Court has increasingly resorted to purely formal rhetoric, empty of any explanatory content, settling nothing and generating confusion. To the contrary, the internal meaningfulness of legal argument requires the recognition of continuity between present cases and a contested past, not an ahistoric past. Explaining the mediating function of adjudication thus requires relating the relevance of past conflict to the present case, an inherently factual representation, before a formalistic rule should be extended. The more fact, the more supportable the continuation or change of legal power in the present litigation. Law is made undemocratic in a step-by-step process that reduces each complex struggle to a formal contest over a rule. In the next episode or case this rule appears as a settled part of the now natural background that forms the context of the next ruling. As Judith Shklar has noted, confusing this procedure for having factually ended the past case's stakes commits the naturalistic fallacy, confusing language for truth, and is therefore inherently conservative as a practice. It conservatively overemphasizes the power of past prevailing parties and their relative power, and dismisses the relevance of losing parties. This is, of course, entirely counterfactual to modern notions of economics, history, and political choice theory. Legal meaning, and therefore, legal power is contested, and should be produced on that basis. Legislation in itself does not end conflict even as it codifies conflict for further legal politics.

Third, since democracy-in-fact depends upon the participation of relative equals, the courts should acknowledge the conditions of society that tie each of us to the others of our communities. The courts should seek the most appropriate democratic interpretation of legal text available as measured by its contribution to overcoming the alienation of unjustified force, that is subordination. The stark failure of the twentieth century has been witnessing those who would impose their own utopias upon vast segments of the world's population. Subordination fuels the will to democracy rising across the world. It is not a utopian vision of justice driving that force. Rather, it is the will to overcome the conditions of injustice in each location which demands the sharing of power and equalizing the conditions sanctioning suffering. Before we have to worry about formal conditions of justice in order to define the deserving, we have plenty of injustice to correct, to overcome.

Each of these counters to the present Court are consistent with our present constitutional text and its generation. Democracy is the decisional politics of free individuals. Free individuals, however, depend on the conditions of their interdependency within a complex division of labor. If each self takes the measure of their power from their relations to the others within a system capable of social stability, indeed social advance, then a kind of equivalency is necessary for democracy in fact. That equality is not a license or a subsidy to consume goods or cultural experience. Here lies liberalism's fatal concession and mistake. Making distribution of wealth available for consumption the key framework of social analysis, misses the point that we make ourselves, we don't just buy our identities. Rather, it is equal access to produce and contribute within a division of labor based on mutual recognition of one's own self in the conditions experienced by all others which is necessary to democracy in fact. Furthermore, it is the risks of being subordinated in a prevailing, thus historical, division of labor which leads us to demand democracy, and then authentic democracy, as the only structure by which to solve social conflict over the terms of social production.

> If the system of rights is elaborated and extended under such favorable circumstances, each citizen can perceive, and come to appreciate, citizenship as the core of what holds people together, of what makes them at once dependent upon, and responsible for each other. They see that private and public autonomy presuppose each

> other in maintaining and improving necessary conditions for preferred forms of life. They intuitively realize that they can succeed in fairly regulating their private autonomy only by making an appropriate use of their civic autonomy, and that they are in turn empowered to do so only on a social basis that makes them, as private persons, sufficiently interdependent. They learn to conceive citizenship as the frame for that dialectic between legal and actual equality from which fair and preferable living conditions for all of them can emerge. [Jurgen Habermas, *The European Nation State: Its Achievements and its Limitations: On the Past and Future of Sovereignty and Citizenship*, 9 Ratio Juris 125, 135 (1996).]

Notes and Questions

1. Casebeer's call for courts to be mindful of losers echoes Guinier's story of her son who learned about voting from *Sesame Street* and resisted the hypothetical's implicit "winner-take-all" approach. Are courts or the electoral process preferable modes to establish such protection? Can majoritarian democracy protect minorities? *See* John Hart Ely, *Democracy and Distrust: A Theory of Judicial Review* (1980) (assessing the role of courts in the democratic process).

2. Is a right to protection from harm part of the vital functioning of a democracy? Robin West has argued that the state must protect individuals against private harm. Much of West's argument relies on the work of philosopher Martha Nussbaum and economist Amartya Sen:

> Nussbaum argues [that] for many or even all of us, [the material] preconditions [that make fully human lives possible] cannot be met without considerable state and community assistance, or more pointedly, without considerable state-run redistribution and regulation. These are not preconditions readily satisfied in either a state of nature or a minimally regulated social order. * * * All states, particularly liberal states, ought to regard their obligation to secure the preconditions of basic human capabilities as fundamental and as required by justice. Liberal states should regard their obligation to secure the minimal material preconditions of the basic human capabilities to be a basic *constitutional* duty.

Robin West, *Rights, Capabilities, and the Good Society*, 69 Fordham L. Rev. 1901, 1903 (2001).

In addition to the work of Sen and Nussbaum, West finds support for state protection against private violence in the work of Thomas Hobbes:

> The rationale of * * * [the right to security against private violence] is essentially Hobbesian * * * . As Hobbes claimed, our nature is such that the state must monopolize the tools and instruments of violence if our lives are to be relatively secure. Security against private violence is the core, material precondition of our capability for living safely and free of fear, and hence of meaningfully partici-

> pating in a good life or good society. In terms of modern utopianists, we cannot lead 'fully human lives' without such a right. In Hobbesian terms, we would not have a state without it—it is the right for which we relinquish natural freedoms. The state therefore has an obligation—a first duty—to protect citizens against private violence and aggression, including private sexual violence and aggression. It has that obligation, or first duty, because such an obligation is necessary to the creation of a good society. Again, we cannot lead 'fully human' lives otherwise.
>
> A liberal state that fails to provide such protection violates the individual's right to that protection, as well as the state's "first duty" to provide it. What might follow from the existence of such a right? A state that failed to criminalize, or failed to enforce existing laws that criminalize, domestic violence, for example, or marital rape, or violence against lesbians and gay men, or people of color, would violate those citizens' right to protection, and not just equal protection, of the law. Likewise, a state that turned its police force on its citizenry, rather than employed it in their protection, would violate positive rights to protection as well as a negative right to be free from unwarranted state intrusion. These would be clear, unequivocal violations of the citizen's most fundamental right and the state's most fundamental duty. Less blatant, and even unintentional or neglectful failures to protect citizens from violence, however, might also violate such a right. A failure, for example, to enact adequate gun control legislation so as to ensure the safety of school children, women, or urban residents, might constitute a failure to provide for the safety of citizens, and hence violate their rights to protection of the law. A consistent pattern of punishing violence against a group of citizens more leniently than the same crimes committed against another more favored group might also constitute such a violation, as Randall Kennedy argued some time ago.

Id. at 1922–23.

3. How can social justice activists respond to decisions like *DeShaney*? Judicial selection, explored in chapter 10, influences the direction of the Court.

Another answer lies in seeking legislation that imposes a duty to protect by statute. Under a Reconstruction-Era civil rights statute, the Third Circuit held the police liable for failure to protect an interracial crowd from a racist attack in Pennsylvania:

> A small pack of white thugs storms into a small town on Harley-Davidsons on a hot midsummer evening, intent on ridding the town of the young African-Americans who have been congregating on the town square that summer. Joined by a swarm of hundreds of angry townspeople, the vigilantes scream racial epithets and threats at the interlopers ("Get the n____," "N___, get out of town," et cetera). They are particularly enraged at the relationships that have developed between the young black men and local white women. The mob

chases and attacks the black youths and their white friends, finally driving them out of the square after several terrifying hours. Only a few police officers are on the scene. They stand by idly, despite town officials' advance knowledge of the impending confrontation.

The violence continues the next night. The mob is unrestrained despite an onslaught of racially charged threats and assaults. An exchange of rocks and bottles ensues between the factions. The police finally intervene. They arrest the entire interracial group, rather than their attackers, on disorderly conduct charges notwithstanding a complete lack of evidence of individual guilt (the charges are later dismissed on appeal). Nearby, the mob blocks, threatens ("Kill the n____. Get the f___ing n___ out of town before we kill them."), and descends upon two black men and two white women attempting to enter a car and drive away. Police drag off and arrest the four occupants of the car, ignoring the mob. Elsewhere in town, a crowd hurls threats at an interracial couple sitting quietly in their home. The police only urge the couple to move out of town.

This scene occurred neither in the 1800s, nor in the South in an early decade of * * * [the 20th] century, but in the town of Hanover, Pennsylvania during July of 1991, only a few months after videotapes of the Rodney King beating were nationally televised. The event, however, is eerily reminiscent of the much earlier Reconstruction era when the Ku Klux Klan and local white militia groups similarly intimidated the newly freed slaves from exercising their democratic rights. * * *

While the interracial group members in this case clearly had legal claims against the white bikers who instigated the riot, the nonresponsiveness of the police is to me the most shocking aspect of the story. Their liability, however, is less than apparent, because the police did not join directly in any racist activity, and because the crux of their dereliction was a failure to protect the riot's victims. Tort law does not normally impose a duty to protect, nor do the police ordinarily have a duty to render assistance to any particular member of the public.

The interracial youth group probably would have no legal recourse against the police were it not for the 1871 Civil Rights Act, also denominated the Ku Klux Klan Act (Act), which Congress passed to address similar conduct. The Act includes provisions now codified at 42 U.S.C. §§ 1985 and 1986 that provide a cause of action against both perpetrators of class-based conspiracies and individuals who fail to protect victims of such conspiracies. Section 1986 claims are important tools for civil rights litigators attempting to deter and punish racial violence. * * *

Section 1986 * * * imposes perhaps the strongest affirmative duty of any piece of legislation arising from the Civil War. It demonstrates the extent to which Congress reached, pursuant to the enforcement clause of the Fourteenth Amendment, to attempt to

> eradicate Ku Klux Klan violence during Reconstruction. Section 1986 imposes a "Good Samaritan" duty to protect upon police, bystanders, or others who have knowledge of impending execution of a racist conspiracy as defined by § 1985 of the Act and have the ability to prevent the conspirators from carrying out their objectives. Section 1986 provides:
>
> > Every person who, having knowledge that any of the wrongs conspired to be done, and mentioned in section 1985 of this title, are about to be committed, and having power to prevent or aid in preventing the commission of the same, neglects or refuses so to do, if such wrongful act be committed, shall be liable to the party injured . . . for all damages caused by such wrongful act, which such person by reasonable diligence could have prevented; and such damages may be recovered in an action on the case.
>
> Thus, knowledge of a § 1985 conspiracy, power to protect its victims, and neglect or refusal to protect results in liability under § 1986. Section 1986 * * * [inculpates] bystander defendants who are not themselves conspirators under § 1985. * * * A negligent failure to protect by an actor with knowledge of a § 1985 conspiracy and power to protect its victims is actionable. [Clark v. Clabaugh, 20 F.3d 1290, 1298 (3d Cir.1994)] The statute creates a legal duty. In effect, it "deputizes" local actors in a position to intervene in prohibited conspiracies and renders them liable to victims of conspiratorial violence, thus focusing on those in the best position to stop the violence. * * *

Linda E. Fisher, *Anatomy of an Affirmative Duty to Protect: 42 U.S.C. Section 1986*, 56 Wash. & Lee L. Rev. 461, 461–64 (1999) (noting that "few civil rights litigators are aware of the statute's existence and its utility in fighting racist conspiracies").

B. Domestic Violence and Rights to Protection Against Harm

Cases after the *DeShaney* decision reveal the impact of that decision on domestic violence cases. In one case, police officers who responded to a call for help were "rude, insulting, and unsympathetic" to an injured domestic violence victim. One officer said that the victim deserved the beating; another pressured her into agreeing not to press charges. She got a restraining order enjoining her former husband from contact or making harassing phone calls. When he crashed his car into the garage in violation of the order, the police who arrived would not arrest him. Police ridiculed her further complaints about harassment and vandalism. She complained of inadequate investigation after a firebomb was thrown through the window of her house. Balistreri v. Pacifica Police Dept., 855 F.2d 1421 (9th Cir.1988). In 1988, the Ninth Circuit Court of Appeals held that the restraining order could create an affirmative state commitment to protect her which, combined with police awareness of her complaints, could have established a special relationship that would impose a duty to protect on the state. In 1990, the appellate court withdrew its decision and held instead that, under *DeShaney*, no duty to protect was created despite the restraining order. Balistreri v. Pacifica Police Dept., 901 F.2d 696 (9th Cir.1988).

When the state has placed the person in a dangerous situation or increased their danger, some courts have imposed a duty to protect. The cases are inconsistent in this area, however, with some courts holding the state liable for failure to protect when other courts hold the opposite on similar facts. For example, in Monfils v. Taylor, 165 F.3d 511 (7th Cir.1998), an anonymous informant told police about a planned theft from a factory. Although the informant immediately sought to keep police from releasing the tape of his call, the man he had accused of theft obtained the tape from police and recognized his voice. The informant was brutally murdered. The court noted:

> Two "exceptions" have grown out of *DeShaney*. One exists if the state has a "special relationship" with a person, that is, if the state has custody of a person, thus cutting off alternate avenues of aid. *See Youngberg v. Romeo*, 457 U.S. 307 (1982) (requiring services to involuntarily committed mental patients); *Revere v. Massachusetts Gen. Hosp.*, 463 U.S. 239 (1983) (requiring medical care for suspects in police custody); *K.H. Through Murphy v. Morgan*, 914 F.2d 846 (7th Cir.1990) (holding that a child in state custody has a liberty interest in not being placed in an abusive foster home). The other is the state-created danger exception. The Court said in *DeShaney*, "While the State may have been aware of the dangers that Joshua faced in the free world, it played no part in their creation, nor did it do anything to render him any more vulnerable to them." From that statement courts have concluded that liability exists when the state "affirmatively places a particular individual in a position of danger the individual would not otherwise have faced." *Reed v. Gardner*, 986 F.2d 1122, 1125 (7th Cir.1993), *cert. denied*, 510 U.S. 947 (1993). In *Wallace v. Adkins*, 115 F.3d 427 (7th Cir.1997), we recognized that an order that a prison guard remain at his especially dangerous post, while at the same time offering him false assurances that he would be protected, qualifies as an affirmative act for purposes of a state-created danger claim.

165 F.3d at 516.

In contrast, in Pinder v. Johnson, 54 F.3d 1169 (4th Cir.1995), Pinder's boyfriend, recently released from ten months in prison for the attempted arson of her home, broke into her home, punched her, pushed her, threw objects at her, and threatened to murder her children. Pinder called police for help, explained the facts to the officer, and asked whether it would be safe for her to return to work. The policeman assured her that her ex-boyfriend would be in police custody overnight, and Pinder returned to work based on that promise. However, when the officer took the defendant to his initial court appearance, he was charged only with malicious destruction of property and trespassing. He was released the same night and merely warned to stay away from Pinder's residence. He returned to her home and set fire to it, causing the death of her three sleeping children. The Fourth Circuit held against Pinder, reasoning that "[t]he affirmative duty that the Supreme Court rejected in *DeShaney* is precisely the duty Pinder relies on in this case. * * * *DeShaney* makes clear, however, that no affirmative duty was clearly established in these circumstances. * * * Promises do not create a special relationship—custody does." 54 F.3d at 1174–75.

A dissenting opinion argued that the state placed Pinder and her children in a position of danger: "Pinder's children were left alone at home, vulnerable to the rampage of a violent, intemperate man, and deprived of their mother's protection because of the hollow word of an irresponsible, thoughtless police officer." 54 F.3d at 1182.

In a footnote to the *DeShaney* opinion above, Justice Rehnquist stated, "The State may not, of course, selectively deny its protective services to certain disfavored minorities without violating the Equal Protection Clause. See *Yick Wo v. Hopkins,* 118 U.S. 356 (1886)." 489 U.S. 189, 197, n. 3. However, proving invidious discrimination has been difficult in domestic violence cases, as the following case illustrates.

SOTO v. FLORES

103 F.3d 1056 (1st Cir.1997)

LYNCH, Circuit Judge.

[Flor Maria Soto sued defendants Carlos Flores, a police officer, and Ismael Betancourt-Lebron, Puerto Rico's superintendent of police, under 42 U.S.C. § 1983 claiming a violation of her due process and equal protection rights. She had gone to the police, for the first time in nine years of abuse, to report her husband's battering, even though he had threatened to kill her or other members of her family if she went to the police.]

* * *

Soto's effort to get police assistance came a year and a half after a new law aimed at curbing domestic violence had gone into effect. In November 1989, the Puerto Rican legislature enacted one of the nation's most comprehensive domestic violence laws, the Domestic Abuse Prevention and Intervention Act, known popularly as "Law 54." In addition to defining criminal domestic violence broadly, Law 54 makes arrest of an abuser mandatory whenever an officer has grounds to believe that Law 54 has been violated. P.R. Laws Ann. tit. 8, §§ 631–635, 638 (Supp. 1995). Police officers are required to take all steps necessary to prevent abuse from recurring, including providing the complainant with information about social services and, if she expresses concern for her safety, with transportation to a safe place. *Id.* § 640. Law 54 also requires that police officers file a written report on all domestic violence incidents, whether or not any charges are ever filed. *Id.* § 641. The police superintendent is charged with establishing "norms to guarantee confidentiality with regard to the identity of the persons involved in incidents of domestic violence." *Id.* Implementing regulations issued by the superintendent of police detail the officer's responsibilities, and instruct that arrest determinations are not to be affected by irrelevant factors, including victim reluctance. The regulations explicitly state that police attempts at mediation or reconciliation shall not substitute for arrest. The regulations require that domestic violence reports be kept confidential, in separate files, and that copies only be issued upon a court order. These regulations explicitly recognize that:

> Domestic violence . . . frequently ends in intra-family homicide and it affects all the components of the family, including the children.

Despite this legal framework, at the conclusion of his interview with Soto, [Officer] Carrasquillo took no action. Carrasquillo did not tell Soto about the availability of battered women's shelters or about procedures for obtaining an order of protection. Nor did he prepare a domestic violence report. Instead, Carrasquillo wrote up an "other Services Report," which falsely indicated that Soto had visited the police solely for advice relating to child custody. * * *

Carrasquillo discussed Soto's complaint with his supervisor, Sergeant Orta, that evening. When Sergeant Orta signed the Other Services Report he did so despite information that this was a Law 54 situation and that the men under his supervision were not doing what the law required. * * * [The Sergeant discussed the report with another officer who was a friend of Soto's husband. This officer told the husband of his wife's visit to the station, despite knowing of the husband's threats to commit murder. Several days later, when Soto went to retrieve her children from a visit with their father, the husband shot and killed both children before turning the gun on himself.]

* * *

Soto alleges an equal protection violation in her assertion that "[d]efendants have a custom, policy and practice of treating complaints from, or on behalf of, women threatened with violence in domestic disputes differently from other complaints of violence. Defendants have discriminated on the basis of the sex of the complaining victim." The district court measured Soto's equal protection claim under the standard for such claims brought by domestic violence victims that was first articulated by the Tenth Circuit in *Watson v. City of Kansas City*, 857 F.2d 690 (10th Cir.1988), and subsequently adopted by several other circuits. Under the *Watson* standard, a plaintiff seeking to defeat a motion for summary judgment must:

> proffer sufficient evidence that would allow a reasonable jury to infer that it is the policy or custom of the police to provide less protection to victims of domestic violence than to other victims of violence, that discrimination against women was a motivating factor, and that the plaintiff was injured by the policy or custom.

Ricketts v. City of Columbia, 36 F.3d 775, 779 (8th Cir.1994) (citing *Watson*, 857 F.2d at 694), *cert. denied*, 514 U.S. 1103 (1995).

The district court found that Soto had adduced sufficient evidence to create a genuine issue as to whether the police force had a custom or policy of providing less protection to victims of domestic violence than to other assault victims. We agree. The court also found that plaintiff had failed to meet her burden in opposing summary judgment on either the discriminatory intent prong or the causation prong of the *Watson* standard.

In a matter of first impression for this court, we adopt the *Watson* standard for section 1983 equal protection claims brought by domestic violence victims. Several other circuits have considered similar claims. These tragedies follow a sadly similar pattern; an abuse victim, after repeatedly seeking police protection from her abuser, is gravely injured or killed. The victim, or her next of kin, claims under section 1983 that law enforcement policies provide lesser protection to victims of domestic violence and discriminate on the basis of gender.

Under the standard we adopt today, Soto must show that there is a policy or custom of providing less protection to victims of domestic violence than to victims of other crimes, that gender discrimination is a motivating factor, and that Soto was injured by the practice. Soto has adduced evidence sufficient to create an issue as to whether there was a custom or policy of providing less protection to domestic violence victims. Closer questions are whether Soto adduces evidence sufficient to permit the drawing of the necessary inference of an intent to discriminate against women and whether Soto provides sufficient evidence that her injuries were *caused* by the alleged custom or policy.

Soto's argument may be summarized as follows: (1) that the Preamble to Law 54 explicitly recognizes that "women are usually the victims of . . . conjugal abuse" and that Law 54 expresses a legislative intent to protect women and children from domestic violence; (2) that, although 95% of domestic violence complaints involve females as victims and males as perpetrators, one out of every four persons in jail in Puerto Rico for domestic violence is female; (3) that statements of the individual in charge of the police in Puerto Rico, Betancourt-Lebron, demonstrate both that Law 54 is not enforced as are other laws and that his disagreement with the law, which may reasonably be understood to be gender motivated, has led to non-enforcement by subordinate officers; (4) that there was no police training on domestic violence prior to the events at issue; (5) that statements by Sergeant Orta, and Officers Flores and Carrasquillo acknowledge that police officers in the Rio Grande precinct in 1991 did not enforce Law 54; (6) that statements by individual officers demonstrate gender bias and stereotyping, indicating that the Law was not enforced for discriminatory reasons; (7) that the non-discriminatory reasons offered for the non-enforcement are pretextual; (8) that differential enforcement of Law 54 therefore permits an inference of an intent to discriminate; and (9) that her injuries were caused by the non-enforcement of the domestic violence law.

Defendants argue that no intent to discriminate can be inferred from mere non-enforcement of a law. It is a truism that under current Equal Protection Clause jurisprudence, a showing of disproportionate impact alone is not enough to establish a constitutional violation. *See Washington v. Davis*, 426 U.S. 229, 242 (1976). While "impact provides an important starting point" for a court seeking to determine if the adverse effect reflects invidious gender-based discrimination, "purposeful discrimination is 'the condition that offends the Constitution.'" *Personnel Administrator v. Feeney*, 442 U.S. 256, 274 (1979) (citation omitted) (upholding a veteran's preference in civil service hiring where 98% of veterans were male). "[T]he mere existence of disparate treatment—even widely disparate treatment—does not furnish adequate basis for an inference that the discrimination was [impermissibly] motivated." *Dartmouth Review v. Dartmouth College*, 889 F.2d 13, 19 (1989); *see* Siegel, *"The Rule of Love": Wife Beating as Prerogative and Privacy*, 105 Yale L.J. 2117, 2190–94 (1996) (modern doctrines of equal protection have encouraged the development of facially neutral policies that are difficult to challenge on constitutional grounds).

A domestic violence victim seeking to prove an equal protection violation must thus show that the relevant policymakers and actors were motivated, at least in part, by a discriminatory purpose. *Feeney*, 442 U.S. at 274. The Supreme Court has defined discriminatory purpose as being:

> more than intent as volition or intent as awareness of consequences.... It implies that the decisionmaker ... selected or reaffirmed a course of action at least in part "because of," not merely "in spite of" its adverse effects upon an identifiable group.

Id. at 279.

Without the smoking gun of an overtly discriminatory statement by a decisionmaker, it may be very difficult to offer sufficient proof of such a purpose. *See, e.g., Eagleston*, 41 F.3d at 878 (statistics showing that domestic violence complaints were less likely to result in arrest than were stranger assault complaints and evidence of under-enforcement of official domestic violence policy did not constitute evidence of discriminatory intent or purpose); *Ricketts*, 36 F.3d at 781 (although over 90% of victims of domestic abuse are women, and police statements offered support for discriminatory intent toward domestic disputes, plaintiff presented no evidence of intent to discriminate against women). It is true, as Soto points out, that some courts have allowed the equal protection claims of domestic violence victims to proceed on an arguably lesser showing. *See Balistreri*, 901 F.2d at 701 (remark of officer that plaintiff's husband was entitled to hit her because she was "carrying on" suggested an animus against women sufficient to allow plaintiff's complaint to survive motion to dismiss); *Thurman v. City of Torrington*, 595 F.Supp. 1521, 1528–29 (D.Conn.1984) (viewing equal protection claim of domestic violence victim in terms of "increasingly outdated misconception" of husband's prerogative to discipline his wife). However, we think that the stringent standards imposed by the majority of circuit courts are more in keeping with the Supreme Court's approach to equal protection challenges to facially neutral policies. It is in this light that we evaluate Soto's equal protection claim.

This is not the usual case in which plaintiffs seek to prove discriminatory intent from the mere fact of differential impact. Nor is this the more common case where a plaintiff in a civil rights action seeks to use the courts to upset the majoritarian preferences expressed through the legislative process. Rather, plaintiff here seeks the benefit of the protection afforded by that majoritarian legislative process and argues that she has been deprived of that protection by the actions of individual public officials motivated by a contrary, gender-discriminatory intent.

The statutory language of Law 54, and the legislative intent evident from its preamble, serve to differentiate this case from the typical disparate impact case. The Law's prefatory "Statement of Motives" states that:

> Although men as well as women may be victims of conjugal abuse, studies show that women are usually the victims of the aggressive and violent conduct that we call conjugal abuse.... The investigators figure that 60% of all married women in Puerto Rico are victims of conjugal abuse.

Statement of Motives, Domestic Abuse Prevention and Intervention Act, Act No. 54 (Aug. 15, 1989). This recognition that the problem of domestic violence impacts women most heavily is reiterated in the text of Law 54 itself:

> In developing the public policy on this matter, we must give attention to the handling of the difficulties that domestic abuse presents, *especially for women and children*.

P.R. Laws ann. tit. 8, § 601 (Supp.1995) (emphasis added). Law 54 also explicitly recognizes that discrimination has impeded institutional responses to domestic violence:

> Domestic abuse is one of the most critical manifestations of the effect of inequities in the relationships between men and women. The discriminatory ideas, attitudes, and conduct also *permeate those social institutions called upon to resolve and prevent the problem of domestic abuse and its consequences*. The efforts of these institutions to identify, understand and handle abuse have been limited, and often inadequate.

Id. (emphasis added).

In the more usual equal protection case, a plaintiff will present evidence of disparate impact upon a disfavored group in an attempt to provide an "important starting point" for proof of discriminatory intent. Here, the Statement of Motives of Law 54 contains an explicit legislative finding that domestic violence has a greater impact on women and the Law expresses an intent to ameliorate that impact. This legislative finding is evidence that under-enforcement of Law 54 would indeed have a greater impact on women and might therefore be motivated by gender discrimination.

Moreover, the express legislative desire to assist women victims of domestic violence and recognition of the problem of discrimination within responsible institutions are important factors to be considered in the "give and take" of the situation. The Supreme Court has said that the discriminatory intent inquiry should look not only at the different impact a policy has on a disfavored group, but also at the history behind the development of a policy, including looking at the problems it was intended to address. *See Arlington Heights*, 429 U.S. at 266–68.

To the extent that decisions such as *Feeney* and *Arlington Heights* are rooted in an appropriate judicial deference to democratic processes and rational legislative preferences, the rationale of deference is less compelling here. *See, e.g., Feeney*, 442 U.S. at 271 ("The calculus of effects, the manner in which a particular law reverberates in a society, is a legislative and not a judicial responsibility.... [I]t is presumed that 'even improvident decisions will eventually be rectified by the democratic process....'" (citations omitted)); *Arlington Heights*, 429 U.S. at 265 ("[I]t is because legislators and administrators are properly concerned with balancing numerous competing considerations that courts refrain from reviewing the merits of their decisions, absent a showing of arbitrariness or irrationality."). With Law 54, the legislature of Puerto Rico has expressed, through the democratic process, an intent to protect the female victims of domestic violence *and* has noted that enforcement agencies have been discriminatory and part of the problem. Thus, under-enforcement of Law 54 by those charged with administering the law may in fact be a subversion of majoritarian processes for individual, illegitimate motives. We believe, in this context, that action by officials leading to non-enforcement of Law 54 may be *some* evidence of discriminatory intent by those individuals. The policy Soto challenges is, of course, not Law 54, but the decision not to implement the Law when she sought its protections. In determining what, if anything, motivated that decision, the factfinder may consider the purposes of the Law itself, and draw appropriate inferences about what might motivate a decision not to effectuate those purposes. As the Law expressly seeks to aid women victims and eradicate institutional discriminatory attitudes, a decision not to implement the Law may well have been motivated not "in spite of," but "because of" the resulting impact on women. We review the record to see whether there is *sufficient* evidence of intent as to each of named defendants.

1. *The Rio Grande Precinct*

In reviewing whether the failure to enforce Law 54 was motivated by discriminatory intent, we look first to the actions of the officers in the Rio Grande precinct. The key actor at the precinct level was Sergeant Orta. Orta was told Soto was making a Law 54 complaint, yet he [did not file a complaint under Law 54; rather, he] signed an Other Services

Report in violation of Law 54 and took no steps to have Rodriguez arrested. Nor did he take any steps to remove Soto and her children from harm's way. He knew that Flores was going to talk to Rodriguez and did not try to stop him. He thus ratified and condoned the officers' disregard of Law 54.

Orta's statements, as described below, suggest a discriminatory attitude towards women; this attitude may have been one of the reasons behind the lack of enforcement of Law 54 at the Palmer substation of the Rio Grande precinct. Sergeant Orta made statements which a trier of fact could easily find reveal gender-discriminatory stereotypes and biases. He testified as follows:

> Q: What is your opinion of Act 54?
>
> A: I told you the first time, and I remit myself to the record, that I am in total disagreement with that Act. I believe that it is very unjust related to aggressions against women and I do not agree with that.
>
> Q: Why do you believe it is very unjust with relation to aggressions against women?
>
> A: Sometimes men, including myself of course, but sometimes one drinks on the outside or has a woman on the side or a friend on the side, and one has an argument with one's lady friend and goes home and takes it out on the wife. And I believe that is not just.
>
> . . .
>
> Q: Then I ask you, again, what is your opinion with relation to the law?
>
> A: Well, the thing is that the law, in spite of it mentioning both parties as being able to complain, the woman is always the person who is injured. Credibility is given to the woman, where there are occasions when that doesn't happen that way.

The weight to be given to Sergeant Orta's comments depends upon many factors. See *National Amusements*, 43 F.3d at 743 (ambiguous comments standing alone are insufficient to raise an inference of racial animus). The defendants here have not offered a plausible alternative interpretation for comments which in context suggest discrimination. *See Alexis v. McDonald's Restaurants, Inc.*, 67 F.3d 341, 348 (1st Cir.1995) ("[A] rational factfinder would be hard-pressed to glean a more plausible inference [than discriminatory intent], particularly since [defendant] has tendered no alternative interpretation supported by the present record."). The comments were made by a person whose actions allegedly contributed to the plaintiff's injury.

Sergeant Orta's statements are very troubling. His hostility to enforcing the domestic violence law could certainly be understood as arising from archaic stereotypes which assume that men enjoy certain prerogatives towards women, including beating them. Gender-based "classifications may not be used, as they once were, to create or perpetuate the legal, social, and economic inferiority of women." *United States v. Virginia*, ___ U.S. at ___, 116 S.Ct. at 2275 (citation omitted). Although Sergeant Orta is not a defendant here, he was a supervisor and his attitudes are evidence of whether the failure to enforce Law 54 at the precinct level was based on discrimination.

Law 54 was enforced sporadically, at best, in the precinct in 1991. Officer Flores testified that almost everyone in his police detachment "shied away from" Law 54 complaints. Asked what happened to the victims when the officers did not want to take complaints, Flores responded, "Well, they had to continue complaining." Flores testified that proper Law 54 procedures were followed only about 75% of the time, and then just by certain officers. Sergeant Orta, Flores's direct supervisor, stated that, despite Law 54, domestic violence complaints were not given great importance in 1991 and were commonly handled in the station as "Other Services" reports. There would certainly be enough facts to raise a reasonable inference that the failure to enforce Law 54 at the precinct level was based on gender discrimination.

That, however, does not answer the question as to whether Officer Flores, who is the defendant here, acted out of gender-based discriminatory intent in talking to Rodriguez. It was not within Flores's responsibilities to take Soto's complaint or to arrest Rodriguez. We find no evidence to suggest that Flores's motivation in talking to Rodriguez was based on gender discrimination. There is no evidence that Flores himself attempted to avoid enforcement of Law 54 at all, much less for discriminatory reasons. Flores, despite the lack of official training, undertook to get some training for himself. When Soto came to the Palmer substation, Flores called in the two patrol officers, whose responsibility it was to take the complaint and act on it. Flores described Soto's complaint as a Law 54 complaint to the patrol officers, as he did to Sergeant Orta. There is no evidence that Flores intervened and talked to Rodriguez because of a gender-discriminatory motive; rather, the relationship between the two men provides a strong inference that Flores believed his friendship could provide a basis to resolve the matter. Sadly, he was wrong. That he was wrong does not turn his action into one motivated by gender discrimination.

2. *Police Superintendent Betancourt-Lebron*

Plaintiff asserts that Betancourt-Lebron, the superintendent of police for the Commonwealth of Puerto Rico, should be held responsible because he failed to provide adequate training, and because that failure was due to gender-discriminatory bias. This claim is based largely on Betancourt-Lebron's public statements. For example, when Law 54 had been in effect for eight months, Betancourt-Lebron, was quoted in the press as saying:

> I don't believe that [Law 54] is solving anything because it has not lessened the fights between husbands and wives. On the contrary, there is evidence that it continues to increase.

He went on to say that domestic violence should not be treated with laws that punish the aggressors, but with psychologists and social workers. This statement of disagreement with the law's decision to criminalize such conduct is not, in itself, a statement of discriminatory intent. Plaintiff posits that the statement in context should be read as discriminatory.

Soto's expert witness, Mercedes Rodriguez, opined that, because one of the most dramatic changes achieved by Law 54 was the criminalization of domestic violence, this statement by Betancourt-Lebron was "one of the most severe blows, that a public official of [his] stature" could give to the law. Rodriguez called these statements "a deviation on the part of the institutional leadership." It was the position of the Women's Affairs Commission that Betancourt's public statements "would promote rank and file's negative attitudes toward women victims and their rights under Law 54." The Superintendent's public statements, in opposition to a law he was charged with enforcing, were widely disseminated. It is reasonable to infer, as Soto's expert and the Women's Affairs Commission suggest, that they influenced many of the rank and file in the police. But that the statements had influence does not mean that they were motivated by discrimination.

Additionally, Betancourt-Lebron acknowledged that he foresaw that police officers would have problems implementing Law 54 because its procedures differed from other laws, and because "of active resistance from some members of the Force toward the law." There is no evidence, however, that he was aware of discriminatory attitudes at the Rio Grande precinct, much less that, in the face of such knowledge, he failed to act to curb those attitudes. Nor is there any comparative evidence as to what, if any, training Betancourt-Lebron implemented when other new laws went into effect. Evidence that Law 54, which was specifically intended to assist abused women, was handled differently than other new major law enforcement initiatives could, perhaps, support an inference of discriminatory intent. But the record is devoid of such evidence.

Somewhat more probative of Betancourt-Lebron's intent is his relationship with the Women's Affairs Commission. Betancourt-Lebron declined to meet, for a year after approval of Law 54, with the Women's Affairs Commission. Law 54 directs the Commission to evaluate implementation of the law and to promote the response of law enforcement agencies to victims. *See* P.R. Laws ann. tit. 8, § 651 (Supp.1995). The initial report of the Commission, covering the first year of implementation, noted: "Coordination with the Police of Puerto Rico to train personnel as to domestic violence problems and Law 54 has been virtually impossible." In fact, Betancourt-Lebron returned none of the numerous phone calls or letters to him from the Executive Director of the Commission, who was concerned about the Police Department's apparent lack of interest in implementing the law.

In the end, this evidence, while painting an unwholesome picture, is not enough to meet the strict standards imposed by the Supreme Court for showing discriminatory intent in equal protection claims. As *Feeney* says, the intent to be shown must be more than an "awareness of consequences." *Feeney*, 442 U.S. at 279. The defendant must have "selected . . . a course of action at least in part 'because of' not merely 'in spite of' its adverse effects on an identifiable group." An expression of disagreement with Law 54 and a failure to meet with the Women's Affairs Commission, while some evidence of discriminatory intent on the part of Betancourt-Lebron, is too slender a stalk on which to rest.

Thus, we conclude that plaintiff has fallen short of her difficult burden of proving discriminatory intent against these defendants as required to establish a constitutional tort. * * *

Accordingly, the grant of summary judgment against plaintiff is *affirmed*.

Notes and Questions

1. The standard adopted by the court in *Soto* was set forth in Watson v. City of Kansas City, Kan., 857 F.2d 690 (10th Cir.1988). In *Watson*, a domestic violence victim alleged that the police department followed an unwritten policy or custom of responding differently and thus affording less protection to domestic violence victims than to nondomestic violence victims. The court reasoned that the victim "presented evidence showing that out of 608 nondomestic assault cases in Kansas City, Kansas, from January 1, 1983, to September 8, 1983, where there was a known perpetrator, there were 186 arrests for an arrest rate of 31%. Out of 369 domestic assaults, there were only 69 arrests for a rate of 16%." Furthermore, the victim also presented evidence that the officers received training that encouraged officers to use arrest as only a last resort and that they should attempt to "defuse" domestic violence situations. *Id.* at 695–96. Did *Soto* correctly apply the standard of *Watson*?

2. Could a plaintiff like Ms. Soto ever prove discriminatory intent? What facts would be sufficient to meet the test set forth by the court?

Consider this critique of equal protection doctrine:

> The *Soto* case illustrates the poverty of the sameness/difference problem in equality theory which relies on a comparison model to find discrimination. In the domestic violence context, no mirror image comparison exists; the police conduct cannot be compared to other corresponding situations. Unable to make the comparison, the court fails to find a sex discriminatory purpose.

Stephanie M. Wildman, *Ending Male Privilege: Beyond the Reasonable Woman*, 98 Mich. L. Rev. 1797, 1821 (2000).

Is any other theory of equal protection viable?

> *Soto* provides another shocking illustration of gendered views of reality. * * * [T]he court dismisses a man's friendship network as

> personal, separate, and distinct from sex discrimination or discriminatory purpose. * * *
>
> Could a privilege analysis help? If equal protection means not maintaining male privilege and ensuring women can be full societal participants, then Soto's right to equal protection was violated. These male actors are not simply private men, buddies getting together to complain about women and the domestic violence act. They are also police officers, the representatives of the state, and they act in that capacity to undermine the law and maintain male privilege. Naming the harm Ms. Soto suffered by the police refusal to take her claim seriously or to take Law 54 seriously, despite its language directed at such violent situations, confronts a system of state permission for domestic abuse. The gendered nature of the harm is apparent and systemic, not accidental.

Id. at 1816–17.

3. G. Kristian Miccio criticizes the cases that applied *DeShaney* to limit responsibility to domestic violence victims, noting the irony of this doctrinal development in a period of great activism and law reform work on domestic violence:

> I wonder why the courts chose to relieve the state of any accountability. I am mindful collective accountability now stops at the threshold of the home and developing conceptions of accountability create caveats that exempt the state from scrutiny. I am also aware that the policy shift away from collective responsibility is a consequence of material concerns or priorities. But neither these facts nor cultural realities adequately explain why we would impose limitations on collective responsibility especially when balanced against the known harm, to family, community and our collective souls.
>
> The moral paucity of *Benavidez* [which found no duty to protect a woman who told police present at her house that her ex-husband was returning to attack her] is overwhelming when contrasted with the political rhetoric of the early 1990s concerning domestic violence. Federal and state legislators adopted the lexicon of feminists within the battered women's movement who were calling for zero tolerance for domestic violence. Legislation proliferated at the state and federal levels constructing a paradigm that placed safety of battered mothers and children at center stage. Yet, it was the same politicians who appropriated domestic violence for their political platforms that either passed legislation to immunize municipalities from accountability, or when court decisions such as *DeShaney* * * * limited battered women's legal recourse, refused to legislatively correct the meager rights paradigm constructed by the court.
>
> An insuperable chasm has developed between our rhetoric and our reality. * * *

G. Kristian Miccio, *Male Violence—State Silence: These and Other Tragedies of the 20th Century*, 5 J. Gender Race & Justice 339, 348–49 (2002).

4. Why has the right to bodily integrity not been understood as central to democratic participation? Is a gendered vision responsible? Consider this comment:

> [B]ecause the right to bodily integrity is intrinsic to conceptions of liberty and to women's personhood, it is the appropriate rights paradigm within which to hold the state accountable for its failure to protect battered women from male violence within the family. Furthermore, the right to bodily integrity contextualizes those rights that flow from it—not the least of which is intimate association. Indeed, within the context of association the right to associate with one's self, free from harm, is deeply rooted in conceptions of personhood and liberty. When the state not only fails to protect against male violence but also facilitates such violence, it disrupts those conceptions so central to liberty and our view of nationhood.

G. Kristian Miccio, *Notes from the Underground: Battered Women, the State, and Conceptions of Accountability*, 23 Harv. Women's L.J. 133, 164 (2000).

*

Chapter 10

THE JUDICIARY AND ACCESS TO COURTS

In Bush v. Gore, 531 U.S. 98 (2000), the historic U.S. Supreme Court case involving the 2000 presidential election, Justice John Paul Stevens, dissenting, wrote: "Although we may never know with complete certainty the identity of the winner of this year's Presidential election, the identity of the loser is perfectly clear. It is the nation's confidence in the judge as an impartial guardian of the law." 531 U.S. at 128–29. The role of judges and courts as interpreters or makers of law has been long contested. This chapter examines the judiciary and considers its role in the struggle for social justice. Has the judiciary always been another politicized faction of government or are judges apolitical decision makers in the struggle for social justice?

Several important trends in today's political and judicial climate raise the question of access to courts. Recent congressional legislation in the areas of immigration, habeas corpus, and the provision of legal services has resulted in shrinking federal jurisdiction. Furthermore, during the last few years the expansion of the sovereign immunity doctrine in Supreme Court decisions under the Eleventh Amendment has limited the right to sue states in federal court, and other decisions have limited congressional power to ensure the guarantee of equal protection of the laws under Section 5 of the Fourteenth Amendment.

Commenting in an earlier era on the trend to decrease access to federal courts, Justice William J. Brennan said:

> It is true, of course, that there has been an increasing amount of litigation of all types filling the calendars of virtually every state and federal court. But a solution that shuts the courthouse door in the face of the litigant with a legitimate claim for relief, particularly a claim of deprivation of a constitutional right, seems to be not only the wrong tool but also a dangerous tool for solving the problem. The victims of the use of that tool are most often the litigants most in need of judicial protection of their rights—the poor, the underprivileged, the deprived minorities. The very lifeblood of courts is popular confidence that they mete out evenhanded justice and any

> discrimination that denies these groups access to the courts for resolution of their meritorious claims unnecessarily risks loss of that confidence.

William J. Brennan, Jr., *State Constitutions and the Protection of Individual Rights*, 90 Harv. L. Rev. 489, 498 (1977).

Consider the contexts in which courts strive to "mete out evenhanded justice" in this examination of judicial selection, the role of the judiciary, and access to federal courts.

SECTION 1. THE JUDICIARY: WHO ARE THE JUDGES AND HOW ARE THEY CHOSEN?

The federal judiciary is a branch of the national government that is co-equal with the executive and legislative branches. As part of government, the judiciary is a political entity, although its political nature is often denied or obscured. At the state level, judicial officers are also part of a government structure that is political.

The United States Constitution assigns to the president the responsibility of nominating federal judges. Subject to the advice and consent of the Senate, federal judges are life-tenured. For a detailed description of the modern day selection process, see Sheldon Goldman, *Picking Federal Judges: Lower Court Selection From Roosevelt Through Reagan* (1997). This selection process involves political value judgments. Describing the appointment of women and African Americans to the federal bench, Carl Tobias explains:

> Presidents Franklin Roosevelt, Harry Truman, and Dwight Eisenhower expressly instructed their aides responsible for judicial selection to find highly qualified men while displaying disinterest in, if not hostility to, the idea of seriously considering African Americans. * * * Presidents John F. Kennedy, Lyndon Johnson, Richard Nixon and Gerald Ford made essentially token appointments of female and minority judges, even as each achieved breakthroughs. * * * President Jimmy Carter was the first Chief Executive who treated naming many women and minorities as a significant policy priority. * * * [President Reagan] * * * did appoint numerous women to the bench. President George Bush correspondingly instituted special efforts to appoint female judges and succeeded in placing unprecedented numbers of women on the federal courts.

Carl Tobias, *Modern Federal Judicial Selection* (reviewing Sheldon Goldman, *Picking Federal Judges: Lower Court Selection From Roosevelt Through Reagan* (1997)), 67 U. Cin. L. Rev. 527, 530–31 (1999).

Tobias noted that "Fewer than two percent of the judges whom President Reagan chose were African-Americans, while President Bush named one Asian-American, nine Latinos, and ten African-Americans." Carl Tobias, *Leaving a Legacy on the Federal Courts*, 53 U. Miami L. Rev. 315, 328 (1999). Tobias found this paucity particularly troubling in light of the increasingly larger pools of women and minority attorneys. *Id. See also* Tracey E. George, *Court Fixing*, 43 Ariz. L. Rev. 9 (2001) (describing Clinton's judicial appointments); Becky Kruse, *Luck and Politics: Judicial Selection Methods and Their Effect on Women on the Bench*, 16 Wis. Women's L.J. 67 (2001) (detailing the value of nominating committees to the selection of women and value of appointing women and minorities to positions responsible for selecting judges).

While the political process surrounding appointment of U.S. Supreme Court judges has always been scrutinized, increasing media attention focuses on lower federal court appointments and the accompanying political battles. *See, e.g.*, Howard Mintz, *Fletchers, Hatch Make Judgeship Deal; 9th Circuit's Betty Fletcher Agrees to Senior Status, Lifting Block on Son's Confirmation*, The Recorder, May 9, 1996 (reporting political "trade-off" forced by Senator Hatch); David G. Savage, *Federal Benches Left Vacant Over Utah Tug of War*, L.A. Times, May 10, 1999 (relating Senator Hatch's demand that conservative Ted Steward be named to federal bench, and the senator's refusal to hold confirmation hearings for other judges in connection with that demand); Otto Kreisher, *Wait May Be Over For Two California Judge Nominees*, Copley News Service, Mar. 3, 2000 (recounting lengthy, politicized confirmation processes for Hon. Richard Paez and Hon. Marsha Berzon). *See also* The Alliance for Justice website which provides demographics for African-American, Latina/o, and Asian-American judges at <http://www.afj.org (visited Dec. 16, 2002).

State court judicial selection processes vary. Historically states used legislative appointment, now used only by four states. The trend toward the use of elections has been tempered by nominating commissions, also known as merit plans. *See* Kruse, *supra* at 75.

Whatever selection method is used in either state or federal jurisdiction, judges continue to garner increased attention by political processes: Stephen B. Bright observed:

> Immediately after Justice Penny White was voted off the Tennessee Supreme Court last August in a retention election which became a referendum on the death penalty, the Governor of Tennessee, Don Sundquist, said: "Should a judge look over his shoulder [when making decisions] about whether they're going to be thrown out of office? I hope so." Sundquist's statement contrasts sharply with one made by Supreme Court Justice John Paul Stevens at the American Bar Association meeting in Orlando the same month: "[I]t was 'never contemplated that the individual who has to protect our individual rights would have to consider what decision would produce the most votes.' "

Judges are increasingly coming under fire in the political system. When Judge Harold Baer suppressed cocaine and heroin seized by New York City police officers, Republican presidential candidate Robert Dole called for his impeachment and the Clinton White

House suggested it would ask for his resignation if Judge Baer did not reverse his ruling. Judge Baer reversed himself.

Stephen B. Bright, *Political Attacks on the Judiciary: Can Justice Be Done Amid Efforts to Intimidate and Remove Judges from Office for Unpopular Decisions?*, 72 N.Y.U. L. Rev. 308, 310–11 (1997).

In this section, Kathryn Abrams and Anthony Lewis contemplate the implications of judicial elections and the politicization of the judiciary, and Hon. Joseph R. Grodin offers a personal reflection on his own state court judicial appointment.

KATHRYN ABRAMS

Some Realism about Electoralism: Rethinking Judicial Campaign Finance
72 S. Cal. L. Rev. 505, 512–13, 516–17, 519–22, 533–34 (1999)

Nearly eighty-two percent of state appellate judges and almost eighty-seven percent of state trial court judges stand for election of some type. While the majority of these elections are uncontested, contested races have become considerably more frequent over the last two decades. Involvement of state judiciaries in such contentious areas as the death penalty, criminal law enforcement, and reproductive choices has meant that even the formerly still waters of retention elections have become roiled in controversy in some states. More pointedly, some prominent jurists have acknowledged recently that the process of facing election has the power to influence judicial thinking on controversial issues. The late California Supreme Court Justice Otto Kaus argued that judicial elections were the "alligator in the bathtub" of the judicial consciousness. He also acknowledged that electoral pressures may well have affected his decisionmaking in several controversial cases. His statement prompted a similar acknowledgment by Joseph Grodin, one of three California Supreme Court Justices unseated in 1986.

* * *

* * * [A]ttorneys are often important contributors to judicial campaigns. Attorneys may give funds, or donate materials or time because they genuinely admire a particular judicial candidate. However, both patterns of giving and direct statements by benefactors make clear that other motives often play a role. The starkest example is of individual lawyers or law firms making contributions during a pending case under circumstances that suggest an effort to curry favor with a judge who has been, or may be, assigned to the case. The dismal story of the Pennzoil litigation has been repeated many times, but it still retains its power to shock. During the Pennzoil-Texaco lawsuit, a lawyer from Pennzoil contributed $10,000 to the re-election campaign of the trial judge initially assigned to the case. Texaco objected and demanded a new trial, while simultaneously contributing $72,700 to seven Texas Supreme Court justices who were in a position to make the final ruling on the case, including three justices not up for re-election. Pennzoil then contributed

more than $300,000 to the campaigns of the supreme court justices and eventually became the victor in the lawsuit. More prevalent patterns are less stark, but still suggestive of opportunistic motives. Some firms or particular segments of the bar contribute to judges whose campaigns are uncontested; others contribute to both competitors in order to hedge their bets concerning the outcome; still others send a contribution as a "show of support" after a particular candidate has been elected. As one veteran attorney put it, " 'People who make substantial contributions do so with the thought of gaining a responsive ear.' " This may be true even in cases where contributors doubt a judge's qualifications. Finally, in some segments of some bars, contribution has become such a prevalent norm that lawyers pay in order to avoid "jeopardizing . . . [their] clients in [a particular] judge's courtroom" or to avoid looking cheap. * * *

* * *

* * * Judges are not detached, disinterested "others" who deduce legal answers from a logically complete and coherent system of rules. They are actors whose judgment and discretion must give shape and application to an often indeterminate body of rules. Moreover, they are human beings whose life experiences, affiliations, predilections, psychic needs, and accidents of fate push and pull against each other to influence the way they exercise this discretion. As proponents of critical legal studies have suggested, these more particularized perspectives may render some judges unable or unwilling to disrupt dominant frameworks. They may also render others more responsive to the plight of those made marginal * * *. Moreover, the potential for judicial identification—be it experiential or imaginative—with claims placed before the bench may not necessarily be a bad thing. It prevents the detachment that can make judges oblivious to their power over others, as well as their potential for wreaking change and violence on individual lives.

* * *

In contrast with the diffuse, plural, cross-cutting messages communicated by group-based affiliation or shaped by prevailing political discourses, the messages communicated by attorneys' financial support are likely to be more explicit, more readily subject to quantification and comparison, and clearer in their import for particular cases. A judge is likely to know what the trial lawyers' association that contributed to his campaign believes about particular issues or particular kinds of cases, because it is part of their purpose as an organization to articulate views on such matters. A contribution made by a firm that represents a particular client or category of clients is likely to be equally clear in its import. A contribution made while litigation is pending is even less equivocal in the message it directs.

A second distinction concerns the different sources of (or motivations for) decisions influenced by social groups or discourses, and decisions influenced by campaign contributors. One of the central premises of post-realist critical scholarship is that group-based affiliations, or dominant or dissonant social discourses, are powerful engines of social construction: They are as constitutive of those humans who ascend to the bench as they are of any others. Judges most often do not understand influences of this sort to arise from outside themselves. These influences are part of the way a self is formed, and, while critical scholars counsel judicial cognizance or awareness of these constitutive forces, these scholars find it unrealistic, and in many cases undesirable, for judges to strive for separation from such influences in decisionmaking.

Influences from within the profession can also be constitutive of oneself as a judge or private citizen. A judge who has been president of a trial lawyers' association or who has consistently represented a particular kind of client is likely to be shaped to some degree by the perspective of that organization or that kind of client. But when a trial lawyers' association, or a law firm representing a particular kind of client makes a large contribution to a judicial campaign, they are not manifesting a willingness to rest simply on that constitutive association. They are at the very least seeking to remind a judge of an association in a manner that makes as much of an appeal to the judge's immediate or impending financial needs as to his sense of being affiliated or constituted by that connection. Moreover, in the probably more frequent case where the judge has no prior constitutive affiliation with a category of contributor, a contribution reflects an effort to secure a relationship of a different kind; one that offers financial support in exchange for solicitude or receptiveness to the contributor's future legal claims. Money has been understood to make a claim of a particular kind on a judge's attention—this is one reason, for example, the Constitution provides that the compensation provided to federal judges may not be diminished during their service in office. It invokes a distinct set of fears and aspirations. A judge who acts on the basis of a contributor's preference may not be acting on a self-generated normative vision that gives determinate meaning to the ambiguities in the law; she may instead be acting from a fear of the withdrawal or transfer of support, or about the solvency of future campaigns.

This last point also relates to the argument made by some feminist scholars that it is productive for a judge to experience some identification with, or become aware of, her power over the litigants before her. The process endorsed by feminists is one of imaginative identification, which makes the judge alert to the implications of her decision on the lives of litigants and third parties. The process experienced by a judge deciding a case involving a campaign contributor is in no way an extension of imagination. The interests of this judge are in fact intertwined with those of the litigant in the sense that the litigant's defeat may affect support for the judge in future campaigns. She acts not simply with an awareness of the implications of her decision for others, but also of the implications of her decision for her own professional well-being.

* * *

* * * Judicial elections were, in their Jacksonian heyday, considered a device for ensuring the popular responsiveness of judges, who were otherwise likely to be responsive only to the politicians or bureaucracies responsible for their appointment. Not only have our own understandings about judges altered to the point where many observers would regard this electoral accountability as a cure worse than the disease, but judges must also face the twin challenges of escalating campaign costs and lawyer and litigant contributions to judicial campaigns. The result is not judicial independence of political leaders, or even broader responsiveness to the public, but judicial dependence of a particularly acute sort on the opinions and goodwill of a comparatively narrow range of campaign contributors. Realists concerned with the shifting political meanings underlying a particular rule or practice can no longer afford to let the practice of electing judges go unchallenged.

ANTHONY LEWIS

The Quiet of the Storm Center
40 S. Tex. L. Rev. 933, 933–39 (1999)

Those of us who lived through the years after the Supreme Court held public school segregation unconstitutional in 1954 saw ferocious attacks on judges who carried out the law. The assault came from ideological groups and public officials. There were billboards in the South urging "Impeach Earl Warren," and other judges had to have security protection. What we have today is less obvious but in a sense more insidious. For it is an attack on the independence of judges—their right, no, their duty, to decide cases without regard to political pressures. The attack is not limited to one kind of case, such as racial segregation, and it is occurring around the country.

* * *

In the spring of 1997 Representative Tom DeLay of Texas, the majority whip in the United States House, made a series of speeches calling for impeachment of judges who make improper decisions. What kind of decisions? Ones, he said, that evidenced "judicial despotism" or "judicial activism," ones in which "judges exercise power not delegated to them by the Constitution." Those condemnatory phrases are not self-explanatory. But Representative DeLay gave some examples. He deplored a decision by a federal judge in California temporarily enjoining enforcement of the state's initiative barring the use of race in state university admissions and other official actions. He said, critically: "Judges have created a right to die. Judges have prohibited states from declaring English an official language. Judges have extended the right of states to withhold taxpayer-funded services from illegal aliens, all without sound constitutional basis." And he said, "[t]he American people are frustrated when one person . . . subverts their will, expressed in a democratic election."

That last statement by Mr. DeLay seems to me quite revealing. It evidently means that if the voters of a state or locality approve some policy, it is insulated from review by the courts. So when the voters of Alabama elected George Wallace and endorsed his cry of "segregation forever," that should have trumped the Supreme Court's repeated decisions that racial segregation violated the constitutional guarantee of "the equal protection of the laws."

When Representative DeLay spoke as he did two years ago, many people—including me—interpreted his talk of impeachment as a threat: a way of intimidating judges out of making decisions that he and other conservatives would not like. That response did not trouble him. Judges "need to be intimidated," he said. "If they don't behave, we're going to go after them in a big way."

We should not take that threat lightly. Mr. DeLay's idea of impeaching judges because of the nature of their decisions is a radical notion. It was tried at the very beginning of the Republic, with the impeachment of Supreme Court Justice Samuel Chase by the Jeffersonians in Congress because of decisions embracing Federalist beliefs. But Justice Chase was acquitted in the Senate: a result that Chief Justice Rehnquist has said assured the independence of federal judges. To go back to impeachment as a way of punishing unpopular judicial decisions would be surprising, but we must not think it impossible. * * *

* * *

Now "activist" is a term of art—not in the legal but in the political sense. It is used mostly by conservatives to disapprove of what they regard as liberal judicial decisions. But if an "activist" judge is, as Senator Hatch said, one who bends the law to reach a desired result, then I put it to you that the most activist judges today are on the conservative side—the ones who pay the least heed to stare decisis, who are the readiest to go beyond the rules. * * * I think the word "activist" is simply political slang.

* * *

The Federal Constitution's model of judicial independence was drawn from the first constitution of Massachusetts. It was drafted by John Adams and came into effect on October 25, 1780—seven years before the Constitutional Convention in Philadelphia. And it is still, with amendments, the Constitution of Massachusetts. It provides that judges be appointed by the governor, with the consent of his council, to serve during good behavior. The purpose, it says, is that judges should be "as free, impartial and independent as the lot of humanity will admit."

Something like that is what Americans generally expect of judges. We have high expectations. More than any other people, we rely on judges to vindicate our needs and beliefs. When we feel wronged in life, we look to the law. We demand justice, above all, when we encounter official abuse or neglect. We believe that any bureaucrat, any government that mistreats us can be called to account in court.

But the principle that government officials are accountable at law for their actions is being nibbled away. In 1996, Congress passed legislation that drastically limits the right of prisoners to challenge the constitutionality of their convictions and sentences by seeking writs of habeas corpus in federal courts. Habeas corpus goes back hundreds of years in English history as the great engine of freedom: the device that enables anyone to challenge the authority that has imprisoned him. There is no law of habeas corpus in totalitarian states. In this country, the role of federal courts in habeas corpus was defined by Justice Holmes in 1923 in the case of *Moore v. Dempsey*. Five black men in Arkansas were convicted of murder in a forty-five minute trial dominated by a mob. Justice Holmes said for the Court that they must have an opportunity to show in federal court that they were swept to conviction and death sentences without a semblance of fair trial: unconstitutionally.

Federal habeas corpus has saved the lives of a considerable number of people who ended up on death row because of racial discrimination or hopelessly inadequate legal representation, or other constitutional violations. State officials complained of abuses in repetitious habeas petitions that delayed executions for years—and there were abuses. But it was not necessary to strip away virtually all the protection of the writ in order to correct abuses, and that is what Congress and President Clinton did. We know that innocent men have been on death row. In Illinois, in this decade, ten of twenty-one prisoners scheduled for execution have been freed after investigations showed them to be innocent.

* * *

Immigrants and prisoners have little if any political influence, so it is perhaps not surprising that they should be the first targeted for removal of the right to go to court. But I do not think they will be the last. The principle has been established; a terrible principle, in my judgment. It will not take much ingenuity for members of Congress to think of stripping the protection of courts away from other people and other subjects. The possibility will be in the air when a judge has to decide a claim against a politically influential official or agency. If the judge decides in favor of the individual claimant, will Congress strip the courts of jurisdiction in that whole class of cases? Like the threat of impeachment or political denunciation, it is a way of putting pressure on judges—of menacing their independence.

* * *

State judges face political pressure of a more direct kind. In most states, unlike Massachusetts, they are elected. Judicial elections have an honorable tradition going back to the populism of Andrew Jackson. But populism can conflict with the premise of our system that some things—constitutional rights—are too fundamental to be decided by elections, that the majority must not always have its way.

* * *

Americans are so keen for capital punishment that any judge subject to election takes a risk if he votes to set aside a verdict or death sentence, however appalling the circumstances. Given that reality, it is perhaps not surprising that appellate courts have approved capital convictions in which trial counsel for the defendant was grossly incompetent—drunk or asleep during the trial, for example. It seems to me that judges have simply hardened their hearts to even the most egregious injustice.

JOSEPH R. GRODIN

Pursuit of Justice: Reflections of a State Supreme Court Justice 3–10 (1989)

People, especially lawyers, frequently ask me how one gets to be a judge. That can be an easy or difficult question to answer, depending on what it is that the questioner wants to know.

The mechanics, for any one state, are easy enough to describe. There is, however, considerable variation among states, and even among different courts within the same state. Roughly, there are four models: popular election, selection by the legislature, selection by other judges, and selection by the governor.

On paper, popular election is the most common mode; the constitutions of forty-three states provide for election of at least some judges, forty of them for most or all judges. In the majority of these states, however, vacancies are filled initially by the governor, and though the appointee must appear on the ballot at election time, there will often be no opposition. Running against an incumbent is one way to become a judge, but relatively few judges acquire their robes in that manner.

Selection of judges by the legislature is rare, now confined to South Carolina, Virginia, and Rhode Island. Selection by other judges is even rarer; it is used to fill temporary judicial vacancies in Illinois and Louisiana, and in a few states to fill minor positions such as magistracies.

In most states, and for most judges, the path to judicial office is through the governor's door. More than half the states now have a system by which the governor's discretion is limited to candidates who are nominated by some form of commission; and in those states that do not have such a system the governor's appointment must be confirmed by some body—usually a commission or a branch of the state legislature—but it is still the governor who does the appointing.

The California system is mixed. A lawyer may become a trial court judge either by running for office in a popular election or by gubernatorial appointment, but to serve on the Court of Appeal or the Supreme Court appointment by the governor is the only way. The governor must submit the names of prospective appointees to the state bar for its evaluation, and the appointment must be confirmed by the Commission on Judicial Appointments, but otherwise (subject to eligibility requirements such as at least ten years in the state bar) there is no legal limitation on the governor's choice. Once appointed, a judge must stand for a "retention" vote at the next gubernatorial election * * * .

Those who ask me how one becomes a judge usually have something other than these legalities in mind. They know it is the governor who does the appointing in a state like California; they want to know how he or she does it, or, if they are lawyers hankering after the robes, how to get him or her to do it, and that is a much more difficult question.

Honesty compels me to say that appointment is not simply a matter of merit. I recognize there were many lawyers, including many fine trial court judges, whose academic and professional records were at least as good as mine, and I am sure they would have performed at least as well on the appellate court.

Nor, in my case, was it a matter of being particularly friendly with or supportive of the governor. My acquaintance with Governor Jerry Brown was in fact quite thin when he appointed me to the Court of Appeal. Our paths had crossed during Eugene McCarthy's campaign for the presidency in 1968, in which we were both active, but our contacts then were minimal. I had not been particularly active in mainstream Democratic politics. I supported his candidacy for the governorship in 1974, but not in any way that he or his advisers are likely to have noticed; I think I contributed a total of two hundred dollars to his campaign.

* * *

What, then, accounted for the lightning that eventually struck? My best guess—and I think it a good one—is that the governor and I had a mutual friend.

I first met Mathew Tobriner in 1951 when I was a senior at the University of California, Berkeley. * * * Like most idealistic young people of that period I was intrigued with the labor movement, and a family friend suggested that I speak with Tobriner, who was at that time a well-known and highly respected labor lawyer. I did so; we took an instant liking to one another, and thereby began one of the most rewarding relationships of my life. * * *

* * *

[Justice Grodin describes his friendship with Justice Tobriner, leading to Grodin's work in labor law. He characterizes Justice Tobriner as] * * * dedicated to his clients, and they to him. It was in some ways an odd alliance—this thoughtful, intellectual, gentle man and those Teamster business agents, rough and tough and worldly wise—but Mat believed fervently in their cause, and they knew it. * * *

In 1959, four years after I came to the firm, Mat was appointed by the newly elected governor, Edmund G. ("Pat") Brown—Jerry Brown's father—to the California Court of Appeal. That appointment came as no surprise. Mat and Pat Brown had been friends since boyhood, and they had worked together within the Democratic party in San Francisco ever since the early Franklin Roosevelt days when Mat convinced Pat—in the men's room of their office building, the story goes—to switch from the Republicans.

Shortly thereafter Pat Brown appointed the other half of Tobriner & Lazarus, Leland Lazarus, to the trial bench, leaving the firm without a name, and leaving me, at age twenty-nine, a de facto partner in a successful and highly regarded labor law firm, the largest west of the Mississippi. * * * I did not believe that the goddess of justice was always on my clients' side—there were occasions when I thought I saw her hovering over my opponents' shoulders—but she was there enough to keep my conscience clear. * * *

Meanwhile, Mat's judicial career had taken off. After two years on the Court of Appeal, Pat Brown had appointed Mat to the California Supreme Court, and there he quickly established a reputation as one of the outstanding state court judges in the country. To summarize his contributions briefly is difficult—in 1977 an entire issue of the *Hastings Law Journal* was devoted to his work—but there are a number of opinions for which he is particularly well known. These include cases holding that a mother who suffers emotional trauma from witnessing an accident involving her child may sue the person who negligently caused the accident for her emotional distress (*Dillon v. Legg)*; that a psychotherapist who becomes aware that his or her patient poses a risk of physical harm to another person has a duty to warn that person or the police (*Tarasoff v. Board of Regents*); and that a tenant may withhold rent from a landlord who fails to maintain the premises in a habitable condition (*Green v. Superior Court*). He was also the author of opinions establishing or expanding constitutional rights for welfare recipients and for practitioners of unconventional life-styles, and he broke new ground in protecting consumers against boilerplate contracts that purported to limit or waive their reasonable expectations in the transaction or relationship. Many of Mat's opinions appeared in law school casebooks. * * *

* * *

* * * Tobriner began an indefatigable campaign to have the governor appoint me to the Court of Appeal. I had not seriously considered a judicial appointment before then, and I was not sure at first that I wanted one; but once I began talking about the idea, my enthusiasm grew. Mat, who always had a way of making people feel good about themselves, insisted that I had the perfect qualifications for the bench and that the state would be lucky to have me. I know that he carried that message to the governor more than once—I fear more often than the governor cared to hear it. Eventually, he succeeded.

Notes and Questions

1. What is the professional responsibility of a lawyer who sees the goddess of justice hovering over the other side of a case? How does the

goddess of justice relate to social justice? Was Justice Tobriner an example of a judge who applied a social justice framework when he decided cases? *See* Derrick Bell, *"Here Come de Judge": The Role of Faith in Progressive Decision-Making,* 51 Hastings L. J. 1 (1999) (describing "courageous commitment" of Justice Tobriner).

2. Were you surprised by Justice Grodin's statement that becoming a judge was not simply a matter of merit? Does this reality comport with popular conceptions about becoming a judge? What effect does the emphasis on merit as a basis for judicial appointment have on judges' views of themselves and on the public's view of the legal system? Are there any alternatives to this emphasis on merit? What does merit mean in the context of judicial selection?

3. Justice Grodin lost his seat on the California Supreme Court in a controversial election that also unseated his colleagues, Justices Rose Bird and Cruz Reynoso. This removal of a woman and a Latino judge from a state supreme court by election generated much attention. Does the judicial election mechanism present special issues for women or minority judges? Grodin, for the sake of argument, presents the view supporting judicial elections:

> Elections * * * provide a valuable means by which the public may exercise ultimate control over the judicial branch and in the process validate the functions that that branch performs, especially the function of constitutional review. An election may be traumatic to the participants and the institution, and it may result in the removal of some judges who are doing a fine job, but * * * public confidence in the judiciary is likely to be enhanced.

Grodin, *supra* at 182.

Justice Grodin explains he is unpersuaded by this argument, preferring the lifetime appointments model used in the federal courts. He proposes as a second choice a fixed term of fourteen years. *Id.* at 183.

4. Peter D. Webster voices his concern over "an apparent trend toward politicization of retention elections, as special interest groups begin to recognize that judges standing in such elections are at a tremendous disadvantage when it comes to conducting a campaign." Peter D. Webster, *Selection and Retention of Judges: Is There One "Best" Method?*, 23 Fla. St. U. L. Rev. 1, 35 (1995). He explains the political context of the California retention election:

> In 1977, Rose Bird was appointed Chief Justice of the California Supreme Court. * * * In 1978, she stood for retention. "Several conservative 'law-and-order' groups, agribusiness organizations, and a coalition of public officials, marshalled opposition...." She managed to win retention, but only by a mere two percentage points.
>
> By 1986, when Bird was again required to stand for retention, her opponents were ready. A coalition consisting of district attorneys and other law enforcement groups, "law-and-order" proponents, anti-abortion groups, agribusiness interests and Republicans, unhap-

> py with rulings emanating from the supreme court, mounted a massive campaign to portray Bird (and Justices Reynoso and Grodin, who were also on the ballot) as ultra-liberal. They placed particular emphasis upon the votes of the three justices in death penalty cases, contending that the justices were "soft on crime." Because of ethical restraints and other factors, the justices were ill-prepared to do battle. The result was an overwhelming defeat for all three. According to Justice Grodin, he and the other two justices "raised nearly $4 million," and their opponents "raised approximately $7 million." Of course, virtually all of this money came from lawyers and special interest groups.

Id. at 36.

5. Chief Justice Shirley S. Abrahamson, of the Wisconsin Supreme Court, comments concerning judicial elections:

> In Wisconsin, all judges must stand for election in nonpartisan elections, that is, judicial candidates are not identified with a political party. I stood for election in 1979 and every ten years thereafter. Each of my three elections—1979, 1989, and 1999—was hotly contested, which might very well be a record in Wisconsin. The last campaign involved such lofty issues as the appropriateness of my sponsoring a staff aerobic class in the courtroom after hours, my decision to hang a portrait of the first woman to be admitted to the Wisconsin Supreme Court bar, and the removal of computer games from justices' computers. I was also the target of television ads challenging my votes in specific cases involving a school locker search, a * * * [probable cause] stop, and the sexual predator law. More than $1 million was raised by both candidates, and the election set a record for Wisconsin judicial campaign spending. The most fun thing about the race was winning it.
>
> * * * With my election experiences, you might think I would be unalterably opposed to the elective system of selecting judges—both in practice and theory. But I am not—that is, I am not opposed to electing judges in a state like Wisconsin.
>
> There is no perfect system for selecting judges. No system guarantees the best qualified judges, even if we could agree on qualifications. Each selection method has its strengths and weaknesses, and each presents problems and opportunities. People will evaluate the pluses and minuses differently and choose a selection system that most closely meets their comfort level. Furthermore, although the strengths and weaknesses, and problems and opportunities, of a selection method can, and should, be discussed in the abstract, the system chosen as best will depend to a large extent on the legal, historical, and political culture of the jurisdiction.
>
> * * *

> * * * [I]n any judicial selection system, the best way to ensure judicial independence is to develop the public's understanding of, and respect for, the concept of judicial independence. * * *

Shirley S. Abrahamson, *The Ballot and the Bench*, 76 N.Y.U. L. Rev. 973, 975–77 (2001).

6. Which method of judicial selection do you prefer? *See* Judith L. Maute, *Selecting Justice in State Courts: The Ballot Box or the Backroom?*, 41 So. Tex. L. Rev. 1197 (2000) (examining selection formats and considering independence and accountability). Do any judicial selection models ensure that an aspiration for social justice is part of the selection process? Do any models provide protection for a judge who views achieving social justice as part of the job?

SECTION 2. THE ROLE OF THE JUDICIARY

What attributes describe a good judge? What cultural attributes are assigned to the word "judge" when it is used as a verb? Consider, as you read this section, how judges can perform the task of judging with integrity, in light of the political context of the courts.

The role of the trial judge is often romanticized in depictions of the legal system. Yet most cases do not result in a trial. As Judith Resnik explains in the next excerpt, judges play a political role when they influence decisionmaking about the role of the judiciary. Should judges play a political role, openly? Jack M. Balkin and Sanford Levinson, in the subsequent excerpt, suggest the outrage that can result when judges decline to acknowledge that political role.

JUDITH RESNIK

Trial as Error, Jurisdiction as Injury: Transforming the Meaning of Article III

113 Harv. L. Rev. 924, 926–27, 969, 974–76, 993–95, 1003–08, 1035 (2000)

The internal rhetoric and rules *of* the federal judiciary stand in contrast to discussions in law, politics, and popular culture *about* the federal judiciary. Since the country's founding, the federal courts have been identified as an important participant in national governance. The United States Constitution sets the judiciary apart as a distinct branch of government charged with exercising judicial power under a tripartite system of separated powers. Judges and lawyers fly the globe to propose that other nations adopt constitutions that guarantee similar structural protection for judges. Since the Civil War, Congress has authorized the federal judiciary to rule on a widening range of problems. Over the course of this century, law schools have come to emphasize the centrality of the federal judiciary and to stress that one of its distinctive features, life-tenure, is exemplary of the principle of judicial independence. Legal and popular culture portray federal judges as solemn and deliberate—sometimes assuming heroic proportions.

* * *

* * * Federal judges describe their courts as the venue for "important" matters, as contrasted (implicitly and sometimes explicitly) with "ordinary," "routine," "run of the mill," "run of the mine," "garden variety" (pick your metaphor) litigation.

The turn to such contrasts between the ordinary and the important is not intrinsic in role differentiation. Difference does not necessarily entail superiority. One might have a political theory of multiple spheres of governance that relies on distinctive mandates to create and preserve specific identities. But the construction of federal judicial distinctiveness has not rested only on "neutral" differences (you do torts, we'll take contracts; you do fraud, we'll do bank robbery). Superiority is claimed.

Another wrinkle: "More important" could (simply) be equated with whatever is "federal." If Congress assigns a particular kind of case to the federal courts ("makes a federal case out of it"), then that case could be deemed more important than if sent to state courts. Federal judges might thus see their docket as a perfect fit, matching their own conceptions of import. But federal judges seek not only to *receive* federal cases, but also to *define* the meaning of "the federal"—to have only the "right" federal cases sent their way. To that end, in both their adjudicatory and administrative capacities, federal judges worked during the later part of the twentieth century to circumscribe what *should* be federal.

* * *

One variable in the developing sense of the federal courts as distinct from (and eventually as more important than) state courts is the creation in the 1930s of nationwide federal rules of civil procedure. * * * The relevance of the Federal Rules here is that they became one means by which federal courts began to differentiate themselves from state courts.

With the promulgation of the Federal Rules of Civil Procedure in 1938 and the Supreme Court's decision of the same year in *Erie Railroad Co. v. Tompkins*, the idea that federal and state courts were different because they had different procedures and controlled different arenas of law started to become embedded. *Erie's* prohibition on federal lawmaking in diversity cases constrained federal judges by placing them in the role of surrogate state judges, obliged to conform their rulings to those of the state judiciary. Add another event—collection within the federal courts of data that attempted to evaluate the time that each case took and identified "private cases" ("a considerable fraction of them brought under the jurisdiction based on diversity of citizenship") as a particular burden—and a sense of state cases as different and potentially uninteresting or burdensome for federal judges began to develop.

But the now familiar and essentializing response—that a subject matter was intrinsically "federal" as contrasted with "state"—was (in the 1940s) not yet an intuitive response for the U.S. Judicial Conference. Other cultural and political changes provided more of the context for that assumption to develop. During the 1940s and 1950s, habeas corpus and civil rights became the focus of Conference discussion and of Supreme Court adjudication. The era of *Brown v. Board of Education* and the beginning work of the Warren Court brought yet other forms of pressure to members of the federal judiciary. The idea of "state" as contrasted to "federal" functions began to be both formed and freighted as scenes of resistance by state officers to federal authority made national news. Workload demands continued to grow, and * * * , the Judicial Conference began in the 1950s to consider asking Congress not to enact certain proposed legislation.

* * *

Two aspects of the judicial posture thus come into focus. First, while conceptually distinct, in recent decades the federal judiciary's institutional and adjudicatory modes have blurred. Ideas of the judiciary as an administrative agenda-setter are not insulated from its work as a constitutional adjudicator; rather, they are intertwined. For example, with increasing insistence beginning in the 1980s, members of the judiciary began to campaign against "federalization of crime." These views obtained corporate status in 1995 in the *Long Range Plan*. In the same year, the Supreme Court imposed such a limit in one arena as a matter of constitutional law—in *United States v. Lopez*, which held that Congress lacked the power to confer federal jurisdiction over crimes of gun possession within 1000 yards of a school. Similarly, although federal judges have not (as policy makers) been able to persuade Congress to refrain from creating or to repeal certain civil causes of action, they have (as judges) found unconstitutional some of the applications of rights that Congress has articulated. Moreover, even when pending litigation about such statutes raises constitutional questions, some federal judges comment on those statutes and the desirability of retrenchment.

Second, the judiciary's posture towards its institutional role in shaping its own jurisdiction has shifted. Individual members of the federal judiciary have long complained, in opinions and essays, and through committee reports, about being required to adjudicate particular kinds of cases, such as those arising under diversity jurisdiction or under specific statutory grants, or filed by prisoners. Further, as discussed above, since the middle of the twentieth century, the Judicial Conference has objected to specific proposed jurisdictional grants and has endorsed limitations on extant provisions. What is different—and new—is the emergence of a broad objection at the institutional level. The federal judiciary now counsels Congress against creation of new federal rights in general, if these rights are to be enforced in federal courts. This theme has been powerfully articulated by the Chief Judge of the Fourth Circuit in his testimony to Congress: "Uncontrolled growth in judges and jurisdiction is the single greatest problem the federal judiciary has to confront."

For those enamored with "The Federal Courts" because they assume that inherent in the charter of life-tenured judges is a commitment to guarding rights, it may well be time to leave behind that romance. As an educational and rulemaking organization, the federal judiciary has adopted an anti-adjudication and pro-settlement agenda. As a lobbying organization, the federal judiciary has chosen to oppose creation of new federal rights, to support retrenchment of the roles of life-tenured judges, and to propose delegation of many of their tasks to other judges.

* * *

The federal judiciary's delineation of its identity by attempting to limit the kinds of cases that the federal courts "should" decide prompts criticism of a different sort, predicated on a mixture of interpretation of the constitutional powers of both the courts and the Congress and contemporary appreciation for the capacious qualities of federalism theory. As described above, federal congresses since the Civil War have pulled an array of topics—from civil rights to labor relations, from health and welfare to guns and education—into the federal net.

The federal judiciary has, in turn, ruled on the scope of congressional authority under the Commerce Clause, the Spending Clause, the Eleventh and Fourteenth Amendments, and how these provisions interact with aspects of federalism theory. Once past the struggles of the New Deal, the Supreme Court generally found that Congress had the power to make an array of issues "federal," thus enabling growth of the federal courts' docket. In the last few years, however, the Court has shifted, concluding in a few decisions that Congress has exceeded its charter either because of Commerce Clause boundaries or because of prohibitions that reside in the penumbra of the Eleventh Amendment, in the vague text of the Tenth, or in a more general but non-text-specific constitutional structure. The federal judiciary as agenda-setter has adopted a parallel set of positions, making "policy" arguments that certain problems should not become federal cases but belong to the states.

Here, the very judges who in their settlement mode have veered toward the postmodern (reluctant to fix precise meanings of law and fact and welcoming of multiple and blurred roles) return to essentialist claims when discussing the allocation of cases between state and federal courts—arguing that certain issues intrinsically constitute a "state" as compared to a "federal" case. An example comes from the contemporary controversy over the constitutionality of the Violence Against Women Act (VAWA), which some federal judges have located as relevant to family law, and have argued both in case law and in Congress to be intrinsically a matter for state, not federal, governance.

By essentializing both categories of law and the proper spheres of governance of state and federal courts, such claims reduce each to a caricature. A binary assumption, that an issue is either "state" or "federal," misses the rich complexity of governance, in which shared and overlapping work is commonplace. Self-conscious avoidance of such an approach should stem from recalling parallel and unsuccessful efforts earlier in the nineteenth and twentieth centuries, when the line-drawing battles were about federal involvement in the regulation of insurance, corporations, labor-management relations, welfare, and family life. Moreover, efforts to locate violence within familiar relationships as a part of a legal category "family law" obscure the role of the government in creating family life and licensing violence within its parameters, as well as the role of violence in marking status within a polity. Ignored in the intimate image of the family is the web of state and federal economic regulations that affect interpersonal relationships.

My goal is to shift the discussion away from constructions of the "essence" of federal power, as if it existed ex ante or were fixed, and toward a different question: is a particular problem one for which judges employed by the federal government could usefully participate in development of national norms? Rather than naturalizing a set of problems as intrinsically and always "federal," I urge an understanding of "the federal" as (almost) whatever Congress deems to be in need of national attention, be it kidnapping, alcohol consumption, bank robbery, fraud, or nondiscrimination.

This approach (which I term "non-categorical federalism") does not require that federal judges (life-tenured or not) ignore workload problems. Rather, the advice is threefold: first, Congress should have a presumption in favor of jurisdictional grants vesting concurrently in state and federal courts so as to avoid essentializing either jurisdiction and to seek assistance in norm development from different sets of judges; second, such grants should be accompanied by resources for both sets of court systems; and, third, Congress should consider de-accessing categories of cases within the federal docket in which either Congress has not sought national norm development or the work of national norm development has been sufficiently accomplished so that exchanges between state and federal courts have limited utility.

Categories plausibly to be eliminated under this formulation include some that might have significant effects on the federal docket (such as diversity litigation) and others in which the numbers of filings are smaller (such as the federal crimes of kidnapping and bank robbery). Diversity jurisdiction is a candidate because, given *Erie*, federal adjudicatory generativity is limited. Unless Congress provides mandates for federal lawmaking, such cases have (in terms of norm development) a weaker claim for a place on the docket than do other issues. Federal crimes like bank robbery could also be considered for de-accession because little norm development remains to be done; we all believe it is bad to rob banks.

In contrast, "we"—members of this polity—are in deep discord about the rights, wrongs, and import of other behaviors, such as possessing guns, using drugs, and doing physical harm to women. Therefore, until shared norms have been developed and stabilized, federal and state judicial resources can be reasonably and well spent. Under this conceptualization, when Prohibition existed, the federal judiciary was usefully a part of the enforcement mechanism because it provided a venue in which to debate anti-alcohol policies.

Non-categorical federalism shifts the focus from either the dollar value of disputes (to find "important" cases) or their frequency (to sort "garden variety" or "routine" cases from the "exotic"). Instead, the questions are about the political and symbolic meaning of issues and the work to be done to develop normative commitments. Non-categorical federalism helps move the tenor of discussion away from claims of hierarchical superiority (with remission of low-value or routine work to non-Article III adjudicators, including state judges) to a focus on the exchange of ideas needed for the process of norm development. The goal is co-venturing, in which federal judges (both constitutional and statutory) are engaged with state judges in adjudication of issues of fact, law, and in-between.

Notes and Questions

1. Does the fact that judges are chosen from the ranks of lawyers suggest another reason why education in social justice must be part of every attorney's professional education?

2. Judging is a situated activity. Justice Cardozo wrote:

> There is in each of us a stream of tendency * * * which gives coherence and direction to thought and action. Judges cannot escape that current any more than other mortals. All their lives, forces which they do not recognize and cannot name, have been tugging at them—inherited instincts, traditional beliefs, acquired convictions * * * . In this mental background every problem finds its setting. We may try to see things as objectively as we please. None the less, we can never see them with any eyes except our own.

Benjamin N. Cardozo, *The Nature of the Judicial Process* 12–13 (1921).

Consider Catharine Wells' view about the art of judging:

> [E]very legal judgment is made from a particular perspective. * * * [I]f judging is a situated activity, then judges should attend to their situation in a conscientious way. While "we can never see with any eyes except our own," we can broaden our situation in such a way that our "stream(s) of tendency" are more receptive to the different perspectives that exist in the world we are seeking to judge.

Catharine Pierce Wells, *Improving One's Situation: Some Pragmatic Reflections on the Art of Judging*, 49 Wash. & Lee L. Rev. 323, 323 (1992).

Might legal education play a role in helping judges attend to their situations in those formative years when they are law students?

3. Does race play a role in judging? What arguments support the need for a diverse judiciary? Sherrilyn Ifill writes that arguments for increased racial diversity on the bench have been hindered by a focus on

the function of jurists of color as role models. She urges attention to the role minority judges might play in enriching judicial decisionmaking as representatives of outsider perspectives:

> Put simply, judges can be impartial representatives. This means that in approaching, analyzing, and deciding legal and factual issues, judges can at once decide cases without prejudgment and yet represent values and perspectives. The representative function does not run afoul of the need for impartiality because the representation function expresses itself in the *process* of decision-making, rather than in a judge's ultimate decision about criminal guilt or innocence, sentencing, or the civil liability of a litigant.
>
> A judge can represent by expressly including alternative perspectives in the deliberative process. Justice Thurgood Marshall is the prime example of this kind of judicial representation. He often represented the perspectives of African Americans, women, prisoners, and other marginalized groups by bringing the stories of these groups to Supreme Court deliberations. In so doing, Marshall enriched the Court's process of judicial decision-making by insisting that the Justices consider "outsider" narratives and perspectives in their deliberations. Judges can represent impartially by affirmatively including and engaging the perspective of constituent communities in judicial decision-making.
>
> An important step in accepting this exercise of judicial representation lies in acknowledging that white judges also function as representatives. They articulate, engage and affirm narratives with which they are familiar and with which they share with their constituent communities. Certainly some data suggests that this is true in discrimination cases. This does not mean that white judges are "biased" or "partial;" instead, they are "situated." They are steeped in and bound by narratives which appear not to be narratives at all because they are cloaked in the transparency of whiteness.
>
> * * * [W]e must be prepared to acknowledge that race makes a difference in how judges develop a "sense of justice," and we must look for opportunities for judges with disparate "senses" to interact with one another in judicial decision-making.

Sherrilyn A. Ifill, *Racial Diversity on the Bench: Beyond Role Models and Public Confidence*, 57 Wash. & Lee L. Rev. 405, 468–69 (2000).

Is Ifill correct that one can serve as both an impartial judge and a judicial "representative?" For additional discussion of the notion of "white transparency," see Barbara Flagg, *Was Blind But Now I See* (1998). *See also* Stephanie M. Wildman (with contributions by Adrienne D. Davis, Margalynne Armstrong & Trina Grillo), *Privilege Revealed: How Invisible Preference Undermines America* (1996), for a discussion of existing systems of privilege, such as whiteness, generally unacknowledged by society.

4. For another view of the complexity race adds to the judicial role see Tom Tso, *Indian Nations and the Human Right to an Independent Judiciary*, 3 N.Y. City L. Rev. 105, 113 (1998).

> I know from personal experience that the job of an Indian-nation judge is very frustrating and discouraging. Aside from the normal difficulties of acting as a judge, such as complex legal issues or high caseloads, we are confronted with situations in which non-Indian offenders get away with their crimes and corporate defendants evade their responsibilities to Indian nations. While there is legislation before Congress that would permit non-Indians to sue Indian nations in a state court, this legislation is deeply flawed because it is not reciprocal: Indians are not usually permitted to sue non-Indians in the appropriate Indian court.

5. Addressing the role of judges, particularly at the Supreme Court level, in a pluralistic, democratic society, Sylvia R. Lazos Vargas comments:

> The Supreme Court plays a critical role in resolving clashes between majority and minority interests and perspectives. * * * The Court's ability to resolve such majority-minority disputes in a manner that furthers democratic values is key to our polity's ability to be inclusive and equitable as it becomes increasingly diverse.
>
> * * * The Court's privileging of majority views over those of the minority (or the "other") is critical, not so much because it causes the Court to reach the "wrong" result in key battleground civil rights cases, nor even because the Court has adopted the "wrong" view of the world, but instead because the Court has failed to recognize the multitude of views and perspectives that exist in our society. * * * [The author] faults the Court not so much for its selection of the majority perspective, but for its failure even to recognize that it has made a choice and for its failure to attempt to reason with the alternative point of view.

Sylvia R. Lazos Vargas, *Democracy and Inclusion: Reconceptualizing the Role of the Judge in a Pluralist Polity*, 58 Md. L. Rev. 150, 152–54 (1999).

Lazos, writing before *Bush v. Gore*, was prescient in noting that the masking by the court of its choosing a perspective for decisionmaking undermines the credibility of the office. In this next article Jack M. Balkin and Sanford Levinson pose the question of political judging and reveal the outrage that masking generates as they examine contemporary constitutional revolution.

JACK M. BALKIN & SANFORD LEVINSON

Understanding the Constitutional Revolution
87 Va. L. Rev. 1045, 1045–53, 1066–67, 1083–88,
1094–97, 1099–1103, 1107–09 (2001)

We live in extraordinary times. In the past year the Supreme Court of the United States has decided an election and installed a president. In the past ten years it has produced fundamental changes in American constitutional law. These two phenomena are related. Understanding the constitutional revolution that we are living through means understanding their connections.

The new occupant of the White House—we will call him "President" after he has successfully prevailed in an election conducted according to acceptable constitutional norms—has taken the oath of office and has begun to govern. But his claim to the presidency is deeply illegitimate. He and the political party that he leads seized power through the confluence of two important events that would have caused widespread outrage and produced vigorous objections from neutral observers if they had occurred in a third world country.

The first is the disenfranchisement of black voters in Florida in violation of the Voting Rights Act of 1965. Concerned about alleged voter fraud in the 1997 Miami mayoral election, Florida state officials hired Database Technologies, a private firm with Republican connections, to purge the voter rolls of suspected felons. "Suspected," it turned out, is the key word, because a substantial number of the purged voters turned out to be guilty of nothing more than the crime of being African-American. Although Database Technologies repeatedly warned that their methods would produce many false positives, Florida officials insisted on eliminating large numbers of suspected felons from the rolls and leaving it to county supervisors and individual voters to correct any inaccuracies. Clay Roberts, director of the state's division of elections, explained that "(t)he decision was made to do the match in such a way as not to be terribly strict on the name." Indeed, the list was so inclusive that one county election supervisor found that she was on it.

It is estimated that at least fifteen percent of the purge list statewide was inaccurate, and well over half of these voters were black. When these unsuspecting voters arrived at their precincts on November 7 in order to exercise their "fundamental political right" to the franchise, they were turned away. Any protests were effectively silenced by the bureaucratic machinery of Florida law. As the U.S. Civil Rights Commission put it, "(p)erhaps the most dramatic undercount in Florida's election was the nonexistent ballots of countless unknown eligible voters, who were turned away, or wrongfully purged from the voter registration rolls by various procedures and practices and were prevented from exercising the franchise." Those voters, wrongfully excluded from the rolls, were almost certainly more than enough to overcome George W.

Bush's 537 vote margin in Florida. In addition, many African-Americans who did vote nevertheless had their ballots spoiled and thus left uncounted because they lived in counties with antiquated and unreliable voting equipment. The Civil Rights Commission estimated that black voters were nine times more likely to have their votes rejected than white voters.

* * *

Yet even the purging of black voters was not enough to swing the election to George W. Bush. The second act of dubious legality occurred on December 9, 2000, when five members of the United States Supreme Court issued a stay halting recounts in Florida, recounts which almost all observers at the time believed would put Al Gore ahead. On December 12, the same five members of the Court halted the recounts for good in *Bush v. Gore*. The opinion was hastily written and poorly reasoned. Its conclusion—that all recounts should stop—did not easily follow from its premise—that the recounts should be conducted according to principles of equal protection of the laws. Nevertheless, the opinion had the desired effect. The recounts stopped. Gore conceded. Bush took the oath of office.

* * * Five members of the United States Supreme Court, confident of their power, and brazen in their authority, engaged in flagrant judicial misconduct that undermined the foundations of constitutional government. * * * The election is like the stinking carcass of a pig dumped unceremoniously into a parlor. The smell of rot is everywhere. How can you avoid talking about it? * * *

The Supreme Court's decision in *Bush v. Gore* did not occur in a vacuum. It occurred against the background of a veritable revolution in constitutional doctrine that has been going on for some fifteen years. We are in the middle of a paradigm shift that has changed the way that people write, think, and teach about American constitutional law. Those changes are still ongoing; their full contours have yet to be determined. Black disenfranchisement and *Bush v. Gore* seem revolutionary, if only because they occurred over a relatively short period of time. But there is a larger revolution going on of which they are only a part—one that has occurred slowly over the course of a decade. * * *

* * *

In the past ten years, the Supreme Court of the United States has begun a systematic reappraisal of doctrines concerning federalism, racial equality, and civil rights that, if fully successful, will redraw the constitutional map as we have known it. * * * And, not surprisingly, this same bloc of five conservatives handed the presidency to George W. Bush in *Bush v. Gore*. By doing so, they helped ensure a greater probability for more conservative appointments and more changes in constitutional doctrine. * * *

* * *

[The authors describe the long term transformation in constitutional doctrine begun by this court.] * * * That transformation involves a fairly consistent application of a core set of ideological premises: limitations on federal power, promotion of states' rights, narrow construction of federal civil rights laws, a theory of neutrality in religion cases, and colorblindness as a theory of racial equality.

* * *

* * * To understand judicial review one must begin by understanding the role of political parties in the American constitutional system. Political parties are among the most important institutions for translating and interpreting popular will and negotiating among various interest groups and factions. Political parties are both influenced by and provide a filter for the views of social movements. Both populism and the Civil Rights Movement influenced the Democratic Party, for example, which, in turn, accepted some but not all of their ideas. The same is true of the popular insurgency that accounted for much of Senator Barry Goldwater's support in 1964, which became the base for the ultimate takeover of the Republican Party by conservatives rallying around Ronald Reagan.

* * *

* * * [I]n *Bush v. Gore*, we have the totally unprecedented spectacle of five members of the Court using their powers of judicial review to entrench their party in the Presidency, and thus, in effect, in the judiciary as well, because of the President's appointments power. It is perfectly normal for Presidents to entrench members of their party in the judiciary as a means of shaping constitutional interpretation. That is the way most constitutional change occurs. It is quite another matter for members of the federal judiciary to select a president who will entrench like-minded colleagues in the judiciary. In our system of divided powers, the appointments process gives the political branches a check on the actions of the judiciary. The judiciary is not permitted to pick its own members, either directly or indirectly.

Thus, *Bush v. Gore* offers a bizarre variation on the problem of self-perpetuating majorities discussed in *United States v. Carolene Products* and its famous footnote four. In *Carolene Products*, Justice Harlan Fiske Stone cautioned that courts should be particularly suspicious of attempts by political insiders to pass laws that hobble their political opponents and prevent them from serving as effective participants in the political process. The theory of footnote four is predicated on an elemental fear of political parties or other factions using legislative power to further entrench themselves in legislatures. In *Bush v. Gore*, however, the danger of entrenchment comes not from the legislature but from the Supreme Court itself. The five Justice majority used the power of judicial review to short circuit the processes of democratic representation, install a president of their choice, and help keep their constitutional revolution going.

We hasten to add that this is normally not how judicial review works, even when ideologically driven. Sometimes the work of a majority of Justices does help their party's fortunes. By lowering barriers to the exercise of the franchise—particularly by blacks and the poor—the Warren Court's decision in *Harper v. Virginia Board of Elections* [see chapter 9] probably worked to the benefit of Democrats. But the danger of judicial self-entrenchment is considerably more indirect and attenuated than we see in *Bush v. Gore*, where the five conservatives stopped an ongoing election contest and all but handed George W. Bush the keys to the White House front door. Unlike the scenario in *Bush v. Gore*, the Warren Court's liberal majority in *Harper* was not intervening in an ongoing presidential election and effectively determining its outcome. Second, its decision in *Harper* seems entirely consistent with its larger ideological agenda of promoting racial equality and open access to the political process. By contrast, in *Bush v. Gore* we do not see a bold attempt to further the conservative revolution's ideological principles. Rather we see the narrowest possible holding moving in the opposite direction from which the conservatives usually innovate, a holding that is designed primarily to stop the election.

* * *

Understanding how constitutional revolutions occur allows us to understand the proper response to them. The most common and obvious way that people object to constitutional revolutions is to make arguments about the judicial role: They argue that past precedents are not being respected or that lawyerly professional norms are not being obeyed. They argue for judicial caution and judicial restraint. * * *

But in an important sense these procedural or process-based objections are beside the point. As Mao Tse-tung succinctly put it, a revolution is not a dinner party. One would hardly expect that in times of great constitutional change courts would observe all the niceties that cautious jurists would espouse. That is not the point of a revolution. And in hindsight, the quality of a constitutional revolution will not be judged by how well older precedents were respected or how minimally or moderately courts acted during revolutionary times. It will be judged by the political justice of the substantive principles that the courts expound in their new doctrines. No one thinks that the Warren Court was good because of its cautious respect for precedents or that the *Lochner* Court was bad because it failed to avoid constitutional questions through artful statutory interpretation. Chief Justice Roger Taney's poor reputation is not based on his embrace or rejection of minimalism, but on his support for slavery. Justice William Brennan's towering reputation rests not on his treatment of precedents or his embrace of judicial restraint but on the fact that he was on the politically progressive side of most controversies concerning civil liberties and civil equality. Stated more correctly, he was on the right side as judged by subsequent history (at least so far), whereas Taney was not. Judicial revolutions, like political revolutions, are judged in terms of their results and what they say about the meaning of America. We know the quality of a constitutional revolution by the politics that it keeps.

If this is so, it suggests that the proper way to criticize a constitutional revolution, whether one still in the making or in the full flower of its audacity, is in terms of the constitutional principles that it espouses and the vision of the country that it summons. * * * [O]ne should consider and criticize it from the standpoint of * * * the larger political principles that one believes animate and should animate the Constitution.

Those political principles are hardly foreign to law. Indeed, they are what constitutional law is made of. Debating the political principles that one believes underlie America's higher law means that one must debate the meaning of the country and what it stands for. To participate in this sort of debate involves summoning a conception of "We the People" and a conception of the principles that our country and our Constitution should be devoted to. This criticism is "political," but it is a criticism from *constitutional politics*. And a debate about constitutional politics, we think, is the only kind of debate worth having in moments of profound constitutional change.

* * *

In the constitutional imagination of the five conservatives, the federal government is large, intrusive, and distant, constantly forgetting the fact that it is a government of limited and enumerated powers. The people are well represented in state legislatures, which are closer to their interests, but they are not well represented in Congress. The Congress is unruly and unthoughtful, always trying to aggrandize itself and interfere with more and more aspects of daily life. Its work must be carefully scrutinized and narrowly construed to avoid usurping the role of the courts on the one hand, and the states on the other. The states, by contrast, are the primary guarantors of liberty in the United States. Decentralization of decisionmaking authority increases human freedom. Indeed, courts must protect the "dignity" of states as distinct sovereigns from suits for damages based on federal causes of action. Only by immunizing states when they violate federal rights can states serve their function as protectors of individual liberty.

Ordinary politics is messy and unprincipled, often little more than the play of special interests. Contemporary politics features selfish grabs for power and influence, not public-spirited aspiration toward larger ideals. Politicians, especially at the federal level, cannot restrain themselves from misbehaving and sacrificing public interest to private concerns. They cannot be trusted to save the public from a genuine national crisis.

Congress has undoubted power to regulate the national economy. But it is not generally free to regulate noneconomic questions or inherently local subjects. Congress has no general power to pass civil rights laws affecting private actors. Civil rights is a national subject of regulation only to the extent that it affects economic interests like employment or involves instrumentalities of interstate commerce or things or people that have moved across state lines. So-called civil rights statutes that concern noneconomic harms or invade "traditional" areas of state regulation are beyond the power of the federal government.

All too often civil rights laws reflect congressional grandstanding and the influence of special interests rather than the public interest. Courts must restrain Congress from creating ever new forms of interference with state autonomy under the guise of protecting civil rights. "New" forms of asserted discrimination—like those against the disabled or the aged—are less important than older forms based on race or gender, which the Court has long recognized merit heightened scrutiny. Therefore states may rationally discriminate on the basis of these "new" categories.

These days whites are just as likely to be victims of official discrimination as members of racial or ethnic minorities. Indeed, so-called affirmative action laws are really examples of special interest legislation trying to pass themselves off as civil rights laws. They are a sort of racial and ethnic spoils system and must be viewed with the highest level of scrutiny. Any attempt to give racial minorities special treatment will only harm them because it will generate racial hostility by whites and reinforce stereotypes of inferiority. It will generate racial polarization and reinforce the notion that we are not a unified nation and that race matters in everything that people do. This can only heighten racial tensions and cause unhappiness for everyone.

Last but not least, in the new conservative constitutional vision, courts are the final authority on the meaning of the Constitution. The Congress has no authority to interpret the Constitution differently from the Courts. It may only remedy demonstrated violations of constitutional rights by states, and the Court will carefully scrutinize Congress's work to determine whether it is really enforcing rights in the same way that the Court interprets them. Congress is not the Supreme Court's partner in interpreting the Constitution. It is its subordinate. Pushed and pulled as it is by special interests, Congress cannot be trusted to respect the separation of powers or the inherent sovereignty and dignity of the states.

* * *

There is a better way to interpret the Constitution, one that is more consistent with the meaning of our history as a people. As a result of the Civil War and the Civil Rights Movement, the movement for women's suffrage and the women's movement of the 1960s and 1970s, it should be abundantly clear that the creation and protection of civil rights is a national commitment. It is as central to Congress's work as the regulation of the national economy. In our view Congress has the power to pass laws that protect the equal citizenship of Americans. The opening sentence of the Fourteenth Amendment says that "[a]ll persons born or naturalized in the United States, and subject to the jurisdiction thereof, are citizens of the United States and of the State wherein they reside." The Citizenship Clause was designed to overrule the *Dred Scott* decision, which held that blacks could not be citizens and "had no rights which the white man was bound to respect." It establishes a principle of equal citizenship: The United States cannot create first- and second-class citizens. Equally importantly, it contains no state action requirement.

When Congress passes regulations of private conduct under its power to enforce the Citizenship Clause, courts should uphold them—not as economic regulations but as civil rights laws. When Congress specifically extends those laws to state governments, states should not be allowed to violate them. The proper question for courts should be whether Congress has reasonably concluded that legislation promotes equal citizenship or prevents or forestalls the maintenance of second-class citizenship. Unless the Court can plausibly believe that Congress was unreasonable, the legislation should be upheld. This is, of course, the basic test of national legislation established by Chief Justice John Marshall in *McCulloch v. Maryland*.

The idea of equal citizenship and equal rights has evolved over the years, shaped by the many social movements that followed the Civil War. Today few people think that blacks would truly be equal before the law if they were not protected from private discrimination. After all, the Civil Rights Movement of the 1960s was not just about constitutional violations by states; it was about private discriminations at lunch counters. Just as the reach of Congress's commerce power has grown in response to our developing economy, the reach of its civil rights power grows as our nation gradually comes to terms with old outmoded prejudices and inequalities. Understanding what it means to be a free and equal citizen in a democracy is an ongoing project.

This approach has three distinct advantages. First, it obviates the need to tie civil rights legislation to a story about cumulative effects on interstate commerce. Second, it locates civil rights law under the Fourteenth Amendment, which was intended to be and should be its natural home. Third, when Congress acts to protect the ideal of equal citizenship, it is not necessarily enforcing judicially recognized constitutional rights, any more than when it clears the channels of interstate commerce through economic regulations under its commerce power. Rather, it is doing what it reasonably believes is necessary and appropriate to protect equal citizenship. Thus, legislation under the Citizenship Clause does not require that Congress remedy prior violations of rights by states. Like Congress's authority under the Commerce Clause, its authority to enforce the Citizenship Clause is positive, not remedial. * * *

Taken together, Congress's civil rights power and its commerce power give the national government the effective equivalent of a general police power. Probably very few things will fall outside the scope of these two powers. But by the beginning of the twenty-first century, it is not clear why this should matter. We are, after all, one nation, declared to be "indivisible, with liberty and justice for all."

The choice between the theory we offer here and the theories that the Court offers * * * can be played out through the traditional modalities of text, intentions, structure, consequences, and precedent. There is obviously much more that both sides could say. But at the end of the day the choice between them is really a choice between two visions of constitutional politics, two narratives about the American experiment. It is a choice about who we are and what it means to be an American.

* * *

Bush v. Gore * * * undermines the very mechanisms that keep judicial interpretations of the Constitution roughly in sync with the broad understandings of the American public. By seizing control of the election, the five conservatives severed the connections between their constitutional revolution and popular will. They insulated themselves from the normal checks and balances between the political branches and the judiciary. Their self-entrenching behavior created a real danger that their constitutional revolution would be propelled forward into the future without sustained and continuing popular support.

* * *

* * * [T]he remedy for *Bush v. Gore* lies in electoral politics. The only way to oppose *Bush v. Gore* is to oppose the constitutional revolution it furthers. The great irony of Justice Thomas's sanctimonious insistence that the decision in *Bush v. Gore* had nothing to do with politics is that politics is the only means by which the American people can discipline the misbehavior of its highest court. The battle over the fate of *Bush v. Gore* and indeed, over the fate of the constitutional revolution itself, will not be decided in the courts. It will be decided through the next several election cycles and through the fight over judicial appointments during the administration of George W. Bush. Politics, and not legal reasoning, will determine what becomes of the constitutional revolution.

* * *

Shortly after *Bush v. Gore*, the *New Yorker* ran a cartoon featuring a scruffy, thuggish-looking man sitting at a bar with a huge bag of money beside him. He is having a drink and speaking cheerfully to another customer. The caption reads: "Oh, sure, it's stolen, but now we have to get on with our lives." The point of the joke, of course, is that if somebody does something very bad, we normally do not think that we should simply accept it and just move on. The wrong should be corrected and the wrongdoer punished. Yet the message from many quarters these days is that we should forget about it: The Supreme Court has spoken, Bush won the election, he is in the White House, and one should get over it. Let's move on. We do not doubt the emotional conflict that many Americans now face. It is hard to admit that one lives in a country that has just suffered through a judicial coup. And many people will do almost anything to avoid recognizing that very unsettling fact. But the problem is that if the Supreme Court acted wrongfully, then to move on is to sanction something illegal and unjust. It is to turn what is illegitimate into something legitimate. And that may constitute its own form of injustice.

There is a moral obligation, if there is not a legal obligation, to name what is unjust as unjust, to say that people have done wrong even if there is nothing that one can do about it at present. Of course, to say such things may lead one to be thought unpleasant or a crank. But to refuse to name the unjust, and to move on for fear of being thought unreasonable may condemn one to a form of cravenness that is even worse.

The Rule of Law and constitutional government are worthy values, but we should not confuse either the Supreme Court or the flesh and blood members of that body with those values. Law schools in particular are well known for fawning over Supreme Court Justices and devoting their considerable resources to shoring up the Court's credibility. But when those Justices betray principles of constitutional government, their proper and just reward should not be even more fawning and flattery, even more bowing and scraping. We do not live in a monarchy. We overthrew that form of government long ago. Perhaps the King can do no wrong. But the Justices of the Supreme Court certainly can. In a democracy, they must be called to account when they do.

We well realize that the desire to reduce cognitive dissonance is strong. It is easy to understand why most lawyers and legal academics, like most people in the country more generally, do not want to accept the possibility that five Justices fundamentally betrayed their oaths of office and helped to place in the White House someone who does not deserve the title of President. But if one says nothing, and accepts the Court's actions and the Presidency as fully normal in all respects, then the injustices will be forgotten or, perhaps worse, accepted as simply the way "we" do things in America. One will end up bowing to authority not because it is honest or just, but simply because it is stronger. Submitting to power in this way is the most abject betrayal of the American constitutional tradition.

Notes and Questions

1. Are political parties important to social movements, as Balkin and Levinson claim? What role should the judiciary play in relation to social movements? Jerome Frank suggested that judges should not wear the robes that serve as a symbol of judicial neutrality. Jerome Frank, *Courts on Trial* 254–61 (1973) (originally published 1949). Has *Bush v. Gore* effectively removed the robes from judges in the collective social consciousness or has the nation continued business as usual as the *New Yorker* cartoon, described above, suggests?

2. Would *Bush v. Gore* have been a better decision if the Court had made explicit its selection of the vision of the Constitution that Balkin and Levinson ascribe to them? Is belief in judicial impartiality crucial to democratic government?

3. For another vision of the Constitution, see John Denvir, *Democracy's Constitution: Claiming the Privileges of American Citizenship*

(2001) (arguing for an inclusive interpretation of the privileges and immunities clause).

Bradley Joondeph comments on the place of *Bush v. Gore* in the Rehnquist Court's constitutional vision: "*Bush v. Gore* embraced a novel and rather expansive understanding of equal protection that seems largely out of character for the Rehnquist Court. But the decision to intervene and resolve the election dispute was not inconsistent with this Court's general approach to constitutional federalism." Bradley W. Joondeph, Bush v. Gore*, Federalism, and the Distrust of Politics,* 62 Ohio St. L.J. 1781, 1827 (2001). He notes further:

> [T]he Rehnquist Court did precisely what it has done throughout its major federalism decisions * * * . Namely, the Court determined that these important questions of constitutional meaning must be resolved by the judiciary, not the political process. To paraphrase the Chief Justice, the lawfulness of the manual count ordered by the Florida Supreme Court was "ultimately a judicial rather than a legislative question, and [could] be settled finally only by this Court." Once again—and in the most dramatic fashion possible—the Court found itself responsible for providing the definitive constitutional answers.

Id. at 1826–27.

4. Justice Clarence Thomas, speaking shortly after *Bush v. Gore*, said "the work of the Court was not in any way influenced by politics or partisan considerations." Jack M. Balkin, Bush v. Gore *and the Boundary Between Law and Politics*, 110 Yale L.J. 1407, 1407 (2001). Balkin commented: "Afterwards the question on many legal scholars' minds was not whether Justice Thomas had in fact made these statements. The question was whether he also told the students that he believed in Santa Claus, the Easter Bunny, and the Tooth Fairy." *Id.* Is judicial impartiality a myth?

Five African-American law professors at the University of North Carolina were condemned in their local press for publicly criticizing Supreme Court Justice Clarence Thomas. *Editorial: Five Petulant Profs*, The Herald-Sun, Mar. 6, 2002, at A16. The professors had written in part:

> Justice Thomas is not just another Supreme Court justice with whom we disagree. Rather, as a justice, he not only engages in acts that harm other African Americans *like* himself, but also gives aid, comfort, and racial legitimacy to acts and doctrines of others that harm African Americans *unlike* himself—that is, those who have not yet reaped the benefits of civil rights laws, including affirmative action, and who have not yet received the benefits of the white-conservative sponsorships that now empower him.
>
> The Supreme Court opinions of Justice Thomas are inevitably linked to those of Chief Justice Rehnquist and Associate Justices Scalia, O'Connor, and Kennedy. Thus, since Justice Thomas's ap-

pointment to the Court, replacing Justice Thurgood Marshall, he has provided the critical fifth vote in a number of decisions that have set back the quest for racial equality and social justice in this country. While these five justices attempt to mask their entrenched partisanship, we know better than to see their expressions as mere judicial philosophy. They articulate a conservative politics that drives a conservative jurisprudence to obstruct the quest for long-delayed racial equality and the increasingly urgent need for broad-based social justice.

> * * * [W]e want to be clear that we reject not only the jurisprudence of Clarence Thomas, but also the politics of Clarence Thomas—just as over 90 percent of African-American voters rejected the politics of George W. Bush in the last presidential election. We oppose the de facto, if not intentional, linkage of conservative political themes and racial injustice. * * *

> * * *

> * * * While the political right does not need Justice Thomas to push its agenda against social justice and equality, it does need him to put a black face on that agenda. Justice Thomas operates as powerfully on a symbolic register as on a jurisprudential one. For all its talk of color-blindness, the political right realizes that Justice Thomas will not be an effective icon of racial conservatism until African Americans ourselves accept and embrace him. * * *

Charles E. Daye, Marilyn V. Yarbrough, John O. Calmore, Adrienne D. Davis & Kevin V. Haynes, *Statement by the African-American Faculty of the UNC School of Law Regarding the Visit of Justice Clarence Thomas* (February 28, 2002) (www.unc.edu/student/orgs/blsa/documents/Thomas_Final.pdf). *See also* A. Leon Higginbotham, Jr., *An Open Letter to Justice Clarence Thomas from a Federal Judicial Colleague*, 140 U. Pa. L. Rev. 1005 (1992) (urging Justice Thomas not to dilute gains made in the struggle for racial equality).

5. In the wake of *Bush v. Gore* some called for senators to refuse judicial appointments proposed by President Bush. *See, e.g.*, George M. Kraw, *Behind Closed Doors the "Nonpartisan" Plan for Picking California's Federal Judges Is Nonsensical*, Recorder, May 9, 2001, at 4 (reporting Bruce Ackerman's call for Democrats to refuse Supreme Court nominees until the next presidential election). Is it realistic to think that senators will refuse judicial appointments made by Bush?

For more critical commentary on *Bush v. Gore* see Pamela S. Karlan, *The Newest Equal Protection: Regressive Doctrine on a Changeable Court*, in *The Vote: Bush, Gore, and the Supreme Court* 77 (Cass R. Sunstein & Richard A. Epstein eds., 2001); Michael J. Klarman, Bush v. Gore *Through the Lens of Constitutional History*, 89 Cal. L. Rev. 1721 (2001); Frank I. Michelman, *Suspicion, or the New Prince*, 68 U. Chi. L. Rev. 679 (2001); David A. Strauss, Bush v. Gore: *What Were They Thinking?*, 68 U. Chi. L. Rev. 737 (2001); Cass R. Sunstein, *Order Without Law*, 68 U. Chi. L. Rev. 757 (2001).

SECTION 3. ACCESS TO FEDERAL COURTS

The Rehnquist Supreme Court, often labeled as conservative, has engaged in an unprecedented spate of activism related to limiting access to federal courts. These decisions by the Supreme Court have been coupled with congressional legislation to limit access. Consider, in contrast, the early role of federal courts in affirming the Civil Rights Movement. It is hard to ignore the racialized conduct of the modern court and legislative actions which are directed at redefining the balance of power in the federal system.

Congress has attacked access to federal courts in a series of statutes, taking federal court jurisdiction away in legislation involving immigrants, prisoners, the death penalty, and legal services. As Adrien Katherine Wing explains:

> In the 1980s, conservative members of Congress such as Senator Jesse Helms attempted to strip the federal courts of authority over issues like abortion, school prayer, school desegregation, and the armed services, but failed. The recent efforts to limit judicial independence have included proposals for constitutional amendments that would end life tenure, hearings on judicial activism, delay of Senate confirmations, defining good behavior, and impeachment of officials. The recent attacks are so severe that Senator Russell Feingold has stated, "I think we are close to being able to say this is an unprecedented series of threats toward the independence of the judiciary." Four of these court-stripping bills were passed in 1996. Along with the IIRIRA [Illegal Immigration Reform and Immigrant Responsibility Act of 1996, Pub. L. No. 104–208, div. C., 110 Stat. 3009 (1996)], these included the Prison Litigation Reform Act of 1995 [Pub. L. No. 104–134, 110 Stat. 1321–66], restrictions on the Legal Services Corporation [Omnibus Consolidated Rescissions and Appropriations Act of 1996, Title VIII, Pub. L. No. 104–134, 110 Stat. 1321–66], and the Antiterrorism and Effective Death Penalty Act of 1996 [Pub. L. No. 104–132, 110 Stat. 1214 (1996)]. Interestingly, all of these laws affect the most disadvantaged groups in our society—the poor, prisoners, and aliens.

Adrien Katherine Wing, Reno v. American-Arab Anti-Discrimination Committee: *A Critical Race Perspective*, 31 Colum. Hum. Rts. L. Rev. 561, 568 (2000). *See also* Leti Volpp, *Court-Stripping and Class-Wide Relief: A Response to Judicial Review in Immigration Cases after* AADC, 14 Geo. Immigr. L.J. 463 (2000).

During the same time the U.S. Supreme Court, in a series of cases, has questioned congressional power to enact legislation giving access to federal courts. Sylvia Law explains this recent history concerning constitutional constraints on federal power:

> Since 1995, the Supreme Court has sharply limited the power of Congress to regulate interstate commerce. Art. I, Section 8 of the

Constitution gives Congress the authority to "regulate Commerce . . . among the several states." Initially the Supreme Court, in an opinion by Chief Justice Marshall, interpreted this power broadly, allowing Congress to regulate commercial activity having any interstate impact, however indirect. Gibbons v. Ogden, 22 U.S. (9 Wheat.) 1, 194, (1824). Until 1887, Congress rarely exercised this broad power. When Congress began to regulate interstate commerce, the Supreme Court applied formalistic distinctions, for example, between commerce and manufacture, or between production and trade, to limit the power of the Congress. In the 1930s, as the New Deal Congress sought to find national solutions to the Great Depression, the Court's constraint on congressional power produced a national crisis. In 1937, the Supreme Court returned to the older view of broad congressional power under the commerce clause. *See* NLRB v. Jones & Laughlin Steel Corp., 301 U.S. 1 (1937) (upholding the National Labor Relations Act); United States v. Darby, 312 U.S. 100, 118–119 (1941) (upholding the wage and hour provisions of the Fair Labor Standards Act); Wickard v. Filburn, 317 U.S. 111 (1942) (upholding the application of wheat price controls as applied to grain grown for home consumption because the cumulative effect may affect interstate demand).

From 1937 until 1995, the Court never struck down an act of Congress for exceeding its powers under the Commerce Clause. Indeed because economic relations were increasingly national and global, and the lines between commercial and other activities so difficult to draw, some respected scholars urged the Court to renounce completely any role in policing the boundaries of the commerce power. Jessie H. Choper, *Judicial Review and the National Political Process* 171–259 (1980).

In 1995, for the first time in over half a century, the Court found that an act of Congress exceeded its power under the Commerce Clause. In *United States v. Lopez*, 514 U.S. 549 (1995), the Court held, 5–4, that Congress lacked power under the Commerce Clause to adopt the Gun-Free School Zones Act of 1990 that made it a federal crime for any individual "knowingly to possess a firearm at a place that the individual knows, or has reasonable cause to believe, is a school zone." 18 U.S.C. § 992(q)(2)(A). The *Lopez* majority asked whether the federally prohibited activity "substantially affects," rather than tangentially affects interstate commerce. 514 U.S. 564–566. The Court also suggests concern about whether the underlying activity is "commercial" or "economic." *Id.* at 567.

Sylvia A. Law, *Families and Federalism,* 4 Wash. U. J. L. & Pol'y 175, 226–27 (2000). *See also* Sylvia A. Law, *In the Name of Federalism: The Supreme Court's Assault on Democracy and Civil Rights*, 70 U. Cin. L. Rev. 367 (2002) (describing the Supreme Court's role in diminishing the power of Congress to address national problems).

UNITED STATES v. MORRISON

529 U.S. 598 (2000)

CHIEF JUSTICE REHNQUIST delivered the opinion of the Court.

In these cases we consider the constitutionality of 42 U.S.C. § 13981, which provides a federal civil remedy for the victims of gender-motivated violence. The United States Court of Appeals for the Fourth Circuit, sitting en banc, struck down § 13981 because it concluded that Congress lacked constitutional authority to enact the section's civil remedy. Believing that these cases are controlled by our decisions in *United States v. Lopez*, 514 U.S. 549 (1995), *United States v. Harris*, 106 U.S. 629 (1883), and the *In re Civil Rights Cases*, 109 U.S. 3 (1883), we affirm.

I

Petitioner Christy Brzonkala enrolled at Virginia Polytechnic Institute (Virginia Tech) in the fall of 1994. In September of that year, Brzonkala met respondents Antonio Morrison and James Crawford, who were both students at Virginia Tech and members of its varsity football team. Brzonkala alleges that, within 30 minutes of meeting Morrison and Crawford, they assaulted and repeatedly raped her. After the attack, Morrison allegedly told Brzonkala, "You better not have any . . . diseases." In the months following the rape, Morrison also allegedly announced in the dormitory's dining room that he "like[d] to get girls drunk and. . . . " The omitted portions, quoted verbatim in the briefs on file with this Court, consist of boasting, debased remarks about what Morrison would do to women, vulgar remarks that cannot fail to shock and offend.

Brzonkala alleges that this attack caused her to become severely emotionally disturbed and depressed. She sought assistance from a university psychiatrist, who prescribed antidepressant medication. Shortly after the rape Brzonkala stopped attending classes and withdrew from the university.

[Ms. Brzonkala pursued a remedy through the campus sexual assault policy. After two hearings and appeals, the university administration set aside Morrison's punishment.]

* * *

* * * After learning from a newspaper that Morrison would be returning to Virginia Tech for the fall 1995 semester, she dropped out of the university.

In December 1995, Brzonkala sued Morrison, Crawford, and Virginia Tech in the United States District Court for the Western District of Virginia. Her complaint alleged that Morrison's and Crawford's attack violated § 13981 * * * . Morrison and Crawford moved to dismiss this complaint on the grounds that it failed to state a claim and that

§ 13981's civil remedy is unconstitutional. The United States * * * intervened to defend § 13981's constitutionality.

*

Section 13981 was part of the Violence Against Women Act of 1994, § 40302, 108 Stat. 1941–1942. It states that "[a]ll persons within the United States shall have the right to be free from crimes of violence motivated by gender." 42 U.S.C. § 13981(b). To enforce that right, subsection (c) declares:

> "A person (including a person who acts under color of any statute, ordinance, regulation, custom, or usage of any State) who commits a crime of violence motivated by gender and thus deprives another of the right declared in subsection (b) of this section shall be liable to the party injured, in an action for the recovery of compensatory and punitive damages, injunctive and declaratory relief, and such other relief as a court may deem appropriate."

Section 13981 defines a "crim[e] of violence motivated by gender" as "a crime of violence committed because of gender or on the basis of gender, and due, at least in part, to an animus based on the victim's gender." § 13981(d)(1). It also provides that the term "crime of violence" includes any

> "(A) . . . act or series of acts that would constitute a felony against the person or that would constitute a felony against property if the conduct presents a serious risk of physical injury to another, and that would come within the meaning of State or Federal offenses described in section 16 of Title 18, whether or not those acts have actually resulted in criminal charges, prosecution, or conviction and whether or not those acts were committed in the special maritime, territorial, or prison jurisdiction of the United States;" and
>
> "(B) includes an act or series of acts that would constitute a felony described in subparagraph (A) but for the relationship between the person who takes such action and the individual against whom such action is taken." § 13981(d)(2).

Further clarifying the broad scope of § 13981's civil remedy, subsection (e)(2) states that "[n]othing in this section requires a prior criminal complaint, prosecution, or conviction to establish the elements of a cause of action under subsection (c) of this section." And subsection (e)(3) provides a § 13981 litigant with a choice of forums: Federal and state courts "shall have concurrent jurisdiction" over complaints brought under the section.

Although the foregoing language of § 13981 covers a wide swath of criminal conduct, Congress placed some limitations on the section's federal civil remedy. Subsection (e)(1) states that "[n]othing in this section entitles a person to a cause of action under subsection (c) of this section for random acts of violence unrelated to gender or for acts that cannot be demonstrated, by a preponderance of the evidence, to be motivated by gender." Subsection (e)(4) further states that § 13981 shall not be construed "to confer on the courts of the United States jurisdiction over any State law claim seeking the establishment of a divorce, alimony, equitable distribution of marital property, or child custody decree."

Every law enacted by Congress must be based on one or more of its powers enumerated in the Constitution. "The powers of the legislature are defined and limited; and that those limits may not be mistaken or forgotten, the constitution is written." *Marbury v. Madison*, 1 Cranch 137, 176 (1803) (Marshall, C. J.). Congress explicitly identified the sources of federal authority on which it relied in enacting § 13981. It said that a "Federal civil rights cause of action" is established "[p]ursuant to the affirmative power of Congress ... under section 5 of the Fourteenth Amendment to the Constitution, as well as under section 8 of Article I of the Constitution." 42 U.S.C. § 13981(a). We address Congress' authority to enact this remedy under each of these constitutional provisions in turn.

II

Due respect for the decisions of a coordinate branch of Government demands that we invalidate a congressional enactment only upon a plain showing that Congress has exceeded its constitutional bounds. See *United States v. Lopez*, 514 U.S., at 568, 577–578 (KENNEDY, J., concurring); *United States v. Harris*, 106 U.S., at 635. With this presumption of constitutionality in mind, we turn to the question whether § 13981 falls within Congress' power under Article I, § 8, of the Constitution. Brzonkala and the United States rely upon the third clause of the section, which gives Congress power "[t]o regulate Commerce with foreign Nations, and among the several States, and with the Indian Tribes."

As we discussed at length in *Lopez*, our interpretation of the Commerce Clause has changed as our Nation has developed. We need not repeat that detailed review of the Commerce Clause's history here; it suffices to say that, in the years since *NLRB v. Jones & Laughlin Steel Corp.*, 301 U.S. 1 (1937), Congress has had considerably greater latitude in regulating conduct and transactions under the Commerce Clause than our previous case law permitted.

Lopez emphasized, however, that even under our modern, expansive interpretation of the Commerce Clause, Congress' regulatory authority is not without effective bounds.

> "[E]ven [our] modern-era precedents which have expanded congressional power under the Commerce Clause confirm that this power is subject to outer limits. In *Jones & Laughlin Steel*, the Court warned that the scope of the interstate commerce power 'must be considered in the light of our dual system of government and may not be extended so as to embrace effects upon interstate commerce so indirect and remote that to embrace them, in view of our complex society, would effectually obliterate the distinction between what is

national and what is local and create a completely centralized government.' "

As we observed in *Lopez*, modern Commerce Clause jurisprudence has "identified three broad categories of activity that Congress may regulate under its commerce power." "First, Congress may regulate the use of the channels of interstate commerce." (citing *Heart of Atlanta Motel, Inc. v. United States*, 379 U.S. 241, 256 (1964); *United States v. Darby*, 312 U.S. 100, 114 (1941)). "Second, Congress is empowered to regulate and protect the instrumentalities of interstate commerce, or persons or things in interstate commerce, even though the threat may come only from intrastate activities." (citing *Shreveport Rate Cases*, 234 U.S. 342 (1914); *Southern R. Co. v. United States*, 222 U.S. 20 (1911) * * *). "Finally, Congress' commerce authority includes the power to regulate those activities having a substantial relation to interstate commerce, ... *i.e.*, those activities that substantially affect interstate commerce." (citing *Jones & Laughlin Steel*, *supra* at 37).

Petitioners do not contend that these cases fall within either of the first two of these categories of Commerce Clause regulation. They seek to sustain § 13981 as a regulation of activity that substantially affects interstate commerce. Given § 13981's focus on gender-motivated violence wherever it occurs (rather than violence directed at the instrumentalities of interstate commerce, interstate markets, or things or persons in interstate commerce), we agree that this is the proper inquiry.

Since *Lopez* most recently canvassed and clarified our case law governing this third category of Commerce Clause regulation, it provides the proper framework for conducting the required analysis of § 13981. In *Lopez*, we held that the Gun-Free School Zones Act of 1990, 18 U.S.C. § 922(q)(1)(A), which made it a federal crime to knowingly possess a firearm in a school zone, exceeded Congress' authority under the Commerce Clause. Several significant considerations contributed to our decision.

First, we observed that § 922(q) was "a criminal statute that by its terms has nothing to do with 'commerce' or any sort of economic enterprise, however broadly one might define those terms." Reviewing our case law, we noted that "we have upheld a wide variety of congressional Acts regulating intrastate economic activity where we have concluded that the activity substantially affected interstate commerce." Although we cited only a few examples, including * * * *Katzenbach v. McClung*, 379 U.S. 294 (1964) and *Heart of Atlanta Motel*, *supra*, we stated that the pattern of analysis is clear. "Where economic activity substantially affects interstate commerce, legislation regulating that activity will be sustained."

Both petitioners and Justice SOUTER's dissent downplay the role that the economic nature of the regulated activity plays in our Commerce Clause analysis. But a fair reading of *Lopez* shows that the noneconomic, criminal nature of the conduct at issue was central to our decision in that case. * * * *Lopez's* review of Commerce Clause case law demonstrates that in those cases where we have sustained federal regulation of intrastate activity based upon the activity's substantial effects on interstate commerce, the activity in question has been some sort of economic endeavor.

* * *

Finally, our decision in *Lopez* rested in part on the fact that the link between gun possession and a substantial effect on interstate commerce was attenuated. The United States argued that the possession of guns may lead to violent crime, and that violent crime "can be expected to affect the functioning of the national economy in two ways. First, the costs of violent crime are substantial, and, through the mechanism of insurance, those costs are spread throughout the population. Second, violent crime reduces the willingness of individuals to travel to areas within the country that are perceived to be unsafe." The Government also argued that the presence of guns at schools poses a threat to the educational process, which in turn threatens to produce a less efficient and productive work force, which will negatively affect national productivity and thus interstate commerce.

We rejected these "costs of crime" and "national productivity" arguments because they would permit Congress to "regulate not only all violent crime, but all activities that might lead to violent crime, regardless of how tenuously they relate to interstate commerce." We noted that, under this but-for reasoning:

> "Congress could regulate any activity that it found was related to the economic productivity of individual citizens: family law (including marriage, divorce, and child custody), for example. Under the[se] theories ... , it is difficult to perceive any limitation on federal power, even in areas such as criminal law enforcement or education where States historically have been sovereign. Thus, if we were to accept the Government's arguments, we are hard pressed to posit any activity by an individual that Congress is without power to regulate."

With these principles underlying our Commerce Clause jurisprudence as reference points, the proper resolution of the present cases is clear. Gender-motivated crimes of violence are not, in any sense of the phrase, economic activity. While we need not adopt a categorical rule against aggregating the effects of any noneconomic activity in order to decide these cases, thus far in our Nation's history our cases have upheld Commerce Clause regulation of intrastate activity only where that activity is economic in nature.

* * *

In contrast with the lack of congressional findings that we faced in *Lopez*, § 13981 *is* supported by numerous findings regarding the serious impact that gender-motivated violence has on victims and their families. But the existence of congressional findings is not sufficient, by itself, to sustain the constitutionality of Commerce Clause legislation. As we stated in *Lopez,* " '[S]imply because Congress may conclude that a particular activity substantially affects interstate commerce does not necessarily make it so.' " Rather, " '[w]hether particular operations affect interstate commerce sufficiently to come under the constitutional power of Congress to regulate them is ultimately a judicial rather than a legislative question, and can be settled finally only by this Court.' "

In these cases, Congress' findings are substantially weakened by the fact that they rely so heavily on a method of reasoning that we have already rejected as unworkable if we are to maintain the Constitution's enumeration of powers. Congress found that gender-motivated violence affects interstate commerce

> "by deterring potential victims from traveling interstate, from engaging in employment in interstate business, and from transacting with business, and in places involved in interstate commerce; ... by diminishing national productivity, increasing medical and other costs, and decreasing the supply of and the demand for interstate products." H.R. Conf. Rep. No. 103–711, at 385, U.S.Code Cong. & Admin.News 1994, pp. 1803, 1853.

Given these findings and petitioners' arguments, the concern that we expressed in *Lopez* that Congress might use the Commerce Clause to completely obliterate the Constitution's distinction between national and local authority seems well founded. The reasoning that petitioners advance seeks to follow the but-for causal chain from the initial occurrence of violent crime (the suppression of which has always been the prime object of the States' police power) to every attenuated effect upon interstate commerce. If accepted, petitioners' reasoning would allow Congress to regulate any crime as long as the nationwide, aggregated impact of that crime has substantial effects on employment, production, transit, or consumption. Indeed, if Congress may regulate gender-motivated violence, it would be able to regulate murder or any other type of violence since gender-motivated violence, as a subset of all violent crime, is certain to have lesser economic impacts than the larger class of which it is a part.

Petitioners' reasoning, moreover, will not limit Congress to regulating violence but may, as we suggested in *Lopez,* be applied equally as well to family law and other areas of traditional state regulation since the aggregate effect of marriage, divorce, and childrearing on the national economy is undoubtedly significant. Congress may have recognized this specter when it expressly precluded § 13981 from being used in the family law context. See 42 U.S.C. § 13981(e)(4). Under our written Constitution, however, the limitation of congressional authority is not solely a matter of legislative grace.

We accordingly reject the argument that Congress may regulate noneconomic, violent criminal conduct based solely on that conduct's aggregate effect on interstate commerce. The Constitution requires a distinction between what is truly national and what is truly local. In recognizing this fact we preserve one of the few principles that has been consistent since the Clause was adopted. The regulation and punishment of intrastate violence that is not directed at the instrumentalities, channels, or goods involved in interstate commerce has always been the province of the States. *See, e.g., Cohens v. Virginia*, 6 Wheat. 264, 426, 428 (1821) (Marshall, C.J.) (stating that Congress "has no general right to punish murder committed within any of the States," and that it is "clear ... that congress cannot punish felonies generally"). Indeed, we can think of no better example of the police power, which the Founders denied the National Government and reposed in the States, than the suppression of violent crime and vindication of its victims. * * *

III

Because we conclude that the Commerce Clause does not provide Congress with authority to enact § 13981, we address petitioners' alternative argument that the section's civil remedy should be upheld as an exercise of Congress' remedial power under § 5 of the Fourteenth Amendment. As noted above, Congress expressly invoked the Fourteenth Amendment as a source of authority to enact § 13981.

The principles governing an analysis of congressional legislation under § 5 are well settled. Section 5 states that Congress may " 'enforce' by 'appropriate legislation' the constitutional guarantee that no State shall deprive any person of 'life, liberty or property, without due process of law,' nor deny any person 'equal protection of the laws.' " *City of Boerne v. Flores*, 521 U.S. 507, 517 (1997). Section 5 is "a positive grant of legislative power," *Katzenbach v. Morgan*, 384 U.S. 641, 651 (1966), that includes authority to "prohibit conduct which is not itself unconstitutional and [to] intrud[e] into 'legislative spheres of autonomy previously reserved to the States.' " *Flores, supra* at 518 (quoting *Fitzpatrick v. Bitzer*, 427 U.S. 445, 455 (1976)). However, "[a]s broad as the congressional enforcement power is, it is not unlimited." *Oregon v. Mitchell*, 400 U.S. 112, 128 (1970). In fact, as we discuss in detail below, several limitations inherent in § 5's text and constitutional context have been recognized since the Fourteenth Amendment was adopted.

Petitioners' § 5 argument is founded on an assertion that there is pervasive bias in various state justice systems against victims of gender-motivated violence. This assertion is supported by a voluminous congressional record. Specifically, Congress received evidence that many participants in state justice systems are perpetuating an array of erroneous stereotypes and assumptions. Congress concluded that these discriminatory stereotypes often result in insufficient investigation and prosecution of gender-motivated crime, inappropriate focus on the behavior and credibility of the victims of that crime, and unacceptably lenient punishments for those who are actually convicted of gender-motivated violence. See H.R. Conf. Rep. No. 103–711, at 385–386; S.Rep. No. 103–138, at 38, 41–55; S.Rep. No. 102–197, at 33–35, 41, 43–47. Petitioners contend that this bias denies victims of gender-motivated violence the equal protection of the laws and that Congress therefore acted appropriately in enacting a private civil remedy against the perpetrators of gender-motivated violence to both remedy the States' bias and deter future instances of discrimination in the state courts.

As our cases have established, state-sponsored gender discrimination violates equal protection unless it " 'serves "important governmental objectives and . . . the discriminatory means employed" are "substantially related to the achievement of those objectives." ' " *United States v. Virginia*, 518 U.S. 515, 533 (1996) (quoting *Mississippi Univ. for Women v. Hogan*, 458 U.S. 718, 724 (1982), in turn quoting *Wengler v. Druggists Mut. Ins. Co.*, 446 U.S. 142, 150 (1980)). See also *Craig v. Boren*, 429 U.S. 190, 198–199 (1976). However, the language and purpose of the Fourteenth Amendment place certain limitations on the manner in which Congress may attack discriminatory conduct. These limitations are necessary to prevent the Fourteenth Amendment from obliterating the Framers' carefully crafted balance of power between the States and the National Government. Foremost among these limitations is the time-honored principle that the Fourteenth Amendment, by its very terms, prohibits only state action. "[T]he principle has become firmly embedded in our constitutional law that the action inhibited by the first section of the Fourteenth Amendment is only such action as may fairly be said to be that of the States. That Amendment erects no shield against merely private conduct, however discriminatory or wrongful." *Shelley v. Kraemer*, 334 U.S. 1, 13, and n. 12 (1948).

Shortly after the Fourteenth Amendment was adopted, we decided two cases interpreting the Amendment's provisions, *United States v. Harris*, 106 U.S. 629 (1883), and the *Civil Rights Cases*, 109 U.S. 3 (1883). In *Harris*, the Court considered a challenge to § 2 of the Civil Rights Act of 1871. That section sought to punish "private persons" for "conspiring to deprive any one of the equal protection of the laws enacted by the State." We concluded that this law exceeded Congress' § 5 power because the law was "directed exclusively against the action of private persons, without reference to the laws of the State, or their administration by her officers." In so doing, we reemphasized our statement from *Virginia v. Rives*, 100 U.S. 313, 318 (1879), that " 'these provisions of the fourteenth amendment have reference to State action exclusively, and not to any action of private individuals.' "

We reached a similar conclusion in the *Civil Rights Cases*. In those consolidated cases, we held that the public accommodation provisions of the Civil Rights Act of 1875, which applied to purely private conduct, were beyond the scope of the § 5 enforcement power. 109 U.S., at 11 ("Individual invasion of individual rights is not the subject-matter of the [Fourteenth] [A]mendment"). See also, *e.g.*, * * * *United States v. Cruikshank*, 92 U.S. 542, 554 (1875) ("The fourteenth amendment prohibits a state from depriving any person of life, liberty, or property, without due process of law; but this adds nothing to the rights of one citizen as against another. It simply furnishes an additional guaranty against any encroachment by the States upon the fundamental rights which belong to every citizen as a member of society").

* * *

* * * We believe that the description of the § 5 power contained in the *Civil Rights Cases* is correct:

> "But where a subject has not submitted to the general legislative power of Congress, but is only submitted thereto for the purpose of rendering effective some prohibition against particular [s]tate legislation or [s]tate action in reference to that subject, the power given is limited by its object, and any legislation by Congress in the matter must necessarily be corrective in its character, adapted to counteract and redress the operation of such prohibited state laws or proceedings of [s]tate officers." 109 U.S., at 18.

Petitioners alternatively argue that, unlike the situation in the *Civil Rights Cases,* here there has been gender-based disparate treatment by state authorities, whereas in those cases there was no indication of such state action. There is abundant evidence, however, to show that the Congresses that enacted the Civil Rights Acts of 1871 and 1875 had a purpose similar to that of Congress in enacting § 13981: There were state laws on the books bespeaking equality of treatment, but in the administration of these laws there was discrimination against newly freed slaves. The statement of Representative Garfield in the House and that of Senator Sumner in the Senate are representative:

> "[T]he chief complaint is not that the laws of the State are unequal, but that even where the laws are just and equal on their face, yet, by a systematic maladministration of them, or a neglect or refusal to enforce their provisions, a portion of the people are denied equal protection under them." Cong. Globe, 42d Cong., 1st Sess., App. 153 (1871) (statement of Rep. Garfield). * * *

But even if that distinction were valid, we do not believe it would save § 13981's civil remedy. For the remedy is simply not "corrective in its character, adapted to counteract and redress the operation of such prohibited [s]tate laws or proceedings of [s]tate officers." *Civil Rights Cases*, 109 U.S., at 18. Or, as we have phrased it in more recent cases, prophylactic legislation under § 5 must have a "congruence and proportionality between the injury to be prevented or remedied and the means adopted to that end." *Florida Prepaid Postsecondary Ed. Expense Bd. v. College Savings Bank*, 527 U.S. 627, 639 (1999); *Flores*, 521 U.S., at 526. Section 13981 is not aimed at proscribing discrimination by officials which the Fourteenth Amendment might not itself proscribe; it is directed not at any State or state actor, but at individuals who have committed criminal acts motivated by gender bias.

In the present cases, for example, § 13981 visits no consequence whatever on any Virginia public official involved in investigating or prosecuting Brzonkala's assault. The section is, therefore, unlike any of the § 5 remedies that we have previously upheld. For example, in *Katzenbach v. Morgan*, 384 U.S. 641(1966), Congress prohibited New York from imposing literacy tests as a prerequisite for voting because it found that such a requirement disenfranchised thousands of Puerto Rican immigrants who had been educated in the Spanish language of their home territory. That law, which we upheld, was directed at New York officials who administered the State's election law and prohibited them from using a provision of that law. In *South Carolina v. Katzenbach*, 383 U.S. 301 (1966), Congress imposed voting rights requirements on States that, Congress found, had a history of discriminating against blacks in voting. The remedy was also directed at state officials in those States. Similarly, in *Ex parte Virginia*, 100 U.S. 339 (1879), Congress criminally punished state officials who intentionally discriminated in jury selection; again, the remedy was directed to the culpable state official.

Section 13981 is also different from these previously upheld remedies in that it applies uniformly throughout the Nation. Congress' findings indicate that the problem of discrimination against the victims of gender-motivated crimes does not exist in all States, or even most States. By contrast, the § 5 remedy upheld in *Katzenbach v. Morgan*, *supra*, was directed only to the State where the evil found by Congress existed, and in *South Carolina v. Katzenbach*, *supra*, the remedy was directed only to those States in which Congress found that there had been discrimination.

For these reasons, we conclude that Congress' power under § 5 does not extend to the enactment of § 13981.

IV

Petitioner Brzonkala's complaint alleges that she was the victim of a brutal assault. But Congress' effort in § 13981 to provide a federal civil remedy can be sustained neither under the Commerce Clause nor under § 5 of the Fourteenth Amendment. If the allegations here are true, no civilized system of justice could fail to provide her a remedy for the conduct of respondent Morrison. But under our federal system that remedy must be provided by the Commonwealth of Virginia, and not by the United States. The judgment of the Court of Appeals is

Affirmed.

* * *

Justice SOUTER, with whom Justice STEVENS, Justice GINSBURG, and Justice BREYER join, dissenting.

The Court says both that it leaves Commerce Clause precedent undisturbed and that the Civil Rights Remedy of the Violence Against Women Act of 1994, 42 U.S.C. § 13981, exceeds Congress's power under that Clause. I find the claims irreconcilable and respectfully dissent.[1]

I

Our cases, which remain at least nominally undisturbed, stand for the following propositions. Congress has the power to legislate with

1. Finding the law a valid exercise of Commerce Clause power, I have no occasion to reach the question whether it might also be sustained as an exercise of Congress's power to enforce the Fourteenth Amendment.

regard to activity that, in the aggregate, has a substantial effect on interstate commerce. See *Wickard v. Filburn*, 317 U.S. 111, 124–128; *Hodel v. Virginia Surface Mining & Reclamation Assn., Inc.*, 452 U.S. 264, 277 (1981). The fact of such a substantial effect is not an issue for the courts in the first instance but for the Congress, whose institutional capacity for gathering evidence and taking testimony far exceeds ours. By passing legislation, Congress indicates its conclusion, whether explicitly or not, that facts support its exercise of the commerce power. The business of the courts is to review the congressional assessment, not for soundness but simply for the rationality of concluding that a jurisdictional basis exists in fact. Any explicit findings that Congress chooses to make, though not dispositive of the question of rationality, may advance judicial review by identifying factual authority on which Congress relied. Applying those propositions in these cases can lead to only one conclusion.

One obvious difference from *United States v. Lopez*, 514 U.S. 549 (1995), is the mountain of data assembled by Congress, here showing the effects of violence against women on interstate commerce. Passage of the Act in 1994 was preceded by four years of hearings, which included testimony from physicians and law professors; from survivors of rape and domestic violence; and from representatives of state law enforcement and private business. The record includes reports on gender bias from task forces in 21 States, and we have the benefit of specific factual findings in the eight separate Reports issued by Congress and its committees over the long course leading to enactment. Compare *Hodel*, 452 U.S., at 278–279 (noting "extended hearings," "vast amounts of testimony and documentary evidence," and "years of the most thorough legislative consideration").

With respect to domestic violence, Congress received evidence for the following findings:

> "Three out of four American women will be victims of violent crimes sometime during their life."
>
> "Violence is the leading cause of injuries to women ages 15 to 44. . . ."
>
> "[A]s many as 50 percent of homeless women and children are fleeing domestic violence."
>
> "Since 1974, the assault rate against women has outstripped the rate for men by at least twice for some age groups and far more for others."
>
> "[B]attering 'is the single largest cause of injury to women in the United States.' "
>
> "An estimated 4 million American women are battered each year by their husbands or partners."
>
> "Over 1 million women in the United States seek medical assistance each year for injuries sustained [from] their husbands or other partners."

"Between 2,000 and 4,000 women die every year from [domestic] abuse."

"[A]rrest rates may be as low as 1 for every 100 domestic assaults."

"Partial estimates show that violent crime against women costs this country at least 3 billion—not million, but billion—dollars a year."

"[E]stimates suggest that we spend $5 to $10 billion a year on health care, criminal justice, and other social costs of domestic violence."

The evidence as to rape was similarly extensive, supporting these conclusions:

"[The incidence of] rape rose four times as fast as the total national crime rate over the past 10 years."

"According to one study, close to half a million girls now in high school will be raped before they graduate."

"[One hundred twenty-five thousand] college women can expect to be raped during this—or any—year."

"[T]hree-quarters of women never go to the movies alone after dark because of the fear of rape and nearly 50 percent do not use public transit alone after dark for the same reason."

"[Forty-one] percent of judges surveyed believed that juries give sexual assault victims less credibility than other crime victims."

"Less than 1 percent of all [rape] victims have collected damages."

" '[A]n individual who commits rape has only about 4 chances in 100 of being arrested, prosecuted, and found guilty of any offense.' "

"Almost one-quarter of convicted rapists never go to prison and another quarter received sentences in local jails where the average sentence is 11 months."

"[A]lmost 50 percent of rape victims lose their jobs or are forced to quit because of the crime's severity."

Based on the data thus partially summarized, Congress found that

"crimes of violence motivated by gender have a substantial adverse effect on interstate commerce, by deterring potential victims from traveling interstate, from engaging in employment in interstate business, and from transacting with business, and in places involved, in interstate commerce . . . [,] by diminishing national productivity, increasing medical and other costs, and decreasing the supply of and the demand for interstate products. . . ."

Congress thereby explicitly stated the predicate for the exercise of its Commerce Clause power. Is its conclusion irrational in view of the data amassed? True, the methodology of particular studies may be challenged, and some of the figures arrived at may be disputed. But the sufficiency of the evidence before Congress to provide a rational basis for the finding cannot seriously be questioned.

Indeed, the legislative record here is far more voluminous than the record compiled by Congress and found sufficient in two prior cases upholding Title II of the Civil Rights Act of 1964 against Commerce Clause challenges. In *Heart of Atlanta Motel, Inc. v. United States*, 379 U.S. 241, and *Katzenbach v. McClung*, 379 U.S. 294 (1964), the Court referred to evidence showing the consequences of racial discrimination by motels and restaurants on interstate commerce. Congress had relied on compelling anecdotal reports that individual instances of segregation cost thousands to millions of dollars. Congress also had evidence that the average black family spent substantially less than the average white family in the same income range on public accommodations, and that discrimination accounted for much of the difference.

While Congress did not, to my knowledge, calculate aggregate dollar values for the nationwide effects of racial discrimination in 1964, in 1994 it did rely on evidence of the harms caused by domestic violence and sexual assault, citing annual costs of $3 billion in 1990. Equally important, though, gender-based violence in the 1990's was shown to operate in a manner similar to racial discrimination in the 1960's in reducing the mobility of employees and their production and consumption of goods shipped in interstate commerce. Like racial discrimination, "[g]ender-based violence bars its most likely targets—women—from full partic[ipation] in the national economy."

If the analogy to the Civil Rights Act of 1964 is not plain enough, one can always look back a bit further. In *Wickard*, we upheld the application of the Agricultural Adjustment Act to the planting and consumption of homegrown wheat. The effect on interstate commerce in that case followed from the possibility that wheat grown at home for personal consumption could either be drawn into the market by rising prices, or relieve its grower of any need to purchase wheat in the market. The Commerce Clause predicate was simply the effect of the production of wheat for home consumption on supply and demand in interstate commerce. Supply and demand for goods in interstate commerce will also be affected by the deaths of 2,000 to 4,000 women annually at the hands of domestic abusers, see S.Rep. No. 101–545, at 36, and by the reduction in the work force by the 100,000 or more rape victims who lose their jobs each year or are forced to quit, see *id.*, at 56, H.R.Rep. No. 103–395, at 25–26. Violence against women may be found to affect interstate commerce and affect it substantially.

II

The Act would have passed muster at any time between *Wickard* in 1942 and *Lopez* in 1995, a period in which the law enjoyed a stable understanding that congressional power under the Commerce Clause, complemented by the authority of the Necessary and Proper Clause, Art. I. § 8 cl. 18, extended to all activity that, when aggregated, has a substantial effect on interstate commerce. As already noted, this understanding was secure even against the turmoil at the passage of the Civil Rights Act of 1964, in the aftermath of which the Court not only reaffirmed the cumulative effects and rational basis features of the substantial effects test, see *Heart of Atlanta, supra* at 258; *McClung, supra* at 301–305, but declined to limit the commerce power through a formal distinction between legislation focused on "commerce" and statutes addressing "moral and social wrong[s]," *Heart of Atlanta, supra* at 257.

The fact that the Act does not pass muster before the Court today is therefore proof, to a degree that *Lopez* was not, that the Court's nominal adherence to the substantial effects test is merely that. Although a new jurisprudence has not emerged with any distinctness, it is clear that some congressional conclusions about obviously substantial, cumulative effects on commerce are being assigned lesser values than the once-stable doctrine would assign them. These devaluations are accomplished not by any express repudiation of the substantial effects test or its application through the aggregation of individual conduct, but by supplanting rational basis scrutiny with a new criterion of review.

Thus the elusive heart of the majority's analysis in these cases is its statement that Congress's findings of fact are "weakened" by the presence of a disfavored "method of reasoning." This seems to suggest that the "substantial effects" analysis is not a factual enquiry, for Congress in the first instance with subsequent judicial review looking only to the rationality of the congressional conclusion, but one of a rather different sort, dependent upon a uniquely judicial competence.

This new characterization of substantial effects has no support in our cases (the self-fulfilling prophecies of *Lopez* aside), least of all those the majority cites. Perhaps this explains why the majority is not content to rest on its cited precedent but claims a textual justification for moving toward its new system of congressional deference subject to selective discounts. Thus it purports to rely on the sensible and traditional understanding that the listing in the Constitution of some powers implies the exclusion of others unmentioned. The majority stresses that Art. I, § 8, enumerates the powers of Congress, including the commerce power, an enumeration implying the exclusion of powers not enumerated. It follows, for the majority, not only that there must be some limits to "commerce," but that some particular subjects arguably within the commerce power can be identified in advance as excluded, on the basis of characteristics other than their commercial effects. Such exclusions come into sight when the activity regulated is not itself commercial or when the States have traditionally addressed it in the exercise of the general police power, conferred under the state constitutions but never extended to Congress under the Constitution of the Nation.

The premise that the enumeration of powers implies that other powers are withheld is sound; the conclusion that some particular categories of subject matter are therefore presumptively beyond the reach of the commerce power is, however, a non sequitur. From the fact that Art. I, § 8, cl. 3 grants an authority limited to regulating commerce, it follows only that Congress may claim no authority under that section to address any subject that does not affect commerce. It does not at all follow that an activity affecting commerce nonetheless falls outside the commerce power, depending on the specific character of the activity, or the authority of a State to regulate it along with Congress. * * *

Justice BREYER, with whom Justice STEVENS joins, and with whom Justice SOUTER and Justice GINSBURG join as to Part I–A, dissenting.

No one denies the importance of the Constitution's federalist principles. Its state/federal division of authority protects liberty—both by restricting the burdens that government can impose from a distance and by facilitating citizen participation in government that is closer to home. The question is how the judiciary can best implement that original federalist understanding where the Commerce Clause is at issue.

I

The majority holds that the federal commerce power does not extend to such "noneconomic" activities as "noneconomic, violent criminal conduct" that significantly affects interstate commerce only if we "aggregate" the interstate "effect[s]" of individual instances. * * * [T]he majority's holding illustrates the difficulty of finding a workable judicial Commerce Clause touchstone—a set of comprehensible interpretive rules that courts might use to impose some meaningful limit, but not too great a limit, upon the scope of the legislative authority that the Commerce Clause delegates to Congress.

A

Consider the problems. The "economic/noneconomic" distinction is not easy to apply. Does the local street corner mugger engage in "economic" activity or "noneconomic" activity when he mugs for money? See *Perez v. United States*, 402 U.S. 146 (1971) (aggregating local "loan sharking" instances); *United States v. Lopez*, 514 U.S. 549, 559 (1995) (loan sharking is economic because it consists of "intrastate extortionate credit transactions") * * * . Would evidence that desire for economic domination underlies many brutal crimes against women save the present statute?

The line becomes yet harder to draw given the need for exceptions. The Court itself would permit Congress to aggregate, hence regulate, "noneconomic" activity taking place at economic establishments. See *Heart of Atlanta Motel, Inc. v. United States*, 379 U.S. 241 (1964) (upholding civil rights laws forbidding discrimination at local motels); *Katzenbach v. McClung*, 379 U.S. 294 (1964) (same for restaurants)

* * * . Given the former exception, can Congress simply rewrite the present law and limit its application to restaurants, hotels, perhaps universities, and other places of public accommodation? * * *

Notes and Questions

1. Catharine MacKinnon has observed that *Morrison* prevented "the federal government from legislating equality rights in an area that states have inadequately protected." She continues:

> There may be a more direct relation between the denial of equality and the Court's new view of the formal doctrine of federalism. On a deeper level of law and politics, and against an historical backdrop of the use of federalism to deny racial equality and enforce white supremacy, *Morrison* can be seen to employ ostensibly gender-neutral tools to achieve a substantive victory for the social institution of male dominance. Read substantively, *Morrison* is not an abstract application of neutral institutional priorities, but a refusal to allow Congress to redress violence against women—a problem the Court declined to see as one of economic salience or national dimension. In *Morrison*, the Court revived and deployed against women the odious "states' rights" doctrine, the principal legal argument for the maintenance of slavery that was used to deny equality rights on racial grounds well into * * * [the twentieth] century. Combined with the Court's equal protection jurisprudence—the "intent" requirement of which has made it increasingly difficult to hold states responsible for equal protection violations committed by state actors—*Morrison* leaves women who are denied the equal protection of criminal laws against battering and rape without adequate legal recourse.

Catharine A. MacKinnon, *Disputing Male Sovereignty: On* United States v. Morrison, 114 Harv. L. Rev. 135, 136–37 (2000).

2. Is *Morrison* an example of the need for Resnik's non-categorical federalism? Are community norms about violence against women being contested if some view it as not having economic impact or within equal protection norms? Is the majority persuasive in finding that violence against women does not impact interstate commerce? Why do the dissenting justices fail to address the claims relating to Section 5 of the Fourteenth Amendment?

3. The prevalence of violence against women was well supported by the congressional findings that were part of the record in the case. Does the Court's decision surprise you, in light of that overwhelming evidence? Why does this violence remain unremedied? Consider this view:

> Most rape victims, like Christy Brzonkala, are women or girls. There are a great many of them. One in four women in America reports having been raped, with forty-four percent reporting having been subjected to completed or attempted rape at least once in their lives. Almost one in ten women between the ages of fifteen and forty

four who has had sexual intercourse reports that her first act of sexual intercourse was "not voluntary." * * * Like Christy Brzonkala, many young women are raped while they are at a college or university. In one large probability sample, eighty-three women in every thousand attending college or university in a six month period in 1987 reported being raped.

Again like Christy Brzonkala, most rape victims share a context, or some degree of acquaintance, with their rapists. * * *

Unlike Christy Brzonkala's rapes, most sexual assaults remain entirely unreported. This is because the victims anticipate, with reason, that the authorities will not believe them or that they will be revictimized in the legal process. Sexual abuse survivors dread the legal system. Women are routinely disbelieved, humiliated, harassed, and shunned as a result of reporting sexual assault to officials. The police practice of "unfounding," in which police decide that a rape report is without foundation, resembles Virginia Polytechnic's treatment of Ms. Brzonkala's allegations in changing Mr. Morrison's conviction from sexual assault to verbal insult. Many women who bring rape charges feel violated by their encounter with the justice system: "The second rape is exemplified most dramatically when the survivor is strong enough, brave enough, and even naive enough to believe that if she decides to prosecute her offender, justice will be done. It is a rape more devastating and despoiling than the first."

Most rape, like Christy Brzonkala's, is unremedied. Most reported rapes are not prosecuted. Most prosecuted rapes do not result in convictions. Sentences for rapes are often short. The vast majority of rapists are never held to account for their acts in any way.

The most atypical feature of Christy Brzonkala's rapes is that they were interracial—she is white and the men accused of raping her are African American—and the assailants went unpunished. Most rapes occur within rather than across racial groups, even as the American legal system has often had an exaggeratedly punitive reaction to accusations of rape of white women by Black men. The more typical pattern is that Black men are stereotyped as sexual predators and found to have raped white women whether or not they did. In extending effective impunity to African American men, the *Morrison* case was exceptional. Whether in this respect it represents progress against racism, or an extension of misogyny's standard rules to Black men, or both is worth asking.

MacKinnon, *supra* at 141–44. *See also* chapter 14 describing the movement to end violence against women in the context of domestic violence.

4. The heart of the dissent suggests that the majority has changed the law by modifying the sort of scrutiny applied to the commerce clause. If one aspect of judging and judicial review is the selection of standards of scrutiny, have judges changed the law?

ROBERT C. POST & REVA B. SIEGEL

Equal Protection by Law: Federal Antidiscrimination Legislation After Morrison *and* Kimel

110 Yale L.J. 441, 441–44, 446–55, 474–77, 481–82, 485–86, 496–97, 501–02, 506, 508, 523–26 (2000)

Last Term, the Supreme Court sent ominous signals about the future of federal antidiscrimination law. The Court twice ruled that Congress lacked power under Section 5 of the Fourteenth Amendment to enact laws prohibiting discrimination. In *Kimel v. Florida Board of Regents*, [528 U.S. 62 (2000)] the Court concluded that Section 5 did not give Congress the power to abrogate state Eleventh Amendment immunity for suits under the Age Discrimination in Employment Act of 1967, and in *United States v. Morrison*, [529 U.S. 598 (2000)] the Court held that Congress was without power under either the Commerce Clause or Section 5 to enact a provision of the Violence Against Women Act of 1994 (VAWA) creating a federal civil remedy for victims of gender-motivated violence.

Both *Kimel* and *Morrison* are written in forceful and broad strokes that threaten large stretches of congressional authority under Section 5. Yet the Court's Section 5 holdings were rendered without dissent. Although in *Kimel* there were four Justices prepared to disagree strenuously with the decision's liberal interpretation of Eleventh Amendment immunity, and although in *Morrison* there were four Justices prepared to disagree strenuously with the decision's restrictive interpretation of federal Commerce Clause power, not a single Justice in either case was ready to vote to sustain congressional power under Section 5, even as Justice Breyer identified key deficiencies in *Morrison*'s justification for its Section 5 holding.

This silence is remarkable, yet explicable. Since the New Deal, the Commerce Clause has shaped core understandings of the contours of national power. In the early 1960s, the Supreme Court took the consequential step of upholding the public accommodations provisions of the Civil Rights Act of 1964 on Commerce Clause grounds alone, despite the fact that Congress had asserted authority to enact the legislation under both the Commerce Clause and Section 5 of the Fourteenth Amendment. We have ever since grown habituated to the use of Commerce Clause power to sustain federal antidiscrimination law, never definitively resolving the shape and reach of Section 5 authority.

What might be called the "jurisdictional" compromise of the 1960s was forged at a time when the Commerce Clause seemed to offer boundless support for Congress's authority to enact antidiscrimination laws. But this no longer appears to be the case. Given the Court's current determination to impose limits on Congress's authority to enact antidiscrimination legislation under the Commerce Clause, the time has come to examine thoroughly, at long last, a question that the Court has now rendered inescapable: the extent of Congress's power to enact antidiscrimination legislation under Section 5 of the Fourteenth Amendment.

* * * This past Term represents the first time since Reconstruction that the Court has declared that Congress lacked power to enact legislation prohibiting discrimination. Yet the impact of last Term's decisions is still not clear. The decisions are rife with ambiguity. After *Kimel*, for example, it is uncertain whether and to what extent Congress can exercise its power under Section 5 to redress forms of discrimination that differ from those that courts prohibit in cases arising under Section 1 of the Fourteenth Amendment. It is equally unclear after *Morrison* whether and to what extent antidiscrimination legislation enacted under Section 5 can regulate the conduct of private actors. Depending upon how *Kimel* and *Morrison* are interpreted in subsequent decisions, the Court's Section 5 jurisprudence could develop in quite different directions.

* * *

In the aftermath of *Brown*, the Court invited Congress's participation in vindicating equality norms, both because Congress could secure popular acceptance of the Court's decisions interpreting the Equal Protection Clause and because the representative branches of government were an important resource for the Court as it struggled to learn from and speak to the American people about the meaning of the Fourteenth Amendment's guarantee of "equal protection of the laws." In this era, the Court established a relationship with Congress that was fluid and dynamic, and that could not be adequately comprehended by mechanical criteria like "congruence and proportionality." This institutional relationship enabled the Court to interpret the Equal Protection Clause in a manner that was attentive to evolving and contested social norms. The framework of the Court's recent Section 5 decisions represents a fundamental break with the forms of interaction that the Warren and Burger Courts cultivated with Congress in this formative period of the modern antidiscrimination tradition.

At stake in the framework of analysis advanced by *Kimel* and *Morrison*, therefore, is the survival of the very institutional ecology in which legal and social understandings of equality have provoked, inspired, and shaped each other over the last four decades. Yet at no point in last Term's cases did the Court identify or weigh the potential costs of disrupting this ecology, which its newfound interest in limiting the ways that Congress may enforce the Equal Protection Clause threatens to do. Restricting the participation of the representative branches in enforcing the Equal Protection Clause does not necessarily enhance the authority of the Court or the Constitution and, we argue, may ultimately diminish the authority of both.

* * *

The history of federal antidiscrimination law in the twentieth century features two momentous events. The first is *Brown v. Board of*

Education, when the Supreme Court breathed new life into Section 1 of the Fourteenth Amendment. The second is the passage of the Civil Rights Act of 1964, the first major federal antidiscrimination legislation enacted since 1875. In debating and drafting the 1964 Act, Congress invoked its power under both the Commerce Clause and Section 5 of the Fourteenth Amendment. But when the Supreme Court came to determine the Act's constitutionality in *Heart of Atlanta Motel v. United States*, it shied away from a confrontation with its own Section 5 precedents, which dated from the first Reconstruction, and chose instead to build on the case law of the New Deal settlement, which ceded very broad powers to Congress to legislate under the Commerce Clause. It translated the question of congressional authority into the relatively simple issue of whether "Congress had a rational basis for finding that racial discrimination . . . affected commerce."

The decision fixed a fateful pattern. While Congress, in what might be called a second Reconstruction, continued to invoke its powers to enact antidiscrimination legislation under Section 5 of the Fourteenth Amendment, *Heart of Atlanta* set a precedent that invited judicial ratification of this legislation on alternative grounds, most notably on the basis of the Commerce Clause. This pattern persisted during the ensuing years, progressively obscuring the relationship of federal antidiscrimination legislation to Section 5, even as Congress and the Court continued to reason about antidiscrimination legislation as enforcing the equality values of the Fourteenth Amendment. * * *

Recently, however, three lines of decision have combined to disturb this arrangement. First, the Court has signaled its intention to abrogate the New Deal settlement and reassert judicial control over the scope of Commerce Clause power. In *United States v. Lopez*, [514 U.S. 549 (1995)] the Court struck down the Gun-Free School Zones Act of 1990 as exceeding Congress's authority to regulate interstate commerce. [The authors here describe *Morrison*.] * * *

* * *

* * * The Court's recent limitations on Congress's powers under the Commerce Clause thus focus renewed attention on Section 5 as an alternative source of constitutional authority, one adequate to the task of combating discrimination in whatever social forms or settings it happens to manifest itself.

This reinvigorated focus on Section 5 has been intensified by a second line of recent decisions. In its 1996 opinion in *Seminole Tribe v. Florida*, [517 U.S. 44 (1996)] the Court held that congressional legislation enacted pursuant to Article I powers, such as the Commerce Clause, cannot abrogate the Eleventh Amendment immunity of states, which "prevents congressional authorization of suits by private parties against unconsenting States" in federal courts. Two years later, in *Alden v. Maine*, [527 U.S. 706 (1999)] the Court held that this immunity also prohibited the federal government from subjecting "nonconsenting States to private suits for damages in state courts."

The contours of Eleventh Amendment immunity are extremely complex, but suffice it to say that the Amendment bars suits by private parties that seek money or damages "resulting from a past breach of a legal duty." Since large stretches of federal law are ordinarily enforced by exactly such suits, it is fair to conclude that the "net result" of *Seminole Tribe* and *Alden* will be "that Congress may regulate the states, but in the end will lack the practical tools necessary to do so with maximum effectiveness." This would certainly be true of most federal antidiscrimination law, which is normally enforced by private suits against the states. In fact, federal antidiscrimination law that cannot be sustained as an exercise of Section 5 power will probably be enforced against the states primarily through the cumbersome and unwieldy interventions of federal agencies.

Eleventh Amendment immunity, however, can be abrogated by legislation enacted "pursuant to Congress's § 5 power." The upshot is that the scope of Section 5 power has now become the measure of what federal antidiscrimination legislation may effectively be applied to the states. The Court's evasion in *Heart of Atlanta* has thus come home to roost. In the past thirty years, Congress has exercised its commerce authority to develop a rich and complex jurisprudence of federal antidiscrimination legislation, which is in many of its particulars in tension with judicial enforcement of Section 1 of the Fourteenth Amendment. The question of whether this law may properly be applied to the states will depend upon how the Court chooses to conceptualize the relationship between Section 5 and Section 1.

Much is at stake in this issue. So, for example, the Court has interpreted Section 1 to require a showing of "discriminatory purpose" as a prerequisite for a judicial finding of constitutional invalidity, yet a violation of Title VII can be established merely upon a showing of "disparate impact." In order to uphold the application of the disparate impact standard of Title VII to a state, the Eleventh Circuit recently felt itself obliged to reconcile these two standards by concluding that "although the form of the disparate impact inquiry differs from that used in a case challenging state action directly under the Fourteenth Amendment, the core injury targeted by both methods of analysis remains the same: intentional discrimination."

If the conclusion of the Eleventh Circuit were taken seriously, it would suggest a fundamental reworking of an important area of Title VII jurisprudence. We might then imagine Title VII divided between those standards suitable for application to states, because duplicative of judicial practice under Section 1, and those standards suitable for application to private parties, because developed under the aegis of the Commerce Clause. Or we might imagine an incremental judicial reworking of the body of Title VII law so as to bring it into line with the constricted set of standards constitutionally applicable to states. Neither alternative is attractive. They can be avoided, however, only if we are able to distinguish congressional power under Section 5 from judicially enforceable standards under Section 1.

But it is just this possibility that appears to be threatened by the Court's newly developing case law on the scope of Congress's powers under the enforcement clause of the Fourteenth Amendment. We are referring, of course, to a third line of decisions, initiated by the Court's 1997 decision in *City of Boerne v. Flores*, [521 U.S. 507 (1997)] holding that the Religious Freedom Restoration Act of 1993 (RFRA) was not a constitutional exercise of Section 5 power. *Boerne* was the first significant decision explicitly to address the scope of Section 5 in almost twenty years.

Congress enacted RFRA "in direct response" to the Court's decision in *Employment Division v. Smith*, [494 U.S. 872 (1990)] which had sharply constricted the approach of *Sherbert v. Verner* [374 U.S. 398 (1963)] by holding that constitutional rights of free exercise of religion would not, for the most part, be violated by neutral, generally applicable regulations of conduct. Congress disagreed and passed RFRA "to restore the compelling interest test as set forth in *Sherbert v. Verner* ... and to guarantee its application in all cases where free exercise of religion is substantially burdened." RFRA was justified as an exercise of Congress's Section 5 power "to enforce" First Amendment free exercise rights as incorporated in the Due Process Clause of Section 1 of the Fourteenth Amendment.

In *Boerne*, the Court declared that Congress lacked power under Section 5 to enact RFRA. It began its analysis by observing "that § 5 is 'a positive grant of legislative power' to Congress" and that its "scope" was therefore to be interpreted in "broad terms." Reaffirming *Katzenbach v. Morgan*, [384 U.S. 641,] the Court stated that "[i]t is for Congress in the first instance to 'determin[e] whether and what legislation is needed to secure the guarantees of the Fourteenth Amendment,' and its conclusions are entitled to much deference." But the Court then distinguished between the power "to enforce" the provisions of the Fourteenth Amendment and "the power to determine what constitutes a constitutional violation." It held that Section 5 authorized the former, but not the latter:

> Congress's power under § 5 ... extends only to "enforc[ing]" the provisions of the Fourteenth Amendment. The Court has described this power as "remedial[.]" The design of the Amendment and the text of § 5 are inconsistent with the suggestion that Congress has the power to decree the substance of the Fourteenth Amendment's restrictions on the States. Legislation which alters the meaning of the Free Exercise Clause cannot be said to be enforcing the Clause. Congress does not enforce a constitutional right by changing what the right is.

The Court initially argued that maintaining the distinction between the power to remedy constitutional violations and the power to determine the nature of constitutional rights was necessary in order to preserve the supremacy of the Constitution. "If Congress could define its own powers by altering the Fourteenth Amendment's meaning, no longer would the Constitution be 'superior paramount law, unchangeable by ordinary means.' It would be 'on a level with ordinary legislative acts, and, like other acts, ... alterable when the legislature shall please to alter it.' "

But because the Constitution remains "superior, paramount law" whether interpreted by the Court or by Congress, so long as either institution chooses to regard it as such, what really seems to be at stake for the Court in the distinction between remedial and substantive legislation is the preservation of judicial control over the ultimate meaning of the Constitution, at least in the context of cases properly litigated before the Court. In *Boerne*, the Court was plainly provoked by Congress's openly expressed purpose to nullify the Court's own interpretation of the First Amendment in *Smith*. RFRA posed a direct challenge to the Court's interpretation of the Free Exercise Clause, a challenge that the Court was determined to resist:

> When the Court has interpreted the Constitution, it has acted within the province of the Judicial Branch, which embraces the duty to say what the law is.... When the political branches of the Government act against the background of a judicial interpretation of the Constitution already issued, it must be understood that in later cases and controversies the Court will treat its precedents with the respect due them under settled principles, including *stare decisis*, and contrary expectations must be disappointed.... [I]t is this Court's precedent, not RFRA, which must control.

Boerne thus reasserts the basic precept of *Marbury*: In the last instance, it is for "the Judicial Branch ... to say what the law is."

Boerne frankly concedes that "the line between measures that remedy or prevent unconstitutional actions and measures that make a substantive change in the governing law is not easy to discern, and [that] Congress must have wide latitude in determining where it lies." But in a context in which "common sense" suggested that RFRA was "a congressional effort to overrule the Supreme Court on a point of constitutional interpretation," the Court insisted that the line "exists and must be observed."

To ensure that Congress would not exceed its legitimate powers under the Fourteenth Amendment, *Boerne* proposed that the line be discerned by a test of "congruence and proportionality between the injury to be prevented or remedied and the means adopted to that end. Lacking such a connection, legislation may become substantive in operation and effect." The Court concluded that:

> RFRA cannot be considered remedial, preventive legislation, if those terms are to have any meaning. RFRA is so out of proportion to a supposed remedial or preventive object that it cannot be understood as responsive to, or designed to prevent, unconstitutional behavior. It appears, instead, to attempt a substantive change in constitutional protections.

The Court's new interest in constraining Section 5 power, when considered in light of the developments in Commerce Clause and Eleventh Amendment jurisprudence we have just discussed, raises disconcerting questions for the future of federal antidiscrimination law. Limitations on Commerce Clause power, imposed in the name of federalism by *Lopez* and *Seminole Tribe*, have reemphasized the importance of congressional Section 5 power, while *Boerne* has simultaneously imposed a new and uncertain restriction on the nature of that power. When the 1999 Term began, the Court had not yet applied either its resurgent federalism or its intensified solicitude for separation of powers to federal antidiscrimination legislation. But this restraint ended in January 2000, when *Kimel* held that Congress was without power under Section 5 to enact the Age Discrimination in Employment Act of 1967 (ADEA). Five months later, *Morrison* held that Congress was without power under either the Commerce Clause or Section 5 to create in VAWA a civil cause of action for victims of gender-motivated violence.

It is in fact quite difficult to ascertain the scope and grounds of *Morrison*'s Fourteenth Amendment holding. The Court begins its analysis by acknowledging that Congress had exercised its power to enforce the Fourteenth Amendment on the basis of a "voluminous ... record" establishing "that many participants in state justice systems are perpetuating an array of erroneous stereotypes and assumptions" that "often result in insufficient investigation and prosecution of gender-motivated crime, inappropriate focus on the behavior and credibility of the victims of that crime, and unacceptably lenient punishments for those who are actually convicted of gender-motivated violence." The Court concedes that such "state-sponsored gender discrimination" might very well violate the Equal Protection Clause, but it notes that there are "certain limitations on the manner in which Congress may attack discriminatory conduct," limitations that "are necessary to prevent the Fourteenth Amendment from obliterating the Framers' carefully crafted balance of power between the States and the National Government." The Court mentions the "state action" requirement of Section 1 as "[f]oremost among these limitations."

The Court then cites *United States v. Harris* and the *Civil Rights Cases*, two 1883 decisions striking down Reconstruction-era legislation as beyond Congress's Section 5 power, for the proposition that Section 5 legislation cannot be " 'directed exclusively against the action of private persons, without reference to the laws of the State, or their administration by her officers.' " Claiming to yield to "[the] force of the doctrine of *stare decisis* behind these decisions," the Court refuses to let "dicta" in either *United States v. Guest* or *District of Columbia v. Carter* interfere with its view that Congress cannot "under § 5 prohibit actions by private individuals."

The Court's reasoning is very difficult to follow. It seems to conflate the state action requirement of Section 1 with some form of limitation on Section 5 power. There may in fact be questions after *Boerne* about what kind of state action is necessary in order to establish a violation of the Equal Protection Clause for purposes of Section 5 legislation, but in *Morrison* the Court explicitly acknowledges that Congress had extensively documented unconstitutional state action in the discriminatory response of state criminal justice systems to gender-motivated violence. *Morrison* therefore goes beyond a separation-of-powers analysis to intimate that even properly "remedial" Section 5 legislation cannot "prohibit actions by private individuals." It claims to derive this limitation on Section 5 power from *Harris* and the *Civil Rights Cases*.

But these precedents do not support this conclusion. The *Civil Rights Cases* have long been read as standing for the proposition that state action is prerequisite for constitutional violations of the Equal Protection Clause. In both *Harris* and the *Civil Rights Cases*, the Court struck down legislation that prescribed "rules for the conduct of individuals in society toward each other" without being "corrective of any constitutional wrong committed by the States." The *Civil Rights Cases*, which invalidated the Civil Rights Act of 1875, specifically held that the Act was not "predicated" on "any supposed or apprehended violation of the Fourteenth Amendment on the part of the States." It explained:

> [U]ntil some State law has been passed, or some State action through its officers or agents has been taken, adverse to the rights of citizens sought to be protected by the Fourteenth Amendment, no legislation of the United States under said amendment, nor any proceeding under such legislation, can be called into activity.

Although both *Harris* and the *Civil Rights Cases* insist that Section 5 legislation must be "corrective of [a] constitutional wrong committed by the States," neither opinion purports to impose a restriction on Section 5 legislation that is otherwise properly remedial. They are each fully consistent with federal regulation of private parties, so long as that regulation is properly "corrective," which is to say "adapted to counteract and redress the operation of . . . prohibited State laws or proceedings of State officers." As the Court made plain: "It is not necessary for us to state, if we could, what legislation would be proper for Congress to adopt. It is sufficient for us to examine whether the law in question is [corrective in] character."

Perhaps apprehensive about leaning so heavily on stare decisis in the context of largely irrelevant precedents, *Morrison* then proceeds to argue that "even if" its conclusion were not compelled by *Harris* or the *Civil Rights Cases*, VAWA's civil remedy would be impermissible under Section 5 because it fails the congruence and proportionality test of *Boerne*. Section 13981 "is directed not at any State or state actor, but at individuals who have committed criminal acts motivated by gender bias." Furthermore, § 13981 "applies uniformly throughout the Nation," whereas "Congress' findings indicate that the problem of discrimination against the victims of gender-motivated crimes does not exist in all States, or even most States."

But this section of the Court's opinion is also unclear, for *Morrison*'s use of the congruence and proportionality test is conceptually quite different from *Boerne*'s. *Boerne* explicitly employed the congruence and proportionality test to determine whether "the goal" of Section 5 legislation was "to prevent and remedy constitutional violations" or instead to redefine the nature of constitutional obligations. *Kimel* employed the test for the same purpose. The Court in *Morrison*, however, applies the test on the assumption that Congress's "goal" in enacting § 13981 is to counteract bona fide violations of the Equal Protection Clause, violations inhering in the discriminatory actions of state criminal justice systems. *Morrison* thus employs the congruence and proportionality test to impose limitations on Section 5 legislation that both *Boerne* and *Kimel* would deem properly remedial.

Boerne and *Kimel* each begin with the premise "that § 5 is 'a positive grant of legislative power' to Congress," and that it is therefore "for Congress in the first instance to 'determin[e] whether and what legislation is needed to secure the guarantees of the Fourteenth Amendment,' and its conclusions are entitled to much deference." Yet *Morrison* uses the congruence and proportionality test to fasten tight restrictions on the exercise of otherwise legitimate Section 5 legislation, restrictions that seem analogous to the narrow tailoring required by strict scrutiny. We know of no other positive constitutional grant of power to Congress that is treated with such suspicion and hostility by the Court. The general rule is quite otherwise. Congressional enactments within the domain of positive constitutional grants of power are normally treated with a "deference" that reflects a "presumption of constitutionality."

* * *

In point of fact, the Court never pauses to explain what it finds so very alarming in Congress's use of Section 5 power to create a civil cause of action for victims of gender-motivated violence. The closest it comes is by referring to the constitutional function of the state action requirement of Section 1, which the Court notes is "necessary to prevent the Fourteenth Amendment from obliterating the Framers' carefully crafted balance of power between the States and the National Government." This theme of federalism is reinforced by *Morrison*'s unusual tribute to the "force of the doctrine of stare decisis" carried by the Court's 1883 decisions in *Harris* and the *Civil Rights Cases*. In these decisions of the first Reconstruction, the Court was centrally concerned with interpreting the Fourteenth Amendment to prevent Congress from adopting "general legislation upon the rights of the citizen," limiting the scope of Section 5 instead to "corrective legislation, that is, such as may be necessary and proper for counteracting . . . such acts and proceedings as the States may commit or take, and which, by the [fourteenth] amendment, they are prohibited from committing or taking." The *Civil Rights Cases* held that Congress could not "establish a code of municipal law regulative of all private rights between man and man in society," for that "would be to make Congress take the place of the State legislatures and to supersede them." Constitutional concern about preserving the "distinction between what is truly national and what is truly local" is of course also a central theme in *Morrison*'s account of why § 13981 cannot be justified under Congress's Commerce Clause power.

It is federalism, then, that drives *Morrison*'s dismissive treatment of congressional Section 5 power. Having worked so hard in the first section of its opinion to preserve the regulation of violence in domestic relations from the reach of national Commerce Clause power, the Court in *Morrison* was not about to turn around and let federal authority return through the back door of Section 5. This raises the question, however, of whether federalism constraints imposed on Section 5 should be construed *in pari materia* with those imposed on the Commerce Clause. As we have discussed, there is every reason to reject this supposition, because Section 5 has its own particular purposes and priorities that differ from the "commercial concerns that are central to the Commerce Clause."

The relationship between national and state governments in our federal system is not static. One cannot simply extract an account of the national government's powers from cases decided in 1883 and mechanically apply it to a federal civil rights statute enacted more than one hundred years later. As our Commerce Clause jurisprudence so richly illustrates, the practical implications of our federalism commitments change over time, because federalism itself is a dynamic system, expressed in institutional relationships that evolve in history. So, for example, the economic upheavals of the Great Depression fundamentally altered our "practical conception" of the necessity of national economic regulation "in this interdependent world of ours." Although the Court initially and infamously resisted the implications of these altered understandings, it eventually changed its constitutional conception of the scope and range of Congress's power to regulate commerce. Today, the employment relationship, which the Court once confidently declared beyond Congress's power to regulate, now appears to us as quintessentially a sphere of "national" regulatory concern.

The same historically and institutionally attentive approach ought to inform any serious effort to understand the questions of federalism presented by Congress's Section 5 power to enact antidiscrimination legislation. Just as our understanding of federal economic regulatory power has changed dramatically since 1883, so has our understanding of federal civil rights authority. The Court, however, invokes *Harris* and the *Civil Rights Cases* as definitive accounts of how federalism ought to restrict national efforts to protect civil rights, without pausing to inquire whether any intervening historical developments might have qualified the descriptive or prescriptive understandings on which these nineteenth-century decisions are premised. The Court's assumption that national authority to enforce civil rights has remained unaltered since the nineteenth century is all the more remarkable given the dramatic changes in our understanding of the Equal Protection Clause. One would think that a Court that has enshrined Justice Harlan's dissent in *Plessy* might at least pause before invoking the *Civil Rights Cases* as an authoritative account of federal power to regulate discrimination, given that Justice Harlan dissented just as passionately from the Court's judgment in the *Civil Rights Cases* as he did from the notorious ruling of *Plessy*.

One cannot reason about the scope of the national government's authority to enforce civil rights without addressing the history of the second Reconstruction, which profoundly altered the federal government's role in combating discrimination. That history is now institutionalized in judicial precedents, congressional enactments, and executive agencies. It has been incorporated into the common sense and experience of the country. * * *

* * *

By the end of the 1960s, in short, the landscape of federalism had been fundamentally altered. Social activism had forced the question of discrimination by private actors to the top of the national agenda, and Congress had responded with major legislation to address the problem. This legislation was ratified by the Court, whether based upon the Commerce Clause, the Thirteenth Amendment, or the spending power. One way or the other, what would have been unimaginable in prior decades had come to pass: The struggle against discrimination by private actors had become a legitimate end of the federal government.

* * *

Although we cannot understand the full range of concerns that led the Court to rely on the Commerce Clause and Section 2 of the Thirteenth Amendment to vindicate Congress's power to enact antidiscrimination legislation during the 1960s—while reserving decision about the scope of Congress's powers under Section 5 of the Fourteenth Amendment—this lingering question should not obscure what is perfectly clear about the Court's commitment during the 1960s. Through a combination of interpretive stratagems, the Court decisively freed federal antidiscrimination legislation from the state action requirement it preserved for its own Section 1 cases. It encouraged Congress to decide when and how the federal government would enforce antidiscrimination norms against private actors—authority Congress exercised in enacting the violence and housing provisions of the 1968 Civil Rights Act. The Court's deference to Congress helped to consolidate a new consensus about the federal government's role in enforcing civil rights. By the end of the decade, Congress, the Court, and the American people all expected the federal government to lead the fight against discrimination in the public and private sectors. This is the momentous fact that *Morrison* ignores by citing the *Civil Rights Cases* as an authoritative account of the meaning of federalism in the context of federal antidiscrimination legislation.

No doubt the Court has the raw power to deny this historical transformation by seeking to revive older notions of federalism. Federalism is, as we have said, a dynamic system, and since the days of the second Reconstruction there has certainly been a renewed interest in restricting the power of the federal government. But the decisive question raised by *Morrison*'s appeal to federalism is whether the nation has retreated from the view that a central mission of the federal government is to protect individuals against discrimination by public and private actors.

* * *

A test of congruence and proportionality would mandate case-by-case inquiry into the question of whether Section 5 power may be used to regulate the conduct of private actors. Rather than defining a distinct sphere of private action that must remain free from federal regulation, the test would focus judicial attention on whether federal regulation is an appropriate means of redressing particular Section 1 violations that Congress is otherwise authorized to remedy. This use of the congruence and proportionality test would be distinct from *Kimel*'s deployment of the test, because its purpose would not be to ensure that Section 5 legislation is remedial. Its purpose would instead be to protect the values of federalism by restricting undue federal interference with states and private actors. The question of what federal interference should be regarded as "undue" would depend upon two questions: the precise values of federalism the test is designed to safeguard, and the Court's apprehension of the proper role of the federal government in remedying unconstitutional discrimination. *Morrison*, however, does not discuss either question.

* * *

Morrison was apparently unwilling explicitly to challenge this consensus understanding. It refused to acknowledge, much less to criticize, the role the federal government has played in remedying discrimination during the last half of the twentieth century. The opinion offered no plausible alternative account of the proper role of the federal government in enforcing civil rights. It did not argue, for example, that the consensus of the 1960s concerned only the role of the federal government in redressing racial discrimination, rather than protecting broader norms of equality. It did not even claim that this consensus extended only to the specific forms of discrimination prohibited by the Civil Rights Act of 1964. Any such view of our national commitments would be highly controversial, of course, but at least it would articulate the actual set of national equality values that the Court was prepared to permit Congress to implement pursuant to Section 5. Without such an explanation, *Morrison*'s deployment of the congruence and proportionality test can only be arbitrary.

* * *

The dangers of the Court's new juricentric approach to Section 5 are abundantly illustrated by the *Morrison* opinion. *Morrison* concludes its account of why VAWA's civil rights remedy is unconstitutional with an ominously ambiguous observation. Summarizing its case for invalidating the statute, the Court remarks that if the facts concerning the "brutal assault" alleged in the case "are true, no civilized system of justice could fail to provide [the petitioner, Christy Brzonkala,] a remedy for the conduct of respondent Morrison. But under our federal system that remedy must be provided by the Commonwealth of Virginia, and not by the United States."

Is the Court saying that Virginia *will* provide Christy Brzonkala a remedy if the facts she alleges are true, or merely that it *should*? It is telling that we cannot discern the answer to this question from the opinion the Court writes striking down the statute Congress enacted in an effort to ensure that Christy Brzonkala *would* have a remedy if she proved the brutal assault she alleged.

That this question remains unanswerable at the end of the *Morrison* opinion, even after several readings, reveals something very important about the way the Court decided the case. *Morrison* declares unconstitutional Congress's efforts to remedy gender bias in the criminal justice system without demonstrating that the Court understood the constitutional concerns that moved Congress to enact the statute in the first instance.

The *Morrison* opinion recounts, with citations to the record, Congress's rationale for enacting the civil rights remedy. It reports that the "§ 5 argument is founded on an assertion that there is pervasive bias in various state justice systems against victims of gender-motivated violence." It accepts that "[t]his assertion is supported by a voluminous congressional record," noting that "Congress received evidence that many participants in state justice systems are perpetuating an array of erroneous stereotypes and assumptions." The Court acknowledges that Congress "concluded that these discriminatory stereotypes often result in insufficient investigation and prosecution of gender-motivated crime, inappropriate focus on the behavior and credibility of the victims of that crime, and unacceptably lenient punishments for those who are actually convicted of gender-motivated violence."

But if the Court recites Congress's rationale for enacting § 13981, it evinces no interest in remedying the constitutional wrong that Congress identified. Instead, the Court announces that "the language and purpose of the Fourteenth Amendment place certain limitations on the manner in which Congress may attack discriminatory conduct" even if "there has been gender-based disparate treatment by state authorities." What, then, do we make of the Court's capacity (1) to recount Congress's findings of gender bias in state administration of the criminal law; (2) to invalidate VAWA's civil rights remedy; and then, in the face of these findings, (3) to send Christy Brzonkala back to Virginia for the remedy that "no civilized system of justice could fail to provide her" if the facts of the "brutal assault" she alleges are true? Does the Court not credit the evidence of pervasive gender bias in state criminal justice systems that Congress gathered? Or does the Court simply not judge this gender bias to be of constitutional moment?

The Court sees questions of constitutional significance in Congress's decision to supply Brzonkala a federal forum so that her claim will be heard even if state fora are infected by gender bias. But it appears not to see a question of constitutional importance in the possibility that gender bias in state fora might leave a victim of a "brutal assault" without a remedy. At root, the Court seems to be denying that such gender bias is a problem in the United States, which, we are to presume, the Court considers to have a "civilized system of justice."

This refusal to entertain the possibility of systemic constitutional wrong informs and organizes the whole of the *Morrison* opinion, from its insistence on treating VAWA's civil rights remedy as a species of domestic relations or criminal law in its discussion of congressional commerce power, to its elevation of federalism over gender equality values in its treatment of congressional Section 5 power. The Court undertakes to pronounce on the constitutionality of VAWA's civil rights remedy without truly grappling with the systemic nature and breadth of the constitutional violation that Congress was undertaking to remedy.

To have faced this question openly would have been to acknowledge the civil rights remedy, not as a species of family or criminal law, but as an antidiscrimination statute with deep roots in the Court's own Section 1 jurisprudence. This *Morrison* never does. Section 13981 grows directly out of the Court's own sex discrimination jurisprudence, taking its normative ends from the strengths of that jurisprudence and its practical urgency from its weaknesses. Yet throughout *Morrison* the Court never acknowledges the relationship of this Section 5 statute to the Court's own Section 1 case law.

What then explains the Court's cavalier treatment of the constitutional concerns that moved Congress to enact the civil rights remedy? *Morrison* betrays the Court's conviction that, at least where matters of equal protection are concerned, the Court has little to learn from Congress. The Court brusquely denies Congress's Section 5 power to enact the civil rights remedy, without cultivating even the appearance of a respectful working relationship with the institution that is equally responsible under the Fourteenth Amendment for enforcing the "provisions of this article." In explaining its decision, the Court mentions, but does not discuss, the voluminous record compiled during years of hearings and debates in which Congress gathered evidence of gender bias in the criminal justice system and discussed how it should be remedied. The Court does not treat the innovative features of VAWA's civil rights remedy as meriting careful consideration, but instead as prima facie reasons for the statute's invalidation.

At root, the Court seems to view the enforcement of the Equal Protection Clause as primarily a matter for the judiciary, treating Congress's efforts to implement the Clause as superfluous or even suspect. This juricentric approach to enforcing the Equal Protection Clause carries with it the risk of institutional insularity, and *Morrison* well exemplifies this danger. The gender conventionalism of the Court's reasoning about federalism is striking, as is the Court's failure to evince any appreciation of why Congress had concluded that the criminal justice system's traditional methods of handling violence against women presented grave problems of sex discrimination. In the hearings and debates leading up to the enactment of VAWA, citizens and their congressional representatives repeatedly asserted that the failures of the criminal justice system to protect women from assault betrayed the nation's commitment to equal citizenship for women. *Morrison* simply ignores these claims. The contrast with the manner in which the Court in the 1970s attended to and learned from congressional understandings of the harm of sex discrimination, understandings that differed from the Court's own decisions, could not be sharper.

The abstract criteria of the *Boerne* test invite courts to dismiss Section 5 antidiscrimination legislation with the same spirit of unsympathetic insularity that characterizes *Morrison*. The test of congruence and proportionality flattens and effaces the myriad subtle and complex ways that Congress has participated in the development of our modern equal protection tradition. The mechanical application of the test to Section 5 legislation promises to stunt the ability of Congress to participate in the future development of that tradition. Applied without an appreciation of the actual evolution of modern equal protection jurisprudence, the *Boerne* test could easily invalidate large stretches of federal antidiscrimination law and suppress the lively relationship between Congress and the courts that has in the past animated our vision of what equal protection demands.

And that, for reasons we have tried to explain, threatens forms of institutional dialogue within which Americans have attempted to work out the meanings of national citizenship during the past half century.

Notes and Questions

1. Should issues involving discrimination be the province of the federal government? What are the potential advantages and disadvantages of being part of a strong federal government from the perspective of local efforts aimed at forging social justice?

2. Are Post and Siegel correct in concluding that the court's decision is steeped in "gender conventionalism"? If so, what role could a social justice litigator play in presenting this argument to the same court? What strategies would you employ in carrying out this role?

3. Should social justice advocates seek to use the spending power as a way to encourage federal regulation in light of limits set by recent interpretations of the commerce clause, sovereign immunity, and Section 5 of the Fourteenth Amendment? Sylvia Law has commented:

> Even though the Court has sharply constrained the power of Congress to act under the Commerce Clause and under Section 5 of the Fourteenth Amendment, many of the goals Congress seeks to achieve may still be pursued through the federal spending power, if such goals are carefully cast as conditions on federal funding. *South Dakota v. Dole*, 483 U.S. 203 (1987), upheld a federal program withholding a percentage of otherwise available federal highway

funds from states that failed to adopt a twenty-one year-old minimum drinking age, even though the regulation of alcohol is assigned to the states under the Twenty-first Amendment. The Court suggested that the spending power is subject to four restrictions. First, "the exercise of the spending power must be in pursuit of 'the general welfare.' " Second, if Congress conditions the states' receipt of Federal funds, it "must do so unambiguously . . . , enabl[ing] the States to exercise their choice knowingly, cognizant of the consequences of their participation." Third, the conditions on federal grants must be related "to the federal interest in particular national projects or programs." Finally, conditions on spending may not violate other substantive constitutional norms. The *Dole* Court also acknowledged that financial inducements offered by Congress may be "so coercive as to pass the point at which 'pressure turns into compulsion.' "

The eight hundred pound gorilla in the room is whether the Court will interpret the Constitution to restrict the power of Congress to act under the spending power. For now, at least, the Court has not done so. Professor Laurence H. Tribe suggests that "the scope of the spending power would seem to extend to virtually any secular activity." * * * *But see* Lynn A. Baker, *Conditional Federal Spending After* Lopez, 95 Colum. L. Rev.1911, 1916 (1995) (arguing that the spending clause power should be re-interpreted to prohibit "conditional offers of federal funds in order to regulate the states in ways [Congress] could not directly mandate"); Ann Laquer Estin, *Federalism and Child Support*, 5 Va. J. Soc. Pol'y & L. 541, 595 (1998) (arguing that Congress and the Supreme Court need to consider whether the allocation of family and policy-making authority away from states is a sensible choice).

Sylvia A. Law, *Families and Federalism*, 4 Wash. U. J. L. & Pol'y 175, 232–33 (2000).

Is Congressional action under the spending power an adequate response to the shrinking access to federal courts described in this section? What other strategies might be employed?

4. This chapter has described a trend away from access to federal courts for civil rights related claims. In this context consider the Indian Civil Rights Act (ICRA) of 1968, Pub. L. No. 90-284, Tit. II–VII, §§ 201–701, 82 Stat. 77 (codified as amended at 25 U.S.C. §§ 1301–1341 (1994)). Describing conflicting positive and negative visions of the tribal court system, one commentator characterized ICRA as "a complex compromise intended to guarantee that tribal governments respect civil rights while minimizing federal interference with tribal culture and tradition." Robert J. McCarthy, *Civil Rights in Tribal Courts: The Indian Bill of Rights at Thirty Years*, 34 Idaho L. Rev. 465, 467 (1998) (concluding "the cause of civil rights would be better served if greater resources were to be made available for advocacy in tribal courts" *id.* at 468).

Are Native-American litigants more likely to find social justice in tribal courts or in federal courts? For the view of the Honorable Chief Justice Emeritus of the Navajo Nation, see Tso, *supra.*

> Presently, there are massive violations of Indian rights in the United States. Individual Indians are the victims of hate crimes, and Indian nations are suffering at the hands of the United States Courts and Congress. Individual states are targeting Indian-nation authority over issues of gaming, taxation, hunting and fishing, economic development, land use regulation, and a wide range of other issues. The purpose of these attacks is to chip away at the inherent powers of Indian nations so that they will eventually have little political authority; except perhaps, to the extent of enrollment, member conduct, member-on-member crimes, or child welfare within the Indian nation.

Id. at 107.

5. 42 U.S.C. § 1983, enacted in 1871, provides in relevant part:

> Every person who, under color of any statute, ordinance, regulation, custom, or usage, of any State or Territory or the District of Columbia, subjects, or causes to be subjected, any citizen of the United States or other person within the jurisdiction thereof to the deprivation of any rights, privileges, or immunities secured by the Constitution and laws, shall be liable to the party injured in an action at law, suit in equity, or other proper proceeding for redress * * *.

Litigation under Section 1983, like efforts to utilize other Reformation Era enactments such as the equal protection and privileges and immunities clauses of the Fourteenth Amendment, was not initially very successful. *See, e.g.*, Brawner v. Irvin, 169 F. 964 (C.C. Georgia 1909) (Plaintiff, an African-American woman sued the police chief who whipped her in her front yard. Court denied her claim for federal relief as based on rights secured by state law.).

Thus, "Section 1983 litigation is a fairly recent phenomenon." Daniel J. McDonald, *A Primer on 42 U.S.C. § 1983*, 12 Utah Bar J. 29, 29 (1999). He continues:

> Before the landmark United States Supreme Court decision of *Monroe v. Pape* [365 U.S. 167] in 1961, "§ 1983 was remarkable for its insignificance." "Indeed, one commentator found only 21 suits brought under this provision in the years between 1871 and 1920." However, in *Monroe* the Court overturned a long-standing assumption that § 1983 reached only misconduct either officially authorized or so widely tolerated as to amount to a "custom or usage" of government by holding that § 1983 was "meant to give a remedy to parties deprived of constitutional rights, privileges and immunities by an official's abuse of his position." [365 U.S. at 172] Since *Monroe*, there has been a literal explosion of § 1983 litigation,

> ranging from suits brought by prisoners to land use cases brought by wealthy corporate developers.
>
> Section 1983 now encompasses any action taken "under color" of state or local law, even when the actor is not, himself, a state or local official. Additionally, deprivations of non-constitutional, federal law are also remediable under § 1983. However, with each expansion of § 1983 liability there has been concomitant contractions, including a host of immunities and procedural hurdles such as heightened pleading requirements. In the wake of these developments, a complicated and often counterintuitive patchwork of precedents has emerged under § 1983. This patchwork contains many traps for the unwary § 1983 litigant.

Id. at 29–30.

Some of the issues contested in the effort to use § 1983 to secure constitutional rights include: definition of the rights that can be vindicated, definition of who is subject to suit, immunity, pleading requirements and other procedural barriers, damages, and attorneys' fees. Section 1983 is also central in the federalism battle currently being waged in the Supreme Court. As Martin A. Schwartz explains:

> Section 1983 raises, if not always on the surface, certainly below the surface, federalism issues. Section 1983 is a federal congressional remedy authorizing claims for relief against state and local government. In a very high percentage of the cases, the Section 1983 battle takes place in the federal courts.

Martin A. Schwartz, *Supreme Court Section 1983 Developments: October 1998 Term*, 16 Touro L. Rev. 753, 753–54 (2000). Will § 1983 litigation be another frontier where access to federal courts is denied?

PART III

A SYSTEM OF POLITICS: LEGAL WORK AND SOCIAL CHANGE

The following chapters explore issues that arise when lawyers work toward community empowerment and transformation. Movements for transformation take place through the lives and work of people and communities for whom lawyers are at most a small part of the story. Therefore, an important question for lawyers working on social justice issues is how to carry out their professional work in ways that empower the people whose lives are involved.

Chapter 11 examines the consciousness about power and the self-awareness about the attorney's role that are both necessary to this work. Will the community's concerns, which may have many political and social aspects, be reframed around claims that can be taken to court? What will be gained and lost through such an approach? Will the lawyer become the spokesperson, the media figure, or the political adviser? Is the goal of legal work for social justice to win recognition of rights, such as passing a statute against discrimination, or is the ultimate goal a change in the culture and practice in a society that brings about greater equality for all? If far-reaching transformation is the goal, social justice lawyers need to discern when it is most effective to turn to courts to seek legal change and when their main role is to defend the ability of their clients to work for social and political change.

This part examines in depth three areas of lawyering for social justice that have seen both gains and setbacks. Chapter 12 considers the quest for racial equality and just urban development; chapter 13, the struggle for gay and lesbian liberation; and chapter 14, the movement against domestic violence. In all three areas, the questions facing social justice lawyers are not simply doctrinal, though they are sometimes fought in courts and through contests about legal rules. Rather, social justice lawyers find ways to work with people who are organizing for social change, reorganizing after defeats, and working to sustain victories.

What can lawyers do when systems of oppression are deeply interrelated and no single intervention can adequately address structural injustice? Residential segregation is the linchpin that perpetuates and strengthens racial inequality in jobs, schools, municipal services, and other areas of life. Educational inequality is so closely linked with residential segregation that intervention may seem an overwhelming challenge. How can lawyers, scholars, and activists raise demands that continue to focus broadly on racial injustice while building particular struggles? How can work with community activists give depth to those demands and mobilize residents in ways that strengthen their position locally as well as coordinating legal and political battles?

How can a longstanding form of oppression be rendered so socially and politically unacceptable that courts and legislatures become convinced they must act to end it? In the context of domestic violence, could it possibly be enough to win a legal decision stating that battering must be treated as a crime? Even if high damages for plaintiffs do persuade municipalities that they face liability if their police forces do not respond to domestic violence calls, what measures will be necessary to ensure that officers change their practices? If a lawsuit is settled, will the community be organized enough to know whether promises are being kept—and, if they are not kept, to respond appropriately?

What should be done when the courts, the legislatures, and the executive branches at the state and federal level are all hostile to new claims for social justice? Gay men and lesbians in the United States in the 1950s and 1960s faced this situation. What if each advance, such as a court decision mandating equality, brings a new round of reaction? Law and lawyers become *part* of a struggle for transformation, so that legal setbacks can be answered with political activism, and political setbacks, such as the repeal of an anti-discrimination ordinance, can be addressed through legal challenges.

Reva Siegel describes a process of "preservation-through-transformation" based on a review of changes in law in the nineteenth and twentieth centuries. In this period, the legal system responded to demands for the equality of women and the equality of African Americans with modifications that began to treat people as equal under law who had formerly appeared in law only in hierarchical relationships. Nonetheless, the legal changes did not eradicate "foundational status structures":

> In gender, race, and class relationships, the legal system continued to allocate privileges and entitlements in a manner that perpetuated former systems of express hierarchy. Analyzed from this vantage point, the rise of liberal and capitalist systems of social organization did not result in the dismantlement of status relationships, but instead precipitated their evolution into new forms.
>
> This process of transformation is well worth examining. In the middle decades of the nineteenth century, the American legal system sought, as it never had before, to repudiate bodies of law that for centuries had defined African Americans and white women as subordinate members of the polity. That this effort to disestablish entrenched bodies of status law was fitfully pursued, energetically resisted, and soon abandoned does not detract from its significance. For in this period of sweeping sociolegal change, we can examine the disestablishment dynamic as it actually unfolds in history. In the tug and haul of politics, the process of dismantling an entrenched system of status relations may well transform the regime without abolishing it.

Reva Siegel, *Why Equal Protection No Longer Protects: The Evolving Forms of Status-Enforcing State Action,* 49 Stan. L. Rev. 1111, 1116 (1997).

Knowing the contemporary manifestations of the processes described by Siegel, social justice lawyers and community activists work to make transformation mean more than mere legal reorganization. In chapters 12, 13, and 14, the phenomena of change, readjustment, and ongoing struggle are consistent themes. Consider what additional themes these movements have in common and what lessons can be drawn by lawyers who seek to make sure that systems of subordination are dismantled rather than reorganized.

*

Chapter 11

LAWYERS AND POLITICAL STRUGGLES TOWARD TRANSFORMATION

Lawyering for community empowerment and transformation, one aspect of social justice lawyering, involves consciousness about power and self-awareness as to the attorney's role. This chapter explores both the meaning of power consciousness in the context of legal practice and the role of the lawyer. Recall chapter 3 on social justice lawyering in context and chapter 5 concerning the lawyer-client relationship. Those chapters raised issues about the potential tensions between representing individuals and representing groups, which are reprised here. This chapter also presents examples of community empowerment practice. It concludes by examining the role of law and the social justice lawyer in relation to the possibility of societal transformation. *See* chapters 12–14 for examples of lawyers working with social movements and communities in the contemporary United States.

SECTION 1. CONSCIOUSNESS ABOUT POWER AS A GOAL OF LEGAL PRACTICE

In a classic article, Peter Gabel and Paul Harris reflect on the lawyer's role in empowering clients and causes. They urge that legal strategies beyond "rights consciousness" must necessarily be employed in a law practice seeking client empowerment. Recall that chapter 7 addressed the efficacy of rights claims. Does claiming legal rights undercut the goal of gaining consciousness about power?

PETER GABEL & PAUL HARRIS

Building Power and Breaking Images: Critical Legal Theory and the Practice of Law
11 N.Y.U. Rev. of L. & Soc. Change 369, 375–76, 379–81, 389–94, 405 (1982–83)

A first principle of a "counter-hegemonic" legal practice must be to subordinate the goal of getting people their rights to the goal of building an authentic or unalienated political consciousness. This obviously does not mean that one should not try to win one's cases; nor does it necessarily mean that we should not continue to organize groups by appealing to rights. * * *

A legal strategy that goes beyond rights-consciousness is one that focuses upon expanding political consciousness through using the legal system to increase people's sense of personal and political power. * * * [T]his can mean many different things depending upon the political visibility of any given case and the specific social and legal context within which a case arises. But in any context a "power" rather than a "rights" approach to law practice should be guided by three general objectives that are as applicable to minor personal injury cases as to major cases involving important social issues. First, the lawyer should seek to develop a relationship of genuine equality and mutual respect with her client. Second, the lawyer should conduct herself in a way that demystifies the symbolic authority of the State * * * . Third, the lawyer should always attempt to reshape the way legal conflicts are represented in the law, revealing the limiting character of legal ideology and bringing out the true socioeconomic and political foundations of legal disputes. Reaching these objectives may have a transformative impact not only upon the lawyer and client working in concert, but also upon others who come into contact with the case, including the client's friends and family, courtroom participants such as jurors, stenographers, and public observers, and, in some cases, thousands or even millions of people who follow high-visibility political cases through the media. Of course, any particular lawyer's actions in a single case cannot lead to the development of an anti-hierarchical social movement; we believe, however, that if lawyers as a group begin to organize themselves around the realization of these goals, their impact on the culture as a whole can be much greater than they currently believe is possible.

* * *

Although * * * all legal cases are potentially empowering, the classic political case remains one that receives widespread public attention because it emerges from a social conflict that has already achieved high visibility in the public consciousness. Examples of such cases in recent years include the political trials that arose out of the student and anti-war movements, and the many Supreme Court cases that have emerged from the civil rights and women's movements. Such cases contain unique possibilities and also difficulties for the lawyers and clients involved in them, because the aim is not only to win on the legal issues raised by the case, but to speak for the movement itself. Precisely because the State's objective is in part to defuse the political energy that has given rise to the case, the legal issue is often one that deflects attention from and even denies the political nature of the conflict.

Perhaps the clearest example of this "deflection" was the so-called "conspiracy" trial of the Chicago Eight, in which the issue as defined by the prosecutor was whether the defendants who had helped to organize the antiwar demonstrations outside the Democratic National Convention in 1968 had conspired to cross state lines with the intent to incite a riot. The political meaning of the demonstrations was to challenge the morality of the Vietnam War and the political process that served to justify it, but this meaning was, of course, legally irrelevant to the determination of whether the alleged conspiracy had taken place.

Using a case like this to increase the power of an existing political movement requires a systematic refusal to accept the limiting boundaries which the State seeks to impose on the conflict. Had the lawyers and clients in the Chicago Eight trial presented a legal defense in a normal professional way, they would have deferred to the authority of Judge Hoffman and politely tried to show, perhaps with success, that the defendants did not "intend" to incite a riot or did not "conspire" to cross state lines to do so. But the lawyers and clients understood very well that even a legal victory on these terms would have meant a political defeat for their movement. They understood that the prosecutor's real purpose was to channel the political struggle in the streets into an official public chamber, to recharacterize the protestors as hooligans, and to substitute a narrow and depoliticized legal description of the meaning of the Chicago events for their true meaning. In this context State power consists not so much in the use of direct force, but in the use of the sanctity of the legal process to recast the meaning of the disruption that took place.

In concert with their courageous clients, William Kunstler and Leonard Weinglass were able to reverse the government's strategy and cause it to backfire, seizing upon the media's coverage of the trial to strengthen the resistance that had begun in the streets. By openly flaunting the hierarchical norms of the courtroom and ridiculing the judge, the prosecutor, and the nature of the charges themselves, they successfully rejected the very forms of authority upon which the legitimacy of the war itself depended. As Judge Hoffman gradually lost the capacity to control "his" room, he was transformed on national television from a learned figure worthy of great respect into a vindictive old man wearing a funny black tunic. In the absence of an underlying popular movement, the tactic of showing continuous contempt for the proceedings might simply have been an unproductive form of "acting out." But within its concrete historical context, this tactic was the most effective way to affirm to millions of supporters following the trial that their version of the meaning of the Chicago protests was right and could not be eroded by the State's appeal to a mass belief in authoritarian imagery.

* * *

In 1971 the Latin community in San Francisco's Mission District was experiencing "brown power" and intense organizing by radical and liberal groups. The most effective radical organization was called "Los Siete" ("The Seven"), named after seven young men who had been acquitted of murdering a policeman after a long, contested trial. Los Siete ran a community clinic, organized a formidable labor caucus, pushed for community control of police, and published a community newspaper.

Los Siete's members were often harassed by police who operated out of the then infamous Mission police station. On a busy shopping day, two of Los Siete's most active members, a latin man and a black woman, were selling their newspaper *Basta Ya* on the sidewalk in front of the largest department store in the Mission. The store manager called the police. When the police arrived they berated the young man, called him "wetback" and told him to go back to Mexico. The police confiscated the papers and arrested both the man and the woman for trespass, obstructing the sidewalk, and resisting arrest.

There was no publicity of the arrest. The store owners saw the arrest as a vindication of their right of private property. The police viewed it as a demonstration of their power in the Mission district and a warning to community groups. The district attorney's office treated the case as a routine misdemeanor. The defendants felt the arrests had been an act of intimidation and racism. The woman was treated as a prostitute at the City Jail, examined for venereal disease and put in quarantine for two days while awaiting the results of the test. The excuse given for such treatment was that she had been charged with obstructing the sidewalk, an offense associated with prostitution.

Los Siete asked the Community Law Collective, a local law office which acted as "house counsel" to many community organizations, to defend their members and to help them develop a legal-political analysis of the case. The attorneys explained that although there was a first amendment issue present, it was doubtful that such a right could be vindicated at the lower court level. At trial, it would be the defendants' testimony against the testimony of two policemen, a security guard, and possibly the store manager. Even though the defendants had sold their newspapers on the sidewalk without harassing store customers, the State's witnesses would place them on store property obstructing customers, and the police would swear the latin man had pushed them and refused arrest. The jury would be almost all white and predisposed toward the State's witnesses. If the trial was before one of the few liberal municipal court judges, the defendants might receive thirty days in jail if convicted; if before one of the many conservatives, the sentence would probably be six months in jail. If, on the other hand, the defendants were to plead guilty, the district attorney would drop all the charges except trespass, and would offer a sixty-day suspended sentence.

If the lawyers had acted as apolitical professionals in this situation, they almost certainly would have advised their clients to plea bargain. First, it makes sense to accept probation in the face of a likely jail sentence. Second, preparation and trial would be quite time-consuming and remuneration would be small. But for the lawyers to have given such "normal" advice in this context would have made them mere extensions of the system. It is not in the interests of the State in this situation to send defendants to jail and risk an increase of organized anger in the community. Rather, the State's strategy is to break the spirit and limit the options of the community movement. It is the plea bargain which best accomplishes this purpose, by simultaneously vindicating the police, legitimating the store owner's property rights, and making community activists feel powerless and humiliated. Moreover, in offering defendants a six-month suspended sentence, the State is also offering them a two-year probation period, the obvious effect of which is to inhibit any future activism. In this context the plea bargain becomes the iron fist in the velvet glove, and the defense lawyer who passively participates in arranging such an outcome becomes partly responsible for its consequences.

Understanding the dangers of "copping a plea," the lawyers and clients attempted to define what was really at issue and to explore a radical approach to the case. The issue was the exercise of political power, in the form of selling *Basta Ya* on the streets of the Mission community. Selling the newspaper served three purposes. First, the person-to-person contact was an effective organizing tool for Los Siete, helping them to build support for their community programs. Second, the street-corner sales were the primary means of distributing the paper and therefore of getting the information in the paper out to the community. Third, the very act of selling their paper in the streets of the Mission district made the activists feel some power in the face of overwhelming police authority, and the sight of young latinos passing out their radical newspaper helped to create a vague but important sense of indigenous power in the community residents as well. To maintain this sense of power it seemed necessary to reject the psychological defeat inherent in the plea bargain, and to risk a trial.

The tasks facing the lawyers in this case were, first, to empower their clients and Los Siete as an organization and, second, to win the trial. Both goals would be furthered by an overtly political defense, the first because a political defense would insist that the defendants were right to be reaching out to the community; the second because this particular trial could be won only by challenging the narrow "legal" definition of their action as criminal obstruction and trespass.

The lawyers' first tactic was to go on the offensive by filing a motion to suppress the seized newspapers on the grounds that the arrest and seizure violated the first amendment. This tactic was no different from one that any good defense lawyer would use once plea bargaining had been rejected, but here the purpose was not so much to vindicate a legal right as such, but rather to force the State to *defend* its actions. Surprisingly, the municipal court granted the motion, much to the irritation of the district attorney, who was then forced into the defensive posture of filing an appeal. The defense lawyers asked a young corporate attorney interested in "pro bono" work to prepare the appeal. The coalition of community lawyers and corporate lawyer increased the ideological pressure on the district attorney's office. Although the corporate attorney wrote an excellent brief and argued the case, the municipal court decision was reversed.

Next came the trial plan. The first strategic issue was whether to try to pack the courtroom with community people. Traditional lawyers are wary of this tactic for fear that the presence of third world and "radical" people will frighten the jury and create subconscious hostility. However, lawyers can often use crowded courtrooms to their advantage by dealing with the jury's anxiety and hostility toward the community presence in voir dire, and by openly discussing any negative preconceptions the jurors might have in opening and/or closing arguments. Due to a lack of publicity it was not possible in this case to fill the courtroom with community supporters, but enough were present to prevent the defendants from feeling isolated.

The second issue related to the clients' participation in the preparation and conduct of the trial. In the traditional view of the lawyer-client relationship, the lawyer is defined as the professional who "handles" all legal aspects of the case without client participation. By treating the client as someone who cannot understand the conduct of her own trial, the traditional approach increases the client's sense of powerlessness in the face of the intimidating spectacle going on in the courtroom. In this case the lawyers took the opposite approach, asking the clients to take an active part in all aspects of the case where prior legal training was not absolutely required. Thus the defendants wrote voir dire questions and assisted in the selection of jurors. The lawyers discussed each aspect of the case, explaining their tactics and incorporating many of the suggestions of the clients. In this manner the clients began to feel some control over the process which the State had forced them into.

As for the trial itself, a traditional approach would have been to argue the client's version of the facts against the State's version, relying on a reasonable doubt defense and keeping the content of the newspaper itself out of evidence. A more liberal approach would have been to focus on the first amendment aspects of the case, emphasizing the abstract right of dissenters to freedom of speech. The radical approach was to stress the political realities involved; to admit and defend the true nature of *Basta Ya*, and to expose the police department's racism and its attempts to harass and intimidate members of Los Siete.

The trial ended successfully for the defendants despite the judge's persistent attempts to ridicule the attorneys and to prohibit their making any mention of the first amendment. Instead of feeling that they had won by disguising the politics through either the traditional or liberal approaches, the defendants felt a sense of power and truth because the political meaning of their actions had been presented and vindicated. After the trial the defendants went back with other members of Los Siete to distribute newspapers in the same location, while the police and storeowner looked on. "Basta Ya" means "Enough Already." The case delivered to the arresting officers, the local police station, and the conservative merchants a clear message: if you mess with Los Siete, they have the spirit and resources to hit back.

* * *

Low-visibility cases that contain political elements, such as *Basta Ya*, are presented in courtrooms throughout the country on a frequent basis. What is critical to understand is that one can transform a "solely criminal" case into a political case by making a few simple changes in approach and technique. This is possible because the courtroom is a small, closed, intensified experience for the jury and for the participants. Everything that takes place is magnified. Since the district attorney and judge will almost always define the case as nonpolitical, and will attempt to create an atmosphere of neutral application of objective laws, any injection of political and social reality will have a powerful impact. Using the *Basta Ya* trial, we can look at voir dire, opening statement and cross examination to illuminate this analysis.

The two young lawyers in the *Basta Ya* trial had a combined experience of less than four trials. They could not carry off a week-long antiracist voir dire as Charles Garry did in many of the Black Panther cases; their clients faced only misdemeanors and there was very little visible community support in the courtroom itself. An extensive voir dire in this context may have been viewed as overkill. However, it was simple to ask a few questions that had the effect of setting a political tone to the trial. For example, the first juror was asked the following: "The community newspaper that was being passed out was called *Basta Ya*, which means 'Enough Already!' Have you ever heard of it?" Since the juror's answer was no, the next question, spoken with enough clarity and strength to grab the attention of all the jurors, was, "*Basta Ya* has articles very critical of the police for harassing latinos and Mission residents. Would that prejudice you against Raul Flores?" By the fourth or fifth juror, this question became shortened to, "Would the articles criticizing police brutality make it hard for you to evaluate the evidence with an open mind?" One of the jurors, an older Italian man, was asked the following series of questions: "Mr. Flores speaks both English and Spanish. Are you familiar with people who have the ability to speak two languages?" Answer: "Of course; in my family, my wife and I, and son do." Question: "Do you take pride in your heritage, your culture?" Answer: "Very much. It's important." Question: "Would you think badly of Mr. Flores if, when he testifies, he speaks with a heavy Spanish accent?" Answer: "No, not if I can understand him." These types of questions give jurors some understanding of the racial and political issues behind the formal charges.

In opening statement, one need not give a political lecture to the jury, nor are most judges likely to allow such an approach. However, a few sentences can inform both the jury and the judge as to the actual nature of the case. For example, the following was one of two or three political comments in the *Basta Ya* opening statement: "Raul Flores will take the stand and testify. You will see that he is 23 years old, married, with one small child. He has been active for many years in community groups, militantly organizing against police abuse and brutality in the Mission district." At the very least, this type of statement puts the jury on notice as to the political context of the trial.

Cross-examination is the most overrated aspect of the trial. In a low-visibility case it is quite difficult for a lawyer to be able to expose the racism and bias of police officers. Consequently, one must try to shed light on that bias rather than attempt to tear the mask off:

Question: "Officer, you are assigned to the Mission police station, correct?" Answer: "Yes." Question: "For two years you have worked out of the Mission station, right?" Answer: "That's right." Question: "You've seen people selling *Basta Ya* up and down the streets of the Mission, haven't you?" Answer: "Yes, I have." Question: "And you have see *Basta Ya* in the little newsboxes on the corners?" Answer: "I've noticed them occasionally." Question: "Before you arrested Mr. Flores and confiscated his papers, you were aware that the front page photo and headline were about police brutality in the Mission, weren't you?" Answer: "No, I don't think I was aware of that." These questions gave the jury some insight into the political motivations of the police, even though they did not fit the romanticized notion of a great political cross-examination.

One does not have to be defending the Chicago Eight * * * to bring political reality into the courtroom. * * * If we remember that behind each case there is a social reality that the law is trying to hide and suppress, we can find acceptable and practical methods to politicize our cases.

* * *

Many lawyers assume that it is dangerous to be political in the courtroom because it will reduce their chances of winning. This is incorrect as a general principle, particularly if "political" is understood to mean demonstrating the underlying social reality of the case. Although there are undoubtedly many instances when a traditional legalistic approach is the most appropriate course of action, it is also true that as a general rule, judges, prosecutors, and lawyers feel a loss of power when the roles within which they exercise control are revealed to be artificial and manipulative. The greater the extent to which conditioned images of the courtroom are undermined by honest spontaneity and moral authenticity in speech and action, the more likely it is that the jury will react to the totality of the event with a free and human response.

Notes and Questions

1. Can lawyers build power for their clients, as Gabel and Harris, suggest? Gabel and Harris note that "behind each case there is a social reality that the law is trying to hide and suppress." Is politicizing cases by revealing that reality desirable? Who should make that decision? Does case politicization empower litigants or communities?

2. What did you learn about conflict and confrontation from your family upbringing or from your educational experiences? How do you deal with conflict and confrontation now? Do your personal experiences with conflict impact your view of the desirability of politicizing cases?

3. Were the techniques that Gabel and Harris described during the voir dire in the *Basta Ya* case politicizing or merely examples of good trial technique that would be used by any good advocate? Is politicization of a case just another weapon in the advocate's arsenal of effective representation? What professional responsibility does a lawyer have in advising a client about politicization of a case? Does it matter if the client is an individual or a group? For a personal reflection on the tensions in politicized cases when the lawyer believes in the cause, see Nancy D. Polikoff, *Am I My Client?,* excerpted in chapter 5.

SECTION 2. COMMUNITY EMPOWERMENT AND THE ROLE OF THE LAWYER

Legal scholars have long noted the danger that the actions of lawyers who are trying to help community activists may actually harm them directly or indirectly. For example, Stephen Wexler commented: "The lawyer for poor individuals is likely, whether he wins the case or not, to leave his clients precisely where he found them, except that they will have developed a dependency on his skills to smooth out the roughest spots in their lives." Stephen Wexler, *Practicing Law for Poor People*, 79 Yale L.J. 1049, 1053 (1970). What steps can lawyers take to avoid weakening their clients' capacity for organization and action?

William P. Quigley, who has represented community organizations for more than two decades, presents the insights of community organizers and identifies themes of lawyering toward empowerment that are derived from the organizers as well as his own experience. He names: building up the community (rather than winning on an issue) as the primary goal of the lawyer's work; avoiding the dangers of disempowering groups by creating dependency; treating litigation as only one of many means to pursuing goals; learning about community organizing and leadership development; involving the community in everything the lawyer does; never becoming the leader of the group; understanding how much the lawyer is taking as well as giving; being wary of speaking for the group; confronting the lawyer's own comfort with an unjust system; and being willing to "journey with the community."

WILLIAM P. QUIGLEY

Reflections of Community Organizers: Lawyering for Empowerment of Community Organizations
21 Ohio N.U. L. Rev. 455, 455–79 (1995)

> Poverty will not be stopped by people who are not poor. If poverty is stopped, it will be stopped by poor people. And poor people can stop poverty only if they work at it together. The lawyer who wants to serve poor people must put his skills to the task of helping poor people organize themselves. [Wexler, *supra* at 1053.]

Empowerment lawyering with organizations of the poor and powerless differs from corporate lawyering or criminal defense lawyering in purpose, substance and style. It also differs from traditional public interest lawyering in significant respects.

The purpose of empowerment lawyering with community organizations is to enable a group of people to gain control of the forces which affect their lives. The substance of this lawyering is primarily the representation of groups rather than individuals. This style calls for lawyering which joins, rather than leads, the persons represented.

Community organizing is *the* essential element of empowering organizational advocacy. Unless the lawyer recognizes that advocacy with groups cannot proceed without community organizing, there can be no effective empowering advocacy. In fact, if an organization could only have one advocate and had to choose between the most accomplished traditional lawyer and a good community organizer, it had better, for its own survival, choose the organizer.

Community organizers are in an important position to observe and evaluate lawyers in community organizations. Because lawyers ask doctors and engineers to help shape and evaluate their legal product, lawyers should also consider the insights of community organizers in developing approaches to lawyering with organizations where the goal is empowerment of the organization's members. * * *

* * *

Reflections by Community Organizers

Ron Chisom, an African-American community organizer, has worked over three decades with dozens of community organizations in the southern United States, including public housing tenants, people opposing police brutality, neighborhood preservationists, and civil rights groups. He consults with numerous groups and is a national trainer with The People's Institute for Survival and Beyond. Here are his reflections on the role of lawyers in community organizations:

Lawyers have killed off more groups by helping them than ever would have died if the lawyers had never showed up.

Most organizations when they come up with a problem—they turn it into an issue and then they get stumped and then they call a lawyer. A lawyer steps in, in what is essentially a technical role and shows some real authority and expertise by even simple things like taking notes which most people in the community do not do.

People in the organization look up to the lawyer because of their writing skills, their reading skills, their education, their speaking skills and it really makes the lawyer look like they are doing something. People then tend to transfer their interest in the issue and the problem to the lawyer to have the lawyer solve it and this creates dependency.

Total dependence on a lawyer by an organization is not good because most lawyers are "career oriented." They will usually help the community, but they also later hurt the community by making money off the contacts in the community, by political aspirations and by leaving the community stranded. In many cases, they actually leave the community in a worse condition had they never been involved.

Most lawyers do not understand about organizing. Lawyers do not understand that the legal piece is only one tactic of organizing. It is not the goal.

In my 25 years of experience, I find that lawyers create dependency. The lawyers want to advocate for others and do not understand the goal of giving a people a sense of their own power. Traditional lawyer advocacy creates dependency and not interdependency. With most lawyers there is no leadership development of the group.

If lawyers get involved, they create a lot of problems. Most lawyers have never been through the consistent frustration of community building with its petty disputes, confusion, personality problems and the like. Most lawyers get frustrated with that, have a low degree of tolerance with people problems, and will walk away from the effort of community building.

The legal dimension of community organizing is only one piece of the overall strategy. Commonly, lawyers are not clear about strategy. They don't understand community, they don't understand organizing, they don't understand leadership development.

Lawyers, if they understand the process, can play a major role in the development of the community. If lawyers understand the dynamics of community leadership and development, this understanding can also work to reduce the frustration level of the lawyer because the people involved will not call the lawyer for every little problem that they have in the struggle.

As an example, when the organization goes to court or to confront the government, the people must play a major role in the choices of where to go and how to go. The people must also participate in the investigation and speaking out on the issue.

At a certain level, groups will need a lawyer. What the groups really need is a lawyer with understanding and an analysis of the community group—who they are, what are their problems and what is their history. If the lawyer does not understand how the group fits into the larger part of society and community, the lawyer will only see this organization as just another case. This is particularly true when the group itself does not understand the big picture either.

Big problems develop when the lawyer becomes the leader. The lawyer ends up almost as a god to the group and that will kill off the momentum and emotionalism that brought the group that far. The people lose interest as the lawyer becomes the momentum. The lawyer can stimulate the group, pacify the group or walk out at any time. This effectively kills the leadership and power of the group.

The lawyer is "credentialized." The lawyer is structured, disciplined, succinct, and trained. He or she is closer to and understands the system better than anybody in the group. Then, the lawyer becomes the focal point of the group and becomes leader of the group. More mature groups will not let this happen, but when it does happen the collective power of the group is transferred from the individuals to the lawyer. The group is then susceptible to any action or lack of action that the lawyer takes rather than the direction and leadership being given by the organization.

In tactics, the legal piece is only one tactic of many. There is the legislative, legal, demonstration, picketing, fund-raising, community building, leadership development and many other pieces. Lawyers do not usually understand that.

Lawyers tend to focus only on the case and want the organization to bend itself to the case rather than the other way around. Lawyers think in terms only of what will help or hurt the case, but they do not understand that "the case" is not the point of building up the community.

Another problem is that most community lawyers, especially white lawyers, do not want to confront or agitate the power structure. This is primarily because of the role of racism in all of these conflicts. Lawyers, particularly white lawyers, are trained to understand and be comfortable with the system even when they criticize it. Almost all lawyers, including community lawyers, want to succeed in the system. They want money, power, political advantage, respect or whatever their individual dreams are. Therefore, confronting the system or raising hell makes the lawyer very uncomfortable because it is not how the lawyer was trained to deal with the system, and the lawyer, without realizing it, is challenged individually because the lawyer is part of the system.

> The white legal system perpetuates the white power system. Reliance on that system is a contradiction to the development of collective power in a community organization. I also find that black lawyers also have serious problems confronting the system because they don't really want to challenge the system because black lawyers gain advantage and reap rewards from the system so, therefore, they cannot challenge it the way it needs to be challenged.
>
> The lack of understanding is not confined to lawyers because * * * [frequently, the group itself and] inexperienced organizers themselves do not understand the demands of leadership development.
>
> Leadership development is the key to solving problems locally. If the lawyer does not understand leadership development and the group does not understand leadership development then certainly leadership development is not going to happen. There may well be some flurry of activity on a problem, perhaps even the problem will be solved, but the community will be left with as little, or sometimes even less power and understanding of power than they had before they started the fight.

Wade Rathke is Chief Organizer of Local 100, Service Employees International Union (SEIU) and one of the founders of the Arkansas Community Organization for Reform Now (ACORN). He has been an organizer for twenty years, first with the Welfare Rights Organization movement, and later as a founder and chief organizer for ACORN. ACORN has created a national organization of low and moderate income members, with active local organizations in twenty states. He speaks about the experiences of the organizations with which he has worked:

> The fundamental challenge in finding good organizational lawyers is to find out whether or not a lawyer is willing to see their role as similar to an organizer or researcher who is employed by an organization as a helper toward the process of helping the organization gain power. Empowerment must be the lawyer's goal; not breaking the new legal ground which changes a particular statute or right.
>
> I remember a top lawyer who worked with us in the early days of the ACORN organization who used to take new volunteer lawyers and the first thing he would make them do, for as long as a month, was make them run the mimeograph machine and put out mailings. He would take them door to door canvassing and train them like organizers. He believed that unless lawyers for organizations understood that there is different training to work with organizations than the training they had in law school then there would always be problems. Lawyers have to be able to understand that organizing an issue is a process where an individual problem changes and becomes a political issue.
>
> ACORN has found that the lawyers who are most accessible to organizations tend to be ones who come out of the union lawyer tradition. In union lawyers there is still a strong culture that says

the organization's membership must bear the control of final decisions. Because that tradition is not as common in either civil rights or in poverty law, we have tended to find that we do better in working with lawyers who come out of thc union tradition of membership and organizational leadership and service than those coming out of classically trained legal services lawyers who, we have found, more want to create law than create power.

One thing that you just do not find much in lawyers is people who are sensitive enough to understand organizations and their dynamics well enough to be able to look at the structures of law and figure out how you can attack some laws to open up vital organizational opportunity and authority. You know, it is not necessarily a colorful area of law, but there is a tremendous amount of work that needs to be done in areas like access to public records and opening up payroll and other deduction systems.

In the ACORN experience we have seen substantial legal precedents in law won through organizational activity joined with lawyers. At the same time, there is a level of what some call "gonzo law" that is essential to allow organizations to pursue campaigns. This law may pursue new ideas in the law but may not [be] pursued to create precedent at all, and in some non-organizational view may be almost totally frivolous. As an example, it is certainly not news that it is a common organizational tactic in trying to pursue issue campaigns, that, when you are unable to win all the objectives of the campaign and it has been a fierce struggle, the organization may try to exit the campaign by filing a suit. The filing of a lawsuit may make it appear that the issue is not totally lost and gives the losing issue an afterlife where something may or may not come down the legal avenue, but it at least gives it a public viability that it is being pursued. If something comes of it, great, if not, it was a way to get out of a losing situation.

This is a tactical use of law. There are some lawyers who are comfortable with this sort of use of the law, but I think it is a rare talent.

Barbara Major, an African American organizer, works with numerous low income women's groups in the southern United States. She is also a trainer with the People's Institute for Survival and Beyond. She has suggested the following:

Empowerment is when a person or a group of people know who they are, accept who they are, and refuse to let people make them anything else.

Lawyers, like any other profession, can be a really good resource in the community that is seeking to empower itself. An excellent resource and always a necessary one. Especially when you look historically in terms of the need—not only to change attitudes, but to change policy and legislation to really make access available to resources for everybody. I think lawyers have always played a key role, especially in the civil rights movement, the worker's rights movement, and the women's rights movements in this country.

I think one of the things that lawyers have to understand is the reality of the community that it deals with. I think oftentimes lawyers come in with their own reality, their own world view, and think or assume that this is everybody's reality and they just start moving along. That is not the case because a lot of times, especially when you are dealing in a struggling community, their reality is very different from the reality that people who have been educated have, or their world view is very different from the people at the bottom that they will be working with.

People used to work "in community" but I think now people should think a little more about working "with community." This means lawyers have to learn how, with all of their skills, to journey with the community. This journey has to involve the community really getting a sense of who they are, in the sense of beginning to understand their own power. In working with community the wisdom or the knowledge of the lawyer does not outweigh the wisdom and the knowledge of the community, about itself especially.

I think also when you talk about lawyers you must help them have a reality check, in my experience lawyers don't often do that. You know, they often believe in the system—that the system is going to work because it's the right thing to do. I do not think they understand that, when you are dealing with challenging power, that the system works on the side of power. The lawyers do not realize they need another tool to challenge the system, one that lawyers do not know about, and that is the power of the community. Because no matter how good you might be in court, the power of the people in the street weighs mighty heavily on the decision of the power brokers, sometimes more heavily than the law itself. One lawyer, I don't care how good she is, how well she argues or whatever, the power brokers will take that same lawyer and beat her to death one day, unless, the people in the street say this is not legal, this is not fair.

I think a lot of times lawyers have come into the community and only created another entity to be dependent on. Their communities begin to believe that all they have to do is bring their problems to court and they forget that they must continue to organize and educate the people. * * * [P]eople will lay back and just think well "I'll just sue 'em." This will not lead to permanent change. Because even if the community wins the suit, what are they going to do the next time there is a problem? Sue again?

Problems can be headed off if the powerful know there is an organized community willing to fight them. That is better than the best suit.

Another problem is when the lawyer comes in and just takes over and becomes the leader and the spokesperson and it disempowers the community. The lawyer becomes the one everyone wants to interview and everybody wants to talk to. Then the media and the powerful don't ever talk directly to the people any more. The community's struggle becomes the lawyer's struggle and not the people's struggle.

Who becomes the spokesperson is real important because the community starts out so weakened. It's not destroyed, but it's weakened. The community needs to feel its own power and continue to be built back up in the sense that says you not only have the right to speak for yourself, but you can speak for yourself. The community needs to be allowed to demonstrate as many times as possible its capabilities and abilities to do and to be itself, its own power source, its own leadership. I find it real destructive when outside people speak for the community. It is the simple folk that sustain us as a people—not some lawyer or nun or hot shot organizer who comes in and does works in the community. It is very important for the community to feel its own power, and part of that power is the ability to speak for itself.

If lawyers want to work with the community, they must first do some thinking. If they come in with a sense of not only just coming in to say they want to work, they want to help the community, but coming in and saying that I, too, have something to gain from this, then I think the community will welcome them. Because, then the building up will not be one-sided. As the community builds its power and self confidence, the lawyer will also reach new heights. I know as an organizer when I see the community moving up and I am connected to them, it's like hey, I am moving too. You know they are not leaving me behind and I can't leave them behind. So we are moving together. It's a different kind of relationship.

It is not a matter to me of where you live, or whether you are poor yourself. The lawyer can live in a nice house, as long as they are struggling for folk in that community to have nice houses too. See, I don't think poverty is a damned virtue. It's your becoming a part of that human family is what you are really becoming a part of in that community. I have had problems out of all kinds of lawyers—Black male, Black female, White male, White female and everything in between. So, their race and gender does not matter to me. It is the ability of that person to see the human capacity in the community. Unfortunately, a lot of people don't see it—all they see is that depressed community that I am coming in and giving something to.

Only when they understand that they will not only be the only one giving, but they will also be receiving, then it can roll. And it will be a growing and learning process for everybody.

Themes in Community Empowerment Lawyering

1. The primary goal is building up the community.

[As Chisom suggested, if leadership development does not happen, even if the problem is solved, the community will be left with as little, or sometimes even less power and understanding of power than they had before they started the fight.]

* * *

In his very first meeting with the residents of a neighborhood, Joe Lewis, a community organizer hired by the Atlanta Project as a coordinator for the area, was asked by residents what he was going to do for the community. He said, "I don't know. You haven't told me yet."

As one author has suggested, "Organizing in its simplified form is people working together to get things accomplished. Organizing is about people taking a role in determining their own future and improving the quality of life not only for themselves but for everyone." Educate, activate, and build the membership of the organization. These are the goals of organizational empowerment lawyering.

2. *Lawyers can disempower groups by creating dependency.*

Empowerment is a term that has been given several slightly differing conceptual meanings. In all meanings, it involves an attempt to give the acted upon the right to decide for themselves or act in their own interests. What does traditional public interest lawyering say to the goal of empowerment? Not much.

There are two traditional methods of public interest lawyering: providing individual legal services to the indigent, usually in a government-funded setting, and providing reform or impact litigation which targets particular issues for focused high intensity litigation. Neither of these traditional forms of public interest lawyering is well suited to empowering. Both focus the power and the decision-making in the lawyer and the organization which employs the lawyer. The lawyer decides if she will take the case. The lawyer decides what is a reasonably achievable outcome. The lawyer and her employer decides how much time and resources can be committed to the effort. Both approaches individualize or compartmentalize the problems of the poor and powerless by not addressing their collective difficulties and lack of power.

While both approaches employ many hard-working and dedicated advocates, even when successful in achieving their defined mission they define for themselves, empowerment will not occur. * * * If empowerment is the end, creating dependence on a lawyer is not the means.

3. *Litigation is only one of many means to the end.*

The clash in problem-solving approaches between the lawyer and the organizer highlights one of the inherent difficulties in using litigation in an empowering fashion. Consider the following:

> Lawyers and organizers tend to approach problems differently, with often marked implications. For example, consider an intersection where the lack of a stop sign is causing traffic hazards and threatening children. A lawyer would solve this problem by going to court to get the stop sign put into place. From this process people either do

> not know how the stop sign got there or learn that lawyers produce change. Both results aggravate people's perceptions of their powerlessness, which is disastrous from an organizer's perspective. In contrast to the lawyer, the organizer would knock on all the doors in the neighborhood, organize a meeting of interested people, and help them collectively deal with the problem. They would probably hold a mass demonstration, meet with a city official, and successfully pressure her to provide the stop sign. From this experience, people in the neighborhood would learn that they can have power if they organize, and coordinate their efforts. Because so many individuals participated in producing the sign, nearly everyone in the neighborhood would learn this lesson. Suddenly an aspect of the neighborhood is the product of the residents' personal actions.

This example sharply contrasts two ways to approach the same problem. If the goal is getting a stop sign, then litigation may well be the superior method to use. If the goal is taking, developing, and sharing power, then litigation is not effective.

Other than the circumstances discussed below, it is a good rule to avoid litigation in empowerment advocacy. The goal of this advocacy is to help the group and its members take, develop, and share their rightful power. Litigation usually does not further that goal. There are literally scores of other actions that groups can take that will highlight the problem, call for solutions, and involve the community members in leading their own fight. At its worst, litigation on behalf of an emerging organization of people may well be harmful to the growth and development of the organization.

When lawyers are confronted with a wrong, they are tempted to draw on their litigation skills. Also, people tend to seek out lawyers for their litigation skills as opposed to their organizational assistance. In advocacy with an organization, litigation can be considered helpful in three situations: defending the organization and its members; serving the organization's development; and terminating causes from which the organization has no other way to exit.

Law reform litigation should be undertaken only reluctantly in organizational advocacy and only after considerable thought by the organization. Litigation should be avoided in most other situations because lawyering and organizational development do not often go together. * * * Many lawyers have tried to achieve justice for poor and powerless people and organizations and victims of discrimination. As even most successful lawyers will ruefully admit, there was often more victory in the courtroom than in reality.

One of the weaknesses of litigation is the inherent limitation of the judicial system when called upon to produce social reform. The judiciary is far more disposed to and capable of stopping something from happening than it is to force something positive to occur. If the organization needs to stop something and can figure no other way to do it, or, better yet, is trying all other ways to stop it, then litigation may prove helpful if properly constrained and directed. However, the real work of organizational development is to take the members' rightful share of power and redistribute it. The judicial system has fundamental problems with such positive actions. And even where the judicial system takes a modest step or two forward, it can only make change and was probably prodded to those modest achievements in the first place, with significant support from other parts of society. Thus, litigation, particularly litigation as the sole approach to a problem, will not likely be effective in solving the problem.

* * *

Further, even when reform-minded lawyers participate on behalf of the poor and the powerless, too frequently a gap in understanding and common priorities prevents even infrequent, well-intentioned litigation from succeeding in actually empowering those on whose behalf the litigation is brought. This failure is a result of the different priorities that litigation has, by its nature, opposed to the priorities of helping people gain power. As Professor White ironically notes in her analysis of the empowerment shortcomings of public interest litigation,

> The gap between what poor people want to say and what the law wants to hear often seems enormous. Legal education does not prepare lawyers for this daunting task, and the profession does not encourage or reward such efforts. Reform-oriented lawyers have been taught to read statutes, question bureaucrats, and analyze policy. They have not learned to listen and talk to poor people....
>
> Therefore, in practice, welfare litigators often subordinate their clients' perceptions of need to the lawyers' own agendas for reform. They rarely design litigation to respond to their clients' own priorities and ideas. Rather, litigation is designed to effect broad reforms that will benefit the whole class of welfare recipients.... Not only do clients feel incapable of speaking and acting freely in the strange language and culture of the courtroom; in addition, their own lawsuits are often framed to render their perceptions and passions irrelevant to the legal claims.

Thus, traditional public interest reform, or impact litigation, is of very limited value in actually helping the poor and powerless. While identifiable progress may well be made on a particular issue, the progress will be made by lawyers in an environment unsympathetic to poor people. If empowerment is the end, this type of legal public interest work is rarely the means.

4. *Learn community organizing and leadership development.*

The challenge of the community organization process is to help the people recognize common challenges and fashion common, workable strategies to address the common problems. While most people, including the powerless, are fairly cognizant of common challenges to themselves and their communities, it takes strategy and skill to develop realistic, achievable approaches to combat the problems. Without such community organizing, there can be spontaneous protest, a flare of activity, and minimal progress. But this progress will be short-lived and likely reversed once the immediate crisis passes, unless there is good community organizing in between these moments of passion.

* * *

In the context of an organization of poor or powerless people lawyering has as its goal the reallocation of power from those who have an unfair share to those who lack their rightful share. The organization lifts the concerns of the individuals together beyond the concerns of any one individual. Individual desires and energies are fused to secure greater power, voice, and influence for those who are individually undervalued by the present system. Therefore, lawyering involves not advocacy for individual interests, but advocacy with a group of people organized to reclaim what is rightfully theirs, their own power. That is empowerment. Lawyers interested in learning more about organizing and leadership development have a variety of sources from which to choose.

5. *The community must be involved in everything the lawyer does.*

Martin Luther King, Jr. once said,

> [W]e've got to understand people, first, and then analyze their problems. If we really pay attention to those we want to help; if we listen to them; if we let them tell us about themselves—how they live, what they want out of life—we'll be on much more solid ground when we start 'planning' our 'action,' our 'programs,' than if we march ahead, to our own music, and treat 'them' as if they're only meant to pay attention to us, anyway.

There is a tendency to consider work with organizations as volunteer or pro bono work that is somehow governed by different dynamics than work for paying clients. It should not be so considered. If the lawyer takes the community organization's problem as her own task and begins to independently prepare and execute a legal strategy, the organization immediately loses control of its own actions. No lawyer would consider independently creating and implementing a legal strategy for a big corporation. Community organizations demand the same respect. Since empowerment by definition means controlling one's own destiny in as many ways as possible, even the most well-intentioned lawyer who works independent from the organization is undercutting the life of the organization.

The organization should work with the attorney to decide what the attorney should be involved in, how the legal strategy should proceed, and when the lawyer's assistance is needed. If a legal strategy is developed, the organization should decide what are the first steps taken, what forum should those steps be taken in, what resources should be committed to the task, and what realistic goals and timetables should be communicated to the members of the organization. * * *

6. *Never become the leader of the group.*

Consider the advice of another veteran organizer: "You don't need a lawyer to talk to politicians for you. Hiring a lawyer to deal with politicians would be a waste of your money. You can say it better than them—from the heart and from your own experience." Empowerment means people seizing control of their own life choices. Following a lawyer is not empowerment. As was once said so succinctly, "[t]he lawyer should be on tap, and not on top."

7. *Be willing to confront the lawyer's own comfort with an unjust legal system.*

* * * Ultimately every group of people who seeks power must face those with the power. Seeking a rightful share of power means demanding the return of that power from the powerful. This is confrontation. It can happen in the legislatures, on the streets, in the courts, in the media, or in the banks, but it is confrontation. It is certainly one of the options that those without power must consider. The lawyer for an organization can assist in the inevitable confrontation by either of two approaches: shut up and get out of the way and/or help the group discuss the best options to provoke or defend the resulting confrontation.

The lawyer's comfort level with the current legal, political, economic and social system comes to the forefront at certain points in organizing, even when there is confrontation. Lawyers participate and reap benefit from these systems even while apparently challenging them. Lawyers profit by their education in and participation in the legal system, even while they self-identify themselves as "standing outside the system." This participation cannot be denied but need not paralyze the lawyer of an organization seeking its rightful share of power. This participation must first be consciously recognized as an investment in the current system and then, to the degree the lawyer can do so, it must be consciously set aside while assisting the organization in confronting those who unjustly have their power.

In analyzing options in confrontation strategies, the lawyer's comfort level with some types of confrontation and lack of comfort with others must be identified and, to the degree possible, set aside. Since some lawyers have substantial experience in controlled legal confrontation, there is the tendency of the lawyer to try to control and direct the confrontation to conform to the confrontation style to which the lawyer is accustomed. This tendency usually seeks for more polite, ordered confrontation that follows the rules of polite, ordered society. This tendency is usually a mistake for those who have been shut out of the polite, ordered society. The point of confrontation is not to persuade the quiet and ordered powerful to generously provide a donation of excess power, but to assist the powerless in finding their own voice to demand what is justly theirs.

Subjecting the powerless to the rules of the powerful in a confrontation over the just reallocation of power is contradictory and counterproductive. This is not to say that thoughtless stridency is the best approach to confront the powerful, rather the lawyer must be prepared for the group to consciously adopt and utilize methods of confrontation which the lawyer would never choose for herself.

Take the simple example of deciding whether to be quiet when ordered to do so in a public meeting of the city council. Continuing to speak beyond the allotted time or on topics not allowed on the agenda or directly to members of the government who do not wish to be so addressed will likely result in being requested or ordered to sit down and be quiet. The polite, ordered response of those who follow the rules would be to reluctantly sit down and ponder other ways to get the point across. For the purposes of development of the group, it may well be most effective to continue to speak and either be physically expelled or even arrested to demonstrate the unwillingness of the powerful to even give an airing to the group's concerns. The lawyer's tendency to seek ordered results has to be subordinated to the development of progress on the organization's goals.

In working with organizations, the goal of all action, legal and nonlegal, is to empower the members of the group so they are able to be as self-directed as possible. * * * A further challenge involves the entire concept of de-lawyering current systems so the members of the organization can better learn to advocate for themselves.

The lawyer has a delicate and paradoxical role to play in empowerment advocacy. The primary role is to help the organization and its members take, develop, and share their rightful power. In contemporary society, the lawyer holds a position of power partly because the law has drawn away from regular people and become a system unto itself, unaccessible to a nonlawyer, with its own language, and its own liturgies of practice. In this sense, the ignorance of the client enriches the lawyer's power position. Thus, the lawyer, even the well-intentioned public interest lawyer, has a share of power that is only the result of others not having access to it. The lawyer pursuing the goals of empowerment advocacy is called to a higher form of advocacy than "doing for" her client. Rather, the lawyer is called to assist her client to escape the need of being anyone's client and learning to advocate for herself. This demands that the lawyer undo the secret wrappings of the legal system and share the essence of legal advocacy. Doing so lessens the mystical power of the lawyer but, in practice, enriches the advocate in the sharing and developing of rightful power.

8. Be wary of speaking for the group.

There are only two instances when it is appropriate for a lawyer to speak to the media about the organization. First, if the organization asks the lawyer and [gives] specific instructions on how to proceed, and second, in an emergency. The lawyer should not speak for the organization unless that is the only way the organization's position will be reported, all the organization's members are unavailable, or the organization's message is already decided and communicated to the lawyer. Consider how the powerful deal with the media. Does a lawyer for Proctor & Gamble assume she has the authority to comment on anything for Proctor & Gamble without explicit permission and direction? No, and neither should the organizational lawyer.

* * *

9. Understand how much the lawyer is taking as well as giving.

It has been suggested that "the challenge of responding to others, especially across great distances of life experience, inevitably leads us to confront more deeply the uncertainty—the possibility—that is ourselves." Anyone who has worked with vital community organizations in a fight against those who oppress the members of the organization knows it can be one of life's peak experiences. Along the way it will also likely be one of the most frustrating experiences in which they will ever participate.

The essence of working with a community organization is harnessing the powers of the individuals involved into a team. When the lawyer is part of that team, and the team wins an uphill battle, there is no big fee, no precedent-setting case, no pro bono award, that can ever substitute for the enduring sense of fulfilling friendship that binds those who were there and met the challenge.

The lawyer gives, no doubt about it. But the lawyer receives, too, no doubt about it.

10. Be willing to journey with the community.

* * *

Learning to join rather than lead, learning to listen rather than to speak, learning to assist people in empowering themselves rather than manipulating the levers of power for them, these are the elements of lawyering for empowerment. By mastering their elements, a lawyer can help people join together and control those forces influencing their daily lives. By helping people in a community organized process to recognize common challenges, they can work together to formulate common strategies to combat these challenges.

Notes and Questions

1. What skills have you learned that will help meet Ron Chisom's comment that most lawyers have never experienced the challenges of community building, which entails "petty disputes, confusion, personality problems, and the like"? How would you feel if you went to work for a community group that asked you to begin by operating the copying machine or by going door to door to learn about the work of your clients?

2. The organizers talk about "empowerment." Does law school actually work against this needed training by being anti-empowerment?

Does legal education equate the power to win a legal decision with the power to change a social problem? What is the difference between that concept of power and the concepts discussed by the organizers?

Gerald López argues that "[t]hough millions in this country live in social and political subordination and though lawyers have worked to help challenge these conditions, law schools only rarely have understood their job to include designing a training regimen responsive to this situation and this task." Gerald P. López, *Training Future Lawyers to Work with the Politically and Socially Subordinated: Anti-Generic Education*, 91 W. Va. L. Rev. 305, 306 (1988–89). López proposes a curriculum for legal education designed to train students to work with, and for, the poor and powerless.

3. Ron Chisom states that attitudes of people in community groups can result in dependency, and that the lawyers' attitudes also create dependency. How can a lawyer avoid this dynamic? What training could be offered in law school that would help law students prepare for this task? Could legal training involve additional skills that would help avoid the dangers identified by community organizers?

4. Barbara Major says that what matters is not whether the lawyer lives within the community or shares an identity with the members of the community, but rather "the ability of that person to see the human capacity in the community." Is it possible to see that capacity for agency and mobilization from the perspective of a distant outsider? If not, how can law students or lawyers achieve this view of the community? Can it be done quickly? Does anything in law school prepare you for investing time in developing such relationships and understandings?

5. A focus on litigation really means a focus on the courtroom as the crucial location for social change:

> Litigation validates the perception that ordinary people of low and moderate income have nothing to do with law reform and social change, and that such reform and change result only from efforts of well-heeled attorneys and judges. Litigation perpetuates the notion that significant change occurs "by magic," because ordinary people of low and moderate income frequently do not know or care what happens in the court rooms. When ordinary people perceive that they can change nothing or that they have to rely on "experts" or "magic" to solve their problems, they come to believe they are powerless * * * which is to say, their original condition of limited capability for societal change is only exacerbated. The deplorable conditions of the status quo are intensified, not ameliorated.

Steve Bachmann, The Hollow Hope*: Can Courts Bring About Social Change*?, 19 N.Y.U. Rev. L. & Soc. Change 391, 391–92 (1992) (reviewing Gerald N. Rosenberg, *The Hollow Hope* (1991)).

What advantages and disadvantages accompany a focus on the courtroom? Why does Quigley say that if organizations can have only one advocate they "had better, for their own survival, choose the organizer?"

Do you agree or does his statement mean that lawyers must play a greater role as organizers? In the remainder of this section Lucie E. White, Scott L. Cummings, and Ingrid V. Eagly reflect on lawyers as organizers.

6. Consider the dynamic interactions between communities, lawyers, and power. As Luke Cole and Sheila Foster have explained, in the context of environmental justice:

> Individuals are transformed through the process of struggle by learning about, and participating in, a decision that will fundamentally affect their quality of life. Using lawyers and other technicians, residents in embattled communities both build upon their knowledge of their community's environmental problems and acquire knowledge about the substantive and procedural aspects of environmental decision making. Their home-grown, and acquired, expertise empowers local residents and helps them to develop a grassroots base to influence environmental decision making.
>
> The community is transformed by the grassroots environmental justice groups established in the midst of environmental struggles. These groups help to transform marginal communities from passive victims to significant actors in environmental decision-making processes. * * *
>
> Part of what also empowers individuals and communities to demand participation in decisions that fundamentally affect their lives is the realization that power relationships within a decision-making structure are fluid and open to contestation. Once this realization takes hold, community residents can move from a reactive mode to one in which they take the initiative and decision makers begin to respond to their concerns. In this way, decision-making bodies—government institutions and corporations—are also transformed. This mutually transformative power dynamic in disaffected communities reveals an important facet of environmental justice politics. That disaffected communities are both vulnerable to disproportionate siting practices and, simultaneously, often successful at halting those practices suggests a paradoxical combination of socially oppressive sociopolitical constraints and self-determining capacities at work in these communities.

Luke W. Cole & Sheila R. Foster, *From the Ground Up: Environmental Racism and the Rise of the Environmental Justice Movement* 14–15 (2001). Does the transformative dynamic that Cole and Foster describe occur in other areas of lawyering? How might it best be nurtured?

7. Dean Rivkin discusses the theoretical challenges of lawyers interacting both with structures of power and social control and with subordinated people and their struggles:

> The rhetoric and the rules of a society are something a great deal more than sham. In the same moment they may modify, in profound ways, the behaviour of the powerful, and

> mystify the powerless. They may disguise the true realities of power, but, at the same time, they may curb that power and check its intrusions. And it is often from within that very rhetoric that a radical critique of the practice of the society is developed.... [E.P. Thompson, *Whigs and Hunters: the Origin of the Black Act* 265 (1975).]
>
> Social theorists have long grappled with the concept of power and its impact on both citizen action and inaction. An essential question in these theories persistently emerges: what prompts citizens, who have been adversely affected by government or corporate action, to mobilize opposition? Phrased differently, what processes empower people to resist government or corporate decisions that harm their perceived or inchoate interests?

Dean Hill Rivkin, *Lawyering, Power, and Reform: The Legal Campaign to Abolish the Broad Form Mineral Deed,* 66 Tenn. L. Rev. 467, 473 (1999).

In this framework, the question of empowerment goes beyond addressing the grievances that people have already framed as social or legal demands. Rather identifying the ways in which subordination breeds further disempowerment and reframing understanding is part of challenging subordination. Rivkin discusses John Gaventa's study of inequality:

> "Power serves to create power. Powerlessness serves to re-enforce powerlessness. Power relationships, once established, are self-sustaining." [John Gaventa, *Power and Powerlessness: Quiescence and Rebellion in an Appalachian Valley*, 256 (1980)] To break this cycle, Gaventa prescribes "a process of issue and action formulation" [*id.* at 257] in which the powerless share grievances among themselves and construct their own ranking of interests. Next, using resources within their control, the powerless must take action to create their own agenda and to challenge the barriers to participation in decision-making that will affect these issues. In this process of reallocation, the powerless must constantly be vigilant, for, until the mechanisms of power are altered, the power holders—whether on a national or local level—possess the potential to erect new and more insidious barriers to participation and challenge.

Rivkin, *supra* at 476.

How can lawyers be part of this process of exploration and empowerment? Lucie White explains Steven Lukes' understanding of three dimensions through which power is exercised and, applying Lukes' theory, describes three images of the work of lawyers. The first part of White's article, omitted here, is a complex and nuanced case study of the struggle of a small farming community called Driefontein against forced relocation under the apartheid regime in South Africa. The article details the community's resistance to removal and the help of two white outsiders, an organizer and a lawyer, who worked with them, providing examples of how legal work can be part of organizing against subordination.

LUCIE E. WHITE

To Learn and Teach: Lessons from Driefontein on Lawyering and Power
1988 Wis. L. Rev. 699, 747–52, 754–65, 768–69

* * * [Political scientist Steven Lukes] sets out three mechanisms through which political power is exercised and maintained in society. Using Lukes' framework, I specify three ideal images of change-oriented lawyering, each of them addressing a different mechanism of domination. In the first image, official channels for political expression are assumed to work for everyone. In most instances, the lawyer can work through those traditional channels. Only occasionally must the lawyer take action to unplug an episodic obstruction in them. In the second image, domination means the systematic exclusion of certain interests from traditional channels for political expression. The lawyer devises strategies that will both expose the exclusion process and give voice to the excluded claims. In the third image, the lawyer's focus expands beyond those systematic barriers to include her own clients. Recognizing that the conditions of subordination force people to suppress their own interests and discount their own power, the lawyer seeks to engage her clients in a process that will help them reclaim their power.

* * *

A. *Three Levels of Subordination*

The first dimension of power that Lukes identifies is that of interest group contestation that has been analyzed by Anglo-American pluralist political scientists. In this dimension, power is exercised as groups contest their interests through established channels of political disputing. A group gains power when it wins a particular contest; it is momentarily disadvantaged when its interests do not prevail. On this level, people are assumed to recognize their interests and their grievances. They are assumed to make informed, rational choices about whether or not to act on those interests in particular circumstances. In this dimension, the analysis focuses on the official, public political contests that groups enter, how those contests are conducted, and, most importantly, who wins.

This first dimension does not comprehend several phenomena that might be viewed as features of political and social domination. It cannot respond when certain interests or groups are repeatedly defeated in the political arena. Nor can it explain in terms of political power why some people habitually fail to assert their interests in public settings. Rather, the "first-dimensional" analysis fails to comprehend systemic mechanisms that affect the outcome of political contests or the capacity of groups to enter those contests at all.

Lukes' second dimension of power addresses this failure to account for the dynamics of exclusion at work in the political system. In contrast to the first-dimensional analysis, which looks only at the contests which *are* fought, the analysis in the second dimension focuses on the barriers—the social values and institutional practices—that keep certain interests and issues out of the political sphere altogether.

The most overt of these barriers is the formal exclusion of certain groups or issues from the political process. Many barriers are more subtle, however. For example, one common barrier to participation is the threat of retaliation—physical, emotional, or economic—if an issue is contested. For example, a tenant may know that his landlord is breaking the law by failing to make repairs and may want to protest. Yet his fear of eviction may prevent him from complaining. A claimant may also risk social sanction if he protests. Thus, an employee might not support a union if he fears he will be ostracized by coworkers or disfavored by management.

Another kind of barrier is found in institutional structures and cultural patterns which make it hard for the state to implement measures that benefit certain interests, even when change has been mandated. For instance, a coalition of civil rights groups might succeed in getting a legislature to make housing discrimination illegal. Yet in spite of this formal victory, the actual practice of residential discrimination might persist for years. A judge might find that an agency is out of compliance with the law in its day-to-day practices toward the poor. Yet institutional and cultural factors may nonetheless prevent that judge from devising a remedy that will solve the problem.

Another kind of barrier exists when the prevailing norms do not identify a particular experience as a legitimate legal or political claim. In that circumstance, a person or group may feel an injury and may even try to complain about it. However, because there is no legitimate concept for translating that injury into a public concern, the effort will fail. Only with change in shared norms about the boundaries of the political and the appropriate criteria for dignity and fairness will the old categories expand, and new ones emerge.

These barriers operate together to deflect, submerge, or conceal the wants or preferences of subordinated groups. In most cases, group members are discouraged from raising their voices at all, or the polity has no language for comprehending or responding to their claims. In the rare instances where a group's claim is acknowledged by legislative or judicial action, social practice may not readily change to comply with that mandate. As a result, challenges to the existing allocation of benefits are "suffocated before they are even voiced; or . . . maimed or destroyed in the decision-implementing stage of the policy process."

In this second dimension, the analysis searches for factors that cause the *suppression* of conflict, rather than overt political defeat. Like the first dimension, however, the second is also limited. It can offer a power-oriented analysis when a person feels an injury but fails to raise it as a political claim. It has no analysis, however, for the more vexing case of the apparent absence of grievance from consciousness altogether. What are the mechanisms of power that work within the consciousness of an individual or group to cause apparent acquiescence to the status quo? * * *

In the third dimension, the analysis * * * [focuses] on the subtle mechanisms of power that place individuals and communities in circumstances where they are constrained from clearly asserting their own interests. The focus is on those social processes through which subordinated groups construct their experience and give it meaning. Perhaps the most basic of these processes is the socialization of subordinated groups into the norms and practices of the dominant culture. Through their learning of the language and beliefs of the dominant culture, subordinated people are taught how to interpret their experience. They are taught to perceive, remember, imagine the world as though things cannot—and should not—change.

Also at play in the third dimension are the mechanisms through which information is packaged and disseminated and public opinion is molded—the "engineering of consent." Through these processes, the subordinated are persuaded that the dominant group has their interests at heart. Other social groups are led to despise and fear the most subordinated sectors and to act in ways that stigmatize those groups.

Finally, the third dimension of power includes a psychological process that is triggered by the experience of subordination itself. John Gaventa describes this process in *Power and Powerlessness: Quiescence and Rebellion in an Appalachian Valley*, which analyzes social subordination in Appalachia. The repeated experience of domination and defeat leads to psychic withdrawal from the public sphere. Such withdrawal engenders even greater feelings of fatalism, self-deprecation, and apathy, especially if community bonds are weak within the subordinated group. * * * Those values that would ground resistance are driven deep within the consciousness of the subordinated.

The process feeds upon itself. As individuals become more alienated from their own community and from activities that might nurture and strengthen self-esteem and cultural identity, they sink deeper into a state of passivity and silence. Those in power point to this silence to legitimate their regime. The subordinated person himself begins to believe the argument.

* * *

B. Three Visions of How the Lawyer Promotes Change

* * *

In this section, I suggest three "ideal types" of activist lawyering, to correspond to Lukes' three dimensions of subordination. * * *

1. The First Image: The Contest of Litigation

The first image of lawyering corresponds to the first dimension of power. In this image, the role of the public interest lawyer is straightforward and familiar. He is charged with designing and winning lawsuits that will further the substantive interests of client groups. The lawyer "translates" client grievances into legal claims. He crafts the lawsuit so that the judicial remedy, if granted, will directly remove, or at least ameliorate, those grievances.

Within this image, the lawyer assumes that client groups perceive their suffering as injuries that can be redressed, and stand willing to share these perceptions with their lawyers. It is not the lawyer's role to question the structure of the law itself, asking whether it sometimes prevents the lawyer from translating his clients' grievances into good legal claims. Nor is it his role to question the judicial system, asking whether it sometimes prevents him from securing remedies that really work.

* * * [T]he lawyer assumes that the powerful have dominated the courts in the past because they have been the most effective at litigation. * * * By mobilizing massive professional lawyer-power behind his clients' claims, the first-dimensional lawyer seeks to use the courts as a direct mechanism for redressing the injuries of class, race, and gender, and for redistributing power to subordinated groups.

In order to frame claims that could do justice to their clients' injuries, first-dimensional lawyers must often seek very sweeping, very innovative remedies from the courts. They must ask judges and courts to get involved in the funding, design, or management of public institutions. Yet, in litigating these unconventional cases, first-dimensional lawyers play an essentially traditional professional role.

Because the lawyer relies on the *court*, finally, to effect change, he must, first and foremost, be a good litigator. He must be creative at manipulating and extending accepted doctrine. He must assume a personal style that makes him credible to the judge. He must strive to have the other lawyers accept him as a person who plays to win, but whose ultimate loyalty is to the game itself.

In this image, the lawyer's primary foci are the adversary, the judge, and the courtroom. The client must be sufficiently acculturated to that world to be a good witness when facts are at issue. But apart from the moments when facts are contested, the client is in the background.

Public interest litigation has brought about substantial change, and continues to do so. However, in some circumstances where institutional practices are challenged, courts have difficulty fashioning effective remedies. * * *

* * * [T]here is a deeper limitation in the litigation-centered approach to public interest lawyering. Recall that in the one-dimensional understanding of the process of social subordination, the existing arenas for political contest were assumed to be adequate to accommodate the

interests of all groups in society. In the first-dimensional image, the lawyer makes the same assumption about the law. He thus places great pressure on subordinate groups to formulate their interests in forms that the law can "process."

In order to get into court, litigants must present their claims as similar to precedent claims that courts have already accepted. In order to get relief, litigants must propose remedies that are coextensive with these confined claims and that can be feasibly administered by the courts. The result of these pressures is the oft-observed risk that litigation will co-opt social mobilization. Through the process of voicing grievances in terms to which courts can respond, social groups risk stunting their own aspiration. Eventually, they may find themselves pleading for permission to conform to the *status quo*.

2. The Second Image: Law as a Public Conversation

In the second image of lawyering, the lawyer acknowledges that litigation can sometimes work directly to change the allocation of social power. However, she sees these effects as secondary to law's deeper function in stimulating progressive change. In addition to generating remedies that can coerce change, litigation is also public action with political significance. The law and its practice has cultural meaning; it constitutes a discourse about social justice.

Recall that second-dimension mechanisms work to shape political institutions and public values so that subordinated groups are excluded from asserting their interests in the official channels of political contest. Lawyers can use litigation to challenge these mechanisms of exclusion. Even when it does not succeed, well-crafted litigation can reveal the law systematically working to contain grievances. Litigants, by reformulating legal norms in light of their intuitions and experience, can project visions that expand the range of social options.

* * * Under the second-dimensional approach, the lawyer is not indifferent to victory in court. * * * But the measure of the case's success is not who wins. Rather, success is measured by such factors as whether the case widens the public imagination about right and wrong, mobilizes political action behind new social arrangements, or pressures those in power to make concessions. To accomplish these goals, the lawyer must design the case with the audience—the subordinated group and the wider public—in mind.

Within this second dimension, the lawyer must, first and foremost, be able to produce public happenings that "work." Most trials are open to the public; this fact inevitably affects any lawyer's advocacy decisions. However, in order to make the case into an effective vehicle for changing public consciousness, the audience is not merely on the periphery. It becomes the focus of the lawyer's attention. The client will "win," ultimately, only if the lawyer moves the audience to action.

The lawyer must learn to read public sentiment, framing cases in which the public will readily see injustice and can be led to see that conventional legal remedies do not really right the wrong. Furthermore, the lawyer must be able to coordinate the lawsuit with any direct political action that the litigation might spark. She must support such mobilization when it arises without either diverting its energy into litigation support or confining its own demands to the legally feasible remedies. Thus, she must at the same time be fluent in the law and attuned to the feelings and beliefs of the relevant audiences.

All litigation has both direct and indirect effects. In many cases, the lawyer can seek simultaneously to persuade the judge and to mobilize the public. The two goals—of winning a legal remedy and influencing public consciousness—do not work at cross purposes. On some occasions however, typically in high visibility political trials, lawyer and client may choose to spurn the legal ground rules and sacrifice a favorable outcome precisely in order to make the litigation speak most effectively to public consciousness. It is on these occasions that the contrast between first- and second-dimensional lawyering is most dramatic.

* * *

If third order mechanisms of power do indeed operate, the clients that are most fully subordinated never get the second-dimensional lawyer's attention. These are the people who feel cheated but have no clear sense of who is responsible, people who describe their suffering to outsiders as their lot in life, or people who distrust the "system" and the remedial processes that it offers. Such people will not give the right answers when the well-meaning lawyer innocently asks, "What's wrong?"

The lawyer then has three choices. She can work for more assimilated groups, those who ask for help in terms that lawyers more readily understand. She can set her own priorities for social change, recruiting token clients to stand for the issues that her own political analysis has led her to pursue. Or, finally, she can take on the dangerous project of listening carefully to the answers that at first might seem "non-responsive." She can work with those groups in a joint project of translating felt experience into understandings and actions that can increase their power. This is the project of lawyering on the third dimension.

3. The Third Image: Lawyering Together Toward Change

If a lawyer wants to stimulate change on the level of consciousness, she has much to learn from the writings of Paulo Freire and the parallel feminist methodology of consciousness raising. Freire's work shows how an active, critical consciousness can re-emerge among oppressed groups as they reflect together about concrete injustices in their immediate world and act to challenge them. He views this liberation of consciousness as fundamentally a pedagogic process. It is an unconventional, non-hierarchical learning practice in which small groups reflect together upon the immediate conditions of their lives. The groups first search their shared reality for feelings about that reality that have previously gone unnamed. They then attempt to re-evaluate these common understandings as problems to be solved. They collectively design actions to respond to these problems and, insofar as possible, to carry them out. They then continue to reflect upon the changed reality, thereby deepening their analysis of domination and their concrete understanding of their own power.

* * * [The analysis of shared reality and alternatives may proceed in a straight-forward, immediate way, through discussions of shared conditions of life that deepen a sense of injury and lead to the beginning of ideas on how to seek possibilities for change.]

Through this dialogic process of reflection and action, subordinated communities can, Freire contends, gradually liberate their consciousness from internalized oppression. Their private methods of surviving and resisting their common oppression can be brought to the surface and their lessons shared. Fatalism and passivity can be transformed into a common recognition of the skills that people already possess and into a shared willingness to risk change. The lawyer must learn how to engage with her clients in a conversational process of naming and critiquing their immediate reality. This process, as laborious as it may seem to the result-oriented lawyer, must be the center of a third-dimensional practice of law.

In Freire's model of learning, no one monopolizes the teacher role. Yet the outsider with professional skills does have a distinct role to play in the mutual learning practice. In the third-dimensional image, the lawyer aspires to learn this role. The outsider helps to bring people together, sets a tone in which collective learning can take place, and teaches a practice of critical reflection by leading the group through its first sessions and helping it plan its first actions. In contrast to the conventional professional, however, the outsider—the lawyer working in the third dimension—does not claim to possess privileged knowledge about politics or reality. "Dialogue, as the encounter of men addressed to the common task of learning and acting, is broken if the parties (or one of them) lack humility."

* * *

Challenging subordination on the level of consciousness entails educational work in the broadest sense, working with people to engender changes in how all participants view themselves and the world. * * *

In addition to pedagogy, lawyering in the third dimension also includes strategic work. The lawyer must help the client-group devise concrete actions that challenge the patterns of domination that they identify. This strategizing is also a learning process. Through it, the group learns to interpret their relationship with those in power as an ongoing drama rather than as a static condition. They learn to interpret the particular configurations that the oppressor's power takes on over time and to respond to those changing patterns with pragmatism and creativity. They learn how to design context-specific acts of public resistance, which work, not by overpowering the oppressor, but by revealing the wrongness and vulnerability of its positions to itself and to a wider public.

Thus, third-dimensional lawyering involves helping a group learn how to interpret moments of domination as opportunities for resistance. The lawyer cannot simply dictate to the group what actions they must take. Neither the lawyer nor any single individual is positioned to know what actions the group should take at a particular moment. Sound decisions will come only as those who know the landscape and will suffer the risks deliberate together. The role of the lawyer is to help the group learn a *method* of deliberation that will lead to effective and responsible strategic action.

This image of lawyering bears little resemblance to traditional professional practice. * * * Freire's writing suggests a parallel between the "outsider" and the radical cleric from the tradition of Liberation Theology. The outsider might also be compared to an organizer. But he is less directive than familiar models of organizing advise. [*See, e.g.*, Saul Alinsky, *Reveille For Radicals* (1969); Saul Alinsky, *Rules For Radicals: A Practical Primer For Realistic Radicals* (1972).] Rather than leading clients to engage in pre-scripted actions that will give them the momentary illusion of confrontation and victory, he seeks to enable group members to speak for themselves, both as critics and as strategists.

Why should this "third-dimensional" work be thought of as lawyering at all? It certainly can be done without an attorney's license and, indeed, without any legal training at all. Nevertheless, fluency in the law—that is, a deep practical understanding of law as a discourse for articulating norms of justice and an array of rituals for resolving social conflict—will greatly improve a person's flexibility and effectiveness at "third-dimensional" work. * * * It is also possible, however, that professional identification as a lawyer can narrow one's strategic imagination. Perhaps the best arrangement is for lawyer-outsiders to work side by side with outsiders trained in other fields.

This third-dimensional image of lawyering may seem very remote from our conceptions of lawyering, even lawyering specifically directed toward social change. Yet some writers, in exploring alternative visions of lawyering, have pointed toward it. Its outlines were suggested in 1970 in an article by Steven Wexler. He observed that the problems of poor people are fundamentally social rather than individual in nature and concluded that in order to effect lasting change, the poor must organize and act for themselves. In order to support that process, poor people's lawyers must depart radically from the traditional lawyer's role. They must act more like teachers, turning every moment into an occasion for clients to practice skills and build connections that will enable them to make change.

* * *

Such a practice places enormous demands on its participants. Both lawyer and client must accept, indeed invite, repeated challenge from the other; no longer are the lawyer's supposed skills or the client's claimed desires entitled to deference. Even more problematic, however, is the moral risk that attends this practice. The process simultaneously demands committed action and insists that there can be no secure, external grounding for the consequent choices that must be made.

* * *

Yet, if domination does indeed penetrate within consciousness and if we sense that domination is wrong, we cannot escape that risk. We have no choice but to proceed tentatively, attentively in our work, never escaping from the uncertainty of our action. We cannot construct a frame of reference beyond the particular situations in which we find ourselves and our own shared deliberation, our shared judgment, our "step by step . . . reflection . . . on given situations." Perhaps the biggest challenge, given our culture's particular myths, is to accept that our choices are inevitably situated and inevitably ambiguous, and that our most powerful theory, in the end, may be our practice of deliberating together on our experience and our action.

Notes and Questions

1. Rivkin notes that, in the theories that informed the modern public interest law movement, lawyers "viewed themselves as surrogate representatives of under-represented people. Overcoming the barriers to participation in decision-making channels that were the exclusive province of strong, organized corporate interests, public interest lawyers sought to combine the second face of power with the first face, creating an expanded, two-dimensional view of power. They believed that such a structural transformation would breathe life into the rhetoric of the traditional pluralists." Rivkin, *supra* at 474–75.

2. The "first dimension" lawyers described by White rely not only on a vision of law as adequate to the contest—they also rely on courts as an adequate theater for combat or resource for justice. *See* chapter 10, on the selection of judges and access to federal courts.

Is the following example of "political lawyering" an example of White's "second dimension" or "third dimension?"

> Wasco is a little town off the freeway at the southern end of California's San Joaquin Valley. Its residents are largely poor farmworkers; most are black—unusual for that area—and Chicano. One day when Gary Bellow worked as an attorney at California Rural Legal Assistance, several people from Wasco came in to complain about the mud in their household tap water and the utility company's failure to respond to their complaints. After researching the relevant law establishing standards for potable water, Gary went to a local church in Wasco to meet with more members of the community. He explained two options available to them: bringing a complaint to the state public utilities commission or complaining directly to the utility company. In response, the townspeople expressed an overwhelming desire to deal directly with the previously unrespon-

sive utility company. Gary agreed to try to get representatives of the company to come to Wasco and created a committee of town residents to spearhead the effort.

Another committee organized to develop the evidence: everyone in the community would collect samples of tap water in jars and label them with date and place. For the next several Sunday nights, community members gathered back at the church to check in and discuss their plans. Gary reported that company representatives had agreed to come to Wasco after he presented them with the alternative of complaining to the state public utilities commission. The Sunday night before the scheduled meeting, Gary and the community members planned how they would present the evidence.

When the day arrived, three men in suits came and sat in the front of the room behind a table, appearing poised to give a public relations speech. One by one, members of the community stood up to tell their stories, with tales of how for fifteen years they had to boil the water because it was so dirty and how they could not allow their children to drink the water. As each person finished, he or she would walk to the back of the room where the bottles of muddy water were stacked and carry his or her bottles over to the table where the company men sat. By the end of the testimonials, the table was piled high with bottles of filthy water.

The men in the suits looked at each other and responded that the company would dig out the water pipes and put in new ones. "But what about the past?" Gary asked, "What about compensation for the past?" Arguments ensued. Another resident committee was organized to document the history of the problem and the numbers of people affected.

Again, the company representatives came to the church, and one claimed that the company had never received a formal complaint about the dirty water. A community member stood up and responded, "I think you gentlemen should remember we saved the bottles." Ultimately the company agreed to pay compensation to each of sixty households at a level comparable to the annual income of a farmworker at that time.

Martha Minow, *Political Lawyering: An Introduction*, 31 Harv. C.R.-C.L. L. Rev. 287, 287–88 (1996).

Is Gary Bellow's work here "second dimension" lawyering? Community involvement and decision-making transformed the community's sense of its own power, left the group stronger, and achieved remedies. Does White's "third dimension" describe people who do not realize that they are oppressed by the delivery of muddy water, people who fail to believe that anything can be done about it, or both? Do some people suppress the ability to make complaints when they believe that change is not possible? What is the role of the lawyer in a context where people feel too defeated to even complain?

White's third image of lawyering is distinguished by its focus on the consciousness of the clients. Where does Julie Su's practice (*see* chapter 3) with Asian and Latina garment workers fit in White's typology? Is William Quigley (excerpted in this chapter) trying to change the consciousness of his clients? What about Paul Harris and Peter Gabel (excerpted in this chapter)?

3. Another example of creative lawyering can be found in Gary Blasi's description of advocacy for the homeless. Blasi reviews empirical evidence showing that, "While most people blame poverty on the poor, most people blame homelessness on society." Gary Blasi, *Advocacy and Attribution: Shaping and Responding to Perceptions of the Causes of Homelessness*, 19 St. Louis U. Pub. L. Rev. 207, 208 (2000). Blasi suggests that societal understanding was transformed by the brilliant work of advocates for homeless people during the 1980s that helped to frame a structural understanding of "homelessness" rather an asocial perception that this phenomenon was caused by personal failings of poor people:

> Organizing people to collective action requires, among many other things, altering their understandings of their own circumstances and the alternatives. Advocacy requires, among many other things, changing how more powerful people understand the circumstances of the less powerful. * * * In both instances, a crucial aspect of understanding itself is the perception of the causes of behavior and of social facts—what psychologists call "social attribution." * * *
>
> * * *
>
> One possible explanation for the attributions of causes of homelessness is that these pervasive public attitudes are the product of conscious advocacy, aided by the mass media, during the time that "the homeless" took shape in contemporary American popular culture. * * * [T]he modern construction of homelessness began in New York City and Washington, D.C. in late 1970s and early 1980s. In Washington, D.C., Mitch Snyder, Mary Ellen Hombs and others at the Center for Creative Non-Violence (CCNV) brought homelessness into public view with a series of brilliantly conceived acts of civil disobedience and public education. * * * [Litigation in New York City by the Coalition for the Homeless, and sympathetic articles in the media, increased consciousness about the problem] and gave voice to one view of its causes.

Id. at 207, 220. Blasi also describes the work of lawyer Robert Hayes, of the National Coalition for the Homeless, who said there were three reasons people were homeless, "housing, housing, and housing." *Id.* at 221.

Does the work of organizing among homeless people, litigating, and using the media fit into the frameworks of consciousness raising about power? Can other issues be similarly reframed through activism and legal advocacy?

4. For further exploration of these dimensions in the context of examining power, see Lani Guinier & Gerald Torres, *The Miner's Canary: Enlisting Race, Resisting Power, Transforming Democracy* 109–11 (2002). Guinier and Torres observe that power is about control.

> Those with control maintain control because they set the agenda. With no voice in the process that distributes power, those out of power have a hard time wresting control. And they become further isolated and alienated because the stories that the winners tell the losers make the losers feel as though they deserve their condition and do not have a legitimate right to complain.

Id. at 110. Have you been a "winner" or "loser" in the dynamic that Guinier and Torres describe? How might the awareness gained from your position in that power dynamic inform your work as a lawyer?

5. Have you been trained to work as a "second-dimension" lawyer, with consciousness of power and skill at collaborating with people to change a situation? Or has your education emphasized analyzing rules to reach a legal result? Have you been trained for "third-dimension" lawyering? Is a law school the best place to seek this training? If not, how could you get such training while in school?

6. Why does White argue that the pressure of law can make people's aspirations so stunted that they may find themselves pleading to conform to the status quo? In the omitted portion of her article on Driefontein, White describes a village that had no legal rights to resist removal. If they had pursued their legal rights, they would have lost. Instead, they engaged in many creative forms of resistance through organizing and raised legal claims where possible—as when a leader from the village was shot by authorities at a public meeting—and avoided removal. Julie Su (*see* excerpt chapter 3) believes that "we succeeded in getting the workers released in just over a week in part because we did not know the rules, because we would not accept procedures that made no sense either in our hearts or to our minds," and that formal education "might, at times, actually make us less effective advocates for the causes we believe in and for the people we care about." Given the danger that law will shape work against subordination conservatively, is "fluency in the law" really an advantage in organizing?

The landscape of legal rights includes lost battles—in which people failed to carve out legal protections—as well as successful ones. *See, e.g.*, chapter 7 (describing the effort to vindicate claims for land by freed slaves after the Civil War and the mobilization of collective memory through rights claims regarding the internment of Japanese Americans during World War II). Working only within those rights which have been won may confine mobilization to limited terrain.

7. Commitment to the goal of transforming consciousness of clients is very different from the usual conception of the role of a lawyer. Are you concerned about the time involved in this project? How does White's call for lawyers to help change consciousness compare with the cautions

about the role of lawyers in organizing expressed by Diamond (*see* excerpt chapter 3) and Quigley? Does client-centered counseling, as discussed in chapter 5, help or hinder achieving the goal of transforming client consciousness?

8. What are the "familiar models of organizing" that White describes as involving "pre-scripted actions that will give them the momentary illusion of confrontation and victory"? Cummings and Eagly describe the recent history of community organizing in the United States, pointing to the many forms of work referred to as "organizing," and call for further exploration of the priorities and possibilities for lawyers involved in organizing work. The portion of this article that deals with legal ethics in the context of organizing is excerpted in chapter 6.

SCOTT L. CUMMINGS & INGRID V. EAGLY

A Critical Reflection on Law and Organizing
48 UCLA L. Rev. 443, 460–69, 479–93, 498, 500 (2001)

By the early 1990s, legal scholars had rejected the law as a vehicle for social transformation, challenged the privileged position of lawyers in social change strategies, and actively encouraged lawyers to work with other community members to seek local, nonlegal solutions to poverty. The collective force of these multilayered critiques of conventional practice ignited the search for alternative models of progressive lawyering. Beginning with the work of [Gerald] López and [Lucie] White, the vision of community-based advocacy that emerged held out community organizing as a critical component.

Over the past several decades, community organizing has emerged as a self-conscious social justice movement with the primary goal of "community building." The movement has focused on fostering grassroots participation in local decision making, coordinating the strategic deployment of community resources to achieve community-defined goals, and building community-based democratic organizations led by local leaders who advocate for social and economic change. In practice, community organizations have worked at the local level to create more equitable social and economic policies, redistribute resources to low-income communities, and empower marginalized constituencies by giving voice to their concerns. As a result of the community organizing movement, there are now more than six thousand community organizations in the United States. Movement historians have pointed to its many accomplishments, including the development of skilled community-based leaders and national community organizing networks, the refinement of replicable community organizing models, and numerous successful campaigns that have effectively shifted the balance of power toward disadvantaged communities.

The birth of the modern community organizing movement is generally associated with the work of Saul Alinsky. Beginning in the 1930s, Alinsky's "Back-of-the-Yards" organization in Chicago focused on organizing poor people through the development of neighborhood "organizations of organizations" that brought together local unions, churches, and service clubs. Central tenets of "Alinskyism" included building local power through the strategic mobilization of poor people, developing indigenous leadership to articulate specific community interests, and ensuring that organizing efforts evolved organically out of the needs of local communities. Alinsky's organizing efforts were focused on geographically discrete neighborhoods and sought to influence the decisions of local governments regarding the allocation of resources. The Alinsky model was extended by Fred Ross, the director of Alinsky's Industrial Areas Foundation, who developed the Community Service Organization in the 1940s to organize Latinos in the Southwest. Ross, who later worked alongside César Chávez in the farm worker organizing effort, is credited with instituting an organizing approach based on issues—which was distinct from the Alinsky model of organizing local institutions—and developing innovative organizing structures.

Despite the work of these early community organizing pioneers, it was not until the advent of the political and cultural ferment of the 1950s and 1960s that community organizing emerged as a "full-scale movement." During this period of intense social change, increased private funding for community organizations and a decline in municipal services created an atmosphere ripe for local organizing efforts. As a result, the number of organizations serving low-income constituencies grew significantly and community organizing emerged as a potent political force. Most significantly, the civil rights movement highlighted the grassroots organizing work of a diverse array of groups working to end Jim Crow segregation and achieve political and economic equality—the Congress of Racial Equality, the Student Nonviolent Coordinating Committee, the Southern Christian Leadership Conference, Students for a Democratic Society, and the Black Panthers. Due to the national prominence achieved by these organizations and the success of grassroots campaigns such as the Montgomery Bus Boycott, community organizing came to be recognized as an important social change strategy.

The contours of community organizing shifted in the 1970s. Community organizers, faced with corporate opposition to reform, shrinking institutional resources, and flagging memberships, sought to broaden their constituencies by building coalitions beyond neighborhood boundaries. In particular, some organizers worked to develop national organizing campaigns to align the majority of Americans against the narrow interests of powerful corporations and their government sponsors. This "majority-strategy" was adopted by the National Welfare Rights Organization (NWRO) and was central to the development of groups such as the Association of Community Organizations for Reform Now (ACORN). Although the turbulence of the 1970s led to the evolution of different approaches to community organizing, the trend was toward building large-scale organizations that would advance national agendas.

The 1980s ushered in an era of neoconservative politics that shifted the direction of community organizing away from large-scale mobilization and toward less confrontational local strategies, such as community economic development and the cultivation of alliances with economic and political elites. In response to declining public services, this period also gave rise to a proliferation of diverse community organizations seeking to shoulder the burden created by dwindling government funds. In the 1990s, as the number of community organizations continued to grow, increasing diversity in urban areas, combined with a groundswell of reactionary political initiatives targeted at communities of color, led to the expansion of organizing activities around issues of race and other identity categories. The heightened focus on organizing in communities of color, especially in immigrant communities, resulted in the adoption of innovative organizing techniques that drew upon international models. Toward the end of the decade, activists began to discuss local community organizing strategies in the context of increasing globalization, and a new effort emerged to organize multiracial coalitions to press a unified economic and political agenda against corporate interests.

The Fusion of Law and Organizing

In the late 1980s and early 1990s, as the community organizing movement confronted the challenges posed by Reagan-era cutbacks and demographic change, it also began to generate increased attention from progressive legal scholars and practitioners. Although the idea that lawyers should facilitate community organizing was not entirely new, this period was characterized by a different orientation toward organizing practice. Organizing became the centerpiece of a new theory of progressive lawyering that sought to empower low-income communities, and an emerging base of scholarship began to focus on studying international and domestic law and organizing projects.

* * *

As it has evolved, the law and organizing model represents a set of disparate approaches, rather than a unified theory of progressive legal practice. That is, there have been varied descriptions of what it means to engage in law and organizing. * * * [According to Steve Bachmann, describing his work on behalf of ACORN,] the promise of legal assistance could be used to encourage people to join an organizing group, while litigation was sometimes necessary to defend an organization against a lawsuit or help it exit from an unproductive campaign. David Luban offered another incipient version of law and organizing practice, arguing that lawyers must maintain a "subordinate role" when working with organizing groups, emerging to assist only when "a legal strategy fits in with a street strategy." He claimed that a "lawyer *qua* lawyer" could play an important role in "political organizing" by using legal action to accomplish specific group aims, augment the group's morale by attaining a legal victory, and catalyze collective action.

More recently, scholars have departed from these conceptions, suggesting that lawyers should not only use their legal skills to assist organizing groups, but that they should also engage directly in organizing activities to empower client communities. For example, López and White have promoted community organizing in an attempt to loosen lawyers' affinity for traditional legal practice and to encourage them to "think outside the box" by embracing a more diverse set of organizing skills. Thus, in many instances, they depict lawyers employing organizing techniques, instead of legal ones.

[Jennifer] Gordon has offered a particularly comprehensive vision of law and organizing practice. She argues that there are "three interesting and under-explored possibilities for how to use law" in grassroots organizing work. First, law can be used "as a draw" to bring new members into an organization that has larger organizing and reformist goals. The promise of legal assistance on a discrete case can motivate a worker to come to a workers' meeting at which she will be exposed to the broader educational and organizing activities of the group. Second, the law can be used as a "measure of injustice." For instance, as part of educational efforts, workers can be asked to analyze how their own experiences may diverge from what the law defines as basic legal protections. In this way, a discussion of legal issues can highlight discrepancies between the law as written and the law as lived by marginalized workers. The gap between the legal ideal and practical reality can then be used to chart a course for political action and community mobilization. Finally, the law can be used as "part of a larger organizing campaign" in which the ultimate goal is not to win a particular lawsuit, but rather to achieve specific organizing objectives and build power among unrepresented groups. According to this conception, the law serves as a strategic mechanism to support or advance organizing campaigns in practical ways—for example, by filing a lawsuit to call attention to a broader structural issue or to put pressure on an employer or industry to undertake systemic reforms.

* * * The law and organizing movement has created a decisive break in poverty law scholarship and firmly established the idea that building connections with community organizing campaigns is a critical component of social change advocacy. Over the last decade, the proponents of law and organizing have successfully incorporated scholarship from diverse sources to develop what is now one of the most influential models of progressive legal practice. The evolution of law and organizing has infused a new energy into debates about poverty law advocacy by urging practitioners to move away from conventional modes of practice and challenging them to measure the results of their efforts by the extent to which they are successful in shifting power to the poor. * * * [T]he emergence of the law and organizing paradigm has prompted the formation of new collaborations, the implementation of innovative advocacy projects, and the direct participation of increasing numbers of clients in successful social change efforts.

* * *

The development of law and organizing has fundamentally altered the terrain of progressive legal practice. By highlighting the value of organizing, the model has challenged the ingrained habits of legal services practitioners and has led to a more flexible and multifaceted vision of effective lawyering for the poor. Furthermore, by questioning the privileged position of lawyers within social movements, law and organizing proponents have reclaimed the centrality of community members in shaping social change. Most significantly, law and organizing has forced poverty lawyers to evaluate the effect of their efforts using a new calculus—one that defines success by asking whether legal advocacy has empowered client communities.

* * *

In the law and organizing scholarship, organizing itself is promoted as a technique that can effectively advance social justice in a way that conventional lawyering cannot. Law and organizing proponents argue that if lawyers can learn to integrate organizing into their day-to-day legal practice, radical change is more likely to occur. However, while its advantages have been richly detailed, the limitations and complexities of organizing have not been sufficiently addressed. * * *

Unpacking Organizing

One of the critical issues that law and organizing practitioners must grapple with is the ambiguous meaning of organizing. * * *

Organizing is often used as shorthand for a range of community-based practices, such as organization building, mobilization, education, consciousness raising, and legislative advocacy. * * * [I]t is useful to examine the distinction between community mobilization and organizing articulated by Frances Fox Piven and Richard Cloward. During the welfare rights movement, they argued that institutional change would most likely occur if welfare recipients were mobilized to engage in disruptive tactics, such as descending upon local welfare offices in large numbers to demand benefits. They contrasted this vision of mobilization with the model employed by George Wiley, head of NWRO, who sought to organize the poor through the development of a stable institutional structure with dues-paying members who could exert their collective power to challenge welfare policies. This distinction between mobilization as short-term community action and organizing as an effort to build long-term institutional power, while perhaps obscuring areas of overlap between the two concepts, nevertheless provides an initial framework for beginning to identify different roles for law and organizing practitioners. For instance, lawyers in the mobilization context might advise activists on the legality of different tactics, while lawyers in the organization-building context might counsel groups on the steps necessary to establish membership associations.

Distinctions have also been made between organizing and popular education. In particular, the defining feature of the Alinsky organizing model popularized in the 1940s is organizing to win, despite the fact that winning might involve the organizers making the key decisions about how to achieve the desired end. Popular education, on the other hand, has evolved as a process of nonhierarchical learning through which people analyze problems on their own so that they may arrive at a more critical understanding of the mechanisms of power and oppression. This understanding may then form the basis for collective action; however, it is the process of arriving at this understanding, rather than the action taken as a result, that constitutes the core of the popular education technique. * * *

Another practice frequently associated with community organizing is legislative advocacy. Although many efforts to influence legislation have an organizing component, it is important to disaggregate the concepts in order to better understand the different levers for applying political pressure. An example of effective legislative advocacy by the Workplace Project highlights this point. By organizing aggrieved Latino workers and building political coalitions with sympathetic constituencies, Workplace Project organizers were able to help win the passage of stringent employer penalties for nonpayment of wages. In this effort, the Workplace Project relied on a variety of community-based techniques, including education, media pressure, and signature gathering. In addition, organizers and community members worked together to draft legislation and conduct lobbying visits with key legislators. These varied practices suggest different roles for lawyers engaged in legislative work. In particular, practitioners supporting the efforts of a community-based organization to change the law might explain the technical aspects of the existing legal regime, research how other jurisdictions have dealt with similar issues, assist in drafting legislation, and help the organization understand and negotiate the legislative process.

Not only does organizing practice comprise a range of different techniques, it also takes place within disparate institutional contexts. In his recent work on organizing, Gary Delgado, one of the founders of ACORN, highlights three principal community organizing structures: (1) the direct membership model, (2) the coalition model, and (3) the institutionally based model. * * * Groups using the direct membership model are generally small, geographically based organizations of low-and moderate-income members that aim to increase their political power through direct action, including organized protests, strategic pressure, and media campaigns. Coalitions, in contrast, are issue-based groupings of existing organizations that seek to mobilize their members to change public policy through lobbying, public hearings, and electoral work. Institutionally based organizations, which tend to be affiliated with religious institutions, focus on developing strong indigenous leaders who use public pressure and negotiation strategies to influence local politics.

Law and organizing practice can vary depending on the type of institutional arrangements chosen by community groups. In a direct membership organization the lawyer might be asked to provide limited legal assistance to members. Frequently such services are promoted as a benefit of membership and used as a method to draw new members. For instance, a group focused on welfare reform might offer a free consultation with a lawyer on benefits issues in order to attract welfare recipients as members. Coalition organizations, in contrast, might find it useful for lawyers to share their knowledge of a particular specialized issue. For example, a coalition focused on immigrant rights would need a lawyer to explain existing immigration laws and interpret new legislative proposals. Finally, lawyers working with an institutionally based organization might be asked to analyze local redevelopment laws or the rules governing municipal decision making in order to strengthen the organization's ability to influence political decisions affecting the allocation of local resources.

Organizing must therefore be understood as encompassing a diverse range of methods and institutional forms. * * * Sophisticated practitioners have already begun * * * providing models of coordinated law and organizing advocacy that deftly integrate different community-based techniques to achieve clearly defined strategic goals. * * *

Limitations of Local Organizing as a Social Change Strategy

The law and organizing model privileges local organizing as the centerpiece of social change practice. Relying significantly on postmodern conceptions of political action, which have emphasized small-scale resistance against subordination, law and organizing proponents have viewed organizing as capable of fostering the type of local grassroots participation that leads to community empowerment. Yet, while the ideal of local action has appealed to progressive scholars and activists, it has also been the subject of criticism by those who contend that, as a political strategy, it fails to offer a coherent challenge to the larger institutional structures that produce poverty and inequality.

Critics of localism have expressed concern about measuring the success of political action by an empowerment standard and have wondered whether local, neighborhood-based efforts can ultimately generate a viable progressive social movement. Carl Boggs, for example, has questioned the effectiveness of local organizing in light of the increasing consolidation of corporate power and the growing importance of global economic and political decision-making structures. He argues that "[o]ne of the great ironies of the past two decades is that large-scale, macro, and global issues are increasingly met with local, often individual or privatized, outlooks and 'solutions' which is yet another testament to political futility." Handler has put forth a similar critique of the "new social movements," which he describes as "the archetypal form of postmodern politics—grass roots, protest from below, solidarity, collective identity, affective processes—all in the struggle against the established order outside the 'normal' channels." Handler suggests that these grassroots initiatives lack a comprehensive alternative social vision, which ultimately prevents them from developing institutional structures and challenging the hegemony of liberal capitalism. Community development scholars have leveled similar critiques against localism, arguing that social change strategies focused on geographically discrete communities cannot sufficiently address the problems of racial isolation and poverty concentration that are generated by broader regional dynamics.

Community organizers have also voiced concerns about the limitations of place-based neighborhood action strategies.

These criticisms raise legitimate questions about the efficacy of local organizing movements. How can local victories be leveraged into systemic, long-term changes in political and economic structures? How can local efforts be forged into a broader social movement? Although much attention has been focused on the benefits that grassroots organizing has produced for low-income communities, scholars and practitioners must begin to think more expansively about how community-based action can be linked to large-scale reform.

Increasingly, activists are working to connect local efforts to larger social change goals in ways that point to new directions in community organizing practice. For example, Fran Ansley has described the efforts of the Tennessee Industrial Renewal Network to address the impact of economic globalism on vulnerable factory workers by cultivating cross-border alliances and engaging in grassroots advocacy around issues of free trade. In Los Angeles, groups such as the Figueroa Corridor Coalition for Economic Justice and the Metropolitan Alliance have initiated organizing initiatives to address housing and job creation issues on a regional level. Community and student organizing against sweatshops has also produced large-scale change by forcing some multinational clothing companies to take steps toward reforming labor practices. * * *

The challenge facing law and organizing practitioners is to build upon these efforts in order to define more precisely the ways community-based organizing can change broader political and economic structures to benefit marginalized communities. * * *

Hierarchy and Identity Conflicts in Organizing Practice

* * * [W]hile there has been a discussion of the ways that conventional legal advocacy reinforces power inequality among different groups, there has been little examination of racism and other forms of subordination in the context of an organizing-centered approach.

Despite its progressive orientation, community organizing has not been immune from the same type of bias and discrimination prevalent in the dominant society. Commentators have criticized traditional organizing tactics that marginalize the concerns of people of color, women, gays, lesbians, and disabled persons. The labor organizing movement, which has focused on creating class solidarity among the working poor, also has a history of ignoring identity-based interests. Similarly, the civil rights movement, another precursor of modern organizing practice, has often been criticized for its patriarchal structure and its marginalization of black women's issues. * * *

[The Alinsky model of organizing was historically dominated by white male organizers. However, women and people of color have increasingly assumed leadership in organizing groups, groups have increasingly taken up issues of racial injustice, including police violence, environmental racism, immigrant rights, and workplace discrimination; also, community-based groups have formed around the issues of women of color. But change has been slow and hierarchy persists. There is also a danger that stereotypes and prejudices will be expressed by group members during the group discussions that are a frequent technique of popular education efforts.]

* * *

* * * [L]awyers should not assume that grassroots practice will deliver them from the grips of identity conflict. To the contrary, like their regnant counterparts, law and organizing practitioners must exercise constant vigilance in navigating the shoals of racism, sexism, and homophobia.

Law Versus Organizing: The Perils of Privileging an Organizing-Centered Approach

The law and organizing movement has evolved from a critique of litigation-centered poverty law practice. Scholars have argued that, rather than focus on piecemeal litigation for individual clients, lawyers should engage in grassroots political interventions to challenge injustice. To achieve this end, organizing has been privileged as a social change strategy while the relative importance of traditional lawyering has been de-emphasized. Thus, descriptions of model law and organizing programs have presented a narrow and arguably inconsequential role for conventional lawyers, while highlighting the community empowering methods of organizers. Although this critique of the regnant model has succeeded in breaking the spell of lawyer-driven social change, it has done so by diminishing the viability of traditional practice. The attenuation of the connection between conventional legal services and social change raises two major concerns.

First, exaggerating the ineffectiveness of traditional legal interventions minimizes the significant institutional restructuring that legal advocacy has achieved. Indeed, creative litigation and court-ordered remedies have changed many aspects of the social, political, and economic landscape. An analysis that obscures this fact truncates progressive legal practice by closing off potential avenues for redress.

In addition, the suggestion by proponents of law and organizing that lawyers should act as organizers, facilitators, and educators would require that less time be spent providing conventional representation to low-income clients, who are already drastically underserved. As it stands, there are only six thousand full-time legal services staff lawyers to meet the legal needs of the forty-five million persons who are income-eligible for free legal services. Each day, poor people flood legal services offices seeking assistance in accessing welfare benefits, contesting discriminatory employment terminations, petitioning for political asylum, resisting unlawful evictions, obtaining restraining orders from abusive spouses, and recovering illegally withheld wages. Given the scarcity of resources in legal aid programs, a shift toward an organizing-centered approach would result in a reduction of basic services to these clients.

In the end, this type of resource reallocation may be beneficial—it may, as law and organizing advocates argue, ultimately allow poverty lawyers to effect greater institutional reform. However, it would be short-sighted to undertake such a shift without a careful evaluation of how law and organizing relates to existing legal services priorities. This evaluation should be grounded in an empirical analysis of the relative effectiveness of conventional legal practice and law and organizing activities. Thus, to advance the dialogue on social change lawyering, scholars and practitioners must move beyond discussions of law and organizing that merely magnify the deficiencies of traditional legal tactics and instead begin to articulate a new type of interdisciplinary collaboration.

* * *

The Practical Difficulties of Law and Organizing

* * *

[There are also practical difficulties with law and organizing. Some groups of clients historically served by poverty lawyers are hard to organize, including substance abusers and people with severe disabilities or health problems. People who are the sole providers for their families may have scheduling problems, and very poor populations may be transient, making it difficult to reach them through traditional techniques such as mailings and home visits. It can be difficult for community groups to provide support such as child care, free transportation, and disability accommodations. As lawyers continue to experiment with organizing-centered approaches, they must do so with a keen awareness of the context-specific nature of their advocacy.]

Lawyers working in organizing contexts also face unique challenges related to the nontraditional nature of their practice. One of the most frequently cited concerns among lawyer-organizers is that it is extremely difficult to coordinate legal and organizing work. Law practice, whether litigation or transactional, has its own special pressures and deadlines. When legal work needs to get done, a lawyer's ethics will require that it takes priority over any organizing obligations, creating inevitable tensions. Furthermore, as organizers cannot engage in the practice of law, the dual role of "law and organizing" necessarily falls on the lawyers. * * * [Balancing time management and prioritizing work assignments] can be especially difficult when organizers are not entirely supportive of a community-based lawyer's legal work and put pressure on her to abandon some aspects of her legal assistance in order to attend organizing meetings and events.

Notes and Questions

1. Do you agree with Cummings and Eagly that lawyers playing traditional roles have won victories that have played an important part in social justice struggles in the United States?

2. How do you assess the importance of lawyers, working as organizers, to social justice struggles? Can lawyers work for community empowerment without being organizers? Recall Sophie and Amos, introduced by Gerald López in chapter 3. Are they attractive models because of the organizing component of their practices? Should all community-oriented law offices include community organizers as part of the staff or should lawyers retain that role?

3. The articles by White and by Cummings and Eagly both emphasize the role of education in lawyering for transformation. Recall Dale Minami, excerpted in chapter 2, also stressed education as an important role of his social justice practice. Is the role of lawyer as educator inextricably linked to organizing? How can a lawyer handle the danger that stereotypes and prejudices will be expressed by group members during popular education sessions?

4. Cummings and Eagly comment on three community organizing models: direct membership, coalition, and institutionally based. What similarities or important differences do these models share? How might the lawyers' role be different within these three contexts?

SECTION 3. COMMUNITY EMPOWERMENT IN PRACTICE

Virginia Coto and Jennifer Gordon report examples of lawyering toward community empowerment. They describe legal practices with similarities to lawyers depicted by Lucie White and discussed as positive examples of law and organizing by Scott Cummings and Ingrid Eagly. Consider the lawyers engaged in these projects in relation to the arguments and critiques of the preceding authors.

VIRGINIA P. COTO

LUCHA, The Struggle for Life: Legal Services for Battered Immigrant Women
53 U. Miami L. Rev. 749, 753–58 (1999)

Traditional practice hurts poor people by isolating them from each other, and fails to meet their need for a lawyer by completely misunderstanding that need. Poor people have few individual legal problems in the traditional sense; their problems are the product of poverty, and are common to all poor people. The lawyer for poor individuals is likely, whether he wins cases or not, to leave his clients precisely where he found them, except that they will have developed a dependency on his skills to smooth out the roughest spots in their lives.

Unlike traditional litigation techniques, community education offers a significant opportunity for clients to participate in discussions, learn new information, and play an active role in solving problems that affect them. Because clients are brought together through educational work, learning occurs in collaborative, dynamic ways that are not possible within the confines of the attorney's office.

Grassroots legal education and empowerment projects nonetheless offer an important means for expanding the boundaries of the traditional attorney-client relationship. Attorneys can learn to effectively facilitate, educate, and organize, and can create an environment that empowers members of historically marginalized communities. Clients can begin to take a greater role in making decisions within their individual legal cases, and can work together to solve their own problems. In addition, empowered clients can be more effective in building community organizations and coalitions dedicated to bringing about fundamental social change.

One example is the *Hermanas Unidas* program at *Ayuda*, Inc. located in Washington, D.C. *Ayuda* offers an additional route to its clients; a route that enables them to do for themselves what we as attorneys cannot and should not do. *Hermanas Unidas* provides a vehicle for addressing many of the "non-legal" concerns confronting our clients. The members not only improve their access to desperately needed social services, but also learn to advocate for one another. The women gain independence, and avoid relying on professionals who are often not as effective as another *compañera*.

Those clients who believe that they are alone in their struggle against domestic violence discover that they are not alone. With other women, they "share their stories" and offer emotional support to one another. This support enables participants to build self-esteem and confidence. They begin to exchange opinions, debate issues, and critically examine the world around them. With this increasing confidence, they turn outward and begin educating and organizing others in the community.

Another example is the Workplace Project located in Hempstead, New York. The Workplace Project is a community-based membership organization that organizes workers to fight widespread labor exploitation. The Workplace Project works in the Latino community and its goal is to organize immigrant workers. It is an active grassroots organization that is run democratically by low-income immigrant workers. The Workplace Project chose not to work with all workers, because the Project gains strength from having deep roots in a single community, creating the potential for effective alliances with other communities. The Workplace Project also conducts outreach in the Latino community to provide information about workers' rights and a Worker Course designed to develop legal knowledge, organizing skills, and leadership ability in its participants.

* * * *LUCHA* [THE STRUGGLE]: A Women's Legal Project was formed in 1997 as a grassroots membership organization that would address battered immigrant women's individual struggles of domestic violence, while providing the vehicle for them to become involved in the larger struggle on behalf of other women. *LUCHA*'s approach requires

the active involvement of battered immigrant women. Women become *LUCHA* members by taking a six-part course on women's rights, and committing their time to assisting other women. Members are then eligible to receive free legal representation in immigration matters. *LUCHA*'s main activities fall into three categories: education, legal services, and organizing.

LUCHA provides a six-part course on women's issues. The participative course covers topics selected by low-income immigrant women, such as immigration law, workers' rights, domestic violence, public benefits, victim's rights, community resources and how to be heard by your government. The class setting provides battered immigrant women with an emotional and social support system consisting of other women in the same situation as themselves, thus alleviating the isolation that they endured in their abusive relationship. Moreover, the course empowers the women by educating them about their rights and how to ensure that these rights are not infringed upon. Completion of the *LUCHA* course is a prerequisite for *LUCHA* membership.

We wanted the women to feel comfortable and encouraged them to attend classes. To allow for maximum participation, the classes are held in Spanish, and childcare is provided for them. Perhaps the most important element of the course was establishing a sense of community among participants. We tried to generate a group feeling by conducting some exercises to get to know one another and by initiating communication. As a result, the women were very active and interacted with each other as well as the class speaker. They took notes and used that resource to follow up on their individual legal cases as well as for areas of concern of their family and friends.

Informal and formal evaluations are conducted at the end of the course in the form of a group brainstorming session. The results indicated that the members wanted more than six classes and wanted them to be longer than the two hours scheduled. Also, the members felt that they wanted to implement what they learned through the formation of committees.

Upon completion of each *LUCHA* course, graduates join a women's organization which conducts outreach activities, examines public policy, and shares responsibility for *LUCHA*'s Spanish language radio show, "*La Voz de la Mujer*" (The Voice of Women). Class graduates have participated in *LUCHA* activities in various forms. Members' commitment to assisting other victims of domestic violence range from exchanging phone numbers, or assisting each other with transportation by car pooling to classes, or by attending a court hearing with a fellow member. Moreover, graduates have made presentations to incoming classes on the *LUCHA* support network, to church groups or at informal gatherings in their homes, and have assisted in formatting "*La Voz de la Mujer*." New members are encouraged to participate in *LUCHA* activities and commit to assisting other women who have survived domestic violence.

The commitment to helping other victims of domestic violence has resulted in the creation of committees. One such committee is the community education committee. Its purpose is to provide access to information to battered immigrant women so they too can escape the intolerable situation of violence in their homes. The committee's efforts focus on speaking out on domestic violence in the media including radio, television, and newspaper. As part of its goal, the committee will take over the radio show in its entirety and be responsible for its programming.

In exchange for their participation, *LUCHA* members receive free legal services in immigration matters. However, in a world where free legal services are more and more restricted we felt that we wanted to develop a system for delivery of legal services. Although Miami has several nonprofit organizations dedicated to assisting poor immigrants in immigration matters there are none that specifically address the needs of this most vulnerable population, abused women and children. A significant portion of *LUCHA*'s educational work focused on training domestic violence service providers about battered immigrant women needs and the relief available under immigration law. Because domestic violence service providers work directly with the community, they are often the first contact for persons in domestic violence situations. It is therefore vital that these providers develop the ability to give basic problem-solving advice and to have a basic understanding of immigration law.

Soon after *LUCHA* opened its doors we found ourselves overwhelmed with the amount of clients that needed our legal representation. We realized that we lacked the resources to provide legal representation for all those who required our assistance. It became crucial to train pro bono lawyers and domestic violence advocates in assisting battered immigrant women. Trainings have been conducted in an attempt to reach this goal. Domestic violence advocates are given the tools necessary to assist battered immigrant women in accessing services and gathering evidence. One of the barriers that battered immigrant women face is the ability to establish their case under immigration law. Thus, advocates become central in assisting attorneys representing battered women. The idea is that domestic violence advocates work together with attorneys thus facilitating successful legal representation.

* * *

In Miami, *LUCHA* was an innovative means of providing services to an under-served population while at the same time providing education and empowerment. However, *LUCHA* received much opposition in the community as to the way it provides legal services to clients. The opposition felt that it was unreasonable to force battered women to participate in a six-part course and to request a commitment to help other domestic violence victims in order to receive legal services. Battered women already have so much on their plate and this was one more thing among several that was imposed on them. They have to deal with their social worker, participate in groups at the shelter, take parenting classes, and a long list of other potential obligations. This was not fair. Women need legal services and not education they said.

We adhered to the project's original design and explained that like other legal services organizations which ration out services this was just a different way to do it in this community. Legal services for the poor are rationed out in a variety of ways already, such as by geographic location, income eligibility, immigration status, and project funding levels. We felt that when legal service programs provide assistance to indigent clients without charging for those services, we are unwittingly transmitting a message: "Nothing you have and nothing you can provide is of any value to me, the poverty lawyer." That is not only patronizing; it is wrong and it is self-defeating. It is a strategy more likely to generate frustration and a sense of powerlessness than progress. Helping the poor with legal representation will not work if it does not enable our clients to produce and to contribute. If we are to be true to our commitment to the client community, we must understand that we need them at least as much as they need us.

JENNIFER GORDON

We Make the Road by Walking: Immigrant Workers, the Workplace Project, and the Struggle for Social Change
30 Harv. C.R.-C.L. L. Rev. 407, 428–32 (1995)

* * * [The Workplace Project is] an organization through which Latino immigrant workers on Long Island could address the myriad problems that they face at their jobs and in their communities. The Project, also known as "Centro de Derechos Laborales," is now one of a small but growing number of workers centers around the country.

Workers centers are community-based membership organizations that organize workers to fight widespread labor exploitation. Workers centers organize at a grassroots level, across trades and industries, in communities of working-class people. In addition to confronting systematic exploitation in the workplace, the centers also focus their attention on the economic, social, and political concerns of their members. These centers are part of an effort to build a new labor movement, to lead the fight against exploitation of immigrants and other working-class people.

Currently, the Project works in the Latino community. For the Project's first two years, we worked exclusively with Central Americans. As the Workplace Project grew, we expanded our work to the entire Latino community, because we realized that immigrants from many Latin American countries were working side by side all over Long Island; checking passports at our center's door would only reduce the potential for solidarity in the workplace. We chose not to work with *all* workers, because the Project gains strength from having deep roots in a single community, creating the potential for effective alliances with other communities. Additionally, we wanted to ensure that our ambition did not outstrip our resources.

The Project is located in the center of Hempstead, a poor and working-class town of about 50,000 people—mostly African American and Salvadoran—with a smattering of older white people and immigrants from other countries. Hempstead has one of the largest communities of Latino immigrants on Long Island. The Workplace Project office is in a three-story building behind the state district courthouse. The building sits in the middle of a string of Salvadoran-owned businesses and is well-known to the Latino community. It is home to several lawyers that serve the community as well as the Central American Refugee Center (CARECEN), a nonprofit legal services center which sees approximately 8000 Central Americans with immigration questions each year.

For the Workplace Project's first year of operation, I was the sole staff person based in the office of CARECEN. During the second year, I raised sufficient funds to hire Omar Henriquez, a Salvadoran man and fifteen-year resident of Long Island, as a full-time organizer. By the end of the second year, we moved the Workplace Project to a new office and became an independent nonprofit corporation with a membership and board of directors made up entirely of immigrant workers. In this, our third year, the center will be hiring a second organizer to focus on the popular education of women workers.

During the first two years of its existence, we thought of the Workplace Project as housing three distinct programs: (1) a legal clinic for immigrants with labor problems; (2) a community outreach and education program on workers' rights; and (3) an organizing project. We have come to realize that this is not how we want the Project to function. Instead, we now see organizing immigrant workers as both our end goal and our core strategy. Our community education programs and legal clinic are part of this organizing effort. Both of these programs are designed to deepen workers' involvement in the Workplace Project and their analysis of the position of immigrants in the United States economy. As a whole, the programs support and train workers as they turn these analyses into strategies for change.

The Project has two goals for its organizing program. The first is to build an active, grassroots organization that is run democratically by low-income immigrant workers. Because of this, the Project has an all-worker membership from which the board of directors is elected as well as several worker committees. We see this organizational development work as an essential component of our second goal, mobilizing workers for structural change.

As part of the organizational development work, we sponsor a central workers committee, C-POL (the "Committee for Labor Organizing" or "Comite Pro-Organización Laboral" in Spanish). This group was founded in order to promote the education and organization of other workers by workers attending our Workers Course. The C-POL has developed educational events for community members in churches and other gathering places. The members of C-POL also actively participate in the planning and execution of Workplace Project events such as marches, dances, and organizing campaigns.

Although we encouraged women to join C-POL from the beginning, few did. Those who came to meetings felt uncomfortable and soon dropped out. In the summer of 1994, a group of women who had recently graduated from the Workers Course formed a women workers committee, Fuerza Laboral Femenina (Women's Labor Force). The committee met several times, but was divided on whether or not to merge with C-POL or remain a separate group that would focus exclusively on the needs of women workers. They voted, in the end, to join C-POL. When the first joint C-POL/Fuerza meeting fizzled, Fuerza also disbanded as a regular committee.

In general, we have found that men are much more likely than women to participate in our organizing and educational efforts. We attribute this trend to a variety of factors. First, compared to men who tend to work either in large factories or as landscapers waiting on a crowded street corner for work, immigrant women often labor in isolation. For example, many women are domestic workers or sew piecework at home. Their isolation makes outreach difficult. Second, women carry the double load of working outside the home and keeping the family together, leaving them too exhausted to take on other responsibilities. They may feel uncomfortable about bringing their children to a meeting. Husbands and boyfriends are often opposed to their wives' and girlfriends' participating in activities outside the family. Moreover, many women who neither drive nor have access to a car may feel unsafe waiting at a bus stop in Hempstead at night. Third, the immigration patterns in the Central American community also contribute to the predominance of men in organizing activities. Because men usually migrate first, their numbers far exceed those of the women. Because women face significant barriers to participating in organizing work, the Project has decided to create and fund a position for a woman to coordinate organizing, outreach, and education among Latina immigrant women.

Notes and Questions

1. What characteristics of *LUCHA* and the Workplace Project make them successful in the goal of community empowerment? Are these characteristics unique to these particular programs or could a social justice lawyer apply these attributes in other settings?

2. Virginia Coto argues, in an omitted portion of her article, that battered immigrant women are trapped in abusive relationships by a lack of knowledge and resources. Barriers include "language, a lack of domestic violence service providers, a legal system that lacks cultural sensitivity, and a lack of information about legal relief that is available."

Coto, *supra* at 751. "Large numbers of immigrant women are trapped in violent homes by abusive husbands who use the promise of legal status or the threat of deportation as a means to exert power and to maintain control over their wives' lives." *Id.* Therefore, domestic violence fits within Coto's argument that the problems of poor people come largely from their poverty. She treats domestic violence not as an individual matter but as a matter of resources and information. Do you agree?

3. Coto states that "Traditional practice hurts poor people by isolating them from each other" and that traditional practice misunderstands the needs of poor people as individual rather than as systemic and related to their poverty. Do you agree? What characteristics of "traditional" practice for poor people lead her to this conclusion? Do you agree with her statement? Recall the struggles of legal services lawyers to deliver both law reform work as well as legal assistance, detailed in chapter 2.

SECTION 4. LAWMAKING AND TRANSFORMATION: CHANGING CULTURE, POWER, AND SOCIAL RELATIONS

Recall the views of Nancy Fraser and Iris Marion Young in chapter 1 discussing whether an emphasis on identity politics has displaced attention from material conditions in the struggle for social change or whether this dichotomy is overstated. Reconsider the dilemma posed by Charles Lawrence (*see* excerpt, chapter 1) about seeking progressive change within a liberal framework. These discussions provide a backdrop for this dialogue between Thomas Stoddard and Nan Hunter about the role of legal change in shifting culture and social practices. Is there an identifiable relationship between the outcome of social justice legal battles and political climate?

THOMAS B. STODDARD

Bleeding Heart: Reflections on Using the Law to Make Social Change
72 N.Y.U. L. Rev. 967, 969–87, 990–91 (1997)

[The author describes traveling to New Zealand, which he had viewed as a kind of utopia for gay rights because formal legal rules promised legal equality, unlike the situation in the United States. However, Stoddard found that New Zealand was just beginning to experience the emergence of a collective gay consciousness paralleling that of the United States of twenty years earlier.] * * * New Zealand was not utopia—it merely had the formal rules that ought to govern any utopia that includes lesbians and gay men. * * *

I was confounded by my discovery. As a lawyer working for social change, I had assumed—and hoped—that changes in the rules that governed a society would inevitably lead to some form of larger cultural transformation. Protecting gay people from discrimination under the law would, for example, cause gay people to cast off the centuries of persecution that are their history, at least in the English-speaking world, and promote a flowering of gay culture, whatever that may be. But my trip to New Zealand suggested that I was mistaken in my assumptions about the ways that the law acts as a catalyst for social or cultural change.

* * * When and how, if ever, can the law change a society for the better? Are there more successful and less successful ways to make social change? Is the law an effective tool for social change? (Or should I have become a social worker instead of a lawyer?) Are there any lessons to be learned from the attempt by so many lawyers of my own generation to make social and cultural change through the formal rulemaking mechanisms of the law?

* * *

I begin, concededly, with several assumptions. I assume, first of all, that this society needs and deserves significant change—as well as more people, including lawyers, committed to that change, according to their individual and collective conceptions of the good society. The country's problems are large and numerous, but they are not insoluble. Second, I assume that employing the law to make change—cultural as well as formalistic—is appropriate. The law is not now, and never has been, simply a set of formal rules; it is also the most obvious expression of a society's values and concerns, and it can and ought to be used to improve values and concerns.

* * *

* * * [S]ocial change and legal change do not always walk hand-in-hand. One does not always stimulate the other. Attempts to reform the law may succeed as a formal matter but have only modest effects on the larger cultural context into which they fit. When can the law make cultural change—change that is effective and enduring? What are its limitations? And what works and doesn't work?

Lawmaking has at least five general goals:

(1) To create new rights and remedies for victims;

(2) To alter the conduct of the government;

(3) To alter the conduct of citizens and private entities;

(4) To express a new moral ideal or standard; and

(5) To change cultural attitudes and patterns.

The first three goals comprise the traditional role of the law in expressing the formal rulemaking function for a society. The law sets and alters rules; if it is effective, it also enforces those rules. I will call this the law's "rule-shifting" capacity. But lawyers of my generation, inspired by Supreme Court decisions like *Brown v. Board of Education*, *Baker v. Carr*, and *Roe v. Wade*, and by the success of the African American civil rights movement and companion movements for political change, have sought to do more with the law than make rules. We have, in the last half of this century, adapted the law's traditional mechanisms of change to a newfangled end: making social change that transcends mere rulemaking and seeks, above and beyond all the rules, to improve the society in fundamental, extralegal ways. In particular, we have sought to advance the rights and interests of people who have been treated badly by the law and by the culture, either individually or collectively, and to promote values we think ought to be rights. I will call this concept the law's "culture-shifting" capacity.

The fourth and fifth items on my list of lawmaking's aims reflect the conception of the law as a "culture-shifting" tool. The law has always been an instrument of change, of course, but in recent decades it has become, through the deliberate, indeed passionate, efforts of a new breed of lawyer-activists, a favored engine of change. The law has thus become increasingly "culture-shifting."

The Civil Rights Act of 1964, enacting probably the most famous reform statute of the twentieth century, may be the statutory paradigm of legal reform intended to make social change. The Act established new rules of law, but it accomplished much more, and its full effects are still being felt—and I do mean "felt"—throughout the society. The new rules were simply stated. The Act banned "discrimination or segregation" in the provision of goods and services, even by private entities, on the basis of "race, color, religion, or national origin," and outlawed discrimination or segregation in employment because of a person's "race, color, religion, sex, or national origin." It also forbade discrimination by the federal government on the ground of "race, color, or national origin" in any of its programs and activities.

The new law did not represent a simple recrafting of the applicable rules and remedies. It did not merely rewrite the canons of employment law. It did not mean only that in the future, employers, merchants, and the government (if law-abiding) would have to adhere to a new set of guidelines. The Act brought into being a whole new model of conduct that, consciously and deliberately, overturned doctrines embedded in American culture—and, more widely speaking, European culture—for several centuries. These doctrines carried different articulations and emphases over time—black inferiority, "separate but equal," and "states' rights" are but three—but, when reduced to their essentials, they resulted in the basic notion of white privilege. Enactment of the Civil Rights Act of 1964 constituted a formal, national rebuke of this detestable, but time-honored concept.

The Act was, as already stated, far more than an employment manual or sales guide. It put forward new ideas about everyday relations between individuals—not only in the workplace or in stores, but, implicitly, in all aspects of human interaction. The ideas were essentially two: (1) that each human being has rights equal to any other, at least in the public realm, and (2) that segregation by race is wrong.

The Act, put into its full historical context, constituted "culture-shifting" as well as "rule-shifting," attaining simultaneously all five aims of legal reform. It gave victims of discrimination new rights and remedies. It instructed the government to promulgate and enforce new rules of conduct for itself. It altered the conduct of private entities and citizens—dramatically, in the South. It expressed a new moral standard. And—I believe, although I cannot easily document my belief—it changed cultural attitudes.

There is no sure way to measure changes in cultural attitudes. Legal and economic statistics about jobs and income may help somewhat, but they reflect external rather than internal realities—formalities rather than conceptions. Even opinion polls are not especially instructive, because respondents to such polls often are not truthful, especially when the subject is race. I offer merely my own sense of things. But I see signs of the change all around me. Perhaps the most credible monitor is television—the cultural medium that binds together more Americans than any other. On the American television screen of 1996, black and brown faces are everywhere: on situation comedies, in dramas, on talk shows, on sports programs, at news desks, and in advertisements; in 1966—when I was in high school—integrated depictions on television were exceedingly rare. Many forces have helped to integrate the world of television—and the world of television is admittedly not an imitation or reflection of the day to day experiences of Americans off the screen—but the change does seem attributable, at least in part, to changes in the law that sent new cultural signals, primary among them the Civil Rights Act of 1964. Americans may not yet live fully in a world of equal opportunity and integration, but their principal cultural medium suggests that they have at least embraced the ideals—the desiderata—of equality and integration. "Chicago Hope" depicts an integrated world, even if the real Chicago does not.

I cannot, as I said, prove my point about cultural change, and I realize that there is plenty of evidence to show deterioration rather than improvement of relations between blacks and whites in the United States, such as the increase in rates of poverty among African Americans. I would never contend that the Civil Rights Act of 1964, even three decades after its passage, ended discrimination or racism. * * * But this point seems instinctively right, at least to someone who has seen the evolution of American culture over the past fifty years: cultural ideals have changed, even if cultural realities still lag. At least in part because of the Civil Rights Act of 1964—the most important statutory embodiment of the ideal of racial justice—American culture, American government, and the American people have absorbed the concepts of equality and integration embodied in the Act as the proper ethical framework for the resolution of issues of race. Outright segregationists like David Duke, and genetic supremacists like William Shockley, are remarkable for their contemporary scarcity; in 1954, views similar to theirs were widely held and admired, both within and without government.

Let me also suggest this: the Civil Rights Act of 1964 has had such a powerful cultural impact not just because of what it said, but also because of how it came into being. The Act was the product of a continuing passionate and informal national debate of at least a decade's duration (beginning, vaguely, with the Supreme Court's decision in *Brown v. Board of Education* invalidating the concept of "separate but equal" in the public schools) over the state of race relations in the United States. The debate took place every day and every night in millions of homes, schools, and workplaces. It is this debate—not the debate in the Congress—that really made the Act a reform capable of moral force. Through a continuing national conversation about race, ordinary citizens (especially white citizens) came to see the subject of race anew.

The arena of change may also have influenced the scope and power of the result. Imagine that the new rules enacted by the Civil Rights Act of 1964 had, instead, emanated from a ruling of the U.S. Supreme Court. * * * Imagine further no substantial difference between the provisions of the Civil Rights Act of 1964 as enacted and the holdings of one or several hypothetical decisions from the Supreme Court. Would American history have evolved in the same way? Would the difference in the forum of decisionmaking have resulted in a different public reaction to the new rules of law?

I think history would have been different. The new rules of law were widely disliked, especially by whites in the South, but the opponents of the Civil Rights Act of 1964 never rose in rebellion, either formal or informal, against enforcement of the statute. If the new rules had come down from on high from the Supreme Court, many Americans would have probably considered the change of law illegitimate, high-handed, and undemocratic—another act of arrogance by the nine philosopher-kings sitting on the Court. Because the change emanated from Congress, however, such sentiments of distrust (whether grounded in principle or in simple racism) never came to affect the legitimacy of this stunning change in American law and mores. The Civil Rights Act of 1964 came into being because a majority of the members of the national legislature believed it represented sound policy and would improve the life of the country's citizens as a whole; the ideas motivating the Act must therefore have validity behind them. In general, then, not only did the historical fact of the continuing national debate on race facilitate the public's acceptance of the Civil Rights Act of 1964, even in the South, but so did the additional (I believe crucial) fact that the change came through legislative consideration rather than judicial or administrative fiat—lending it "culture-shifting" as well as "rule-shifting" power.

The astonishing effectiveness of the Civil Rights Act of 1964—the breathtaking sweep of its cultural tailcoats—suggests that it should be a model for social change in other settings. It also indicates that how change is made matters almost as much as what is, in the end, done.

Most forms of law, statutory, judicial, or administrative, do not have social and cultural resonance. They merely set forth governing rules. Those rules affect conduct, individual and institutional, perhaps even in a way that is important and widespread, but they do not reverberate throughout the society, as did the Civil Rights Act of 1964. Nor do they mark a shift in fundamental values or concerns. They touch only specialized audiences, or constitute incremental variations on established themes, or both. Lawyers notice and care, bureaucrats notice and care, and accountants notice and care, as do other discrete and insular audiences, but most people neither notice nor care, and the overall tone of the society remains largely undisturbed. "Culture-shifting" laws, by contrast, alter basic principles, and alter them in ways that are inescapable—indeed, transformational. They remake culture.

The Civil Rights Act of 1964 is different from most forms of law in this way. Part of its effect emanated from the importance of its underlying theme and the history of that theme. At bottom, the Civil Rights Act of 1964 concerned a subject that is one of the central themes of this country's culture and history: racism. Part of its effect stemmed from the sheer size of the shift in rules; the Act overturned centuries of personal habits and customs, as well as set rules. It influenced every person in the United States in some fashion—not just African Americans, not just Southerners, and not just employers and shopkeepers. It set a new standard of conduct for the nation as a whole in the transaction, moment by moment and day by day, of the ordinary affairs of ordinary people.

My analysis of the Civil Rights Act of 1964 and other "culture-shifting" forms of law suggests that four factors determine when "rule-shifting" becomes "culture-shifting" as well. For "culture-shifting" to take place, all four factors must be engaged. The four factors are these:

(1) A change that is very broad or profound;

(2) Public awareness of that change;

(3) A general sense of the legitimacy (or validity) of the change; and

(4) Overall, continuous enforcement of the change.

In general, "culture-shifting" requires all four; anything less amounts to a form of "rule-shifting."

Some forms of "rule-shifting" are so grand or so pervasive that they cannot be ignored. Some affect so many people in such fundamental ways that they seem inherently "culture-shifting." Thus, while the breadth of change is not by itself dispositive, the very scope of a new law may by itself create the potential for "culture-shifting."

The Civil Rights Act of 1964 is such a form of lawmaking. It did not merely change the applicable rules; it transformed basic beliefs about relations between people of different races across the United States, and it did so in a way that no American (except hermits and misanthropes) could escape. Even other civil rights statutes, regardless of their value and importance, do not necessarily entail "culture-shifting." * * *

* * *

"Rule-shifting" cannot possibly become "culture-shifting" without public awareness both that a change has taken place, and that that change will affect daily life. Ordinary citizens must know that a shift has taken place for that shift to have cultural resonance. * * *

* * *

Changes that occur through legislative deliberation generally entail greater public awareness than judicial or administrative changes do. Public awareness is, indeed, a natural concomitant of the legislative process. A legislature—any legislature—purports to be a representative collection of public delegates engaged in the people's business; its work has inherent public significance. Judicial and administrative proceedings, by contrast, involve private actors in private disputes. Those disputes may or may not have implications for others, and they are often subject to the principle of *stare decisis*, but they are not public by their very nature. (Administrative rulemaking is a different animal, akin—at least in theory—to legislative activity, but it is still typically accorded less attention than the business of legislatures.)

Legislative lawmaking is, by its nature, open, tumultuous, and prolonged. It encourages scrutiny and evaluation. Thus, it is much more likely than other forms of lawmaking to promote public discussion and knowledge. For that reason alone, such lawmaking possesses a special power beyond that of mere rulemaking. Indeed, the real significance of some forms of legislative lawmaking lies in the debate they engender rather than the formal consequences of their enactment.

Between 1971 and 1986, the New York City Council had before it every year a bill that would amend the city's human rights laws to protect lesbians and gay men from discrimination in employment, housing, and public accommodations. * * * As a perennial lobbyist for the gay rights bill, and a gay man to boot, I publicly bemoaned the bill's failure year after year. However, in hindsight, I am not unhappy that enactment of the bill took fifteen years.

Over those fifteen years, the city council and the citizens of New York more generally had to confront continually the issue of discrimination against lesbians and gay men. They had to hear again and again the assertions made by my colleagues and by me that gay people exist; that gay people encounter constant scorn, disapproval, and prejudice; and that gay people deserve protection from discrimination in the basic necessities of life. The city council, for a full decade and one-half, became a city-wide civic classroom for a course on sexual orientation discrimination—an intracity teach-in, if you will. If we had our platform during the fifteen years of the bill's pendency, so did our opponents, but in many ways the other side's comments (especially the more rancorous observations) bolstered our advocacy, for the comments prolonged the discussion—and also helped to demonstrate our claims of the existence of prejudice.

Immediate passage of New York City's gay rights bill as early as 1971 or 1972 would have afforded immediate political gratification to me and my colleagues (I would have been very gratified indeed), but immediate passage would also have deprived the city and its residents of the extended exploration of the subject of gay people and their rights. And, I am now convinced, it is the city-wide debate of the subject, rather than mere passage itself, that has helped to open eyes and hearts. Mere passage would have added up to "rule-shifting" when "culture-shifting" is what this controversial and often misunderstood issue really required. Mere passage would have given lesbians and gay men who suffered discrimination (and who could prove their assertions) a form of redress, and it would probably have led some especially principled employers to adopt implementing guidelines, but enactment of the gay rights bill would have eluded the attention of many, if not most, non-gay New Yorkers. The fifteen years of struggle, however, made the subject ultimately inescapable to New Yorkers—and led to genuine and deep "culture-shifting."

From my experience on the gay rights bill, and my experience as an activist more generally, I harbor a bias in favor of legislative reform. Legislative reform makes real change—"culture-shifting"—more probable, since it is much more likely than other forms of lawmaking to engage the attention of the public. "Rule-shifting" has its merits and advantages, but it is simply less potent than "culture-shifting" in accomplishing the things I want to accomplish.

Awareness of change is never enough to assure compliance with a new law, whether that law has "rule-shifting" or "culture-shifting" capacity. Awareness must be accompanied by public acceptance—which must inevitably be grounded in a sense of legitimacy or validity.

* * *

The Civil Rights Act of 1964, as noted already, encountered surprisingly little public resistance, even though it overturned centuries of well settled law, custom, and habit. Why is that? The Supreme Court's decision ten years earlier in *Brown v. Board of Education*, by contrast, provoked widespread defiance among southern whites and the state and local governments purporting to represent them; southern officials tried to stop implementation of *Brown* and subsequent federal decisions requiring integration of the public schools, and southern parents withdrew their children from public schools and enrolled them in newly created private schools for white students alone. Why such a difference between the public reception of the two events when both, at bottom, concerned the same subject—integration?

There can be no single or definitive answer. Yet, one instance of lawmaking—the Civil Rights Act of 1964—carried an aura of legitimacy that fostered public acceptance, while the other—the Court's decision in *Brown*—did not. I see at least three explanations for the aura of legitimacy that accompanied the Act that help to illuminate the different contexts of the two related developments.

One element is timing. The Act came ten years after *Brown*, and during the decade between the two events, the entire country had an opportunity, in part because of *Brown* itself, to examine and reflect upon the issue of integration. The Act was able to gestate before its birth. This period of gestation allowed individuals, in the South and elsewhere, to reflect upon the subject and accommodate themselves to imminent realities.

Secondly, the African American civil rights movement, over the decade from 1954 to 1964, was especially active and effective at influencing public opinion against Jim Crow laws and other expressions of discrimination. Through continual demonstrations, protests, and public statements, Dr. Martin Luther King, Jr., and his colleagues and allies, forced the American public to face up to the question of racial inequality. Dr. King and the movement not only kept the issue on the front page of the country's newspapers, but also repeatedly framed it in a way that highlighted its moral dimensions. Statements like Dr. King's *Letter from the Birmingham Jail* appealed to the largest possible audience—whites as well as blacks, Northerners as well as Southerners—by making universal assertions about the civil rights of all people, not just black Americans. The deliberate universality of his declarations greatly enhanced the sense of legitimacy that accompanied the civil rights movement and, inevitably, the laws attendant on its success, like the Civil Rights Act of 1964.

The fact that the Act emanated from Congress rather than the Supreme Court may also have enhanced its legitimacy and promoted its public acceptance. To many white Southerners, *Brown* seemed thrust on them suddenly from above. They were not prepared for it, and they had little opportunity to participate in its formulation or implementation. The Act, however, came about only after much debate at all levels of government, in all segments of the society, and in every region of the country. And it came about only after a formal vote of the one body that can lay claim to be representative of the nation as a whole—the Congress. White Southerners had a chance to enter into both the debate and the vote; they could make their claims and express their views. In the end, those views were examined and rejected by the country overall.

By virtue of timing, context, and method of enactment, then, the Civil Rights Act of 1964 carried a presumption of democratic legitimacy (one might say "validity") that was absent from *Brown*, at least in the imaginations of some white Southerners. This sense of legitimacy fostered public acceptance, even in the South, and made possible the Act's "culture-shifting" potential.

Commentators for 200 years, from John Locke to Robert Bork—especially those, in recent years, identified with conservative politics—have asserted the superiority of legislative change. (Locke portrayed the legislature as the "supreme power of the commonwealth ... sacred and unalterable in the hands where the community have once placed it.") I find, after twenty years of work as a lawyer purporting to promote the public interest, that I have come to share the partiality for legislative lawmaking—but for reasons different from those of most other observers. I prefer legislative lawmaking because I view it as the avenue of change most likely to advance "culture-shifting" as well as "rule-shifting"—the method of lawmaking most likely to lead to absorption into the society of new ideas and relationships.

Judicial lawmaking, however, ought not to be abandoned by public interest lawyers like me. Like so many of my colleagues, I do not always trust legislatures, and I would certainly not want them to have sole lawmaking authority in this or any other legal system—but judicial lawmaking ought to be employed with greater cunning and precision. Lawsuits are effective at highlighting problems. They may be effective at forcing government to face up to problems. But they are often ineffective at the long-term resolution of issues with deep cultural roots, for they focus on rules rather than the culture that sustains those rules, and as a result frequently fail to engage or connect with the public.

The fourth prerequisite for legal change that accomplishes "culture-shifting" as well as "rule-shifting" is overall and continuous enforcement of the new rule by the government. Rules that are not enforced, particularly if they are dramatic or controversial, will simply be disregarded by all or part of the public.

I use the word "enforcement" in its broadest possible sense. "Enforcement" to me is not simply the imposition of penalties, civil or criminal. It is also the systematic notification—or lack of notification—of the new rule, and the provision of civil remedies to aggrieved individuals. Effective enforcement of a new law ought to incorporate mechanisms to promote public awareness and adherence as well as provide appropriate punishment; "culture-shifting" may be impossible without multiple systems of enforcement.

* * *

* * * Enforcement does not ensure "culture-shifting," of course, but it greatly enhances the likelihood.

"Rule-shifting"—the formal adoption by government of new rules to govern all or part of a society—is not always a prerequisite to "culture-shifting," in my experience. In unusual circumstances, "culture-shifting" may take place even without a formal change in rules.

* * *

I have stated * * * a personal preference for legislative change, since in general I believe that legislative activity is more likely than judicial or administrative lawmaking to lead to "culture-shifting" in addition to "rule-shifting." The story of *Baehr v. Lewin*, [*see* chapter 13] however, demonstrates the power and value of litigation to make social change, when that litigation is cunningly prosecuted. *Baehr* brought national attention to an issue previously overlooked or belittled. It began the "culture-shifting" necessary for ultimate success.

Many of my colleagues seeking social justice have deliberately avoided legislatures in recent decades, both because of the difficulty of making change there and because of the perception that politicians will not be receptive to their claims. They have turned by and large to the courts. While applauding the changes these lawyer-activists have helped to bring about, and while acknowledging the shortcomings and frustrations of legislative change, I submit that those of us in the business of "culture-shifting" should upend our traditional preference for judicial activity and embrace the special advantages of legislative change.

* * * If we lawyer-activists truly seek deep, lasting change, we have to "connect" with the public. We have to accord as much attention to public attitudes as we do to the formal rules that purport to guide or mold those attitudes. That means thinking as concertedly about process as we do about substance. Process matters. How a new rule comes about may, in the end, be as important as what it says.

The world yearns for change—and for changemakers. But those of us who try to make change ought to think more systematically about what we do and why. For the world deserves effective change, not just new rules.

NAN D. HUNTER

Lawyering for Social Justice
72 N.Y.U. L. Rev. 1009, 1011–13, 1017–22 (1997)

I do not believe that as a general rule one can ascribe culture-shifting moments to one arena—legislation or litigation—more than the other. Breakthrough moments in law occur rarely but not randomly, regardless of arena. They usually follow long periods of incremental, often nearly imperceptible, social change occurring at a glacial pace. When they do occur, they crystallize what has gone before at the same instant that they propel social structures forward. Law is unique in that it has the power of coercion: it seeks to lock in the very change that it signifies.

It is impossible to completely separate these arenas analytically, for multiple reasons. I agree that majoritarian legislative victories can be more politically stable than judicial interpretations of the Constitution, despite the fact that enactment of any statute is subject to nullification by the process of judicial review. Note, however, that the distinction between the arenas of change (legislative or judicial) is not the same as the distinction between sources of law: statutory, or legislature created, versus constitutional, or (mostly) judge created. [Tom Stoddard's] *Bleeding Heart* invokes as archetypes the enactment of a statute versus the interpretation of the Constitution. In my view, however, the single most common and powerful activity within social change lawyering has become the use of litigation to secure enforcement and expansive interpretation of statutes.

The primary example of a culture-shifting statute cited in *Bleeding Heart* is the 1964 Civil Rights Act. At the time of its enactment, the Civil Rights Act was culture-shifting for the South, but became so nationally because of judicial interpretation primarily. Congress and the public viewed the new statute as one that would end racial apartheid, which most of the country saw as a problem of the South.

As the bill went through the legislative process, most public attention focused on the sections dealing with voting, public accommodations, and the authority of the Attorney General to enforce equal protection of the laws. The public accommodations section "was easily its most controversial provision, and arguably its most radically transforming one for the South." As a result of that portion of the statute, "the destruction of Jim Crow in public accommodations would occur with surprising speed and virtually self-executing finality." The continuing nationwide impact of this statute thirty-five years later, long after the end of de jure segregation, flows from such judicial decisions as *Griggs v. Duke Power Co.*, in which the Court interpreted the statute to reach widespread employment practices that were facially neutral, but racially subordinating in their effects.

Although the 1964 Civil Rights Act prohibited sex as well as race discrimination, it was not culture-shifting on the basis of sex. As *Bleeding Heart* points out, the addition of "sex" to the prohibited bases for discrimination was a ploy to derail the bill by legislating for a form of equality that its opponents thought would be viewed as absurd.

Structural factors determine whether legislation or litigation dominates an equality movement at any given moment: the roles of the state and the market as allies or foes; the nature of the rights being sought; and the broader political climate in each arena. * * *

* * *

One of the most controversial arguments in *Bleeding Heart* is implicit: underlying a call for a shift to prioritizing legislative strategy is the belief that gay equality claims *can* be achieved, with a regular if not inevitable degree of success, by majoritarian means. This is a provocative premise.

Until now, advocates for lesbian and gay rights have asserted that homosexual citizens meet the indicia for political powerlessness associated with the requisite criteria for recognition as a suspect class in equal protection law. Indeed, advocates have argued that lesbians and gay men often constitute "pariahs" in the pluralist bazaar, invoking Bruce Ackerman's description of groups so stigmatized that the ordinary give and take of coalition politics cannot afford them a fair opportunity to protect their interests. *Bleeding Heart* does not relinquish that claim, but it does raise the question of whether a group that can function effectively in the normal political process can invoke a suspectness claim based on process failure.

There are signs that opponents of equality are finding increased difficulties in using anti-gay electoral strategies. Indeed, perhaps the most significant, least noticed, aspect of the controversy surrounding the Colorado anti-gay initiative, declared unconstitutional by the Supreme Court in *Romer v. Evans*, was how *a*typical it was. Most anti-gay voter initiatives in the 1990s have been defeated at the polls or have failed to obtain the necessary number of signatures to qualify for placement on the ballot; the Colorado provision was an exception. One can contrast that to the late 1970s, when a wave of newly enacted civil rights provisions were repealed by popular vote.

The obvious response is that advocates for lesbian and gay equality have made enormous strides, but this success is fragile and highly uneven. The most stunning variation is geographic: laws guaranteeing equal rights for sexual minorities have become standard in urban settings, but are still atypical in states that are not highly urbanized. * * *

The need for heightened scrutiny remains strong in most situations, but it may be that the lesbian and gay rights claim of a systematic political process breakdown, such as to trigger heightened scrutiny, is no longer viable in certain local jurisdictions.

* * *

Tom [Stoddard, in *Bleeding Heart*,] posits four criteria for when rule-shifting becomes culture-shifting: a genuinely significant change in the law; public consciousness of the change and its impact; a sense of legitimacy behind the new law; and continuous enforcement. I have no quarrel with any of these, but I think a fifth necessary ingredient is missing: public engagement. By engagement, I mean more than consciousness and more than passive support, even legitimacy. Unless there is significant public engagement in some form, beyond a small cadre of litigators or lobbyists, in the effort to change the law, there is no basis for culture-shifting.

* * *

In my view, the lesser degree of legitimacy that *Bleeding Heart* ascribes to judge made rather than legislative decisions is better captured by the distinction between an engaged constituency and a passive audience. Consider the Massachusetts gay rights bill, enacted in 1989, and skillfully managed by legislative advocates who sought to minimize public awareness of or involvement in the legislative debates. The strategy worked and may have been necessary to achieve victory, but its price was that "[t]he impact of the struggle to enact the Bill on a *cultural* level was virtually nonexistent."

I would change the injunction in *Bleeding Heart* to prioritize legislative work into one to use any arena for lawyering also as a vehicle for mobilization. Both legislative and litigation arenas have the potential to mobilize and demobilize by empowering those who seek legal assistance or by imposing the role of passive client onto persons who were initially engaged. Both arenas reward repeat players. In the realm of public interest and civil rights law, one goal should be consciously using one's legal skills to strengthen the constituency or community organization one represents, to make them more effective as repeat players.

For a social justice lawyer, repeat clients are groups of people active in the relevant community (which may be an issue constituency or an identity group or a geographic community) who regularly confront hostile policies. They may be repeat clients for litigation work or legislative advocacy or, more likely, for a mixture of both. Because they seek equality as a social result, rather than solely reform of the law, they are not constrained by doctrinal thinking. If such a group is unconcerned or dismissive of the importance of law, there is little basis for a synergistic linkage. But if law figures prominently, if not predominately, in a group's approach, the lawyer who links with such a group has the best opportunity to use law as a conscious culture-shifting strategy.

At issue here is not a split between arenas for lawmaking but between models of social justice lawyering. The two major American models have been doctrinal development and client advocacy, one emphasizing the achievement of a certain new principle of law, the other undertaking to serve the legal needs of some defined group. The classic First Amendment test case strategy undertaken by the American Civil Liberties Union illustrates the former, and the in-house organizational lawyer epitomizes the latter (e.g., labor union lawyers). Community legal services offices fall somewhere between, often beginning as the latter but shifting to the former as budget reductions force greater prioritization of impact litigation. Many organizations have developed hybrids. Some in-house legal units function as both corporate counsel and law reform units (e.g., Planned Parenthood Federation of America), while others perform legal services and law reform work, leaving organizational legal matters to retained counsel (e.g., Gay Men's Health Crisis). A number of stand alone test case groups develop ongoing relations with client groups whom they repeatedly represent (e.g., the ACLU Reproductive Freedom Project and the Center for Reproductive Law and Policy).

My concern is not with declaring one specific format to be the correct one, but with the trend of law reform (litigation and lobbying) groups proliferating without linkages to non-law defined groups. Consider the historical progression from the NAACP Legal Defense Fund (LDF), which began as a part of the National Association for the Advancement of Colored People, then separated for tax and organizational reasons; to the NOW Legal Defense Fund, which, learning the lessons of the NAACP LDF's history, began in tandem with, but always separate from, the National Organization for Women; to the Lambda Legal Defense and Education Fund, which began solely as a law reform group and never had an organizational affiliation with a national political group. Lambda's stand alone origin was a development quite representative of the time in which it was formed (1973), the glory days for judicial breakthrough cases in the Supreme Court.

A new literature on "critical lawyering," deriving primarily from clinical law teachers, emphasizes linkages to organized client groups among its other precepts. This literature and *Bleeding Heart* need to be read together. Both arc incomplete. In my view, the engagement principle is the most important predictor of culture-shifting. The critical lawyering literature concurs on that point, but is virtually mute on lawyering in the legislative realm. To critical lawyers, *Bleeding Heart* should serve as a powerful reminder that such an oversight reflects and helps to perpetuate a long outdated understanding of the full parameters of social justice law.

Notes and Questions

1. Hunter describes the rewards for repeat players, in both the judicial and legislative arenas. *See* chapter 2 for a discussion of repeat players and the advantages that accompany litigating from that posture.

2. Hunter asserts "the single most common and powerful activity within social change lawyering has become the use of litigation to secure enforcement and expansive interpretation of statutes." Do you agree? Or do you share Stoddard's view that a legislative focus is a more promising avenue for social change? How would you respond to Hunter's concern that a legislative focus makes the assumption that success can be achieved by majoritarian means? Is reliance on majority approval always dangerous for discrete and insular minorities?

3. Hunter identifies public engagement and the need to link to non-law defined groups as missing ingredients in Stoddard's analysis. She resists the call to a legislative focus and urges that social justice advocates, rather than prioritizing legislation, "use any area for lawyering also as a vehicle for mobilization." Is her prescription appealing?

4. Urvashi Vaid, former head of the National Gay and Lesbian Task Force, argues that the process of legislative reform at the federal level has significant tensions with the work of political organizing. Vaid describes the lobbying process involved in achieving the inclusion of data on hate crimes based on sexual orientation. The campaign, waged by the Anti-Violence Project of the National Gay and Lesbian Task Force and lobbyists from the American Psychological Association, involved making the problem visible, creating a broad coalition, educating Congress, generating constituent support. Urvashi Vaid, *Virtual Equality* 141–43 (1995). They were fortunate to encounter relatively little serious opposition, because "no civil rights group has been able to match the ability of the right wing to elicit constituent letters on any topic." *Id.* at 143. Based on this experience, Vaid cautions that the processes of getting legislation enacted can actually work against the goal of organizing for social change:

> [T]he process of passing [federal] legislation differs markedly from the process of building a social change movement. Indeed, the two are antithetical. The former requires a fairly obsessive and insular

> focus on 535 members of Congress, on several hundred staff members, and on the media and opinion-shaping elite that determines the meaning of whatever legislative measure one is pushing. Legislative enactment requires enormous discretion, secretiveness, the shrewdness to play off one political player against another, the ability to compromise and horse-trade on particulars. The building of a movement requires the involvement of large numbers of people in a political process from which they feel estranged. It calls for the motivation of the electorate, openness and candor, and the demystification of insider language into colloquial and commonsense phrases. It works best when ordinary people have an easy way to get involved and when they believe that their leaders stand for principles that will not be compromised away.
>
> [A tension in legislative strategy is that lobbyists and lawmakers are intently focused on the passage of a piece of legislation, seen as the ultimate win. This limited goal leads them to enter the legislative process ready to bargain and compromise.]
>
> * * *
>
> Finally, legislative strategies are more vulnerable than any kind of activism to becoming insular, self-referential, and separated from the interests of the broader community. There is something inherently limiting in the legislative strategy; it requires a kind of conformity to the status quo that neither political organizing, public education, legal argument, nor cultural work demands. To pass a piece of legislation, one has to focus on the needs and self-interest of a handful of lawmakers. They, not the constituents, are the focal point of the effort, and they dictate the terms and outcome.

Vaid, *supra* at 146.

If work with legislatures—like work with courts—is subject to pressures that can work against community empowerment, what are the lessons for social justice lawyers? *See* chapter 12 (describing the efforts of community groups to expand the meaning of fair housing legislation to redress urban injustice and spatial inequality), chapter 13 (describing role of activists, courts, and legislatures in creating "civil unions" enabling gay men and lesbians to have the privileges associated with marriage in Vermont) and chapter 14 (describing the achievements of the Violence Against Women Act and its creation of new possibilities for changing culture and society as well as the compromises involved in enacting that statute).

5. This chapter offers the opportunity to reflect "What have I learned about social justice lawyering and social justice law?" As you single out important lessons, consider whether those insights are worth teaching to others. How might you teach them? What are some visions of "justice" that you encountered? Do some of these visions conflict? What is the role of the lawyer, especially when litigation is not the focus of the lawyers' work?

*

Chapter 12

THE MOVEMENT TOWARD A NEW FAIR HOUSING: REDRESSING SPATIAL INEQUALITY AND INJUSTICE

The twin evils of housing discrimination and imposed residential segregation represent both a condition and process of inequality and injustice. Urban development and city life are particularly plagued by this inequality and injustice. *See generally The Urbanization of Injustice* (Andy Merrifield & Erik Swyngedouw eds., 1997). The importance of space and one's place within it is a persistent concern. Accordingly, Lawrence Bobo views residential segregation as the " 'structural lynchpin' of America's racial inequality." Melvin L. Oliver & Thomas M. Shapiro, *Black/White Wealth: A New Perspective on Racial Inequality* 33 (1995). Literally, a linchpin is "a pin that goes through the end of an axle outside the wheel to keep the wheel from coming off." *Webster's Seventh New Collegiate Dictionary* 491 (1969). In this sense, the linchpin of residential segregation empowers and enables racial inequality to keep rolling. Thus, the structural inequality cannot be dismantled without removing this linchpin of residential segregation and its complementary evils of discrimination, exclusion, exploitation, and subordination. As John Calmore notes, "Racial inequality, with the linchpin intact, rolls on, carrying with it denied or diminished opportunity in education, employment, and wealth accumulation. The wheels are much more than merely where the rubber meets the road—rather, these wheels are instead vicious cycles of subordination." John O. Calmore, *Race/ism Lost and Found: The Fair Housing Act at Thirty*, 52 Miami L. Rev. 1067, 1118 (1998).

In another sense, a "linchpin" is "something that serves to hold together the elements of a situation." *Webster's Dictionary, supra* at 491. This meaning reminds one that within the context of imposed, constraining segregation, the oppressive elements of the situation will often coalesce and people experience them in simultaneity. David Harvey,

Class Relations, Social Justice and the Politics of Difference, in *Place and the Politics of Identity* 41, 56–57 (Michael Keith & Steve Pile eds., 1993).

The modern era of housing discrimination law dates back only to 1968, a time when urban disorders forced race and the city to be joined as a pressing national concern. *See generally* John Charles Boger, *Race and the American City: The Kerner Commission Report,* in *Race, Poverty, and American Cities* 3 (John Charles Boger & Judith Welch Wegner eds., 1996). The primary legal apparatus for redressing the injustice of housing discrimination and residential segregation is Title VIII of the Civil Rights Act of 1968, known as the Fair Housing Act, 42 U.S.C. §§ 3601–3619, 3631. *See generally* Robert Schwemm, *Housing Discrimination: Law and Litigation* (1996) and James Kushner, *Discrimination in Real Estate, Community Development and Revitalization* (2d ed., 1995). The Act was passed in April 1968, one week after the assassination of Martin Luther King, Jr.

In June of 1968, two months after passage of the Fair Housing Act, the Supreme Court held that the Civil Rights Act of 1866 (42 U.S.C. §§ 1981–1982) prohibited not only public, but also private discrimination in housing. Jones v. Alfred H. Mayer Co., 392 U.S. 409 (1968). Section 1982 provides: "All citizens of the United States shall have the same right, in every State and Territory, as is enjoyed by white citizens thereof to inherit, purchase, lease, sell, hold, and convey real and personal property." Writing for the majority, Justice Stewart declared:

> Just as the Black Codes, enacted after the Civil War to restrict the free exercise of those rights,were substitutes for the slave system, so the exclusion of Negroes from white communities became a substitute for the Black Codes. And when racial discrimination herds men into ghettos and makes their ability to buy property turn on the color of their skin, then it too is a relic of slavery.

392 U.S. 442–43. *See also* Douglas L. Colbert, *Liberating the Thirteenth Amendment,* 20 Harv. C.R.-C.L. L. Rev. 1 (1995). In a concurring opinion, Justice Douglas advanced this theme, stating: "This Act [of 1866] was passed to enforce the Thirteenth Amendment which * * * abolished slavery. * * * Enabling a Negro to buy and sell real and personal property is a removal of one of many badges of slavery. * * * Some badges of slavery remain today. While the institution has been outlawed, it has remained in the minds and hearts of many white men. Cases which have come to this Court depict a spectacle of slavery unwilling to die.* * * Today the black is protected by a host of civil rights laws. But the forces of discrimination are still strong." 392 U.S. at 444–445.

While Section 1982 prohibits racial discrimination, the Fair Housing Act prohibits discrimination because of race, color, religion, sex, familial status, or national origin. Complemented by Section 1982, the Fair Housing Act should be seen not only as an equal-opportunity law, but also as an open-society law. James P. Chandler, *Fair Housing Laws: A Critique,* 24 Hastings L. J. 159 (1973). The Act was substantially amended in 1988. *See* James Kushner, *The Fair Housing Amendments Act of 1988: The Second Generation of Fair Housing*, 42 Vand. L. Rev. 1049 (1989). Although "fair housing" is declared in the Act to be "our national policy," the meaning of "fair housing" is ambiguous, complex, contested, and inherently contradictory. Charles E. Daye, *Whither "Fair" Housing: Meditations on Wrong Paradigms, Ambivalent Answers, and a Legislative Proposal*, 3 Wash. U. J. L. & Pol'y 241 (2000).

According to Daye:

> [S]ome policies—nondiscrimination, individual rights, process, means, and micro perspective—tend to be related and correlated, though not exclusively or completely. Similarly, policies such as desegregation, group fairness, outcomes, ends, and macro perspective tend to correlate one with the other. While each policy can have a distinct emphasis in a particular context, on the whole, they have a tendency to overlap. Each policy group also tends to point in the opposite direction from the other group. In this sense they seem to have oppositional tendencies.

Id. at 261.

Section 1 of this chapter provides a brief treatment of the Fair Housing Act's response to discriminatory dual housing markets. Section 2 analyzes the conditions and processes of constraint that are associated with spatial inequality and injustice. Finally, section 3 sets out materials that respond to John Calmore's call for "spatial reparations" as a matter of "justice in place." The call was made at the closing plenary session of the Association of American Law Schools Workshop on Property, Wealth, and Inequality, at the AALS Annual Meeting in San Francisco, January 4, 2001. Many of the themes of the AALS workshop have been developed in legal scholarship since then. *See generally Symposium: Property, Wealth, & Inequality*, 34 Indiana L. Rev. 1199–1443 (2001).

SECTION 1. THE FAIR HOUSING RESPONSE

DOUGLAS MASSEY

Housing Discrimination 101
28 Population Today 1, 4 (Aug.-Sept. 2000)

Racial discrimination is a topic that undergraduate sociology students expect to study. Few of them, though, expect to encounter it as part of a class project. So when students in my research methods course conducted a housing audit, they got more out of it than they had anticipated.

I came up with the idea of using undergraduates to carry out a housing audit partly because, at my university, pressure to involve undergraduates in research is mounting. But I wanted to go beyond assigning research for research's sake, which students see through and which doesn't generate data for social scientists. The audit project proved so successful that it could be applied widely in classrooms throughout the country to produce valuable data, sharpen students' research skills, and teach them a life lesson.

For many years, I have followed the results of racial housing audits. The design of these audits is simple: Teams of white and black auditors are assigned similar identities and characteristics. Realtors are usually sampled from some listing, such as the real estate section of a major newspaper. The auditors then visit selected agents to inquire about the availability of housing. After the encounter, the auditors fill out forms describing their treatment. When all agents have been contacted, the investigator compares the findings of black and white auditors to see whether they were treated differently. Systematic differences in treatment are taken to reflect racial discrimination.

My plan was to have students do a housing audit to study racial discrimination over the telephone. Many African Americans speak a dialect known by sociolinguists as Black English Vernacular, and even more speak standard English with an accent that most listeners identify as "black." If people can attribute race by voice alone, phone-based discrimination can occur.

To examine this hypothesis, I offered an undergraduate course called "Research Design: Measurement of Discrimination." As I had hoped, a racially diverse group of students registered, and among them were speakers of Black English Vernacular (BEV), Black Accented English (BAE), and White Middle Class English. With male and female speakers in each group, I had six treatment categories for the study.

In class, we designed profiles that gave each auditor an identity and standard sociodemographic characteristics. We then designed a script that asked about the availability of an advertised unit and other units that might be available, as well as the terms and conditions of the rental. We translated the standard script into BEV.

Under the supervision of a postdoctoral fellow, the class applied this design to audit 79 rental units advertised in newspapers and rental guides. The study was done blindly; white students did not know how black students were treated, and vice versa. After the study, I analyzed the data and organized results into tables that students used in writing papers for a final grade.

The analysis revealed phone-based racial discrimination. Compared with whites, African Americans were less likely to speak to a rental agent (agents could screen calls using answering machines), less likely to be told of a unit's availability, more likely to pay an application fee, and more likely to have credit mentioned as an issue. These racial effects interacted with and were exacerbated by gender and class. Typically, students posing as lower-class blacks (speakers of BEV) experienced less access to rental housing than those who represented middle-class blacks (speakers of BAE), and black females experienced less access than black males * * * . In general, students playing the part of lowerclass black females were most disadvantaged.

Students enjoyed participating in the study and writing the papers, and they learned something not only about research, but also about the reality of race in America * * *. Our experience suggests that telephone audits constitute a potentially cheap, easy, and efficient way of measuring and studying processes of racial discrimination in urban housing markets. All that is needed to accurately measure racial discrimination is access to a local newspaper or rental guide, a telephone, and people capable of using linguistic styles associated with race and ethnicity. * * *

The reaction of the students to the experience varied:

White students were shocked at the degree of discrimination against blacks. Most said they wouldn't have believed it beforehand.

Black students were not surprised. It simply confirmed their experience.

The women in the class were most shocked. Although black women expected the racial discrimination, they were dismayed at how much worse they were treated even than black men, and they were horrified at some remarks made to them, which hinted at sexual promiscuity, drug use, and welfare receipt. No other group had to endure this kind of stereotyping. White women were shocked, and then outraged, that they were treated differently than white males. Like many women of their generation, they assumed that gender bias was a thing of the past.

Notes and Questions

1. Have you ever experienced housing discrimination? How did it make you feel? Often the harms of housing discrimination are non-pecuniary injuries such as humiliation, embarrassment, and mental anguish. Do you think that the embarrassment and humiliation deter people from telling others about how deeply hurt they were by the experience? How could you make a jury really feel the sense of dignitary harm that is experienced? How would you make it real—not abstract—for the jury?

2. Few things are more personal than where and with whom we chose to live—where we are at home. Okainer Christian Dark, a successful African-American law professor, describes the experience of hurt when she was denied an opportunity to rent an apartment because she was black. It was like "someone taking a piece of paper with everything on it that describes you—more than a resume, because it includes your essence—and crumpling it up because the reader didn't like the color." She goes on to say that she is still trying to smooth out the paper, but it never again will be wrinkle-free. Margalynne Armstrong, *Privilege in Residential Housing*, in Stephanie M. Wildman with contributions by Margalynne Armstrong, Adrienne D. Davis & Trina Grillo, *Privilege Revealed: How Invisible Preference Undermines America* 43, 43–44 (1996).

3. Patricia Williams, another African-American law professor, tells of going Christmas shopping in New York City to buy a sweater for her mother. It was two Saturdays before Christmas at 1 o'clock in the afternoon when she pressed the buzzer to gain entry to a Benetton's store, only to be denied by a youthful clerk, who mouthed the words, "We are closed." Williams observes, however, "there were several white people in the store who appeared to be shopping for *their* mothers." She describes her reaction to this incident of discrimination:

> I am still struck by the structure of power that drove me into such a blizzard of rage. There was almost nothing I could do, short of physically intruding upon him, that would humiliate him the way he humiliated me. No words, no gestures, no prejudices of my own would make a bit of difference to him, his refusal to let me into the store * * * was an outward manifestation of his never having let someone like me into the realm of his reality. He had no compassion, no remorse, no reference to me; and no desire to acknowledge me even at the estranged level of arm's length transactor. He saw me only as one who would take his money and therefore could not conceive that I was there to give him money.

Patricia J. Williams, *The Alchemy of Race and Rights* 44–45 (1991).

4. The experiences of Professors Dark and Williams are not unique to them. They are not over-sensitive, over-emotional women. As Richard Delgado explained 20 years ago, "The psychological harms caused by racial stigmatization are often much more severe than those created by other stereotyping actions. Unlike many characteristics upon which stigmatization may be based, membership in a racial minority can be considered neither self-induced, like alcoholism or prostitution, nor alterable. Race-based stigmatization is, therefore, 'one of the most fruitful causes of human misery.' " Richard Delgado, *Words that Wound: A Tort Action for Racial Insults, Epithets, and Name-Calling*, 17 Harv. C.L.-C.R. L. Rev. 133, 136 (1982). Delgado also points out:

> The psychological responses to such stigmatization consist of feelings of humiliation, isolation, and self-hatred. Consequently, it is neither unusual nor abnormal for stigmatized individuals to feel ambivalent about their self-worth and identity. This ambivalence arises from the stigmatized individual's awareness that others perceive him or her as falling short of societal standards, standards which the individual has adopted. Stigmatized individuals thus often are hypersensitive and anticipate pain at the prospect of contact with "normals."

Id. at 137. Why should the harm that is described by Professors Dark, Williams, and Delgado be a concern of federal housing policy? Why not leave these matters to the tort of infliction of emotional distress and not make "a federal case" out of it? *See* Judith Resnik's discussion, in chapter 10, of the need for federal cases to establish cultural norms.

5. When people perpetrate housing discrimination are they simply exercising their freedom of association? The argument that this discrimi-

nation is not wrongful when it is simply a form of the right to associate with whomever one pleases was debated in connection with President Reagan's nomination of Judge Robert Bork to become a justice of the United States Supreme Court. In 1963, Judge Bork wrote an article attacking the proposed legislation of the Civil Rights Act of 1964, which prohibits, *inter alia*, discrimination in employment, public accommodations, and programs that receive federal financial assistance. In Judge Bork's view:

> Of the ugliness of racial discrimination there need be no argument (though there may be some presumption in identifying one's own hotly controverted aims with the objective of the nation). But it is one thing when stubborn people express their racial antipathies in laws which prevent individuals, whether white or Negro, from dealing with those who are willing to deal with them, and quite another to tell them that as individuals that they may not act on their racial preferences in particular areas of life. The principle of such legislation is that if I find your behavior ugly by my standards, law or aesthetic, and if you prove stubborn about adopting my view of the situation, I am justified in having the state coerce you into more righteous paths. That is itself a principle of unsurpassed ugliness.

Robert Bork, *Civil Rights—A Challenge*, The New Republic, Aug. 31, 1963, at 22. While this position may have contributed to the defeat of Bork's nomination, can you imagine other sitting federal judges sharing his view? Do you think that antidiscrimination laws like the Fair Housing Act represent intended state coercion into more righteous paths? According to two social scientists, a distinctive feature of antidiscrimination law in the area of housing "is the call to use the force of law to back the principle of equal treatment in a 'private' context—to intervene in decisions which people would ordinarily take to be their own business." Paul M. Sniderman & Thomas Piazza, *The Scar of Race* 124–25 (1993). *See also* Marie Failinger, *Remembering Mrs. Murphy: A Remedies Approach to the Conflict Between Gay/Lesbian Renters and Religious Landlords*, 29 Cap. U. L. Rev. 383 (2001) (discussing the difficult compromises that may be part of constructing viable remedies in fighting religiously motivated discrimination against gay and lesbian renters in the private housing market).

6. The notion of wanting the government to stay out of one's personal business is a strong sentiment among those who oppose fair housing laws. According to Douglas Massey and Nancy Denton,

> Although 88% of whites in 1978 agreed that blacks have a right to live wherever they want to, only 40% in 1980 were willing to vote for a community-wide law stating that "a homeowner cannot refuse to sell to someone because of their race or skin color." That is, as recently as 1980, 60% of whites would have voted against a fair housing law, even though one had been on the federal books for a dozen years.

Douglas S. Massey & Nancy Denton, *American Apartheid: Segregation and the Making of the Underclass* 92 (1993). In a 1995 survey replication, the percentage of those favoring the open-housing law rose to 64%. But 36% still opposed it even though the Fair Housing Act had existed for over 25 years at the time. Howard Shuman et al., *Racial Attitudes in America: Trends and Interpretations* 302–03 (rev. ed., 1997).

7. Is freedom of association an answer to the question: "How does it happen that so many black teenagers end up at the same cafeteria table during lunch time?" Beverly Daniel Tatum, *"Why Are All the Black Kids Sitting Together in the Cafeteria?": And Other Conversations About Race* 52 (1999). Should black kids be forced to sit with white students? How is neighborhood integration different, other than the fact that more is at stake on both sides?

Is integration generally a *forced* fit? Shortly after Christmas in 1962, Martin Luther King, Jr. noted that "[t]rue integration will be achieved by true neighbors who are willingly obedient to unenforceable obligations." Martin Luther King, Jr., *The Ethical Demands for Integration*, in *A Testament of Hope: The Essential Writings and Speeches of Martin Luther King, Jr.* 117, 124 (James Melvin Washington ed., 1986). What do you think he meant? Would Judge Bork agree with King? Do you?

8. Although most fair housing cases and commentary focus on whites discriminating against blacks, Asians and Latina/os also experience housing discrimination. *See generally* John Yinger, *Closed Doors, Opportunities Lost: The Continuing Costs of Housing Discrimination* (1995). For example, in 1998, five Asian students at Stanford University recovered $300,000 to settle a fair housing claim against a landlord who refused to rent them a dwelling in Menlo Park, California. The lessor allegedly told the women that she already had "good white American applicants" and that "you people are ruining this country." Carolyne Zinko, *Stanford Students Settle Housing Suit over Racial Slurs*, S.F. Chron., Feb. 11, 1998, at A17. As this instance illustrates, for Asians and Latina/os, xenophobia, nativism, and racial antipathy may combine to serve as the joint bases of discrimination.

9. It is clear that the media create negative stereotypes that block fair housing access. Is it possible that positive media images are, ultimately, more important than fair-housing litigation in efforts to achieve that access? Robert Schwemm asserts, "to take a more positive example of the media's influence, it may be that one 'Bill Cosby Show' can accomplish as much encouragement of residential integration as scores of Title VIII lawsuits. * * * The point is that effective litigation, though a necessary element in the effort to accomplish Title VIII's goal of making race truly irrelevant in America's housing decisions, is only one piece of the puzzle. Those outside the legal community may have as much to offer as those in law enforcement." Robert G. Schwemm, *The Future of Fair Housing Litigation*, 26 J. Marshall L. Rev. 745, 772 (1993). *See also* the remarks of Robert Ellickson, discussing Thomas Schelling, *Micromotives and Macrobehavior* (1978), in *The Fair Housing*

Act After Twenty Years: A Conference at the Yale Law School 59–60 (Robert G. Schwemm ed., 1989). Professor Ellickson has stated that:

> It is possible that someone like Bill Cosby will do more for fair housing than will all the lawyers in this room put together. The Bill Cosby Show is a highly popular television series. And by gosh, Bill Cosby's family is just like every other family, except, of course, that the family members are funnier and have more interesting things happen to them. Because the Cosby family is an ordinary family, a lot of white viewers who might otherwise think, "Gee, we don't want blacks in our neighborhood," might decide, "Hey, the members of the Cosby family would be dynamite neighbors!" This sort of change in household preferences would alter the likelihood of neighborhood tipping.

Id. at 61. What is your response to what John Calmore has characterized as "this Huxtable family syndrome"? *See* John O. Calmore, *Race/ism Lost and Found: The Fair Housing Act at Thirty,* 52 Miami L. Rev. 1067 (1998). Calmore finds this strategy of "integration warriors" to be troubling, because the Huxtables were no "ordinary family." Claire was an attorney, Cliff was a physician, and their five children were bright, high-achieving, and, yes, they were "dynamite neighbors." As Calmore argues, "Thus, the Schwemm-Ellickson view requires an extraordinary black family * * * to meet white acceptance as just an ordinary family." Calmore also argues that this reinforces tokenism, because very few black families fit the Huxtable profile.

10. What does "integration" mean to you? Is it "race mixing"? Do you equate it with "assimilation"? According to john powell, "Integration can be a tough concept to embrace when one considers that it cannot claim many examples. One obstacle, especially for those who would otherwise support the idea of integration, is the association of integration with assimilation." john a. powell, *Living and Learning: Linking Housing and Education*, 80 Minn. L. Rev. 749, 753 (1996). *See also* George A. Martinez, *Latinos, Assimilation and the Law: A Philosophical Perspective*, 20 UCLA Chicano-Latino L. Rev. 1 (1999), and Jerome M. Culp, Jr., *Black People in White Face: Assimilation, Culture, and the* Brown *Case*, 36 Wm. & Mary L. Rev. 665 (1995).

SECTION 2. THE CONTEXT AND CONDITIONS OF SPATIAL INEQUALITY AND INJUSTICE

In 1993, Cornel West wrote of the remarkable residential separation between blacks and and whites, noting that 86% of white suburbanites lived in residential neighborhoods where the percentage of black residents was less than 1%. Cornel West, *Race Matters* 4 (1993). Did you live in such a neighborhood? In that same year, Douglas Massey and Nancy Denton argued, "Residential segregation has become the forgotten factor of American race relations * * * ." Massey & Denton, *supra* at 16. Indeed, residential segregation is pretty much a fact of life, viewed as normal and unremarkable. The nation just takes it for granted. Segregation, however, is not normal and the federal government has played a significant role in creating, sponsoring, and perpetuating the racially segregated dual housing markets that divide the nation. As you read the following article by Florence Roisman, note whether the story of the government's involvement is familiar to you.

FLORENCE WAGMAN ROISMAN

Teaching About Inequality, Race, and Property
46 St. Louis U. L. J. 665, 667–86 (2002)

> From Tennessee an army officer asked for a copy of the last issue [of The Liberator] "as a relic * * * that our tale is true." Without such proofs, he said future generations would never believe "that there was once such a thing as slavery."
>
> * * *

There is no question that in the United States there are large differences between whites and minorities, particularly African-Americans, with respect to control over property. These gaps characterize all measures of property control: income, wealth, and the particular form of wealth represented by homeownership.

The incomes of blacks and Hispanics lag behind those of whites "by wide margins." This is true not only for wages and salaries but also for income from self-employment, farming, rents, interest, dividends, royalties, and government transfers. Moreover, the racial income gap, like inequality generally, has increased in recent years.

The racial wealth gap is even more dramatic. In 1998, for example, "the median wealth of black and Hispanic households was less than one-fifth the median wealth of white households."

The disparities are particularly striking with respect to characteristics of residence: whether one is a homeowner or a tenant, and the value of the home, in financial and other respects. The United States is called "a nation of homeowners," but minority homeownership is substantially lower than white homeownership. In the year 2000, the white homeownership rate was 73.8 percent; Asian/other, 53.9 percent; Black, 47.6 percent; and Hispanic, 46.3 percent. Although minority homeownership experienced the fastest growth, the racial gap narrowed only slightly from previous years.

Moreover, "even among homeowners, . . . African Americans consistently own homes of lower value, regardless of their socioeconomic status and household structure." And much of the minority homeownership is precarious, because of the state of the economy in general and the prevalence of subprime and often predatory lending. The households most vulnerable to loss of their homes by foreclosure are minority households.

This racial disparity means that minorities are disadvantaged with respect to what is for most middle-class households in the United States the greatest source of household wealth. Homeownership affects the ability to finance education, self-employment, and other capital development. It is the principal source of family wealth that is transmitted from one generation to another, and family wealth, in turn, largely determines whether and to what extent homeownership is possible.

The location of the home—in particular, whether or not it is in a predominantly minority neighborhood—has a substantial impact in determining the value of the home, both financially and with respect to whether the household lives in a well-served neighborhood with good schools, safe streets, and access to employment, or in an ill-served neighborhood with inadequate schools, high crime rates, and diminished employment opportunities.

Minorities are segregated into predominantly minority neighborhoods. This segregation is particularly pervasive for African-Americans, who have been described as "hyper-segregated"—that is, scoring high levels on at least four of the five dimensions by which demographers measure racial segregation. In predominantly minority neighborhoods, houses are less valuable. Recent studies show that "both blacks and whites are penalized for living in neighborhoods that are heavily black."

Whether the neighborhood is a predominantly minority neighborhood thus determines the extent to which individuals may accumulate property during their lifetimes. "Residential segregation limits individual accumulation of human capital via education and the job market." "By preventing residents of segregated neighborhoods from obtaining high quality educations and jobs, segregation imposes limits on how much wealth and property they can amass as a result of their own efforts. . . ." Segregation also limits the extent of wealth accumulation by property appreciation.

The direct advantages of homeownership are enhanced by tax preferences. There are four principal tax benefits for homeowners—the deductions for mortgage interest and real estate taxes, the exclusion of gain (within limits) on the sale of a home, and the fact that owner occupants do not have to include the rental value of the home as part of taxable income.

The tax advantages associated with homeownership are by far the largest federal housing subsidies, many times greater than the housing subsidies for low-income people. The tax advantages accrue more to whites than to minorities.

[S]ince blacks are less likely to own homes, they are less likely to be able to take advantage of these benefits. Furthermore, since black homes are on average less expensive than white homes, blacks derive less benefit than whites when they do utilize these tax provisions. And finally, since most of the benefits in question are available only when taxpayers itemize their deductions, there is a great deal of concern that many black taxpayers may not take advantage of the tax breaks they are eligible for because they file the short tax form.

Thus, racial property disparities are maintained by everything in our property regime that makes minorities disproportionately renters rather than homeowners, or segregates them in neighborhoods where property values appreciate relatively little, and schools, safety and employment opportunities are relatively poor.

The causes of the racial disparities have been the subject of considerable analysis and discussion. Although some argue that the racial disparities are due to choices or attributes for which minorities are responsible, substantial scholarship shows that concepts of white supremacy, racial dominance, and similar racial attitudes, their implementation in racial discrimination and segregation, and their embodiment in social structures, all contribute to the racial disparities in control of property. Thus, for example, a recent interdisciplinary, multi-year study of four metropolitan areas concluded that race is a major "shaping force in the distribution of opportunity" and works "in complex and varied ways that go beyond individual attitudes or acts of discrimination," operating "even more pervasively at the institutional and structural level—especially in the form of highly segregated housing and labor markets, along with the practices that keep them that way."

* * *

The United States did not become a "nation of homeowners" by accident. Homeownership was promoted by deliberate government policy—deliberate government policy that provided homeownership much more for whites than for people of color and restricted homeownership to racially segregated communities.

Until the 1930s, "home loans had been short-term affairs available primarily to the relatively well-to-do[;] ... barely 45 percent of U.S. housing units were owner-occupied." In the wake of the Great Depression, President Roosevelt

> modernized the concept of Jeffersonian democracy by broadening it to include homeowners in an industrial society as well as the idealized yeoman farmer. Building on the Lockean notion of propertied citizenship, Roosevelt's New Deal sought stability and security in a time of turmoil by making it easier to purchase—and keep—a house.

This was accomplished through the Home Owners Loan Corporation (HOLC), the FHA, and the VA.

These homeownership programs contrasted dramatically with the public housing program that was enacted in 1937. As Gail Radford has documented, the federal government created a two-tiered housing policy, with FHA/VA the upper, homeownership tier and public housing, a "stingy, alienating, and means-tested" rental program, the lower. The two tiers "held racial significance; the upper tier nourished a growing, virtually all-white constituency while public housing struggled to support primarily a fragment of the minority community with which it became identified."

The HOLC introduced longer term, fully amortized mortgages and the practice of "redlining." It was followed by the FHA, created by the National Housing Act of 1934. The role of FHA was not to make mortgage loans, but to insure them. (One needs to emphasize to students that FHA insured the lender against loss of money, not the borrower against loss of the home.) Because FHA insured lenders against loss, lenders were willing to make loans on terms that were acceptable to FHA; and the terms that FHA set made homeownership affordable to middle-income people for the first time. When the VA was created in 1944, it "very largely followed FHA procedures and attitudes...."

In Kenneth Jackson's words, the FHA and VA "revolutionized the home finance industry" in five ways. FHA made three major financing changes: low downpayments, a long repayment period (twenty-five or thirty years), and full amortization rather than balloon payments. Fourth, FHA focused its mortgage insurance on "new residential developments on the edges of metropolitan areas, to the neglect of core cities." FHA insurance required appraisals of the property, the borrower, and the neighborhood, and FHA instructed its underwriters that the characteristics of existing city neighborhoods made insuring housing in those neighborhoods unacceptably risky.

The final important FHA policy was reflected in the appraisal standards. The FHA Underwriting Manual specifically instructed that the presence of "inharmonious racial or nationality groups" made a neighborhood's housing undesirable for insurance. The Underwriting Manual explicitly recommended racially restrictive covenants, and warned: "If a neighborhood is to retain stability, it is necessary that properties shall continue to be occupied by the same social and racial classes...." As Charles Abrams wrote:

> FHA adopted a racial policy that could well have been culled from the Nuremberg laws. From its inception FHA set itself up as the protector of the all white neighborhood. It sent its agents into the field to keep Negroes and other minorities from buying houses in white neighborhoods.

FHA "not only insisted on social and racial 'homogeneity' in all of its projects as the price of insurance but became the vanguard of white supremacy and racial purity—in the North as well as the South."

Even after the Supreme Court ruled, in *Shelley v. Kraemer*, that racially restrictive covenants were judicially unenforceable, FHA and VA continued to require the covenants. Initially, FHA Commissioner Franklin D. Richards asserted that the Court's action would "in no way affect the programs of this agency." Later, Richards elaborated, stating that it was not "the policy of the Government to require private individuals to give up their right to dispose of their property as they [saw] fit, as a condition of receiving the benefits of the National Housing Act."

After vigorous advocacy by the NAACP, "FHA grudgingly agreed, ... only after Presidential intervention, ... to drop its flat ban against integrated projects...." Solicitor General Perlman announced in December 1949 that FHA would refuse to issue mortgage insurance on properties "bound by racially restrictive covenants recorded after February 15, 1950." But "that did not signify that [FHA] encouraged open occupancy...." As former housing administrator Nathan Straus noted, "the new policy in fact served only to warn speculative builders who had not filed covenants of their right to do so, and it gave them a convenient respite in which to file."

"This new policy could not, however, undo the damage already done, and it said nothing about barring aid to builders who practiced discrimination by other means." Three days after Perlman's announcement, "the FHA's executive board met and agreed that 'it should be made entirely clear that violation [of the new rules] would not invalidate insurance.' " By 1951, responding to the charge that the FHA engaged in a "clear evasion" of the president's intent, a high agency official blandly responded that "it was not the purpose of these Rules to forbid segregation or to deny the benefits of the National Housing Act to persons who might be unwilling to disregard race, color or creed in the selection of their purchasers or tenants." President Truman rejected a request that he "bar FHA aid to any segregated housing...." The Eisenhower Administration also continued to "reject ... demands that FHA require open occupancy in its insured projects...." Thus, long after FHA revised its Underwriting Manual, "FHA continued to deny housing insurance to Negroes except in Negro neighborhoods and commitments in such areas were rare."

The FHA and VA support for homeownership almost exclusively for whites in exclusively white communities continued at least until 1962, when President Kennedy issued Executive Order 11063.

The FHA/VA standards had immense impact. "By the start of the 1970s, eleven million Americans had purchased dwellings thanks to FHA-VA financing." The influence of the FHA-VA policies extended to housing financed otherwise than through those agencies. "A developer might sell just a few houses in a subdivision through the FHA-VA, but only if the whole subdivision met federal standards. As a result, FHA-VA ideas quickly became the accepted wisdom among American developers and ordinary home buyers as well and as such remained in force long after federal policy officially changed."

Almost all of those millions of federally-insured and federally-guaranteed home mortgage loans went to whites; almost all of those millions of homes were available only to whites. "[L]ess than 2 percent of the housing financed with federal mortgage assistance from 1946 to 1959 was available to Negroes."

The exclusion of African-Americans from the FHA and VA programs not only deprived them of the advantages of particular homes and property appreciation, but also, to a very large extent, excluded them from suburban areas. Since FHA and VA were deeply committed to financing housing in the suburbs, not in cities, by excluding blacks from FHA and VA assisted housing, the federal government excluded blacks from suburbs. The exclusion of blacks and other minorities from the FHA- and VA-financed homes—and from subdivisions that had some FHA- and VA-financed homes—had immense significance for whites and for minorities:

> FHA's racial policies meant that whites who previously lacked the means to remove themselves to racially homogeneous communities could now do so with public support. As Gunnar Myrdal concluded in *An American Dilemma* (1944), New Deal programs extended racial " 'protection' to areas and groups of white people who were earlier without it." The result was that the emergent sense of entitlement that appeared after World War II embraced not merely the fact of property ownership, but a broader conception of homeowners' rights that included the assumption of a racially exclusive neighborhood.

The houses that whites bought with FHA and VA help provided an extraordinary opportunity for wealth appreciation—an opportunity that was denied to non-whites.

> White homeowners who had taken advantage of FHA financing policies saw the value of their homes increase dramatically, especially during the 1970s when housing prices tripled.... Those who were locked out of the housing market by FHA policies and who later sought to become first-time homebuyers faced rising housing costs that curtailed their ability to purchase the kind of home they desired. The postwar generation of whites whose parents gained a foothold in the housing market through the FHA will harvest a bounteous inheritance in the years to come. Thus the process of asset accumulation that began in the 1930s has become layered over and over by social and economic trends that magnify inequality over time and across generations.

As this quotation suggests, even if those who were locked out of the FHA/VA subdivisions managed to buy homes elsewhere, they were losing out on a particularly advantageous opportunity. For example, the Levittown houses, the prototype of the FHA/VA financed homes, were known as "the buy of the century." "*Life* magazine reported that it was cheaper to move out to Levittown and buy a new house than to keep renting an existing apartment in the city, an astonishing testimonial to the power of the federal mortgage subsidy." The Levittown and other FHA/VA financed houses increased dramatically in value. The basic house in Levittown, New York, more than doubled in value by 1957; "improved houses almost tripled in value." Blacks did not share in this appreciation.

As Oliver and Shapiro concluded:

> The FHA's actions have had a lasting impact on the wealth portfolios of black Americans. Locked out of the greatest mass-based opportunity for wealth accumulation in American history, African Americans who desired and were able to afford home ownership found themselves consigned to central-city communities where their investments were affected by the "self-fulfilling prophecies" of the FHA appraisers: cut off from sources of new investment their homes and communities deteriorated and lost value in comparison to those homes and communities that FHA appraisers deemed desirable.

The personal impact of the exclusion was substantial and long-lived. In 1952, Frank Horne visited the Pennsylvania Levittown. Arnold Hirsch, whose research in the federal archives enables him to paint a vivid picture, tells us that

> Horne, an exceptionally fair-skinned African American, reported that a Levittown sales agent leaned over a counter to confide to him in a whisper: "You know, we've got to keep the colored out." Horne repeatedly brought the situation to Foley's attention and claimed that the slur placed both himself and the agency in an "untenable position." "[I]t is more than an anomaly," Horne wrote, "that a representative of the Federal agency is subject to affront and insult by a developer who is receiving assistance from the same Federal agency." Like [Thurgood] Marshall, he urged that federal aid "be withheld from Levitt until he shall cease and desist from his brazen racial discrimination." Horne's complaints, like Marshall's, were brushed aside.

On the fiftieth anniversary of the Long Island Levittown, in 1997, the *New York Times* reported the reaction of Mr. Eugene Burnett, a retired Suffolk County police sergeant, "who was among thousands of military veterans who" sought housing in Levittown "[b]ut ... was turned away because he is black." "The anniversary leaves me cold," Mr. Burnett is quoted as saying. "He said he still stings from 'the feeling of rejection on that long ride back to Harlem.' " Similar stories were told by others. Ms. Ann Gilmore recalled that "she and her husband had taken two different buses to get to the model homes in Levittown [New York], only to receive the cold shoulder":

> "It was a Sunday, ... sometime in 1948, well, it was strange, because when we finally approached a salesman to ask for an application, well, he didn't say anything, but just walked away from us. It was as if we were invisible...."
>
> In 1997, Mr. Burnett recalled the 1949 visit that he and his wife had made to Levitttown New York:
>
> "I found the salesman and said, 'I like your house and I'm considering buying one. Could you give me the application?' "
>
> "He said, 'It's not me. But the owners of this development have not yet decided to sell to [N]egroes.' I was shocked out of my shoes."

The drive back to Harlem was grim. "I don't know how I didn't start World War III that day."

Levittown's refusal to allow black homeownership "proved potent and long-lasting.... Decades after [the racially exclusionary clause in the deed] lost any legal force, it might as well remain in effect." In 1990, the Levittown on Long Island, New York, "remain[ed] overwhelmingly white—97.37 percent." "The black population has never neared 1 percent." One white resident expressed "a feeling there's a stigma related to Levittown.... A kind of 'They didn't want us; we don't want them.'" This is buttressed by another recent report: "[A]sk Ann Gilmore about Levittown [in 1997] and she still bristles. 'If they gave me a Levittown house today,' she said, 'I wouldn't take it.'"

I teach the case of *Levitt & Sons v. Division Against Discrimination*, [158 A.2d 177 (N.J. Super. Ct. App.Div. 1960)] which illustrates nicely the way in which the FHA process worked, the importance of the FHA financing, and the ordinary, matter-of-fact exclusion of "Negroes." The case also illuminates the absence of any federal protection from racial discrimination: in states that did not have fair housing laws, "Negroes" would have no recourse from the refusal to allow them to purchase homes until 1968, when Congress enacted Title VIII of the 1968 Civil Rights Act, and the Supreme Court held in *Jones v. Alfred H. Mayer Co.* that the 1866 Civil Rights Act prohibited private discrimination.

The case involves three African-Americans, Franklin D. Todd, Willie R. James, and Luther Gardner. Each sought to purchase a home in a large development of FHA-insured homes, Todd and James from Levittown, in Burlington County, and Gardner from Green Fields Village, in Gloucester County. Each alleged that he was rejected as a purchaser because of his race. The three men then filed complaints with the New Jersey Division Against Discrimination (DAD), charging that the defendants had violated the New Jersey Law Against Discrimination, which prohibited racial discrimination in publicly assisted housing. The Division found probable cause to process the complaints.

Levittown and Green Fields filed suit, challenging the jurisdiction of the DAD to hear these complaints and attacking the constitutionality of the New Jersey law. The New Jersey Supreme Court discussed the nature of the two developments and their close association with the FHA, quoting the Congressional testimony of William Levitt, president of the corporation, that "We are 100 percent dependent on Government." The court held that the housing was publicly assisted housing, the DAD did have jurisdiction, the law was constitutional, and the developments could not lawfully exclude African-Americans.

Notes and Questions

1. Florence Roisman, a former chair of the Property Section, Association of American Law Schools, explains that she teaches inequality as part of her first-year property course:

> Many cases that appear in all parts of the Property curriculum illuminate ways in which white supremacist ideology and action have been a substantial cause of racial disparities in control of property. These involve, among other things: conquest; slavery; disposition of public lands to predominantly white, male, Anglo beneficiaries; explicit racial zoning; racially restrictive covenants; "manifest destiny"; "Negro removal" by the urban renewal and interstate highway programs; racially discriminatory donative transfers; the implementation of the public housing program; the treatment of farmworkers; and the use of zoning to establish and maintain exclusively white, Anglo settlements. In addition to these cases and related material, I teach a class that explicitly "explor[es] the forces driving the larger distribution of advantage...." and the "structural underpinnings of inequality," seeking to focus attention on "the ways in which th[e] opportunity structure has disadvantaged blacks [and other minorities] and helped contribute to massive wealth inequalities between the races."

Roisman, *supra* at 675. Was any of this material addressed in your property course? It is appropriate as well to address these issues in other courses? *See, e.g.*, Veryl Victoria Miles, *Raising Issues of Property, Wealth and Inequality in the Law School: Contracts and Commercial Law School Courses*, 34 Ind. L. Rev. 1365 (2001); Frances Lee Ansley, *Race and the Core Curriculum in Legal Education*, 79 Cal. L. Rev. 1511 (1991); Reginald Leamon Robinson, *Teaching From The Margins: Race as a Pedagogical Sub-Text: A Critical Essay*, 19 W. New Eng. L. Rev. 151 (1997). At the Association of American Law Schools Annual Meeting in New Orleans, on January 4, 2002, the Poverty Law Section presented a panel on this topic that included Dean Jeffrey S. Lehman's discussion of raising issues of inequality in tax courses. For materials that raise these and other social justice issues in Property, Housing Law, Homelessness and the Law, and Housing Discrimination and Segregation, see the Appendix to Florence Wagman Roisman, *Teaching About Inequality, Race, and Property*, 46 St. Louis L. J. 665, 687 (2002).

2. A social justice perspective extends from domestic to global issues of wealth inequality. *See, e.g.*, Lucy A. Williams, *Poverty, Wealth and Inequality through the Lens of Globalization: Lessons from The United States and Mexico*, 34 Ind. L. Rev. 1243, 1244–46 (2001) (discussing global inequality); Salih Booker & William Minter, *Global Apartheid*, The Nation, July 9, 2001, at 11 (discussing "global apartheid," "an international system of minority rule whose attributes include: differential access to basic human rights; wealth and power structured by race and place; ... and the international practice of double standards that assumes inferior rights to be appropriate for certain 'others,' defined by location, origin, race or gender"); Congressional Budget Office, *A CBO Study: Historical Effective Tax Rates 1979–1997* (2001); Isaac Shapiro et al., Center on Budget and Policy Priorities, *Pathbreaking CBO Study Shows Dramatic Increases in Income Disparities in 1980s and 1990s: An Analysis of the CBO Data* 1 (2000), available at http://www.cbpp.org/5–

31–01tax.htm. According to this study, there were "dramatic increases in income disparities ... in both the 1980s and 1990s." It further states: "[I]ncome disparities grew more sharply between 1995 and 1997 ... than in any other two-year period since 1979. This suggests the possibility that the growth in disparities in after-tax income may have accelerated in the latter half of 1990s." *Id.* at 5. *See also* William Julius Wilson, *The Bridge Over the Racial Divide: Rising Inequality and Coalition Politics* 27 (1999) ("[T]he United States has had the most rapid growth of wage inequality in the Western world.").

3. As Roisman points out, wealth inequality is tied to homeownership. Given the increasing income gap as well, do you see any way to close the gap in inequality? *See* Katherine Q. Seelye, *Poverty Rates Fell in 2000, But Income Was Stagnant*, N.Y. Times, Sept. 26, 2001, at A12; Carmen DeNavas Walt et al., United States Census Bureau, *Money Income in the United States 2000* at 4 (2001), at http:// www.census.gov/hhes/www/income00.html (last revised Dec. 03, 2001) (stating that the average median incomes for 2000 were: Asian/Pacific Islanders, $55,521; non-Hispanic whites, $45,904; whites, $44,226; Hispanics, $33,447; blacks, $30,439); Dalton Conley, *Being Black, Living in the Red* 11 (1999) ("in 1997, the median income for black families was 55 percent that of white families ($26,522 compared to $47,023)"). Gaps persist between black and white the middle classes as well. *See* Oliver & Shapiro, *supra* at 7, n.10 ("[M]iddle-class blacks ... earn seventy cents for every dollar earned by middle-class whites but they possess only fifteen cents for every dollar of wealth held by middle-class whites."); William A. Darity & Samuel K. Myers, Jr., *Persistent Disparity: Race and Economic Inequality in the United States since 1944* 136 (1998) ("Even larger gaps between blacks and whites are found in asset holding and wealth. While black families may receive about 60 cents for every dollar of income whites receive, they hold seven cents of wealth for every dollar of wealth held by whites."); Conley, *supra* at 25 ("[T]he typical white American family in 1994 had a nest egg of assets totaling a median of $72,000. With a median net worth of approximately $9,800 in that year, the typical black family had no significant nest egg to speak of."); *id.* at 26–27 ("[A]t every income level, blacks have substantially fewer assets than whites."); *id.* at 28 ("median assets for blacks, excluding home equity, total $2,000; the corresponding figure for whites is $28,816"). This inequality traces to residential segregation.

MELVIN OLIVER

The Social Construction of Racial Privilege in the United States: An Asset Perspective
in *Beyond Racism: Race and Inequality in Brazil, South Africa and the United States* 251, 255, 258–59, 267 (Charles V. Hamilton, Lynn Huntley et al. eds., 2001)

Most observers measure the character of racial justice in the United States through the lens of income. * * *

A focus on wealth changes the picture of racial inequality and our notion of progress. * * *

* * *

A focus on wealth or assets allows us to deconstruct the origins and maintenance of racial privilege. It helps us uncover the footprints of the past that weigh heavily on the present. Economists often emphasize that wealth is a consequence of a combination of factors: inheritance, rates of savings, and income. I do not so much disagree with this calculus, as I am concerned that economists have not properly appreciated the social context in which the processes in question take place. I want to suggest another perspective that posits that it is the social structure of investment opportunity, a process that has been racially constructed to provide privilege and opportunity for whites in general, and the middle and higher classes in particular, that is responsible for driving these differences. Blacks and whites have faced an opportunity to create wealth that has been structured by the intersection of class and race. Economists rightly note that blacks' lack of desirable human capital attributes places them at a disadvantage in the wealth accumulation process. However, those human capital deficiencies can be traced, in part, to barriers that denied blacks access to quality education, job-training opportunities, and other work-related factors. In order to deconstruct this process you must investigate public policies and private actions that determine how people have been able to make asset accumulation a part of their lives.

Three concepts help organize a whole set of findings that give us an opportunity to look at how this kind of disparity is socially constructed. First, the notion of the racialization of state policy, that is, how state policy has actually created opportunities—differential opportunities for blacks and whites to be part of asset accumulation. Second, the notion of an economic detour that is quite peculiar to African Americans as an ethnic group in America. Where all ethnic groups have come to the United States and seen entrepreneurship and business opportunities as an economic possibility, African Americans have taken an economic detour. It is not the African Americans have not been involved in business and entrepreneurship but that their level and extent of involvement has been so much less when compared to other ethnic groups. Finally, there is a synthetic notion—the sedimentation of inequality—that pulls all this together in a way that integrates the intergenerational consequences of having low net worth over a long historical period of time. * * *

* * *

This process reveals a key to understanding how past inequality is linked to the present and how present inequalities will project into the next generation. * * *

RAYMOND A. MOHL

Planned Destruction: The Interstates and Central City Housing in *From Tenements to the Taylor Homes: In Search of an Urban Housing Policy in Twentieth-Century America* 226, 226–29, 236–41 (John F. Bauman et al. eds., 2000)

Few public policy initiatives have had as dramatic and lasting impact on the late twentieth-century urban United States as the decision to build the Interstate Highway system. Virtually completed over a fifteen-year period between 1956 and the early 1970s, the building of the new Interstates had inevitable and powerful consequences for the U.S. urban housing policy—consequences that ranged from the rapid growth of suburban communities to the massive destruction of inner-city housing in the path of the new urban expressways. Housing and highways were intimately linked in the post-World War II United States. In fact, * * * postwar policymakers and highway builders used Interstate construction to destroy low-income and especially black neighborhoods in an effort to reshape the racial landscapes of the U.S. city.

In metropolitan areas, the coming of urban expressways led very quickly to a reorganization of urban and suburban space. The Interstates linked central cities with sprawling postwar suburbs, facilitating automobile commuting while undermining what was left of inner-city mass transit. They stimulated new downtown physical development and spurred the growth of suburban shopping malls, office parks, and residential subdivisions. Oriented toward center cities, urban expressways also tore through long-established inner-city residential communities, destroying low-income housing on a vast and unprecedented scale. Huge expressway interchanges, clover leafs, and on-off ramps created enormous areas of dead and useless space in the central cities. The new expressways, in short, permanently altered the urban and suburban landscape throughout the nation. The Interstate system was a gigantic public works program, but it is now apparent that freeway construction had enormous and often negative consequences for the cities. As Mark I. Gelfand noted, "No federal venture spent more funds in urban areas and returned fewer dividends to central cities than the national highway program."

Almost everywhere, the new urban expressways destroyed wide swaths of existing housing and dislocated people by the tens of thousands. Highway promoters and highway builders envisioned the new Interstate Highways as a means of clearing "blighted" urban areas. These plans actually date to the late 1930s, but they were not fully implemented until the late 1950s and 1960s. Massive amounts of urban housing were destroyed in the process of building the urban sections of the Interstate Highway system. According to the 1969 report of the National Commission on Urban Problems, at least 330,000 urban housing units were destroyed as a direct result of federal highway building between 1957 and 1968. In the early 1960s, federal highway construction dislocated an average of 32,400 families each year. "The amount of disruption," the U.S. House Committee on Public Works conceded in 1965, was "astoundingly large." A large proportion of those dislocated were African Americans, and in most cities the Interstates were routinely routed through black neighborhoods.

Dislocated urbanites had few advocates in the state and federal road-building agencies. The federal Bureau of Public Roads and the state highway departments believed that their business was to finance and build highways and that any social consequences of highway construction were the responsibility of other agencies. One federal housing official noted in 1957: "It is my impression that regional personnel of the Bureau of Public Roads are not overly concerned with the problems of family relocation." Indeed, during most of the expressway-building era, little was done to link the Interstate Highway program with public or private housing construction or even with relocation assistance for displaced families, businesses, or community institutions such as churches and schools.

The victims of highway building tended to be overwhelmingly poor and black. A general pattern emerged, promoted by the state and federal highway officials and by private agencies such as the Urban Land Institute, of using highway construction to eliminate "blighted" neighborhoods and to redevelop valuable inner-city land. This was the position of Thomas H. MacDonald, director of the U.S. Bureau of Public Roads (BPR) during the formative years of the Interstate system. It was also the policy of New York's influential builder of public works projects, Robert Moses. Highway builders were clearly conscious of the social consequences of Interstate route location. It was quite obvious that neighborhoods and communities would be destroyed and people uprooted, but this was thought to be an acceptable cost of creating new transportation routes and facilitating urban economic development. In fact, highway builders and downtown redevelopers had a common interest in eliminating low-income housing and, as one redeveloper put it in 1959, freeing "blighted" areas "for higher and better uses."

The federal government provided most of the funding for the Interstate Highway construction, but state highway departments working with local officials selected the actual Interstate routes. The consequence of state and local route selection was that urban expressways could be used specifically to carry out local race, housing, and residential segregation agendas. In most cities, moreover, the uprooting of people for central-city housing triggered a spatial reorganization of residential neighborhoods. Black population pressure on limited inner-city housing meant that dislocated blacks pressed into neighborhoods of "transition," generally working-class white neighborhoods on the fringes of the black ghetto where low-cost housing predominated. These newer "second ghettos" were already forming after World War II, as whites began moving to the suburbs and as blacks migrated out of the South into the urban North. Interstate Highway construction speeded up this process of second-ghetto formation, helping mold the sprawling, densely populated ghettos of the modern American city. Official housing and highway policies, taken together, helped to produce the much more intensely concentrated and racially segregated landscapes of contemporary urban America.

* * *

* * * A few examples should serve to demonstrate the destructive impact of urban expressways.

In Miami, Florida, state highway planners and local officials deliberately routed Interstate-95 directly through the inner-city black community of Overtown. An alternative route using an abandoned railroad corridor was rejected, as the highway planners noted, to provide "ample room for the future expansion of the central business district in a westerly direction," a goal of the local business elite since the 1930s. Even before the expressway was built, and in the absence of any relocation planning, some in Miami's white and black press asked: "What About the Negroes Uprooted by Expressway?" The question remained unanswered, and when the downtown leg of the expressway was completed in the mid-1960s, it tore through the center of Overtown, wiping out massive amounts of housing as well as Overtown's main business district, the commercial and cultural heart of black Miami. One massive expressway interchange took up twenty square blocks of densely settled land and destroyed the housing of about 10,000 people. By the end of the 1960s, Overtown had become an urban wasteland dominated by the physical presence of the expressway. Little remained of the neighborhood to recall its days as a thriving center of black community life, when it was known as the Harlem of the South.

In Nashville, Tennessee, highway planners went out of their way to put a "kink" in the urban link of Interstate-40 as it passed through the city. The expressway route gouged a concrete swath through the North Nashville black community, destroying hundreds of homes and businesses and dividing what was left of the neighborhood. The decision for the I-40 route had been made quietly in 1957 at a nonpublic meeting of white business leaders and state highway officials. By 1967, after years of denying that the expressway would adversely affect the community, the state highway department began acquiring right of way displacing residents, and bulldozing the route. Outraged blacks in Nashville organized the Nashville I-40 Steering Committee to mount an opposition campaign, charging that routing an Interstate expressway through a black community could be legally classified as racial discrimination.

The I-40 Steering Committee won a temporary restraining order in 1967, the first time a highway project had been halted by claims of racial discrimination. The Steering Committee's attorney alleged that "the highway was arbitrarily routed through the North Nashville ghetto solely because of the racial and low socio-economic character of the ghetto and its occupants without regard to the widespread adverse effects on the land uses adjoining the route." Ultimately, the I-40

Steering Committee lost its case in federal court, and the I-40 expressway was completed through Nashville's black community. However, the legal controversy in Nashville starkly revealed, if not a racial purpose, at least a racial outcome experienced by many cities.

In New Orleans, enraged freeway opponents successfully waged a long battle against an eight-lane elevated expressway along the Mississippi River and through the edges of the city's historic French Quarter. The Riverfront Expressway originated in a 1946 plan proposed for New Orleans by the New York highway builder Robert Moses. The planned expressway was part of an inner-city beltway of the type that Moses favored and that the BPR had incorporated into its Interstate planning. After several years of hot debate and controversy, historic preservationists succeeded in fighting off the Riverfront Expressway plan. In 1969, the Department of Transportation secretary, John A. Volpe, terminated the I-10 loop through the Vieux Carré.

However, while white New Orleans residents were fending off the highway builders, the nearby mid-city black community along North Claiborne Avenue was less successful. Highway builders there leveled a wide swath for Interstate-10. At the center of an old and stable black Creole community, boasting a long stretch of magnificent old oak trees, North Claiborne served a variety of community functions such as picnics, festivals, and parades. The highway builders rammed an elevated expressway through the neighborhood before anyone could organize or protest. Some of the preservationists who fought the Riverfront Expressway gladly suggested North Claiborne as an alternative. By the 1970s, Interstate-10 in New Orleans rolled through a devastated black community, a concrete jungle left in the shadows by a massive elevated highway.

* * *

In Birmingham, Alabama, where three Interstates intersected, a black citizens' committee complained to the Alabama state highway department and the BPR in 1960 that proposed Interstate freeways "would almost completely wipe out two old Negro communities [in] eastern Birmingham with their 13 churches and three schools." Moreover, the public hearing held on the highway proposal had been segregated, and blacks were unable to present their grievances. In 1963, as the start of Interstate construction neared in Birmingham, opposition flared again in the city's black community. A resident, James Hutchinson, protested to Alabama Senator John Sparkman that the Interstate (I-59) "bisects an exclusive colored residential area. In addition, it has a large interchange in the heart of this area." In the early days of the Interstates, the racial routing of the Birmingham expressway noted by Hutchison was rather typical. So was the response of Federal Highway Administrator Rex M. Whitton to Senator Sparkman. The route had been chosen by the Alabama state highway department and approved by the Bureau of Public Roads, Whitton wrote, "based on a thorough evaluation of all engineering, economic, and sociological factors involved." If that was the case, then it would seem that the destruction of the Birmingham black community was indeed a planned event.

A similar pattern of planned destruction took place in Camden, New Jersey, bisected in the 1960s by Interstate-95, with the usual consequences for low-income housing. In 1968, the Department of Housing and Urban Development sent a task force to Camden to study the impact of highway building and urban renewal. It found that minorities made up 85 percent of the families displaced by the North-South Freeway—some 1,093 of a total of 1,289 displaced families. For the five-year period 1963–1967, about 3,000 low-income housing units were destroyed in Camden, but only about 100 new low-income housing units were built during that period.

The Civil Rights Division of the New Jersey State Attorney General's Office prepared a second report on Camden. Entitled "Camden, New Jersey: A City in Crisis," the report made a similar case for the racial implications of expressway construction in Camden. As the report stated: "It is obvious from a glance at the renewal and transit plans that an attempt is being made to eliminate the Negro and Puerto Rican ghetto areas by two different methods. The first is building the highways that benefit white suburbanites, facilitating their movement from the suburbs to work and back; the second is by means of urban renewal projects which produce middle and upper income housing and civic centers without providing adequate, decent, safe, and sanitary housing, as the law provides, at prices which the relocatee can afford." The central argument of the New Jersey civil rights report was that this out come was purposely planned and carried out.

The experience of Camden during the expressway-building era of the late 1950s and 1960s was duplicated in cities throughout the nation. A Kansas City, Missouri, midtown freeway originally slated to pass through an affluent neighborhood ultimately sliced through a racially integrated Model City area. It destroyed 1,800 buildings there and displaced several thousand people. In Charlotte, North Carolina, Interstate-77 leveled an African American community, including four black schools. Highway officials pushed ahead with a three-and-one-half-mile inner-city expressway in Pittsburgh, even though it was expected to dislocate 5,800 people. In St. Paul, Minnesota, Interstate-94 cut directly through the city's black community, displacing one-seventh of St. Paul's black population. As one critic put it, "very few blacks lived in Minnesota, but the road builders found them." Despite the fact that the Century Freeway in Los Angeles would dislocate 3,550 families, 117 businesses, and numerous schools and churches, mainly in black Watts and Willowbrook, the Department of Transportation approved the new expressway in 1968.

The story was much the same in other cities. In Florida, Interstates in Tampa, Saint Petersburg, Jacksonville, Orlando, and Pensacola routinely ripped through, divided, and dislocated black neighborhoods. In Columbus, Ohio, an inner-city expressway leveled an entire black community. In Milwaukee, the North-South Expressway cleared a path through sixteen blocks in the city's black community, uprooting 600 families and ultimately intensifying patterns of racial segregation. A network of expressways in Cleveland displaced some 19,000 people by the early 1970s. In Atlanta, according to the historian Ronald H. Bayor, highways were purposely planned and built "to sustain racial ghettos and control black migration" in the metropolitan area.

* * *

* * * The new lily-white suburbs that sprouted in the postwar automobile era were unwelcoming to blacks. Essentially, most uprooted African American families found new housing in nearby low- and middle-income white residential areas, which themselves were experiencing the transition from white to black. The expressway building of the 1950s and 1960s ultimately produced the much larger, more spatially isolated, and more intensely segregated second ghettos characteristic of the late twentieth century.

Notes and Questions

1. Above, Oliver discusses inequality from an asset perspective that focuses on wealth. In drawing a link, for example, between historical housing discrimination and the gap in homeownership and equity, he suggests a form of compensatory reparations to develop community assets: "Taken together, these forms of contemporary bias cost the current generation of blacks about $82 billion dollars. If these biases continue unabated, they will cost the next generation of black homeowners $93 billion. On the basis of this logic, one could take the $93–billion figure as the minimal target of public and private initiatives needed to help create housing assets in the black community." Oliver, *supra* at 268. *See generally* Nancy A. Denton, *The Role of Residential Segregation in Promoting and Maintaining Inequality in Wealth and Property*, 34 Ind. L. Rev. 1199 (2001).

2. In discussing wealth inequality, Oliver & Shapiro state:

> Racial difference in inheritance is a key feature of our story. * * * The grandparents and parents of blacks under the age of forty toiled under segregation, where education and access to decent jobs and wages were severely restricted. Racialized state policy and the economic detour constrained their ability to enter the post-World War II housing market. Segregation created an extreme situation in which earlier generations were unable to build up much, if any, wealth.

Melvin L. Oliver & Thomas M. Shapiro, *Black Wealth/White Wealth: A New Perspective on Racial Inequality* 6–7 (1995). Did an inheritance aid you in accumulating wealth? Did it aid your parents or grandparents?

3. The analyses of Roisman, Oliver, and Mohl implicate the federal government in creating, maintaining, and perpetuating urbanized injustice. Prior to reading this material, what was your view on the causes of

residential segregation? Were you aware of the federal government's role?

4. Oliver states that "a focus on wealth changes the picture of racial inequality and our notion of progress." Do the historical analyses of Roisman and Mohl do the same?

5. Oliver and Shapiro, *supra* at 23, state, " '[S]ocial inequality' means patterned differences in people's living standards, life chances, and command over resources." How does a focus on prohibiting current discrimination in housing and mortgage lending reduce this social inequality? Can it be reduced without taking into account past discrimination? What is the significance for fair housing if past discrimination's legacy is taken into account—that is, what are the remedial ramifications? Who would be accountable for this social inequality?

NANCY A. DENTON

The Persistence of Segregation: Links Between Residential Segregation and School Segregation
80 Minn. L. Rev. 795, 819–22 (1996)

The literature on residential and school segregation share a focus on the situation of African-Americans, which reflects both the *Brown* decision and the civil rights movement of the 1960s generally. However, population data reveal that metropolitan areas in the United States are increasingly becoming multi-ethnic, and projections reveal that by the year 2050 the United States as a whole will only barely be a white majority. Therefore, efforts to desegregate either schools or neighborhoods will occur in a more multi-ethnic framework than was true in the past. What are the implications of this multi-ethnicity? In a recent study, Bridget Anderson and I examined the patterns of neighborhood transition in five metropolitan areas between 1970 and 1990: Philadelphia, Miami, Chicago, Houston, and Los Angeles. We chose these five cities to reflect different regions and different combinations of racial/ethnic groups, in order to provide five mini-laboratories for detailed examination of the process of neighborhood change. Neighborhoods occupied by a single group were relatively uncommon throughout the years studied, with two dramatic exceptions: white-only neighborhoods were substantial in Philadelphia (55% in 1970, declining to 34% in 1990); and in Chicago white-only and black-only neighborhoods were 31% and 11% of the total in 1970, but declined to 6% and 19% by 1990. The most common type of two group neighborhoods contained whites and Hispanics only: 63% of Miami's neighborhoods in 1970 were of this type, as were 42% of Los Angeles's, 33% of Houston's, and 29% of Chicago's.

Over time, however, two-group neighborhoods declined in importance. Three-and four-group multi-ethnic neighborhoods became the norm: white-Hispanic-Asian, white-black-Hispanic, or white-black-Hispanic-Asian. The presence of Asians in the city determines how often the four-group type of neighborhood can emerge. Thus, nearly half of Los

Angeles's neighborhoods contained all four groups by 1990, whereas in Philadelphia (with a much smaller Asian population) only 11% did. We found similar results in the New York metropolitan area over the same time period. Further analysis revealed that these multi-ethnic neighborhoods are not confined to center cities only, were generally formed by the entry of minorities, and that their white population did not decline precipitously on average.

While more detailed study of the stability of these new multi-ethnic neighborhoods remains to be done, their existence in substantial numbers offers a new possibility to proponents of both school and neighborhood integration. Historically, integrated neighborhoods often have turned out to be "on [the] road to re-segregation": public policy has enhanced re-segregation by condoning real estate steering and financial discrimination. This process was further enhanced by municipal fragmentation, thereby facilitating the availability of all-white enclaves. To the extent that these all-white enclaves are diminishing in number and to the extent that multi-ethnic neighborhoods can be preserved, this new kind of neighborhood change could support integrated schools as well as building integrated neighborhoods.

To capitalize on the growth of multi-ethnic neighborhoods requires that we begin to tie together social policy designed to desegregate schools and neighborhoods. First, it is necessary to establish formal institutional ties between organizations fighting school segregation and those fighting neighborhood segregation, with a specific focus on these neighborhoods. Such cooperation is easy to suggest, of course, while the organizations involved in combatting both types of segregation are frequently underfunded, understated, and overworked. Organizations that focus on specific neighborhoods, however, could promote creative policies, such as eliminating from busing requirements schools that are already serving integrated neighborhoods. This would re-establish the importance of neighborhood schools at the same time as promoting residential integration.

Focusing on multi-ethnic neighborhoods in linking school and neighborhood desegregation efforts also provides the opportunity to actively promote specific examples of *successful* schools and neighborhoods. Too often we focus only on conflict or on failures, thus increasing the sense of despair that frequently pervades discussion of these issues. While there is evidence of the positive effects of metropolitan-wide school desegregation in reducing housing segregation patterns, changing demographics are not accepted by the courts as a cause of school segregation and that must be attacked. There are many arguments for the continued importance of integration even while there is concern for the difficulties inherent in doing so. The importance of having experience with members of other race and ethnic groups from an early age is vital to the increasingly multi-ethnic society that the United States is becoming, and as we increasingly interact closely in a world where most of the people are not white.

In addition to focusing on multiethnic neighborhoods to revise and strengthen both school and neighborhood desegregation policies, other cross-linkages exist as well. First, we could link the building of new schools or the remodeling of old schools to the building of racially and economically integrated housing. A new school is a boon to developers trying to sell houses, and Florida has had success in allowing developers to build one, but only if they meet certain housing requirements. Second, we could link the building of housing to particular schools, for example by offering incentives to builders to improve neighborhoods with reasonably good schools in danger of decline due to demographic changes. There are, of course, obstacles to such linkages and state and federal housing and education departments remain both institutionally separated and shackled by obsolete policies and constraining case law. Identifying the linkages between housing and school segregation and the *possibilities* for cooperation and reform, however, are a necessary step in breaking down these institutional and political barriers to change.

MARTHA R. MAHONEY

Segregation, Whiteness, and Transformation
143 U. Pa. L. Rev. 1659, 1659–69, 1677–80 (1995)

Residential segregation is both cause and product in the processes that shape the construction of race in America. The concept of race has no natural truth, no core content or meaning other than those meanings created in a social system of white privilege and racist domination. * * *

Although America has a long history of racial subordination, social and legal fictions continue to equate formal legal equality with equality in fact. In the context of residential segregation, this formalism leads to de-emphasizing the ongoing existence and harms of segregation and to emphasizing legal and economic mechanisms that could theoretically correct it. Professor [Alex] Johnson * * * therefore rightly criticizes both the idea that the market will naturally end discrimination and the idea that the existence of antidiscrimination law in housing will be sufficient to end segregation. Civil rights scholars necessarily put a great deal of energy into revealing past and present structures of subordination. We prove (again and again) that subordination has happened and does happen, that segregation reflects and creates inequality, and that white privilege is real. The metaphor of a "property right in whiteness" helps emphasize that privilege exists and that law protects it. While necessarily repeated, the reiteration of the existence of subordination and privilege tends to take our eyes off the question of transformation. * * *

As recent critical scholarship has shown, race is a social construction in which whiteness is a distinct, socially constructed identity. Since race is a phenomenon always in formation, then whiteness—like other racial constructions—is subject to contest and change. Whiteness is historically located, malleable, contingent, and capable of being transformed. Arguments about the malleability and contingency of white privilege, and its dysfunctionality for white working people, seem counterintuitive in today's legal and social discourses. These discourses generally emphasize what whites gain—the existence and benefits of privilege—or what whites lose—the costs of change for whites—rather than looking at transformative interests for whites. Yet historical struggles characterized by antiracist, multiracial struggle in defense of shared class interests have historically won significant successes, even under the apparently impossible conditions of formal segregation, fomentation of race hatred, exploitation, and abuse. One important goal in the transformative project is therefore to identify those points about whiteness that are most susceptible to working for change—especially those points that reveal potential for undermining the construction of privilege and subordination and for uniting whites, along with people of color, in opposition to privilege.

Race is a social construction, not "a natural division of humankind." As a concept or an ideology, however, race derives much of its power from seeming to be a natural or biological phenomenon or, at the very least, a coherent social category. For whites, residential segregation is one of the forces giving race a "natural" appearance: "good" neighborhoods are equated with whiteness, and "black" neighborhoods are equated with joblessness. The construction of race in America today allows whiteness to remain a dominant background norm, associated with positive qualities, for white people, and it allows unemployment and underemployment to seem like natural features of black communities. As I tell my Property students, when you wake up in the morning and go to the kitchen for coffee, you do not feel as if you hold partial interests or particular sticks in a bundle of rights in the structure you inhabit, nor does it feel as if land-use regulation shaped your structure, street, and community. This is *home*, where you roll out of bed, smell the coffee, reach for clothing, and inhabit the "reality" of the house. The physicality of home and community—that apparently natural quality from which Property professors must detach students to teach legal concepts—tends to make our lived experience appear natural. The appearance that this is "the way things are" in turn tends to make prevailing patterns of race, ethnicity, power, and the distribution of privilege appear as features of the natural world.

Race is a relational concept. It describes at least two social and cultural groups in relation to each other. The concept of race acquires meaning only in the context of historical development and existing race relations. Therefore, the construction of whiteness as "naturally" employed and employable, and blackness as "naturally" unemployed and unemployable, are both examples of the way in which concepts of whiteness and blackness imply whiteness as dominant and blackness as "other." Both become part of the way of thinking about race in America.

Race is a powerful concept, even though it is neither natural nor fixed. Social constructions acquire power because we inhabit their landscape and see through their lenses. Therefore, change cannot be achieved by a decision not to act racially, given the patterns of privilege and exclusion, dominance, and subordination that characterize individual and collective life in a racialized society. Large-scale patterns of urban development have shaped patterns of privilege for mostly white areas and subordination, including economic decline, for many mostly black areas and have made these patterns part of the space we inhabit. In the context of residential segregation and urban/suburban development, therefore, the challenge of ending subordination involves changing widespread patterns of residence and economic development and changing the social meanings attached to these patterns.

Recently, social and legal theorists have begun to "interrogate whiteness." There are several parts to this project. The dominant norm, the transparency phenomenon, must be made visible and cognizable to those within its sphere. Whiteness is historically and culturally specific. It has changed over time and continues to change. Whites need to find antiracist ways in which whiteness can be identified and changed. The point of inquiry is to identify how the concept "white" can be explored and understood, a project made difficult in part because explicit discussion of whiteness is usually associated only with white supremacists. We especially need to identify those moments in time and points in social understanding at which shared social interests exist, rather than treat white privilege as a fixed and frozen artifact.

Ruth Frankenberg divides whiteness into a set of "linked dimensions": a location of structural advantage and race privilege; a "standpoint" from which white people look at ourselves, at others, and at society; and a set of cultural practices that are usually unmarked and unnamed. Frankenberg explores the ways in which material existence and the way we understand and describe it are interconnected in the construction of whiteness. The interaction of the material world and the ways we explain and understand it "generates experience" and, therefore, the "experience" of lived whiteness is something continuously constructed, reconstructed, and transformed for white people. Frankenberg's description of the relationship between the material world and our understanding of our experience helps explain the ways in which urban segregation itself becomes a force in constructing social concepts of race. For whites, white neighborhoods become part of the "natural" world, helping to keep their whiteness unnoticed and undisturbed, and helping to equate whiteness with something that reflects positive values and feels like home.

Whites have difficulty perceiving whiteness, both because of its cultural prevalence and because of its cultural dominance. Anthropologist Renato Rosaldo describes "culture" as something perceived in someone else, something one does not perceive oneself as having. "Culture" is a feature that marks a community in inverse proportion with power, so that the less full citizenship one possesses, the more "culture" one is likely to have. What we ourselves do and think does not appear to us to be "culture," but rather appears to be the definition of what is normal and neutral, like the air we breathe, transparent from our perspective.

Like culture, race is something whites notice in ourselves only in relation to others. Privileged identity requires reinforcement and maintenance, but protection against seeing the mechanisms that socially reproduce and maintain privilege is an important component of the privilege itself. Peggy McIntosh conceptualizes white privilege as "an invisible weightless knapsack" of provisions, maps, guides, codebooks, passports, visas, compasses, and blank checks. The privilege that facilitates mobility and comfort in ordinary life is particularly difficult for whites to see. Opening a bank account appears routine, as does air travel without police stops, or shopping without facing questions about one's identification—unless the absence of suspicion is a privilege of whiteness.

White privilege therefore includes the ability to not-see whiteness and its privileges. Whites fail to see ourselves clearly, and we also fail to see the way white privilege appears to those defined into the category of "Other." Among other whites, white people generally perceive that no race at all is present. "Race" itself comes to mean "Other" or "Black." In the context of housing and urban development, terms like "racially identifiable" are generally used to refer to locations that are racially identifiably black. Similarly, "impacted" or "racially impacted" are terms that refer to black neighborhoods—not white neighborhoods. There is no "impact" to whiteness because it defines the norm. Dominant culture remains transparent to those inside it.

Because the dominant norms of whiteness are not visible to whites, whites are free to see ourselves as "individuals," rather than as members of a culture. Individualism in turn becomes part of white resistance to perceiving whiteness and indeed to being placed in the category "white" at all. The shift in vision that makes whiteness perceptible is thus doubly threatening for whites: It places us in a category that our whiteness itself requires us to be able to ignore, and it asks us to admit into our perception of ourselves the perceptions of those defined outside the circle of whiteness.

Ruth Frankenberg identified discursive repertoires in the way white women were "thinking through race," essentialist racism, color and power evasion, and race cognizance. Color and power evasion are the key strategies in the colorblind ideology that characterizes most legal opinions and predominates in most areas of public discourse in the United States today. Color evasion is similar to what Neil Gotanda calls the myth of "non-recognition." Noticing a person's color, and noticing differences between another person's color and one's own, is equated with being "prejudiced." Whites are color evasive about people of color, often declining to identify the race of someone who is "other" than white in an effort to avoid appearing prejudiced. Notably, whites are also color evasive when describing a white self in relation to people of color. For whites, noticing race is not nice for whites because the meaning of "race" itself is "Other," inferior, and stigmatized. The colorblind approach, which is generally adopted by whites to avoid being racist, therefore implicitly preserves much of the power structure of essentialist racism. Power evasion, in Frankenberg's terms, is color evasion with a different edge. Whites notice difference but do not allow into consciousness those differences that threaten white self-perceptions or make whites feel bad.

Race cognizance, Frankenberg's third category, means recognizing difference on the basis of cultural autonomy and empowerment for people of color. Because white privilege and whiteness are not visible, whites can only recognize "racism" or animus—but we recognize this quality in others more than ourselves. Therefore, most whites perceive racism as something that a second party (the racist actor) does to a third party (the subordinated person of a minority race). For white Americans of middle-class and elite status—the people who write the books and do the social analysis—racism is something that working-class whites (particularly Southerners) do to blacks and other people of color. Although racism is capable of being recognized in this framework, it appears as an unchanging artifact that is assigned to a social location within the white working class.

When racism becomes a feature possessed by "other" whites, whites of more elite status acquire a double layer of protection. First, they are protected racially. Because the focus on racism avoids the problems inherent in exploring privilege, this approach tends to exonerate the elite from responsibility for the reproduction of racial power and subordination. Second, blaming less elite whites for racism protects elite whites in class terms as well: racism becomes evidence against the potential for working-class solidarity, and therefore class privilege exists not because of a system that produces and distributes wealth to the advantage of elite whites, but because of the failures of white working-class people themselves.

Whiteness is visible to whites, however, when it appears to be the basis on which well-being is threatened. Whites perceive racism against ourselves when, through interventions in the norm of transparency, we are forced to experience the consciousness of whiteness. In the logic of white privilege, making whites feel white equals racism. A recent poll of young people between the ages of fifteen and twenty-four (called the "post-civil-rights" generation) showed that 68% of blacks felt that blacks were discriminated against on the basis of race, 52% of Hispanics felt Hispanics were discriminated against on the basis of race, and 49% of white people felt that whites were being discriminated against on the basis of race. Many whites explain the gap between black and white earnings not by invoking inequality and prejudice, but by relying on "individualistic" explanations about thrift, hard work, and other factors—all of which tend to explain white success through white merit and equate whiteness with stability and employability.

In the context of desegregation and urban development, the routine acceptance of whiteness as a dominant background norm is apparent in attitude surveys that inquire about the percentage of blacks whom whites would be willing to tolerate as neighbors. Whites are seldom asked how many whites they require as neighbors in order to feel comfortable. The accepted concept of "neighbors" or "area residents" is one that is white. On the other hand, defensive white self-awareness manifests itself quickly during times of racial transition in an area, or in relation to nearby groups in "other" neighborhoods.

* * *

In the context of residential segregation, antidiscrimination law is part of the attack on whiteness as a dominant norm. Whiteness has been constructed by excluding blacks, by defining white areas as superior, and by allocating to white areas the resources that reinforce privilege. Housing discrimination perpetuates segregation. It reflects the social construction of race—blacks as undesirable residents for white areas, whites as desirable residents for those areas—and perpetuates the processes that concentrate black poverty and continue to reproduce race and racism in America. A straight-forward attack on housing discrimination is therefore vital to break down walls of exclusion and begin the process of including people of color into formerly all-white or mostly white areas. Fighting housing discrimination is an important part of transforming whiteness in America.

Antidiscrimination law by itself, however, even when combined with a ban on employment discrimination, is insufficient to undo the processes by which residential life is segregated by race and racial concentration of blacks is linked with poverty. The many areas of selective investment and divestment that continue to reproduce segregation and exclusion and protect white privilege are larger social processes than can be attacked through antidiscrimination law. Therefore, the processes that reproduce whiteness and blackness must be deprived of their apparently natural quality, revealing the multiple forces and factors linking whiteness with access and economic development, and linking blackness with exclusion and impoverishment.

Land-use decisions affect the development of jobs and housing and the racialized allocation of resources and economic access—even when those decisions appear to have nothing to do with race. Decisions like highway planning, industrial-park location, bridge development, and other decisions should all be evaluated for their impact on the perpetuation of current patterns of racial segregation in housing and employment. All decisions should then be scrutinized for their effect on the racial reproduction of power and access in employment and on residence as well. Reports evaluating potential decisions would project the impact of any development on residential and employment segregation.

The idea of this proposal is to undo the apparently natural quality that accompanies the reproduction of whiteness, leaving a paper trial of land-use decision-making in the reproduction of power that can be identified and disputed. Unlike an environmental impact report, which embodies a more straightforward weighing of environmental factors, the emphasis here would be on revealing the reproduction of power and making it possible to trace causality when differential impacts ensue (or do not achieve what their proponents hope or promise)—rather than on evaluating whether certain regulatory standards have been met. The success of this measure, therefore, would not be measured directly because the actions taken might not always be those with the most beneficial impact on current patterns of segregation and economic concentration. Rather, the entire "natural" quality that makes white privilege and concentrated black poverty seem features of a physical landscape as inevitable as mountains or rivers would be challenged by showing the very processes of the construction of power and reproduction of racial exclusion and privilege. This proposal carries the danger that the discussion will become inflammatory and that power will be reproduced anyway, but it would have the helpful effect of revealing the production of white privilege and revealing some of the processes by which black communities are separated from opportunity and access.

Overall, the project of revealing power helps show the difference between treating race as a social construction and treating it as a natural phenomenon. Many discussions of race and poverty emphasize deconcentrating black people and black communities. These approaches treat race as a natural phenomenon. They have been criticized by scholars such as John Calmore, who emphasizes "spatial equality," economic and social access, and development for black communities, rather than integration. Arguments about spatial equality tend to reveal the ongoing exercise of power and dominance. This approach attacks the link between blackness and inferiority (the social construction of blackness) by revealing the power that reproduces inequality, rather than by emphasizing deconcentration of black people's residential locations.

Because the social construction of race is not symmetrical, and because blackness is not simply the mirror image of whiteness, there is a difference between the effects of deconcentration on blacks compared to the effects on whites. For whites, the concentration of blacks somewhere other than white neighborhoods is the spatial phenomenon that allows whiteness to remain both exclusive (that is, physically populated mostly by white persons) and a dominant norm (unnoticed except when threatened). Breaking down the walls of exclusion therefore has the effect of breaking down white dominance as well as making white spaces less white. Residence in white neighborhoods obviously has some advantages for those black individuals who find that it detaches some of the social construction of blackness (including identification with "inner-city" or "unemployable") for some of the privileges of whiteness ("suburban" and, often, "employable"). But, as Calmore points out, part of contesting the social construction of blackness involves defending the strengths and potential of black people and neighborhoods. * * *

Notes and Questions

1. What is residential "segregation"? How does Mahoney provide a "thicker" description than most people seem to mean when referring to "segregation"? How does residential segregation interact with white privilege?

2. According to Mahoney, whites have a "property interest in whiteness." *See* Cheryl I. Harris, *Whiteness as Property*, 106 Harv. L. Rev. 1709, 1745–57 (1993) (discussing the property interest in whiteness as a legal doctrine). How does this property interest in whiteness manifest itself in the creation, maintenance, and perpetuation of our "built environment," the environment that includes "the totality of physical structures—houses, roads, factories, offices, sewage systems, parks, cultural institutions, educational facilities, and so on" that society must create? *See, e.g.*, Raymond A. Mohl, *Planned Destruction: The Interstates and Central City Housing*, in *From Tenements to the Taylor Homes: In Search of an Urban Housing Policy in Twentieth-Century America* 226 (John F. Bauman et al. eds., 2000); Joseph Seliga, *Gautreaux a Generation Later: Remedying the Second Ghetto or Creating the Third?*, 94 Nw. U. L. Rev. 1049 (2000); Terenia Urban Guill, *Environmental Justice Suits Under the Fair Housing Act*, 12 Tul. Envtl. L. J. 189 (1998); and Jon C. Dubin, *From Junkyards to Gentrification: Explicating a Right to Protective Zoning in Low-Income Communities of Color*, 77 Minn. L. Rev. 739 (1993).

3. Joe Feagin and Hernan Vera note at the end of their analysis of white racism that: "Whites support the cause of equality and justice for blacks only when it is in their interest to do so. The difficult and necessary task, in our view, is to bring whites to a recognition that the destruction of racism is in their interest." Joe R. Feagin & Hernan Vera, *White Racism: The Basics* 191 (1995). How might whites come to this recognition? John Calmore sees racial separateness in living patterns as an extremely high hurdle in the path of whites in coming to this recognition. He writes: "Empathetic understanding is a rare gift, so I imagine it is very difficult for whites to appreciate the pain, the hurt, the humiliation, and the insult of housing discrimination. Likewise, I imagine it is difficult for whites to appreciate the dehumanizing constraints and isolation of imposed segregation. * * * The compoundedness of race and space, I imagine, is for whites taken for granted; white space is not problematic and black space is somewhere else." John O. Calmore, *Racialized Space and the Culture of Segregation: "Hewing a Stone of Hope from a Mountain of Despair,"* 143 U. Pa. L. Rev. 1233, 1234 (1995). If you are white, do you see your space as not problematic and black space somewhere else? If you are black, do you live in a racially mixed neighborhood? If so, are your neighbors, Asian, Latina/o, white? If you are Asian or Latina/o, in what kind of neighborhood(s) have you lived?

4. Is racial progress dependent on "a convergence of interest" between blacks and powerful whites? Many critical race theorists think so. *See* Derrick A. Bell, Jr., Brown v. Board of Education *and the Interest-Convergence Dilemma*, 93 Harv. L. Rev. 518 (1980). Do you believe that preferences to be with other nonwhites, rather than racial constraints, are becoming more important in explaining why we have segregated neighborhoods?

5. Jennifer Hochschild uses an analysis of survey data by race and class to demonstrate both the continuing power of and the internal

inconsistencies in the American Dream. Jennifer L. Hochschild, *Facing Up to the American Dream: Race, Class and the Soul of the Nation* (1995). She argues that because the American Dream focuses on individuals rather than structures, it is difficult to see the true obstacles that frustrate achieving the dream for many people, especially "estranged poor." *Id.* at 252–53. Hochschild thinks that the alternatives to the dream—white denial and black separatism—would be unfortunate for the fabric of the nation. *Id.* at 259–60. In what senses might it be unfortunate?

6. Do you see how housing discrimination and racial segregation diminish our humanity? Consider the following two observations. According to Roberta Achtenberg, a former Assistant Secretary for Fair Housing and Equal Opportunity, U. S. Dept. of Housing and Urban Development: "What does it mean for America when we hold fast to our values of openness and acceptance? It means we are all saved—saved from having our humanity diminished. There is no rigid doctrine in this. There is no particular standard of political correctness. There is only common sense and basic human decency." Roberta Achtenberg, *Symposium Keynote Address*, 143 U. Pa. L. Rev. 1191, 1201 (1995). According to Kenneth Clark, "Racial segregation, like all other forms of cruelty and tyranny, debases all human beings—those who are its victims, those who victimize, and in quite subtle ways those who are mere accessories." Kenneth B. Clark, *Epigraph* to Douglas S. Massey & Nancy A. Denton, *American Apartheid: Segregation and the Making of the Underclass* xi (1993). Is it your opinion that most white people in the United States do not see themselves fitting into either of Dr. Clark's categories—victimizers or mere accessories? If so, is that why they would not find the appeals to rehabilitated humanity very compelling? Personally, do you find them compelling?

7. Linking school segregation and residential segregation is necessary in many contexts, but does the linking of these problems of segregation make redress seem to be overwhelming? Denton sees opportunities among the challenges: "Since people of all races care deeply about both their neighborhoods and the education of their children, perhaps the strategy of combating both school and neighborhood segregation simultaneously in a multi-ethnic neighborhood context will be in everyone's interest. The limited success seen in the two spheres of residential segregation and [school] segregation separately makes approaching them together even more challenging. But as long as these two systems of segregation mutually reinforce each other, it may prove easier—and indeed necessary—to combat them together. And combat them we must." Denton, *supra* at 823.

8. To most, "segregation" is a term that connotes black isolation from whites. This black-white segregation remains the most extreme form of segregation. Yet, the picture grows complex as the changing demography of many metropolitan areas may call for some rethinking. *See* Janny Scott, *Rethinking Segregation Beyond Black and White*, N.Y. Times, July 29, 2001, Sec. 4, at 1, 6. Scott reports: " 'In some ways, we

have become a far more mixed, multicultural community,' Professor [Philip] Kasinitz said of New York. He pointed out that the number of places that whites share with Asians and that blacks share with Latinos increased. 'But the old, core segregation problem in the United States, the distance between blacks and whites, hasn't changed.' " For an analysis of segregation of particular Asian and Latina/o ethnic groups, see Douglas S. Massey, *The Segregation of Blacks, Hispanics, and Asians,* in *Immigration and Race: New Challenges for American Democracy* 44 (Gerald D. Jaynes ed., 2000), and John O. Calmore, *Race/ism Lost and Found: The Fair Housing Act at Thirty*, 52 Miami L. Rev. 1067, 1108–17 (1998).

SECTION 3. MOVING BEYOND FAIR HOUSING TOWARD JUSTICE IN PLACE

The Fair Housing Act has been the least effective of the modern-day civil rights acts. In one sense, it is inadequate because it promotes a weak, individualized equality of opportunity without really addressing structural racism and historic wrongs. Margalynne Armstrong, *Desegregation through Private Litigation: Using Equitable Remedies to Achieve the Purposes of the Fair Housing Act*, 64 Temp. L. Rev. 909 (1991). Thus, to advance social justice, the topic of justice in place explores issues related to establishing a stronger concept of opportunity. For instance, James Nickel defines opportunities as "states of affairs that combine the absence of insuperable obstacles with the presences of means—internal or external—that give one a chance of overcoming the obstacles that remain." Iris Marion Young, *Justice and the Politics of Difference* 26 (1990).

In this sense, fair housing would mean much more than a right to formal "equality of opportunity." In Iris Young's view, "Opportunity is a concept of enablement rather than possession; it refers to doing more than having. A person has opportunities if he or she is not constrained from doing things, and lives under the enabling conditions for doing them. * * * Evaluating social justice according to whether persons have opportunities, therefore, must involve evaluating not a distributive outcome but the social structures that enable or constrain the individuals in relevant situations." *Id.* The movement toward a new fair housing is animated by this stronger sense of opportunity that enables one to be free from oppressive constraints.

The call for "spatial reparations" recognizes that progressive fair housing advocacy must extend itself beyond the rights-based framework and normative push of formal equality of opportunity and additionally move to attack oppression. The call for spatial reparations recognizes the attack must be more deliberate, more strategic, and more persistent. Oppression is commonly a group-based harm that is structural, multifaceted, and systemic. Thus, extending beyond disparate treatment, oppression is "the inhibition of a group through a vast network of everyday practices, attitudes, assumptions, behaviors, and institutional rules." Iris Young, *Five Faces of Oppression*, in *Power, Privilege and Law* 66, 67 (Leslie Bender & Dann Braveman eds., 1995). As Young points out, "[t]he difference between the concept of discrimination and the concept of oppression emerges most clearly with the insight that oppression often exists in the absence of overt discrimination." *Id.* at 68. Social justice advocacy moves beyond discrimination as a matter of individual treatment. In doing so, attention is drawn to institutional racism as it was analyzed above by Roisman, Oliver, and Mohl in section 2.

The call for spatial reparations pays particularly close attention to this form and process of racism because, as Joseph Barndt points out, "[i]nstitutional racism as practiced today with sublety and sophistication often seems both innocent and innocuous unless it is recognized as the successor in disguise to the deliberate and direct institutional racism of the past. Rather than being eliminated, racism has been driven underground. * * * The results, however, are no less harmful. Today's racism cannot be understood without comprehending its deliberate and intentional origins." Joseph Barndt, *Dismantling Racism: The Continuing Challenge to White America* 83 (1991). As Ian Haney López also points out, institutional racism theory provides a compelling critique of fundamental facets of the contemporary Supreme Court's equal protection jurisprudence—"its exclusive fascination with purposeful racism, and its increasingly strict equation of purposeful racism with the open consideration of race. Institutional analysis demonstrates that the current Supreme Court's reasoning is exactly backward: Racism occurs frequently—and perhaps predominantly—without any specific invocation of race, while the explicit consideration of race may have as its aim racism's amelioration rather than perpetuation." Ian F. Haney López, *Institutional Racism: Judicial Conduct and a New Theory of Racial Discrimination*, 109 Yale L.J. 1717, 1730 (2000).

Against the background of today's frequent institutional racism—"as the successor in disguise to the deliberate and direct institutional racism of the past"—the importance of space attaches to the call for reparations. As geographer Edward Soja argues,

> [A]ll social relations become real and concrete, a part of our lived social existence, only when they are spatially "inscribed"—that is, *concretely represented*—in the social production of social space. Social reality is not just coincidentally spatial, existing "in" space, it is presuppositionally and ontologically spatial. *There is no unspatialized social reality*. There are no aspatial social processes.

Edward Soja, *Thirdspace: Journeys to Los Angeles and Other Real-and-Imagined Places* 46 (1996). Reparations to people may adopt the individualist remedial posture of liberal antidiscrimination advocacy. In that sense, against the horrors of slavery, no compensation would be adequate, no apology would be meaningful. Charles J. Ogletree, *Litigating the Legacy of Slavery*, N.Y. Times, Mar. 31, 2002, Section 4, at 9. As many legal scholars have recently demonstrated, individualized opportunity and redress—even reparations to enhance asset formation—would fall far short of redressing the deeper issues of systemic, synergistic, and structural racism that justice in place and spatial reparations seek to redress. *See* Deborah Kenn, *Institutionalized, Legal Racism: Housing Segregation and Beyond*, 11 B.U. Pub. Int. L.J. 35 (2001); Cassandra Jones Havard, *Invisible Markets Netting Visible Results: When Sub-Prime Lending Becomes Predatory*, 26 Okla. City U. L. Rev. 1057 (2001); Audrey G. McFarlane, *When Inclusion Leads to Exclusion: The Uncharted Terrain of Community Participation in Economic Development*, 66 Brook. L. Rev. 861 (Winter 2000/Spring 2001); David Dante Troutt, *Ghettoes Made Easy: The Metamarket/Antimarket Dichotomy and the Legal Challenges of Inner-City Economic Development*, 35 Harv. C.R.-C.L. L. Rev. 427 (2000); Terenia Urban Guill, *Environmental Justice Suits Under the Fair Housing Act*, 12 Tul. Envtl. L.J. 189 (1998); Margalynne Armstrong, *Race and Property Values in Entrenched Segregation*, 52 U. Miami L. Rev. 1051 (1998); Florence Wagman Roisman, *Mandates Unsatisfied: The Low Income Housing Tax Credit Program and the Civil Rights Laws*, 52 U. Miami L. Rev. 1011 (1998); Michelle Adams, *Separate and [Un]equal: Housing Choice, Mobility, and Equalization in the Federally Subsidized Housing Program*, 71 Tul. L. Rev. 1343 (1996); Justin D. Cummins, *Recasting Fair Share: Toward Effective Housing Law and Principled Social Policy*, 14 Law & Ineq. 339 (1996); and Paula Beck, *Fighting Section 8 Discrimination: The Fair Housing Act's New Frontier*, 31 Harv. C.R.-C.L. L. Rev. 155 (1996). While the focus here is on the urbanization of spatial inequality, spatial reparations should extend to rural contexts as well. *See* Cassandra Jones Havard, *African-American Farmers and Fair Lending: Racializing Rural Economic Space*, 12 Stan. L. & Pol'y Rev. 333 (2001).

Why then reparations? As Ogletree observes, "A full and deep conversation on slavery and its legacy has never taken place in America; reparations litigation will show what slavery meant, how it was profitable and how it has continued to affect the opportunities of black Americans." *Id.* Regarding spatial reparations, there are at least four responses to the question that fit into the stage-setting context discussed in the previous two sections of this chapter. First, the claim for reparations is appropriate to avoid cheapening the suffering of black people and it demands redress that is commensurate to the harm of spatial inequality and injustice. Second, as a concept of enablement, reparations demands repair and rebuilding as much as it demands compensation or restitution. Third, reparations opens the way for the nation to acknowledge the harm done and the racialized state's full responsibility for a significant degree of that harm. Fourth, reparations brings to the surface the unjust enrichment that has accrued to the nation and many people at the expense of black people and communities. The benefits of that unjust enrichment include the inter-generational wealth accumulated through homeownership and suburban development, the ease with which people and commerce travel the nation's interstate highway systems, the enjoyment of city life that is part of the built environment through urban renewal and gentrification—these are some of those benefits, and, as described by Peggy McIntosh, they are items that are to be found in the large "weightless, invisible knapsack of white privilege."

Thus, the claim for spatial reparations joins the larger movement for reparations for slavery, but the focus is on places and communities rather than individuals per se. While the legacy of slavery—a crime against humanity—is a lived experience among many whose ancestors were slaves, the claim for spatial reparations does not rest on a legacy of generations of discrimination. Instead, as Dennis Judd has argued, the claim for spatial reparations rests on the ground that "within the past half century the federal government helped to create the present pattern of residential segregation and therefore is obligated to enact policies of equal force to reverse the effects of its own racist policies." Dennis R. Judd, *Segregation Forever,* Nation, Dec. 9, 1991, 740, at 742. *See also* James A. Kushner, *Apartheid in America: An Historical and Legal Analysis of Contemporary Racial Segregation in the United States*, 22 How. L.J. 547 (1979).

As Melvin Oliver indicated, the black-white gap in wealth provides a more meaningful analysis than that which one derives from focusing merely on the black-white gap in income. It changes the "whole gestalt of inequality" and we assess racial progress, or the lack thereof, more critically. Complementing claims for asset formation subsidies to individuals, there is a necessary and proper call for place-based reparations as well. Hence, spatial reparations is a justice claim. With respect to critical theory, advocates for spatial reparations can learn from scholars who have advocated reparations for Japanese Americans, Mexican Americans, and Native Americans. *See, e.g.*, Rebecca Tsosie, *Sacred Obligations: Intercultural Justice and the Discourse of Treaty Rights*, 47 UCLA L. Rev. 1615 (2000); Chris Iijima, *Reparations and the "Model Minority" Ideology of Acquiescence: The Necessity to Refuse the Return to Original Humiliation*, 19 B.C. Third World L J. 385 (1998); Eric Yamamoto, *Racial Reparations: Japanese American Redress and African American Claims*, 19 B.C. Third World L.J. 477 (1998); and Mari J. Matsuda, *Looking to the Bottom: Critical Legal Studies and Reparations*, 22 Harv. C.R.-C.L. L. Rev. 323 (1987). Mari Matsuda characterizes reparations as a "critical legalism," which is a legal norm that reflects and reinforces the interests and the perspectives of the subordinated. Eric Yamamoto points out that reparations is a remedy of repair and an invitation to open new lines of inquiry and consideration of just redress. Thus, spatial reparations is part of a connected set of advocacy efforts and tenets; it is no silver bullet. Justice claims are not to be constrained by causes of actions or judicial forums. The nation should commit to repair harmed *places* for people who, *in place*, have been harmed by the assault on their community. *See, e.g.*, this chapter's closing excerpt that presents the story of Ms. Olivia Brown and her community's battle to save their neighborhood in Cocoa, Florida. Judith Koons, *Fair Housing and Community Empowerment: Where the Roof Meets Redemption*, 4 Geo. J. on

Fighting Poverty 75 (1996). *See also Voices Focus: Litigation and Community Empowerment*, 4 Geo. J. on Fighting Poverty 199 (1996).

KEITH AOKI

Space Invaders: Critical Geography, the "Third World" in International Law and Critical Race Theory
45 Vill. L. Rev. 913, 917–24, 938–39, 956 (2000)

Critical geographers ask: "Where do the poor and working class people go; where are their spaces; what is their lived experience of place in the brave new world of the new world economic order?" * * *

Over the past two decades, critical geographers have been transforming our understanding of how geographic "space" and experiences of "place," on both the individual and community level, are strongly influenced by and, in turn, strongly influence dynamic social processes. Traditionally, geography was devoted to studying cultural descriptions of places and given to technical, economic analyses. New geographers writing from a critical perspective, those such as David Harvey, Edward Soja, James Duncan, Yi–Fu Tuan and Alexander Murphy, have been examining the role of space in political economy and culture. These critical geographers have been looking at how spatial distribution in our neighborhoods, towns, cities and regions has been consciously shaped by both local governments and private businesses. These organizations create, circulate and maintain new levels of profits within our late capitalist economy, determining what effects such spaces have on people's sense of place. Spatial distance or proximity can be used to create affinities among people as well as to create and maintain social distance, such as the distance between those living in decaying areas of our inner cities and those in the posh suburbs ringing those cities. In turn, posh suburbs, high-tech office parks, deteriorated inner cities and dense urban centers produce a sense of place for their inhabitants that are often extremely divergent.

Spaces are produced and maintained by a dynamic set of factors. For example, critical geographers show how investment capital may be distributed very unevenly to certain neighborhoods of cities, regions of the nation or throughout the global market. New configurations of public and private partnerships, either express or implicit, emerge to reconfigure former industrial cities of factories and working-class neighborhoods into global administrative and information centers with gentrified, but historical, "yuppie" demographic residential and work districts. Critical geographers argue that chronic underdevelopment of regions or nations is not merely accidental, but follows a certain logic. As the economies of the developed nations of the North shift from an industrial to a post-industrial economy, centered around the provision of financial services and information moving swiftly across increasingly porous borders, new types of spaces are created and older understandings of place are transformed. The development of certain regions is dependent on the underdevelopment of others. Particular nations, regions, cities and areas within cities prosper and thrive, while others decline and wither.

* * *

* * * Beginning in the 1980s, many critical geographers began "reading" the cultural narratives of space (which required thinking of urban and suburban spaces as "texts") to uncover hidden underlying power relationships between macro decisions about space and micro understandings of experiential place. Cities, as the sites where major corporate and governmental decisions are made, were particularly important places in which to analyze how culture and power are produced, represented and circulated. Critical geographic analysis might look at ways in which the building styles used in earlier historical periods, for example, turn of the century cast-iron building fronts in the SoHo area of New York City, were commodified, repackaged and resold as desirable and possessing historic "ambiance." Soon these areas became filled with pricey lofts for galleries, boutiques and upscale bohemians, driving the SoHo real estate market sky-high. Such gentrification also meant that the inhabitants of a former trucking district of Manhattan, like SoHo, were displaced as their revalued spaces were sold out from beneath them. Who were these displaced people? Where did they go? What effects did gentrification in one area have on neighboring property values and demographics? How does this spatial reordering use proximity or distance to embody "progress" and simultaneously, through use of exclusion, segregation and enclosure, create areas where "others" (defined as "other" on class, racial, ethnic, linguistic bases, etc.) live or work? Although race was one of the identifiable axes that urban demographic change turned on, note that the critical geographers' main focus was not on race per se, but on the operations of capital moving people around. What were the politics of such transformed spaces and places?

The second analytical move among critical geographers has been to connect mappings and understandings of these newly-transformed urban and suburban places and spaces with the political and economic configurations of the post-industrial economic order that have been referred to as the processes of globalization. This new world, post-industrial order may be characterized by the dissolution of large, centralized factory systems ("Fordism") in favor of hyper-mobile capital engaged in exploiting cost differences among and between different regions, or even between different nations in terms of lower environmental or regulatory burdens. Rapid advances in communications and transportation technologies make planning and allocation decisions by corporate CEOs and top-level managers able to be implemented among manufacturing sites located throughout the world. Part of the labor in the new global workforce involves subcontracting and temporary labor regimes such as sweatshops and homework and piecework (particularly in the garment industry), which exist outside the traditional collective bargaining framework of the developed world. These new and pervasive regimes are underwritten by neoliberal ideology that promotes deregulation and privatization, which benefits the swift investment and disinvestment of capital across increasingly porous borders. This creates environmental and labor regulation "races-to-the bottom," in which capital flight is driven elsewhere (or enticed) by the presence of ever cheaper labor and low or nonexistent regulation.

The consequences of this increased flexibility of capital include increasing competition among cities, regions and nations for private investment. The flows of capital and investment follow political concessions by competing regions or nations, such as lower wages and taxes, and lower or nonexistent labor or environmental regulation. Capital flight also works to drive down wages within the United States and to significantly hinder environmental regulation, labor regulation and union organizing. Uneven economic development between regions within nations, and between nations and global regions, becomes increasingly pronounced—opening up a widening gap between newly-gentrified areas and economically depressed inner-city neighborhoods, between city centers and suburbs, and, on the international level, between the nations of the developed and developing world. The idea that the world is increasingly the same, yet increasingly filled with difference, begins to capture a sense of this paradox of uneven development.

Using an interdisciplinary set of tools culled from philosophy, social theory, economic geography, political economics and postmodern theory, Soja insists that space is not merely an inert residue left in the wake of decisions governing capital accumulation by top-level managers or a *tabula rasa* on which investment decisions are made, but that spatial outcomes possess a strikingly political meaning. Space defines political boundaries as well as private property—constructing, ratifying and reproducing community and individual identities as well as pre-existing distributive inequities—and then, importantly, making those outcomes seem "natural." Wall Street thrives and South Central Los Angeles seethes—that's just the way things are.

Residences, neighborhoods, cities and regions are also control centers of power, places or sites for what Michel Foucault has referred to as "the little tactics of the habitat," embodied by geographies of confinement, partitioning, enclosure and spatial differentiation. If white middle-class suburbanites are able to relocate work and residence to outlying areas, they may completely avoid inner-city neighborhoods occupied by racialized others, except as presented by the mass media, who are themselves an important part of the contemporary political economy of spatial differentiation.

* * *

* * * One area to which the critical geographers have given relatively little attention [however] is the construction of "race." * * *

* * *

Some work being done by legal scholars using spatial analysis involves mapping out the spatial (and often cross-boundary, whether national or local governmental) consequences for communities of color of injuries to a community's "right" to a clean environment or to electoral representation. An important additional aspect of some of this new spatial/legal work is the recognition of the complexity and contingency of political boundaries—the very units of political representation that may have arisen in response to earlier overt racial segregation. Imagining and articulating what might be the preconditions for democratic empowerment and process of people and communities that have been historically disempowered by imposition of dominant understandings of race, space and place is yet another link in the project of forcing the articulation of a coherent link between events occurring on the local level and events occurring on the global level.

In terms of legal articulations of place and analyses of the contemporary political economy of space, legal scholars have two things to add. First, critical legal scholars * * * bring a sense of the nuance of the law, how there are places of unexpected indeterminacy and "give" in legal doctrine that may be exploited. This corrects and supplements the project of critical geography, which tends to overestimate the fixedness of legal doctrine, considering the legal rules in force as another input to the creation and shaping of space.

Second, critical legal scholars bring a consciousness of how race within the United States occupies an important, but contentious, social place. This critical awareness of the fluidity of race, when combined with the emerging critique of the macro and micro global political economies of space, challenges us to analyze both maps of the globe and maps of urban regions within the United States. Through revealing new lenses in areas such as local government law, access to housing, investment patterns in urban areas and redevelopment within and without the United States, the means whereby "race-ed" bodies are produced in segregated spaces in turn become manufactories for the media spectacle of "black criminality."

* * *

* * * As Italo Calvino points out, each "invisible city" holds its opposite within itself. Hopefully, some of the dystopian features of the currently racially and spatially segregated cities of this country hold within themselves potential for their opposites as well. * * *

Notes and Questions

1. Among the legal scholarship that Aoki characterizes as that of space invaders, see John O. Calmore, *Racialized Space and the Culture of Segregation: "Hewing a Stone of Hope from a Mountain of Despair,"* 143 U. Pa. L. Rev. 1233 (1995), and *Random Notes of an Integration Warrior*, 81 Minn. L. Rev. 1441 (1997); Anthony Paul Farley, *The Black Body as Fetish Object*, 76 Or. L. Rev. 457 (1997); Richard Thompson Ford, *The Boundaries of Race: Political Geography in Legal Analysis*, 107 Harv. L. Rev. 1841 (1994), and *Geography and Sovereignty: Jurisdictional Formation and Racial Segregation*, 49 Stan. L. Rev. 1365 (1997); Elizabeth M.

Iglesias, *Human Rights in International Economic Law: Locating Latinas/os in the Linkage Debates*, 28 U. Miami Inter-Am. L. Rev. 361 (1996); Audrey G. McFarlane, *Race, Space and Place: The Geography of Economic Development*, 36 San Diego L. Rev. 295 (1999); and Chantal Thomas, *Globalization and the Reproduction of Hierarchy,* 33 U.C. Davis L. Rev. 1451 (2000).

2. According to Aoki, these scholars "raise questions about how to move beyond liberal individualism, communitarianism or nostalgic images of romanticized organic community; how to rethink, critique (but not necessarily abandon) and transform received ideas about sovereignty, autonomy, democracy and community, and how to inhabit a world of multiplied, splintered, mutating, overlapping and conflicting spaces and places." Aoki, *supra* at 956.

JOHN O. CALMORE

Spatial Equality and the Kerner Commission Report: A Back-to-the-Future Essay
71 N.C. L. Rev. 1487, 1487–88, 1490–1501, 1504–09 (1993)

In tracing the development of race consciousness, particularly during the period from the mid-1960s to the mid-1970s, Gary Peller observed that the national commitment to a centralized policy of integration virtually ignored the integrity and health of black institutions. In his words, "[i]ntegration of dominant institutions, rather than reparations from one community to another, became the paradigm for racial enlightenment." The demand for spatial equality [and spatial reparations] is a call for a paradigm shift in these terms and for a new day of racial enlightenment.

Twenty-five years ago [in 1968], the *Kerner Commission Report* concluded that the future of our cities would be enhanced only through the combination of enrichment programs designed to improve the quality of life in black communities and programs designed to encourage integration of substantial numbers of blacks into American society beyond the ghetto. The *Report* warned us that integration would not occur quickly and, therefore, that enrichment had to be an important adjunct to any program of integration. Spatial equality recognizes the continuing validity of this warning. It thus demands, as a matter of justice, that the enrichment program finally receive the policy attention and financial commitment necessary to compensate for decades of neglect and active exploitation.

* * *

The basic truth told in the *Kerner Commission Report* is more often than not denied now: "What white Americans have never fully understood—but what the Negro can never forget—is that white society is deeply implicated in the ghetto. White institutions created it, white institutions maintain it, and white society condones it." Until dominant society re-recognizes, acknowledges, and takes responsibility for this fact, denial and neglect will continue to stand in the way of establishing a coherent urban policy that addresses not only matters of housing and community development, but also the larger issues of social, economic, and racial justice. For now, the nation continues to run scared and time continues to run out.

The Kerner Commission stated that America was moving toward a deepening racial division, "two societies, one black, one white—separate and unequal." The Commission expressed great faith, however, in the reversibility of this trend. In lieu of either "blind repression or capitulation to lawlessness," it urged "the realization of common opportunities for all within a single society." Today, the nation's growing multicultural population displaces the propriety of continuing to view race relations as simply black and white, but the necessary commitment described by the Commission remains pertinent: "national action—compassionate, massive and sustained, backed by the resources of the most powerful and the richest nation on this earth." Accordingly, the Commission called upon every American to approach the task with "new attitudes, new understanding, and, above all, new will."

* * *

Integrationists, black and white, traditionally have focused on an individualized equality of opportunity. In an ideal world, society would be race-neutral. Individuals could transcend the race-conscious framework of our world, a framework that structures social stratification along race lines. This stratification, however, merges the race question with that of class. In most of our cities with a significant black population, the stratification has been spacialized. A unique, historical subjugation is perpetuated as race, class, and space intersect to compound the disadvantage that now determines the status of black society. Blacks occupy an inferior position that is reflected in the quantitative and qualitative differences between the respective class structures of blacks and whites. Aside from spatial containment, the inferior status of blacks is constantly regenerated by economic forces, along with the legal, cultural, political, and social apparatuses that support them.

Integrationists have never really accepted community enrichment as an appropriate prelude to broad-scale integration. Their early reaction to the terrible de jure segregation in the South extended itself to the de facto segregation in the urban North. They blurred the distinction between a compulsory ghetto and a voluntary black community, and accepted as true the proposition that in all areas of life separate was inherently unequal. Civil rights advocates were simply "unable to argue simultaneously against Jim Crow and for the improvement of the Negro community." Moreover, influential white liberals argued that the ghetto enrichment strategy was politically infeasible because the strategy incorrectly assumed sufficient white goodwill and continued willingness to commit great resources. Ghetto enrichment and integration were viewed as competing strategies and the integrationists claimed consistently that "in a white-dominated society, separate is inevitably unequal both in terms of the resources that go into a community and in terms of the way in which society values that community, its institutions, and its people." As time has told, however, in a white-dominated society, part of the domination has been to persist in blocking black entry into white residential areas or to flee from significant entry.

Title VIII of the Civil Rights Act of 1968 declared that it was national policy "to provide . . . for fair housing throughout the United States." Although "fair housing" was not expressly defined in the Act, its primary objective was initially interpreted to be "the replacement of ghettos by truly integrated and balanced living patterns." This "integration imperative" legitimated the emphasis on desegregation rather than on simple nonsegregation and free choice as to where to live. This imperative has proven futile, especially for those who live under the double bind of racial subordination and economic class subjugation. As it has turned out, integration presupposes relatively affluent black families effectively buying their way out of segregation. Success has been modest even here, however.

* * *

* * * Fair housing must be reconceptualized to mean not only increased opportunity for blacks to move beyond their socio-territorial disadvantage but also to mean enhanced choice to overcome opportunity-denying circumstances while continuing to live in black communities. Spatial equality is a group-based remedy that focuses on opportunity and circumstances within black communities and demands that both be improved, enriched, and equalized. Short of this, blacks, as a group, will be left with the inadequate "remedy" of individuals choosing, or being forced, to move to "better" space somewhere else.

Spatial equality compensates for past discrimination by legitimately combining the most effective features of affirmative action with expanded housing opportunity and choice. In many ways, it is analogous to educational equity advocacy. If we really care about a more effective fair housing policy, we must expand its scope. Remedies limited to nondiscriminatory free access to housing and to desegregating the ghetto are insufficient given the intersectional features of race and class oppression, the extensive and persistent segregation with which we live, and the historical legacy of denied opportunities associated with that oppression and segregation. Redefining fair housing would include providing housing "in forms and locations that address the special situation of oppressed groups, including the right to remain in place or to move to other neighborhoods of choice." While we certainly must attempt to control and eliminate finally the housing market's pervasive discrimination and exclusion, we certainly must also target housing resources to revitalize existing communities of color "in order to protect and affirm the right of minority residents to enhance their social and political cohesiveness by remaining in place if they choose to do so." The expansion of increased housing opportunity in other neighborhoods cannot diminish the "prior commitment to neighborhood revitalization."

* * *

It is now time to rethink integration and examine its fundamental context-setting assumptions. In examining the progress of black-white integration since World War II, the National Research Council characterized "integration" as a broad term that refers to "the nature of intergroup relations, to the quality of group treatment or interaction that exists." In an interracial or multiracial context, integration means that each group is (1) significantly represented, (2) broadly distributed, and (3) sharing power and equality.

After World War II, integration theory was influenced by a contact hypothesis that integration would be optimal when there was equal status between blacks and whites who pursued common, mutually supportive goals and when there was authoritative sanction and support for this process. This hypothesis was implicit in Dr. King's dream. In the early 1960s, integration was responsive to both political demands and moral claims. Today, it is antagonistic to political demands, and its moral claims are rejected by whites who deny responsibility for segregation.

Because of the extent of exclusion of blacks from dominant institutions, integration packaged itself in a comprehensive way. Integrationists early on assumed a linear, coherent, and symbiotic process whereby integrated schooling would provide children with a better education and training, which would in turn enable them to secure good jobs in an integrated labor market, which would in turn provide them sufficient economic resources to buy good housing in an integrated residential neighborhood. As the races got to know each other under these circumstances, they would come to appreciate each other as individuals who would be judged on the content of their character rather than the color of their skin. This process then would be enhanced and repeated for subsequent generations. What has occurred, however, is not coherent and packaged integration, but rather segmented integration. By this I mean that fragments of integration in education, primarily at the college and graduate level, in politics and governance, in the employment and business sectors, and in social interaction have been attained in most cases without having been linked to residential integration.

Although it is frequently paid lip service, integration cannot be said to have been a broadly shared value within dominant America. Integration has always been a tight, forced fit; too much so for the whole notion to work. For instance, when the school busing controversy raged during the 1970s, those advocating racially balanced public schools may have feared that to abandon busing would constrict the expanding civil rights movement. To these people, the debate over busing as a means to desegregate schools was viewed as a test of national commitment to continued civil rights progress. To sound a retreat on busing was deemed to be an abandonment of the commitment to integration and a re-embracing of the evils of segregation. Under a kind of "domino theory," establishment civil rights leaders feared that failure on the busing issue would trigger a string of defeats that would curtail the civil rights quest for integrated jobs, housing, public accommodations, and so on.

Today, given the recognition of integration as a segmented rather than as a coherently packaged process, the domino theory should be rejected. Blacks of all socio-economic classes still are forced to measure their progress in all areas of life primarily within the context of segregated housing and public education for their children. Each area of life must be analyzed separately to evaluate the connection between integration and concrete payoffs. We can no longer presume the linear progress that leads from an integrated neighborhood, to integrated school, to integrated workplace.

Although the meaning of integration and its value in various contexts are contested matters, most blacks remain committed to it as a pragmatic matter. The integration imperative still drives many civil rights strategies, social and public policy deliberation and formulation, and moral and ethical discourse. It does so, however, primarily through wishful thinking and excessive loss of faith in black institutional and community capacity. Spatial equality does not presume that benefits automatically are associated with integration, and it does not denigrate black capacity. It sees "nonsegregation" as an alternative to integration: "Nonsegregation implies both the right of people to remain indefinitely where they are, even if in ghetto areas, and the elimination of restrictions on moving into other areas.... Only white ethnocentrism could lead to the belief that all blacks would want to live in predominantly white areas."

Integrationists too often see segregation as a result of mere discrimination; I see it as primarily a result of domination and exclusion. The evil of Jim Crow segregation began with the fact that whites chose to impose the separation on blacks. The invidious nature of the discrimination stemmed not simply from individual perpetrators engaged in the disparate treatment of individual blacks, but from a white group disposition to dominate and exclude blacks. The white desire to exercise this power remains strong today, especially when directed to poor, urban blacks. Hence, large gaps exist between black and white perceptions on the degree of integration that is acceptable. According to Reynolds Farley, even when whites endorse the ideal of integrated housing, they would be uncomfortable if more than a token number of blacks was to enter their neighborhood. In other words, whites accept integration only if black representation is minimal. Twenty-five percent of the whites surveyed by Farley in 1978 stated that they would feel uncomfortable if blacks constituted just seven percent of the area population. Additionally, if the black percentage were twenty, then over forty percent of the whites would feel uncomfortable, and twenty-four percent would try to move. Blacks, by contrast, viewed integration as desirable only if they constituted a sizeable percentage—"a number that [would] not only make whites uncomfortable, but [would] terminate white demand for housing in the neighborhood."

Since Farley's 1978 study, racial polarization has increased greatly, and the prospects for integration are less promising. Consider a 1985 study of white, working-class defectors from the Democratic Party. The study's findings indicate the following:

> These ... defectors express a profound distaste for blacks, a sentiment that pervades almost everything they think about government and politics. Blacks constitute the explanation for their vulnerability and for almost everything that has gone wrong in their lives; not being black is what constitutes being middle class; not living with blacks is what makes a neighborhood a decent place to live ... These sentiments have important implications, ... as virtually all progressive symbols and themes have been redefined in racial and pejorative terms.

Among liberal integrationists, Gary Orfield is a consistently articulate voice. In 1988, however, two years after concluding that integration was the only real alternative to ghettoization, even he had harsh words for his own white liberal tradition. Orfield claimed that white liberals failed to develop a coherent program of reform in response to the urban ghetto crisis that was brought into sharp focus during the mid-1960s. By the beginning of the 1970s, each branch of the federal government rejected efforts to make structural changes in the ghetto, and racial separation was accepted as natural. Anyone who suggested more than incremental changes was subjected to intense political and intellectual attack. Liberals thus focused on other issues.

As liberals turned away from a structural analysis of urban inequality and racial oppression, the conservatives captured the policy agenda. They recharacterized compensatory programs as being based on the fact that the ghetto's inhabitants were in a subordinate position because of their own inherent personal behavior and group inferiority. In the urban North during the early 1970s, and within a few years after the *Kerner Commission Report* found that white institutions were fundamentally responsible for urban racial inequality, there developed a totally different dominant understanding—the black community was responsible for its own problems, and significant governmental action was no longer necessary: "[T]he perception of the late 1960s that America faced a fundamental racial crisis was replaced by the belief that everything reasonable had been done and that, in fact, policies had often gone so far as to be unfair to whites." Those who held these views included the officials who took charge of the principal social policy and civil rights agencies in the federal government.

The acceptance of the ghetto system as natural was accompanied by the denunciation of policies aimed at challenging the color line, including aggressive fair housing enforcement and the dispersion of subsidized, low-income housing to the suburbs. The Nixon, Ford, and Reagan Administrations adopted as a basic policy of the federal government the preservation of the racial status quo in metropolitan areas. * * * [T]his preservation of the racial status quo has adversely affected blacks of varied socio-economic classes.

* * *

It is rare for blacks and whites to experience both integrated housing and a sense of community. Blacks demonstrate a history of integrating for a better housing package, not in quest of community. Integrated housing seldom represents "a path to belonging." It is usually at the expense of community that blacks improve their housing package in integrated settings dominated by whites. The integration imperative is predicated on white dominance and virtual assimilation by blacks as preconditions to whites accepting blacks into their communities. When these preconditions are not met, blacks who serve as the agents of integration risk living a life that lacks context and community. As Blair Stone indicates, "[t]o be a part of a community one must feel 'at home' there. One must have a sense of attachment, both emotional and physical." In the absence of these circumstances, affluent blacks who maximize the quality of their housing bundle do so at the expense of finding a home and community in the same space.

In light of the difficulty of linking home and community in the context of residential integration, there is evidence that even middle-class blacks increasingly value black community attachment and affiliation at the expense of integration. This is a controversial matter because opponents to fair housing often have cited voluntary segregation in denying the existence or extent of racial discrimination. The theory that "blacks prefer to live among their own kind" is advanced to delay or prevent efforts toward decreasing black residential segregation. In turn, this rationale can support a community's efforts to " 'maintain the ethnic purity of its neighborhood without racist guilt.' "

Nevertheless, I believe that a growing segment of the black middle class is voluntarily attaining housing in black areas. This may stem in part from the increase in black alienation from white society that has developed from the late 1960s and into the early 1980s among all segments of the black community. According to the National Research Council's survey, "[q]uestions concerning white intentions or basic trust in whites elicit some of the most alienated responses." Also, for the black middle class, it has been possible to attain the benefits of socio-economic mobility without living in integrated neighborhoods.

Motivation aside, for the black middle class the existence of adequate housing alternatives to the most impoverished black areas has come about within the context of persistent racial segregation from whites and the reduced push to move to all-white or integrated areas. The push to move to these areas apparently was more valued when they represented the only viable options to deplorable living conditions. Moreover, given the past history of white resistance to residential integration—including acts of intimidation, harassment, and violence—"voluntary" segregation may "simply reflect the judgment that entry into all-white communities is just not worth the risk or aggravation; and it is certainly no longer necessary to achieve a decent standard of living."

Those who emphasize integration either as a value per se or as a pragmatic means of access to improved lifestyles and life chances often discount the growing importance of black cultural and community affinities. Take, for example, the black community of Los Angeles' View Park: "To the outside observer, it may seem ironic that this group of professional blacks, who have successfully assimilated into mainstream white society, choose to live in this mostly black neighborhood—especially one that is situated a quick drive away from the gang-scarred neighborhoods east of Crenshaw." Residents offer various explanations. According to a black airline pilot, the presence of black role models for his two pre-adolescent children outweighed negative factors associated with living in an urban area: "In this community, they can see black doctors, writers, lawyers, artists, craftsmen, law-enforcement officials. They're all within a hundred yards of where we live."

Many of the View Park residents reportedly experience relief upon returning home to a black environment after having endured the job stress of "competing on a white playing field all day." Black parents, whose children attend predominantly white private schools, expressed a critical need to have their children come home to a black neighborhood where it is the norm to be black; otherwise the children could lose a social and cultural grounding that would militate against their growing up "lost, not knowing who they are."

In spite of the growing class schism among blacks, spatial equality's group-based remedial orientation presents the potential to build black community and cultural life in ways that integration simply cannot. The integration imperative is a skimming-off process that disperses from the community many of the very people who are needed as resources, often leaving behind in isolated circumstances those who are the most disabled and dislocated socially and economically. Spatial equality enables a relinking of black interests across class lines.

A decade ago, Eric Schnapper wrote that the central discrimination issue of the 1980s would be to end the perpetuation of past discrimination. In considering the remedy for black America's housing predicament, it is important to move beyond individual acts of racial discrimination and address the government rules, policies, and practices "that perennially reenforce the subordinate status of any group." The urban oppression now experienced by so many blacks is neither natural nor inevitable. In assessing responsibility, little is gained by searching out individual perpetrators. A regime sustains subordination through generating "devices, institutions, and circumstances that impose burdens or constraints on the target group without resort to repeated or individualized discriminatory actions." Through contextualizing the historical development of federal housing policies, we can look back to the future and see the nation's continuing responsibility for furthering the racist adventure that now plagues so many blacks in urban settings. * * *

In *Milliken v. Bradley*, the 1974 Detroit school desegregation case, Justice Potter Stewart concluded that the segregative disadvantages associated with spatial inequality had been caused "by unknown and perhaps unknowable factors." This view badly misreads the historical role of the federal government since the 1930s. It is now clear that the dual housing market that undergirds racial demography and residential segregation has been preserved and expanded by the federal government's express endorsement of racism. * * * It is virtually impossible to overstate the significance of this involvement in creating, sponsoring, and perpetuating the racially segregated dual housing markets that divide America. The federal government should acknowledge its role and move to right these tragic wrongs.

Notes and Questions

1. Toward the end of 2001 the *New York Times Magazine* characterized the "return to segregation" as one of the "ideas ... and hindsight reckonings that made a difference in 2001." James Traub, *Return to Segregation*, N.Y. Times, Dec. 9, 2001, Section 6, at 96. The continuing failure of integration for blacks is noted: "It is not assimilation that has failed; it is integration—the word we use specifically for the incorporation of African Americans into the mainstream." According to George Galster, a professor of urban affairs at Wayne State University, "Despite conventional wisdom, the upper-income group of black Americans by many indexes is as segregated from white Americans as lower-income blacks are." *Id.*

2. Do you think that the black-middle class segregation is voluntary? The *New York Times* reports:

> Implicit within the new residential data is the idea that while immigrants are finding their way into the larger culture in much the same way as they have in generations past, blacks remain a special case. Scholars do disagree about whether middle-class black segregation should be understood as a matter of choice—a conscious repudiation of the integration ethic—or as a consequence of such discriminatory practices as "racial steering."

Id. Calmore, however, suggests that this distinction is probably too schematic and he "would put the 'voluntary' in quotes." *Id.* Does Calmore's description of integration as sequential, rather than coherently packaged help to explain so-called voluntary residential segregation? As indicated by Sheryll Cashin, however, living in an affluent all-black suburban community may present a very problematic alternative to integration. She points out:

> African Americans fare better—at least in terms of government services, local taxes, and access to educational and economic opportunity—in integrated settings. While middle-class black enclaves may be premised on a confident separatism, the rightfully proud residents of these communities must face a painful reality. Try as

they might, they cannot completely control their own destiny simply by gaining political control of a suburban locality. Externalities beyond their control are inevitable—a chief external factor being the race-laden private decisions of people and institutions not to invest in, locate in, or cooperate with all-black communities. Try as they might, residents of these black enclaves also cannot completely escape their lower-income brethren or the social distress associated with low-income minority communities.

This reflects a larger conundrum most affluent or middle-class blacks in America face. They cannot live the American suburban dream if that dream means replicating exclusive white suburbs—that is, an enclave of "one's own" with high-quality schools, low property taxes, and desired amenities. The evidence * * * suggests that this dream will elude black Americans. The evidence also suggests that blacks with economic means are faced with a stark choice: racial segregation versus living in communities where they are vastly outnumbered by whites, a kind of integration they may not want.

Sheryll D. Cashin, *Middle-Class Black Suburbs and the State of Integration: A Post-Integrationist Vision for Metropolitan America,* 86 Cornell L. Rev. 729, 733 (2001).

3. If you are a person of color, in choosing to live in a residential neighborhood, what features do you want it to have: privacy, good schools, access to jobs, shopping, and transportation, green space, and recreational sites? How important is living in a neighborhood with a racially heterogeneous mixture of people? What are the difficulties with the various options you see? John Goering notes that Huxtable-like integration warriors have choices that "reflect a complex overlay of fears of white rejection and hostility, desires for better residential services for themselves and their children, preferences for those like themselves, and the dislike of deteriorating conditions in older, segregated neighborhoods." Joe R. Feagin & Melvin P. Sikes, *Living with Racism: The Black Middle-Class Experience* 269–70 (1994). Among the web of forces contributing to residential segregation are actually experienced discrimination and "the hostility that blacks anticipate receiving upon moving into predominantly white areas." Reynolds Farley, Elaine L. Fielding & Maria Krysan, *The Residential Preferences of Blacks and Whites: A Four-Metropolis Analysis*, 8 Housing Pol'y Debate 763, 796 (1997). Do you think that Asians and Latina/os experience their own "complex overlay" of factors in choosing where to live? If so, what are some of the factors?

4. Cashin argues that localism—"the ideological commitment to local autonomy"—is an impediment to regional solutions. Thus, in her view, "because localism adherents view participatory self-determination as a near-sacred value, they are willing to accept the often high degree of homogeneity that results from fragmented local governance." Cashin, *supra* at 753–54. She cites the following support:

> Richard Thompson Ford, *The Boundaries of Race: Political Geography in Legal Analysis*, 107 Harv. L. Rev. 1841, 1908–09 (1994) (arguing that regional administration makes it difficult for politically engaged communities to form and alienates citizens from decision-making processes, and that having many small communities nourishes cultural differences); Jerry Frug, *Decentering Decentralization*, 60 U. Chi. L. Rev. 253, 257 (1993) (noting that the "values of decentralization" include "the freedom gained from the ability to participate in the basic societal decisions that affect one's life"); Georgette C. Poindexter, *Collective Individualism: Deconstructing the Legal City*, 145 U. Pa. L. Rev. 607 (1997) (arguing that small communities foster citizen participation, efficiency, government responsiveness to citizen needs, and a sense of community).

Id. at 754, n. 142. *See also* john a. powell, *Addressing Regional Dilemmas for Minority Communities*, in *Reflections on Regionalism* 218 (Bruce Katz ed., 2000). Could an aspect of spatial reparations include the incorporation of metropolitan solutions? Why do you think that metropolitan solutions are not more prevalent? Is the primary obstacle more than a matter of valuing localism? *See* Sheryll D. Cashin, *Drifting Apart: How Wealth and Race Segregation Are Reshaping the American Dream*, 47 Vill. L. Rev. 595 (2002); Drew S. Days, III, *Rethinking the Integrative Ideal: Housing*, 33 McGeorge L. Rev. 459 (2002); Gerald E. Frug, *Beyond Regional Government*, 115 Harv. L. Rev. 1763 (2002); and Mary Jo Wiggins, *Race, Class, and Suburbia: The Modern Black Suburb As a "Race-Making Situation,"* 35 U. Mich. J. L. Reform 749 (2002).

5. Would the following respective excerpts of Sheila Foster and Judith Koons on the grass-roots movements to secure environmental justice and to save black homes in the context of community redevelopment, fit within the call for spatial reparations? How do these excerpts help us to understand the experience of injustice rather than merely the naming of it?

SHEILA FOSTER

Justice from the Ground Up: Distributive Inequities, Grassroots Resistance, and the Transformative Politics of the Environmental Justice Movement
86 Calif. L. Rev. 775, 776–80, 786–89, 791, 807–11, 826, 838–41 (1998)

The environmental justice movement is one of the fastest growing social justice movements in the United States. The movement has emerged from a primarily local, grassroots response to the presence and continued siting of hazardous waste facilities in poor communities and communities of color. For the last two decades, these communities have fought back against the injustice they perceive that permeates environmental decision-making. In doing so, they seek justice in environmental policy-making and administration.

What is the *injustice* they experience? What is the *justice* they seek? There is no clear-cut answer to such questions, especially given the diversity of the various local struggles. Any attempt to answer such theoretically complex questions must, however, consider the movement at its source. As many books on the subject illustrate, grassroots struggles form the core of any epistemological understanding of the movement and the content of its claims. By studying the movement at its source and talking to those actually leading these struggles, we can begin to understand the normative content of their claims of injustice and their corresponding struggle for justice.

Both national and regional studies have attempted to "measure" the phenomenon of environmental injustice. These studies have both benefited and imperiled the movement. While studies documenting the connection between race and environmental hazards raised national consciousness about local struggles, they also begged for further examination of the underlying phenomenon. As Iris Marion Young warns, social research and analysis should "aim to evaluate the given in normative terms. Without such a critical stance, many questions about what occurs in society and why, who benefits and who is harmed, will not be asked, and social theory is liable to reaffirm and reify the given social reality." Recently, scholars have attempted to articulate the normative premises underlying the empirical conclusions. These articulations have helped shift the focus away from a strictly empirical assessment to a more qualitative analysis of the problem—one that ascertains the social relations and processes behind the statistics.

* * * I will recount in detail the struggle of the Chester Residents Concerned for Quality Living (CRCQL) in Chester, Pennsylvania, and its efforts to stop the clustering of commercial waste facilities in this predominantly poor African-American community. Although only one case study, Chester is not unique as a magnet for toxic waste facilities. Chester shares a similar social, political, and economic history with other areas experiencing a proliferation of unwanted toxic waste facilities—the community is a former industrial town, now populated by low-income people of color. Moreover, Chester residents' struggle to save their community from the proliferation of unwanted facilities is similar to many other struggles. I invoke the Chester case study to illustrate and explore the contours of environmental injustice in places like Chester, the efficacy of reforms in the siting process, and the political strategies and possibilities of locally-based movements for environmental justice. * * *

Chester, Pennsylvania is an urban city of 39,000 residents. Located along the Delaware River, approximately fifteen miles southwest of Philadelphia, Chester is a small enclave of people of color within predominantly white Delaware County. While Delaware County, excluding Chester, is only 6.2% African American, Chester is 65% African American. The median family income in Chester is 45% lower than in Delaware County and its 25% poverty rate is more than three times the rate in

Delaware County. Unemployment and crime are high in Chester, as is the rate of health problems. Chester has a mortality rate 40% higher than the rest of Delaware County, as well as the state's highest child mortality rate.

Waste facilities that once promised needed jobs have instead brought many forms of pollution. From 1986 to 1996, the Pennsylvania Department of Environmental Protection (DEP) issued seven permits for commercial waste facilities in Delaware County, five of which were in Chester. All of the municipal waste and sewage in Delaware County is processed in Chester, even though only 7.5% of the county population lives in Chester. Moreover, over 60% of the waste-processing industries in Delaware County are located in Chester.

Living in Chester today can best be described as an assault on the senses—a toxic assault. During the summer, the stench and noise force residents to retreat into their dwellings. Recent visitors to Chester are quoted as saying that the "air is thick with acrid smells and, often, smoke. Dump trucks rumble through throughout the day," and "the first thing you notice is the smell."

These conditions have prompted a citizen uprising against the facilities. Concerned residents began meeting privately in 1992, spurred by the noise and dust generated by trucks that brought trash to one of the largest garbage incinerators in the country—located only eighty feet from the closest homes in Chester's West End neighborhood. The residents were most irritated by the huge trucks that would rumble through their neighborhoods at all times of the day and night, disturbing their sleep and their children's recreational time, and damaging the overall character and peace of their community. Noise and vibration from the constant stream of waste trucks have caused the foundations of nearby houses to crack and property values to plummet. Residents have felt imprisoned in their own community. Only later would they fully appreciate the damaging effects these facilities might have on the health of their community. "We are not against profit or gain, but we want to gain in our own areas," said one resident, "we want to live."

Today, the toxic assault on Chester continues. Remarkably, even with knowledge of the community's poor health and stringent opposition from local officials, in 1995 the DEP granted a permit to yet another facility, Soil Remediation Systems (SRS). SRS proposes to treat 960 tons of petroleum-contaminated soil each day at very high temperatures in order to burn off contaminants so the soil can be landfilled. Subsequently, the Cherokee Environmental Group applied for a permit to process petroleum-contaminated soil by a process called "bio-remediation," in which microorganisms digest the contaminants in the soil. If allowed to operate, Cherokee will bio-remediate 900 tons of contaminated soil per day. Thus far, the residents have successfully defeated efforts by both SRS and Cherokee to build their facilities in Chester.

The long history of environmental degradation, coupled with the relatively recent assault on Chester by the waste industry, led the community to ponder what could be done to stop waste facility permits in Chester. This question led CRCQL to file a lawsuit against the Pennsylvania DEP alleging environmental racism. In May 1996, Chester residents invoked Title VI of the Civil Rights Act, claiming that the DEP's pattern of granting permits in Delaware County is racially discriminatory. As evidence, they pointed to the clustering of waste facility permits in Chester's predominantly African-American community. The Chester lawsuit is one of only three lawsuits ever filed against a state agency in federal court alleging discrimination in the permit-granting process of waste facilities. The lawsuit, however, was not filed directly under Title VI. Instead, the residents claimed that the DEP violated regulations, implemented to enforce Title VI, which mandate that any jurisdiction receiving federal EPA money "shall not use criteria or methods of administering its program which have the *effect* of subjecting individuals to discrimination because of their race, color, national origin, or sex. . . ."

If successful, the Title VI lawsuit would establish legally what has already been determined empirically. As many studies document, commercial waste facilities are disproportionately located in poor communities of color. This disparate impact and its empirical basis have provided substance to claims of environmental racism and environmental injustice. Highlighting the empirical results, even without legal imprimatur, has been an important political rallying point for environmental justice advocates.

But the weight placed on empirical studies as the defining characteristic or indicia of environmental injustice has also imperiled the progress of the movement. * * * [T]he conception of injustice established by these studies, and the subsequent heavy reliance upon them in framing the problem, were fraught with risks from the beginning. Although focusing on the national distributive inequities provided a starting point for inquiring about the injustice, it provided little else in the way of a substantive understanding of environmental racism. As Laura Pulido argues, the hidden assumption underlying empirical work on environmental racism is that racism is a specific thing whose effects can be neatly isolated. Limiting the concept of environmental racism to discrete and measurable discriminatory acts fosters an incomplete understanding of racism and injustice.

The movement for environmental justice has existed on a local grassroots level since the 1970s. It was not until the release of two studies documenting the connection between race, class, and the distribution of environmental hazards, however, that the issue received national recognition. In 1983, a study by the United States General Accounting Office (GAO) found that three out of four landfills in the Southeastern region of the United States are located in predominantly poor and African-American communities. The United Church of Christ (UCC) found similar disparities on a national level in its 1987 study. The UCC study measured the demographic patterns associated with commercial hazardous waste facilities and uncontrolled toxic waste sites. As for the demographic characteristics of communities with commercial hazardous waste facilities, the study found that race proved to be the most significant variable in determining the location of commercial hazardous waste facilities. Communities with the greatest number of commercial hazardous waste facilities had the highest percentage of non-white residents. Its study of uncontrolled waste sites produced similar findings: Three out of every five African-American and Latino residents lived in communities with uncontrolled toxic waste sites. Furthermore, African-Americans were heavily over-represented in the populations of metropolitan areas with the largest number of such sites. These studies further galvanized an already active grassroots movement, and, by highlighting the national scope of the problem, added to the already impressive array of regional studies. Since the 1980s, numerous empirical studies have continued to document the disproportionate impact of environmental hazards on poor people of color.

* * *

This is not to say that distributive patterns are irrelevant or not critical to the social justice inquiry. For many issues of social justice, the evaluation of distributive patterns over time is indeed an important starting point. In answering the question, "Why is this general pattern [being] reproduced?" we must evaluate the "matrix of rules, attitudes, interaction, and policies as a social process that produces and reproduces that pattern."

Distribution thus should be seen not as the *sine qua non* of environmental racism, but instead as a crucial entry point for exploring the justice of social processes underlying distributional patterns, including environmental decision-making processes. * * *

* * * Grassroots struggles are a window into the social relations and processes underlying distributive outcomes. To be sure, they are not the only window into this process. Importantly, however, grassroots accounts tell a crucial narrative that "reveals the particular experiences of those in social locations, experiences that cannot be shared by those situated differently but that they must understand in order to do justice to the others." * * * [M]any books on the subject illustrate that narratives of disaffected communities are important to our understanding of the normative content of claims of injustice in environmental decision-making. As importantly, grassroots struggles can help policy-makers understand the way in which individuals in disaffected communities experience the very social and structural constraints upon which the siting process relies. Such an understanding, one hopes, will help reconceptualize grassroots efforts as more than mere attempts to disrupt the decisions of private corporations and state agencies. Rather, grassroots struggles are a crucial arena of restructuring social relations in systems of localized environmental decision-making.

* * *

Feminist scholars have recently articulated a view of power and agency, applicable to grassroots environmental justice struggles, which goes beyond the traditional dominant-subordinate model. Collective resistance in communities such as Chester, amidst social and structural constraints, reflects individuals operating with "incomplete agency." Viewed within the context of incomplete agency, the choices and actions of individuals in grassroots struggles are "neither fully free nor completely determined." Instead, they are influenced by independent self-conceptions, or internal agency, and the reality of broader patterns of oppression.

This richer, more complex view of power and agency in vulnerable, yet resistant, communities forces us to scrutinize the forces, or mechanisms, which render the agency of some actors incomplete. For instance, such scrutiny will require an analysis of those forces that mediate between agents in a social relationship, so-called "third agents," which allow the "powerful" to enact and reproduce their power. This analysis, in turn, necessitates an analysis of the legal and regulatory context in which these struggles take place. The legal and/or regulatory context either independently may constrain the agency of disaffected individuals or, alternatively, facilitate the constraints imposed by others in the social structure.

A close study of grassroots struggles helps unmask the social and structural constraints operating in a local system of environmental decision-making and underlying the distributive outcomes. We can see the many dimensions of power struggles, the relationships of actors within that struggle, and the role of the siting process in structuring those relationships. Focusing on the structural dynamics of a grassroots struggle, particularly as they interact with the state/public apparatus, also shifts the focus away from individual actors and the fruitless search for clearly identified perpetrators and victims. The focus appropriately shifts toward the structured nature of decision-making power. This more structural focus, in turn, can lead to fruitful discussions about the role of siting process reforms in achieving environmental justice.

* * *

Despite the recent and potential setbacks, CRCQL has created a venerable legacy—it is now a political force to be reckoned with in Chester. What began as a small group of residents concerned with their quality of life and their health, has grown into an organization with the power to engage decision-makers on issues that fundamentally affect the residents' material livelihood. Indeed, CRCQL's biggest victory may be that it is a cohesive, healthy group and is still fighting in coalition with C4 [Campus Coalition Concerning Chester]. A self-taught community organizer, Zulene Mayfield recognizes that the importance of CRCQL's struggle goes beyond the individual victories and defeats in their campaign against the toxic facilities in Chester. "Historically, black people haven't realized the power they have. The people who have realized it, who have the knowledge, have to teach the others. We have to start using our own power."

* * *

Grassroots groups such as CRCQL have not had the time to await reforms in environmental decision-making processes. Even while operating under the influence of various social and structural constraints, Chester residents have been able to construct a direct political strategy and establish a grassroots base to influence environmental decision-making in their community. However, as the current situation in Chester indicates, the residents' success remains tentative and subject to the same constraints that threaten to overwhelm their resistance. An ever-changing political landscape further frustrates reform efforts. Nevertheless, groups such as CRCQL already have begun to transform environmental politics and the representation of marginalized communities in the environmental decision-making process.

One of the ways in which this transformation is occurring is that groups such as CRCQL are practicing a strong version of participatory democracy, whereby "self-governing citizens ... participate in the talk through which questions are formulated and given a decisive political conception." The process of strong participatory democracy in Chester progressed through various stages of evolution, in which they "creat[ed] greater political consciousness among the potential participants, directly confront[ed] entrenched economic and statist powers, present[ed] their cause to the larger public, cultivat[ed] support among various constituencies, and develop[ed] sufficient internal and external resources so that they could mobilize large numbers when necessary." CRCQL's struggle also evolved from a confrontational mode in which they demanded answers from decision-makers, to a more sophisticated deliberative mode which included the mastery of technical language, and finally to a coalition mode in which they drew upon the resources of other citizens. As importantly, CRCQL became an effective political actor in the decision-making process by affecting the local decision-making processes through protesting and lobbying for ordinances.

In the process of building its strong democratic movement, CRCQL created what Harry Boyte and Sara Evans have called *free spaces*, "settings which create new opportunities for self-definition, for the development of public and leadership skills, for a new confidence in the possibilities of participation, and for wider mappings of the connections between the movement members and other groups and institutions." Part of what sustains these free spaces—in which ordinary people move from complainers and victims to participants in the processes which govern their lives—is the realization by local groups that power relationships within a decision-making structure are fluid and contestable. Once this realization takes hold, as it did in Chester, participants move from a reactive to a proactive mode in which decision-makers respond to their concerns.

What do the strategies of these grassroots groups mean for the future of environmentalism? Grassroots activists, such as the members of CRCQL, create a level of environmental self-determination once non-existent in their communities. It is not that these communities are just beginning to care about environmental issues. Rather, these communities have come to realize that the mainstream environmental movement has constructed a notion of environmentalism which fails to address the material concerns of low-income communities of color. Grassroots environmental justice activists recognize this neglect and hope to construct a new meaning of environmentalism, linking environmental preservation to their material environment and community.

The notion of "environment" for environmental justice groups and networks has come to mean "home" and "community." These are the places that need to be preserved and protected from pollutants and other harms. This "community preservation" principle recognizes that the harms resulting from the disenfranchisement of the most vulnerable communities from environmental decision-making are not only health-related, but include non-health-related consequences—such as the reduction of community cohesion and socioeconomic damage, resulting from the loss of businesses, homes, and schools. The initial rallying point for many communities is the destruction of their quality of life—from the invasion of trucks, dust, and noise that accompany the existence of a waste facility in their neighborhood. Only later do residents see the link to actual health effects.

However, to reduce grassroots struggles to a new consciousness about environmental concerns—even as that term is construed broadly—would be a mistake. As Giovanna Di Chiro explains:

> The notion that grassroots, community-based, social and racial-justice driven organizations are composed of "new environmentalists" is contested terrain. Questions of the importance of self-representation, definitional clarity, and the agency inherent in "speaking for ourselves" are key issues for movement activists. What is "new" about the environmental justice movement is not the "elevated environmental consciousness" of its members but the ways that it is transforming the possibilities for fundamental social and environmental change through processes of redefinition, reinvention, and construction of innovative political and cultural discourses and practices. This includes, among other things, the articulation of concepts of environmental justice and environmental racism and the forging of new forms of grassroots political organization.

Indeed, the next phase in the transformation of environmental justice participants, and their local communities, lies in forging partnerships and networking with grassroots organizations across substantive areas. As CRCQL has done in Chester, environmental justice groups are networking with other groups to provide information and technical expertise to grassroots constituencies on various issues of interest to disenfranchised communities. Because of these networks, residents in marginal communities will continue to shape environmental policy and create more opportunities for community input into the spectrum of policy-making which affect their material conditions. Only the future will prove whether, and to what extent, these networks can consolidate the power of varied local organizations such as CRCQL and implement an agenda for environmental and social justice for society's most vulnerable members. Until then, the success of groups such as CRCQL suggests that the goal is not out of reach.

* * *

As Chester illustrates, the environmental injustice phenomenon goes beyond the racial and class maldistribution so well documented in numerous empirical studies. Environmental injustice manifests itself through environmental decision-making processes. Thus, policy-makers should continue to reexamine the foundations of both substantive criteria and participatory processes in reforming the siting process. While current and proposed reforms are a step toward a more equitable siting process, environmental justice in communities such as Chester will require stronger participatory norms in the siting process. Until then, groups such as CRCQL in Chester will continue to build a grassroots base to influence local environmental decision-making processes, even while operating under severe social and structural constraints which render their victories so tentative.

Notes and Questions

1. The environmental justice movement is broad and includes a multifaceted approach to redress. For an overview of legal claims, see Terenia Urban Guill, *Environmental Justice Suits Under the Fair Housing Act*, 12 Tul. Envtl. L. J. 189 (1998); Kathy S. Northern, *Battery and Beyond: Tort Law Response to Environmental Racism*, 21 Wm. & Mary Entvl. L. & Pol'y Rev. 485 (1997); Luke Cole, *Environmental Justice Litigation: Another Stone in David's Sling*, 21 Fordham Urb. L.J. 523 (1994). As Sheila Foster states above, however, "grassroots struggles form the core of any epistemological understanding of the movement and the content of its claims." *See also Confronting Environmental Racism: Voices from the Grassroots* (Robert D. Bullard ed., 1993); *Unequal Protection: Environmental Justice and Communities of Color* (Robert D. Bullard ed., 1994); Laura Pulido, *Environmentalism and Economic Justice: Two Chicano Struggles in the Southwest* (1996).

2. The literature on environmental justice and environmental racism is immense, including Vicki Been, *Locally Undesirable Land Uses in Minority Neighborhoods: Disproportionate Sting or Market Dynamics?*, 103 Yale L.J. 1383 (1994); Luke Cole, *Macho Law Brains, Public Citizens, and Grassroots Activists: Three Models of Environmental Advocacy*, 14 Va. Envtl. L.J. 687 (1995); Kelly Michelle Colquette & Elizabeth A. Henry Robertson, *Environmental Racism: The Causes, Consequences, and Commendations,* 5 Tul. Envtl. L.J. 153 (1991); Peter L. Reich, *Greening the Ghetto: A Theory of Environmental Race Discrimination*, 41 Kan. L. Rev. 271 (1992); Gerald Torres, *Introduction: Understanding Environmental Racism*, 63 U. Colo. L. Rev. 839 (1992); Eric K. Yamamoto & Jen-L W. Lyman, *Racializing Environmental Justice*, 72 U. Colo. L. Rev. 311 (2001).

3. Part III of this book emphasizes the acts of struggle in the quest for social justice. What does the word, "struggle," mean to you? How is hope tied to the concept of struggle? What is the role of struggle in relation to legal advocacy? How does a lawyer's participation in community struggles possibly enhance what Foster discussed as "incomplete agency" among vulnerable parties? Keep these questions in mind as you read this extended excerpt by Judith Koons, who gives voice to the enhanced notion of humanity and connection that social justice lawyering must support and advance.

JUDITH KOONS

Fair Housing and Community Empowerment: Where the Roof Meets Redemption
4 Geo. J. on Fighting Poverty 75, 77–90, 92–105, 109, 118–20, 123 (1996)

Wiping her hands on her apron, Olivia Brown opened the screen door and beckoned her guests in. "Well *hello*, Miss Beatrice and Miss Roni, come in, come in," she exclaimed, beaming widely at her neighbors who had brought a stranger to visit. "Charlie's taking a nap in the other room, but we can visit." In a few minutes, Beatrice Houston and her daughter, Roni Houston McNeil, had told their friend about a zoning ordinance that the City Council had just passed that looked like it was designed to destroy their neighborhood. The threat of displacement was no stranger to the women who lived in the African-American neighborhood that traced its origins to the first days of the small central Florida town. However, this ordinance, which had rezoned their land as high density residential and which had used phrases like "aggregation of parcels" and "transferable development rights," seemed to carry the threat to a new, ominous level.

As the women quietly talked, shadows of an old sadness seemed to stalk the corners of the modest frame house. Words like "redevelopment," "condominiums," and "relocation" were passed among the women like pieces of a dismantled grenade. Miss Olivia kept shaking her head, at first in hopeful disbelief and then with determination. * * *

After leaving Ms. Brown's house that day, Beatrice Houston and Roni Houston McNeil had a lot more walking and talking to do. Over the next few days, they went from door to door in the neighborhood, telling the residents about the zoning ordinance and the threat of displacement. Out of the community, a fighting spirit arose. The residents, mostly poor and many aging, launched a series of proceedings to preserve their homes and their neighborhood from the forces of municipal destruction. * * *

Civil rights is essentially a spiritual struggle. It is expressed, at heart, in the stories, dreams, and songs of the dispossessed. * * *

The "problem of the color-line" persists despite two decades of the twentieth century that chiseled deep changes in the law—from the school desegregation cases of 1954 to the Housing and Community Development Act of 1974. One of the overarching pieces of legislation enacted during this period was the Fair Housing Act of 1968. In retrospect, perhaps more than other civil rights acts of its era, scholars view the Fair Housing Act as flawed and ineffective to remedy national problems of segregated and unaffordable housing. To millions of Americans, the promise of civil rights, made in 1863 and sought to be actualized in the civil rights acts, seems as dry as a valley of old bones.

Every so often, though, a case emerges that enlivens those bones. In the plain rigor of southern communities, where the daily struggle of African-Americans to live is played out in small town anonymity, there sometimes is a convergence of people and forces that has great moment and meaning: a veil is pulled aside as if viewing a nighttime full of stars. New constellations appear to take form. Racial imbalance seems righted, for a while. Racial healing takes place, for a while. What happened in this community is what has happened in every community that has, for whatever period of time, become a site of transformation. In these places, large and small, known and unknown, the law became animated with the spirit of people and became a structure for spiritual change. The law became a bridge spanning the constellation of time—from redemption of past wrongs to the creation of new worlds. A symbol of promise crosses the span—the wheels of the chariot of Yahweh smoke like a freedom train—bearing the certainty that "sometime, somewhere" justice will be done.

One of those times was 1990; one of those places was Cocoa, Florida.

To challenge the City's threatened destruction of her neighborhood, Beatrice Houston stepped into the shoes of community organizer and lead plaintiff in a series of three formal proceedings. Roni Houston McNeil used her magnetic leadership to forge a community protest and client support organization called Save Our Neighborhood. The litigation, generically referred to as *Houston v. City of Cocoa*, was formally conducted in state and federal judicial and administrative arenas, but was grounded in the community. * * *

* * * [E]mpowerment finds its home in the individual and collective spirit and reaches beyond the political into the spiritual dimension. Empowerment is the means of transforming oppression into freedom. It crosses an initial threshold of awareness of subordination and gathers force by claiming the ability to name oneself and one's reality. Speaking, petitioning, and honoring individual and community narratives are critical dialogic components of empowerment. Dialogue, when combined with confrontation and resistance, creates a channel of power and transformative opportunities through which subordinated people break free, sometimes quickly, sometimes slowly, of internal and external oppression and cross into liberation.

The goal of empowerment may be accorded a long-term view that resists a win or lose approach. Stripped of a four-quarter, event-driven identity, litigation may be part of a transformative process for a given community. The point of empowering litigation is to create a channel of opportunities for poor people to bring power, resources, and an improved quality of life to their communities. With this approach, the triumph of empowerment would be possible even with the loss of a lawsuit.

* * *

[This article] addresses how the goal of empowerment of poor communities may be served through a model of lawyering that includes traditional legal strategies. That model, called "community empowerment lawyering," includes both attorney-client and strategic components. Within the attorney-client relationship, the primary dynamic elements reflected in the Cocoa case are those featured in the theoretics scholarship—collaboration, shared power and decision-making, reliance on client expertise and labor, and use of client and community narratives. Paired with strategies of community mobilization on the front end and strategies of community economic development at the remedy stage, traditional legal strategies employed in Cocoa achieved greater empowerment potential.

The Cocoa clients mobilized the community by forming a community protest group, fully engaging the media, organizing at the grassroots and electoral levels, collaborating with a spectrum of community groups, and educating the community, decision-makers, and the public. * * *

Three traditional legal strategies were adopted in *Houston v. City of Cocoa*: a federal class action, federal administrative proceedings, and state administrative proceedings. The litigation pieces were constructed out of the disciplines of civil rights, affordable housing and poverty law, zoning and land use planning, environmental protection, and historic preservation. As a multiple-forum, interdisciplinary effort, the case invited doctrinal innovations, such as the successful marriage of civil rights and environmental theories. [*See* Order Denying Motion to Dismiss, *Houston v. City of Cocoa*, 2 Fair Housing-Fair Lending (P-H) P15,625 (M.d. Fla. Oct. 26, 1990).]

Admittedly, the legal tools, even with lawyerly innovations, seemed inadequate to the task of preserving the Cocoa neighborhood. And those legal tools, perhaps best described as "blunted," were raised in the struggle for survival by mostly elderly, low-income residents. Yet there seemed to be a strength in the arms wielding those tools that redressed inadequacy. In the alchemy of law, poverty, spirituality, and civil rights that moved this case, the legal tools and the community seemed to be mutually empowered. With a process of snowballing synergy, the litigation in *Houston v. City of Cocoa* empowered the community as the community spurred on the litigation. Years after the conclusion of the legal proceedings, the litigation found its greatest legacy in the community organization that it spawned.

The final strategic component of the model of community empowerment lawyering derived from the case is that of community economic development. * * *

* * * [T]he thesis of empowerment [is joined] with two subthemes. The first subtheme speaks to the role of community vigilance. The undermining of a community takes place over time, marked by changes that are so gradual and on such a small scale that they are all but invisible to those who live and work in the community. Among the termites quietly eating away at neighborhoods are governmental policies and practices that, by themselves, seem to be benign, if not helpful, creatures of the state. It is a sad irony that governmental programs designed to improve communities are sometimes employed as instruments of destruction. For example, the Community Development Block Grant (CDBG) program, originally fashioned by the federal government to improve affordable housing and to expand economic opportunities for low-and moderate-income persons, and the Enterprise Zone program, conceived by the state to boost weak local economies, were active agents in the assault on the neighborhood in Cocoa. Consequently, the signs of incremental community destruction are identified so that community awareness may be raised to enhance preservation efforts. Moreover, the description of the governmental forces at play is transmitted for policymakers who wish to avert the sacrifice of residential communities in the name of non-community economic development.

The second subtheme recognizes the traditions of redemption and civic humanism. The people of color of Cocoa combined the faith of prayer warriors with the actions of humanists to save their land. The rallying charge of the Cocoa residents was to "save black heritage land." As facts were uncovered, it became clear that, in the abundance of local history, precious little of preserved history was that of the black community. Here, too, history was sifted through a selective pan. Due to the absence of records, the African-Americans of Cocoa had lost their history twice—first their African history, and then their history in America. As counsel and residents dug for facts, they churned up some of the unrecorded history of the people of color of Cocoa. * * *

* * *

Cocoa is a sleepy little town, resting with one eye open on the banks of the Indian River near the east central coast of Florida. The open eye watches those in its population of 17,722 who toil and those who are or who may become political enemies. It is a town where everyone chooses a political camp, knowingly or unknowingly, and then becomes a Saint or a Sinner, depending on the camp colors chosen. The watchful eye also remains steadfast on the neighboring town of Rockledge which, if it were a twin, would quietly be called the prettier, smarter, and richer one. Some might note a trace of jaundice in Cocoa's gaze.

Less than ten miles due east of Cocoa sit the beach communities of Cape Canaveral and Cocoa Beach. An hour directly west are Orlando and central Florida attractions such as the Magic Kingdom. Paralleling the Indian River is U.S. 1, running north twenty miles to Titusville and south twenty miles to Melbourne and Palm Bay. Cocoa shares the distinction with its neighbors in Brevard County of being a bedroom community of Cape Kennedy, the growth of which rocketed the area forever away from the pristine land of palmetto brush and scrub jays.

Local historians gauge the settlement of Cocoa in the 1880s. The naming of Cocoa is often attributed to an African-American woman, sometimes referred to as Mrs. James, who is purported to have saved the day by pointing out a box of baking chocolate as the city fathers were stumped for a name. Early pioneers fought the mosquitos to claim the land. White settlers built their homes and stores on the shoreline of the Indian River. By 1886, a sizeable black community had arisen several blocks west, on the other side of Florida Avenue and the railroad tracks. Growth of Cocoa, white and black, was spurred by Henry Flagler's railroad and the Florida Land Boom of the 1920s.

In the African-American community, the favorable economy was reflected in the construction of modest single-family homes on small lots. Money was saved in small portions from laborer jobs. Women typically worked for ten cents an hour scrubbing floors in riverfront homes. Men usually labored in the groves for up to fifty cents an hour. Land was often bought outright, followed sometime later by the building of a home.

Laced throughout the homes in the oldest part of the neighborhood were black-owned businesses serving the residents. Dr. B.C. Scurry's office, J.C. Ager's Grocery, Evelyn's Beauty Shop, and Rosa Marie's Coffee Shop were among the neighborhood businesses catering to residents during the 1940s. Two churches—the historic Mt. Moriah A.M.E. Church and the widely attended Greater St. Paul's Baptist Church—were the cornerstones of the community. Neighborhood children like Roni Houston McNeil who grew up in the 1950s and 1960s fondly recall a cookie and candy store midway in the block between these two churches. Here the children congregated each week during that sweet period between Sunday school and church services.

By 1980, the neighborhood was home to 536 people living in 276 homes. Approximately 22% of the residents were homeowners and 78% were tenants. Virtually all of the residents were African-American. Severe poverty marked the neighborhood: 76% of the residents earned less than $5,000 per year. Yet the neighborhood supplied affordable housing to its residents. Mortgages were a rarity among the homeowners, over half of whom were elderly. For the tenants, rents averaged $130 per month, when $250 stood as the minimally expected rent for a standard unit. Although two out of every five households did not own an automobile, the neighborhood was within walking distance of many stores and services.

In 1980, the neighborhood also was occupied by heavy commercial enterprises that were neither owned by nor serving the residents. Auto body shops, construction storage yards, and a paint manufacturing operation squatted in the area along with a number of vacant lots. At the center of the neighborhood was the central facility for cable trucks of a major utility company. These "Wholesale Commercial" (WC) businesses were the daily companions of the residents.

As Cocoa entered the 1980s, the City pondered its financial future. Since the turn of the century, six of eight decades had been marked by growth. The economic decline after the Florida Land Boom had been followed in the 1940s by the construction of Patrick Air Force Base and the growth of the space program. Wildfire prosperity marked the 1950s and 1960s. Cocoa was then at the hub of steamrolling development. * * * In the wake of the end of the Apollo program and the ensuing lay-offs at Cape Kennedy, the whole of Brevard County, including Cocoa, went dead in the economic waters. But, by the mid-1970s, the Space Shuttle program propelled much of the County out of that economic slump. Except Cocoa. Negative growth was Cocoa's calling card during the 1970s, while economic recovery was being touted by Rockledge and other municipal neighbors.

Rankled by its economic failure, the City began exploring plans to "redevelop" Cocoa. Few in the African-American community were aware that their historically rooted neighborhood had become the focus of considerable attention at Cocoa City Hall. Like urban renewal plans of the 1960s, the price of redevelopment of the 1980s was to be borne by the black community—the historic neighborhood was targeted for elimination.

Although rising out of economic desperation, the idea of redevelopment seemed to start benignly enough. A three-by-four block area in downtown Cocoa with some historic charm bore the potential of being enhanced for tourism. Enchanted with the prospect of dollars flowing from historic preservation, a group of businessmen organized an ad hoc committee with the blessing of Cocoa City Council. Just as the committee was poised to advance a historic Cocoa Village tourism plan, a consultant arrived with tales of remarkable turnarounds in cities such as Pasadena through the power of *Redevelopment*.

The Florida Legislature had adopted the Community Redevelopment Act in 1969, but local governments had not been enticed. Following amendments to the Act in 1977 that provided for local funding of redevelopment through revenue bonds and tax increment financing, the first redevelopment agency in Florida was formed in Miami Beach. At the end of 1980, the Florida Supreme Court upheld the constitutionality of redevelopment financing. The floodgates then opened. As of the mid-1980s, forty-one community redevelopment agencies had been created in the state.

Cocoa was one of the first municipalities in Florida to follow the lead of Miami Beach. In July 1980, the Cocoa City Council adopted a Resolution that "one or more slum or blighted areas" of the City needed redevelopment. * * *

* * *

When the Redevelopment Plan was presented for adoption over a year later, it confirmed a plan of wholesale displacement of the historic African-American community. * * * In a pull-out diagram of Project 12, all of the Core Area homes were gone, including those owned by Beatrice Houston and Olivia Brown. In their stead were townhouses, shopping centers, professional offices, and a city park. Assessing the impact of Project 12, the Redevelopment Plan Supplement stated: "Clearly the greatest impact to occur in the core area project will be the relocation. A total of 276 residential units representing 536 persons will require relocating to other suitable housing as well as 46 businesses." With the implementation of all twelve Redevelopment projects, the total anticipated "residential workload" for displacement was 326 households, at least 276 of which were African-American.

* * *

Several years into the redevelopment business, Cocoa's far-reaching plans remained fallow. At the end of 1985, the Agency had yet to land any big-ticket projects. Cocoa then recruited a mover and shaker to head its Community Improvement Department. Her mission: to bring the Redevelopment Plan to life. Within a year, the Agency was reviewing plans for a four-hundred-slip marina and had engaged the services of a top-flight, out-of-state law firm to revise the zoning of the Redevelopment Area.

* * *

* * * Community Improvement Director Rochelle Lawandales described her vision of the neighborhood as follows: "I see a One Harbor Place, the 1900 Building. I see the Hilton at Rialto Place.... If we have one holdout property owner and something like a Hilton wants to come in ... you're darn tootin' we'd do everything to get that property." The Redevelopment Coordinator, Merrill Ladika, echoed that statement, reasoning, "If we're going to have a development come in, you can't have Mrs. Smith in her little shack on the corner.... She's going to have to go somewhere else too." In Ms. Ladika's assessment, "It's not like they're leaving the good old days. The good old days are long gone for those people." The staff member credited with authoring the Redevelopment Plan offered this summary: "The core area, in pragmatic, cold dollars and cents, should be very valuable."

Opposition by residents rested on a common theme. "I own this house," said resident Omega Austin. "My daddy built this house and that makes it special.... We had so many Christmases in this house, big feasts with all the grandchildren. There's so many memories, I'm talking about fifty years." To those finding no value in her neighborhood, Ms. Austin replied, "Everybody still looks out for each other. If you miss somebody a couple of days, you go check on them. You walk across the street and say, 'Are you all right, Miss Rosa? Is there anything I can do for you?' " Evaluating the purported relocation benefits, resident Glanville Bethel stated, "It would make no sense to take $40,000 or $50,000 if it's not enough to go buy another house. Because then you have to rent, and when you're out of money you're out on the streets."

* * * Ms. Houston and Roni Houston McNeil met with the local Legal Services attorney. Ms. Houston's goal was clear: her home and her neighborhood must be preserved. A soft-spoken and unassuming grandmother in her sixties, Ms. Houston presented some initial contrast to her charismatic and politically astute daughter. Two less apparent qualities they shared were unwavering determination and faith. The mother-daughter team proved to be an uncommon force in the history of Cocoa.

In the 1940s, Ms. Houston and her now-deceased husband, Jeff Houston, had built their home and had begun to raise their children in the neighborhood. * * *

Forty years later, Roni Houston McNeil expressed pride in her heritage and in the contribution African-Americans had made to the City. Cocoa was built on the backs of blacks, according to Ms. McNeil. She proudly relayed the story of her great grandfather, who was the first postman of Cocoa. Neither Ms. Houston nor her daughter could countenance the City's tearing down what their family had helped to build. Preserving their land and their heritage was the overriding goal that drew Ms. Houston's neighbors together. While a number of residents were skeptical about opposing the City, no resident expressed a desire to wage a legal battle against the City in an effort to obtain more money to relocate.

A preliminary review of the facts and the law convinced Central Florida Legal Services that the Redevelopment Plan and Ordinance 7-88 were at odds with the Fair Housing Act, at least by virtue of a disproportionate adverse impact on black residents. Recognizing that the case would smother the two-attorney, one-paralegal office and that the requisite expertise was not available in the local market, Central Florida Legal Services called Florence Roisman of the National Housing Law Project. The NAACP Legal Defense & Educational Fund, Inc., soon joined the Legal Services program, attracting Berle, Kass & Case, a New York City firm specializing in environmental and land use law.

* * *

Counsel for the residents submitted a request to appear on the City Council agenda for the March 22, 1988, meeting for the purpose of discussing Ordinance 7-88. Rejecting the request, the City Manager proffered that the City Council would be disinclined to reconsider adopted action. Counsel was assured that an opportunity to raise the issue would arise during the delegations portion of the meeting.

During the afternoon of March 22nd, the residents held a press conference at the home Ms. Houston and her husband had built. Seated in her front yard were fifty elderly homeowners and younger tenants. One at a time, they rose to defend their homes. Ms. Houston stood first to welcome everyone, stating:

> I have been your neighbor for 40 years. We have watched each others' children grow. We have taken care of each other when we have been sick. We have shared our sorrow when burying our dead. We are family, and one of the last true neighborhoods in the county.... I will not move from this neighborhood until and if the sad day comes when the last court in the land tells me I must move.

Roni Houston McNeil joined her mother in declaring that the redevelopment and rezoning "would wipe this neighborhood off the face of this earth, uprooting elderly black homesteaders and low-income tenants and destroying our heritage."

* * *

In June 1988, residents filled the Council chambers to hear Roni Houston McNeil and counsel address a Special City Council meeting. Holding the sign from the wagon her great-grandfather had driven through dirt roads in Cocoa as he delivered mail, Ms. McNeil eloquently gave voice to the history, work ethic, and dignity of the neighborhood:

> Blacks had a lot of input in the building of the city. Maybe they weren't doctors and lawyers and bankers, but they provided the support services—they were the maids and the groundskeepers and the shoeshiners.... This was undesirable land 100 years ago—it was swampy. We cleared it and filled it and built a community. And as soon as you get roots down, here come these politicians who want you to move.... These were old people ... They fought the good fight their whole lives. And it wasn't for riches or gold, it was to hold onto their little corner of the world.

John Charles Boger, appearing with Jon Dubin of the NAACP Legal Defense Fund, advised the City: "We're down here because we think there's a serious problem...." Pressure on the City had reached a churning point. Calling the issue a "durned bucket of worms," the City agreed to a ninety-day extension of Ordinance 7-88 in exchange for the submission by the Legal Defense Fund of a memorandum explaining the illegality of the City's rezoning and redevelopment plans and activities. Residents and counsel then continued to maintain pressure on the City to revise the ordinances by mobilizing the community on several fronts. Cocoa's bucket was indeed overflowing.

* * *

As other community groups in Cocoa expressed dissatisfaction with the growth-inducing policies of the City Council, Save Our Neighborhood joined a coalition to engage in grassroots political activism. At every election and in between, every block of pavement in Cocoa was pounded by members of the coalition. Time and time again, Save Our Neighborhood and the coalition moved the people of Cocoa to public meetings and to the polls.

Invoking Florida's Public Records Act, counsel submitted regular requests to inspect and copy the City Council and Redevelopment Agency files. Counsel visited City Hall several times a week, reviewed thousands of documents, then copied and circulated relevant documents to co-counsel. At the same time, counsel made similar requests of the Department of Housing and Urban Development (HUD) under the federal Freedom of Information Act. The synoptic cover memos became the basis for workfiles, the organizational backbone of the case. Key documents were copied and discussed at Save Our Neighborhood and community meetings.

The Legal Defense Fund used the summer rezoning extension to develop key legal theories. In September, counsel submitted a memorandum to the city government discussing, in general but persuasive terms, the applicability of the Fair Housing Act to the zoning and redevelopment plans for the neighborhood. The City took the memo and did not pause as Ordinance 7-88 went into effect. With the goals of the Redevelopment Plan as its beacon, the City appeared to be set on its plan to destroy the neighborhood. However, the residents and the legal team were prepared to catapult the case into its next stage—the filing of three formal proceedings against the City.

Late Friday afternoon, September 16, 1988, counsel for the residents received a call from Community Improvement Director Rochelle Lawandales. Ms. Lawandales advised that the City had prepared necessary CDBG documents for the upcoming grant year by publishing a Finding of No Significant Impact (FONSI) based on Environmental Review Records (ERRs). Comments were due to the City Manager on Monday, September 19th. Calling from the telephone booth outside City Hall, counsel managed to extract key documents after 5:00 p.m. that Friday. The next day, Karl Coplan, Jean McCarroll, and Steve Kass of Berle, Kass & Case hammered out comments to the FONSI and ERR which were delivered to the Cocoa City Manager and to HUD on Monday, September 19th.

Presented on behalf of twenty-five residents of the Core Area, the CDBG comments challenged the ERR and FONSI as failing to consider the impact of the entire Redevelopment Plan as a single major federal action with significant impact on the human environment, thus requiring an Environmental Impact Statement (EIS). Among other grounds, the comments cited the failure of the City to consider the impact of its activities on structures eligible for inclusion in the National Register of Historic Properties. In addition, the comments raised the City's failure to deliver a copy of the FONSI to counsel for the residents at the time of its publication while being on notice of counsel's interest in the City's CDBG program and activities. In December, after the City dismissed the comments and requested release of the funds, counsel for the residents filed objections with HUD on the noted environmental, historic, and procedural grounds.

Later in December, attorneys with the Legal Defense Fund filed another set of objections with the Secretary of HUD based on violations of Title VI of the Civil Rights Act and the Housing & Community Development Act of 1974. Four objections were lodged:

1. The City's use of CDBG funds to bring about the total displacement of the residents of the neighborhood had the purpose and effect of discriminating on the basis of race and demonstrated the failure to take affirmative steps to remedy past race discrimination;

2. The City's actions and inactions violated the requirements of one-for-one replacement of housing and the preparation of an anti-displacement plan;

3. The use of federal funds by the City triggered the obligation to minimize displacement or to mitigate the adverse effects of displacement. The City failed to adopt any such policy; and

4. The City violated its 1985–1988 Housing Assistance Plan (HAP) and the proposed 1988–1991 HAP did not satisfy the Housing and Community. Development Act.

HUD dispatched an investigative team to Cocoa to inquire into the civil rights complaint. In response to the environmental objections, HUD froze the City's CDBG funds. The usually mild winter air in Cocoa took on a distinct chill.

* * *

On the first day of Black History Month in 1989, a complaint was filed in federal court asserting twelve claims for relief against the City and the Redevelopment Agency. Eight named residents sought relief on behalf of a class of past, present, and future homeowners and tenants of the Core Area. Relief was sought from a discriminatory pattern and practice of destructive actions toward the neighborhood, having the purpose and effect of undermining the residents' quality of life, encouraging deterioration of their homes and tenancies, and causing their displacement. To describe the pattern and practice, the complaint identified four sets of activities of defendants:

1. Adopting and implementing the Redevelopment Plan targeting the neighborhood for clearance;

2. Redlining the neighborhood and Redevelopment Area by declaring the moratorium on the use of federal housing rehabilitation funds;

3. Rezoning the neighborhood to provide development incentives designed to encourage the conversion of low-income housing to upscale residential and commercial development; and

4. Imposing incompatible commercial zoning on the neighborhood to precipitate the intrusion of noxious nonresidential uses into the area while providing protective residential zoning for white neighborhoods.

The complaint alleged five counts of race-based discrimination under Title VIII of the Civil Rights Act of 1968, Title VI of the Civil Rights Act of 1964, the Civil Rights Act of 1866, and the Thirteenth and Fourteenth Amendments to the United States Constitution. Residents challenged defendants' use of CDBG funds under the Housing and Community Development Act of 1974, the National Environmental Policy Act of 1969, and the National Historic Preservation Act of 1966. The complaint joined two state and federal due process claims with two state notice and Redevelopment Act claims, rounding out the twelve grounds for relief.

The City Attorney advised the City Council that defense of the suit would likely be successful. In fact, he doubted that the case would be certified as a class action. Not long thereafter, $50,000 was transferred from the City's contingency account to the budget line item for legal fees after the $100,000 budgeted for legal expenses for the year had been spent. Having initiated the litigation, counsel and the residents then were challenged to maintain pressure on each informal front and to make progress in each formal proceeding while tending to the quiet labor of building the case, brick by brick, fact by fact.

To build the case, the legal team for the residents shaped theories of discriminatory intent and impact while sifting through decades of data and weighing strategies to achieve projected remedies. Central to this case development effort was collaboration with the client community.

* * *

Since 1976, when the Supreme Court announced its decision in *Washington v. Davis*, the standard for a successful race-based Equal Protection challenge has been clear: Fourteenth Amendment Equal Protection is offended where racial categories are employed with the intent to discriminate. The following year, the Court made clear that *Washington v. Davis* would not be confined to employment discrimination. In *Village of Arlington Heights v. Metropolitan Housing Development Corporation (Arlington Heights I)*, the Court applied the same intent requirement to an exclusionary zoning action. Although the Court remanded the Fair Housing claim for consideration of discriminatory impact, the constitutional inquiry ended when the Court found insufficient proof of discriminatory purpose.

Much debate has been aired over the propriety of the discriminatory intent requirement. Among the reasons advanced for the requirement are questions of alternative standards, issues of remedies, and concerns about invalidating hosts of laws and practices designed to serve neutral ends. In *Arlington Heights I*, zoning was highlighted as one such law of neutral design. Curious. From its inception, zoning was designed to and has been used to segregate uses by economics and race. Zoning may wear a face of neutrality, but its heart beats in a history of segregative intent.

Intent remains an indelible figure in constitutional civil rights law, but the Fair Housing Act extends to practices that have a discriminatory impact. A plaintiff may prove discriminatory effect by either an "adverse racial impact," meaning that the conduct has a greater negative impact on one racial group than on another, or an "ultimate effect" discrimination, meaning that the practice harms the community generally by perpetuating segregation. Even though the circuit courts of appeals disagree on the precise test to analyze impact, a successful Fair Housing claim will include essentially the same components. With the burden at each stage varying by circuit, a plaintiff must produce some quantum of evidence in the following areas: disparate impact (either in terms of "adverse racial impact" or "ultimate effects" discrimination); the strength of that impact; whether there is evidence of discriminatory intent; the defendant's interest in the challenged action; the nature of the relief sought; and, with respect to any proffered justification, whether the reasons are legitimate and whether any less discriminatory alternatives are available. Discriminatory intent is always relevant in a Fair Housing case, but the strength of a disproportionate impact is also a leading factor for courts to consider. Where the disparity is significant, even practices "neutral" on their face may be invalidated.

The Supreme Court has outlined the following indicia of unlawful purpose: the impact of the action; the historical background of the decision; the sequence of events leading to the action; any departures from normal procedural sequence; any deviation from normal substantive criteria; and the legislative or administrative history of the decision. Although the necessity and wisdom of requiring proof of motive remain controversial, three strong ameliorative factors persist. First, the sole motive need not be discriminatory. Race need only be *a* motivating factor. Second, direct evidence of intent is not necessary. Race-based motive may be inferred from circumstantial evidence. Third, evidence of wrongful purpose often will be available simply because discrimination pervades our history, our institutions, and our consciousness.

The language of the Redevelopment Plan provided initial evidence of intent: the Plan was race-conscious. And Project 12, as depicted in the Redevelopment Supplement, schematically eliminated the neighborhood. Complications arose when the Council disavowed Project 12 in response to the residents' challenge and then passed a new ordinance repealing Project 12. The residents and legal team doubted that the City's plans really had changed. Because the infrastructure of displacement was retained in the operative zoning and land use designations, it seemed evident that the City Council was merely pursuing a more subtle, *de facto* Project 12.

With a healthy suspicion of the City Council's motives, the residents and legal team followed two trails of evidence. First, they explored whether the City was engaged in ongoing plans and activities to eliminate the neighborhood. To counsel, any race-conscious displacement efforts with a significant disparate impact on African-Americans provided compelling evidence of discriminatory intent. Second, they pursued evidence of race-based motivation under the criteria outlined by the Supreme Court.

To examine data of discriminatory intent as well as of disparate impact, counsel continued to visit City Hall on a weekly basis and reviewed every document on file in the Planning and Development Department. Of the thousands of reviewed documents, five sets of documents substantiated an original and ongoing race-conscious intent to displace the residents.

First, beginning in March 1982, the Redevelopment Agency had obtained appraisals of every parcel in the Core Area. The appraisals seemed strikingly low. Second, the City had adopted an indefinite moratorium on the use of housing rehabilitation funds in the Redevelopment Area. A former employee of the City frankly advised counsel that the purpose of the moratorium was to diminish property values in the Core Area so that properties could be acquired less expensively. Third, an analysis made of the rezoning ordinance by the Planning Director advised that zoning and infrastructure improvements would be conducive to attracting private development. According to the memo, such rezoning was of "particular importance" in the Core Area.

Fourth, representatives of the City attempted to explain the installation of pipes in the Core Area on Hughlett Avenue as improvements to the residential community. But a number of City documents also discussed securing easements from residents where to give an easement would also mean to lose a front yard. Another memo by a City employee observed that the Hughlett Avenue streetscape would create a "drawing and retention mechanism" for business enterprise. Even more revealing was an interdepartmental memo by the utilities director indicating that commercial service lines had been used in the streetscape and had been placed along residential lots with "development potential." This evidence demonstrated to counsel that, public disclaimers aside, the City was literally laying the foundation in the streetscape to attract developers to the neighborhood.

Finally, a number of documents suggested ongoing efforts to finance the acquisition of property in the neighborhood. The prohibitive expense of such efforts led to the private displacement plan of Ordinance 7-88, but public relocation also remained an option, as reflected in a handwritten note discovered in city files. While the City disclaimed plans to displace or relocate residents, the Planning Director had affixed a note to a report on HUD Section 108 loans stating, "I think this may be a way to purchase core properties."

Section 108 is a loan guarantee program in which a local government that receives CDBG funds may pledge those funds as collateral for a loan of three to five times the grant amount. Such loans are used to fund property acquisition costs, relocation payments, clearance, and demolition. The amount of the loan may have provided sufficient leverage for the City to procure other funds to finance the destruction of the neighborhood. Counsel became more convinced that removing the residents and their homes from the neighborhood, with or without relocation benefits, was paramount in the City's mind.

The second trail of evidence sought to identify evidence of race-based intent according to the criteria outlined by the Supreme Court. Most striking were preparatory steps to establish Redevelopment Area Number Two in the other predominately African-American community on the west side of the railroad tracks. Also significant was the City's designation of an historic district only in the white Redevelopment Area. The western boundary of the historic district ran down Florida Avenue, the dividing line between black and white Cocoa. A half-block away, century-old homes of African-Americans were completely overlooked. The historic district purported to protect historic resources, apparently only in the white area, from encroaching development. The City not only had ignored the neighborhood and its historic homes, but also had taken pains to protect white residential structures from the displacement effects of nearby development.

In a written discourse instructive of intent and luxury development, a City staff member observed that areas known for slum, blight, and having "a majority of minority residents" deter incoming businesses. Even though two white residential areas were also the recipients of high density residential zoning, a memorandum by the City's rezoning consultant stated that there would be no forced removal of homes in these areas.

The manner of giving notice of the appraisal and rezoning also illustrated to counsel the City's discriminatory intent. City files contained letters to white business owners in the City of the opportunity to be present during an appraiser's inspection. For the Core Area appraisals, City staff apparently recognized requirements for such notice, but bypassed them. Unlike white property owners in the area, African-American residents were not given notice of the Core Area appraisals.

Another aberration in notice was demonstrated when the rezoning ordinance was coursing toward adoption. White property owners in the WC district loudly objected to the absence of grandparented status. Although the Ordinance was designed to attract more refined uses than those in the WC category, the City capitulated.

The City then mailed individual written notices of meetings on the ordinance to eighty predominantly white owners of commercial property in and around the neighborhood. In contrast, the City did not send notice to any black residents of the neighborhood. At meetings on the rezoning ordinance, City staff and WC owners concocted a "great-grandparent clause" to allow all permissible commercial uses then in operation to continue despite their nonconformity. No accommodation was made by the City for the homes of black residents. Counsel viewed the background and events leading to the rezoning, the dual system of notification, the deviations from procedure governing notice, and the differences in substantive criteria between white-owned and black-owned property as compelling evidence of discriminatory intent.

Counsel expected the City to reply that its motive was only economic. Anticipating that explanation, the Legal Defense Fund prepared to show the alignment of economic and racial factors. Efforts were underway to demonstrate that the redevelopment and rezoning plans, with their race-based market factors, struck at the heart of Title VIII.

A plaintiff may prove a Fair Housing case based upon discriminatory effect by demonstrating either "adverse impact," where the conduct has a greater negative impact on one racial group, or "ultimate effects," where the community is harmed by the perpetuation of segregation. Adverse impact on a particular racial group may be shown in one of three ways: (1) more minorities than whites are affected; (2) minorities are disproportionately affected; or (3) minorities incur more harm than whites.

The basic building blocks of any disparate racial impact case are population, income, and housing statistics. Professor John Calmore advised that statistics are necessary to show that African-Americans in a geographic area are not only those most in need of improved housing but also those most affected by the challenged conduct which interferes with the development of low-income housing. Population data in the Cocoa area supported a showing of the adverse racial impact of the City's zoning and redevelopment activities. Surveys in local government files denoted that 536 African-Americans and 44 white persons lived in the Redevelopment Area. While all of the blacks in the Redevelopment Area would be displaced by Project 12, the City had tailored the Plan to lead to relocation of white residents only in selected projects. Even if all 44 white residents were to be displaced, the Plan would affect 12% of black Cocoa and only 0.33% of the white residents of the City.

Income data depicted the breadth and depth of poverty in black Cocoa. Black residents simply did not possess the economic standing of whites. Nearly one-quarter of black homeowners and two-thirds of black tenants lived in poverty. In contrast, less than one-twentieth of white families in Cocoa lived below the poverty line.

Combining the housing and income statistics provided an evidentiary foundation for the disparate impact analysis. According to Yale Rabin, the residents' planning expert, the median single-home value was $23,330 in the Core Area and $48,330 in the white residential sections of the Redevelopment Area. Consequently, the inducements of Ordinance 7-88 would provide a far greater return to developers in the Core Area than in the more costly white neighborhoods. Therefore, the likelihood of displacement in the Core Area was substantially greater than in the comparable white districts. Similarly, the adverse impact on Core Area tenants was much greater than that on white tenants because black renters were more dependent on their current housing location and did not possess the financial resiliency to cope with displacement.

Counsel recognized troublesome issues in the "ultimate effects" case. Because the neighborhood was segregated, counsel anticipated that the defendants would attempt to justify their actions as promoting integration. Three theories were developed to defeat the expected justification. First, although dispersing an all-black community may initially appear integrative, income and housing data indicated that such effect would be temporary at best and most likely resegregative. Data demonstrated that the plans were likely to perpetuate segregated living patterns by forcing African-Americans to move to areas outside the city limits, where the affordable housing market was predominately black.

Second, the legal team considered an affirmative use of the ultimate effects standard. Counsel developed an argument that the ultimate effect of the City's conduct was segregative because it would remove all black residents from the section of the City between the railroad tracks and the downtown area. White Cocoa would then be at greater distance from the remaining black residential area of Cocoa. Advancement of housing segregation by this displacement would be injurious to the community as a whole.

The third, and perhaps most substantial, response to the City's expected argument was to proffer in public hearings a variety of housing and community rehabilitation plans which not only were less discriminatory but also promoted rebuilding and integration of the community. By illustrating that the City's legitimate goals could be accomplished while preserving and enhancing the community, counsel and the residents sought to produce evidence satisfying the legal standard for the impact case and to raise public awareness of the availability of more appropriate housing rehabilitation programs. Roni Houston McNeil advanced this sound bite in the press for the residents' position: "Improve, not remove; rebuild, not destroy."

Despite preparation, the City's offered justification was a bit unnerving. With the density bonus provision of the rezoning, the City suggested it could just as readily encourage the construction of low-income housing as luxury condominiums. The choice was left to private enterprise. Counsel never resolved whether the rationale was brilliant or simply peculiar, but did conclude that the proffered justification was neither bona fide nor legitimate. If the City really wished to induce the development of low-income housing, that goal could certainly be accomplished in many less discriminatory ways. There was no "choice" when the City had stacked the deck to induce upscale development.

Documents in City files suggested to counsel that the City's underlying goal was to create a predominately white mini-Manhattan. The sales pitch for Ordinance 7-88 included the message that a revitalized Cocoa would mean "no more public housing." Two Planning and Zoning Board members recounted public discussions about high-cost and high-amenity condominiums which would be constructed in the Core Area after the adoption of Ordinance 7-88. In the final analysis, the legal team believed that the history of the adoption of the Redevelopment Plan and Ordinance 7-88, when read in light of the development inducements, would carry sufficient strength to rebut the City's argument.

To prevail on its pattern and practice discrimination case, much more was required than several approaches to prove intent and impact. A wide-ranging examination of Cocoa's economic and sociopolitical history in areas such as education, employment, voting, precinct-setting, electoral politics, insurance and mortgage redlining, and municipal services was necessary. That factual investigation warrants separate discussion.

While developing the case of intent and impact, counsel secured a planning expert to plumb the City's history for historical evidence of discrimination. Days prior to his agreement to participate in the case, Yale Rabin had released a draft of his most recent article, "Expulsive Zoning: Another Inequitable Legacy of Euclid." The Professor Emeritus of Planning at the University of Virginia explained that while zoning has been widely used as an exclusionary mechanism, it has also been used by local governments to promote the intrusion of low-grade and incompatible uses into low-income African-American neighborhoods, diminishing the quality and the stability of the communities. Allowing the incompatible uses in residential areas caused a piecemeal replacement of the residents by the superimposed low-grade uses. Professor Rabin characterized zoning that ousted people of color from their neighborhoods as "expulsive zoning."

In examining the origins of expulsive zoning, Professor Rabin traced the law from the Supreme Court's rejection of racial zoning in 1917 to the striking phenomenon of municipal zoning of black residential areas for industrial or commercial uses. Looking at twelve cities, Professor Rabin found expulsive zoning to be one among many discriminatory practices. Few of the cities had attracted litigious attention due to their zoning. The displacement plans of Ordinance 7-88 had placed Cocoa in the expulsive zoning spotlight.

With Professor Rabin's assistance, the team for the residents developed the Fair Housing and civil rights claims in five key areas. First, the team conducted a thorough assessment of housing conditions in the community. Next, an analysis of the Cocoa housing market was undertaken to evaluate the adequacy of alternative housing to accommodate Core Area displacees.

Third, the legal team examined the impact of the Redevelopment Plan on Cocoa and the Core Area. Lines of inquiry included anticipated demographic changes, extent of secondary displacement, net reduction in the black population of Cocoa, likely segregative consequences, feasibility of the Plan, consequences of a "failed" Plan, and the comparative degree of development experimentation in white residential areas. Fourth, the team prepared to survey the zoning and land use history of the City, including perceived causes of blight, indicia of boundary gerrymandering, and racial demography of use districts. Finally, the team was primed to follow any evidence of historic displacement of African-Americans in the City.

On July 4, 1988, Professor Rabin arrived in Cocoa to review existing land uses and housing conditions in the neighborhood. Rabin first assessed whether a "critical mass" of housing in the neighborhood supported a proposal for rehabilitation as a less discriminatory alternative. Professor Rabin determined that residential uses predominated—73% of the uses were residential. Thus, the neighborhood was not so infiltrated with commercial uses as to render preservation efforts futile. Because 87% of the occupied structures were in good or fair condition, the residents had a sound factual basis to assert neighborhood rehabilitation.

In the second area of factual inquiry, the team scoured all available housing data and discovered that the market was incapable of providing comparable replacement housing for low-income displacees. In its thirteen-year history with the CDBG program, the City had sought funds by emphasizing the unavailability of decent, safe, and sanitary housing for low-income persons. That this claim was not hollow was substantiated by data gathered from the Census, current and former Comprehensive Plans, waiting lists for subsidized housing, County housing plans, and local housing task forces. This stockpile of information was amassed to rebut any argument the City may have offered that replacement housing for the residents was readily available.

The third area of examination called for a more expansive analysis of the impact of the redevelopment and rezoning plans on the residents. Aerial photographs taken by the County and by the Department of Agriculture in the 1960s, 1970s, and mid-1980s were collected. These time-delineated documents showed the chronology of the intrusion of incompatible uses into the neighborhood as well as the degree of change in the area following the adoption of the Redevelopment Plan.

In addition, since the neighborhood was within walking distance of community services, shops, businesses, and churches, a careful review was conducted of locational losses to be suffered by displacement. Human losses were also considered, as reflected by the grieving of elderly people who are moved from their homes. By any assessment, the losses which would come to the residents and to the community from displacement were immense.

Then counsel and Professor Rabin shoveled into the fourth area—the zoning history of the City. A multi-layered world of race-based discrimination was uncovered. In Cocoa's excavated zoning history, the uppermost layer consisted of a major rezoning undertaken in 1974. The Core Area had then been zoned for heavy commercial use. At the next level down, another comprehensive rezoning had taken place in 1959. In this rezoning, the City had grafted intense commercial zoning onto the Core Area. The earliest zoning of Cocoa appeared in the bottom layer. In 1940, with its first zoning ordinance, the City had zoned the residential portions of the Core Area for heavy commercial use.

Counsel requested a copy of the City's 1974 zoning map. Because maps of the 1940 and 1959 zonings no longer existed, a patient paralegal reconstructed those maps from a 1939 County plat map and legal descriptions. Together, the three maps told the story: From the dawn of zoning in Cocoa, white residential areas were given protective residential zoning while the Core Area was given incompatible expulsive zoning.

As the zoning history coalesced and more historic facts surfaced, it became apparent that displacement for the African-American population of Cocoa did not originate with the Redevelopment Plan. Black residents of Cocoa had been displaced on five earlier occasions. Incompatible zoning had been the City's pre-Redevelopment Plan displacement tool. Such zoning had likely led to the deterioration of black-owned single family homes which had been replaced by auto body shops and junk-yards. That hypothesis was supported by census data: between 1970 and 1980, the number of occupied dwelling units in the Core Area had declined from 290 to 244 and the black population had fallen from 734 to 591.

* * *

Professor Rabin opined that the neighborhood may have become a target for expulsive zoning with the first relocation of Florida East Coast Railway. Until that time, the railroad had marked the symbolic and geographic boundary between black and white Cocoa. When the railroad moved, Florida Avenue remained the sole line between the races. The neighborhood may then have seemed uncomfortably close to downtown Cocoa and the white riverfront homes. This may have been when the City began to focus its instruments of displacement on the community that was now on the "wrong side of the tracks." Such a notion did not seem odd to Rabin. For, in Rabin's experience, the 1927 realignment of the railroad left the Core Area in the rare and vulnerable position among east coast African-American neighborhoods of standing on the east side of the railroad tracks.

The last encountered displacement bore signs of irony. A black residential neighborhood had grown up in Cocoa on the western side of the newly relocated tracks. In 1959, many of these residents were moved several miles west, outside the City limits, to make room for scattered-site public housing. Affordable single family homes owned by black residents had been destroyed to provide sites for assisted housing which came to be occupied by black tenant households. Displacement had resulted in the replacement of African-American homeowners with poorer African-American tenants.

Six months of case development had led to the discovery not only of Redevelopment-era discriminatory practices, but also of pre-Redevelopment expulsive zoning and race-based displacement. Of perhaps greater significance to the community, though, was the participation by the residents in the factual development of the case. That participation continued to mobilize the community through the long period of case development.

Due to the breadth and depth of the factual investigation, counsel was forced to look to the client community for assistance. Save Our Neighborhood assumed roles in two key areas—gathering information from meetings of City boards and tracking down data in designated areas. Save Our Neighborhood members were assigned to attend meetings and act as watchdogs of the City Council, Redevelopment Agency, Planning and Zoning Board, Code Enforcement Board, and CDBG Advisory Board. Counsel regularly made requests for follow-up information to community watchdogs. For example, the member serving as the watchdog of the Code Enforcement Board may also have been tracking down data about past or anticipated demolitions in the Redevelopment Area.

Neighborhood watchdogs attended the meetings armed not simply with single-sheet agendas but, courtesy of the public record requests, with the same agenda packages that were given to board members. Save Our Neighborhood members poured over the packages before the meetings and then actively participated during the public sessions. Board meetings became community events. The telephone grapevine kept the community apprised of upcoming meetings. Chambers were packed at City Council and Redevelopment Agency meetings. Residents were also visible at other public meetings. Every so often, Save Our Neighborhood called a community meeting to discuss significant happenings. The meetings served many community-nourishing purposes. Save Our Neighborhood members had educated themselves through counsel, the agenda packages, the public meetings, and the factual investigation. Then, as Roni Houston McNeil explained, "We came back to the community as teachers to share the information and make sure people understood."

Information exchanged at neighborhood meetings initially focused on pending zoning and redevelopment plans. But as the factual investigation began to unearth historic facts about the neighborhood and the history of race-based discrimination, the effect on the community was galvanizing. The record, the real record, verified the community's claims and more. The history of the neighborhood, which had never been acknowledged, was now undeniable. Knowledge of discrimination had existed in the community's heart for generations. Now the residents possessed proof of that discrimination. Newly discovered and verified facts validated the pain of generational discrimination. In the neighborhood meetings, residents examined documents showing the first commercial zoning of the City. Residents also exchanged stories about earlier days in Cocoa, stories describing the early reach of the black community into the north and west areas of the City and accounts of the former black-owned grove land on Smith Lane in the neighborhood.

As the investigation produced evidence of discrimination, selected facts were fired back at the City during public hearings. New information about historical discrimination kept the story in the press, continued to educate the public, and maintained pressure on the City. Residents continued to be outspoken in the press. Roni Houston McNeil was a dynamic spokeswomen for the cause. But other residents also developed reputations for "telling it like it is." Among those was Omega Austin, one of the Named Plaintiffs, who told the press that if the City did not change its ways, "In the next 10 years, the whole of downtown Cocoa is going to be one big shopping center." Grace Edwards, another resident nearing the age of ninety, advised: "You know the one thing that will move me? The Florida militia! Yes, that's right. I say with authority and all my heart that I ain't going." Ms. Edwards also painted this picture of the growth of the neighborhood:

> None of them wanted anything to do with this place because it was all wilderness.... Snakes and alligators. Lord, how we struggled, and when it rained, the streets were so flooded you had to use a boat. The blacks built this place up. Negroes didn't have to go downtown for nothing because we had everything we needed right here in our own neighborhood. Grocery stores, dress shops, and butcher shop—we cared for our own. And now the whites want to develop this place and turn it into something else. Where could I live that would make me as happy as this?

Save Our Neighborhood members, with counsel and Yale Rabin, also quietly talked with elderly residents to gather historic anecdotal evidence and to search for individuals who had been direct victims of discrimination. Among the stories that surfaced were three, set forth below, that illuminated the personal wreckage resulting from the City's efforts to destroy the neighborhood.

After newspaper editor Dorothy Sweetwine's family lost their home in 1960 to make room for the re-routing of State Road 520, she moved in with her sister. Then she went to stay with her cousin in the Elmer Silas homestead at 104 St. Charles Street in the neighborhood. The two-story home, believed to be fifty or sixty years old, had two bedrooms upstairs, a storage area under the porch, and avocado trees in the yard. The house was built of the hardest wood Ms. Sweetwine had ever seen. The wood was so hard that she had to call a carpenter to drill nail holes when she wanted to hang pictures. Ms. Sweetwine acquired the home by devise in 1969.

During the period of the moratorium on rehabilitation funds in the early 1980s, Ms. Sweetwine visited City Hall to obtain a permit to refurbish the house. She was directed to the Planning Department. When she expressed her desire to repair the home, an official began rubbing his head and said, "I'm not sure I know what to do with that property yet." She thought the comment was odd, but she went on to explain that she had heard about a program that improved the outside of a person's house and she thought she would like to do the inside, too, with a loan or matching money or just a permit. The man who rubbed his head said he would contact her.

After a while, when Ms. Sweetwine did not hear from the man, she tried to find help from someone else in City Hall. After several attempts, she gained the attention of the Building Official who sent a man over to the house. This man toured the house with a knife, chipping at the wood, and saying, "See, termites ..." That statement surprised Ms. Sweetwine because she had "termited" the house and because the house was made of such hard wood.

Then the Building Official told her the bad news: the house had to come down. The City put a sign on it that said "Unsafe." When Ms. Sweetwine said she could not move right away and did not have the money to tear down the house, the Building Official told her to take her time in moving and not to worry about the money, he would make sure the City tore the house down without charging her.

It took Ms. Sweetwine over a year to move. She and her sister found a house in nearby Rockledge. The City came to tear down her old house in late 1987 or early 1988. On that day, she went to the house and watched, trying to keep from crying. After they took it down, the workmen left a lot of junk around the yard. The lot looked worse than when the house had stood there. In fact, Ms. Sweetwine advised that they never did take care of the lot.

Down the street from the Silas/Sweetwine homestead, Mary Dorn's parents had built a home at 128 St. Charles Street in the early 1950s. Cocoa Public Housing had provided Ms. Dorn and her children a home for twenty years. But in 1973, after her parents died, Ms. Dorn moved into the family homestead. She was happy to have her own home, but had difficulty maintaining it because she was a widow on a small veteran's pension.

By the mid-1980s, Ms. Dorn was dismayed about the condition of her home. The roof was rotting and cracked, letting in air from the outside. So, Ms. Dorn went to City Hall to find out about the rehabilitation program. There she was told that she would not be able to obtain assistance because the property was jointly owned by Ms. Dorn and her six brothers and sisters. Ms. Dorn decided to put money aside to formalize her title. After some difficulty, she retained a lawyer and was able to have title consolidated in her name.

Jubilant, Ms. Dorn returned to City Hall with the papers showing her to be the sole owner. A worker in the housing office told her they could not help her: the program was no longer available. Ms. Dorn returned home and made the few repairs she could afford. Cold air continued to come in through the cracks. But, as she had for many years, Ms. Dorn wrapped up to keep warm during the winter months.

A few blocks away on Stone Street, "Josie Baker" had lived alone in her seventy-five year old home since her husband, "Harry," died. The house, a small shotgun-style bungalow, was deteriorating. The CDBG Housing Rehabilitation program would have been ideal for Ms. Baker. However, because of the moratorium, those funds were not available for Ms. Baker and other neighborhood residents. Borrowing money was, to Ms. Baker, the only feasible way to obtain the needed repairs. In the mid-1980s, she approached a local finance company that, despite her inability to repay the loan on an income of $241 per month, loaned her nearly $9,000.

Some local men did the work, not very well, but well enough to keep the house together. Ms. Baker faithfully paid the finance company every month, often going without other things to do so. But the day came when Ms. Baker could not pay the finance company. She decided the best course of action was to borrow more money to make the loan payments. And she did make those payments for a while. When she arrived at the end of her resources again, she took another loan. By the late 1980s, Ms.

Baker's debt remained at $9,000. She made monthly payments that amounted to over half of her monthly income. Again, her home needed repairs. In her eighties, Ms. Baker carried enormous debt and worry. Neighbors did what they could to help with her bills. But Ms. Baker lived daily with the fear of losing her home and being unable to pay the debt.

Residents exchanged these stories privately, out of respect for their neighbors and as an acknowledgment of the pain underlying each narrative. The community's resolve to press forward deepened. Even though the legal remedies seemed inadequate to redress the level of harm that had been suffered, the residents embraced the imperative of taking action. For Save Our Neighborhood and the residents, a sense of enabling power grew as they continued to rise in community action.

* * *

That December, as the parties were approving the settlement agreement, the federal court issued its order on the defendants' motion to dismiss. To the defendants, settlement probably seemed an even wiser course than before: the court upheld each of the challenged claims for relief. Key rulings affirmed the plaintiffs' standing and theory of the case. In the court's view, standing had been met by allegations of threatened injury, such as defendants' encouraging discriminatory redevelopment of the neighborhood by attracting developers to the area.

In addition, the court readily acknowledged the application of the Fair Housing Act to discriminatory activities other than those connected with the actual sale or lease of housing, including discriminatory zoning. In approving the more novel claims, the court found the Thirteenth Amendment's prohibition of badges and incidents of slavery was fairly alleged and enforceable under 42 U.S.C. § 1983, as were the claims arising under other federal statutes, including the National Environmental Policy Act (NEPA) and the National Historic Preservation Act of 1966 (NHPA). To uphold the latter two claims, the court affirmed NEPA's protection of the urban as well as the natural environment and NHPA's protection of residents' enjoyment of the historic character of areas where some properties may be eligible for inclusion in the National Register. As to the pendent claim under the Redevelopment Act, the court determined that nine of the alleged procedural violations could be construed to cause, directly or indirectly, the threatened injury of dislocation. Finally, in upholding the claim for punitive damages, stayed by the order on class certification, the court noted the allegations of purposeful discrimination.

* * *

As this chronicle of the fight for survival of the historic African-American community of Cocoa draws to a close, an assessment is due of the degree to which the community has been empowered and transformed. * * * Power has been considered a force—fluid, dynamic. Empowerment begins with an awareness of its absence and finds its movement in claiming one's name, one's home, one's experience. Empowerment fills narrative with meaning that opens eyes and hearts and doors that are concurrently opened by confrontation and collective action. Passing through those channels, empowerment works its magic, leaving its bearer enabled, making decisions, attracting resources, and charged with an enlivened spirit.

* * * Roni Houston McNeil answers:

* * *

> It effected a great change in me. The lawsuit encouraged me. I didn't know that was in me. When the fight for the neighborhood started, there I was. I grew up as a stutterer, afraid to stand up and talk, throughout young adulthood. But this lawsuit brought a need to stand up before the City powers and tell them what they were not going to do and tell them how wrong they were. It was a shock; I had no idea that I could speak so well.... So much was beyond us, I had to stop focusing on my problems and go on the great need. The stakes were so high, I didn't have the luxury of being afraid.
>
> I re-enrolled in the University of Central Florida in Public Administration. I choose the degree because of the lawsuit and the need for humanitarians to be a part of the political process, defenders of the people—to be a voice.

The case gave a soft-spoken grandmother the confidence to confront a City and made her a force to be reckoned with as a person of standing and political influence. The case gave her daughter the platform she needed to leave behind a history of stuttering and to step up to the podium of public speaking. There the daughter developed leadership as she confronted the City and elegantly narrated the story of her family and her community which was instrumental to preserving the neighborhood.

When asked whether her community was empowered, Beatrice Houston chuckled and remembered that several of her neighbors had told her that it was just as well for her to go home and sit down, not to try to do anything, the City wasn't going to do anything for her, stop asking them, the City was going to get what they wanted anyhow. Then she related: "Now some of the same people come here and say, 'This is *nice*....' And I say, 'This is the same place you told me to come and sit down and not do anything.' " Roni Houston McNeil explained the story: "It made a skeptical community a believing community. I see the confidence in people. We see with our eyes what can be done. There was so much hopelessness. Hopelessness is replaced with hope." For the residents, the case opened a channel through which came belief, not in the City and perhaps not in lawyers or legal tools, but in themselves.

Some may rightly query to what extent the people of Cocoa were empowered by prevailing in the legal proceedings, and consequently were equally vulnerable to the danger of disempowerment had the legal weapons backfired. Roni Houston McNeil responded that winning was not crucial to empowerment because "a people had come together.... Winning was standing no matter the cost and accepting the consequences.... The Lord gave us Win Number One by empowerment and Win Number Two was the legal battle." While the legal strategies reaped additional resources for the community, to McNeil the empowerment had already taken place.

A separate question is whether and the degree to which the community has been transformed by this case. The neighborhood remains steeped in poverty. The age and deterioration of the area has led some to call the neighborhood "arthritic," like many of its residents. Some may note with an air of prophesy that many of the homes are built on sand. And to seasoned lawyers and scholars dedicated to the cause of social justice, the lesson from years of struggle and study may be that transformation, while a worthwhile goal, may be attainable only in a way that is partial and passing.

Residents point to the eighteen new and rehabilitated homes, with another one on its way, as perhaps the clearest examples of the transformation in the community. Changes in people, leadership, policies and ordinances, political influences, and social structures are also noted. * * *

A stone's throw across Hughlett Avenue from the Silver Dollar Bar lot is the home of Olivia Brown. Passing through the neighborhood on any given day, one is likely to see her on the porch.

> *Olivia Brown was sweeping her doorstep, a reflective but competitive ritual in the neighborhood. It was hard to say who had the cleanest doorstep in the area, but Miss Olivia was certainly in the top two. Maybe not so much these days with her arthritis, but today was a good day. She felt like she could sweep for a while. As she swept, the light in her face moved with the rhythm, sweeping back and forth over its contours of love and pain. There were additional furrows in her face these days. Charlie had passed. The family and the community had mourned. Now Miss Olivia was sweeping and thinking....*
>
> *... Thinking perhaps of the days when she and Charlie were courting, how he looked after the baseball game in Morgan, Georgia, with his cap in his hand. Thinking how she waited nine years to decide to marry him, to see if he meant business. Oh, he meant business—he worked hard picking beans in Virginia and then cutting cane in the Everglades. He did mean business and they were married in the courthouse in Georgia. That was sixty years ago. She missed Charlie so. Thinking, too, of the day he bought the lot from Rev. Parker. Thinking of her dream about the house. That was over forty years ago. She looked up. The roof was brand new. They had done such a nice job on it. That and sealing the house real good so the wind wouldn't come in. And sealing up the porch real tight, too. They say the City is building a new home for Betty Ann Wilson. That will be real nice. They also say the City might try to put in a new City Hall over across the way. "Lord, save our land," she murmured. "No, I ain't moving for nobody. You gave me this house and I ain't...." Shaking her head, she swept with determination in the*

late afternoon sun. As her sweeping slowed, she reminded herself, "Blessings ... count your blessings, Olivia."

Satisfied with her work, she put aside the broom and wiped her hands on her apron. * * *

Notes and Questions

1. How does the Cocoa experience, as described by Koons, illustrate how litigation such as that crafted in Cocoa may serve the goals of client and community empowerment? Does this story help you to explain to others what social justice lawyering is about?

2. How might the call for spatial reparations appeal to base building at the grass-roots level? As a call for spatial reparations takes form, what adversarial and community-building issues might arise based on the excerpts from Foster and Koons?

3. Review the readings in the chapter and respond to the following: What normative and legal theories might support a call for spatial reparations? Who would be key defendants? What are the most compelling facts of national history and current empirical data that would support a claim for relief? What problems would you anticipate? For a review of the normative, legal, and practical issues, see Adjoa A. Aiyetoro, *The Development of the Movement for Reparations for African Descendants,* 3 J. L. & Soc'y 133 (2002); Alfred L. Brophy, *The World of Reparations: Slavery Reparations in Historical Perspective*, 3 J. L. & Soc'y 105 (2002); Anthony E. Cook, *King and the Beloved Community: A Communitarian Defense of Black Reparations*, 68 Geo. Wash. L. Rev. 1021 (2000); Kevin Hopkins, *Forgive U.S. Our Debts? Righting the Wrongs of Slavery*, 89 Geo. L. J. 2531 (2001) (reviewing Randall Robinson, *The Debt: What America Owes to Blacks* (2000)); Alberto B. Lopez, *Focusing the Reparations Debate Beyond 1865*, 69 Tenn. L. Rev. 653 (2002); and Robert Westley, *Many Millions Gone: Is It Time to Reconsider the Case for Black Reparations*?, 19 B.C. Third World L.J. 429 (1998).

4. In Cato v. United States, 70 F.3d 1103 (9th Cir.1995), the court denied a claim for monetary damages based on reparations. If litigating the claim for spatial reparations is not viable, what other avenues are available for claimants? How about legislation? Since 1989 Congressman John Conyers has submitted a bill, H.R. 40, or the Commission to Study Reparation Proposals for African-Americans Act. *See* Sanford Cloud Jr., *The Next Bold Step Toward Racial Healing and Reconciliation: Dealing With the Legacy of Slavery*, 45 How. L. J. 157 (2001); Tuneen E. Chisolm, Comment, *Sweep Around Your Own Front Door: Examining the Argument for Legislative African-American Reparations*, 147 U. Pa. L. Rev. 677 (1999). In 2002, the Chicago City Council passed an ordinance requiring certain companies doing business with the city to reveal any involvement with slavery. Fran Spielman, *Firms Must Come Clean on Slavery, City's Insurers to Be Subject to Requirement*, Chi. Sun-Times, Sept 13, 2002, at 3. This follows state legislation in California where the

law "resulted in a groundbreaking report that named 433 slaveholders who purchased policies, 614 slaves who were covered and three insurers that sold coverage." *Id.*

5. Is community economic development a movement that advances spatial reparations. *See* Audrey G. McFarlane, *Race, Space and Place: The Geography of Economic Development*, 36 San Diego L. Rev. 295, 300 (1999) (declaring that, as a social ideal, development envisions community self-determination and invokes images of improvement, progress, and social justice).

How does the lawyer engaged in community development, for instance, balance the need to respond to the community's initiatives and provide expertise and leadership where appropriate, such as dealing with broad social and policy issues? *See* Louise G. Trubek, *Foreword*, in *Symposium Issue: Lawyering for a New Democracy*, 2002 Wis. L. Rev. 271, 272–73 (describing practices that "are a creative response to the critique that preoccupation with client participation and community involvement reduces the crucial leadership role of the lawyer in working on broad social and policy issues"). Would the claim for spatial reparations involve such issues?

For a discussion of a variety of current issues in community development and economic justice, see Susan Bennett, *Little Engines That Could: Community Clients, Their Lawyers, and Training in the Arts of Democracy*, 2002 Wis. L. Rev. 469; Susan Jones, *Current Issues in the Changing Roles and Practices of Community Economic Development Lawyers*, 2002 Wis. L. Rev. 437; William H. Simon, *The Community Economic Development Movement*, 2002 Wis. L. Rev. 377; and Gregory L. Volz, Keith W. Reeves & Erica Kaufman, *Higher Education and Community Lawyering: Common Ground, Consensus, and Collaboration for Economic Justice*, 2002 Wis. L. Rev. 505.

6. The issue of reparations is so divisive, one might question the wisdom of even bringing it up. But as Chicago Alderman Dorothy Tillman says, "We will shine the light on this grim chapter of our history that continues to infect, poison and divide us as a nation.... I don't think America can heal without doing this." *Id.* Do segregated living patterns, spatial inequality, and urbanized injustice, created in large part by governmental actions, continue to "infect, poison and divide us as a nation"? What can the social justice lawyer do about this predicament? *See* Note, *Bridging the Color Line: The Power of African-American Reparations to Redirect America's Future*, 115 Harv. L. Rev. 1689 (2002).

Chapter 13

SEXUAL MINORITIES: THE MOVEMENT FOR EQUALITY AND LIBERATION

Encompassing actions from the local level to the national, and from popular mobilization through state and federal courts, the movement for lesbian, gay, bisexual, and transgender (LGBT) equality and liberation marks an important case study in contemporary law and social change. LGBT victories grew out of a national mass movement that was set back, but not extinguished, by the decision in *Bowers v. Hardwick,* 478 U.S. 186 (1986). Successes in communities around the United States at enacting antidiscrimination ordinances were followed by reactionary statewide initiatives banning these ordinances; the Supreme Court then struck down the Colorado anti-gay rights initiative in *Romer v. Evans,* 517 U.S. 620 (1996). The pattern of activism, change, and reaction continues today in legislative action in state and local governments on issues of domestic partnership, hate crimes, and bans on discrimination, and in state and federal courts on issues of marriage, family law, and challenges to the criminalization of sodomy. This chapter traces the relationship between social movements and law reform in the context of the LGBT movement.

"[T]he invention and construction of sexual minority identity has always sparked naming issues." Francisco Valdes, *Queers, Sissies, Dykes, and Tomboys: Deconstructing the Conflation of "Sex," "Gender," and "Sexual Orientation" in Euro-American Law and Society,* 83 Calif. L. Rev. 1, 346 (1995). Because identities are social constructions and language is ever-changing, this chapter reflects the wide range of terms used to identify sexual minorities within the evolving LGBT movement.

SECTION 1. THE GROWTH OF A MOVEMENT

Drawing on the work of gay historians, Patricia Cain explains the development of the political and legal movement for gay rights:

PATRICIA A. CAIN

Litigating for Lesbian and Gay Rights: A Legal History
79 Va. L. Rev. 1551, 1557–59, 1561–65,
1567, 1580–84, 1586 (1993)

Gay Rights Before Stonewall

* * *

The post-World War I era in America was * * * a time of censorship, especially with respect to the topic of sex. Although lesbian and gay subcultures existed during this period, hostility toward "difference" prevented the formation of any widespread gay or lesbian movement against anti-gay discrimination.

After World War II, a number of homophile organizations began to spring up around the country. The Mattachine Society was formed in Los Angeles around 1950. * * * The repressive climate of the early 1950s, especially the attacks on communists and other radicals, led these organizers to opt for secrecy in their organizing tactics. But they never kept the mission of their organization secret: to liberate the homosexual minority from the oppression of the majority and to call on other minorities to fight with them against oppression.

The first legal case backed by Mattachine involved one of its founders, Dale Jennings, who had been arrested for lewd behavior in a Los Angeles public park. The charges arose from an incident fairly described as entrapment. The trial, which began in June of 1952, was historically significant because it was one of the first times that a gay man had been willing to stand up in court and say, "Yes, I am gay, but I nonetheless have legal rights." The trial ended in a hung jury, which, given the attitudes of the times, was a clear victory for gay rights. Shortly thereafter, the District Attorney dropped all charges.

* * *

* * * In 1955, Del Martin and Phyllis Lyon formed the first lesbian organization, the Daughters of Bilitis ("DOB"), in San Francisco. * * * [Neither organization was particularly radical during this era.]

* * *

In 1961, the homophile movement took a turn toward militant activism when Frank Kameny formed the Mattachine Society of Washington, D.C., as a last recourse in his legal battle to keep his job with the federal government, a job he lost solely because he was gay. * * *

Kameny's militant stand in favor of the right of homosexuals to keep their jobs attracted the attention of Barbara Gittings, founder and president of the New York chapter of DOB. They worked together in the East Coast Homophile Organizations ("ECHO"), an umbrella group made up of the New York DOB chapter and the Mattachine groups from New York, Washington, D.C., and Philadelphia.

In the mid 1960s, Kameny, Gittings, and other militants took the position that ECHO members should engage in picketing activities calling for recognition of gay rights. DOB's national board rejected this position and directed the New York chapter to withdraw from ECHO. ECHO members, led by Frank Kameny, demonstrated in front of the White House, the men conservatively attired in suits and the women in skirts. Kameny's militancy, which so angered the old guard lesbians and gay men, was nonetheless tempered by his demand for respectability. Kameny's main contribution to the movement was to shift efforts away from education and pleas for tolerance and understanding in favor of strategies that boldly asserted the worth of homosexual people as citizens.

While Frank Kameny and his East Coast coalition of militant homophile organizations were becoming more aggressive in their fight for equal rights, a new group was being formed on the West Coast, with similarly militant inclinations. The Society for Individual Rights ("SIR") was formed in San Francisco in 1964 and quickly became the largest pre-Stonewall gay rights organization in the country. * * *

All of these pre-Stonewall organizations were grass-roots organizations of gay men and lesbians. Although some homophile organizations focused more on civil rights issues than others, none of them were specifically legal organizations. In addition, those organizations that did focus on civil rights issues nonetheless adopted assimilationist arguments and accommodationist tactics. They were reluctant to challenge gender roles or to assert the right to a public sexual identity different from the gender norms of the times.

The Legal Condition of Gay People: Pre-Stonewall

It has never been illegal to be gay. But, in the pre-Stonewall era, the legal consequences of choosing a gay lifestyle were sufficiently severe to make lesbians and gay men think of themselves as criminals just for being who they were.

Various sorts of laws have been used to harass gay people. Charges, mostly against gay men, have been brought under vagrancy statutes for loitering or for wearing a disguise (e.g., dressing in "drag"). In the pre-Stonewall era, policemen raided gay bars and arrested patrons for engaging in "lewd acts." Often the patrons were too frightened of publicity to demand a jury trial to challenge the charges.

The 1950s marked the arrival of McCarthyism and a heightened concern with homosexuals. "Sexual perverts" were equated with communists as security risks. * * *

* * *

Despite the repressive social and political climate, lesbians and gay men began to win some protections in court. * * * [Victories came in cases attempting to close gay bars—with decisions holding that something other than the status of the patrons would be required to demonstrate good cause for revoking a license—and cases holding that discharged government employees were entitled to due process, and that dismissing an employee for "unspecified homosexual conduct" was improperly vague.]

* * *

The Significance of Stonewall

Most lesbian and gay rights activists cite June 27, 1969, as the beginning of the modern gay liberation movement. On that evening, when the New York police raided the Stonewall Inn, a gay bar in Greenwich Village, something unusual happened. The patrons, mostly gay men, resisted police harassment, thereby sparking three days of riots known as the Stonewall riots (or, the Stonewall Rebellion). Gay solidarity throughout the country generated many similar demonstrations of gay pride.

The Stonewall riots did not create the modern gay liberation movement. The movement's origins * * * can be traced to the formation of the Mattachine Society in Los Angeles in the early 1950s, the concentrated litigation efforts in Washington, D.C. against the federal government, and the growing resistance to police raids of gay bars and gay social events in San Francisco in the 1950s and 1960s.

Nor can the gay liberation movement be viewed in isolation from the other radical movements of the 1960s. Martin Luther King preached nonviolent opposition to the racist power structure and led civil rights marches to protest the inequality between black and white Americans. Student radicals in Berkeley challenged the authorities in charge of the University of California by claiming their free speech rights. Students exercised these rights by protesting the war in Viet Nam. Students for a Democratic Society was formed in the early 1960s in Michigan and launched a new left political movement. The second wave of feminism began in the early 1960s, and by the late 1960s had spawned several radical organizations. In 1968, protesters at the Democratic convention in Chicago were beaten by police officers. It was within this broader context of resistance and public challenges to governmental authority that the Stonewall riots began.

The Stonewall riots provided a symbolic radical shift in lesbian and gay arguments for civil rights. No longer would the movement be primarily about obtaining the right, so long as lesbians and gay men looked and acted like heterosexuals, to be treated just like heterosexuals in public. The symbolic power of Stonewall lay in the fact that it was the drag queens and the nellies—the most unassimilated—who were the most visible and the most vocal. They were demanding respect and they were demanding the right to be different.

Just four years earlier, the Supreme Court had made its own contribution to this new gay and lesbian movement. The Court's decision in *Griswold v. Connecticut* [381 U.S. 479 (1965)], recognized a right to privacy in the context of marital sex and gave lawyers the necessary foothold to begin challenging the criminalization of homosexual conduct. * * * Despite the hope of *Griswold* and the legal challenges that it inspired, however, Stonewall has proven to be the more important event of the late 1960's for lesbians and gay men.

Social and Political Organizations

Stonewall was quickly followed by the formation of new gay liberation organizations. Inspired by the radical politics of the 1960s, these new groups broke rank with the older homophile organizations and their leaders. Gay liberation in the post-Stonewall days was not a civil rights movement to gain equality for homosexuals. Rather, it was a movement focused on the sexual oppression of all people, with the goal of liberating the "homosexuality" in everyone. In this regard, gay liberation resembled the more radical forces in the women's liberation movement.

The new gay liberation groups did not turn immediately to the courts, but rather turned out into the streets. Two of the most active groups were the Gay Liberation Front and the Gay Activists Alliance. In addition to demonstrating against anti-gay policies and homophobic employers, gay activists showed up at political forums to question candidates about their position on gay issues. The silence of the closet was broken by this new visibility as the ranks of persons willing to stand up and be counted as lesbian and gay swelled significantly.

Perhaps the most successful challenge by these new activists was the assault mounted against the American Psychiatric Association to remove homosexuality from its list of mental disorders [in late 1973] * * * . Because the medical profession's definitions of illness can have meaningful legal consequences, this victory within the American Psychiatric Association was equivalent to winning an important test case in the courts.

By the early 1970s, the movement began to split into radical and conservative camps, a not uncommon event in the life of social and political movements. The Gay Activists Alliance had become more structured and separated itself from the more radical Gay Liberation Front. Eventually the Alliance dissolved and began anew in 1973 as the National Gay Task Force (now the National Gay and Lesbian Task Force). Overall, the defining characteristics of the gay movement in the immediate post-Stonewall years were its increasing visibility and the vitality of its more radical demands for the freedom to be different.

* * *

In 1973 a new gay liberation organization was formed, a public interest law firm to be run by lesbians and gay men to serve the lesbian and gay community. * * *

[Conceived in 1972, the Lambda Legal Defense and Education Fund was at first denied the right to incorporate as a public interest law firm, when a New York state court held that Lambda did not meet the state requirement that it be "organized for benevolent or charitable purposes, or for the purpose of assisting persons without means in the pursuit of any civil remedy." Although the court admitted that the gay community suffered from discrimination, no proof showed that discrimination prevented gay and lesbian clients from obtaining adequate legal representation.]

The New York Court of Appeals reversed the lower court's denial of Lambda's application. * * * [In October 1973] Lambda Legal Defense and Education Fund was officially incorporated and authorized to practice law.

* * * Together with the ACLU, Lambda has helped to shape gay rights litigation across the country. * * *

Notes and Questions

1. The new movement was both similar to and different from previous waves of civil rights movements that had brought social change in America:

> [T]he fundamental feeling, the bias which defined this population to begin with, is more subtle, more personal * * * . It is sexual. That dynamic sets up an emotional conflict, both within gay men and lesbians and within the broader culture, which is unique to the character and path of this movement. The kinds of oppression that homosexuals have experienced, the role that religion played in it, the psychological effect of it, the way gay men and lesbians do and don't relate to each other, the fractious nature of the movement, its difficulty in finding leaders and a voice—and the transcendent experience of AIDS—have all made this struggle for civil rights different from the others. * * *
>
> * * * [I]t was not until homosexuals began to adopt the tactics of other, more radical movements after the riots in New York that the struggle for gay rights gained momentum, and quicker change began to come. * * *

Dudley Clendinen & Adam Nagourney, *Out for Good: The Struggle to Build a Gay Rights Movement in America* 13–14 (1999).

2. Urvashi Vaid describes different trends at work within the gay rights movement:

> Throughout the history of our resistance to prejudice, gay people have clashed over a fundamental question about the overall goal of our movement. Are we a movement aimed at mainstreaming gay and lesbian people (legitimation), or do we seek radical social change out of the process of our integration (liberation)? * * * Legitimation and liberation are interconnected and often congruent; the former makes it possible to imagine the latter. But our pursuit of them takes different roads and leads to very different outcomes.

> For some gay and lesbian people, mainstream integration is the paramount goal of our political movement. For others, the transformation of mainstream culture holds the key to genuine gay and lesbian equality. Some of us believe that our political movement exists solely to fight antigay and antilesbian prejudice. Others believe that the elimination of homophobic prejudice is intimately related to the end of gender inequality, the end of racial prejudice, and the institution of a moral economic system.
>
> Gay and lesbian legitimation seeks straight tolerance and acceptance of gay people; gay and lesbian liberation seeks nothing less than affirmation, represented in the acknowledgment that queer sexuality is morally equivalent to straight sexuality. Legitimation seeks to change hearts and minds by educating the general public to understand that gay and lesbian people are human beings. Liberation seeks that same shift in consciousness, but it also looks for a transformation in social institutions—in government, family, religion, and the economy. Legitimation strategies stem from the discrimination that gay and lesbian people face as a minority; the goal of our movement is to end that discrimination and protect our rights. The movement for gay and lesbian liberation, on the other hand, focuses on the suppression of sexuality itself. Viewing categories like gay and straight as constraining, gay liberation seeks to "liberate an aspect of the personal lives of all people—sexual expression." * * *
>
> Proponents of legitimation argue to the straight world that gay people are "just like" straights, that we are merely a minority, and that prejudice against us is, therefore, irrational and unconstitutional. * * *
>
> Proponents of liberation argue that gay, lesbian, bisexual, transgendered, and straight people are all subject to an oppressive sexual and political order, what Adrienne Rich calls "compulsory heterosexuality." Liberationists devised the strategies of visibility and coming-out to challenge the cultural stereotypes that flourished because of gay invisibility. * * *
>
> As a formal political movement, gay and lesbian liberation was short-lived. Having emerged in the post-Stonewall period, it had largely disappeared as a national force by the early 1980s. But the ideas, values, and criticisms made by gay and lesbian liberationists survived and flourished in queer culture. This dissonance between a gay culture that embodies values more radical than the political movement that defends it continues to be a source of tension within the contemporary gay and lesbian movement.

Urvashi Vaid, *Virtual Equality* 37–38 (1995).

3. The visibility and public presence of sexual minorities became a significant component of the politics of transformation. Although *variations from gender roles* are often visible and become the target of discrimination, abuse, and violence in American society, *sexual orienta-*

tion and sexual practices are relatively easier to conceal. *See, e.g.*, Kenji Yoshino, *Covering*, 111 Yale L.J. 769 (2002).

> As one of its chief tactics for accomplishing its goals, gay liberation adopted the notion of "coming out." In its older, original meaning, "coming out" referred to the acknowledgment of one's homosexuality to oneself and other gay people. Gay liberationists transformed it into a public avowal. A critical step on the road to freedom, coming out implied a rejection of the negative social meaning attached to homosexuality in favor of pride and self-acceptance. The men and women who took the plunge had to overcome the fear of punishment and be willing to brave the ostracism of society that might result. In the process, they would also shed much of the self-hatred that they had internalized. Thus, the act became both a marker of liberation and an act of resistance against an oppressive society. * * *
>
> * * * With the range of penalties that exposure promised to homosexuals, it was radical youth, contemptuous of the rewards that American society offered for conformity, who were most likely to rally to the banner of gay liberation. Exclusion from the military or a civil service career, ostracism by society, and the threat of arrest held little power over these self-styled revolutionaries. And, coming out promised the movement an army of permanent recruits. By discarding the protection that came from hiding, gay men and lesbians invested heavily in the successful outcome of their struggle.
>
> But coming out signified something more. As the gay movement grew and gathered strength in the 1970s, the example of radical activists proved infectious, and many conventional homosexuals imitated this simple act of pride. Coming out of the closet was incorporated into the basic assumptions of what it meant to be gay. As such, it came to represent not simply a single act, but the adoption of an identity in which the erotic played a central role. * * *

John D'Emilio & Estelle B. Freedman, *Intimate Matters: A History of Sexuality in America* 322–23 (1988).

4. The new movement faced questions of equality and of inclusion. Equality for lesbians became an increasingly important issue. In the 1950s and 1960s, lesbians were expected to fulfill traditional women's roles within groups; "lesbian attempts to shape the political agenda were largely unsuccessful, and gay men tended to downplay the differences between the two groups." Jean Reith Schroedel & Pamela Fiber, *Lesbian and Gay Policy Priorities: Commonalities and Differences* in *The Politics of Gay Rights* 99 (Craig A. Rimmerman, Kenneth D. Wald & Clyde Wilcox eds., 2000). In time, lesbians became impatient with having their needs ignored. Lesbian feminism promoted solidarity among women. *Id.* at 99–100. Lesbian issues were not automatically included either within feminism or within gay organizations. "As a lesbian, I am constantly reminded of the myriad ways in which both gay liberation and feminism

have often 'forgotten' the existence of non-heterosexual women. It is, of course, not surprising that even movements critical of mainstream culture and politics tend nonetheless to adopt many mainstream assumptions (such as sexism and heterosexism)." Christine A. Littleton, *Double and Nothing: Lesbian as Category*, 7 UCLA Women's L.J. 1, 3 (1996).

In many discussions of sexual orientation, bisexuals become invisible even though they are at least as numerous as people who identify as gay or lesbian. *See generally* Kenji Yoshino, *The Epistemic Contract of Bisexual Erasure,* 52 Stan. L. Rev. 353 (2000). Yoshino argues that both people who self-identified as gay and those who identify as straight may have an investment in a view of sexuality as organized around polar opposites. *Id.* at 391–96.

The contemporary term "transgender," which came into use in the mid–1990s, "encompasses anyone whose identity or behavior falls outside of stereotypical gender norms," including transsexuals, cross dressers, and "men and women, regardless of sexual orientation, whose appearance or characteristics are perceived to be gender atypical." Paisley Currah & Shannon Minter, *Transgender Equality: A Handbook for Activists and Policymakers* 3–4 (June, 2000), available at http://www.nclrights.org/publications/pubs/transeq.pdf (last viewed August 11, 2002). The use of the LGBT umbrella has been contested as gay advocacy groups have struggled to determine whether to represent transgender people and transgender issues. *See* Shannon Minter, *Do Transsexuals Dream of Gay Rights? Getting Real About Transgender Inclusion in the Gay Rights Movement*, 17 N.Y. L. Sch. J. Hum. Rts. 589 (2000).

Some theorists today use "queer" as an umbrella term. *See* Laurie Rose Kepros, *Queer Theory: Weed or Seed in the Garden of Legal Theory?*, 9 Law & Sex. 279 (1999–2000). Urvashi Vaid discusses this terminology:

> A false assumption underlies all gay and lesbian organizing: that there is something at once singular and universal that can be called gay or lesbian or bisexual or even transgendered identity. (In fact, homosexual and bisexual people are enormously diverse. The notion that we constitute one community and can coalesce into a unified movement is both a fiction and a prayer.) * * *
>
> John D'Emilio terms this the "myth of the eternal homosexual." * * *
>
> Belief in this universal gay or lesbian identity informs the work of many activists. They see their work as ensuring the security, safety, and freedom of the status queer, which becomes the unifying project of the gay and lesbian movement. * * * I think this desire for some unification around our sexual identity explains why so many people embrace the word *queer* in this decade. * * * [T]he term *queer* provides a new anchor to ground us * * *, defined as much by the contrast and challenge we present to hetero-normativity as by our sexual identity.

> In fact, gay and lesbian identity is far from a unitary thing. It is mediated by our race, gender, economic status, history, and other conditions of life. * * * I can be at once all or three or four of the identities I embody: a lesbian, an immigrant, a Hindu, an Indian-American, a feminist, an organizer, a lawyer. My identification as a lesbian allies me with other homosexual men and women, but it may or may not ally me with everyone who claims to be gay. * * *

Vaid, *supra* at 286–87.

5. The movement developed a national strategy to eradicate state sodomy laws after the ACLU and Lambda Legal Defense Fund hosted a meeting of gay and lesbian legal organizations in November 1983. Cain, *supra* at 1586–87. Patricia Cain explains the importance of the sodomy issue:

> Mainstream lawyers and activists have not always understood why gay and lesbian legal organizations focus their attention on sodomy laws. After all, sodomy laws are rarely enforced against consenting adults in private. Surely fear of prosecution is not the main concern of most gay men and lesbians. * * *
>
> In answer to these questions, which came both from without and within the gay and lesbian community, Lambda's legal director, Abby Rubenfeld, stressed the fact that "sodomy laws are the bedrock of legal discrimination against gay men and lesbians." Associating homosexuals with sodomy and thus with criminal activity had been at the core of earlier governmental action against gay men and lesbians. Raids on gay bars were often justified on grounds that criminal activity might result where gay persons congregate. The 1950 Senate Subcommittee report recommending that all homosexuals be dismissed from government service relied in large part on the fact that same-sex sexual conduct was both criminal and immoral. Persons who engaged in such conduct were presumed to be morally weak and thus unfit for employment in responsible positions. So long as consensual same-sex sodomy remained a crime, these justifications for discrimination against gay people were more difficult to attack.
>
> The role played by sodomy laws in anti-gay discrimination in the 1980s was much the same as in earlier decades. * * *
>
> Within the gay and lesbian community, sodomy challenges were often perceived as a male issue. Lesbians were more concerned with family issues such as custody and domestic partner benefits. Lambda's Rubenfeld spoke to lesbian activists about the importance of sodomy challenges to lesbian issues. To illustrate her point, she described a Tennessee custody case in which her lesbian client was branded as a criminal in open court by counsel for the husband. The effect of this claim was to diminish the positive impact of expert testimony as to the mother's fitness. Nor should lesbians assume that sodomy statutes are not enforced against private lesbian sexual conduct. * * *

> The campaign to erase sodomy statutes from the books was consistent with the impulses of gay liberation. Gay liberation was always about sexual freedom and the breaking down of stereotypes. So long as state laws criminalizing lesbians and gay men for engaging in intimate sexual behavior remained on the books, the state's repressive power was legitimated. This state power to define good and bad sex was a barrier for those gay and lesbian individuals who sought to redefine themselves publicly as good, moral, and noncriminal.

Patricia A. Cain, *Litigating for Lesbian and Gay Rights: A Legal History*, *supra* at 1587–89.

SECTION 2. "WHAT ARE YOU DOING IN MY BEDROOM?": SEXUALITY, EQUALITY, AND PRIVACY

The stage was set for a historic decision by the U.S. Supreme Court. Michael Hardwick explains how his arrest for engaging in private, consensual sex in his own bedroom came before the Court.

PETER IRONS

Michael Hardwick v. Michael Bowers
in *The Courage of Their Convictions* 392–403 (1988)

I was born in Miami in 1954 and raised in Miami. * * * My parents divorced when I was twelve years old and I lived with my mom until I was seventeen. I went to high school here and it was pretty normal, just like high school anywhere. * * *

* * *

* * * I told my mother and my sister I was gay, and they were very supportive. I was twenty-one years old at the time. And I've been out since then. My mother was very accepting. * * *

* * *

* * * [I went to Atlanta to visit a friend] which is how this whole case started. I had been working for about a year, in a gay bar that was getting ready to open up a discothèque. I was there one night until seven o' clock in the morning, helping them put in insulation. When I left, I went up to the bar and they gave me a beer. I was kind of debating whether I wanted to leave, because I was pretty exhausted, or stay and finish the beer. I decided to leave, and I opened the door and threw the beer bottle into this trash can by the front door of the bar. I wasn't really in the mood for the beer.

Just as I did that, I saw a cop drive by. I walked about a block, and he turned around and came back and asked me where the beer was. I told him I had thrown it in the trash can in front of the bar. He insisted

I had thrown the beer bottle right as he pulled up. He made me get in the car and asked me what I was doing. I told him that I worked there, which immediately identified me as a homosexual, because he knew it was a homosexual bar. He was enjoying *his* position as opposed to *my* position.

After about twenty minutes of bickering he drove me back so I could show him where the beer bottle was. * * * I told him it was in the trash can and he said he couldn't see it from the car. I said fine, just give me a ticket for drinking in public. He was just busting my chops because he knew I was gay.

Anyway, the ticket had a court date on the top and a date in the center and they didn't coincide; they were one day apart. Tuesday was the court date, and the officer had written Wednesday on top of the ticket. So Tuesday, two hours after my court date, he was at my house with a warrant for my arrest. This was Officer Torick. This was unheard of, because it takes forty-eight hours to process a warrant. What I didn't realize, and didn't find out until later, was that he had personally processed a warrant for the first time in ten years. So I think there is reason to believe that he had it out for me.

I wasn't there when he came with the warrant. I got home that afternoon and my roommate said there was a cop here with a warrant. I said, that's impossible; my court date isn't until tomorrow. I went and got my ticket and realized the court date was Tuesday, not Wednesday. I asked my roommate if he'd seen the warrant and he said he hadn't. So I went down to the county clerk and showed him the discrepancy on the ticket. He brought it before the judge, and he fined me $50. I told the county clerk the cop had already been at my house with a warrant and he said that was impossible. He said it takes forty-eight hours to process a warrant. He wrote me a receipt just in case I had any problems with it further down the road. * * * I thought I had taken care of it and everything was finished, and I didn't give it much thought.

Three weeks went by, and my mom had come up to visit me. I came home one morning after work at 6:30 and there were three guys standing in front of my house. I cannot say for *sure* that they had anything to do with this, but they were very straight, middle thirties, civilian clothes. I got out of the car, turned around, and they said "Michael" and I said yes, and they proceeded to beat the hell out of me. Tore all the cartilage out of my nose, kicked me in the face, cracked about six of my ribs. I passed out. I don't know how long I was unconscious. When I came to, all I could think of was, God, I don't want my *mom* to see me like this!

I managed to crawl up the stairs into the house, into the back bedroom. What I didn't realize was that I'd left a trail of blood all the way back. My mom woke up, found this trail of blood, found me passed out, and just freaked out. I assured her that everything was okay, that it was like a fluke accident, there guys were drunk or whatever. They weren't drunk, they weren't ruffians, and they knew who I was. I convinced her everything was okay and she left to go visit a friend in Pennsylvania.

I had a friend come in a few days later who was from out of town, in Atlanta to apply for a government job. He waited for me to get off work, we went home, and then my roommate left for work. That night at work, another friend of mine had gotten really drunk, and I took his car keys, put him in a cab, and sent him to my house, so he was passed out on the couch in the living room. He did not hear me and my friend come in. I retired with my friend. He had left the front door open, and Officer Torick came into my house about 8:30 in the morning. He had a warrant that had not been valid for three weeks and that he didn't bother to call in and check on. Officer Torick came in and woke up the guy who was passed out on my couch, who didn't know I was there and had a friend with me.

Officer Torick then came to my bedroom. The door was cracked, and the door opened up and I looked up and there was nobody there. I just blew it off as the wind and went back to what I was involved in, which was mutual oral sex. About thirty-five seconds went by and I heard another noise and I looked up, and this officer is standing in my bedroom. He identified himself when he realized I had seen him. He said, my name is Officer Torick. Michael Hardwick, you are under arrest. I said, For what? What are you doing in my bedroom? He said, I have a warrant for your arrest. I told him the warrant isn't any good. He said, It doesn't matter, because I was acting under good faith.

I asked Torick if he would leave the room so we could get dressed and he said, There's no reason for that, because I have already seen you in your most intimate aspect. He stood there and watched us get dressed, and then he brought us over to a substation. We waited in the car for about twenty-five minutes, handcuffed to the back floor. Then he brought us downtown; brought us in and made sure everyone in the holding cells and guards and people who were processing us knew I was in there for "cocksucking" and that I should be able to get what I was looking for. The guards were having a *real* good time with that.

There was somebody to get me out of jail within an hour, but it took them twelve hours to get me out. * * *

I was contacted about three days later by a man named Clint Sumrall who was working in and out of the ACLU. For the last five years, he would go to the courts every day and find sodomy cases and try to get a test case. By this time, my mom had come back into town and found out what had happened. We had a typical mother conversation—she was saying, I *knew* I shouldn't have left! So she went with me to meet with Sumrall and this team of ten lawyers. I asked them what was the worst that could happen, what was the best that could happen? They explained to me that the judge could make an example out of me and give me twenty years in jail. * * * [T]hey said, Just think about it for two or three days.

I realized that if there was anything I could do, even if it was just laying the foundation to change this horrendous law, that I would feel pretty bad about myself if I just walked away from it. One thing that influenced me was that they'd been trying for five years to get a perfect case. Most of the arrests that are made for sodomy in Atlanta are of people who are having sex outside in public; or an adult and a minor; or two consenting adults, but their families don't know they are gay; or they went through seven years of college to teach and they'd be jeopardizing their teaching position. There's a lot of different reasons why people would not want to go on with it. I was fortunate to have a supportive family who knew I was gay. I'm a bartender, so I can always work in a gay bar. And I was arrested in my own house. So I was a perfect test case.

* * *

* * * I went to the Supreme Court and was there for the hearing. No one knew who I was. At that point, I had not done any interviews or speaking in public. The issue was privacy, and I wanted to keep it a private issue. My lawyers had informed me from the very beginning that it would be better to keep a low profile because we did not want the personal aspects of the case to come into it, which I agreed with. They thought that if there was a lot of personal publicity it would affect the decision of the Supreme Court.

It was an education to be there. I had forty-two lawyers working on my case, plus Laurence Tribe of Harvard Law School arguing the case for me. * * * I was going to be sitting with one of the people who wrote the *amicus* brief for Lambda, which does gay legal defense in New York, and they once again assured me that no one knew who I was. So I sat in the Supreme Court as a completely anonymous person. The whole omnipresence of the room, the procedure of the judges coming in, is sort of overpowering. * * *

The guy from the state came up first and argued for about five minutes and he was an idiot. He kept going on about how the state *did* have a justified government interest in continuing to enforce the law because it prevented adultery and retarded children and bestiality, and that if they changed the law all of those things would be legal. He made absolutely no sense. I think it was Justice Burger who asked why, if they had my head on a silver platter, if they had such a justified government interest in enforcing this law, did they refuse to prosecute me. At which point, his answer was that he wasn't at liberty to discuss that. The nine justices and the whole place cracked up and he pretty much ended his argument.

Then Laurence Tribe got up and articulately argued for about forty-five minutes. He was incredible. * * * When he got done, everyone was very much pre-victory. They were *sure* I would win. About forty of us went to lunch around the corner, and everything seemed very positive and optimistic, and I flew back to Miami to work. Then came the waiting period. That was the worst phase for me, because we never knew when the decision was coming. I would be on pins and needles, and every time the phone rang I'd be jumping. They made it the last decision of the year, of course. They waited until just after all of the Gay Pride parades around the country.

I was at work when I heard the decision. I cater a complimentary buffet for about a hundred people a day, so I go into work about four or five hours before anyone else gets there to do all my prep work. On this particular morning I could not sleep, and I got to work about nine o'clock. A friend of mine had been watching cable news and had seen it and knew where to find me and came over. When I opened the door he was crying and saying he was sorry, and I didn't know what the hell he was talking about. Finally I calmed him down and he told me what had happened: that I had lost by a five-to four vote.

I was totally stunned. My friend took off and I was there for about four hours by myself and that's when it really sunk in. I just cried—not so much because I had failed but because to me it was frightening to think that in the year of 1986 our Supreme Court, next to God, could make a decision that was more suitable to the mentality of the Spanish Inquisition. It was frightening and it stunned me. I was scared. I had been fighting this case for five years and everyone had seemed so confident that I was really *not* expecting this decision the way that they handed it down.

* * * I learned later that I originally *had* five votes in my favor on the Supreme Court. Justice Powell came out a week later and said to the press that he had originally decided in my favor. I *still* don't understand why Powell changed his mind in my case. * * *

About two days went by where I was just kind of stunned. There wasn't anything I could do to change the way I feel, and I'm normally a very positive person. It wasn't that I was negative, I was just nonresponsive to anything. Then all of a sudden I started getting pissed off, angry. Kathy called me two days later and she said that *Newsweek* magazine just came out with a national poll that said 57 percent of the people were opposed to the decision. And she said, By the way, Phil Donahue called and wants to know if you'll do his show. She was very clever, letting me know the nation was behind me, and then hitting me with the Donahue show. Up until then, they had all advised me to keep it private. But she said, This is one approach you can take: You can come out and let people know this was not a homosexual decision, as they tried to put it out, but that it affects everyone as individuals, as consenting adults. And the only way you're going to get that across to them is to use this opportunity.

That was the first time I'd ever spoken publicly. Donahue called and said he was putting me on with Jerry Falwell, and I said I wouldn't do the show—it wasn't a religious issue. So he called back and said, We got rid of Falwell, but you'll have to do the whole show by yourself. Okay. So I flew up there and did that, and that was probably the hardest thing I've ever done in my life. But it went very well, and everyone who saw the program said I was a good spokesman. That started something I had never anticipated. I did a lot of talk shows after that, a lot of newspaper interviews.

They told me after Donahue that in a month I'd be old news, but this has been the most hectic year of my life. Just about the time the whole thing died out, we started on the two hundredth birthday of the Constitution. I did a special with Bill Moyers on PBS, and one with Peter Jennings. And I've been speaking at a lot of rallies.

In the last three months, I've done about twenty-four round trips to various areas, usually in one day. It's very draining, because I work two full-time jobs. I bartend full time to support myself, and I also have my work as a sculptor. I just started about a year ago, but I'm doing very well with my art, getting a lot of exposure. So that right there is about seventy hours a week. And usually on the weekends I'm going to New York or Washington or Columbus, Ohio. I consider this an obligation on my part. It's something I started, and I had no idea it would go to the Supreme Court. * * *

* * *

When I started this case, people had never heard of AIDS, and that all developed as my case developed. And all the negative impressions that society and the media have been producing for the last three years had just about reached a high point when the decision came down and they asked me to come out nationally. That affected me a lot. When I first started speaking I thought that some crazy fundamentalist was going to blow my head off. Once I overcame that fear and a month to two went by, people would stop me and say, I'm not a homosexual but I definitely agree with what you're doing. This is America and we have the right to privacy, and the Constitution should protect us. They were supportive once they understood the issue and how it affected them.

* * * It would be easy to say that I've done my bit and now I'm going on with my personal life. But as long as there is a need for me to speak, as long as I can help work towards changing the negative impression society has right now about gays, I'll continue to work in that direction.

Gays are just a step up from drug addicts in the way society treats us. We're second-class citizens. I would fight to my dying day to defend my rights as a homosexual. I am a perfectly well adjusted person. I am very productive, I am very talented. I refuse to be suppressed, I refuse to be treated as a second-class citizen. There's no *way* the Supreme Court can say that I can't have sex with a consenting adult in the privacy of my own bedroom.

* * * I have a tendency to dwell on the positive instead of the negative. I feel very fortunate I was given the opportunity to do it. Speaking and coming out nationally was a very healthy experience for me, because it made me develop a confidence I never would have had if I had gone along with my individual life. It also gave me a sense of importance, because right now there is a very strong need for the gay

community to pull together, and also for the heterosexual community to pull together, against something that's affecting both of us. I feel that no matter what happens, I gave it my best shot. I will continue to give it my best shot.

BOWERS v. HARDWICK

478 U.S. 186 (1986)

Justice WHITE delivered the opinion of the Court.

In August 1982, respondent Hardwick (hereafter respondent) was charged with violating the Georgia statute criminalizing sodomy[1] by committing that act with another adult male in the bedroom of respondent's home. After a preliminary hearing, the District Attorney decided not to present the matter to the grand jury unless further evidence developed.

Respondent then brought suit in the Federal District Court, challenging the constitutionality of the statute insofar as it criminalized consensual sodomy.[2] He asserted that he was a practicing homosexual, that the Georgia sodomy statute, as administered by the defendants, placed him in imminent danger of arrest, and that the statute for several reasons violates the Federal Constitution. The District Court granted the defendants' motion to dismiss for failure to state a claim * * * .

A divided panel of the Court of Appeals for the Eleventh Circuit reversed. * * * [The Eleventh Circuit held] that the Georgia statute violated respondent's fundamental rights because his homosexual activity is a private and intimate association that is beyond the reach of state regulation by reason of the Ninth Amendment and the Due Process Clause of the Fourteenth Amendment. * * *

* * *

This case does not require a judgment on whether laws against sodomy between consenting adults in general, or between homosexuals in particular, are wise or desirable. It raises no question about the right

1. Georgia Code Ann. § 16–6–2 (1984) provides, in pertinent part, as follows:

"(a) A person commits the offense of sodomy when he performs or submits to any sexual act involving the sex organs of one person and the mouth or anus of another....

"(b) A person convicted of the offense of sodomy shall be punished by imprisonment for not less than one nor more than 20 years...."

2. John and Mary Doe were also plaintiffs in the action. They alleged that they wished to engage in sexual activity proscribed by § 16–6–2 in the privacy of their home, and that they had been "chilled and deterred" from engaging in such activity by both the existence of the statute and Hardwick's arrest. The District Court held, however, that because they had neither sustained, nor were in immediate danger of sustaining, any direct injury from the enforcement of the statute, they did not have proper standing to maintain the action. The Court of Appeals affirmed the District Court's judgment dismissing the Does' claim for lack of standing, and the Does do not challenge that holding in this Court.

The only claim properly before the Court, therefore, is Hardwick's challenge to the Georgia statute as applied to consensual homosexual sodomy. We express no opinion on the constitutionality of the Georgia statute as applied to other acts of sodomy.

or propriety of state legislative decisions to repeal their laws that criminalize homosexual sodomy, or of state-court decisions invalidating those laws on state constitutional grounds. The issue presented is whether the Federal Constitution confers a fundamental right upon homosexuals to engage in sodomy and hence invalidates the laws of the many States that still make such conduct illegal and have done so for a very long time. The case also calls for some judgment about the limits of the Court's role in carrying out its constitutional mandate.

We first register our disagreement with the Court of Appeals and with respondent that the Court's prior cases have construed the Constitution to confer a right of privacy that extends to homosexual sodomy and for all intents and purposes have decided this case. The reach of this line of cases was sketched in * * * [cases dealing with child rearing and education, family relationships, procreation, marriage, contraception, and abortion.] * * * [Three of these cases were] interpreted as construing the Due Process Clause of the Fourteenth Amendment to confer a fundamental individual right to decide whether or not to beget or bear a child.

Accepting the decisions in these cases and the above description of them, we think it evident that none of the rights announced in those cases bears any resemblance to the claimed constitutional right of homosexuals to engage in acts of sodomy that is asserted in this case. No connection between family, marriage, or procreation on the one hand and homosexual activity on the other has been demonstrated, either by the Court of Appeals or by respondent. Moreover, any claim that these cases nevertheless stand for the proposition that any kind of private sexual conduct between consenting adults is constitutionally insulated from state proscription is unsupportable. * * *

Precedent aside, however, respondent would have us announce, as the Court of Appeals did, a fundamental right to engage in homosexual sodomy. This we are quite unwilling to do. It is true that despite the language of the Due Process Clauses of the Fifth and Fourteenth Amendments, which appears to focus only on the processes by which life, liberty, or property is taken, the cases are legion in which those Clauses have been interpreted to have substantive content, subsuming rights that to a great extent are immune from federal or state regulation or proscription. Among such cases are those recognizing rights that have little or no textual support in the constitutional language. * * *

Striving to assure itself and the public that announcing rights not readily identifiable in the Constitution's text involves much more than the imposition of the Justices' own choice of values on the States and the Federal Government, the Court has sought to identify the nature of the rights qualifying for heightened judicial protection. In *Palko v. Connecticut,* 302 U.S. 319, 325, 326 (1937), it was said that this category includes those fundamental liberties that are "implicit in the concept of ordered liberty," such that "neither liberty nor justice would exist if [they] were sacrificed." A different description of fundamental liberties appeared in

Moore v. East Cleveland, 431 U.S. 494, 503 (1977) (opinion of POWELL, J.), where they are characterized as those liberties that are "deeply rooted in this Nation's history and tradition."

It is obvious to us that neither of these formulations would extend a fundamental right to homosexuals to engage in acts of consensual sodomy. Proscriptions against that conduct have ancient roots. See generally, Survey on the Constitutional Right to Privacy in the Context of Homosexual Activity, 40 U. Miami L. Rev. 521, 525 (1986). Sodomy was a criminal offense at common law and was forbidden by the laws of the original thirteen States when they ratified the Bill of Rights. In 1868, when the Fourteenth Amendment was ratified, all but 5 of the 37 States in the Union had criminal sodomy laws. In fact, until 1961, all 50 States outlawed sodomy, and today, 24 States and the District of Columbia continue to provide criminal penalties for sodomy performed in private and between consenting adults. Against this background, to claim that a right to engage in such conduct is "deeply rooted in this Nation's history and tradition" or "implicit in the concept of ordered liberty" is, at best, facetious.

Nor are we inclined to take a more expansive view of our authority to discover new fundamental rights imbedded in the Due Process Clause. The Court is most vulnerable and comes nearest to illegitimacy when it deals with judge-made constitutional law having little or no cognizable roots in the language or design of the Constitution. That this is so was painfully demonstrated by the face-off between the Executive and the Court in the 1930's, which resulted in the repudiation of much of the substantive gloss that the Court had placed on the Due Process Clauses of the Fifth and Fourteenth Amendments. There should be, therefore, great resistance to expand the substantive reach of those Clauses, particularly if it requires redefining the category of rights deemed to be fundamental. Otherwise, the Judiciary necessarily takes to itself further authority to govern the country without express constitutional authority. The claimed right pressed on us today falls far short of overcoming this resistance.

Respondent, however, asserts that the result should be different where the homosexual conduct occurs in the privacy of the home. He relies on *Stanley v. Georgia,* 394 U.S. 557 (1969), where the Court held that the First Amendment prevents conviction for possessing and reading obscene material in the privacy of one's home: "If the First Amendment means anything, it means that a State has no business telling a man, sitting alone in his house, what books he may read or what films he may watch."

Stanley did protect conduct that would not have been protected outside the home, and it partially prevented the enforcement of state obscenity laws; but the decision was firmly grounded in the First Amendment. The right pressed upon us here has no similar support in the text of the Constitution, and it does not qualify for recognition under the prevailing principles for construing the Fourteenth Amendment. Its limits are also difficult to discern. Plainly enough, otherwise illegal conduct is not always immunized whenever it occurs in the home. Victimless crimes, such as the possession and use of illegal drugs, do not escape the law where they are committed at home. *Stanley* itself recognized that its holding offered no protection for the possession in the home of drugs, firearms, or stolen goods. And if respondent's submission is limited to the voluntary sexual conduct between consenting adults, it would be difficult, except by fiat, to limit the claimed right to homosexual conduct while leaving exposed to prosecution adultery, incest, and other sexual crimes even though they are committed in the home. We are unwilling to start down that road.

Even if the conduct at issue here is not a fundamental right, respondent asserts that there must be a rational basis for the law and that there is none in this case other than the presumed belief of a majority of the electorate in Georgia that homosexual sodomy is immoral and unacceptable. This is said to be an inadequate rationale to support the law. The law, however, is constantly based on notions of morality, and if all laws representing essentially moral choices are to be invalidated under the Due Process Clause, the courts will be very busy indeed. Even respondent makes no such claim, but insists that majority sentiments about the morality of homosexuality should be declared inadequate. We do not agree, and are unpersuaded that the sodomy laws of some 25 States should be invalidated on this basis.

Accordingly, the judgment of the Court of Appeals is

Reversed.

Chief Justice BURGER, concurring.

I join the Court's opinion, but I write separately to underscore my view that in constitutional terms there is no such thing as a fundamental right to commit homosexual sodomy.

As the Court notes, the proscriptions against sodomy have very "ancient roots." Decisions of individuals relating to homosexual conduct have been subject to state intervention throughout the history of Western civilization. Condemnation of those practices is firmly rooted in Judeo-Christian moral and ethical standards. Homosexual sodomy was a capital crime under Roman law. During the English Reformation when powers of the ecclesiastical courts were transferred to the King's Courts, the first English statute criminalizing sodomy was passed. Blackstone described "the infamous *crime against nature*" as an offense of "deeper malignity" than rape, a heinous act "the very mention of which is a disgrace to human nature," and "a crime not fit to be named." The common law of England, including its prohibition of sodomy, became the received law of Georgia and the other Colonies. In 1816 the Georgia Legislature passed the statute at issue here, and that statute has been continuously in force in one form or another since that time. To hold that the act of homosexual sodomy is somehow protected as a fundamental right would be to cast aside millennia of moral teaching.

This is essentially not a question of personal "preferences" but rather of the legislative authority of the State. I find nothing in the Constitution depriving a State of the power to enact the statute challenged here.

Justice POWELL, concurring.

I join the opinion of the Court. I agree with the Court that there is no fundamental right—*i.e.*, no substantive right under the Due Process Clause—such as that claimed by respondent Hardwick, and found to exist by the Court of Appeals. This is not to suggest, however, that respondent may not be protected by the Eighth Amendment of the Constitution. The Georgia statute at issue in this case authorizes a court to imprison a person for up to 20 years for a single private, consensual act of sodomy. In my view, a prison sentence for such conduct—certainly a sentence of long duration—would create a serious Eighth Amendment issue. Under the Georgia statute a single act of sodomy, even in the private setting of a home, is a felony comparable in terms of the possible sentence imposed to serious felonies such as aggravated battery, first-degree arson, and robbery.

In this case, however, respondent has not been tried, much less convicted and sentenced. Moreover, respondent has not raised the Eighth Amendment issue below. For these reasons this constitutional argument is not before us.

Justice BLACKMUN, with whom Justice BRENNAN, Justice MARSHALL, and Justice STEVENS join, dissenting.

This case is no more about "a fundamental right to engage in homosexual sodomy," as the Court purports to declare, than *Stanley v. Georgia* was about a fundamental right to watch obscene movies, or *Katz v. United States* was about a fundamental right to place interstate bets from a telephone booth. Rather, this case is about "the most comprehensive of rights and the right most valued by civilized men," namely, "the right to be let alone."

The statute at issue denies individuals the right to decide for themselves whether to engage in particular forms of private, consensual sexual activity. The Court concludes that § 16–6–2 is valid essentially because "the laws of ... many States ... still make such conduct illegal and have done so for a very long time." But the fact that the moral judgments expressed by statutes like § 16–6–2 may be " 'natural and familiar ... ought not to conclude our judgment upon the question whether statutes embodying them conflict with the Constitution of the United States.' " Like Justice Holmes, I believe that "[i]t is revolting to have no better reason for a rule of law than that so it was laid down in the time of Henry IV. It is still more revolting if the grounds upon which it was laid down have vanished long since, and the rule simply persists from blind imitation of the past." I believe we must analyze Hardwick's claim in the light of the values that underlie the constitutional right to privacy. If that right means anything, it means that, before Georgia can prosecute its citizens for making choices about the most intimate aspects of their lives, it must do more than assert that the choice they have made is an " 'abominable crime not fit to be named among Christians.' "

I

* * * [T]he Court's almost obsessive focus on homosexual activity is particularly hard to justify in light of the broad language Georgia has used. Unlike the Court, the Georgia Legislature has not proceeded on the assumption that homosexuals are so different from other citizens that their lives may be controlled in a way that would not be tolerated if it limited the choices of those other citizens. Rather, Georgia has provided that "[a] person commits the offense of sodomy when he performs or submits to any sexual act involving the sex organs of one person and the mouth or anus of another." The sex or status of the persons who engage in the act is irrelevant as a matter of state law. In fact, to the extent I can discern a legislative purpose for Georgia's 1968 enactment of § 16–6–2, that purpose seems to have been to broaden the coverage of the law to reach heterosexual as well as homosexual activity.[1] I therefore see no basis for the Court's decision to treat this case as an "as applied" challenge to § 16–6–2, or for Georgia's attempt, both in its brief and at oral argument, to defend § 16–6–2 solely on the grounds that it prohibits homosexual activity. Michael Hardwick's standing may rest in significant part on Georgia's apparent willingness to enforce against homosexuals a law it seems not to have any desire to enforce against heterosexuals. But his claim that § 16–6–2 involves an unconstitutional intrusion into his privacy and his right of intimate association does not depend in any way on his sexual orientation.

* * *

II

"Our cases long have recognized that the Constitution embodies a promise that a certain private sphere of individual liberty will be kept largely beyond the reach of government." In construing the right to privacy, the Court has proceeded along two somewhat distinct, albeit complementary, lines. First, it has recognized a privacy interest with reference to certain *decisions* that are properly for the individual to make. Second, it has recognized a privacy interest with reference to certain *places* without regard for the particular activities in which the individuals who occupy them are engaged. The case before us implicates both the decisional and the spatial aspects of the right to privacy.

1. Until 1968, Georgia defined sodomy as "the carnal knowledge and connection against the order of nature, by man with man, or in the same unnatural manner with woman." In *Thompson v. Aldredge,* 187 Ga. 467, 200 S.E. 799 (1939), the Georgia Supreme Court held that § 26–5901 did not prohibit lesbian activity. And in *Riley v. Garrett,* 219 Ga. 345, 133 S.E.2d 367 (1963), the Georgia Supreme Court held that § 26–5901 did not prohibit heterosexual cunnilingus. Georgia passed the act-specific statute currently in force "perhaps in response to the restrictive court decisions such as *Riley,*" Note, The Crimes Against Nature, 16 J.Pub.L. 159, 167, n. 47 (1967).

A

The Court concludes today that none of our prior cases dealing with various decisions that individuals are entitled to make free of governmental interference "bears any resemblance to the claimed constitutional right of homosexuals to engage in acts of sodomy that is asserted in this case." While it is true that these cases may be characterized by their connection to protection of the family, the Court's conclusion that they extend no further than this boundary ignores the warning in *Moore v. East Cleveland,* 431 U.S. 494, 501 (1977) (plurality opinion), against "clos[ing] our eyes to the basic reasons why certain rights associated with the family have been accorded shelter under the Fourteenth Amendment's Due Process Clause." We protect those rights not because they contribute, in some direct and material way, to the general public welfare, but because they form so central a part of an individual's life. "[T]he concept of privacy embodies the 'moral fact that a person belongs to himself and not others nor to society as a whole.' " And so we protect the decision whether to marry precisely because marriage "is an association that promotes a way of life, not causes; a harmony in living, not political faiths; a bilateral loyalty, not commercial or social projects." We protect the decision whether to have a child because parenthood alters so dramatically an individual's self-definition, not because of demographic considerations or the Bible's command to be fruitful and multiply. And we protect the family because it contributes so powerfully to the happiness of individuals, not because of a preference for stereotypical households. The Court [has] recognized * * * that the "ability independently to define one's identity that is central to any concept of liberty" cannot truly be exercised in a vacuum; we all depend on the "emotional enrichment from close ties with others."

Only the most willful blindness could obscure the fact that sexual intimacy is "a sensitive, key relationship of human existence, central to family life, community welfare, and the development of human personality." The fact that individuals define themselves in a significant way through their intimate sexual relationships with others suggests, in a Nation as diverse as ours, that there may be many "right" ways of conducting those relationships, and that much of the richness of a relationship will come from the freedom an individual has to *choose* the form and nature of these intensely personal bonds.

In a variety of circumstances we have recognized that a necessary corollary of giving individuals freedom to choose how to conduct their lives is acceptance of the fact that different individuals will make different choices. * * * The Court claims that its decision today merely refuses to recognize a fundamental right to engage in homosexual sodomy; what the Court really has refused to recognize is the fundamental interest all individuals have in controlling the nature of their intimate associations with others.

B

The behavior for which Hardwick faces prosecution occurred in his own home, a place to which the Fourth Amendment attaches special significance. The Court's treatment of this aspect of the case is symptomatic of its overall refusal to consider the broad principles that have informed our treatment of privacy in specific cases. Just as the right to privacy is more than the mere aggregation of a number of entitlements to engage in specific behavior, so too, protecting the physical integrity of the home is more than merely a means of protecting specific activities that often take place there. Even when our understanding of the contours of the right to privacy depends on "reference to a 'place,' " "the essence of a Fourth Amendment violation is 'not the breaking of [a person's] doors, and the rummaging of his drawers,' but rather is 'the invasion of his indefeasible right of personal security, personal liberty and private property.' "

The Court's interpretation of the pivotal case of *Stanley v. Georgia* is entirely unconvincing. *Stanley* held that Georgia's undoubted power to punish the public distribution of constitutionally unprotected, obscene material did not permit the State to punish the private possession of such material. * * * [T]he *Stanley* Court anchored its holding in the Fourth Amendment's special protection for the individual in his home:

> " 'The makers of our Constitution undertook to secure conditions favorable to the pursuit of happiness. They recognized the significance of man's spiritual nature, of his feelings and of his intellect. They knew that only a part of the pain, pleasure and satisfactions of life are to be found in material things. They sought to protect Americans in their beliefs, their thoughts, their emotions and their sensations.'
>
> * * *
>
> "These are the rights that appellant is asserting in the case before us. He is asserting the right to read or observe what he pleases—the right to satisfy his intellectual and emotional needs in the privacy of his own home."

* * * "The right of the people to be secure in their ... houses," expressly guaranteed by the Fourth Amendment, is perhaps the most "textual" of the various constitutional provisions that inform our understanding of the right to privacy, and thus I cannot agree with the Court's statement that "[t]he right pressed upon us here has no ... support in the text of the Constitution." Indeed, the right of an individual to conduct intimate relationships in the intimacy of his or her own home seems to me to be the heart of the Constitution's protection of privacy.

III

The Court's failure to comprehend the magnitude of the liberty interests at stake in this case leads it to slight the question whether petitioner, on behalf of the State, has justified Georgia's infringement on these interests. * * *

* * *

* * * Essentially, petitioner argues, and the Court agrees, that the fact that the acts described in § 16–6–2 "for hundreds of years, if not thousands, have been uniformly condemned as immoral" is a sufficient reason to permit a State to ban them today.

I cannot agree that either the length of time a majority has held its convictions or the passions with which it defends them can withdraw legislation from this Court's scrutiny.[5] As Justice Jackson wrote so eloquently for the Court in *West Virginia Board of Education v. Barnette*, "we apply the limitations of the Constitution with no fear that freedom to be intellectually and spiritually diverse or even contrary will disintegrate the social organization.... [F]reedom to differ is not limited to things that do not matter much. That would be a mere shadow of freedom. The test of its substance is the right to differ as to things that touch the heart of the existing order." It is precisely because the issue raised by this case touches the heart of what makes individuals what they are that we should be especially sensitive to the rights of those whose choices upset the majority.

The assertion that "traditional Judeo-Christian values proscribe" the conduct involved, Brief for Petitioner 20, cannot provide an adequate justification for § 16–6–2. That certain, but by no means all, religious groups condemn the behavior at issue gives the State no license to impose their judgments on the entire citizenry. The legitimacy of secular legislation depends instead on whether the State can advance some justification for its law beyond its conformity to religious doctrine. Thus, far from buttressing his case, petitioner's invocation of Leviticus, Romans, St. Thomas Aquinas, and sodomy's heretical status during the Middle Ages undermines his suggestion that § 16–6–2 represents a legitimate use of secular coercive power. A State can no more punish private behavior because of religious intolerance than it can punish such behavior because of racial animus. "The Constitution cannot control such prejudices, but neither can it tolerate them. Private biases may be outside the reach of the law, but the law cannot, directly or indirectly, give them effect." *Palmore v. Sidoti,* 466 U.S. 429, 433 (1984). No matter how uncomfortable a certain group may make the majority of this Court, we have held that "[m]ere public intolerance or animosity cannot constitutionally justify the deprivation of a person's physical liberty."

* * * [T]he mere fact that intimate behavior may be punished when it takes place in public cannot dictate how States can regulate intimate behavior that occurs in intimate places.

5. The parallel between *Loving* [*v. Virginia* 388 U.S. 1 (1967)] and this case is almost uncanny. There, too, the State relied on a religious justification for its law. * * * There, too, defenders of the challenged statute relied heavily on the fact that when the Fourteenth Amendment was ratified, most of the States had similar prohibitions. There, too, at the time the case came before the Court, many of the States still had criminal statutes concerning the conduct at issue. Yet the Court held, not only that the invidious racism of Virginia's law violated the Equal Protection Clause, but also that the law deprived the Lovings of due process by denying them the "freedom of choice to marry" that had "long been recognized as one of the vital personal rights essential to the orderly pursuit of happiness by free men."

This case involves no real interference with the rights of others, for the mere knowledge that other individuals do not adhere to one's value system cannot be a legally cognizable interest, let alone an interest that can justify invading the houses, hearts, and minds of citizens who choose to live their lives differently.

IV

* * * I can only hope that here, too, the Court soon will reconsider its analysis and conclude that depriving individuals of the right to choose for themselves how to conduct their intimate relationships poses a far greater threat to the values most deeply rooted in our Nation's history than tolerance of nonconformity could ever do. Because I think the Court today betrays those values, I dissent.

Notes and Questions

1. Do you think that Michael Hardwick's original decision to play an anonymous role affected the outcome of the case? Is his transformation to public spokesperson unusual? Did his lawyers help or hinder that process? What role should a lawyer in that situation play?

2. Justice Lewis F. Powell conceded, after he retired from the Court, that he had made an error in joining the *Bowers* majority. Anand Agneshwar, *Ex-Justice Says He May Have Been Wrong: Powell on Sodomy*, The National Law Journal, Nov. 5, 1990, at 3. Powell's indecision about the case, chronicled in Joyce Murdoch & Deb Price, *Courting Justice: Gay Men and Lesbians v. the Supreme Court* (2001), provides an example of the relationship between visibility for gays and lesbians and reasoning about gay rights. While the case was pending before the court, Powell had a long conversation with one of his law clerks about the case. Powell remarked, "I don't believe I've ever met a homosexual." The clerk responded that just couldn't be right, and explained that "One could work next to a homosexual for years and a gay person would choose never to disclose that aspect of his private life." *Id.* at 273. The clerk with whom Powell was speaking was gay, and in fact Powell had previously employed several gay or lesbian law clerks. *Id.* at 342–43.

Lynne Henderson criticized the overall failure to describe the lives of gay people, oppose the stereotypes that appeared in the Georgia brief, and build empathy for Hardwick and his situation. "Mr. Hardwick never appeared in the briefs or arguments as a human being. * * * He became another disembodied person onto whom fears, prejudices, and false beliefs could be projected." Lynne N. Henderson, *Legality and Empathy*, 85 Mich. L. Rev. 1574, 1639 (1987). She argues that the focus on privacy—which linked the situation of gay people to that of heterosexuals—did nothing to broaden understanding or rebut prejudice, permitting erroneous concepts such as that held by Justice Powell to shape the Court's reasoning. *Id.* at 1638–46. *See also* Marc A. Fajer, *Can Two Real Men Eat Quiche Together? Storytelling, Gender-role Stereotypes, and*

Legal Protection for Lesbians and Gay Men, 46 U. Miami L. Rev. 511, 513–14 (1992) (emphasizing empathy arguments).

Do you believe that empathic arguments could have changed Justice Powell's vote? Could more open acquaintance with gay, lesbian, and bisexual people have changed his mind?

3. Marc Fajer explains how questions of identity and behavior are often confused in legal reasoning:

> [Some courts have held that sodomy is the "conduct that defines the class" of homosexuals.] Similarly, some anti-gay advocates insist that "sexual orientation is not an identity, it's a behavior." However, saying that one's sexual orientation is defined by one's sexual conduct raises obvious questions like "Which conduct?" and "How much of it?"
>
> * * * [W]hich same-sex sexual activities are sufficient to cross the threshold into becoming a "homosexual"? Kissing? Heavy petting? Oral sex?
>
> Even if everyone agreed on the precise sexual conduct that warrants the label "homosexual," we still would need to have rules regarding how frequent the conduct must be both in absolute terms and relative to the amount of sexual activity with persons of the other sex. Is there some minimum amount of same-sex sexual activity required? * * * [I]s everyone who has engaged in some sexual activity with both men and women therefore "bisexual"? Conversely, if one really wants to engage in same-sex sexual behavior but has never engaged in any sexual activity at all, is he or she simply an undifferentiated "virgin"?
>
> Related problems emerge because people's behavior changes over time. Many men have same-sex sexual experiences with peers during adolescence and never repeat them as adults. [Almost 2% of adult men in one large study * * * reported this pattern. Edward O. Laumann et. al., *The Social Organization of Sexuality: Sexual Practices in the United States* 296 (1994)] Is there a statute of limitations?[67] Is pre-majority sexual activity voidable like a contract or does a same-sex experiment by two fifteen-year-olds "vest" their status as "homosexuals"? Can a person "divest" the label with a lot of heterosexual sex? As these rather absurd questions suggest, relying on behavior alone yields difficult line-drawing problems and strange results.

67. The New Hampshire Supreme Court believes there is. It excluded from the definition of "homosexual" people who had committed homosexual acts not "reasonably close in time" to the point at which the state has to make the determination. *In re Opinion of the Justices*, 525 A.2d [1095, 1098 (N.H.1987).] For those who have a well-developed les/bi/gay identity, the answer is probably no. As one lesbian comic put it, "If I never had sex with another woman again, I would still be a lesbian. I wouldn't be a very happy lesbian, but I would still be a lesbian." Robin Tyler, *Still a Bridesmaid, Never a Groom*, in Ed Karvoski, Jr., *A Funny Time to Be Gay* 25, 26 (1997).

On the other hand, relying on self-identification instead of sexual conduct also can be problematic. People have frequently responded to the stigma attached to homosexuality by living lives of contradiction. Some engage only in heterosexual sexual activity that they may not particularly desire or enjoy, and limit their same-sex sexual activity to fantasies. Are they "homosexuals" or "bisexuals" if they so define themselves? Others engage in same-sex sexual acts but protect themselves by holding fast to the notion that they themselves are not "homosexuals." * * *

* * *

Some human beings desire to engage in sexual activity with others of the same sex; some do not. There is no very strong evidence about why this is so. Despite this lack of evidence, the debate about whether homosexuality is "chosen" or not consumes a large part of the discussion about the inclusion of sexual orientation in antidiscrimination laws. The debate is rhetorically important because if sexual orientation is "chosen," it can be distinguished from characteristics like race or sex that are viewed as outside an individual's control, thus arguably weakening the claim that the fight for gay rights is simply an extension of earlier civil rights movements. Viewing homosexuality as "chosen" is also more consistent with anti-gay advocates' claim that it is "unnatural"; an innate characteristic would likely be viewed as "natural."

* * * [A]nti-gay advocates generally argue that homosexuality is a "choice." However, conservative opponents of gay rights may not be as sure about this characterization as their rhetoric would suggest. Their frequent use of the odd phrase, "practicing homosexual" indicates this uncertainty. In context, the phrase clearly refers to someone who engages in same-sex sexual activity. But if homosexuality itself merely consists of chosen behavior, what then is a "non-practicing homosexual"? Within the rhetoric of "choice," someone who chooses to refrain from homosexual behavior would seem not to be a "homosexual" at all. However, the phrase inherently suggests the possibility of someone who is a "homosexual" but does not engage in same-sex sexual conduct. Yet this is the very separation of conduct and identity that the rhetoric of choice denies.

Unsurprisingly, many advocates for gay rights argue that sexual orientation is beyond a person's control. Although to date this position is not strongly supported by biological evidence, it is bolstered by the perception of almost all gay men and many lesbians that they can not control which people they find sexually attractive, and by the common cultural understanding that love strikes in uncontrollable ways. However, this argument does not take into account the perception of some lesbians that they *have* chosen their orientation. In any event, the lack of control argument only can take one so far. Assuming that people cannot control desire, they still can control how they act in response to desire. To flirt, to seduce, to

> make love, and to rape are all choices people make for which they should be held responsible. The claim of the moral correctness of same-sex sexual intimacy must rest on some foundation other than compulsive desire.

Marc A. Fajer, *A Better Analogy: "Jews," "Homosexuals," and the Inclusion of Sexual Orientation as a Forbidden Characteristic in Antidiscrimination Laws*, 12 Stan. L. & Pol'y Rev. 37, 41, 42–43 (2001).

4. In the last paragraph of the *Bowers* opinion, moral condemnation of *homosexuality* (a status, not an act) was held to provide a rational basis for a law that criminalized *sodomy* (an act, not an identity) in terms that were not limited to same-sex conduct:

> [T]he *Bowers* holding ignores the status/conduct distinction. In fact, the Court's opinion blithely skips back and forth between "homosexual sodomy" and "homosexuals" as if conduct and status were fungible. * * *
>
> Despite this confusion, *Bowers* has been applied, either explicitly or implicitly, as if it had spoken consciously and coherently *both* about "homosexuals" as people, as well as about sodomy as an act. This interpretation turns on the premise that sodomy as a behavior defines the person as a being. In other words, this interpretation presumes that sodomy is something that only homosexuals do, and that to speak about one is to speak about the other. This interpretation thus is rooted in the notion that status *is* conduct, or at least compelling evidence of conduct. Of course, this view disregards the obvious fact that sodomy is a type of specific conduct that demonstrably is performed by heterosexuals, bisexuals, and homosexuals.

Francisco Valdes, *Sexual Minorities in the Military: Charting the Constitutional Frontiers of Status and Conduct*, 27 Creighton L. Rev. 381, 432–33 (1994).

5. How important is it to the holding of *Bowers* that the Does were dismissed from the case? Is it possible that some heterosexual couples *only* practice acts described in the Georgia statute? Janet Halley argues that a focus on "homosexual sodomy" protected heterosexual sodomists:

> *Heterosexual* acts are prohibited by the Georgia sodomy statute and, notably, by virtually identical statutes in force when the Justices rendered their decision not only in Washington D.C., but also in Virginia and in Maryland, where presumably several of the majority Justices spent their most intimate hours. By reasoning that the Georgia statute plausibly supports an anti-homosexual morality, the Justices engage in masking their own status as potential sodomites *even if* they never stray from the class of heterosexuals. Invisibility here is immunity * * * .

Janet E. Halley, *Reasoning about Sodomy: Act and Identity in and After* Bowers v. Hardwick, 79 Va. L. Rev. 1721, 1769–70 (1993).

Halley concludes that a focus on acts defined as sodomy, rather than on identity and sexual orientation, would bring alliance between the

LGBT movement and anti-homophobic heterosexuals. She also argues that a focus on acts "forces heterosexual identity to share some of the glaring light that shines, thanks to *Hardwick*'s privacy holding, on the profane homosexual bed * * *." *Id.* at 1772. Would forcing heterosexuals to share the "glaring light" help courts and the public face the privacy and equality arguments about sodomy?

> Attorney General Bowers failed to tell the justices what he knew firsthand about the degradation of marriage and extramarital heterosexual sodomy. He was then in the midst of a 15-year extramarital affair. In 1997, while running for governor, Bowers admitted the illicit liaison. His former mistress, Anne Davis, then told the world: "As far as sodomy is concerned, Mike Bowers is a hypocrite." Bowers lost the election.

Murdoch & Price, *supra* at 287.

Adultery was also against the law in Georgia. Is the electoral defeat of Michael Bowers a victory for LGBT people?

6. Would better information about sexual practices in the United States change the minds of judges and the public? An ongoing debate surrounds the interpretation of data gathered in studies of sexuality. Adult men and women in the United States have a wide variety of sexual contacts. *See generally* Edward O. Laumann et. al., *The Social Organization of Sexuality: Sexual Practices in the United States* (1994). Many gay and lesbian activists have long cited the Kinsey report as showing that approximately 10% of the population is gay or lesbian. Vaid, *supra* at 28. Laumann notes that the 10% figure is widely accepted. *Id.* at 286–87. The Laumann study, however, found that 9.1% of the men and 4.3% of the women reported some same-sex sexual behavior since puberty. *Id.* at 294–96, 305. A much lower figure, 2.8% of the men and 1.4% of the women, reported a homosexual or bisexual identity. *Id.* at 305. There was a marked difference between urban and rural locations, with many more people reporting same-sex contact or identifying as homosexual or bisexual in central cities than in suburbs or rural areas. *Id.*

Antigay activists cite low statistics as proof that homosexuality is less widespread than many gay advocates have claimed. On the other hand, same-sex sexual contact is more widespread than any figure reported for gay or lesbian identity. Figures vary somewhat in different studies. For example, a Harris Poll conducted in 1988 found that 4.1% of the men reported exclusively same-sex sexual contact; an additional 1.9% of men had same-sex contact "fairly often," and another 3.6% of men had such contact "rarely"—a total of 9.6% who had some homosexual contact after the age of fifteen. Vaid, *supra* at 27–28. For women, the comparable numbers were 2.3% having exclusively same-sex contact, 1.2% "fairly often," and 2.9% "rarely," for a total of 6.4 percent. However, a much larger number of persons either had homosexual attraction or experience since the age of fifteen—18.3% of men and 17.4% of women. *Id.* Kenji Yoshino reviewed five sexuality studies and found that they "all came to roughly the same conclusion about the relative incidence of bisexuality to homosexuality—namely, that the incidence of bisexuality was greater than or comparable to the incidence of homosexuality." Kenji Yoshino, *The Epistemic Contract of Bisexual Erasure,* 52 Stan. L. Rev. 353, 386 (2000).

What do these figures say about sexual norms? About the reasoning of *Bowers*?

7. After *Bowers*, several states reconsidered their sodomy laws. In Commonwealth v. Wasson, 842 S.W.2d 487 (Ky.1992), Jeffrey Wasson had been charged with soliciting an undercover police officer to engage in deviate sexual intercourse, a misdemeanor. The court explained that there was no suggestion that the sexual activity would take place other than in the privacy of Wasson's home, between consenting adults; no money was offered or solicited.

Seven expert witnesses testified in support of Wasson's case: a cultural anthropologist, who "testified about the presence of homosexuals in every recorded human culture"; a Presbyterian minister who offered a modern interpretation of Biblical statements; a sociologists and sex researcher, co-author of the Kinsey Report on homosexual behavior, who testified that homosexuality was not a choice and could not be cured, and that oral and anal sex, prohibited to homosexuals by the sodomy statute, are widely practiced by heterosexuals; a psychologist who testified that homosexuality is no longer classified as a disorder; a therapist who testified that the criminalization of sodomy had an adverse impact on homosexuals and interfered with therapy for any who need it; and a professor of medicine who testified about the origin and spread of AIDS, expressing the opinion that the sodomy statute offered no benefit in preventing the spread of AIDS and could be a barrier to getting accurate medical histories, therefore having an adverse effect on public health.

The state of Kentucky offered no witnesses but argued that the majority of citizens, through the government, had the right to criminalize sexual activity deemed immoral even if conducted in private between consenting adults and not inherently harmful to the participants or others, at least when Biblical and historical traditions supported criminalization.

The Kentucky Supreme Court analyzed the statute under the Kentucky constitution:

COMMONWEALTH v. WASSON

842 S.W.2d 487 (Ky.1992)

LEIBSON, Justice.

* * *

* * * [The court distinguished the current sodomy statute from an older state sodomy statute that existed before the Kentucky constitution. The current statute defined] "deviate sexual intercourse" [as including]

"any act of sexual gratification involving the sex organs of one (1) person and the mouth or anus of another;" [the earlier statute had been limited to anal intercourse between men.] Unlike the present statute our common law tradition punished *neither oral copulation nor any form of deviate sexual activity between women.* * * *

* * *

Thus the statute in question here punishes conduct which has been historically and traditionally viewed as immoral, but much of which has never been punished as criminal.

* * * [The lower courts struck down the statute as unconstitutional because it] "clearly seeks to regulate the most profoundly private conduct and in so doing impermissibly invades the privacy of the citizens of this state" [and because the statute] unjustifiably discriminates, and thus is unconstitutional under Sections 2 and 3 of our Kentucky Constitution. These sections are:

> "§ 2. Absolute and arbitrary power over the lives, liberty and property of freemen exists nowhere in a republic, not even in the largest majority.
>
> § 3. All men, when they form a social compact, are equal...."]

These Sections, together with Sections 59 and 60 of our Kentucky Constitution which prohibit "local or special" legislation, express the guarantee of equal treatment provided by the law in our Kentucky Constitution. The lower courts' judgments limit their finding of unconstitutionality to *state* constitutional grounds. *Bowers v. Hardwick, supra,* speaks neither to rights of privacy under the state constitution nor to equal protection rights under either federal or state constitutions. * * *

* * *

I. RIGHTS OF PRIVACY

* * * We are not bound by decisions of the United States Supreme Court when deciding whether a state statute impermissibly infringes upon individual rights guaranteed in the State Constitution so long as state constitutional protection does not fall below the federal *floor,* meaning the minimum guarantee of individual rights under the United States Constitution as interpreted by the United States Supreme Court. * * *

* * *

* * * Kentucky has a rich and compelling tradition of recognizing and protecting individual rights from state intrusion in cases similar in nature, found in the Debates of the Kentucky Constitutional Convention of 1890 and cases from the same era when that Constitution was adopted. * * *

* * *

* * * [In a case criminalizing possession of intoxicating liquor, even for "private use," our Court has] interpreted the Kentucky Bill of Rights

as defining a right of privacy, even though the constitution did not say so in that terminology:

> "Man in his natural state has the right to do whatever he chooses and has the power to do. When he becomes a member of organized society, under governmental regulation, he surrenders, of necessity, all of his natural right the exercise of which is, or may be, injurious to his fellow citizens. This is the price that he pays for governmental protection, but it is not within the competency of a free government to invade the sanctity of the absolute rights of the citizen any further than the direct protection of society requires.... It is *not within the competency of government to invade the privacy of a citizen's life and to regulate his conduct in matters in which he alone is concerned,* or to prohibit him any liberty the exercise of which will not directly injure society. *Id.* [Emphasis added.] * * *"

* * *

The right of privacy has been recognized as an integral part of the guarantee of liberty in our 1891 Kentucky Constitution since its inception. * * *

* * *

The clear implication [of our previous cases] is that immorality in private which does "not operate to the detriment of others," is placed beyond the reach of state action by the guarantees of liberty in the Kentucky Constitution.

* * *

We view the United States Supreme Court decision in *Bowers v. Hardwick, supra,* as a misdirected application of the theory of original intent. To illustrate: as a theory of majoritarian morality, miscegenation was an offense with ancient roots. It is highly unlikely that protecting the rights of persons of different races to copulate was one of the considerations behind the Fourteenth Amendment. Nevertheless, in *Loving v. Virginia,* 388 U.S. 1 (1967), the United States Supreme Court recognized that a contemporary, enlightened interpretation of the liberty interest involved in the sexual act made its punishment constitutionally impermissible.

According to *Bowers v. Hardwick,* "until 1961, all 50 States outlawed sodomy, and today, 25 States and District of Colombia continue to provide criminal penalties for sodomy performed in private and between consenting adults." 478 U.S. at 193–94. In the space of three decades half the states decriminalized this conduct, some no doubt in deference to the position taken by the American Law Institute in the Model Penal Code Sec. 213.2:

> "Section 213.2 of the Model Code makes a fundamental departure from prior law in excepting from criminal sanctions deviate sexual intercourse between consenting adults."

* * *

* * * [Other states have held homosexual sodomy statutes of this nature unconstitutional for reasons similar to those stated here.] Thus our decision, rather than being the leading edge of change, is but a part of the moving stream.

* * *

II. EQUAL PROTECTION

* * * [I]n *Bowers v. Hardwick, supra,* the Equal Protection Clause was not implicated because the Georgia statute criminalized both heterosexual and homosexual sodomy. Unlike the Due Process Clause analysis provided in *Bowers v. Hardwick,* equal protection analysis does *not* turn on whether the law (KRS 510.100), transgresses "liberties that are 'deeply rooted in this Nation's history and tradition.' " 478 U.S. at 191–92.

In *Watkins v. U.S. Army,* 875 F.2d 699 (9th Cir.1989), involving the constitutionality of an Army regulation which made homosexuality a nonwaivable disqualification for reenlistment, Judge Norris, concurring in the judgment, explained the difference between Due Process Clause analysis and Equal Protection Clause analysis, as follows:

> "The due process clause, as the Court recognized in *Hardwick,* protects practices which are 'deeply rooted in this Nation's history and tradition.' The Equal Protection Clause, in contrast, protects minorities from discriminatory treatment at the hands of the majority. Its purpose is not to protect traditional values and practices, but to *call into question* such values and practices when they operate to burden disadvantaged minorities.... [Emphasis original.]
>
> The Equal Protection Clause, by contrast ... protect[s] disadvantaged groups from discriminatory practices, however deeply ingrained and long-standing." *Id.,* 875 F.2d at 718.
>
> * * *

Certainly, the practice of deviate sexual intercourse violates traditional morality. But so does the same act between heterosexuals, which activity is decriminalized. Going one step further, *all* sexual activity between consenting adults outside of marriage violates our traditional morality. The issue here is not whether sexual activity traditionally viewed as immoral can be punished by society, but whether it can be punished solely on the basis of sexual preference.

The Commonwealth's argument against permitting sexual behavior preferred by homosexuals the protection of the Equal Protection Clause has centered solely on denying homosexuals status as a protected class, claiming society has a right to discriminate so long as such discrimination is not race related or gender related and this law punishes the act and not the preference of the actor. In *American Constitutional Law,* 2d ed. 1988, Laurence H. Tribe, p. 1616, the author answers the Commonwealth's claims:

"Not only is the characteristic of homosexuality or heterosexuality central to the personal identities of those singled out by laws based on sexual orientation, but homosexuals in particular seem to satisfy all of the Court's implicit criteria of suspectness. As subjects of age-old discrimination and disapproval, homosexuals form virtually a discrete and insular minority. Their sexual orientation is in all likelihood 'a characteristic determined by causes not within [their] control (noting *Mathews v. Lucas,* 427 U.S. 495, 505 (1976), describing illegitimacy),' and is, if not immutable, at least 'extremely difficult to alter * * *.' "

* * *

We do not speculate on how the United States Supreme Court as presently constituted will decide whether the sexual preference of homosexuals is entitled to protection under the Equal Protection Clause of the Federal constitution. We need not speculate as to whether male and/or female homosexuals will be allowed status as a protected class if and when the United States Supreme Court confronts this issue. They are a separate and identifiable class for Kentucky constitutional law analysis because no class of persons can be discriminated against under the Kentucky Constitution. All are entitled to equal treatment, unless there is a substantial governmental interest, a rational basis, for different treatment. The statute before us is in violation of Kentucky constitutional protection in Section Three that "all men (persons), when they form a social compact, are equal," and in Section Two that "absolute and arbitrary power over the lives, liberty and property of free men (persons) exist nowhere in a republic, not even in the largest majority." We have concluded that it is "arbitrary" for the majority to criminalize sexual activity solely on the basis of majoritarian sexual preference, and that it denied "equal" treatment under the law when there is no rational basis, as this term is used and applied in our Kentucky cases.

* * *

The Commonwealth has tried hard to demonstrate a legitimate governmental interest justifying a distinction, but has failed. Many of the claimed justifications are simply outrageous: that "homosexuals are more promiscuous than heterosexuals, ... that homosexuals enjoy the company of children, and that homosexuals are more prone to engage in sex acts in public." The only proffered justification with superficial validity is that "infectious diseases are more readily transmitted by anal sodomy than by other forms of sexual copulation." But this statute is not limited to anal copulation, and this reasoning would apply to male-female anal intercourse the same as it applies to male-male intercourse. * * *

In the final analysis we can attribute no legislative purpose to this statute except to single out homosexuals for different treatment for indulging their sexual preference by engaging in the same activity heterosexuals are now at liberty to perform.* * * The question is whether a society that no longer criminalizes adultery, fornication, or deviate sexual intercourse between heterosexuals, has a rational basis to single out homosexual acts for different treatment. Is there a rational basis for declaring this one type of sexual immorality so destructive of family values as to merit criminal punishment whereas other acts of sexual immorality which were likewise forbidden by the same religious and traditional heritage of Western civilization are now decriminalized? If there is a rational basis for different treatment it has yet to be demonstrated in this case. We need not sympathize, agree with, or even understand the sexual preference of homosexuals in order to recognize their right to equal treatment before the bar of criminal justice.

To be treated equally by the law is a broader constitutional value than due process of law as discussed in the *Bowers* case. We recognize it as such under the Kentucky Constitution, without regard to whether the United States Supreme Court continues to do so in federal constitutional jurisprudence. "Equal Justice Under Law" inscribed above the entrance to the United States Supreme Court, expresses the unique goal to which all humanity aspires. In Kentucky it is more than a mere aspiration. It is part of the "inherent and inalienable" rights protected by our Kentucky Constitution. * * *

The purpose of the present statute is not to protect the marital relationship against sexual activity outside of marriage, but only to punish one aspect of it while other activities similarly destructive of the marital relationship, if not more so, go unpunished. Sexual preference, and not the act committed, determines criminality, and is being punished. Simply because the majority, speaking through the General Assembly, finds one type of extramarital intercourse more offensive than another, does not provide a rational basis for criminalizing the sexual preference of homosexuals.

For the reasons stated, we affirm the decision of the Fayette Circuit Court, and the judgment on appeal from the Fayette District Court.

Notes and Questions

1. In 2002, the Arkansas Supreme Court struck down that state's sodomy law, which applied only to same-sex sodomy, and reviewed recent changes among the states:

> According to *Bowers v. Hardwick,* all fifty states outlawed sodomy prior to 1961. At the time of *Bowers,* twenty-five states and the District of Columbia criminalized private, consensual sodomy by adults. Today, twenty-six states and the District of Columbia have legislatively repealed their sodomy laws * * * .
>
> Nine states have invalidated sodomy laws by judicial decision * * *.
>
> Six states, including Arkansas [until July 2002], maintain "same-sex" sodomy statutes * * *.
>
> Nine states and Puerto Rico maintain statutes prohibiting same-sex and opposite-sex sodomy * * *.

Jegley v. Picado, 349 Ark. 600, 80 S.W.3d 332, 346, n. 4 (2002).

2. After the decision in *Bowers v. Hardwick*, the Supreme Court refused to hear an appeal in *Baker v. Wade*, 774 F.2d 1285 (5th Cir.1985), a case concerning the Texas sodomy statute:

> After Texas lawmakers revised their state penal code in 1974 some traditional sex "crimes," including fornication and adultery, were no longer illegal. Bestiality was forbidden only in public. Sodomy was downgraded to a $200 misdemeanor and applied only to same-sex couples. So, by the end of 1974, Don Baker could legally have had private oral or anal sex with a woman or even a dog but not with another man.

Price & Murdoch, *supra* at 346.

In 2002, Lambda Legal Defense Fund again challenged the criminalization of sodomy in the United States Supreme Court, filing a petition for certiorari in *Lawrence v. State of Texas*, 41 S.W.3d 349 (2001) *cert. granted*, 123 S.Ct. 661 (2002). John Lawrence and Tyron Garner were convicted of deviate sexual conduct for violating the Texas sodomy law in one of their homes. Citing *Bowers v. Hardwick*, the appellate court sitting *en banc* upheld the constitutionality of the law. The court reasoned that the statute did not discriminate on the basis of sex or gender: "[W]e find nothing in the history of Section 21.06 to suggest it was intended to promote any hostility between the sexes, preserve any unequal treatment as between men and women, or perpetuate any societal or cultural bias with regard to gender." *Id.* at 357–58. The court also held that the statute did not punish people for their orientation rather than conduct: "While homosexuals may be disproportionately affected by the statute, we cannot assume homosexual conduct is limited only to those possessing a homosexual 'orientation.' Persons having a predominately heterosexual inclination may sometimes engage in homosexual conduct. Thus, the statute's proscription applies, facially at least, without respect to a defendant's sexual orientation." *Id.* at 353.

3. What was the "rational basis" identified by Justice White in the last paragraph of his *Bowers* opinion to support the Georgia sodomy statute? Since the analysis in *Bowers* relied heavily on popular morality, concepts of rights "implicit in idea of ordered liberty," and the history of laws prohibiting sodomy, has the reasoning of *Bowers* been undermined by the changes in state sodomy law? *See* Jay Michaelson, *On Listening to the* Kulturkampf, *Or, How America Overruled* Bowers v. Hardwick, *Even Though* Romer v. Evans *Didn't*, 49 Duke L.J. 1559 (2000) ("There is no need for innovative readings of the Constitution or expansions of notions of personal liberty to see how Bowers v. Hardwick has ceased to be good law. * * * Bowers is obsolete." *Id.* at 1617.).

SECTION 3. DISCRIMINATION ON THE BASIS OF SEXUAL ORIENTATION AND GENDER NONCONFORMITY

In an omitted portion of his dissent in *Bowers v. Hardwick*, Justice Blackmun had pointed to an Eighth Amendment problem with the statute. In Robinson v. California, 370 U.S. 660 (1962), the Supreme Court relied on the Eighth Amendment to hold that the state could not punish the *status* of being a drug addict, reasoning that addiction was "apparently an illness which may be contracted innocently or involuntarily." *Id.* at 667. In Powell v. Texas, 392 U.S. 514 (1968), the Court distinguished conduct from status and held that the defendant in that case, a habitual alcoholic, had been punished for the *act* of being drunk in public, rather than for the *status* of being an alcoholic.

A. Status, Conduct, and Discrimination: The Example of Gays in the Military

The status/conduct distinction has been important to several cases concerning gay men and lesbians who were discharged from military service. If the members of the armed forces had openly stated that their sexual orientation was homosexual—but there was *no* evidence that any conduct had involved same-sex sexual contact—then only their *orientation* (or status) and not their acts was the basis for discharge.

FRANCISCO VALDES

Sexual Minorities in the Military: Charting the Constitutional Frontiers of Status and Conduct
27 Creighton L. Rev. 381, 406–11 (1994)

* * * [Perry Watkins] joined the Army when he was nineteen years old, and over the next fourteen years became, in the words of his commanding officer, "one of our most respected and trusted soldiers" who built an exemplary service record. Nonetheless, he was discharged just a few years before becoming eligible for retirement benefits.

The *Watkins* litigation, spanning nearly a decade, is based on Perry Watkins' induction into the United States Army in 1967. At that time, he truthfully and affirmatively answered the question on the Report of Medical History that inquired whether he "had homosexual tendencies or had experienced homosexual tendencies." A psychiatrist then examined him and found him "qualified for admission." During his tour of duty, Watkins did not hide his sexual orientation; in fact, in November 1968 he stated to an Army investigator that he "had been a homosexual since the age of 13 and had engaged in homosexual relations with two servicemen." However, the Army did not discharge Watkins, and in 1971 he re-enlisted for a period of three years.

During his re-enlistment period, and with the approval of his commanding officers, Watkins performed as a female impersonator in highly publicized military venues on several occasions though in 1972 he was denied a security clearance based on his 1968 comments regarding homosexual status and relations. Nonetheless, Watkins finished his second tour of duty, re-enlisted for an additional period of six years, and was re-assigned as a company clerk to a post in South Korea. While there, his new commander initiated elimination proceedings because Watkins was gay. In 1975, a discharge hearing convened. The commander testified that he had discovered Watkins' sexual orientation status through a background records check, but that Watkins was "the best clerk I have known." Others in Watkins' company testified that "everyone in the company knew that plaintiff was a homosexual and that [it] had not caused any problems or elicited any complaints." Therefore, Watkins was retained, but his duties were limited to clerical or administrative positions.

Following this incident, Watkins went through several re-assignments and in 1977 received a security clearance from his commanding officer for information classified as "Secret," which qualified him for new positions. Watkins therefore applied for a new position but was rejected because his "medical records showed he had homosexual tendencies." Watkins appealed this rejection, supported by his new commander, who requested Watkins' re-qualification because of Watkins' outstanding professional attitude, integrity, and suitability for assignment. Moreover, Watkins' commander pointed out the earlier incidents and hearings, and noted that Watkins always had been medically cleared and retained for service. When an examining physician concluded that Watkins' sexuality "appeared to cause no problems" and that earlier proceedings and investigations had concluded with "positive results," the Army relented and in 1978 approved his eligibility for the Nuclear Surety Program.

However, Watkins' repose was short-lived. In 1979, he was notified that his security clearance was being revoked because he had acknowledged his homosexuality at yet another interview earlier that year. * * * The Army * * * initiated another discharge action and convened a new hearing to investigate Watkins' [homosexual activity subsequent to the previous proceedings.] * * *

* * *

Because Watkins' statement acknowledging that he was a homosexual during the 1979 interview took place after his 1975 discharge hearing, the Army took the position that his words constituted "subsequent conduct" and moved to discharge him on that basis. Watkins * * * filed suit in federal court to halt his discharge and remain in the Army. The district court held in Watkins' favor, indirectly incorporating into its analysis key status/conduct considerations. * * * Five months later, * * * the district court further held that [the Army was estopped from discharging Watkins because it had retained him after his previous admissions.]

* * *

Initially, the [Ninth Circuit Court of Appeals] noted that the Army's regulations used the term "homosexuality" rather than phrases such as "sexual conduct" to describe what was proscribed, and that they defined a "homosexual" as a "person, regardless of sex, who desires bodily contact between persons of the same sex." The court further noted that, "under the regulations any homosexual act or statement of homosexuality gives rise to a presumption of homosexual orientation, and anyone who fails to rebut that presumption is conclusively barred from Army service." * * * [T]he court in *Watkins* also took notice of the regulation's special caveat for the benefit of the sexual majority: "Persons may still qualify for the Army despite their homosexual conduct if they prove to the satisfaction of Army officials that their *orientation* is heterosexual rather than homosexual." The court therefore reasoned that the regulations targeted homosexual orientation itself.

More pointedly, the court emphasized that the regulation expressly stated that the exemption for heterosexuals who committed homosexual acts was intended to "permit retention only of nonhomosexual soldiers." Therefore, the court explained, "[i]f a straight soldier and a gay soldier of the same sex engage in homosexual acts because they are drunk, immature, or curious, the straight soldier may remain in the Army while the gay soldier is automatically terminated" even though both had engaged in identical and mutual conduct. In short, the court concluded that "the regulations do not penalize soldiers for engaging in homosexual acts; they penalize soldiers who have engaged in homosexual acts only when the Army decides that those soldiers are actually gay."

Though insightful, this passage, which assumes the occurrence of homosexual acts as a prerequisite for the penalization of soldiers who are actually gay, overlooked that the record of "subsequent conduct" in Watkins' case was devoid of any "homosexual acts." * * * [O]nly a statement acknowledging homosexual status was present. Thus, the Army's scheme was even more pernicious than the court seemed to appreciate. The Army's regulations contemplated the excuse of same-sex acts if committed by soldiers with a cross-sex status, the punishment of identical acts if committed by soldiers with a same-sex status, *and* the discharge of soldiers with a same-sex status despite the absence of *any* act.

Despite this oversight, the Ninth Circuit's analysis concluded with a finding of unconstitutionality. Reasoning that the Army's regulatory scheme effectively created classifications based on status, the court held that status-based classifications were suspect and struck down the regulations as violative of equal protection. However, instead of grounding itself in the reasoning of *Robinson* and *Powell*, the Ninth Circuit in *Watkins* engaged in a conventional equal protection analysis of the status-based classification. The discussion * * * created a mixed precedent based technically on equal protection grounds but grounded conceptually in status/conduct considerations. * * *

[Ultimately, the en banc court withdrew the appellate opinions and held for Watkins on the estoppel theory.]

Notes and Questions

1. The stories of four exemplary servicemembers who challenged the ban on sexual minorities in the military appear in R.L. Evans, *U.S. Military Policies Concerning Homosexuals: Development, Implementation, and Outcomes*, 11 Law & Sexuality 113 (2002) (describing the cases of Keith Meinhold, Richard Watson, Zoe Dunning, and Steve May). All continued to serve during while being open about their sexual orientation during their legal challenges. "These servicemembers maintained collegial relationships with co-workers, received outstanding evaluations, won awards, and were promoted during their periods of open service. They also maintained high levels of responsibility, managing personnel, overseeing military budgets, and commanding troops." *Id.* at 192.

2. The new regulations adopted in 1993 and popularly known as "Don't Ask/Don't Tell" were described to the public as distinguishing status from conduct and making only conduct the basis for discharge from the military. However, Janet Halley explains that under these regulations, the statement "I am gay," or "I am a lesbian" is not simply a description of status but an indicator of the propensity to engage in prohibited homosexual conduct. "[T]he servicemember can stay in the military only if she shows that she in fact lacks *a propensity* to engage in homosexual conduct." Janet E. Halley, *Don't: A Reader's Guide to the Military's Anti-Gay Policy* 57 (1999). Halley argues that the new regulations force all military personnel to strictly avoid using any gesture or statement that could be understood as manifesting a propensity to commit homosexual conduct. "Doing things that make your commander think you are gay—like making pro-gay statements, or cutting your hair a certain way, or not fitting the gender stereotype of the sex you belong to—can be the basis for an inference that you have engaged in or might someday engage in homosexual conduct; and once your commander draws that inference you can be discharged from the military unless you prove that you have *no propensity* to engage in such conduct." *Id.* at 2.

How can military personnel prove that they have no propensity to engage in homosexual acts? Will the wise course of action be to continually make anti-gay statements to establish the *lack* of propensity?

3. William Rubenstein analyzes the issues that faced activists and lawyers as the LGBT organizations and individuals confronted—and worked around—*Bowers v. Hardwick*:

WILLIAM B. RUBENSTEIN

Divided We Litigate: Addressing Disputes Among Group Members and Lawyers in Civil Rights Campaigns
106 Yale L.J. 1623, 1623–33, 1635–44, 1680 (1997)

Groups are messy. They are, by definition, comprised of many individuals and thus encompass a range of desires and agendas. Any group must generate ways to reach decisions among these competing possibilities. * * *

* * *

* * * Why is any individual group member able to step forward in the litigation arena and unilaterally claim to represent, and indeed bind, all similarly situated group members to a particular legal position? Further, why can any single attorney litigating one of many cases brought on behalf of a group decide alone what tactics and strategies to employ in pursuing that case? There is one immediate answer to both of these questions: Group decisions about litigation are structured by the rules of litigation, that is, by the rules of civil procedure and professional ethics, and those rules currently adhere to an individualist model. The rules of procedure structure group member disputes about litigation because they dictate who can represent the group in court, and how. They generally enable any individual to appoint herself the representative of the group's litigative desires. Similarly, the rules of professional ethics dictate the professional responsibilities of lawyers pursuing a group's cases; they generally require the attorney to be, above all else, loyal to her individual client's desires. Decisions about litigation are currently not made through more formal political processes because our rules of civil procedure and professional ethics promote individualist decisionmaking, even where the consequences of litigative decisions affect entire groups of people.

* * * [O]ur current procedural and ethical rules too heavily favor individualism alone. Community member disputes concerning the goals of litigation are inherently political in nature and therefore call for more democratic forms of decisionmaking; attorney disputes about the methods of litigation are often technical disputes and therefore call for more expertise-reliant forms of decisionmaking. * * *

Scholars have, of course, written about the challenges that groups pose to our adjudicatory system. Derrick Bell's pathbreaking article, *Serving Two Masters*[: *Integration Ideals and Client Interests in School Desegregation Litigation*, 85 Yale L.J. 470 (1976), excerpted in chapter 5], introduced a consideration of these issues that many scholars have since joined. As is evident from the title of Professor Bell's article, however, the exploration he inaugurated has largely focused on the ethical conflict of interest problem that arises when a single attorney (or law firm) attempts to represent a divided group. * * * Rather than considering how groups challenge traditional notions of lawyering, this Article examines how litigation challenges conventional ways that groups make political decisions. Why do we promote, vis-a-vis litigation, methods of group decisionmaking that would never be tolerated for other type of political decisions?

The Story of *Shelley v. Kraemer*

In the spring of 1947, Thurgood Marshall was annoyed. The source of his frustration was an attorney from St. Louis named George Vaughn. Vaughn had just done something Marshall did not want him to do: He had filed a petition for certiorari with the United States Supreme Court in a case called *Shelley v. Kraemer*, one of the many cases pending throughout the country in which the constitutionality of racially restrictive housing covenants was at issue. Marshall did not want Vaughn to file this petition because he did not think that the black community's legal position in the many restrictive covenant cases was sufficiently developed to be heard by the Supreme Court; Marshall and his NAACP colleagues had been working on developing that position for many years. Marshall also did not believe Vaughn's factual record in the *Shelley* case was the best that could be brought before the Court; he and the NAACP attorneys had been working closely with social scientists to generate a compelling policy analysis of the effects of these covenants.

Marshall was also worried about Vaughn's legal abilities. Vaughn was not a constitutional scholar. He was an able municipal court lawyer in St. Louis, and, in part because of his political influence within the Democratic party, had prevailed in the *Shelley* case in municipal court. But Vaughn's 1945 victory was shortlived; by the end of 1946, the Missouri Supreme Court had overturned it. What may have worried Marshall most of all was that Vaughn thought that he had a good Thirteenth Amendment argument in his restrictive covenant case. The antislavery amendment was, of course, not unknown to Marshall, but it may have been more immediate to Vaughn. Vaughn was proud of telling people that he was the son of a slave. Born in Kentucky, Vaughn had graduated from Lane College in Jackson, Tennessee, and received his law degree from Nashville's Walden University. He had worked his way into the local ranks of the Missouri Democratic Party and the local NAACP. In the latter capacity, he attended a conference that the NAACP held in Chicago in 1945 to help coordinate the many restrictive covenant cases that were percolating throughout the country.

Marshall's intent in convening this conference was to try to develop the right theory and case for Supreme Court review. In the following year, however, the cases reached uniformly bad outcomes in the lower courts. Marshall grew worried and called a second conference in January of 1947. By the end of the conference, Marshall was convinced that the ideal case had not yet been developed and that the time was still not right. Vaughn did not attend Marshall's second conference; he was busy preparing his petition for *certiorari* in *Shelley* at the time. Vaughn's filing of the petition that spring forced Marshall's hand. He and other NAACP staff took over the appeal of a case pending in Michigan, which Marshall had deemed not the right test case at the January conference, and filed a petition for certiorari. Better to argue a less than perfect Michigan case than to have Vaughn argue the issue alone in the Supreme Court.

To Marshall's relief, the Court consolidated the cases when it granted certiorari in June of 1947. * * * The one significant boost Marshall received that summer came from the government, which filed an amicus brief in support of the civil rights position.

The restrictive covenant cases were argued for seven hours in the Supreme Court. Philip Elman, an attorney in the Solicitor General's office who helped produce the government's brief in *Shelley v. Kraem-*

er—and who would write the government's brief in *Brown v. Board of Education*—was present for the argument. He tells this story of George Vaughn's argument:

> [H]e made an argument that as a professional piece of advocacy was not particularly distinguished. You might even say it was poor. He mainly argued the thirteenth amendment, which wasn't before the Court. He tried to distinguish cases when it was clear that the cases were indistinguishable and the only way to deal with them was to ignore or overrule them. He didn't cut through all the underbrush; he got caught in it. And the Justices didn't ask many questions. It was a dull argument until he came to the very end. He concluded his argument by saying . . . "Now I've finished my legal argument, but I want to say this before I sit down. In this Court, this house of law, the Negro today stands outside, and he knocks on the door, over and over again, he knocks on the door and cries out, 'Let me in, let me in, for I too have helped build this house.' "
>
> All of a sudden there was drama in the courtroom, a sense of what the case was really all about rather than the technical legal arguments. . . . [It was] the most moving plea in the Court I've ever heard.

Vaughn's speech was so compelling that he was invited to repeat it at the 1948 Democratic National Convention.

In May 1948, the Supreme Court ruled in the black litigants' favor, holding in *Shelley v. Kraemer* that court enforcement of racially restrictive covenants would violate the Equal Protection Clause of the Constitution. Legend has it that Thurgood Marshall argued *Shelley*. Legend does not say much about George Vaughn.

The story of the litigation campaign that culminated with *Shelley* exemplifies * * * central concerns [about] the difficulty the NAACP attorneys had "controlling" civil rights litigation even at a time when so few lawyers were involved that control seemed plausible, and, more importantly, the intriguing question of what values are furthered by such control. Before turning to the exploration of these themes, it is necessary to state several key premises, each of which also flows from the *Shelley* story. First, this Article talks of "communities" pursuing "goals," despite the fact that civil rights campaigns are not waged by easily identifiable "communities" pursuing settled, concrete goals. The restrictive covenant cases reflected the interests of a particular segment of the African-American community, the black middle-class home-buyers, and the extent to which such cases represented an important element of the civil rights struggle was contested among the various factions struggling to define that movement. Similarly, there is not a fixed "lesbian and gay 'community.' " Indeed, if anything, the fact that lesbians, gay men, and bisexuals are generally not visually identifiable makes the boundaries of this "community" especially amorphous. This limitation does not, however, frustrate this Article's central purpose. Without insisting on coherent notions of "identity" and "community," this

Article simply aims to examine the disputes that arise among individuals and groups pursuing legal rights.

Second, this Article employs the term "litigation campaigns" because its concern is the relationships among cases, clients, and lawyers that emerge in the course of a social enterprise. The piecemeal litigations that constituted the restrictive covenant campaign demonstrate that the disputes at issue here are not confined to the class action context nor to single cases. The significant unifying factor of the cases discussed in this Article is that they are brought with the intention of establishing a legal precedent that will improve a group's social situation and thus they aim to have an effect on other pending cases or on future cases. They constitute "impact" litigation or "test" cases brought over time as part of larger litigation "campaigns."

* * * [T]he lawyers waging these campaigns fall roughly into two distinct categories: professional public interest litigators like Thurgood Marshall and the occasional pro bono attorneys like George Vaughn. Within the lesbian/gay community, the primary public interest law firm is Lambda Legal Defense and Education Fund, Inc. (Lambda), based in New York. The American Civil Liberties Union (ACLU), through its affiliate offices and its national Lesbian and Gay Rights Project in New York, is the other largest provider of legal representation for lesbian/gay impact litigation. The National Center for Lesbian Rights in San Francisco also employs several impact litigators, as does a regional gay legal group, Gay and Lesbian Advocates and Defenders, based in Boston. The professional pro-gay advocates attempt to coordinate their work through biannual meetings known as the "Lesbian/Gay Litigators Roundtable." Like their predecessors in other social movements, these litigators typically (though not invariably) conduct litigation in conjunction with pro bono counsel, who are usually lawyers drawn from private law firms. Private attorneys like George Vaughn may also litigate pro-gay impact cases without the assistance of public interest firms (either for money or on a pro bono basis). I refer to these nonprofessional impact litigators as "occasional civil rights lawyers" to distinguish them from lawyers in professional civil rights organizations. While disputes occur among professional attorneys or among occasional pro bono attorneys, this Article is particularly concerned with disputes like the Marshall/Vaughn interaction that are between professional civil rights litigators on the one hand and occasional pro bono attorneys on the other. Such disputes provide an opportunity for considering the extent to which professional civil rights litigators have "expertise" that should be valued in particular ways in litigation campaigns at the expense of attorney individualism or group decisionmaking.

* * *

Disputes About Goals: Lessons from the Same-Sex Marriage Debate

In the fall of 1989, a lesbian/gay intellectual journal called *Out/Look* published a debate concerning same-sex marriage. On one side of the debate was Tom Stoddard, then the executive director of Lambda; on the other side of the debate was Paula Ettelbrick, then Lambda's legal director. Stoddard's contribution, entitled *Why Gay People Should Seek the Right to Marry*, set forth a practical, political, and philosophical argument for gay marriage and urged the gay community to give marriage priority as an issue: "I believe very strongly," Stoddard wrote, "that every lesbian and gay man should have the right to marry the same-sex partner of his or her choice, and that the gay rights movement should aggressively seek full legal recognition for same-sex marriages." Ettelbrick dissented. In her article, entitled, *Since When Is Marriage a Path to Liberation?*, Ettelbrick stated that:

> [M]arriage will not liberate us as lesbians and gay men. In fact, it will constrain us, make us more invisible, force our assimilation into the mainstream and undermine the goals of gay liberation.... Marriage runs contrary to two of the primary goals of the lesbian and gay movement: the affirmation of gay identity and culture; and the validation of many forms of relationships.
>
> . . .
>
> The moment we argue, as some among us insist on doing, that we should be treated as equals because we are really just like married couples and hold the same values to be true, we undermine the very purpose of our movement and begin the dangerous process of silencing our different voices.
>
> . . .
>
> We will be liberated only when we are respected and accepted for our differences and the diversity we provide to this society. Marriage is not a path to that liberation.

The Stoddard/Ettelbrick exchange was a "marriage announcement" of sorts, a declaration that the issue of marriage was moving from the margin to the center of the lesbian/gay movement. Yet from the moment of its reintroduction, the marriage issue produced controversy among community members. The Stoddard/Ettelbrick debate exposed one fissure, whether the community ought to prioritize and pursue marriage at all, and reflected a discussion within Lambda about how the organization should respond to increasing demands that it file a same-sex marriage case. This was not the only contentious issue. The community also disputed when such cases ought to be filed, where such filings might be made, and on whose behalf. The community generally, and the lawyers at Lambda specifically, were confronted by a significant conundrum: What constituted a satisfactory response to these divisions?

Stoddard and Ettelbrick's response was to air their debate publicly, first in the pages of *Out/Look* and then "on the road." The two leaders traveled around the United States to debate in front of community audiences. By taking their debate to the community, Stoddard and Ettelbrick apparently envisioned that some resolution of their disagreement would emerge from the community discussion, perhaps that some consensus would evolve to guide their actions.

A similar attempt to gauge community consensus occurred at the outset of a marriage challenge in Hawaii. In 1990, some individuals in Hawaii approached the ACLU affiliate in that state, asking the organization to file a challenge to Hawaii's marriage laws on their behalf. The local ACLU affiliate contacted the ACLU's National Lesbian and Gay Rights Project in New York seeking guidance. Nan Hunter, then Director of the Project, suggested that the Hawaii affiliate measure support for the case within the lesbian and gay community in Hawaii before pursuing the issue. The ACLU's Hawaii affiliate translated Hunter's advice into an informal poll of gay community leaders. By letter, the Hawaii affiliate attorney sought input from the community about whether there was "broadly based support for such litigation" in Hawaii, writing that the "ACLU would not want to act in a manner inconsistent with the opinion of a substantial number of gays and gay rights activists." The ACLU was attacked for taking this approach: A community activist in Hawaii wrote that "[i]ndividuals or civil rights should never be construed as a popular opinion issue, but rather a right of each human being."

The internal community debate largely subsided after lesbians and gay men, without support from the legal experts, proceeded with their own legal actions. In late 1990, Craig Dean, a gay lawyer, filed his own case challenging the District of Columbia's marriage law on behalf of himself and his lover. In May 1991, three lesbian and gay male couples in Hawaii filed an action in Hawaii state court without the support of the ACLU; they were represented by a former staff attorney at the ACLU of Hawaii. After the cases were filed, the community legal organizations ultimately provided support for them, thus quelling the internal community drama. All of the actors had different perspectives on how this resolution was accomplished: The professionals viewed it as a rebuke of their expertise, or of some community consensus, by rogue individuals; the individuals defended their actions either as in the best tradition of courageous individuals, or as capturing a community consensus while their leaders fiddled. Notwithstanding these differing perspectives, what seems clear is that the legal capacity of any individual, or group of individuals, within the community to end the debate *about* litigation by resorting *to* litigation proved to be an important factor in concluding the community's marriage debate. Once filed, such litigation changed the terms of the debate from an intracommunity struggle of self-definition to an intercommunity struggle of self-preservation.

Disputes About Means: Lessons from "Litigating Around Hardwick"

Debate about and interest in the nature of sexual orientation is nothing new. Several factors collided, coincidentally or not, in the late 1980s and early 1990s to bring these questions to the center of discourse within the lesbian/gay community. One was the increasing search for biological evidence of homosexuality. Simultaneously, the central dispute in the emerging field of lesbian/gay (or queer) studies was the essentialist/social constructionist argument. Essentialists argue that the categories of sexual orientation are descriptive of "real" human behavior anterior to culture. The social constructionist position holds that the process of creating and defining categories itself establishes the ways in which humans behave. Beyond its scientific and academic bases, this debate about the nature of sexual orientation has had an important foothold in law. Since the Supreme Court's 1986 decision in *Bowers v. Hardwick* that homosexual sodomy could be constitutionally criminalized, pro-gay litigators have struggled to "litigate around *Hardwick*." The primary strategy for doing so has been to rely on equality, rather than liberty, arguments. In turning to equal protection jurisprudence, pro-gay litigators have argued that government classifications disadvantaging persons on the basis of their sexual orientation are suspect and should trigger heightened judicial scrutiny. Two important problems have developed: First, the litigators have had to demonstrate why *Hardwick*'s ruling about sodomy does not preclude heightened constitutional protection for groups of persons allegedly defined by the fact that they engage in criminalizable conduct; second, the litigators have had to struggle with whether to argue that sexual orientation is an "immutable" characteristic.

From the moment of their appearance in legal discourse, these identity issues produced controversy among pro-gay litigators. On the one hand, distinguishing status from conduct seemed like the best way around *Hardwick*, and the growing body of biological materials clearly mattered to judges. On the other hand, some expressed apprehension about the artificiality of the status/conduct distinction, anxiety about the fact that only celibate homosexuals would be protected by such rulings, and hesitation about introducing preliminary and problematic biological evidence.

Two of the key cases challenging the military's "don't ask, don't tell" policy exemplify the conflict. In *Able v. Perry*, Lambda and the ACLU's Lesbian and Gay Rights Project represent a group of six servicemembers drawn from each of the services and from across the country. In framing the issues, the plaintiffs and their counsel have not argued that their clients' acknowledgement of their sexual identities is unrelated to their sexual conduct, but rather have attacked the "acts" portions of the military's policy as itself discriminating on the basis of sexual orientation. The second case was brought by an individual servicemember, Paul Thomasson, represented by attorneys at a large corporate law firm. In Thomasson's case, the litigators utilized the status/conduct distinction. The different approaches in these two cases can be seen in the way each deals with the precedent of *Steffan v. Perry*. In *Steffan*, the D.C. Circuit reasoned that because homosexual sodomy was criminalizable, regulations that discriminated against persons because they were apt to engage in such conduct were not unconstitutional. The *Thomasson* brief in the Fourth Circuit distinguished *Steffan* as concerned with conduct, and thus inapplicable to Thomasson's status-based challenge. Thomasson argued that:

> Whether a classification on the basis of sexual orientation alone, *irrespective of conduct*, is constitutionally suspect remains an open question in this and every other circuit. The D.C. Circuit, for example, has approached this issue on a number of occasions, including in its recent *Steffan* decision, but it has always ultimately declined to address it and, like a number of other courts, has held only that classifications predicated on homosexual *conduct* are not inherently suspect.

Rather than frame their case as being about status, as opposed to conduct, appellees' brief in *Able* challenged the underlying assumption in *Steffan*—that homosexual conduct could be criminalized in the manner the military did so. The plaintiffs thus wrote of *Steffan*:

> The court deemed the plaintiff to have conceded that "homosexual conduct" could be constitutionally punished by the then-applicable Directives. Here, in contrast, plaintiffs challenge the entire Act, including the constitutionality of the gay-only, more severe "acts" regulation. . . .

The "immutability" issue has been similarly divisive, most critically creating discord about the wisdom of introducing expert testimony to demonstrate that homosexuality is genetic in origin. Given the conflicting opinions on these subjects among the litigators, they face a dilemma: How are they to decide which depictions of gay identity to present in the cases that they litigate?

Several possibilities are evident. One approach would be to yield decisionmaking to the individual clients, allowing those persons to determine how to present homosexuality to the courts in their own cases. By contrast, the professional litigators have largely approached the issue as appropriate for debate, consultation, and consensus among themselves; for example, the Lesbian/Gay Litigators Roundtable regularly discussed the issue throughout the late 1980s and early 1990s, reaching a formal consensus—embodied by the approach to the *Able* case—in 1994. A third approach, espoused by many attorneys not involved in the professional meetings, has been to view the decision as one requiring the application of their own technical "expertise." The different approaches in the *Able* and *Thomasson* cases may therefore reflect not only different tactics, but also different theories about how these tactical disputes should be addressed. Just as the procedural rules enabled any individual to opt out of community goal debates about filing, the professional capacity of each attorney to frame her own tactics as she desires similarly provides the definitive norm for disputes among attorneys. Such individual authority grants each attorney the right to end the internal strategy debate at any moment simply by pursuing her own tactics regardless of the recommendations of her fellow attorneys.

Within social groups that are striving for their civil rights, disputes are inevitable. Community members disagree about which goals should be pursued, lawyers about the strategies that should be employed. Such disagreements can be constructively undertaken and productive for the community, or can be destructively waged and become bitterly divisive. * * * [M]ore attention needs to be paid to the ways that disputes are conducted in the shadow of the law, so as to ensure, as much as possible, their productivity. * * *

Notes and Questions

1. In an omitted portion of the article, Rubenstein proposes that procedural and ethical rules should "promote more democratic means of client goal-setting and more expertise-driven norms of attorney decision-making in group litigation." *Id.* at 1668. He proposes innovations in procedural rules to facilitate these processes.

2. Rubenstein explains how debates about immutability arguments have challenged gay rights litigators. Gay rights litigators have frequently attempted to win recognition from courts that homosexuality should be treated as a "suspect classification" under the federal constitution, arguing the existence of a history of discrimination, the exhibition of immutable characteristics that define them as members of a discrete group, and political powerlessness. Immutability is sometimes recognized as a characteristic deserving protection in other legal contexts. For example, in *Hernandez-Montiel v. INS*, 225 F.3d 1084 (2000), the Ninth Circuit held that a man who dressed and behaved as a woman in Mexico belonged to an identifiable social group of people who share a common, immutable characteristic. "Sexual orientation and sexual identity are immutable; they are so fundamental to one's identity that a person should not be required to abandon them. * * * Sexual identity is inherent to one's very identity as a person." *Id.* at 1093 (reversing Board of Immigration Appeals holding that effeminate appearance was not immutable because he could have changed his dress).

Janet Halley argues against this strategy, stating that when immutable characteristics are identified courts do not always protect them against invidious classifications through strict scrutiny. Further, although many people do experience their sexuality as something they did not choose and cannot change, that is not true for many others to whom LGBT issues are important:

> As long as people who suffer anti-gay discrimination differ about whether they were born or became gay—indeed, about whether they *are* gay—neither a purely essentialist nor a purely constructivist approach can adequately ground pro-gay legal theory. And differ we do, media reports to the contrary notwithstanding. Immutability offers no theoretical foundation for legal protection of those gay men and lesbians who experience their sexual orientation as contingent, mutable, chosen. This exclusion will only get worse as a distinctive movement of bisexuals takes shape: The fairness theory of pro-gay essentialism does not explain why bisexuals—by hypothesis capable of satisfactory sexual encounters with members of the so-

called "opposite" sex—should not be encouraged or forced to do so. But building a new foundation for legal protection on the contrary assumption—that sexual orientation is constructed and *not* biologically determined—would risk the same exclusion in reverse. An adequate legal theory should protect the entire social class on whose behalf it is articulated.

The argument from immutability responds to a particularly contemptuous and dismissive form of anti-gay animus with elegant simplicity and plangent appeal. It also works. Indeed, it often is the *only* effective resource available to gay men, lesbians, and bisexuals seeking to persuade their parents, coworkers, and neighbors that they can love someone of the same sex and remain fully human. Moreover, for most of the gay children, workers, and neighbors who use the argument from immutability in these settings, it is absolutely true: They can't change their sexual orientation.

When the argument from immutability leaves those settings and becomes a legal strategy, however, the terms by which we should judge its plausibility and effectiveness shift. While it may be entirely responsive to the particular form of personal criticism faced by many gay men, lesbians, and bisexuals ("Why don't you just change?"), it is not fully or even coherently responsive to the forms of anti-gay argument used to justify state-sponsored discrimination against all of us. Three new elements need to be taken into account.

First, anti-gay public policy is complex and flexible, and finds ways to justify itself even on the assumption that homosexual orientation in many, most, or all its bearers is immutable. Second, the reasons why the *state* should not discriminate against gay men, lesbians, and bisexuals are different in important ways from the reasons why parents should not think ill of their gay children. Suspect class analysis (when given its best reading) asks whether the resources of the state are being used to enforce, confirm, and validate social hierarchies. The argument from immutability has never attained the preeminence in suspect class analysis that some pro-gay advocates attribute to it * * * . And third, the argument from immutability, when advanced on behalf of a complex movement, many of whose members *can* change some aspect of their sexuality that is targeted by anti-gay policy, is less directly responsive to the problem we face. Moreover, the argument becomes burdened with an ethical problem it does not have when used privately: When pro-gay advocates use the argument from immutability before a court on behalf of gay men, lesbians, and bisexuals, they misrepresent us.

Even worse, when the pro-gay argument from immutability annexes recent scientific findings to bolster its empirical claim that homosexual orientation is immutable, it becomes simply incoherent. * * * [B]iologically caused traits can change; there is as yet no proof that human sexual orientation has a biological cause; and even if a

> biological cause of human sexual orientation were eventually identified, the conceptually distinct question whether it causes *homosexuality* and *heterosexuality* would remain outstanding.

Janet E. Halley, *Sexual Orientation and the Politics of Biology: A Critique of the Argument from Immutability*, 46 Stan. L. Rev. 503, 528, 567–68 (1994) (reviewing studies of biology and sexual orientation).

Should the possibility of change be the focus of legal inquiry on LGBT issues? How else could the issues be framed?

B. Rights Against Discrimination: State and Local Ordinances

As the gay civil rights movement developed, activists sought and sometimes won the passage of local ordinances banning discrimination. In reaction to these ordinances, voter initiatives in several states sought to make it impossible for local governments to prohibit sexual orientation discrimination. Opponents of gay rights ordinances characterized them as creating special rights for homosexuals. The majority of the Supreme Court rejected this position in Romer v. Evans, 517 U.S. 620 (1996), seeing anti-gay rights initiatives as instead imposing disadvantage born of animosity. The dissent, in contrast, characterized antidiscrimination ordinances as a form of special favor and preferential protection. The dissent would also argue that passage of antidiscrimination laws proved that, although they were a minority, gays and lesbians were politically powerful and did not need protection by the courts.

JAMES W. BUTTON, BARBARA A. RIENZO, & KENNETH D. WALD

The Politics of Gay Rights at the Local and State Level in *The Politics of Gay Rights* 269, 272–74 (Craig A. Rimmerman, Kenneth D. Wald & Clyde Wilcox eds., 2000)

The Stonewall rebellion of 1969 sparked the beginning of an active gay political movement for civil rights protections. Prior to this time there were no laws or policies that prohibited discrimination on the basis of sexual orientation in any public or private organization in the country. The post-Stonewall gay movement, however, was relatively small with few significant supporters. Politically organized lesbians and gay men resided primarily in large cities and liberal university communities.

It is not surprising, therefore, that many of the initial adoptions of gay rights ordinances took place in university settings. In the early 1970s antidiscrimination laws were passed in Berkeley, Palo Alto, Boulder, Ann Arbor, East Lansing, Austin, and Madison, Wis. By 1977 two-thirds of the twenty-eight communities with gay rights legislation were university-dominated cities or counties. As in the case of the black civil rights and women's movements, liberal students and faculty were often in the vanguard of the quest for gay rights.

Large cities with sizable and organized gay populations were also among the first communities to adopt legislation to protect against discrimination based on sexual orientation. These cities included Detroit, Minneapolis, San Francisco, Seattle, and Washington. Other large cities with similar characteristics * * * had at least initiated political discussion of such laws by 1975. Thus the pioneers of gay rights laws or policies were localities with significant supportive constituencies consisting typically of liberal university populations and mobilized gay citizens.

Progressive states also began to consider civil rights protections for gays. * * *

The legal successes of gays in the early 1970s were also achieved because of the lack of organized resistance. While the Catholic Church offered modest opposition in a few cities, other potential opponents seemed caught off guard by the sudden emergence of this political issue. Traditional religious groups and other opponents began to mobilize, however, and in 1977 they won a major victory by repealing via referendum the Dade County, Florida ordinance protecting gays. It was the first defeat of gay rights in a major U.S. community. Anita Bryant, a popular singer and devout Baptist, led the coalition of right-wing (primarily religious) forces in Dade Count. She contended that such ordinances were a religious abomination and a license for gays to molest children. Bryant's success attracted national attention and propelled her onto an antigay rights crusade that was effective in rescinding similar local laws in Eugene, St. Paul, and Wichita. Moreover, this antigay initiative, with its focus on children, kept proponents from seeking similar protections on behalf of youth in school settings for years to come.

The conservative opposition to gay rights sparked a further politicization of lesbians and gay men. Gay activists successfully parlayed the attacks on them into greater publicity and increased support for their grievances. In California, for example, a controversial 1978 proposition that would have permitted school boards to expel gay teachers was soundly defeated in a voter referendum. In addition, the steady trend of local adoptions of legal protection for gays continued, and by 1980 forty U.S. communities could claim such legislation.

The decade of the 1980s marked a shift to a more conservative time in American politics. The new Christian Right emerged as an organized constituency with a strong antigay agenda. The AIDS epidemic broke out, and the stigma of an often fatal disease was conferred on gay men, encouraging many Americans to become less tolerant of homosexuals. However, the disease also pushed a number of gays out of the closet and into the political arena in order to gain government help and protection and in time most Americans, in spite of their attitudes that the gay subculture was immoral, came to support basic civil rights protections for lesbians and gay men. As a result, the 1980s saw some forty additional cities and counties pass gay rights legislation [including a mix of large cities, suburban communities adjacent to major cities, and ten counties].

* * *

* * * In 1982, after seven years of debate, Wisconsin became the first state to enact legislation protective of gays. * * * In 1989, after a legislative battle of nearly two decades, Massachusetts became the second * * * .

Notes and Questions

1. In reaction to these legislative gains, in the early 1990s, voter initiatives in several states sought to enact statutes or amend state constitutions to make it impossible for local governments to ban discrimination on the basis of sexual orientation. Most such efforts did not gain enough support to qualify for the ballot. Stephanie L. Witt & Suzanne McCorkle, *Anti-Gay Rights: Assessing Voter Initiatives* 142–43 (1997). The antigay initiatives went to voters but lost in Idaho in 1994, Oregon in 1992 and 1994, and Maine in 1995; the initiative succeeded in Colorado in 1992. *Id.* at 142–43, 160.

The voter initiatives were a way of attacking the antidiscrimination ordinances directly, and they played a role in general political mobilization as well.

> Even an initiative doomed to failure at the ballot box or in the courts can generate a wealth of media attention and serve to mobilize supporters. The initiative itself may turn out to be a secondary goal for an interest group. As Kelly Walton, head of the Idaho Citizens Alliance (proponents of the anti-gay initiative), remarked * * * , "one of the main results [of the initiative effort] is we were able to rob left-wing candidates of precious campaign money that was devoted to this initiative, and the election night results * * * clearly shows that to be true."

Id. at 6.

2. Does the city in which you are living have an antidiscrimination ordinance that protects gays and lesbians? Does it also protect bisexuals, transgendered people, and heterosexuals from discrimination on the basis of sexual orientation?

3. In *Romer v. Evans*, the Supreme Court addressed the constitutionality of the anti-gay rights amendment to the Colorado constitution.

ROMER v. EVANS

517 U.S. 620 (1996)

Justice KENNEDY delivered the opinion of the Court.

One century ago, the first Justice Harlan admonished this Court that the Constitution "neither knows nor tolerates classes among citizens." *Plessy v. Ferguson,* 163 U.S. 537, 559 (1896) (dissenting opinion). Unheeded then, those words now are understood to state a commitment to the law's neutrality where the rights of persons are at stake. The Equal Protection Clause enforces this principle and today requires us to hold invalid a provision of Colorado's Constitution.

I

The enactment challenged in this case is an amendment to the Constitution of the State of Colorado, adopted in a 1992 statewide referendum. The parties and the state courts refer to it as "Amendment 2," its designation when submitted to the voters. The impetus for the amendment and the contentious campaign that preceded its adoption came in large part from ordinances that had been passed in various Colorado municipalities. For example, the cities of Aspen and Boulder and the city and County of Denver each had enacted ordinances which banned discrimination in many transactions and activities, including housing, employment, education, public accommodations, and health and welfare services. What gave rise to the statewide controversy was the protection the ordinances afforded to persons discriminated against by reason of their sexual orientation. See Boulder Rev.Code § 12–1–1 (defining "sexual orientation" as "the choice of sexual partners, i.e., bisexual, homosexual or heterosexual"); Denver Rev. Municipal Code, Art. IV, § 28–92 (defining "sexual orientation" as "[t]he status of an individual as to his or her heterosexuality, homosexuality or bisexuality"). Amendment 2 repeals these ordinances to the extent they prohibit discrimination on the basis of "homosexual, lesbian or bisexual orientation, conduct, practices or relationships." Colo. Const., Art. II, § 30b.

Yet Amendment 2, in explicit terms, does more than repeal or rescind these provisions. It prohibits all legislative, executive or judicial action at any level of state or local government designed to protect the named class, a class we shall refer to as homosexual persons or gays and lesbians. The amendment reads:

> "No Protected Status Based on Homosexual, Lesbian or Bisexual Orientation. Neither the State of Colorado, through any of its branches or departments, nor any of its agencies, political subdivisions, municipalities or school districts, shall enact, adopt or enforce any statute, regulation, ordinance or policy whereby homosexual, lesbian or bisexual orientation, conduct, practices or relationships shall constitute or otherwise be the basis of or entitle any person or class of persons to have or claim any minority status, quota preferences, protected status or claim of discrimination. This Section of the Constitution shall be in all respects self-executing." *Ibid.*

Soon after Amendment 2 was adopted, this litigation to declare its invalidity and enjoin its enforcement was commenced * * * .

* * *

II

The State's principal argument in defense of Amendment 2 is that it puts gays and lesbians in the same position as all other persons. So, the State says, the measure does no more than deny homosexuals special rights. This reading of the amendment's language is implausible. We rely not upon our own interpretation of the amendment but upon the authoritative construction of Colorado's Supreme Court. * * * The critical discussion of the amendment, set out in *Evans I,* is as follows:

> "The immediate objective of Amendment 2 is, at a minimum, to repeal existing statutes, regulations, ordinances, and policies of state and local entities that barred discrimination based on sexual orientation. * * *
>
> "The 'ultimate effect' of Amendment 2 is to prohibit any governmental entity from adopting similar, or more protective statutes, regulations, ordinances, or policies in the future unless the state constitution is first amended to permit such measures." 854 P.2d, at 1284–1285, and n. 26.

Sweeping and comprehensive is the change in legal status effected by this law. So much is evident from the ordinances the Colorado Supreme Court declared would be void by operation of Amendment 2. Homosexuals, by state decree, are put in a solitary class with respect to transactions and relations in both the private and governmental spheres. The amendment withdraws from homosexuals, but no others, specific legal protection from the injuries caused by discrimination, and it forbids reinstatement of these laws and policies.

The change Amendment 2 works in the legal status of gays and lesbians in the private sphere is far reaching, both on its own terms and when considered in light of the structure and operation of modern antidiscrimination laws. That structure is well illustrated by contemporary statutes and ordinances prohibiting discrimination by providers of public accommodations. "At common law, innkeepers, smiths, and others who 'made profession of a public employment,' were prohibited from refusing, without good reason, to serve a customer." *Hurley v. Irish-American Gay, Lesbian and Bisexual Group of Boston, Inc.,* 515 U.S. 557, 571 (1995). The duty was a general one and did not specify protection for particular groups. The common-law rules, however, proved insufficient in many instances, and it was settled early that the Fourteenth Amendment did not give Congress a general power to prohibit discrimination in public accommodations, *Civil Rights Cases,* 109 U.S. 3, 25 (1883). In consequence, most States have chosen to counter discrimination by enacting detailed statutory schemes.

Colorado's state and municipal laws typify this emerging tradition of statutory protection and follow a consistent pattern. The laws first enumerate the persons or entities subject to a duty not to discriminate. The list goes well beyond the entities covered by the common law. The Boulder ordinance, for example, has a comprehensive definition of entities deemed places of "public accommodation." They include "any place of business engaged in any sales to the general public and any place that offers services, facilities, privileges, or advantages to the general public or that receives financial support through solicitation of the general public or through governmental subsidy of any kind." The Denver ordinance is of similar breadth, applying, for example, to hotels, restaurants, hospitals, dental clinics, theaters, banks, common carriers, travel and insurance agencies, and "shops and stores dealing with goods or services of any kind."

These statutes and ordinances also depart from the common law by enumerating the groups or persons within their ambit of protection. Enumeration is the essential device used to make the duty not to discriminate concrete and to provide guidance for those who must comply. In following this approach, Colorado's state and local governments have not limited antidiscrimination laws to groups that have so far been given the protection of heightened equal protection scrutiny under our cases. Rather, they set forth an extensive catalog of traits which cannot be the basis for discrimination, including age, military status, marital status, pregnancy, parenthood, custody of a minor child, political affiliation, physical or mental disability of an individual or of his or her associates—and, in recent times, sexual orientation.

Amendment 2 bars homosexuals from securing protection against the injuries that these public-accommodations laws address. That in itself is a severe consequence, but there is more. Amendment 2, in addition, nullifies specific legal protections for this targeted class in all transactions in housing, sale of real estate, insurance, health and welfare services, private education, and employment.

Not confined to the private sphere, Amendment 2 also operates to repeal and forbid all laws or policies providing specific protection for gays or lesbians from discrimination by every level of Colorado government. The State Supreme Court cited two examples of protections in the governmental sphere that are now rescinded and may not be reintroduced. The first is Colorado Executive Order D0035 (1990), which forbids employment discrimination against " 'all state employees, classified and exempt' on the basis of sexual orientation." Also repealed, and now forbidden, are "various provisions prohibiting discrimination based on sexual orientation at state colleges." The repeal of these measures and the prohibition against their future reenactment demonstrate that Amendment 2 has the same force and effect in Colorado's governmental sector as it does elsewhere and that it applies to policies as well as ordinary legislation.

Amendment 2's reach may not be limited to specific laws passed for the benefit of gays and lesbians. It is a fair, if not necessary, inference from the broad language of the amendment that it deprives gays and lesbians even of the protection of general laws and policies that prohibit arbitrary discrimination in governmental and private settings. * * * At some point in the systematic administration of these laws, an official must determine whether homosexuality is an arbitrary and, thus, forbidden basis for decision. Yet a decision to that effect would itself amount to a policy prohibiting discrimination on the basis of homosexuality, and so would appear to be no more valid under Amendment 2 than the specific prohibitions against discrimination the state court held invalid.

If this consequence follows from Amendment 2, as its broad language suggests, it would compound the constitutional difficulties the law creates. The state court did not decide whether the amendment has this effect, however, and neither need we. In the course of rejecting the argument that Amendment 2 is intended to conserve resources to fight discrimination against suspect classes, the Colorado Supreme Court made the limited observation that the amendment is not intended to affect many anti-discrimination laws protecting nonsuspect classes,. In our view that does not resolve the issue. In any event, even if, as we doubt, homosexuals could find some safe harbor in laws of general application, we cannot accept the view that Amendment 2's prohibition on specific legal protections does no more than deprive homosexuals of special rights. To the contrary, the amendment imposes a special disability upon those persons alone. Homosexuals are forbidden the safeguards that others enjoy or may seek without constraint. They can obtain specific protection against discrimination only by enlisting the citizenry of Colorado to amend the State Constitution or perhaps, on the State's view, by trying to pass helpful laws of general applicability. This is so no matter how local or discrete the harm, no matter how public and widespread the injury. We find nothing special in the protections Amendment 2 withholds. These are protections taken for granted by most people either because they already have them or do not need them; these are protections against exclusion from an almost limitless number of transactions and endeavors that constitute ordinary civic life in a free society.

III

The Fourteenth Amendment's promise that no person shall be denied the equal protection of the laws must coexist with the practical necessity that most legislation classifies for one purpose or another, with resulting disadvantage to various groups or persons. We have attempted to reconcile the principle with the reality by stating that, if a law neither burdens a fundamental right nor targets a suspect class, we will uphold the legislative classification so long as it bears a rational relation to some legitimate end.

Amendment 2 fails, indeed defies, even this conventional inquiry. First, the amendment has the peculiar property of imposing a broad and undifferentiated disability on a single named group, an exceptional and, as we shall explain, invalid form of legislation. Second, its sheer breadth is so discontinuous with the reasons offered for it that the amendment seems inexplicable by anything but animus toward the class it affects; it lacks a rational relationship to legitimate state interests.

Taking the first point, even in the ordinary equal protection case calling for the most deferential of standards, we insist on knowing the relation between the classification adopted and the object to be attained. The search for the link between classification and objective gives substance to the Equal Protection Clause; it provides guidance and discipline for the legislature, which is entitled to know what sorts of laws it can pass; and it marks the limits of our own authority. In the ordinary case, a law will be sustained if it can be said to advance a legitimate government interest, even if the law seems unwise or works to the disadvantage of a particular group, or if the rationale for it seems tenuous. * * * By requiring that the classification bear a rational relationship to an independent and legitimate legislative end, we ensure that classifications are not drawn for the purpose of disadvantaging the group burdened by the law.

Amendment 2 confounds this normal process of judicial review. It is at once too narrow and too broad. It identifies persons by a single trait and then denies them protection across the board. The resulting disqualification of a class of persons from the right to seek specific protection from the law is unprecedented in our jurisprudence. The absence of precedent for Amendment 2 is itself instructive; "[d]iscriminations of an unusual character especially suggest careful consideration to determine whether they are obnoxious to the constitutional provision."

It is not within our constitutional tradition to enact laws of this sort. Central both to the idea of the rule of law and to our own Constitution's guarantee of equal protection is the principle that government and each of its parts remain open on impartial terms to all who seek its assistance. " 'Equal protection of the laws is not achieved through indiscriminate imposition of inequalities.' " *Sweatt v. Painter,* 339 U.S. 629, 635 (1950) (quoting *Shelley v. Kraemer,* 334 U.S. 1, 22 (1948)). Respect for this principle explains why laws singling out a certain class of citizens for disfavored legal status or general hardships are rare. A law declaring that in general it shall be more difficult for one group of citizens than for all others to seek aid from the government is itself a denial of equal protection of the laws in the most literal sense. "The guaranty of 'equal protection of the laws is a pledge of the protection of equal laws.' " *Skinner v. Oklahoma ex rel. Williamson,* 316 U.S. 535, 541 (1942) (quoting *Yick Wo v. Hopkins,* 118 U.S. 356, 369 (1886)).

* * *

* * * [L]aws of the kind now before us raise the inevitable inference that the disadvantage imposed is born of animosity toward the class of persons affected. "[I]f the constitutional conception of 'equal protection of the laws' means anything, it must at the very least mean that a bare . . . desire to harm a politically unpopular group cannot constitute a *legitimate* governmental interest." Even laws enacted for broad and ambitious purposes often can be explained by reference to legitimate public policies which justify the incidental disadvantages they impose on certain persons. Amendment 2, however, in making a general announcement that gays and lesbians shall not have any particular protections from the law, inflicts on them immediate, continuing, and real injuries that outrun and belie any legitimate justifications that may be claimed for it. We conclude that, in addition to the far-reaching deficiencies of Amendment 2 that we have noted, the principles it offends, in another sense, are conventional and venerable; a law must bear a rational relationship to a legitimate governmental purpose, and Amendment 2 does not.

The primary rationale the State offers for Amendment 2 is respect for other citizens' freedom of association, and in particular the liberties of landlords or employers who have personal or religious objections to homosexuality. Colorado also cites its interest in conserving resources to fight discrimination against other groups. The breadth of the amendment is so far removed from these particular justifications that we find it impossible to credit them. We cannot say that Amendment 2 is directed to any identifiable legitimate purpose or discrete objective. It is a status-based enactment divorced from any factual context from which we could discern a relationship to legitimate state interests; it is a classification of persons undertaken for its own sake, something the Equal Protection Clause does not permit. "[C]lass legislation ... [is] obnoxious to the prohibitions of the Fourteenth Amendment...." *Civil Rights Cases,* 109 U.S., at 24.

We must conclude that Amendment 2 classifies homosexuals not to further a proper legislative end but to make them unequal to everyone else. This Colorado cannot do. A State cannot so deem a class of persons a stranger to its laws. Amendment 2 violates the Equal Protection Clause, and the judgment of the Supreme Court of Colorado is affirmed.

It is so ordered.

Justice SCALIA, with whom THE CHIEF JUSTICE and Justice THOMAS join, dissenting.

The Court has mistaken a Kulturkampf for a fit of spite. The constitutional amendment before us here is not the manifestation of a " 'bare ... desire to harm' " homosexuals, but is rather a modest attempt by seemingly tolerant Coloradans to preserve traditional sexual mores against the efforts of a politically powerful minority to revise those mores through use of the laws. That objective, and the means chosen to achieve it, are not only unimpeachable under any constitutional doctrine hitherto pronounced (hence the opinion's heavy reliance upon principles of righteousness rather than judicial holdings); they have been specifically approved by the Congress of the United States and by this Court.

In holding that homosexuality cannot be singled out for disfavorable treatment, the Court contradicts a decision, unchallenged here, pronounced only 10 years ago, see *Bowers v. Hardwick,* 478 U.S. 186 (1986), and places the prestige of this institution behind the proposition that opposition to homosexuality is as reprehensible as racial or religious bias. Whether it is or not is *precisely* the cultural debate that gave rise to the Colorado constitutional amendment (and to the preferential laws against which the amendment was directed). Since the Constitution of the United States says nothing about this subject, it is left to be resolved by normal democratic means, including the democratic adoption of provisions in state constitutions. This Court has no business imposing upon all Americans the resolution favored by the elite class from which the Members of this institution are selected, pronouncing that "animosity" toward homosexuality is evil. I vigorously dissent.

I

Let me first discuss Part II of the Court's opinion, its longest section, which is devoted to rejecting the State's arguments that Amendment 2 "puts gays and lesbians in the same position as all other persons," and "does no more than deny homosexuals special rights." The Court concludes that this reading of Amendment 2's language is "implausible" under the "authoritative construction" given Amendment 2 by the Supreme Court of Colorado.

* * *

Despite all of its hand wringing about the potential effect of Amendment 2 on general antidiscrimination laws, the Court's opinion ultimately does not dispute all this, but assumes it to be true. The only denial of equal treatment it contends homosexuals have suffered is this: They may not obtain *preferential* treatment without amending the State Constitution. That is to say, the principle underlying the Court's opinion is that one who is accorded equal treatment under the laws, but cannot as readily as others obtain *preferential* treatment under the laws, has been denied equal protection of the laws. If merely stating this alleged "equal protection" violation does not suffice to refute it, our constitutional jurisprudence has achieved terminal silliness.

The central thesis of the Court's reasoning is that any group is denied equal protection when, to obtain advantage (or, presumably, to avoid disadvantage), it must have recourse to a more general and hence more difficult level of political decisionmaking than others. The world has never heard of such a principle, which is why the Court's opinion is so long on emotive utterance and so short on relevant legal citation. And it seems to me most unlikely that any multilevel democracy can function under such a principle. For *whenever* a disadvantage is imposed, or conferral of a benefit is prohibited, at one of the higher levels of democratic decisionmaking (*i.e.,* by the state legislature rather than local government, or by the people at large in the state constitution rather than the legislature), the affected group has (under this theory) been denied equal protection. * * *

II

I turn next to whether there was a legitimate rational basis for the substance of the constitutional amendment—for the prohibition of special protection for homosexuals. It is unsurprising that the Court avoids discussion of this question, since the answer is so obviously yes. The case most relevant to the issue before us today is not even mentioned in the Court's opinion: In *Bowers v. Hardwick,* 478 U.S. 186 (1986), we held that the Constitution does not prohibit what virtually all States had done from the founding of the Republic until very recent years—making homosexual conduct a crime.* * * If it is constitutionally permissible for a State to make homosexual conduct criminal, surely it is constitutionally permissible for a State to enact other laws merely *disfavoring* homosexual conduct. (As the Court of Appeals for the District of Columbia

Circuit has aptly put it: "If the Court [in *Bowers*] was unwilling to object to state laws that criminalize the behavior that defines the class, it is hardly open . . . to conclude that state sponsored discrimination against the class is invidious. After all, there can hardly be more palpable discrimination against a class than making the conduct that defines the class criminal." *Padula v. Webster,* 822 F.2d 97, 103 (1987).) And *a fortiori* it is constitutionally permissible for a State to adopt a provision *not even* disfavoring homosexual conduct, but merely prohibiting all levels of state government from bestowing *special protections* upon homosexual conduct. Respondents (who, unlike the Court, cannot afford the luxury of ignoring inconvenient precedent) counter *Bowers* with the argument that a greater-includes-the-lesser rationale cannot justify Amendment 2's application to individuals who do not engage in homosexual acts, but are merely of homosexual "orientation." Some Courts of Appeals have concluded that, with respect to laws of this sort at least, that is a distinction without a difference. * * *

But assuming that, in Amendment 2, a person of homosexual "orientation" is someone who does not engage in homosexual conduct but merely has a tendency or desire to do so, *Bowers* still suffices to establish a rational basis for the provision. If it is rational to criminalize the conduct, surely it is rational to deny special favor and protection to those with a self-avowed tendency or desire to engage in the conduct. Indeed, where criminal sanctions are not involved, homosexual "orientation" is an acceptable stand-in for homosexual conduct. A State "does not violate the Equal Protection Clause merely because the classifications made by its laws are imperfect," *Dandridge v. Williams,* 397 U.S. 471, 485 (1970). Just as a policy barring the hiring of methadone users as transit employees does not violate equal protection simply because *some* methadone users pose no threat to passenger safety, and just as a mandatory retirement age of 50 for police officers does not violate equal protection even though it prematurely ends the careers of many policemen over 50 who still have the capacity to do the job, Amendment 2 is not constitutionally invalid simply because it could have been drawn more precisely so as to withdraw special antidiscrimination protections only from those of homosexual "orientation" who actually engage in homosexual conduct. * * *

Moreover, even if the provision regarding homosexual "orientation" *were* invalid, respondents' challenge to Amendment 2—which is a facial challenge—must fail. "A facial challenge to a legislative Act is, of course, the most difficult challenge to mount successfully, since the challenger must establish that no set of circumstances exists under which the Act would be valid." It would not be enough for respondents to establish (if they could) that Amendment 2 is unconstitutional as applied to those of homosexual "orientation"; since, under *Bowers,* Amendment 2 is unquestionably constitutional as applied to those who engage in homosexual conduct, the facial challenge cannot succeed. Some individuals of homosexual "orientation" who do not engage in homosexual acts might successfully bring an as-applied challenge to Amendment 2, but so far as the record indicates, none of the respondents is such a person.

III

The foregoing suffices to establish what the Court's failure to cite any case remotely in point would lead one to suspect: No principle set forth in the Constitution, nor even any imagined by this Court in the past 200 years, prohibits what Colorado has done here. * * *

* * * [A]s to its eminent reasonableness. The Court's opinion contains grim, disapproving hints that Coloradans have been guilty of "animus" or "animosity" toward homosexuality, as though that has been established as un-American. Of course it is our moral heritage that one should not hate any human being or class of human beings. But I had thought that one could consider certain conduct reprehensible—murder, for example, or polygamy, or cruelty to animals—and could exhibit even "animus" toward such conduct. Surely that is the only sort of "animus" at issue here: moral disapproval of homosexual conduct, the same sort of moral disapproval that produced the centuries-old criminal laws that we held constitutional in *Bowers.* The Colorado amendment does not, to speak entirely precisely, prohibit giving favored status to people who are *homosexuals;* they can be favored for many reasons—for example, because they are senior citizens or members of racial minorities. But it prohibits giving them favored status *because of their homosexual conduct*—that is, it prohibits favored status *for homosexuality.*

But though Coloradans are, as I say, *entitled* to be hostile toward homosexual conduct, the fact is that the degree of hostility reflected by Amendment 2 is the smallest conceivable. The Court's portrayal of Coloradans as a society fallen victim to pointless, hate-filled "gay-bashing" is so false as to be comical. Colorado not only is one of the 25 States that have repealed their antisodomy laws, but was among the first to do so. But the society that eliminates criminal punishment for homosexual acts does not necessarily abandon the view that homosexuality is morally wrong and socially harmful; often, abolition simply reflects the view that enforcement of such criminal laws involves unseemly intrusion into the intimate lives of citizens.

There is a problem, however, which arises when criminal sanction of homosexuality is eliminated but moral and social disapprobation of homosexuality is meant to be retained. * * * The problem (a problem, that is, for those who wish to retain social disapprobation of homosexuality) is that, because those who engage in homosexual conduct tend to reside in disproportionate numbers in certain communities, and, of course, care about homosexual-rights issues much more ardently than the public at large, they possess political power much greater than their numbers, both locally and statewide. Quite understandably, they devote this political power to achieving not merely a grudging social toleration, but full social acceptance, of homosexuality. See, *e.g.,* Jacobs, The Rhetorical Construction of Rights: The Case of the Gay Rights Movement, 1969–1991, 72 Neb. L. Rev. 723, 724 (1993) ("[T]he task of gay rights proponents is to move the center of public discourse along a continuum from the rhetoric of disapprobation, to rhetoric of tolerance, and finally to affirmation").

By the time Coloradans were asked to vote on Amendment 2, their exposure to homosexuals' quest for social endorsement was not limited to newspaper accounts of happenings in places such as New York, Los Angeles, San Francisco, and Key West. Three Colorado cities—Aspen, Boulder, and Denver—had enacted ordinances that listed "sexual orientation" as an impermissible ground for discrimination, equating the moral disapproval of homosexual conduct with racial and religious bigotry. The phenomenon had even appeared statewide: The Governor of Colorado had signed an executive order pronouncing that "in the State of Colorado we recognize the diversity in our pluralistic society and strive to bring an end to discrimination in any form," and directing state agency-heads to "ensure non-discrimination" in hiring and promotion based on, among other things, "sexual orientation." I do not mean to be critical of these legislative successes; homosexuals are as entitled to use the legal system for reinforcement of their moral sentiments as is the rest of society. But they are subject to being countered by lawful, democratic countermeasures as well.

That is where Amendment 2 came in. It sought to counter both the geographic concentration and the disproportionate political power of homosexuals by (1) resolving the controversy at the statewide level, and (2) making the election a single-issue contest for both sides. It put directly, to all the citizens of the State, the question: Should homosexuality be given special protection? They answered no. The Court today asserts that this most democratic of procedures is unconstitutional. Lacking any cases to establish that facially absurd proposition, it simply asserts that it *must* be unconstitutional, because it has never happened before. * * * What the Court says is * * * demonstrably false at the constitutional level. The Eighteenth Amendment to the Federal Constitution, for example, deprived those who drank alcohol not only of the power to alter the policy of prohibition *locally* or through *state legislation,* but even of the power to alter it through *state constitutional amendment* or *federal legislation.* The Establishment Clause of the First Amendment prevents theocrats from having their way by converting their fellow citizens at the local, state, or federal statutory level; as does the Republican Form of Government Clause prevent monarchists.

* * *

IV

* * * I think it no business of the courts (as opposed to the political branches) to take sides in this culture war.

But the Court today has done so, not only by inventing a novel and extravagant constitutional doctrine to take the victory away from traditional forces, but even by verbally disparaging as bigotry adherence to traditional attitudes. To suggest, for example, that this constitutional amendment springs from nothing more than " 'a bare . . . desire to harm a politically unpopular group,' " is nothing short of insulting. (It is also nothing short of preposterous to call "politically unpopular" a group which enjoys enormous influence in American media and politics, and which, as the trial court here noted, though composing no more than 4% of the population had the support of 46% of the voters on Amendment 2.)

When the Court takes sides in the culture wars, it tends to be with the knights rather than the villeins—and more specifically with the Templars, reflecting the views and values of the lawyer class from which the Court's Members are drawn. How that class feels about homosexuality will be evident to anyone who wishes to interview job applicants at virtually any of the Nation's law schools. The interviewer may refuse to offer a job because the applicant is a Republican; because he is an adulterer; because he went to the wrong prep school or belongs to the wrong country club; because he eats snails; because he is a womanizer; because she wears real-animal fur; or even because he hates the Chicago Cubs. But if the interviewer should wish not to be an associate or partner of an applicant because he disapproves of the applicant's homosexuality, *then* he will have violated the pledge which the Association of American Law Schools requires all its member schools to exact from job interviewers: "assurance of the employer's willingness" to hire homosexuals. Bylaws of the Association of American Law Schools, Inc. § 6–4(b); Executive Committee Regulations of the Association of American Law Schools § 6.19, in 1995 Handbook, Association of American Law Schools. This law-school view of what "prejudices" must be stamped out may be contrasted with the more plebeian attitudes that apparently still prevail in the United States Congress, which has been unresponsive to repeated attempts to extend to homosexuals the protections of federal civil rights laws and which took the pains to exclude them specifically from the Americans with Disabilities Act of 1990.

* * *

Today's opinion has no foundation in American constitutional law, and barely pretends to. The people of Colorado have adopted an entirely reasonable provision which does not even disfavor homosexuals in any substantive sense, but merely denies them preferential treatment. Amendment 2 is designed to prevent piecemeal deterioration of the sexual morality favored by a majority of Coloradans, and is not only an appropriate means to that legitimate end, but a means that Americans have employed before. Striking it down is an act, not of judicial judgment, but of political will. I dissent.

Notes and Questions

1. Were you surprised that the majority opinion did not mention *Bowers v. Hardwick*? Does this omission mean that the Court has firmly distinguished between the *status* of gay or lesbian "sexual orientation" and the *conduct* involved in same-sex sexual acts?

Does the majority in *Romer* think that "sexual orientation" is a term defined by status or by conduct? How may times in the dissenting opinion does Justice Scalia treat "sexual orientation" as defined by acts or conduct—including "sodomy"—rather than by desire, identity, or status? *See* Janet E. Halley, *Romer v. Hardwick*, 68 U. Colo. L. Rev. 429 (1997) (contrasting status and conduct approaches of majority and dissent).

2. Would the emphasis on antigay animus in *Romer* make it unconstitutional for a municipality to amend its charter to repeal an antidiscrimination ordinance by forbidding the creation of any "special class status" defined by sexual orientation?

3. What is the special privilege that Justice Scalia believes gays and lesbians have established after *Romer v. Evans*? How does the majority address this?

The ordinances in Denver and Boulder banned discrimination on the basis of sexual orientation against homosexuals, bisexuals, and heterosexuals. In other words, they applied to heterosexuals as well as to sexual minorities. When an ordinance bans discrimination on the basis of "religion," it is not usually criticized for creating special rights for Jews, Buddhists, or other minority religions. Why has the "special rights" argument become part of legal and popular discourse in the area of sexual orientation?

For a critical review of the framework of advocacy on this issue, *see* Karen Engle, *What's So Special About Special Rights?*, 75 Denv. U. L. Rev. 1265 (1998). *See also* Jane S. Schacter, *The Gay Civil Rights Debate in the States: Decoding the Discourse of Equivalents*, 29 Harv. C.R.-C.L. L. Rev. 283 (1994) (arguing that the attack on "special rights" for gays invokes conservative attacks on civil rights generally, including affirmative action).

4. Did the court's discussion conceal a different issue of sexual orientation?

> Bisexual invisibility manifests itself in the studied omission of bisexuality in discussions of sexual orientation. * * * This elision carries over into the law, where discussions of sexual orientation almost invariably privilege the straight/gay binary. One example among many is the recent Supreme Court opinion in *Romer v. Evans*. In that case, the Court found that Amendment 2 of Colorado's state constitution violated the federal Equal Protection Clause. Amendment 2 stated that there would be "No Protected Status Based on Homosexual, Lesbian or Bisexual Orientation." The Amendment thus took the class of bisexuals seriously, probably because the municipal ordinances it overrode explicitly protected bisexuals. The Court, however, subsumed bisexuals into the homosexual category, noting that it would refer to the "named class" protected by the ordinances "as homosexual persons or gays and lesbians." Thus, the only references to bisexuals in the opinion occur in the quoted language of the ordinances and Amendment 2;

> when the Court speaks for itself, it speaks solely about homosexual persons.

Kenji Yoshino, *The Epistemic Contract of Bisexual Erasure,* 52 Stan. L. Rev. 353, 367 (2000).

C. Discrimination, Gender, and Sexual Orientation: Protecting Gay and Lesbian Youth

In the 1970s and 1980s, courts generally treated discrimination based on failure to conform to gender stereotypes as discrimination based on sexual orientation, which they held not to be protected under Title VII. *See, e.g.*, Francisco Valdes, *Queers, Sissies, Dykes, and Tomboys: Deconstructing the Conflation of "Sex," "Gender," and "Sexual Orientation" in Euro-American Law and Society,* 83 Calif. L. Rev. 1, 138–147 (1995) (discussing *Smith v. Liberty Mut. Ins. Co.*, 569 F.2d 325 (5th Cir.1978), in which plaintiff stated that he was heterosexual but had been denied a job because of effeminate appearance). In *Price Waterhouse v. Hopkins*, 490 U.S. 228 (1989), the Supreme Court held that an employer who subjects someone to adverse employment decisions because she does not conform to gender stereotypes violates Title VII. Hopkins, a female employee who had been denied partnership in an accounting firm, could establish a case of sex discrimination based on comments of partners that she was too "macho" and needed to "walk more femininely, talk more femininely, dress more femininely, wear make-up, have her hair styled, and wear jewelry." *Id.* at 234–35. Following *Price Waterhouse*, courts have begun to apply antidiscrimination law prohibiting sex discrimination to cases of gender nonconformity. *See Nichols v. Azteca Restaurant Enterprises, Inc.*, 256 F.3d 864 (9th Cir. 2001) (holding that harassment of male employee by coworkers and a supervisor because he was effeminate and failed to conform to male stereotype was discrimination based on sex under Title VII). This approach to antidiscrimination law has opened the door to protecting gay and lesbian youth—and youth perceived as gay or lesbian—under Title IX, the federal civil rights act that prohibits disparate treatment of male and female students.

> In recent years, anti-gay harassment and violence in schools has received much national attention, with the media reporting incidents, each more terrifying than the last. For example, Alana Flores, a student in Northern California, received a barrage of death threats in her school locker because a fellow student thought she was a lesbian. Included among these threats was a pornographic picture of a woman bound and gagged with her throat slit. Several Washington state students raped and then urinated on a lesbian student on school grounds, forcing another female student, the girlfriend of one of the perpetrators, to watch because the two girls had kissed. Another California student was beaten unconscious in his high school, and his attackers carved the word "fag" into his skin. It is no wonder that many gay, lesbian, bisexual and transgendered students

live in constant fear of their classmates, unable to fully partake of the educational opportunities to which they are entitled.

Vanessa H. Eisemann, *Protecting the Kids in the Hall: Using Title IX to Stop Student-on-Student Anti-Gay Harassment*, 15 Berkeley Women's L.J. 125, 125–26 (2000).

JOAN E. SCHAFFNER

Approaching the New Millennium with Mixed Blessings for Harassed Gay Students
22 Harv. Women's L.J. 159, 159–61, 164, 171–76 (1999)

The parents of sixteen-year-old William removed their son from public school because they feared for his life. For two years, William "was constantly jeered by students with epithets like 'fucking faggot,' was taunted about wanting sex with other boys, and had drawings passed around of him in sexual acts." To make matters even worse, teachers who saw the harassment "usually said nothing and occasionally laughed." The principal's response to the problem was "[William] ha[s] made a bad choice to be Gay.... Kids will be kids."

Mark Iversen was also a victim of continuous abuse from his peers. While in junior high "he was pushed into lockers with a broomstick and called 'fag' while two teachers sat by and did nothing.... a classmate slammed a handwritten note on Mark's chest threatening 'You're dead fag'.... When Mark reported to a teacher the abuse he had been suffering, the teacher became antagonistic toward him, banned him from her classroom, and failed him." The violence continued through high school and culminated in October 1996 when Mark "was brutally beaten and kicked in his high school classroom by at least eight classmates, who yelled epithets such as 'faggot' and 'queer' as they struck him. More than 30 other students watched the assault, and many actively encouraged the violence."

* * *

* * * While no federal laws are specifically targeted to protect harassed gay students, Title IX is designed to protect students from discrimination on the basis of sex while involved in school activities. Such discrimination includes sexual harassment. The courts recognize two "types" of sexual harassment: quid pro quo sexual harassment and hostile environment sexual harassment. Quid pro quo sexual harassment occurs when threats are carried out unless the student succumbs to sexual overtures. Hostile environment sexual harassment involves unwelcome attention or sexual remarks that are sufficiently severe or pervasive to create an offensive environment. * * *

* * *

Title IX states that "[n]o person ... shall, on the basis of sex, be excluded from participation in, be denied the benefits of, or be subjected to discrimination under any educational program or activity receiving

Federal financial assistance." Congress enacted Title IX with two primary goals in mind: "to avoid the use of federal resources to support discriminatory practices [and] to provide individual citizens effective protection against those practices." Providing broader coverage than Title VII, Title IX, as the Supreme Court has declared, "is to be given 'a sweep as broad as its language.' " Title IX focuses on the protected class, providing that "no person . . . shall . . . be subjected to discrimination." In contrast, Title VII focuses on the particular wrongdoer, stating that it is unlawful for "an employer [and its agent] . . . to discriminate." Moreover, while Title VII limits liability to employers and their agents only, Title IX requires that "no person . . . be subjected to discrimination *under* any educational program." Because of the statute's broad language and its focus on the protected class, courts should interpret "under" to mean "in," not "by" the educational program. Thus, schools are under an affirmative obligation to protect students from sex discrimination, regardless of the source, while employers only agree not to discriminate.

* * *

In order for behavior to rise to a level of *actionable* harassment under Title IX, it must be sufficiently severe, persistent, or pervasive that it adversely affects a student's education or creates a hostile or abusive educational environment. This definition is derived from the Court's Title VII definition of actionable sexual harassment. * * *

* * *

The second requirement is that the harassment be "based on sex." Because Title IX does not protect gay and lesbian students from discrimination on the basis of sexual orientation, a gay student must prove that the harassment was based on sex, *not* sexual orientation. Just three years ago, a gay student successfully proved this in a widely acclaimed case from the Seventh Circuit. Jamie Nabozny suffered constant harassment and physical abuse by his peers, beginning in eighth grade and continuing through high school because he was gay. His classmates regularly called him a faggot, struck and spit on him, performed a mock rape of him in a science class, as well as pushed him, forcing him to fall into a urinal. The aggression became so severe that Jamie collapsed from internal bleeding. These events led Jamie to attempt suicide twice. Nabozny and his parents reported each of these incidents to the principal, who gave them the following response: "boys will be boys"; besides, "if he was going to be so openly gay, he should expect such behavior from his fellow students." School officials failed to enforce the anti-harassment policies to protect Nabozny. Consequently, Nabozny filed a complaint under 42 U.S.C. § 1983 ("Section 1983") claiming that his equal protection and due process rights had been violated. The trial court dismissed all claims and Nabozny appealed. The appellate court dismissed his due process claims on appeal, but upheld the equal protection claims. [Nabozny v. Podlesny, 92 F.3d 446, 451–52 (7th Cir.1996).]

Nabozny had brought equal protection claims on two grounds: sex and sexual orientation. A Section 1983 sex discrimination claim requires a similar showing as a claim under Title IX for sexual harassment: the victim received different treatment because of his sex. Nabozny successfully demonstrated that while the school officials aggressively punished male-on-female harassment, they failed to address his complaints of male-on-male harassment. In fact, Nabozny introduced evidence that the defendants laughed at his requests for help. According to Nabozny, this departure from the school's established anti-harassment practices proved discrimination "on the basis of sex." He explained that the school treated him differently because he was male—the school would have taken action on his complaints had he been female. This evidence supported a reversal of the district court's decision dismissing his equal protection claim based on sex. Nabozny's equal protection claim based on sexual orientation also survived. The court, applying the most deferential standard, rational basis, found that the defendants could offer no rational basis for permitting a student to attack another student based on the victim's sexual orientation. * * *

The Nabozny decision represents a victory for harassed gay students. Although it unfortunately does not establish a heightened scrutiny standard for evaluating discriminatory behavior based on sexual orientation, it does reinforce the fact that discriminatory treatment of harassed gay students' complaints will not even survive rational basis review. Further, the court acknowledged that sexual orientation discrimination can be characterized as sex discrimination. The Seventh Circuit appropriately compared Nabozny's treatment with the treatment of female students in a similar circumstance rather than with that of a lesbian student. Under the proper comparison, Nabozny was able to demonstrate that the school officials would have treated his complaints differently had he been female; thus they discriminated against him because he was male. If the court had compared Nabozny's fate with that of a lesbian student, Nabozny probably would have been unable to prove that his complaints were treated any differently. As a result, he would have failed to prove sex discrimination.

Notes and Questions

1. The *Nabozny* court relied on the equal protection clause. One federal court has followed the reasoning of *Nabozny* and gone further to extend Title IX protection to peer harassment based on perceived sexual orientation. The plaintiff, Jesse Montgomery, described a pattern of taunting and physical assaults including continual teasing by other students beginning in kindergarten and recurring almost daily through tenth grade. Much of the taunting appeared to have been directed at him because of his perceived sexual orientation, including "fag," "gay," "Jessica," "girl," "princess," "fairy," "homo," "freak," "lesbian," "femme boy," "gay boy," "bitch," "queer," "pansy," and "queen." *Montgomery v. Independent School District No. 709*, 109 F.Supp.2d 1081,

1084 (D.Minn.2000). Beginning in sixth grade and escalating through middle school, students also directed physical violence against Jesse, including punching him, kicking him, knocking him down, and other assaults. In high school, the threats and assaults became more sexual in nature, including grabbing his legs, inner thighs, chest, crotch, and buttocks. The students who committed the physical and sexual assaults were all male.

> One of the students grabbed his own genitals while squeezing plaintiff's buttocks, and on other occasions would stand behind plaintiff and grind his penis into plaintiff's backside. The same student once threw him to the ground and pretended to rape him anally, and on another occasion sat on plaintiff's lap and bounced while pretending to have intercourse with him. Other students watched and laughed during these incidents.

Id. at 1084–85.

Although Jesse reported these assaults to a variety of School District officials, including teachers, bus drivers, principals, assistant principals, playground and cafeteria monitors, locker room attendants, and school counselors, the office of the School District superintendent, only inconsistent disciplinary action was taken against the students who harassed him, often no more than a verbal reprimand. Eventually, after tenth grade, Jesse transferred to another school district for his last two years of secondary education. *Id.* at 1085, 1086.

The court found for Jesse under the Minnesota Human Rights Act (MHRA), the due process and equal protection clauses of the federal constitution, and Title IX of the Civil Rights Act. The MHRA's prohibition on "sexual harassment" included unwelcome sexual advances, requests for sexual favors, sexually motivated physical contact or other verbal or physical conduct or communication of sexual nature when that conduct or communication has the purpose or effect of substantially interfering with an individual's education. *Id.* at 1087. "Plaintiff not only asserted that the students called him derogatory sexual names such as 'faggot' and 'queer,' but also that students approached him and asked to see him naked." *Id.* at 1088. The sexual requests fell within the prohibition on sexual harassment even if they were meant to humiliate him rather than to express desire.

As in *Nabozny*, the court also held that the school district had offered no rational basis for permitting students to assault Jesse on the basis of his sexual orientation while protecting other students from similar forms of harassment. The court could "conceive of no legitimate government interest for doing so." *Id.* at 1089.

Finally, relying on a series of Supreme Court cases on sex discrimination and sexual harassment, the court held that Montgomery had stated a claim under Title IX. The court cited *Davis v. Monroe County Bd. of Educ.*, 526 U.S. 629 (1999), in which the Supreme Court held that student-against-student harassment may violate Title IX, and noted that same sex harassment can be a form of employment discrimination under

Title VII, *Oncale v. Sundowner Offshore Servs., Inc.*, 523 U.S. 75 (1998). The court also noted that *Price Waterhouse* had recognized that discrimination based on the failure to meet gender norms can be a form of sex discrimination. The crucial question for Montomery was whether the same-sex threats and assaults he had experienced were "based on sex."

> Plaintiff contends that the students engaged in the offensive conduct at issue not only because they believed him to be gay, but also because he did not meet their stereotyped expectations of masculinity. The facts alleged in plaintiff's complaint support this characterization of the students' misconduct. He specifically alleges that some of the students called him "Jessica," a girl's name, indicating a belief that he exhibited feminine characteristics. Moreover, the Court finds important the fact that plaintiff's peers began harassing him as early as kindergarten. It is highly unlikely that at that tender age plaintiff would have developed any solidified sexual preference, or for that matter, that he even understood what it meant to be "homosexual" or "heterosexual." [Indeed, as of the date of his deposition in this matter, plaintiff testified that he was still confused about his sexual orientation.] The likelihood that he openly identified himself as gay or that he engaged in any homosexual conduct at that age is quite low. It is much more plausible that the students began tormenting him based on feminine personality traits that he exhibited and the perception that he did not engage in behaviors befitting a boy. Plaintiff thus appears to plead facts that would support a claim of harassment based on the perception that he did not fit his peers' stereotypes of masculinity.

Montgomery, 109 F.Supp.2d at 1090.

2. Some states have passed laws prohibiting student-on-student sexual harassment; a smaller number of states specifically prohibit peer harassment of gay students. Some states have statutes barring discrimination in education or hate crime statutes that could protect gay students. But in most states, gay students must rely on Title IX. Eisemann, *supra* at 33.

> Some school districts, individual schools, and individual teachers have created and implemented educational programs that emphasize the value of diversity. Some of these programs use films or local speakers bureaus to address misinformation, confusion, and even hostility toward gay issues and people. Other programs teach students about the contributions of gay people and the discrimination gay people face. Despite the beneficial effects these programs may have for gay and non-gay students alike, the programs are usually labeled "controversial" and are subject to the opposition of parents and the community at large. Some states even have anti-gay educational statutes that ban teachers from addressing homosexuality in schools or from expressing the view that homosexuality is acceptable. Even when school board officials or members of state legislatures win the uphill battle of gaining approval for a program, they

> run the risk of being voted out of office and replaced by people who will promptly remove the program from school curricula. * * *
>
> Other schools have formed support groups and gay-straight alliances in an attempt to help gay students. * * * [However,] gay students may be too afraid to attend meetings out of fear of "outing" themselves and being subjected to harassment.

Id. at 136–37. *See also* Jennifer C. Pizer & Doreena P. Wong, *Arresting "The Plague of Violence": California's Unruh Act Requires School Officials to Act Against Anti-Gay Peer Abuse,* 12 Stan. L. & Pol'y Rev. 63 (2001) (reproducing amicus curiae brief of Lambda Legal Defense and Education Fund, Inc.; Asian Pacific American Legal Center of Southern California; Gay Asian Pacific Support Network; the L.A. Gay & Lesbian Center in a suit by Jamie Bigornia, a young gay Filipino man, against the college which failed to act against his harassers); Jenny Casciano et al., *Client-Centered Advocacy on Behalf of At-Risk LGBT Youth*, 26 N.Y.U. Rev. L. & Soc. Change 221 (2000–2001) (describing advocacy programs).

3. Were you surprised that harassment of youth perceived as gay and lesbian has been such a difficult issue under existing civil rights law? What explains the reluctance of school officials to discipline students for attacks on sexual orientation or gender nonconformity? Is it possible to effectively distinguish attacks based on gender from those based on sexual orientation?

SECTION 4. FAMILY LIFE

Legal inequality affects the ability of LGBT people to protect family relationships. Lesbian mothers, in particular, have faced the threat of losing their children when they divorce or end relationships. Domestic partnership laws began to provide some protection for same-sex relationships, and the issue of same-sex marriage drew debate and litigation in several states during the 1990s. Political and legal efforts to win protection for LGBT families has continued, but change has proceeded unevenly.

A. Child Custody

"Lesbian and gay parenting did not appear on the original agenda of either women's or gay liberation." Nancy D. Polikoff, *Raising Children: Lesbian and Gay Parents Face the Public and the Courts*, in *Creating Change: Sexuality, Public Policy, and Civil Rights* (John D'Emilio, William B. Turner & Urvashi Vaid eds., 2000). In 1972, Del Martin and Phyllis Lyon included a chapter on lesbian mothers in their groundbreaking book, *Lesbian/Woman*. "Child custody became the first lesbian issue addressed at the National Conference on Women and the Law in 1974, and later it became the first primarily lesbian issue addressed by the nascent gay legal and policy organizations." Id. at 308.

Custody litigation can be devastating to lesbian mothers and challenging for lawyers. But since many lesbian mothers do encounter custody issues, it is important for lawyers to learn to work both with the family law and civil rights aspects of the cases. National Center for Lesbian Rights, *Lesbian Mother Litigation Manual* 3 (2nd ed., 1990).

DAVID L. CHAMBERS & NANCY D. POLIKOFF

Family Law and Gay and Lesbian Family Issues in the Twentieth Century
33 Fam. L.Q. 523, 532–35, 539–40, 542 (1999)

Many gay men and lesbians have children. They have them in the course of marriages and other relationships with a person of the opposite sex. They have them, by artificial insemination or adoption, when single or during relationships with a same-sex partner. There is very little statutory law explicitly addressing the gay parent. Lesbians and gay men who are parents or who want to become parents come into contact with the law in the same way that most heterosexuals do: when they divorce or become involved in a custody struggle with another person who claims the rights of a parent and when they apply for adoption or seek to become foster parents. Over the last thirty years, as more and more women and men have revealed themselves as lesbian or gay, these encounters with the legal system have become more frequent.

A parent's homosexuality was explicitly acknowledged in a handful of reported cases going back to 1952, but custody cases involving a homosexual parent first began appearing with some frequency in the early and mid-1970s, as the women's liberation movement and changing attitudes towards divorce made it easier for all women to leave marriages and as the gay liberation movement enabled substantial numbers of gay men and lesbians to embrace an identity they had earlier been taught to despise.

When the cases first arose in the 1970s, courts applying the prevailing "best interests of the child" standard ruled both for and against lesbian and gay parents. For example, in 1972, a lesbian couple in Seattle was permitted to keep custody of six children between them, despite a joint effort by the children's fathers to secure a modification. * * * In the first, and still one of the few, victories for transsexual parents, in 1973 a Colorado appeals court told a trial court it was wrong to remove custody of four children from a mother simply because she had undergone a sex change operation and become a man.

Unsurprisingly, during the same period, cases in which lesbian mothers lost custody of their children were more numerous. For example, an Oregon case involved a custody struggle between a father and a lesbian mother over three children, ages fifteen, twelve, and ten. All of the children wanted to live with the mother and her partner. The judge permitted the oldest to live where she wished, but ordered the younger two into the custody of their father. When the younger children ran away and later told the judge they would not live with their father, the judge placed them in a juvenile detention center and subsequently with their married half-sister. In an Ohio case, a judge found the father unfit because he had once attempted suicide in front of the children, but awarded custody to the paternal grandmother, who had not testified in the case nor expressed a willingness to raise the children, rather than place them with their lesbian mother.

[Developments in the 1970s assisted advocates for gay and lesbian parents. In 1973, the American Psychiatric Association removed homosexuality from its Diagnostic and Statistical Manual of mental disorders, and in 1976 the American Psychological Association recommended against using sexual orientation as a as a primary component in custody, adoption, or foster parenting determinations. During the late 1970s, mental health research disproved negative myths about lesbian mothers such as the likelihood of sexual molestation by the mother and the fear that children raised by lesbian mothers would themselves become homosexual. During the following decades, the number of reported cases of custody and visitation disputes between a heterosexual parent and a gay or lesbian parent increased; most courts continued to rule against gay parents. During the 1990s, gay and lesbians became increasingly visible in the media and in the courts. The American Psychological Association published additional studies showing no disadvantages for children of gay and lesbian parents, and the American Bar Association opposed using sexual orientation as a basis for denying custody.]

* * *

With increased visibility came increased political volatility. Legislatures had more opportunities to debate lesbian and gay parenting. Related issues concerning children and homosexuality, such as the content of school curricula, the sexual orientation of teachers and school board members, and whether gay men can serve as Boy Scout leaders, increasingly became subjects of public controversy. The debates over same-sex marriage often included heated discussion of childrearing by lesbians and gay men. Courts today considering the fate of lesbian and gay parents issue their rulings in this volatile context. * * *

* * *

Although childrearing by openly gay men and women has become increasingly common, and although young gay men and lesbians have an increasing number of positive images and role models that allow them to affirm their sexual orientation, large numbers of adults still do not come out as gay or lesbian until after they have married and had children within heterosexual marriages. Their life stories look strikingly like those of their counterparts in the 1970s, and, as in earlier decades, their fate will be determined more than anything else by the state in which they live and the judge who hears their case.

* * *

The continuing vulnerability of lesbian and gay parents in some parts of the country was reinforced by a series of state supreme court decisions in 1998 and 1999 from Indiana, Missouri, North Carolina, Alabama, and Mississippi. Each affirmed either a change in custody or a severe restriction on visitation rights based upon the parent's homosexuality. In one of the Alabama cases, custody was transferred from a mother who had raised her daughter with her partner for six years to a father who had remarried, in spite of the recommendation of the child's therapist that custody remain with the mother. The court condemned the mother for establishing "a two-parent home environment where their homosexual relationship is openly practiced and presented to the child as the social and moral equivalent of a heterosexual marriage," and concluded that the mother was exposing her daughter "to a lifestyle that is neither legal in this state, nor moral in the eyes of most of its citizens."

To be sure, there were positive court decisions during the 1990s. A 1998 opinion from the highest court in Maryland overturned a trial judge's order that a gay father's partner be prohibited from being present during the father's visitation with his children, in the process citing similar 1990s decisions from Illinois, Pennsylvania, and Washington. Nonetheless, a review of reported disputes between gay and straight parents in the 1990s demonstrates that neither the increased visibility of lesbian and gay families, nor the mental health research on the well-being of children raised by lesbian and gay parents, nor the successes in the areas of adoption and foster-parenting have decreased the risks to a lesbian mother or gay father battling a heterosexual former spouse over custody or visitation. It is as true at the turn of the millennium as it was in the 1970s that the result of such a dispute depends largely on where the case goes to court.

Notes and Questions

1. Cases involving lesbian mothers require close cooperation between the lawyer and client. The *Litigation Manual* published by the National Center for Lesbian Rights cautions that the strategic decisions involved in these cases can have a profound impact on the lives of the mother and the children and advises attorneys that "[T]he mother must make the ultimate decisions. She is the person who will have to live with the consequences." Are you being trained for this sort of lawyering? How is it like the lawyering skills you are learning?

B. Marriage and Its Privileges

The first application by a gay couple seeking a marriage license was filed in Minnesota in 1970:

> The pioneers of the same-sex marriage movement were civil rights rebels, activists inspired by the foment of the 1960s and the fires of Stonewall. Many of the early advocates for same-sex marriage saw their struggle as part of a larger cultural upheaval. Jack

> Baker and Michael McConnell, the two gay men who in 1970 filed the first same-sex marriage case, were committed activists with a broad political agenda. Jack Baker, a "crusader with a twinkle in his eye," made national news by becoming the first openly gay student elected president of the University of Minnesota Student Association. With the marriage lawsuit, Baker hoped to "cause a cultural revolution!" He predicted that "within five years we can turn the whole institution of marriage upside down!" His lover, Michael McConnell, agreed: "We want to cause a re-examination and re-evaluation of the institution of marriage. We feel we can be the catalyst for that. Our getting married would be a political act with political implications."
>
> * * *
>
> The pioneers of the same-sex marriage movement often paid dearly for their advocacy. After Jack Baker and James Michael McConnell made the news by filing their marriage suit, McConnell lost his job as a librarian at the University of Minnesota. McConnell filed suit to get his job back but lost before the Eighth Circuit Court of Appeals. The court acknowledged that McConnell was fully qualified for the job, but concluded that the University could fire him because of his activism. * * *
>
> * * *
>
> * * * The pioneers of the same-sex marriage movement put their lives and livelihoods on the line for a cause we hold dear. Their cases, while not ultimately successful, made the issue of same-sex marriage real.

Greg Johnson, *Vermont Civil Unions: The New Language of Marriage*, 25 Vt. L. Rev. 15, 20–22 (2000).

Thomas Stoddard describes the effect of the first victory for advocates of same-sex marriage in a state supreme court:

> In 1993 the Supreme Court of Hawaii, in *Baehr v. Lewin* [852 P.2d 44 (Haw.1993)], issued the startling ruling that the equal protection clause of the state's constitution appeared to compel the state government to issue marriage licenses to lesbian and gay couples as well as heterosexual couples. It remanded the case to the trial court for that tribunal to consider justifications offered by the state government for the distinction between homosexual and heterosexual couples. The state would have to show, said the supreme court, that the distinction between couples furthered "compelling state interests" and, in addition, was "narrowly drawn to avoid unnecessary abridgements of constitutional rights."
>
> This decision was the first of its kind in the United States—indeed, the entire world. * * *
>
> Yet this breakthrough, if that is what it was initially, was very rapidly transformed into an audacious step backwards. In response to the decision of the Hawaii Supreme Court, conservative legisla-

tors in statehouses around the country offered bills to deny recognition to same-sex marriage licenses that might eventually be issued by Hawaii (or any other state). And then, one by one, states began to enact those bills—even though the litigation in Hawaii had not yet reached a definitive resolution, and no state, including Hawaii, had yet to extend marriage licenses to male-male or female-female couples. Utah was the very first to act, in 1995. In its wake came South Dakota and several other states.

The litigation in Hawaii * * * also affected national politics. It provoked a "marriage protection" rally in Des Moines, Iowa, on the eve of that state's presidential caucuses, an event that attracted candidate Patrick Buchanan in person and the support of three other candidates—Bob Dole, Steve Forbes, and Lamar Alexander—in writing. Even more disturbingly, it led to the introduction in both houses of Congress of a federal bill to limit the validity of same-sex marriages that might ultimately be accorded recognition by Hawaii. This bill, given the sanctimonious title of the "Defense of Marriage Act" (DOMA), declared that no state would be required to "give effect to any public act, record, or judicial proceeding, or tribe respecting a relationship between persons of the same sex that is treated as a marriage." The bill also asserted that under federal law the word "marriage" would mean "only a legal union between one man and one woman."

The House of Representatives approved the Defense of Marriage Act on July 12, 1996, by the overwhelming margin of 342 to 67. The Senate followed suit, by a vote of 85 to 14, on September 10, 1996. And President Clinton, despite his professed support of equal rights for gay people, signed the bill shortly afterwards. (The White House did, however, express regret that he had been presented with such a measure.)

In short, one encouraging judicial decision in only one of the fifty states—a decision that was merely tentative, since the case in which it was issued was still unresolved—touched off a national political and legal avalanche with horrifying consequences for gay people. One tentative, halting step toward same-sex marriage had incited a nationwide political riot against same-sex marriage. As a formal matter and from a national perspective, *Baehr v. Lewin*—regardless of the ultimate outcome in Hawaii—seemed a complete disaster.

Yet, while acknowledging the technical losses in Congress and the various statehouses, I am still heartened by the developments to date overall—because of their profound "culture-shifting" potential. DOMA and its state analogues did not really change the rules applicable to would-be same-sex marriages; they merely fortified the existing rules, since no jurisdiction in the United States has ever permitted such marriages. And, despite the formal defeat they represent, they helped, I believe, to herald a world in which same-sex marriages will eventually be lawful and commonplace.

The subject of same-sex marriage is novel to the public at large. Until the lawsuit in Hawaii, the issue was no more than a political curiosity, except to advocates and troublemakers like me. *Baehr*, however, in conjunction with the reaction in Washington and other legislative centers, legitimated the issue, making it fit for general discussion. Whether two men or two women should have the right to marry was—at last—accorded serious attention in the country's newspapers and political journals.

The vote in Congress was a loss. I do not pretend otherwise. But it was a loss containing the seeds of eventual victory. * * *

Thomas B. Stoddard, *Bleeding Heart: Reflections on Using the Law to Make Social Change*, 72 N.Y.U. L. Rev. 967, 987–89 (1997).

A major victory came six years later in Vermont, in litigation based on the state constitution. In *Baker v. State of Vermont*, 170 Vt. 194, 744 A.2d 864 (1999), the Vermont Supreme Court recognized that marriage conferred many benefits unavailable to couples who could not marry. Among these were the right to receive a portion of the estate of a spouse who dies intestate and protection against disinheritance through elective share provisions; preference in being appointed as the personal representative of a spouse who dies intestate; the right to bring a lawsuit for the wrongful death of a spouse; the right to bring an action for loss of consortium; the right to workers' compensation survivor benefits; the right to spousal benefits statutorily guaranteed to public employees, including health, life, disability, and accident insurance; the opportunity to be covered as a spouse under group life insurance policies issued to an employee; the opportunity to be covered as the insured's spouse under an individual health insurance policy; the right to claim an evidentiary privilege for marital communications; homestead rights and protections; the presumption of joint ownership of property and the concomitant right of survivorship; hospital visitation and other rights incident to the medical treatment of a family member; and the right to receive, and the obligation to provide, spousal support, maintenance, and property division in the event of separation or divorce. 744 A.2d at 883–84. *Baker* addressed a challenge by gay and lesbian couples under the Common Benefits clause of the state constitution to their exclusion from the legal privileges associated with marriage.

DAVID CHAMBERS

Couples: Marriage, Civil Union, and Domestic Partnership in *Creating Change: Sexuality, Public Policy, and Civil Rights* 281, 296 (John D'Emilio, William B. Turner & Urvashi Vaid eds., 2000)

In the Vermont litigation, unlike the marriage litigation in other states, national legal organizations and local attorneys collaborated from the outset. Susan Murray and Beth Robinson, law partners in a firm in Middlebury, Vermont, worked with Mary Bonauto of Gay and Lesbian Advocates and Defenders in Boston. They found three Vermont couples, Peter Harrigan and Stan Baker, Holly Puterbaugh and Lois Farnham, and Stacy Jolles and Nina Beck, who were eager to marry. In 1996, the three couples applied for a marriage license in the usual manner, and when it was denied in the usual way, Bonauto, Murray, and Robinson filed a lawsuit on their behalf.

The plaintiffs claimed that the Vermont marriage statute violated the Vermont state constitution and, to prevent eventual review by the United States Supreme Court, made no allegations under the U.S. Constitution. They relied on a two-hundred-year-old Vermont provision that declares that "government is, or ought to be, instituted for the common benefit, protection, and security of the people, nation, or community, and not for the particular emolument of any single man, family or set of persons who are a part only of the community." This clause was originally intended to prohibit the giving of privileges to a landed aristocracy, but had been interpreted by the Vermont Supreme court as a general protection against unjust discriminations of all sorts in much the same manner that the U.S. Supreme Court has interpreted the Equal Protection Clause.

The state of Vermont found itself in an awkward position in defending the marriage statute. The Attorney General, a liberal, was unwilling to argue that same-sex couples should be excluded from marriage simply because Vermonters considered their relationships immoral, but had difficulty coming up with other plausible explanations for the law. The state came up with seven possible justifications. In its ruling in December 1997, the trial court rejected six of them, but held that the statute was justified on the ground that sanctioning same-sex marriage would diminish the perception of the link between marriage and procreation and thus reduce men's and women's sense of responsibility for childrearing.

The plaintiffs appealed to the Vermont Supreme Court. In November 1998, Beth Robinson argued the case for the plaintiffs to a sympathetic court. She began by drawing an analogy to a case from the 1950s in which the California Supreme Court became the first appellate court to strike down a statutory ban on interracial marriage. She said that, in the California case, the state had made the same sorts of unfounded claims about harms to children and families that Vermont was making here, and she bravely acknowledged that a positive decision by the Vermont justices would require much the same courage that had been shown by the California justices a half century before, at a time when interracial marriage was regarded by the public even more hostilely than same-sex marriage is regarded today. The justices seemed to hear her message. When counsel for the state began her presentation by claiming that the California case was quite different (because some states had never prohibited interracial marriages while all states prohibit marriage between persons of the same sex), one of the justices interrupted her and asked rhetorically, as to same-sex marriage, "Some state court has to go first, doesn't it?" And, as the state's lawyer groped for a response, another justice asked her whether the uniformity among the states regarding same-sex marriage might not simply demonstrate the depth of the hostile feelings toward gay people in our country. It was not a good day for the state's attorney.

Thirteen months later, in December 1999, the Vermont Supreme Court issued its decision, unanimously holding unconstitutional the state's exclusion of same-sex couples from marriage. The majority opinion, written by Chief Justice Jeffrey Amestoy, rejected all the justifications offered by the state. It found no empirical support or logical plausibility for the claim that only by limiting marriage to one man and one woman could the state sustain in the public mind the link between procreation and parental responsibility. It supported its conclusions for equal treatment by pointing out that the state legislature itself had recently prohibited employment discrimination on the basis of sexual orientation and had permitted adoption by same-sex couples. In a stirring conclusion, the court declared that "The extension of the Common Benefits Clause to acknowledge plaintiffs as Vermonters who seek nothing more, nothing less, than legal protection and security for their avowed commitment to an intimate and lasting human relationship is simply, when all is said and done, a recognition of our common humanity."

Despite this embracing statement, the court did not then enter an order directing the state to issue marriage licenses to same-sex couples. Instead, in a most unusual disposition, the court held that the state must extend all the legal benefits and responsibilities of married persons to same-sex couples, but that it could do so either by permitting gay people to "marry" or by creating a parallel institution known as domestic partnership or something else. It remitted the case to the legislature, telling the plaintiffs that if the legislature did not provide full benefits within a "reasonable period of time," the court would order specific relief. One justice, Denise Johnson, dissented as to the remedy, asserting that the Court should have provided the relief that the plaintiffs had demanded.

The Vermont legislature reconvened in early January 2000 and immediately began considering how to respond. The House and Senate Judiciary Committees held joint public hearings in the House chamber attended by thousands of people. More than two hundred Vermont citizens, chosen by lot, spoke for and against marriage for two minutes each. Gay people told stories of their own lives. The children of gay couples spoke. So did many others who simply prized Vermonters' tolerance of diversity. Conservatives also testified in large numbers, quoting Leviticus, railing against "Adam and Steve," forecasting the collapse of the American family, and threatening revenge in November.

To the legislator's chagrin, almost no one had anything kind to say about domestic partnership. One side sought marriage; the other urged the legislature to ignore the court and to begin the process of amending the state constitution. Conservative legislators strongly resisted creating an expansive form of domestic partnership, saying it would really be marriage in thin disguise. "If it looks like a duck and walks like a duck and quacks like a duck, it is a duck and we should reject it," fumed one Republican legislator from Northern Vermont. Of course, the gay organizations would have been glad to call the duck a duck, but came to understand that their supporters in the legislature simply couldn't put together enough votes to do so.

In the end, after receiving signals from gay organizations that they would prefer marriage by another name to nothing at all, the House committee created an entity called "civil unions" available solely to same-sex couples and poured into it every benefit and responsibility attaching to marriage. As with the marriage statute, the civil union required not only that the couple register with the state but also that they enter into the relationship in the presence of a minister or a justice of the peace. The bill carried each chamber by a narrow margin and was signed into law by Governor Howard Dean on Thursday, April 27, 2000. The law went into effect on July 1, 2000, and along with many other couples across the state, Lois Farnham and Holly Puterbaugh, joined together that day in a civil union.

GREG JOHNSON

Vermont Civil Unions: The New Language of Marriage
25 Vt. L. Rev. 15, 24–35 (2000)

Until Vermont, the same-sex marriage movement had not had a single lasting victory in the United States. In fact, no state had even come close. In Alaska and Hawaii, voters resoundingly overturned positive judicial decisions, and at the end of the century, state legislatures rushed to follow Congress' lead to pass so-called "Defense of Marriage Acts" (DOMA). In the face of this rather bleak record, a casual observer might have concluded that prospects were slim as the hopes for gay marriage shifted to Vermont. Yet, the world now knows that the result was dramatically different in Vermont. The movement's Dunkirk has become its Normandy Beach.

What makes Vermont so different? How could the drive for equal marriage rights succeed so famously here when it failed so miserably everywhere else? It is a question on everyone's mind, and pundits have been quick to weigh in. The most common—and least imaginative—explanation points to Vermont's "liberal" tradition and its long history of storied "firsts." * * * I find this explanation unsatisfying because * * * it largely describes events occurring literally hundreds of years ago. On such a vexatious and closely-watched issue as civil unions, I doubt that many legislators voted in favor of the bill simply because to do so would uphold a long, liberal tradition.

* * *

* * * [A]s a gay activist who has seen first-hand the rise and fall of same-sex marriage movements in other states, I feel more confident in saying one thing that distinguishes Vermont is the remarkable amount of planning and coordination which preceded and accompanied the push for equal marriage rights. In Alaska, the lawyers working on the same-sex marriage case held to a naive belief in the power and primacy of constitutional rights. Ours was a legal struggle with precious little political planning or outreach. * * * [At the end of February, 1998, Alaska Superior Court Judge Peter Michalski issued a decision stating that two men who had applied for a marriage license had a fundamental right to choose a life partner, and accordingly the state must show a compelling state interest for banning same-sex marriage.]

I believe the Alaska Supreme Court would have affirmed if given a chance, but the Alaska Legislature made sure the court was never given that chance. With lightning speed, the legislature considered and passed a resolution putting to a popular vote a constitutional amendment to overturn Judge Michalski's decision. Since little grassroots or legislative work had been done on the marriage issue prior to Judge Michalski's decision, despite enormous efforts to assemble a political coalition to challenge the anti-marriage amendment, supporters of same-sex marriage were largely playing catch-up throughout the campaign.

Contrast this with Vermont, where significant grassroots and legislative work was occurring a full decade before the suit was even filed. Even though Vermont is thought of as the last state in the second wave of marriage cases, work began on the suit "well before Hawaii's Supreme Court issued its ruling in 1993." In 1985, the Vermont Coalition for Lesbian and Gay Rights (VCLGR) was formed. It was initially organized "to provide social activities for [gays/lesbians] who felt isolated in rural Vermont, but [it] soon developed a political identity/consciousness." In 1986 Vermont Governor Madeleine Kunin established "Co-Liaisons to the Governor" for gay and lesbian issues. The positions were filled by VCLGR members. The liaisons "nurtured personal relationships" with the governor and other elected officials. They sat in on legislative hearings, and "spoke up in [the] legislature in support of issues of importance to non-gay groups (e.g., Commission on Women, Human Rights Commission), thereby gaining respect and support of non-gay allies."

The "ground laying work" of the Co-Liaisons and of the VCLGR bore fruit. In 1990 Vermont enacted a hate crimes law that included sexual orientation; a number of laws were passed to protect and support those with HIV; and in 1992 Vermont passed an anti-discrimination law prohibiting discrimination in employment, housing and public accommodations. Flush with these successes, lesbian and gay Vermonters were ready to take on marriage in earnest.

In 1993, VCLGR held its first statewide conference. The conference included a keynote debate between Professor David Chambers and Paula Ettelbrick (then Legal Director at Lambda Legal Defense) on the "pros and cons'' of marriage for same-sex couples. Chambers spoke in favor of marriage and Ettelbrick spoke for giving marriage a low priority. In 1994, local advocates met with lawyers at Gay and Lesbian Advocates and Defenders (GLAD) in Boston and other "national leaders organizing and establishing strategies for freedom to marry." In 1995, still a full two years before *Baker* was filed, the VCLGR created a thirty-five page set of "speaking points" on the marriage issue. The "Marriage Speaking Points" Manual includes suggestions on speaking style and specific words to use and avoid in speaking about marriage.

In late 1995, the Vermont Freedom to Marry Task Force was founded. The Task Force established a speakers bureau; it created a seventeen-minute video about marriage; it worked with skeptics of marriage within the gay and lesbian community; it secured some positive media coverage; and it met with political leaders, including "the governor, both candidates for lieutenant governor, [the] speaker of [the] house, president of [the] senate, majority and minority leaders and important committee chairs, including [the] Judiciary Committee." Shortly before *Baker* was filed, the Task Force created a media team "whose names would be given to the news media as a source of information." The team consisted of the chairs of the task force, several gay and lesbian couples, two people from religious organizations and two Parents and Friends of Lesbians and Gays (PFLAG) members. The team met on at least three occasions to practice being interviewed. Team members "familiarized themselves with the speaking points" and "critiqued each other's answers thoroughly." They "attended [a] press conference to announce the filing of the suit and made [them]selves available for interviews."

All of this planning and promotion created a positive media buzz about the issue of same-sex marriage even before the suit was filed. When the suit was filed, on July 21, 1997, the media responded with more positive coverage. The case moved rapidly through the trial court. * * * On December 19, 1997, less then five months after the suit was filed, Superior Court Judge Linda Levitt granted the State's motion and dismissed the plaintiffs' complaint. Judge Levitt rejected six of the seven reasons offered by the state for banning same-sex marriage, but grudgingly accepted the State's argument that banning same-sex marriage "further[s] the link between procreation and child-rearing." So although the plaintiffs appeared before the Supreme Court as appellants, they could correctly claim to have prevailed at the trial court on virtually all of the state's justifications for banning same-sex marriage.

* * *

The court deliberated for over a year, perhaps because, as Justice Dooley said, *Baker* was "the most closely-watched opinion in this Court's history...." The court ultimately ruled in favor of the plaintiffs, but stopped short of requiring the state to issue the plaintiffs a marriage license. The court directed the enactment of legislation providing same-sex couples with all the benefits and protections of marriage, but the court left it to the legislature to decide whether this meant "inclusion within the marriage laws themselves ... or some equivalent statutory alternative...." The court described its mandate as "broadly deferential to the legislative prerogative to define and advance governmental ends...."

In the thirteen long months it took the court to reach a decision, the Freedom To Marry Task Force continued to build broad-based support for same-sex marriage. One group who came to the aid of the cause was women. In July 1999, the Vermont Governor's Commission on Women honored the six *Baker* plaintiffs with an award to recognize "their courage, commitment and willingness to open their private lives to public scrutiny for what is simply a civil rights issue." Women's support proved crucial after the Court handed the issue to the legislature. Women representatives made the difference when the House voted on the civil unions bill.

> Male representatives voted against the bill by a margin of 60–41, but women voted in favor of the bill 35–9. All but one of 32 female Democrats voted for the bill. And four of 12 Republican women voted for it. * * * More than half of the Democrats voting yes were women, and more than a quarter of the Republicans voting yes were women—even though women make up relatively smaller proportions of each caucus.

* * *

Support for the bill came also from another, somewhat more surprising corner: Republicans. It is true that most Republicans voted against the bill; however, the bill could not have passed the House without Republican support. While only two Republicans voted in favor of the bill in the Senate, many more Republicans voted against the two constitutional amendments that were proposed. Moreover, individual Republicans rose to the challenge when the cause really needed them. * * *

* * * The Committee took testimony from about fifty expert witnesses in addition to the hundreds of Vermonters who testified before two joint sessions of the House and Senate Judiciary Committees. The Committee's pace was so deliberate that at one time its thoughtful work threatened to stall the passage of the bill in the 1999 session. In the end, all five Republicans on the Committee voted in favor of the bill. According to Beth Robinson, the 10–1 vote * * * [which the Republican head of the Judiciary Committee helped engineer,] "was 'completely crucial' in assembling the 78–69 margin by which the bill cleared the full House." For this, the movement has a Republican to thank.

It is also worth noting that, with only one openly gay representative in the Vermont Legislature, the civil unions law owes its passage almost entirely to straight people. That is quite a testament, given the thunderstorm of protest that accompanied the bill's passage and the very real chance that some of these legislators would lose their seats in November because of their votes. * * *

Notes and Questions

1. The Justices of the Vermont Supreme Court all found for the plaintiffs, but their opinions had three different rationales. The majority looked to the state constitution as a unique declaration of rights with a strong guarantee of equality for all Vermont citizens. The concurrence by Justice Dooley reasoned that classification on the basis of sexual orientation was suspect and demanded strict scrutiny by courts. Justice Johnson, concurring and dissenting, opined that refusal to award a marriage license on the basis of the sex of the partners constituted sex discrimination.

> Under * * * [the argument of the state and the majority opinion,] there can be no sex discrimination here because "[i]f a man wants to marry a man, he is barred; a woman seeking to marry a woman is barred in precisely the same way. For this reason, women and men are not treated differently." C. Sunstein, *Homosexuality and the Constitution,* 70 Ind. L.J. 1, 19 (1994). But consider the following example. Dr. A and Dr. B both want to marry Ms. C, an X-ray technician. Dr. A may do so because Dr. A is a man. Dr. B may not because Dr. B is a woman. Dr. A and Dr. B are people of opposite sexes who are similarly situated in the sense that they both want to marry a person of their choice. The statute disqualifies Dr. B from marriage solely on the basis of her sex and treats her differently from Dr. A, a man. This is sex discrimination. *Baker*, 744 A.2d at 906.

Justice Johnson would therefore have granted the couples a marriage license rather than permitting the creation of civil unions.

On the importance of the right to marry, see William Eskridge, *The Case for Same-Sex Marriage: From Sexual Liberty to Civilized Commitment* (1996). On the sex discrimination argument for same-sex marriage, see Sylvia A. Law, *Homosexuality and the Social Meaning of Gender*, 1988 Wis. L. Rev. 187 (1988); Fajer, *Can Two Real Men Eat Quiche Together?*, *supra*; Andrew Koppelman, *The Gay Rights Question in Contemporary America* (2002).

2. Some LGBT scholars have pointed to the demand for same-sex marriage as a demand for formal equality rather than substantive equality, which would involve greater social transformation on many fronts including race and gender. *See, e.g.,* Darren Lenard Hutchinson, *"Gay Rights" for "Gay Whites"?: Race, Sexual Identity, and Equal Protection Discourse*, 85 Cornell L. Rev. 1358 (2000) (criticizing emphasis in gay movement activism on formal equality rather than substantive equality and describing the demand for same-sex marriage as a formal equality demand); Sheila Rose Foster, *The Symbolism of Rights and the Costs of Symbolism: Some Thoughts on the Campaign for Same-Sex Marriage,* 7 Temp. Pol. & Civ. Rts. L. Rev. 319 (1998) (criticizing emphasis on symbolism of marriage).

Other scholars have emphasized the positive "symbolic" value of the right to marry:

> Vermont has moved to treat same-sex civil unions the same as mixed-sex civil marriages. The state has adopted a separate legal status of "domestic partnership" that is virtually identical to marriage except in name, as even opponents of civil union in Vermont have recognized. "Mere" symbolic or expressive difference between mixed-sex civil marriage and same-sex civil unions thus has to a degree become reality in the United States.

David B. Cruz, *"Just Don't Call it Marriage": The First Amendment and Marriage as an Expressive Resource,* 74 S. Cal. L. Rev. 925, 953 (2001). If civil unions can provide most or all of the substantive rights and privileges of marriage, is the symbolic value of "marriage" still important to the struggle for equality?

3. According to David Chambers, the victory in *Baker* came through carefully crafted legal work. Greg Johnson emphasizes that, in Vermont, activists had done years of organizing including work at the grass roots and with the legislature and governor. If both scholars are right, what are the lessons for work on gay rights in the future? Might these lessons apply to other efforts at legal change?

4. Beginning in the 1970s, the lack of legal recognition of lesbian and gay couple relationships led advocates to invent a new status, "domestic partnership," which involves a public registration system for same-sex and sometimes unmarried opposite-sex couples. The registration may merely recognize the relationship or it may provide legal privileges and benefits to registrants. Domestic partner recognition programs may focus on a particular benefit, such as health care, making it available to same-sex couples as well as to married couples. By the late 1990s, "at least one municipality or county in over half the states adopted some form of domestic partner registration and many provide benefits to their employees' partners." Some states offer domestic partner benefits to employees; others have domestic partner registries; some states have both. Many employers and institutions offer partner benefits. *See* Chambers & Polikoff, *supra* at 529–32.

5. In June 2002, Lambda Legal Defense Fund sued in New Jersey state court on behalf of seven same-sex couples who had been denied marriage licenses. Groups opposed to gay marriage said that they would push for legislation to prohibit same-sex marriages, the method used in Hawaii after the *Baehr* decision. Lambda had been drafting the suit for more than a year, but "the group said it was spurred to act now after the surviving partners of people killed in the Sept. 11 World Trade Center attack often went unacknowledged by governmental and charitable organizations." Andrew Jacobs, *New Jersey Likely to be Gay Marriage Battleground*, New York Times, June 26, 2002, at B–5.

6. Nancy Ota summarizes the progress and struggles of the past thirty years:

One state has granted legal status to same-sex civil unions. On the other hand, voters in thirty-five states have adopted anti-same-sex marriage measures, including Hawaii, which once held so much promise for gays and lesbians interested in marriage. Anti-gay rights organizations continue to lobby state legislatures, and they have introduced various anti-same-sex marriage measures in other states.

Although eighteen states and the federal government protect public employees from discrimination on the basis of sexual orientation, only eleven states prohibit discrimination based on sexual orientation in public *and* private employment. Also, several of the jurisdictions that protect public employment do so on the basis of an executive order, not legislative or constitutional protection. Few jurisdictions provide legal protection from discrimination based on sexual orientation in public accommodations, education, housing, extension of credit, and union practices.

Four states, plus the District of Columbia, have hate crime laws that include sexual orientation and gender identity, nineteen others include sexual orientation, and sixteen do not include sexual orientation as a basis for hate crimes. Two states, Texas and Georgia, address crimes motivated by "bias or prejudice" without listing categories, and ten states do not have hate crimes laws.

Six states, including New York, offer domestic partnership benefits to government employees, and in other states these benefits may be available to public employees in many counties and cities or may be made available to employees of private organizations * * *.

* * * Although enforcement of [sodomy] * * * laws is not common, these and other sex laws are frequently used in a discriminatory fashion to harass members of the LGBT community. If officials choose to enforce the laws, the legal regime allows officials to impose harsh penalties, such as up to fifteen years in prison. Moreover, the criminalization of consensual sex acts is a basis for other legal consequences such as custody denials, restrictions on visitation, prohibition on adoption, removal of children from stable homes, and the military's "Don't Ask, Don't Tell" policy.

Numerous courts, including the Supreme Court in *Romer v. Evans*, have delivered opinions with a positive outcome for LGBT litigants. But many courts, including the Supreme Court, and administrative agencies continue to uphold discriminatory policies, deny custody and visitation to otherwise qualified LGBT parents, disallow adoption by LGBTs, disrespect long-term relationships by refusing to recognize them for purposes of property rights, and deny legally recognized relationships for purposes of asserting or enforcing legal rights.

The legal landscape is changing, but at the same time we are witnessing backlash through courts and popular referenda, and this backlash continues to fuel social enforcement of oppression of lesbians, gays, bisexuals, and transgender people using harassment, terror, and murder.

Nancy K. Ota, *Queer Recount*, 64 Alb. L. Rev. 889, 893–96 (2001).

The regime of local, state, and federal laws on sexuality and sexual orientation is subject to rapid change and development. Current information on marriage, domestic partnership, and other legal issues can be found at the Lambda Legal Defense and Education Fund website: www.lambdalegal.org (last visited August 13, 2002).

SECTION 5. GAY RIGHTS, CIVIL RIGHTS: ANALOGIES BETWEEN RACE AND SEXUAL ORIENTATION

Analogies between African-American civil rights and the rights of gays and lesbians appear in many judicial opinions, scholarly articles, and political debates. Justice Blackmun stated in his dissent in *Hardwick*: "The parallel between *Loving* and this case is almost uncanny," comparing sodomy laws to anti-miscegenation laws; the Kentucky Supreme Court made the same analogy in *Wasson*, striking down their state sodomy law. The opinions in *Baker* made comparisons to *Loving* in addressing the rights of gay men and lesbians to marry. Analogies between civil rights struggles have been made to support arguments against discrimination in jobs, housing, and other fields. Debates about gays in the military also use the race analogy.

These analogies invoke both empathy and logic. Implicitly or explicitly, they point to the destructive nature of prejudice and the fundamental equality of persons. They also emphasize the ability of law to transcend longstanding prejudice, recognize the human commonality of love and committed relationships, and remove bars to equality.

Opponents of LGBT rights often make arguments differentiating racial oppression from discrimination against LGBT people. Some argue that race is an involuntary status which may not be the basis for discrimination but that sexual behavior involves voluntary choices which society may rightfully condemn. Others argue, similar to Justice Scalia's dissent in *Romer v. Evans*, that LGBT people are privileged or politically powerful, and that this privilege differentiates them from the situation faced by racial minorities. Gay rights advocates have answered by emphasizing the ways in which sexual desire is difficult or impossible to change, as well as by rebutting the arguments about power and privilege.

Devon Carbado challenges the assumptions about black identity and gay identity that underlie both the claim that "blacks are like gays" and the opposing claim that "blacks are not like gays." He urges that, when making analogies between civil rights struggles, gay rights advocates avoid the dangers of failing to address racism in the gay and lesbian community and homophobia in the black community.

DEVON W. CARBADO

Black Rights, Gay Rights, Civil Rights
47 UCLA L. Rev. 1467, 1468–69, 1472–75,
1478–89, 1492–97 (2000)

In the context of the "Don't Ask, Don't Tell" controversy, some gay rights proponents argued that the military's historical discriminatory policies against blacks are like the military's current discriminatory policies against gays and lesbians. They insisted that the rhetoric the military employed to justify and legitimize the politics of racial segregation in the armed forces is the same as the rhetoric the military employs today to justify and legitimize the politics of "the closet" in the armed forces.

Several black antiracist proponents who joined the public debates about "Don't Ask, Don't Tell" challenged these black/gay analogies. Specifically, they argued that blacks are *not* like gays; therefore, the military's discrimination against blacks is *not* the same as the military's discrimination against gays and lesbians. * * * [T]he pro-gay rights employment of, and the responses of black antiracists to race/sexual orientation analogies marginalized black gays and lesbians. Both the deployment of the analogies and the antiracist responses privileged white homosexuality and black heterosexuality. Throughout the debates about "Don't Ask, Don't Tell," black identity was represented as heterosexual and gay identity was represented as white.

The invisibility of black gays and lesbians in both gay rights and black antiracist discourses about "Don't Ask, Don't Tell," raises serious questions about the legitimacy of civil rights agendas that fail to address intragroup differences. Not all black people are straight. Not all gay people are white. Both of these points seem obvious enough. Yet, black antiracism and white gay and lesbian civil rights advocacy continues to reflect essentialized notions of black and gay identity. This essentialism reifies the idea that, in fashioning a civil rights agenda, all of the black people (who matter) are straight and all of the gay people (who matter) are white. * * * [A]n antihomophobic intervention into black civil rights advocacy and an antiracist intervention into gay rights advocacy [is necessary.] * * *

* * *

The notion that blacks are not like gays takes several rhetorical forms in black antiracist discourse. * * * [T]hese arguments [are]: (1) Homosexuality is unblack, and (2) Race, unlike homosexuality, is biologically determined and homosexuality, unlike race, is freely chosen. Most of the discussion focuses on the second claim, for it is clearly reflected in and reproduced by some black public responses to race/sexual orientation analogies.

Perhaps the most problematic argument about the relationship between black identity and homosexuality is the idea that in a biological, cultural, and "natural" sense, homosexuality is fundamentally unblack. This notion has deep roots in black social and political culture, and it provides a backdrop for the emergence of the more nuanced arguments some antiracist proponents advanced in the context of the "Don't Ask, Don't Tell" controversy. Stated directly, the claim is that blacks are not like gays because homosexuality is a white phenomenon. Nathan and Julia Hare, for example, argued almost twenty years ago that there is "no[ ] need to engage in endless debates about the pros and cons of homosexuality.... [H]omosexuality does not promote black family stability and ... it historically has been a product largely of the Europeanized society." More recently, Louis Farrakhan suggested to gay black men that "you weren't born that way brother.... You never had a strong male image."

The idea "that homosexuality is something that white people 'do' [and something that Black people should not 'do'] has been circulated and reified in black communities at least since the 1960s." This helps to explain why in 1963 Bayard Rustin, a gay black man and one of the main organizers of the March on Washington, was not accepted by some members of the civil rights movement. Rustin was not supposed to be a homosexual. And certainly, as a homosexual, he was not supposed to represent the black community, that is to say, assume the role of a "race man"—a man with racial standing to articulate a political vision for black community building and uplift. To the extent that Rustin was to participate in the civil rights movement, his sexuality would have to be contained; he would have to be invisibly out. * * *

* * *

The more sophisticated, though not unproblematic, antiracist argument that gays are not like blacks is reflected in black civil rights participation in the public debates concerning the "Don't Ask, Don't Tell" policy. To a large extent, the purpose of the intervention was to critique the Gay Movement's "appropriation" of black civil rights symbols, heroes, and rhetoric. Some of those who intervened opposed the black/gay analogies the gay rights proponents employed to challenge "Don't Ask, Don't Tell." * * * [The argument made by] John Butler, perhaps the most distinguished black American military sociologist * * * reflects the simplistic notion that race is a static identity and that homosexuality is a changeable lifestyle. * * *

According to Butler, one should not compare homosexuality, which is colorblind and "run[ning] through all racial groups," with race, which arranges individuals into different groups. To illustrate the nature of the difference between race—read here: straight blacks—and sexual orientation—read here: white gays and lesbians—Butler asks the following rather pointed and rhetorical question: "Where did these people drink water during the days of segregation? If the answer is that they drank from the 'Whites Only' fountain, instead of the 'Coloreds Only' fountain, then their oppression should be seen in a different historical light than that of black Americans."

Interestingly, Butler seems to want to both recognize and deny black gay identity. He understands that homosexuality is not race specific, that "it runs through all racial groups." Yet, in thinking about blacks and segregation he normalizes heterosexuality—it is his black identity starting point. Further, he racializes homosexuality as white. Thus, his question, "Where did these [gay] people drink water during the days of segregation?" The question presupposes a white gay sexual identity, otherwise his query is not meaningful. Most of us know from which water fountains black people drank in the segregated south.

* * *

The rhetorical strategy at work in Butler's analysis is clear: "white" and "black" are deployed to convey identity (conceptualized as static and fixed), and "homosexual" and "lesbian" are deployed to convey a lifestyle (conceptualized as fluid and fixable). From this, we are to conclude that there is agency in homosexuality but not in race. Race is a given; homosexuality is a choice. Race is the noun, homosexuality the verb. Thus, for Butler, a black lesbian is really just another black person with a different lifestyle.

Butler's conception of blackness normalizes heterosexuality. * * *

* * * Butler's behavorialist conceptualization of homosexuality allows him to conceive of race as an essential category, unmodified by sexuality. * * * [Butler argues that] "Black homosexuals, like all blacks, have had a different experience in the workplace [than whites]." Although I share Butler's observation, his reasoning obscures the fact that heterosexual blacks and openly gay and lesbian blacks have different workplace experiences as well. Butler's racial essentialism ignores the extent to which the sexualization of race affects the nature and extent of discrimination against black lesbians and gays.

I should be clear to point out that my critique of the claim that "blacks are not like gays" is not intended to legitimize race/sexual orientation analogies. * * * [T]he analogizing of race to sexual orientation, the argument that blacks are like gays, is buttressed by some of the same assumptions about black identity and gay identity that support the notion that blacks are not like gays. * * *

During the "Don't Ask, Don't Tell" controversy, gay rights proponents sought to legitimize a sexual identity antidiscrimination norm by analogizing to historical race discrimination. Specifically, gay activists compared the military's current discriminatory practices against gays and lesbians to the military's historical discriminatory practices against blacks. Thus, the following syllogism emerged: Because it is illegal and immoral for the military to discriminate against blacks, it should be illegal and immoral for the military to discriminate against gays and lesbians.

In a sense, the gay rights proponents were engaged in what Jane Schacter refers to as a "discourse of equivalents." This discourse is constituted by inquiries into "whether gay men and lesbians are sufficiently 'like' other protected groups, and whether sexual orientation is sufficiently 'like' race." Schacter is critical of a "discourse of equivalents" because, among other reasons, "[c]urrent civil rights laws are held out as the normative baseline against which the gay civil rights claim is tested." Importantly, when Schacter speaks of a discourse of equivalents she does not have pro-gay rights discourse in mind. Rather, she is referring to the rhetorical strategy deployed by opponents of gay rights initiatives and legislation, who invoke the analogy to delegitimize and undermine claims for gay equality and equal protection.

Yet, a discourse of equivalents—blacks are like gays—is also problematic in the context of gay rights advocacy. In this arena as well, this discourse must be "decoded." Not only does a discourse of equivalents suggest that gay and lesbian civil rights claims are legitimate only to the extent that gays and lesbians are perceived to be like blacks or other racial minorities, it also falsely disaggregates race and sexuality. At least two consequences flow from this disaggregation. For one thing, the disaggregation entrenches the perception that black identity and gay identity are mutually exclusive categories with separate and distinct social realities. For another, it contributes to the normalization of white gay and black heterosexual identities. * * * Moreover, the rhetorical force of the analogies derived, in part, from the lack of attention gay rights proponents paid to history and social context.

To support the claim that the rationales proffered for the segregation of blacks in the military are the same as the rationales proffered for the exclusion of gays and lesbians from the military, gay rights proponents often invoke the anti-integration argument Admiral W.R. Sexton made in a 1942 memorandum to the Secretary of the Navy (Navy Memorandum).

> The close and intimate conditions of life [in the armed forces], the necessity for the highest possible degree of unity and the esprit-de-corps; the requirement of the morale—all these demand that nothing be done which may adversely affect the situation. Past experience has shown irrefutably that enlistment of the Negroes other than for mess attendants leads to disruptive and undermining conditions. It should be pointed out in this connection that one of the principle objectives by subversive agents in this country attempting to break down the existing efficient organization is by demanding participation of minorities in all aspects of defense, because such participation tends to disrupt present smooth working organizations.... The loyalty and patriotism should be such that there be no desire on their part to weaken or disrupt present organization.

According to David Smith, the spokesperson for Campaign for Military Service, a gay and lesbian coalition group, substituting the words "gay" and "lesbian" for the word "Negro" reveals the similarities between the rationales the military offered to justify black racial segregation in the armed forces, on the one hand, and the rationales the military advances today to legitimize sexual orientation discrimination on the other.

Smith's argument has more force if we examine two additional texts: (1) a Department of Defense Directive (Defense Directive) justifying the military's discrimination against gays and lesbians, and (2) a 1942 statement from the Secretary of the Navy (Navy Statement) supporting racial segregation in the armed forces. Consider first the Defense Directive, which reads, in part:

> Homosexuality is incompatible with military service. The presence in the military environment of persons who engage in homosexual conduct or who, by their statements, demonstrate a propensity to engage in homosexual conduct, seriously impairs the accomplishment of the military mission. The presence of such members adversely affects the ability of the Military Services to maintain discipline, good order, and morale; to foster mutual trust and confidence among servicemembers; to ensure the integrity of the system of rank and command; to facilitate assignment and worldwide deployment of servicemembers who frequently must live and work under close conditions affording minimal privacy; to recruit and retain members of the military services; to maintain the public acceptability of military service.

Now consider the Navy statement, which reads, in part:

> Men on board ships live in particularly close association; in their messes, one man sits beside another; their hammocks or bunks are close together; in their tasks such as those of gun crew, they form a closely knit, highly coordinated team. How many white men would choose, of their own accord, that their closest associates in sleeping quarters, at mess, and in gun crews should be of another race? How many would accept such conditions, if required to do so, without resentment and just as a matter of course? The General Board believes that if the issue were forced, there would be lowering of contentment, teamwork and discipline in the service.

These texts suggest that at different historical moments in America the armed forces have employed military necessity arguments to justify racial segregation in and the exclusion of gays and lesbians from the military. Blackness and homosexuality threaten military discipline, organization, morale, and readiness.

Given the use of military necessity rhetoric to enforce and legitimize heterosexism and racism in the military, one might reasonably advance what I refer to as "language comparability argument" to connect racially and sexually oriented military practices. The argument would go something like the following: The language the military employs to justify the exclusion of gays and lesbians from the military is the same as or similar to the language the military employed in the past to legitimize black racial segregation. Vis-à-vis race, this language has been discredited. Thus, it should have no force with respect to sexual orientation.

There are several problems with language comparability arguments. First, facial comparisons of language obscure the political and historical context in which the language is or was deployed. Second, in the context of the "Don't Ask, Don't Tell" controversy, comparability arguments about language became comparability arguments about identity (black and gay) and discrimination (racism and homophobia). Third, comparability arguments about language, identity, and experience erase black gay and lesbian identities and, simultaneously, obscure white gay and lesbian racial privilege. This erasure and obfuscation of the racial dimensions to sexual identity, helped to produce and to legitimize a white gay and lesbian civil rights campaign.

Facial comparisons of language tell us nothing about the political and historical context of the language—that is to say, when and politically why the language was written. * * *

* * *

* * * [W]hat difference do history and social context make? In other words, how does the context of 1940s America help us understand the language from the military statements justifying racial discrimination and exclusion?

Consider again the Navy Statement, written in the context of Jim Crow. The prosegregation military officials who promulgated this document were not worried about black (presumptively heterosexual) men cruising white (presumptively heterosexual) men. The concern was not about the gay gaze or gay bodies, though bodies certainly mattered—especially black bodies. Instead, the Navy Statement reflects the then pervasive notion of the black body as contaminated and contaminating, and the notion of black people as inferior. When, for example, Congressman Stephen Pace from Georgia argued, in a letter to the Secretary of the Navy, against racial integration of the armed forces on the ground that "white boys [would be] forced to sleep with . . . negroes," his fear was not about gay men homosexually sleeping with heterosexual men; rather, he was worried about black men interracially sleeping with white men. Here, *racial* penetration is at stake. Military officials and politicians were worried about the "amalgamation of the races"—that is to say, interracial intimacy. In this sense, racial segregation in the armed forces was an important part of the disciplinary apparatus of Jim Crow; it reflected and reinforced the racial logic of *Plessy v. Ferguson*; it signified and reproduced black second-class citizenship.

In fact, the military often justified racial discrimination against blacks by arguing that such discrimination was normative—an acceptable aspect of American social, political, and legal culture. * * *

Military officials and politicians understood perfectly well that integrating the armed forces would create racial precedent for a broader-based racial integration movement. They knew, in other words, that racial integration in the armed forces would highlight, challenge, and call into question racial segregation in American life. Black antiracist proponents knew this as well—that military participation, especially combat, undermines societal discrimination, especially racial discrimination. The thinking was that if black people performed a citizenship duty, perhaps they would be granted citizenship rights. In short, black civil rights proponents attempted to exploit, and white military officials and politicians worked racially to control, the citizenship-conferring possibilities of military service.

To be sure, this exploit/control citizenship dynamic was reproduced in the public debates about "Don't Ask, Don't Tell." That is to say, gay rights activists attempted to exploit and military officials attempted to control the citizenship-conferring possibilities of military service. People on both sides of the "Don't Ask, Don't Tell" controversy understood that sexual orientation equality in the military would create precedent for sexual orientation equality in all aspects of American life. More was at stake than the narrow, though important, question of whether gays and lesbians should be permitted to serve openly in the military. The debates about sexual orientation and military service, like the debates about race and military service, are really about citizenship.

* * * Because the military has employed both race and sexual orientation to police military membership, it makes sense that, with respect to civil rights strategy, there would be some convergence between gay rights and black antiracist challenges to military discrimination.

* * * Of course, there are similarities. Thus, I am not suggesting we should never advance language comparability arguments. I am simply urging caution. Facial comparisons of race and sexual orientation obscure important history. David Smith's invocation of the Navy Memorandum does precisely that. Specifically, his analysis does not attend to an important and uncontestable historical reality: The language in the Navy Memorandum reflects the military's unwillingness to challenge the racial logic of Jim Crow. In this sense, it is formative and reflective of a segregationist regime that enforced racial hierarchy. Substituting the words "gay" or "lesbian" for the word "Negro" in the Navy Memorandum obscures this racial history. More than that, the black/gay rhetorical substitution does discursive violence to black peoples' subordinating experiences under Jim Crow.

* * *

* * * [Another] problem with facial comparability arguments about language * * * is that they easily become or are interpreted as comparability arguments about identity (black and gay) or discrimination (racism and homophobia).

Notes and Questions

1. Trina Grillo and Stephanie Wildman criticized analogies between racial oppression and other forms of oppression for "obscuring the importance" of race in the United States. Although analogies might seem to build empathy and may be made in an effort to increase understanding, Grillo and Wildman argue that they can be misleading:

> The "analogizer" often believes that her situation is the same as another's. Nothing in the comparison process challenges this belief, and the analogizer may think that she understands the other's situation in its fullness. The analogy makes the analogizer forget the difference and allows her to stay focused on her own situation without grappling with the other person's reality.

Trina Grillo & Stephanie M. Wildman, *Obscuring the Importance of Race: The Implication of Making Comparisons Between Racism and Sexism (or Other-Isms)* in Stephanie M. Wildman et. al., *Privilege Revealed: How Invisible Preference Undermines America* 86 (1996). *See also* Margaret M. Russell, *Lesbian, Gay and Bisexual Rights and "The Civil Rights Agenda,"* 1 Afr.-Am. L. & Pol'y Rep. 33 (1994) (criticizing analogies); Jane S. Schacter, *The Gay Civil Rights Debate in the States: Decoding the Discourse of Equivalents*, 29 Harv. C.R.-C.L. L. Rev. 283, 291 (1994) (criticizing "discourse of equivalents" in antigay rhetoric).

Should advocates for social justice abandon analogies, or is there a way to use them that does not appropriate the experience of others in misleading ways?

2. Legal reasoning generally depends on analogies and distinctions between situations. Are analogies between different types of legal inequality fundamental to legal reasoning about gay rights? Can social justice advocates avoid making general analogies between rights struggles that may lose important particularities related to identity and oppression while still using the power of analogies to convince courts of important parallels in combating inequality? Is it possible to argue for same-sex marriage or an end to the ban on sodomy without looking to precedent such as *Loving*?

Is Carbado's call for caution in "language comparability" arguments a call against use of analogies in general, or does he also recognize the relevance of similarities in structures of exclusion and struggles for citizenship?

Are there important claims about human equality that are part of arguing for the applicability of *Loving* to cases on marriage or sodomy? Is it important to continue to make claims about the fundamental equality of different forms of love and desire?

3. Darren Hutchinson criticizes arguments that overlook the particular needs and experience of people of color and poor people who are gay, lesbian, bisexual, and transgendered. Darren Lenard Hutchinson, *"Gay Rights" for "Gay Whites"?: Race, Sexual Identity, and Equal Protection Discourse*, 85 Cornell L. Rev. 1358 (2000).

Hutchinson criticizes the effect of single-issue politics on the LGBT movement, exemplified by the endorsement in 1998 of then-Senator Alfonse d'Amato by the Human Rights Campaign (HRC), the nation's largest gay and lesbian civil rights organization. "Many individuals voiced opposition to the endorsement, citing the generally more hostile attitudes toward gay, lesbian, bisexual, and transgender equality among

Republicans and D'Amato's own conservative politics, including his opposition to abortion rights.'' Darren Lenard Hutchinson, *Identity Crisis: "Intersectionality," "Multidimensionality," and the Development of an Adequate Theory of Subordination*, 6 Mich. J. Race & L. 285, 285–86 (2001). The HRC explained that its endorsement decisions depended on two primary factors: a preference for pro-gay and lesbian incumbents and a commitment to supporting only one candidate in each race. Charles Schumer, the Democratic challenger, had an "excellent record" on gay and lesbian equality, but because D'Amato had cast votes for some gay issues and was the incumbent he won the group's endorsement. *Id.* at 285–87.

Hutchinson argues that the reasoning of the HRC is at the center of an ongoing conflict over the direction of identity politics: whether single-issue commitments should dominate social equality movements, or whether those movements should embrace a broader understanding of subordination and discrimination and engage in the difficult work of building political coalitions.

> HRC's endorsement of D'Amato is essentialist (as well as racist, sexist, and classist) because it defines gay and lesbian politics in white, upper-class, and male terms. The organization endorsed D'Amato despite his utter lack of support among persons of color, feminists, and even the larger population of gays and lesbians (who are not, of course, completely separate communities). These communities undoubtedly withheld their support from D'Amato due to his political positions disfavoring the poor, women, and persons of color; they also opposed the broader racism, sexism and homophobia within the Republican party. HRC, nevertheless, overlooked these critical issues and selected D'Amato over Schumer because D'Amato cast scattered votes for "gay" issues. Thus, HRC's position placed gay and lesbian equality in tension with racial, class, and gender justice. * * *

Id. at 287–88.

Do "gay and lesbian" issues mean issues that apply *only* to LGBT people? How can those issues be clearly distinguished, since many people experience same-sex desire or contact who do not define themselves as lesbian, gay, bisexual, or transgendered?

Hutchinson argues that single-issue political strategies effectively address only the interests of LGBT people who are otherwise the most privileged. Do you agree?

4. Peter Kwan describes the "cosynthesis" of racial, sexual, gender, and economic privileges that enabled participation, without objection, in a LGBT charity auction in which a date with an African-American man in a grass skirt was sold to the highest bidder. Peter Kwan, *Complicity and Complexity: Cosynthesis and Praxis*, 49 DePaul L. Rev. 673 (2000) Auction participants, mostly white, failed to grasp the parallel of the proceedings to a slave auction. "To call it simply racism also is to ignore the gendered way in which the spectacle 'normalized'

the depiction of racial dominance." *Id.* at 684. Kwan explains that "the cross-dressing and therefore feminizing effect of putting the African American male into a grass skirt, in an already homosexualized context," *id.*, illustrates the need to examine the interaction of identity categories and emphasizes the urgency of working in coalitions. *Id.* at 689. Can you think of examples of the interaction of identity categories?

5. How can a movement that grows up around an issue such as gay rights incorporate antiracism into its perspective and work? Recall Mari Matsuda's alternative to single-issue movements, excerpted in chapter 1:

> The way I try to understand the interconnection of all forms of subordination is through a method I call "ask the other question." When I see something that looks racist, I ask, "Where is the patriarchy in this?" When I see something that looks sexist, I ask, "Where is the heterosexism in this?" When I see something that looks homophobic, I ask, "Where are the class interests in this?" Working in coalition forces us to look for both the obvious and non-obvious relationships of domination, helping us to realize that no form of subordination ever stands alone.

Mari J. Matsuda, *Beside My Sister, Facing The Enemy: Legal Theory Out of Coalition,* 43 Stan. L. Rev. 1183, 1189 (1991).

How does Matsuda's approach differ from analogies between forms of oppression?

6. For further reading on sexual orientation and law, see William M. Eskridge Jr. & Nan D. Hunter, *Sexuality, Gender and the Law* (1997); William B. Rubenstein, *Cases and Materials on Sexual Orientation and the Law: Lesbians, Gay Men and the Law* (1996).

*

Chapter 14

THE MOVEMENT AGAINST DOMESTIC VIOLENCE

The movement to end the battering of women developed within a larger social movement against gender inequality. Most domestic violence had been socially invisible, some had been acceptable, and the efforts of women to survive and resist abuse had been unnoticed or misrepresented. The women's movement identified the role of battering in the subordination of women and began creating support for survivors of violence and seeking legal reforms. Feminist law reform work challenged widespread stereotypes about women and domestic violence and sought changes in many areas including criminal law and family law. This chapter explores the social and legal efforts to end domestic violence and empower battered women, including issues of law enforcement, the ability of battered women and their lawyers to explain women's experiences in court, the debates over mandatory arrest and no-drop prosecution policies, and the difficulties facing battered mothers of dependent children in their interactions with their partners and the state.

SECTION 1. BUILDING A MOVEMENT AND IDENTIFYING BATTERED WOMEN

DARLENE FUREY

Foreword, in *Feminists Negotiate the State: The Politics of Domestic Violence* vii-viii (Cynthia R. Daniels et al. eds., 1997)

I grew up in a house where my father's violence against me was an accepted part of daily living. My mother's one concession to this occurrence was to close the windows so the neighbors would not hear my screams. I have never been easily controlled, and my father's violence was clearly an effort to obtain such control. At 17, I escaped, going to live with my married cousin and her family. My cousin and her husband were supers in an apartment building. They offered me an empty room in the basement as a refuge in exchange for babysitting. As the mother of a six month old and an eighteen month old, only nineteen herself, she desperately needed the help and I, being employed in a fast food restaurant, desperately needed the free room. The sense of relief I felt was overwhelming, but it was not to last. Not long after moving in, I was awakened by screams. I opened my door to my cousin, babies in tow, running from her apartment. We wound up barricaded in my room for the rest of the night. When the pounding on the door subsided, and the babies fell asleep, she confided the extent of the violence she had been subjected to over the past years. I begged her to leave, to go somewhere safe. She had nowhere to go, she said. It was 1974, there was no place to go.

In the ensuing twenty or so years, I have been involved in the battered women's movement in some way, sometimes as a volunteer, sometimes as a staff member in a shelter program. I have talked with women on the hotline; met them in court, and in emergency rooms with crying children hiding behind huge plastic garbage bags that contain all that they have been able to salvage. I have heard tales of unspeakable horror and cruelty. I have wrestled, along with other activists, with the brutal truth that women are not safe anywhere, even in shelters, following two rapes that occurred at knife point within the shelter. I have seen women so battered and bruised that there was no place on their bodies to put a comforting hand without inflicting further pain. I have watched women frantically trying to get housing before their shelter time was up. I have helped women pack up to go back, carefully reviewing safety plans, respecting their decision, but silently wondering if their partners will kill them the next time. Because they do, although it is true that women are most at risk when they try to end the relationship.

On a glorious April morning, one year ago, as I stood in my driveway packing the car for a trip, I heard my neighbor, Alison, scream. I froze. More screams, three funny sounding pops, breaking glass, then silence. On her front step, thirty minutes after our daughters had left for school, the abusive boyfriend whose relationship she had severed the previous day, ended her life.

In the past twenty years everything has changed and nothing has changed. These are the voices I carry with me. I have only to close my eyes to hear Alison's screams. Finally, there is someplace to go, a refuge exists, but it cannot keep women safe or even alive. Yesterday morning, almost a year after Alison's murder, in the next town, a young woman was shot to death by her boyfriend, two days after she ended the relationship. On Thursday, he sent her roses, the paper said. On Friday, he killed her. . . .

Notes and Questions

1. Darlene Furey's story includes many elements that are common to domestic violence narratives and important to working on the prob-

lem: the lack of resources for battered women; the danger that violence may become most lethal when the woman tries to leave; the fact that shelters provide some safety but have limited resources compared to the needs of women and children; the fact that women who achieve temporary shelter sometimes return to their previous relationships; and the particular difficulties facing battered mothers and their children.

"There was virtually no public discussion of wife beating from the turn of the century until the mid-1970s. Wife beating was called 'domestic disturbance' by the police, 'family maladjustment' by marriage counselors and social caseworkers." Elizabeth Pleck, *Domestic Tyranny: The Making of Social Policy Against Family Violence from Colonial Times to the Present* 182 (1987). No article on family violence appeared in the sociological *Journal of Marriage and the Family* until 1969, and psychiatrists regarded battered women as masochists who provoked their husbands into beating them. *Id.*

When Furey and her cousin barricaded themselves in a basement room in 1974, they had nowhere else to go. "As late as 1976, New York City, with a population estimated at more than 8 million people, had 1000 beds for homeless men and 45 for homeless women." Susan Schechter, *Women and Male Violence: The Visions and Struggles of the Battered Women's Movement* 11 (1982). Minneapolis-St. Paul had only a few beds before the first shelter for battered women opened in 1974, and Los Angeles had 30 beds for women and children but 5000 for men in 1973. *Id.*

In the early 1970s, shelters for battered women opened in several cities. Schechter, *supra* at 56–57. The social climate was "alive with feminist organizing and community self-help projects," *id.* at 58, and the women who founded the shelters challenged prevailing ideology that accepted mild forms of chastisement and assumed that "real men keep their women under control;" "she needed to be brought to her senses;" or "women like men who dominate." *Id.* One of the founders of Women's Advocates, a shelter in Minneapolis, explained their opposition to hiring professionals to work at the shelter and their collective work methods: "A shelter is not a treatment center, residents are not described as clients, battering is not described as a syndrome. Women are not thought of as victims except of a crime requiring redress." Pleck, *supra* at 189. Transition House, a shelter in Boston, hired former victims of domestic violence so that the experience of the staff would remain close to that of the women seeking shelter. Schechter, *supra* at 66. By 1982, there were hundreds of shelters in the United States, and by 1989, 1,200 battered women's programs sheltered 300,000 women per year. Elizabeth Felter, *A History of the State's Response to Domestic Violence*, in *Feminists Negotiate the State: The Politics of Domestic Violence* 15 (Cynthia R. Daniels et al. eds., 1997). Battered women's organizations became important sites of political activism and organizing. As task forces and coalitions formed at the state and national levels, the battered women's movement began to shape public debate. Elizabeth Schneider, *Battered Women and Feminist Lawmaking* 21 (2001).

ELIZABETH FELTER

A History of the State's Response to Domestic Violence
in *Feminists Negotiate the State: The Politics of Domestic Violence*
5, 16–19 (Cynthia R. Daniels et al. eds., 1997)

Arguably, the most significant organization that grew out of the movement was the National Coalition Against Domestic Violence. Organized in 1978, it provides financial aid to shelters and services, shares information, and supports research. The Coalition also aims to educate the public about domestic violence and supports changes in sex-role expectations for women. In 1980, it developed an agenda that included fighting racism at every level of the battered women's movement. They also took a public stance against homophobia.

The battered women's movement and the shelters that proliferated defy generalization. Perhaps the most complex dynamic is that shelters are dependent on the society which they have been trying to change. Some shelters are more institutional because of financial pressures, yet some shelters have resisted such institutionalization. * * *

Because it relies on state money, the battered women's movement often is forced to meet the state's terms, and women's energies are devoted to clamoring for more money. Susan Schechter talks about the terms entailed in accepting state money. She calls money "the mixed blessing." While it provides training, salaries, legitimization of the cause, better record keeping, and the ability of shelters to operate continuously without interruptions, it is also a source of controversy. Money creates a split between administration and service, destroys nonhierarchical structures, and facilitates professionalization of the work. * * *

* * *

Clearly, shelters perform an integral role in women's early steps to establishing violence-free lives. * * * However, we need to question the over-reliance on service which many shelters provide, whether by their own choice or not. * * * Counseling services are more available to women than material opportunities that allow women to change their lives with a new job, and permanent, safe, housing, for instance. * * *

In the battered women's movement, women have engaged in a struggle between accepting the state's parameters and defining their own solutions. Battered women's advocates had to develop strategies to win in the political arena—to get a slice of the funding pie and a piece of lawmakers' attention. * * *

Our ever-changing political and social culture restricts the range of politically viable solutions available at any one time. Making demands of the state and developing strategies to win concessions means that women must confine their arguments within certain parameters, or risk being ignored and marginalized. Imagine that after World War II a group of women went to talk to a Member of Congress. They told him that male violence in the home was unacceptable. They argued that the men who returned from fighting in Europe and the Pacific could not break away from their war mentality and were too aggressive towards their wives and children. They asked the Member of Congress to pass a law that would require all veterans to attend mandatory anti-violence training sessions.

Imagine that another group of women came the next day to talk to the Congressman. They, too, were concerned with male violence, but did not articulate their concern the same way as the first group. They also argued that the men who returned from fighting were too violent, but they linked the violence to the high unemployment rate in their neighborhood. They asked the Congressman to create more jobs in the area.

The second group of women would be more likely to succeed precisely because their request would not upset traditional gender roles. Indeed, it would strengthen them by reinforcing traditional definitions of the husband as breadwinner and the wife as dependent. More employment for their husbands would be an acceptable solution. In the post-World War II era, male violence in the home was not considered deviant behavior, and therefore, the Congressman would have been reluctant to focus his energies there. What kind of electoral payoff would this have provided him? It might have been an electoral liability. While change is not impossible, it most often occurs within parameters that maintain masculine bias.

ELIZABETH M. SCHNEIDER

Battered Women and Feminist Lawmaking 21–24, 27–28 (2001)

The theoretical approach to battering that developed from the battered women's movement was explicitly political. * * * First, "battered women" were set forth as a definable group or category, with battering regarded within the larger context of "power and control"; physical abuse was a particular "moment" in a larger continuum of "doing power," which might include emotional abuse, sexual abuse and rape, and other maneuvers to control, isolate, threaten, intimidate, or stalk. Battering, and the problem of power and control, were understood within a systemic framework as part of the larger dilemma of gender subordination, which included gender role socialization; social and economic discrimination in education, workplace, and home; and lack of access to child care. Battered women and battered women's experiences were the focal point of strategies for change; battered women were viewed as "sisters," actors, participants in a larger struggle. Their needs for safety, protection, refuge, and social and economic resources drove the movement.

* * *

Today, some of this has changed. In the United States, the trend within battered women's organizations has been toward a service orientation and away from explicitly feminist organizing. Although many groups that began as feminist organizations are still actively involved in battered women's work, many newer groups that have organized around battering see themselves primarily as service providers. They do social service work and perceive battered women as "clients," not "sisters"—as persons to be helped, not participants in a larger struggle.

The battered women's movement defined battering within the larger framework of gender subordination. Domestic violence was linked to women's inferior position within the family, discrimination within the workplace, wage inequity, lack of educational opportunities, the absence of social supports for mothering, and the lack of child care. Traditionally, however, intimate violence had been viewed from a psychological perspective. This approach, which predated the feminist analysis of the 1960's, had been concerned with how violence is linked to specific pathology in the individual's personality traits and psychological disorders.

Significantly, even since the advent of the battered women's movement, this psychological perspective has not focused primarily on the pathology of male batterers. Although violent men are commonly labeled "sick" or "emotionally disturbed," in the public mind this perspective of pathology focuses largely on the woman who is battered. Those who are battered and who remain in battering relationships are regarded as more pathological, more deeply troubled, than the men who batter them. Some psychiatrists have attributed domestic violence to the victim's inherent sexual and biological problems, or regarded battering as related to women's masochism, a construct within which women are seen first to provoke battering and then to remain in battering relationships.

* * *

A second perspective, a sociological approach, rests on the premise that social structures affect people and their behaviors. This approach, which exploded as a focus of research on battering in the early 1980's, focuses on the problem of family violence—the way the institution of the family is set up to allow and even encourage violence among family members. Proponents of this view look at violence as a result of family dysfunction and examine how all participants in the family may be involved in perpetuating the violence.

Research on family violence further deflected attention from the crucial link to gender, and shifted focus onto research tools that deeply challenged feminist approaches. In a review of the family violence literature in 1983, Wini Breines and Linda Gordon perceived the dangers in this approach: "First, all violence must be seen in the context of wider power relations; violence is not necessarily deviant or fundamentally different from other means of exerting power over another person. Thus, violence cannot be accurately viewed as a set of isolated events but must be placed in an entire social context. Second, the social contexts of family violence have gender and generational inequalities at their heart. There are patterns to violence between intimates which only an analysis of gender and its centrality to the family can illuminate."

Yet one of the consequences of this shift to family violence theory has been the move to gender-neutral explanations, highlighting the long-standing and continuing debate surrounding the question whether women are as violent as men. Some researchers, notably Murray Straus and Richard Gelles, have resuscitated the view that violence against husbands is as prevalent as violence against wives. Spousal violence has been said to be symmetrical in its extent, severity, intentions, motivational contexts, and even its consequences. Prominent violence researchers R. Emerson Dobash and Russell Dobash, along with many others, have rebutted these arguments, saying that women use violence primarily in self-defense. * * *

* * *

Work on issues concerning battered women is now at a turning point. Some reforms have been institutionalized, and the problems of battered women have achieved credibility and visibility. To some degree, a public dimension to the problem is now recognized. Although federal, state, and private resources devoted to these reform efforts have increased substantially, they are still minimal, and the culture of female subordination that supports and maintains abuse has undergone little change. At the same time, there is a serious backlash to these reform efforts, and many of the reforms that have been accomplished are in jeopardy.

Today, then, there are profound contradictions. Domestic violence has been widely recognized as a "social problem"; President Clinton * * * brought battered women's advocates to the White House. Stories about battered women, shelters, homicides, and police and judges who fail to enforce protective orders appear in newspapers and magazines and on television and radio. Public service announcements on television dramatize the seriousness of the problem and affirm the public's responsibility to report it. October has been officially named Domestic Violence Awareness Month. There is a federal Office of Violence Against Women in the Justice Department. But the issue of domestic violence has been decontextualized from the larger issue of gender subordination that animated the movement. Elizabeth Pleck has observed that today, "as in the nineteenth century, feminism questioned the nature of the family and espoused greater options for women. Nonetheless, for reform on behalf of abused women to succeed, feminism—a controversial ideology—had to be tamed."

Domestic violence is now treated as a problem in isolation, with neither history nor social context. It is viewed as though it can be "solved" or "treated" through legal remedies or mediation or therapy alone, without considering the issues of women's equality and gender subordination. In this way, the concept of battering has been unmoored from its historical roots of gender subordination and feminist activism.

Paradoxically, it is the exciting development of an explicitly feminist international human rights campaign on gender violence that has garnered worldwide attention. This campaign, which began in a series of conferences in the 1990's and led to the Beijing Declaration and Platform Action in 1995, continues today and has mobilized women around the world. This human rights framework places women at the center, defines the problem of intimate violence as "gender violence," and recognizes the indivisibility of violence, reproductive choice and sexual equality, workplace discrimination, wage equity, child care, and health care. Consequently, the rallying cry for many feminists who continue to do trailblazing work on battering in the United States has been, as women's international human rights scholar Rhonda Copelon has put it, to "bring Beijing home," to reshape domestic violence work in this country with the explicitly feminist political and expansive social vision that first inspired the issue's advocates.

Notes and Questions

1. Schneider distinguishes between a feminist activist approach to the problem of battering and a social services orientation in which battered women are not sisters but clients to be helped. What does the difference between these approaches mean in practice?

Think of a battered woman holding the hands of two children, with $20 in her pocket, walking into a shelter. Is her situation a product of the social, psychological, and economic subordination of women in society? Or is it the result of her individual bad choices, since the partner she selected has turned on her? Do you believe that her partner was probably naturally abusive, that she probably could have controlled his behavior if she tried, or that the attitudes that encourage violence against women are part of society that can be changed? Is she really there because of a lack of resources—if she were sufficiently wealthy, could she have checked into a hotel or driven to another state to stay with relatives? Besides shelter for the night, what will be necessary to change her situation: access to social services, individual consciousness raising, community organizing, a job with adequate pay to support herself and her family, a lawyer, a psychotherapist? Do your answers to these questions depend on whether you define the "problem" as the set of needs presented by each woman client who needs emergency assistance, or as the difficult task of transforming society so that women have economic and social equality and are less vulnerable to the dangers of abuse?

Is it possible to achieve economic and social equality for women without ending domestic violence? Is it possible to end domestic violence without ending economic and social inequality?

2. Domestic violence is widespread in the United States, but estimating its incidence is difficult. People are reluctant to discuss domestic violence, and discussing it with interviewers may be dangerous for victims. There is as yet no consensus among scholars and policymakers on this question. *See* Patricia Tjaden & Nancy Thoennes, *Prevalence and Consequences of Male-to-Female and Female-to-Male Partner Violence as Measured by the National Violence Against Women Survey*, 6 Violence

Against Women 142, 142–46 (2000) (reviewing studies) [hereinafter *Prevalence and Consequences*].

In the early days of the battered women's movement, several experts and advocates estimated that 50% of relationships or more involved some domestic violence. *See, e.g.,* Martha R. Mahoney, *Legal Images of Battered Women: Redefining the Issue of Separation*, 90 Mich. L. Rev. 1, 10–11, 14 (1991) (comparing estimates by different sources, finding 50% credible, working with an estimate of 25%). One study in the 1970s interviewed all women who sought divorce through a Legal Aid office in a five-day period, finding that 40% were "battered women" and that a total of 66% had experienced violence by their husbands at least once. Barbara Parker & Dale N. Schumacher, *The Battered Wife Syndrome and Violence in the Nuclear Family of Origin: A Controlled Pilot Study*, 67 Am. J. Pub. Health 760–61 (1977).

Patricia Tjaden and Nancy Thoennes, who produced the report on the National Violence Against Women Survey (NVAWS) conducted pursuant to the Violence Against Women Act, summarize the findings of other studies as well as their own, Tjaden & Thoennes, *Prevalence and Consequences, supra* at 142–46, 154–59. The questions that show the most divergent findings and have caused most debate relate to the prevalence of intimate partner violence perpetrated by men compared with that perpetrated by women, and to the severity of violence perpetrated against women compared with that against men. *Id.* at 152–53.

The NVAWS report found that 7% of the men and 20.4% of the women reported being physically assaulted by a current or former intimate partner at some time, and .5% of the men and 4.1% of the women reported being stalked. *Id.* at 150–51. Further, 0.2% of the men and 4.5% of the women reported being raped by a current or former partner of the opposite sex at some time in their lifetime. *Id.* Women experienced more frequent victimization (7.1 incidents for women who had been victimized, compared with 4.7 incidents for men). Female victims experienced "significantly more life threats and fear of bodily injury than did their male counterparts," and women were significantly more likely than men to report injury, medical treatment, lost time from work, and other indicia of serious consequences. *Id.* at 152–54. "Nearly three-quarters (72.1 percent) of the women who reported being physically assaulted as an adult were assaulted by a current or former husband, cohabiting partner, boyfriend, or date * * * ." Patricia Tjaden & Nancy Thoennes, *Full Report of the Prevalence, Incidence, and Consequences of Violence Against Women: Findings From the National Violence Against Women Survey* 45 (U.S. Dep't of Justice, National Institute of Justice, 2000). Similarly, among adult female rape victims, more than 60% had been raped by an intimate partner. *Id.* at 43. In contrast, only 16.6% of men who had experienced physical assault had been assaulted by a current or former wife, cohabiting partner, girlfriend, or date. *Id.* at 45.

"Most intimate partner victimizations are not reported to the police. Approximately one-fifth of all rapes, one-quarter of all physical assaults, and one-half of all stalkings perpetrated against female respondents by intimates were reported to the police." Patricia Tjaden & Nancy Thoennes, *Extent, Nature, and Consequences of Intimate Partner Violence: Findings from the National Violence Against Women Survey* v (U.S. Dep't of Justice, National Institute of Justice July, 2002). Even fewer victimizations of men were reported to police. Most victims thought the police could do nothing on their behalf. *Id.*

3. Felter argues that a congressman would be willing to pass a jobs program because it does not threaten gender roles. Might some women believe that a jobs program would be *fundamental* to controlling violence against women in their community? Could they be correct? Are these approaches mutually exclusive, or could *both* be correct? *See* Kimberlé Crenshaw, *Mapping the Margins: Intersectionality, Identity Politics, and Violence Against Women of Color*, 43 Stan. L. Rev. 1241 (1991), excerpted below (emphasizing the ways in which violence combines with poverty, racism, or immigrant status in the lives of women).

4. One stereotypical image of battered women is that they have a tendency to repeatedly choose abusive partners. In Matter of Farley, 437 Mich. 992, 469 N.W.2d 295 (1991), the state terminated the parental rights of Sharon Benn, a woman whose husband had beaten her and attacked her children. Although the state later said she had failed to protect the children, the violence had usually occurred when she was absent, and the children were told not to tell her about it. She had completed parenting classes, had a clean home for the children, was divorcing the abuser, and was working toward an associate's degree at the community college. The court terminated her parental rights, clearing the way for adoption by another family, relying mostly on testimony by a psychologist that Sharon *might* enter another abusive relationship at some time in the future. Justice Levin, dissenting from the denial of review by the Michigan Supreme Court, collected several authorities to explain the destructive power of myths and stereotypes of battered women:

> It appears that the testimony of the professionals expressing concern that Sharon would enter into another abusive relationship, with resulting damage to her children if they were to be returned to her, is based on the view that "once a battered woman, always a battered woman":
>
> "This myth is the reason why many people have not encouraged women to leave their battering relationships. They think she will only seek out another violent man. Though several of the women in this sample had a series of violent relationships, this pattern did not hold true for most of those interviewed. While they wanted another intimate relationship with a man, they were extremely careful not to choose another violent one. There was a low rate of remarriage for older women who had left battering relationships. Most of them had left a marriage by going against the advice of their families and friends. They preferred being single rather than trying to make the

male-female relationship work again. *Women who had received some beneficial intervention rarely remarried another batterer.*" Walker, *The Battered Woman* (1979), p. 28. (Emphasis supplied [in dissent].)

Another author reports concerning a follow-up study of battered women that "*[f]ive years later none of the women interviewed have put up with physical abuse from a man after leaving a violent relationship.* Furthermore, they all made explicit statements affirming their determination never to tolerate physical abuse again. Even the two who attempted reconciliations with their husbands took the lead in finally ending the relationship when these reconciliations failed." Hoff, *Battered Women as Survivors* (1990), p. 241.

The author of another article, Russell, *Wife Assault Theory, Research, and Treatment: A Literature Review,* 3 Journal of Family Violence 193, 203 (1988), reports:

> "[A study of women in shelters] analyzed factors predicting subsequent abuse, and found that it was only when seeking shelter was used in conjunction with other help-seeking behaviors (in an attempt to gain control over one's life) that the likelihood of subsequent abuse decreased. [A study] of factors associated with leaving an assaultive relationship, found economic factors, associated with women's employment status, to have the greatest predictive value."

A researcher, in describing clinical profiles of battered women and the men that batter them, wrote:

> "It is too often assumed that the battered woman's personality characteristics are causal or predisposing to her being battered. This grows out of the usual assumption of abnormal psychology that a profile of symptoms composing a given syndrome represents—at least in part—causal or predisposing factors. For example, a symptom such as a hand-washing compulsion is seen as either revealing underlying causative neurotic dynamics and/or as reflecting past experiences in which the symptom was learned. The symptoms—the individual's problems in living—thus give important clues about her/his history and personality. No such assumption should be made about battered women's condition of being battered.
>
> "No one has yet presented convincing evidence of factors which predispose women either to be battered or to abide in violent relationships. Given the epidemic extent of woman-battering, it is more than possible that random factors unrelated to individual psychology are the key determinants of which women become battered and which do not." Okun, *Woman Abuse, Facts Replacing Myths* (Albany: State University of New York Press, 1986), pp. 65–66.

* * *

> "Court-appointed social workers or conventionally trained psychologists, psychiatrists, and counselors often lack the special training needed to identify domestic violence and its causes and treatment." Sun & Thomas, *Custody Litigation on Behalf of Battered Women,* 21 Clearinghouse Review 563, 569 (1987).
>
> "Battered women themselves usually do not come from violent homes; batterers do. In fact, most battered women's first exposure to domestic violence is with their husbands. Thus, violent behavior and tolerance for violence is less ingrained in the mothers than in the fathers. Most former victims of violence are extremely careful not to choose another violent man for an intimate relationship, and therefore are likely to lead violence-free lives after separating from the children's father. Abusers, on the other hand, are poor candidates for counseling, are unlikely to believe their conduct is wrong or should be changed, and therefore are less likely than their mates to break the pattern of violence." *Id.,* p. 565.

Farley, 469 N.W.2d at 299–300.

5. Another widely held stereotype concerns separation from abusive relationships. Even though Sharon Benn was divorcing her husband, and even though some authorities had encouraged her to reunite with him, she was seen as an incompetent parent because she failed to leave him soon enough. Stereotypes about women's failure to leave are of crucial importance when battered women kill their abusers. Courts sometimes hold that the women could have left rather than kill in self defense. *See, e.g.*, State v. Norman, 324 N.C. 253, 378 S.E.2d 8, 12 (1989); Martha R. Mahoney, *EXIT: Power and the Idea of Leaving in Love, Work, and the Confirmation Hearings*, 65 S. Cal. L. Rev. 1283 (1992). The next section discusses the development of expert testimony on domestic violence and its relationship to the widely-held perception that women fail to leave abusive relationships.

SECTION 2. EXPLAINING INEQUALITY AND THE EXPERIENCE OF WOMEN

Feminist activists faced a double problem when they sought to explain women's experience in court or when seeking reforms from legislatures. First, there were widely held social stereotypes about battered women and their experiences; second, there was an uneasy fit between the doctrinal categories in legal cases and those social stereotypes of battered women. Feminists responded by seeking to introduce evidence of battering in court proceedings—directly, through testimony by the victim, and also indirectly, through expert testimony. The introduction of expert testimony, however, was affected by stereotypes about battered women's "failure to leave" violent relationships. In the same period, feminists also sought to emphasize the widespread dangers of domestic violence to women and to counter the stereotypes that treated domestic violence primarily as a problem of poor, working class, or minority families. But each of these interventions encountered further resistance and difficulty.

Elizabeth Schneider explains the ways in which self defense claims for battered women encountered resistance to equality. Martha Mahoney explores several ways in which stereotypes about women's failure to leave violent relationships—and the efforts to answer those stereotypes—mischaracterized the struggles in the lives of women who encountered violence from intimate partners. Kimberlé Crenshaw describes the ways in which emphasizing universal dangers of domestic violence tended to conceal particular dangers to minority and immigrant women.

ELIZABETH M. SCHNEIDER

Resistance to Equality

57 U. Pitt. L. Rev. 477, 483, 489–90, 495–99, 505–08 (1996)

The insight that first generated legal work on this issue almost twenty years ago was that, for a variety of different reasons, women who were battered and faced criminal charges for homicide or assault of their assailant were likely to be denied equal rights to trial, that is, equal rights to present the circumstances of their acts in the framework of the criminal law. The equal rights problem in this context flows from an equal rights problem in the criminal law generally: what Stephen Schulhofer has described as the fact that "the criminal justice system is dominated (incontrovertibly so) by a preoccupation with men and male perspectives." * * *

* * *

* * * [We now know that states that have fewer resources devoted to battered women have a higher rate of homicides committed by battered women.] We understand that a history of battering, previously invisible, can now be seen in women's criminal conduct in a wide variety of circumstances, and that many women who are in jail on charges that are seemingly unrelated to battering have been battered.

* * *

* * * The crux of self-defense is the concept of reasonableness. In order for a defense lawyer to believe that a battered woman has a credible claim of self-defense, the lawyer will first have to overcome sex-based stereotypes of reasonableness, understand enough about the experiences of battered women to be able to fully consider whether the woman's actions are reasonable, and be able to listen to the woman's experiences sensitive to the problems of gender-bias. * * *

The next step was to make sure that battered women's experiences were heard * * * . [Thus feminists emphasized] the crucial role of admission of evidence on battering, first from the woman and others who might have observed or known about the violence, and then from experts who might be able to explain those experiences and assist factfinders to overcome myths and misconceptions that might impede their consideration. Admission of evidence at trial concerning battering was deemed crucial, because of the view that the social relations of domination, the history and experience of abuse, were not only relevant but essential to the determination of guilt.

* * *

* * * [T]he term "battered woman" itself is rigid and static, and implies that there is one model, which excludes women with diverse experiences who do not fit a particular mold or stereotype. * * * [T]he phrase "battered woman" connotes victimization, perhaps because of its association with the concept of "battered woman syndrome." However, women who are battered are also survivors, active help-seekers who find little help and protection from the state, with extraordinary abilities to strategize in order to keep themselves and their families safe under terrible circumstances. * * * [S]ome battered women who kill have been deprived of the opportunity to seek jury instructions at trial, or to get the issue of self-defense to the jury, because the judge decided that they were not "real" battered women.

This duality can be understood as flowing from the notion of what I have called the victimization-agency dichotomy. Battered women are simplistically viewed as either "victims" or "agents." This significantly contributes to confusion about appropriate legal defense strategies for women in a number of ways. A battered woman cannot be victimized if she is an agent or survivor; nor can she be responsible if she is a victim. Judges and scholars reflect this dichotomized approach in analyses that make claims about the criminal liability of battered women in general in totalistic ways. But women who are battered and particularly battered women who kill, are simultaneously both victims and agents. Indeed it is the very complexity of their situations, the simultaneity of being both victim and agent that makes these cases so difficult from both a moral and legal perspective. It is the more complex and nuanced situation of "situated agency" that the equal rights framework tries to grapple with in the concrete context of individual cases. However, the way that the law has developed in this area tends to make this more complex accommodation difficult.

* * *

The common and undifferentiated use of the term "battered woman syndrome" has heightened general confusion about domestic violence and battered women and the likelihood of misapplication of the law to these women. Battering relationships share characteristics which arise from the common cultural and historical roots of male violence against women, as well as from the subordination of women both in intimate relationships and in the world. However, the experiences of battered women are highly diverse and complex, and battered women defendants do not all fit into the same legal mold. The term "battered woman syndrome" also tends to shift the focus of—and the blame for—intimate violence to the woman away from the perpetrator. Its widespread use, even in common parlance, has tended to reinforce traditional attitudes about women's responsibility for their own abuse.

There are many descriptions of the battering relationship and battered women's experiences which emphasize a wide range of dynamics and behavior. "Battered woman syndrome," a term originally coined by psychologist Lenore Walker, is one particular description of battered women's experiences, one which carries a connotation of psychological impairment of the woman. However, because the term is frequently used as shorthand for "evidence of a battering relationship" by judges, legislators, and legal scholars, it is not clear in any particular context what is actually meant by use of the term "battered woman syndrome." "Battered woman syndrome" was originally a clinical description of certain psychological effects produced by the trauma of battering, most notably "learned helplessness" resulting from the cyclical nature of woman abuse, but it has been used in courtrooms to describe a range of issues. Expert testimony on "battered woman syndrome" may be used to describe a woman's prior responses to violence, and the context in which those responses occurred or to describe the dynamics of the abusive relationship. Other experts have claimed "battered woman syndrome" as a subcategory of posttraumatic stress disorder. "Battered woman syndrome" may also include a description of woman abuse as a larger social problem.

The use of expert testimony on "battered woman syndrome" highlights this confusion. It can be admitted in court to demonstrate the reasonableness of women's acts in support of claims of self-defense and to demonstrate their "irrationality" in support of insanity defenses. It has been used by courts for many different purposes, to explain why a woman stayed in an abusive relationship, to rebut common myths and misconceptions about battered women, to describe battered women's responses to violence in a general way, and to explain why a specific battered woman responded in the way that she did. However, the term and its interpretive framework have been widely criticized. Significantly, other interpretive frameworks to describe battering that have been proposed, such as "coercive control," do not focus exclusively on the woman who has been battered, but on the batterer or the relationship.

Notes and Questions

1. The term "battered woman" defines a woman by her experience of violence. Thc focus on physical acts of battering may make deadly threats, stalking, and patterns of controlling behavior less apparent. Further, women may resist applying the term to themselves. One scholar summarized the debates about the term:

> Because the term "battered woman" focuses on the woman in a violent relationship rather than the man or the battering process, it creates a tendency to see the woman as the problem. There are

> other options: at one conference, several women described themselves with the phrase "a woman who used to be married to a battering man." However, many feminists insist on using "battered woman" in preference to terms such as "spouse abuse" which are not gender specific in order to emphasize that women, not men, are almost always the target of intraspousal abuse. The very substantial psychic damage done through the experience of violence may be minimized or denied through less woman-focused terminology. Although the term "battered woman" is unfortunate in its potential for stigma, no less specific term can capture this damage; the search for different language may lose a sense of the harm.

Martha R. Mahoney, *Legal Images of Battered Women: Redefining the Issue of Separation*, 90 Mich. L. Rev. 1, 25–26 (1991).

2. There are several psychological and sociological frameworks through which experts explain the violence in intimate relationships. Elizabeth Schneider discusses "battered woman syndrome," a term developed by Lenore Walker to explain the impact of battering on women. Walker described a "cycle of violence" including stages of tension-building, explosive rage and violence, and a period of contrition in which the batterer was loving and apologetic to his partner. Drawing on psychological studies of animals subjected to repeated shocks in laboratories, she identified "learned helplessness" in women's failure to be able to escape from violent relationships. *See* Lenore Walker, *The Battered Woman Syndrome* 86–87, 95 (1984).

Other experts have, in contrast, emphasized the batterer's controlling behavior or the woman's attempts at resistance and problem-solving. Evan Stark focuses on "coercive control" as a model for understanding domestic violence and its effects, emphasizing the abuse of power as well as physical abuse in the relationship. Evan Stark, *Re-Presenting Woman Battering: From Battered Woman Syndrome to Coercive Control*, 58 Alb. L. Rev. 973 (1995). Mary Ann Dutton proposed "a redefinition of battered woman syndrome in three ways:" by describing the subject of psychological expertise as "expert testimony on battered women's experiences" rather than "battered woman syndrome"; by framing testimony about battered women's experiences "within the overall social context that is essential for explaining battered women's responses to violence"; and by incorporating into the evaluation and testimony about battered women's psychological reactions to violence the "diverse range of traumatic reactions described in the scientific literature," and not limiting psychological expertise to "an examination of learned helplessness, PTSD, or any other single reaction or 'profile.'" Mary Ann Dutton, *Understanding Women's Responses to Domestic Violence: A Redefinition of Battered Woman Syndrome,* 21 Hofstra L. Rev. 1191 (1993). Dutton outlines four key components of the woman's experience that should be analyzed by the expert witness: a) the cumulative history of violence and abuse; b) the woman's psychological reactions to the batterer's violence; c) the strategies that the battered woman used or did not use in response to prior violence and abuse, and the consequences of those strategies; and d) the contextual factors that influenced both the battered woman's strategies for responses to prior violence and her psychological reactions. *Id. See also* Mary Ann Dutton, *Empowering and Healing the Battered Woman: A Model for Assessment and Intervention* (1992).

3. Holly Maguigan analyzed the appellate cases on battered women who killed in self defense and disproved two stereotypes about cases involving battered women who kill their abusers. The first was a widespread belief that most such killings arose in a "nonconfrontational" setting—for example, when the man was asleep. Maguigan found that at least 75% of the cases involved situations where battered women killed during an ongoing attack or under an imminent threat. The second assumption was that the existing law of self-defense could not accommodate cases of battered women who kill their batterers, and that the basic criminal law of self defense must be rewritten to accommodate the context of battering. Maguigan found instead that self-defense law was being poorly applied to battered women at trial, and that these cases were frequently reversed on appeal. Expert testimony that provided evidence about the social context of battering had been excluded by trial judges; also, judges had failed to instruct juries adequately on the law of self defense. *See* Holly Maguigan, *Battered Women and Self-Defense: Myths and Misconceptions in Current Reform Proposals,*140 U. Pa. L. Rev. 379 (1991).

4. There are nearly 40,000 women in prison in the United States, and approximately 2,000 of these women have been convicted for killing a husband, ex-husband, or boyfriend. Of those women, "a number of studies have concluded that at least forty-five percent and perhaps as many as ninety-seven percent were abused by the person they killed." Schneider, *Resistance to Equality*, 519–20.

> It is not known exactly how many of these women may not have even gone to trial, consenting to plea bargain arrangements on the advice of attorneys who were unaware of the fact that their clients were battered and the role battering may have played in their cases, or who were ignorant of the possible legal significance of evidence of battering. Of those who did go to trial, many may have received unfair trials, either because of attorney ineffectiveness or judicial error in applying the law where evidence of battering was present. * * *

Id. at 520.

Through executive clemency, the head of a state can commute sentences or pardon convicted offenders. *See* Linda L. Ammons, *Discretionary Justice: A Legal And Policy Analysis of a Governor's Use of The Clemency Power in The Cases of Incarcerated Battered Women*, 3 J. L. & Pol'y 1 (1994) (describing clemency process and the role of executive clemency). A movement for clemency for battered women emerged in response to inequality manifested in trials of battered women who killed their abusers, particularly in resistance to the admission of expert testimony on domestic violence and ineffective assistance from counsel who did not understand domestic violence issues.

> National recognition of what has been called the "clemency movement" occurred in October 1990, when the former Governor of Ohio, Richard Celeste, issued a mass clemency of twenty-five battered women who had been convicted of killing or assaulting their batterers, just before he left office. * * * By 1993, governors in seven states * * * had granted clemency to thirty-eight formerly battered women convicted of killing or assaulting their batterers. At least twenty-six states have since set up committees to review the cases of incarcerated battered women. In recent years, however, the trend toward granting clemency to battered women appears to have slowed. * * *

Schneider, *Resistance to Equality*, 519.

Law students were involved in clemency efforts in several states. *See, e.g.*, Cynthia Grant Bowman & Eden Kusmiersky, *Praxis and Pedagogy: Domestic Violence*, 32 Loy. L.A. L. Rev. 719 (1999) (describing course taught at Northwestern University School of Law in 1993, in which the students brought clemency petitions on behalf of women incarcerated in Illinois prisons for having killed their abusers, and which included an activist component drawing on professor's involvement in domestic violence movement); Jacqueline St. Joan & Nancy Ehrenreich, *Putting Theory into Practice: A Battered Women's Clemency Clinic*, 8 Clinical L. Rev. 171 (2001) (describing clemency clinic at Denver University School of Law and experience of student attorneys and professors with the clemency process).

MARTHA R. MAHONEY

Victimization or Oppression? Women's Lives, Violence, and Agency in *The Public Nature of Private Violence: The Discovery of Domestic Abuse*, 59, 60–61, 63–64, 73–79 (Martha Albertson Fineman & Roxanne Mykitiuk eds., 1994)

All work with subordinated people confronts, at least to some extent, the challenge of analyzing structures of oppression while including an account of the resistance, struggles, and achievements of the oppressed. * * *

Women live under conditions of unequal personal and systemic power that affect all aspects of our lives. On this uneven terrain, we find whatever we achieve of love, productivity, and resources to care for ourselves and our dependents. The experience of structural inequality is, for each woman, the experience of her life: race and culture, sexuality, work and family are aspects of her life, struggles, and consciousness. When women work for wages, our lives as workers are shaped not only by the workplace but by the needs of our children, the social assignment of household care to women, and the power structures of our intimate relationships. The unmarked backdrop at work and at home is an absence of rights to either shelter or employment.

Violence at the hands of intimate partners, a relatively common event for women, is experienced in this context of love and responsibility, work and obligation, commitment and uncertainty. * * * Women's responses to battering are shaped by the needs, struggles, and commitments of our lives. Our previous experiences, the batterers' quest for control, and the inevitable social context of power are all crucial factors in our decisions about relationships.

Social stereotypes and cultural expectations about the behavior of battered women help to hide women's acts of resistance and struggle. Both law and popular culture tend to equate agency in battered women with separation from the relationship. Women who seek love and survival for ourselves and our families are treated as if our only choices are to "stay" or "leave." Staying is a socially suspect choice—often perceived as acceptance of violence—though "leaving" is often unsafe. In fact, women often assert ourselves by attempting to work out relationships without battering. Separation assault, the violent and sometimes lethal attack on a woman's attempt to leave a relationship, proves that the power and control quest of the batterer often continues after the woman's decision to leave. The prevalent social focus on leaving conceals the nature of domestic violence as a struggle for control, pretends away the extreme dangers of separation, and hides the interaction of social structures that oppress women.

* * *

I agree with [Elizabeth] Schneider's concern [that emphasizing helplessness and victimization creates problems for battered women.] * * * Even when feminists do not emphasize helplessness and passivity in battered women, courts have imposed the cultural stereotypes held by judges, social workers, and other legal actors to recreate concepts of battered women as victims without agency. Even when battered women energetically seek to protect themselves and their children, their actions are often misinterpreted as pathological or incompetent.

* * *

Why is it so difficult to see both agency and oppression in the lives of women? Why did society and law respond to a movement against battering with a concept of "battered woman" that defined the woman by the harm that had been done to her? I have come to believe that the problem lies in part in prevailing social and legal concepts of agency. In our society, agency and victimization are each known by the absence of the other: you are an agent if you are not a victim, and you are a victim if you are in no way an agent. In this concept, agency does not mean acting for oneself under conditions of oppression; it means *being without oppression*, either having ended oppression or never having experienced it at all. This all-agent or all-victim conceptual dichotomy will not be easy to escape or transform.

* * *

When women experience violence in intimate relationships, we assert ourselves in a variety of ways. We attempt to change the situation and improve the relationship; we seek help formally or informally from friends, family, or organizations; we flee temporarily and make return conditional upon assurances of care and safety; we break off relationships. Continuing the relationship may therefore be part of a pattern of resistance to violence on the part of the woman.

On the other hand, a woman may continue the relationship because of uncertainty about other options or her ability to subsist or care for dependents, because of depression and dislocation that come with intimate loss and harm, or because she is afraid that leaving will trigger lethal danger—because, essentially, she is held captive. When a woman encounters the grave lethality that characterizes some batterers, survival is her primary concern; resistance becomes the project of staying alive, which will *only* involve flight when it seems either possible or safer than staying. The physical acts and relocations which are summarized in the concepts of "staying" or "leaving" therefore do not necessarily support conclusions about whether a woman is functioning as an agent in her life.

Discussions of domestic violence often treat "staying" as identical with victimization. * * *

Assumptions about staying and leaving, and the concepts of agency and victimization that underlie them, need to be challenged and transformed. But women's lives intersect the legal system at moments of great urgency, when remaking social expectation is too large a task. We therefore explain "failure" to leave rather than attempting to reckon with all the ways women struggle to protect themselves and assert themselves in abusive situations. This concedes a concept of agency that is doubly misleading: its individualism fails to describe the multiple responsibilities women face, and its pretense that women are free actors *after* separation is contradicted by frequent news reports of women attacked and killed by former partners.

* * *

Violence usually begins after a woman has made a deep investment of her love, energy, and self into the relationship. Violence often begins after marriage, sometimes during pregnancy. The first incident of violence is *always* a surprise, a departure from what went before either absolutely (he never showed this kind of temper before) or at least qualitatively (he was angry before, but never angry in this way.) Violence and coercion are not committed by someone the woman calls a "batterer," but by her lover, husband, or partner—often, the father of her children. Deciding whether a loved one must be redefined as a "batterer" raises questions about the deepest structures of the woman's intimate life, her safety, and needs of her children. This decision can be particularly difficult because society vests in women a great deal of responsibility for the relationship between children and their fathers. * * *

* * *

Relationships involve many incidents of betrayal of trust, negotiations of solutions, and attempts to rebuild and continue. Many (perhaps most) relationships also involve abuses of male power. Yet social expectations and many legal standards impose on the battered woman an obligation to leave that is not present in other abusive circumstances. If a woman's husband pushes her to the floor and tells her he just had an affair with her best friend, it is not clear which betrayal will be more painful to her or which will seem the greater danger to the relationship. If she tries to change his behavior—tells him to stop, seek counseling, and extracts assurances from him—and later he is unfaithful again, friends and family will probably comfort her: Well, you tried to work it out. If he hits her again, however, and violates his promises to stop, people will ask: Why didn't you leave? Love is an acceptable reason for trying to work out infidelity, but women who love their partners and hope to get them to stop battering are treated as crazy or masochistic.

* * *

The question "why didn't you leave?" implies that exit is always the appropriate response to violence, and tends to hide all the things women actually do to cope with violence and to resist the batterer's quest for control. This "shopworn question" implicitly asserts both that leaving is possible and that it will bring safety. In truth, either staying or leaving are often dangerous acts for women. * * *

The categories of "staying" and "leaving" collapse women's actions into categories that hide many acts of self-assertion. A woman might tell her partner to stop, seeking counseling, make him promise not to do it again. But these acts of agency are subsumed into the category of "staying" and seen as a problematic failure to leave. A woman whose partner is violent may go stay with family of friends, or take formal or informal shelter, for a few days. Retrospectively, this will also be categorized as "staying" with a batterer because the separation was only temporary. Legal and social inquiry then turn to investigation of "staying" as a problem, rather than giving attention to the help and support a battered woman needs to effectuate her goals.

If the woman succeeds in continuing the relationship without further violence—if he does not hurt her again—no one will know it. She disappears from the radar screen: no shelter requests, no emergency calls, no police reports. This will be defined socially as a normal relationship, regardless of whether other forms of control and nonphysical abuse continue. There will seldom be inquiries about past histories of violence in any relationship that does not present itself as currently violent. If anyone does interview this woman, she will appear as a successful strategist. She will be seen as an agent in her life if his violence has stopped *even if these same acts in another woman would be called "staying" and treated as lack of agency.*

Women's successes at ending violence are virtually invisible, perpetuating the concept that "staying" is irrational. * * * [Studies of the recurrence of violence show that 27% of women who reunite with batterers experience violence within six weeks, and 57% within six months—but they also reveal that more than 40% of women report no violence for six months after returning to a relationship.]

* * *

In an original and thoughtful study, Lee Bowker interviewed women who had "solved the problem of violence" without leaving their relationships. He asked these women to describe their experience in detail and had them describe the strategies they used when their husbands became violent. The women had threatened divorce, sought formal and informal help, left temporarily, hidden, and fought back. Some had complied with the batterer's demands to avoid further confrontations, and some tried to persuade the men to change. Bowker found that certain strategies had been more effective than others at stopping violence. More than half the husbands had ended their violence either from fear of divorce or from desire to rebuild and regain a relationship.

The women in Bowker's study are the success stories that become invisible in studies of recurrent violence. Their action tracked the actions of many battered women. Of course, at the moment those women decided to give their partners one more chance, they actually had no way to know if they would ever be praised for strategizing or treated as dysfunctional for "staying." Women who "succeed" in stopping violence without permanently leaving the relationship have made decisions that are not treated as legitimate or intelligent in women who "fail" to halt the violence of their lovers. Inside the framework imposed by the question "why didn't she leave," women become socially defined as strong or weak depending on what their batterers do next.

The social insistence that the woman should leave treats the actions women often take as illegitimate unless those actions succeed in stopping violence. * * * This view actually *increases inequality* by stripping legitimacy and social respect from the very things most women do.

* * * Failure to exit is often treated, in law and elsewhere in society, as evidence against the woman's account of the facts, her competence, even her honesty. Either the abuse never happened (if it really happened, she would have left), or it was not severe (if things were that bad, she would have left)—and in either instance, her veracity is subject to challenge. In custody evaluations, when a woman's account of violence is not believed, she may be regarded as manipulative or disruptive of the parental relationship of the children's father by the professional performing the assessment.

When it is clear that violence actually has occurred, but leaving is considered the appropriate act of agency by the woman, failure to exit becomes an indication that something is wrong with the battered woman. * * * A woman's lack of resources becomes an explanation for "failure to leave," when in fact all her choices, including the relationship she forged, the compromises she has made in the past, and her decisions after physical abuse begins, have been affected by the lack of social rights to a job, income, child care, and housing.

* * *

Violence does not end when a woman decides to leave a relationship. The recognition of danger is essential to challenging the equation of agency with exit from violent relationships. Separation assault is the violent attack on a woman's body and volition by which a batterer seeks to keep her from leaving, force her to return, or retaliate against her departure. These attacks take place when the batterer feels his control eroding. The most dangerous moment may come when a woman makes a decision to leave, at the moment she actually walks out, or shortly after she has left. Because the key issue is control, flight might even create a temporarily enhanced sense of power in the batterer, which would turn to loss of control (and acts of violence to reassert control) later, when the woman refused to return and began building a new life.

Separation assault is an easy concept to grasp. Reports of women killed by ex-partners appear regularly in local newspapers all over the country. We recognize this attack instinctively: this is what most orders for protection seek to prevent, and the reason most shelters have secret addresses and telephone numbers. * * *

Separation is often the moment when the batterer's quest for control becomes lethal. One study of interspousal homicide found that more than half of the men who killed their wives did so after the partners had separated. * * * Close examination of police reports and supplementary records reveals that many more women are killed by former partners than are reported in police or FBI statistics. One author estimates that more than half of the women who leave abusive relationships are followed, harassed, or further attacked after separation.

Identifying separation assault helps * * * [demonstrate] both oppression and resistance in battered women. * * *

Notes and Questions

1. Advocates working with battered women often emphasize women's struggles and resourcefulness, describing women as "survivors" rather than "victims." In ironic contrast to theories of "learned helplessness" in battered women, Edward Gondolf and Ellen Fisher describe "learned helplessness" among the helping professions as a phenomenon which occurs when a systemic lack of resources gives rise to the inability of professionals to meet the needs of battered woman, resulting in the erosion of hope and initiative among professionals. Edward N. Gondolf & Ellen R. Fisher, *Battered Women as Survivors: An Alternative to Treating Learned Helplessness* 22–23, 99 (1988).

If "women's lives intersect the legal system at moments of great urgency, when remaking social expectation is too large a task," as Mahoney claims, how can stereotypes about battered women be transformed into understanding of how women confront violence and subordination? Training and education are crucially important for judges, social workers, and other decision makers throughout the civil and criminal justice systems, including for attorneys who work in the fields of family law, child custody, and criminal defense and prosecution. *See, e.g.*, Kathleen Waits, *Battered Women and Family Lawyers: The Need for an Identification Protocol,* 58 Alb. L. Rev. 1027 (1995) (discussing the need for lawyers to identify battered women among their clients and the ongoing need to train lawyers about battering).

2. Asking why women failed to leave a relationship implies that, if women had left, they would have been safe. Recognizing that separation can be dangerous revealed special issues in legal processes such as divorce and custody disputes. *See, e.g.,* Barbara J. Hart, *Gentle Jeopardy: The Further Endangerment of Battered Women and Children in Custody Mediation*, 7 Mediation Q. 317, 324 (1990) (noting study finding that up to three-quarters of domestic assaults occur after the victim has left the batterer). On particular issues facing battered mothers and their children, *see* section 5.

3. Opinion polls suggest that "tolerance for gender-based violence has decreased significantly" in recent years, and feminist activism has achieved "a considerable shift in public consciousness with regard to the problem of violence against women." Beth E. Richie, *A Black Feminist Reflection on the Antiviolence Movement*, 25 Signs: Journal of Women in Culture and Society 1133, 1134 (2000).

> Arguably, a critical dimension of the public awareness campaign * * * is the assertion that violence against women is a common experience, that any woman or child can be the victim of gender violence. In fact, many of us who do training, public speaking, teaching, and writing on violence against women traditionally begin our presentations by saying, "It can happen to anyone." This notion has become a powerful emblem of our rhetoric and, some would argue, the basis of our mainstream success. Indeed, many people in this country finally understand that they and their children, mothers, sisters, coworkers, and neighbors can be victimized by gender violence—that it really *can* happen to anyone.

Id. This reflects a strategic attempt by early activists to resist "the stigmatization of race and class commonly associated with mainstream responses to social problems" and helped foster "an analysis of women's vulnerability as both profound and persistent, rather than as particular to any racial/ethnic community, socioeconomic position, religious group, or station in life." *Id.*

Kimberlé Crenshaw argues that the efforts to show that violence is a problem that affects all women tended to hide the ways in which violence combines with poverty, racism, or immigrant status in the lives of women:

KIMBERLÉ CRENSHAW

Mapping the Margins: Intersectionality, Identity Politics, and Violence Against Women of Color
43 Stan. L. Rev. 1241, 1244–46, 1252–53, 1255–61 (1991)

In an earlier article, I used the concept of intersectionality to denote the various ways in which race and gender interact to shape the multiple dimensions of Black women's employment experiences. [Kimberlé Crenshaw, *Demarginalizing the Intersection of Race and Sex*, 1989 U. Chi. Legal F. 139.] My objective there was to illustrate that many of the experiences Black women face are not subsumed within the traditional boundaries of race or gender discrimination as these boundaries are currently understood, and that the intersection of racism and sexism factors into Black women's lives in ways that cannot be captured wholly by looking at the race or gender dimensions of those experiences separately. I build on those observations here by exploring the various ways in which race and gender intersect in shaping structural, political, and representational aspects of violence against women of color.

* * *

I observed the dynamics of structural intersectionality during a brief field study of battered women's shelters located in minority communities in Los Angeles. In most cases, the physical assault that leads women to these shelters is merely the most immediate manifestation of the subordination they experience. Many women who seek protection are unemployed or underemployed, and a good number of them are poor. Shelters serving these women cannot afford to address only the violence inflicted by the batterer; they must also confront the other multilayered and routinized forms of domination that often converge in these women's lives, hindering their ability to create alternatives to the abusive relationships that brought them to shelters in the first place. Many women of color, for example, are burdened by poverty, child care responsibilities, and the lack of job skills. These burdens, largely the consequence of gender and class oppression, are then compounded by the racially discriminatory employment and housing practices women of color often face, as well as by the disproportionately high unemployment among people of color that makes battered women of color less able to depend on the support of friends and relatives for temporary shelter.

* * *

That the political interests of women of color are obscured and sometimes jeopardized by political strategies that ignore or suppress intersectional issues is illustrated by my experiences in gathering information for this article. I attempted to review Los Angeles Police Department statistics reflecting the rate of domestic violence interventions by precinct because such statistics can provide a rough picture of arrests by racial group, given the degree of racial segregation in Los Angeles. L.A.P.D., however, would not release the statistics. A representative explained that one reason the statistics were not released was that domestic violence activists both within and outside the Department feared that statistics reflecting the extent of domestic violence in minority communities might be selectively interpreted and publicized so as to undermine long-term efforts to force the Department to address domestic violence as a serious problem. I was told that activists were worried that the statistics might permit opponents to dismiss domestic violence as a minority problem and, therefore, not deserving of aggressive action.

The informant also claimed that representatives from various minority communities opposed the release of the statistics. They were concerned, apparently, that the data would unfairly represent Black and Brown communities as unusually violent, potentially reinforcing stereotypes that might be used in attempts to justify oppressive police tactics and other discriminatory practices. These misgivings are based on the familiar and not unfounded premise that certain minority groups—especially Black men—have already been stereotyped as uncontrollably violent. Some worry that attempts to make domestic violence an object of political action may only serve to confirm such stereotypes and undermine efforts to combat negative beliefs about the Black community.

This account sharply illustrates how women of color can be erased by the strategic silences of antiracism and feminism. The political priorities of both were defined in ways that suppressed information that could have facilitated attempts to confront the problem of domestic violence in communities of color.

Within communities of color, efforts to stem the politicization of domestic violence are often grounded in attempts to maintain the integrity of the community. The articulation of this perspective takes different forms. Some critics allege that feminism has no place within communities of color, that the issues are internally divisive, and that they represent the migration of white women's concerns into a context in which they are not only irrelevant but also harmful. At its most extreme, this rhetoric denies that gender violence is a problem in the community and characterizes any effort to politicize gender subordination as itself a community problem. * * *

* * * The recourse to violence to resolve conflicts establishes a dangerous pattern for children raised in such environments and contributes to many other pressing problems. It has been estimated that nearly forty percent of all homeless women and children have fled violence in the home, and an estimated sixty-three percent of young men between the ages of eleven and twenty who are imprisoned for homicide have killed their mothers' batterers. And yet, while gang violence, homicide, and other forms of Black-on-Black crime have increasingly been discussed within African-American politics, patriarchal ideas about gender and power preclude the recognition of domestic violence as yet another compelling incidence of Black-on-Black crime.

* * * [T]he political or cultural interests of the community are interpreted in a way that precludes full public recognition of the problem of domestic violence. While it would be misleading to suggest that white Americans have come to terms with the degree of violence in their own homes, it is nonetheless the case that race adds yet another dimension to why the problem of domestic violence is suppressed within nonwhite communities. People of color often must weigh their interests in avoiding issues that might reinforce distorted public perceptions against the need to acknowledge and address intracommunity problems. Yet the cost of suppression is seldom recognized in part because the failure to discuss the issue shapes perceptions of how serious the problem is in the first place.

* * *

* * * Where information about violence in minority communities is not available, domestic violence is unlikely to be addressed as a serious issue.

The political imperatives of a narrowly focused antiracist strategy support other practices that isolate women of color. For example, activists who have attempted to provide support services to Asian- and African-American women report intense resistance from those communities. At other times, cultural and social factors contribute to suppression. Nilda Rimonte, director of Everywoman's Shelter in Los Angeles, points out that in the Asian community, saving the honor of the family from shame is a priority. Unfortunately, this priority tends to be interpreted as obliging women not to scream rather than obliging men not to hit.

Race and culture contribute to the suppression of domestic violence in other ways as well. Women of color are often reluctant to call the police, a hesitancy likely due to a general unwillingness among people of color to subject their private lives to the scrutiny and control of a police force that is frequently hostile. There is also a more generalized community ethic against public intervention, the product of a desire to create a private world free from the diverse assaults on the public lives of racially subordinated people. The home is not simply a man's castle in the patriarchal sense, but may also function as a safe haven from the indignities of life in a racist society. However, but for this "safe haven" in many cases, women of color victimized by violence might otherwise seek help.

There is also a general tendency within antiracist discourse to regard the problem of violence against women of color as just another manifestation of racism. In this sense, the relevance of gender domination within the community is reconfigured as a consequence of discrimination against men. Of course, it is probably true that racism contributes to the cycle of violence, given the stress that men of color experience in dominant society. It is therefore more than reasonable to explore the links between racism and domestic violence. But the chain of violence is more complex and extends beyond this single link. Racism is linked to patriarchy to the extent that racism denies men of color the power and privilege that dominant men enjoy. When violence is understood as an acting-out of being denied male power in other spheres, it seems counter-productive to embrace constructs that implicitly link the solution to domestic violence to the acquisition of greater male power. The more promising political imperative is to challenge the legitimacy of such power expectations by exposing their dysfunctional and debilitating effect on families and communities of color. Moreover, while understanding links between racism and domestic violence is an important component of any effective intervention strategy, it is also clear that women of color need not await the ultimate triumph over racism before they can expect to live violence-free lives.

Not only do race-based priorities function to obscure the problem of violence suffered by women of color; feminist concerns often suppress minority experiences as well. Strategies for increasing awareness of domestic violence within the white community tend to begin by citing the commonly shared assumption that battering is a minority problem. The strategy then focuses on demolishing this strawman, stressing that spousal abuse also occurs in the white community. Countless first-person stories begin with a statement like, "I was not supposed to be a battered wife." That battering occurs in families of all races and all classes seems to be an ever-present theme of anti-abuse campaigns. First-person anecdotes and studies, for example, consistently assert that battering cuts across racial, ethnic, economic, educational, and religious lines. Such disclaimers seem relevant only in the presence of an initial, widely held belief that domestic violence occurs primarily in minority or poor families. Indeed some authorities explicitly renounce the "stereotypical myths" about battered women. A few commentators have even transformed the message that battering is not *exclusively* a problem of the poor or minority communities into a claim that it *equally* affects all races and classes. Yet these comments seem less concerned with exploring domestic abuse within "stereotyped" communities than with removing the stereotype as an obstacle to exposing battering within white middle- and upper-class communities.

Efforts to politicize the issue of violence against women challenge beliefs that violence occurs only in homes of "others." While it is unlikely that advocates and others who adopt this rhetorical strategy intend to exclude or ignore the needs of poor and colored women, the underlying premise of this seemingly universalistic appeal is to keep the sensibilities of dominant social groups focused on the experiences of those groups. * * * [T]he displacement of the "other" as the presumed victim of domestic violence works primarily as a political appeal to rally white elites. * * * This strategy permits white women victims to come into focus, but does little to disrupt the patterns of neglect that permitted the problem to continue as long as it was imagined to be a minority problem. The experience of violence by minority women is ignored, except to the extent it gains white support for domestic violence programs in the white community.

* * * As long as attempts to politicize domestic violence focus on convincing whites that this is not a "minority" problem but *their* problem, any authentic and sensitive attention to the experiences of Black and other minority women probably will continue to be regarded as jeopardizing the movement.

Notes and Questions

1. Kimberlé Crenshaw argues that women of color are "erased by the strategic silences of feminism and antiracism." A feminist strategy which was undertaken with the goal of treating domestic violence as a universal problem—to rebut stereotypes that it was a problem of "other," less-elite or non-white people—proved to have high costs for many women. What assumptions are prevalent today about who is "supposed to be a battered woman"?

2. Crenshaw's critique helped stimulate a reexamination of the particular needs of women of color and the interaction of domestic violence with other aspects of the oppression of women. *See, e.g.*, Linda L. Ammons, *Mules, Madonnas, Babies, Bathwater, Racial Imagery and Stereotypes: The African-American Woman and the Battered Woman Syndrome*, 1995 Wis. L. Rev. 1003; Zanita E. Fenton, *Domestic Violence in Black and White: Racialized Gender Stereotypes in Gender Violence*, 8 Colum. J. Gender & L. 1 (1998).

SECTION 3. THE CHALLENGE OF LAW REFORM

A. Enforcing Existing Laws

As the movement against domestic violence developed, it was increasingly frustrated by the failure of police to arrest even husbands who had committed felony assaults. Restraining orders were difficult to obtain in the early 1970s—available only to married women against their husbands, and not easily enforceable. As remedies became more broadly available, battered women and their advocates moved to improve the effectiveness of law enforcement.

JOAN ZORZA

The Criminal Law of Misdemeanor Domestic Violence, 1970–1990,
83 J. Crim. L. & Criminology 46, 47–48,
50–52, 54–55, 59–60 (1992)

Domestic disturbance incidents constitute the largest category of calls received by police each year. This is not surprising given the number of women who are abused by their intimate partners. * * * The U.S. Surgeon General found that battering of women by husbands, ex-husbands or lovers "is the single largest cause of injury to women in the

United States," accounting for one-fifth of all hospital emergency room cases. * * *

* * *

In most communities police officers may be the only meaningful contact citizens have with "the law." * * * Throughout the 1970s and early 1980s, officers believed and were taught that domestic violence was a private matter, ill suited to public intervention. Police departments also consider domestic violence calls unglamorous, nonprestigious, and unrewarding. Until recently, police frequently ignored domestic violence calls or purposefully delayed responding for several hours. Even when they eventually arrived on the scene, police rarely did anything about domestic violence, and some actually responded by laughing in the woman's face. Other officers talked to the abuser, possibly removing the batterer from the home temporarily to cool off. Some police officers removed the abused woman from "his" home. * * * [P]olice virtually never arrested the abuser. * * *

[For example, Michigan's policy, as taught in its Police Training Academy, directed officers to avoid arrest if possible and suggested several measures that discouraged complainants, including appealing to women's vanity, explaining that court was not in session and no judge was available, explaining that attitudes usually change by court time, and instructing them not to "be too harsh or critical."]

* * *

* * * The responding officer often admonished the woman to be a better wife or asked, or at least wondered, why she did not leave. Some officers concluded that she must enjoy the beatings, or at least not mind them. These officers conveniently ignored the fact that their failure to protect the woman, her lack of money, and the far greater risk of being beaten or killed if she tried to separate herself from her abuser all combined to make her decision logical. Women's fears of retaliation for leaving are rational; divorced and separated women, who comprise only ten percent of all women, account for fully seventy-five percent of all battered women, and they report being battered fourteen times more often than do women still living with their partners.

Battered women who reported assaults have typically represented a small portion of the total number of victims. * * * Victims sadly learned that reporting spouse abuse was futile.

* * *

Police frequently rationalized their refusal to intervene in domestic violence cases on the ground that domestic violence work was highly dangerous. Restoring peace while maintaining control was seen as the best way to minimize the risk to the responding officer with an emphasis on maintaining control. * * *

The reality, however, is that domestic disturbance incidents, which account for thirty percent of police calls, account for only 5.7% of police deaths, making domestic disturbances one of the least dangerous of all police activities. * * *

* * *

[In late 1976, lawsuits in California and New York forced changes in police policy. The suits were filed by attorneys in legal aid and legal services, who had observed the impact of domestic violence on their women clients, and by the Center for Constitutional Rights in New York. *Scott v. Hart* was a class action suit against the chief of the Oakland Police Department] * * * on behalf of "women in general and black women in particular who are victims of domestic violence." * * * [T]he named plaintiffs were black women who had repeatedly called the Oakland police for protection when they were beaten up by their husbands, ex-husbands or boyfriends. The officers had either failed to respond or had responded in an ineffectual or, in one case, a threatening manner. * * * [The complaint alleged denial of equal protection under the Fourteenth Amendment and a breach of duty to arrest abusers when a felony had been committed. The New York lawsuit, *Bruno v. Codd*, involved extensive preparation and hundreds of pages of affidavits showing that police failed to respond or to protect women, that women were desperate to stop the abuse, and that they had tried numerous times to do so. The affidavits explained the economic and societal pressures that the women faced, such as a lack of day care, shelter beds or housing, and increased violence from their husbands; along with the absence of police protection, these factors combined to prevent women from leaving their husbands. The Oakland lawsuit settled in an agreement that reformed police practices. The New York lawsuit reached a similar settlement after the court denied a motion to dismiss, commenting that if the allegations in the complaint and hundreds of pages of affidavits were true, "only the written law has changed; in reality, wife beating is still condoned, if not approved, by some of those charged with protecting its victims." *Bruno v. Codd*, 90 Misc.2d 1047, 396 N.Y.S.2d 974 (Sup. Ct. 1977)]

The Oakland and New York City lawsuits made clear to police departments throughout the United States that they were vulnerable to being sued if they failed to protect the rights of battered women. Battered women's advocates soon learned how many police chiefs knew that both of the departments had "lost." As a result, police departments in many towns and cities agreed to revamp their policies and practices without any suit having to be filed. * * *

The caselaw took one more important step forward in *Thurman v. City of Torrington*, Conn. [595 F.Supp. 1521 (Dist. Conn. 1984)], where a federal jury awarded Tracey Thurman and her son $2.3 million because the police were negligent in failing to protect her from her abusive husband. The court found that Torrington's policy of indifference amounted to sex discrimination.

The effect of the case was dramatic. * * *

> The *Thurman* case was widely reported in the popular press and in academic journals. It graphically confirmed the extreme financial penalty that could be imposed on police departments when they abjectly fail to perform their duties. * * * [I]t confirmed that in appropriate cases, these massive liability awards would be upheld.

Many police departments that did not get the message from *Scott* and *Bruno* were forced by *Thurman*'s threat of huge liability to change their policies.

Notes and Questions

1. Why was it so difficult to win protection of the law for battered women? If the only problem was that the police thought of this particular crime as a private matter, why did they see it that way?

2. Do you know the current practices of the police department in the community in which you live? How could you find out whether they respond appropriately to domestic violence reports?

B. The Violence Against Women Act

The first efforts at national domestic violence bills were proposed and defeated in 1977 and 1978. In 1979, President Jimmy Carter established the Office of Domestic Violence with a budget of $900,000, but it was closed by President Ronald Reagan in 1981. Two federal statutes in 1984 provided some money for shelters, counseling, and law enforcement training, and a significant amount of money for grants to aid survivors of crimes including domestic violence, sexual assault, and child abuse. From 1990, when it was introduced by Senator Joseph Biden, the Violence Against Women Act [VAWA] went through repeated drafting and revisions. Rachelle Brooks, *Feminists Negotiate the Legislative Branch: The Violence Against Women Act*, in *Feminists Negotiate the State*, *supra* at 65–74. Deborah Weissman provides an overview of VAWA:

> In September 1994 Congress passed the Violence Against Women Act, a historic legislative enactment which recognized the nexus between gender-based violence and women's equality, and addressed the persistent failure of the states' legal systems to provide adequate legal redress to victims. VAWA incorporated measures designed to respond to the wide-ranging consequences of domestic violence: It funded a variety of programs, including women's shelters, a national domestic abuse hotline, rape education and prevention programs, and training for federal and state judges.
>
> In addition to funding services and improving existing legal responses to domestic violence, the Act expanded legal remedies for gender-based violence. It created new relief measures designed for immigrants whose abusive spouses obstructed access to lawful status in the United States. It criminalized the crossing of state lines for the purpose of "harassing, intimidating, or injuring a spouse or

intimate partner," and provided for interstate enforcement of orders of protection. * * *

The Act had an extensive legislative history. For more than four years, Congress assembled a voluminous record of oral testimony and written documentation about the problem of gender-based violence. Over one hundred witnesses testified during the course of at least nine hearings. Experts provided research findings and evidence documenting the consequences of violence against women. In public testimony, victims of violence detailed their horrific experiences. Witnesses included battered women, rape victims, shelter and rape crisis program advocates, law enforcement officials, lawyers with expertise in domestic violence, state attorneys general, judges, legal and other academic scholars, social scientists, and physicians. Documentation of the extensive nature and consequences of gender-based violence was introduced from businesses and professional associations, judicial organizations, medical groups, feminist research centers, and other women's groups.

Deborah M. Weissman, *Gender-Based Violence as Judicial Anomaly: Between "The Truly National and the Truly Local,"* 42 B.C. L. Rev.1081, 1088–89 (2001).

JENNY RIVERA

The Violence Against Women Act and the Construction of Multiple Consciousness in the Civil Rights and Feminist Movements
4 J.L. & Pol'y 463, 464–66, 492–97, 503–08, 510–11 (1996)

The enactment of the Violence Against Women Act ("VAWA") in 1994 was, ostensibly, a success of historic proportions on various political and social fronts. It has significantly furthered efforts to legitimize a feminist anti-violence agenda within the political mainstream by providing federal criminal and civil legal remedies for female survivors of violence. Indeed, significant portions of the VAWA were originally viewed as highly controversial, in part because of their feminist origin. * * * When the VAWA was finally signed into legislation, it marked the end of a protracted political and educational campaign conducted in Congress and across the country on gender-motivated violence.

While the enactment of the VAWA is undeniably a victory for feminism, and as such served as a vehicle for a sophisticated national discourse on violence between intimate partners, the passage of the VAWA is also a civil rights victory. * * * [A]t a time when the hard-won gains of civil rights and feminist struggles are being challenged and dismantled, both movements must work together cooperatively. * * * The VAWA represents an important opportunity for civil rights activists and feminists to identify common goals and philosophies of their respective social and legal reform movements, and an opportunity to convert their doctrines into practice through joint action.

The recognition that the civil rights movement can be gender-conscious and gender-responsive, and that the feminist movement can speak to issues of race and ethnic discrimination—that both movements can be constructed in such a way as to account for and respond to the particular issues and concerns of women of all races and ethnic backgrounds—allows for collaboration between the proponents of these two movements. As a consequence, both movements will benefit and can fully pursue their mutual goals of equity and justice. * * *

* * *

One of the primary aspects of the legislation is its ambitious attempt to respond to the particular ways women experience violence. First, it recognizes the prevalence of violence between intimate partners, and, because it applies to former intimate partners, it also recognizes that violence does not necessarily terminate when the relationship ends. Second, the VAWA avoids making the all too common mistake of judging women who stay in violent relationships by adversely characterizing them as "failing" to take aggressive steps to curtail the batterer's conduct, or otherwise blaming women for their abusers' conduct. Rather, the VAWA provides for the establishment of programs and law enforcement strategies that will, at least in theory, create an environment in which women can feel they have real options to negotiate the violence. If these programs and strategies are effectively established and enforced, women will have more resources, such as shelters and support services, and police will be better able to respond appropriately to domestic violence with education and enhanced resources.

Another way in which the VAWA incorporates the experiential and doctrinal foundations of civil rights and feminist antidiscrimination theory and activism is by providing for the installation and integration of programs and services responsive to the different situations faced by women of color. This ensures the applicability of particular VAWA projects to a diverse population of women, and also enhances the VAWA's overall vitality. For example, in several sections the VAWA mandates the inclusion of representatives from various communities, including communities of color, in the development and strategic planning of VAWA mandated or facilitated enforcement, education and research projects. Thus, the VAWA discreetly, but effectively, recognizes that women of color have available to them different and often fewer options than do many White women because of their race, ethnicity, culture and language.

* * * [L]aw enforcement and prosecution federal grants are available for, *inter alia*, purposes of "developing or improving delivery of victim services to racial, cultural, ethnic, and language minorities. . . ." Further, states must set forth in their grant applications the demographics of the service population, including information on "race, ethnicity and language background . . ." in order to qualify for a grant. Applicants for the National Domestic Violence Hotline grant had to provide a plan for servicing "non-English speaking callers," such as by employing

Spanish-speaking hotline personnel, and had to demonstrate a commitment to "diversity, and to the provision of services to ethnic, racial, and non-English speaking minorities...." * * *

[In developing a research agenda, VAWA requires the inclusion of expertise on services to ethnic and language minority communities, and a focus on the needs of underserved populations.] Such data is critical because there is little information about domestic violence and its impact on women within communities of color. * * *

Several sections of the VAWA are most likely to provide assistance to Latinas and other non-English speaking or immigrant groups of women in particular * * * . [One provision] * * * amends the Immigration and Nationality Act, and authorizes immigrant women and children who are survivors of domestic violence to petition for legal status on their own. As a result, Latina immigrant survivors and other immigrant women survivors of domestic violence may apply for legal status without relying on an abusive spouse or parent. In effect, [this] * * * removes leverage the abuser may have against a woman previously available to him because of the abuser's legal petitioning standing.

* * *

The VAWA also establishes a fund for community projects on domestic violence. Under the "Demonstration Grants for Community Initiatives" section, the VAWA authorizes grants to nonprofit organizations to "establish projects in local communities involving many sectors of each community to coordinate intervention and prevention of domestic violence." Community leaders must be involved in the program planning and development process.

* * *

* * * [T]here are VAWA sections which seek to influence state-based initiatives by applying federal policies directly to the state VAWA appropriations grantees. The VAWA provision which requires the adoption and implementation of mandatory arrest procedures reflects current feminist preference for and utilization of this strategy. * * * [To be eligible for VAWA grants, states must certify that their laws or policies encourage or mandate arrests of domestic violence offenders based on probable cause that an offense has been committed, and when a valid protection order has been violated. State and local governments must also certify that they prohibit dual arrest (the practice of arresting both the abuser and the woman) and mutual restraining orders (restraining orders issued against both parties.)]

* * *

Support and opposition to mandatory arrest policies and laws is contentious and the issues surrounding the implementation of mandatory arrest policies remain unresolved. * * *

The task of analyzing and critiquing the utility and effect of mandatory arrest policies on women of color is difficult because of the lack of research and evaluation of the subject. However, I have previously articulated my deep concern with the utility and implementational effects of mandatory arrest as applied to Latinas. These concerns are founded on two aspects of mandatory arrest.

First, because it is a law enforcement model which is only effective to the extent that the woman has no control over the actions taken by police officers, it is philosophically in opposition to feminist and civil rights doctrines which have been founded on notions of individual and community empowerment and community-based control. While some supporters have argued that mandatory arrest is itself an empowering mechanism, the lack of information on the experiences of women of color with mandatory arrest policies, belies reliance on prior evaluations of mandatory arrest practices and procedures. Even without such information we can, nevertheless, consider theoretical and historical observations and arguments concerning communities of color and women within those communities.

A second troubling aspect of mandatory arrest is that it adopts and furthers an invasive state law model. Dependence on initiatives which are strategies for authorizing state involvement in individual relationships have proved debilitating for communities of color and women. * * * Uncertainty as to the application of mandatory arrest to communities of color, and the general failure to contextualize law enforcement strategies in such a way as to reflect the history of abuse by police and the state is a significant problem with the VAWA.

* * *

While the shelter system has provided many services to women of color, * * * [the VAWA grants money to an existing system that has serious institutional problems which] have resulted in the failure to provide sufficient, culturally appropriate services for women of color, especially women who do not speak English.

* * * [State grantees under VAWA must give] special emphasis to the support of community-based projects of demonstrated effectiveness carried out by nonprofit organizations, the primary purpose of which is to operate shelters for victims of family violence and their dependents, and those which provide counseling, advocacy, and self-help services to victims and their children.

To the extent that funding of shelters and services is prioritized in such a way as to benefit organizations and entities with a history of this work, programs developed by women of color which are community-based may proceed in the funding process at a disadvantage because of their inexperience and insufficient history with the contract bidding process. There may be an adverse impact on Latino community-based programs which do not have a history of working on domestic violence issues.

* * *

Recommendations for the increased utilization of all sections of the VAWA by women of color must promote the integration of women of color into the political system and into civil rights and feminist movements. The collaborative agenda that can be developed together by participants in the civil rights movement and the feminist movement is possible so long as women of color have an equal voice in the political dialogue. * * * Legislation that purports to address gender-based violence must also address the concerns and issues of women of color specifically. This requires addressing discrimination based on race, national origin, culture and language. The passage of the VAWA brings us part of the way towards addressing these issues. Through the cooperative efforts of civil rights activists and feminists, the VAWA can fulfill its obligation to all women, and can become part of a more fully collaborative activism that is the culmination of the struggles of women and people of color against violence as systemic oppression.

Notes and Questions

1. Rivera emphasizes the potential problems in funding only organizations that directly provide domestic violence services in immigrant communities. Her argument is supported by a study of battered immigrant Latinas in the Washington, D.C. area. The women were isolated from many sources of help, and were very unlikely to call domestic violence organizations for assistance. They got most of their information about domestic violence, and most of their support, within close female relationships. Mary Ann Dutton, Leslye E. Orloff & Giselle Aguilar Hass, *Characteristics of Help-Seeking Behaviors, Resources and Service Needs of Battered Immigrant Latinas: Legal and Policy Implications,* 7 Geo. J. on Poverty L. & Pol'y 245, 284–85 (2000). They did, however, reach out to other sorts of organizations: "The top four services, used by between one fourth and one fifth of the battered immigrant women surveyed, were immigration, maternal health, public benefits, and health insurance. The next most highly ranked services used by abused women were emergency medical services, English as a second language classes, child care, and reproductive health." *Id.* at 286. Therefore, community education was vital, so that when women reached out to each other, they would receive accurate information about available resources; education of all service providers on the particular needs of battered women was also necessary, since those providers, rather than police, lawyers, shelters, or advocacy services, would be the first contact or the only contact for many battered women. *Id.* at 286–87.

2. One of the most innovative sections of VAWA created a federal civil rights remedy, modeled on other civil rights statutes, for acts of gender-motivated violence:

> The principal contribution of VAWA's civil rights remedy was to reconceptualize violence against women as part of a social pattern rather than a series of isolated events. This approach reflects the insights of feminism into the pervasiveness of male violence in the lives of women and its role in maintaining women's disadvantaged social status. Gender-motivated violence, like other forms of discrim-

> ination, is a collective injury, a social wrong carried out on an individual level. Since their inception in the 1970s, the modern battered women's movement and anti-rape movement have struggled to convey the ways in which individual acts of violence grow out of and reinforce an overarching structure of unequal power between the sexes. The civil rights provision of the Violence Against Women Act put that vision into practice. By recognizing that violence is inflicted on women because of their membership in a group defined by their gender, that such violence erodes women's status as equal citizens, and that women are entitled to protection from such violence as a matter of federal civil rights, VAWA achieved what Professor Catharine MacKinnon has described as "a conceptual overhaul from the ground up."

Sally F. Goldfarb, *"No Civilized System of Justice": The Fate of The Violence Against Women Act,* 102 W. Va. L. Rev. 499, 509 (2000).

In United States v. Morrison, 529 U.S. 598 (2000), the Supreme Court held the VAWA civil rights remedy unconstitutional. *See United States v. Morrison*, excerpted in chapter 10. The rest of the Violence Against Women Act remains in effect, however, and its wide variety of grants and programs have vastly increased knowledge about violence against women and programs aimed at helping battered women and ending abuse. Goldfarb, *supra* at 540–43.

3. Passage of the VAWA was the product of years of work by feminists and the battered women's movement. Feminists fought for the inclusion of the civil rights remedy and for particular remedies for immigrant women, with the NOW Legal Defense and Education Fund playing a leading role. Brooks, *supra* at 65–74; *see also* "How Do Social Movements Shape Civil Rights Legislation for Women? The 1994 Violence Against Women Act," at http://womhist.binghamton.edu/vawa/intro.htm (last viewed July 13, 2002) (history of VAWA, documents, and social and legal analysis assembled by historian Kathryn Kish Sklar).

Winning passage of the bill included compromises. In 1994, VAWA was incorporated into the Crime Bill, which also included the Racial Justice Act. The Racial Justice Act confronted racial inequality in the imposition of the death penalty by allowing courts "to consider evidence of a consistent pattern of racially discriminatory death sentences in the sentencing jurisdiction." Don Edwards & John Conyers, Jr., *The Racial Justice Act—A Simple Matter of Justice*, 20 U. Dayton L. Rev. 699, 700 (1995); *see also, id.* at 703–04 (explaining that the Act responded to McCleskey v. Kemp, 481 U.S. 279 (1987), in which the Supreme Court had held that statistics showing racial sentencing disparities did not prove intentional discrimination against a particular defendant). When the Racial Justice Act was later removed from the Crime Bill, feminists faced a dilemma:

> [Feminists who supported VAWA were] forced to choose between fighting for a policy dealing with racism and a measure to alleviate the amount of violence committed against women. In supporting the

> final version of the crime bill feminists implicitly endorsed both the removal of the Racial Justice Act and what many consider to be inherent racism in our current system of justice. Domestic violence and racial justice became competing policies, rather than complementary ones * * *.

Brooks, *supra* at 80.

Placing VAWA in the Crime Bill also framed domestic violence as a criminal problem and allowed the state to "ignore the many other roots of this violence." *Id.* at 79.

> [I]ssues such as women's health or their economic vulnerability are also important for alleviating the problem and are not addressed by this legislation. For example, a law which proposed to address women's health concerns and included domestic violence in the measure would provide very different solutions to the problem. Likewise, if a law created greater economic equality for women, many would be better able to sustain themselves financially upon leaving an abusive relationships and would be less likely to return to their batterers. * * * As long as domestic violence against women continues to be framed as a crime issue, the solutions the state can offer will necessarily be limited.

Id.

4. Immigrant battered women faced new difficulties after 1996. Among a series of restrictive changes to immigration law, Congress enacted new provisions that specifically addressed domestic violence issues. Conviction for domestic violence became a deportable offense. This new rule had unintended consequences. Battered women now faced deportation of their partners—an extreme result—if they called for police protection in response to misdemeanor level violence; also, mandatory arrest laws had resulted in the arrest of many more women, who themselves faced deportation because of the new laws. *See generally* Cecelia M. Espenoza, *No Relief for the Weary: VAWA Relief Denied for Battered Immigrants Lost in the Intersections*, 83 Marq. L. Rev. 163 (1999). The impact of these provisions was ameliorated by the enactment of the Battered Immigrant Women Protection Act of 2000, which gives the attorney general the discretion to waive deportation for immigrants who were "not the primary perpetrator of violence in the relationship" and were "acting in self-defense." *See* Donna Coker, *Crime Control and Feminist Law Reform in Domestic Violence Law: A Critical Review*, 4 Buff. Crim. L. Rev. 801, 831 (2001).

5. Jenny Rivera identified concerns about the impact of mandatory arrest policies on Latinas. The following section reviews contemporary debates about mandatory arrest and prosecution policies.

SECTION 4. MANDATORY ARREST AND PROSECUTION POLICIES: DEBATES ABOUT INEQUALITY AND EMPOWERMENT

Arguments about protecting individual women and transforming gender inequality are made on both sides of the policy debates about mandatory arrest and prosecution. Supporting mandatory arrest, Evan Stark focuses on the ways in which the structures which oppress women include interpersonal violence by their partners, which affects all aspects of women's participation in society. Cheryl Hanna supports mandatory prosecution to control vacillation both by victims of domestic violence and by prosecutors in law enforcement. Opposing mandatory policies, Linda Mills emphasizes the harm to individual women that can occur in the process of interaction between the prosecutor and the victim of domestic violence; Donna Coker emphasizes the danger that mandatory policies can become part of structural inequality in American society. The following section first presents contrasting arguments regarding the interaction between prosecutors and victims of domestic violence, followed by contrasting arguments about the impact of mandatory policies on structural inequality.

CHERYL HANNA

No Right to Choose: Mandated Victim Participation in Domestic Violence Prosecutions
109 Harv. L. Rev. 1849, 1850–54, 1859–68, 1873, 1892, 1897 (1996)

If Nicole Brown Simpson had lived in Duluth, Minnesota, we might have seen a very different O.J. Simpson trial. For had she lived in Duluth in October 1993, when Mr. Simpson broke into her home and terrorized her, Mr. Simpson might have been tried much earlier—for domestic violence. The Los Angeles District Attorney's Office dropped the 1993 prosecution because Ms. Simpson did not want to press charges. In Duluth, she would not have had a choice.

One of the defining moments in the O.J. Simpson murder trial came when the prosecution introduced the 911 tape from October 1993 that vividly illustrated prior abuse in the Simpson marriage. On the tape, Ms. Simpson's terrified voice begs the operator to send the police, as Mr. Simpson had just smashed the door. She says she fears that he will "beat the shit" out of her. O.J. Simpson is heard screaming in the background—threatening her, taunting her. The operator's voice sounds surprised when she learns that the suspect is O.J. Simpson. "I think you know his record," Ms. Simpson tells the operator. Mr. Simpson was never arrested or prosecuted for the 1993 incident because Ms. Simpson did not want to press charges.

Under these same circumstances, the Duluth District Attorney would likely have initiated charges against Mr. Simpson, signing the complaint and requesting an arrest warrant. A proper investigation of the case would have been conducted and might have lead to a wealth of physical evidence. Under established police protocols for handling domestic violence calls, the police could have photographed the door that Mr. Simpson allegedly broke. They could also have photographed both Ms. Simpson and Mr. Simpson to document the physical condition of each of them. Neighbors who may have heard Mr. Simpson break in and threaten Ms. Simpson could have been questioned and subpoenaed to testify. Admissions allegedly made by Mr. Simpson when police arrived could have been introduced against him at trial. The 911 tape would have been particularly damaging. With this evidence, the state could have charged Mr. Simpson with assault, battery, breaking and entering, malicious destruction of property, and trespass.

In Duluth, Ms. Simpson would not have been asked if she wanted to proceed. She would not have had a choice. She would have been interviewed in the early stages of the case and subpoenaed to testify. If she refused after being counseled, she could have been held in contempt. If Ms. Simpson recanted at trial, prosecutors could have used statements that she made at the scene to police and to the 911 operator to impeach her testimony. With the proper investigation, it is unlikely that the state would have had to go that far to elicit her cooperation; the case would have been strong enough either to end in a plea bargain or to proceed regardless of her testimony.

* * *

Tremendous progress has been made in the last twenty years in providing services and legal remedies for battered women. Prosecutors have begun treating domestic violence as a serious crime. Routine dismissal of domestic violence cases is becoming less acceptable, and many jurisdictions have implemented special procedures for domestic violence cases. However, although the clear trend has been toward more aggressive prosecution, the domestic violence advocacy community has not reached a consensus on the extent to which the state should use its powers to compel women to help prosecute their batterers. What should prosecutors do when faced with cases in which the victim does not want to cooperate?

As a former assistant state's attorney in an urban domestic violence prosecution unit, I struggled daily with cases like Nicole Brown Simpson's. Abused women often will not cooperate and refuse to appear in court. Sometimes they change their stories to protect their batterers or to shield themselves and their families from outside intervention. Despite our unit's aggressive "no-drop" prosecution policy of pursuing cases regardless of the victims' wishes, I often resisted holding individual women responsible to the state. For example, if a women who had been subpoenaed to testify about being abused refused to appear, I rarely requested a body attachment or an arrest warrant. If my attempts to convince her to proceed failed, I would dismiss or "STET" the case rather than send a police officer to arrest her. I faced a troubling inability to reconcile my responsibility to prosecute aggressively with my concern that forcing her to participate would hold her responsible for stopping the abuse and disempower her from responding to the abusive relationship on her own.

* * *

In 1984, the United States Attorney General recommended arrest as the standard police response to domestic violence. This recommendation resulted from a landmark Minneapolis study that compared the deterrent effects of arresting the suspect, mediating the dispute, and requiring the batterer to leave the house for eight hours. The study found that arrest more effectively deterred subsequent violence than did the other courses of action. This study, followed by the Attorney General's recommendation, provided the foundation for nationwide legal reform. By 1988, all but two states had created an exception to the in-presence requirement to permit warrantless arrest when the officer has probable cause to believe that someone has committed a misdemeanor or violated a restraining order. All fifty states now provide for warrantless misdemeanor arrests in domestic violence cases.

Since arrest statutes have been broadened, many jurisdictions have moved toward mandatory and pro-arrest policies. Under these policies, an arrest is either required or preferred if there is probable cause to believe that a domestic battery has taken place. Although these policies have received mixed reviews, the clear trend in police practice is to arrest the batterer at the scene, regardless of the victim's wishes.

Once police started to arrest alleged batterers, advocates began to focus reform efforts on prosecution practices. Prosecutors often fail to initiate charges and to follow through with criminal prosecution in domestic violence cases. Victim noncooperation, reluctance, or outright refusal to proceed are often cited as the major reasons for this lack of criminal prosecution. Prosecutors may also resist pursuing cases because they believe that battering is a minor, private crime. Within the past ten years, domestic violence advocacy groups have urged prosecutors to follow through with legal intervention. Law reform efforts have also aided and encouraged more aggressive prosecution. Perhaps most importantly, more women are becoming District Attorneys, bringing with them new perspectives on women's issues and prompting internal change.

Specialized domestic violence units are being established throughout the country. Although policies vary among jurisdictions, many offices now have pro-prosecution or "no-drop" policies. Some states have adopted pro-prosecution legislation, and many others have officially endorsed its adoption. Pro-prosecution policies check prosecutorial discretion and actively encourage women to proceed through the criminal justice system. Prosecutors cannot routinely dismiss charges at a woman's request, but are required to pursue cases and elicit the victim's cooperation. Moreover, the prosecutor usually signs the charge, relieving the woman of responsibility. Thus, pro-prosecution policies treat domestic violence as a serious crime and recognize the ambivalence that abused women bring to the process. These policies also provide guidelines on how to handle cases in which the victim is reluctant to proceed. Policies range from formal protocols requiring that all victims be subpoenaed to informal practices against routinely dismissing cases at the victim's request.

The term "no-drop" is something of a misnomer. Pro-prosecution policies are often characterized as either "hard" or "soft" no-drop policies. Under "hard" policies, cases proceed regardless of the victim's wishes when there is enough evidence to go forward. In Duluth, Minnesota, for example, prosecutors subpoena all victims to testify and have standard procedures for dealing with uncooperative victims. Many more cases are prosecuted as a result of this hard no-drop policy. * * *

Although no nationwide survey of prosecution policies currently exists, the limited available research suggests that most jurisdictions that give special attention to domestic violence cases employ "soft" no-drop policies. Under soft policies, prosecutors do not force victims to participate in the criminal process; rather, victims are provided with support services and encouraged to continue the process. * * *

Many domestic violence advocates emphasize the importance of listening to women and their concerns before taking action against their batterers. Numerous state programs employ or work closely with victim advocates. In Alexandria, Virginia, for example, a victim can drop charges after appearing before a counselor or a judge to explain her refusal. In other soft no-drop jurisdictions, a victim who fails to appear, refuses to testify, or recants her testimony is not sanctioned or forced to participate. * * *

* * *

* * * Just how far the state should go in forcing women to participate before dismissing charges remains an issue of intense debate.

Pro-prosecution advocates argue that aggressive policies take the burden off the victim by removing her as the "plaintiff." They contend that the batterer has less incentive to try to control or intimidate his victim once he realizes that she no longer controls the process. They also argue that because domestic violence is a public crime, the state has a responsibility to intervene aggressively. For these advocates, this response communicates and follows through on the message that the state will not tolerate violence of any sort. These arguments are rooted in the feminist principle that, when the state refuses to intervene under the rationale that domestic violence is a private family matter, the state not only condones but, in fact, promotes such violence.

However, many advocates for battered women * * * are * * * concerned that if arrest leads to automatic prosecution, women will be less likely to call the police for help or protection. Critics of no-drop policies further argue that the state should not place the woman at any greater risk of harm or substitute itself for the batterer by taking control of the woman's life. In order to preserve her autonomy and promote her sense of empowerment, the victim ought to have the final decision. * * *

Reactions by battered women's advocates to a 1983 Alaska case illustrate this debate. After Maudie Wall filed an abuse complaint against her husband, she changed her mind and decided that she did not want to testify. Under the Anchorage no-drop policy, Mrs. Wall was jailed overnight for her refusal to cooperate. She was released when her husband agreed to accept a probation and counseling. The prosecutor reasoned:

> [W]hen the police get called and a complaint is filed, it is no longer a private matter.
>
> . . . .
>
> Our only alternative was to drop the case and thereby show defense attorneys and defendants we will not stick to our guns, and the long-range consequences for our [no-drop] policy would be disastrous.

Many in the domestic violence advocacy community * * * argued that forcing Ms. Wall to participate and jailing her for refusing to do so went a step too far, regardless of the long-term consequences for the legitimacy of the no-drop program.

* * *

[My proposal for] a mandated participation policy is more consistent with the approaches taken in hard no-drop jurisdictions. * * * This policy can require a woman to sign statements; be photographed to document injuries; be interviewed by police, prosecutors, or advocates; provide the state with other evidence or information; produce her children if subpoenaed; and appear in court throughout the proceedings. Mandated participation may also involve forced testimony if the case proceeds to trial—although such extreme measures are unlikely given that 90% to 95% of all criminal cases end in plea bargains. * * *

Mandated participation ensures that the prosecution has enough evidence to move beyond the presumption of innocence. It does not remove prosecutorial discretion over cases that lack adequate proof that a crime has been committed. Decisions to prosecute are based on the quality of the evidence and the seriousness of the case, not the victim's reluctance or refusal to proceed. Like hard no-drop policies, this policy ultimately gives the woman no right to choose whether the state criminally prosecutes her partner.

* * *

Although their formal client is the state, domestic violence prosecutors often see themselves as advocates for abused women. They choose this area of law, as I did, because they want to reform the system. When faced with a battered but reluctant victim, however, the prosecutor, rather than the batterer, may become the person who is "ruining the victim's life." The battered victim may accuse the prosecutor of making things worse by pursuing the case. Often, the most psychologically comfortable decision is to abide by the victim's wishes.

* * *

In my experience as a prosecutor, the fact that the state was not likely to request a body attachment for victims who failed to appear for trial traveled very quickly by word-of-mouth. Defense attorneys often informed women that if they did not appear in court, they would probably not be arrested. Day after day, women would not appear and defense attorneys would request dismissals. Many times I could not locate the victim by phone or mail and did not know if the batterer or his attorney had ensured her absence. Judges rarely allowed me to postpone the case unless I had an explanation for the victim's absence. I do not mean to suggest that all defense attorneys advised women to ignore their criminal subpoenas. My example illustrates that prosecutors must be willing—in at least some instances—to mandate participation, including having women picked up by police officers and brought to court if they refuse to appear. Otherwise, the state response to domestic violence is unacceptably undermined.

Although these strategies can be criticized as punitive and victimizing, such concerns are often overstated. Feminists overwhelmingly criticized the prosecutor who jailed Maudie Wall overnight, claiming that the state had gone too far. Much of that criticism is misplaced. First, Ms. Wall's overnight stay in jail may have been the first time that she recognized the seriousness of the abuse against her. Second, her inaction had consequences for the state. Resources had been expended in the case against the abuser. If such cases are dismissed, "wasting" resources on cases never pursued, already tight prosecutors' budgets could come under further attack. Third, if Mr. Wall knew that he could get away with his abusive behavior, he would have been much more likely to batter his wife again. Ms. Wall's long-term situation would be worse, not better.

* * *

* * * [W]e do more harm than good by trying to protect women from the criminal justice system. Domestic violence reflects not only a psychological problem in individual men or women, but also a deeper problem of state-condoned violence. Shielding women who do not want to proceed through the criminal system reinforces the idea that domestic violence is a private crime without social consequence and, ultimately, marginalizes and isolates women who are not expected to respond to the violence on a broader scale.

LINDA G. MILLS

Killing Her Softly: Intimate Abuse and the Violence of State Intervention

113 Harv. L. Rev. 550, 552–55, 563–68, 696, 697, 612 (1999)

Laura entered the emergency room with some trepidation. Her eye was bruised and her head was pounding. When she was finally seen, she told the doctor that Thomas, her husband, had pushed her. They had fought and she had accidentally fallen into a lamp. It had bruised her eye and she had a migraine. Thomas and Laura had been married for four years and he had never been violent before. Within moments, the doctor told Laura that under California's mandatory reporting law, he would have to call the police.

Laura was horrified. "What about what I want to do?" she asked. "What about my rights?" Laura explained that she did not want Thomas arrested; he was a good man and a fine provider, and she was not worried that his behavior was or would become dangerous. The doctor had no choice—he would be held personally liable if he failed to report the abuse.

The doctor called the police. Laura warned Thomas by phone that the police were coming. Laura arrived home just as the police showed up. She tried to convince the officers not to arrest him—to no avail. The officers informed her that the Los Angeles Police Department has a mandatory arrest policy. If the officers have "probable cause" to suspect that domestic violence has occurred, they must arrest the suspect regardless of the woman's objections or protestations.

Thomas spent three days in jail. Having been arrested on Friday night, he missed work on Monday and worries that he may be fired if he is convicted of a crime. He also awaits prosecution on a domestic violence charge.

Laura has spoken with the prosecutor and has begged her not to prosecute. She has explained that Thomas may lose his job and that their daughter, who suffers from multiple disabilities, relies on both parents for her care. Thomas's employer-provided health insurance covers their daughter's health care.

The prosecutor does not listen. She informs Laura that the Los Angeles City Attorney's office adheres to a no-drop prosecution policy. The prosecutor assigned to the case will proceed against Thomas regardless of Laura's objections or her reluctance to testify. If she refuses to testify, the City Attorney's office will subpoena her. And, to prove the case against Thomas, the prosecutor will use the statements Laura made to the emergency room doctor.

* * * Technically speaking, emotional abuse is "the nonphysical degradation of the self which lowers worth and interferes with human development and productivity." It can be experienced in a wide variety of ways by the recipient or victim. * * *

* * *

* * * [T]he state's regulation of domestic violence in the United States has become tinged with emotional violence. * * * [S]uch policies as mandatory arrest, prosecution, and reporting, which have become standard legal fare in the fight against domestic violence and which categorically ignore the battered woman's perspective, can themselves be forms of abuse. * * * [I]ronically, the very state interventions designed

to eradicate the intimate abuse in battered women's lives all too often reproduce the emotional abuse of the battering relationship. In these instances, state policies have the inadvertent effect of rendering battered women less, rather than more, safe from violence. Proceeding on the assumption that battered women are as often survivors as they are victims, I argue that mandatory state interventions rob the battered woman of an important opportunity to acknowledge and reject patterns of abuse and to partner with state actors (law enforcement officers, prosecutors, and medical professionals) in imagining the possibility of a life without violence. Therefore, I propose an empowerment model that reverses the violent dynamic imposed on the battered woman by the batterer, a method that nurtures the survivor's need for emotional support and helps heal the wounds inflicted by the abuser.

* * *

* * * [Advocates of mandatory arrest and prosecution argue that mandatory policies force state actors to treat crimes against women in the same manner in which they treat other crimes, and] that these approaches keep battered women safe. They rely on the results of the Minneapolis arrest study to claim that when the police intervene regardless of the battered woman's wishes, the impact is positive. They argue that arrest, on balance, deters future incidents of violence.

Finally, and in some respects most significantly, advocates believe that these proactive policies structurally alter the politics of gender violence. * * * In policy and practice, police officers, prosecutors, and medical personnel no longer collude with batterers by ignoring violence inflicted on women. This approach or attitude, proponents argue, dismantles sexism at the level of institutions and achieves the overarching goal of altering discrimination against women. * * *

There are, however, significant costs associated with mandatory interventions. For example, the empirical evidence suggests that individual battered women suffer when mandatory intervention policies go awry. Indeed, mandatory arrest may actually increase the incidence of violence in some battered women's lives. In 1992, Lawrence Sherman conducted a study in Milwaukee on the effects of arrest on batterers in that city. * * * Sherman found that * * * [arrest] had a short-term deterrent effect. However, over the long term there was a trend that violence increased in cases in which the perpetrator had been arrested. * * * Sherman concluded, based on this study, that mandatory arrest policies are highly problematic.

* * * Very few studies have tested the effectiveness of mandatory prosecution policies in eliminating violence in battered women's lives. * * *

A recent study on the effects of prosecution on recidivism presented striking results. After reviewing a large sample of domestic violence misdemeanor cases (1133), the researchers found that prosecution had no effect on the likelihood of re-arrest of the batterer within a six-month period. * * * [R]ecidivism was unaffected by whether a case was dropped, dismissed, or prosecuted. While the authors warned that their findings were tentative, they nevertheless concluded that "there is little support for the idea that law enforcement responses to domestic violence misdemeanors reduce or eliminate violence." * * *

* * *

[Not only might mandatory policies increase the incidence of physical abuse against victims by their intimate partners, but these policies also visit upon these victims an entirely distinct violent interaction, one that contains many of the emotionally abusive elements of the victim's relationship with the batterer.]

From the accumulated evidence, a dynamic between the state and the battered woman emerges that distinctly mimics the violent dynamic in the battering relationship. Three correlative themes are the most problematic. First, mandatory interventions reinforce the battered woman's psychic injury and encourage feelings of guilt, low self-esteem, and dependency. Mandatory interventions are predicated on the assumption that state actors are incapable of distinguishing between battered women who are truly suffering from "learned helplessness" and battered women who are capable of making reasoned decisions about which healing strategies to pursue. * * * [T]his disinterest, or even laziness, on the part of the state in developing a person-by-person approach to domestic violence intervention causes the state to replicate unwittingly the behavior of the batterer in some cases.

Second, mandatory interventions may have the ironic effect of realigning the battered woman with the batterer. Some studies suggest and numerous authors have surmised that when the battered woman has a negative interaction with the state, she is less likely to rely on governmental assistance in the future. Indeed, * * * if a battered woman is given the choice between abuse by the batterer, which is familiar, and abuse by state actors, which is unfamiliar, she is likely to choose the abuse she knows best.

Finally, mandatory interventions deny the battered woman an important opportunity to partner with the state to help ensure her future safety. * * *

* * *

To counteract the destructive dynamics of the current relationship between the state and battered women * * *, I have developed a Survivor-Centered Model of state response to domestic violence. This approach assumes that the victim of domestic violence is searching for a path toward healing, that state actors should help facilitate her psychological health as well as her physical safety, and that the victim of domestic violence is in the best position to dictate the terms of her healing. * * *

* * *

[The Survivor-Centered Model includes an element of accepting the battered woman "as she is" and learning more about her specific emotional and physical needs, including the possibility that she may need to return to the batterer because of love that developed when he was not violent, or because he is the father of her children, or she may need to return before concluding that the violence is likely to persist, regardless of her efforts to repress or overcome it. This model also includes elements of respect (choosing with her a strategy that responds to her complex and sometimes conflicting concerns); reassurance (safety planning and helping her weigh arrest and prosecution options); engagement (countering social isolation, and changing the rules so that financial assistance to victims is not conditioned on her cooperation with the prosecution); resocialization; empowerment; and emotional responsiveness.]

Rather than employ one-dimensional responses in every case, we need to enhance the clinical ability of law enforcement personnel, prosecutors, and other professionals, including doctors, who are in a position to help battered women. These professionals need to learn skills that draw on the rich clinical literature and that address the trauma of each specific victim. * * *

DONNA COKER

Crime Control and Feminist Law Reform in Domestic Violence Law: A Critical Review
4 Buff. Crim. L. Rev. 801, 802–05, 823–27, 830–32, 840–46, 849, 858–60 (2001)

The last several years have seen an explosion of domestic violence law reform. While significant changes have occurred in civil law provisions, much of the recent law reform has focused on a number of far-reaching changes in criminal law. This focus on criminal law reform is the result of a confluence of factors. First, many advocates for battered women have urged a stronger criminal response, in part as a corrective for the history of profoundly inadequate and sometimes hostile response of the criminal justice system to domestic violence cases.

Second, crime control politics makes criminal law a particularly attractive area of law reform. Politicians who oppose increased government spending on "social programs" have been happy to spend funds on "fighting crime." Fighting crime has political appeal to legislators in part because it is one of the few concerns that reaches across differences in fractious American politics. As Jonathan Simon argues, citizen disillusionment with government's ability to provide for other aspects of communal life has strengthened this focus on crime control. The result, what Simon refers to as "governing through crime," is increasing reliance on surveillance, control, punitive measures, and fear of crime to shape social behavior.

Millions of dollars are now being spent on domestic violence criminal interventions. Battered women's advocates spend much of their time monitoring police and prosecutor response to battered women. There is nothing obvious or necessary about this allocation of dollars or human capital. Poor women are more vulnerable to repeat violence, yet relatively few dollars are allocated for measures that would render them less vulnerable such as transportation, or education and job training. Without legal representation, women are unable to benefit from much of domestic violence law reform, yet women have no legal right to a state subsidy for an attorney and there are too few free lawyers for the number of domestic violence cases. Without adequate resources, women are unable to relocate and therefore, they are unable to escape the reach of controlling, violent ex-partners. Yet few dollars are allocated for emergency relocation and long-term housing. Women who are escaping well-funded or well-connected dangerous men need the equivalent of a witness-protection program (regardless of whether or not they testify in a criminal proceeding), but no such program exists.

Not only does a focus on crime control deflect attention from other anti-domestic violence strategies, crime control policies result in greater state control of women, particularly poor women. Further, under policies that do not allow victims to choose whether or not to arrest and prosecute their abuser, battered women are unable to leverage the potential of criminal prosecution in return for agreements from the batterer.

* * *

The danger is that feminist law reformers will both overestimate the state's power to do good and underestimate the power of the state to do harm. Further, women's decisions whether or not to support criminal intervention *are* often related to whether or not they can afford to prioritize prosecution over other more immediate concerns such as food, employment, and childcare. Thus, the second danger is that feminist law reformers will overlook the importance of women's material resources in the calculus of whether or not state intervention is likely to do harm or good.

Overestimating the Power of the State to Do Good

* * *

Cheryl Hanna, in reflecting on her experiences as a domestic violence prosecutor, describes a case in which the judge dismissed charges at the complainant's request. When Hanna next encounters this woman, the woman has a broken nose, severe bruising, and has lost forty pounds from the stress. Women often experience renewed violence, despite the promises of batterers to reform, but the point of Hanna's story is not merely that domestic violence sometimes escalates. The implicit message of the narrative is that the woman would have been safe (or safer) if only the judge had refused to drop charges. Hanna sets up a dichotomy: Women can be allowed to make the "wrong" decision (against prosecution) or the state can protect their interests in stopping the violence (and proceed with prosecution). This unfairly stacks the deck in favor of mandated prosecution policies.

Any choice a battered woman makes is, to some extent, playing the odds. Narratives like Hanna's rest on two implicit and questionable assumptions. The first is that cooperation with the system is more likely to increase a woman's safety than is non-cooperation. The second assumption regards the relevant universe of choice: A woman chooses either to be wholly cooperative with prosecution or she chooses to be wholly uncooperative with prosecution.

The assumption that the criminal justice system offers the best chance of increasing a woman's safety overstates the efficacy of the system in stopping the violence while simultaneously understating the importance of the availability of women's other resources. * * * Prosecution (or other state intervention) is no guarantee that the violence will stop. A woman who opposes prosecution is taking a calculated risk, as is the woman who actively pursues prosecution. Neither she, nor the judge or the prosecutor, can know with certainty which action will result in less violence. The problem is not that the batterer's coercion is not real, but rather that it is not always clear that the criminal justice system offers a better alternative.

The assumption that women are safest when they cooperate with prosecution also ignores the stories of the women who are successful in stopping the violence in their lives. * * *

* * * Recent research regarding the effects of a pro-arrest policy found that two groups of women were the most likely to be strongly opposed to mandatory arrest. The first were those who had experienced minor violence and who accurately predicted that they were not in danger. The second were those women who were in extreme danger from very violent partners and who predicted *accurately* that arrest and prosecution would not make them any safer.

* * *

Underestimating the Power of the State to do Harm

Mandatory policies make battered women more vulnerable to state control. * * *

The first set of risks for increased state control flow from the increased risk that battered women will be arrested. When mandatory and pro-arrest policies are adopted, more women are arrested for domestic violence. Strong anecdotal evidence suggests that most of the women arrested are victims of battering who are acting in self-defense or who are responding to a pattern of abuse.

Arrests of battered women present serious collateral risks that go beyond the threat of criminal punishment. For example, conviction for domestic violence can result in the deportation of a non-citizen. Recent immigration law reform allows the Attorney General to waive deportation in the case of battered women who can prove that they are "not the primary perpetrator of violence in the relationship" and that they were "acting in self-defense." The difficulty with this standard is that many women who are violent in response to ongoing battering may not meet the legal requirements for self-defense in a particular incident. For example, Cecelia Espenoza relates the story of Paula, a battered immigrant woman from Mexico, who received support from Lideras Campensinas. Paula, determined not to take her husband's abuse any longer and, with a baseball bat in hand, told him to leave the home. He tried to return three times. Each time, he left after Paula threatened him with the bat. In many jurisdictions, Paula's actions would render her criminally liable for domestic violence assault and thereby subject her to mandatory arrest. Since Paula was not in immediate danger when she threatened her husband, it is not clear that she would meet the self-defense requirements for the waiver of deportation.

* * * [B]attered women who are arrested often lose the protection otherwise afforded by special domestic violence legislation. For example, evidence of an arrest, even if the women are not charged, is sufficient in many states to prevent them from benefiting from child custody laws that disfavor a violent parent.

* * *

Rather than the result of batterer intimidation or persuasion, women's cooperation with mandatory policies, particularly with prosecution, is often a product of their access to material resources and the quality of their interactions with actors in the criminal justice system. Cooperation with prosecution often requires women to take time off from work, to acquire transportation and childcare, or to make other sometimes costly and difficult arrangements. Thus, women who have family or friends who will watch the children, help them with chores, or provide transportation or emergency loans, are more likely to cooperate with prosecution than women who do not have access to these informal sources of tangible support. * * * [W]omen's lack of access to material resources can make them more vulnerable to battering. Criminal interventions coupled with assistance directed at alleviating the sources of women's vulnerability are likely to be more effective. Without this assistance, mandatory policies are likely to be harmful.

* * *

Controlling the State: The Organizing Dilemma

* * * The enactment of mandatory policies, particularly mandatory arrest, may be a particularly well-suited goal for feminist organizing. Mandatory arrest provides a bright-line standard for police behavior, which makes it easier for battered women's advocates to hold police accountable when they fail adequately to protect battered women. Additionally, mandatory policies that are the result of feminist activism may result in agreements that place battered women's advocates within the courts and police stations on a regular basis, thus providing an ongoing institutional voice for the concerns of battered women.

The concern that the absence of mandatory policies will result in further police minimization or maltreatment is well grounded. The most common complaint of battered women regarding police response is that the police do not do enough. Women complain that unless they are seriously injured, police underestimate their danger and treat them with disrespect. * * *

Ensuring that the state responds to battered women is critical, but it is not clear that mandatory policies are the only or best manner in which to control police and prosecution response. * * * [C]urrent "soft" no-drop prosecution policies suggest the possibilities of more flexible standards. * * * Police response can also be more flexible, while still incorporating a standard for police conduct. For example, Lawrence Sherman proposes that police be subject to "mandatory action" policies that require that they choose from a list of options including:

> offering to transport the victim to a shelter, taking the suspect or victim to a detoxification treatment center, allowing the victim to decide if an immediate arrest should be made, [and] mobilizing the victim's social networks to provide short-term protection.

A second difficulty with reliance on mandatory policies to ensure police and prosecutorial response is that the effectiveness of these policies depends, in large part, on the existence of an effective battered women's organization. But mandatory policies are sometimes adopted for reasons unrelated to feminist organizing, such as the desire to appease "tough on crime" constituencies while also currying favor with female voters, or the desire to be eligible for federal funds that require that state grantees adopt a pro-arrest policy.

A number of battered women's advocates believe that mandatory policies should be adopted *only* when the policies are a part of a "coordinated community response" that includes significant advocacy and services for battered women. Melanie Shepard, for example, argues that the following essential services for battered women must be in place before engaging in "institutional reform": emergency housing, legal advocacy, support groups for battered women, and financial resources for battered women. "[W]ithout . . . [these] essential services, battered women may be placed in greater danger when the criminal justice system responds to the offender's violence."

Even the availability of services for battered women may not be adequate to ensure that advocates engage in ongoing monitoring of the criminal justice system. Battered women's advocates should be "the stewards of [the service and legal] infrastructure as they direct, guide, and support battered women while confronting and challenging obstacles to their safety." Many advocacy programs are simply not prepared to take on this monitoring role. Yet, the availability of such advocacy may be a critical determinant in the quality of battered women's experiences with mandatory policies. Advocates act in two important roles: as institutional reformers—monitoring police, prosecutor, and judicial responses to domestic violence; and, as advocates for individual women. They often act to soften the effects of mandatory policies when those policies threaten to harm individual women. As one advocate notes, "[t]he criminal justice process does not always effectively address the individual needs of women and does not work well for many[,]" thus, advocates frequently find themselves "hav[ing] argued for policy reforms (e.g., prosecution of cases) only to turn around and ask for exceptions for individual battered women."

* * *

* * * [F]eminist law reformers are faced with a dilemma. Mandatory policies can provide some measure of control over police and prosecutorial response, but such policies may also increase the state's control of women. This risk of increased state control is particularly true for those women who are otherwise most vulnerable to state control: poor women, particularly poor women of color, and women who are engaged in minor crimes, *many* of which *are* directly related to battering. The ability of mandatory policies to control state action is related to the political strength of the battered women's movement in a given locale and the available services for battered women, but mandatory policies are implemented in jurisdictions with weak or non-existent advocacy communities. Activists who support mandatory policies frequently presume that battered women's advocates will play an ongoing monitoring role and will mediate the effects of mandatory policies in circumstances where women are endangered, yet there is no guarantee that such advocacy is available or that the advocacy community will adequately represent the interests of all women.

* * *

Poor women are subject to a dual vulnerability: the private coercion and violence of abusive men and the public coercion and violence of the state. When battered women's advocates negotiate with the state, the challenge is to develop strategies that ensure a positive state response, while limiting the risk that these interventions will result in increased state control *of women*.

How might we diminish the risk that increasing state intervention against domestic violence will increase state control of women? First, we must organize for more material assistance for battered women. Crime control policies are costly, but lawmakers continue to be willing to allocate funds for purposes that sound like "fighting crime." We must begin to articulate that economic justice for women and children is part of domestic violence prevention. Bundling services within crime control programs does not adequately address this need. This is true both because of the limitations of the programs and because many battered women do not come to the attention of the criminal justice system. A focus on economic justice requires that battered women's advocates work to strengthen coalitions with activists and organizations that attend to the broader picture of violence against women in inner cities and the broader picture of women's economic status.

Second, we must recognize that universal policies are unlikely to be successful. Rather, effective policies must derive from local struggles and local organizing efforts.

Third, we must explore alternatives to mandatory policies for establishing control of the state's response to domestic violence. For example, elsewhere, I suggest the establishment of domestic violence citizen review panels that would evaluate police response to domestic violence calls and hear complaints from individuals regarding inadequate responses.

Finally, in developing anti-domestic violence strategies, we must attend to the coercive power of the state, as well as the coercive power of battering men.

EVAN STARK

Mandatory Arrest of Batterers, A Reply to Its Critics,
in *Do Arrests and Restraining Orders Work?*
115, 120–24, 145 (Eve S. Buzawa and Carl G. Buzawa eds., 1996)

* * * [V]iolence against women is a political fact. This means that everything about it—when, how, why, and where it is used, whom it affects, the nature of intervention, and most important, the consequences of intervention for all involved—reflects the relative power of men over women and the struggles by particular men to assert and women to escape this power. Whether this violence is expressed through child sexual abuse, harassment, rape, or battering, the key is the selection of females as victims on the basis of their gender. Because of its roots in sexual inequality, whatever occasions violence in a given encounter, the ultimate cause of "battering" (as well as its consequence) is the denial of women's *civil rights*. When men, children, or the elderly are victimized, this is not structural inequality. * * *

Understanding violence against women as a civil rights issue goes to the very heart of the abusive experience. What distinguishes violence that exploits the structural inequality between men and women from acts of violence generally is neither the greater physical strength of men nor their greater propensity to aggress, both of which have been exaggerated. Rather, its distinctive character derives from how the convergent supports for male authority "enter" an actual conflict and merge with the batterer's pattern of control during and *after* a conflict arises, regardless of who initiates physical violence, particularly if women try to leave the relationship or seek outside help. * * *

In trying to conceptualize battering, we need to picture ongoing forms of control that are at once both personal and social, including economic exploitation, isolation from family and friends, intimidation, and a host of rules governing everyday activities. Ann Jones and Susan Schechter use the term *coercive control* to describe the systemic fusion of social and individual dominance that undermines the physical, psychological, or political autonomy of even the strongest, most aggressive and capable woman.

Because the control elements in battering are visible only negatively, coercive control gives a particular man far more power in the eyes of his mate than an outsider without expert knowledge of the situation can perceive. This is why the risks inherent in abusive situations are consistently underestimated even after helpers have been sensitized to intervene. * * *

Coercive control is the proper frame for understanding male violence against women * * *. By contrast, little of the essential reality is captured by models that rely on a "discourse of injury" in which the location, nature, and severity of physical "damage" provides the basis for assessment, arrest, or disposition and assignment to a specialist. In any case, when we speak about "battering," we refer to both the pattern of violent acts and their political framework, the pattern of social, institutional, and interpersonal controls that usurp a woman's capacity to determine her destiny and make her vulnerable to a range of secondary consequences—attempted suicide, substance abuse, mental illness, and the like. The term *entrapment* describes the cumulative effects of having one's political, social, and psychological identity subordinated to the will of a more powerful other who controls resources that are vital to one's survival.

How does conceptualizing *battering, the social phenomenon*, in terms of sexual inequality, coercive control, and entrapment help us understand *battering, the crime*? Most notably, it highlights the contrast between criminal acts of domestic violence and the pattern of coercion and control that is not currently proscribed by law. Intuitively, it shifts from the class of crimes associated with assault (in which injury is emphasized) to those associated with a history of restraint, such as kidnapping or hostage taking. * * * [Murray] Straus reminds us that domestic violence abrogates the basic trust implied by family connections, hence the term *abuse*. * * * [Straus's] analogy to child abuse and his belief in the sanctity of family connections lead him to question legal sanctions in any but the most extreme instances of spousal violence. But highlighting coercive control and entrapment moves us from an abuse model, in which otherwise legitimate authority is exercised illegitimately, to a model in which violent restraint is placed on a continuum with the normative authority men exercise over women. Whatever informal modes of trust it offends, battering also violates women's affirmative rights to liberty and equality, rights that children do not possess. To reiterate, the civil rights violation is to exploit sexual inequality and obstruct women's self-determination as legally independent adults.

The emphasis on restraint also underlies the social interest in criminalizing battering. [Nineteenth century feminist Frances Power] Cobbe assumed that women possess affirmative rights to liberty and equality and that society reaps the benefits of women's contribution only when these rights are protected. Starting here shifts the rationale for antibattering laws from protecting the innocent—an emphasis that relies heavily on paternalistic stereotypes of women—to removing an obstacle to social progress.

We may anticipate what this frame implies for policy. Because sexual inequality is not merely an unpleasant sociological fact, but rather a condition of existential risk, women's safety is always contingent and context specific, their "fear" chronic, and their self-inhibition of desired social activities routine. Thus, although safety and the reduction of fear remain important goals, their realization depends on making women's "empowerment" the ultimate standard against which the efficacy of various interventions is judged.

* * * *[B]attering, the social phenomenon*, occurs at three levels simultaneously: the political level of female subordination, the level of interpersonal assault, and the level of coercive control at which women's social vulnerability is exploited for personal gain. *Battering, the experience* arises from the particular ways in which these three levels interrelate in a given relationship over time. The challenge is for criminal justice to recontextualize the sorts of disembodied acts of assault recorded by medicine, such as "punched with fist," * * * in terms of entrapment and control. * * * Lacking a conceptual frame to understand the historical nature of battering, police, judges, physicians, and other professionals fall back on kitsch psychology or on cultural stereotypes to explain the patterns they observe among individuals, families, or entire groups who appear "violence prone." Absent a theory of coercive control, the traumatic effects of battering seem to be derived from victim psychology.

The question is how to bring these three levels of causality to bear in a criminal justice response to *battering, the crime*, and in making and assessing arrest decisions. A democratic society is unlikely to punish normative behaviors as such, even when these reproduce social inequalities and evoke consistent emotional and social harms. Thus, the law acknowledges only extraordinary harms, no matter how pathological the standard. We may not be ready to imprison the physician who abandons his wife after she puts him through medical school, but we have reached a level of social development consistent with sanctioning those who forcibly exploit the inequalities that result from discrimination—even in their homes—to deny minorities such personal liberties as the right to go and come freely, to exercise sexual self-determination, or to freely access helping services, family and friends, money, food, and other personal resources, services, education, and so forth.

Because the element of control is what links the assaultive dimensions of abuse to the political fact of female inequality, there can be no hope of preventing battering simply by regulating the degree of violence. This is why we call for "zero tolerance" of force in interpersonal relationships and oppose basing police intervention on a calculus of physical harm. At the same time, no level of "treatment" (for women or men) will substantially reduce force until the political dimensions of sexuality are addressed. * * *

Asking police to help free women from a historical process of entrapment and control by men involves them directly in the politics of gender. * * * Ethnographic descriptions of the informal codes governing how police function on the street and theoretical pictures of how policing reproduces social inequality may add substantially to other dimensions of criminal justice thinking. But they can also obscure what is, at bottom, a political process of negotiation that involves every aspect of law enforcement, from personal attitudes and departmental priorities through who sits on local police boards. * * * [Implementing mandatory arrest] is inextricably linked to a range of challenges to basic police functions. As [Barbara] Hart makes clear, we see laws against battering as part of a broad strategy of justice for women. But before we can debate the wisdom of this strategy or the role of police in its implementation, we must reach a consensus that an affirmative conception of women's rights is the proper basis for reform.

* * *

[Does mandatory arrest disempower women?] The conflicting realities of coercive control and empowerment through victim preference [with regard to arrest decisions] raise what is undoubtedly the most difficult dilemma about mandatory arrest. Too often in women's lives, the question of who speaks in their name has been dealt with fatuously. For battered women, in particular, there is no more important issue in recovery than the restoration of "voice"; the essence of empowerment, we like to say, is allowing women to make the *wrong* decision. At the same time, and although all choices are constrained by an implicit calculus of costs and benefits to a certain extent, for women who are seriously injured or for those whose decisions reflect ignorance of their danger or psychological, material, economic, or racial deprivation, it is hard to see how the benefits of individual choice outweigh the interest in stopping the use of illegitimate power. Only in situations where there are no injuries and where there is an expressed desire *not* to arrest despite probable cause to believe an assault has taken place is it likely that the arrest decision will be experienced as demeaning. Because this profile may describe the *most* as well as the least dangerous situations, I would prefer to mandate arrest than leave assessment to police.

Notes and Questions

1. Does Hanna imply that O.J. Simpson was guilty of killing his wife, and that Nicole Brown Simpson would not have died if O.J. had been prosecuted for beating her? How crucial to Hanna's support of mandated participation is her belief that prosecution increases the safety of women? How do Mills and Coker respond to this argument?

2. Hanna argues that it is the state's responsibility to prosecute crimes regardless of whether or not prosecution helps the victim. Mills argues that the state has a responsibility to use its power to help the victim heal. What are the strengths and weaknesses of these arguments? Would you weigh them in the context of prosecution differently than in the context of arrest?

Hanna suggests that "Ms. Wall's overnight stay in jail may have been the first time that she recognized the seriousness of the abuse against her." In contrast, Mills would argue that, in jail, Ms. Wall would have been "recognizing" abuse by the state. Coker would raise the corollary effects of putting her in jail: she might lose her job or have the state take custody of her children. Which argument poses the sharpest challenge for domestic violence policymaking today?

3. Jonathan Simon argues that "advanced industrial societies (particularly the United States) are experiencing not a crisis of crime and punishment but a crisis of governance that has led them to prioritize crime and punishment as the preferred contexts for governance." Jonathan Simon, *Governing Through Crime*, in *The Crime Conundrum: Essays on Criminal Justice* 173 (Lawrence M. Friedman & George Fisher eds., 1997). For much of the 20th century, "punishment of crime was displaced as the key to urban governance by a focus on housing, public health, social work, and education." *Id.* at 176. Recently, however, "[t]he United States and other advanced industrialized societies have found themselves reevaluating systems of collective risk distribution like welfare, public education, unemployment insurance, and worker's compensation. The failure of modest national health insurance in the United States in 1993 was a potent reminder of how muddled the basic narratives and rationalities supporting these governance modalities have become." *Id.* at 178. Simon's criticisms of governing through crime include arguments that it is too costly, as the explosion of spending on police and prisons is a drag on the economy and higher education; that it does not work; that it makes communities less governable through the impact on people and communities of the large number of people passing through the penal system; and that it is corrosive of democracy.

By comparing contemporary crime control politics in domestic violence reform to Simon's concept of "governing through crime," Donna Coker criticizes the emphasis on punishment over other strategies and methods for transforming danger into empowerment and safety for women. How does Coker's concern about the ways in which the coercive power of the state will fall most harshly on low-income women compare with Linda Mills's emphasis on the state's duty to help women heal rather than hurt them, using clinical evaluations of whether the woman is capable of acting for herself? What would Coker's alternative policies be, compared with the alternatives envisioned by Mills?

4. Mills's theories are part of a school of thought known as therapeutic jurisprudence which seeks to engage the power of courts for psychological growth and rehabilitation. Examples include programs that emphasize treatment for addiction over punishment, efforts to make divorce less traumatic for the separating parties, and other innovative programs. *See, e.g.*, *Practicing Therapeutic Jurisprudence: Law as a Helping Profession* (Dennis Stolle, David B. Wexler & Bruce J. Winick eds., 2000). Even among those who strongly believe in the power of law to help with healing, however, mandatory policies are subject to intense debate. *See, e.g.*, Bruce J. Winick, *Applying the Law Therapeutically in*

Domestic Violence Cases, 69 U.M.K.C. Law Rev. 33, 80 (2000) (summarizing debates over psychological impacts of mandatory policies and advocating presumptive arrest rather than mandatory arrest).

5. According to Coker, defenders of mandatory policies often assume that well organized advocates will be available to provide support for victims, bringing experience and care into the legal process. Duluth, Minnesota, where an influential early study of the deterrent effect of mandatory arrest was carried out, is also the location of a nationally distinguished center for advocacy work against domestic violence. The center had achieved extensive criminal justice reform, which was integrated with programs providing support for women and intervention and training programs in which batterers could learn new responses and behaviors. Should adoption or implementation of mandatory policies depend upon whether a well-developed network of domestic violence advocates is available locally? Recalling Elizabeth Schneider's description at the beginning of this chapter of a shift toward a service orientation and away from feminist organizing, should it matter which perspective is adopted by advocacy programs in that area?

6. An early study in Duluth, Minnesota, showed a drop in subsequent attacks on women when abusers were arrested rather than when police mediated between the parties. This study helped persuade many jurisdictions to adopt mandatory arrest policies. Later, several follow-up studies were conducted in other cities, attempting to replicate the findings of the Duluth arrest study. A study in Milwaukee, Wisconsin found a marked difference in the effects of arrest on recidivism which correlated with both race and unemployment. When unemployed men and African-American men were arrested, they were more likely to commit abuse again than were men who were white and men who were employed.

No consensus has yet been reached on data interpretation or policy recommendations based on the data gathered in the arrest studies. The differential effects of mandatory policies on different racial groups have been the subject of debate among scholars, including an extended exchange between Linda Mills and Evan Stark. In arguing against mandatory arrest, Linda Mills pointed to a study in Milwaukee in which the frequency of repeat violence increased when the persons arrested were unemployed, unmarried, high school dropouts, or African-American; in contrast, repeat violence decreased when the persons arrested were employed, married, and white. She concluded that, under these circumstances, a mandatory arrest policy saves harm to some women, most of whom are white, at the cost of increased harm to other women, most of whom are African-American. *See* Mills, *supra* at 565–66. Evan Stark argued in response that the replication studies took place during an economic downturn with accompanying unemployment, stress, and poverty for minorities and the working poor; "The correlation between crimes of violence (including assault) and the business cycle has been well known in criminology for some time." Stark, *supra* at 131.

7. Beth Richie argues for "a reassessment of the responses that have been central to antiviolence work—in particular, the reliance on law enforcement as the principal provider of women's safety." Beth E. Richie, *A Black Feminist Reflection on the Antiviolence Movement*, 25 Signs: Journal of Women in Culture and Society 1133, 1136 (2000).

> For over a decade, women of color in the antiviolence movement have warned against investing too heavily in arrest, detention, and prosecution as responses to violence against women. Our warnings have been ignored, and the consequences have been serious: serious for the credibility of the antiviolence movement, serious for feminist organizing by women of color, and, most important, serious for women experiencing gender violence who fall outside of the mainstream.
>
> The concern with overreliance on law enforcement parallels a broader apprehension about the expansion of state power in the lives of poor women of color in this country. Just as the antiviolence movement is relying on legal and legislative strategies to criminalize gender violence, women in communities of color are experiencing the negative effects of conservative legislation regarding public assistance, affirmative action, and immigration. And, while the antiviolence movement is working to improve arrest policies, everyday safety in communities of color is being threatened by more aggressive policing, which has resulted in increased use of force, mass incarceration, and brutality. The conflict between the antiviolence movement's strategy and the experiences of low-income communities of color has seriously undermined our work as feminists of color fighting violence against women.

Id. at 1136–37.

8. Should empirical studies be the basis of law enforcement policies? "We do not consider eliminating arrest for other crimes (e.g., robbery), however, because it may not deter a particular individual or class of individuals." Zorza, *supra* at 66. Further, if a businessperson is robbed, prosecution will usually not depend on studies about the effect of prosecution on the businesses of crime victims.

In what ways is domestic violence like other crimes—a wrong against society, which must be taken seriously by the state? In what ways is it different? If you were determining your community's policy on this issue, how would you know which policy is best? If you could not be sure which is best, how would you make a decision, and which policy would you pursue? If you would need more information before making a decision, what information would you want, and how would you obtain it?

9. The following section discusses both the dangers of state control and the effort to win standards that protect battered women in domestic relations law.

SECTION 5. BATTERED MOTHERS AND THEIR CHILDREN

As battering of women became more widely recognized as a social problem, the safety of children became an issue in divorce and custody proceedings. Most states made changes to their child custody laws to consider the issue of domestic violence. The focus on the dangers to children of intimate partner violence raised questions about issues of child protection outside the context of divorce. Judges, legislators, advocates, psychologists, and other professionals debated the appropriate policies to protect both women and children. Aggressive intervention by child protection services when mothers were assaulted by intimate partners brought legal challenges as well.

A. Protection From Physical Harm: Child Abuse and Woman Abuse

Traditionally, a father's violence against the mother had not been considered a threat to children and therefore not an issue in custody. Gradually, the antiviolence movement won recognition that the abuse of mothers can be dangerous to the wellbeing of children both psychologically and physically. "In families where the mother is beaten, sixty-two percent of sons over the age of fourteen are injured trying to protect their mothers. A son who sees his father beat his mother is more likely to become a delinquent or a batterer himself than if his father beat him instead." Zorza, *supra* at 47. Men who abuse women are more likely to abuse children as well. "Between fifty-three and seventy percent of men who abuse women also beat their children, and a significant number sexually abuse the children, especially daughters. Many children also suffer serious injuries as a result of the reckless conduct of their fathers' while beating their mothers." *Id.*

As the effects of domestic violence became more widely recognized, attention to child abuse also increased, placing additional focus on the difficulties that battered mothers faced in protecting their children. Mary Becker describes the resulting tensions:

MARY E. BECKER

Double Binds Facing Mothers in Abusive Families: Social Support Systems, Custody Outcomes, and Liability for Acts of Others
2 U. Chi. L. Sch. Roundtable 13, 13–15, 20–23, 25–32 (1995)

Child abuse is an awkward topic for feminists and feminism. Feminists and feminist theory tend to focus on problems women face in society and in the legal system, on the ways in which both need to change to give women a more equitable share of the good things in life. Thus, the central question is identifying and analyzing ways in which women are, in some sense, victimized, i.e., treated unfairly by current social or legal systems. But women are not only victims in homes in which children are abused; they are often guilty themselves as agents who abuse children or fail to protect them.

* * *

* * * [C]hild abuse is [also] a difficult topic because gender bias operates on many levels. Because of this bias, mothers are likely to be found liable for abuse and neglect regardless of the identity of the actor. If one looks at who is charged with abuse and neglect in juvenile courts, this worry is verified: it is almost always only the mother, though often the mother is charged with failing to protect and the active abuser was a man. * * *

There is a profound tendency in our culture to blame mothers (not fathers) for all problems children face (and all problem children). Mother-blaming has deep roots and persists to the present in modern disciplines such as psychology and psychiatry. In legal proceedings, this bias operates as an unspoken and unconscious double standard for mothers and fathers, such that mothers are expected to be much better and more powerful parents than fathers, always putting their children's needs above their own and protecting their children from all harm. Mothers are likely to be held liable in tort and criminal law for harm caused by men under circumstances in which, were the situation reversed, the father would *not* be regarded as responsible. * * *

Double Binds: Legal Responsibility for Staying Without Legal or Social Support for Leaving

A parent who stays in a home in which children are abused by the other parent or someone else can, of course, lose custody and even parental rights. Mothers are often held criminally accountable for their children's abuse by another, typically a father, stepfather, or boyfriend. Yet social and legal supports for their leaving are absent; indeed, often existing social and legal systems encourage or require their staying in households with abusive men. * * *

* * * [A]n affirmative duty to care for the child may be the basis for holding a parent criminally liable for an act committed by another. Not all states impose criminal liability for another's abuse, but a few do, and the trend seems to be toward increased parental liability for failure to protect. Most states have criminal child-abuse statutes that apply to acts of omission as well as commission. In some states, parents have been held criminally liable under general assault or battery, manslaughter, or second-or first-degree murder statutes as well as under child abuse statutes, for acts committed by another. * * *

Adults in a household should be responsible for injury to the child if they knew or should have known about the abuse and could have taken steps to prevent the abuse by leaving with the children or reporting the abuse to the authorities. The assumption should be that the adult who was not literally a hostage—not literally coerced at every available second—*could* have acted to end abuse. Although the adult might have found herself or himself in circumstances such that protection of the child seemed impossible, the child is still a child. No matter how weak the mother, she is in a much better position than the child to prevent abuse and owes a duty of care to her children. As Alice Miller, the contemporary Swiss psychologist who has done much work on child abuse, has pointed out, "[t]he situation of an adult woman confronted by a brutal man is not the same as that of a small child."

The adults around the child are necessarily responsible for the child's well-being. In extreme cases, such responsibility should carry with it criminal penalties, even if the adult did not herself or himself perform abusive acts. And an adult's obligations to a child do not diminish because the adult herself is also abused by the perpetrator. * * * Unless we are willing to recognize a general *diminished* capacity defense—a defense easier to establish than incapacity, duress, and insanity—criminal liability is appropriate under generally applicable standards. * * *

True, such liability is likely to be imposed unevenly, given pervasive class, race, and gender biases in our culture. Yet bias against mothers cannot preclude maternal responsibility unless we are willing to ignore harm to children (half of whom are girls) as a remedy for systematic biases in our culture. * * *

Holding an abused adult liable criminally or civilly is not, however, likely to be an effective way to protect living children from future abuse. And even for the adult who is not abused herself, there may be more effective ways to protect children than vicarious maternal liability. * * *

Escape

If mothers, even abused mothers, are civilly and criminally liable for the abuse of their children by fathers, husbands, or boyfriends, then social and legal systems must support their efforts to escape to safety with their children. But these systems today present women with a number of double binds because the mother's removal of her children from an abusive household may increase her problems, rather than eliminate them. * * *

During divorce proceedings, when a woman alleges that her spouse has abused her or their children, she faces two particular problems. The judge and other professionals involved in the case may disbelieve her allegations, believing instead that the allegations were made for a strategic purpose: to strengthen her bargaining position in divorce negotiations. And to the extent she alleges abuse of *herself*, the judge and experts involved in the proceeding may conclude that the abuse is irrelevant to the father's fitness as a custodial parent. * * *

* * *

Yet if the mother whose children are being abused will not be believed if she seeks custody at divorce, she may well be right in concluding that the children are best off with her continued silence. Accusing the father leads to divorce in most circumstances, and the children are probably better off with her in the home with the father, rather than in the sole or joint custody of the father. Our inability to believe mothers when they do complain of paternal sexual or physical abuse of children is inconsistent with holding mothers criminally and civilly responsible for a father's injuries to the children.

Actually, what empirical evidence there is suggests that even at divorce most allegations of paternal sexual abuse are true. Such allegations are actually rare, probably only somewhere between two and fifteen out of every one thousand divorce filings involve allegations of sexual abuse. * * *

There are many reasons for such allegations to arise only at or after a divorce, since few marriages could survive thereafter. [Also, these allegations make it possible that the mother will be regarded as unfit, either because she did not prevent earlier abuse, or because if her allegations are disbelieved she will be seen as lying, vindictive, and hostile.] * * *

* * *

If she is regarded as hostile to the father, the mother will be disfavored for custody under the friendlier-parent provisions in many state custody statutes. Under these provisions, a court considers how receptive each parent is toward the other parent's continued involvement with the child. * * * [I]f her allegations of abuse are disbelieved—regarded as fabricated to give her an edge in divorce or custody proceedings—she will be seen as a less appropriate custodial parent for having voiced them. And if she does lose custody because she is not believed, custody is likely to go to the abuser.

* * *

Women will be empowered (and children in violent households thereby protected) by a number of reforms in divorce laws needed by most women, particularly poor ones. Women and children need better economic protection at divorce, including higher support and maintenance standards as well as more effective collection methods, particularly for self-employed fathers and fathers who switch jobs often. State agencies already required to enforce child support for mothers (under federal law) need to develop far more effective and efficient procedures.

The discretionary best-interest standard—which applies in almost all American jurisdictions—does not require trial judges to give particular weight to the parent who has been the child's primary caretaker in the past. As a result, mothers who have been primary caretakers and who therefore have an extremely strong commitment to post-divorce custody, will trade post-divorce economic well-being (for themselves and their children) for a maternal custody agreement, rather than risk losing custody when it is determined in the judicial black box of the discretionary best-interest standard. This problem is exacerbated by the parents' relative economic strength. The person who has been primary caretaker of the children will, for that very reason, tend to have fewer economic resources to use in a judicial battle for custody, a battle whose outcome is fairly uncertain under such a discretionary standard. And the expense of the battle is maximized by the open-ended nature of this standard and the routine use of expensive "experts."

For the mother who has been married to an abusive man (abusive to his wife or to the children), these fears are likely to be particularly strong. Violent men routinely use children as hostages, threatening their wives with loss of the children if they leave them. Strengthening the mother's bargaining position at divorce with a custody standard—such as West Virginia's primary caretaker provision—that protects with greater reliability her relationship with her children, will make it easier to escape an abusive household, and will thereby serve to lower violence and abuse against children in such households. [Presumptions in favor of joint custody also create problems in the context of domestic violence.] * * *

* * *

On a systemic basis, empowerment of mothers (rather than fathers) is likely to improve the well-being of children for a number of reasons. In general, in our culture women are primarily responsible for children. The well-being of mothers and children is therefore more closely linked in general than is the well-being of fathers and children. Empowered mothers will have more assets and hence be better able to care for their children. Children are likely to be physically safer if mothers themselves can escape abusive men. Although mothers should be criminally and civilly responsible for harm to their children as a result of their own abuse or their failure to protect their children from the abuse of others (given that the mother knows, or should know, of the abuse), society cannot show a meaningful commitment to children without other changes designed to empower women and, hence, indirectly empower children.

* * *

Given the high correlation between child abuse and maternal abuse, as a society we need to do what is possible to facilitate women's safe exit with their children from abusive households. If we are truly committed to children's welfare, then we cannot simply rely on mothers who are likely themselves to be abused as well as economically dependent on the abuser. As one commentator has noted, "[o]ur society must take some responsibility for the inability of some women to leave abusive partners."

This means spending scarce resources in a time of severe budgetary constraints on state and federal governments. But unless we are *only* willing to impose responsibility for children's welfare on women likely to be themselves abused, we must spend resources to make it easier for women to leave. Shelter space is limited in most parts of the country. Often there is a time limit at a shelter, such as thirty days, which is far too short a period for an effective transition to an independent establishment, particularly for a mother (like most) without sufficient economic resources. For an effective exit, most mothers of abused children are likely to need longer-term transitional low-cost housing, job training, child care, health care, health insurance, and adequate economic support during the transitional period.

* * * In a long-term study of children of abused mothers who had stayed in shelters in the past, most of the reduction in abuse of the children "resulted from women no longer living with abusive men." According to this study, for the abused mothers who in turn abused their children, the mother's successful escape from an abusive relationship was the most effective way to lower levels of violence against the children by the mothers as well as by the men. And, of course, women need to be empowered in order to be able to protect themselves as well as their children.

Notes and Questions

1. For many years, judges paid little attention to questions of violence unless the child was the target. No-fault divorce tended to make domestic violence less visible in custody contests. *See* Martha R. Mahoney, *Legal Images of Battered Women: Redefining the Issue of Separation*, 90 Mich. L. Rev. 1, 45–46 (1991); Naomi R. Cahn, *Civil Images of Battered Women: The Impact of Domestic Violence on Child Custody Decisions*, 44 Vand. L. Rev. 1041, 1083–84 (1991). Nancy Lemon describes the gradual transition in the approach of lawmakers:

> By the 1980's, the domestic violence movement had become a vocal presence, and was developing some sophistication in terms of changing entrenched policies. Advocates began to call for legislators and courts to protect children from batterers. Feminists stressed the harmful effects of exposure to domestic violence on children, and stated that it is not actually possible to be a violent husband and a good father.
>
> At the same time, there was a strong trend toward trying to keep fathers close to their children. Father's rights groups pushed for, and succeeded in getting, legislation stressing the importance of joint custody. Families were no longer seen as "broken," but instead were "in transition," with the goal being that both parents were still involved in their children's lives. In some cases, courts gave fathers more time with their children than they had generally spent with them while living with the children's mother; in these cases the goal was not merely to continue the father/child relationship, but to try to strengthen it.
>
> Legislatures started to respond to both these groups. Some states enacted laws stating that domestic violence could be taken into account in making custody decisions, but leaving the decision up to the judge whether or not to even admit such evidence. Other states went further, actually mandating that judges consider domestic violence.
>
> * * *

Meanwhile, many states were also enacting laws allowing for or preferring joint custody of children. * * *

In all too many cases, these two trends worked at cross-purposes. * * * Starting in 1991, some states resolved this conflict by enacting statutes creating a presumption against custody to batterers.

* * * The first U.S. national policy statement supporting a rebuttable presumption in domestic violence cases was H. R. Congressional Resolution 172 [sponsored by Rep. Constance Morella and passed unanimously on Oct. 25, 1990]: "It is the sense of Congress that, for purposes of determining child custody, credible evidence of physical abuse of a spouse should create a statutory presumption that it is detrimental to the child to be placed in the custody of the abusive spouse." While Congress does not have the authority to tell states how to handle custody decisions, this Resolution was intended to encourage states to pass their own statutes establishing such presumptions.

In 1994, the National Council of Juvenile and Family Court Judges released the Model Code on Domestic and Family Violence. This Code was developed in conjunction with legislators, the American Bar Association, the American Medical Association, domestic violence experts, prosecutors, and defense counsel over a period of three years. Section 401 of the Model Code states:

> In every proceeding where there is at issue a dispute as to the custody of a child, a determination by the court that domestic or family violence has occurred raises a rebuttable presumption that it is detrimental to the child and not in the best interest of the child to be placed in sole custody, joint legal custody, or joint physical custody with the perpetrator of family violence.

Nancy K. D. Lemon, *Statutes Creating Rebuttable Presumptions Against Custody to Batterers: How Effective Are They?*, 28 Wm. Mitchell L. Rev. 601, 604–07 (2001).

By the spring of 2001, forty-eight state statutes used domestic violence as a factor in custody decisions, and twenty states had enacted some form of presumption in their statutes. *Id.* at 610–13. The presumption statutes vary greatly, in terms of (1) whether the presumption applies to all types of custody or only to joint custody; (2) how domestic violence is defined—what type of violence triggers the presumption; (3) what evidentiary standard is required to trigger the presumption; (4) what type of evidence is required to rebut the presumption; and (5) what evidentiary standard is required to rebut the presumption. They also vary in terms of what the court is to do if both parents appear to have been abusive, and what standard should be applied if the presumption is found inapplicable. *Id.* at 614.

2. When divorce and custody agreements are negotiated between the parties rather than resolved by courts, men and women are often on unequal ground, and battered women face additional difficulties. The battered wife has often established a pattern of compliance with the demands of the abuser which make it difficult for her to make her own demands in negotiations. The history of abuse may have compromised her work performance, depleting her financial resources and leaving her unable to obtain legal counsel. Even if the battered woman has an attorney, she is at a disadvantage in negotiations because attorneys and judges often minimize the abuse and sometimes, perversely, blame women for allowing it to occur. Because of the secretive nature of domestic violence, women often have difficulty producing witnesses or evidence of the abuse. Penelope Eileen Bryan, *Women's Freedom to Contract at Divorce: A Mask For Contextual Coercion*, 47 Buff. L. Rev. 1153, 1156–57, 1220, 1226–30 (1999).

3. Becker emphasizes the need to facilitate escape for women. Donna Coker explains that separation often requires careful planning:

> * * * Despite well-documented evidence that battered women are at greater risk of harm from their abusers during separation, the child protection system's traditional approach has been to require battered women to leave their abusers immediately or face the loss of their children. Separation also requires resources. Women who separate need money for new housing—first and last month rent plus deposit, new childcare arrangements, new school enrollments, and a new job. Many women must make these arrangements while using inadequate and unreliable public transportation. When women separate they often require a restraining order. They must then distribute copies of the order, along with a picture of the abuser, to the children's schools and childcare providers and to the security personnel at their work site.
>
> The failure of child protection workers to understand the dangers of separation and the importance of women's material resources to their safety results in a failure to provide the resources and support that battered women most require. Women are often coerced into signing "voluntary" plans that include agreements to participate in such services as parenting classes and battered women's support groups but are not given assistance with the resources needed to separate safely.

Coker, *Crime Control*, 835–36.

Many homeless women and children have experienced battering, and many of the women who are unsuccessful at meeting the work requirements of welfare are being undermined by domestic abuse. *See, e.g.,* Jody Raphael, *Saving Bernice: Battered Women, Welfare, and Poverty* (2000). Recognizing that battered women often cannot depend on the state to meet needs such as housing, subsistence, or child care assistance, Coker suggests that programs for battered women be evaluated through a "material resources test" which examines the likelihood that a particular program will move resources directly or indirectly into the hands of women. For example, when police come to the door after a domestic violence call, they may simply decide whether or not to make an arrest, or alternatively they may offer rides to shelters, or bring with them information on services and counseling. This test could direct material support toward battered women and also help to shift consciousness about their needs and struggles. *See* Donna Coker, *Shifting Power for Battered Women: Law, Material Resources, and Poor Women of Color*, 33 U.C. Davis Law Rev. 1009 (2000).

4. When children have been physically harmed, Becker would hold all adults around them criminally responsible, whether they committed the acts of violence or failed to save the children from harm. Some scholars emphasize the danger to women in violent relationships and the coercive control of batterers, questioning the fairness of punishing women who fail to successfully prevent abuse of children. *See, e.g.*, V. Pualani Enos, *Prosecuting Battered Mothers: State Laws' Failure to Protect Battered Women and Abused Children*, 19 Harv. Women's L.J. 229, 229–30 (1996) (proposing that "when determining whether a woman is responsible for harm done to her child by a third person, courts should employ an objective standard. A mother should only be held responsible for situations which she can control or affect.")

5. While some battered mothers have been held criminally liable for abuse committed against their children by their abusive partners, the state more frequently intervenes through child protection agencies. These agencies are responsible for responding to allegations of child abuse and neglect and have the authority to initiate the removal of children from the custody of a parent or to remove parents from the home. Child protection agencies have become increasingly concerned with the danger to children in violent households who may be at risk of emotional harm even if they are not physically harmed. One of the most searching debates in the field of domestic violence today involves the question of how and when to intervene—and of the appropriate focus for intervention—when children witness the abuse of a parent but have not been physically harmed themselves.

B. Child Witnessing of Domestic Violence

Aggressive child protection interventions responded to increased knowledge about the dangers of domestic violence to children, but these interventions often lacked an understanding of the dynamics of domestic violence that had been developed by professionals and advocates helping battered women. Because of changes in child protection laws and policies, there has been a dramatic recent increase in child abuse investigations founded solely or primarily on the fact that a child's mother has been the victim of domestic violence. Some child protection organizations have expanded the definition of child abuse to include residing in a home in which domestic violence has taken place. Also, "[s]ome police departments have developed policies that require officers to report to child protection services every case in which a child is present at a domestic violence call." Coker, *Crime Control*, 833. "Children are removed even when the violence was a one-time occurrence, and sometimes even when they did not witness the violence." *Id.* at 834. These child protection policies often implicitly assume that battered women could avoid or control the violence. But, as Coker points out, this is often untrue: "Battering is often unpredictable: Women are beaten for 'failure' to have the proper demeanor, for 'failure' to prepare the 'right' meal, for 'failure' to desire sex at the 'right' times." Coker, *Crime Control, supra* at 835.

"Increasingly a unique type of case is coming before the juvenile court, a case in which the child is alleged to have been victimized by watching or being exposed to one parent being beaten by another adult in the home." National Council of Juvenile and Family Court Judges Family Violence Department, *Effective Intervention in Domestic Violence & Child Maltreatment Cases: Guidelines for Policy and Practice* 109 (1999) [hereinafter *Effective Intervention*]. Aggressive interventions revealed tensions between the goals of protecting children and empowering women. Advocates working with mothers affected by these policies also raised questions about whether the interventions placed women at increased risk from batterers and whether taking children away from battered mothers helped children or caused them further problems.

Scholars, advocates, and judges increasingly debated what interventions were appropriate and how to both support abused mothers and protect children. The *Effective Intervention* guidelines were compiled for the National Council of Juvenile and Family Court Judges through extensive consultation by judges and experts. *Id.* at 4–5. Their "overriding" first principle is that batterers should be held accountable and victims should be protected:

> Leaders of the community and its institutions should join together to establish responses to domestic violence and child maltreatment that offer meaningful help to families, including protections for all victims from physical harm; adequate social and economic supports for families; and access to services that are respectful, culturally relevant, and responsive to the unique strengths and concerns of families. Simultaneously, the community should hold violent perpetrators responsible for their abusive behavior and provide a variety of legal interventions and social services to stop this violence.

Id. at 14.

Effective Intervention suggests that child welfare services sometimes blame victimized mothers for "failure to protect" children because of the "system's inability to hold the actual perpetrator of violence accountable." *Id.* at 66. Battered mothers, like non-battered mothers, may themselves abuse or neglect their children and should be held accountable if they do so. However, strategies that blame a non-abusive parent for the violence committed by others should be avoided. *Id.*

> Blaming a battered mother for being abused, for not leaving the domestic violence perpetrator, or for not stopping his violence is

> simply counterproductive. The battered woman cannot change or stop the perpetrator's violence by herself. If she does not have adequate support, resources, and protection, leaving him may simply make it worse for the children. * * *

Id. at 19.

In most cases, juvenile court jurisdiction should not be established solely on the basis that the children have witnessed domestic violence. Court intervention is recommended only if the evidence shows that the children "suffered significant emotional harm from that witnessing and that the caretaker or non-abusing parent is unable to protect them from that emotional abuse even with the assistance of social and child protection services." *Id.* at 109.

"Service plans are developed most commonly for mothers of children in the child protection system. Perpetrators of violence against women and children often are missing from the child protection response" because fathers may not living in the home, or may be an inconsistent presence in the home; abusers who do live in the home may not be legally or biologically related to the children. *Id.* at 64–65. In addition, the abuser may make child protection workers feel unsafe. Nonetheless, "child protection services must initiate efforts to reach violent perpetrators and hold them accountable." Child welfare services should engage batterers directly, develop service plans for them, and monitor their compliance. *Id.* at 65.

Effective Intervention notes that "Many women take strong steps toward developing safe environments only to be defeated by the lack of community support structures and the inadequate response to repeatedly violent men." *Id.* at 57. A dynamic and responsive array of services should be designed collaboratively to ensure the safety of battered mothers and their children. *Id.* Victims should not be reflexively required to take particular actions, such as obtaining an order of protection or moving into a shelter, because there are cases in which these actions are neither helpful nor appropriate. *Id.* at 22. "Success and safety require added assistance in the form of subsidized childcare, transportation, transitional housing, job training, employment and substance abuse services, health and mental health care, and access to advocacy in key systems including police, courts, and child protection services." *Id.* at 57.

Separating children from their mother can be harmful: "Because these children may be attached significantly to the victim, to remove them would re-victimize both the children and the non-abusive parent." *Id.* at 109. Therefore, "[a]s a way to ensure stability and permanency for children, child welfare administrators and juvenile court personnel should try to keep children affected by maltreatment and domestic violence in the care of their non-offending parent (or parents), whenever possible." *Id.* at 19. This recommendation promotes the best interests of the child because, in most cases, "trying to make mothers safe does make children safer and offers children their best hope for stability." *Id.*

According to the guidelines in *Effective Intervention*, the court should make a priority of removing the abuser before it removes a child from a battered mother:

> the court should remove a child from the non-abusive parent's care only if it is proven by clear and convincing evidence that the caretaking parent is unable to protect the child, even with the assistance of social and child protection services. To this end, the court must be prepared to insist that services such as safe housing be available for the victim-parent and the children.

Id. at 109.

Despite these recommendations, advocates in many states continued to find conflicts in the interactions between child protection systems and battered women. In child protection cases, the emphasis is usually on family reunification after the removal of children; measures such as parenting classes, contracts to perform certain tasks or go to counseling, are routine tools used to rehabilitate families and teach parenting skills. Domestic violence advocates, recognizing that leaving may be more dangerous than staying, emphasize careful safety planning.

The following descriptions of the experience of families in New York are summarized from the factual findings of a civil rights case, Nicholson v. Williams, 203 F.Supp.2d 153 (E.D.N.Y.2002), brought on behalf of battered mothers by lawyers from a social service agency, Sanctuary for Families, and a small civil rights law firm:

Sharwline Nicholson was a thirty-two year old mother of two children who worked full-time as a cashier at Home Depot and also took classes full-time at Mercy College. While she worked, the children were at school and daycare; when she went to college, she took her son with her and left her infant daughter with a baby sitter. The baby's father never lived with Nicholson but traveled from South Carolina to visit on a monthly basis for nine months after the baby was born. He had never assaulted or threatened Nicholson until, during one of his visits in early 1999, she told him that she was breaking off their relationship because they lived so far apart. He flew into a rage, punched her, kicked her, and threw objects at her. During the assault, their daughter was in her crib in another room, and Nicholson's son was at school. Nicholson suffered a broken arm, fractured ribs, and head injuries. When the baby's father left the apartment, Nicholson called 911. Before the ambulance arrived, she arranged for child care from a baby-sitter who had cared for the children in the past. *Nicholson*, 203 F.Supp.2d at 168–69.

Police officers came to the hospital and said that it would be better if her children could stay with a family member. She gave them telephone numbers for family members and information about the assault. At the direction of the Administration for Children's Services (ACS), police took the children from the babysitter to a nursery that evening. The next day, an ACS worker told Nicholson that the agency had possession of her children but would not say where they were; if she wanted to see them, she had to appear in court the following week.

Nicholson was "very upset . . . [and] devastated." She demanded to be discharged from the hospital so that she could get more information about her children and went to stay with a cousin because the police had left word with the hospital that she was not to return to her apartment. *Id.* at 169–70.

The Child Protective Manager (CPM) in charge of overseeing child protection work on the case believed that the children were in "imminent risk if they remained in the care of Ms. Nicholson because she was not, at that time, able to protect herself nor her children because Mr. Barnett had viciously beaten her." The CPM did not look into the case but feared that return to her apartment would be unsafe—in fact, her assailant had never lived at the Brooklyn apartment, did not have a key, and lived in South Carolina. ACS filed a neglect petition regarding the children. Even though the CPM did not believe she was actually neglectful, the neglect petition alleged against both parents that "[r]espondents engage in acts of domestic violence in the presence of the subject child * * *. As a result of one such fight, * * * the respondent mother suffered a broken left arm and a head injury * * *." This count made no distinction between the culpability of batterer and victim. Another count, directed solely against Nicholson, alleged that she "fails to cooperate with offered services designed to insure the safety of the children" but did not state any services with which she had failed to cooperate, or how any failure constituted neglect. *Id.* at 170–71.

Despite repeated appearances at Family Court, Ms. Nicholson was not allowed to see her children for eight days. When she finally saw them, her daughter had a rash and pus running from her nose; her son had a swollen eye and reported that the foster mother had slapped his face. ACS moved them to a different foster care setting but did not return them to their mother until twenty-one days after the separation and fourteen days after the Family Court had ordered them returned to her. *Id.* at 172.

Other plaintiffs had similar stories. After reporting an assault by Michael Gamble, April Rodriguez's two children and her stepdaughter were removed without a court order. Rodriguez was told that she would have to move into a shelter for abused women in order to keep her children. She refused because the shelter would have required her to give up her job as an assistant manager at a video rental store. Originally, a caseworker said that she could live at her grandmother's house with the children. ACS then forced her to transfer custody to Michael Gamble but later blamed her for giving custody to him after they discovered a fact that neither ACS nor Rodriguez had known—that Gamble had been charged with child sexual abuse in the past. Ultimately, ACS placed the children in foster care until Rodriguez agreed to move to a shelter. When she was finally reunited with her children, almost two months after the initial assault, they required hospital treatment for medical problems acquired while in foster care. Ironically, the shelter in which Rodriguez was placed was not a domestic violence shelter, and it did not have a confidential location or services for victims and their children. Rodriguez could not meet the strict curfew of the shelter while working. Although she had previously been entirely self supporting, at the time of litigation, Rodriguez was receiving public assistance. The Child Protective Manager from the case testified that neither the caseworker nor the case supervisor did anything wrong in handling this case—everything was "in conformance with regular practice." *Id.* at 173–76.

Sharlene Tillett was pregnant when she was attacked by Jamie Gray. Her newborn baby, Uganda, was removed by ACS without a court order after Tillett reported the abuse. The CPM ignored a report by the caseworker that the baby was healthy, clean and well cared for. ACS charged Tillett with neglect, alleging that she "engage[d] in acts of domestic violence in the presence of the subject child." At trial, the CPM conceded that, as an unborn baby, Uganda could not have witnessed the violence. Tillett complied with ACS's demands by obtaining a new residence, getting a bassinet for Uganda, becoming self-supporting, and attending domestic violence and parenting classes as well as one on one counseling sessions but ACS further demanded a psychological examination before releasing Uganda to her mother. Tillett refused to undergo the psychological examination, and Uganda was not returned to her until two months after the assault. None of the charges against Sharlene Tillett were ultimately proven. *Id.* at 180–82.

Michele Garcia, a dental assistant with three children, was charged with neglect and had her children removed by ACS without a court order. She had been attacked by her son's father after she ended a seven year relationship. She was hospitalized for a week and a half; he was never arrested. The domestic violence specialist assigned to her case found no signs of harm to the children, described Michele Garcia as "a strong woman who would do anything to protect her children," and determined that removal of the children was unnecessary. Nevertheless, the CPM charged Michele Garcia with neglect and removed the children without a court order because she believed that they were in "imminent danger" because they were not receiving counseling. Ironically, the children were placed with the batterer's family and never received counseling. *Id.* at 182–85.

These women and many others became the named plaintiffs in a federal class action lawsuit brought against the city of New York.

NICHOLSON v. WILLIAMS

203 F.Supp.2d 153 (E.D.N.Y.2002)

WEINSTEIN, Senior District J.

The evidence reveals widespread and unnecessary cruelty by agencies of the City of New York towards mothers abused by their consorts, through forced unnecessary separation of the mothers from their children on the excuse that this sundering is necessary to protect the children. The pitiless double abuse of these mothers is not malicious, but is due to benign indifference, bureaucratic inefficiency, and outmoded institutional biases.

This class action is brought on behalf of abused mothers and their children who are separated from each other because the mother has suffered domestic abuse and the children are for this reason deemed neglected by the mother. Three sometimes conflicting principles control: First, as a parent, a mother has rights to uninterrupted custody of her children and a child has rights to remain with parents; within wide limits, adults and children in a household are immune from state prying and intrusion. Second, domestic abuse—particularly if physical—of a mother or child will not be tolerated. Third, the state has the obligation to protect children from abuse, including, where clearly necessary to protect the child, the power to separate the mother and child. It is this third element that the defendants are misusing in unjustified reliance on the second and in violation of the first. The resulting denial of constitutional rights of both mothers and children cannot go unchecked.

[The court described the facts of cases involving ten women and their children, all victims of domestic violence, whose children were removed by the Administration for Children's Services, or ACS.]

* * *

In many other cases petitions in Family Court allege neglect and domestic violence against the mother even when she has herself committed no violence and is separated from the batterer, and is caring for her child with no evidence of harm to the child.

* * *

At trial substantial expert evidence was presented on the subject of how children are affected by the presence of domestic violence in the home. Two general topics were addressed in detail: the effect that witnessing domestic violence has on children, and the connection between domestic violence in the household and direct abuse against the children.

The consensus of the experts was that the children can be—but are not necessarily—negatively affected by witnessing domestic violence. The experts agreed that children who witness domestic violence exhibit a broad range of responses. * * *

* * *

In a 1999 study by Jeffrey L. Edleson surveying existing research on how children respond to witnessing domestic violence, he addressed how this evidence should influence decisions about child maltreatment. In his conclusion Edleson warned against automatically defining a child's witnessing battery of the mother as maltreatment by her; he observed that there is

> great concern [regarding] how increased awareness of children's exposure [to domestic violence] and associated problems is being used. Concerned about the risk adult domestic violence poses for children, some child protection agencies in the United States appear to be defining exposure to domestic violence as a form of child maltreatment.... Defining witnessing as maltreatment is a mis-

take. Doing so ignores the fact that large numbers of children in these studies showed no negative development problems and some showed evidence of strong coping abilities. Automatically defining witnessing as maltreatment may also ignore battered mothers' efforts to develop safe environments for their children and themselves. A careful assessment of the risks and protective factors in every family is necessary before drawing conclusions about the risks and harm to children. * * *

Several expert witnesses * * * testified about the primacy of the parent-child bond and the effect on a child if he or she is separated from a parent. * * * [T]he attachment between parent and child forms the basis of who we are as humans and the continuity of that attachment is essential to a child's natural development. * * *

* * *

* * * [P]laintiffs' expert Dr. Stark noted the importance of a consistent relationship with a primary caretaker to a child's health development. For those children who are in homes where there is domestic violence, disruption of that bond can be even more traumatic than situations where there is no domestic violence. Dr. Stark asserted that if a child is placed in foster care as a result of domestic violence in the home, then he or she may view such removal as "a traumatic act of punishment ... and [think] that something [the mother] has done or failed to do has caused this separation." [Another expert] testified that when a child is separated from a mother because of domestic violence, the separation is even more traumatic because the child "is terrified that a parent might not be OK, may be injured, may be vulnerable.... They feel that they should somehow be responsible for the parent and if they are not with the parent, then it's their fault."

* * *

Another serious implication of removal is that it introduces children to the foster care system which can be much more dangerous and debilitating than the home situation. Dr. Stark testified that foster homes are rarely screened for the presence of domestic violence, and that the incidence of abuse and child fatality in foster homes in New York City is double that in the general population. Children in foster care often fail to receive adequate medical care. Foster care placements can disrupt the child's contact with community, school and siblings.

* * *

The limiting factor on what a battered mother does to protect herself or her children from the batterer is usually a lack of viable options, not a lack of desire. Dr Richard Gelles, the City defendants' expert witness, has written, "[t]he typical battered wife is hardly passive. She actively seeks to prevent further victimization and is handicapped, not by her own psychological limitations, but by the *lack of concrete and effective remedies available from agencies of social control or other institutions*." Usually the mother is doing everything she believes is possible to protect herself and her children. The problem is that often her options are severely limited.

Accusing battered mothers of neglect aggravates the problem because it blames the mother for failing to control a situation which is defined by the batterer's efforts to deprive her of control. * * * Counter-productively, one of the outcomes of accusing the battered woman of neglect is that the power of the batterer in the household may be reinforced.

* * *

Dr. Stark testified that best practices establish that the batterer should be held accountable for his actions, and that the victim is in a particularly bad position to perform this task. Thus, every state now requires that police arrest batterers, rather than making the victim responsible for deciding whether the arrest should occur. *See* New York Commission on Domestic Violence Fatalities, *Report to the Governor* at 40 (1997) (Charging victims of domestic violence with neglect "implicitly places responsibility for stopping the violence on the victim, rather than on the violent partner who is committing the acts.").

* * *

Dr. Stark testified that * * * [b]atterers often try to separate the mother from the child, and services should focus on "strengthening the bonds between mother and child," rather than exacerbating the damage. Dr. Stark reported that while removal must remain an option available to ACS [the Administration for Children's Services] in domestic violence cases, it is justified to prevent risk to the child only when three conditions have been met: [1.] ACS has engaged in joint safety planning with the victim that includes an offer of services geared to the dynamics and risks identified in a specific case. [2.] Criminal Justice intervention has been aggressively pursued. At a minimum, this would include support for the victim in obtaining a protective order, arrest of the batterer where appropriate, and an offer of services to the offender, including education. [3.] There is a demonstrable safety risk to the child that outweighs the risks associated with foster placement.

When agencies remove children from battered mothers, they put the mothers in a terrible dilemma. Dr. Stark testified that when a mother believes that if she reports domestic violence her children's well-being will be endangered because they will be removed from the home and put in foster care, then she is unlikely to report the violence until it reaches an extreme level where public notice is unavoidable. As a result agencies that remove children from battered women aggravate the occurrence of domestic violence by discouraging women from reporting it at early stages. "Knowing that they may be investigated by child protective services, or charged with neglect, and that they may lose their children to foster care, battered mothers are more likely to remain in the abusive home, isolated and afraid, so that they can remain with their children." * * *

* * *

Much of the actual policies as applied by ACS are driven by fear of an untoward incident of child abuse that will result in criticism of the agency and some of its employees. The concern over institutional self-protection, rather than children's best interests, explains a good deal of ACS's predisposition toward counterproductive separation of abused mothers and their children.

* * *

[ACS files a petition of neglect or abuse in 11.8 percent of cases involving domestic violence. Of these cases, the victim is one of the respondents in 92.3 percent of the cases, and the victim is the *sole* respondent in 53.8 percent of the cases. The batterer is not listed at all in 46.2 percent of the cases. ACS prosecutes the victim of domestic violence for neglect in Family Court in approximately 935 cases each year. The petition explicitly charges the victim with having failed to protect the child from witnessing domestic violence in 23.1 percent of cases. The abusive partner, by contrast, is charged with causing harm to the child by engaging in domestic violence in only 15.4 percent of cases. It appears that ACS explicitly charges victims of domestic violence with neglect for having failed to protect children from witnessing domestic violence in approximately 234 cases each year. Although during the litigation of this case ACS eventually criticized the phrase "engaged in domestic violence" as misstating the role of the victim, ACS did not address the broader question of whether a woman who has been abused should be charged with neglect on the grounds that she somehow permitted her children to witness the violence inflicted upon her.]

The practice and policies of ACS often lead to the abuser being left unaccountable because it is administratively easier to punish the mother by separating her from her children.* * *

* * *

Plaintiffs' expert Laura M. Fernandez opined that part of the reason ACS targets mothers who are victims of domestic violence is that the system is "set up to view mothers as the focal point." Historically, fathers have not been given much attention and were not expected to participate in referral services.

> The battered mother ... may easily be engaged and seen as the parent who is more willing and interested in complying with services to prevent removal of her children or to get them returned from foster care. This creates a situation in which a child welfare case is opened due to the father's beating of the mother in the presence of the children, and she is sent for domestic violence education, parenting classes, individual counseling, and drug testing, among other possible referrals. In addition, she may be told she must go into shelter—while, meanwhile, the father is sent to either an anger

management class or, perhaps parenting [classes] and nothing further. This unequal treatment sends a message that the mother is more responsible for getting help and is more "sick" for being in an abusive relationship than the actual person who committed the violence. As part of their mental abuse, many fathers will tell a woman that if she seeks help to escape the home, the system will turn against her, that she will be blamed for the break up of the family, that she will lose everything and that the abuser will get away with everything because he is in control—the system often perpetuates this belief and reinforces to women that they are powerless and will be punished, no matter what they do.

There is no indication that ACS effectively and systematically pursues removal of the abuser before seeking removal of the battered victim's child. ACS has the power to petition the Family Court for an order that removes the perpetrator of abuse or neglect from a household if that would enable the children to remain with or return to the non-offending parent. * * *

* * *

All findings of fact in this memorandum and order have been established by clear and convincing evidence—a standard far higher than the preponderance standard required in this civil case. The * * * findings of fact may be summarized as follows:

1) ACS unnecessarily routinely prosecutes mothers for neglect and removes their children where the mothers have been the victims of significant domestic violence, and where the mothers themselves have done nothing wrong. ACS unnecessarily routinely does so without having previously ensured that the mother has access to the services she needs to protect herself and her children. ACS unnecessarily routinely removes children without a court order. ACS unnecessarily routinely fails to return these children to their mothers promptly after being ordered to do so by a court. Even as it unnecessarily prosecutes the mother and demands that she participate in often ill-advised services, ACS unnecessarily routinely fails to engage the batterer, demand that the batterer participate in needed services, attempt to remove the batterer from the household, or otherwise hold the batterer accountable.

2) ACS caseworkers and case managers who make decisions about what services to provide and when to remove children do so without adequate training about domestic violence. ACS practice is to unnecessarily separate the mother from the child when less harmful alternatives involving non-separation are available.

* * *

[The court found violations of procedural and substantive due process and violations under the equal protection clause and the Fourth, Ninth, Thirteenth, and Nineteenth Amendment. The Fourth Amendment holding was based on the seizure of the child. The due process holdings emphasized the right of the family to remain together without the coercive interference of the awesome power of the state. The court also emphasized the role of ACS as prosecutor in child protection cases. While prosecutors enjoy broad discretion in the conduct of their office, the discretion to prosecute is not absolute but subject to constitutional constraints. Prosecutorial discretion extends only so far as "the prosecutor has probable cause to believe that the accused committed an offense defined by statute." "To punish a person because he has done what the law plainly allows him to do is a due process violation of the most basic sort." "Prosecutors, both governmental and specially appointed, have an ethical duty to ensure that justice [is] done, and, while responsible for prosecuting the guilty, they must also make sure that the innocent do not suffer." As to the equal protection issue, "Separating her from her children merely because she has been abused—a characteristic irrelevant to her right to keep her children—treats her unequally from other parents who are not abused." The Thirteenth Amendment holding was based on the forcible removal of children from mothers without adjudication, their placement in state or private custody, and discipline by those not their parents.]

As a matter of policy and practice, when ACS prosecutes a woman for neglecting her child when she has done nothing but suffer abuse at the hands of another, it does so under what might at best be termed false assumptions and findings. It infers from the fact that a woman has been beaten and humiliated that she permitted or encouraged her own mistreatment. As a matter of policy and practice ACS presumes that she is not a fit parent and that she is not capable of raising her children in a safe and appropriate manner because of actions which are not her own. * * * [A]pplying this presumption violates constitutional rights.

It desecrates fundamental precepts of justice to blame a crime on the victim. * * *

Notes and Questions

1. At the beginning of this chapter, Elizabeth Schneider contrasted a feminist activist approach to ending the subordination of women with a client services approach, noting that new groups perceive battered women as "persons to be helped, not participants in a larger struggle." Schneider, *Battered Women and Feminist Lawmaking*, *supra*. Do you think that the dynamics between women and the state recounted in *Nicholson* may be affected by the orientation of battered women's organizations? Or do the debates over child protection policy simply recognize the hard facts that ending violence is difficult and protecting children is a necessary measure?

Under the approach taken by ACS in New York, what would a good mother have done if attacked by her partner? Should state intervention into the mother-child relationship be permitted even if she has done everything possible for her children's safety and her own? Given the prevalence of domestic violence, if all cases of domestic violence were reported to authorities, would it be it appropriate for a society to have more than 20% of mother-child relationships under the supervision of the state?

2. If society does not blame the woman for the attack on her and does not seek to take her children away, then what is the best policy to protect children? Lois Weithorn makes a comprehensive examination of the psychological harm to children from domestic violence and concludes:

> Whereas there clearly may be situations in which a protective services agency must use the neglect ground to proceed against a domestic violence victim for failures to protect the child, these situations are far less frequent than agency practices suggest. More frequently, state intervention to protect and support adult victims and children together, and to promote their positive functioning, will create the most promising short- and long-term prospects for both. * * *

Lois A. Weithorn, *Protecting Children from Exposure to Domestic Violence: The Use and Abuse Of Child Maltreatment Statutes*, 53 Hastings L.J. 1, 136–37 (2001)

Are there policy alternatives that can protect both battered women and their children? When *safety*, not *separation*, is the focus of intervention, battered women are not required to leave their homes, and children are not removed from their mothers; rather, batterers are arrested and removed from the home. The practices of ACS in New York were in ironic contrast with pilot projects which had "demonstrated dramatic drops in removal rates and subsequent abuse and neglect allegations where ACS and the criminal justice resources were cooperating effectively and abusers were being regularly arrested." *Nicholson*, 203 F.Supp.2d at 210.

3. When child protection workers believe stereotypes of battered women, those stereotypes can intersect with and reinforce stereotypes based on race and class:

> Poor women and particularly poor African-American women are far more likely to be the subject of charges of child neglect than are other women. "In child welfare cases, where the individual is pitted against the vast power and resources of the state, the power imbalance is extreme. And in the vast majority of cases, the fact that the parent is female, poor, uneducated, and nonwhite, exacerbates this inherent power disparity."

Donna Coker, *Crime Control, supra* at 833, 837 (quoting Amy Sinden, *"Why Won't Mom Cooperate?": A Critique of Informality in Child Welfare Proceedings*, 11 Yale J. L. & Feminism 339, 385 (1999)).

Dorothy Roberts explains the race and class implications of moving from their homes and into the foster care system.

> The class and race dimensions of foster care magnify this problem [of the large number of children removed from their homes]—virtually all of the parents who lose custody of their chil-

dren are poor, and a startling percentage are black. More than 200,000 children are removed from their homes and placed in foster care annually. In 1998, black children made up 45% of the foster care population while comprising only 15% of the general population under age eighteen. In the nation's urban centers, the racial disparity is even greater. Chicago's foster care population, for example, is almost 90% black. Of 42,000 children in foster care in New York City in 1997, only 1300 were white. Moreover, once black children enter foster care, they remain there longer, are moved more often, and receive less desirable placements than white children. Even if all of the thousands of black children in foster care were adopted tomorrow, there would still be cause for concern. Acquiring permanent out-of-home placements for all these children would do nothing to stem the tide of family disruption.

Dorothy E. Roberts, *Is There Justice in Children's Rights?: The Critique of Federal Family Preservation Policy*, 2 U. Pa. J. Const. L. 112, 125–26 (1999)

Roberts argues that the majority of children are removed from their homes because of problems related to poverty. *Id.* at 120. "The intersection of * * * federal welfare [reform] and adoption reform laws marks the first time in this nation's history that 'states have a federal mandate to protect children from abuse and neglect but no corresponding mandate to provide basic economic support to poor families.' " *Id.* at 132 (quoting Martha Matthews, *Assessing the Effect of Welfare Reform on Child Welfare*, 32 Clearinghouse Rev. 395, 397 (Jan.-Feb. 1999)). Citing the example of Wisconsin, in which 5% of mothers removed from public assistance have reportedly been forced to "abandon their children," Roberts warns that welfare reform may cause a net increase in the number of children entering foster care. Roberts, *supra* at 133.

Were the children in *Nicholson* safe within the foster care system?

5. Why did the New York child protection agency require that mothers move into shelters, rather than requiring that batterers live elsewhere? "It is a peculiarity of the abuse of women that we are expected to 'leave' the very centers of our lives whether or not we have anywhere else to go." Martha R. Mahoney, *EXIT: Power and the Idea of Leaving in Love, Work, and the Confirmation Hearings*, 65 S. Cal. L. Rev. 1283, 1300 (1992). Is this policy an implicit admission that it is easier to control the mother than to control an abusive man?

6. A woman who reports violence to the police may ultimately be involved in separate, ongoing legal actions: in civil court to obtain a restraining order, in criminal court as a witness in the case against the batterer, in a different civil court action for her divorce, and in dependency or juvenile court on the issue of protecting children from the harm of witnessing abuse. Meanwhile, she must work, shop, cook, and care for her family; frequently, she also must seek housing and move, or fulfill conditions imposed by child protection services, such as attendance at parenting classes or seeking counseling. How can she work and maintain

this schedule? How can she support and care for children if she does not work? Would she have been better off if she did not seek help from the police?

7. Would it be better if all services for women and children were combined into a single court or agency? In 1981, as part of a debate that has continuing relevance, Susan Schechter argued against a proposal to combine child protection programs with programs for battered women under an umbrella of services related to "family violence":

> * * * [B]attered women exist today as a social category only because former battered women and feminists insisted that safety for women had to be provided as a priority. A political movement, formed through the will and hard work of grassroots women, created this safety, funding over 500 programs in seven years. The model of service developed was significantly different from that used in child protection. It assumes that battered women are in a situational crisis caused by the repeated violence that this society has allowed men to carry out. Battered women are not disabled; they and their children are facing violence, pain, fear, and major dislocations. Women regain control over their lives through finding safety, emotional support from other women, and advocacy. Children experience the same support and advocacy within many shelters. These shelters articulate a vision that sees violence as a result of the unequal power between men and women and sees adult women as competent to control their own lives.
>
> Child abuse and violence against women are different phenomena with different historical roots. A major goal of child protection services is to keep the family united, hopefully free from violence. Our goal is to support a woman in creating a violence-free life for herself and her children in whatever way she chooses. You must provide a form of protection and caretaking that is necessary for children but demeaning and debilitating for adults. Child protection services were organized because children are dependent. Battered women's service provision fundamentally challenges women's dependence, asserting the necessity of independence in order to be free from violence. Two clearly different forms of intervention are required. To use only one means women will be treated as incompetent and denied the very autonomy needed to escape victimization.

Susan Schechter, *Against Consolidation with Child Abuse Services*, in Susan Schechter, *Women and Male Violence: The Visions and Struggles of the Battered Women's Movement* 323 (1982).

8. How did society and culture in the United States move from no shelters or support for battered women in 1974, through the widespread existence of domestic violence shelters and support services and the passage of the Violence Against Women Act in 1994, to the removal of children because of attacks on their mothers in 2001? Are the New York child protection policies produced by an old view of women that blames them for the violence against them? By a misplaced focus on the

woman's failure to separate rather than on the batterer's failure to refrain from using violence? Are they products of a popular image of the battered woman as helpless, dysfunctional, and irresistibly drawn to abusive men? Are these policies an effort to avoid the sort of harm to children caused by a careless bureaucracy in DeShaney v. Winnebago County, 489 U.S. 189 (1989), excerpted in chapter 9? Are they produced by an overworked, underfunded bureaucracy that will do anything to avoid the scandal it will experience if a child is injured or killed? If the New York policies could be the product of all these factors, how should law reform intervene today?

SECTION 6. PROGRESS AND CHALLENGES: DOMESTIC VIOLENCE LAWYERING TODAY

LINDA L. AMMONS

Dealing with the Nastiness: Mixing Feminism and Criminal Law in the Review of Cases of Battered Incarcerated Women—A Tenth-Year Reflection

4 Buff. Crim. L. Rev. 891, 892, 909–12, 914–17 (2001)

During my law school matriculation, the number of women students was beginning to increase dramatically. The words "affirmative action" were just beginning to be used as code words to indicate that some students, primarily black but also sometimes women, had somehow fooled administrators into allowing them access to legal education. New courses like Sex Discrimination Law were being added to the curriculum. Before taking this class, I thought I fully understood what discrimination was all about. I am an African-American woman, a child of the fifties and sixties, and I had often been the first of my kind in many (particularly career) situations. Feminism and women's studies were not new topics for me. On my own and in graduate school, I had read many of the books in the emerging feminist canon. I was not afraid to be identified with a group of persons who believed that women were fully human and had the God-given right to determine for themselves their destinies. I was probably drawn to the sex discrimination class for a variety of reasons, not really sure of what to expect but willing to be open to whatever I could learn.

I do not remember how much time we spent on the topic of battered women. Textbooks on gender or women and law were scarce. The professor had to compile handouts on current issues. Employment discrimination and reproductive freedom were the hot topics then, and the core of feminist jurisprudence was equality theory. What I do remember is being one of a handful of women who were challenged by a thoughtful, tough female law professor first to learn and then to question the rules, the analysis and the obvious. I left law school thankful that I had been exposed to an expanding area of law that would or should help women in their quest of full citizenship. [The author later worked extensively on clemency for battered women as an aide to Governor Celeste of Ohio.]

* * *

Whatever progress has been made on the issue of battered women is directly attributed to those feminist lawyers, scholars, advocates, and crusaders who insisted that the criminal law must be written, interpreted, or revised and fairly applied in ways that takes into account the plight of abused women without stigmatizing them. In 1990, releasing a woman from prison when the criminal justice system had unjustly imposed too harsh a sentence on her because she decided to protect her own life rather than be the victim of death or grievous bodily injury was a revolutionary, feminist, humanitarian, legal, and just act. If feminist practical reasoning is "expand[ing] traditional notions of legal relevance to make legal decision making more sensitive to the features of a case not already reflected in legal doctrine," freeing oppressed, tortured, and wrongly convicted, incarcerated women was feminism in action. However, providing clemency for incarcerated battered women after the fact is like ending slavery by granting emancipation to one slave at a time. The better solution is to grant relief to battered women before the violence escalates to homicide. There is no quick fix to this universal problem.

There are those who will recoil at the notion that public policy and the criminal justice system should be informed and influenced by feminist theory. Today some view even the label feminist as something akin to a four-letter word. Unfortunately, those who have benefited the most from the hard won battles to treat women as equals and human often try to distance themselves the farthest from being associated with the politics or responsibilities of feminism. Criminal law, a type of public law, is not made in a vacuum. This body of law that so preoccupies our legislators, ties up our courts, and fills our jails is influenced by ideas (good and bad), theories, and notions that have been passed down for millennia. Feminism and feminist theory had to be created because the stories were only half told. Because "absolute power corrupts absolutely," those in power failed to make sure that all of the laws worked for all of the people, including the female people. Feminist legal theory is an attempt to set the record straight and straighten out the law.

Over the past ten years, I have watched as fewer students, men and women, express any interest in gender and law classes. Students have told me that they fear that having such courses on their transcripts might make employers hesitant to hire them. Women who might, under other circumstances, be open to studying the gender issue are intimidated by the possibility of being labeled "feminazi" or worse yet, lesbian if they express too much interest in "women's" issues. This trepidation is tragic. One never knows from where the next idea of liberation will spring. I cannot recount all of the things I learned and took with me from that women's law class, but I do believe that my perspective and analysis concerning male supremacy at law were sharpened, and I was prepared to use this much-needed tool when the time came. My interest in how the law affects half of humanity has led directly and indirectly to the freedom of scores of women, who had been punished enough. Perhaps the pressure to conform was not as great when I was a student, or maybe I just understood that we had not yet overcome.

Gains have been made in most areas of society relative to women. Hopefully, the world will never be as it was for women just thirty years ago. However, to declare that victory has been won because privileged women are enrolled in professional schools in equal numbers to men, get jobs in traditionally male segregated fields, and earn almost as much as men is premature and shortsighted.

* * *

* * * We now understand that a good, just government does not allow its citizens (male or female) to be tortured either by public institutions or by private (albeit intimate) associates. Hopefully, we have concluded that when a woman defends her life or herself from grievous bodily harm, she should not be unjustly penalized for trying to survive. In the year 2000, we have a better understanding of the myriad ways of intervening and assisting persons being victimized by familial violence, either through the courts, police authorities, social service agencies, public health institutions, or community-based forums. We are better equipped to handle such crisis and more alert to the signs of domestic terrorism. But our remedies are far from perfect. We seem to be stymied as to what really works in getting abusers to change their behavior. * * *

While we try to determine just what formula is best, women continue to die at the hands of those who are supposed to love them. * * * While law, and criminal law in particular, can deter inappropriate behavior, law is not enough. Something more needs to be added to the mixture. Intractable domestic violence is only symptomatic of a much larger problem which law alone cannot resolve. When policy makers, clergy, social service providers, lawyers, athletes, legislators, entertainers, homemakers, laborers, teachers, medical personnel, and others really begin to act on the belief that women are equal citizens and valuable human beings and that violence, against women—real, simulated, or virtual—harms us all, then and only then will the need to review and challenge our theories and practices regarding domestic violence cease. In the meantime, the nastiness continues.

Notes and Questions

1. Linda Ammons says that granting executive clemency to battered woman was a "revolutionary, feminist, humanitarian, legal, and just act." Nonetheless, she argues, "providing clemency for incarcerated battered women after the fact is like ending slavery by granting emancipation to one slave at a time." How can the work of attorneys on domestic violence cases—or the work of law students—contribute to the

sort of equality for women that Ammons argues is fundamental to solving domestic violence? *See* Virginia Coto, *Lucha, The Struggle For Life: Legal Services For Battered Immigrant Women,* 53 U. Miami L. Rev. 749 (1999) (excerpted in chapter 11).

2. Social justice lawyers have learned to link domestic violence with issues of poverty as well as gender equality. In the early days of legal services representation, the New Haven legal services program, staffed by the poverty lawyering pioneer Jean Camper Cahn, "sought to bridge the gap between instrumental and affective styles by addressing each client as a 'whole person.'" Peter Margulies, *Representation of Domestic Violence Survivors as a New Paradigm of Poverty Law: In Search of Access, Connection, and Voice*, 63 Geo. Wash. L. Rev. 1071, 1087 (1995). However, the scarcity of legal services lawyers and restrictions on their practice pushed domestic violence off the agenda of most legal services offices. For example, restrictions on client income may block services: "Typically income and asset ceilings are judged by looking at the household in which the prospective client is located. This means that if a victim is still living with her abusive partner, and the partner makes above a certain income, the woman may not be eligible for assistance. Yet this means that a woman must become homeless first and only then become eligible." *Id.* at 1090.

In recent years, new poverty law scholarship and practice have made domestic violence work a priority. Louise Trubek and Jennifer Farnham describe the work of Jill Davies, who has "spent her career as a lawyer for people with low income at Greater Hartford Legal Assistance (GHLA) in Connecticut." Louise G. Trubek & Jennifer J. Farnham, *Social Justice Collaboratives: Multidisciplinary Practices for People,* 7 Clinical L. Rev. 227 (2000). Davies has a broad vision of law and its relationship to larger society, and a humble approach to her own role as a lawyer, recognizing that legal solutions do not always provide outcomes that clients want. "[S]he has been at the forefront of the movement to see the battered woman as the expert on her own situation and lawyers and advocates as providing information and support. She has a leadership role nationally as part of an effort to consider the interconnections between domestic violence and poverty." Davies credits advocates and battered women with having taught her how best to use legal skills to respond to domestic violence.

> GHLA began this work in the late 1970s in Hartford doing family law around domestic violence issues. Davies started as staff attorney in the Domestic Violence Unit at GHLA in the early 1980s. She began to feel like the work she was doing was essentially freeing batterers to abuse other women. She felt that while her work was important to her individual clients, it was not really helping in a larger sense. So, she began to reach out to domestic violence organizations in her area. At first she concentrated on building relationships, initially just spending time with them, learning what they did and seeing how she could be useful. In the late 1980s the Connecticut laws surrounding domestic violence changed and GHLA

and the Connecticut Coalition Against Domestic Violence started a legal advocacy program to help train the advocates provided for in the new legislation. These advocates would be employed by shelters but work in criminal court. Davies directed this program out of an office in the Coalition while still an employee of GHLA. During this time she had to deal with the skepticism of her colleagues, at least one of whom commented that she was not doing "real lawyering."

* * * [In the late 1990s GHLA received Civil Legal Assistance funding under VAWA to expand their existing collaborative relationships with domestic violence advocates.] The VAWA-funded attorneys let the advocates decide when to refer cases to them, deferring to their experience. In addition to this, Davies wrote a book in collaboration with an advocate and a sociologist about woman-defined advocacy: the battered woman herself is the "expert" and the advocate's role is to provide her with the information, advocacy, and support she needs to plan her safe future. GHLA leads the New England Network on Domestic Violence & Poverty, which is part of a national initiative to build comprehensive solutions to domestic violence. * * *

* * *

* * * Attempting to deal with battering situations often means disrupting households in a way that raises many civil as well as criminal legal issues. These include family law issues such as divorces, child custody and probate, and consumer issues such as landlord/tenant matters, debt collection, bankruptcy and so on. Employment issues also arise. * * * Native American reservations have their own sets of laws and customs which can introduce complicating factors. Depending on the economic situation of the family there may be public benefits issues involved. Thus, dealing with domestic violence brings up many potential civil legal issues while simultaneously involving the criminal justice system as well. The Hartford domestic violence program reports spending ninety to ninety-five percent of attorney time on family law issues, with some juvenile court work, outstanding abuse or neglect issues, and employment and benefits matters taking up the rest of the attorneys' time.

Domestic violence advocates often accompany victims to court and help with obtaining protection and restraining orders. [The mothers also may need lawyers in divorces, custody and visitation battles, and to defend them against failure-to-protect charges.] * * * Legal counseling may also be helpful in safety planning in terms of showing women what their options for government benefits can be if they choose to leave permanently.

* * *

The domestic violence movement is collaborative by design: it emphasizes that violence is a community problem and that collaboration will be necessary to address it. * * * This means understand-

> ing the context of domestic violence survivors, working with other advocates and service providers to help individual clients, and working for system reform.
>
> The types of people who collaborate with lawyers in this sector are most often victim advocates, who are generally trained by shelters or others in the battered women's movement in addition to whatever other training and experience they have. Empowerment through victim advocates and peer support is a key element of support for battered women. In addition, a broad cross section of health, mental health, and social work professionals collaborate as well.
>
> The physical arrangements of collaborations vary. In some cases lawyers are employed by shelters; others have a referral relationship. In most cases intake is done through advocates, who are often trained to help women through some legal processes but will need to refer to an attorney for others. The centrality of advocates in service provision means that the location of attorneys may not be significant as long as they are available and accessible to clients. Lawyers in shelters have the advantage of proximity to clients, but have the potential disadvantage of less mentoring and professional support as a result of being isolated from other lawyers.

Id. at 241–42, 244–45, 247–48.

Ethical challenges facing collaborative practice on domestic violence include confidentiality problems with mandated reporting of child abuse by advocates. Advocates must also avoid giving legal advice or face problems with the unauthorized practice of law. *Id.* at 248–49. A description of innovative funding and practice structures that bring shelters in Wisconsin together with staff lawyers and legal services providers appears in Louise G. Trubek, *Embedded Practices: Lawyers, Clients, and Social Change,* 31 Harv. C.R.-C.L L.Rev. 415 (1996), excerpted in chapter 2.

3. For further reading on domestic violence, see Clare Dalton & Elizabeth M. Schneider, *Battered Women and the Law* (2001); Nancy K.D. Lemon, *Domestic Violence Law* 2001; and Beverly Balos & Mary Louise Fellows, *Law and Violence Against Women: Cases and Materials on Systems of Oppression* (1994).

Index

References are to Pages

References are to Pages

References are to Pages

References are to Pages

†